U.S. and CANADA LITERATU

NAME: ______

COMPANY: ______

ADDRESS: ______

CITY: ______ STATE: ______ ZIP: ______

COUNTRY: ______

PHONE NO.: (   ) ______

ORDER NO.	TITLE	QTY.		PRICE		TOTAL
			×		=	
			×		=	
			×		=	
			×		=	
			×		=	
			×		=	
			×		=	
			×		=	
			×		=	
			×		=	

Subtotal ______

Must Add Your Local Sales Tax ______

Include postage:
Must add 15% of Subtotal to cover U.S. and Canada postage. (20% all other.) → Postage ______

Total ______

Pay by check, money order, or include company purchase order with this form ($200 minimum). We also accept VISA, MasterCard or American Express. Make payment to Intel Literature Sales. Allow 2-4 weeks for delivery.

☐ VISA ☐ MasterCard ☐ American Express Expiration Date ______

Account No. ______

Signature ______

Mail To: Intel Literature Sales
P.O. Box 7641
Mt. Prospect, IL 60056-7641

International Customers outside the U.S. and Canada should use the International order form on the next page or contact their local Sales Office or Distributor.

For phone orders in the U.S. and Canada
Call Toll Free: (800) 548-4725

Prices good until 12/31/92.
Source HB

INTERNATIONAL LITERATURE ORDER FORM

NAME: ______________________________

COMPANY: ______________________________

ADDRESS: ______________________________

CITY: ______________ STATE: ________ ZIP: ________

COUNTRY: ______________________________

PHONE NO.: (   ) ______________________________

ORDER NO.	TITLE	QTY.		PRICE		TOTAL
			×		=	
			×		=	
			×		=	
			×		=	
			×		=	
			×		=	
			×		=	
			×		=	
			×		=	
			×		=	

Subtotal ________

Must Add Your Local Sales Tax ________

Total ________

PAYMENT

Cheques should be made payable to your ***local*** Intel Sales Office (see inside back cover).

Other forms of payment may be available in your country. Please contact the Literature Coordinator at your ***local*** Intel Sales Office for details.

The completed form should be marked to the attention of the LITERATURE COORDINATOR and returned to your ***local*** Intel Sales Office.

Intel Corporation is a leading supplier of microcomputer components, modules and systems. When Intel first introduced the microprocessor in 1971, it created the era of the microcomputer. Today, Intel architectures are considered world standards. Intel products are used in a wide variety of applications including, embedded systems such as automobiles, avionics systems and telecommunications equipment, and as the CPU in personal computers, network servers and supercomputers. Others bring enhanced capabilities to systems and networks. Intel's mission is to deliver quality products through leading-edge technology.

MICROCOMPUTER PRODUCTS HANDBOOK

1992

Additional copies of this manual or other Intel literature may be obtained from:

Intel Corporation
Literature Sales
P.O. Box 7641
Mt. Prospect, IL 60056-7641

INTEL SERVICE

INTEL'S COMPLETE SUPPORT SOLUTION WORLDWIDE

Intel Service is a complete support program that provides Intel customers with hardware support, software support, customer training, and consulting services. For detailed information contact your local sales offices.

Service and support are major factors in determining the success of a product or program. For Intel this support includes an international service organization and a breadth of service programs to meet a variety of customer needs. As you might expect, Intel service is extensive. It can start with On-Site Installation and Maintenance for Intel and non-Intel systems and peripherals, Repair Services for Intel OEM Modules and Platforms, Network Operating System support for Novell NetWare and Banyan VINES software, Custom Integration Services for Intel Platforms, Customer Training, and System Engineering Consulting Services. Intel maintains service locations worldwide. So wherever you're using Intel technology, our professional staff is within close reach.

ON-SITE INSTALLATION AND MAINTENANCE

Intel's installation and maintenance services are designed to get Intel and Intel-based systems and the networks they use up and running—fast. Intel's service centers are staffed by trained and certified Customer Engineers throughout the world. Once installed, Intel is dedicated to keeping them running at maximum efficiency, while controlling costs.

REPAIR SERVICES FOR INTEL OEM MODULES AND PLATFORMS

Intel offers customers of its OEM Modules and Platforms a comprehensive set of repair services that reduce the costs of system warranty, maintenance, and ownership. Repair services include module or system testing and repair, module exchange, and spare part sales.

NETWORK OPERATING SYSTEM SUPPORT

An Intel software support contract for Novell NetWare or Banyan VINES software means unlimited access to troubleshooting expertise any time during contract hours—up to seven days per week, twenty-four hours per day. To keep networks current and compatible with the latest software versions, support services include access to minor releases and "patches" as made available by Novell and Banyan.

CUSTOM SYSTEM INTEGRATION SERVICES

Intel Custom System Integration Services enable resellers to order completely integrated systems assembled from a list of Intel386™ and Intel486™ microcomputers and validated hardware and software options. These services are designed to complement the reseller's own integration capabilities. Resellers can increase business opportunities, while controlling overhead and support costs.

CUSTOMER TRAINING

Intel offers a wide range of instructional programs covering various aspects of system design and implementation. In just three to five days a limited number of individuals learn more in a single workshop than in weeks of self-study. Covering a wide variety of topics, Intel's major course categories include: architecture and assembly language, programming and operating systems, BITBUS™, and LAN applications.

SYSTEM ENGINEERING CONSULTING

Intel provides field system engineering consulting services for any phase of your development or application effort. You can use our system engineers in a variety of ways ranging from assistance in using a new product, developing an application, personalizing training and customizing an Intel product to providing technical and management consulting. Working together, we can help you get a successful product to market in the least possible time.

DATA SHEET DESIGNATIONS

Intel uses various data sheet markings to designate each phase of the document as it relates to the product. The marking appears in the upper, right-hand corner of the data sheet. The following is the definition of these markings:

Data Sheet Marking	Description
Product Preview	Contains information on products in the design phase of development. Do not finalize a design with this information. Revised information will be published when the product becomes available.
Advanced Information	Contains information on products being sampled or in the initial production phase of development.*
Preliminary	Contains preliminary information on new products in production.*
No Marking	Contains information on products in full production.*

*Specifications within these data sheets are subject to change without notice. Verify with your local Intel sales office that you have the latest data sheet before finalizing a design.

intel®

intel®

Table of Contents

Table of Contents (Continued)

Table of Contents (Continued)

Table of Contents (Continued)

Alphanumeric Index

Alphanumeric Index (Continued)

Alphanumeric Index (Continued)

Multibus II Single Board Computers

1

intel®

iSBC® 486/133SE* SINGLE BOARD COMPUTER

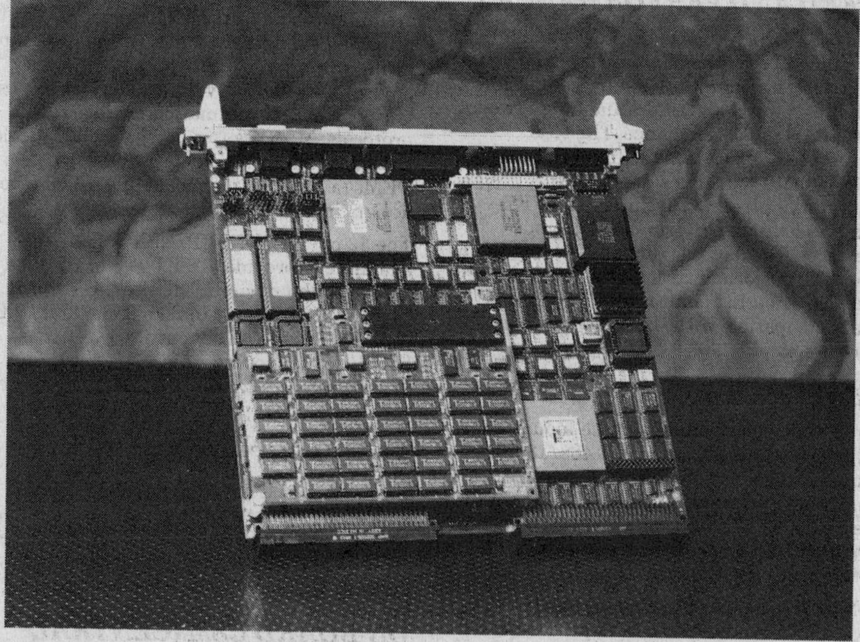

281108-1

SAVES MONEY AND SLOTS: ONE CPU BOARD FEATURES i486™, SCSI AND ETHERNET*

The iSBC® 486/133SE is a high-integration single board computer that provides a 33 MHz i486™ microprocessor, SCSI and Ethernet* on Multibus II, the industry standard multiprocessing system bus. High CPU performance combined with an extensive on-board set of I/O offerings, makes the iSBC 486/133SE an impressive single board system. The iSBC 486/133SE reduces a three-board set to one board while continuing to provide equal functionality. The single board solution saves you money and valuable slots.

FEATURES

- i486 CPU operating at 33 MHz with on-chip FPU and cache
- 4, 8, 16 or 32 MB on-board DRAM with parity
- 82258 ADMA operating at 10.0 MHz
- 82596CA high-performance 32-bit LAN Coprocessor operating at 33 MHz
- One small computer system interface (SCSI) port
- Two 32-pin JEDEC DIP sites preconfigured with full MSA firmware in two 27020 EPROMs
- Two 32-pin PLCC sites that support EPROMs or Flash Memory devices
- Supports iRMX® III Operating System Software
- Supports UNIX* V.4 Operating System Software

*Ethernet® is a registered trademark of Xerox Corporation.

October 1991
Order Number: 281108-002

FEATURES

i486™ MICROPROCESSOR SPEED AND PERFORMANCE

The i486 microprocessor, the newest and fastest member of the popular INTEL386™ 32-bit processor family, is binary compatible with 386™ microprocessors and offers two to three times the performance. The i486 microprocessor provides the highest level of performance through a state-of-the-art design containing a pipelined architecture, 8 KB cache, and a high-performance local bus interface. Frequent instructions execute in one cycle. The performance is further enhanced by an on-chip floating point unit (FPU) that is binary compatible with the 387™ numerics coprocessor.

WEALTH OF I/O

Through extensive use of surface mount technology and ASIC, the iSBC 486/133SE board increases the on-board I/O features compared to previous Multibus II CPU boards. The wealth of I/O features provides the user a variety of I/O interfaces in a single board. Slots are saved without limiting I/O.

- Ethernet — On-board using the Intel 82596 LAN Coprocessor running at 33 MHz
- SCSI — Single-ended SCSI interface through the P2 connector
- iSBX™ — Compliance Level: D16/16 DMA
- Serial Ports — Based on Intel's 82530 Serial Communications Controller and RS-232 compatible
- Parallel Port — Centronics compatible

HIGH-SPEED MEMORY INTERFACE OPTIMIZES i486™ CPU PERFORMANCE

The iSBC 486/133SE comes with 4, 8, 16 or 32 MBytes of byte-parity protected fast-page DRAM which minimizes the memory access time seen by the i486 CPU and thereby maximizes the CPU performance. The memory interface is designed to support up to 64 Mbytes.

MSA FIRMWARE

MSA is a complete hierarchy of hardware, firmware, and software interfaces and protocols that builds on and extends the basic Multibus II (IEEE/ANSI 1296) bus standard. Specifically, MSA defines message passing, system boot and initialization, system and board level diagnostics, and automatic board configuration in a multiprocessor system environment. By providing a standardized set of powerful programmatic interfaces and protocols, MSA assures a high level of vendor and board compatibility. This, in turn, provides OEMs faster time to market due to a shorter design/integration cycle.

The 32-pin JEDEC (DIP) EPROM sites are available to provide 512 KBytes of EPROM for 27020, 2 Mbit devices. The sites, as shipped, contain BISTS (Built-in-Self-Tests) and IDX (Initialization and Diagnostics eXecutive) power-up diagnostics residing in two preprogrammed 27020 EPROMs. These sites can also support programmed flash devices.

FLASH SUPPORT

Two 32-pin PLCC sites are available which support 512 Kbytes of on-board programmable FLASH memory when using 28F020 devices. FLASH may be used for user-specific firmware space or for non-volatile memory.

ON-BOARD CSM (CENTRAL SERVICES MODULE) CAPABILITY

An iSBC CSM/002 connector on the iSBC 486/133SE provides an on-board CSM option. The iSBC CSM/002 module performs all CSM functions required by the IEEE/ANSI 1296 specification when the iSBC 486/133SE is installed in slot 0. The CSM also provides, a battery backed time-of-day clock, periodic alarm function, and 20 bytes of non-volatile RAM.

FULLY COMPATIBLE

The iSBC 486/133SE is fully compatible with the iSBC 486/125, iSBC 386/133, and 120 members of the Multibus II CPU family as well as with the iSBC 386/258 SCSI Controller Board and iSBC 186/530 Ethernet Communications Engine. The table on the next page shows the iSBC 486/133SE feature set. The high level of integration allows you two distinct benefits: You can upgrade your existing CPU to a higher performance level or you can use a single board where previously you used three boards: CPU, SCSI and Ethernet.

FEATURES

DEVELOPMENT AND OPERATING SYSTEM SUPPORT

Operating System support includes the 32-bit iRMX® III Real-Time Operating System and UNIX* V.4 operating system.

ONE YEAR WARRANTY

All Intel board level products have a one year mail in warranty on both parts and labor.

WORLDWIDE SERVICE AND SUPPORT

Should any Intel board ever need service beyond the warranty period, Intel maintains a world wide network of service and repair facilities to keep you and your customers up and running.

INTEL QUALITY — YOUR GUARANTEE

The iSBC 486/133SE boards are designed and manufactured to meet Intel's strict standards, assuring reliability and high quality.

	CPU Speed (MHz)	FPU Speed	Cache	Max DRAM (MByte)	Ethernet	SCSI	Parallel Port	Two EPROM Sockets	Supports Flash Memory	ADMA	Serial Ports	iSBX™ Connector	iLBX™ II Interface	BIST and IDX	CSM Option	Local Access to PSB Memory and I/O	PSB Access to On-Board Memory	iRMX® III UNIX Support
SBC 486/133SE	33	On Chip	On Chip	64	✓	✓	✓	✓	✓	✓	2	✓		✓	✓	✓		✓
SBC 486/125	25	On Chip	On Chip	64				✓		✓	2	✓	✓	✓	✓	✓		✓
SBC 386/133	33	387/33	64 KB	64				✓		✓	2	✓	✓	✓	✓	✓		✓
SBC 386/120	20	387/20	64 KB	16				✓		✓	1 (8751)	✓		✓		✓	✓	✓

SPECIFICATIONS

CPU CLOCK RATE

i486 CPU @ 33.3 MHz

CACHE MEMORY

8 Kbytes on-chip, 0 wait-state on read hit

DMA CLOCK RATES/MAXIMUM BANDWIDTH

82258 ADMA is 10 MHz 20 MB per second. (Assumes transfer between local DRAM and MPC)

ON-BOARD DRAM MEMORY

Model	Supplied
SBC486133SE004	4 MB
SBC486133SE008	8 MB
SBC486133SE016	16 MB
SBC486133SE032	32 MB

Memory expansion possible with one additional memory module. Maximum on-board memory capacity is 64 MB.

EPROM MEMORY

Two Jedec sites provide the following capacity:

Devices	Capacity
27010	256 KBytes
27020	512 KBytes
27040	1 MByte

FLASH MEMORY

Two PLCC sites provide the following capacity:

Devices	Capacity
28F010	256K
28F020	512K

INTERFACES

Multibus II PSB:	32-bit parallel System Bus (ANSI/IEEE 1296) interface with full message passing capability
iSBX Bus:	Compliance Level: D16/16 DMA
Serial I/O:	RS232C DTE ASYNC
SCSI:	Single-ended
Ethernet:	82596CA 32-bit LAN Coprocessor operating at 33 MHz
Parallel Port:	Centronics Compatible

SERIAL I/O PORT

- Channel A & B: RS232C Compatible DTE Asynchronous interface
- 9-pin D-Shell Shielded Connector
- Configurable Baud Rates: 300, 600, 1200, 2400, 4800, 9600, 19200, and 38400

PHYSICAL CHARACTERISTICS

Standard Multibus II Board

4 MB, 8 MB and 16 MB Boards take a single slot in a Multibus II Chassis—32 MB and 64 MB Boards take two slots.

Physical Dimensions

Height:	233 mm (9.18 inches)
Depth:	220 mm (8.65 inches)
Front Panel Width:	19.2mm (0.76 inches)

ELECTRICAL CHARACTERISTICS

Power Requirements

DC Power Requirements (Typical):
+5V, 12A
±12V, 250mA

Note: Does not include power for iSBX module, or added iSBC memory modules.

REFERENCE MANUALS

The following manuals provide necessary information when using the iSBC 486/133SE board:

Multibus II Interconnect Interface Specification,
Order Number: 149299-003*

Introduction to Multibus II System Architecture,
Order Number: 508305-001

MSA Firmware User's Guide,
Order Number: 506090-001

iSBC® 486/133SE Single Board Computer Users Guide,
Order Number: 506085-001

* recently revised, be sure to order new -003 manual.

SPECIFICATIONS

ORDERING INFORMATION

Order Code	Description
SBC486133SE004	33 MHz 486 CPU Board with 4 MB DRAM, SCSI and Ethernet
SBC486133SE008	33 MHz 486 CPU Board with 8 MB DRAM, SCSI and Ethernet
SBC486133SE016	33 MHz 486 CPU Board with 16 MB DRAM, SCSI and Ethernet
SBC486133SE032	33 MHz 486 CPU Board with 32 MB DRAM, SCSI and Ethernet
SBCMM3008	8 MB Memory Module
SBCMM3016	16 MB Memory Module
SBCMM3032	32 MB Memory Module

For more information or the number of your nearest Intel sales office, call 800-548-4725 (good in the U.S. and Canada).

intel®

iSBC® 486/125 AND 386/133* SINGLE BOARD COMPUTERS

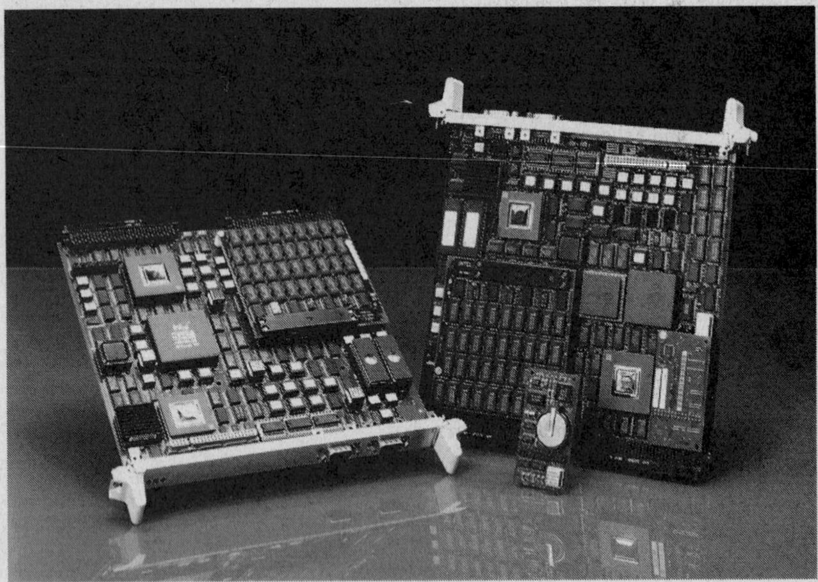

281007-1

ADDING i486™ AND 386™ CPU POWER TO MULTIBUS II

The iSBC® 486/125 and iSBC 386/133 Single Board Computers provide immediate access to the i486™ and 386™ 32-bit microprocessors on Multibus II, the industry standard multiprocessing system bus. These boards are fully compatible, offering different price performance points for users to choose from. Boasting the 25 MHz i486 and 33 MHz 386 processors and a feature set compatible with their predecessors, the iSBC 486/125 and 386/133 boards also offer an immediate performance boost for current Multibus II designs.

FEATURES

iSBC® 486/125
- i486™ CPU operating at 25 MHz with on-chip FPU and cache
- 2–64MB on-board DRAM with parity

iSBC® 386/133
- 386™ CPU operating at 33 MHz
- 387™ Numeric Coprocessor
- 64KB SRAM zero wait-state cache
- 1–64MB on-board DRAM with parity

iSBC® 486/125 AND iSBC® 386/133
- 82258 ADMA with 16-byte "blast" mode
- Two 32-pin JEDEC EPROM Sites with Built-in-self-test (BIST)
- iLBX™ II interface
- Two RS-232 asynchronous serial ports
- One iSBX™ connector
- 3 programmable interval timers, 15 levels of interrupt
- Full 32-bit Multibus II (IEEE/ANSI 1296) Parallel System Bus interface
- Connector for on-board CSM option
- Full Operating Systems Support: iRMX® II, iRMX III, and UNIX** System V/386 operating systems, and iRMK™ I real-time kernel

*The iSBC 386/133 board is also manufactured under product code pSBC386/133 by Intel Puerto Rico, Inc.
The iSBC 486/125 board is also manufactured under product code pSBC486/125 by Intel Puerto Rico, Inc.
**UNIX is a registered trademark of AT&T in the U.S.A. and other countries.

September 1991
Order Number: 281007-003

iSBC® 386/133 FEATURES

386™ MICROPROCESSOR SPEED AND PERFORMANCE

The iSBC 386/133 Single Board Computer features the highest speed 386™ microprocessor available today—33 MHz. It also includes a 387™ floating-point coprocessor running at 33 MHz. The 121-pin, extended math coprocessor socket could also house a WEITEK 3167 floating-point unit (FPU) instead of the 387 FPU.

HIGH-SPEED ON-BOARD MEMORY

For optimum CPU performance, the iSBC 386/133 board includes a 64K Byte cache memory resulting in zero wait-state read accesses on cache hits. The iSBC 386/133 board provides 1–64MB of parity protected, fast-page DRAM memory.

This board also includes two 32-pin JEDEC sites for up to 512KB of EPROM using 27020, 2 Mbit EPROM devices. These sites, as shipped, contain BIST (Built-In-Self-Test) and IDX (Initialization and Diagnostics eXecutive) power-up diagnostics residing in two pre-programmed 27010 EPROMs.

82258 ADMA COPROCESSOR WITH 16-BYTE "BLAST" MODE

The 82258 Advanced DMA coprocessor provides 4 DMA channels. Two channels are allocated to data transfers to/from the iSBX™ bus interface. The remaining two channels handle data transfers between the MPC and on-board memory. Special logic on the board allows the 82258 to transfer data to and from the MPC 4-bytes ("fly-by") or 16-bytes ("blast" mode) at a time; or at a sustained rate of 13.3M bytes/sec or 20.0M bytes/sec.

iLBX™ II INTERFACE FOR MEMORY MAPPED I/O EXPANSION

The iLBX™ II interface on P2 provides expansion for 64M Bytes of off-board memory or memory mapped I/O. It operates at 8 MHz and is completely compatible with the iLBX II interface on the iSBC 286/100A and the iSBC MEM/340 memory board.

ON-BOARD CSM (CENTRAL SERVICES MODULE) CAPABILITY

An iSBC CSM/002 connector on the iSBC 386/133 provides an on-board CSM option. The iSBC CSM/002 module performs all CSM functions required by the IEEE/ANSI 1296 Specification. It also provides a battery-backed time-of-day clock, periodic alarm function, and 28 bytes of non-volatile RAM. The iSBC 386/133 with CSM module is installed in slot zero of a Multibus II chassis and requires only one slot.

FULLY COMPATIBLE WITH iSBC® 386/116,120 AND iSBC® 486/125

The iSBC 386/133 board is fully compatible with the INTEL386 family of Multibus II boards, namely the iSBC 386/116, 386/120 and 486/125. Table 1 shows that the iSBC 386/133 feature set, with the exception of PSB access to on-board memory, is a super set of the iSBC 386/116, 120 feature set and matches that of the iSBC 486/125. Your 16 MHz and 20 MHz designs may be upgraded to 33 MHz for an immediate system performance boost with a simple board swap.

iSBC® 386/133 FEATURES

COMPREHENSIVE DEVELOPMENT AND OPERATING SYSTEM SUPPORT

Operating system support includes the 16-bit iRMX® II and 32-bit iRMX III Real-Time operating system and UNIX System V/386 operating system. The iRMK™ I real-time kernel is available for 32-bit embedded applications. All three include Multibus II transport for full message passing support. To ease Multibus II modules development, Intel offers both the iRMX and UNIX operating system versions of the System 520 Development System which can support on-target and/or cross-hosted software development in one chassis.

BALANCED SET OF ON-BOARD I/O: TWO SERIAL PORTS, iSBX™ CONNECTOR

Through extensive use of surface mount technology, the iSBC 386/133 board has increased the on-board I/O features over previous Multibus II CPU boards. It provides two serial ports based on Intel's 82530 Serial Communications Controller and one iSBX connector, capable of supporting a single- or double-wide, 8- or 16-bit iSBX MULTIMODULE™ board.

PLUG-AND-PLAY WITH SYSTEM 520

Conforming to the Multibus II Systems Architecture (MSA), this board integrates cleanly into the System 520. Just plug the iSBC 386/133 into an empty slot, and start the system. It's that simple.

iSBC® 486/125 FEATURES

i486™ MICROPROCESSOR: THE HIGHEST PERFORMANCE COMPATIBILITY PROCESSOR

The heart of the iSBC 486/125 board is the i486™ microprocessor, the newest and fastest member of the popular INTEL386™ 32-bit processor family. It is binary compatible with 386 microprocessors and offers two to three times the performance. The i486 microprocessor provides the highest level of performance through a state-of-the-art design containing a pipelined architecture, 8KB cache, and a high-performance local bus interface. Frequent instructions execute in one cycle. The performance is further enhanced by an on-chip floating-point unit (FPU) that is binary compatible with the 387 numerics coprocessor.

HIGH-SPEED MEMORY INTERFACE OPTIMIZES i486™ CPU PERFORMANCE

The iSBC 486/125 board comes with 2, 8 or 32 MBytes of byte-parity protected DRAM. On-board memory access is optimized via a two way interleaved memory design. This on-board memory can be expanded to a maximum of 64 Mbytes through the addition of an iSBC MMFC memory expansion module.

COMPLETELY COMPATIBLE WITH THE iSBC® 386/133

As shown in Table 1, all the I/O and Multibus II architecture support features of the iSBC 386/133 are also provided on the iSBC 486/125 for full compatibility with the iSBC 386/133. Both boards are supported by the iRMX II, iRMX III, iRMK and UNIX operating systems.

TABLE 1

INTEL386™ architecture based Multibus II CPU Boards' Feature Set Comparison:

	CPU/Speed (MHz)	FPU/Speed	Cache	Max DRAM (MByte)	Two EPROM Sockets	ADMA	Serial Ports	iSBC™ Connector	iLBX™ II Interface	BIST and IDX	CSM Option	Local Access to PSB Memory and I/O	PSB Access to On-Board Memory	iRMX® II, III, iRMK™ I, UNIX Support
iSBC® 486/125	486™/25	On chip	On chip	64	✓	✓	2	✓	✓	✓	✓	✓		✓
iSBC® 386/133	386™/33	387™/33	64KB	64	✓	✓	2	✓	✓	✓	✓	✓		✓
iSBC® 386/120	386™/20	387™/20	64KB	64	✓	✓	1(8751)	✓		✓		✓	✓	✓

iSBC® 486/125 FEATURES

WORLD WIDE SERVICE AND SUPPORT

Should these or any Intel board ever need service, Intel maintains a world wide network of service and repair facilities to keep you and your customers up and running. For unique applications requiring customization of our products, the Intel Custom Board and Systems Group is available to modify, integrate and test Intel boards and system components to your requirements.

INTEL QUALITY—YOUR GUARANTEE

The iSBC 386/133 and iSBC 486/125 boards are designed and manufactured to meet Intel's strict standards, assuring their reliability and high quality.

ONE YEAR WARRANTY

All Intel board level products have a one year mail in warranty on both parts and labor.

SPECIFICATIONS

CPU CLOCK RATE

386/133:	386™ CPU @ 33.3 MHz 387™ FPU @ 33.3 MHz
iSBC 486/125:	i486™ CPU @ 25 MHz

CACHE MEMORY

iSBC 386/133:	64K bytes 0 wait state on read hit
iSBC 486/125:	8K bytes on-chip 0 wait state on read hit

DMA CLOCK RATES/MAXIMUM BANDWIDTH*

82258 ADMA 10 MHz/20 MB per second

*assumes transfer between local DRAM and MPC.

ON-BOARD DRAM MEMORY

Model	Supplied
iSBC 486/125 C02	2MB
iSBC 486/125 C08	8MB
iSBC 486/125 C32	32MB
iSBC 386/133 F01	1MB
iSBC 386/133 F02	2MB
iSBC 386/133 F04	4MB
iSBC 386/133 F08	8MB

- Single-bit parity error detection per byte
- Memory expansion possible with one additional iSBC MM0xFC or iSBC MM0xFP module. Maximum on-board memory capacity = 64MB

NOTE: iSBC 386/133 F02 and F08 require two Multibus II card slots.
iSBC 486 C02, C08 and C32 fit in one Multibus II slot.

EPROM MEMORY

Two JEDEC sites provide following capacity:

Devices	Capacity
27010	256K byte (supplied)
27020	512K byte

INTERFACES

- Multibus II PSB: 32-bit Parallel System Bus (ANSI/IEEE 1296) interface with full message passing capability
- iSBX Bus: Compliance Level: D16/16 DMA
- iLBX II Bus: Compliance Level: PRQA
- Serial I/O: RS232C DTE ASYNC

SERIAL I/O PORT

- Channel A & B: RS232C compatible DTE Asynchronous interface
- 9-pin D-shell shielded connector
- Configurable baud rates: 300,600,1200,2400,4800,9600,19200, and 38400

PHYSICAL DIMENSIONS

Height:	233 mm (9.18 inches)
Depth:	220 mm (8.65 inches)
Front Panel Width:	19.2 mm (0.76 inches)

ELECTRICAL CHARACTERISTICS

DC Power Requirements (Typical):	+5V, 13A ±12V, 200mA

NOTE: Does not include power for iSBX module, or added iSBC MM0x modules.

For the second iSBC MM0x module, add:

iSBC MM01-FP or iSBC MM04-FP	+5V, 0.71A
iSBC MM02-FP or iSBC MM08-FP	+5V, 0.96A

REFERENCE MANUAL

iSBC 386/133 Single Board Computer User's Guide (order number 457629)

iSBC 486/125 Single Board Computer User's Guide (order number 459600)

ORDERING INFORMATION

Order Code	Description
SBC486125C02	25 MHz 486 CPU board w/ 2MB DRAM
SBC486125C08	25 MHz 486 CPU board w/ 8MB DRAM
SBC486125C32	25 MHz 486 CPU board w/ 32MB DRAM
SBC386133F01	33 MHz 386 CPU board w/ 1MB DRAM
SBC386133F02	33 MHz 386 CPU board w/ 2MB DRAM
SBC386133F04	33 MHz 386 CPU board w/ 4MB DRAM
SBC386133F08	33 MHz 386 CPU board w/ 8MB DRAM

SPECIFICATIONS

SBCMM02FC	2MB memory expansion module for 486/125
SBCMM08FC	8MB memory expansion module for 486/125
SBCMM32FC	32MB memory expansion module for 486/125
SBCMM01FP	1MB memory expansion module for 386/133
SBCMM02FP	2MB memory expansion module for 386/133
SBCMM04FP	4MB memory expansion module for 386/133
SBCMM08FP	8MB memory expansion module for 386/133
SBCMM16FP	16MB memory expansion module for 386/133
SBCMM32FP	32MB memory expansion module for 386/133

iSBC® 386/120* MULTIBUS II SINGLE BOARD COMPUTER

- High Performance 32-bit 386™ Processor Operating at 20 MHz
- 80387 Numerics Co-Processor Providing IEEE 754 Floating Point Instruction Set, Operating at 20 MHz
- 64K byte Static RAM Cache Providing Zero Wait State Reads
- 2, 4 or 8M Bytes of On-Board Dual-Ported Dynamic RAM Memory with Parity Error Detection, Expandable to 16M Bytes
- One RS 232C Serial I/O Port
- 82258 DMA Controller Providing 4 High Performance DMA Channels
- 32-Bit Multibus II Parallel System Bus (IEEE 1296) Interface with Full Message Passing Capability
- 8-, 16-Bit iSBX™ Bus (IEEE P959) Interface with DMA for I/O Expansion
- Resident Firmware to Support Built-In-Self-Test (BIST) Power-Up Diagnostics
- Multibus II Interconnect Space for Software Configurability and Diagnostics

1

The iSBC® 386/120 Multibus II Single Board Computer is based on Intel's 386™ high performance 32-bit microprocessor. The 386 CPU maintains software compatibility with the entire 8086 microprocessor family and delivers new performance standards for microcomputer-based systems. Three versions of the iSBC 386/120 board is offered: the M02, which contains 2M bytes of DRAM; the M04, which includes 4M bytes of DRAM; and the M08 which contains 8M bytes of DRAM. An optional memory expansion module can be added to expand the iSBC 386/120 board's resident memory to a maximum of 16M bytes.

The 64K byte static RAM cache enables the 386 CPU to execute at its full potential performance, while the Multibus II bus provides an interface for reliable, high performance multiprocessing.

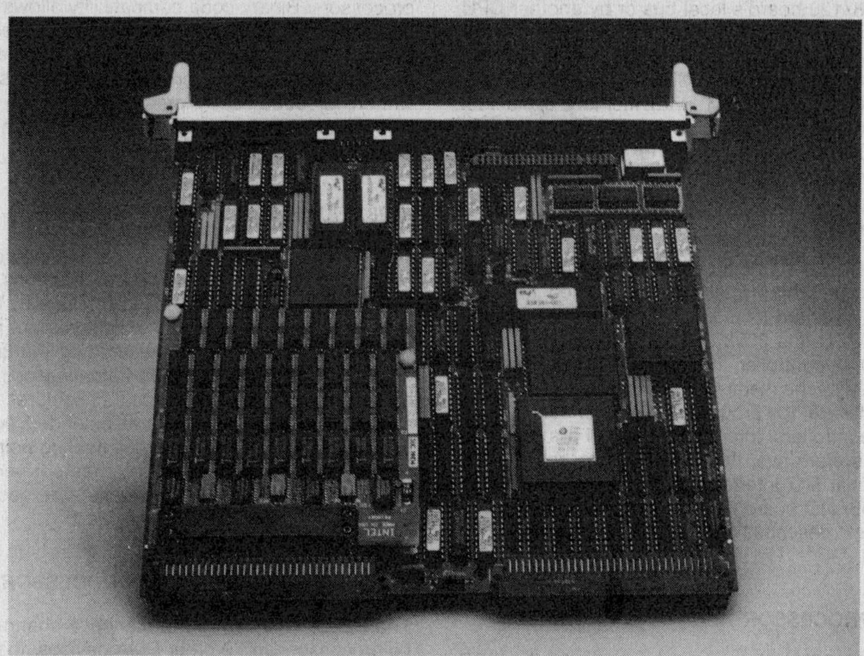

280631-1

The iSBC® 386/120 is also manufactured under product code pSBC386120 by Intel Puerto Rico, Inc.

September 1991
Order Number: 280631-004

FUNCTIONAL DESCRIPTION

Overview

The iSBC 386/120 board utilizes Intel's 386 32-bit microprocessor. The advanced capabilities of the Multibus II architecture coupled with the high performance and compatibility features of the 386 CPU, provide the designer with a superior 32-bit solution for multiprocessing applications. By using the Multibus II architecture, multiprocessing systems are enhanced through advanced bus features including: 21-board distributed arbitration, virtual interrupts, hardware-assisted message passing, bus parity for high reliability, and software configurability using interconnect address space. The Multibus II parallel system bus (iPSB) interface on the iSBC 386/120 board supports full message passing and dual-port architectures and is fully compatible with other SBCs based on the Multibus II (IEEE 1296) bus specification.

The iSBC 386/120 board is offered in three versions: M02, M04 and M08 which contain 2, 4 and 8M bytes of resident DRAM memory respectively. This memory is physically located on an expansion board, and can be accessed directly from the iSBC 386/120 board's local bus or by another CPU over the iPSB bus. This dual-port memory can be expanded to a maximum of 16M bytes though the addition of a second Intel iSBC MM02FP, MM04FP or MM08FP (2, 4 or 8M byte) memory expansion module. Parity error detection is included on all resident DRAM memory.

Architecture

The iSBC 386/120 logic consists of eight resource modules and three interfaces connected together over an on-board local bus. The resources include the 386 CPU, the 80387 numeric co-processor, the 82258 DMA controller, the dual-port DRAM memory, the SRAM cache memory, the EPROM memory with BIST software, the programmable timers and the interrupt controllers. Interfaces included are the iPSB parallel system bus, the iSBX I/O bus and the RS 232C serial I/O interface. A block diagram of the iSBC 386/120 board is shown in Figure 1. The following text describes each of the resources and interfaces.

386™ PROCESSOR

Intel's 386 CPU is the central processor for the iSBC 386/120 board. This is the first 32-bit member of Intel's 8086 family of microprocessors. At 20 MHz, the 386 is capable of executing at sustained rates of 5 million 32-bit instructions per second. This performance is made possible through a state-of-the-art design combining advanced VLSI semiconductor technology, a pipelined architecture, address translation caches and a high performance local bus interface.

The 386 processor provides a rich, generalized register and instruction set for manipulating 32-bit data and addresses. Features such as scaled indexing and a 64-bit barrel shifter ensure the efficient addressing and fast instruction processing. Special emphasis has been placed on providing optimized instructions for high-level languages and operating system functions. Advanced functions, such as hardware-supported multitasking and virtual memory support, provide the foundation necessary to build the most sophisticated multitasking and multiuser systems. Many operating system functions have been placed in hardware to enhance execution speed. The integrated memory management and protection mechanism translates virtual addresses to physical addresses and enforces the protection rules necessary for maintaining task integrity in a multiprocessing environment.

The 386 CPU provides access to the large base of software developed for the 8086 family of microprocessors. Binary code compatibility allows execution of existing 16-bit applications without recompilation or reassembly, directly in a virtual 8086 environment. Programs and even entire operating systems written for 8086 family processors can be run as tasks under 32-bit operating systems written for the 386 CPU.

80287 NUMERIC CO-PROCESSOR

The 80387 is a high-performance floating-point co-processor that takes numerics functions which would normally be performed in software by the 386 microprocessor and instead executes them in hardware. The instruction set executed by the 80387 is compatible with the IEEE 754 floating point standard, with high-precision 80-bit architectures and full support for single, double and extended precision operations. The 80387 executes floating point operations at a rate of 1.5M Whetstones per second at 16 MHz, and 1.86M Whetstones per second at 20 MHz.

82258 ADVANCED DMA CO-PROCESSOR

The 82258 is a high performance 4 channel DMA co-processor. Unlike other DMA devices, the 82258 has processing capabilities. Its command chaining feature and data manipulation capabilities (compare, verify, translate), allow the 82258 to execute simple

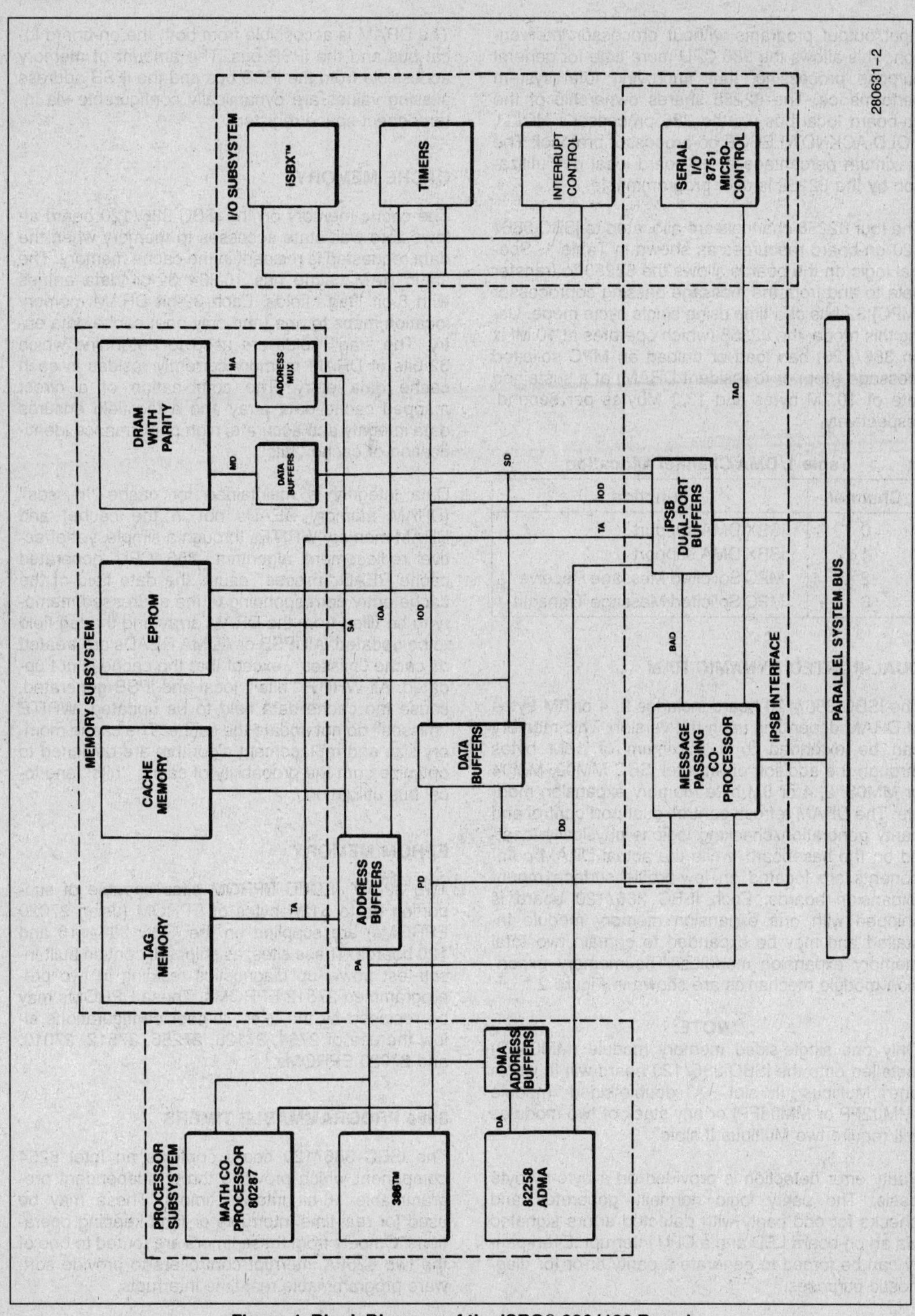

Figure 1. Block Diagram of the iSBC® 386/120 Board

input/output programs without processor intervention. This allows the 386 CPU more time for general purpose processing, thus improving total system performance. The 82258 shares ownership of the on-board local bus via the 386 processor's HOLD, HOLD ACKNOWLEDGE co-processor protocol. The maximum percentage of on-board local bus utilization by the 82258 is user programmable.

The four 82258 channels are allocated to iSBC 386/120 on-board resources as shown in Table 1. Special logic on the boards allows the 82258 to transfer data to and from the message passing coprocessor (MPC) 32-bits at a time using single cycle mode. Using this mode, the 82258 (which operates at 10 MHz on 386/120) can load or unload an MPC solicited message (from or to resident DRAM) at a sustained rate of 10.7M bytes and 13.3 Mbytes per second, respectively.

Table 1. DMA Channel Allocation

Channel	Function
0	iSBX DMA support
1	iSBX DMA support
2	MPC Solicited Message Receive
3	MPC Solicited Message Transmit

DUAL-PORTED DYNAMIC RAM

The iSBC 386/120 board includes 2, 4 or 8M bytes of DRAM depending upon the version. This memory can be extended to a maximum of 16M bytes through the addition of an Intel iSBC MM02, MM04 or MM08: 2, 4 or 8M byte memory expansion module. The DRAM refresh control, dual-port control and parity generation/checking logic is physically located on the baseboard, while the actual DRAM components are located on low-profile surface mount expansion boards. Each iSBC 386/120 board is shipped with one expansion memory module installed and may be expanded to contain two total memory expansion modules. The memory expansion module mechanics are shown in Figure 2.*

***NOTE:**
Only one single-sided memory module (MM04FP) installed onto the iSBC 386/120 board will fit within one Multibus II slot. A double-sided module (MM02FP or MM08FP) or any stack of two modules will require two Multibus II slots.

Parity error detection is provided on a byte-by-byte basis. The parity logic normally generates and checks for odd parity with detected errors signaled via an on-board LED and a CPU interrupt. Even parity can be forced to generate a parity error for diagnostic purposes.

The DRAM is accessible from both the on-board local bus and the iPSB bus. The amount of memory accessible from the iPSB bus and the iPSB address aliasing values are dynamically configurable via interconnect space registers.

CACHE MEMORY

The cache memory on the iSBC 386/120 board allows zero wait-state accesses to memory when the data requested is resident in the cache memory. The static RAM cache has 16,384 32-bit data entries with 8-bit "tag" fields. Each 32-bit DRAM memory location maps to one (and only one) cache data entry. The "tag" fields are used to determine which 32-bits of DRAM memory currently resides in each cache data entry. The combination of a direct mapped cache data array and a tag field ensures data integrity and accurate, high performance identification of cache "hits".

Data integrity is maintained for cache "misses" (DRAM memory READs not in the cache) and DRAM memory WRITEs through a simple, yet effective replacement algorithm. 386 CPU generated cache READ "misses" cause the data field of the cache entry corresponding to the addressed memory to be filled from the DRAM array and the tag field to be updated. All iPSB or ADMA READs are treated as cache "misses", except that the cache is not updated. All WRITE "hits", local and iPSB generated, cause the cache data field to be updated. WRITE "misses" do not update the cache. The cache memory size and replacement algorithm are designed to optimize both the probability of cache "hits" and local bus utilization.

EPROM MEMORY

Two 32-pin JEDEC EPROM sites capable of supporting up to 512K bytes of EPROM (using 27020 EPROMs) are supplied on the iSBC 386/116 and 120 boards. These sites, as shipped, contain built-in-self-test power-up diagnostics residing in two pre-programmed 27512 EPROMs. These EPROMs may be replaced by the user. Jumper configurations allow the use of 2764, 27128, 27256, 27512, 27010, and 27020 EPROMs.

8254 PROGRAMMABLE TIMERS

The iSBC 386/120 board contains an Intel 8254 component which provides three independent programmable 16-bit interval timers. These may be used for real-time interrupts or time keeping operations. Outputs from these timers are routed to one of the two 8259A interrupt controllers to provide software programmable real-time interrupts.

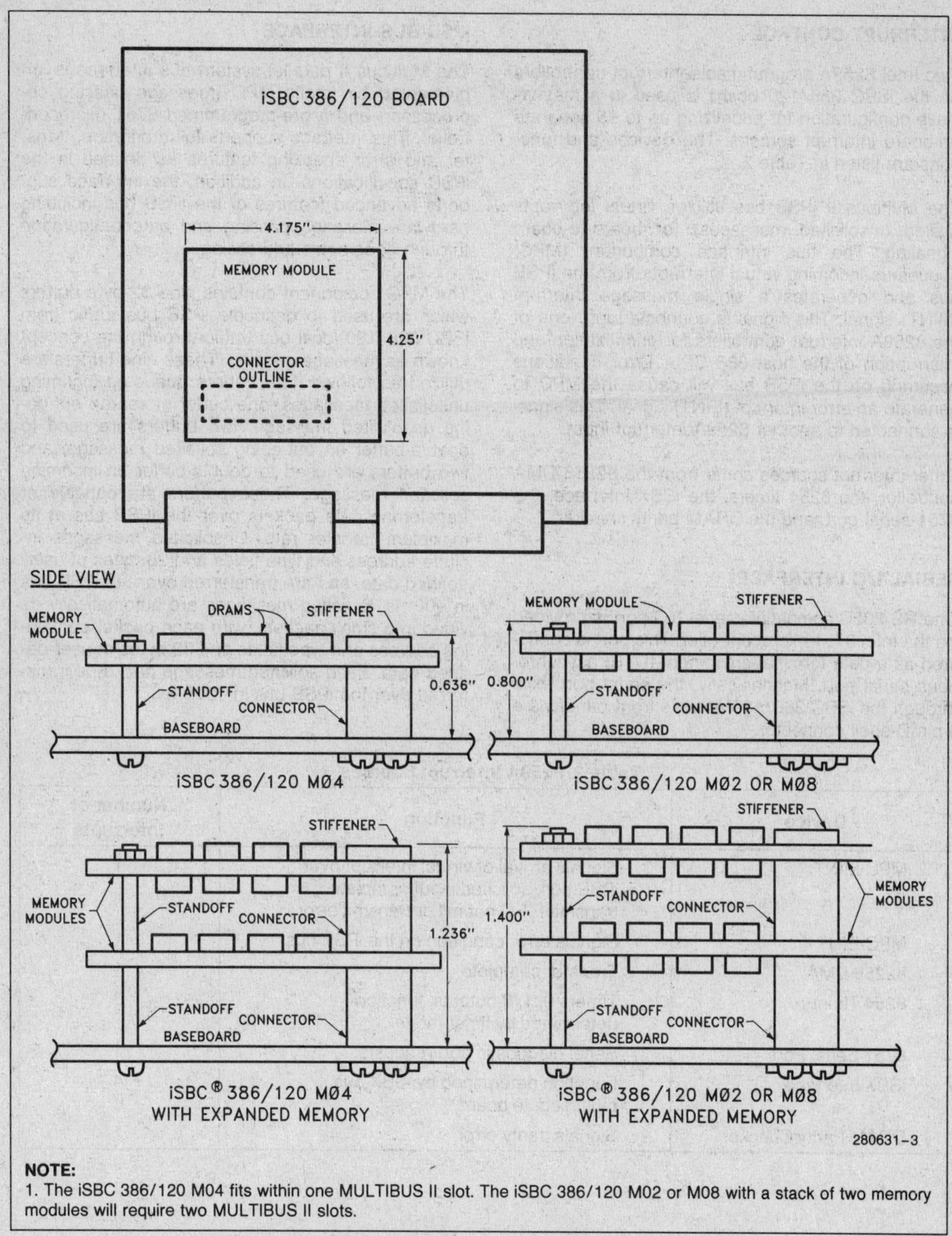

NOTE:
1. The iSBC 386/120 M04 fits within one MULTIBUS II slot. The iSBC 386/120 M02 or M08 with a stack of two memory modules will require two MULTIBUS II slots.

Figure 2. iSBC® 386/120 Board Memory Module Mechanics

INTERRUPT CONTROL

Two Intel 8259A programmable interrupt controllers on the iSBC 386/120 board is used in a master-slave configuration for prioritizing up to 15 separate on-board interrupt sources. The devices and functions are listed in Table 2.

The Multibus II iPSB bus utilizes virtual interrupts (called unsolicited messages) for board-to-board signaling. The bus interface component (MPC) queues-up incoming virtual interrupts from the iPSB bus and generates a single message interrupt (MINT) signal. This signal is connected into one of the 8259A interrupt controllers for prioritization and interruption of the host 386 CPU. Error conditions occurring on the iPSB bus will cause the MPC to generate an error interrupt (EINT) signal. This signal is connected to another 8259A interrupt input.

Other interrupt sources come from the 82258 DMA controller, the 8254 timers, the iSBX interface, the 8751 serial port, and the DRAM parity checker.

SERIAL I/O INTERFACE

One RS 232C compatible serial I/O port is provided via the Intel 8751 microcontroller. This port is configured as a data terminal equipment (DTE) asynchronous serial port. Mechanically, the serial port exits through the iSBC 386/120 board's front panel via a 9-pin D-shell connector.

iPSB BUS INTERFACE

The Multibus II parallel system bus interface is implemented by Intel's MPC (message passing coprocessor) and a pre-programmed 8751 microcontroller. This interface supports full arbitration, transfer and error checking features as defined in the iPSB specifications. In addition, the interface supports advanced features of the iPSB bus including hardware message passing and autoconfiguration through geographic addressing.

The MPC component contains nine 32-byte buffers which are used to decouple iPSB bus traffic from iSBC 386/120 local bus traffic through the concept known as message passing. These nine buffers are utilized as follows: four buffers queue-up incoming unsolicited messages, one buffer stores an out-going unsolicited message, two buffers are used to double-buffer an out-going solicited message, and two buffers are used to double-buffer an incoming solicited message. These buffers are capable of transferring data packets over the iPSB bus at its maximum transfer rate. Unsolicited messages include address and type fields and 28 bytes of user-defined data, and are transferred over the iPSB bus in 900 ns. Solicited messages are automatically divided into small packets, with each packet containing address and type fields and 32 bytes of user-defined data. Each solicited message packet is transferred over the iPSB bus in 1000 ns.

Table 2. 8259A Interrupt Sources

Device	Function	Number of Interrupts
MPC-MINT	Signals arrival of virtual interrupt over iPSB bus, solicited input complete, transmit FIFO not full or transmit error	1
MPC-EINT	Signals error condition on the iPSB bus	1
82258 DMA	Transfer complete	1
8254 Timers	Timers 0, 1, 2 outputs, function determined by timer mode	3
8751 Serial Port	Serial diagnostic port requests	1
iSBX Interface	Function determined by iSBX bus multimodule board	4
DRAM Parity Checker	Signals parity error	1

The 8751 component implements the iPSB geographic addressing feature called Interconnect space. Read-only registers are used to hold information such as board type and revision level. Software configurable registers are used for auto-configurability, local or remote diagnostics and software controlled reset. In addition, the 386 CPU executes power-up built-in self tests of the various resources on the iSBC 386/120 board. The results of these tests are reported via registers in interconnect space. After successfully completing its BIST routines, the 386 CPU must clear the reset-not-complete register. If, after 30 seconds, the reset-not-complete has not been cleared, the 8751 resets the local bus and holds it in a reset state. In this way, only a few components on the iSBC 386/120 board must be functional to allow the iPSB bus to operate.

iSBX™ BUS INTERFACE

One iSBX connector, capable of supporting one single- or double-wide, 8- or 16-bit iSBX MULTIMODULE board, is provided on the iSBC 386/120 board for the addition of an optional I/O module. Two DMA channels from the 82258 can be used with iSBX modules which require DMA support.

SPECIFICATIONS

Word Size

Instruction — 8-, 16-, 24-, 32-, 40-bit

Data — 8-, 16-, 32-bit

Floating Point Data — 80-bit

Clock Rates

	386/120
386™ CPU	20 MHz
80387 Numeric Co-processor	20 MHz
82258 DMA	10 MHz

Dual-Port DRAM Memory

DEFAULT CAPACITY

iSBC 386/120 M02—2M byte

iSBC 386/120 M04—4M byte

iSBC 386/120 M08—8M byte

EXPANSION MODULES

iSBC MM02FP—2M byte

iSBC MM04FP—4M byte

iSBC MM08FP—8M byte

MAXIMUM CAPACITY—16M BYTES

EPROM Memory

Default — 128K byte using two pre-programmed 27512 EPROMs

Capacity — Two 24-, 28- or 32-pin JEDEC-compatible devices

EPROM	Memory Capacity
2764	16 KB
27128	32 KB
27256	64 KB
27512	128 KB
27010	256 KB
27020	512 KB

Timers

Capability — Three independently programmed 16-bit interval timers

Input Frequency — 1.25 MHz ±0.1%

Output Period — 1.6 μs to 52.4 ms

Interrupt Capability

Incoming Interrupts — 255 individual and 1 broadcast from iPSB bus 12 local sources (see Table 2)

Outgoing Interrupts — 255 individual and 1 broadcast to IPSB bus

Serial Port Interface

RS 232C Electrical
Asynchronous, DTE only
9-pin D-shell connector
Baud rates: 9600, 4800, 2400, 1200, 300, 110 bits/sec

iSBX Interface

Capability — One 8- or 16-bit, single- or double-wide iSBX module

Compliance Code — D16/16 DMA

iPSB Interface

Capability— Requesting and replying agent supporting 8-, 16-, 24- and 32-bit transfers, parity bit generation and checking, unsolicited and solicited message passing, and autoconfiguration through interconnect space.

Physical Dimensions

Length:	220 mm (8.6 in.)
Width:	233 mm (9.2 in.)
Front Panel Height:	19.2 mm (0.76 in.)

Power Requirements

5V:	11.14 Amps
12V:	0.046 Amps
−12V:	0.041 Amps
	Voltage tolerance ±5%

Temperature Range and Airflow Requirements

Storage Temperature:	−40°C to +70°C
Operating Temperature:	0°C to +55°C
Airflow:	200 LFM minimum

ORDERING INFORMATION

Part Number	Description
SBC386120M02	20 MHz 386 CPU-based Multibus II CPU board with 2M byte memory
SBC386120M04	20 MHz 386 CPU-based Multibus II CPU board with 4M byte memory
SBC386120M08	20 MHz 386 CPU-based Multibus II CPU board with 8M byte memory
SBCMM02FP	2M byte memory expansion module
SBCMM04FP	4M byte memory expansion module
SBCMM08FP	8M byte memory expansion module
451833	iSBC 386/120 Single Board Computer Users Guide

iSBC® 286/100A* Multibus II SINGLE BOARD COMPUTER

- **8 MHz 80286 Microprocessor with Optional 80287 Numeric Data Co-Processor**
- **Multibus II PSB (Parallel System Bus) Interface with Full Message Passing Capabilities and up to 4 Gigabytes of Memory Addressability on the Bus**
- **High-Speed Memory Expansion with Multibus II iLBX II (Local Bus Extension) Interface Addresses up to 16 MBytes of Local and/or Dual Port Memory**
- **Two iSBX Bus Interface Connectors for I/O Expansion Bus**
- **Four DMA Channels Supplied by the 82258 Advanced DMA Controller with 8 MBytes/sec Transfer Rate**
- **Multibus II Interconnect Space for Software Configurability and Self-Test Diagnostics**
- **Resident Firmware Supports Self-Test Power-Up Diagnostics and On-Command Extended Self-Test Diagnostics**
- **Two Programmable Serial Interfaces, one RS232C (DCE or DTE), the other RS232C or RE422A/RS449 Compatible**
- **Two 28-pin JEDEC Sites for up to 128 KBytes of Local Memory Using SRAM, NVRAM, EEPROM, and EPROM**
- **24 Programmable I/O Lines Configurable as SCSI Interface, Centronics Interface, or General Purpose I/O**

1

The iSBC 286/100A Single Board Computer is part of Intel's family of Multibus II CPU boards that utilizes the advanced features of the Multibus II System Architecture. It is ideally suited for a wide range of OEM applications. The combination of the 80286 CPU, the Message Passing Coprocessor (MPC), the Multibus II Parallel System Bus (PSB bus), and the Local Bus Extension (iLBX II bus) makes the iSBC 286/100A board suited for high performance, multiprocessing system applications in a multimaster environment. The board is a complete microcomputer system on a 220mm x 233mm (8.7 x 9.2 inch) Eurocard form factor with pin and socket DIN connectors.

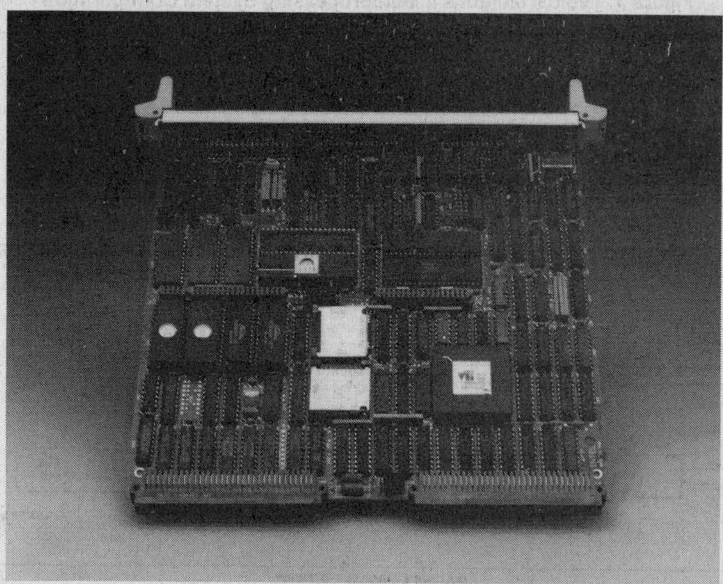

280076–1

*The iSBC® 286/100A is also manufactured under product code pSBC286100A by Intel Puerto Rico, Inc.

October 1990
Order Number: 280076-005

Overview

The iSBC 286/100A Single Board Computer combines the 80286 microprocessor with the Message Passing Component (MPC) on a single board within the Multibus II system architecture. This offers a message passing based high performance multiprocessing solution for system integrators and designers. Figure 1 shows a typical Multibus II multiprocessing system configuration. Overall system performance is enhanced by the Local Bus Extension (iLBX II) which allows 0 wait state high speed memory execution.

Architecture

All features of the Multibus II architecture are fully supported by the iSBC 286/100A board including the Parallel System Bus (PSB), interconnect space, Built-In-Self-Tests (BIST) diagnostics, and full message passing. These features are described in the following sections. In addition to taking advantage of the Multibus II system architecture, the iSBC 286/100A board has complete single board computer capability including two iSBX bus expansion connectors, 80287 numeric data coprocessor option, advanced DMA control, JEDEC memory sites, SCSI configurable parallel interface, serial I/O, and programmable timers. Figure 2 shows the iSBC 286/100A board block diagram.

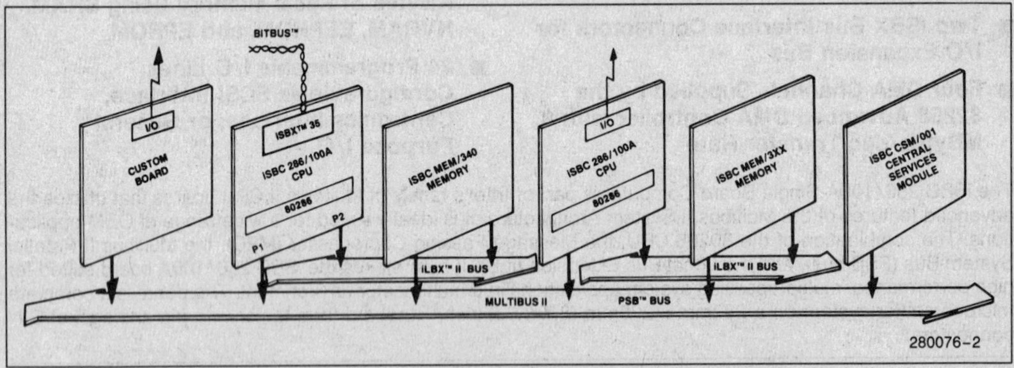

Figure 1. Typical Multibus II Multiprocessing System Configuration

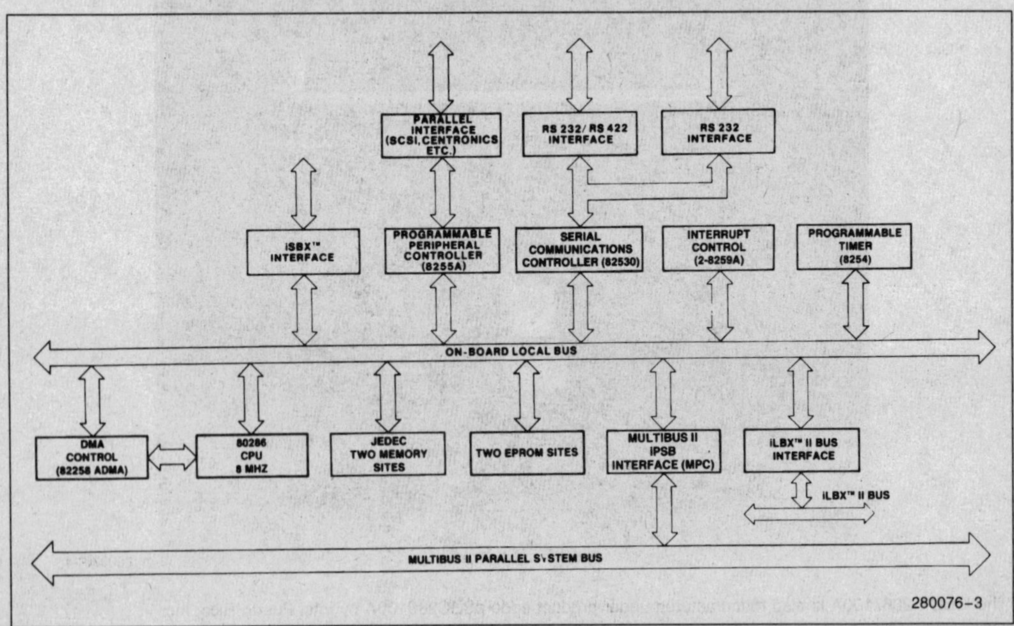

Figure 2. iSBC® 286/100A Board Block Diagram

Central Processing Unit

The central processing unit for the iSBC 286/100A board is the 80286 microprocessor operating at 8.0 MHz clock rate. The 80286 runs 8086 and 80186 code at substantially higher speeds (due to a parallel chip architecture) while maintaining software compatibility with Intel's 8086 and 80186 microprocessors. Numeric processing power may be enhanced with the 80287 numeric data coprocessor. The 80286 CPU operates in two modes: real address mode and protected virtual address mode. In real address mode, programs use real addressing with up to one megabyte of address space. In protected virtual address mode, the 80286 CPU automatically maps 1 gigabyte of virtual address per task into a 16 megabyte real address space. This mode also provides the hardware memory protection for the operating system. The operating mode is selected via CPU instructions.

PSB Bus Interface

The iSBC 286/100A board has a Message Passing Coprocessor (MPC) component on the base board that contains most of the logic required to operate the Parallel System Bus (PSB bus) interface. Some of the key functions provided by the MPC include bus arbitration, transfer control, parity generation and checking, and error detection and reporting.

Data transfers between processors via the PSB bus is defined in the Multibus II architecture through a transfer protocol, a reserved address space, and an information/data block. This interprocessor communication convention is known as message passing. Operations occurring within the reserved address space are called message space operations.

Message passing allows PSB bus agents to transfer variable amounts of data at rates approaching the maximum bandwidth of the bus. Message passing permits a sustained transfer rate of 2.2 Mbytes per second, and a single message may transfer up to 16 Mbytes from one agent to another. The MPC fully supports message space operations, executes PSB bus arbitration and executes the message passing protocol independent of the host CPU, leaving the host free to process other tasks.

The MPC supports both solicited and unsolicited message passing capability across the PSB. An unsolicited message can be thought of as an intelligent interrupt from the perspective of the receiving agent because the arrival of an unsolicited message is unpredictable. Attached to an unsolicited message is one of 255 possible source addresses along with 28 bytes of data attached to the message data field. A solicited message moves large blocks of data between agents on the PSB bus. The arrival of a solicited message is negotiated between the sending and receiving agents. Data is sent in "packets" with each packet containing four bytes of control information and up to 28 bytes of data. There is no specific limit to the number of packets that may be sent in a single message, but the total message may not transfer more than 16 Mbytes.

The iSBC 286/100A also includes a feature called the PSB window register that allows the user to selectively access under software control any 256K byte block of memory within the 4 Gigabytes of memory space on the PSB bus interface.

INTERCONNECT SPACE SUPPORT

Interconnect space is one of four Multibus II address spaces, the other three being memory space, I/O space, and message space. Interconnect space allows software to initialize, identify, configure, and diagnose the boards in a Multibus II system. The Interconnect template consists of 8-bit registers, organized into functional groups called records. There are three types of records, the header record, function records, and the End of Template record.

The header record provides board and vendor ID information, general status and control information, and diagnostic control. The function records allow the user to configure and/or read the iSBC 286/100A board's hardware configuration via software. The End of Template record identifies the end of the interconnect template.

BUILT IN SELF TEST (BIST) DIAGNOSTICS

Multibus II's Built in Self Test (BIST) diagnostics improve the reliability and error reporting and recovery capability of Multibus II boards. These confidence tests and diagnostics not only improve reliability but also reduce manufacturing and maintenance costs for the OEM user. The yellow BIST LED (LED 1) on the front panel provides a visual indication of the power-up diagnostics status.

Error Reporting and Recovery

The Multibus II Parallel System Bus and the iLBX II bus provides bus transmission and bus parity error detection signals. Error information is logged in the MPC and a bus error interrupt is generated. Information on the error source for reporting or recovery purposes is available to software through the iSBC 286/100A board interconnect space registers.

INTERRUPT CONTROL

In a Multibus II system, external interrupts (interrupts originating off the CPU board) are messages over the bus rather than signals on individual lines. Message based interrupts are handled by the MPC. Two on-board 8259A Programmable Interrupt Controllers (PICs) are used for processing on-board interrupts. One is used as the master and the other as the slave. Table 1 includes a list of devices and functions supported by interrupts.

iSBX® BUS MULTIMODULE™ ON-BOARD EXPANSION

Two iSBX bus MULTIMODULE connectors are provided, one 16- or 8-bit and the other 8-bit. Through these connectors additional on-board I/O functions may be added. The iSBX bus MULTIMODULE boards optimally support functions provided by VLSI peripheral components such as additional parallel and serial I/O, analog I/O, and graphics control. The iSBX bus connectors on the iSBC 286/100A board provides all signals necessary to interface to the local on-board bus including 16 data lines and DMA for maximum data transfer rates. MULTIMODULE boards designed with 8-bit data paths and using the 8-bit iSBX bus connectors are also supported. A broad range of iSBX bus MULTIMODULE options are available from Intel. Custom iSBX bus MULTIMODULE boards designed for Multibus or proprietary bus systems are also supported provided the IEEE P959 iSBX bus specification is followed.

NUMERIC DATA CO-PROCESSOR

The 80287 Numeric Data Co-Processor can be installed on the iSBC 286/100A board by the user. The 80287 Numeric Data Co-Processor is connected to dedicated processor signal lines which are pulled to their inactive state when the 80287 Numeric Data Co-Processor is not installed. This enables the user to detect via software that the 80287 socket is occupied. The 80287 Numeric Data Co-Processor runs asynchronously to the 80286 clock. The 80287 Numeric Data Co-Processor operates at 8 MHz and is driven by the 8284A clock generator.

Table 1. Interrupt Devices and Functions

Device	Function	Number of Interrupts
Multibus II Interface	Message-based Interrupt Request from the PSB Bus via 84120 Message Interrupt Controller	1 Interrupt from up to 256 sources
8751 Interconnect Controller	BIST Control Functions	1
82530 Serial Controller	Transmit Buffer Empty, Receive Buffer Full and Channel Errors	1 Interrupt from 10 Sources
8254 Timers	Timers 0, 1, 2 Outputs; Function Determined by Timer Mode	3
8255A Parallel I/O	Parallel Port Control	2
iLBX II Bus Interface	Indicates iLBX™ II Bus Error Condition	3
PSB Bus Interface	Indicates Transmission Error on PSB Bus	1
iSBX Bus Connector	Function Determined by iSBX Bus MULTIMODULE Board	2
Edge Sense Out	Converts Edge Triggered Interrupt to a Level	1
Bus Error	Indicates Last PSB Bus Operation Encountered an Error	1
Power-Fail	External/Power-Fail Interrupts	1

DMA CONTROL

Four DMA (Direct Memory Access) channels are supplied on the iSBC 286/100A board by the 82258. The 82258 is an advanced DMA controller designed especially for the 16-bit 80286 microprocessor. It has four DMA channels which can transfer data at rates up to 8 Megabytes per second (8 MHz clock) in an 80286 system. The large bandwidth allows the user to handle very fast data transfer or a large number of concurrent peripherals.

MEMORY CAPABILITIES

The local memory of the iSBC 286/100A board consists of two groups of byte-wide sites. The first group of two sites are reserved for EPROM or ROM and are used for the BIST power-up diagnostic firmware. The second group of two sites support JEDEC standard 28-pin devices.

PARALLEL PERIPHERAL INTERFACE

The iSBC 286/100A board includes a parallel peripheral interface that consists of three 8-bit parallel ports. As shipped, these ports are configured for general purpose I/O. Programmed PAL (Programmable Array Logic) devices and the octal transceiver 74LS640-1 are provided to make it easy to reconfigure the parallel interface to be compatible with the SCSI (Small Computer System Interconnect) peripheral interface. Alternatively, the parallel interface may be reconfigured as a Centronics compatible line printer by adding one PAL and reconfiguring jumpers. Both interfaces may use the 82258 DMA controllers for data transfers.

The SCSI interface allows multiple mass storage peripherals such as Winchester disk drives, floppy disk drives, and tape drives to be connected directly to the iSBC 286/100A board. A sample SCSI application is shown in Figure 3. The SCSI interface is compatible with SCSI controllers such as the Adaptek 4500, DTC 1410, Iomga Alpha 10, Shugart 1601 and 1610, Vermont Research 8403, and Xebec 1410.

The Centronics interface requires very little software overhead since a user-supplied PAL device is used to provide necessary handshake timing. Interrupts are generated for printer fault conditions and a DMA request is issued for every character.

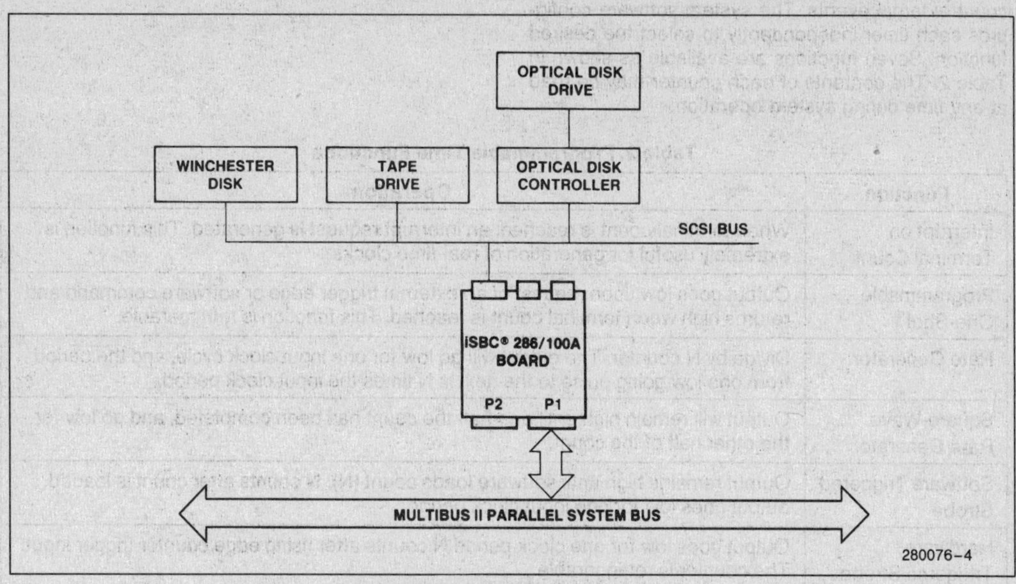

Figure 3. Sample SCSI Applications

SERIAL I/O

The 82530 Serial Communications Controller (SCC) is used to provide two channels of serial I/O. The SCC generates all baudrate clocks and provides loopback capability on both channels. Channel B is RS232C only and is configured as a DCE. Channel A is factory-default configured for DCE RS232C operation. Channel A may be reconfigured by the user for DTE or RS422 operation.

The 82258 ADMA can be programmed to support both channels A and B to perform movement of large bit streams or blocks of data.

PROGRAMMABLE TIMERS

The iSBC 286/100A board provides three independent, fully programmable 16-bit interval timers/event counters utilizing the Intel 8254 Programmable Interval Timer. Each counter is capable of operating in either BCD or binary modes. Three of these timers/counters are available to the system designer to generate accurate time intervals under software control. The outputs may be independently routed to the 8259A Programmable Interrupt Controller to count external events. The system software configures each timer independently to select the desired function. Seven functions are available as shown in Table 2. The contents of each counter may be read at any time during system operation.

SOFTWARE SUPPORT

The iRMX II Operating System software provides the ability to execute all configurable layers of the iRMX II software in the Multibus II environment. The iRMX II Operating System also supports all 80286 component applications.

For on-target Multibus II development, use the iSBX 218A or a SCSI controller and a floppy or Winchester drive, or port iRMX application software developed on the System 310, Series II/III, IV to Multibus II hardware.

Language support for the iSBC 286/100A boards real address mode includes Intel's ASM 86, PL/M 86, PASCAL and FORTRAN as well as many third party 8086 languages. Language support for virtual address mode operation includes ASM 286, PL/M 286, PASCAL and C. Programs developed in these languages can be down-loaded from the Development System to the iSBC 286/100A board via the iSDM 286 System Debug Monitor. The iSBX 218A can be used to load iRMX software developed on a System 310. The iSDM 286 monitor also provides on-target program debugging support including breakpoint and memory examination features.

Table 2. Programmable Time Functions

Function	Operation
Interrupt on Terminal Count	When terminal count is reached, an interrupt request is generated. This function is extremely useful for generation of real-time clocks.
Programmable One-Shot	Output goes low upon request of an external trigger edge or software command and returns high when terminal count is reached. This function is retriggerable.
Rate Generator	Divide by N counter. The output will go low for one input clock cycle, and the period from one low going pulse to the next is N times the input clock period.
Square-Wave Rate Generator	Output will remain high until one-half the count has been completed, and go low for the other half of the count.
Software Triggered Strobe	Output remains high until software loads count (N). N counts after count is loaded, output goes low for one input clock period.
Hardware Triggered Strobe	Output goes low for one clock period N counts after rising edge counter trigger input. The counter is retriggerable.
Event Counter	On a jumper selectable basis, the clock input becomes an input from the external system. CPU may read the number of events occurring after the counter "window" has been enabled or an interrupt may be generated after N events occur in the system.

The Multibus II Interconnect Space Registers allow the software to configure boards eliminating much of the need for jumpers and wire wraps. The iSDM 286 Monitor can initialize these registers at configuration time using user-defined variables. The monitor can also automatically configure memory boards, defining the addresses for each board sequentially in relation to the board's physical placement in the card cage. This feature allows for swapping, adding, and deleting of memory boards on a dynamic basis.

SPECIFICATIONS

WORD SIZE

Instruction— 8-, 16-, 24-, 32-, or 40-bits

Data — 8- or 16-bits

SYSTEM CLOCK

CPU — 8.0 MHz

Numeric Co-Processor— 8.0 MHz

CYCLE TIME

Basic Instruction: 8.0 MHz-375 ns; 250 ns (assumes instruction in queue)

NOTE:
Basic instruction cycle is defined as the fastest instruction time (i.e., two clock cycles)

Memory Capacity (Maximum)

EPROM: 2732, 8K bytes; 2764, 16K bytes; 27128, 32K bytes; 27256, 64K bytes; 27512, 128K bytes

EEPROM: 2817A, 4K bytes

RAM: 2186, 16K bytes

NOTE:
Two local sites must contain BIST or user-supplied boot-up EPROM.

I/O CAPABILITY

Parallel: SCSI, Centronics, or general purpose I/O

Serial: Two programmable channels using one 82530 Serial Communications Controller

Timers: Three programmable timers using one 8254 Programmable Interrupt Controller

Expansion: One 8/16-bit iSBX MULTIMODULE connector and one 8-bit iSBX MULTIMODULE connector

1

INTERRUPT CAPABILITY

Potential Interrupt Sources—255 individual and 1 broadcast

Interrupt Levels — 16 vectored requests using two 8259As and the 80286 NMI line

Serial Communications Characteristics

Asynchronous Modes:
- — 5–8-bit character; odd, even, or parity; 1, 1.5, or 2 stop bits
- — Independent transmit and receive clocks, 1X, 16X, 32X, or 64X programmable sampling rate
- — Error Detection: Framing, Overrun and Parity
- — Break detection and generation

Bit Synchronous Modes:
- — SDLC/HDLC flag generation and recognition
- — Automatic zero bit insertion bit and detection
- — Automatic CRC generation and detection (CRC 16 or CCITT)
- — Abort generation and detection
- — I-field residue handling
- — SDLC loop mode operation
- — CCITT X.25 compatible

Byte Synchronous Modes:
- — Internal or external character synchronization (1 or 2 characters)
- — Automatic CRC generation and checking (CRC 16 or CCITT)
- — IBM Bisync compatible

Common Baud Rates

Baud Rate	Synchronous (x1 Clock)	Asynchronous (x16 Clock)
	Time Constant	Time Constant
64 K	36	—
48 K	49	—
19.2 K	126	6
9600	254	14
4800	510	30
2400	1022	62
1800	1363	83
1200	2046	126
300	8190	510
110	—	1394

Timers

Input Frequencies: 1.23 MHz ±0.1% or 4 MHz ±0.1% (Jumper Selectable)

Output Frequencies/Timing Intervals

	Single Timer/Counter		Dual Timer/Counter (two timers cascaded)	
	Min	Max	Min	Max
Real-Time Interrupt	500 ns	53.1 ms	1.00 ms	57.9 min
Programmable One-Shot	500 ns	53.1 ms	1.00 ms	57.9 min
Rate Generator	18.8 Hz	2 MHz	0.000290 Hz	1 MHz
Square-Wave Rate Generator	18.8 Hz	2 MHz	0.000290 Hz	1 MHz
Software Triggered Strobe	500 ns	53.1 ms	1.00 ms	57.9 min
Hardware Triggered Strobe	500 ns	53.1 ms	1.00 ms	57.9 min
Event Counter	—	5.0 MHz	—	—

INTERFACES

PSB Bus: All signals TTL compatible

iLBX II Bus: All signals TTL compatible

iSBX Bus: All signals TTL compatible

SERIAL I/O

Channel A: RS232C/RS422 compatible, configurable as a data set or data terminal

Channel B: RS232C compatible, configured as a data set

Timer: All signals TTl compatible

Interrupt Requests: All signals TTL compatible

CONNECTORS

Location	Function	Part #
P1	PSB Bus	603-2-IEC-C096-F
P2	iLBX™ II Bus	603-2-IEC-C096-F

PHYSICAL DIMENSIONS

The iSBC 286/100A board meets all Multibus II mechanical specifications as represented in IEEE 1296 specification.

Double-High Eurocard Form Factor:

Depth: 220 mm (8.7 in.)
Height: 233 mm (9.2 in.)
Front Panel Width: 20 mm (0.784 in.)
Weight: 653 g (1 lb. 7 oz.)

ELECTRICAL CHARACTERISTICS

The maximum power required per voltage is shown below. These numbers do not include the power required by the optional memory devices, SCSI PALs, or expansion modules.

Voltage (volts)	Max/Typical Current (amps)	Max Power (watts)	BTU	Gram-Calorie
+5	10.31/8.25A	54.39W	3.13	774.2
+12	50/40 mA	630 mW	0.04	9.0
−12	46/37 mA	580 mW	0.03	8.3

ENVIRONMENTAL REQUIREMENTS

Temperature: (Inlet air) at 200 LFM airflow over boards
Non-operating— −40°C to +70°C
Operating—0 to +55°C

Humidity: Non-operating—95% RH @ 55°C
Operating—90% RH @ 55°C

1

REFERENCE MANUALS

iSBC 286/100A Single Board Manual Computer User's Guide (#149093)

Manual may be ordered from any Sales Representative, Distribution Office, or from the Intel Literature Department, 3065 Bowers Ave., Santa Clara, CA 95051

ORDERING INFORMATION

Order Code	Description
SBC286100A	Multibus II 80286 based Single Board Computer

iSBC® 186/100* MULTIBUS® II SINGLE BOARD COMPUTER

- **8.0 MHz 80186 Microprocessor with Optional High Speed 8087-1 Numeric Data Coprocessor**
- **Optional 82258 Advanced DMA Controller Providing Four Additional High Peformance DMA Channels**
- **On-Board 512K Bytes DRAM Configurable as Dual Port Memory**
- **MPC (Message Passing Coprocessor) Single Chip Interface to the Parallel System Bus with Full Message Passing Capability**
- **Four (Expandable to Eight) 28-Pin JEDEC Sites for PROM, EPROM, or EEPROM**
- **24 Programmable I/O Lines Configurable as SCSI Interface, Centronics Interface, or General Purpose I/O**
- **Two Programmable Serial Interfaces, One RS 232C and the Other RS 422A with Multidrop Capabilities**
- **Resident Firmware Supporting a Reset Operating System, a Program Table, and Build-In-Self-Test (BIST) Diagnostics Including Initialization and Power-Up Tests**
- **8- or 16-bit iSBX™ IEEE 959 Interface Connector with DMA Support for I/O Expansion**

The iSBC® 186/100 Single Board Computer is a member of Intel's family of microcomputer modules that utilizes the advanced features of the MULTIBUS® II system architecture. The 80186-based CPU board takes advantage of VLSI technology to provide economical, off-the-shelf, computer based solutions for OEM applications. All features of the iSBC 186/100 board, including the single chip bus interface (message passing coprocessor), reside on a 220mm x 233mm (8.7 inches x 9.2 inches) Eurocard printed circuit board and provide a complete microcomputer system. The iSBC 186/100 board takes full advantage of the MULTIBUS II bus architecture and can provide a high performance single CPU system or a powerful element for a highly integrated multi-processing application.

280263–1

*The iSBC® 186/100 is also manufactured under product code pSBC 186/100 by Intel Puerto Rico, Inc.

August 1990
Order Number: 280263-002

FUNCTIONAL DESCRIPTION

Overview

The iSBC 186/100 MULTIBUS II Single Board Computer utilizes the 8 MHz 80186 microprocessor to provide a range of solutions for various low cost OEM and end-user applications. Intel's commitment to offering high performance at a cost effective level are evident in the design of the iSBC 186/100 Single Board Computer. The integration of the functions of a general purpose system (CPU, memory, I/O and peripheral control) into a single board computer imply that the total system's board count, power and space requirements, and costs are reduced. Combining these cost advantages with the advanced features of the MULTIBUS II system architecture, the iSBC 186/100 board is ideal for price sensitive MULTIBUS II multi-processing or single CPU applications. Some of the advanced featues of the MULTIBUS II architecture embodied in the iSBC 186/100 board are distributed arbitration, virtual interrupt capabilities, message passing, iPSB bus parity, and software configurability and diagnostics using interconnect address space.

Architecture

The iSBC 186/100 CPU board supports the PSB bus features of interconnect address space, Built-In-Self-Test (BIST) diagnostics, solicited and unsolicited message passing, and memory and I/O references. In addition to supporting the PSB bus architecture, other functions traditionally found on Intel single board computers are included in the iSBC 186/100 board. These traditional capabilities include iSBX bus expansion; high speed 8087-1 numeric coprocessor; advanced DMA control; JEDEC memory site expansion; SCSI; Centronics; or general purpose configurable parallel I/O interface; serial I/O; and programmable timers on the 808186 microprocessor. Figure 1 shows the iSBC 186/100 board block diagram.

Central Processing Unit and DMA

The 80186 is an 8.0 MHz 16-bit microprocessor combining several common system components onto a single chip (i.e., two Direct Memory Access lines, three Interval Timers, Clock Generator, and Programmable Interrupt Controller). The 80186 instruction set is a superset of the 8086 and maintains object code compatiblity while adding additional instructions.

In the basic configuration, Direct Memory Access (DMA) requests are available between the local memory and the bus interface (see Table 1). With the addition of an Advanced DMA (ADMA) 82258 controller, ADMA requests may be generated by either the iSBX interface, the SCSI interface, the bus interface controller, or the serial interface (see Table 2). The addition of the ADMA controller also allows the serial ports to be used in a full-or half-duplex multidrop application.

An additional high performance 8087-1 Numeric Data Coprocessor may be installed by the user to significantly improve the iSBC 186/100 board's numerical processing power. Depending on the application, the high speed 8087-1 will increase the performance of floating point calculations by 50 to 100 times.

1

Table 1. Basic DMA Configuration

80186	Local Bus
DMA Channel 0	Output DMA iPSB Bus Interface
DMA Channel 1	Input DMA iPSB Bus Interface

Memory Subsystem

The 1M byte memory space of the 80186 is divided into three main sections. The first section is the 512K bytes of installed DRAM, the second section is the window into the global 4G bytes memory space of the PSB bus (PSB memory window address space) which starts at 512K bytes and goes up to either 640K bytes or 768K bytes, and the third section is designated for local ROM going from the ending address of the PSB memory window address space up to, if desired, 1M byte (see Figure 2).

The iSBC 186/100 board comes with 512K bytes of DRAM installed on the board. This memory can be used as either on-board RAM or Dual Port RAM by loading the start and end addresses into the appropriate interconnect registers. The lower boundary address to the PSB memory window may begin at any 64K byte boundary and the upper boundary address may end at any 64K byte boundary. Refer to the iSBC 186/100 Single Board Computer User's Guide for specific information on programming address spaces into interconnect registers.

The memory subsystem supports 128K bytes or 256K bytes access to the PSB memory address space. The PSB memory window base address is fixed at address 512K. The position of the window in the iPSB memory address space is programmable and thus allows the CPU to access the complete 4G byte memory address space of the MULTIBUS II PSB bus.

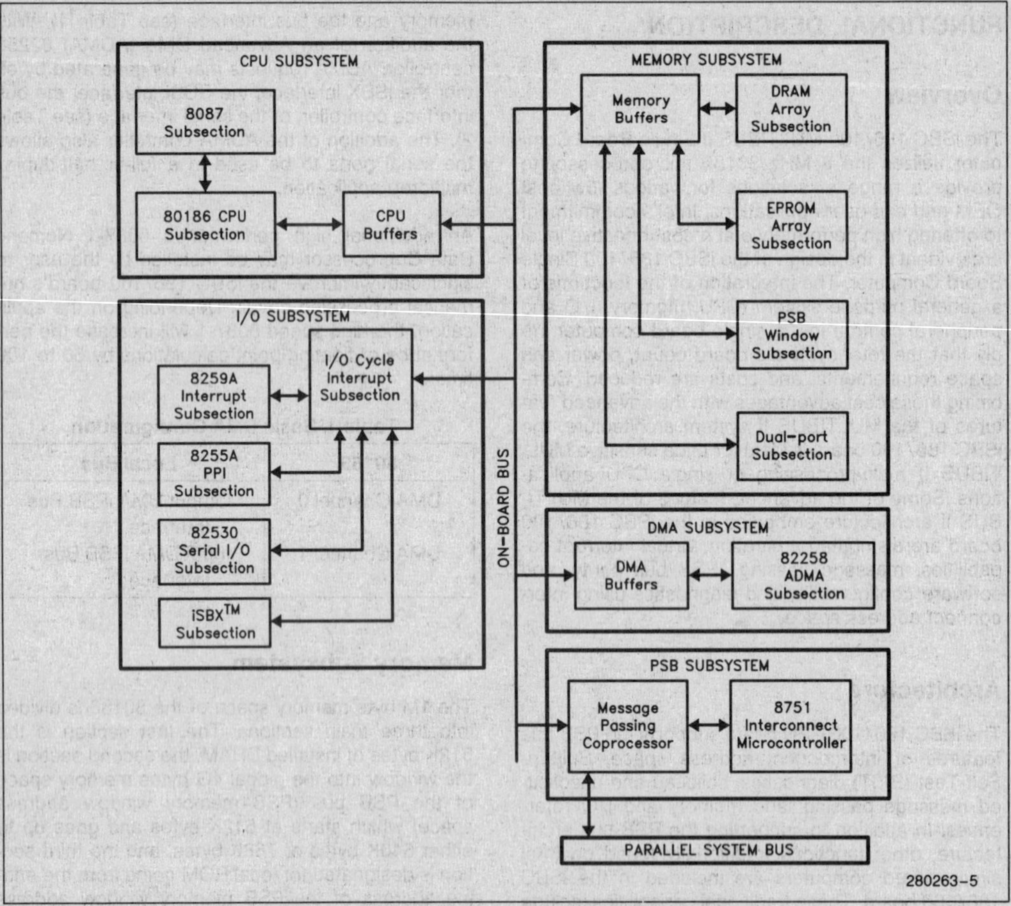

Figure 1. iSBC® 186/100 CPU Board Block Diagram

The ROM space consists of four 28-pin JEDEC sockets which take EPROMs, EEPROMs, or ROMs with 28-pin packages. An iSBC 341 28-pin MULTI-MODULE™ EPROM board can be plugged into 2 of the JEDEC sockets and provide up to 512K bytes of ROM memory. Device capacities, which are jumper selectable, are supported from 8K x 8 up to 64K x 8. Once the device capacity is selected, the capacity is uniform for all sockets.

I/O access from the iSBC 186/100 CPU board across the PSB bus is accomplished by mapping 64K bytes of local I/O access one to one to the PSB I/O address space. However, only the upper 32K bytes are available to access the PSB I/O address space because the lower 32K bytes on the iSBC 186/100 board are reserved for local on-board I/O.

On-Board Local Functions

PROGRAMMABLE TIMERS AND INTERRUPT CONTROL

The 80186 microprocessor on the iSBC 186/100 board provides three independent, fully programmable 16-bit interval timers/event counters. In conjunction, two 8259A Programmable Interrupt Controllers (PIC) on the iSBC 186/100 board are used in a master/slave configuration for processing on-board interrupts. At shipment, the 80186 interrupt controller and one PIC are connected as slaves to the master PIC. The first timer on the 80186 microprocessor is routed to the master Programmable Interrupt Controller and the second CPU timer is routed to the slave PIC. This architecture thus supports software

Table 2. DMA Configuration with ADMA Option

80186	Local Bus
DMA Channel 0 DMA Channel 1	Serial Channel B DMA Serial Channel B DMA or Parallel Port
ADMA 82258	
DMA Channel 0 DMA Channel 1 DMA Channel 2 DMA Channel 3	Input DMA Bus Interface Output DMA Bus Interface Half-duplex Fast Serial Interconnect 1 Channel A or Interrupt 1 from iSBX Bus if Used with an iSBC 341 EPROM MULTIMODULE Board Full-duplex Fast Serial Interconnect 1 Channel A or iSBX Bus DMA Channel if Used with an iSBC 341 EPROM MULTIMODULE board.

NOTE:
When a MULTIMODULE™ expansion board is installed and DMA support is required, then an ADMA controller must also be installed. For additional optional configurations see the *iSBC 186/100 Single Board Computer User's Guide.*

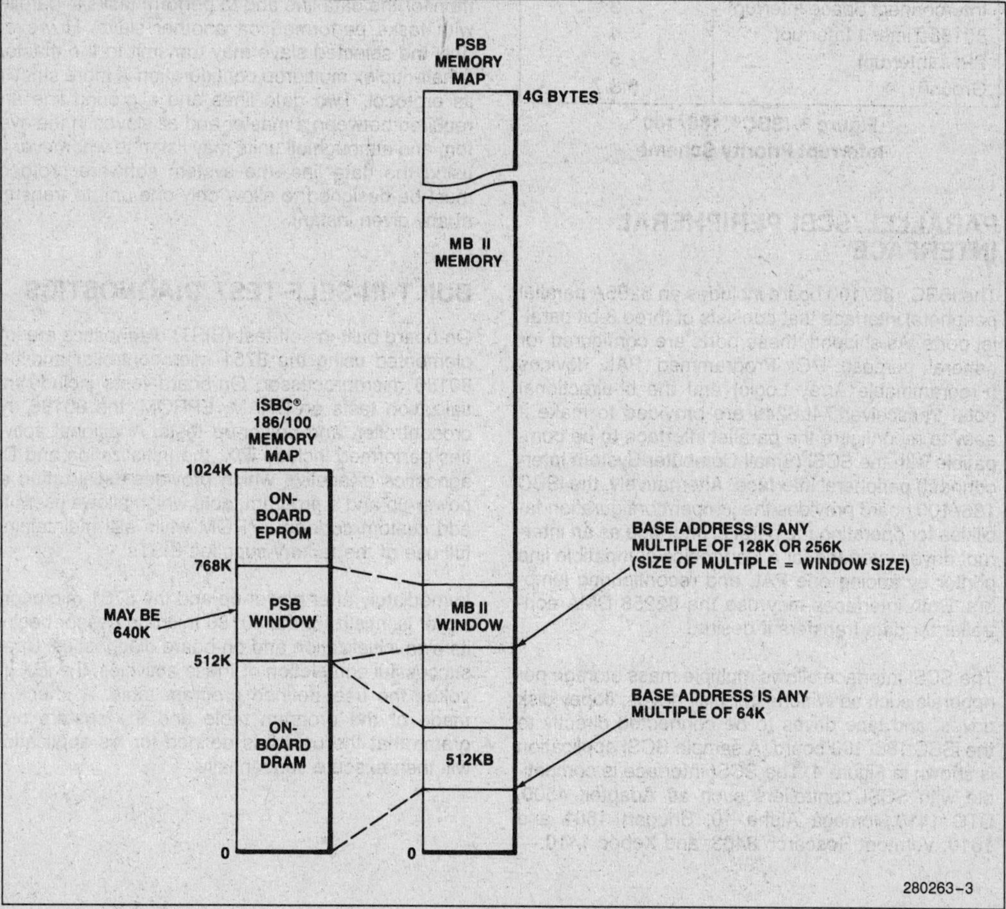

Figure 2. Memory Mapping Diagram

programmable timer interrupts. In addition, direct-vectored interrupt capability of the serial communication controller (SCC) may be used. Figure 3 depicts the interrupts in terms of their priorities.

Interrupt Services	Interrupt Priority
80186 Timer 0	Master Level 0
8087-1 Error Interrupt	1
Message Interrupt	2
iPSB Bus Error Interrupt	3
82530 SCC Interrupt	4
82258 ADMA Interrupt	5
80186 Slave PIC Interrupt	6
8259 Slave PIC Interrupt	7
PPI 0 Interrupt	Slave 0
iSBX Bus Interrupt 0	1
iSBX Bus Interrupt 1	2
Interconnect Space Interrupt	3
80186 Timer 1 Interrupt	4
PPI 1 Interrupt	5
Ground	6 & 7

Figure 3. iSBC® 186/100 Interrupt Priority Scheme

PARALLEL/SCSI PERIPHERAL INTERFACE

The iSBC 186/100 board includes an 8255A parallel peripheral interface that consists of three 8-bit parallel ports. As shipped, these ports are configured for general purpose I/O. Programmed PAL devices (Programmable Array Logic) and the bi-directional octal transceiver 74LS245 are provided to make it easy to reconfigure the parallel interface to be compatible with the SCSI (Small Computer System Interconnect) peripheral interface. Alternatively, the iSBC 186/100 board provides the jumper configuration facilities for operating the parallel interface as an interrupt driven interface for a Centronics compatible line printer by adding one PAL and reconfiguring jumpers. Both interfaces may use the 82258 DMA controller for data transfers if desired.

The SCSI interface allows multiple mass storage peripherals such as Winchester disk drives, floppy disk drives, and tape drives to be connected directly to the iSBC 186/100 board. A sample SCSI application is shown in Figure 4. The SCSI interface is compatible with SCSI controllers such as Adaptek 4500, DTC 1410, Iomega Alpha 10, Shugart 1601 and 1610, Vermont Research 8403, and Xebec 1410.

The Centronics interface requires very little software overhead since a user supplied PAL device is used to provide necessary handshake timing. Interrupts are generated for printer fault conditions and a DMA request is issued for every character.

SERIAL I/O LINES

The iSBC 186/100 board has one 82530 Serial Communciations Controller (SCC) to provide 2 channels of serial I/O. The SCC generates all baudrate clocks and provides loopback capability on both channels. Channel A is configured for RS 422A multidrop DTE application. Channel B is RS 232C only and is configured as DTE.

The multidrop configuration may either full-or half-duplex. A full-duplex multidrop configuration with a single master driving the output lines allow a slave to monitor the data line and to perform tasks in parallel with tasks performed on another slave. However, only the selected slave may transmit to the master. A half-duplex multidrop configuration is more strict in its protocol. Two data lines and a ground line are required between a master and all slaves in the system and although all units may listen to whomever is using the data line, the system software protocol must be designed to allow only one unit to transmit at any given instant.

BUILT-IN-SELF-TEST DIAGNOSTICS

On-board built-in-self-test (BIST) diagnostics are implemented using the 8751 microcontroller and the 80186 microprocessor. On-board tests include initialization tests on DRAM, EPROM, the 80186 microcontroller, and power-up tests. Additional activities performed include iDX, the Initialization and Diagnostics eXecutive which provides initialization at power-up and a program table which allows users to add custom code in EPROM while still maintaining full use of the factory supplied BISTs.

Immediately after power-up and the 8751 microcontroller is intialized, the 80186 microprocessor begins its own initialization and on-board diagnostics. Upon successful completion of these activities, the iDX invokes the user-defined program table. A check is made of the program table and the custom programs that the user has defined for his application will then execute sequentially.

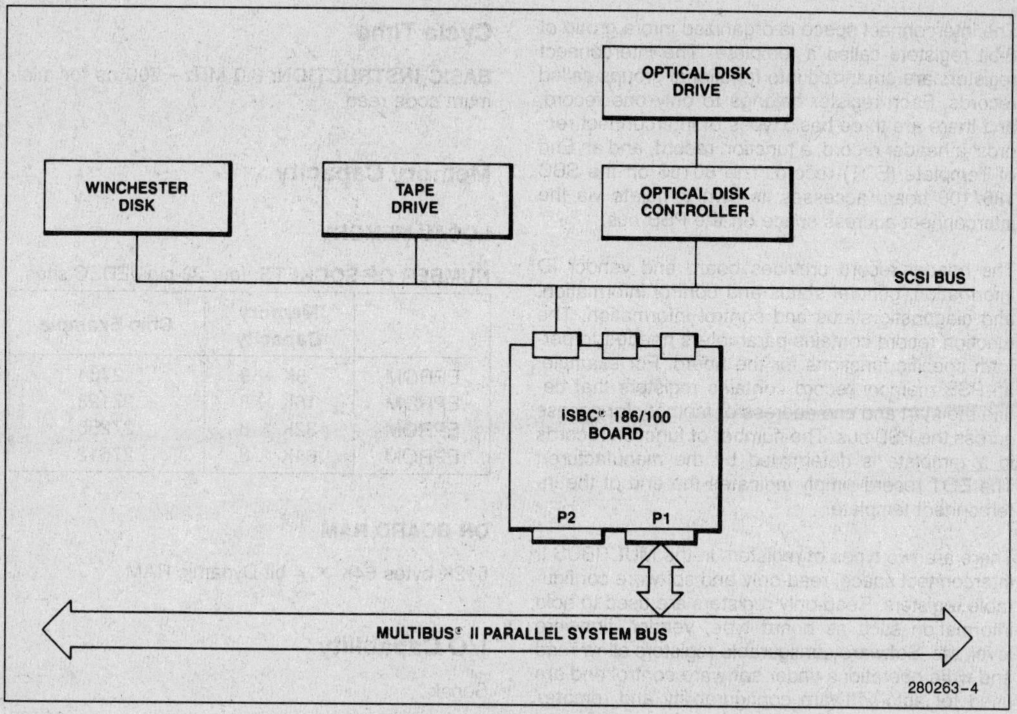

Figure 4. SCSI Application

BISTs improve the reliability, error reporting, and recovery capability of MULTIBUS II boards. In addition, these test and diagnostics reduce manufacturing and maintenance costs for the user. A yellow LED (labeled 'BIST') on the front panel indicates the status of the initialization checks and the power-up tests. It is illuminated if any of the initialization checks fail and remains off if the board successfully completes its tests. The LED also illuminates when the BIST tests start and stays on until the test complete successfully. The results of the BIST diagnostics are stored in the last 6 registers of the Header Record in Interconnect space.

iSBX™ BUS MULTIMODULE™ EXPANSION

One 8-or 16-bit iSBX bus MULTIMODULE connector is provided for I/O expansion. The iSBC 186/100 board supports both 8-bit and 16-bit iSBX modules through this connector. DMA is also supported to the iSBX connector and can be configured by programming the DMA multiplexor attached to the 82258 DMA component. The iSBX connector on the iSBC 186/100 board supports a wide variety of standard MULTIMODULE boards available from Intel and independent hardware vendors. Custom iSBX bus MULTIMODULE boards designed for MULTIBUS or proprietary bus systems are also supported as long as the IEEE 959 iSBX bus specification is followed.

PSB BUS INTERFACE SILICON

The MPC (message passing coprocessor) provides all necessary PSB bus interface logic on a single chip. Services provided by the MPC include memory and I/O access to the PSB by the 80186 processor, bus arbitration, exception cycle protocols, and transfers as well as full message passing support. Dual port architecture may be implemented using the message passing coprocessor.

Interconnect Subsystem

The interconnect subsystem is one of the four MULTIBUS II address spaces, the other three being memory space, I/O space, and message space. The purpose of interconnect space is to allow software to initialize, identify, configure, and diagnose the boards in a MULTIBUS II system. All Intel MULTIBUS II boards support interconnect space.

The interconnect space is organized into a group of 8-bit registers called a template. The interconnect registers are organized into functional groups called records. Each register belongs to only one record, and there are three basic types of interconnect records: a header record, a function record, and an End of Template (EOT) record. The 80186 on the SBC 186/100 board accesses its own template via the interconnect address space on the PSB bus.

The header record provides board and vendor ID information, general status and control information, and diagnostic status and control information. The function record contains parameters needed to perform specific functions for the board. For example, an PSB memory record contains registers that define the start and end address of memory for access across the PSB bus. The number of function records in a template is determined by the manufacturer. The EOT record simply indicates the end of the interconnect template.

There are two types of registers in the MULTIBUS II interconnect space, read-only and software configurable registers. Read-only registers are used to hold information such as board type, vendor, firmware level, etc. Software configurable registers allow read and write operations under software control and are used for auto-software configurability and remote/local diagnostics and testing. Software can be used to dynamically change bus memory sizes, disable or enable on-board resources such as PROM or JEDEC sites, read if an iSBX Board or PROM are installed as well as access the results of Built-In-Self-Tests or user installed diagnostics. Some of the interconnect registers on the iSBC 186/100 board perform functions traditionally done by jumper stakes. Interconnect space support is implemented with the 8751 microcontroller and iPSB bus interface logic.

SPECIFICATIONS

Word Size

INSTRUCTION: 8-, 16-, 24-, 32-, or 40-bits

DATA: 8-or 16-bits

System Clock

CPU: 8.0 MHz

NUMERIC COPROCESSOR: 8.0 MHz (part number 8087-1)

Cycle Time

BASIC INSTRUCTION: 8.0 MHz - 500 ns for minimum code read

Memory Capacity

LOCAL MEMORY

NUMBER OF SOCKETS: four 28-pin JEDEC sites

	Memory Capacity	Chip Example
EPROM	8K × 8	2764
EPROM	16K × 8	27128
EPROM	32K × 8	27256
EPROM	64K × 8	27512

ON-BOARD RAM

512K bytes 64K × 4 bit Dynamic RAM

I/O Capability

Serial:

— Two programmable channels using one 82530 Serial Communications Controller

— 19.2K baud rate maximum in full duplex in asynchronous mode or 1 megabit per second in full duplex in synchronous mode

— Channel A: RS 422A with DTE multidrop capability

— Channel B: RS 232C compatible, configured as DTE

— Parallel: SCSI, Centronics, or general purpose I/O

— Expansion: One 8-or 16-bit IEEE 959 iSBX MULTIMODULE board connector supporting DMA

Serial Communications Characteristics

ASYNCHRONOUS MODES:

- 19.2K baud rate maximum in full duplex
- 5-8-bit character; odd, even, or parity; 1, 1.5, or 2 stops bits
- Independent transmit and receive clocks, 1X, 16X, 32X, or 64X programmable sampling rate
- Error detection: Framing, Overrun, and Parity
- Break detection and generation

BIT SYNCHRONOUS MODES:

- 1 megabit per second maximum in full duplex
- SDLC/HDLC flag generation and recognition
- Automatic zero bit insertion and detection
- Automatic CRC generation and detection (CRC 16 or CCITT)
- Abort generation and detection
- I-field residue handling
- SDLC loop mode operation
- CCITT X.25 compatible

BYTE SYNCHRONOUS MODES:

- Internal or external character synchronization (1 or 2 characters)
- Automatic CRC generation and checking (CRC 16 or CCITT)
- IBM Bisync compatible

Timers

Three programmable timers on the 80186 microprocessor

INPUT FREQUENCIES:

Frequencies supplied by the internal 80186 16 MHz crystal

Serial chips: crystal driver at 9.8304 MHz divide by two

iSBX connector: 9.8304 crystal driven at 9.8304 MHz

Interrupt Capacity

POTENTIAL INTERRUPT SOURCES:

255 individual and 1 broadcast

INTERRUPT LEVELS:

12 vectored requests using two 8259As, 3 grounded inputs, and 1 input to the master PIC from the slave PIC

INTERRUPT REQUESTS:

All signals TTL compatible

Interfaces

PSB BUS:

As per IEEE/ANSI 1296 MULTIBUS II bus architecture specification

iSBX BUS:

As per IEEE 959 specification

CONNECTORS

Location	Function	Part #
P1	PSB Bus	603-2-IEC-C096-F

Physical Dimensions

The iSBC 186/100 board meets all MULTIBUS II mechanical specifications as presented in the MULTIBUS II specification (#146077)

DOUBLE-HIGH EUROCARD FORM FACTOR:

Depth: 220 mm (8.7 in.)

Height: 233 mm (9.2 in.)

Front Panel Width: 20 mm (0.784 in.)

Weight: 743 g (26 oz.)

Environmental Requirements

Temperature: Inlet air at 200 LFM airflow over all boards

Non-operating: −40° to +70°C

Operating: 0° to +55°C

Humidity: Non-operating: 95% RH @55°C, non-condensing

Operating: 90% RH @ 55°C, non-condensing

Electrical Characteristics

The maximum power required per voltage is shown below. These numbers do not include the power required by the optional memory devices, SCSI PALs, or expansion modules.

Voltage (Volts)	Max Current (Amps)	Max Power (Watts)
+5	6.5 mA	34.13W
+12	50 mA	0.06W
−12	50 mA	0.06W

Reference Manuals

iSBC 186/100 Single Board Computer User's Guide (#148732)

Manuals may be ordered from any Sales Representative, Distribution Office, or from the Intel Literature Department, 3065 Bowers Avenue, Santa Clara, CA, 95051.

ORDERING INFORMATION

Part Number	Description
SBC186100	MULTIBUS II 80186-based Single Board Computer

THE MULTIBUS II PC SUBSYSTEM

280673-1

PC AT COMPATIBILITY COMES TO MULTIBUS II SYSTEMS*

The Intel Multibus II PC Subsystem combines the power of the 386™ microprocessor, the multi-processing capabilities of the Multibus II architecture and the large base of DOS compatible software into a high performance IBM PC AT* compatible two board set. When used with a standard PC AT compatible keyboard and VGA compatible monitor this subsystem provides an excellent foundation for a human interface with color graphics for Multibus II systems. Running off-the-shelf software packages it is suitable for data acquisition or process monitoring applications, and can be easily customized using a variety of available PC compatible products.

FEATURES

CPU BOARD

- Fully IBM PC AT compatible subsystem running at 16 MHz 386 32-bit CPU.
- Includes socket for Intel 80387 or Weitek numeric co-processor chip, 64 K of high speed SRAM cache, 2 serial ports, 1 parallel port, keyboard and floppy drive controllers.
- Completely Multibus II systems architecture compatible including ADMA, MPC and 8751 interconnect controller.

PERIPHERAL COMPANION BOARD

- ST-506/ST-412 compatible Hard Disk Controller

Adapter board allows standard PC add-on cards to be used.**

*UNIX is a trademark of AT&T.
*PC-DOS, PC XT, and PC AT are trademarks of International Business Machines.
*MS-DOS is a trademark of Microsoft.
*Hercules is a trademark of Hercules Computer Technology, Inc.

September 1991
Order Number: 280673-002

FEATURES

- VGA graphics controller, with VGA, CGA, EGA, and mono-graphics software compatibility
- Built-in CSM functionality

PART OF THE MULTIBUS II FAMILY

Now PC AT* compatibility has come to a Multibus II CPU. The Multibus II Parallel System Bus is the bus of choice for Real Time multiprocessing. Its advanced bus architecture includes such features as a high speed (32 Mbytes/sec) Parallel Systems Bus (PSB) with message passing and bus parity detection, virtual interrupts, simplified systems configuration through interconnect space, and extensive power-up testing. Now our Multibus II family is even more complete with DOS complementing iRMX®, iRMK™, and UNIX* operating systems, and bringing with it a complete human interface including keyboard controller and VGA graphics.

386™ MICROPROCESSOR SPEED AND PERFORMANCE

The iSBC® 386/PC16 CPU board features a 386™ CPU running at 16 MHz and 64 K of 0 wait state (read hit) cache memory for 32-bit speed and performance. Performance can be even further enhanced by adding an Intel 80387 or Weitek math co-processor in the provided socket.

As much as 16 Mbyte of DRAM can be provided on-board using memory expansion modules. For full IBM PC AT software compatibility the iSBC 386/PC16 comes with an Award BIOS and runs either PC-DOS* or MS-DOS*. As a 386™ microprocessor-based PC platform, UNIX V/386 can also be easily ported to this board.

FULL COMPLEMENT OF PC PERIPHERALS

To minimize the need for add-in cards, the iSBC 386/PC16 CPU board includes 2 serial ports, 1 Centronics compatible parallel port, keyboard controller, and floppy disk controller.

The iSBC PCSYS/100 Peripheral Companion Board adds to that a hard disk controller, and a VGA graphics controller which is software compatible with EGA, CGA, and Hercules* monochrome graphics modes. In addition, it provides built-in Multibus II Central Services Module Functionality.

INTEGRATES EASILY INTO A MULTIBUS II SYSTEM

The iSBC 386/PC16 PCU board was designed to integrate easily into a Multibus II system. Hardware support includes the Multibus II Message Passing Coprocessor (MPC), 8751 interconnect space controller, and 82258 ADMA controller to provide full message passing support. It can also access global memory and I/O on the Parallel Systems Bus.

Conforming to the Multibus II Systems Architecture (MSA) the SBC 386/PC16 includes firmware support for BISTs (Built-In Self Tests), IDX (Initialization and Diagnostics eXecutive), and DOS Multibus II Transport Protocol. The DOS Transport Call Library, available as part of the PC16SWUTILS software package, allows user implementation of communication and data sharing with other Multibus II CPUs and peripherals.

BACKPLANES AND ADAPTOR BOARD

Rounding out the complement of products in the Intel Multibus II PC Subsystem family are 2 and 4 slot backplanes for the P2/aPC bus (the PC bus brought out on the Multibus II P2 connector) and an Adaptor Board. Intended for development purposes, the iSBC PCSYS/900 Adaptor Board plugs into a Multibus II card cage or chassis and accommodates up to four "half size' PC XT* add-on cards or two "half size" PC XT and either two PC AT "full size" or two PC XT "full size" add-on boards.

WORLD WIDE SERVICE AND SUPPORT

Should this or any Intel board ever need service, Intel maintains a world wide network of service and repair facilities to keep you and your customers up and running. In addition, should you need system level design support, our international Systems Engineering organization is available to integrate Intel boards and systems components into your products.

FEATURES

CONFIGURATION GUIDE

A Multibus II PC Subsystem can consist of a CPU board, and one or more optional boards connected together by a P2 backplane. The appropriate backplane to order can be found by finding the CPU board to be used in the left hand column and moving right to the column containing the optional board or boards in your system.

	None*	iSBCPCSYS100 Only	iSBCPCSYS900 Only	iSCPCSYS100 & iSBCPCSYS900
iSBC386PC16F01	iSBCPCSYS602	iSBCPCSYS602	iSBCPCSYS602	iSBCPCSYS604
iSBC386PC16F02	iSBCPCSYS602	iSBCPCSYS602	iSBCPCSYS604	iSBCPCSYS604
iSBC386PC16F04	iSBCPCSYS602	iSBCPCSYS602	iSBCPCSYS602	iSBCPCSYS604
iSBC386PC16F08	iSBCPCSYS602	iSBCPCSYS602	iSBCPCSYS604	iSBCPCSYS604
Any iSBC386PC16 with a stacked MM0xFP	iSBCPCSYS602	iSBCPCSYS602	iSBCPCSYS604	iSBCPCSYS604

*A backplane is not required, but provides a connector for the floppy drive cable.

1

BLOCK DIAGRAMS

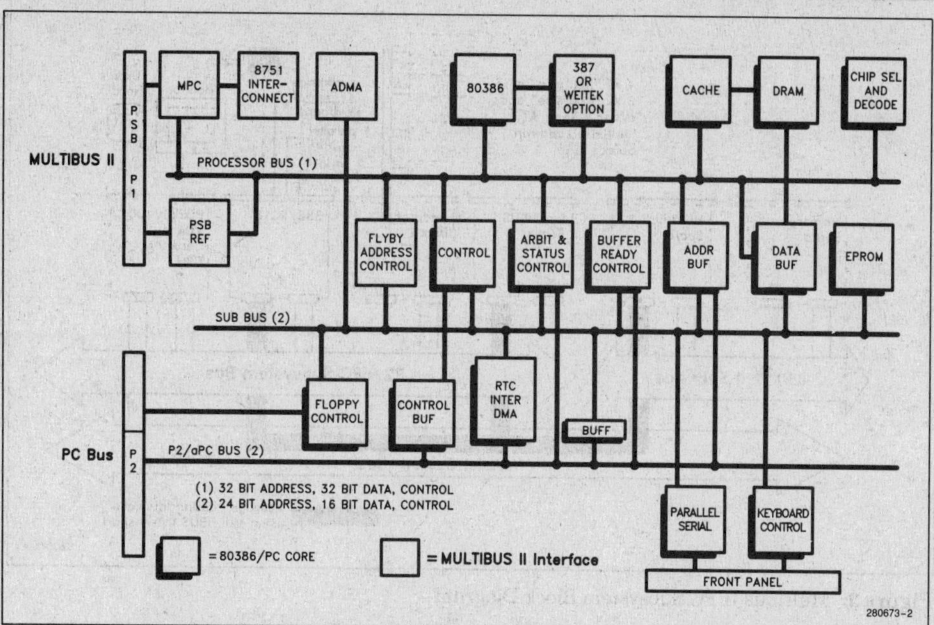

Figure 1: iSBC® 386/PC16 Functional Block Diagram

BLOCK DIAGRAMS

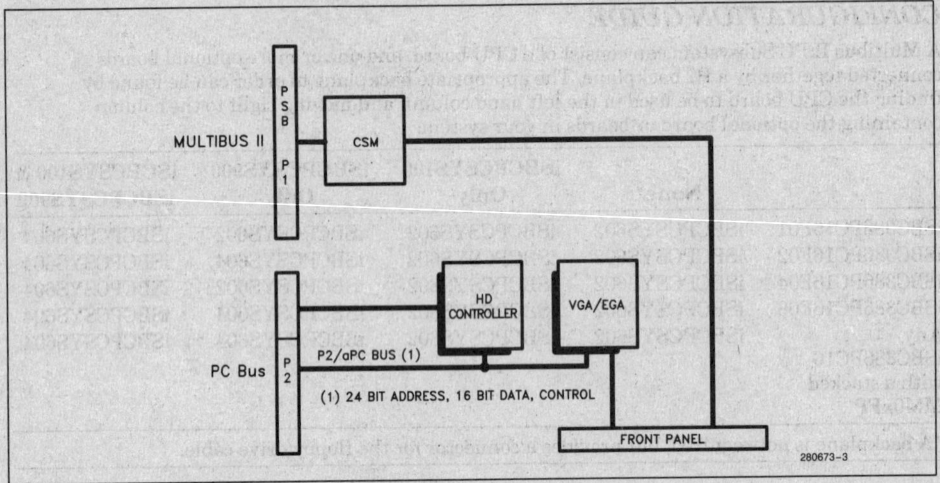

Figure 2: iSBC PCSYS/100 Functional Block Diagram

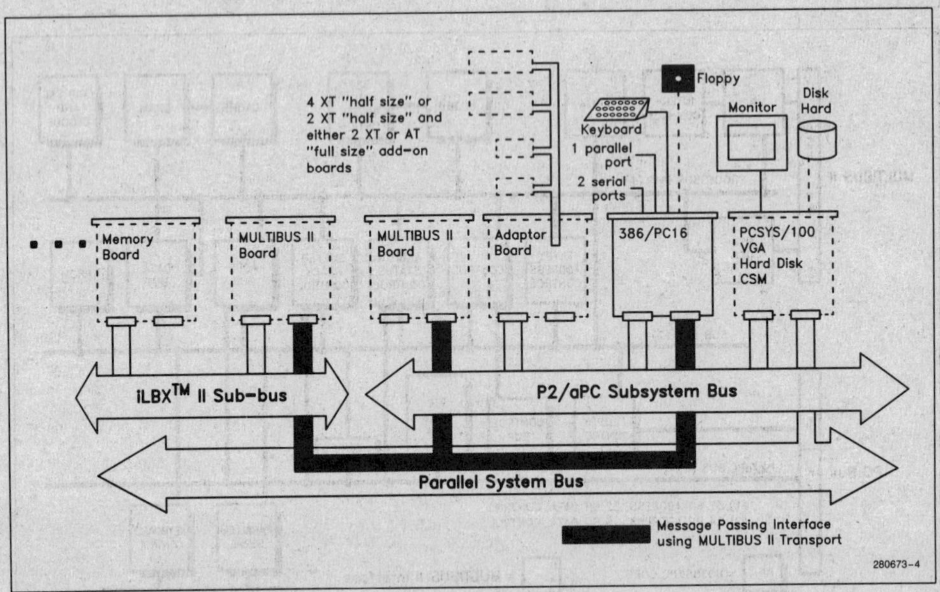

Figure 3: Multibus II PC Subsystem Block Diagram

SPECIFICATIONS

CPU BOARD—SBC 386/PC16

CPU

386™ microprocessor running at 16 MHz

DRAM Memory

32-bit parity protected memory:

Model	*Supplies*
SBC 386PC16 F01	1 Mb
SBC 386PC16 F02	2 Mb
SBC 386PC16 F04	4 Mb
SBC 386PC16 F08	8 Mb

Note: Model suffixes F02 and F08 require two Multibus II card slots, Model suffixes F01 and F04 require only one Multibus II card slot.

Memory expansion modules—one may be added to base models above

Model	*Supplies*
SBC MM01 FP	1 MB
SBC MM02 FP	2 MB
SBC MM04 FP	4 MB
SBC MM08 FP	8 MB

SRAM Cache

Capacity: 64K

Speed: 0 wait state on read hit
2 wait states on write
3 wait states on read miss

EPROM Memory

Two 32-pin JEDEC sites containing 256 K of EPROM memory with Awards BIOS and MSA firmware.

Two additional 32-pin JEDEC sites provided for user EPROM or EEPROM memory. Circuitry is provided to write as well as read EEPROM memory.

PERIPHERAL COMPANION BOARD—SBC PCSYS/100

Hard Disk Controller

- PC AT Compatible Winchester Controller

Graphics

- Supports VGA, EGA, CGA, and Hercules Compatible graphics
- Four text mode resolutions: 40×125, 80×125, 132×125, 132×143
- Graphics Mode Resolution: maximum resolution is 800×1600 pixels in all modes—16 colors, 4 colors, and monochrome

CSM

- Assigns card slot and arbitration IDs at initialization
- Generates system clock for all agents on the PSB
- Provides system wide reset signals for power-up, warm reset, and power failure
- Detects bus timeouts
- Supports up to two ST-506/ST-412 drives

P2/aPC BACKPLANES—SBC PCSYS/602 AND SBC PCSYS/604

- Available in 2 and 4 slot versions

ADAPTOR BOARD—SBC PCSYS/900

- Accommodates up to four "half size" PC XT add-on cards or two "half size" PC XT and either two "full size" PC AT or two PC XT "full size" add-on boards (subject to the mechanical limitations of the chassis)
- Adaptor board is 3 Multibus II card slots wide

ENVIRONMENTAL REQUIREMENTS

Storage Temperature:	−40°C to 70°C (0°F to 158°F)
Operating Temperature:	0°C to 55°C (32°F to 131°F)
Storage Humidity:	5%–95% non-condensing at 55°C
Operating Humidity:	8%–90% non-condensing at 55°C

SPECIFICATIONS

ORDERING INFORMATION

SBC386PC16F01	386-based PC compatible CPU board with 1 Mb of DRAM
SBC386PC16F02	386-based PC compatible CPU board with 2 Mb of DRAM
SBC386PC16F04	386-based PC compatible CPU board with 4 Mb of DRAM
SBC386PC16F08	386-based PC compatible CPU board with 8 Mb of DRAM
SBCPCSYS100	Companion board with VGA graphics, HD controller and CSM functionality
S301K3	101-key enhanced AT-style keyboard
SBCPCSYS602	2-slot Backplane for the P2/aPC bus
SBCPCSYS604	4-slot Backplane for the P2/aPC bus
SBCPCSYS900	Adaptor Board
SBC MM01 FP	1 MB Memory Expansion Module
SBC MM02 FP	2 MB Memory Expansion Module
SBC MM04 FP	4 MB Memory Expansion Module
SBC MM08 FP	8 MB Memory Expansion Module
SBC MM16 FP	16 MB Memory Expansion Module

For more information or the number of your nearest Intel sales office, call 800-548-4725 (good in the U.S. and Canada).

UNITED STATES, Intel Corporation
3065 Bowers Ave., Santa Clara, CA 95051
Tel: (408) 765-8080

Multibus II Memory Expansion Boards

2

iSBC® MM01FP, MM02FP, MM04FP, MM08FP, MM16FP, MM32FP* HIGH PERFORMANCE MEMORY MODULES

- Provides High Speed Parity Memory Expansion for Intel's iSBC® 386/2X, iSBC 386/3X and iSBC 386/1XX CPU Boards
- Available in 1M, 2M, 4M, 8M, 16M and 32M Byte Sizes
- 32 Bits Wide with Byte Parity
- Stackable to Provide up to 16M Bytes of High Speed Memory for MULTIBUS I and MULTIBUS II Boards
- Supports 32-Bit, 16-Bit and 8-Bit Data Paths
- Supports Independent Read/Writes
- Easily Installed

The iSBC MM0XFP DRAM memory modules are members of Intel's complete line of iSBC memory and I/O expansion boards. The MM-Series of memory modules use a dedicated memory interface to maximize CPU/memory performance.

2

Figure 1. iSBC® MM08FP Memory Module

281010–1

*The iSBC® MM01FP, MM02FP, MM04FP, MM08FP, MM16FP, MM32FP memory modules are also manufactured under product code pSBC MM01FP, MM02FP, MM04FP, MM08FP, MM16FP, MM32FP by Intel Puerto Rico, Inc.

October 1991
Order Number: 281010-002

FUNCTIONAL DESCRIPTION

The iSBC MM-Series provide high performance, 32-bit parity DRAM memory for the MULTIBUS I and MULTIBUS II boards. These CPU boards come standard with one MM-Series module installed, with memory expansion available through the addition of a second stackable iSBC MM-Series module.

Memory Access Capabilities

The dynamic RAM memory of the memory modules is accessed through the dedicated memory module interface.

The MM memory module is designed for direct transfer of data between the CPU and the memory module without accessing the MULTIBUS interface.

MM01/MM02/MM04/MM08 Memory Size

The iSBC MM01FP, iSBC MM02FP, iSBC MM04FP, iSBC MM08FP, iSBC MM16FP, and iSBC MM32FP modules can be stacked on the CPU baseboard in any combination.

Data Bus Structure

The MM-Series memory modules use a 32-bit wide data path with storage for byte parity that can accommodate 8-bit byte, 16-bit or 32-bit word data transfers. In addition, the data path is capable of independent byte operations. This means that one byte can be written while the other three bytes (or any other combination) can be read.

Parity

One parity bit is provided for each of the four, 8-bit bytes in the 32-bit wide data path. For special applications, the parity bits can serve as data bits making possible 9-, 18-, or 36-bit data transfers.

Memory Function

The module protocol supports standard dynamic RAM READ, WRITE, RAS* only REFRESH cycles, and CAS* before RAS* REFRESH.

Installation

The iSBC MM-Series memory modules are easily installed by the user. Each module includes all necessary connectors, screws, and other hardware for installation, either as a second stacked module or as a replacement for a module with less memory.

SPECIFICATIONS

Word Size Supported

8-, 16-, or 32-bits

Memory Size

iSBC MM01FP	1,048,576 bytes
iSBC MM02FP	2,097,152 bytes
iSBC MM04FP	4,194,304 bytes
iSBC MM08FP	8,388,608 bytes

Access Time (All Densities)

Read/Write — 107 ns (max)-MM0X

Read/Write — 88 ns (max)-MM0XFP

Power Requirements

Voltage −5 VDC ±5%

Memory addressing for the iSBC MM-Series memory modules is controlled by the host CPU board over the memory module interface. The maximum system RAM size is 64M Bytes.

Top View

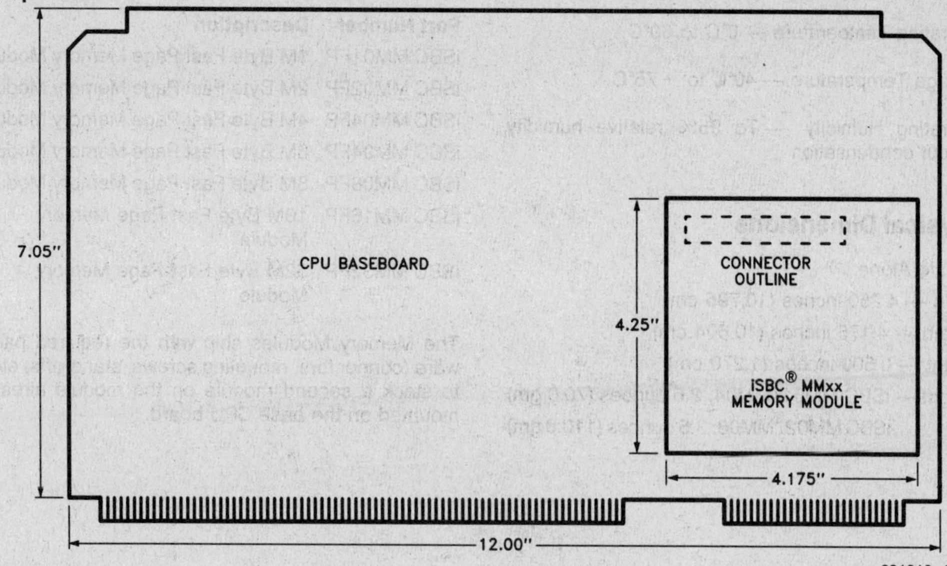

7.05"
CPU BASEBOARD
CONNECTOR OUTLINE
4.25"
iSBC® MMxx MEMORY MODULE
4.175"
12.00"

281010-2

Side View

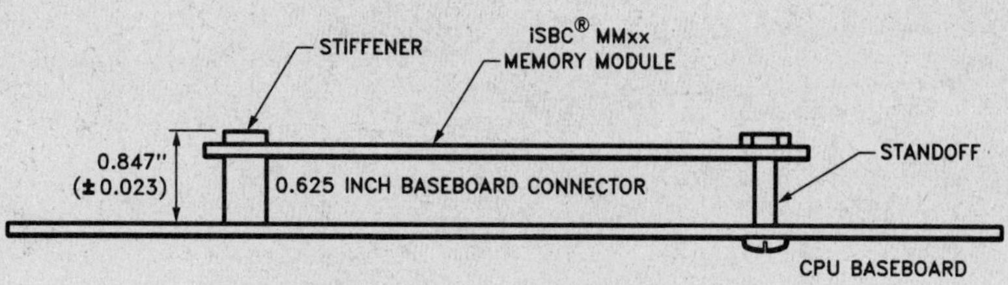

STIFFENER
iSBC® MMxx MEMORY MODULE
0.847" (±0.023)
0.625 INCH BASEBOARD CONNECTOR
STANDOFF
CPU BASEBOARD

281010-3

Single iSBC® MMxx Memory Module

Side View

iSBC® MMxx MEMORY MODULES
STIFFENER
1.564" (±0.033)
0.525 INCH STACKING CONNECTOR
STANDOFFS
0.625 INCH BASEBOARD CONNECTOR
CPU BASEBOARD

281010-4

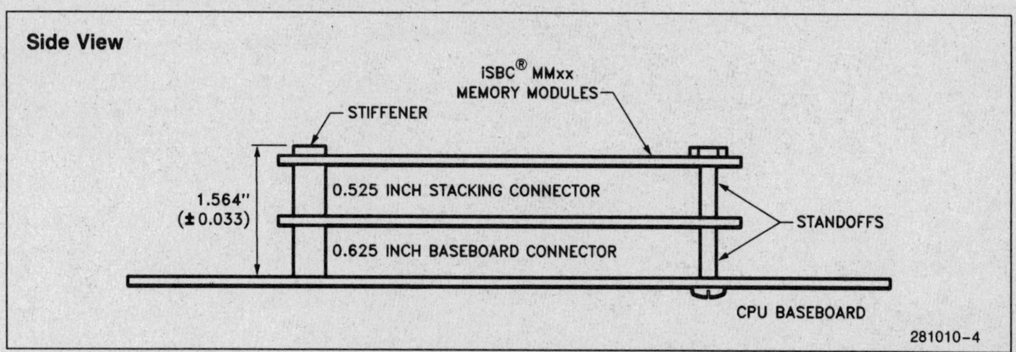

Stacked iSBC® MMxx Memory Modules

Environmental Requirements

Operating Temperature — 0°C to 60°C

Storage Temperature — 40°C to +75°C

Operating Humidity — To 95% relative humidity without condensation

Physical Dimensions

Module Alone:

Width — 4.250 inches (10,795 cm)

Length — 4.175 inches (10,604 cm)

Height — 0.500 inches (1,270 cm)

Weight — iSBC MM01/MM04: 2.5 ounces (70.0 gm)
iSBC MM02/MM08: 3.5 ounces (110.0 gm)

ORDERING INFORMATION

Part Number	Description
iSBC MM01FP	1M Byte Fast Page Memory Module
iSBC MM02FP	2M Byte Fast Page Memory Module
iSBC MM04FP	4M Byte Fast Page Memory Module
iSBC MM04FP	8M Byte Fast Page Memory Module
iSBC MM08FP	8M Byte Fast Page Memory Module
iSBC MM16FP	16M Byte Fast Page Memory Module
iSBC MM32FP	32M Byte Fast Page Memory Module

The Memory Modules ship with the required hardware (connectors, mounting screws, stand-offs, etc.) to stack a second module on the module already mounted on the base CPU board.

iSBC® MEM/340*
CACHE-BASED MULTIBUS II RAM BOARD

- 32-bit Multibus II Parallel System Bus (PSB) and Local Bus Extension II (iLBX™ II Bus) Interface Support
- Zero Wait State Over iLBX™ on a Cache Hit, One Wait State for Cache Misses and Writes at 8 MHz
- 4 MBytes Dual Port Memory
- Multibus II Interconnect Space for Dynamic Memory Configuration and Diagnostics
- Built-In-Self-Test (BIST) Diagnostics On-Board with Both LED Indicators and Software Access to Error Information
- Automatic Memory Initialization at Power-Up and at Power-Fail Recovery
- Byte Parity Error Detection

2

The iSBC MEM/340 is a cache-based memory board that supports the Multibus II architecture. It has a 32-bit architecture throughout, supporting 8-, 16-, and 32-bit central processors. The iSBC MEM/340 memory board is dual-ported, with access to the interfaces of both the Multibus II Parallel System Bus (PSB bus) and the iLBX™ II (Local Bus Extension).

In addition to the 32-bit memory transfer, the iSBC MEM/340 high-speed cache control subsystem is standard on this board. This improves performance by allowing zero wait state read access over the iLBX II at 8 MHz when data requested is in the cache memory.

280071-1

*The iSBC® MEM/340 is also manufactured under product code pSBCMEM340 by Intel Puerto Rico, Inc.

September 1991
Order Number: 280071-004

FUNCTIONAL DESCRIPTION

General

The iSBC MEM/340 high-speed cache-based memory board is physically and electrically compatible with the Multibus II PSB bus standard and the new iLBX II bus (Local Bus Extension) as outlined in the Intel Multibus II specification. Figure 1 illustrates a typical multiprocessing Multibus II system configuration.

Architecture

The four main subsystems of the iSBC MEM/340 board are the cache controller subsystem, the cache memory subsystem, the DRAM memory subsystem, and the interconnect space subsystem (see Figure 2). The following sections describe these subsystems and their capabilities in more detail.

Cache Memory Capabilities

The cache memory system is designed around the 32-bit architecture of the main memory system and reduces read access timers. The 8K Bytes of 45 nsec SRAM allows zero wait state read accesses over the iLBX II bus when data requested is in the cache memory (cache hit). A cache hit takes only two iLBX II bus clocks (250 nsec at 8 MHz).

Each entry in the 8K Byte cache memory subsystem consists of a data field of 32-bits and a tag field of up to 9-bits (depending on board DRAM size). Each byte in the main memory DRAM array directly maps to one and only one entry on the cache array. This direct mapped cache array along with tag labels ensure data integrity and accurate identification of cache hits. The cache memory size and simple but effective replacement algorithm is designed to optimize both the probability of cache hits and the CPU bus utilization. On any miss or write access, the contents of one cache entry are updated to maintain consistency with the corresponding entry in the DRAM memory array.

Dual Port DRAM Capabilities

The MEM/340 module contains 4 MBytes of read/write memory using 256K dynamic RAM components.

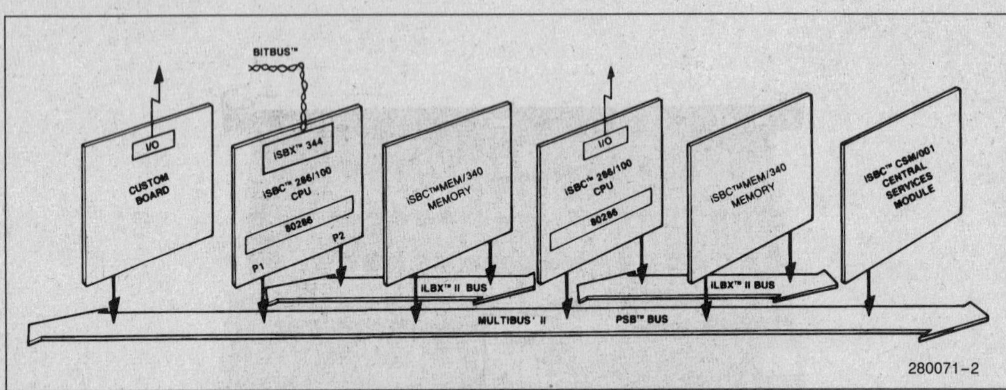

Figure 1. Typical Multibus II System Configuration

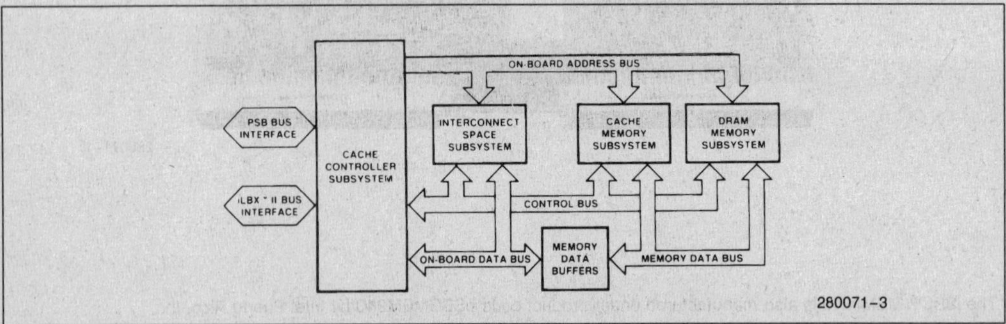

Figure 2. iSBC® MEM/340 Board Block Diagram

The dual port capability of the iSBC MEM/340 boards allows 32-bit access from either the PSB bus interface or the iLBX II bus interface (see Figure 1). Due to the simple arbitration nature of the iLBX II bus interface and the cache memory subsystem, the iSBC MEM/340 family allows optimal access to 20M Bytes of DRAM on the iLBX II bus.

System Memory Size

Using this series of memory boards the maximum system memory capacity based on one CPU board and 19 memory boards is 76M Bytes on the PSB bus. The memory partitioning is independent for the PSB bus interface and the iLBX II bus interface.

The start address can be on any 64K Byte boundary on the PSB bus and any 64K Byte boundary on the iLBX II bus. Software configures the start and ending addresses through the interconnect space. No jumpers are needed.

Interconnect Space Capabilities

The iSBC MEM/340 board module has a set of interconnect registers which allow the system software to dynamically configure and test the status of the memory board, replacing hardwired jumper functions. This interconnect subsystem also provides control and access to the Built-In-Self-Test (BIST) features. During power-up reset, the iSBC MEM/340 board initializes the memory and cache, sets all interconnect registers to their default values and performs a self-test. Error information from both Built-In-Self-Test (BIST) and parity checking is indicated in front panel LEDs and recorded in interconnect space registers accessible to software.

Built-In-Self-Test (BIST)

Self-test/diagnostics have been built into the heart of the Multibus II system. These confidence tests and diagnostics improve reliability and reduce manufacturing and maintenance costs. LED 1 (labelled BIST) is used to indicate the status of the Built-In Self Test. It is turned on when the BIST starts running and is turned off when the BIST completes successfully. The Built-In-Self-Test performed by the on-board microcontroller at power-up or at software command are:

1. **EPROM Checksum:**

   This test performs a checksum test on its internal EPROM to check operation of the 8751 microcontroller.

2. **Cache Data Test:**

   The microcontroller performs a sliding ones test on the cache memory in hit-only mode.

3. **Cache Address Test:**

   This test verifies that the cache address path is working properly.

4. **Refresh Check:**

   This test performs RAM test on a small portion of DRAM with an elapsed time between the write operation and the verification of the data.

5. **Dynamic RAM Address Test:**

   This test performs Address Rippled RAM test on the board memory (MISS ONLY operation mode).

6. **Dynamic RAM Data Test:**

   This test runs an AA-55 data pattern to check the DRAM data path.

7. **Parity Test:**

   This test injects parity errors in the DRAM array and then verifies that the board detects these errors.

These tests are described in detail in the User's Manual, Section 9-23.

Memory Initialization and Reset

Memory is initialized automatically during power-up. All bytes are set to 00.

Error Detection Using Byte Parity

Parity will detect all single bit parity errors on a byte parity basis and many multiple bit errors. LED 2 (labelled Parity) is used to indicate parity errors. LED 2 is turned on when a parity error is detected and turned off when the parity status register within interconnect space is cleared. This same LED turns on and off during power-up to verify operation of the LED.

Error information is recorded in interconnect space so it is accessible to software for error reporting.

2

SPECIFICATIONS

Word Size Supported

8-, 16-, 24-, and 32-bits

Memory Size

4 Megabytes (iSBC MEM/340) board

Access Times (All Densities)

Multibus II Parallel System Bus—PSB (@ 10 MHz)

Read: 562 ns (avg.)
775 ns (max.)

Write: 662 ns (avg.)
775 ns (max.)

NOTE:
Average access times assume 80% cache hit rates

iLBX™ II Bus—Local Bus Extension (at 8 MHz)

Read: 250 ns (min.)
275 ns (avg.)
375 ns (max.)

Write: 375 ns (avg.)
375 ns (max.)

Base Address

PSB Bus—any 64K Bytes boundary
iLBX II Bus—any 64K Bytes boundary

Power Requirements

Voltage: 5V DC ±5%

Product	Current
iSBC MEM/340 Board	4.1 A (typ) 6.7 A (max)

ENVIRONMENTAL REQUIREMENTS

Temperature: (inlet air) at 200 LFM airflow over boards
Non-Operating: −40 to +70°C
Operating: 0 to +55°C

Humidity: Non-operating: 95% RH @ 55°C
Operating: 90% RH @ 55°C

Physical Dimensions

The iSBC MEM/340 board meets all Multibus II mechanical specifications as presented in the ANSI/IEEE 1296 Multibus II specification.

Double High Eurocard Form Factor:

Depth: 220 mm (8.6 in.)
Height: 233 mm (9.2 in.)
Front Panel Width: 20 mm (0.784 in.)
Weight: iSBC MEM/340 board: 10080 gm (36 oz.)

Reference Manuals

iSBC MEM/340 Board Manual (#146707)

Ordering Information

Part Number	Description
SBCMEM340	4M Byte Cache Based Multibus II RAM Board

Multibus II I/O Products

3

MULTIBUS II I/O PRODUCT LINES

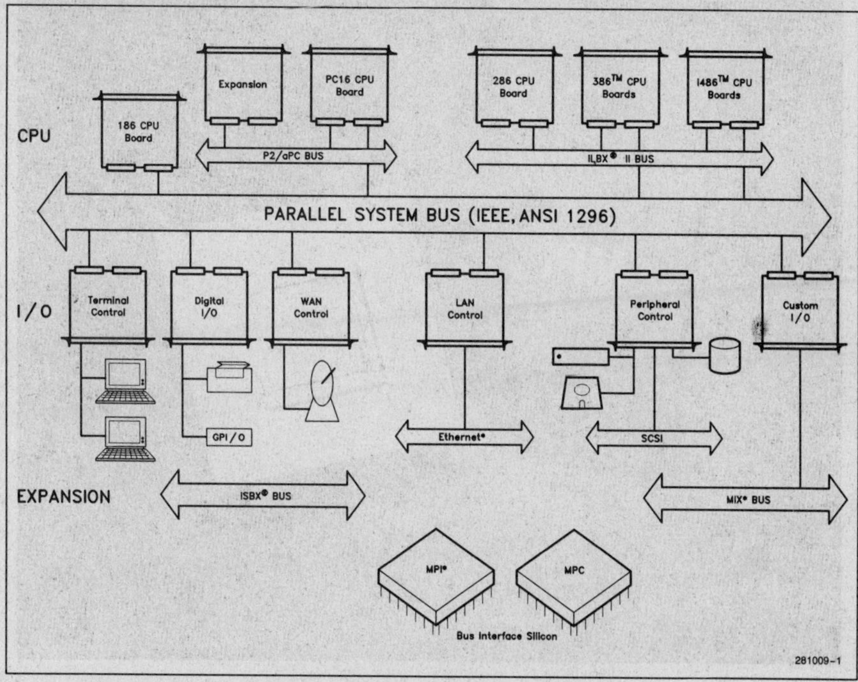

3

A SPECTRUM OF I/O FOR MULTIBUS II DESIGNS

Intel's wide range of Multibus II I/O products is designed to help you easily complete your application. These boards include a variety of standard I/O products, such as terminal controllers, wide area network controllers, Ethernet controllers, SCSI peripheral controllers and Digital I/O boards. Intel also offers a choice of development methods for designing custom I/O boards. Now you can design low-cost, non-intelligent I/O boards based on the Multibus II Peripheral Interface (MPI) silicon, or you can quickly and easily design high-performance, 386™ CPU-based I/O boards based on the Modular Interface eXtension (MIX) architecture. These products are described on the following pages.

TABLE OF CONTENTS

September 1991
Order Number: 281009-003

I/O DEVELOPMENT PRODUCTS

281009-2

MULTIBUS II SILICON PRODUCTS

Intel's Multibus II bus interface device product family has been created to aid the designer in interfacing application modules to the Multibus II Parallel System Bus (PSB). The IEEE/ANSI 1296 specification defines a set of synchronous state machines which are clocked by a central bus clock. Adherence to this type of specification is simple and provably correct. This architectural discipline has resulted in unprecedented compatibility between Multibus II products from all vendors. Intel offers a silicon implementation of the IEEE/ANSI 1296 state machines with the 82389 Message Passing Coprocessor (MPC) component to provide a high capability interface targeted for intelligent board products. The Multibus II Peripheral Interface (MPI) omits the block data transfer capabilities of the MPC and is targeted for non-intelligent, lower cost board products.

The Multibus II Peripheral Interface (MPI) is a Multibus II bus interface device providing PSB interface for non-intelligent I/O applications. The MPI is a replier in I/O and Interconnect space and can be implemented with a minimum of additional logic. The MPI supports the standardized signalling methods of the Multibus II architecture with the ability to send and receive unsolicited messages (without data) as interrupts. An on-board CPU or microcontroller (such as an 8751) is not required for applications using the MPI. Interconnect space may be implemented using a single PAL or PROM.

I/O DEVELOPMENT PRODUCTS

The 82389 Message Passing Coprocessor (MPC) is the premier Multibus II bus interface device for intelligent applications. It provides a complete, full function interface to the PSB, including arbitration, dual port memory recognition and the standardized signalling and data transfer methods of the Multibus II architecture. The MPC component requires the support of an 8751-type microcontroller, and a DMA device is recommended for high performance data transfers. The MPC, in combination with the iSBC® CSM/002 module or additional on-board logic, provides complete Central Services Module support for use in a slot 0 system location.

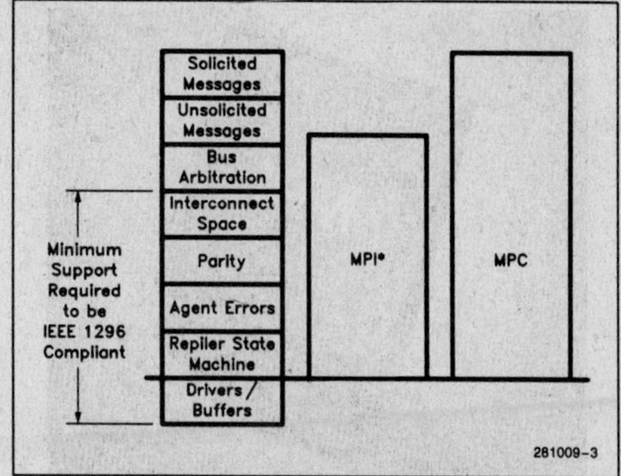

Figure 1: Comparing MPI* and MPC Capability

*MPI is a trademark of Centralp Automatismes, S.A.

MULTIBUS II BUS INTERFACE SILICON PRODUCTS

281009-4

MPI*—MULTIBUS II PERIPHERAL INTERFACE

The Multibus II Peripheral Interface, MPI, is a single chip, "replier only" Parallel System Bus interface device. The MPI implements a IEEE/ANSI 1296 Replier State Machine, seen in Figure 2. All error conditions are monitored and generated if appropriate.

MPI FEATURES

- Replier in I/O Space
  - 2 KBytes address on each board
  - 8/16 bus data width agents
- No application CPU required
- No support microcontroller required
- Supports up to 8 local interrupt sources
- Sends/Receives broadcast messages
- Sends/Receives unsolicited messages (without data)
- Complete arbitration protocol
  - Fair and High Priority modes are supported
- ANSI/IEEE 1296 compliant
- 124-pin plastic PGA package.

DESCRIPTION

The MPI component is a 16-bit integrated CMOS interface component compliant with the IEEE/ANSI 1296 standard and is compatible with other board products using the 82389 Message Passing Coprocessor. It supports data transfer in I/O space, as defined by the IEEE Specification. It is particularly suited to the design of low cost, non-intelligent I/O boards. Since the MPI component incorporates all the interface logic, except for five high current buffer drivers, it simplifies and accelerates I/O board design. The local interface is designed to provide a simple interface to I/O board components. The MPI also includes configuration registers which are programmed from the PSB to suit a variety of applications.

Interconnect Space

The MPI component supports IEEE/ANSI 1296 compliant interconnect space. Its registers are only accessed via the Parallel System Bus. The MPI includes the interface logic to support an external local memory device or PAL to implement most of the interconnect registers. Registers 34 through 38 are internal to the MPI.

I/O Space

The MPI component enables an I/O board to act as a replier in I/O space (as seen in Figure 2). Board address space is programmed through interconnect space which allows multiple MPI-based boards to be used in a Multibus II system with no jumpers. The width of the local I/O data bus can be 8 or 16 bits. Addresses and data for the local I/O is provided on a multiplexed bus.

Message Space

The MPI component enables an I/O board to send and receive interrupt packets, either in standard or Broadcast mode, without data. (Data transfer is carried out in I/O space.) Up to eight local interrupts may generate an interrupt packet onto the PSB; the highest priority interrupt level is encoded into this interrupt packet. The MPI entirely controls the access arbitration procedure for the PSB bus and the interrupt packet transfer. The MPI can receive interrupt packets from the PSB and uses them to generate a local interrupt signal.

The MPI interface supports parity signals when required and is capable of processing all error signals present on the bus.

MULTIBUS II BUS INTERFACE SILICON PRODUCTS

MPI SPECIFICATIONS

Power Supply Voltage: 0 − 5 V

Operating Temperature: 0 − 70°C

Storage Temperature: −65 to +150°C

V_{CC} = 5.0V +10%

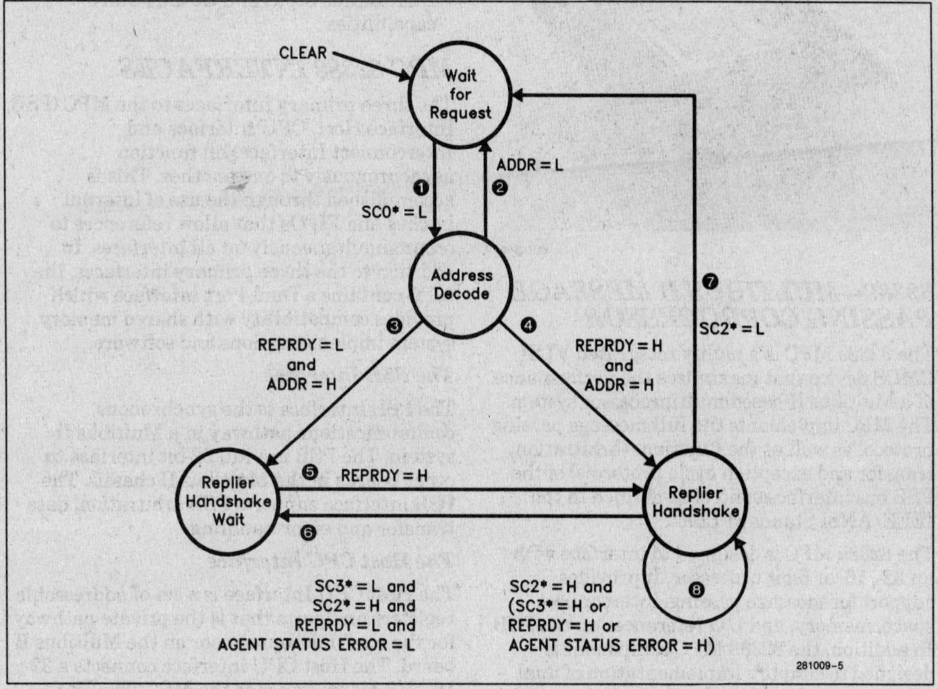

Figure 2: State-Flow Diagram for Replying Agents, from IEEE/ANSI 1296 Specification

MULTIBUS II BUS INTERFACE SILICON PRODUCTS

281009-6

82389—MULTIBUS II MESSAGE PASSING COPROCESSOR

The 82389 MPC is a highly integrated VLSI CMOS device that maximizes the performance of a Multibus II based multiprocessor system. The MPC implements the full message passing protocol as well as the functions (arbitration, transfer and exception cycle protocols) of the PSB bus interface control as defined in the IEEE/ANSI Standard 1296.

The 82389 MPC is designed to interface with an 32-, 16- or 8-bit processor. It provides support for message passing, interconnect space, memory, and I/O references on the PSB. In addition, the 82389 MPC component is designed to simplify implementation of dual port memory functions for those designs which will co-exist with the message passing communications protocol.

MPC FEATURES

- Single Chip Interface for the Parallel System Bus
- 1.0 u CMOS Technology
- 149-pin Ceramic PGA Package (15 × 15 Grid)
- Optimized for Real-Time Response (Maximum 900 ns for 32-byte Interrupt Packet)
- Processor Independent Interface to the Parallel System Bus
- Supports co-existence of dual port and message passing communication protocols
- Dual Buffer Input and Output DMA capabilities

MPC 82389 INTERFACES

The three primary interfaces to the MPC (PSB, Interface Host, CPU Interface and Interconnect Interface) all function asynchronously to one another. This is accomplished through the use of internal latches and FIFOs that allow references to occur simultaneously on all interfaces. In addition to the three primary interfaces, the MPC contains a Dual-Port interface which provides compatibility with shared memory system implementations and software.

The PSB Interface

The PSB Interface is the synchronous, communications pathway in a Multibus II system. The PSB is a full 32-bit interface to other boards in the Multibus II chassis. The PSB interface supports PSB arbitration, data transfer and error handling.

The Host CPU Interface

The Host CPU Interface is a set of addressable registers and ports that is the private pathway for the local microprocessor on the Multibus II board. The Host CPU interface connects a 32-, 16- or 8-bit processor to the MPC. The Host CPU Interface supports direct references to memory, I/O, and interconnect address space on the PSB. The Host CPU Interface also supports DMA operations. The Multibus II PSB and the MPC are defined to be processor independent.

The Interconnect Interface

The Interconnect Interface provides a path for added board functionality that is independent from the host CPU. The Interconnect Interface is an 8-bit communication interface which requires the MPC to be connected to a microcontroller or a simple state machine. A microcontroller will perform tasks such as board configuration at start-up and local diagnostics. All interconnect bus signals are asynchronous to the bus clock and to the local bus signals.

MULTIBUS II BUS INTERFACE SILICON PRODUCTS

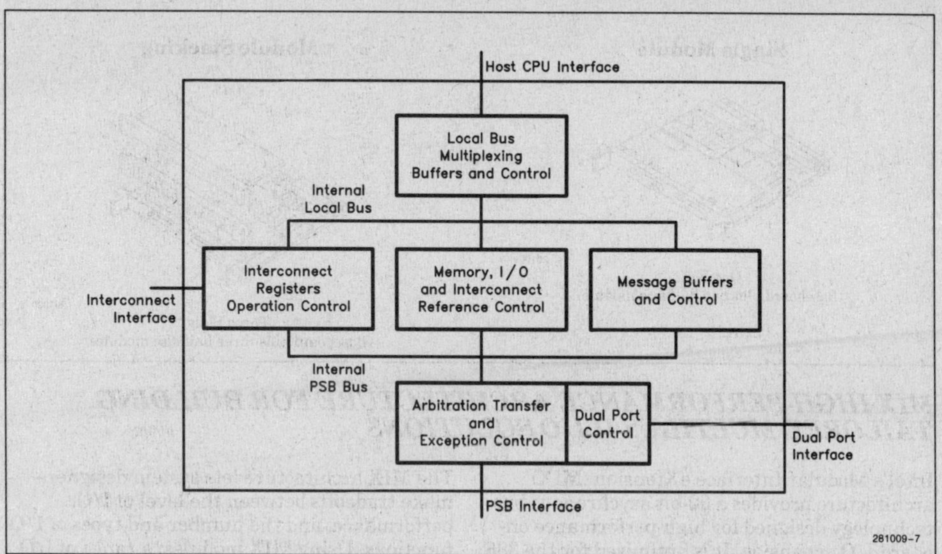

Figure 3: MPC Bus Interfaces

The Interconnect space of an agent is the only required bus space by the IEEE/ANSI 1296 specification and has a 512-byte register range.

The Dual Port Interface

The Dual Port interface supports shared memory accesses between agents on the PSB. The MPC contains programmable address recognizers and PSB cycle control. In order to fully implement dual-port memory, some additional dual-port memory controller logic is required.

MAJOR MPC OPERATIONS

The MPC standardizes the signalling and data transfer between multiple intelligent agents within a Multibus II system. The traditional address spaces of memory and I/O were considered inadequate to accomplish this standardization task, so a new address space, called message space, was added. The movement of information in message space is called message passing. The MPC supports two types of messages: solicited and unsolicited.

Solicited messages are used to transfer large amounts of data. Up to 16 MBytes (less 1 byte) of data can be transferred in a single solicited message transmission sequence. Solicited message transfers require the receiving agent to explicitly allocate a buffer. Data is packetized and reconstructed by the MPC to optimize PSB utililtzation and maintain deterministic performance. Buffer negotiation between sending and receiving agents is handled using unsolicited messages.

Unsolicited messages are short, fixed-length messages that can arrive unexpectedly. Unsolicited messages can be transmitted without explicit buffer allocation and without the cooperation of sending and receiving agents on the PSB. Unsolicited messages are often referred to as intelligent or virtual interrupts, since they are used as a signaling mechanism between boards, replacing traditional system (hard-wired) interrupts and freeing the CPU from having to poll for information. In addition to interrupt generation, unsolicited messages allow for up to 28 bytes of user data.

MPC Specifications

Operating Temperature ....0°C to +70°C

Storage Temperature .... −65°C to +150°C

Voltage on Any Pin ....0.5V to V_{CC} +0.5V

Power Dissipation ....2.5 W

D.C. and A.C. Specifications are available in the 82389, Message Passing Coprocessor Datasheet.
(Intel Order Number 290145-003)

MIX ARCHITECTURE

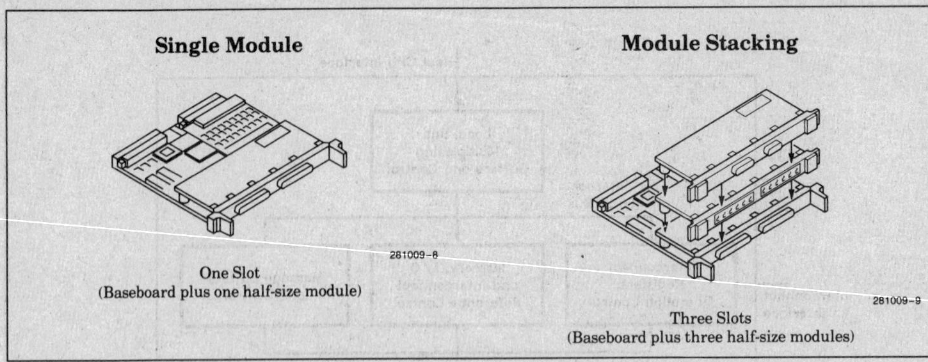

One Slot
(Baseboard plus one half-size module)

Three Slots
(Baseboard plus three half-size modules)

MIX HIGH-PERFORMANCE ARCHITECTURE FOR BUILDING TAILORED MULTIBUS II I/O SOLUTIONS

Intel's Modular Interface eXtension (MIX) architecture provides a 32-bit asychronous bus technology designed for high-performance on-board I/O expansion. It is optimized for the 386 microprocessor family and the Multibus II system architecture. The MIX bus is implemented using a 130-contact surface mount connector and supports stacking of from one to three MIX I/O modules. The I/O module interface to the MIX bus is open, with specifications and documentation available from Intel for the development and implementation of MIX I/O modules.

The MIX architecture lets system designers make tradeoffs between the level of I/O performance, and the number and types of I/O functions. Using MIX modules, a range of I/O solutions can be implemented: from a single-module single-slot high performance I/O controller to a three-module three-slot I/O server subsystem. Now the system designer can select the right combination of I/O and CPU horsepower to effectively manage the system I/O requirements.

MIX ARCHITECTURE FEATURES

- Full compatibility with the Multibus II (IEEE/ANSI 1296) Systems Architecture (MSA).
- Support for stacking up to 3 MIX modules on the baseboard—one of the modules can be full size. A MIX baseboard with a single half-size MIX module fits into a single Multibus II card slot.
- MIX bus data width of 32, 16, or 8 bits.
- Partitioning of I/O SBC architecture into a CPU & Multibus II core and I/O module.
- Multimaster bus ownership for support of master or slave MIX I/O modules.
- Support for like or unlike MIX module stacking with dynamic Built-in Self Test (BIST) and interconnect capabilities.
- Complete documentation available for building MIX I/O modules.

MULTIBUS II COMPATIBILITY

The MIX architecture adds a subsystem bus technology that provides a solution for high performance I/O and brings the capability of a high performance I/O server subsystem to the Multibus II architecture.

MIX ARCHITECTURE FEATURES

PHYSICAL DECOUPLING OF CPU FROM I/O

MIX uses a baseboard plus modules approach to physically decouple the CPU technology of the baseboard from the I/O technology of the module. This decoupling has two benefits for I/O design. First, it allows the CPU and I/O technology to evolve independently so that new technology can be more easily incorporated into system designs. Second, it allows a baseboard to change personality by adding or substituting I/O modules. This provides I/O flexibility while preserving the software investment.

CONNECTING CPU AND I/O VIA A HIGH PERFORMANCE BUS INTERFACE

The MIX architecture provides the high performance bus interface for coupling the CPU baseboard with the I/O modules. Elements of the MIX architecture and bus interface include:

Signal Set

The MIX bus consists of 130 signal, power, and ground connections. There are two types of signals: dedicated and bussed. Dedicated signals belong to specific modules in the MIX stack, while bussed signals are shared by all modules.

Address Capability

The MIX bus supports the full 4 gigabyte physical addressing capability of the 386 microprocessor and other compatible microprocessors.

Data Paths

MIX supports 8, 16, and 32 bit physical data paths on MIX modules. The MIX baseboard data path is 32 bits.

MIX Bus Transfers

The baseboard can perform memory, I/O, and DMA transfers on the MIX bus. The baseboard can also perform a bus vectored interrupt transfer cycle. Bus master modules can perform memory transfers with the baseboard memory.

Arbitration

The MIX bus uses a simple round robin arbitration scheme between the baseboard and master modules to insure that all modules and the baseboard have guaranteed access times to shared baseboard memory and have a guaranteed percentage of the shared memory bandwidth.

Interrupts

Each MIX module has one dedicated interrupt line. Each module also has an option line that can be used as an interrupt line.

DMA

The MIX bus supports DMA transfers between modules and the baseboard memory. Both single-cycle (fly-by) and two-cycle DMA transfers are supported.

Configuration Support

MIX configuration support has been designed to be compatible with the Multibus II interconnect space architecture. MIX modules are viewed as baseboard functions by agents on the parallel system bus. The baseboard microcontroller reads the interconnect information stored in the EEPROM of each module present in the MIX stack to build the function record in baseboard interconnect space.

Built-in Self Test (BIST) Support

MIX provides the capability for BIST code resident in module EPROM to be downloaded and executed as an extension of the baseboard BIST.

OPEN INTERFACE FOR I/O MODULE DEVELOPMENT

MIX provides an excellent platform for building Multibus II I/O solutions. A complete set of manuals, design specifications and design examples for building MIX I/O modules is available from Intel.

MIX BUS INTERFACE SPECIFICATIONS

General

Bus Type:	Asynchronous
Theoretical Bandwidth:	22 MByte/s
Typical Bandwidth:	10 MByte/s
Bus Overhead:	7% Xchange/Refresh
Interrupt Sources:	Any Module
Bus Vector Support:	Yes
Arbitration Scheme:	Fairness (Rd-Robin)
Module Maximum:	3 (master or slave)
Length of Bus Hold:	8 microsec (typical)
Flag Byte Support:	Yes

Lines

130 total signal, power and ground lines:

Number	Functional Group
37	Address
32	Data
7	Transfer Control
6	Arbitration
3	Interrupt
6	DMA
3	Option
7	Configuration
9	+5 VDC
13	GND
2	+12 VDC
2	−12 VDC
3	Reserved

Baseboard Address Range

Memory	4 Gigabytes
I/O	64 Kilobytes

Module Address Range

Memory	256 Megabytes
I/O	1 Kilobyte

Data Path

8, 16, and 32 bit

MIX Connector:

Connector Type:	Surface Mount
Connector Pads:	130

MIX Expansion Module:

Half-Size:	
Height:	8.9 inches
Depth:	3.75 inches
Area:	33 square inches
Full-Size:	
Height:	8.9 inches
Depth:	7.9 inches
Area:	70 square inches
Max Configuration:	1 Baseboard 3 Modules

MIX Bus Power Limits

Voltage (VDC)	Total Current (Amps) Half-Size	Full-Size
+ 5 (+5%, −2%)	9.0	9.0
+12 (+5%, −15%)	1.5	2.0
−12 (+5%, −5%)	1.5	2.0

Module Power Limits

Nominal Voltage (VDC)	Max Current per Module (Amps) Half-Size	Full-Size
+ 5	3.0	9.0
+12	0.5	2.0
−12	0.5	2.0

Thermal Limit (all sources):
20 Watts max per module (half-size);
70 Watts max (full-size)

MIX I/O PLATFORM FAMILY

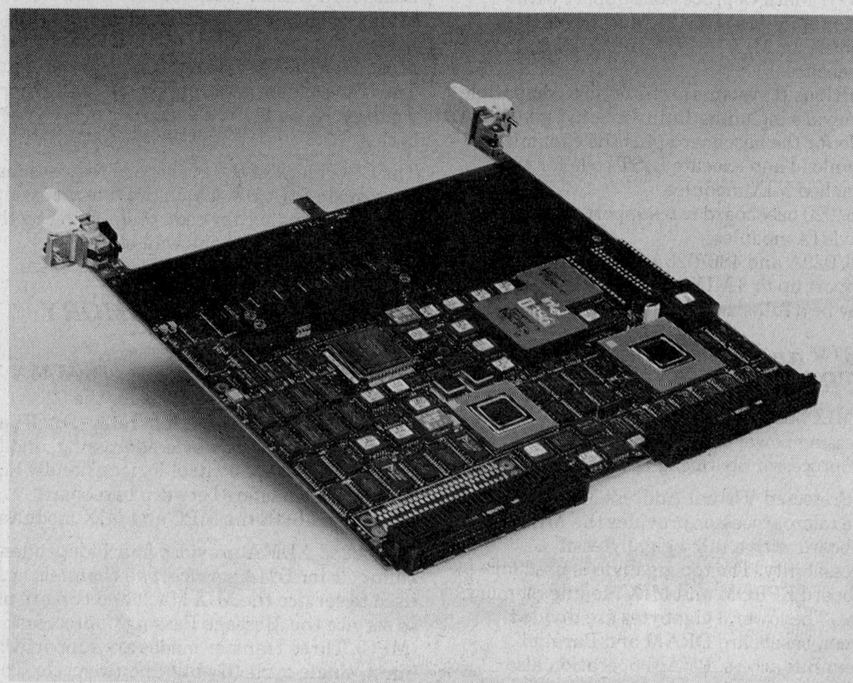

281009-10

i386™ and i486™ CPU-BASED CORES FOR BUILDING INTELLIGENT MULTIBUS II I/O SOLUTIONS

The Intel Modular Interface eXtension (MIX) I/O Platform Family provides the i386 or i486 microprocessor cores, hardware development modules, and documentation needed to build high performance custom I/O solutions for Multibus II systems.

The MIX Baseboards combine a 32-bit microprocessor, Advanced Direct Memory Access (ADMA) controller, and Message Passing Coprocessor (MPC) to provide a significant amount of power for handling I/O processing. In addition, with up to 64 megabytes of DRAM expansion, the baseboards provide enough memory to accommodate on-board execution of large amounts of I/O software. Add to that the I/O expansion capabilities of the MIX interface and you have a versatile, high-performance engine for handling I/O processing.

Three different models are available. The MIX 386/020 features a 20 MHz i386 CPU, 1 MB of on-board expandable memory and support, half-size MIX modules. The MIX 836/02A and MIX 486/02A baseboards feature i386 and i486 CPUs respectively, both support full and half-size MIX modules and include 4 MB of expandable on-board memory.

MIX BASEBOARD FEATURES

- i386 or i486 microprocessor operating at 20 MHz.
- 1 MB (1020) or 4 MB (1020A) of on-board fast page mode DRAM with parity checking.
- Memory expansion up to an additional 16 MB (1020) or 64 MB (1020A) of fast page mode DRAM with parity checking.
- 82258 ADMA for handling data transfers between the baseboard DRAM and the MPC and also between the baseboard DRAM and the MIX modules.

MIX BASEBOARD FEATURES

- 387™ Math Coprocessor support with optional iSBC 387MX25 Math Extension Module for MIX 386/020 and MIX 386/020A baseboards.
- Multibus II systems architecture compatible firmware including Built-In Self-Test (BIST) code for the baseboard plus the capability to download and execute BIST code for the attached MIX modules.
- 386/020 baseboard can support up to 3 half-size MIX modules.
- 386/020A and 486/020A baseboards can support up to 3 MIX modules, one of which may be a full-size module.

i386™ and i486™ MICROPROCESSOR CORES

The MIX baseboards obtain their I/O processing power from a i386 or i486 microprocessor operating at 20 MHz.

The Protected Virtual Address Mode (PVAM) of the microprocessor provides the MIX Baseboard with a full 4 gigabytes of addressability. The top gigabyte is used for baseboard EPROM and MIX Module memory access. The lower 3 gigabytes are divided between baseboard DRAM and Parallel System Bus access. PVAM operation also provides support for code protection, virtual memory and paging mechanisms.

In addition, the microprocessor has a self-test capability which is utilized in the board's power up BIST testing. This function can be disabled via a board jumper option.

FROM 1 TO 68 MEGABYTES OF MEMORY

The DRAM block of the baseboard consists of an asynchronous fast page mode DRAM controller, address multiplexor, data transceivers with parity detection and generation, baseboard DRAM, and DRAM expansion using the MMxx interface.

The MIX 386/020 is designed to accept one or two MMxx DRAM modules. A total of 17 megabytes of DRAM memory is obtained with the installation of two iSBC MM08FP memory modules.

The MIX 386/020A and MIX 486/020A baseboards are supplied with 4 MB of baseboard memory and can accept two MMxx DRAM modules. Maximum total memory is 68 MB using MM 32FP memory modules.

Baseboard DRAM (both on-board and on MMxx modules) is directly accessible to bus masters on the MIX bus. Byte parity protection is used for DRAM error checking on the board. The transceivers generate parity for memory write cycles and check parity for memory read cycles.

The CPU block of the baseboard requires fast page mode DRAMS, which provide zero wait state performance for code prefetching by the microprocessor, and one wait state performance for all other DRAM accesses.

ADMA FOR FAST MEMORY TRANSFERS

The MIX baseboards use the 82258 ADMA operating at 8 MHz, (12 MHz for the 020A modules. DMA Address Generator (DAG) gate array for 32-bit, 4 gigabyte addressing, and fast page mode DRAM control logic to handle high speed data transfers between baseboard DRAM and both the MPC and MIX modules.

The 82258 ADMA provides four independent channels for DMA service; two channels are used to service the MIX stack and two are used to service the Message Passing Coprocessor (MPC). Three transfer modes are supported: burst, single-cycle (fly-by), and two cycle. To the MIX bus, burst mode transfers look like single cycle transfers. Burst mode transfers between the baseboard DRAM and the MPC or MIX modules have a maximum transfer rate of 14.2 MBs and 22.2 MBs for the 1020 and 1020A baseboards respectively.

MULTIBUS II SYSTEMS ARCHITECTURE SUPPORT

The MIX baseboards utilize the 82389 Message Passing Coprocessor (MPC) to provide a full 32 bit interface to the Multibus II Parallel System Bus. Firmware is also provided that contains baseboard Built-In Self Tests (BIST) and Initialization and Diagnostics eXecutive (IDX) code. Also included is the capability to download BIST code from MIX module EPROM and execute the code to test the modules in the MIX stack.

A POWERFUL ENGINE FOR I/O PROCESSING

The MIX 386/020 supports a stack of 1, 2 or 3 MIX I/O modules. The MIX bus supports 32, 16 and 8 bit data transfers and allows MIX modules to be either masters or slaves on the MIX bus.

MIX BASEBOARD FEATURES

A custom gate array device on the baseboard controls the baseboard interface to the MIX bus and implements the MIX bus arbitration logic. The gate array implements the standard MIX round-robin arbitration algorithm which provides guaranteed access to the MIX bus by the baseboard and module bus masters. The capability to modify certain arbitration parameters is also provided.

MIX 386/020 BASEBOARD FEATURES

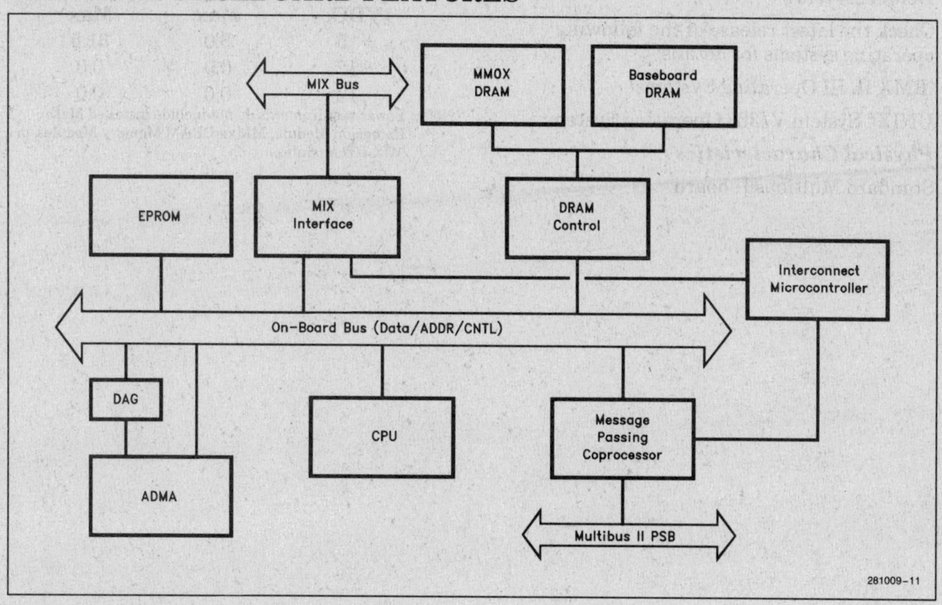

Figure 4: Block Diagram of MIX Baseboards

MIX 386/020 BASEBOARD SPECIFICATIONS

Models

MIX386020	i386 CPU. Supports half-size MIX Modules. 8 MHz ADMA, 1 MByte on-board DRAM
MIX386020A	i386 CPU. Supports full or half-size MIX Modules. 12 MHz ADMA, 4 Mbytes on-board DRAM
MIX486020A	i486 CPU. Supports full or half-size MIX Modules. 12 MHz ADMA, 4 Mbytes on-board DRAM

Note: DRAM memory varies by model. See price list for order codes.

Clock Rates

CPU 1020	20 MHz
82258 ADMA	8 MHz
1020A	12 MHz
8751 Microcontroller	12 MHz
82C54 Timer	(Programmable)

EPROM Memory

Two 32-pin Sites

DRAM Memory

1M byte (1020) or 4 MB (1020A) installed on the baseboard.

Memory may be increased by installing up to two iSBC MM0XFP Memory Expansion Modules. Separate versions are orderable with 1, 4, 8 or 20M bytes already installed.

Interrupt Capabilities

14 programmable interrupts

MIX 386/020 BASEBOARD FEATURES

Interfaces

- P1, Full PSB.
- P2, power only.
- MMxx local memory expansion.
- MIX

Device Drivers

Check the latest release of the following operating systems for details:

iRMX II, III Operating Systems

UNIX* System V/386 Operating System

Physical Characteristics

Standard Multibus II board.

Power Requirements

Maximum values are at nominal voltage plus 5% and at an ambient temperature of 0 degrees C.

Nominal Voltage (VDC)	Current (amps) Max	Power (watts) Max
+ 5	6.0	31.5
+12	0.0	0.0
−12	0.0	0.0

Note: Power requirements do not include installed Math Extension Module, MMxx DRAM Memory Modules, or MIX I/O Modules.

MIX I/O PLATFORM FAMILY

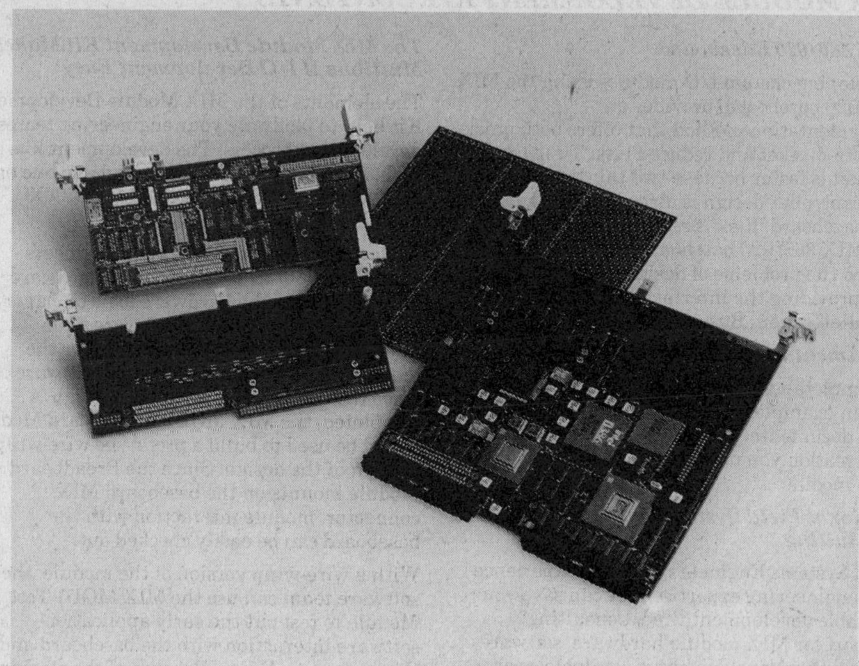

281009-12

A KIT FOR DEVELOPING MIX I/O MODULES

A requirement for many Multibus II designs is the incorporation of custom I/O. This is I/O that may be unique to the application or require an I/O controller not readily available in the market. To date, such a requirement typically would have necessitated the non-trivial task of designing a dedicated Multibus II I/O controller. With the Modular Interface eXtension (MIX) interface and the MIX Module Development Kit, the task of developing a Multibus II I/O solution is simplified.

The MIX bus is a straight-forward, well documented interface for developing MIX I/O modules. In addition, the MIX Module Development Kit provides all the hardware, documentation and optional consulting support needed to easily develop your own MIX I/O module that stacks on a MIX baseboard. This combination greatly simplifies the task of developing your complete I/O solution for Multibus II systems.

MIX MODULE DEVELOPMENT KIT FEATURES

- MIX 386/020 Baseboard used as both the development vehicle and the platform for the final production module
- A set of MIX development modules to facilitate the MIX module development process, including a test module, breadboard module, and debug module.
- Complete documentation set providing all the information needed to develop a MIX module
- Optional Intel Field Systems Engineer consulting to help you better focus your development team and save development time.

MIX I/O PLATFORM FAMILY

MIX MODULE DEVELOPMENT KIT CONTENTS

MIX 386/020 Baseboard

Developing custom I/O modules using the MIX 386/020 baseboard, provides an implementation method that offers both quick time-to-market and reduced risk. Time-to-market is faster because two thirds of the total I/O controller design is already provided by the baseboard. Risk is reduced, because with the MIX 386/020 baseboard, Intel has already solved the problems of designing the CPU core and providing the interface to the Multibus II Parallel System Bus.

Documentation Package

A complete set of manuals, specifications and design examples for building a MIX module. This documentation package provides all the information you need to successfully develop a MIX module.

Optional Field Systems Engineer Consulting

Intel Systems Engineers have the experience and engineering expertise that can save you valuable development time. Consulting support for MIX module hardware, software, or firmware development is available as an optional component of the Module Development Kit.

MIX Development Modules

All the MIX development modules are designed to stack on top of the MIX baseboard or another MIX module.

- **MIX MOD1 Test Module**
  Used for testing of MIX module hardware and software designs. The test module contains a serial interface and an iSBX™ connector for communicating with the MIX baseboard.
- **MIX MOD2 Breadboard Module**
  Used for wire-wrapping and building a prototype module design. The breadboard module provides three separate wire-wrap areas, each surrounded by power and ground connections. In addition, stake pins are provided which give access to the signals from the MIX interface.
- **MIX MOD3 Debug Module**
  Used to mount a MIX module with its component side up (that is, flipped over from its normal mounting orientation). This allows access to the module's components for easy probe connection and debug.

The MIX Module Development Kit Makes Multibus II I/O Development Easy

The elements of the MIX Module Development Kit help to facilitate your engineering teams development process. The development kits include a MIX 386/020 baseboard and one each MIX MOD1, MIX MOD2, and MIX MOD3 modules.

To develop a MIX module, your engineers would start out as usual with the hardware team designing the hardware logic on paper or on a CAD system and the software team developing the preliminary design for the module firmware and application software. Once the preliminary hardware design is completed, the MIX MOD2 Breadboard Module would be used to build a prototype wire-wrap version of the design. Since the Breadboard Module mounts on the baseboard MIX connector, module interaction with the baseboard can be easily checked out.

With a wire-wrap version of the module, the software team can use the MIX MOD1 Test Module to test out the early application software interaction with the baseboard and the wire-wrap design. Because of the stacking capability of MIX, the Test Module and Breadboard Module can both be mounted to the baseboard in a stacked configuration.

Once the breadboard design has been checked out, the engineering team would build the production version of the module. Using the MIX MOD3 Debug Module, the final module can be mounted on the baseboard with its components side up for easy probe access and hardware debug.

Finally, using the Test Module and the Debug Module in a stacked configuration, the engineering team can debug both the final hardware and software to complete the design.

FIRMWARE DEVELOPMENT PACKAGE

281009-13

FIRMWARE DEVELOPMENT PACKAGE

The Multibus II Systems Architecture (MSA) provides the framework and guidelines for the start-up and run-time operation of a multiple board, multiple operating system, heterogeneous microprocessor, Multibus II system. The MSA Firmware Development Package (FDP) enables customers who are developing 386 or i486™ CPU Multibus II boards to easily incorporate firmware on the board that allows it to fully participate in an MSA environment.

The FDP product includes source code in the C language for the generic initialization, diagnostic, and bootstrap elements of the Multibus II Systems Architecture. FDP provides a base level of code on which to begin development of board-specific MSA firmware and the C language source code makes the task of porting the FDP code to other CPU architectures less difficult.

Developing MSA firmware via FDP reduces implementation time and makes the benefits of MSA available at a fraction of the cost of developing a proprietary firmware solution.

FIRMWARE DEVELOPMENT PACKAGE FEATURES

- Source Code and Binary files for: Master Test Handler, Console Controller, Bootstrap Loader, Initialization & Diagnostic Executive, and Core Function Set.
- Complete Documentation: Installation and Generation Guide, Functional Specifications, BIST Writer's Guide, MSA Specifications
- DOS generation environment
- Provided in C language
- Distributed via DOS diskettes, including make files compatible with PolyMake*
- Designed to facilitate customization

*PolyMake is a trademark of SAGE Software.

FIRMWARE DEVELOPMENT PACKAGE FEATURES

INSTALLATION AND GENERATION GUIDE

The FDP Installation and Generation Guide provides an overview of MSA firmware and the FDP product. It also specifies the recommended tools and development environment for FDP.

SOURCE FILES

FDP is a source product. All files necessary to duplicate the MSA firmware functions for diagnostics, initialization, and booting are included in the package. Listings are also included for reference.

BINARY FILES

Binary files of each module are included and may make the generation of unmodified modules unnecessary. These object modules also serve as references in validating the development environment.

EXAMPLE BUILT IN SELF TEST (BIST) CODE

Examples of BIST code commonly used on Intel Multibus II hardware (e.g., RAM tests and message passing tests) are included for reference.

BIST WRITER'S GUIDE

A BIST Writer's Guide is included to aid the process of learning the BIST interfaces and to show the typical organization of BIST code on Intel hardware. Using the guide, the first time BIST writer will quickly come up to speed. Master Test Handler (MTH), Local Test Handler (LTH), and power-up Test Handler (PTH) interfaces to the Initialization and Diagnostics Executive (IDX) are covered.

SPECIFICATIONS PACKAGE

Detailed functional specifications for each FDP module are included. These documents are suitable for implementation purposes and were actually used in the development of base FDP firmware.

AVAILABLE IN C LANGUAGE

Recognizing the need for portability and the popularity of C, the FDP software is provided in the C language.

DISTRIBUTED VIA DOS DISKETTES

Covering the most popular development environment, the distribution media affords easy portability.

INCLUDES MAKE FILES FOR GENERATION

FDP includes a file that may be used with the PolyMake* utility to greatly ease the regeneration process. Only files having modifications are recompiled, which eases the generation process and significantly reduces the time required.

DESIGNED TO FACILITATE CUSTOMIZATION

The FDP code is written for Multibus II boards based on the 386 or i486 microprocessors. However, FDP is an open product which is partitioned and organized to facilitate changes and extensions necessary to support your hardware. In addition, since the source code is provided in the C language, the task of porting the FDP code to other microprocessors is less difficult.

TARGET HARDWARE REQUIREMENTS FOR DEVELOPMENT

Any open system that supports MSA, e.g., the Intel System 520, will provide an adequate hardware environment for firmware validation.

PACKAGE CONTENTS

- FDP software on 5¼ inch DOS diskettes
- FDP Installation and Generation Guide
- BIST Writer's Guide
- FDP module functional specification documents
- MSA specification documents
- FDP-generated sample EPROM devices for the Intel iSBC 386/120 CPU board

*PolyMake is a trademark of SAGE Software

VIM/001: VMEbus TO MULTIBUS II INTERFACE MODULE

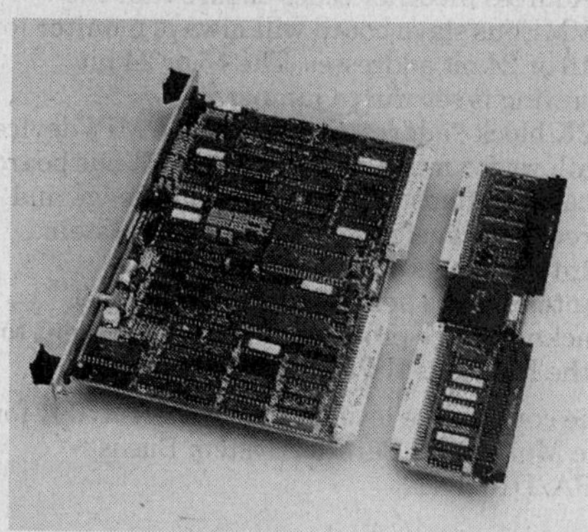

281009-14

The VIM/001 module provides a mechanical and electrical bridging of simple, non-intelligent VMEbus I/O products to the Multibus II environment. Together the VIM/001 and any standard VMEbus compatible board product exactly match the standard Multibus II single board form factor and fit into a standard Multibus II chassis and backplane. Multibus II backplane signals are translated by the VIM/001 into VMEbus signals and vice-versa for complete electrical compatibility.

The VIM/001 supports VMEbus modules rated as Slaves or Interrupters with any combination of the following VMEbus compliance levels: A16, A24, D08(O), D16 (EO), I(1,2,3,4,5,6,7).

FEATURES

- Fully IEEE/ANSI 1296 and IEEE 1014-1987 compliant.
- Data byte swapping maintains coherence between big-endian and little-endian protocols.
- VMEbus memory space accessible through Multibus II I/O space.
- VMEbus interrupts are "translated" into Multibus II unsolicited messages (without data).
- All VMEbus signals on P2, rows A and C pass straight through to the P2 connector for easy access.
- A page register in interconnect space allows the 64K of Multibus II I/O to be mapped anywhere within the 16 MBytes of VMEbus memory.
- Supported with the Multibus II Peripheral Interface (MPI) device.

MULTIBUS II PROTOCOLS SUPPORTED

The VIM/001 supports Multibus II I/O, Message and Interconnect Space in accordance with the IEEE/ANSI 1296 specification.

INTERCONNECT SPACE

A bus master (usually a CPU board) on the Multibus II Parallel System Bus can use interconnect space to initialize the MPI, enable and disable MPI functions or read board description data.

Normally the CPU will access the VIM/001 interconnect space many times after a system reset, both to identify the board and to initialize the MPI. There is no analogous memory space on VME and interconnect accesses do not run any cycles on the VME board.

3

VIM/001: VMEbus TO MULTIBUS II INTERFACE MODULE

MESSAGE SPACE

A Multibus II master on the Parallel System Bus can use message space to receive unsolicited without data (interrupt) messages from the MPI. Solicited messages are not supported (sending or receiving) by the VIM/001 module.

I/O SPACE

The bus master on the Parallel System Bus uses I/O space to communicate with the VME board. All reads and writes to the VME board, as well as interrupt acknowledge cycles, take place through I/O space. I/O space support by the VIM/001 module includes:

- Transparent byte swapping to maintain big-endian, little-endian protocol coherency. VMEbus protocol specifies big-endian data access while Multibus II protocol specifies little-endian data access.
- Address Modifier codes ensure that the VMEbus slave board will always monitor for 16 or 24 bit addresses. The 16 or 24 bit setting is set with a jumper.
- 2K block "addressability" by the MPI device allows for multiple VIM/001-VMEbus board combinations to properly acknowledge and receive transfers in a Multibus II system.
- Interrupt acknowledge for all VME interrupts is achieved via an interrupt acknowledge protocol that is transparent to the Multibus II Parallel System Bus.

The compliance level of the iSBC VIM/001 for the Multibus II Parallel System Bus is RPA/D16/INT.

VIM/001: VMEbus TO MULTIBUS II INTERFACE MODULE

INTERRUPTS SUPPORTED

Any three of the seven interrupts (IRQ1 through IRQ7) on a VMEbus standard module are interpreted and acknowledged appropriately by the VIM/001. Additionally, the priority of the interrupt is passed through. Both the ROAK and RORA varieties of VMEbus interrupts are supported. The unsolicited message created by the MPI translation of a VMEbus interrupt carries the information about which VMEbus interrupt initiated the request. The acknowledge cycle is performed as a normal Multibus II I/O read cycle.

OTHER SUPPORTED CIRCUITRY

The VMEbus SYSCLK circuitry is supported on the VIM/001 module. This 16 MHz signal may be needed for some VMEbus slave boards to function a half size 16 MHz oscillator which drives SYSCLK is included on the VIM/001 board.

Reset signals to the VMEbus slave board and bus error signals for the PSB are supported by the VIM/001 board.

The 64 user-defined signals on the P2 connector of any VMEbus slave board are transferred directly to the P2 connector of the VIM/001 module and are then available for use within the Multibus II chassis.

DESIGN MIGRATION KIT

Offered in conjunction with the iSBC VIM/001 module is a design migration kit for those who desire to migrate a VMEbus board plus VIM/001 combination to a full size Multibus II board. The design migration kit describes the implications of going from a VMEbus to Multibus II single board implementation. Included in the migration kit are a VIM/001 product specification, VIM/001 schematics, PAL codes and an Application Note on "how to" translate your VIM/001-VMEbus module combination into a full height Multibus II module.

SPECIFICATIONS

The VIM/001 supports all VMEbus modules rated as Slaves or Interrupters with any combination of the following VMEbus compliance levels: A16, A24, D08(O), D16 (EO), I(1,2,3,4,5,6,7).

Power Requirements:

Nominal Voltage (VDC)	Current (amps) Max	Power (watts) Max
+ 5	2.0	10
+12	0.0	0
−12	0.0	0

Physical Characteristics:

Height: 23.3 cm (9.18 inches)

Depth: 5.2 cm (2.03 inches)

Width: 1 cm (0.4 inches)

The iSBC VIM/001 meets all mechanical interface specifications to the Multibus II Parallel System Bus. It also meets all mechanical interface specifications to the VMEbus, emulating a one-slot VMEbus backplane.

The iSBC VIM/001 together with a standard double-high VMEbus card exactly matches the form factor for a standard Multibus II full-height card and fits into a standard Multibus II system.

The VIM/001 weighs approximately 200 grams.

Temperature:

Operation: 0 to +55°C at 200 linear feet/minute air velocity

Storage: −40 to +70°C

Humidity:

Operating: 20% to 80% non-condensing

Storage: 5% to 95% non-condensing

Altitude:

Operates normally at altitudes up to 10,000 ft

3

ASYNCHRONOUS TERMINAL CONTROLLERS

281009–15

FAMILY OF MULTIBUS II TERMINAL CONTROLLERS

Asynchronous Terminal Controllers must address such application requirements as terminal access, remote modem access and computer to computer communication while meeting price and performance criteria. The Intel Multibus II terminal controller family addresses these application needs with three boards: iSBC MPI/450, iSBC 186/450 and MIX 386/450. These boards are application compatible, offering a range of price/performance options. The iSBC MPI/450 is a non-intelligent I/O board that provides asynchronous serial I/O port extensions to a host CPU board. The iSBC 186/450 is an intelligent dedicated terminal controller that efficiently performs terminal functions within the system. The MIX 386/450 is a high performance terminal controller, utilizing the power of 386 CPU performance and the flexibility of Modular Interface eXtension (MIX) stacking.

All three boards have been designed stressing compatibility across the product line. In respect to hardware, all physical connections, eg. cabling and connectors, are interchangeable between the boards. The result is that the three boards follow the same front panel design with connectors, each clearly marked with the individual product name. The use of common components result in protocol compatibility. This compatibility is extended into the software structure as well. Standard software support for all three boards maintains a consistent application interface. By adhering to these hardware and software standards, the boards achieve a high degree of interoperability.

ASYNCHRONOUS TERMINAL CONTROLLERS

STANDARD TERMINAL CONTROLLER FEATURES

- Full duplex asynchronous transmission using the 82510 UART
- 12 ports per board, RS232C compatible
- 8 signal support, RJ45 (Phone Jack Style) shielded connectors
- Performance ranging from 110 baud to 288k baud
- Asynchronous Terminal Control Software (ATCS) for interrupt processing, character handling and modem support (max rate = 19.2k baud)

MULTI-TERMINAL ACCESS

Twelve serial I/O ports are provided by each board. Each port is based on the 82510 UART component and supports full duplex asynchronous transmissions. An on-chip baud rate generator allows for independent baud rates on each channel. For applications requiring more than 12 ports, the number of ports can be expanded in three ways: by adding more MPI boards (iSBC MPI/450), by adding more intelligent boards (iSBC 186/450), or by mounting additional MIX450 modules onto the MIX baseboard. The customer may choose their configuration based on price and performance requirements of their application.

EASE OF CABLING

Intel's Terminal Controllers utilize the RJ-45 "phone jack" style connector, which provides shielding and lock in mating. Individual connectors are directly plugged into the front panel mount, hence a break out box is not required. Changing terminal configurations is quick and easy with this versatile connection and the identical front panel mounts on the boards. Cables are available through commercial vendors in both shielded and unshielded specifications. Intel recommends shielded cables for application use.

MODEM SUPPORT

Each channel provides for 8 signal support. Software handshaking (DTR, RTS and CTS), Carrier Detect (DCD), Ring Indicator (RI), Data Relay (RXD and TXD) and Signal Ground (SG) are supported. This support allows for access to remote dial up modems and computer to computer communications.

CONSISTENT APPLICATION INTERFACE

Asynchronous Terminal Control Software (ATCS) provides a standard application interface for all Intel Terminal Controllers. ATCS optimizes the interrupt processing and character handling on an intelligent terminal controller board, offloading this task from the application CPU. ATCS supports full duplex and provides such features as support for multiple hosts, dynamic line switching, and modem support. ATCS achieves these features and high performance by providing input and output buffers of 2K per line (port). These buffers increase serial data throughput on output and allow input bursts to be absorbed. Dependent on the CPU, this capability can result in simultaneous input and output up to 19.2k baud rates. ATCS code is designed to support up to 36 channels per server and multiple ATCS servers may reside in the system.

ASYNCHRONOUS TERMINAL CONTROLLERS

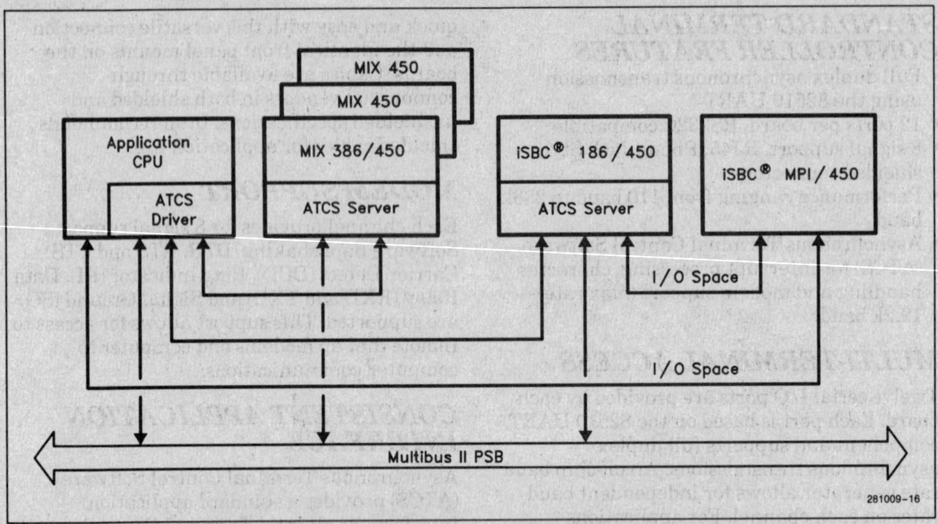

Figure 5: Terminal Controller Configuration Example

ASYNCHRONOUS TERMINAL CONTROLLERS

281009-17

iSBC® MPI/450 TERMINAL CONTROLLER

The iSBC MPI/450 is a non-intelligent 12 channel, RS 232-C compatible, asynchronous terminal controller. The iSBC MPI/450 utilizes the Multibus II Peripheral Interface (MPI) component to add additional I/O capability to an application CPU.

iSBC® MPI/450 FEATURES

- Extension of application CPU by providing offboard asynchronous ports using the 82510 UART
- Slave Multibus II Parallel System Bus Interface provided by the Multibus II Peripheral Interface (MPI)
- 12 ports per board, RS232C compatible
- 8 signal support, RJ45 (Phone Jack Style) shielded connectors
- Performance dependent upon application CPU bandwidth

EXTENSION OF APPLICATION CPU

The iSBC MPI/450 provides 12 offboard asynchronous channels to the application CPU, allowing low cost ports to be easily added to the system. The application CPU accesses the MPI ports via the Parallel System Bus (PSB) I/O space, therefore any intelligent board may host the iSBC MPI/450. The number of MPI boards that can be supported is dependent upon the host CPU bandwidth and application requirements.

MPI FEATURES

The MPI component provides the iSBC MPI/450 with the capability to generate unsolicited messages without data. This feature allows the host CPU boards to interact with the iSBC MPI/450 when prompted by a message rather than requiring continually polling. An interrupt register is provided for servicing the 82510 USARTs, whether a polling or message technique is used.

ASYNCHRONOUS TERMINAL CONTROLLERS

iSBC® MPI/450 CONTROLLER SPECIFICATIONS

Interfaces

P1	Slave PSB
Serial	12 channels, RS232C, 8-pin RJ-45 connectors, 82510 Controller
Signals	DTR, RTS, CTS, CDC, RI, RXD, TXD, SG

Device Drivers

Check the latest release of the following operating systems for details:

iRMX II, III Operating Systems

UNIX* System V/386 Operating System

Physical Characteristics

Standard Multibus II board

Power Requirements

(Excluding user-installed memory devices)

Nominal Voltage (VDC)	Current (amps) Max	Power (watts) Max
+ 5	1.55	7.75
+12	.15	1.8
−12	.15	1.8

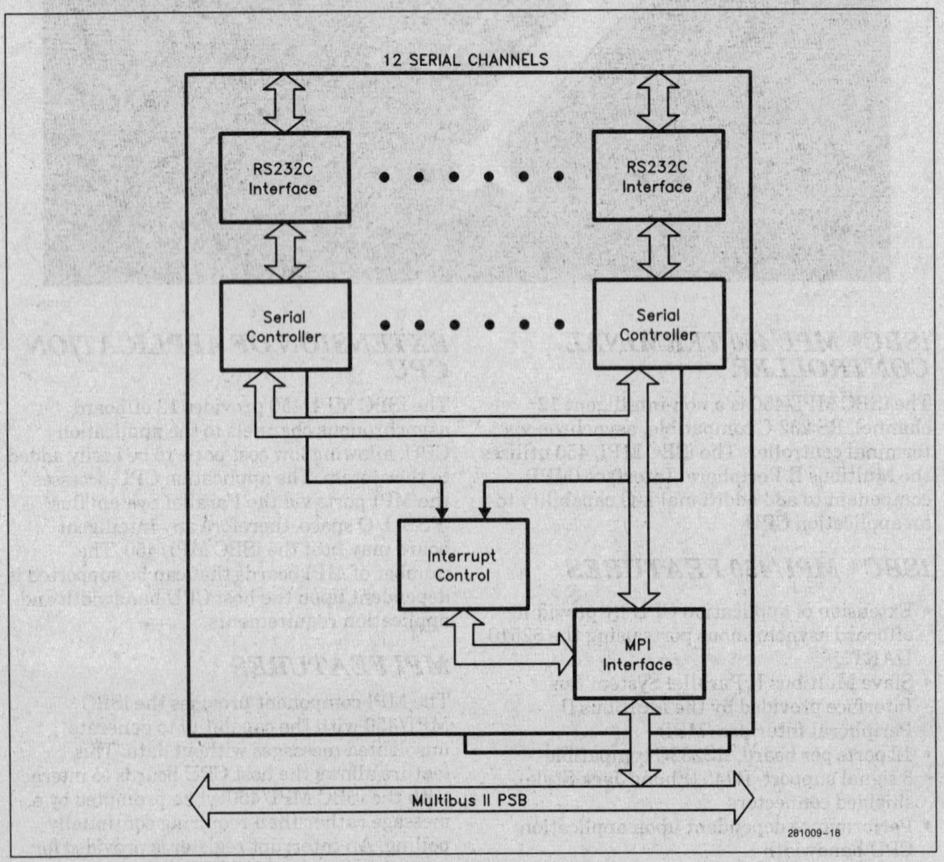

Figure 6: Block Diagram of iSBC®MPI/450 Terminal Controller

ASYNCHRONOUS TERMINAL CONTROLLERS

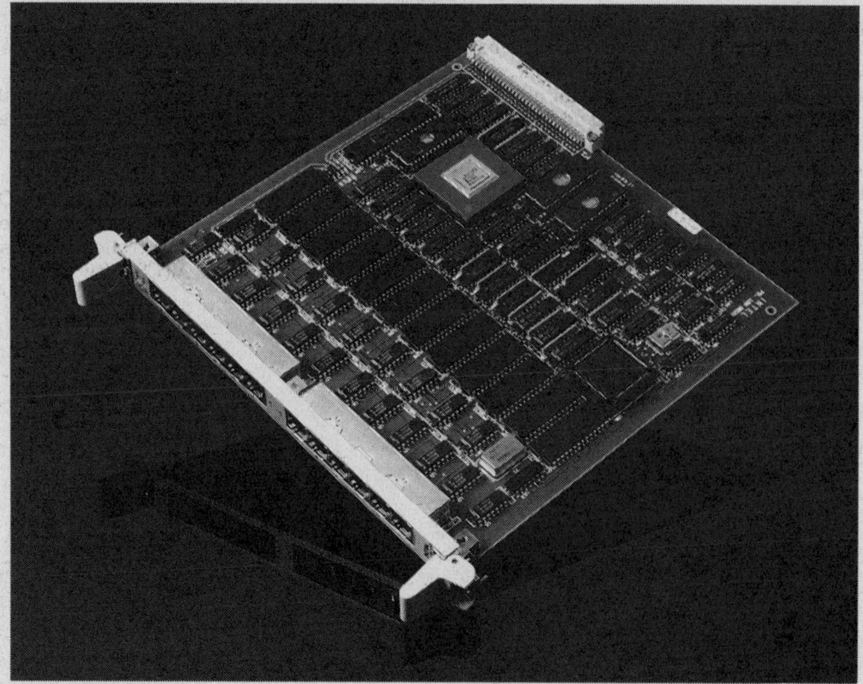

281009-19

iSBC® 186/450 Terminal Controller

The iSBC 186/450 is a high performance intelligent terminal controller. The 80C186 CPU, 512K RAM and ATCS served software allow this board to offload the terminal I/O processing from the Multibus II application CPUs.

iSBC® 186/450 FEATURES

- 80C186-based microprocessor operating at 12.5 MHz
- 512K RAM, 128K or 256K EPROM
- Full Multibus II Parallel System Bus interface provided by the Message Passing Coprocessor (MPC)
- 12 ports, RS232C compatible
- 8 signal support, RJ45 (Phone Jack Style) shielded connectors
- Asynchronous Terminal Control Software (ATCS) for interrupt processing, character handling and modem support
- Multiple host support including dynamic line switching
- Resident firmware to support Built-In-Self-Tests (BIST), host-to-controller software download.

TERMINAL CONTROLLER SUPPORT

The iSBC 186/450 takes the role of dedicated terminal controller in the system by offloading the application CPU of the task of handling terminal interrupts and character processing. This controller can also be the server for the non-intelligent iSBC MPI/450 boards, using the ATCS software resident on the iSBC 186/450 to drive the MPI-based I/O ports.

ASYNCHRONOUS TERMINAL CONTROLLERS

PERFORMANCE

The performance for the 12 channels of the iSBC 186/450 with the ATCS software can be measured at 19.2k baud sustained output, and 19.2k baud input in 2k byte bursts for all channels in a full duplex mode. If additional channels are required, they may be added by introducing additional iSBC 186/450's as additional standalone terminal controllers or by adding additional iSBC MPI/450 boards into the system and utilizing the iSBC 186/450 as a server.

SUPPORT FOR MULTIPLE HOSTS

The ATCS software has the ability to service multiple hosts. The same terminal may be connected to multiple clients and dynamic line switching is supported by the ATCS software.

FIRMWARE

The iSBC 186/450 contains two 32 pin EPROM sites with firmware that includes Built-In-Self-Tests (BISTS) and host-to-controller download code for soft-loading the ATCS software onto the board.

ASYNCHRONOUS TERMINAL CONTROLLERS

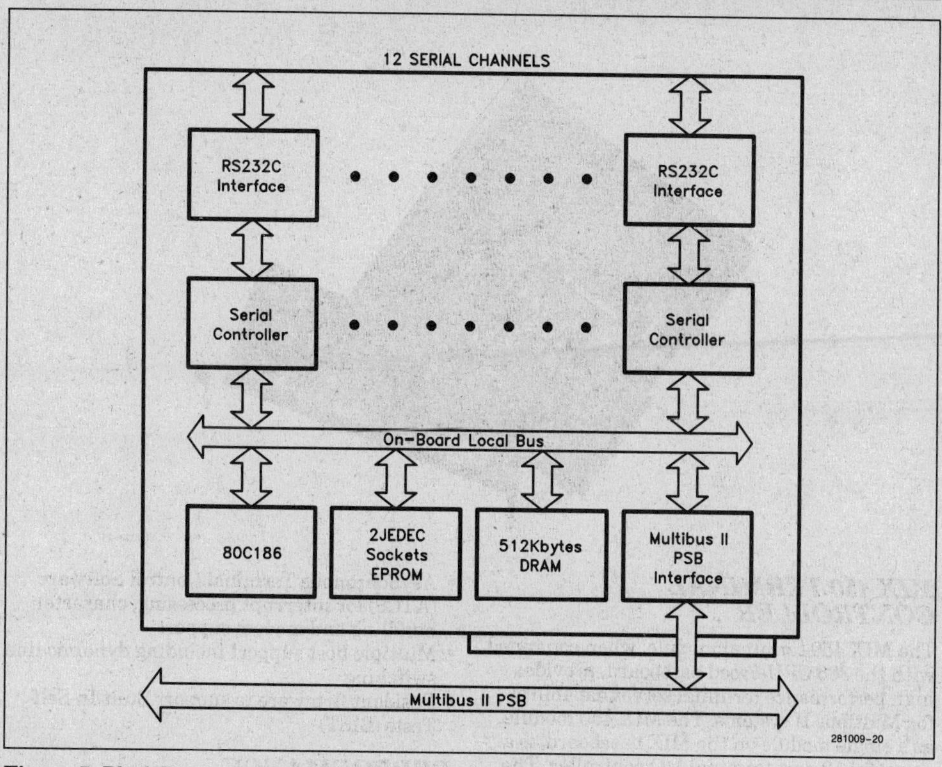

Figure 7: Block Diagram for iSBC® 186/450 Terminal Controller

iSBC® 186/450 CONTROLLER SPECIFICATIONS

Clock Rate

80C186 Microprocessor 12.5 MHz

EPROM Memory

Two 32-pin sites

Supports either 128K bytes or 256K bytes

DRAM Memory

512K bytes installed on the board

Interrupt Capabilities

5 levels with 5 on-board sources

Interfaces

P1	Full PSB
Serial	12 channels, RS232C, 8-pin RJ-45 connectors, 82510 Controller
Signals	DTR, RTS, CTS, RI, CDC, RXD, TXD, SG

Device Drivers

Check the latest release of the following operating systems for details:

iRMX II, III Operating Systems

UNIX* System V/386 Operating System

Physical Characteristics

Standard Multibus II board

Power Requirements

(Excluding user-installed memory devices)

Nominal Voltage (VDC)	Current (amps) Max	Power (watts) Max
+5	4	20
+12	.3	3.6
−12	.3	3.6

ASYNCHRONOUS TERMINAL CONTROLLERS

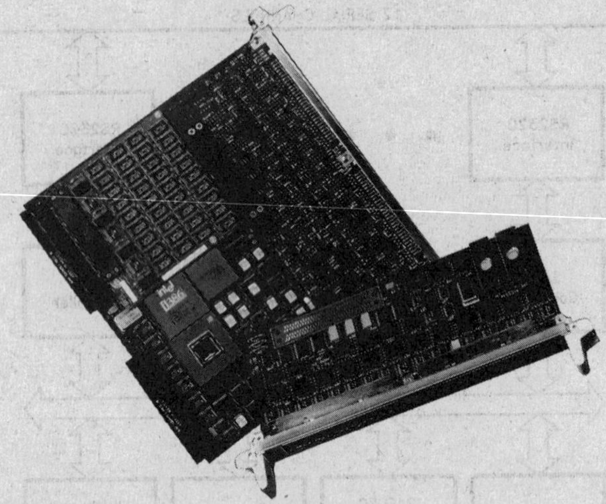

281009–21

MIX 450 TERMINAL CONTROLLER

The MIX 450 terminal module, when combined with the 386 CPU-based baseboard, provides high performance terminal server capability for Multibus II systems. The MIX 450 module, as a single module on the MIX baseboard, is a powerful 12 port terminal I/O controller. The module can also be stacked three high to expand the terminal support to 36 ports. Stacking the MIX 450 with other MIX modules allows the system designer to build to a multi-function I/O server with terminal capabilities.

MIX 450 FEATURES

- 12 ports per board, RS232C compatible
- 8 signal support, RJ45 (Phone Jack Style) shielded connectors
- Asynchronous Terminal Control Software (ATCS) for interrupt processing, character handling and modem support
- Multiple host support including dynamic line switching
- Resident firmware to support Built-In-Self-Tests (BIST)

PERFORMANCE

The MIX 386/450 supplies the highest performance of the terminal controllers offered by Intel. The MIX 386/450 can support 12 channels in fully sustained, simultaneous input and output transmission at 19.2k baud. Two additional modules can be added to the MIX stack for up to 36 channels.

ASYNCHRONOUS TERMINAL CONTROLLERS

SUPPORT FOR MULTIPLE HOSTS

The ATCS software has the ability to service multiple hosts. The same terminal may be connected to multiple clients. Dynamic line switching is also supported.

FIRMWARE

The MIX 450 module contains two 32 pin EPROM sites with firmware that includes Built-In Self Tests (BISTs). Upon power-up, the MIX baseboard copies the MIX 450 BIST code up from the module to the baseboard, where it is executed during initialization.

The MIX baseboard firmware provides the capability of downloading the ATCS software.

MIX ARCHITECTURE

Intel's Modular Interface eXtension (MIX) architecture provides a high-performance terminal controller with built-in high performance, on-board I/O expansion. It is optimized for the *i*386 microprocessor family and the Multibus II System Architecture. The MIX bus allows for easy expansion of terminal support by stacking one, two or three MIX I/O modules. The I/O module interface to the MIX bus is open, with specifications and documentation available from Intel.

ASYNCHRONOUS TERMINAL CONTROLLERS

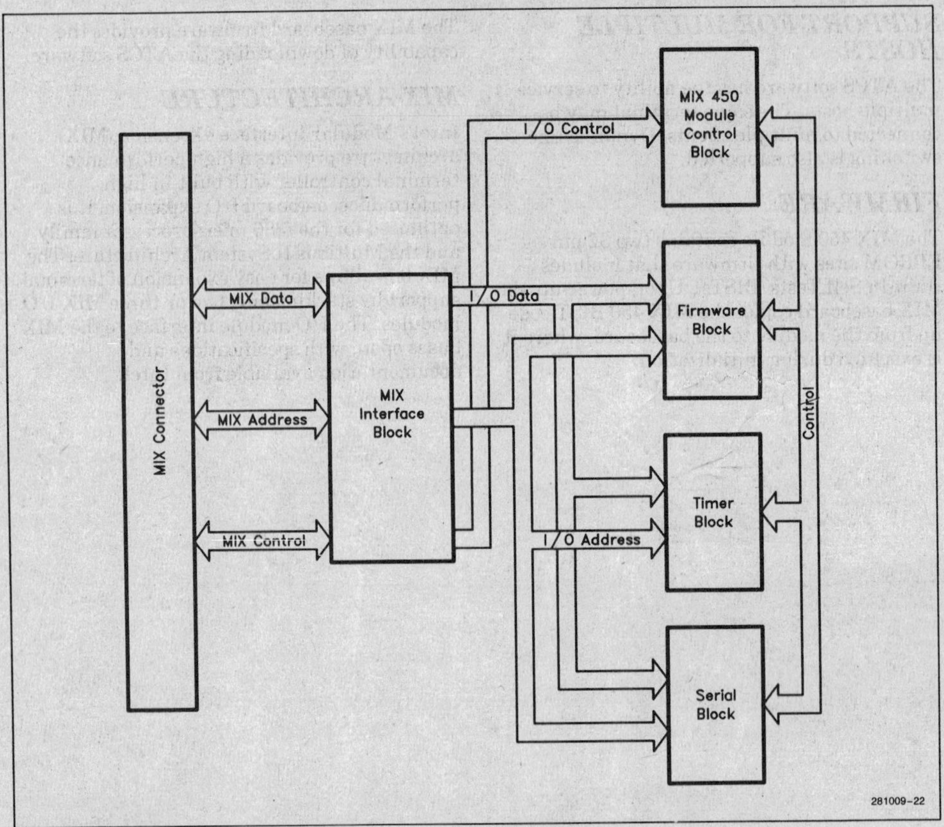

Figure 8: MIX 450 Terminal Controller Module Block Diagram

MIX 450 SPECIFICATIONS†

†For Baseboard specifications, refer to the section on the MIX 386/020 Baseboard

Clock Rates

82C54 Programmable Interval Timer 1.15 MHz

EPROM Memory

Two 32-pin JEDEC sites.

EEPROM

128 bytes installed on the module.

Interfaces

Serial — 12 channels, RS232C, 8-pin RJ45 connector, 82510 Controller

MIX — Bus slave

Signals — DTR, RTS, CTS, CDC, RI, RXD, TXD, SG

Device Drivers

Check the latest release of the following operating systems for details:

iRMX II, III Operating Systems

UNIX* System V/386 Operating System

Physical Characteristics

Standard MIX Module

Power Requirements

Nominal Voltage (VDC)	Current (amps) Max	Power (watts) Max
+5	3.0	15.0
+12	0.02	0.24
−12	0.02	0.24

MULTIBUS II WIDE AREA NETWORK CONTROLLERS

281009-23

A CHOICE OF HIGH PERFORMANCE SYNCHRONOUS CONTROLLERS

Intel provides two synchronous board solutions targeted towards Wide Area Network Applications. Both boards provide the hardware platforms that support commercial Wide Area Network protocols. The two boards provide price and performance options that can be tailored to individual application needs.

The iSBC 186/410 is a standalone communications controller. Within a Multibus II system, the iSBC 186/410 can optimize overall performance by assuming control of the Wide Area Network administration, reducing the primary system CPU overhead.

For applications requiring high speed synchronous control and mainframe communication, the MIX 386/420 provides an optimal solution. The MIX 386/420 combines the intelligence and performance of the MIX 386 Baseboard with the focused synchronous control of the MIX 420 module. The Modular Interface eXtension (MIX) Architecture allows the user to stack up to three modules on the baseboard. This feature can be used to expand up to six channels of high speed synchronous control or to add other I/O capabilities.

WIDE AREA NETWORK CONTROLLER FEATURES

- Two high performance Wide Area Network Controllers address a range of price and performance requirements
- Intelligent controllers based on 80C186 and 386 microprocessors with compatible synchronous serial controllers (82530 and 85C30)
- On board Built-In-Self-Test (BIST) with diagnostics

MULTIBUS II WIDE AREA NETWORK CONTROLLERS

281009-24

iSBC® 186/410 WIDE AREA NETWORK CONTROLLER

The iSBC 186/410 Multibus II Serial Communications Board is an intelligent 6-channel communications processor that addresses the needs of many standard communication applications. The board brings flexibility to the application with its multiple serial channels as well as I/O expansion through the SBX connections.

The iSBC 186/410 is designed to support serial communication within the system. The iSBC 186/410 board supports asynchronous, byte synchronous, and bit-synchronous (HDLC/SDLC) communications on the two full/half duplex RS232C or RS422A channels. On the remaining four channels, only asynchronous mode (RS232C) is supported in either full or half duplex operation. Each serial channel can be individually programmed for different baud rates to allow system configurations with differing terminal types.

iSBC® 186/410 FEATURES

- 8 MHz 80C186 Microprocessor
- Six Serial Communication Channels, Two RS232C or RS422A, Four RS232C Only, Front Panel Connections
- 82258 DMA Controller Provides 4 Independent DMA Channels
- 512K Bytes DRAM Provided, Four 28 Pin JEDEC Sites available for EPROM
- Two iSBX Connector provided for I/O Expansion

MULTIBUS II WIDE AREA NETWORK CONTROLLERS

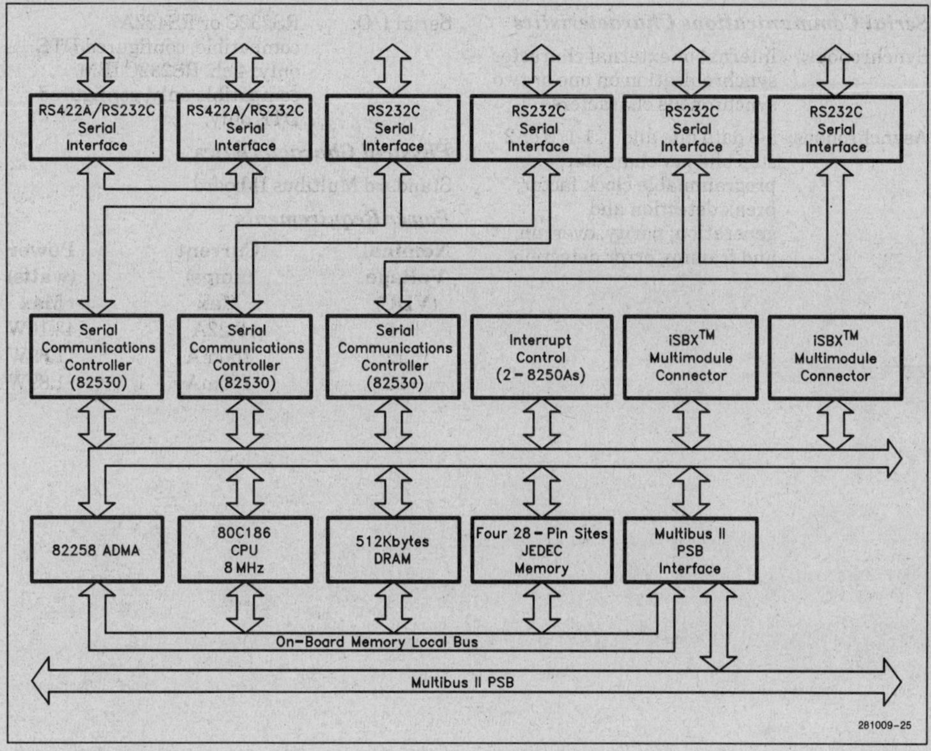

Figure 9: Block Diagram of iSBC® 186/410 WAN Controller

iSBC® 186/410 WAN CONTROLLER SPECIFICATIONS

Clock Rates

80C186 Microprocessor	8 MHz
82258 ADMA	8 MHz
8751 Microcontroller	12 MHz
82C54 Timer	(Programmable)

EPROM Memory

Four 28-pin Socket

DRAM Memory

512K bytes

Programmable Baud Rate

110—19.2 KB (async)
110—1 MB (sync)

Interrupt Capabilities

14 programmable interrupts

Interfaces

P1	Full PSB
Serial	4 Channels, RS-232C only
	2 Channels, RS-232C or RS-422A
iSBX	2 Single Wide

Device Drivers

Check the latest release of the following operating systems for details:

iRMX I, II, III Operating Systems

UNIX* System V/386 Operating System

MULTIBUS II WIDE AREA NETWORK CONTROLLERS

Serial Communications Characteristics

Synchronous: internal or external character synchronization on one or two synchronous characters.

Asynchronous: 5-8 data bits and 1, 1-1/2 or 2 stop bits per character; programmable clock factor; break detection and generation; parity; overrun, and framing error detection.

Serial I/O: RS232C or RS422A compatible, configured DTE only; 4 ch. RS232C IBM compatible only, configured DTE only.

Physical Characteristics

Standard Multibus II board

Power Requirements

Nominal Voltage (VDC)	Current (amps) Max	Power (watts) Max
+ 5	8.22A	43.16W
+12	150mA	1.89W
−12	150mA	1.89W

MULTIBUS II WIDE AREA NETWORK CONTROLLERS

281009-26

MIX 420 WIDE AREA NETWORK MODULE

The MIX 420 module combines two high speed synchronous channels with the 386 CPU-based MIX baseboard to build a high performance Wide Area Network (WAN) platform. The MIX 420 modules can be stacked to a maximum level of three modules for expansion up to six channels. The MIX 420 can be stacked with other MIX modules, allowing the system designer to build a multi-function I/O server with WAN capabilities.

MIX 420 FEATURES

- Two Independent High Speed Synchronous Channels using a 10 MHz 85C30 Serial Communication Controller (SCC).
- High Performance communications capable of 256 kbit/second, with ADMA, and Bypass (slave) speed modes.
- Flexible communications with an 82C54 Programmable Interface Timer and either channel interrupts or hardware interrupts using the 82C59 component.
- "Smart Cable" interface using AT&T General Purpose Synchronous (GPSYNC) Standard.
- Designed as a hardware platform for Synchronous Protocol Support, including SDLC/HDLC, SNA, Bisync/Async, SNA, X.25, X.21, X.21 BIS, LU6.2.
- Firmware containing Built-In Self Test (BIST) code.

MULTIBUS II WIDE AREA NETWORK CONTROLLERS

HIGH PERFORMANCE WIDE AREA NETWORK CONNECTION

The MIX 420 Module provides two independent Wide Area Network interfaces using the 85C30 SCC with resulting transfer rates up to 256 Kbit/sec on each channel simultaneously. Speed is enhanced with an 8 MHz, 82258 ADMA, which supports full duplex DMA access to each serial channel. A Bypass (slave) mode is also supported where the CPU handles the transfers, bypassing the ADMA. This mode allows for the MIX 420 to act as a slave module reducing software complexity or allows for the designer to check the hardware functions of the board.

VERSATILE PROTOCOL SUPPORT

The MIX 420 module provides a hardware platform for synchronous communication protocols. The 85C30 based channels provide standard hardware support for SDLC/HDLC, Bisync and Async. The "Smart Cable" interface provided by the AT&T GPSYNC cable addresses the high level protocols by controlling the electronic specification level via an intelligent cable. This interface allows the designer to switch protocols by merely addressing the software issues and swapping to a new cable. The cable will address the electronic difference between the interfaces such as X.21 RS232, AS449, V.35, V.36 or X.24. Finally, the symmetrical design offers channel independence allowing for unique protocols and baud rates to be run simultaneously on the module.

UTILIZING THE MIX ARCHITECTURE

The MIX 386/420 utilizes the Modular Interface eXtension (MIX) architecture. The MIX architecture provides an intelligent base CPU to be combined with specific I/O modules to create a communication platform. Modular stacking allows for up to three modules to be stacked per baseboard, allowing for up to six high speed synchronous channels through the use of the MIX 420 Module.

FIRMWARE

Two 32 pin EPROM sites reside on the MIX 420 for firmware. Included in the firmware is Built-In-Self-Test (BIST) to check basic functionality of the module and MIX interface. Upon power up, the MIX baseboard copies the MIX 420 BIST from the module to the baseboard where it is executed during initialization

MULTIBUS II WIDE AREA NETWORK CONTROLLERS

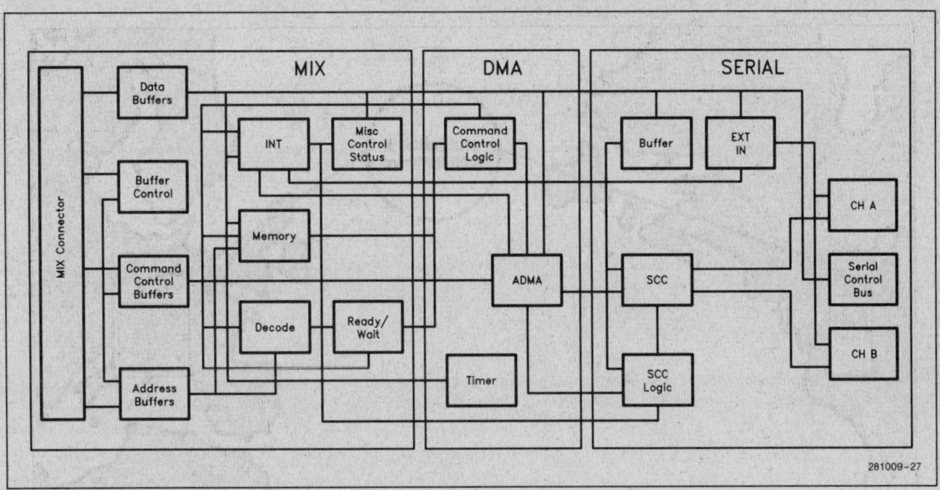

Figure 10: Block Diagram for MIX 420 Module

MIX 420 SPECIFICATIONS†

†For baseboard specifications, refer to the section on the MIX 020A Baseboard

Programmable Baud Rates

110-256 Kbit/sec

Interrupts

Mode	Level
Channel	2
Device	8

Programmable Interval Timer

82C54

EPROM Memory

Two 32-pin JEDEC sites

EEPROM

128 bytes installed

DMA

82258 ADMA 8 MHz

Interfaces

Serial 2 Channels, AT&T GPSYNC Interface, RS-232, RS-449, V.36, V.36, X.24, X.21, 85C30 Controller, 10 MHz

MIX Bus Master

Device Drivers

Check the latest release of the following operating systems for details:

iRMX II, III Operating Systems

UNIX* System V/386

Operating System

Physical Characteristics

Standard MIX module

Power Requirements

Nominal Voltage (VDC)	Current (amps) Max	Power (watts) Max
+5	3.0	15.0
+12	.02	0.24
−12	.02	0.24

MULTIBUS II WIDE AREA NETWORK SOFTWARE

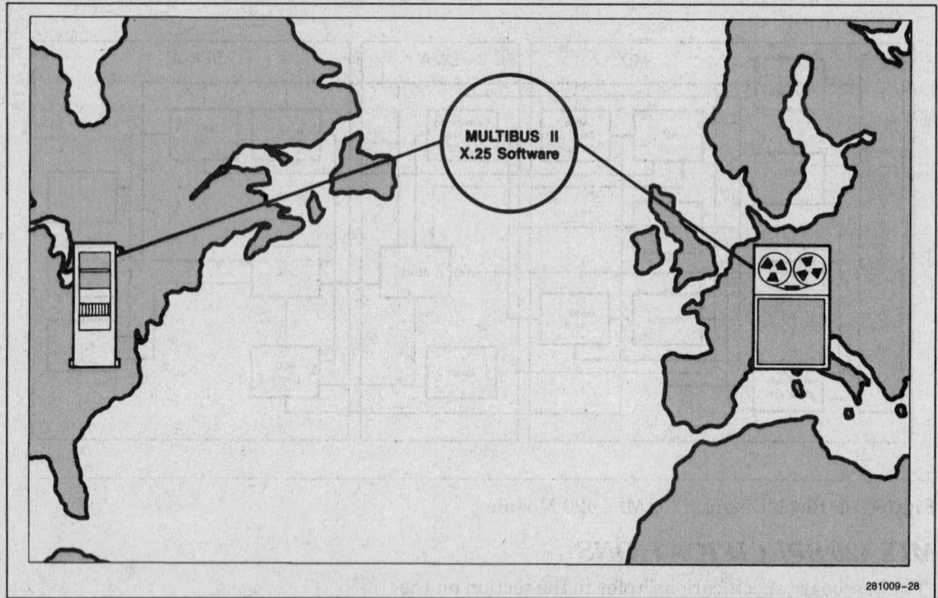

MULTIBUS II X.25 SOFTWARE

X.25 is an international standard synchronous bit-orientated serial communications protocol based on CCITT Recommendations. The protocol provides connection oriented communications, i.e., virtual circuits. The basic unit of transfer is a packet of data. Performance can range with the speeds of the communication lines varying from 110 baud to 256k and above.

X.25 SOFTWARE FEATURES

- Conforms to CCITT Recommendations 1976, 1980, 1984
- Supports LAPX and LAPB protocols at frame level
- Supports Permanent Virtual Circuits (PVC's)
- Supports Switched Virtual Circuits in the following Modes: Incoming-only, Outgoing-only and Two-way
- Supports Networks services such as reverse charging, closed user groups, etc.
- Supports X.32 Dial-up features
- Operating parameters of each line can be dynamically changed (e.g. Baud rates, packet size, timeouts, etc.)
- Modular architecture allows optional functionality to be added (e.g. X.3/X.28, PAD, X.29, QLLC, SNA)

IMPLEMENTATION

The X.25 package is currently available on the iSBC 186/410. The software can co-exits with the Asynchronous Terminal Controller Software (ATCS), allowing the iSBC 186/410 to support two X.25 lines and four terminals. Driver support for the iRMX II operating system is also available.

INSTALLATION AND SUPPORT

Included with the Multibus II X.25 product is on-site installation performed by Intel Customer Support. This service insures that the software is tested and fully functioning. If further service of the network is desired, a support contract may be ordered.

CUSTOMIZATION

Intel Customer Support is available and trained to customize the X.25 to fit various applications. Customization may include parameters such as performance tuning, specific OS drivers or application specific requests.

MULTIBUS II ETHERNET CONTROLLERS

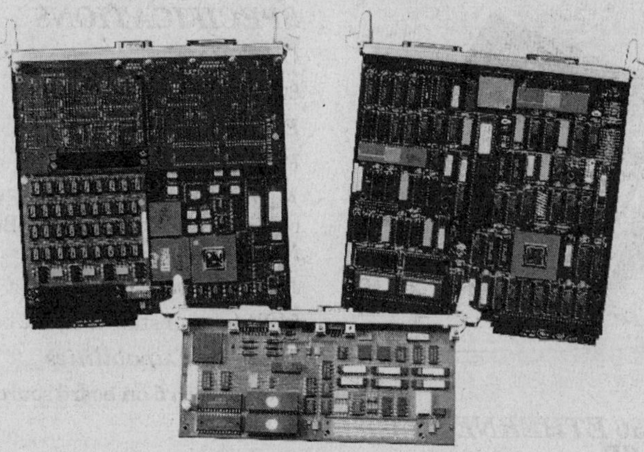

281009-29

A FAMILY OF MULTIBUS II ETHERNET LAN CONTROLLERS WITH OpenNET™ NETWORKING SOFTWARE SUPPORT

The Intel Multibus II Ethernet LAN controller family provides a range of price and performance for handling Multibus II Ethernet communication requirements. The iSBC 186/530 is an 80186 CPU-based Ethernet LAN controller that provides a cost-effective LAN connection for many Multibus II designs.

For high performance, the Modular Interface eXtension (MIX) 560 Ethernet module provides Ethernet I/O capabilities to MIX-based I/O subsystems. A MIX-based I/O subsystem that includes the MIX 560 Ethernet module can span the range from a single MIX 560 module mounted on a MIX baseboard to a MIX 560 module mounted in a stack of three MIX I/O modules to provide a tailored Multibus II I/O solution that includes Ethernet communications.

Ethernet I/O is also available on the iSBC 486/133SE CPU Board.

Intel's iNA 960 networking software provides ISO network and transport layer support for both the iSBC 186/530 and the MIX 386/560.

ETHERNET LAN CONTROLLER FEATURES

- A choice of Ethernet LAN controllers providing a range of price and performance.
- Intelligent controllers based on the 80186 and 386 microprocessors and the 82586 LAN Coprocessor.
- Connection to IEEE 802.3 / Ethernet networks for Multibus II systems.
- Support for downloading of networking software over either the Multibus II Parallel System Bus or the Ethernet network.
- ISO Network and Transport (ISO/OSI Layers 3 and 4) networking software support provided by Intel's iNA 960 software.
- iNA 960 networking software executing on the LAN controllers provides a consistent transport interface to host CPU boards.

MULTIBUS II ETHERNET CONTROLLERS

281009-30

iSBC® 186/530 ETHERNET CONTROLLER

The iSBC 186/530 Multibus II Ethernet Controller is a dedicated IEEE 802.3 compatible front-end processor. The board's 8 MHz 80186, 512K DRAM, and host-to-controller software download capability allows the board to off-load LAN communications functions and I/O software processing from one or all of a Multibus II system's host CPU boards.

iSBC® 186/530 ETHERNET CONTROLLER FEATURES

- Provides IEEE 802.3 / Ethernet compatible networking capability for Multibus II systems.
- Resident firmware to support Built-In Self Test (BIST), Initialization and Diagnostic eXecutive (IDX), and host-to-controller software download.
- Four 28-pin JEDEC sites, expandable to 8 sites with iSBC 341 MULTIMODULE™ for a maximum of 512K bytes of EPROM.
- One RS232C serial port for use in debug and testing or as a system console port.
- Multibus II Parallel System Bus interface with full message passing capability.

iSBC® 186/530 CONTROLLER SPECIFICATIONS

Clock Rate

80186 Microprocessor — 8 MHz

EPROM Memory

Four 28-pin sites.

An additional four 28-pin JEDEC sites may be obtained by installing an iSBC 341 MULTIMODULE.

DRAM Memory

512K bytes installed on the board

Interrupt Capabilities

5 levels with 5 on-board sources

Interfaces

P1	Full PSB
Ethernet	1 channel, 15-pin connector, 82586 LAN Coprocessor
Serial	1 channel, RS232C, 25-pin connector, 8031 Controller

Device Drivers

Check the latest release of the following operating systems for details:

iRMX I, II, III Operating Systems

UNIX* System V/386 Operating System

Physical Characteristics

Standard Multibus II board

Power Requirements

(Excluding user-installed memory devices)

Nominal Voltage (VDC)	Current (amps) Max	Power (watts) Max
+ 5	8.8	44.0
+12	0.05	.6
−12	0.05	.6

MULTIBUS II ETHERNET CONTROLLERS

281009–31

MIX 560 ETHERNET MODULE

The MIX 560 Ethernet Module combines an 82586 LAN Coprocessor, 82501 Ethernet Serial Interface, and 64K bytes of high speed SRAM data buffer to provide high performance Ethernet Modular Interface eXtension (MIX) I/O capabilities. The MIX 560 can be used either in a MIX module stack, to provide Ethernet capabilities to a Multibus II MIX I/O server subsystem, or as a single module on the MIX baseboard, to provide a high performance MIX-based Ethernet controller. Stacking the MIX 560 Ethernet module with other MIX I/O modules allows the system designer to manage the system I/O requirements with a tailored Multibus II I/O subsystem that includes Ethernet communications.

MIX 560 ETHERNET MODULE FEATURES

- 82586 LAN Coprocessor operating at 10 MHz. 82501 Ethernet Serial Interface
- 64K bytes of SRAM data buffer for handling communications from the MIX baseboard to the Ethernet Interface
- Support for 128K-265K EPROM
- Firmware containing Built-In Self Test code
- LED for 82586 Activity
- Serial interface for system console or debug

MIX 560 FEATURES

ETHERNET INTERFACE

The Ethernet interface is implemented using the 82586 Ethernet Coprocessor, the 82501 Ethernet Serial Interface controller, and the standard slide-lock 15 pin IEEE 802.3 connector. The 82501 is software configurable to either Ethernet V1.0 or IEEE 802.3 (Ethernet V2.0). IEEE 802.3 is the default. The Ethernet interface operates at a fixed rate of 10 Mbits per second. An Ethernet station address PROM is also provided.

SERIAL INTERFACE

The serial interface is implemented using the 82510 Asynchronous Serial Controller, an RS232 driver/receiver, and a serial port connector. The connector is an IBM-compatible 9-pin DTE interface (only 3 pins are used). The port is intended for use as the system console or as a debug port. The serial interface supports baud rates up to 19.2K.

TIMERS

Two 16-bit interval timers are provided by an 82C54 for generating timed, independent interrupts at the MIX interface. A third timer, also provided by the 82C54, is used as a 16 bit prescaler to the other two timers. The timers are used by Intel's iNA 960 Networking Software.

STATIC RAM

The MIX 560 contains 64K bytes of Static RAM (SRAM). The memory is shared between the MIX interface and the 82586. Networking software executing on the MIX baseboard can use the SRAM as a buffer to send and receive data over the Ethernet interface as well as issue commands to, and receive status from, the 82586 Ethernet Coprocessor.

FIRMWARE

The MIX 560 module contains two 32 pin sockets, accommodating either two 27512 or two 27010 EPROMS. Firmware provided for the MIX 560 module includes MIX 560 Built-In Self Test (BIST) code and the software load commands.

The MIX 560 BIST code resides in EPROM on the module. On power up, the MIX baseboard copies the MIX 560 BIST code from the module to the baseboard where it is executed during initialization. The MIX 560 BIST contains 12 tests for exercising the module and verification of functionality. The firmware commands also provide the ability to read and set the Ethernet station address and start execution of LAN software code on the MIX baseboard.

MIX 560 FEATURES

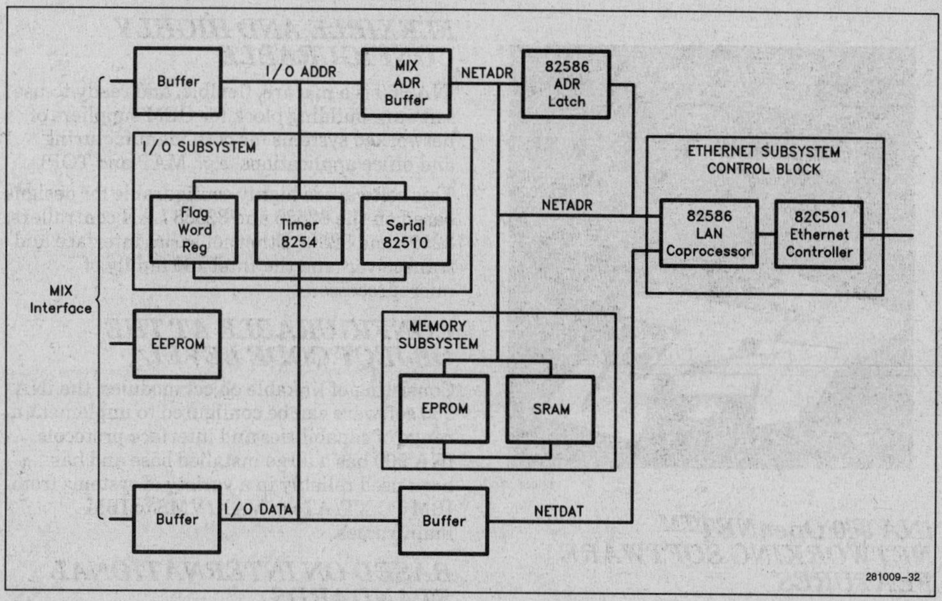

Figure 11: MIX 560 Module Block Diagram

MIX 560 SPECIFICATIONS†

†For Baseboard specifications, refer to the section on the MIX 386/020 or x86/020A Baseboard

Clock Rates

82586 10 MHz

EPROM Memory

Two 32-pin JEDEC sites.

SRAM Memory

64K bytes installed on the module

EEPROM

128 bytes installed on the module

PROM

6 bytes for Ethernet node address

Interfaces

Ethernet	1 channel, 15-pin connector, 82586 LAN Coprocessor
Serial	1 channel, RS232C, 9-pin (IBM-compatible) connector, 82510 Controller
MIX	Bus slave

Device Drivers

Check the latest release of the following operating systems for details:

iRMX II, III Operating Systems

UNIX* System V/386 Operating System

Physical Characteristics

Standard MIX module

Power Requirements

Nominal Voltage (VDC)	Current (amps) Max	Power (watts) Max
+5	3.0	15.0
+12	0.02	0.24
−12	0.02	0.24

The MIX 560 module also passes fused +12 VDC through the Ethernet connector to an external transceiver. The transceiver may require up to an additional 0.5 Amps (max) of +12 V.

MULTIBUS II ETHERNET CONTROLLERS

281009-33

iNA 960 OpenNET™ NETWORKING SOFTWARE FEATURES

- Certified ISO/OSI Transport and Network Layer Software
- ISO 8072/8073 Transport Class 4
- ISO 8602 Connectionless Transport
- ISO 8348/8473 Connectionless Network
- ISO 9542 End System to Intermediate System (ES/IS) Dynamic Routing
- Comprehensive Network Management Functions
- Remote Boot Server for diskless workstations
- Data Link Drivers for iSBC 552A, iSBX 586, iSBC 554, iSBC 186/51, iSBC 186/530, and MIX 386/560

FULLY COMPLIANT ISO/OSI TRANSPORT AND NETWORK LAYER SOFTWARE

iNA 960 is a complete Network and Transport (ISO/OSI Layers 3 and 4) software system plus a comprehensive set of network management functions, Data Link (OSI Layer 2) drivers for IEEE 802.3 Ethernet and IEEE 802.4 Token Bus (MAP), and system environment features.

FLEXIBLE AND HIGHLY CONFIGURABLE

iNA 960 is a mature, flexible, and ready-to-use software building block for OEM suppliers of networked systems for both manufacturing and office applications (e.g., MAP and TOP).

This software is highly configurable for designs based on the 82586 and 82588 LAN controllers, 82501 and 82502 Ethernet serial interface and transceiver, and the Intel x86 family of microprocessors.

CONFIGURABLE AT THE OBJECT CODE LEVEL

Consisting of linkable object modules, the iNA 960 software can be configured to implement a range of capabilities and interface protocols. iNA 960 has a large installed base and has been used reliably in a variety of systems from IBM PC XT/ATs to VAX/VMS to IBM mainframes.

BASED ON INTERNATIONAL STANDARDS

Based on the ISO/OSI seven layer model for network communications, iNA 960 implements ISO 8073 Transport Class 4 providing reliable full-duplex message delivery service on top of the internet capabilities offered by the network layer. The iNA 960 network layer is an implementation of the ISO 8473 Network Class 3 Connectionless Network Protocol and supports ISO 9542 End System to Intermediate System Network Dynamic Routing. iNA 960 also supports ISO 8602 Connectionless Transport Protocol (Datagram).

PRECONFIGURED iNA 961

iNA 960 contains the preconfigured iNA 961 software modules which include support for the iSBC 552A, iSBC 554, iSBC 186/530, and the MIX 386/560.

REMOTE BOOT SERVER SUPPORT

iNA 960 provides basic boot server capabilities that will transmit predefined images to diskless network nodes that request them.

MULTI-SERVER/CONSUMER SUPPORT

iNA 960 supports the powerful Multibus II feature of multiple host and communications boards. This is ideal for LAN load balancing and redundant networks for fault-tolerant systems.

MULTIBUS II PERIPHERAL CONTROLLERS

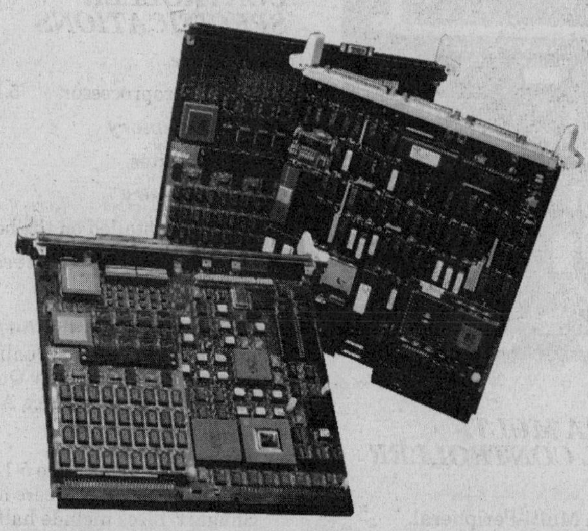

281009-34

A CHOICE OF PERIPHERAL CONTROLLERS

Intel's product line of Multibus II Peripheral Controllers addresses the diverse interfaces of peripheral communications. The iSBC 186/224A, a Multi-Peripheral Controller Subsystem, provides support for up to four ST506/412 Winchester disk drives, up to four SA450/460 floppy drives and quarter inch QIC-02 streaming tape drives. The iSBC 386/258, a versatile high-performance SCSI peripheral controller, provides performance tuning capability for peripheral devices individually for optimum system performance. Additionally, the iSBC 386/258 can complement the host by offloading it with its powerful 386 microprocessor.

PERIPHERAL CONTROLLER FEATURES

- Multiple peripheral interface support:
  SCSI
  ST506/412 Hard Disk
  SA450/460 Floppy Drive
  QIC-02 Tape
- Full PSB interface with complete Message Passing Support
- On-board Built-In-Self-Test (BIST) with Diagnostics

MULTIBUS II PERIPHERAL CONTROLLERS

281009-35

iSBC® 186/224A MULTI-PERIPHERAL CONTROLLER SUBSYSTEM

The iSBC 186/224A Multi-Peripheral Controller Subsystem provides peripheral I/O control for a variety of OEM applications and supports the full message passing protocol of the Multibus II System Architecture. The iSBC 186/224A controller serves as a complete peripheral I/O subsystem and it supports the predominant types of storage media: Winchester disks, floppy disks and quarter-inch streaming tapes. On-board firmware for the board provides improved Winchester disk operation through multiple data track cacheing.

iSBC® 186/224A FEATURES

- 80C186 Microprocessor at 5 MHz
- Controls up to Four ST506/412 Winchester Disk Drives, Four SA450/460 Floppy Drives, and Four QIC-02 Streaming Tape Drives
- 128K Bytes of On-Board SRAM for multiple track cacheing on high speed Winchester data access
- Built-In-Self-Test (BIST) Diagnostics On-Board
- Full Message Passing interface to the Parallel System Bus.

iSBC® 186/224A PERIPHERAL CONTROLLER SPECIFICATIONS

Clock Rate

80C186 Microprocessor 5 MHz

EPROM Memory

Two 28-pin sites.

DRAM Memory

128K bytes installed on the board.

Mass Storage Device Drives

Winchester

ST506/412 compatible 5-1/4″ drives with up to 1024 cylinders. Qualified manufacturers include: Quantum, CMI, CDC, Maxtor, Memorex, Atasi.

Floppy

SA450/460 compatible 5-1/4″ drives. Qualified manufacturers include: Teac and Shugart. Sizes include half height, full height, 48 TPI and 96 TPI.

Tape

QIC-02 compatible, 1/4″ streaming tape drives. Qualified manufacturers include: Archive, Cipher, and Tandberg.

Interfaces

P1	Full PSB
ST506/412	50 pin D-type
SA450/460	25 pin D-type
QIC-02	25 pin D-type

Device Drivers

Check the latest release of the following operating systems for details:
iRMX I, II, III Operating Systems
UNIX* System V/386 Operating System

Physical Characteristics

Standard Multibus II board

Power Requirements

Nominal Voltage (VDC)	Current (amps) Max	Power (watts) Max
+5	7.0	35.0
+12	0.05	.6
−12	0.05	.6

MULTIBUS II PERIPHERAL CONTROLLERS

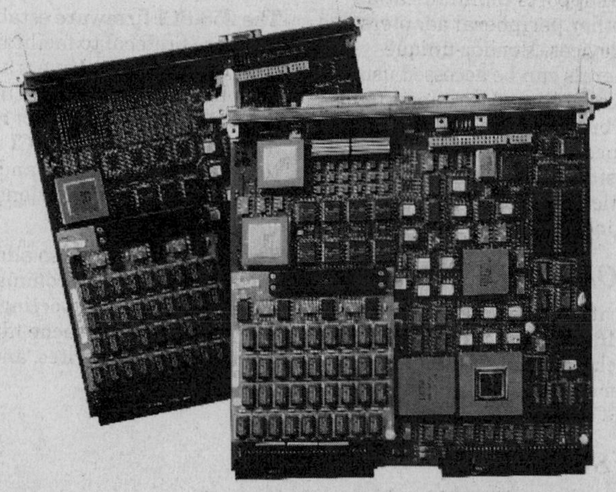

281009-36

iSBC® 386/258 SCSI PERIPHERAL CONTROLLER

The iSBC 386/258 is a high-performance peripheral controller that combines powerful I/O performance and access to SCSI peripherals for Multibus II applications.

Minicomputer-level I/O performance is achieved by utilizing the 386 microprocessor and a large data cache. The added power of the 386 processor gives the iSBC 386/258 the capability of off-loading tasks from other system CPUs as an I/O server. The SCSI standard has achieved wide acceptance because of its extensive capabilities and excellent performance.

iSBC® 386/258 FEATURES

- 16 MHz 386 microprocessor
- 1 or 4 MByte data buffer
- CSM002 module support
- Common Command Set (CCS) SCSI peripheral support
- Asynchronous SCSI to 1.5 MBytes/sec, synchronous to 4.0 MBytes/sec
- Two Versions: single ended SCSI port only or Dual SCSI ports
- Firmware support for BIST, IDX, slave test handler, and downloader
- 258 Peripheral Communications Interface (258-PCI) firmware

MULTIBUS II PERIPHERAL CONTROLLERS

COMPLETE SCSI CAPABILITY

The iSBC 386/258 supports communication with up to seven other peripheral adapters and up to 56 possible devices. Vendor-unique features of peripherals can be accessed using the pass through capability. Also supported is the ability to be a bus initiator, and the use of disconnect/reconnect. Peripherals that support the SCSI standard such as magnetic hard disk, magnetic tape, floppy disk drive, optical disk, and line printers.

HIGH PERFORMANCE

I/O critical applications are accelerated by the combination of a 16 MHz 386 processor, a large data buffer for cacheing (1 or 4 MBbytes), and the 4.0 MBytes per second synchronous transfer rate for SCSI.

FIRMWARE SUPPORT

The iSBC 386/258 includes EPROMs with firmware support for BIST (Built-in Self-Test), IDX (Initialization and Diagnostics Executive), Power up and slave handler, a downloader, and a peripheral communications interface.

The 258-PCI firmware establishes a high level software protocol to facilitate the exchange of data between host drivers and SCSI-based peripheral devices. It also insulates host drivers from knowledge of SCSI bus management. The 258-PCI server manages up to 64 outstanding commands and permits multiheaded I/O operations with up to 56 SCSI peripheral devices.

The 258-PCI server also allows tuning of the cache configuration, command ordering/seek optimization, and reporting of usage statistics, like the number of cache hits and misses, total number of reads, writes, and errors.

MULTIBUS II PERIPHERAL CONTROLLERS

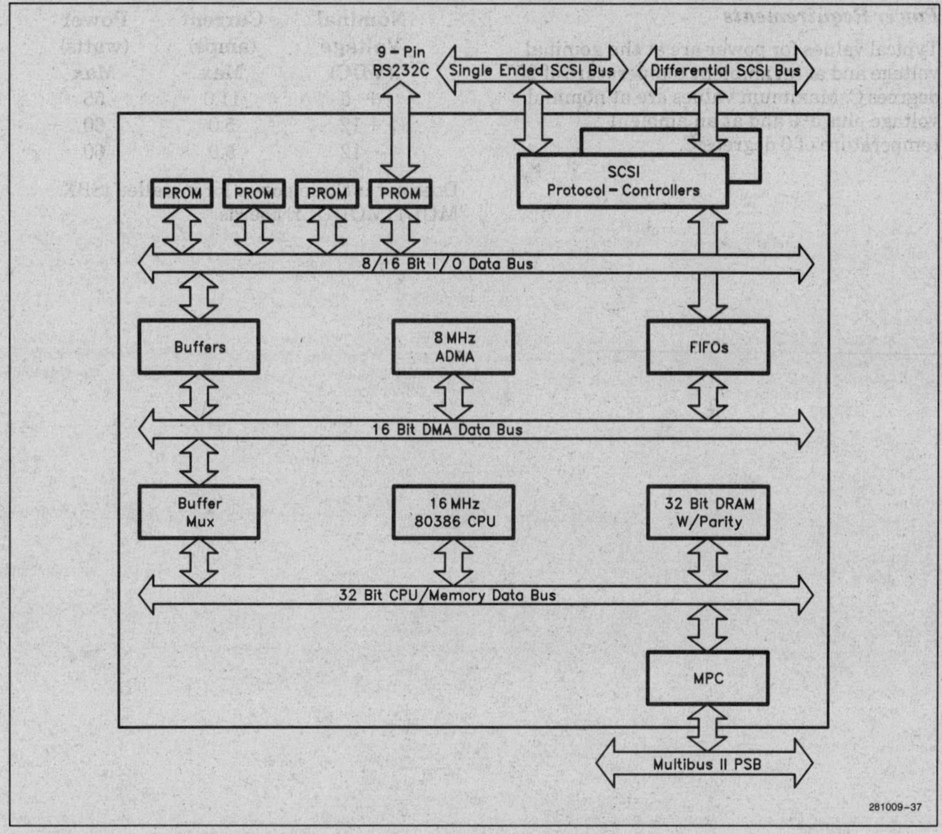

Figure 12: Block Diagram for iSBC® 386/258 Peripheral Controller

iSBC® 386/258 PERIPHERAL CONTROLLER SPECIFICATIONS

Clock Rates

386 DX Microprocessor	16 MHz
82258 ADMA	8 MHz
8751 Microcontroller	12 MHz

EPROM Memory

Two 32-pin Sockets

DRAM Memory

1M or 4M byte installed on the baseboard

Interrupt Capabilities

14 programmable interrupts

Interfaces

- P1, Full PSB
- P2, SCSI: ANSI X3.131—1986, Single-ended or dual versions available.
- iSBX Bus Interface
- Serial I/O Port: RS-232-C (subset)interface (DTE). 9-pin D-shell shielded connector.

Device Drivers

Check the latest release of the following operating systems for details:
iRMX II, III Operating Systems
UNIX* System V/386 Operating System

Physical Characteristics

Standard Multibus II board.

MULTIBUS II PERIPHERAL CONTROLLERS

Power Requirements

Typical values for power are at the nominal voltage and at an ambient temperature of 25 degrees C. Maximum values are at nominal voltage plus 5% and at an ambient temperature of 0 degrees C.

Nominal Voltage (VDC)	Current (amps) Max	Power (watts) Max
+ 5	11.0	55
+12	5.0	60
−12	5.0	60

Does not include power for installed iSBX MULTIMODULE boards.

MULTIBUS II PARALLEL I/O

281009-38

iSBC® MPI/519 72 CHANNEL DIGITAL I/O BOARD

The iSBC MPI/519 is a digital I/O interface board which provides 72 parallel channels of TTL level I/O in Multibus II I/O space. The board is capable of receiving interrupts from other Multibus II agents, as well as generating interrupts from up to 8 sources. It is one of a family of MPI (Multibus II Peripheral Interface)-based I/O boards.

iSBC® MPI/519 FEATURES

- 72 channels of TTL level I/O in banks of 24 channels each
- Banks configurable for general purpose industrial I/O or as Centronics compatible ports
- Output lines may be read back to verify output status
- Socketed buffer drivers and resistor networks for configuring I/O as high or low true
- 8 interrupt request lines
- Precision interval pulse triggering on one of three I/O lines
- Jumperless configuration

FUNCTIONAL DESCRIPTION

The iSBC MPI/519 is a digital I/O board suitable for applications such as industrial automation, printer interface, or for low cost inter-chassis communications requiring multiple parallel I/O lines.

The iSBC MPI/519 board is based on the Multibus II Peripheral Interface (MPI) component which provides all the logic required to interface to the Parallel System Bus (PSB), allows the board to be a replier in I/O and interconnect space, and supports the sending and receiving of interrupt messages.

MULTIBUS II PARALLEL I/O

72 DIGITAL I/O CHANNELS

The 72 channels of TTL (5v) level I/O are arranged in three banks of 24 I/O each (Figure 13). Each bank is implemented using two Intel 82C55 Programmable Peripheral Interface (PPI) components (Figure 14). Port A of each PPI is connected to the front panel through bidirectional buffers. They can be software configured as input or output on a byte basis. Sockets in front of the buffers are provided for the user to add pull-up, pull-down or voltage dividing resistor networks (2.2 K-ohm pull-up resistors are provided). To allow data readback, Port B of each PPI is connected directly to the output side of the Port A buffers, for use in board diagnostics or to ensure the integrity of critical data.

Each bank also has an additional 8 bits I/O implemented through Port C, for use as general purpose I/O or as input and output interrupts.

I/O signals may be interfaced to industry standard signal conditioning and isolation modules through termination panels such as Intel's iRCX910 or OPTO-22's PB24.

CENTRONICS COMPATIBLE

Each bank may be used as a Centronics compatible port. Bank one can automatically generate the data strobe, eliminating an extra bus transaction.

8 INTERRUPT REQUEST LINES

Input interrupts coming from external sources through the front panel are implemented through an 82C59 Programmable Interrupt Controller (PIC) and cause the iSBC MPI/519 to send an unsolicited interrupt message. Up to eight input interrupts are supported. The interrupt source is encoded in the interrupt message. One input interrupt can be configured as a broadcast interrupt, which is sent to all agents. This interrupt is useful to synchronize processors or to alert all processors to an external system event. Output interrupts, received by the iSBC MPI/519 from other agents, cause a 82C54 programmable interval timer to output a precise interval pulse. These pulses can be from 1 μsec to 6.5 msec. in length. There is one output line for output interrupts on each I/O bank.

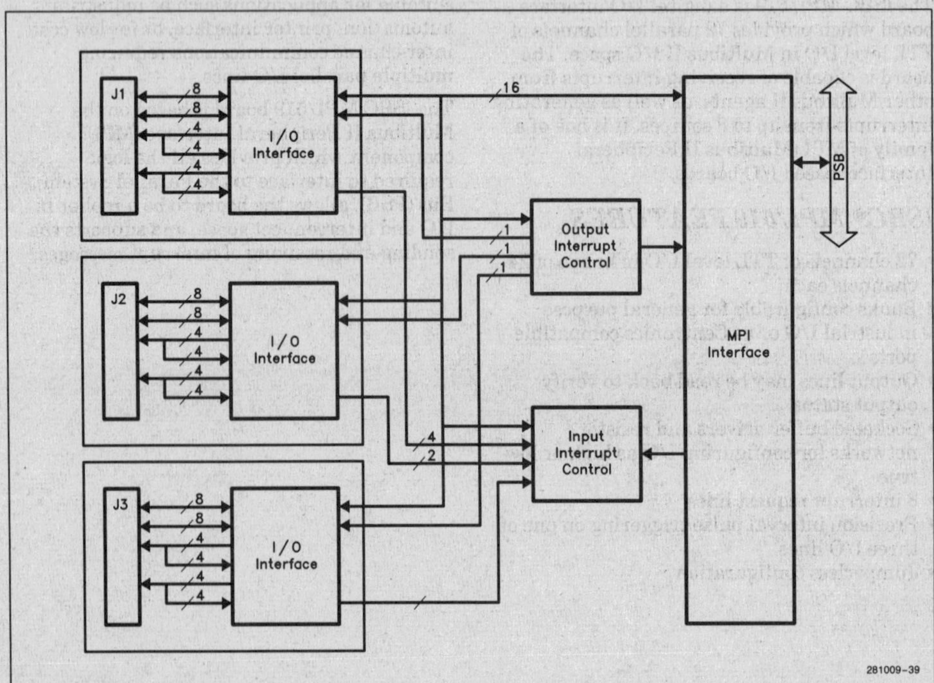

Figure 13: Block Diagram for iSBC® MPI/519 Board

MULTIBUS II PARALLEL I/O

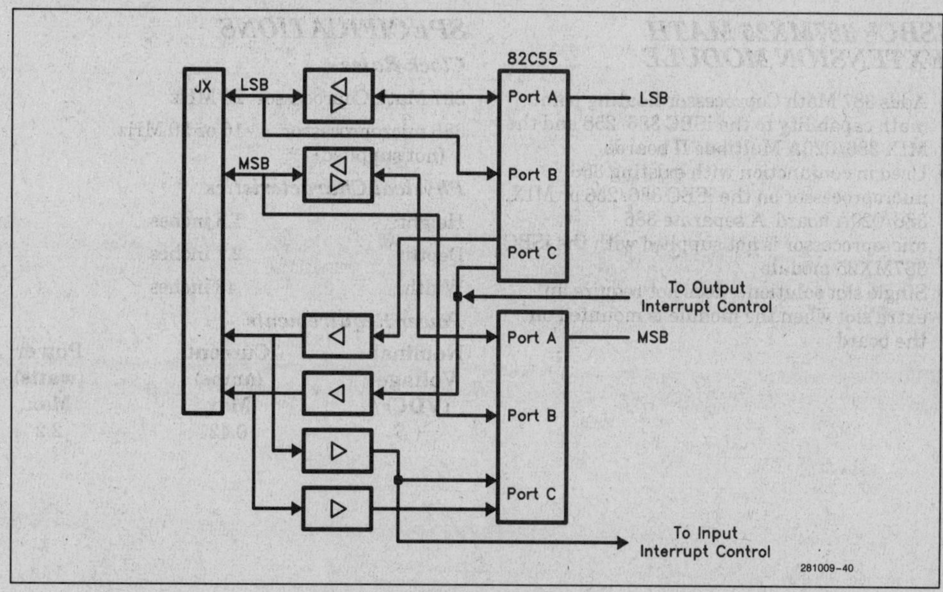

Figure 14: Block Diagram of one iSBC® 519 I/O Bank

iSBC® MPI/519 DIGITAL I/O BOARD SPECIFICATIONS

Interfaces

P1 — Slave PSB

Centronics — Each of the three I/O banks can be used as a Centronics compatible interface. Bank 1 is configurable to minimize handshaking and bus transactions when used as a printer interface.

I/O connector — 3 Positronics ODD44F500TX

Physical Characteristics

Standard Multibus II board

Other Components Supported

Bidirectional Buffers	Unidirectional Buffers	Resistor Networks
74ALS638-74AS638	74ALS00-74AS00	9 or 10 pin SIPs
74ALS639-74AS639	74ALS08-74AS08	all values
		supported
74ALS640-74AS640	74ALS32-74AS32	
74ALS643-74AS643	74ALS37-74AS37	
	74ALS38-74AS38	
or equivalent	or equivalent	

Power Requirements

Nominal Voltage (VDC)	Current (amps) Max	Power (watts) Max
+5 ±5%	3	15

I/O Buffer and Resistors Supplied

Bidirectional Buffers	Unidirectional Buffers	Resistor Networks
74ALS645	74ALS09	2.2 K-Ohm

ACCESSORIES

iSBC® 387MX25 MATH EXTENSION MODULE

- Adds 387 Math Coprocessor floating point math capability to the iSBC 386/258 and the MIX 386/020A Multibus II boards
- Used in conjunction with existing 386 microprocessor on the iSBC 386/258 or MIX 386/020A board. A separate 386 microprocessor is not supplied with the iSBC 387MX25 module
- Single slot solution—does not require an extra slot when the module is mounted on the board

SPECIFICATIONS

Clock Rates

387 Math Coprocessor 25 MHz

386 microprocessor (not supplied) 16 or 20 MHz

Physical Characteristics

Height: 1.8 inches

Depth: 2.7 inches

Width: .43 inches

Power Requirements

Nominal Voltage (VDC)	Current (amps) Max	Power (watts) Max
+5	0.42	2.2

MULTIBUS II ARCHITECTURE STANDARDS

ENVIRONMENTAL REQUIREMENTS

Operating Temperature: 0 to 55°C @ 200 LFM airflow Non-operating: −40 to 70°C
Humidity: 0 to 85% non-condensing

INTERFACES

Full PSB

A full PSB interface is implemented with the 82389 MPC component. This component is Intel's implementation of the IEEE/ANSI 1296 specification cast in silicon. All boards with a full PSB interface have the feature set of the MPC component described in the silicon section.

Slave PSB

A slave PSB interface is implemented with the MPI component. The MPI is a cost and function reduced "little brother" of the MPC component. All boards with the slave PSB interface have the feature set of the MPI component described in the silicon section.

MM0x Memory Expansion

The MM0x interface uses a custom surface mount connector to add expansion local memory to a CPU-based product. The connector allows up to two modules to be added to a baseboard and provide from 1 to 32 MB of memory per module. Memory modules are single-sided or double-sided. A board with a single-sided module consumes a single Multibus II slot, all other combinations require two Multibus II slots (Note: If two MM0X modules are used, then two slots are used).

MIX

The MIX interface is described in the MIX architecture section.

PHYSICAL CHARACTERISTICS

Standard Multibus II Format (Double 6U Eurocard)

Height: 23.3 cm (9.18 inches)
Depth: 22.0 cm (8.65 inches)
Width: 1.92 cm (0.76 inches)

MIX Expansion Module:

Half-Size:

Height: 22.6 cm (8.9 inches)
Depth: 9.5 cm (3.75 inches)
Area: 213 cm (33 square inches)

Full-Size:

Height: 22.6 cm (8.9 inches)
Depth: 2.01 cm (7.9 inches)
Area: 452 cm (70 square inches)

iSBX™ Modules:

Single-Wide

Height: 2.1cm (0.827 inches)
Depth: 7.24cm (2.85 inches)
Width: 9.4cm (3.7 inches)

Double-Wide

Height: 2.1cm (0.827 inches)
Depth: 7.24cm (2.85 inches)
Width: 19.05cm (7.5 inches)

DEVICE DRIVERS

Check the latest release of the following operating systems for details:
iRMX I Operating System
iRMX II Operating System
iRMX III Operating System
UNIX* System V/386 Operating System

COMPREHENSIVE DEVELOPMENT AND OPERATING SYSTEM SUPPORT

Operating system support includes the iRMX II and iRMX III Real-Time operating systems and UNIX* System V/386. The iRMK I real time kernel is available for 32-bit embedded applications. All three—iRMX, iRMK and UNIX operating systems include Multibus II transport for full message passing support. To ease Multibus II modules development, Intel offers both the iRMX and UNIX versions of the System 520 Development System which can support on-target and/or cross-hosted software development in one chassis.

WORLD WIDE SERVICE AND SUPPORT

Should this or any Intel board ever need service, Intel maintains a world wide network of service and repair facilities to keep you and your customers up and running. For unique applications requiring customization of our products, the Intel Systems Group is available to modify, integrate and test Intel boards and system components to your requirements.

*UNIX is a trademark of AT&T in the U.S.A. and other countries.

MULTIBUS II ARCHITECTURE STANDARDS

INTEL QUALITY—YOUR GUARANTEE

All Multibus II I/O products are designed and manufactured to meet Intel's high quality standards. Intel quality is then verified by rigorous testing in our state-of-the-art Environmental Test Laboratory.

PRODUCT AND LITERATURE GUIDE

Product	Description	Manual Number
MULTIBUS II SILICON PRODUCTS		
82389	Message Passing Coprocessor	176526
	Datasheet for 82389 Message Passing Coprocessor	290145
MPI	Multibus II Peripheral Interface	504557
MIX DEVELOPMENT KIT		
MIX386020-1	MIX baseboard w 1MB	503353
MIX386020-1F01	MIX baseboard w 1MB + 1MB module	503353
MIX386020-1F04	MIX baseboard w 1MB + 4MB module	503353
MIX386020A	MIX baseboard for full/half size modules	468229
MIX486020A	MIX baseboard for full/half size modules	468229
MIXMDKIT-1	Kit with baseboard w 1MB	500731
MIXMDKIT-1F01	Kit with baseboard w 1MB + 1MB module	500731
MIXMDKIT-1F04	Kit with baseboard w 1MB + 4MB module	500731
MIXMDKIT-1S	Same as MIXMDKIT-1 w SE support	500731
MIXMDKIT-1F01S	Same as MIXMDKIT-1F01 w SE support	500731
MIXMDKIT-1F04S	Same as MIXMDKIT-1F04 w SE support	500731
MIX EXPANSION MODULES		
MIX 450	MIX Terminal Controller Module	500799
MIX 420	MIX WAN Module	500798
MIX 560	MIX Ethernet Module	459622
MIX MOD1	Test Module	500731
MIX MOD2	Breadboard Module	500731
MIX MOD3	Debug Module	500731
MIX SC10	Ten MIX Stacking Connectors	NA
FIRMWARE DEVELOPMENT		
MSABASEFDP	Firmware Development Package	505480

PRODUCT AND LITERATURE GUIDE

Product	Description	Manual Number

TERMINAL CONTROLLERS

Product	Description	Manual Number
SBCMPI450	MPI-based terminal controller	502200
SBC186450	Mid-range terminal controller	502238
MIX386450-1	MIX Terminal Controller with 1MB	503353 + 500799
MIX386450-1F01	MIX Terminal Controller with 2MB	503353 + 500799
MIX386450-1F04	MIX Terminal Controller with 5MB	503353 + 500799

WIDE AREA NETWORK CONTROLLERS

Product	Description	Manual Number
SBC186410	Mid-range WAN board	148941
MIX386420-1	MIX WAN board with 1MB	503353 + 500798
MIX386420-1F01	MIX WAN board with 2MB	503353 + 500798
MIX386420-1F04	MIX WAN board with 5MB	503353 + 500798

LOCAL AREA NETWORK/ETHERNET CONTROLLERS

Product	Description	Manual Number
SBC186530	Mid-range Ethernet board	149226
MIX386560-1	MIX Ethernet Board with 1MB	503353 + 459622
MIX386560-1F01	MIX Ethernet Board with 2MB	503353 + 459622
MIX386560-1F04	MIX Ethernet Board with 5MB	503353 + 459622

PERIPHERAL CONTROLLERS

Product	Description	Manual Number
SBC186224A	Multi-peripheral controller Subsystem	138272
SBC386258SM01	Single-ended SCSI Controller w 1 MB	149861
SBC386258SM04	Single-ended SCSI Controller w 4 MB	149861
SBC386258DM04	Differential SCSI Controller w 4 MB	149861

PARALLEL I/O

Product	Description	Manual Number
SBCMPI519	Digital I/O Board	502201

SOFTWARE PRODUCTS

Product	Description	Manual Number
INA960J	Networking software	462250
X.25	Communications software	NA

ACCESSORIES

Product	Description	Manual Number
SBC387MX25	Math Extension Module	506056

PRODUCT AND LITERATURE GUIDE

Product	Description	Manual Number

OTHER MULTIBUS II TECHNICAL LITERATURE

Product	Description	Manual Number
	MIX Module Design Specification	500729
	Ap Note: Simple I/O Design Example Using ... MIX ...	281004
	Multibus II: Interconnect Interface Specification	149299
	Multibus II Transport Protocol Specification and Designer's Guide	453508
	Multibus II: Initialization and Diagnostics Specification	454077
	Multibus II Systems Architecture: Bootstrap Specification	455975
	A Multibus II OVERVIEW, Article Reprints and Technical Papers	280684
	ANSI/IEEE 1296	281065
	AP Note: Designing a CPU Module using the 82389, MPC	281022

Multibus II Development Systems and Accessories

4

INTEL SYSTEM 520

280672–1

280672–2

280672–3

UNLOCK THE POWER OF MULTIBUS II WITH AN INTEL OEM SYSTEM

The Intel System 520 makes it easy for OEMs to unlock the power of Multibus II. The System 520 is a family of high performance, multiprocessing OEM systems that combine the Multibus II System Architecture (MSA), the powerful 386™ microprocessor, and UNIX* System V, iRMX® II or iRMX III operating systems. Together, they provide an easily scalable, recomposable open systems for OEMs to build upon.

The System 520 allows users to add to the basic system, or purchase the system's contents separately and repackage them into another enclosure. This capability is provided via the System 520's use of MSA—a standardized set of hardware, firmware, and software interfaces and protocols that builds on and extends the Multibus II (IEEE 1296) bus standard. As a result, the system 520 eases the development and integration efforts of OEM system designers building high-performance multiprocessor systems.

*IBM is a registered trademark of International Business Machines Corp.
*Microsoft and MSDOS are registered trademarks of Microsoft Corporation
*Soft-Scope is a registered trademark of Concurrent Sciences, inc.
*VAX/VMS and DEC are registered trademarks of Digital Equipment Corporation
*386™ is a trademark of Intel Corporation
*UNIX is a registered trademark of AT&T in the U.S.A. and other countries

September 1991
Order Number: 280672-003

FEATURES

- 8 slot enclosure
- 16 or 20 MHz 386 processor
- Multiprocessing support via easy 386 application processor expansion (1 to 4)
- High performance SCSI I/O subsystem
- 80186-based Ethernet and Serial controllers
- Hardware windowed graphics and virtual terminal support
- OpenNET™ transparent remote file sharing & virtual terminal between 386 processors and IEEE 802.3 networked systems
- iRMX II, iRMX III, and System V/386 UNIX* operating systems support

THE MULTIBUS SYSTEM ARCHITECTURE (MSA)

The System 520 is built around the Multibus II System Architecture (MSA) to ease the development and integration work of OEM system designers. MSA is a complete hierarchy of hardware, firmware, and software interfaces and protocols that builds on and extends the basic Multibus II (IEEE/ANSI 1296) bus standard. Specifically, it defines message passing, system boot and initialization, system and board level diagnostics, and automatic board configuration in a multiprocessor system environment. By providing a standardized set of powerful programmatic interfaces and protocols, MSA assures a high level of vendor and board compatibility. This, in turn, provides OEMs quicker time to market with shorter design/integration cycle.

EASILY EXPANDABLE, RECOMPOSABLE SYSTEMS

Using MSA as its foundation, the System 520 boasts easy user expansion and recomposability. MSA allows Intel's full line of Single Board Computer (iSBC®) modules to integrate cleanly into the System 520. OEMs may choose to buy the contents of the system (i.e. the boards, firmware, software, etc.) separately, and recompose all or part of the system's pieces into a different configuration or enclosure. They can also easily add additional iSBC modules to meet their performance and I/O requirements.

The system is available in a series of hardware configurations (See Table 1). The System 520C (Core) serves as the basis for OEMs' production target systems, offering a set of peripherals to which OEMs can add CPU and I/O boards of their choice. The 520B (Base) system, which includes an i386-based SCSI controller and floppy drive, is designed for OEMs who need complete flexibility to select hard disk drives. The System 520BX (Base eXtension) offers the low-end entry point to Intel's Multibus II development system product line. For those OEMs who demand higher compute and I/O performance, the System 520BP (Base Plus I/O) is available.

WINDOWED GRAPHICS AND VIRTUAL TERMINAL SUBSYSTEM

The System 520 hosts the iRMX Graphics Interface driven by Intel's iSBX™ 279 Graphics Board. The graphics subsystem and its companion software provide a windowed virtual terminal console with graphics capabilities. With its onboard processing power and large graphics memory buffer, the iSBX 279 off-loads the application processors of the display processing tasks. The user interfaces to the System 520's subsystem are an RGB color monitor (640 × 480), a mouse, and an AT-style keyboard (purchased separately).

A NETWORK IN THE SYSTEM

Using the Multibus II backplane as an ultra-fast network (40MBytes/sec), multiple peer-to-peer 386 CPU-based application processors operate as independent "networked" iRMX or UNIX* systems over the Multibus II Parallel System Bus (PSB). Each application processor running Intel's OpenNET network software will provide transparent distributed file sharing, file transfer, and virtual terminal capability among all application processors on the backplane—and among IEEE 802.3-based (1.25MBytes/sec) OpenNET networked system nodes. Using the PSB as a network makes the System 520 a high performance "minicomputer" cluster condensed into one multiprocessor system.

The major advantage to the OEM is total network extensibility inside and outside the system, using the same OpenNET software. The key benefits are: reduced cost compared to multiple uni-processor networked systems and servers, drastically reduced physical space requirements, increased overall system throughput and performance, and preserved software investment.

FEATURES

HIGH PERFORMANCE 386™ CPU-BASED I/O SUBSYSTEM

The System 520 uses the iSBC 386/258 module as a dedicated SCSI controller and/or iRMX II/III application processor. In an expanded system, the iSBC 386/258 module can support concurrent disk accesses by multiple application CPUs. It accelerates I/O critical applications by offering a 16 MHz 386 processor, a large (4 MBytes) buffer for data block caching, and sufficient bandwidth to support a 4 MBytes per second SCSI synchronous transfer rate.

UNIX OPERATING SYSTEM*

The System V/386 UNIX operating system provides portability of applications and systems programs from one hardware architecture to another. Integrated with System 520, the UNIX operating system provides a powerful open system platform. The System V/386 product family is ideal as a base for developing custom multi-user systems applications, and multi-purpose network servers requiring open system configurability and flexible packaging.

The System V/386 UNIX operating system delivers full support for Intel's Multibus II System Architecture. Intel has built a complete System V/386 product family providing OEMs, System Integrators and Computing Manufacturers with industry standard UNIX, OpenNET networking, system hardware, and Ada development tools for the Multibus II System Architecture. Together, these elements deliver a rich, complete UNIX development environment.

4

FEATURES

iRMX® II AND iRMX III: FULL FEATURED REAL-TIME OPERATING SYSTEMS

Intel's iRMX family of operating systems is a full featured, stand-alone operating environment, designed to address the unique needs of real-time applications. The 16-bit iRMX II and 32-bit iRMX III operating systems include complete Multibus II facilities supporting Multibus II Transport message passing and Interconnect Space access. The iRMX II/III system software manages all message transmission and reception, making construction of real-time multiprocessor systems easier.

The iRMX operating system family provides a rich set of real-time programming facilities not found in general-purpose operating systems. Some of their key features include preemptive, dynamic priority-based scheduling of application tasks; bounded interrupt latency; multitasking support; inter-task communications and synchronization through priority-based mailboxes, semaphores, and regions; and interrupt management with exception handling. By combining these features with a modular design; quick response; and sophisticated memory protection schemes, the OEM receives a highly configurable, customizable operating system with the high performance and code integrity that real-time applications require.

COMPLETE MULTIBUS II DEVELOPMENT ENVIRONMENT

The System 520 is also available with the iRMX II, iRMX III, or System V/386 UNIX operating system and software. It provides a complete, networked development system for Multibus II modules development, software development and testing of the target applications. The System 520 is unique as a Multibus II development system, because its multiprocessor cluster capability can support both on-target or cross-hosted system and software development in one chassis.

OpenNET™ NETWORKING CAPABILITY

Intel's OpenNET product family provides a complete set of networking software and hardware that follows the International Standards Organization (ISO) Open Systems Interconnect (OSI) seven layer model. The System distributes the ISO/OSI transport protocol processing to intelligent Ethernet controllers hosting Intel's OSI compliant iNA 960 Class 4 Transport software. Intel's OpenNET Network File Access (NFA) protocol provides the upper layer functionality of transparent local or remote file access and file transfer between Intel's complete line of system products, as well as MS-DOS Operating System-based personal computers and VAX/VMS* minicomputers. The OpenNet NFA protocol adheres to the standard IBM*/Microsoft*/Intel Core File Sharing protocol specification.

WORLDWIDE SERVICE AND SUPPORT

The System 520 is fully supported by Intel's worldwide staff of trained hardware and software support engineers. Intel also provides field application assistance, extensive operating system classes, maintenance services, and a help hotline.

The System 520 OEM System products come with a standard 1 year hardware warranty. The System 520 Multibus II Development System products come bundled with a one (1) year service warranty option. This one year warranty includes: hardware installation and one year of on-site maintenance and software installation of the operating system.

INTEL QUALITY AND RELIABILITY

The System 520 is designed to meet the high standards and reliability that users have come to expect from Intel products.

SPECIFICATIONS

SYSTEM 520 CONFIGURATION/OPTIONS—TABLE 1

Product	Model	iSBC 286/258, 4 MB, CSM 002	iSBC 386/120, 4 MB	iSBX 279 Graphics	iSBC 186/410 Terminal Controller	iSBC 186/530 Ethernet Controller	Hard Disk (SCSI)	125/150 MB $^1/_4$" Tape (SCSI)	1.2 MB Floppy and Adapter (SCSI)	Floor Stand Chassis	Table Top Chassis (option)	Power Supply (Watts)	iRMX II Software (option)	iRMX III Software (option)	System V/386 Software (option)
System 520 Base Plus I/O	SYP520R1BP /R1BPT	✓	✓	✓	✓	✓	380 MB	✓	✓	✓	✓	535	✓	✓	✓
System 520 Base eXtension	SYP520R1BX	✓					80 MB	✓	✓	✓		435	✓	✓	
System 520 Base	SYP520R1B /R1BT	✓							✓	✓	✓	535			
System 520 Core	SYP520C1 /C1T						380 MB	✓	✓	✓	✓	535			
Chassis	SYP520FE/TE									✓	✓	535			

SPECIFICATIONS

System 520 Development System Software Contents:

iRMX II or iRMX III operating system
iRMX-Net networking software*
iNA 960 networking transport software*
SYR Language Kit: (PLM 286, ASM 286/386, builder/binder)
C 286/386 compiler*
iRMX Toolbox*
Soft-Scope* II/III Source Level Debugger*
AEDIT Editor
RUN/UDI for 86-based UDI Development Tools
iPPS PROM programmer support
iSBX 279 Graphics Interface Software*
OpenNET Virtual Terminal (VT)*

System V/386 UNIX

System V/386, Release 3.2 operating system
System V OpenNET networking software*
iN⟨KC2⟩A 960 networking transport software*
Virtual terminal*

*Available with SYS520RIDKIT2, SYS520RIDKIT3 or SYS520RIDKITSV only.

REGULATIONS

Meets or exceeds the following requirements:

Safety

US	UL 478 5th Edition
Canada	CSA C22.2 No. 220
Europe	IEC 380 and VDE 0806

EMI/RFI

US & Canada	FCC47 CFR Part 15 Subpart J Class B
Europe	VDE 0871 Level B

ELECTRICAL

DC Power Output	535 watt maximum (B & BP models) 435 watt maximum (BX model)
AC Power Input	88-132 VAC or 176-264 VAC; 47-63 Hz, single phase

OPERATING ENVIRONMENT

Operating Temperature	10°C to 40°C
Relative Humidity	85% non-condensing (operating) 95% condensing (non-operating)
Altitude	Sea level to 10,000 feet

DIMENSIONS

	Floorstand	Table Top
Height	22.25″	8″
Width	8″/12″ at base	17.5″
Depth	23″	22.25″
Weight	Approx. 70 lbs.	Approx. 60 lbs.

ORDERING INFORMATION

Hardware Only

SYP520R1BP	System 520 Base Plus I/O System (floorstand)
SYP520R1BPT	System 520 Base Plus I/O System (tabletop)
SYP520R1BX	System 520 Base eXtension System (floorstand)
SYP520R1B	System 520 Base System (floorstand)
SYP520R1BT	System 520 Base System (tabletop)
SYP520C1	System 520 Core System (tabletop)
SYP520C1T	System 520 Core System (floorstand)
SYP520FE	System 520 Empty Chassis (floorstand)
SYP520TE	System 520 Empty Chassis (tabletop)
CH541C20R	20 slot chassis
CH542R	Peripheral Module

Development Systems

SYS520R1DKIT2	System 520BP w/ iRMX II
SYS520R1DKIT3	System 520BP w/ iRMX III
SYS520R1DKITSV	System 520BP w/ System V/386
SYS520BXDKIT2	System 520BX w/ iRMX II
SYS520BXDKIT3	System 520BX w/ iRMX III
SYS520BXDKITSV	System 520BX w/ System V/386

SYSTEM ENCLOSURES AND BACKPLANES

281029-1

A 20-SLOT MULTIBUS II CHASSIS FOR FLEXIBLE, EXPANDABLE SYSTEMS

Intel's 20-slot 541 CHASSIS provides a basic platform for the integration of large capacity systems. The CH541's modular packaging allows for integration into standard 19-inch rack-mount cabinets and fits in a 24-inch deep rack. Each CH541 chassis is compactly built, ruggedly constructed, and features superior Intel quality and high reliability.

FEATURES

- 20-slot Multibus II (IEEE/ANSI 1296) backplane; EIA, 19-inch rack standard with provision for slide mounting/fits 24-inch deep rack
- Heavy duty bus bars for negligible IR drop across card cage under maximum loading
- 750 Watt multiple output switching power supply with 120A at 5 VDC; jumper selectable for 115/230 VAC
- CH541 Chassis certified as a complete unit to UL, CSA, and TUV safety agency requirements
- High-volume and uniform cooling air flow across all card positions (250 + LFM). Air flow highly independent of adjacent equipment
- P2 backplane at Slot 0 provides "Reset," Remote Diagnostics Serial Port Interface (RSPI) functions and I/O connections
- Unrestricted area behind P2 backplane for user I/O configuration
- One Year Full Warranty

September 1991
Order Number: 281029-002

FEATURES

WORLDWIDE SERVICE AND SUPPORT

Intel provides support for Intel and non-Intel boards and peripherals. Development support options include on-site service, phone support, subscription service, on-site consulting, and customer training.

QUALITY AND RELIABILIITY

The CH541 chassis is designed, tested and manufactured in accordance with Intel's industry leading quality and reliabilty standards.

SPECIFICATIONS

ENVIRONMENTALS

Ambient Temperature	
Operating	0°C to 50°C
Non-Operating	−40°C to 85°C
Relative Humidity	
Operating	<85% Non-condensing
Non-Operating	<95% Non-condensing
Altitude	
Operating	Sea Level to 10,000 feet
Non-Operating	Sea Level to 40,000 feet

ELECTRICAL

DC Power Output	750 watt maximum
+5V	120.0 A maximum
+12V	10.0 A maximum
−12V	10.0 A maximum
AC Power Input	90-132 VAC at 12 A or 180-264 VAC at 6 A 47-63 Hz

REGULATIONS

Chassis complies with safety agency requirements:

US	UL478 5th Edition recognized
Canada	CSA C22.2 No. 220 certified
Europe	TUV, EN60950 certified

Power Supply meets the following EMI requirements:

US/Canada	FCC Class A Conducted emissions
Europe	VDE Limit Class A Conducted emissions

PHYSICAL CHARACTERISTICS

Dimensions

Height	399.2 mm (15.72 in)
Width	482.7 mm (19.00 in)
Depth	497.8 mm (19.60 in)
Weight	15.9 kilograms (35 lbs)

ORDER CODE

CH541C20R

SYSTEM ENCLOSURES AND BACKPLANES

A LOW COST RACKMOUNT PERIPHERAL CHASSIS FOR FLEXIBLE, EXPANDABLE SYSTEMS CONFIGURATIONS

Intel's 542 Rackmount Peripheral Chassis provides a basic platform for integrating large capacity systems. The CH542 chassis is a companion to Intel's CH541 20-slot chassis. However the CH542 chassis may be used with any system where additional peripheral capacity is required. Intel's modular packaging allows for integration into standard 19-inch rackmount cabinets and fits in a 24-inch deep rack. Built into each CH542 chassis is rugged compact construction, superior Intel quality, and high reliability.

FEATURES

- Rigid light weight structure to fit EIA 19-inch rack standard with provision for slide mounting, fits 24-inch deep rack.
- Three full height bays (2 front access, 1 internal) each able to mount two half height devices.
- 300 Watt multiple output switching power supply with 10A at + 12 VDC. Switch selectable for 115/220 VAC.
- CH542 Chassis designed to comply with international safety agency requirements.
- Air flow capable of supporting 40°C operation.
- Power distribution cables provided for all drive positions plus an adaptor board.
- Cable manager with strain relief for rear entry signal cables.
- One year full warranty.

4

FEATURES

ONE YEAR WARRANTY

All Intel board level products have a one year mail-in warranty on both parts and labor.

WORLDWIDE SERVICE AND SUPPORT

Should any Intel enclosure or backplane ever need service beyond the warranty period, Intel maintains a worldwide netork of service and repair facilities to keep you and your customers up and running.

QUALITY AND RELIABILIITY

The CH541 and CH542 are designed, tested and manufactured in accordance with Intel's industry leading quality and reliabilty standards.

SPECIFICATIONS

ENVIRONMENTALS

Ambient Temperature

Operating	0°C to 40°C
Non-Operating	−40°C to 85°C

Relative Humidity

Operating	<85% Non-condensing
Non-Operating	<95% Non-condensing

Altitude

Operating	Sea Level to 10,000 feet
Non-Operating	Sea Level to 40,000 feet

ELECTRICAL

DC Power Output	300 watt maximum
+5V	26.0 A maximum
+12V	10.0 A maximum
AC Power Input	90-132 VAC at 5 A or 180-264 VAC at 2.5 A, 47-63 Hz

REGULATIONS

Chassis designed to comply with international safety agency requirements.

Power Supply meets the following EMI requirements:

US/Canada	FCC Class A Conducted emissions
Europe	VDE Limit Class A Conducted emissions

PHYSICAL CHARACTERISTICS

Dimensions

Height	22.1 cm (8.72 in)
Width	48.3 cm (19.00 in)
Depth	48.0 cm (18.91 in)
Weight	9.1 kilograms (20 lbs)

ORDER CODE

CH542R

iSBC® PKG/902
iSBC® PKG/903
MULTIBUS II iLBX™ II BACKPLANES

- Provides iLBX™ II Interconnect for Fastest CPU/Memory Data Transfers
- Designed to Mount in Multibus II Cardcage Assemblies
- Meets All Electrical and Mechanical Requirements of the Multibus II Specifications
- Uses a 6 Layer, Fully Terminated Backplane
- Includes a 10 Pin Connector for BITBUS™ Applications
- Available in 2 Slot (iSBC® PKG/902) and 3 Slot (iSBC® PKG/903) Sizes

The iSBC PKG/902 and iSBC PKG/903 series of iLBX II backplanes are designed to mount on the P2 side of Intel's Multibus II cardcage assembly or other double Euro (6U) cardcage. One or more backplanes may be installed in a system to allow high speed data transfers between the CPU and memory boards installed in the system. The iLBX II backplane uses a 6 layer PCB with separate power and ground planes and full termination on all signal lines. This design minimizes system noise and ensures reliable operation in all applications.

280074–1

4

September 1991
Order Number: 280074-002

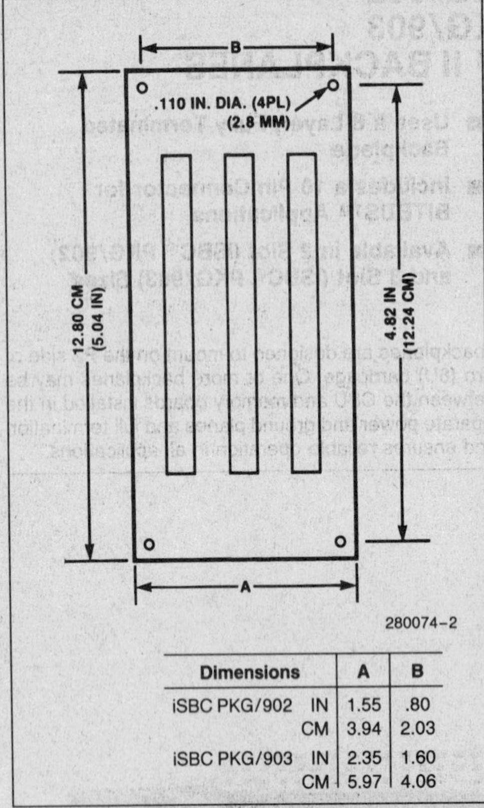

Dimensions		A	B
iSBC PKG/902	IN	1.55	.80
	CM	3.94	2.03
iSBC PKG/903	IN	2.35	1.60
	CM	5.97	4.06

Figure 1. iLBX™ II Board Dimensions (iSBC® PKG/903 Shown)

FEATURES

Mechanical and Electrical

The iSBC PKG/902 and iSBC PKG/903 iLBX II backplanes use a 6 layer printed circuit board (PCB) with separate power and ground layers and a signal lead routing scheme which minimizes ringing, cross-talk, and capacitive loading on the bus. Mounted on the PCB are two (iSBC PKG/902) or three (iSBC PKG/903) 96 pin DIN connectors, one 10-pin BITBUS connector, terminating resistors, decoupling capacitors, and power terminals. The resistors and capacitors are mounted into sockets, and all parts are press-fit into the backplane. The PCB is UL recognized for flammability.

Single In-line Package (SIP) style resistors are used to terminate all address, clock, data, and control lines. Each termination consists of two resistors which connects the line to +VCC and ground. Different size resistors are used according to the type of driver connected to the line in an operating system. The SIP style resistors help make the board compact in size and allows the designer to mount several backplanes directly adjacent to one another in a system without having to skip slots.

Mounted on the rear of the backplane is a 10-pin BITBUS connector. This connector serves as the serial communication interface for any iSBX 344 BITBUS controller boards installed in the system.

The DIN type connectors are female, 96 pins, fully gold plated, and meet IEC standard 603-2-IEC-C096F. The connectors are mounted on 0.8″ centers to match Intel's iPSB (Parallel System Bus) Multibus II backplanes and are keyed to ensure proper mating to the Multibus II board. The connector can provide up to 6 amps of current at +5V to each Multibus II board in addition to the current available over the Parallel System Bus backplane.

Screw terminals on the backplane are provided for connection to +5V power and ground. These terminals, each of which can handle up to 25 amps of current, provide a simple and highly reliable connection method to the power supply.

SPECIFICATIONS

Mechanical and Environmental

Connector Spacing: 20.3 cm (0.8 in)

Number of Slots: iSBC PKG/902: 2 slots
iSBC PKG/903: 3 slots

Board Dimensions: See Figure 1

Weight: iSBC PKG/902—0.2 kg (8 oz)
iSBC PKG/903—0.3 kg (12 oz)

Connectors:

DIN: 96-pin female, gold plated, meets IEC standard 603-2-IEC-C096-F

BITBUS: 10-pin male, gold plated, T&B Ansley 609-1012M, or equivalent

Construction Method: Six layer backplane with separate VCC and ground layers

All connectors, power terminals, and resistor/capacitor sockets are press-fit into the backplane

Mounting Hole Location: See Figure 1

Operating Environment: 0°C–70°C ambient temperature; 0% to 90% relative humidity, non-condensing; 0 ft.–10,000 ft. altitude

Electrical

Backplane Electrical Characteristics and Line Terminations:	Per Intel Multibus II specification 146077, Sec. II, iLBX II

Power Connections

Type: Screw terminal block: AMP P/N 55181-1; Winchester P/N 121-25698-2; or equivalent

Mating Connection: No. 6 locking spade or ring tongue lug

Quantity: 2(VCC, Ground)

Current Rating: iSBC PKG/902: 12 amps; iSBC PKG/903: 18 amps (Power and Ground)

Maximum Current Available Per Slot:	6 amps (over the iLBX II backplane)

REFERENCE MANUAL

Multibus II Cardcage Assembly and iLBX Backplane User's Guide, P/N 146709-001 (not supplied)

ORDERING INFORMATION

Part Number	Description
iSBC PKG/902	2 slot iLBX II Backplane
iSBC PKG/903	3 slot iLBX II Backplane

MULTIBUS® II CENTRAL SERVICES MODULE*

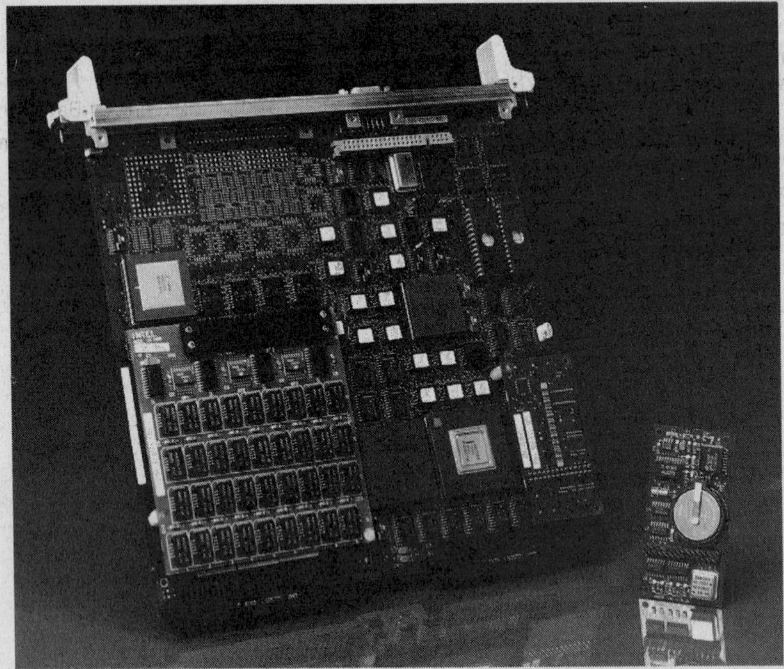

280694-1

COST REDUCED CENTRAL SERVICES MODULE

The iSBC® CSM/002 module is a small, surface mount circuit board which performs all central service module (CSM) functions as required by the IEEE/ANSI 1296 Multibus II specification. This credit card sized module mounts on a compatible base board such as the iSBC 386/258, iSBC 386/133, or iSBC 486/125 single board computer. The combined host board and CSM module require only one card slot. The small size and high functionality of the iSBC CSM/002 module is achieved by taking advantage of silicon support for CSM functions on the MPC (Message Passing Coprocessor) bus interface component. This module reduces system cost while remaining software compatible with the previous iSBC CSM/001 board.

FEATURES

- Full IEEE/ANSI 1296 Compliance for CSM Functions:
  - — Arbitration and slot ID Initialization
  - — BCLK and CCLK Generation
  - — PSB Bus Timeout Monitoring
  - — Reset Sequencing for Warm and Cold Resets
  - — Power Fail Indication and Recovery
- Software compatible with the iSBC CSM/001 board, but saves a card slot
- Battery Backup Time-of-day Clock
- Slot 0 Detection Circuit
- Clock Based Alarm Function for Periodic Interrupt
- 28 Bytes Non-volatile RAM
- Chassis ID for Crate-to-Crate Addressing
- Low Battery and Oscillator Failed Warnings

iSBC®, MULTIBUS®, and iSBX® are registered trademarks of Intel Corporation.
*The Multibus II Central Services Module, iSBCCSM002 is also manufactured under product code pSBCCSM002 by Intel of Puerto Rico, Inc. and sSBCCSM00S by Intel Singapore, Ltd.

December 1990
Order Number: 280694-001

FEATURES

WHAT IS A CENTRAL SERVICES MODULE?

The Central Services Module centralized a variety of bus management tasks in a Multibus II based system, reducing system overhead:

- Sequencing of reset signals on the PSB backplane.
- Assignment of card slot and arbitration IDs.
- Supplies a 10 MHz, system-wide clock signal (BCLK).
- Monitors the PSB bus for time outs, and signals a bus error when a parity error is detected.

FULL IEEE 1296 COMPLIANCE

The iSBC CSM/002 module meets all timing requirements for Central Services Module functions according to the Multibus II specification. This ensures reliable, clean system clock signals and correct reset sequencing for system power-on, power-fail, and front panel warm and cold resets. When used in a system where the power supply is capable of generating an ACLO indicator, the CSM module will signal a non-maskable interrupt to the host CPU shortly before the power goes down.

COMPACT SIZE: NO LONGER REQUIRES A SEPARATE CARD SLOT

The iSBC CSM/002 module reduces total system cost by supporting all CSM functions in an inexpensive, credit card sized module. This module mounts component side down onto compatible baseboards like the iSBC 386/258, iSBC 386/133, or iSBC 486/125 single board computers which have built-in CSM connectors. The combined host board and CSM module occupy only one card slot. The iSBC CSM/002 module is fully software compatible with the earlier iSBC CSM/001 board, and is a direct replacement. Only one CSM module is required per system.

TIME OF DAY CLOCK FUNCTIONS

A battery backed up time-of-day clock is supplied on the iSBC CSM/002 module. This feature is software compatible with existing Time and Date commands supported by various Intel supplied operating systems. In addition a new periodic alarm function is now available. This feature allows the user to generate an interrupt to the local processor based on the system clock. Intervals can be selected ranging from one second to one year. One example of how to use this might be to schedule a disk backup to tape at 1:00 am on Friday of each week.

NON-VOLATILE RAM FUNCTIONS

A two byte chassis ID is stored in an interconnect register in order to identify a particular backplane segment in a network which consists of a large number of nodes distributed in multiple chassis. In addition, there are 28 bytes of user definable non-volatile RAM available. One application might be for a bootstrap password to prevent unauthorized access to a system.

PROGRAMMATIC INTERFACE

All access to the above functions is via a set of function records contained in interconnect address space. These registers are resident on the host in slot space. These registers are resident on the host in slot zero, but are accessible to any agent on the PSB. This allows other boards to query reset status, bus errors, system time, NVRAM contents, and many other centralized functions.

WORLDWIDE SUPPORT AND SERVICE

Assistance in developing and supporting Multibus II applications is available through Intel's network of field application engineers, system engineers, customer training centers and service centers.

INTEL QUALITY—YOUR GUARANTEE

The iSBC CSM/002 module is designed and manufactured in accordance with Intel's high quality standards. Quality is verified by rigorous testing in Intel's state-of-the-art Environmental Test Laboratory.

FEATURES

ORDERING INFORMATION

ORDER CODE: SBCCSM002

DOCUMENTATION: iSBC CSM/002
Hardware Reference
Manual P/N 459706-001

AP NOTE: "Design of a Cost Reduced Central Services Module for Multibus II"

For more information or the number of your nearest Intel sales office, call 800-548-4725 (good in the U.S. and Canada).

iSBC® CSM/001* CENTRAL SERVICES MODULE

- **iSBC® CSM/001 Central Services Module Integrates Multibus II Central System Functions on a Single Board**
- **Multibus II Parallel System Bus Clock Generation for all Agents Interfaced to the Multibus II PSB Bus**
- **System-wide Reset Signals for Power-up, Warm Start, and Power Failure/Recovery**
- **System-wide Time-out Detection and Error Generation**
- **Slot I.D. and Arbitration I.D. Initialization**
- **Multibus II Interconnect Space for Software Configurability and Diagnostics**
- **Built-In Self Test (BIST) Power-up Diagnostics with LED Indicator and Error Reporting Accessible to Software via Interconnect Space**
- **General Purpose Link Interface to Other Standard (Multibus I) or Proprietary Buses**
- **Time-of-day Clock Support with Battery Back-up on Board**
- **Double-high Eurocard Standard Form Factor, Pin and Socket DIN Connectors**

The iSBC CMS/001 Central Services Module is responsible for managing the central system functions of clock generation, power-down and reset, time-out, and assignment of I.D.s defined by the Multibus II specification. The integration of these central functions in a single module improves overall board area utilization in a multi-board system since these functions do not need to be duplicated on every board. The iSBC CSM/001 module additionally provides a time-of-day clock and the general purpose link interface to the other standard (Multibus I) or proprietary buses.

280070–1

*The iSBC® CSM/001 is also manufactured under product code pSBCCSM001 by Intel Puerto Rico, Inc.

September 1991
Order Number: 280070-003

FUNCTIONAL DESCRIPTION

Overall

The iSBC CSM/001 Central Services Module integrates Multibus II central system functions on a single board. Each Multibus II system requires management of these central system functions as defined in the Multibus II specification. To perform its central system functions, the iSBC CSM/001 Central Services Module has a fixed slot I.D. and location in the backplane. The iSBC CSM/001 board additionally provides an interface to the Multibus I Link board and a time-of-day clock.

Architecture

The iSBC CSM/001 board is functionally partitioned into 6 major subsystems. The Central System Wide Control subsystem includes Multibus II PSB bus clock generation and system wide reset signal generation. The Time-Out Control subsystem provides system wide time out detection and error generation. The System Interconnect Space subsystem controls I.D. initialization and software configurable interconnect space. The Link Board interface subsystem provides an interface to the Multibus I Link board or links to other buses. The last two subsystems are of the Time-of-Day clock and the PSB bus interface. These areas are illustrated in Figure 1.

CENTRALIZED SYSTEM-WIDE CONTROL SUBSYSTEM

Parallel System Bus Clock Generation

The CSM generates the Parallel System Bus clocks. The Bus Clock (BCLK*) 10 MHz signal and the Constant Clock (CCLK*) 20 MHz signal are supplied by CSM to all boards interfaced to the Parallel System Bus. These boards use the Bus Clock 10 MHz signal for synchronization, system timing, and arbitration functions. The Constant Clock is an auxiliary clock. The frequency of the Bus Clock and Constant Clock can be halved via jumpers for diagnostic purposes.

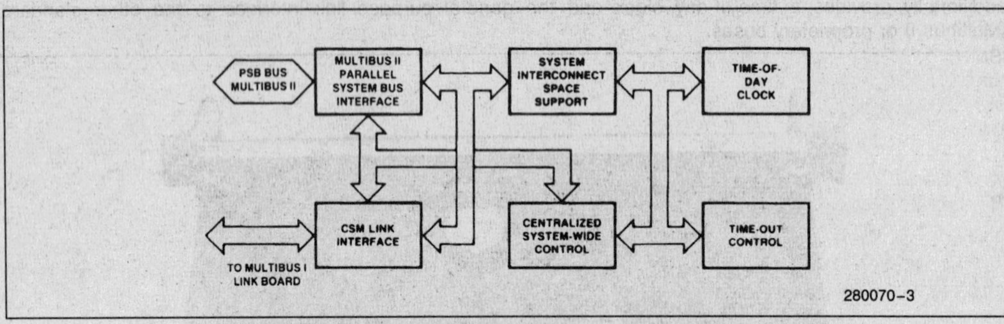

Figure 1. Block Diagram of iSBC® CSM/001 Board

Reset Control and Power-Fail/ Recovery

The CSM sends a system-level reset/initialization signal to all boards interfaced to the Parallel System Bus. The CSM assigns slot I.D. and arbitration I.D. to these boards during this initialization process. It provides this signal upon pressing of the reset switch, restoration of system power or a software request for reset received via the CSM interconnect space. The reset switch may be jumper-configured to cause a power-up or warm reset, with cold reset the default configuration. The reset switch is located on the front panel. Additionally, warm reset and cold reset signals can be input through the P2 connector.

The CSM power supply interface is accomplished via the ACLO input of the P2 connector. ACLO is an open collector input from the power supply which provides advance warning of imminent power fail. If battery backup is not required, a jumper is provided on the CSM to disable the power fail signal ACLO.

TIME-OUT SUBSYSTEM

The TIMOUT* (Time-Out) signal is provided by the CSM whenever it detects the failure of a module to complete a handshake. This TIMOUT* signal is received by all boards interfaced to the PSB bus and may be disabled via the interconnect space.

INTERCONNECT SUBSYSTEM

The CSM Interconnect subsystem provides arbitration I.D., and slot I.D. initialization, software configurable interconnect space, and on-board diagnostics capability.

At reset, the CSM supplies each board interfaced to iPSB bus with its slot I.D. and its arbitration I.D. The slot I. D. assignment allows user or system software to address any board by its physical position in the backplane.

The interconnect space has both read-only and software configurable facilities. The read-only registers hold information such as vendor number and board type, so that this information is available to the system software. The CSM software configurable interconnect space allows write operations to support board configuration and diagnostics under software control. The CSM also uses interconnect space for system wide functions such as providing a time/date record (from time-of-day clock), software access to diagnostics and software control of the system wide functions.

BUILT-IN-SELF-TEST (BIST) DIAGNOSTICS

Self-test/diagnostics have been built into the heart of the Multibus II system. These confidence tests and diagnostics improve reliability and reduce manufacturing and maintenance costs. LED 1 (labeled BIST) is used to indicate the status of the Built-In-Self-Test. It is turned on when the BIST starts running and is turned off when the BIST completes successfully. In addition, all error information is recorded in interconnect space so it is accessible to software for error reporting.

The Built-In-Self-Tests performed by the on-board microcontroller at power-up or at software command are:

1. PROM Checksum Test—Verifies the contents of the 8751 microcontroller.
2. RAM Test—Verifies that each RAM location of the 8751 microcontroller may store 0's and 1's by complementing and verifying twice each RAM location.
3. Real Time Clock Chip RAM Test—Verifies that reads and writes to the RAM locations on Real Time Clock Chip are functional.
4. Real Time Clock Test—Reads and writes all RAM locations of the RTC chip. Not run at power-up due to destructive nature.
5. Arbitration/Slot I.D. Register Test—Verifies that arbitration and slot I.D.s can be read and written from on-board.
6. 8751 Status Test—Verifies that input pins of the 8751 are at correct level.
7. Clock Frequency Test—Tests accuracy of Real Time Clock to 0.2% against bus clock.

CSM LINK INTERFACE

The CSM Link Interface and the Multibus I iSBC LNK/001 board provides a bridge between Multibus I and Multibus II systems. Hybrid systems can be built for development or target. The CSM Link Interface uses the P2 connector on the iSBC CSM/001 module for transferring commands and data from Multibus II to a Multibus I Link board. The Multibus I Link board (iSBC LNK/001) is purchased separately from the iSBC CSM/001 board and includes the cable which connects the iSBC CSM/001 board and the Multibus I Link board (see Figure 3).

The CSM Link Interface supports 8- or 16-bit transfers via a 16-bit address/data path. The iSBC LNK/001 board resides in the Multibus I system and provides a memory and I/O access window to Multibus I from the Multibus II Parallel System Bus. Only one iSBC LNK/001 board can be connected to the iSBC CSM/001 module.

TIME-OF-DAY CLOCK SUBSYSTEM

The Time-Of-Day Clock subsystem consists of a clock chip, battery, and interface circuitry. The clock provides time keeping to 0.01% accuracy of fractions of seconds, seconds, minutes, hours, day, day of week, month, and year. This information is accessible via the interconnect space. The battery backup for the clock chip provides 2 years of operation.

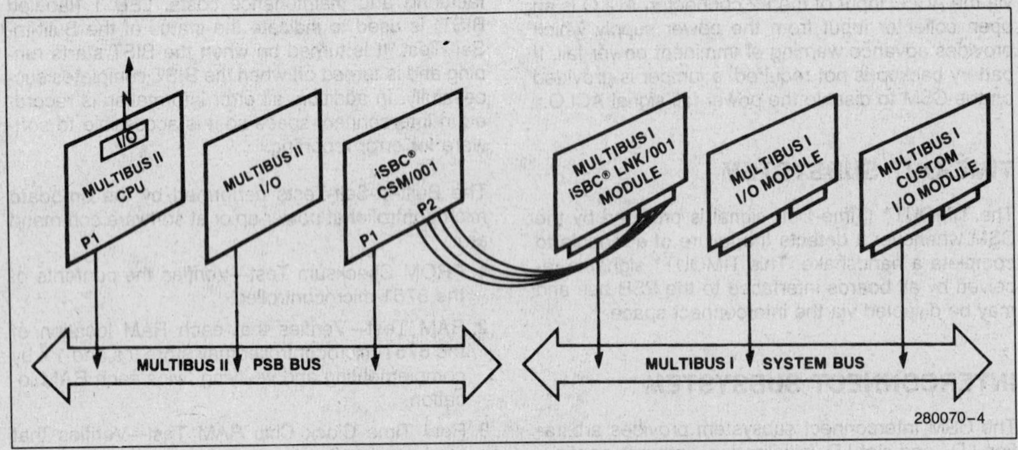

Figure 2. iSBC® CSM/001 Link Interface

SPECIFICATIONS

System Clocks

BCLK* (Bus Clock)	10 MHz
CCLK* (Constant Clock)	20 MHz
LCLK* (Link Clock)	10 MHz

Jumper option available to divide these frequencies in half

Link Cable

The Link cable uses a 64-conductor ribbon cable for interconnecting the CSM board to the Link Board. The maximum length for the cable is 1 meter.

Interface Specifications

Location	Function	Part #
P1	PSB Bus	603-2-IEC-C096F
P2	Link and Remote Services	603-2-IEC-C064-F

PHYSICAL DIMENSIONS

The iSBC CSM/001 board meets all Multibus II mechanical specifications as presented in the Multibus II specification.

Double-High Eurocard Form Factor:

Depth:	22.0 cm. (8.7 in.)
Height:	23.3 cm. (9.2 in.)
Front Panel Width:	2.0 cm. (0.78 in.)
Weight:	0.5 kg. (16.5 oz.)

ENVIRONMENTAL REQUIREMENTS

Temperature: (inlet air) at 200 LFM airflow over boards
Non-operating: −40 to +70°C
Operating: 0 to +55°C

Humidity: Non-operating: 95% RH @ 55°C
Operating: 90% RH @ 55°C

POWER REQUIREMENTS

Voltage (volts)	Current (amps)
+5 V_{CC} +5 (battery)	6A (max.) 0.65A (max.)

BATTERY CHARACTERISTICS

3V nominal voltage; capacity of 160 milliamp hours minimum.

BATTERY DIMENSIONS

Outside dimension	20 mm−23 mm
Height	1.6 mm−3.2 mm

REFERENCE MANUALS

iSBC CSM/001 Board Manual (#146706-001)

Manuals may be ordered from any Sales Representative, Distributor Office, or from the Intel Literature Department, 3065 Bowers Ave., Santa Clara, CA 95051.

ORDERING INFORMATION

Part Number	Description
SBC CSM/001	Multibus II Central Services Module

4

intel®

iSBC® LNK/001* BOARD
MULTIBUS II TO MULTIBUS I LINK BOARD

- Development Vehicle Making Multibus I iSBC® Boards Accessible to Multibus II Board Designers
- On Board 128K Byte Dual Port DRAM Memory
- 16M Bytes of Multibus I Memory Mapped into Multibus II Memory Space Configurable from Multibus II Interconnect Space
- 32K Bytes of Multibus I I/O Mapped into Multibus II I/O Space Configurable from Multibus II Interconnect Space
- Conversion of Multibus I Interrupts to Multibus II Interrupt Messages
- Multibus I Form Factor Board
- Connects to Multibus II Central Services Module (iSBC CSM/001 Board) via a 3 Foot Flat Ribbon Cable

The iSBC® LNK/001 board maps Multibus I memory and I/O space into the Multibus II iPSB bus and converts Multibus I interrupts into Multibus II interrupt messages. Up to 16M Bytes of Multibus I memory and up to 32K Bytes of Multibus I I/O is addressable from Multibus II through the iSBC LNK/001 board. Additionally, 128K Bytes of dual port DRAM memory resides on the iSBC LNK/001 board for use by both Multibus I and Multibus II systems. Multibus II OEM product designers can now speed hardware and software development efforts by using the iSBC LNK/001 board to access standard or custom Multibus I products.

280135-1

*The iSBC® LNK/001 is also manufactured under product code pSBCLNK001 by Intel Puerto Rico, Inc.

September 1991
Order Number: 280135-003

GENERAL DESCRIPTION

The iSBC LNK/001 board makes Multibus I products accessible to Multibus II designers. The iSBC LNK/001 board resides in the Multibus I system and connects to the Central Services Module (iSBC CSM/001 board) via a 3 foot flat ribbon cable. The ribbon cable connects the P2 connector of the iSBC LNK/001 board to the P2 connector on the Central Services Module. The iSBC LNK/001 board supports:

a. 128K Bytes of Dual Port DRAM,

b. 16- and 24-bit addressing into 16M Bytes of Multibus I memory with 8- and 16-bit data paths,

c. 8- and 16-bit addressing into 32K Bytes of Multibus I I/O with 8- and 16-bit data paths,

d. Multibus I interrupt to Multibus II interrupt message conversions of up to eight levels of non bus-vectored interrupts via an 8259A programmable interrupt controller, and

e. initialization tests and Built-In-Self-Test (BIST) using interconnected address space.

APPLICATIONS

The primary application of the iSBC LNK/001 board is in the design development environment. The iSBC LNK/001 board allows designers to start their development efforts by leveraging existing Multibus I products or to begin modular design efforts and preserve investments in custom products. In either case, the use of leverage with existing Multibus I hardware and software allows designers to begin their Multibus II product designs.

MEMORY AND I/O READ/WRITE SEQUENCE

The iSBC LNK/001 board establishes a master/slave relation between a Multibus II system and a Multibus I system. A Multibus II agent requesting a memory transfer involving the iSBC LNK/001 board is directed through the CSM to the iSBC LNK/001 Dual Port memory or a Multibus I slave. If the access address is within the Multibus II Dual Port window, the transaction is acknowledged by the iSBC LNK/001 board and returned to the Multibus II iPSB through the CSM. In the event the address is outside the Multibus II Dual Port window, the transaction is directed to the Multibus I system. Here the iSBC LNK/001 board enters arbitration for the Multibus I system bus to complete the requested transaction. Once the iSBC LNK/001 board is the owner of the Multibus I system bus, data is transferred to or from the iSBC LNK/001 board/Central Services Module connection. The Multibus I slave acknowledges the transfer and the iSBC LNK/001 board passes the acknowledge on through the Central Services Module to the Multibus II iPSB.

Multibus II I/O operations are always directed to the Multibus I I/O slaves and consequently require arbitration for the Multibus I system bus.

INTERCONNECT MAPPING

The function record of the iSBC LNK/001 board, a function record within the Central Services Module interconnect template, appears as a board within a board (see Table 1). The actual iSBC LNK/001 board configuration is done through unique interconnect registers using the same slot ID as the Central Services Module. The iSBC LNK/001 function record begins at an offset of 256 from the start of the CSM template and the EOT (End Of Template) byte is attached as the last function of the iSBC LNK/001 function record.

Dual Port 128K Byte DRAM Memory

A dynamic RAM Dual Port, resident on the iSBC LNK/001 board, provides a 128K Byte media for

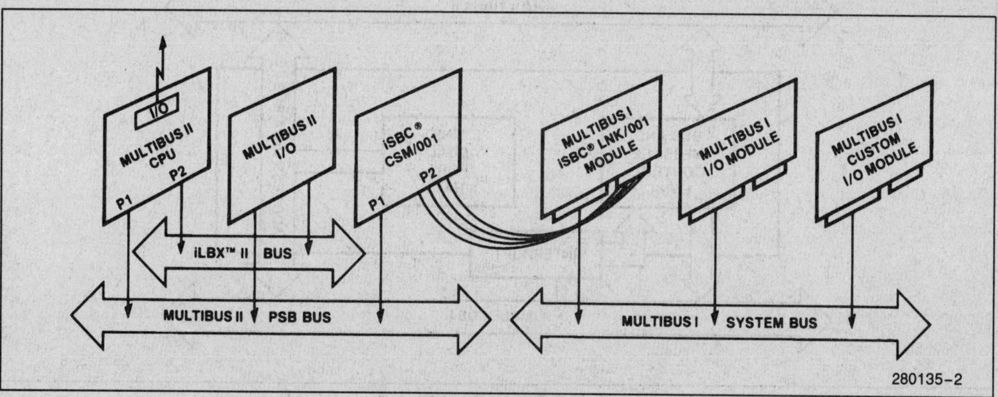

Figure 1. Sequence Diagram

4

Multibus I and Multibus II agents to pass data efficiently. With both buses sharing the Dual Port memory the need for the Multibus II system to continuously arbitrate for Multibus I system access is eliminated. Consequently, each bus can continue operating at its respective speed when accessing the iSBC LNK/001 Dual Port memory.

Multibus I Memory Addressability

The Multibus I system views the iSBC LNK/001 Dual Port as a contiguous 128K Byte memory block mapped into the 16M Bytes of Multibus I memory address space starting at the Dual Port Start Address register value. This memory block, configurable on any 64K Byte boundary within the Multibus I memory address space, is set via interconnect accesses to the iSBC LNK/001 function records from the Multibus II system (see Table 1). The first 16M Bytes of Multibus II memory space can be mapped in the 16M Bytes of Multibus I memory address space (see Figure 3).

Multibus I I/O Addressability

Up to eight 4K Byte blocks of Multibus II I/O space can be mapped into Multibus I I/O space

Table 1. Function Record Overview iSBC® LNK/001 Board

Offset	Description	Offset	Description
0–255	iSBC CSM/001 Header and Function Record	271	MBI Dual Port End Address
		272	MBII Dual Port Start Address
256	Board Specific Record Type	273	MBII Dual Port End Address
257	Record Length	274	MBII Memory Start Address
258	Vendor ID, Low Byte	275	MBII Memory End Address
259	Vendor ID, High Byte	276	I/O 4K Segment Control
260	Link Version Number	277	MBI Interrupt Enable
261	Hardware Revision Test Number	278	Link Interrupt 0 Destination Address
262	Link General Status	279	Link Interrupt 1 Destination Address
263	Link General Control	280	Link Interrupt 2 Destination Address
264	Link BIST Support Level	281	Link Interrupt 3 Destination Address
265	Link BIST Data In	282	Link Interrupt 4 Destination Address
266	Link BIST Data Out	283	Link Interrupt 5 Destination Address
267	Link BIST Slave Status	284	Link Interrupt 6 Destination Address
268	Link BIST Master Status	285	Link Interrupt 7 Destination Address
269	Link BIST Test ID	286	Interrupt Source Address
270	MBI Dual Port Start Address	287	Link Status Register
		288	EOT (End of Template)

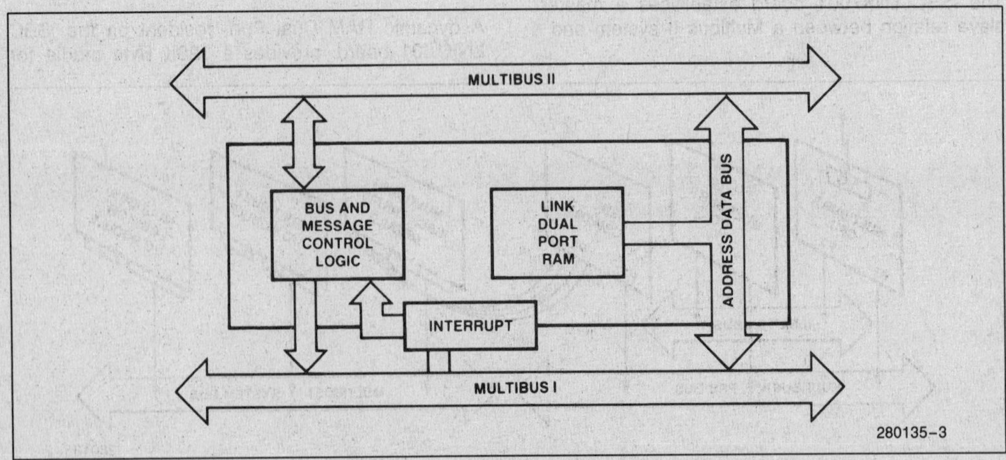

Figure 2. Link Board Dual Port Drawing

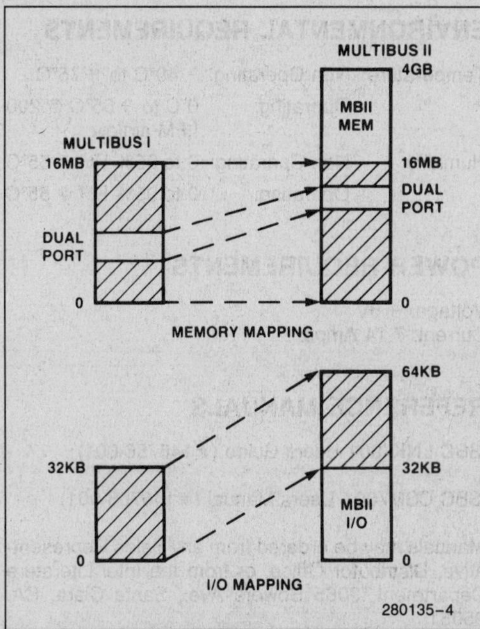

Figure 3. Multibus I Memory and I/O Mapping Diagram

(see Figure 3). Multibus II I/O accesses must be from 32K Byte to 64K Byte in order to be mapped into Multibus I I/O address space. These blocks are specified through an interconnect access to the "I/O 4K Segment Control" register (see Table 1). Each bit in the register represents a 4K Byte block of I/O addresses. When a bit (or bits) is set, the 4K Byte block of Multibus II I/O space represented by that bit will be dedicated to Multibus I I/O space.

Interrupt to Message Conversion

As the iSBC LNK/001 board receives non-bus vectored interrupts from the Multibus I system, the on-board 8259A programmable interrupt controller (PIC) prioritizes the Multibus I interrupts and initiates the Multibus II unsolicited interrupt message generation process. Up to 8 levels of non-bus vectored interrupts are supported by the iSBC LNK/001 board.

The iSBC LNK/001 board generates the Multibus II interrupt messages and is the Interrupt Source. The iSBC LNK/001 board is assigned a Source ID through interconnect space when the Multibus II system is powered up or when the user programs the source ID register via interconnect space. The Interrupt Destination is the Multibus II board to which the interrupt message is being sent. Each of the eight Multibus I interrupt lines can be programmed to generate a unique Multibus II destination address. These destination addresses are initialized through interconnect space by programming the iSBC LNK/001 Interrupt Destination Address Registers. The message source address is also configurable via interconnect space by writing to the Interrupt 0 Source Address Register with a base value. Once the base value of source Address 0 is established, Source Address 1 through 7 are set for incrementing values by the 8751A interconnect processor. The iSBC LNK/001 board recognizes Multibus II Negative Acknowledge agent errors ("NACK") and performs an automatic retry algorithm.

Initialization Tests and BIST

Self test and diagnostics have been built into the Multibus II system. The BIST LED is used to indicate the result of the Built-In-Self-Test and turns on when BIST starts running and turns off when it has successfully executed. BIST test failure information is recorded in the interconnect space and is accessible to software for error reporting.

PHYSICAL CHARACTERISTICS

Form Factor

The iSBC LNK/001 board is a Multibus I form factor board residing in a Multibus I system. Physical dimensions are identical to all standard Multibus I boards.

Connection to Multibus II Bus

The iSBC LNK/001 board connects to the iSBC CSM/001 board in the Multibus II system via a 60 pin conductor flat ribbon cable. The physical connection is made on the P2 connector of both the iSBC LNK/001 board and the iSBC CSM/001 board. The cable termination requirements and DC requirements for the signal drivers and receivers are detailed in the iSBC CSM/001 USERS GUIDE, Section 6.6.4. The maximum length of the cable is 3 feet. The cable and the connectors are shipped unassembled to allow user flexibility.

SOFTWARE SUPPORT

To take advantage of iSBC LNK/001 Dual Port architecture, existing software device drivers may require modification. Device driver changes depend on the specific application and vary in complexity depending upon the device driver.

SPECIFICATIONS

Word Size

16- and 24-bit Address Paths
8- and 16-bit Data Paths
Block transfers are not supported

Cable Characteristics

The cable is a 60 pin conductor flat ribbon cable with a maximum length of 3 feet. The P2 connector to the iSBC LNK/001 board is a 30/60 pin board edge connector with 0.100″ pin centers, KEL-AM Part Number RF30-2853-5. The connector to the P2 DIN connector on the iSBC CSM/001 board is 3M Part Number 3338-000.

Interface Specifications

Location	Function
P1	Multibus IEEE 796 System Bus
P2	Cable connection to P2 connector of iSBC CSM/001 board

PHYSICAL DIMENSIONS

The iSBC LNK/001 board meets all Multibus I mechanical specifications as presented in the Multibus I specification.

Depth: 17.15 cm (6.75 in.)
Height: 1.27 cm (0.50 in.)
Front Panel Width: 30.48 cm (12.00 in.)
Weight: 0.5 kg (20 oz.)

ENVIRONMENTAL REQUIREMENTS

Temperature:	Non Operating:	−40°C to +75°C
	Operating:	0°C to +55°C @ 200 LFM airflow
Humidity:	Non Operating:	0 to 95% RH @ 55°C
	Operating:	0 to 95% RH @ 55°C

POWER REQUIREMENTS

Voltage: +5V
Current: 7.14 Amps

REFERENCE MANUALS

iSBC LNK/001 Users Guide (#148756-001)

iSBC CSM/001 Users Manual (#146706-001)

Manuals may be ordered from any Sales Representative, Distributor Office, or from the Intel Literature Department, 3065 Bowers Ave., Santa Clara, CA. 95051.

ORDERING INFORMATION

Part Number	Description
iSBC LNK/001	Multibus II to Multibus I iSBC LNK/001 Interface Board

intel®

MULTIBUS II HIGH PERFORMANCE SBC GENERAL PURPOSE TEST FIXTURE (GPTF)

- Single Board Computer Tester for Multibus II Boards in a Systems Environment
- Tests up to Four Multibus II Boards Simultaneously in a Range from Ambient Temperature to 70°C — Voltage and Temperature Margins are Software Controlled
- Multiprocessor, Multitesting Functional Tester with Totally Automated Test Sequence, Requiring Minimum Human Intervention
- Powerful Command Language for Troubleshooting and Evaluation
- One STBL (System Test Board Level) Test is Included. Additional Test Programs are Available for Intel Multibus II Boards
- GPTF Includes Video Monitor for Error Message Display and Status of Testing, Also, a Comprehensive Installation Guide and Users Manual
- Bus Drawer Feature on P2 Connector Allows User Flexibility to Test Boards with Different Types of P2 Interfaces
- Available in Either USA, Japan or International Power Configuration
- Safety Features Including Thermal Cut Out at 90°C

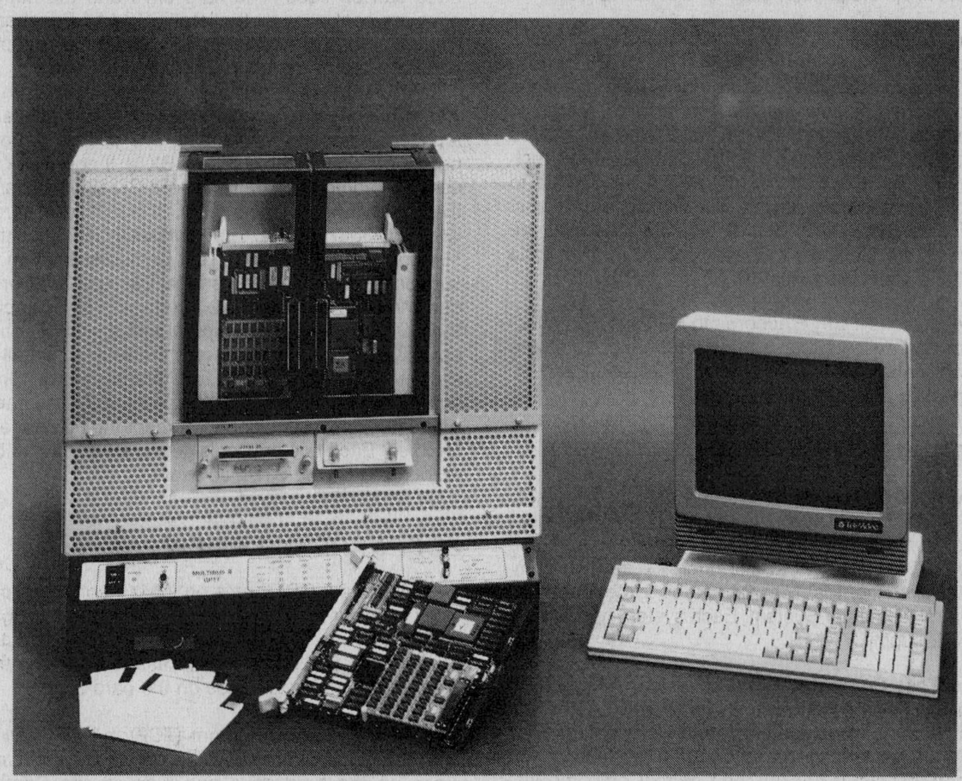

280189–1

4

September 1991
Order Number: 280189-002

TESTER OVERVIEW

The Multibus II General Purpose Test-Fixture (Multibus II GPTF) is a state-of-the-art high performance tester used to test Multibus II boards in a typical systems environment. The System Test Board Level or STBL, as it is usually referred to, is done using the Multibus II GPTF. The STBL is used to validate that the Single Board Computer (SBC) board will perform in a system environment under a variety of temperature and voltage conditions. The Multibus II GPTF is a fully automated tester with minimum operator intervention required. It can test from one to four boards of the same type at a time. A full range of keyboard commands are available for troubleshooting. The human interface is through the Front Panel and the CRT terminal. The Multibus II GPTF requires the use of a Televideo 955 terminal which is included with the GPTF order.

The users manual is written at the operator's level and thus does not require a technician to perform tests. The users manual is written in two parts; operator's instructions and technician's troubleshooting section. An installation guide is also furnished.

The Multibus II GPTF does not require any special Test EPROMs to do the STBL. The STBL can be loaded and stored in the hard drive using either the floppy drive or downloaded from an Intel Series III Development System. Once the STBLs are loaded into the hard drive, reconfiguration time (when testing different types of boards) is typically limited to exchanging the bus drawer. The STBLs for the most part use the Built-In Self Tests (BISTs) which are part of the Multibus II Board Product Firmware, to test the Unit Under Test (UUT).

The Multibus II GPTF adheres to Multibus II architecture and follows the Intel Interconnect Interface Specification (IIS) and the Intel Initialization and Diagnostics eXecutive (IDX).

HARDWARE OVERVIEW

The Multibus II GPTF is uniquely designed for ease of maintainability with three enclosures. The front enclosure is the heat chamber that houses the UUTs. Behind the heat chamber are the two computer systems; the Test Computer System and the Control Computer System. Each system has its own power supply.

The **Test Computer System**, which is Multibus II based, is located immediately behind the heat chamber. It is the slave system to the Control Computer System. Its function is to perform the testing and report test status back to the Control Computer System. The Test Computer System contains three HOST Multibus II boards which always reside in the GPTF.

The **Hot Box Test Chamber** has slots for testing one to four UUT's simultaneously. Both the +5V and temperature can be varied by the Control Computer (or the user) to test the boards in a worst case condition. The +5V voltage can be margined ±10%, and the temperature can be raised from room temperature to 70°C.

The **Control Computer System** is located in the rear of the GPTF and is a Multibus I based system. Its function is to control and manage the Test Computer System. This system controls the AC power to the Test Computer System, has the capability to margin the DC voltages to the Test Comp. Sys., controls the heat chamber heater coils, reset and interrupt lines to the iSBC CSM/001 board, and controls the I/O to the CRT video display, front panel, and the secondary storage. The Control Computer contains an 8-slot Multibus I backplane and five iSBC boards.

The secondary storage consists of a 3.5", 40 Mbyte winchester hard drive and a 5.25", 48 TPI floppy drive. Both iRMX® I and PC-DOS format floppy diskettes can be used. The hard drive and the floppy drive are controlled by the Intel iSBC 214 Peripheral Controller board. Additional 3.5" and 5.25" peripheral bays are designed in for future Intel use.

Variable P2 Interface capability in the Multibus II architecture allows for variable use of the P2 connector on iSBC boards. The iLBX™ II connector is used on some boards, like the iSBC 286/100 and the iSBC MEM/3XX boards, SCSI is used on boards like iSBC 386/258 etc. The Multibus II GPTF has the bus drawer feature in the Test Computer System to support the variable P2 interface. Each bus drawer is designed for a specific P2 interface. For example, the CODE1 bus drawer, shipped with the GPTF, supports iLBX II. The bus drawers are easy to install—slide it in and tighten the two thumb screws. Only two types are shipped with the product. All the parts of the bus drawer are generic except the P2 connector itself. Each bus drawer is coded so that it can be recognized by the STBL software.

SOFTWARE OVERVIEW

The Multibus II GPTF runs on iRMX I software specially configured for the GPTF. The operating system resides on the hard drive in Control Computer System. The DIR command will assist in locating the various directories and files on the hard drive.

The Tester Control Program (TCP), an application program running under iRMX I Operating System, resides on the hard drive and runs on the Control Computer System (iSBC 186/51 board). The TCP resembles a mini operating system. It supports a range of keyboard commands which are useful to run STBL and to troubleshoot suspect boards. A set of ten command strings can be stored in the STBL software and may be invoked at run time by the operator.

Using TCP commands, the operator can control the functions of the GPTF. TCP also responds to the front panel buttons, (START & QUIT) thus, making the GPTF automated. The CRT displays dedicated fields to indicate corresponding status of the testing such as: UUT board ID, UUT power supply status, voltage margin as percent of nominal voltage, and slot location of UUT.

The TCP operates in two modes, PRODUCTION TEST MODE (default) and TROUBLESHOOTING MODE. These modes allow the GPTF to be operated in a fully automated mode or a manually controlled mode. The PRODUCTION TEST MODE is turned off while troubleshooting with just a simple keyboard command.

The TCP works in conjunction with the firmware on the Host CPU board in the Test Computer System. The firmware is usually referred to as Host Firmware (HFW). The HFW is an implementation of the Master Test Handler, as defined in the IDX. The Host firmware under the control of the TCP performs the testing of the UUTs.

The STBL can have tests of three different types. TYPE 1 tests run on the HOST only, TYPE 2 tests run on UUT only and TYPE 3 tests have both UUT and HOST code and can run on both. When testing more than one UUT, the TYPE 2 tests are executed in parallel by the UUTs. A given STBL can have any mixture of these three types of tests.

TESTER BLOCK DIAGRAM

Figure 1 shows a block diagram of the tester, in a level of detail sufficient to understand basic tester operation. The top of the sketch shows the Multibus II system where testing takes place. On the left are the UUT slots, and on the right the host boards. Both iPSB and iLBX II busses are shown. The iLBX II backplane is physically installed in a removable bus drawer. Important communication paths shown are: a fast parallel path between host processor and control computer, and serial channels to the terminal and Series III development system. Details omitted for clarity include the heaters; most cabling; temperature sensors; +5B and heater relays.

4

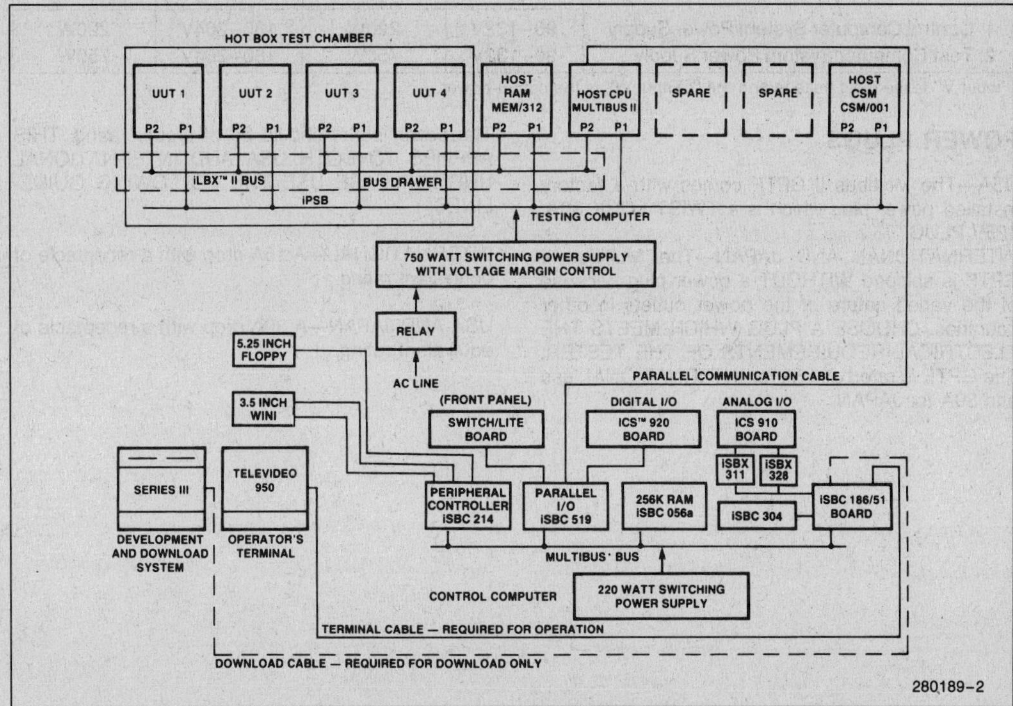

Figure 1. Tester Block Diagram

SPECIFICATIONS

Size: 63.5cm W x 96.5cm D x 62.2cm H (25″ W x 38″ D x 24.5″ H)

Weight: 41 Kg (90 lbs.)

Power Ratings	USA Units	International Units	Japan Units
Nominal Voltage Rating	110 volts	220 volts	100 volts
Current Rating	30 amperes	15 amperes	30 amperes
Frequency Rating	60 hertz	50 hertz	50/60 hertz

FUSE RATINGS

Power Ratings	USA/Japan	International
F1—Heater Coil 1 Fuse	10A @ 250V	5A @ 250V
F2—Heater Coil 2 Fuse	6A @ 250V	3A @ 250V
F3—Multibus I Power Supply Fuse	7A @ 125V	4A @ 250V
F4—Multibus II Power Supply Fuse	15A @ 250V	10A @ 250V

HEATER COIL RATINGS

Power Ratings	USA/Japan	International
Heater Coil 1	1000W 110V	1000W 220V
Heater Coil 2	660W 110V	660W 220V

Heater Coil 1 is to your right when you face the GPTF.

POWER SUPPLY RATINGS

Power Ratings	USA/Japan		International	
	*Input V	Output W	Input V	Output W
1. Control Computer System Power Supply	90–132V	220W	180–264V	220W
2. Test Computer System Power Supply	90–132V	750W	180–264V	750W

*"Input V" is the input voltage and the "Output W" is the output power.

POWER PLUGS

USA—The Multibus II GPTF comes with a factory installed power plug which is a TWIST LOCK 30A, 125V PLUG.

INTERNATIONAL AND JAPAN—The Multibus II GPTF is shipped WITHOUT a power plug because of the varied nature of the power outlets in other countries. CHOOSE A PLUG WHICH MEETS THE ELECTRICAL REQUIREMENTS OF THE TESTER. The GPTF is rated at 15A for INTERNATIONAL use and 30A for JAPAN.

The power outlet should be of proper rating. THIS APPLIES TO BOTH USA AND INTERNATIONAL UNITS. PLEASE USE THE FOLLOWING GUIDELINES:

INTERNATIONAL—A 15A drop with a receptacle of equivalent rating.

USA AND JAPAN—A 30A drop with a receptacle of equivalent rating.

Multibus II Architecture

5

The Multibus II Bus Structure

John Hyde
Multibus II Marketing Manager
Intel Corporation, Hillsboro, OR 97124

INTRODUCTION

Many people equate the phrase "Multibus II" with the Parallel System Bus defined within the IEEE/ANSI 1296 specification. While this over simplification is often useful, the failure to appreciate that *it is a contraction* of a more embracing architecture can lead one astray when comparing the Multibus II bus structure with other buses. Comparisons between the Multibus II Parallel System Bus and other buses are often completed in isolation, without full regard to the framework in which the Multibus II architecture was defined. This chapter rebuilds this framework, describes its hierarchical structure and details how its features are *required* for multiple microprocessor designs of today.

CUSTOMER NEEDS DEFINE THE NEW BUS STRUCTURE

Intel Corporation had had many years experience with the Multibus standard before embarking upon the requirements for a "next generation" bus structure. The first Multibus standard bus was introduced in 1974 and it was fundamentally a CPU/Memory bus. It evolved along with microprocessor technology to become a multi-master shared memory bus capable of solving most real time applications of the 1980s. The silicon trends throughout the 1980s were dramatic with DRAM densities increasing by a factor of two every three years, so projecting exactly what customers would require in the late 1980s and through to the 1990s was particularly difficult. Intel therefore set up a consortium with eighteen of its larger customers and other industry leaders who could see the potential within the single board computer industry, to define the scope and possibilities of what was to be call "Multibus II".

It was known that the rate of silicon integration would allow a complete computer system including CPU, Program Memory, Data Memory, Input/Output and bus interface to be fabricated upon a single board. With such a large transistor budget to be spent upon implementing a single board computer, where would be the optimal places to best utilize the technology? Self test and diagnostics could now be considered—with so much silicon on a board it would be prudent to use some of the transistor count to TEST the remainder of the board. Since board manufacturers are integrating more and more VLSI silicon onto their boards, the user needs some reassurance that the basic board functionality is intact before they load their value added code—the user is *demanding* on-board diagnostics for these highly integrated boards. The bus interface itself, not a traditional candidate for high integration silicon circuitry, could use transistors for added sophistication IF this sophistication could make the single board computers easier to use. A trend began to develop; transistors added to improve ease of use filtered to the top of the implementation list.

With the increased silicon densities available, semiconductor manufacturers turned their focus upon increased capability peripheral components. Their use on single board computers served to compound the boards complexity and the single board computer user was "rewarded" by having to wade through lengthy reference manuals and innumerable jumper options—often arriving at the final solution only by trial and error. Memory mapping options, arbitration priorities, interrupt levels and scores of other "tunable" parameters contributed to the hassle, leaving the systems engineer confused and amazed. Often the only solution was to locate a board which had already been properly configured and was operating and then copy off the jumper list.

Board manufacturers built in numerous options so that their products could be used in the broadest possible spectrum of applications. The number of options offered was not the core of the problem—*but managing them was.* Options allow interrupt routing, memory mapping, EPROM size selection, timing and other user installed components. When the jumper count exceeded 200, it no longer made sense to monopolize board real estate since an inexpensive microcontroller could be used to manage the resources more effectively.

A system bus requires standardized system-wide configuration information to be made accessible to software, opening it to opportunities for centralized control and coordination. Ideally the end-user of these products will be completely unaware of the configuration process. They simply remove the board from it's shipping container, install the proper firmware, plug it into any free slot in the backplane, and apply power. Things work the first time around with no mess, no fuss, and no configuration errors.

Order Number: 281113-001

The consortium therefore placed focus on the system aspects of the single board computer design. The developing model for a typical system built from these highly capable single board computers was based upon functionally partitioned subsystems interacting across a standardized communications channel. This precipitated a change in philosophy for the traditional system development from the single board computer outward to a higher level systems perspective, specified tops-down and bound together by rigid interfaces.

The consortium quickly reached consensus that no single bus could be used to satisfy all aspects of a design of this type—too many variables would have to be compromised, so a *multiple bus* structure was defined in a similar fashion to its Multibus I (IEEE 796) predecessor. Figure 1 shows the four sub- buses defined by the consortium: the iSBX® bus was retained for incremental I/O expansion, a local CPU/Memory expansion bus was proposed and two versions of a SYSTEM bus (serial and parallel) were defined. The concept of a SYSTEM bus is an important one to grasp—all open buses to date were basically CPU/Memory buses with little regard for system aspects. To have an open bus *SPECIFICALLY* designed to be a system bus was a bold step.

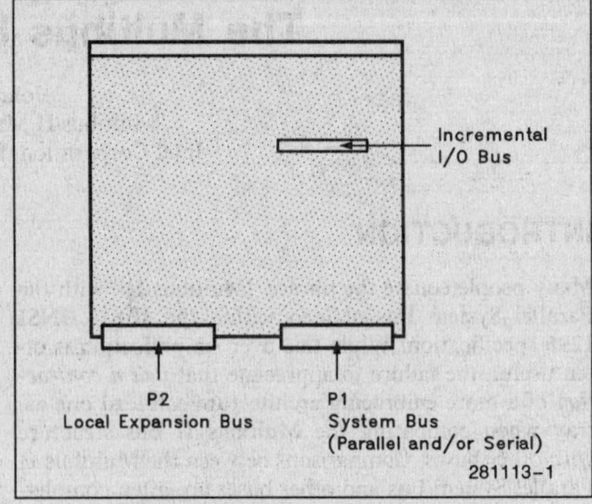

Figure 1. Since no single bus could solve the defined problem set, a multiple bus solution was proposed

FUNCTIONAL PARTITIONING AS A SOLUTION FOR NON-OBSOLESCENCE

Before detailing the attributes of each of the defined buses that make up the Multibus II systems architecture it is important to appreciate the model developed for the bus. Figure 2 shows a typical collection of systems connected to a local area network or LAN. This type of networked systems solution is very popular with

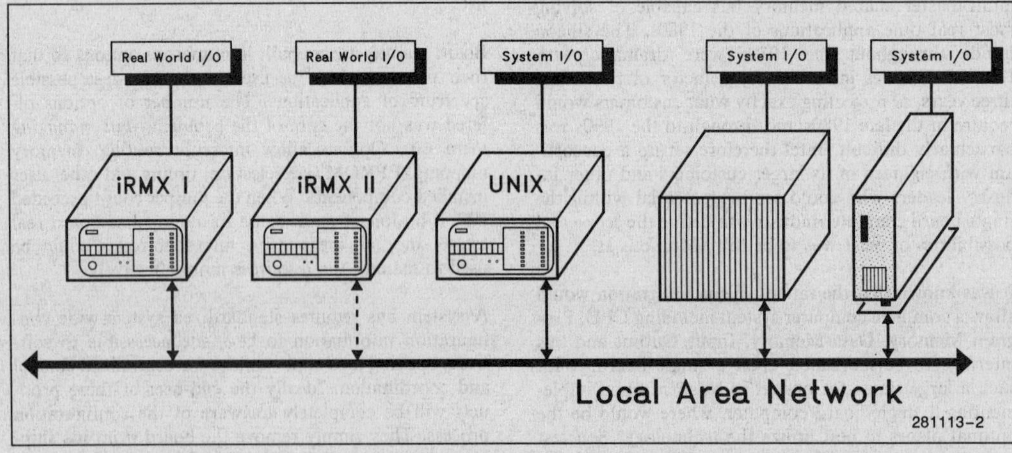

Figure 2. Multiple diverse systems can co-exist on a Local Area Network using defined protocols

systems builders since it boasts a large array of benefits. The solution is functionally partitioned—separate systems are used to tackle different facets of the overall problem. These systems are independent from each other and decisions made to optimize each of them for their individual task may be made in isolation with respect to the other systems in the network. This degree of freedom gives the systems architect an unquestioned edge when engineering tradeoffs are being made. The choice of hardware, options and software may be made with the sole goal of solving the small part of the overall problem currently in focus. Each system is typically tuned for its task using specifically configured hardware and software and it is not uncommon to see multiple different operating systems with a single network. Systems that *MUST* respond in real time, for example, would use Intel's iRMX® Real Time operating system or their iRMK™ Real Time kernel, while a data base manager would use an industry standard operating system such as UNIX® or DOS. The systems would probably contain a diversity of microprocessors.

Each of the systems are individually upgradeable. If something bigger/better/faster/cheaper becomes available it is easy to integrate this into a networked system solution. New technology may be applied at strategic points on the network and no major overhaul of the complete solution is ever required. Since the overall system is continuously upgradeable it will not become obsolete and will serve for many years.

The systems are independent in their own right, capable of completing their assigned task in isolation and need not be connected to the LAN to function. The reason that they are connected to the LAN is to enable the sharing of data. The LAN defines a media type and details certain communications protocols that all the systems on the network must adhere to—in this way the diverse systems may share data in a consistent manner. Each system will require a hardware interface to the media and a software interface to the network protocols. Error recovery and retry algorithms are employed to ensure reliable communications between the individual systems on the network.

The software model for this functionally partitioned solution is "protocol based" with "data movement". In this type of model the computer population is split into server systems and consumer systems. A server system provides facilities and resources to the network such as file systems or access to a communications hierarchy. A consumer system does work using the facilities provided by the network servers. The consumer software model makes defined requests for data that a server will respond to. An inter-system communications standard was developed by the International Standards Organization and its seven-layer model is shown in Figure 3. All interfaces are rigidly defined but the implementation is not—this allows many diverse systems to interact successfully.

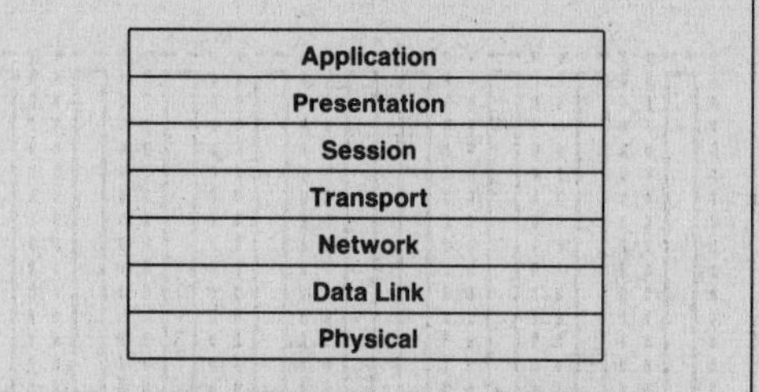

Figure 3. A seven layer inter-system communications model has been defined by the International Standards Organization

A MAJOR BREAKTHROUGH

Imagine now, keeping the same networked topology but using the advances in silicon integration to compress the systems into a single Multibus II chassis as shown in Figure 4. We will use the parallel system bus as the network media. We will use protocols on the parallel system bus very similar to the protocols used over the local area network. Each of the networked systems will become a single board subsystem (or a multi-board subsystem if the circuitry exceeds the area of a single board). We have created a VERY Local Area Network or a "Backplane LAN".

A Multibus II chassis with multiple boards operating as a Backplane LAN is physically similar to a traditional system but its networked-subsystems philosophy realizes many benefits. This use of advanced Multibus II bus technology allows the systems builder to tackle multi-CPU designs with confidence.

Partitioning a multi-CPU application into a set of networked subsystems allows us the opportunity to focus. We are able to break down a complex problem into solvable sub-problems. These sub-problems are also encapsulated, therefore they can be solved independently of the other problems. Encapsulation is an important attribute of a Multibus II subsystem. Encapsulation assumes that a subsystem is intelligent and that it owns most of the resources required to complete its assigned task. These resources are private and are under the sole control of the subsystem CPU(s). In a complex subsystem these resources may be spread over multiple boards as shown in Figure 5. Even though there are three physical boards in this example it is important to appreciate that, at a systems architecture level, they are treated as a single logical subsystem. The boards within a subsystem communicate using a local expansion bus defined on the P2 connector.

5

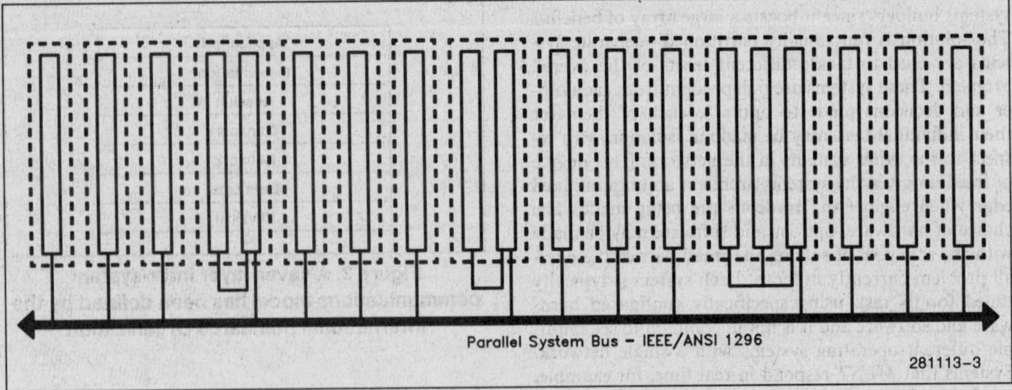

Figure 4. Higher levels of silicon integration allow a network topology to be used within a single system

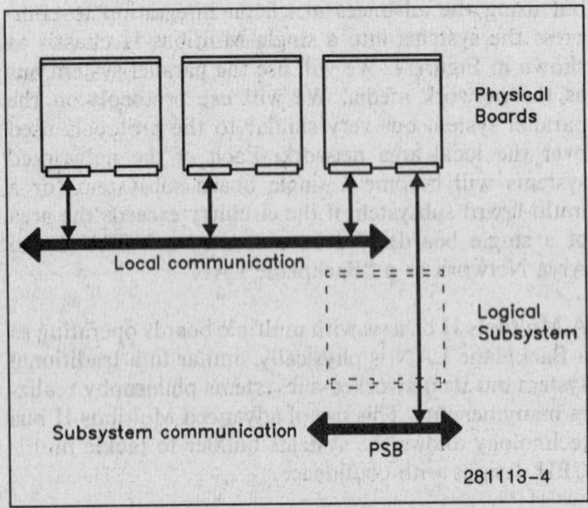

Figure 5. Multi-board subsystems interact with each other across a private P2 bus and appear as a single logical subsystem

IMPLEMENTING THE SUB-BUSES

The realization that a single bus could not solve all of the problems is an important first step. The requirements of each sub-bus are so different that compromising their features will result in sub-optimal system solution. The majority of this chapter will detail the system bus, but the other buses are discussed so that a context for decisions made will be evident.

The Incremental I/O bus needs to be simple. Its role is to allow the addition of a small piece of input/output onto a single board computer to customize it for a particular application. Performance is not an issue but low interfacing costs are. More extensive I/O would be added on the local expansion bus or on the system bus if an accompanying microprocessor was appropriate.

The Local CPU/Memory Expansion bus will always be dependent upon microprocessor technology. The interface between a CPU and its memory needs to be tightly coupled if we are to extract the maximum performance levels from a given microprocessor family. This bus will evolve with microprocessor technology and will typically exist for only two to four years before it has to be redesigned. If the CPU element requires more MIPs then additional identical microprocessors could be closely coupled on this local expansion bus; if these microprocessors had on-chip or local caches, as many of the higher performance offerings do, then this multiple microprocessor CPU/Memory bus must be cache coherent.

A major requirement of the SYSTEM bus is a technology independent communications media. Since this bus will remain constant throughout multiple generations of microprocessors it must be decoupled from the microprocessor technology used on the single board computer. This loosely coupled approach, whereby each single board computer subsystem is independent, will enjoy all of the benefits of the systems networked on a Local Area Network. Global system functions such as initialization, diagnostics and configuration must be added in a standardized way to this long-lived system bus.

PHYSICAL STANDARDS

A reasonably large card size with ample power is key to making the best use of the available levels of silicon integration. While no real data has proven that edge connectors should not be used, there is a definite trend towards gas-tight pin-and-socket connectors. A double Eurocard format, IEEE/ANSI 1101 Standard, with dual 96 pin DIN connectors was chosen for the Multibus II standard. A 'U' shaped front panel, licensed from Siemens, West Germany, was chosen for its enhanced EMI and RFI qualities.

THE INCREMENTAL I/O BUS

The large array of existing iSBX (IEEE 894) modules for the Multibus I family of products encouraged its adoption within the Multibus II standard. The iSBX strategy has proven itself with customers and vendors alike.

THE LOCAL EXPANSION BUS

The exact bus used for local expansion will vary according to the specific requirements and performance levels required in a subsystem design. As far as the IEEE/ANSI 1296 specification is concerned, this is an open option and ANY bus that is suitable may be used. Intel initiated a standard call iLBX™ II which was optimized for a 12 MHz 80286 microprocessor although other manufacturers have implemented this using members of the 68000 family. Siemens have implemented Multibus I on the P2 connector and called it the AMS bus. Intel has also offered the PC AT® bus as a subsystem option on a range of PC compatible products—while this subsystem bus is low performance, it is a low cost method to add dumb I/O to a Multibus II subsystem. The IEEE 896 committee is currently working upon cache coherent extensions to Futurebus; this bus, discussed in Chapter 7, would be a good candidate for a high performance local expansion bus.

Address Space		Address Space Size	Sequence Type	Transfer Width (bits)	Block Transfers	Number of Repling Agents
CPU/Memory Space	Memory	2**32 bytes	Read/Write	8, 16, 24, 32	Supported with increment	One
	Input/Output	2**16 8-bit ports	Read/Write	8, 16, 24, 32	Supported without increment	One
System Space	Message	2**8-1 Agents 1 Broadcast	Write Only	32	Supported without increment	One or All
	Interconnect	2**9 8-bit registers each agent	Read/Write	8	Not supported	One

Figure 6. The Multibus II System Bus has two address spaces each subdivided into two sections

THE SYSTEM BUS

The CPU/Memory bus defined on most buses is inadequate to support "systems-level" requirements so a *SYSTEM SPACE* was added to the definition of the Multibus II System Bus. [A good analogy here, from the software world, is the User/Supervisor Spaces common in advanced operating systems.] This system space is divided into two portions—Interconnect Space to fulfill the initialization, diagnostics and configuration requirements and Message Space to fulfill the standardized communications requirements. Figure 6 shows the four address spaces available on the Multibus II system bus—note that the traditional CPU/Memory space is retained for compatibility with existing buses and to aid migration of existing applications into the Multibus II environment. The system bus is optimized for system space operations but CPU/Memory space operations can perform well in their limited single cycle mode.

Intel's implementation of the Multibus II Parallel System Bus is contained in their VLSI bus interface device, the Message Passing Coprocessor (MPC or 82389), whose functional block diagram is shown in Figure 7. The MPC bus controller is a 70,000 transistor single chip device designed to minimize the board area required by the bus interface circuitry. By standardizing the bus interface in publicly available silicon, all users of the Multibus II standard can look forward to lowering costs and ensured compatibility. This standardization in silicon is similar to Intel's work with IEEE 754 floating point standard implemented in the 8087, 80287 and 80387 components and the IEEE 802.3 Ethernet® standard implemented in the 82586 and 82588 components.

The 70,000 transistors which make up the MPC bus controller implement a variety of functions as shown in Figure 8. As seen from Figure 8 most of the MPC bus controller deals with message space, either interrupt messages or data transfer messages or with interconnect space.

Function	Transistors
Traditional Bus Functions	
Bus Control	4,000
Bus Arbitration	1,000
Dual Port Memory Control	2,000
Off-Board References	1,000
Interrupts	20,000
Advanced Bus Functions	
Parity Generation/Detection	1,000
Interconnect Space	6,000
Built-in-Self-Test	1,000
Message Passing	34,000
Total	70,000

Figure 8. The majority of the 70,000 transistors within the MPC support the System Space functions of the Parallel System Bus

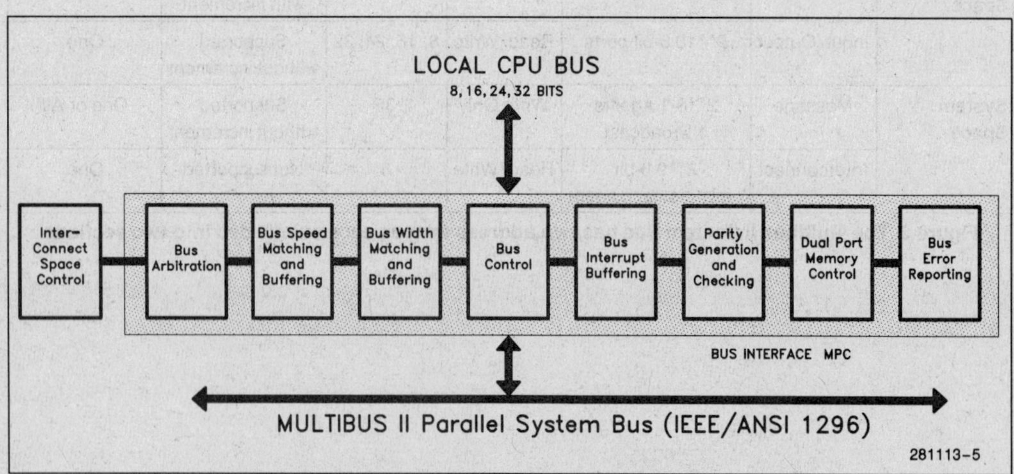

Figure 7. Intel's implementation of the IEEE 1296 specification is cast in silicon as the 82389 component

The MPC bus controller contains almost all of the logic needed to interface any microprocessor to the Parallel System Bus—indeed all of today's popular 32-bit microprocessors are available on Multibus II products. One of the few required external components are the high current bus drivers as shown in Figure 9. Optional external logic to support dual-port memory selection and off-board memory and I/O references may be included if traditional bus functionality is required. All of Intel's Multibus II boards also includes a microcontroller (8751) to implement interconnect space but some members of the Multibus Manufacturers Group have chosen to implement this using the host microprocessor or a simple state machine.

The alternate system bus, the Serial System Bus or SSB, is currently defined but is not implemented in silicon. The goal of this bus was to reduce the cost of coupling multiple boards together and it was specified as a 2 Mb/sec serial link. All software interfaces to an SSB chip would be identical to that of the MPC parallel bus controller so NO SOFTWARE CHANGES would be necessary to use the serial system bus. Performance would be much less using this serial system bus but, for many designs, this would be acceptable. Other designs, however, would benefit from a 200 Mb/sec link and Intel has joined others on the IEEE 1394 serial bus standardization committee to deliver this. This group of multiple vendors is driving for a standard which will allow ALL systems to interoperate. Implementation of the SSB interface chip is on hold pending resolution and recommendation from this IEEE committee.

INTERCONNECT SPACE

Interconnect address space is a fundamental part of the IEEE/ANSI 1296 specification and it addresses three major customer requirements: Board identification, initialization, configuration and diagnostics. Interconnect space is implemented as an ordered set of eight-bit registers on long word (32 bit) boundaries—in this way little endian microprocessors such as the 8086 family and the big endian microprocessors such as the 68000 family access the information in an identical manner. One objective of interconnect address space is to allow higher level software to gain information concerning the environment in which it operates, independent of who manufactured the board, the functions it contains, and the card slot it is in. To accomplish this goal, a comprehensive Interconnect Interface Specification which builds upon the concepts introduced within the IEEE/ANSI 1296 specification has been published by Intel Corporation and is available from the Multibus Manufacturers Group.

Board identification registers are read-only locations containing information on the board type, its manufacturer, what components are installed, and other board

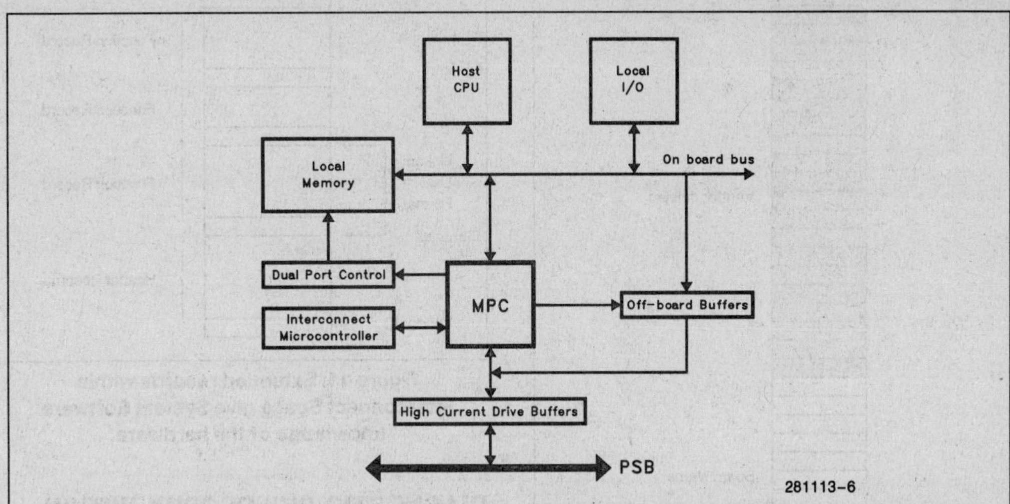

Figure 9. The MPC integrates all of the System Bus functions into a single VLSI component

specific functions. Configuration registers are read/write registers which allow the system software to set and change the configuration of many hardware options. In most cases hard wired jumper options can now be eliminated in favor of software control. Diagnostic registers are used for starting, stopping, and status reporting of self- contained diagnostic routines supplied with each board. These diagnostics are commonly known as Built-in-Self-Tests (BISTs).

Interconnect space is based on the fundamental principle that you can locate boards within a backplane by their physical slot position. This concept, known as geographic addressing, is a very useful tool during system- wide initialization. Each board in the system contains firmware which conforms to a standardized header format as shown in Figure 10. At boot time, the system software will scan the backplane to locate its resources before loading device drivers. This approach eliminates the need for reconfiguring the software every time a new board is introduced to the backplane. It also solves the problem of how to configure multiple controller and processor boards in large multiprocessing systems. Slot independence is achieved by having all boards in the system carry their own initialization and diagnostic functions on-board in firmware. Operating systems can generate a map of where resources are located during initialization time, and then use this list as the basis of message passing addresses.

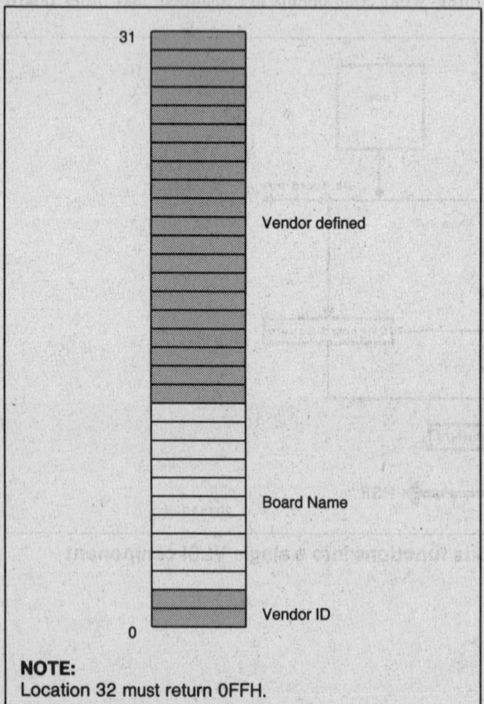

Figure 10. All IEEE/ANSI 1296 compatible boards contain an Interconnect Space Header Record

In addition to the header record, a board manufacturer may also supply additional function records which make other features of the board accessible to the user through interconnect space. An example is shown in Figure 11. Function records begin with a byte specifying the record type, followed by the number of bytes which the function record contains. The data contained in a function record is organized by the manufacturer according to published specifications which accompany the board. Many types of function records have already been defined. Some examples include memory configuration, parity control, serial I/O, and other commonly used functions. If there is no existing record type which adequately describes a given function, new record types can be defined, up to a maximum of 1020 different record types. System software will search for a particular record by starting with register number 32 (end of the header record; start of the first function record), and scanning the record type field, then counting bytes to the next function record until either the correct record is found or an "End of Template" record (hex value 0FFh) is encountered.

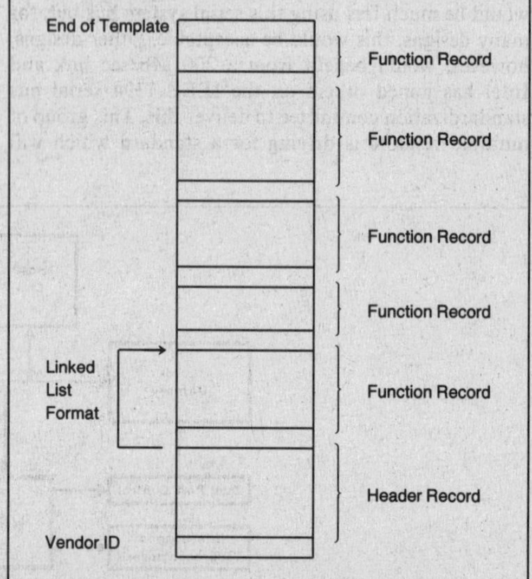

Figure 11. Extended records within Interconnect Space give System Software knowledge of the hardware.

DIAGNOSTIC PHILOSOPHY WITHIN INTERCONNECT SPACE

Intel has taken the usefulness and standardization of interconnect space one step further by embracing a standard diagnostic philosophy. Each intelligent board should have the capability to test itself and report error status in interconnect space if problems exist. There are two occasions when diagnostic testing can be invoked. A subset of the complete on-board diagnostics will be run during power-on initialization, and more extensive testing can be invoked from an operators console. Following power-on, most boards will go through a series of initialization checks, where the basic functioning of the MPC bus controller and microcontroller is verified. These checks are followed by a power-on test suite which is controlled automatically by each local microprocessor. If a hardware failure is detected at this point, a yellow LED on the front panel will illuminate so that the failing module can easily be identified and replaced by an operator, additionally test results are posted in interconnect space to be read across the backplane. Note that a CPU board when scanning interconnect space can now discover the operational status of boards in the backplane as well as their identity.

If further testing is desired, extended diagnostics can be invoked by placing a diagnostic request in the BIST registers of interconnect space. Usually one board will operate as a Master Test Handler, and will request services from other boards in the system which function as Slaves while under test. A menu of available tests is accessible via interconnect space. This test philosophy can be applied on-site by the end-user or service representative, or remotely executed via modem from a regional repair center. In most cases, downtime can be minimized by sending out a replacement board, thus avoiding an expensive repair call.

The firmware content of Multibus II boards is much greater than on previous industry standard buses. In addition to the 8751 microcontroller, there are likely to be EPROMs on board which contain the extended diagnostics, test handlers, reset initialization sequencing, debug monitors, and numerous other functions. The location of diagnostic firmware on a board will depend on the complexity of the code and the speed at which it runs. For simple replier agents, it may be that the on-board EPROM of the 8751 microcontroller contains enough program store for rudimentary diagnostic functions as well as the interconnect core firmware. In contrast, most requestor/replier boards (those capable of becoming bus masters) are more complex, and most diagnostic code is run by the microprocessor from on-board EPROM. In this case, the 8751 serves primarily as the communications interface for diagnostics.

INTERCONNECT SPACE-THE MANUFACTURERS PERSPECTIVE

From the perspective of a board designer, interconnect is a mixed blessing. The board manufacturer is certain to enjoy the benefits of reduced support costs, easier fault isolation in field repairs, and enhanced customer satisfaction, but these advantages do not come for free. One would anticipate longer development times, increased parts count on-board, and configuration in firmware to increase the amount of effort it takes to prepare a Multibus II board for market. Indeed this is so. In order to minimize this development time Intel has produced an Applications Note which details the steps and discusses the options available for a full featured interconnect space implementation. The core microcontroller code is also provided on a DOS diskette and is designed to user extensible. It is now straightforward to add these advanced capabilities to any Multibus II board design.

THE MESSAGE PASSING MECHANISM

While the previously described features make more reliable systems easier to build using the Multibus II standard, it is the innovative message passing scheme that gives the parallel system bus its high performance in a multiple microprocessor application. The underlying theory behind message passing is simple—it decouples activities between the host microprocessor's local bus and the system bus. This decoupled-bus approach provides two major advantages. First, it allows increasing parallelism of operation—resources that would otherwise be held in traditional wait states while arbitration occurs are freed, and second, one bus bandwidth does not limit the transfer rate of another. The local microprocessor bus and the system bus can perform full speed synchronous transfers independently and concurrently. The decoupling is achieved within the MPC bus controller using high speed FIFO circuitry as shown in Figure 12.

Nine 32 byte FIFO's are integrated into the MPC bus controller. Five of them are used for interrupt messages (one transmit and four receive) and four are used for the transfer of data blocks (two transmit and two receive). To understand the impact of message passing, let us consider a simple example of transferring 1K block of data from CPU A to CPU B as shown in Figure 13. We will first use a shared memory method and then a message passing method.

To use a concrete example lets assume that A is a 186 based board and can transfer data at 1 MB/sec and B is a 386™ based board that can receive data at 10 MB/sec. We will ignore DMA controller setup. DMA controller A will put a destination address onto the system bus and the address decode logic on board B will respond. We wait for the address to propagate through the dual-port controller on board B and then wait for the access time of the memory on board B. Data is transferred and once accepted by board B a ready signal will be generated and DMA controller A will move on and generate the next address. This address-wait-data cycle repeats until the full 1 KB of data is trans-

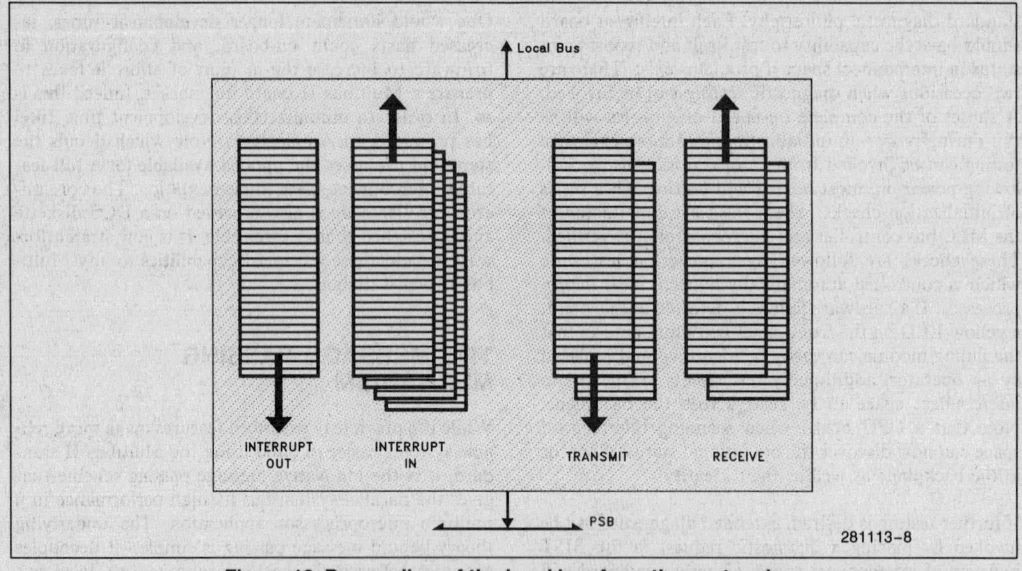

Figure 12. Decoupling of the local bus from the system bus is achieved with nine very high speed FIFOs

ferred. The overall speed of the transfer will be 1 MB/sec (the slower of the two boards) so it will take 1 msec to transfer the complete 1K buffer. If the system bus was required by an alternate CPU then the current data transfer would be delayed or the alternate CPU would have to wait.

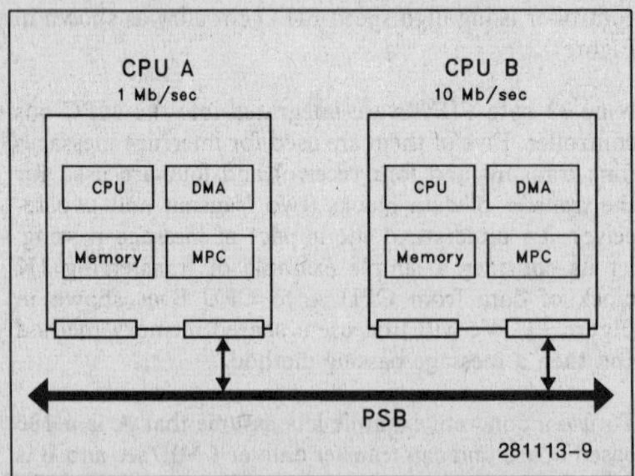

Figure 13. Let us move a 1 Kbyte block of data from Board A to Board B

Now lets consider the message passing case. This time we have to set up both DMA controllers. CPU A could probably transfer data faster than 1 MB/sec into a local I/O port (the MPC bus controller) but we will ignore this potential performance improvement. The speed of this transfer will still be 1 MB/sec, the speed of the slower board, and the total transfer time will still be 1 msec. What did we gain then for the overhead of setting up two DMA controllers?

Let us look in detail at what is happening inside the MPC bus controller. Figure 14 shows a fragment of each board with different areas of each MPC bus controller highlighted. Data is being DMA'ed into MPC-A at 1 MB/sec and flows into one of the transmit FIFO-pairs. Once 32 bytes have been received the MPC automatically switches to the alternate transmit FIFO and starts to fill that. The full transmit FIFO empties across the system bus into a receive FIFO in MPC-B. This transfer of a 32 byte packet occurs at the full bus bandwidth of 40 MB/sec. A data packet has a two clock cycle header which describes the source, destination and type of this packet which reduces the effective data transfer rate to 32 MB/sec. The packet therefore takes 1 microsecond to pass between the two MPC bus controllers. Bus arbitration is done in parallel with the packet transfer so this does not add to the transit time. Once the packet is inside of MPC-B then DMA-B empties its receive FIFO at 10 MB/sec.

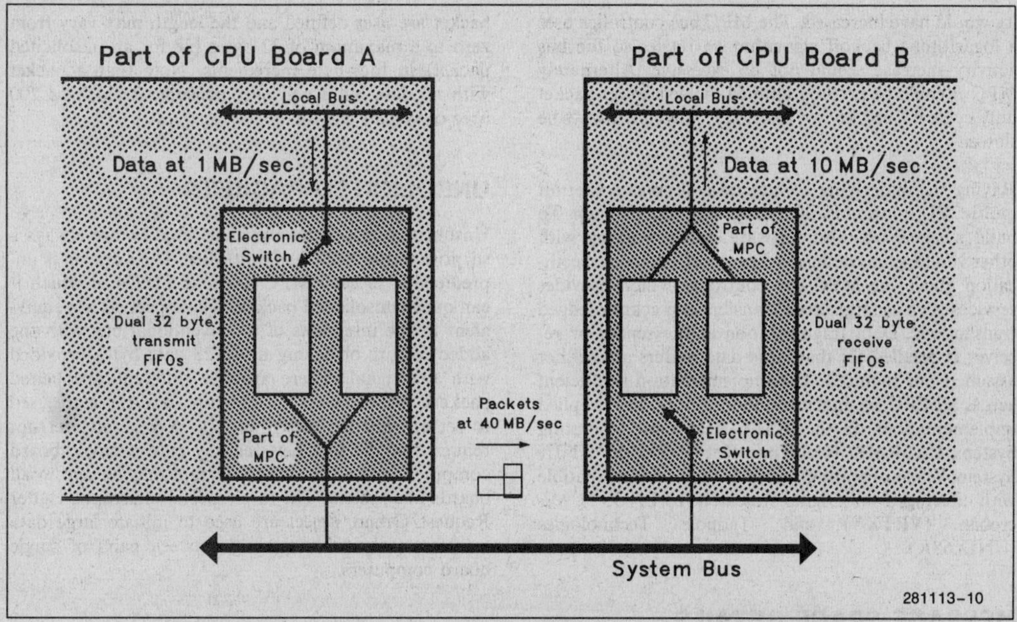

Figure 14. Looking closely at the message based data transfer mechanism

The transmit FIFO-pair of MPC-A alternate between filling from local memory and emptying into MPC-B until the full 1K of data has been transferred. No programming, save the initial setup, is required. If we look at the system bus activity we see that 1 microsecond packets are being transferred at 32 microsecond intervals—the bus is only busy for 3% of the total data transfer. We have gained 97% bus availability. Compare this with the 0% bus availability in the shared memory case. Message passing frees up system bus bandwidth to enable many other single board computer pairs to interchange data at no loss in performance. In a multiple microprocessor application the most precious resource will be system bus bandwidth and the Multibus II message passing scheme gives you more, much more.

We gain a lot more than system bus bandwidth using message passing. Not that CPU A transferred data from its local memory into a local I/O port (the MPC bus controller). CPU A did not have to understand the memory layout or restrictions of memory on CPU B—this also allowed CPU B to do its own memory management and buffer allocations. Similarly CPU B has no concern over how CPU A does its memory management. We have isolated the data away from known memory locations and do not have to deal with semaphore flags or similar mechanisms. This simplifying step make intercommunicating with multiple microprocessors as straight forward as communication with a single microprocessor. This isolation of concerns regarding the local environments of each board, through the use of a standardized data transfer mechanism, is especially important in the general case where each board is running a different operating system (probably on a different microprocessor). A real time operating system can now simply exchange data with, say, UNIX using this standardized message passing mechanism. Message passing also standardizes inter-CPU signalling since interrupts are special TYPEs of packet (more later).

This short explanation has over-simplified the transfer—some setup is required so that the sending MPC bus controller knows the message address of the receiving MPC bus controller, etc. This overhead is more than compensated for by the ignored increase in local transfer data rates. I also simplified the issue by having a receiving board much faster than the transmitting board (10 MB/sec vs. 1 MB/sec)—if I had transferred data in the opposite direction (from B to A) then MPC-A would have rejected some packets because its receive FIFOs would be full and caused MPC B to retry some data transfers. No data would eve be lost but bus activ-

5

ity would have increased. The MPC bus controller uses a logarithmic backoff algorithm on retries so the bus activity increase would not be excessive. Alternately MPC B could be preprogrammed to use a lower packet duty cycle if I had known that MPC A would always be slower.

Having the underlying architectural support to permit multi-CPU solution is, of course, only the first step. To build systems we need software. Intel, working with other vendors, has defined a Transport Protocol specification above the MPC bus controller which provides services such as large block transfers and acknowledged transactions. Data fragmentation at the sender or receiver is detailed sot that large data buffers are neither assumed nor required. The implementation is efficient across all CPU architectures; indeed, Intel has supplied implementations on the iRMX Real Time Operating System, the iRMK Real Time Kernel and the UNIX System V.386 operating systems; these are compatible with offerings from Digital Research (FLEXOS®), Microbar (VRTX®) and Tadpole Technologies (UNIX68K).

MESSAGE SPACE DETAILS

The MPC bus controller introduces a hardware recognized data type called a packet as shown in Figure 15. The MPC contains FIFO circuitry such that these packets may be moved very efficiently between MPCs—data is moved on subsequent clock edges of the 10 MHz synchronous bus; this defines the maximum bus occupancy of a packet to be one microsecond. Each MPC bus controller has an address in message space and these are used in the message header (source and destination fields).

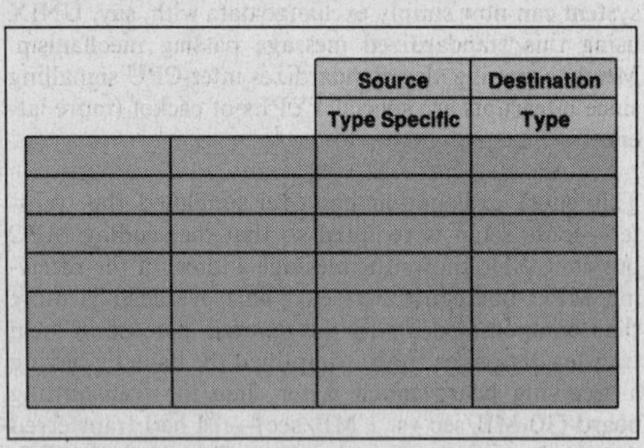

		Source	Destination
		Type Specific	Type

Figure 15. The MPC bus controller introduces a hardware-recognized data type called a packet

Seven different packet types are currently defined and are summarized in Figure 16. These divide into two categories; unsolicited, or interrupt packets and solicited, or data transfer packets. The data fields within a packet are user defined and the length may vary from zero to a maximum of 32 bytes (28 for an unsolicited packet) in four-byte increments. Note that a packet with no data bytes will only consume 2 clock or 200 nsec of system bus time.

UNSOLICITED PACKETS

Unsolicited packets, as the name implies, are always a surprise to the MPC bus controller. Their arrival is unpredictable so each MPC has four FIFOs in which it can queue unsolicited packets. These packets are equivalent to the interrupts of a conventional bus with the added feature of having up to 28 data bytes provided with the signal. There are five different unsolicited packets: two are used for interrupts and three are used to set up solicited data transfers. A general interrupt request may be sent between any pair of single board computers and a broadcast interrupt may be sent to all boards in a system. The three special interrupts, Buffer Request/Grand/Reject are used to initiate large data transfers (solicited messages) between pairs of single board computers.

SOLICITED PACKETS

Solicited packets are never a surprise since their arrival is negotiated—the receiving MPC bus controller knows what to do with them. These packets are used for the transfer of data from one board to another and the transfer is set up using unsolicited packets. To summarize the operation of solicited packets the MPCs cooperate in the moving of blocks of data between boards, they break the data into 32 byte packets, send them across the bus, and reassemble the data transparently to the sending/receiving boards. All operations such as packetization, bus arbitration, error detecting and recovery is handled by the MPC bus controllers—this is done transparently to the local microprocessors. Key to system performance is the packetization of data on the system bus which limits the maximum bus occupancy to one microsecond.

BUS ARBITRATION GUARANTEES LOW BUS LATENCY

The Multibus II system bus uses a distributed arbitration scheme as shown in Figure 17. Each board that requires access to the system bus contains the circuitry of Figure 17 (note that this is contained within the MPC bus controller) and no active components are required on the backplane. The MPC bus controller uses a software assigned identifier to request the bus and the arbitration circuitry will indicate that the MPC is preparing for a bus cycle. The MPC supports two arbitration algorithms, fairness and high priority.

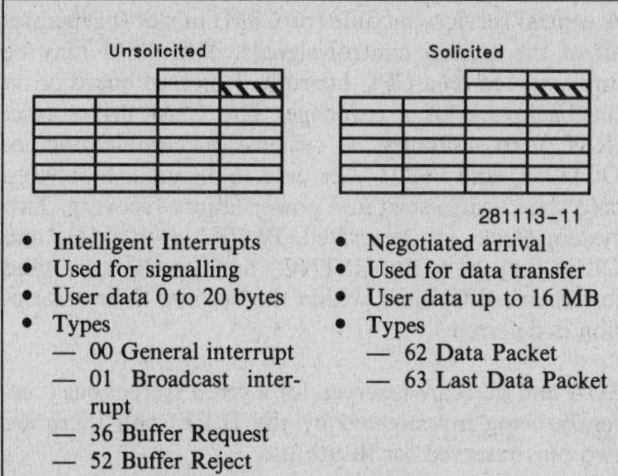

Figure 16. There are seven type of packet subdivided into two categories

The fairness mode is used for data transfers and is "polite". If the bus is being used, the MPC will wait before requesting use of the bus; once the bus is not busy the MPC will request the bus and will wait for it to be granted; once the MPC uses the bus it will not request it again until all other requesters have used the bus. "Parking" on the bus is permitted—if no other board has requested the bus since the last time that this board accessed the bus (remember that the bus is continually monitored) then it may access the bus directly without executing an arbitration cycle. These algorithms assure that a single board cannot monopolize the bus and keep others from using it. Remember that each MPC will only use the bus for a maximum of one microsecond and since the arbitration is being resolved in parallel there are no wasted clocks as bus ownership is transferred; all transfers operate back-to-back.

THE SYSTEM BUS HAS DETERMINISTIC INTERRUPT LATENCY

The high priority mode is used for interrupts and is "impatient". The MPC bus controller, when in this mode, will "barge in" on an arbitration cycle and be guaranteed the next access to the bus. The MPC bus controller can set up interrupt packets specifically to operate in high-priority mode so these will only have a one microsecond latency to access the bus. In the rare instance that two MPCs try to initiate an interrupt packet within the same one microsecond window the highest priority board will be granted the bus and the other board will have to wait a maximum of two microseconds for its bus access.

Interrupt packets and data transfer packets interleave on the bus (actually interleave within a single MPC too) with preference always going to the interrupt packet. A single MPC bus controller will operate with interrupt packets in high priority mode and data transfer packets in fairness mode; this will ensure that interrupt packets have a deterministic bus transit time of 1 μsec (2 μsec sometimes and 20 μsec conceivable worse case when all 21 MPCs try to initiate an interrupt packet within the same one microsecond window, a very, very rare occurrence).

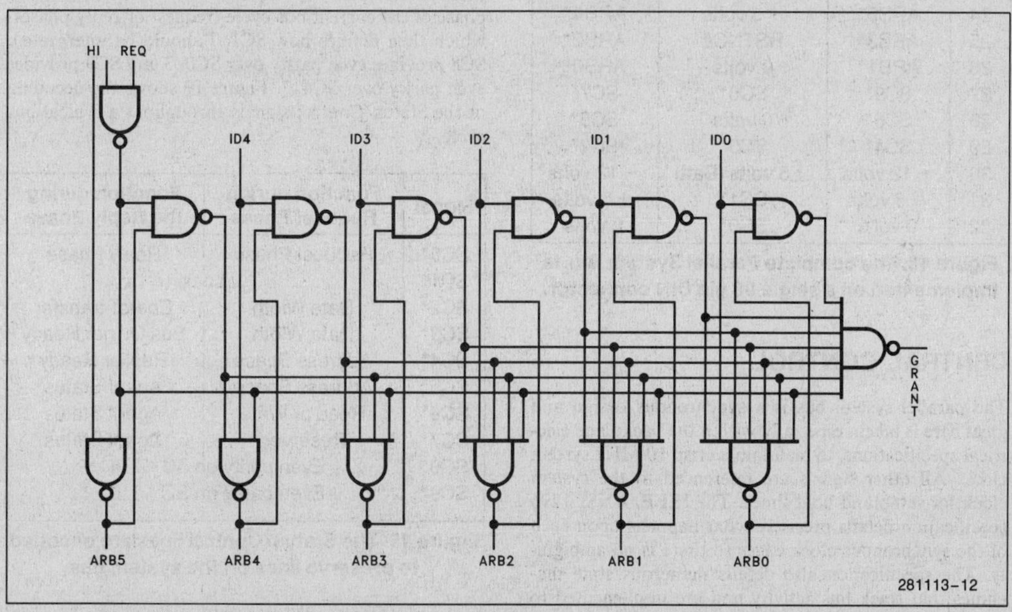

Figure 17. The Multibus II Parallel System Bus uses a distributed arbitration scheme

SYSTEM BUS CHARACTERISTICS

Figure 18 shows the pinout of the P1 connector. The signals can be classified into five groups; 1. Central control, 2. Address/data, 3. System control, 4. Arbitration, and 5. Power.

Pin	Row A	Row B	Row C
1	0 volts	PROT*	0 volts
2	+5	DCLOW*	+5 volts
3	+12 volts	+5 volts (Batt)	+12 volts
4	0 volts	SDA	BCLK*
5	TIMOUT*	SDB	0 volts
6	LACHn*	0 volts	CCLK*
7	AD0*	AD1*	0 volts
8	AD2*	0 volts	AD3*
9	AD4*	AD5*	AD6*
10	AD7*	+5 volts	PAR0*
11	AD8*	AD9*	AD10*
12	AD11*	+5 volts	AD12*
13	AD13*	AD14*	AD15*
14	PAR1*	0 volts	AD16*
15	AD17*	AD18*	AD19*
16	AD20*	0 volts	AD21*
17	AD22*	AD23*	PAR2*
18	AD24*	0 volts	AD25*
19	AD26*	AD27*	AD28*
20	AD29*	0 volts	AD30*
21	AD31*	Reserved	PAR3*
22	+5 volts	+5 volts	Reserved
23	BREQ*	RST*	BUSERR*
24	ARB5*	+5 volts	ARB4*
25	ARB3*	RSTNC*	ARB2*
26	ARB1*	0 volts	ARB0*
27	SC9*	SC8*	SC7*
28	SC6*	0 volts	SC5*
29	SC4*	SC3*	SC2*
30	−12 volts	+5 volts (Batt)	−12 volts
31	+5 volts	SC1*	+5 volts
32	0 volts	SC0*	0 volts

Figure 18. The complete Parallel System Bus is implemented on a single 96 pin DIN connector.

CENTRAL CONTROL

The parallel system bus is a synchronous design and great care is taken, especially within the backplane electrical specifications, to maintain a crisp 10 MHz system clock. All other signals are referenced to the system clock for setup and hold times. The IEEE/ANSI 1296 specification details precisely what happens upon each of the synchronous clock edges so there is no ambiguity. The specification also details numerous state machines that track bus activity and are implemented to guarantee compatibility.

A central services module (or CSM) in slot 0 generates all of the central control signals. This CSM may be implemented on a CPU board, a dedicated board or on the backplane of a cardcage. The CSM drives reset (RST*) to initialize a system; a combination of DCLOW* and PROT* are used to distinguish between cold start, warm start and power failure recovery. Two system clocks are generated, BLCK* at 10 MHz and CLCK* at 20 MHz. RSTNC* and LACHn are used for advanced facilities within the bus and their description is deferred.

SDA and SDB are reserved for a serial system bus (currently being investigated by the IEEE) and there are two pins reserved for future use.

ADDRESS/DATA

The Multibus II parallel system bus is a full 32 bits (AD0..31*) with byte paraty (PAR0..3*). The system control lines will define when address information or data is contained upon these multiplexed lines. Note that all transfers are parity checked and, in the case of message packets, the MPC bus controller will retry an operation that failed due to a parity error. If, after sixteen tries, the error is not recoverable, the MPC bus controller will interrupt its host microprocessor to ask for assistance.

SYSTEM CONTROL

Ten lines (SC0..9*) are used for system control and their functions are multiplexed too. SC0* defines the phase of the current bus cycle (request or reply phases) which then defines how SC1..7 should be interpreted. SC8 provides even parity over SC0..3 and SC9 provides even parity over SC4..7. Figure 19 shows the decoding of the Status/Control signals throughout a typical bus cycle.

Signal	Function during Request Phase	Function during the Reply Phase
SC0*	Request Phase	Reply Phase
SC1*	Lock	
SC2*	Data Width	End-of-transfer
SC3*	Data Width	Bus Owner Ready
SC4*	Address Space	Replier Ready
SC5*	Address Space	Agent Status
SC6*	Read or Write	Agent Status
SC7*	Reserved	Agent Status
SC8*	Even parity on SC<7..4>*	
SC9*	Even parity on SC<3..0>*	

Figure 19. The Status/Control lines are encoded to preserve lines on the system bus

ARBITRATION

All boards request use of the bus through a common bus request line BREQ*. A distributed arbitration scheme is defined which grants the bus to the numerically highest requesting board as identified on lines ARB0..5. Two arbitration algorithms are supported: fairness, which gives each board an even portion of the available bus bandwidth, and priority, which permits a high priority request (such as an interrupt) to be guaranteed the next access to the system bus.

POWER

There are ample power and ground lines defined and these are spread over the length of the P1 connector to minimize ground shift and other problems.

TYPICAL BUS CYCLE

The parallel system bus is particularly easy to interface to. This section will cover the sequencing of a typical REPLIER interface as an illustration of the bus timing. The IEEE/ANSI 1296 specification details numerous state machines that track bus activity and are implemented to guarantee compatibility. An I/O replier need only implement a single "Replying Agent" state machine. This is shown in Figure 3.5-5 in the IEEE/ANSI 1296 standard and repeated here in Figure 20 for reference. Remember that an application CPU (a REQUESTOR) will start the cycle that the REPLIER will respond to.

In order to progress quickly through this discussion, an assumption that the requestor always issues valid requests will be made. Error handling for invalid requests will be added later. Figure 21 summarizes the design task. The logic required to map the multiple signals and protocols from the Multibus II parallel system bus into the simple read strobe, write strobe and chip select of an I/O device must be designed. In this example features will be kept at a design minimum but all essential circuitry will be discussed in detail.

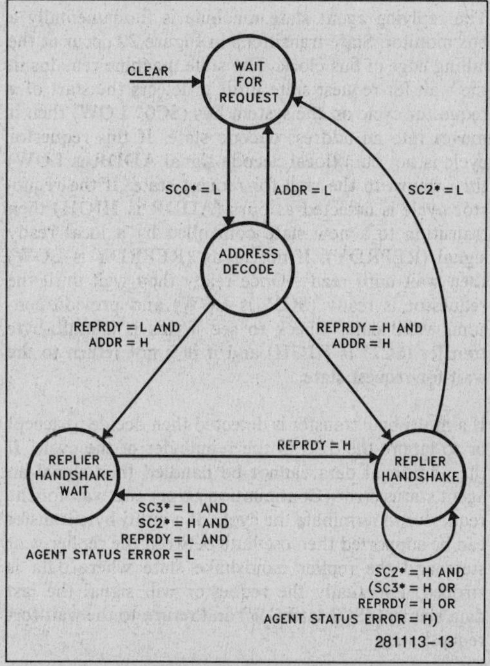

Figure 20. The IEEE/ANSI 1296 Specification details numerous state machines. A replier is shown here.

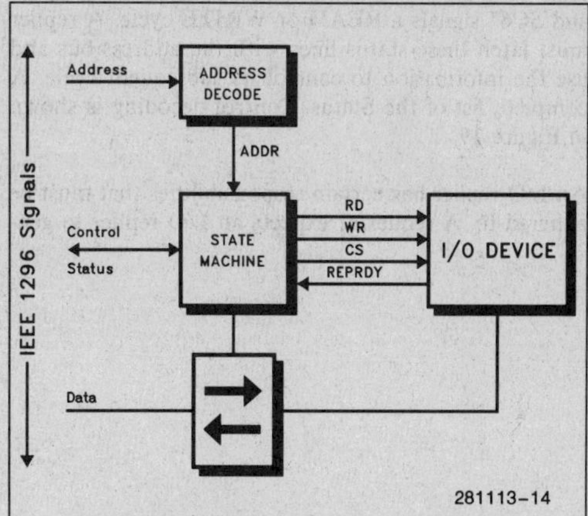

Figure 21. The design of a REPLIER is fundamentally a bus monitor.

5

The replying agent state machine is fundamentally a bus monitor. State transitions in Figure 20 occur at the falling edge of bus clock. The state machine remains in the wait-for-request state until it detects the start of a requestor cycle on the system bus (SC0* LOW) then it moves into an address decode state. If this requestor cycle is not ours (local decode signal ADDR is LOW) then return to the wait-for-request state. If the requestor cycle is detected as ours (ADDR is HIGH) then transition to a new state controlled by a local ready signal (REPRDY). If not ready (REPRDY is LOW) then wait until ready. Once ready then wait until the requestor is ready (SC3* is LOW) and provide/consume valid data. Check to see if this is a multi-byte transfer (SC2* is HIGH) and if it is not return to the wait-for-request state.

If a multi-byte transfer is detected then decide to accept or to ignore the data in the remainder of the cycle. If the additional data cannot be handled then signal an agent status error (Continuation error) and wait for the requestor to terminate the cycle. If a multi-byte transfer can be supported then oscillate between the replier wait state and the replier handshake state where data is strobed. Eventually the requestor will signal the last data element (SC2 set LOW) and return to the wait-for-request state.

At the start of each requestor cycle that status lines (SC1* through SC6*) detail the type of cycle; SC1* signals a locked transfer, SC2* and SC3* encode the data width, SC4* and SC5* encode the address space and SC6* signals a READ or WRITE cycle. A replier must latch these status lines with the address bus and use the information to control its subsequent cycle. A complete list of the Status/Control decoding is shown in Figure 19.

An I/O replier has certain responsibilities that must be adhered to. A requestor expects an I/O replier to generate status information and to signal when ready so that the requestor may proceed with the cycle. The cycle will only terminate once both requestor and replier have signalled that they are ready (the IEEE/ANSI 1296 includes a time out feature which prevents the bus from hanging if both ready signals are not generated). A replier drives SC4* LOW to indicate READY and status information is driven on lines SC5* through SC7*; SC8* must also be driven and identifies parity across lines SC4* through SC7*. If a replier is supplying data to a requestor then correct data parity must also be driven onto the system bus.

SUMMARY

The Multibus II Parallel System Bus was ***DESIGNED*** to implement all of the "systems features" of a single board computer based system. The bus does have some CPU/Memory attributes but these were only included for compatibility and to aid migration into the Multibus II environment—comparing these CPU/Memory features in isolation with those of other buses is a complete disservice to the Multibus II architecture and misses the complete design goals and motivation set forth for this standard.

The silicon revolution forced the design of the Multibus II Parallel System Bus—technology was advancing faster than our abilities to use it so we had to find new implementation strategies to benefit from these advances. Functional partitioning was chosen as the vehicle to embrace the technology; by partitioning the problems into smaller and smaller sub-problems we reach a point where the sub-problems are implementable. The Multibus II consortium chose this path and executed with precision; transistors were applied at strategic points to simplify implementations and encourage ease-of-use. The Multibus II architecture is completely defined, documented and available.

October 1990

Designing a Central Services Module for MULTIBUS® II

JORY RADKE
MODULES DEVELOPMENT ENGINEER

Order Number: 280634-001

5

CONTENTS

PURPOSE

This paper describes and presents methods for implementing the functions provided by the Central Services Module, as defined in the IEEE 1296 specification, and is intended to assist the system designer in understanding and effecting these functions. Function options and other design considerations are discussed. It is assumed the reader is familiar with the terms and definitions used in the IEEE 1296 specification and with basic logic design principles.

1.0 INTRODUCTION

The IEEE 1296 specification, based on the Intel® MULTIBUS®II bus architecture, defines certain general system-wide functions to be provided by a Central Services Module (CSM). These system-wide functions include power-on and power-fail reset sequences, clock generation, bus timeout detection and signal generation, and the assignment of cardslot and arbitration identification (ID) to each board (agent). The communication path between the CSM and the other agents in the system environment is via the Parallel System Bus (PSB) interface.

The implementation of the defined CSM ensures uniformity in providing a single source for those system-wide functions required in an open-bus architecture, such as that established in the IEEE 1296 specification. Centralizing system-wide functions reduces system cost and frees board area for other functions since only one board in the system need contain the CSM logic. The IEEE 1296 specification stipulates that only the agent in cardslot 0 contain the active CSM functions although other system agents may contain CSM functions.

2.0 CSM FUNCTIONS AND PSB SIGNALS

The following paragraphs identify and briefly describe the system-level services and functions supplied by the CSM and the PSB signals generated, monitored or used to implement these services. An asterisk following the signal name indicates that the particular signal or group of signals are active when at their electrical low.

2.1 CSM Functions

The IEEE 1296 specification defines the minimum required functions of a CSM as:

- Generation of system clock signals
- Generation of reset sequences for both cold and warm start and power failure indication
- Cardslot and arbitration ID initialization
- Timeout signal generation for PSB data transfer cycles.

Depending on system requirements, the CSM may additionally provide:

- Power-fail recovery reset
- Bus ownership timeout.

Other system-wide resources, such as a time of day clock or interface to another bus system, may be conveniently implemented with the CSM on the same PSB agent. We shall see that the CSM functions require very little board area to implement.

2.2 PSB Signal Used by the CSM

The CSM utilizes signals from each of the five signal groups defined in the IEEE 1296 specification. These signals are identified and their use by the CSM is described briefly in Table 2-1.

3.0 FUNCTIONAL OVERVIEW

The following sections discuss how to add the CSM functions to a PSB agent. The agent could contain only the CSM and interconnect relier modules and additional functional modules as well. The design example provided in section 4, (excepting the PSB buffers), requires less than six percent of the area on a standard MULTIBUS II board. The CSM module cannot be added to agents which employ Intel's Message Passing Coprocessor, due to the current and capacitive loading requirements of the PSB signals in Table 2-1 which the MPC drives directly.

This paragraph provides a functional overview of the design and discusses signal requirements. A detailed design example is illustrated and discussed in paragraph 4. Additional design considerations are described in paragraph 5.

Functionally partitioning the CSM functions results in the block diagram shown in Figure 3-1. The signal terminations identified on the righthand side of the diagram are the actual PSB pin assignments identified in the IEEE 1296 specification.

3.1 Clock Generator (CLKGEN) Function

Listed in Table 3-1 and depicted in Figure 3-2 are the timing relationships between the **BCLK*** and **CCLK*** signals as specified in the IEEE 1296 specification. The circuits used to develop and supply the **BCLK*** and **CCLK*** signals must guarantee t2 (high time), t4 (low time), and t5 (period). The circuits must also guarantee t6 (clock-to-clock) and the correct phase relationship between clock signals. Signal parameters t1 (rise time) and t3 (fall time) must be met by the buffer device driving the clock signals onto the PSB bus interface.

Table 2-1. PSB Signals Used by the CSM

Signal		CSM Function
Name	**Group**	
BREQ*	Arbitration Cycle	Bus Request. All agents that require access to the PSB assert the **BREQ*** signal. The CSM monitors this signal as part of its bus timeout function.
ARB<5..0>*	Arbitration Cycle	Arbitration lines. The CSM uses these lines during a reset sequence to assign a cardslot ID and an arbitration ID to each agent in the system.
AD<20..1>*	Address/Data Bus	Address/Data lines. See Figure 2-1. Each Address/Data line is connected to the **LACHn*** pin of a cardslot. The **LACHn*** signal is used to latch the cardslot and arbitration IDs to each agent (except cardslot 00) during a reset sequence.
SC<4..2, 0>*	System Control	System Control lines. The CSM monitors these control signals between agents to sense bus timeout during data transfer cycles.
TIMOUT*	Exception Cycle	Bus Timeout. **TIMOUT*** is asserted by the CSM to signal that an agent is taking too much time to respond to a handshake.
BUSERR*	Exception Cycle	Bus Error. An agent activates **BUSERR*** to indicate its detection of a data integrity problem during a transfer. The CSM monitors this signal as part of its bus timeout function.
BCLK*	Central Control	10 MHz Bus Clock. Driven only by the CSM to provide all system timing references.
CCLK*	Central Control	20 MHz Central Clock. Driven only by the CSM as an auxiliary clock for use as an additional timing reference among bus agents.
RST*	Central Control	Reset. Driven only by the CSM as a system-level initialization signal.
DCLOW*	Central Control	DC Power Low. Driven only by the CSM as a warning to system agents of an imminent power failure. Part of the CSM reset generation function.
PROT*	Central Control	Protect. Driven only by the CSM during power-fail sequences. Part of the reset generation function.

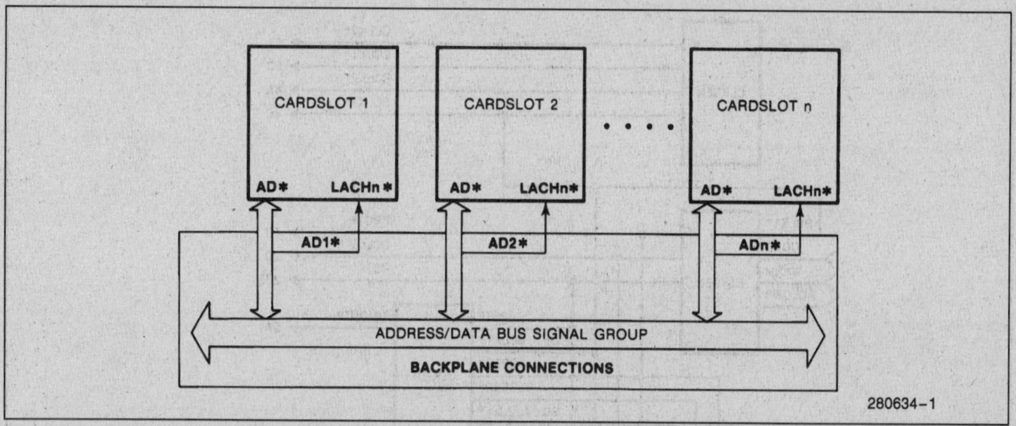

Figure 2-1. Backplane Connection of LACHn*

NOTE:
The **BCLK2*** and **CCLK2*** signals are only required for backplanes containing more than 12 cardslots.

The CSM clock functions can be implemented by use of a crystal oscillator, frequency divider, and two or more bus drivers.

3.2 Reset Generator (RSTGEN) Function

The IEEE 1296 specification defines three types of reset sequences for the CSM: cold, warm and recovery. The **RST***, **DCLOW*** and **PROT*** signals are used to encode the reset type. The **DCLOW*** and **PROT*** signals are defined as being asynchronous while the **RST*** signal is defined as being synchronous.

The **ACLOW*** input is only from the power supply in systems supported by battery backup (VBB) and is required for power fail and recovery resets. The **WARM** and **COLD** inputs represent user-controlled signals for use in generating warm or cold resets. They might be supplied from a system front panel or via a status register in the agent's interconnect space. **BCLK1*** is an input to clock the synchronous **RST*** signal.

Tables 3-2 through 3-4 and Figures 3-3 through 3-5 list and depict the timing specifications for the cold, warm and power-fail recovery resets, respectively.

There are various system and user defined parameters beyond the scope of this article which can be added to the design and implementation of the RSTGEN function. Exploring the flexibility presented by such additional factors as the characteristics of the **ACLOW*** signal, whether or not to support battery backup, the ramp-up time of the power supply, the number of front panel or user inputs, or which options to permit when multiple resets occur simultaneously are left for the design engineer's consideration.

The RSTGEN function described above can be implemented using voltage monitors, timers and basic control logic.

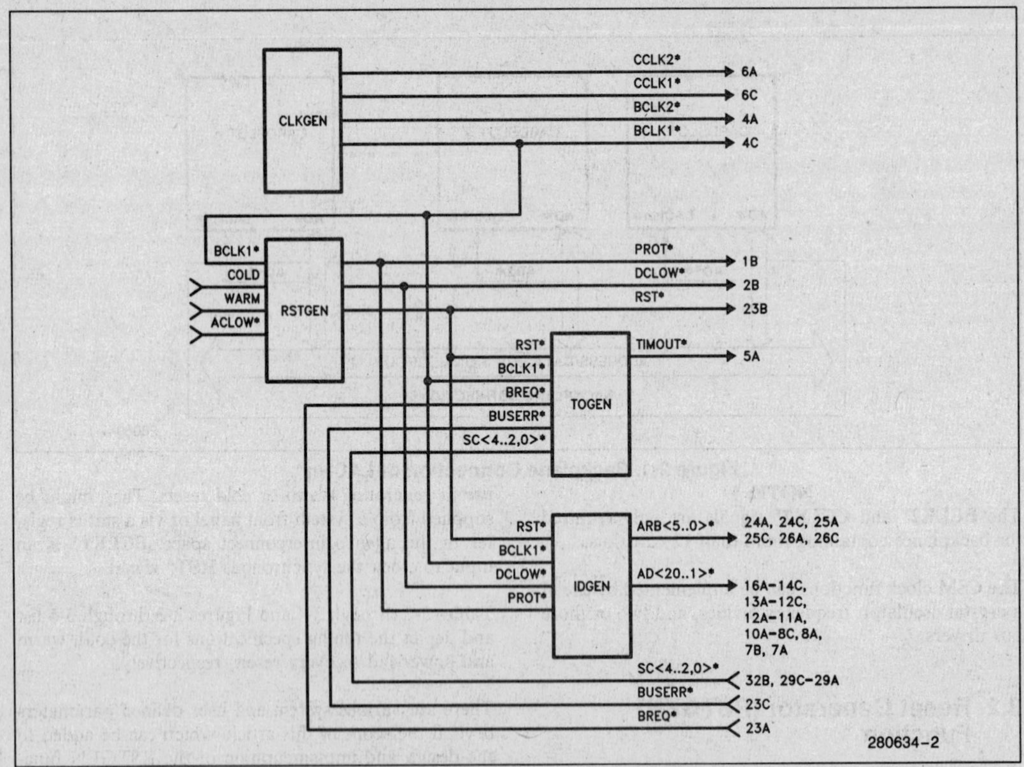

Figure 3-1. CSM Functional Block Diagram

Table 3-1. CSM Clock Timing Specification

Symbol	Parameter	BCLK*		CCLK*		Units
		Min	Max	Min	Max	
t_1	Rise Time		2.0		2.0	ns
t_2	High Time	48.0	52.1	23.0	27.0	ns
t_3	Fall Time		2.0		2.0	ns
t_4	Low Time	48.0	52.1	23.0	27.05	ns
t_5	Period	99.9	100.1	49.95	50.05	ns
t_6	Clock-to-Clock	0	+10			ns

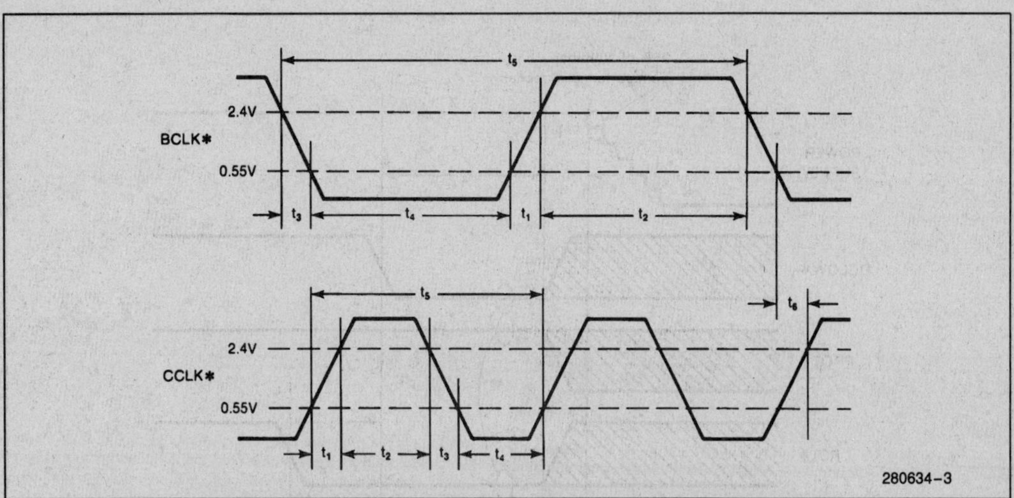

Figure 3-2. Clock Timing Relationships at CSM Connector P1

Table 3-2. CSM Cold Reset Timing Specifications

Symbol	Parameter	Min	Max	Units
t_1	DC Power Setup to **DCLOW***		1.0	ms
t_2	Cold Reset Duration	2.5		ms
t_3	Warm Reset Duration	50.0		ms

5

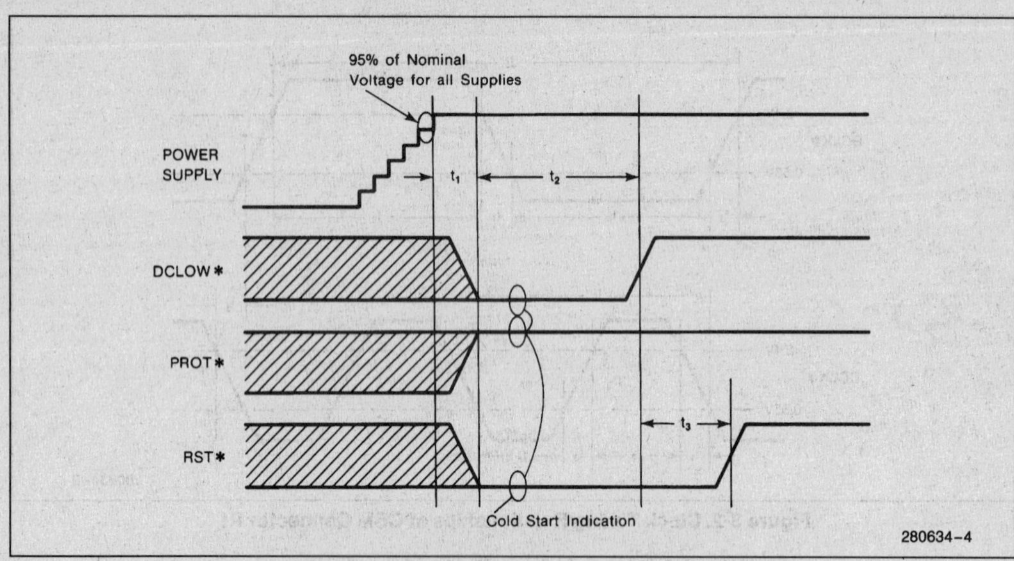

Figure 3-3. Cold Reset Timing on the PSB

Table 3-3. CSM Warm Reset Timing Specifications

Symbol	Parameter	Min	Max	Units
t_1	**RST*** Pulse Width	50.0		ms

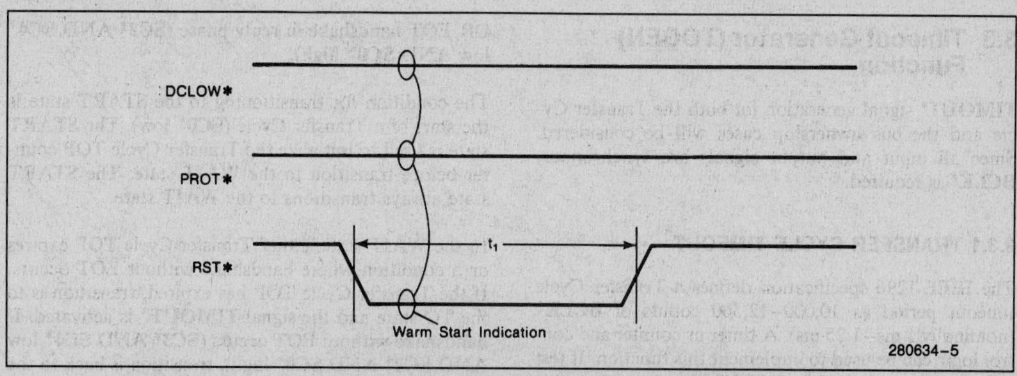

Figure 3-4. Warm Reset Timing on the PSB

Table 3-4. CSM Power Fail and Recovery Timing Specifications

Symbol	Parameter	Min	Max	Units
t_1	DC Power Hold from **DCLOW***	6.5		ms
t_2	**PROT*** Delay from **DCLOW***	6.0	6.25	ms
t_3	DC Power Setup to **DCLOW***	1.0		ms
t_4	**RST*** Delay from **DCLOW***	6.5	7.0	ms
t_5	**RST*** Setup from **DCLOW***	0.5		ms
t_6	**RST*** Active from **PROT***	50.0		ms
t_7	**DCLOW*** Pulse Width	7.5		ms
t_8	**PROT*** Hold from **DCLOW***	2.0	2.5	ms

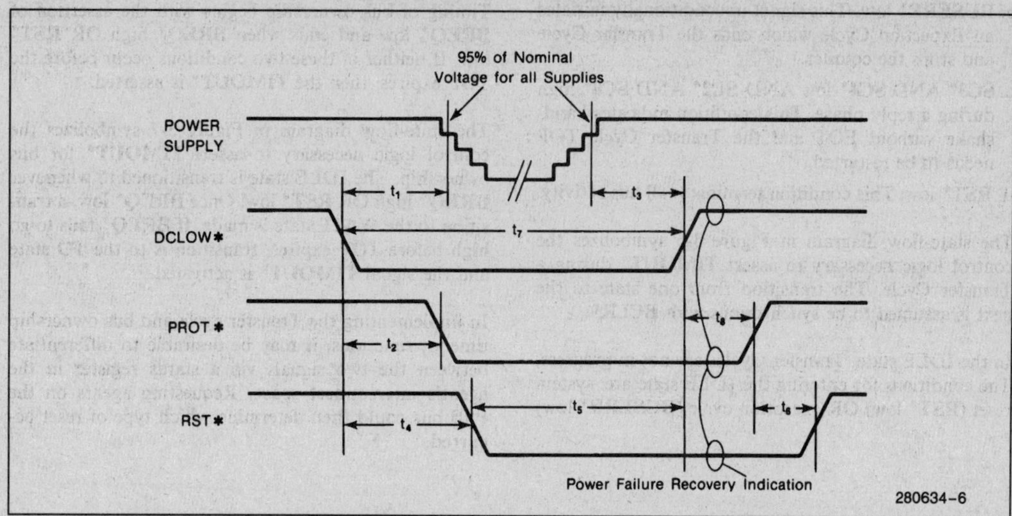

Figure 3-5. Power-Fail Recovery Timing on the PSB

5

3.3 Timeout Generator (TOGEN) Function

TIMOUT* signal generation for both the Transfer Cycle and the bus ownership cases will be considered. Since all input and output signals are synchronous, **BCLK*** is required.

3.3.1 TRANSFER CYCLE TIMEOUT

The IEEE 1296 specification defines a Transfer Cycle timeout period as 10,000–12,500 counts of **BCLK*** (nominally 1 ms–1.25 ms). A timer or counter and control logic can be used to implement this function. If test frequencies are desired for **BCLK***, then a counter may be a more desirable solution so the Transfer Cycle timeout period (TOP) will be a function of **BCLK*** and not fixed at 1 ms.

Timing of the Transfer Cycle begins on the first clock of a request phase; indicated by **SC0*** active. Once initiated and unless one of the following conditions is satisfied, the Transfer Cycle TOP will have expired and the CSM must assert **TIMOUT***:

a. **SC2*** AND **SC4*** low AND **SC0*** high during a reply phase. This condition indicates requester end of transfer (EOT) and replier ready handshake, which terminates Transfer Cycle timing.

b. **BUSERR*** low. This signal unconditionally initiates an Expection Cycle which ends the Transfer Cycle and stops the counter.

c. **SC3*** AND **SC4*** low AND **SC2*** AND **SC0*** high during a reply phase. This condition indicates handshake without EOT and the Transfer Cycle TOP needs to be restarted.

d. **RST*** low. This condition terminates all bus activity.

The state-flow diagram in Figure 3-6 symbolizes the control logic necessary to assert **TIMOUT*** during a Transfer Cycle. The transition from one state to the next is assumed to be synchronous with **BCLK***.

In the IDLE state, Transfer Cycles are not in progress. The conditions for entering the IDLE state are: system reset (**RST*** low) OR exception cycle (**BUSERR*** low) OR EOT handshake in reply phase (**SC2*** AND **SC4*** low AND **SC0*** high).

The condition for transitioning to the START state is the start of a Transfer Cycle (**SC0*** low). The START state is used to initialize the Transfer Cycle TOP counter before transition to the WAIT state. The START state always transitions to the WAIT state.

In the WAIT state, either Transfer Cycle TOP expires or a condition where handshake without EOT occurs. If the Transfer Cycle TOP has expired, transition is to the TO state and the signal **TIMOUT*** is activated. If handshake without EOT occurs (**SC3*** AND **SC4*** low AND **SC2*** AND **SC0*** high), transition is back to the START state to reinitialize the Transfer Cycle TOP counter and then returns to the WAIT state.

The TO state always transitions back to the IDLE state. Thus, in this design, **TIMOUT*** is asserted for one **BCLK***.

3.3.2 BUS OWNERSHIP TIMEOUT

The IEEE 1296 specification identifies the bus ownership timeout as system defined. A timer or counter and control logic can also be used to implement this function.

Timing of bus ownership begins with the assertion of **BREQ*** low and ends when **BREQ*** high OR **RST*** low. If neither of these two conditions occur before the TOP expires; then the **TIMOUT*** is asserted.

The state-flow diagram in Figure 3-7 symbolizes the control logic necessary to assert **TIMOUT*** for bus ownership. The IDLE state is transitioned to whenever **BREQ*** high OR **RST*** low. Once **BREQ*** low, a transition to the WAIT state is made. If **BREQ*** fails to go high before TOP expires, transition is to the TO state and the signal **TIMOUT*** is activated.

In implementing the Transfer cycle and bus ownership timeout functions, it may be desirable to differentiate between the two signals via a status register in the agent's interconnect space. Requesting agents on the PSB bus could then determine which type of reset occurred.

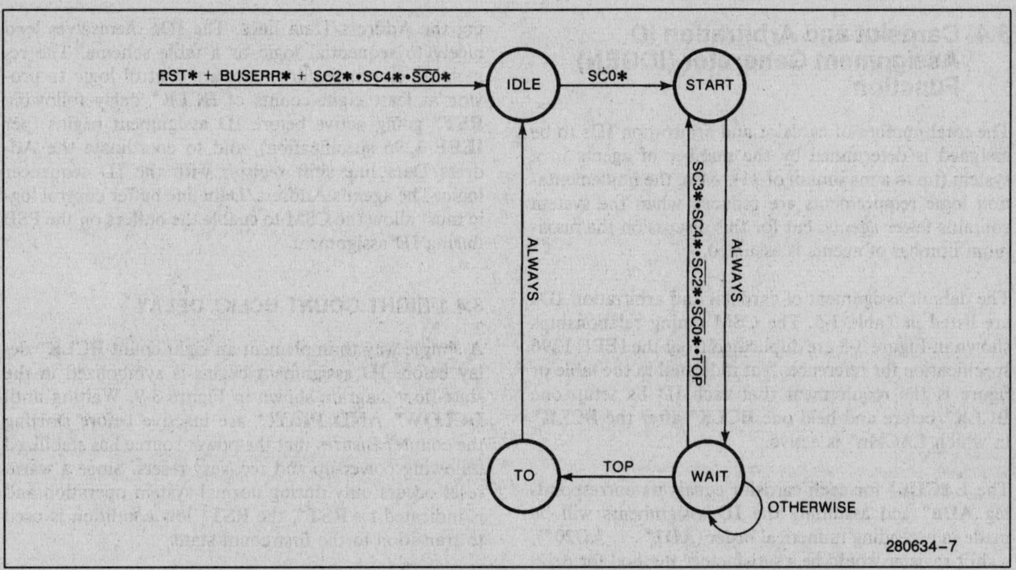

Figure 3-6. State-Flow Diagram for Monitoring Transfer Cycle Timeout

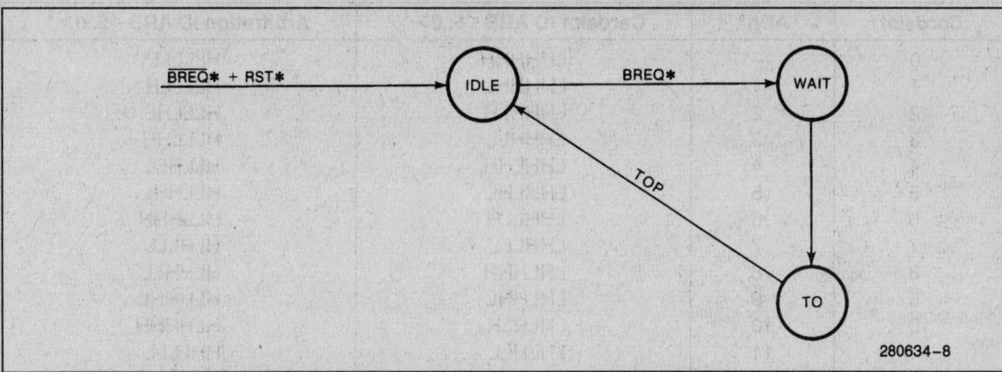

Figure 3-7. State-Flow Diagram for Monitoring Bus Ownership Timeout

5

3.4 Cardslot and Arbitration ID Assignment Generator (IDGEN) Function

The total number of cardslot and arbitration IDs to be assigned is determined by the number of agents in a system (up to a maximum of 21). Also, the implementation logic requirements are reduced when the system contains fewer agents, but for this discussion the maximum number of agents is assumed.

The default assignment of cardslot and arbitration IDs are listed in Table 3-5. The CSM timing relationships shown in Figure 3-8 are duplicated from the IEEE 1296 specification for reference. Not indicated in the table or figure is the requirement that each ID be setup one **BCLK*** before and held one **BCLK*** after the **BCLK*** in which **LACHn*** is active.

The **LACHn*** for each cardslot equals its corresponding **ADn*** and assuming the ID assignments will be made in ascending numerical order (**AD1*** . . . **AD20***), a shift register would be a satisfactory method for driving the Address/Data lines. The IDs themselves lend nicely to sequential logic or a table scheme. The remaining circuit requirements are control logic to provide at least eight counts of **BCLK*** delay following **RST*** going active before ID assignment begins (per IEEE 1296 specification), and to coordinate the Address/Data line shift register with the ID sequencer logic. The agent's Address/Data line buffer control logic must allow the CSM to enable the buffers on the PSB during ID assignment.

3.4.1 EIGHT COUNT BCLK* DELAY

A simple way to implement an eight count **BCLK*** delay before ID assignment begins is symbolized in the state-flow diagram shown in Figure 3-9. Waiting until **DCLOW*** AND **PROT*** are inactive before starting the counter ensures that the power source has stabilized following power-up and recovery resets. Since a warm reset occurs only during normal system operation and is indicated by **RST***, the **RST*** low condition is used to transition to the first count state.

Table 3-5. Default Cardslot and Arbitration ID Values

Cardslot	ADn*	Cardslot ID ARB<5..0>*	Arbitration ID ARB<5..0>*
0	—	LHHHHH	HLLLLL
1	1	LHHHHL	HLLLLH
2	2	LHHHLH	HLLLHL
3	3	LHHHLL	HLLLHH
4	4	LHHLHH	HLLHLL
5	5	LHHLHL	HLLHHL
6	6	LHHLLH	HLLHHH
7	7	LHHLLL	HLHLLL
8	8	LHLHHH	HLHHLL
9	9	LHLHHL	HLHHHL
10	10	LHLHLH	HLHHHH
11	11	LHLHLL	HHLLLL
12	12	LHLLHH	HHLLLH
13	13	LHLLHL	HHLLHH
14	14	LHLLLH	HHLHHH
15	15	LHLLLL	HHHLLL
16	16	LLHHHH	HHHLLH
17	17	LLHHHL	HHHLHH
18	18	LLHHLH	HHHHLL
19	19	LLHHLL	HHHHLH
20	20	LLHLHH	HHHHHL

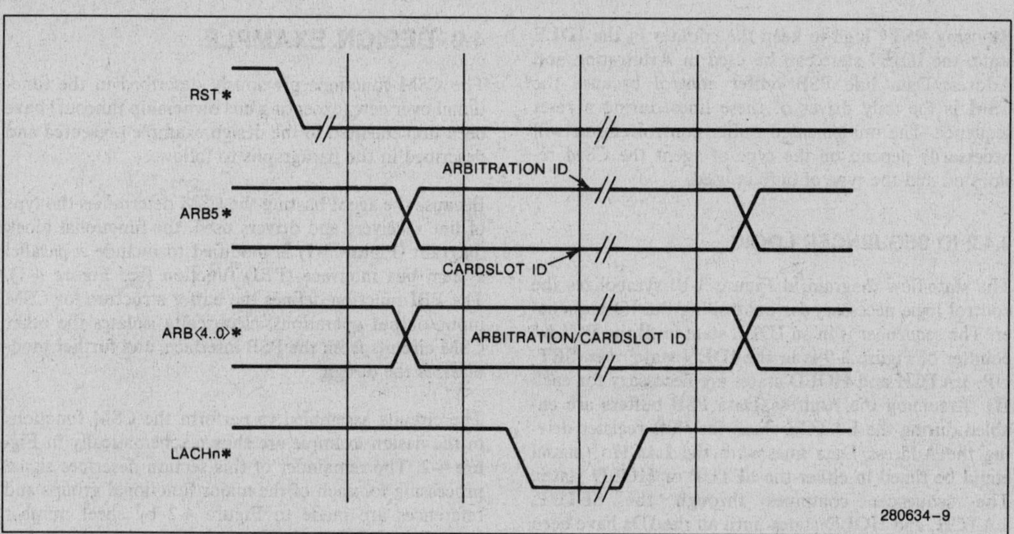

Figure 3-8. Cardslot and Arbitration ID Assignment Timing

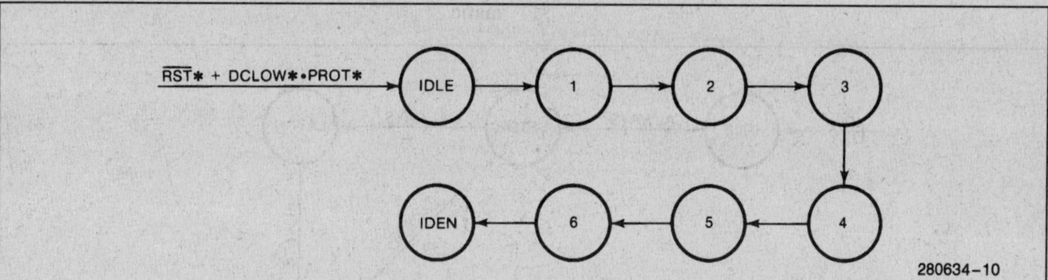

Figure 3-9. State-Flow Diagram for Delaying ID Assignment

5

By using **RST*** high to keep the counter in the IDLE state, the IDEN state can be used in Arbitration and Address/Data line PSB buffer control because the CSM is the only driver of these lines during a reset sequence. The implemented buffer control circuit will necessarily depend on the type of agent the CSM resides on and the type of buffers used.

3.4.2 ID SEQUENCER LOGIC

The state-flow diagram in Figure 3-10 symbolizes the control logic necessary for controlling the ID sequencer. The sequencer is in an IDLE state until the **BCLK*** counter of Figure 3-9 is in the IDEN state; then SETUP, LATCH and HOLD states are necessary for each ID. Assuming the Address/Data PSB buffers are enabled during the LATCH state, the shift register driving the Address/Data lines with the **LACHn*** signal could be timed in either the SETUP or HOLD states. The sequencer continues through the SETUP, LATCH, and HOLD states until all the IDs have been assigned.

4.0 DESIGN EXAMPLE

The CSM functions previously described in the functional overview (excepting bus ownership timeout) have been implemented in the design example presented and described in the paragraphs to follow.

Because the agent hosting the CSM determines the type of line receivers and drivers used, the functional block diagram (Figure 3-1) is modified to include a parallel system bus interface (PBI) function (see Figure 4-1). The PBI function defines the buffer structure for CSM input/output operations, electrically isolates the other CSM circuits from the PSB interface, and further modularizes the design.

The circuits assembled to perform the CSM functions in the design example are shown schematically in Figure 4-2. The remainder of this section describes signal processing for each of the major functional groups and references are made to Figure 4-2 by sheet number only. For usability, the figure is located at the end of this section following Figure 4-8. For simplicity, the decoupling capacities have been omitted from the schematic.

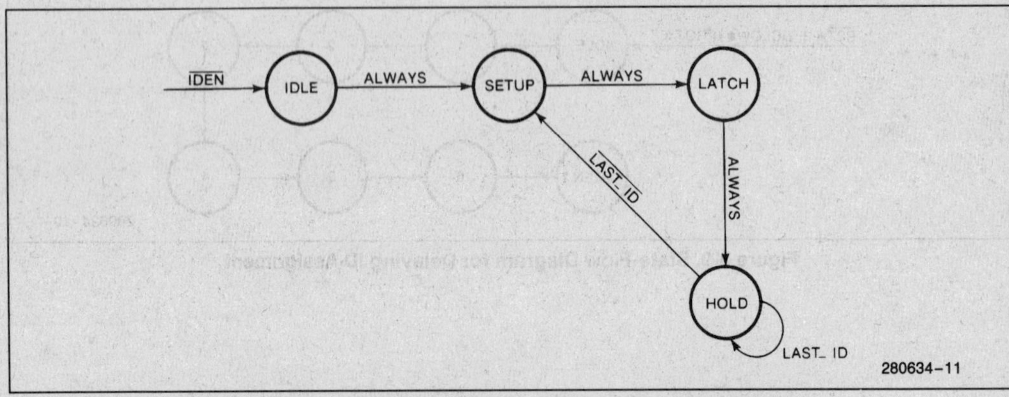

Figure 3-10. State-Flow Diagram for Controlling ID Assignment

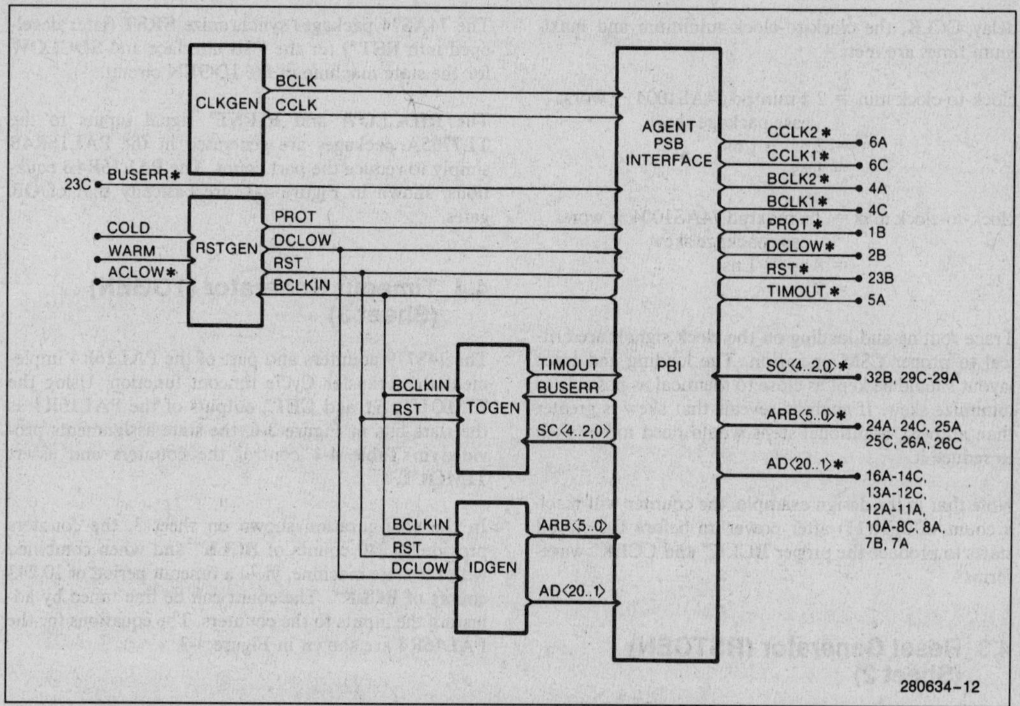

Figure 4-1. CSM Overall Block Diagram

4.1 PSB Buffer Interface (Sheet 1)

The majority of the PSB interface signals are buffered using 74F240 packages. The 74F240 circuitry meets the PSB loading and drive specifications and are satisfactory for this design example. The **ARB<5..0>*** lines are specified to operate open-collector and the 74S38 gates used meet this requirement. The **BUSERR*** input is buffered through a spare 74AS1004 gate simply to keep the part count down.

Since the CSM is the only driver of the clock, reset and timeout signals, their buffer enables are tied active. The **AD<20..1>*** lines are only driven by the CSM during reset sequences and the **ADEN*** signal from the IDGEN circuit is used to enable these lines. Also provided by the IDGEN circuit is the **IDEN** signal to enable the 74S38 gates during ID assignments. **BCLK1*** is buffered through a 74AS1004 gate as **BCLKIN** and provides the on-board timing for the synchronous logic.

4.2 Clock Generator (CLKGEN) (Sheet 2)

The 40 MHz oscillator, 74AS163 package and two 74AS1004 gates form the CLKGEN circuit. Dividing the 40 MHz to 20 MHz and 10 mHz in the same package controls clock-to-clock skew. Since all clock signals are driven by the same 74F240 package (sheet 1) and assuming a less than 0.5 ns same-package skew from both the 74AS163 and 74F240 packages, the worst case clock-to-clock is 1 ns (ignoring trace layout considertions). The IEEE 1296 specification defined clock-to-clock skew is listed in Table 3-1 as parameter t6. By using the 74AS1004 gates in the 20 MHz path to delay **CCLK**, the clock-to-clock minimum and maximum times are met:

clock-to-clock min = 2 x mintpd 74AS1004 − worst case package skew
= 2 ns − 1 ns
= 1 ns

clock-to-clock max = 2 x maxtpd 74AS1004 + worst case package skew
= 8 ns + 1 ns
= 9 ns

Trace routing and loading on the clock signals are critical to proper CSM operation. The loading and trace layout should be kept as close to identical as possible to minimize skew. If analysis reveals that skew is greater than allowed, additional steps would need to be taken to reduce it.

Note that in the design example, the counter will reach a count of 0FH(15) after power-up before the circuit starts to produce the proper **BCLK*** and **CCLK*** waveforms.

4.3 Reset Generator (RSTGEN) (Sheet 2)

As described in paragraph 3.2, the RSTGEN function is influenced by the power supply used and system configuration. For simplicity, the design example assumes the following:

- No battery backup capability
- Equal ramp-up time on all power supply levels
- **ACLOW*** input from the power supply signalling eminent power failure
- Two active high debounced inputs for cold and warm reset invocation by the system user.

The TL7705A and 74AS74 packages on sheet 2 and part of the PAL16R4B programmable logic device on sheet 3 form the RSTGEN circuit. The timing for **DCLOW** and **ARST** are provided by the CT inputs on the TL7705A power supply monitors, which are adjustable to meet different power supply ramp-up times. The timing provided at the CT input can be determined by adding the power supply ramp-up time from the monitor threshold at 90 percent VCC to the minimum pulse width of **DCLOW** or **ARST**. (Note that the pulse width for **ARST** should also include the pulse width for **DCLOW**.) For this example, a 5 ms ramp-up from 4.5- to 4.5-Vdc was assumed.

The 74AS74 packages synchronize **SRST** (later developed into **RST***) for the PSB interface and **SDCLOW** for the state machine in the IDGEN circuit.

The **RIDCLOW** and **RIRST*** signal inputs to the TL7705A packages are generated in the PAL16R4B simply to reduce the part count. The PAL16R4B equations, shown in Figure 4-3, are basically that of OR gates.

4.4 Timeout Generator (TOGEN) (Sheet 3)

The 74S779 counters and part of the PAL16R4 implement the Transfer Cycle timeout function. Using the **TIMOUT, S1** and **CET*** outputs of the PAL16R4 as the state bits in Figure 3-6, the state assignments provided in Table 4-1 control the counters and assert **TIMOUT**.

In the configuration shown on sheet 3, the counters provide 10,240 counts of **BCLK*** and when combined with the state machine, yield a timeout period of 10,243 counts of **BCLK***. The count can be fine tuned by adjusting the inputs to the counters. The equations for the PAL16R4 are shown in Figure 4-3.

4.5 Cardslot and Arbitration ID Generator (IDGEN)

The 63RA481A® PROM (ID sequencer add on sheet 3 and the 74LS164 AD* shift registers and PAL16R8 on sheet 4 form the IDGEN circuit. Note that to keep the part count down, the shift register for driving **AD<17..20>*** is implemented in the PAL16R8. Also implemented in the PAL16R8 is the IDEN state machine depicted in Figure 3-9. The implemented IDEN state machine only provides one **BCLK*** delay instead of eight, but the ID sequencer provides the additional counts required by sequencing through unused cardslot IDs. (The signal to **IDEN2** is identical to **IDEN** and is used to furnish additional D.C. drive for the ID sequencer.)

Table 4-1. TOGEN State Assignments

State	TIMOUT	S1	CET*
IDLE	0	0	1
START	0	0	0
WAIT	0	1	0
TO	1	1	1

```
chip name PAL16R4

BCLKIN SRST SC0 SC2 SC3 SC4 BUSERR /ACLOW /TOP GND
/OE /RIRST /RIDCLOW S1 /CET TIMOUT RST COLD WARM VCC

equations

/TIMOUT     :=  /TOP * /TIMOUT * CET
              + /TIMOUT * /S1
              + TIMOUT * S1 * /CET
              + /SC0 * SC2 * SC4
              + BUSERR
              + RST

/S1         :=  TIMOUT * S1 * /CET
              + /SC0 * SC2 * SC4
              + BUSERR
              + RST
              + /SC0 * SC3 * SC4 * /TOP * /TIMOUT * S1 * CET
              + /TIMOUT * /S1 * /CET

CET         :=  /RST * /SC2 * /BUSERR * /TOP * /TIMOUT * CET
              + /RST * SC0 * /BUSERR * /TIMOUT * /S1
              + /RST * /SC4 * /BUSERR * /TOP * /TIMOUT * CET
              + /RST * SC0 * /BUSERR * /TOP * /TIMOUT * CET
              + /RST * /SC4 * /BUSERR * /TIMOUT * /S1 * CET
              + /RST * /SC2 * /BUSERR * /TIMOUT * /S1 * CET

RIDCLOW :=  COLD
          + ACLOW

RIRST     :=  COLD
          + WARM

/RST      :=  /SRST
```

280634-13

Figure 4-3. Equations for TOGEN PAL16R4B

5

Six outputs of the ID sequencer are used to drive the **ARB<5..0>*** lines and the remaining two outputs are assigned the signal names **LATCH** and **HOLD**. The IDLE state, shown in Figure 3-10, as indicated when all of the ID sequencer outputs are low; the SETUP state by the **ARB<5..0>*** outputs changing to a new ID; the LATCH state when the **LATCH** output is active high and the **HOLD** output is inactive low; the HOLD state when the **HOLD** output is active high and the **LATCH** output inactive low. The ID sequencer remains in the last HOLD state until **IDEN** becomes inactive low and is then reset to the IDLE state.

The state-flow diagrams in Figures 3-9 and 3-10 are modified as shown in Figures 4-4 and 4-5. These modifications take advantage of the design implemented to supply the eight counts of **BCLK*** delay before assigning IDs and to initialize the 74LS164 AD* shift registers.

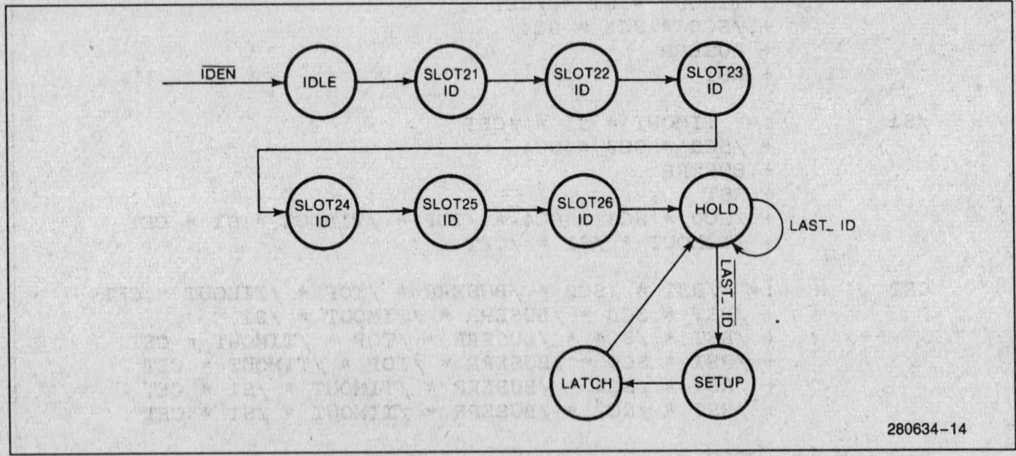

Figure 4-4. Modified State-Flow Diagrams for ID Assignment

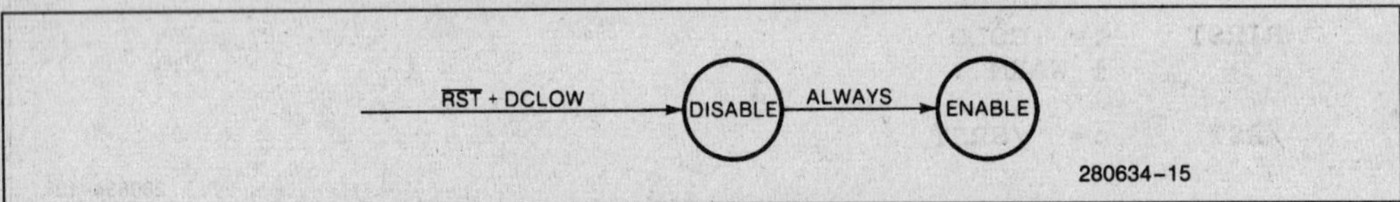

Figure 4-5. Modified IDEN State-Flow Diagram

The AD* shift registers are clocked during the HOLD state of the ID sequencer. Two passes are needed through these registers, one to latch cardslot IDs and one to latch arbitration IDs. The AD* shift registers are initialized at zero while **IDEN** is inactive low. During the HOLD state of unused cardslot ID 26 and the HOLD state of cardslot ID 20, the **SDATA** (Serial Data) output of the PAL16R8A is active high so that a one is shifted into the AD* shift registers at the beginning of each pass.

The **LATCH** output from the ID sequencer is inverted to produce **ADEN***. This signal enables the **AD<20..1>*** buffers (sheet 1) onto the PSB bus during the **LATCH** state.

Figure 4-6 shows the timing produced by the IDGEN circuit. The equations for the PAL16R8 are shown in Figure 4-7. The PROM ID code information is provided in Figure 4-8.

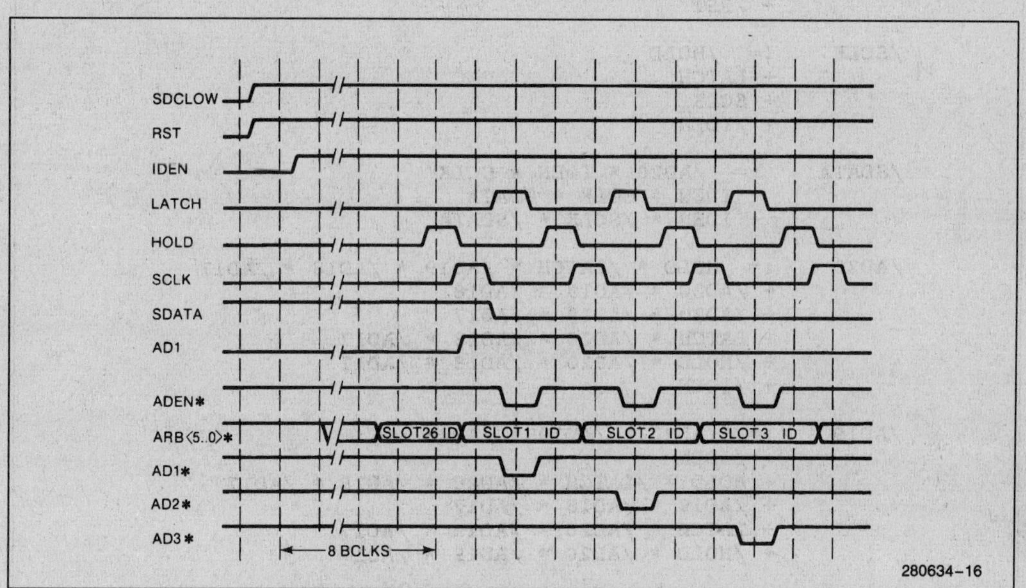

Figure 4-6. IDGEN Timing Diagram

5

```
chip name PAL16R8
BCLKIN RST SDCLOW HOLD LATCH AD16 IC7 IC8 IC9 GND
/OE AD17 AD18 AD19 AD20 SCLK SDATA IDEN2 IDEN VCC
equations
/IDEN       :=  SDCLOW
            + /RST

/IDEN2      :=  SDCLOW
            + /RST

/SCLK       :=  /HOLD
            + LATCH
            + SCLK
            + /IDEN

/SDATA       :=  /AD20 * IDEN * SCLK
             + IDEN * SCLK * SDATA
             + IDEN * /SCLK * /SDATA

/AD20       :=  HOLD * /LATCH * /AD19 * /AD18 * /AD17
            + /AD20 * /AD19 * /AD18
            + /AD20 * /AD19 * /AD17
            + LATCH * /AD20 * /AD18 * /AD17
            + /HOLD * /AD20 * /AD18 * /AD17
            + /IDEN

/AD19       :=  /AD20 * /AD19 * /AD18
            + /IDEN
            + HOLD * /LATCH * /AD20 * /AD18 * /AD17
            + /AD19 * /AD18 * /AD17
            + LATCH * /AD20 * /AD19 * /AD17
            + /HOLD * /AD20 * /AD19 * /AD17

/AD18       :=  /IDEN
            + /AD19 * /AD18 * /AD17
            + HOLD * /LATCH * /AD20 * /AD19 * /AD17
            + /AD20 * /AD18 * /AD17
            + LATCH * /AD20 * /AD19 * /AD18
            + /HOLD * /AD20 * /AD19 * /AD18

/AD17       :=  /IDEN
            + LATCH * /AD20 * /AD19 * /AD17
            + /HOLD * /AD20 * /AD19 * /AD17
            + /AD16 * /AD20 * /AD19 * /AD17
            + HOLD * /LATCH * /AD20 * /AD19 * /AD18 * AD17
            + /AD20 * /AD19 * AD18 * /AD17
            + /AD20 * AD19 * /AD18 * /AD17
            + AD20 * /AD19 * /AD18 * /AD17
```

280634–17

Figure 4-7. Equations for IDGEN PAL16R8A

ADDRESS	DATA	COMMENTS
00000000	00110101	;initial state
00110101	00110110	;setup state for cardslot id 21
00110110	00110111	;setup state for cardslot id 22
00110111	00111000	;setup state for cardslot id 23
00111000	00111001	;setup state for cardslot id 24
00111001	00111010	;setup state for cardslot id 25
00111010	10111010	;setup state for cardslot id 26
10111010	00100001	;hold state for cardslot id 26
00100001	01100001	;setup state for cardslot id 1
01100001	10100001	;latch state for cardslot id 1
10100001	00100010	;hold state for cardslot id 1
00100010	01100010	;setup state for cardslot id 2
01100010	10100010	;latch state for cardslot id 2
10100010	00100011	;hold state for cardslot id 2
00100011	01100011	;setup state for cardslot id 3
01100011	10100011	;latch state for cardslot id 3
10100011	00100100	;hold state for cardslot id 3
00100100	01100100	;setup state for cardslot id 4
01100100	10100100	;latch state for cardslot id 4
10100100	00100101	;hold state for cardslot id 4
00100101	01100101	;setup state for cardslot id 5
01100101	10100101	;latch state for cardslot id 5
10100101	00100110	;hold state for cardslot id 5
00100110	01100110	;setup state for cardslot id 6
01100110	10100110	;latch state for cardslot id 6
10100110	00100111	;hold state for cardslot id 6
00100111	01100111	;setup state for cardslot id 7
01100111	10100111	;latch state for cardslot id 7
10100111	00101000	;hold state for cardslot id 7
00101000	01101000	;setup state for cardslot id 8
01101000	10101000	;latch state for cardslot id 8
10101000	00101001	;hold state for cardslot id 8
00101001	01101001	;setup state for cardslot id 9
01101001	10101001	;latch state for cardslot id 9
10101001	00101010	;hold state for cardslot id 9
00101010	01101010	;setup state for cardslot id 10
01101010	10101010	;latch state for cardslot id 10
10101010	00101011	;hold state for cardslot id 10
00101011	01101011	;setup state for cardslot id 11
01101011	10101011	;latch state for cardslot id 11
10101011	00101100	;hold state for cardslot id 11
00101100	01101100	;setup state for cardslot id 12
01101100	10101100	;latch state for cardslot id 12

280634-18

Figure 4-8. IDGEN PROM Content (Sheet 1 of 3)

5

```
ADDRESS     DATA        COMMENTS
10101100    00101101    ;hold state for cardslot id 12
00101101    01101101    ;setup state for cardslot id 13
01101101    10101101    ;latch state for cardslot id 13
10101101    00101110    ;hold state for cardslot id 13
00101110    01101110    ;setup state for cardslot id 14
01101110    10101110    ;latch state for cardslot id 14
10101110    00101111    ;hold state for cardslot id 14
00101111    01101111    ;setup state for cardslot id 15
01101111    10101111    ;latch state for cardslot id 15
10101111    00110000    ;hold state for cardslot id 15
00110000    01110000    ;setup state for cardslot id 16
01110000    10110000    ;latch state for cardslot id 16
10110000    00110001    ;hold state for cardslot id 16
00110001    01110001    ;setup state for cardslot id 17
01110001    10110001    ;latch state for cardslot id 17
10110001    00110010    ;hold state for cardslot id 17
00110010    01110010    ;setup state for cardslot id 18
01110010    10110010    ;latch state for cardslot id 18
10110010    00110011    ;hold state for cardslot id 18
00110011    01110011    ;setup state for cardslot id 19
01110011    10110011    ;latch state for cardslot id 19
10110011    00110100    ;hold state for cardslot id 19
00110100    01110100    ;setup state for cardslot id 20
01110100    10110100    ;latch state for cardslot id 20
10110100    00011110    ;hold state for cardslot id 20
00011110    01011110    ;setup state for arbitration id 1
01011110    10011110    ;latch state for arbitration id 1
10011110    00011101    ;hold state for arbitration id 1
00011101    01011101    ;setup state for arbitration id 2
01011101    10011101    ;latch state for arbitration id 2
10011101    00011100    ;hold state for arbitration id 2
00011100    01011100    ;setup state for arbitration id 3
01011100    10011100    ;latch state for arbitration id 3
10011100    00011011    ;hold state for arbitration id 3
00011011    01011011    ;setup state for arbitration id 4
01011011    10011011    ;latch state for arbitration id 4
10011011    00011001    ;hold state for arbitration id 4
00011001    01011001    ;setup state for arbitration id 5
01011001    10011001    ;latch state for arbitration id 5
10011001    00011000    ;hold state for arbitration id 5
00011000    01011000    ;setup state for arbitration id 6
01011000    10011000    ;latch state for arbitration id 6
10011000    00010111    ;hold state for arbitration id 6
00010111    01010111    ;setup state for arbitration id 7
```

280634–19

Figure 4-8. IDGEN PROM Content (Sheet 2 of 3) (Continued)

```
ADDRESS     DATE        COMMENTS
01010111    10010111    ;latch state for arbitration id 7
10010111    00010011    ;hold state for arbitration id 7
00010011    01010011    ;setup state for arbitration id 8
01010011    10010011    ;latch state for arbitration id 8
10010011    00010001    ;hold state for arbitration id 8
00010001    01010001    ;setup state for arbitration id 9
01010001    10010001    ;latch state for arbitration id 9
10010001    00010000    ;hold state for arbitration id 9
00010000    01010000    ;setup state for arbitration id 10
01010000    10010000    ;latch state for arbitration id 10
10010000    00001111    ;hold state for arbitration id 10
00001111    01001111    ;setup state for arbitration id 11
01001111    10001111    ;latch state for arbitration id 11
10001111    00001110    ;hold state for arbitration id 11
00001110    01001110    ;setup state for arbitration id 12
01001110    10001110    ;latch state for arbitration id 12
10001110    00001100    ;hold state for arbitration id 12
00001100    01001100    ;setup state for arbitration id 13
01001100    10001100    ;latch state for arbitration id 13
10001100    00001000    ;hold state for arbitration id 13
00001000    01001000    ;setup state for arbitration id 14
01001000    10001000    ;latch state for arbitration id 14
10001000    00000111    ;hold state for arbitration id 14
00000111    01000111    ;setup state for arbitration id 15
01000111    10000111    ;latch state for arbitration id 15
10000111    00000110    ;hold state for arbitration id 15
00000110    01000110    ;setup state for arbitration id 16
01000110    10000110    ;latch state for arbitration id 16
10000110    00000100    ;hold state for arbitration id 16
00000100    01000100    ;setup state for arbitration id 17
01000100    10000100    ;latch state for arbitration id 17
10000100    00000011    ;hold state for arbitration id 17
00000011    01000011    ;setup state for arbitration id 18
01000011    10000011    ;latch state for arbitration id 18
10000011    00000010    ;hold state for arbitration id 18
00000010    01000010    ;setup state for arbitration id 19
01000010    10000010    ;latch state for arbitration id 19
10000010    00000001    ;hold state for arbitration id 19
00000001    01000001    ;setup state for arbitration id 20
01000001    10000001    ;latch state for arbitration id 20
10000001    10000001    ;hold state for arbitration id 20
end
```

280634-20

Figure 4-8. IDGEN PROM Content (Sheet 3 of 3) (Continued)

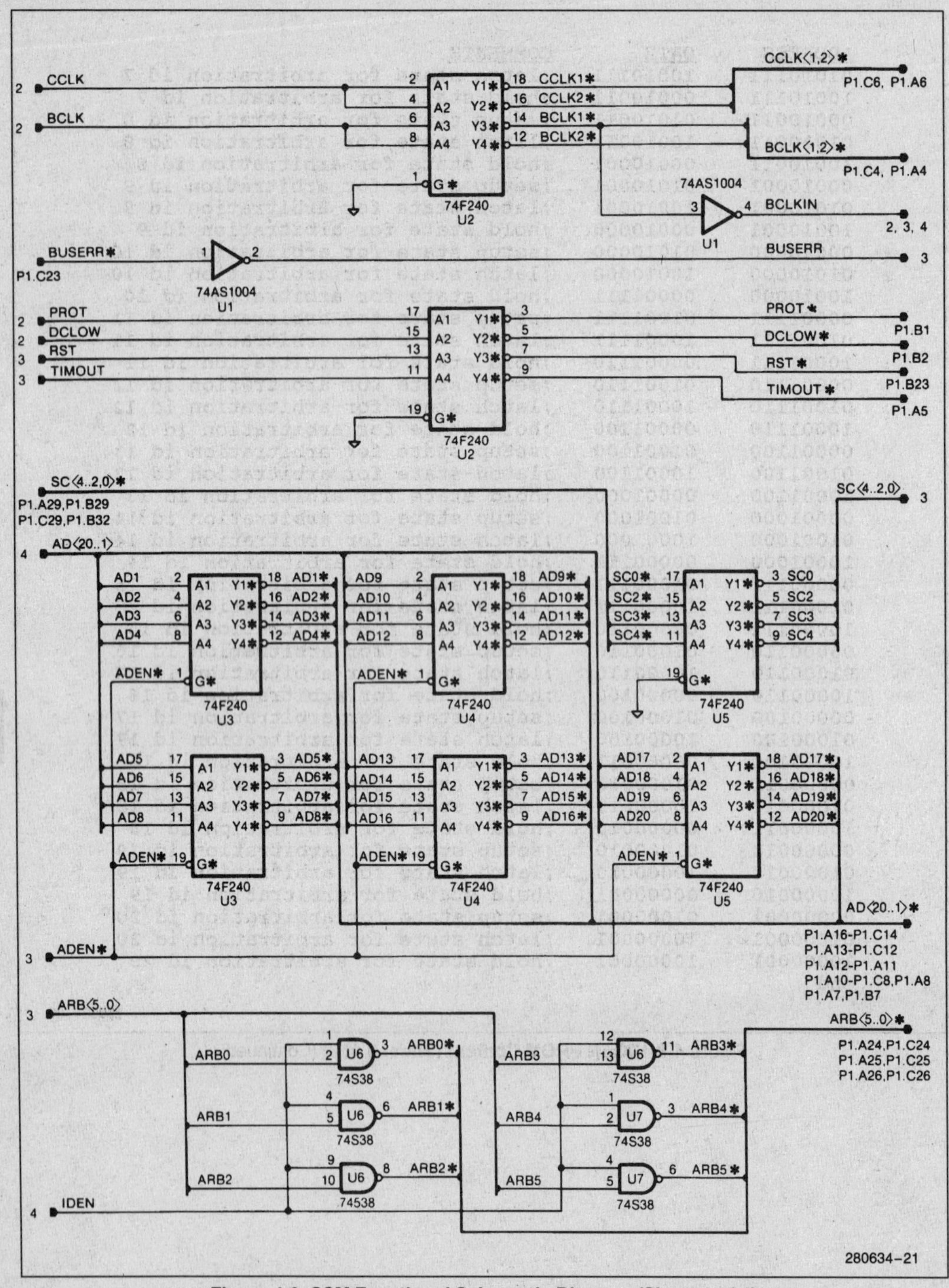

Figure 4-9. CSM Functional Schematic Diagram (Sheet 1 of 4)

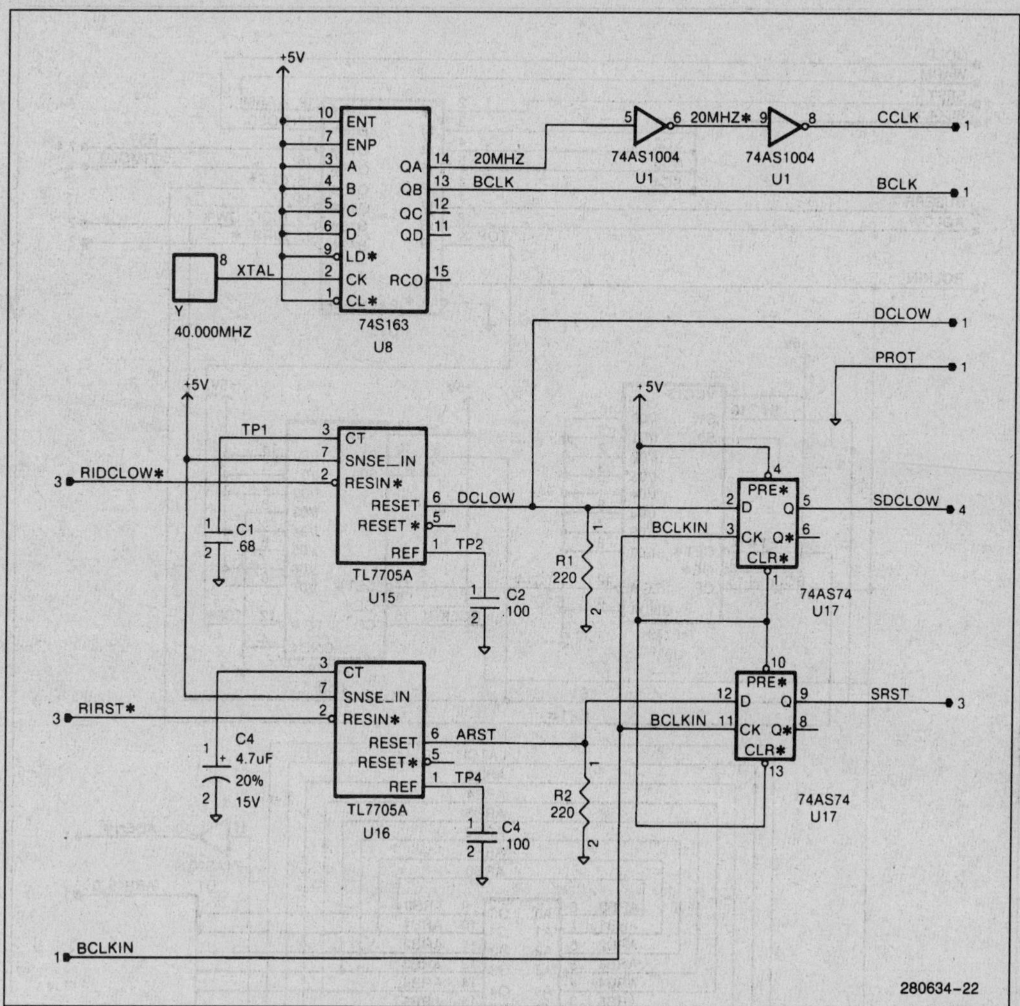

Figure 4-9. CSM Functional Schematic Diagram (Sheet 2 of 4) (Continued)

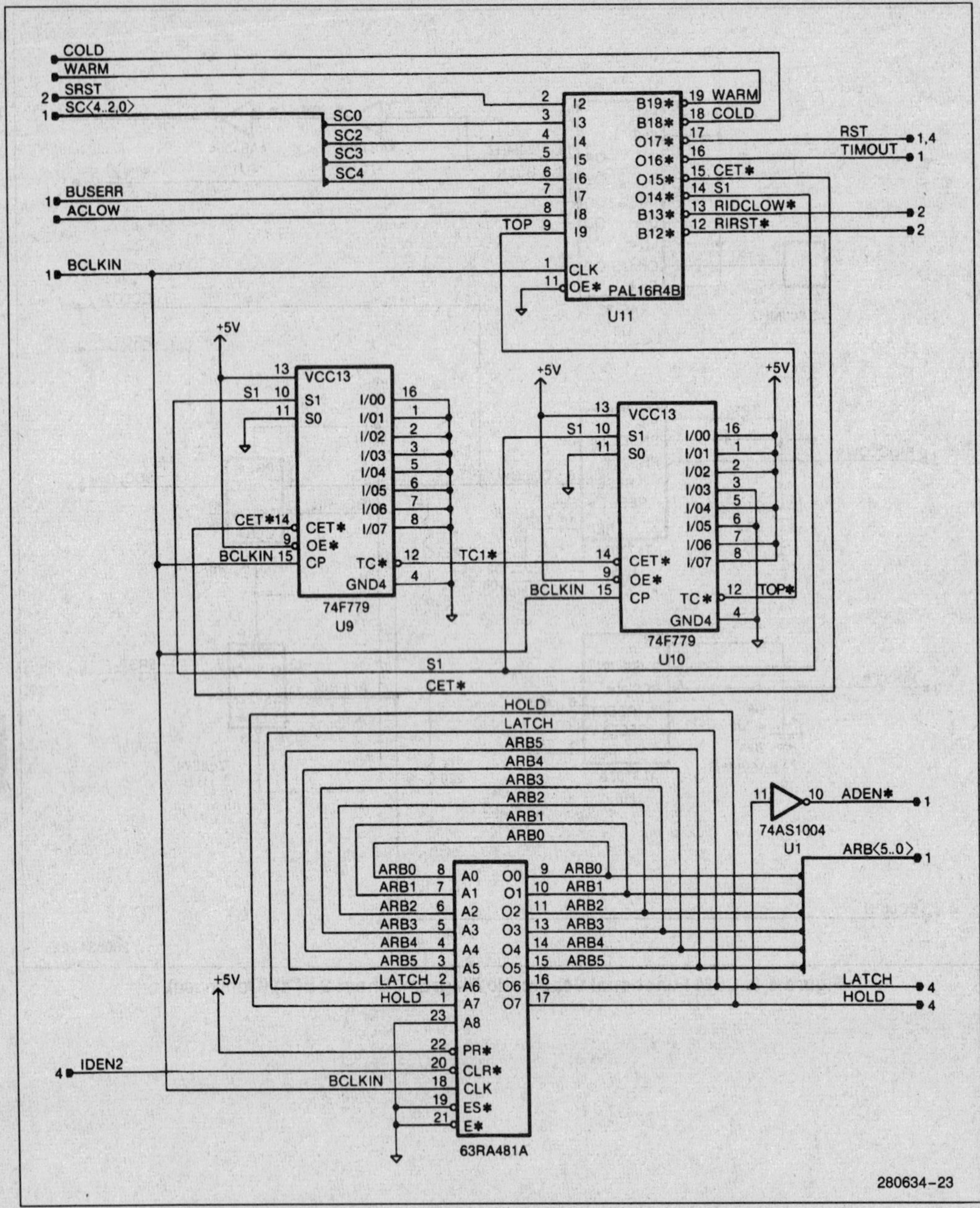

Figure 4-9. CSM Functional Schematic Diagram (Sheet 3 of 4) (Continued)

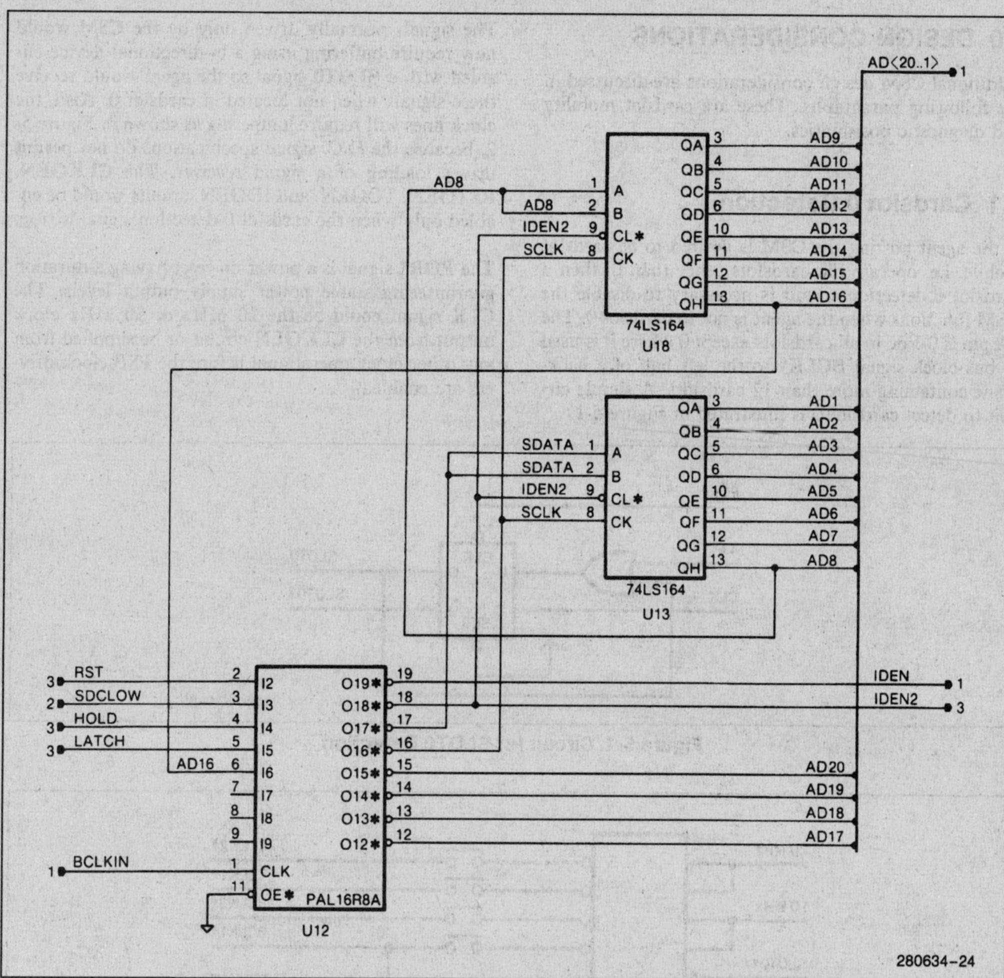

Figure 4-9. CSM Functional Schematic Diagram (Sheet 4 of 4) (Continued)

5

5.0 DESIGN CONSIDERATIONS

Additional CSM design considerations are discussed in the following paragraphs. These are cardslot mobility and diagnostic possibilities.

5.1 Cardslot 0 Detection

If the agent hosting the CSM is desired to be cardslot mobile, i.e. operate the cardslots other than 0; then a cardslot 0 detection circuit is necessary to disable the CSM functions when the agent is not in cardslot 0. The 4A pin is 0-Vdc in all cardslots except 0 where it is used to bus clock signal **BCLK*** to the left half of a backplane containing more than 12 cardslots. A simple circuit to detect cardslot 0 is illustrated in Figure 5-1.

The signals normally driven only by the CSM would now require buffering using a bi-directional device enabled with a **SLOT0** signal so the agent would receive these signals when not located in cardslot 0. Also, the clock lines will require jumpering as shown in Figure 5-2, because the D.C. signal specifications do not permit driver loading of a signal receiver. The CLKGEN, RSTGEN, TOGEN, and IDGEN circuits would be enabled only when the cardslot 0 detection signal is true.

The **POR*** signal is a power-on reset having a duration guaranteeing stable power supply output levels. The **CLK** signal could be the 20 MHz or 10 MHz clock output from the CLKGEN circuit or be supplied from any other clock operational before the PSB clock drivers are enabled.

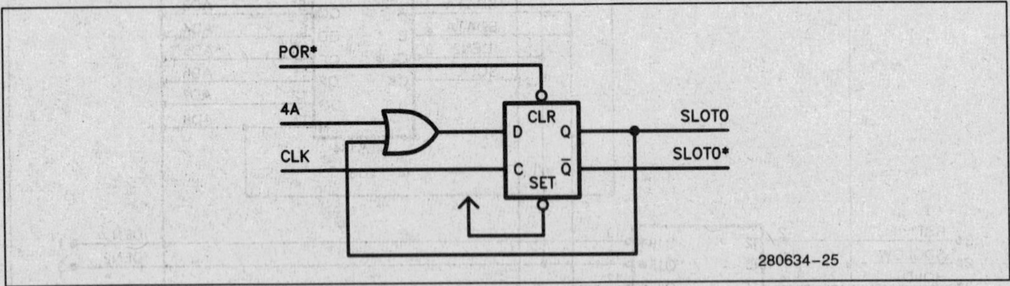

Figure 5-1. Circuit for SLOT0 Detection

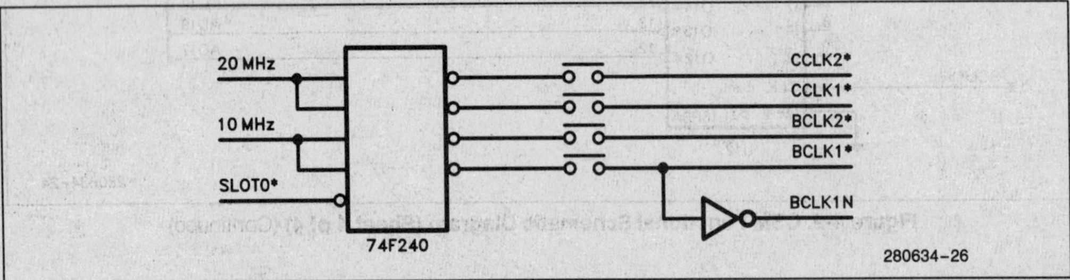

Figure 5-2. CSM Clock Jumper

5.2 System Diagnostic Options

For system test and diagnostic purposes, it may be desirable to provide for the capability of selecting other signal frequencies to exercise the clock drivers. For example, outputs from the frequency divider used in the design example could be selectively jumpered as inputs to the **BCLK*** and **CCLK*** line drivers.

A bus timeout disable function may also be desirable. Such a function can be implemented by providing an additional input to the TOGEN state machine driven by either the interconnect controller or jumper selectable.

5.3 CSM Functions on the Backplane

By removing the PBI function and interfacing directly to an agent's PSB interface, the design example in paragraph 4 could be added to almost any type of MULTIBUS II agent. As mentioned in paragraph 3.0, this agent might be a CPU board or a simple I/O replier device, which may contain other centralized system services.

The IEEE 1296 specification does not preclude putting slot 0 on the reverse side of the backplane. The minimal functionality described here will fit onto a small printed circuit card mounted on the reverse of the backplane—this does, of course require a backplane designed for this application but if you are trying to squeeze an "extra" slot into a 19 inch rack, this can be accomplished.

intel®

APPLICATION NOTE

AP-423

November 1990

The Multibus II Interconnect Design Guide

JORY RADKE
MODULES DEVELOPMENT ENGINEER

ROGER FINGER
MULTIBUS II TECHNICAL MARKETING MANAGER

Order Number: 280640-001

The Multibus II Interconnect Design Guide

CONTENTS PAGE

CONTENTS PAGE

5

CONTENTS PAGE

CONTENTS PAGE

CONTENTS

PAGE

CONTENTS

PAGE

List of Figures

1.0 INTERCONNECT ADDRESS OF SPACE ON MULTIBUS II

1.1 Who Should Read This Document?

The primary audience of this document consists of companies and individuals who are in the process of designing their own Multibus II boards for use with other compatible products. It is assumed that the reader has already studies the Interconnect Interface Specification and has a good working knowledge in the operation of interconnect space on existing Intel products. In addition, portions of the IEEE 1296 specification and the MPC User's Guide are referenced in some detail. A complete bibliography of recommended reading material is contained in Appendix A.

This design package consists of two related items. The first item is the document you are now reading which is a user's guide to the overall design process. The second item, is a diskette containing copyrighted software to be used in generating new firmware for your interconnect subsystem. This package is not intended for users to change the content of microcontrollers already installed on Intel boards.

1.2 Configuration Issues in Microcomputer Based Systems

Over the past few years, microcomputer designs have progressed dramatically in capability and performance. In contrast, little progress has been made in enhancing ease-of-use. Until recently, board users have had to deal with the added complexity of modern single-board computers by wading through lengthy reference manuals and innumerable jumper options—often arriving at the final solution only by trial and error. System integrators often found that the firmware revision number penciled in on the EPROMs they installed did not match the device driver revision and consequently, nothing works! Worse yet, things might work for a little while and then fail; resulting in wasted time debugging the problem to determine what went wrong. Memory mapping options, arbitration priorities, interrupt levels, and scores of other "tunable" parameters contribute to the fray, leaving the system designer befuddled and confused. Often, the only way out of this mess was to locate a board that was already properly configured and copy off the jumper list.

Board designers build in numerous options so their products can be used in the broadest possible spectrum of applications. The number of options offered is not the core of the problem, but managing them is. Multibus II addresses this problem with a special address space known as "interconnect". Now for the first time, system-wide configuration information has been made accessible to software; thereby opening opportunities for centralized control and coordination. In most cases, the end user of these products will be completely unaware of the configuration process. They simply remove the board from its shipping container, install the proper firmware, plug it into a free cardslot in the backplane, and apply power. Things work the first time around with no mess, no fuss, and no configuration errors.

Interconnect is great for end users; it eliminates most of the common configuration errors, speeds up the installation process, and facilitates diagnostics and repair. When considered in the context of an overall system architecture that includes message passing, interconnect is one of the foundation building blocks distinguishing Multibus II as an environment capable of satisfying the most demanding of applications.

1.3 Overview of Interconnect Address Space

Interconnect address space is a fundamental part of the IEEE 1296 specification, which defines Multibus II. Interconnect address space was included in the IEEE 1296 specification to solve three major problems: board identification, configuration, and diagnostics. The board identification registers are read-only locations containing board information such as type, manufacturer, components installed, and other board specific functions. The configuration registers are read/write registers which allow the system software to set and change the configuration of many on-board hardware options. In most cases, hard-wired jumper options can now be eliminated in favor of software control. The diagnostic registers are used for the starting, stopping, and status reporting of self-contained diagnostic routines supplied with each board. These diagnostics are commonly known as Built-In Self Tests (BISTs).

1.3.1 GEOGRAPHICAL ADDRESSING

Interconnect is based on the fundamental principle that you can locate boards within a backplane using a system of cardslot numbering. This concept, known as geographical addressing, is a very useful tool during system-wide initialization. Each board in the system contains firmware which conforms to a standardized header format (Figure 1-1).

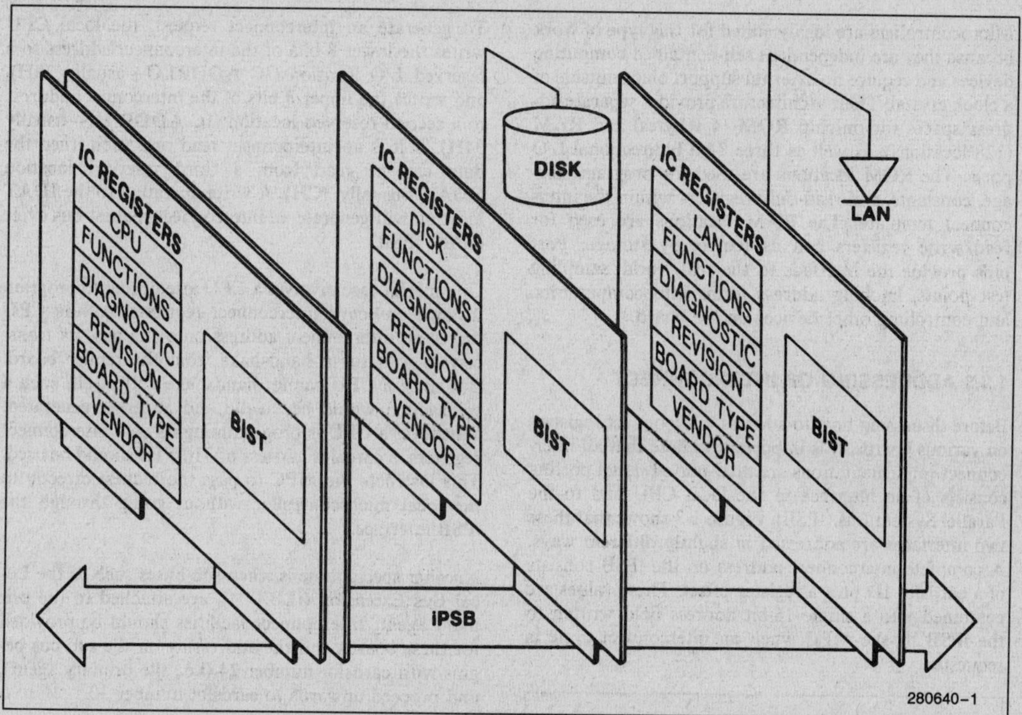

280640-1

Figure 1-1. Interconnect Overview

At boot time, the system software will scan the backplane to locate its resources before loading in the device drivers. This approach eliminates the need for reconfiguring the software every time a new board is introduced into the backplane. It also solves the problem of how to configure multiple instances of controller and processor boards in large multiprocessing systems. Cardslot independence is achieved by having all boards in the system carry their own initialization and diagnostic functions on-board in firmware. Operating systems can generate a map of where resources are located during initialization and then use this map as a base address list for message passing.

1.3.2 MICROCONTROLLERS IN THE BUS INTERFACE

Most Multibus II designs are based on a highly integrated bus interface controller known as the Message Passing Coprocessor (MPC). Special provisions have been made in the bus interface silicon to enable board designers to implement interconnect in a cost effective manner. A typical Multibus II interface consists of the MPC, a small number of bus transceivers, and a microcontroller such as the Intel 8751 or equivalent (Figure 1-2). It is the microcontroller (in association with the MPC) that has the responsibility for all interconnect functions.

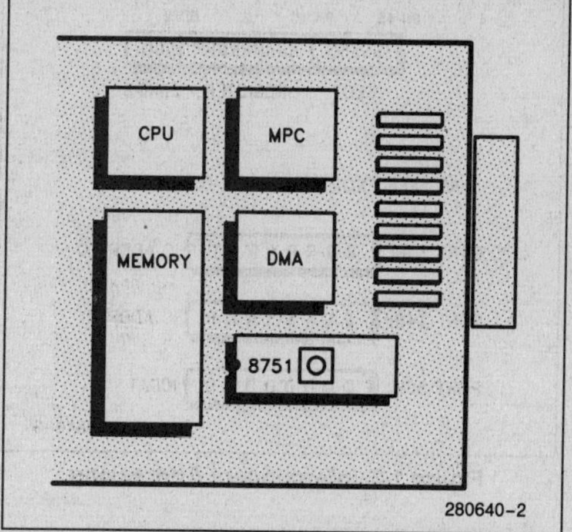

Figure 1-2. Hardware Support for Message Passing

Microcontrollers are idealy suited for this type of work because they are independent self-contained computing devices and require no external support chips outside of a clock crystal. Their architecture provides separate address spaces for on-chip ROM (4 Kbytes) and RAM (128 locations), as well as three 8-bit bidirectional I/O ports. The ROM locations are used for program storage, constants, and read-only registers within the interconnect template. The RAM locations are used for read/write registers and as temporary storage. Port pins provide the interface to the real world; sampling test points, latching address terms into comparators, and controlling other devices on the board.

1.3.3 ADDRESSING OF INTERCONNECT

Before discussing how to address interconnect registers on various boards, it is important to note that all interconnect implementations are dual-ported. Dual porting consists of an interface to the local CPU and to the Parallel System Bus (iPSB). Figure 1-3 shows that these two interfaces are addressed in slightly different ways. A complete interconnect address on the iPSB consists of a cardslot ID plus a register offset. These values are combined into a single 16-bit address field written to the iPSB by the MPC when an interconnect cycle is requested.

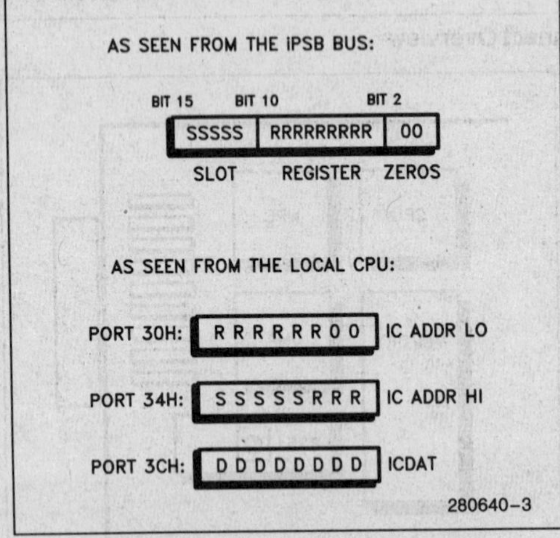

Figure 1-3. Interconnect Addressing

To generate an interconnect request, the local CPU writes the lower 8 bits of the interconnect address to a reserved I/O location (IC ADDRLO—usually 30H), and writes the upper 8 bits of the interconnect address to a second reserved location (IC ADDR HI—usually 34H). If it is an interconnect read operation, then the data can be read from a third reserved location (IDAT—usually 3CH). A write operation to the IDAT location will generate an interconnect request bus cycle on the iPSB.

One special case involves a CPU attempting to program its own on-board interconnect registers. As the CPU drives an interconnect address onto the bus, its transceivers wait for a handshake from the replier board. But since a CPU cannot handshake with itself, such a transaction would be invalid and an error generated. Whenever a CPU is programming its own interconnect registers, a cardslot address of 31(1FH) should be used. This instructs the MPC to pass the request directly to the local microcontroller without going through the iPSB interface.

Another special case is when sub-buses such as the Local Bus Extension (iLBX™), are attached to the primary agent. Interconnect facilities should be provided for these boards and the addressing on the sub-bus begins with cardslot number 24 (i.e., the primary agent), and proceed upwards to cardslot number 30.

1.3.4 DATA STRUCTURES IN INTERCONNECT

The objective of interconnect address space is to allow higher level software to gain information about the environment in which they operate independent of who manufactured the board, what functions it contains, and what cardslot it resides in. To accomplish this goal, an Interconnect Interface Specification has been published and forms the basis for much of the information in this guide. If you have not yet read this document, you should do so before beginning your design effort.

Interconnect functions implemented on Intel's single board computers go beyond the requirements of the IEEE 1296 specification. This specification mandates that all conforming products include an Interconnect Header Record. The header record consists of information regarding board type, its manufacturer, what firmware is installed, and other relevant information. An example header record is shown in Figure 1-4. In addition to the header record, the manufacturer may also supply additional function records which make other features of the board accessible through interconnect.

HEADER RECORD

0 VENDOR ID, LOW BYTE
1 VENDOR ID, HIGH BYTE
2 BOARD ID, CHARACTER 1
3 BOARD ID, CHARACTER 2
4 BOARD ID, CHARACTER 3
5 BOARD ID, CHARACTER 4
6 BOARD ID, CHARACTER 5
7 BOARD ID, CHARACTER 6
8 BOARD ID, CHARACTER 7
9 BOARD ID, CHARACTER 8
10 BOARD ID, CHARACTER 9
11 BOARD ID, CHARACTER 10
12 RESERVED
13 RESERVED
14 RESERVED
15 RESERVED
16 TEST REVISION NUMBER
17 CLASS ID
18 RESERVED
19 RESERVED
20 RESERVED
21 RESET STATUS REGISTER
22 PROGRAM TABLE INDEX
23 NMI ENABLE REGISTER
24 GENERAL STATUS
25 GENERAL CONTROL
26 BIST SUPPORT LEVEL
27 BIST DATA INPUT
28 BIST DATA OUTPUT
29 BIST SLAVE STATUS
30 BIST MASTER STATUS
31 BIST TEST ID

PROTECTION RECORD

32 PROTECTION RECORD TYPE
33 RECORD LENGTH
34 PROTECTION LEVEL REGISTER
35 RESERVED

iPSB CONTROL RECORD

36 iPSB CONTROL RECORD TYPE
37 RECORD LENGTH
38 iPSB SLOT ID NUMBER
39 iPSB ARBITRATION ID NUMBER

LOCAL PROCESSOR RECORD

40 LOCAL PROCESSOR RECORD TYPE
41 RECORD LENGTH
42 LOCAL PROCESSOR CONTROL
43 LOCAL PROCESSOR STATUS
44 RESERVED

END OF TEMPLATE RECORD

45 END OF TEMPLATE RECORD TYPE

280640-4

Figure 1-4. Function Records in the Interconnect Core Firmware

Function records begin with a byte specifying the record type followed by the number of bytes that make up the record. The manufacturer must publish a description of these function records in their reference documentation. Many types of function records have already been defined. Some examples include memory configuration, parity control, serial I/O, and other commonly used functions. If the existing record types do not adequately describe a function, a new record type can be defined—up to a maximum of 1020 different record types are allowed.

The system software initiates the search for a specific function record at interconnect register 32, which is the first function record following the header record. The program first checks the record type field and then counts bytes to the next record type field until either the correct function record is found or the End of Template (EOT) record (hex value 0FF) is encountered.

1.3.5 ACCESS RIGHTS AND PROTECTION RECORDS

Because the interconnect registers are dual-ported, each has a set of static and dynamic access rights that detemine which operations will be allowed on either the local or iPSB bus interface. All interconnect registers can be read from either bus, however, static access rights may place restrictions on whether a register can be written to from either interface. The term "static" is used because these access privileges are predetermined by the designer of the interconnect firmware and will not change during system operation. In other situations it may be desirable to allow a register to be modified during system initialization; then locked against further changes during normal system operation. This capability is essential since many of the functions contained in interconnect are so vital to correct system operation that some means of protecting them from malicious or inexperienced users is required.

Dynamic access rights are determined by protection records which are used to prevent other boards from modifying a local interconnect resource. When activated, all subsequent records become read only so other users can read from interconnect registers, but cannot write to them.

1.3.6 DIAGNOSTIC PHILOSOPHY OF MULTIBUS II

The diagnostic philosophy of Multibus II is that each board should have the capability to test itself and report error status when problems exist. There are two occasions when diagnostic testing is invoked. A subset of the complete on-board diagnostics is run during power-on initialization and more extensive testing can be invoked from the operator's console. Following power-on, most boards go through a series of initialization checks where the basic functioning of the MPC and microcontroller are verified. Initialization is followed by a power-on test suite automatically invoked by each board. If a hardware failure is detected at this point, a yellow LED on the front panel will illuminate so that the failing module can be easily identified and replaced.

If further testing is desired, extended diagnostics can be invoked by placing a diagnostic request packet in the interconnect BIST registers. Usually one board acts as the Master Test Handler and requests services from other system boards functioning as Slaves when under test. A menu of tests is available via interconnect. This test philosophy can be applied on-site by the end-user, service representative, or remotely executed via modem from the regional repair center. In most cases, downtime is minimized by sending out a replacement board and thus avoiding an expensive repair call.

The firmware content of Multibus II boards is much greater than that found on previous industry standard buses. In addition to the 8751 Microcontroller, Multibus II boards normally host EPROMs that contain extended diagnostics (BISTs), test handlers, reset initialization sequencing, debug monitors, and many other functions. The location of diagnostic firmware on a board (Figure 1-5) is dependent on code complexity and execution speed. For simple replier agents, the microcontroller's on-board EPROM may have enough program storage space for diagnostic functions as well as the interconnect firmware. In contrast, the majority of the requester/replier boards (i.e., capable of becoming bus masters), are more complex and most diagnostic code is run on the CPU from on-board EPROM. In this case, the microcontroller primarily serves as the communication interface for the diagnostics.

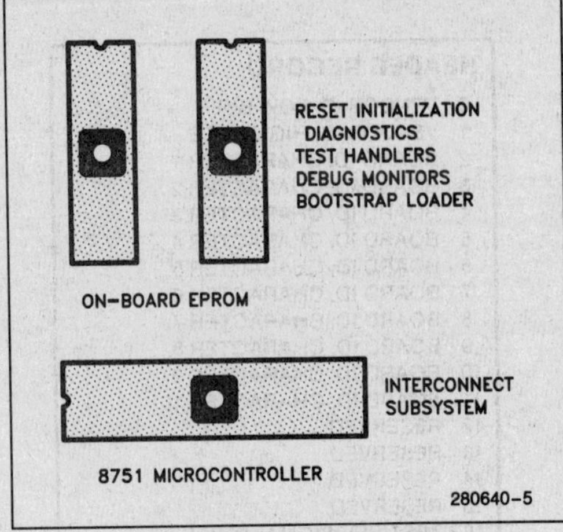

Figure 1-5. Firmware Content of Multibus II Boards

1.4 Interconnect—The Manufacturer's Perspective

From the perspective of a board designer, interconnect is a mixed blessing. The board manufacturer is certain to enjoy the benefits of reduced support costs, easier fault isolation in field repairs, and enhanced customer satisfaction—but these advantages do not come free. One would anticipate longer development time, increased on-board part count, and the firmware configuration to increase the amount of effort it takes to prepare a Multibus II board for market. And indeed this is so. If a competent design team were to tackle the interconnect subsystem (including diagnostics, hardware, and firmware design), it would not be unreasonable to allow six man-months for the job.

Given that this represents an extraordinary investment for the manufacturer, the primary goal of this design package is to reduce the amount of time required to include interconnect in your design from six months to only six days! Another goal is to guarantee compatibility and interoperability of your products by placing common core functions in user extensible firmware in such a way that it is easy to customize the design to fit your own particular needs.

1.5 Assumptions Regarding Your Operating Environment

Although many implementations of interconnect are possible, it was necessary to restrict the scope of this guide to satisfying the broadest and more typical range of users—designs based on the MPC component in association with an 8751 Microcontroller (or equivalent). This design guide is intended as a generic solution that meets the needs of most of these users.

For software development, it will be necessary for you to obtain an IBM™ PC (model XT, AT, or compatible) plus the appropriate Intel programming languages and a PROM programmer to transfer your code into the microcontroller. An in-circuit emulator is not required for this project; however, some users will find it expedient to make use of such a tool since it simplifies debugging and eliminates the need for PROM programming while the code is being developed. A complete list of hardware and software requirements may be found in Section 2. Any departure from the recommended development tools or practices is outside the scope of this document and may lead to unpredictable results.

1.6 Design Methodology—An Overview

The process of designing an interconnect subsystem invariably begins with a high level discussion of what function you intend to support. While the header record is quite easily defined, decisions as to what function records to include should be carefully considered in terms of how much flexibility to give your users, what functions they might be interested in, and how much external hardware will be required. Some of the function records listed in the Interconnect Interface Specification are already implemented in the core firmware and require minimal effort to support. Other functions may be quite complex and could potentially require extensive TTL circuitry external to the microcontroller. As with all engineering designs, you should spend a significant portion of your time making sure that you have a clean workable specification before proceeding into the implementation phase.

The second step in interconnect design is to determine what circuitry is required to gain access to the information in interconnect that you intend to present to the user. This consists of locating all test points, control circuitry, latches, and transceivers external to the microcontroller. Most likely this determination will be made at a point where the overall schematic for the board is near completion and before you begin the layout and develop the prototype. At this stage, all dedicated I/O addresses will be defined and rudimentary PAL equations for the control points will be writen.

The third step of interconnect design consists of evaluating your on-chip resource requirements based on the function records being implemented. At this stage, you will write the functional routines and identify the RAM, ROM, and port requirements for the microcontroller. If your original interconnect specification was overambitious or in appropriately defined, you will discover at this point that you may be forced into external PROM, static RAM, or port expansion logic; and may wish to scale back your design or change over to the 8752 Microcontroller (having 8 Kbytes of ROM and 256 bytes of on-chip RAM). Once you know your resource requirements and have written the functional routines, you are now ready to integrate your custom code with the core interconnect firmware.

The fourth step in the design process consists of loading the tables with data based on the interconnect template you specificed in step one, plus the external declarations for the routines you wrote in step three. The object code supplied on the diskette with this guide contains a table driven collection of routines that provide the core interconnect functions. These give the user some commonly used function records (Figure 1-4) and provide the opportunity for users to add their own routines to this core. Generating the firmware consists of assembling your code and then allowing the table generators to integrate this code into the core module through an ASM-51 macro expansion process. Once complete, the entire package is integrated using RL51 (a relocation linker) to resolve any external references and produce a unified object module for loading into the microcontroller EPROM.

The final step in the process is to program the microcontroller and test every imaginable function and event sequence within interconnect. It is at this stage that the use of an in-circuit emulator, logic analyzer, or oscilloscope may be desirable to help in localizing logic faults or timing related problems. In most cases, debug time is fairly short since the core routines are supplied already and are known to be good.

Once the interconnect subsystem is totally tested, the board can be forwarded to the device driver development team and/or system integrator for initialization software development and further functional testing.

2.0 PREPARATION FOR USE

2.1 Hardware and Software Requirements

Before proceeding with your interconnect design using this guide, the hardware, software, and optional equipment listed below are required (at a minimum).

Hardware Requirements:

- IBM PC (model XT, AT, or compatible) configured with at least 640 Kbytes of internal memory and a 10-Mbyte (or larger) hard disk.

- Intel PROM Programmer, model iUP201, plus the 8751 Microcontroller Personality Module and a serial cable. The IBM PC must have a spare serial port to interface with the PROM Programmer. (Note that other brands of PROM Programmers can be used, but the batch files and object module produced by Intel's development tools are not guaranteed to be compatible.)

Software Requirements:

- DOS Operating System, version 3.0 or greater
- iPPS PROM Programming Software, version 2.2 or greater
- ASM-51 Macro Assembler version 2.2 or greater
- RL51 Relocation/Linkage package version 3.0 or greater

Optional Equipment:

- ICE™ 51 (or ICE 5100) In-Circuit Emulator with IBM PC Interface Card
- Oscilloscope

2.2 Loading Software onto Your System

Before starting, it is assumed that you will have already loaded the ASM-51 and RL51 program files in a common subdirectory of the hard disk and have indicated the route to that subdirectory in a PATH command entered into the AUTOEXEC.BAT file (in the root directory). This will allow you to call these program files from any point in the file structure without having to identify the directory search path to these files.

Install the software supplied with this design guide onto your hard disk by inserting the interconnect firmware diskette into drive A or B. After the C> prompt, type A (or B): to change the default drive. Next type INSTALL and then press **Enter.** The computer will read from the drive specified and immediately start executing the install.bat batch program. When this batch program completes processing, you will find the following added to the subdirectory structure of your hard disk:

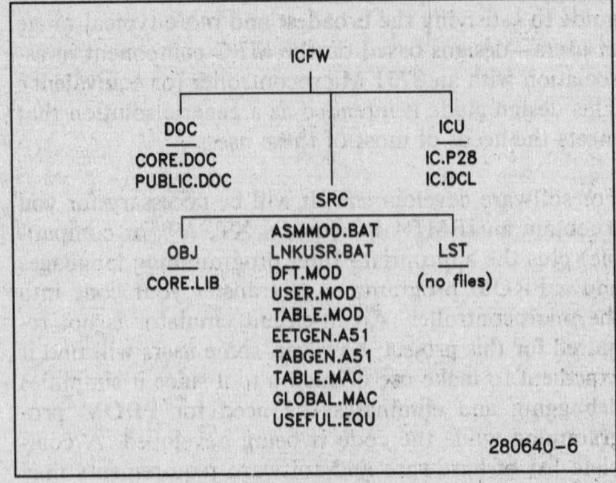

Batch files are supplied to automate the firmware generation process. These files make some assumptions about your hard disk directory structure. It is important to note that all batch files must be called from the \ICFW\SRC directory path, otherwise the DOS command processor will not look beyond your current directory in its search for a file name. Edit the path command in your AUTOEXEC.BAT file to include the \ICFW directory.

2.3 Interconnect the Easy Way

While interconnect is a complex topic, there is an easy way to get a functional interconnect subsystem operational without detailed knowledge of the internal design. To do this, view the file \ICFW\SRC\TABGEN.A51 using the TYPE command or a text editor and notice that the data fields for vendor ID, board ID, hardware test revision, and class ID have been left blank (looking ahead, this is Figure 5-1). Consult the Interconnect Architectural Specification to determine what information to place in these fields. Once you have obtained this information, perform these steps at your computer console:

a. Type CD and then press **Enter** to display the current directory. If \ICFW\SRC is not being displayed, then type CD\ICFW\SRC and press **Enter** to change to the correct directory path.

b. Run the following batch programs in the order listed:

```
ASMMOD  dft
ASMMOD  user
ASMMOD  table
LNKUSR  test
```

The result is a PROMmable object code file (TEST.LNK) that is placed in \ICFW\SRC\OBJ subdirectory. The TEST.LNK object code is ready to burn into the microcontroller EPROM and provides a complete interconnect header record as well as protection, iPSB control, and local processor records.

The core hardware design consists of the minimum interconnect implementation as shown in Figure 4-1. The basic combination of hardware and firmware can be used during prototyping as the starting point for most interconnect designs.

3.0 THEORY OF OPERATION

3.1 MPC to Microcontroller Hardware Interface

Most Multibus II designs use the Message Passing Coprocessor (MPC) component with an 8751 Microcontroller to implement the Parallel System Bus (iPSB) interface. This combination minimizes the number of devices required to implement a full-featured bus interface and provides flexibility in adapting the design to the broadest possible range of functional specifications. The hardware interface between the MPC and the microcontroller is shown in Figure 3-1.

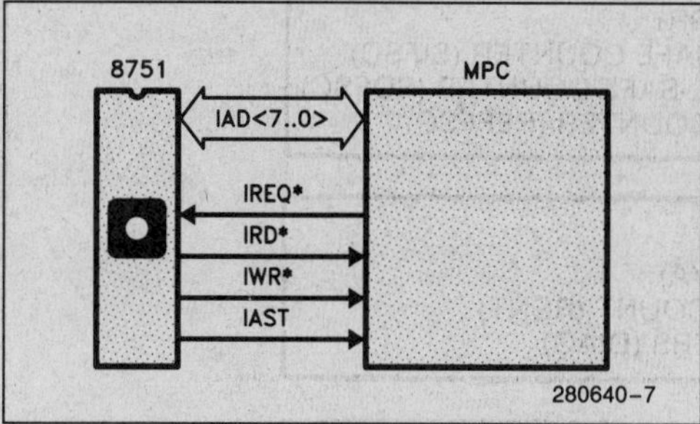

Figure 3-1. MPC to Interconnect Pathway

The MPC is designed to sit directly on the microcontroller's multiplexed Interconnect Address/Data bus (IAD<7..0>). When an interconnect cycle is initiated, the **IREQ*** signal from the MPC interrupts the microcontroller with a request for services. The microcontroller then performs a series of read and write operations to a group of MPC interconnect bus registers to satisfy the interconnect request and complete the operation. In terms of hardware control, the microcontroller acts as the bus master on this interface; generating the read and write signals, and supplying an Interconnect Address Strobe (**IAST**) based on its own Address Latch Enable (**ALE**) signal. The reader is requested to review Sections 4 and 5 of the MPC User's Manaual before continuing further.

3.2 MPC Interconnect Bus Registers

The MPC component contains a set of special function registers that are only accessible via the IAD bus. These registers (Figure 3-2) can be categorized into five functional groups: interconnect reference registers, slot and arbitration ID registers, configuration registers, diagnostic registers, and the no access registers.

The MPC interconnect reference registers serve as the basic communications interface between the microcontroller and the MPC. Whenever the local CPU or iPSB agent generates an interconnect request cycle, the registers actually being accessed (IC ADDR HI, IC ADDR LO, IDAT) physically reside in the MPC rather than in the microcontroller. The MPC asserts the **IREQ*** signal to interrupt the microcontroller which responds by initiating a dialogue of read/write commands to the MPC interconnect reference registers.

The second functional group of MPC interconnect registers are concerned with the cardslot and arbitration ID assignments made by the Central Services Module (CSM) during reset initialization. Note that the Interconnect Interface Specification describes an iPSB Control Record which includes registers for both arbitration and cardslot ID. This allows a CPU to determine in what cardslot it is residing.

The third functional group of MPC interconnect registers control configurable features on the MPC such as dual-port address boundaries, arbitration priority, Reset-Not-Complete (RSTNC) control, error reporting, and fail-safe counter functions. In most implementations, these registers are passed through an interconnect function record to make them user accessible and configurable.

The fourth functional group of MPC interconnect registers control retry and diagnostic functions. These parameters can be used for performance tuning and confidence testing, but are not frequently accessed by users. In general, they can be programmed during initialization with default values and then ignored.

Finally, there is a group of addresses between 0 and 7FH for which the MPC guarantees a tristate condition (no access). Interconnect designers can take advantage of this feature by using these addresses to decode registers and latches residing directly on the IAD bus. This technique provides a convenient way to generate an 8-bit bidirectional bus using user defined addresses as chip enable terms. The reader is encouraged to read all of Section 7 in the MPC User's Guide before proceeding.

REFERENCE REGISTERS
0E1H INTERCONNECT SLOT ADDRESS (IC ADDR HI)
0E2H INTERCONNECT REGISTER ADDRESS(IC ADDR LO)
0E3H INTERCONNECT DATA (IDAT)
0E0H INTERCONNECT STATUS (ISTAT)
0E1H INTERCONNECT COMPLETE (ICMPL)
0E0H INTERCONNECT REFERENCE ARBITRATION (IARB)

ID REGISTERS
0E6H SLOT ID (SID)
0E7H ARBITRATION ID (AID)

CONFIGURATION REGISTERS
0E8H DUAL-PORT LOWER ADDRESS LOW BYTE (LALB)
0E9H DUAL-PORT LOWR ADDRESS HIGH BYTE (LAHB)
0EAH DUAL-PORT UPPER ADDRESS LOW BYTE (HALB)
0EBH DUAL-PORT UPPER ADDRESS HIGH BYTE (HAHB)
0ECH GENERAL PARAMETERS (GEN)
0EFH REFERENCE ERROR (RERR)
0EDH SOLICITED INPUT FAIL-SAFE COUNTER (SIFSC)
0EEH SOLICITED OUTPUT FAIL-SAFE COUNTER (SOFSC)
0F5H REFERENCE FAIL-SAFE COUNTER (REFFSC)

DIAGNOSTIC REGISTERS
0F0H RETRY ALGORITHM (RTYA)
0F1H ACCUMULATED RETRY COUNT (RCNT)
0F2H DIAGNOSTIC PARAMETERS (DIAG)

NO ACCESS REGISTERS
ADDRESSES 00H THRU 07FH

280640-8

Figure 3-2. MPC Interconnect Registers

3.3 Partioning of Functions between the Microcontroller, CPU, and MPC

Because of the close association of the CPU and the microcontroller to the MPC, a number of interdependencies arise—especially during initialization and diagnostic testing. Some of the more complex functions such as dual-port memory control and fail-safe counters actually cross component boundaries. Thus, one must view the complete interface as a functional subsystem. The following discussion highlights the more important interdependencies regarding the interconnect subsystem.

3.3.1 MPC DIAGNOSTIC TESTING

A special feature of the MPC is its ability to simulate message passing operations to itself without presenting data to the iPSB bus interface. This mode is termed "MPC Loopback Testing" and is enabled by the iPSB Diagnostic Register in the iPSB Control Record. This causes the microcontroller to set the Reset-Not-Complete Out (RSTNCOUT) bit in the MPC General Parameter Register. The result is that any messages the local CPU loads into the MPC transmit buffers are routed directly to the MPC receive buffers. While this is happening, the MPC Buffered Address/Data bus

(BAD<31..0>*) is active and it is necessary for the microcontroller to tristate the iPSB buffer logic by preventing the iPSB Transceiver Output Enable (**BTROE***) signal from going active low. Note that MPC loopback testing is only allowed while **RSTNC*** is being asserted by the host agent.

3.3.2 DUAL-PORT MEMORY CONTROL

When another iPSB agent selects your board to participate as a replier in a memory reference, the address recognition function for dual-port memory is performed by the MPC based on the starting and ending addresses programmed into the MPC interconnect registers during initialization. When an address match is found, the MPC will drive the **SEL*** signal to your dual-port memory controller and wait for a **COM*** or **ERR*** signal to be returned before completing the cycle. During this transaction, the MPC provides all parity generation and checking, system control, and wait-state signal generation services to the iPSB bus interface. Valid address selection may occur on any 64-kByte boundary within the 4-Gbyte memory space; however, it is advisable to include value checking in your microcontroller firmware to ensure that the user doesn't enable more memory than is physically present on the board. Only one bank of contiguous memory is supported when using the MPC dual-port functions.

3.3.3 MESSAGE RETRY OPERATIONS

When message traffic is arriving faster than the local CPU can receive it, the MPC FIFO buffers will overflow and some form of flow control must be initiated. The MPC has a special retry mechanism for this condition that is controlled through registers accessible to the microcontroller. Retry is enabled by setting a bit in the MPC Diagnostic Parameters Register and the delay between retries is selected in the Retry Algorithm Register. The Accumulated Retry Count Register indicates how many Negative Acknowledge (NACK) errors have occurred for a given message attempt. The Accumulated Retry Count Register is used with the Retry Algorithm Register to tune system performance by selecting the most effective retry interval.

3.3.4 FAIL-SAFE COUNTER FUNCTIONS

When the MPC issues an iPSB buffer request, there is no guarantee that a buffer grant will be returned in a reasonable amount of time. If enabled, the MPC Reference Fail-Safe Counter will cause an error interrupt if no buffer grant is received by the end of a timeout period (typically 1.5 seconds). Likewise, a similar fail-safe timeout exists for reference operations in the unlikely event that they are unable to acquire the iPSB bus due to arbitration or Bus Clock (BLCK) problems. In either case, the microcontroller acts as a programmable timebase by writing to the MPC fail-safe counter addresses on a periodic basis in response to an internal timer interrupt (Figure 3-3). When the MPC starts the buffer request or reference operation, it enables the fail-safe timeout and waits for the operation to complete. If the microcontroller is able to write to a MPC fail-safe counter address four times before the bus cycle completes; then a timeout interrupt is asserted to alert the CPU to the problem. Note that fail-safe counter functions should be disabled during debugging since breakpoints set by human intervention may prevent the MPC from completing an operation before a timeout occurs.

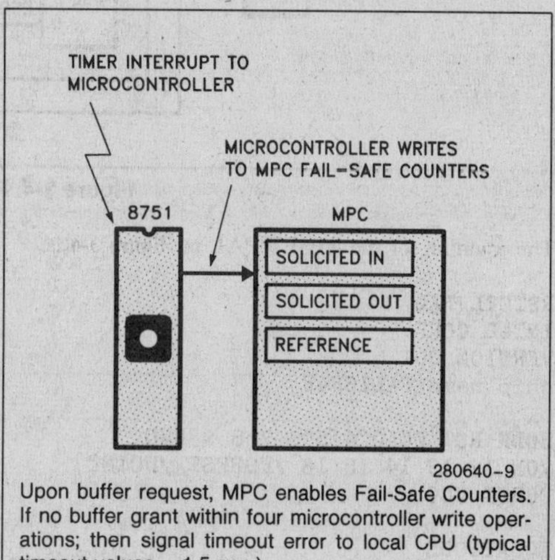

Upon buffer request, MPC enables Fail-Safe Counters. If no buffer grant within four microcontroller write operations; then signal timeout error to local CPU (typical timeout values −1.5 sec.).

Figure 3-3. MPC Fail-Safe Counters

3.4 Multibus II Reset Conditions

In a Multibus II backplane, the **RST*** signal is used for the system-wide reset. Additionally, the **DCLOW*** signal designates power-fail indication and the **PROT*** signal designates an early warning battery back-up control. One of the options available to the board designer is to use combination logic in association with the microcontroller to further define three categories of reset conditions: cold-start, warm-start, and local reset. In Figure 3-4, the reset circuitry that gives a board the capability to distinguish between these events is shown. The reset control logic (in the PAL16R4B) signals a cold-start whenever reset is accompanied by a low power condition and signals a warm-start in all other cases. Local resets are generated by an interconnect operation to the microcontroller, which then pulses the CPU reset line.

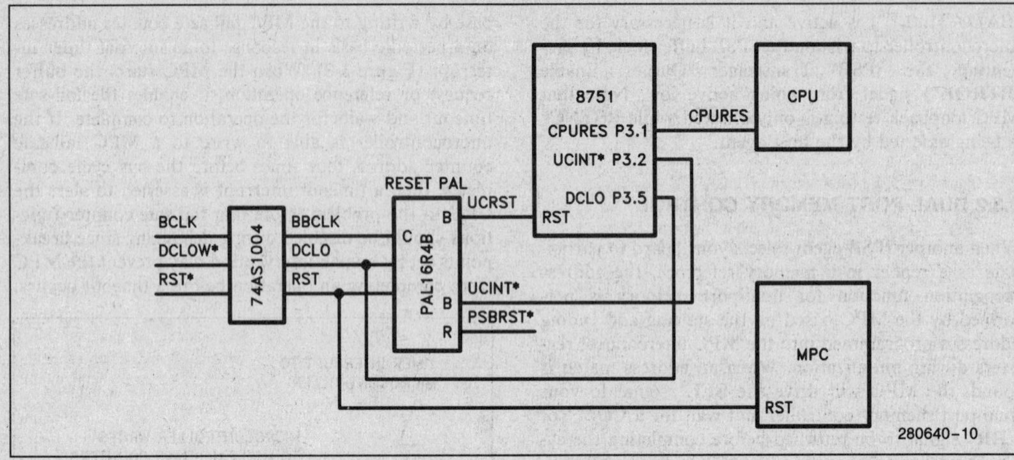

Figure 3-4. Reset Hardware

The equation for the RESET PAL in Figure 3-4 is:

```
RSTCTL PAL
INTeL CORP
VERSION 001
chip name PAL16R4B

BCLK RST DCLO 4 5 6 7 8 9 GND
/OE 12 13 14 15 16 /PSBRST /UCINT
UCRST VCC

EQUATIONS

PSBRST = RST
UCINT = PSBRST * /DCLO * /UCRST
/UCRST = /PSBRST + (/DCLO * /UCRST)
```

3.4.1 COLD-START AND RECOVERY RESET

A cold-start condition represents the state of the backplane following a power-on sequence, while the recovery reset represents the state of the backplane following power failure situations. The CSM will cycle through its normal sequence of assigning cardslot and arbitration IDs during a 50 ms period while the **RST*** signal is active low. The iPSB reset signal is buffered in on each agent and then routed directly to the MPC and the microcontroller. When reset is released from the iPSB, the microcontroller will force a reset to the local CPU and then execute some rudimentary BISTs (initialization checks). The interconnect template will be loaded with default values and the MPC gets initialized to its default state. The CPU is then released from reset to execute its power-on BISTs (some of which are likely to alter the contents of memory by overwriting data previously present).

In the firmware supplied with this guide, the CPU must clear the RSTNC* bit in interconnect within 30 seconds after power-on or else the microcontroller will again assert reset to the CPU on the assumption that something is seriously wrong with the board. (This is done to ensure that the failure of a single system board will not prevent the remainder of the system from coming alive due to **RSTNC*** being held active low.)

3.4.2 WARM-START RESET

A warm-start condition is normally the result of a human operator pressing a front panel reset button or programming the CSM for a system-wide reset via interconnect. The sequence of events is similar to the cold-start except that memory will remain unchanged, BISTs are not run, and all interconnect configuration registers remain unchanged. Warm resets are very useful for recovering from a hung system condition during debugging because the system cycles through reset much more quickly and retains all configuration and error status information.

3.4.3 LOCAL RESET

Local resets selectively return all circuitry behind the bus interface on a single agent to a known condition without effecting any other system boards. Local reset is generatcd through interconnect programming and does not disturb the contents of local memory or the interconnect configuration registers. The microcontroller BIST diagnostics are not run and the agent returns quickly to a known condition. Local resets are often used to recover from a partial system failure condition caused by improper programming or single agent failures.

There are two types of local reset supported: self-toggling and non-toggling. The Interconnect Interface Specification describes a local reset control (bit 7) of the General Control Register in the Interconnect Header Record of each board. This is a non-toggling reset that holds the agent inactive until specifically cleared by further interconnect programming. This feature allows an external agent to clamp reset to that board, thereby taking it off-line until further notice. Note that the board will not respond to other resets (warm or local) until this bit is cleared. This type of local reset is not suitable if the intent is for the agent to reset itself since the board is incapable of returning from the reset condition to clear the bit.

For this reason, many Multibus II boards offer a self-toggling reset control in the Board Specific Record that will clear itself soon after being set (typically 20 ms). One might be tempted to use this register for all local resets in preference to the General Control Register, however, it is not supported on all Multibus II boards and its absolute location in the interconnect template will depend on how many other function records precede it. In common practice, the local reset bit in the General Control Register is a better solution in all cases except self-toggling resets.

3.5 Initialization of the Microcontroller following Reset

Immediately following a cold or recovery reset, all bus interface components must be initialized to a known state. The microcontroller is normally the first to undergo initialization since it will be released from reset before the CPU and has the added responsibility for the MPC interconnect registers. Flowcharts of the program flow in the microcontroller are provided in Appendix B.

The first priority of the microcontroller is to establish its own environment by creating a stack and loading the Special Function Registers (SFR's), which control the on-chip resources such as the ports, timers, and interrupt priorities. Next, the microcontroller initialization checks are run as a basic "sanity check" of itself. There are three BISTs in the initialization sequence:

a. Microcontroller RAM—A simple read/modify/write test to on-chip RAM locations.

b. Microcontroller ROM—A check sum test on the on-chip ROM.

c. IAD Bus and MPC Accessibility—A "walking ones" pattern is written to several MPC registers and read back to verify functionality of the MPC interconnect registers and the IAD bus.

The interconnect registers that reside in RAM (i.e., those that are R/W), are now loaded with their default values. These default values are copied from a ROM-based default table (the DFTABLE), specified at configuration time. Next, the microcontroller on-chip timer/counters and the MPC interconnect registers are initialized. If the user has any unique initialization requirements, a call to the INIT_USER procedure is made at this time. Up to this point, the local CPU has been held in reset and the iPSB transceivers are being held tristate. Now all of these resources are released and timer/counters startup and the CPU has 30 seconds to clear the RSTNC* bit in interconnect. The microcontroller then enters the mainline routine of the firmware.

3.6 Interrupts Driven Firmware Operations

Figure 3-5 illustrates the various interrupt sources which drive the interconnect functions on the microcontroller. The mainline code consists of very simple polling operations that execute with interrupts disabled. These operations consist of polling for the Non-Maskable Interrupt (NMI), BIST, and reset conditions, plus updating the front panel LEDs. At the end of each pass through the mainline code, interrupts are enabled prior to executing the jump instruction that starts the next pass through the mainline code.

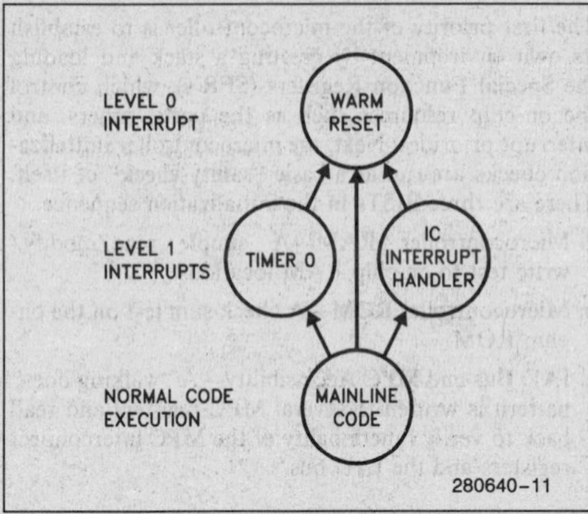

Figure 3-5. Microcontroller Interrupt Sources

Nearly all of the important operations within interconnect are interrupt driven. These include the IC interrupt handler (which services the MPC **IREQ*** signal), a reset interrupt handler, and a group of timer based functions. A general description of these operations follows.

3.6.1 INTERCONNECT INTERRUPT HANDLER

The IC interrupt handler is called whenever the MPC signals to the microcontroller that a request for interconnect service is pending (**IREQ*** has been asserted). The microcontroller responds by reading the MPC's interconnect reference registers to determine which register in interconnect has been requested; whether this is a read or write operation; and whether this is the local CPU or an iPSB agent generating the request. If the register number is beyond the End of Template (EOT) record; then no error status is posted and the interconnect operation is terminated. Otherwise the microcontroller begins a table driven look up of that register and completes the interconnect cycle.

3.6.2 INTERCONNECT READ OPERATIONS

Interconnect read operations are relatively simple because no need exists for checking the access rights or data values (see Figure 3-6). The register number (REGNUM) is used as an 8-bit offset into the read vector table (RVTABLE), which then supplies an offset into the read jump table (RJTABLE) containing a long jump instruction to the address of the read routine. This indirect look up technique is used to allow several different registers to share the same read routine and to improve code compaction. Indirect jump tables also allow the user to add their own read routines to the template following the interconnect core functions.

Once the read operation is complete, the results are available to the IC interrupt handler in the ICDATA register. The data is copied to the MPC IDAT register and completion status is posted. From the IC interrupt handler, control passes back into the mainline code. Note that interrupts were enabled within the IC interrupt handler (just prior to executing the long jump instruction), and that the reset interrupt has a higher priority.

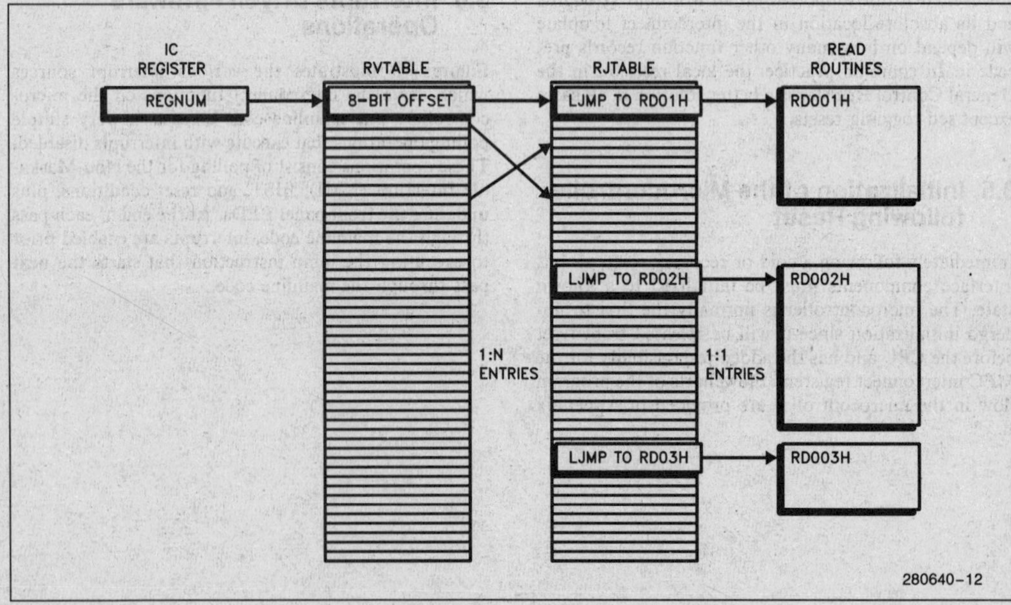

Figure 3-6. Indirect Jump Tables for Read Routines

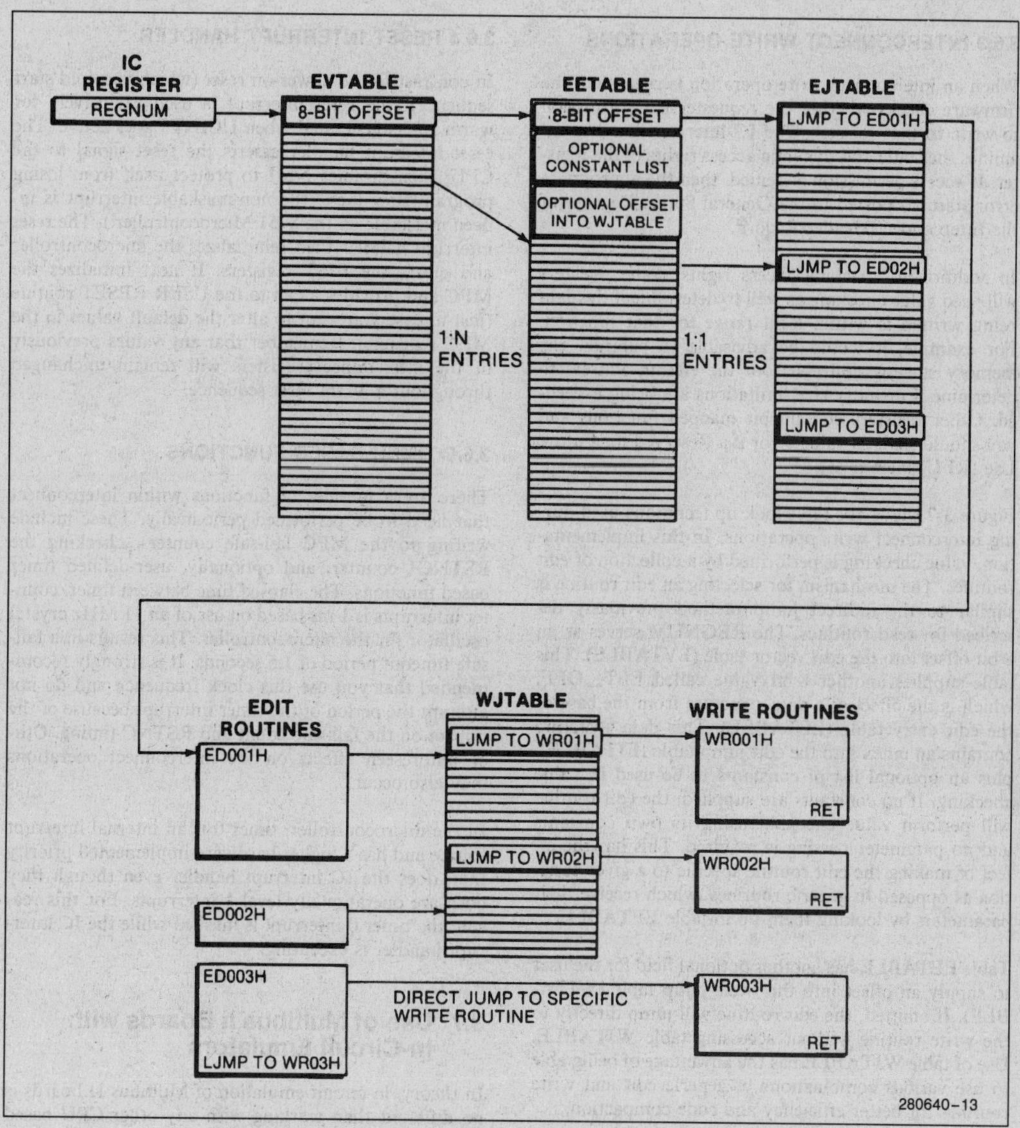

Figure 3-7. Indirect Jump Tables for Edit and Write Routines

3.6.3 INTERCONNECT WRITE OPERATIONS

When an interconnect write operation is requested, the firmware checks whether the requester has permission to write to that register. The IC interrupt handler examines the static and dynamic access rights of the register. If access permission is denied, then the appropriate error status is posted in the General Status Register of the Interconnect Header Record.

In addition to checking access rights, some registers will need value checking as well to determine if the data being written is within legal range for that function. For example, it would be advisable to subtract the memory starting address from the ending address to determine if memory size limitations are being exceeded. Other registers contain bit mapped functions and you should signal a value error if a Reserved for Future Use (RFU) bit was set.

Figure 3-7 shows the table look up technique used during interconnect write operations. In this implementation, value checking is performed by a collection of edit routines. The mechanism for selecting an edit routine is similar to the indirect jump method previously described for read routines. The **REGNUM** serves as an 8-bit offset into the edit vector table (EVTABLE). This table supplies another 8-bit value called EET_OFF, which is the offset of a data structure from the base of the edit entry table (EETABLE). This data structure contains an index into the edit jump table (EJTABLE), plus an optional list of constants to be used in value checking. If no constants are supplied, the edit routine will perform value checking using its own constants and no parameter passing is required. This has the effect of making the edit routine specific to a given function as opposed to generic routines, which receive their parameters by looking them up in table EETABLE.

Table EETABLE has another optional field for the user to supply an offset into the write jump table (WJTABLE). If omitted, the edit routine will jump directly to the write routine without accessing table WJTABLE. Use of table WJTABLE has the advantage of being able to use various combinations of generic edit and write routines for better efficiency and code compaction.

The indirect jump method of read, write, and edit services requires slightly more code space and software overhead than direct calling of register service routines, but offers a simple and extensible mechanism for users to form their own interconnect templates without needing to know the details contained within the core interconnect module. Instructions on how to load these tables and generate the final object code are presented in Section 5.

3.6.4 RESET INTERRUPT HANDLER

In contrast to the power-on reset (which is a cold start sequence), the reset interrupt is used exclusively for warm resets generated when **UCINT*** goes active. The reset interrupt handler asserts the reset signal to the CPU; then disables NMI to protect itself from losing program flow (yes—the non-maskable interrupt is indeed maskable on the 8751 Microcontroller!). The reset interrupt handler then reinitializes the microcontroller and clears the BIST registers. It next initializes the MPC and provides a call to the USER RESET routine (just in case you want to alter the default values in the MPC registers). Remember that any values previously in the interconnect registers will remain unchanged throughout a warm reset sequence.

3.6.5 TIMER BASED FUNCTIONS

There are a number of functions within interconnect that need to be performed periodically. These include writing to the MPC fail-safe counters, checking the RSTNC* counter, and optionally, user-defined timer based functions. The elapsed time between timer/counter interrupts is 1 ms based on use of an 11 MHz crystal oscillator for the microcontroller. This results in a fail-safe timeout period of 1.5 seconds. It is strongly recommended that you use this clock frequency and do not attempt the period of the timer interrupt because of the impact on the fail-safe count and RSTNC timing. Other unforeseen effects on the interconnect operations may also occur.

In the microcontroller, timer 0 is an internal interrupt source and has a higher hardware-implemented priority than does the IC interrupt handler even though they both are operationally level 1 interrupts. For this reason, the timer 0 interrupt is masked while the IC interrupt handler is executing.

3.7 Use of Multibus II Boards with In-Circuit Emulators

In theory, in-circuit emulation of Multibus II boards is no different than working with any other CPU based design. However, due to the indirect reset technique used within the interconnect subsystem, problems with reset initialization of the emulator probe are not uncommon. Most of these can be easily resolved by having the emulator issue port I/O commands to clear the RSTNC* bit in interconnect before a timeout occurs (typically 25 seconds). In some cases even this action will be inadequate because many ICE™ products will not tolerate a condition where reset is held continuously active. The solution to this problem is to disable the RSTNC* timeout function in the microcontroller. The core firmware design includes a jumper selectable option to allow in-circuit emulators to operate without reset problems.

3.8 Avoiding iPSB Timeouts

The reader will by now appreciate that interconnect bus cycles can be potentially long due to the extensive amount of processing a microcontroller completes to satisfy an interconnect reference. Performance within the interconnect address space is not an issue since interconnect bus cycles are run during system initialization and diagnostic tests, but cycles are rarely run during normal system operation because of their affect on the bus bandwidth. If, for any reason an interconnect bus cycle on the iPSB cannot complete within 1 ms; then an iPSB timeout will cancel the transaction and an error status posted. Therefore, users are cautioned not to attempt extensive processing within their interconnect read, write, and edit routines. Worst case timing analysis should be run on all new interconnect function records to avoid unexpected timeouts. More information on this topic is provided along with examples in Section 5.

4.0 INTERCONNECT HARDWARE DESIGN

4.1 Microcontroller Pin Assignments

The 8751 Microcontroller is well configured with I/O port facilities. In addition to the bidirectional Interconnect Address/Data bus (IAD<7..0>) connected to Port 0 (P0), there are 24 additional bidirectional lines and a number of port expansion techniques that can be employed. The core interconnect design will consume some of these resources, but beyond that, the user is free to dedicate the remaining I/O lines in any desired way. A variety of hardware design examples are presented here to satisfy the more typical requirements.

4.1.1 THE INTERCONNECT ADDRESS/DATA BUS

The initial design of the Message Passing Coprocessor (MPC) anticipated that the interconnect subsystem would be partitioned in a microcontroller of the 8751 or 8749 family. For this reason, the MPC provides a directly compatible multiplexed IAD bus requiring no external logic to the microcontroller. From a hardware viewpoint, the MPC is a slave to the microcontroller. The MPC supplies an external interrupt **(IREQ*)** whenever it needs service and the microcontroller satisfies the request. The eight multiplexed IAD lines are taken directly from P0 of the microcontroller and interface timing is based on the microcontroller's Interconnect address strobe **(IAST)**, Read **(IRD*)**, and Write **(IWR*)** control signals. While the primary purpose of the IAD bus is to provide the communications path between the MPC and interconnect subsystem, it should be noted that the MPC will remain tristate for addresses 0 through 7FH. This condition presents an opportunity for I/O port expansion and is discussed later in this chapter.

4.1.2 RESERVED PINS ON THE 8751

In addition to the IAD bus on P0, the eight lines of Port 3 (P3) and two lines on Port 2 (P2) are reserved in support of the core interconnect design. (P3 is completely dedicated to hardware functions.) Figure 4-1 is a simplified schematic of the basic hardware requirements that guarantee proper functioning of the interconnect core. This includes the front panel LED, reset inputs and outputs, interrupt sources, and provisions for MPC loopback testing (discussed in Section 3).

Port function assignments are based on a series of equate statements contained in the program file DFT.MOD. If your interconnect design maintains the configuration shown in Figure 4-1 and defined in DFT.MOD; then there will be no need to modify the equate statements. A total of 14 port pins are available for user-defined I/O schemes. If necessary, the microcontroller pin assignments can be changed by modifying DFT.MOD (contained in the \ICFW\SRC subdirectory).

4.2 External TTL Options

Having completed the hardware design requirements, it is time to include the user hardware support options you have decided on. If your board requires only the core functions, then the hardware design is complete and prototyping can begin. Continued reading of this chapter may give you additional ideas for features you may wish to add. Other readers will already have a well defined functional objective and should be able to satisfy their requirements using one or more of the techniques given below. Bear in mind that the application examples described in this chapter are only suggestions and a combination of techniques are used. This underscores the need for good engineering discipline—always perform the AC/DC timing analysis and loading calculations!

The range of possibilities is limited only by your own imagination, but practical considerations will prevail. Keep aware of board real estate and bus loading requirements, expected implementation costs, and ask yourself if the feature is really worth the effort. With these considerations in mind, we will now examine some of the many options available for hardware design.

5

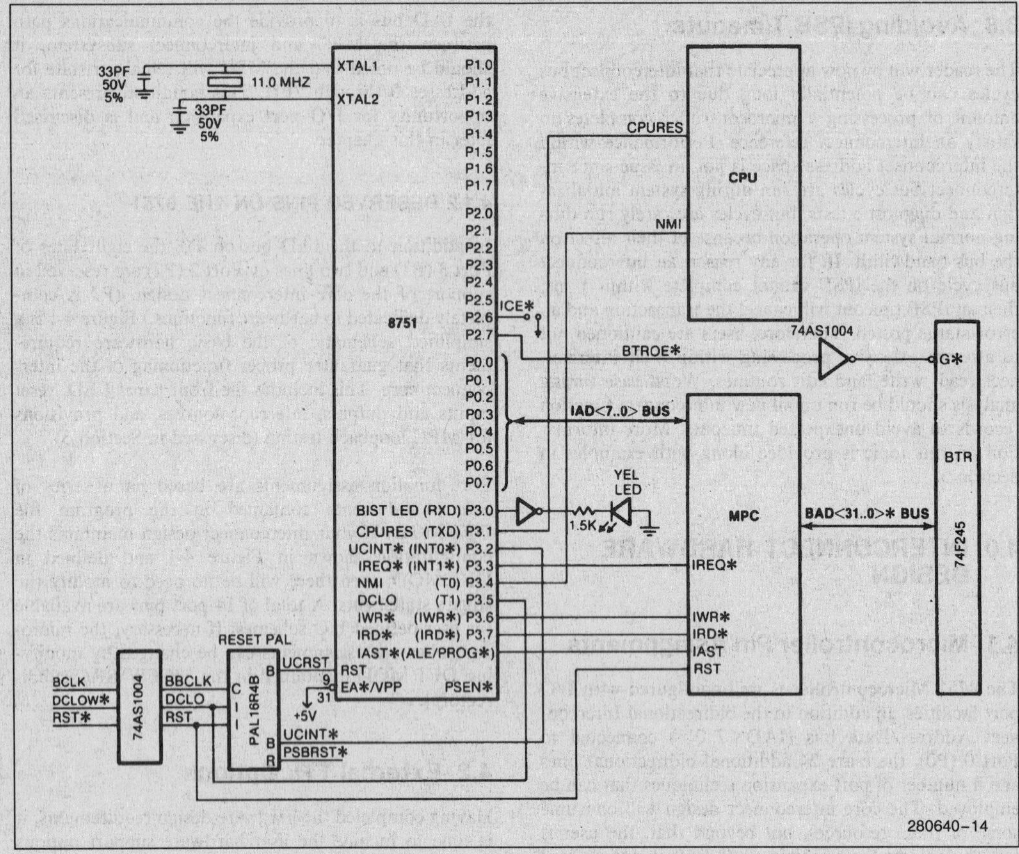

Figure 4-1. Interconnect Core Hardware Design

4.2.1 MICROCONTROLLER INPUT OPTIONS

On boards that contain user-supplied optional devices, it is desirable to include an interconnect status register to report whether or not the device is present. If present, system software can program the device with the appropriate driver. Some common examples include the Single Board Extension Bus (iSBX™) MULTIMODULE™ compatible board products, numeric processors, and DMA controllers.

A technique used to detect a board's presence is to identify a port pin that ties to ground and then have the microcontroller read that pin. The P1 and P2 lines of the 8751 Microcontroller are internally pulled up, which makes module not present for these lines always read a logical "1". Verifying if a chip is present is more difficult since the component needs the ground pin for its own power consumption. The preferred technique here is to ask the user to install a jumper and in that way, the microcontroller can report correct status.

Figure 4-2 schematically diagrams various techniques used to input to an 8751 Microcontroller. A typical technique is to require the microcontroller to read jumper inputs. (Although Multibus II has reduced the number of jumpers required, it hasn't eliminated them.) In cases where jumpers are unavoidable (such as chip select jumpers and component present indicators), it would be helpful to report the state of those jumpers with an interconnect status register. An example is the EPROM size register found on many Intel boards. If you have only a small number of jumpers, then a direct connection to one of the microcontroller's port pins will suffice. For boards with a larger number of jumpers, buffering will be necessary. The buffer output enable term is generated by a port pin in association with the microcontroller's **IRD*** signal.

In the example shown, a read instruction to P2.5 will input data from the jumpers. This could be coded in ASM-51 as:

```
clrb       P2.5  ;activate CS for jumper
                 ;input buffer
mov   R0,  00h   ;load dummy address
movx  A    @R0,  ;read jumper inputs
setb       P2.5  ;deselect buffer
```

4.2.2 MICROCONTROLLER OUTPUT OPTIONS

Outputs from the microcontroller are used at various control points throughout Multibus II boards. Simple functions such as the LED's can use a direct connection to a microcontroller port pin. More complex functions will require a connection to the buffered IAD bus. As a general rule, whenever more than two loads are on the IAD bus, it will need buffering. The MPC must be connected directly to the IAD bus to ensure proper timing. The schematic in Figure 4-3 diagrams some typical applications.

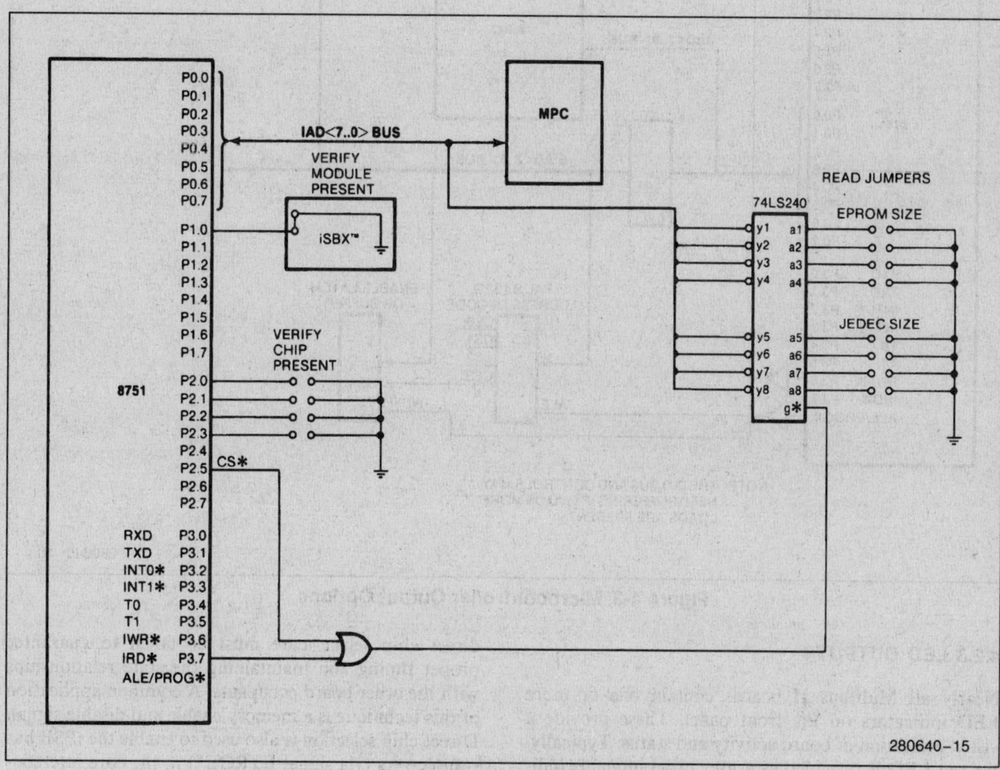

Figure 4-2. Microcontroller Input Options

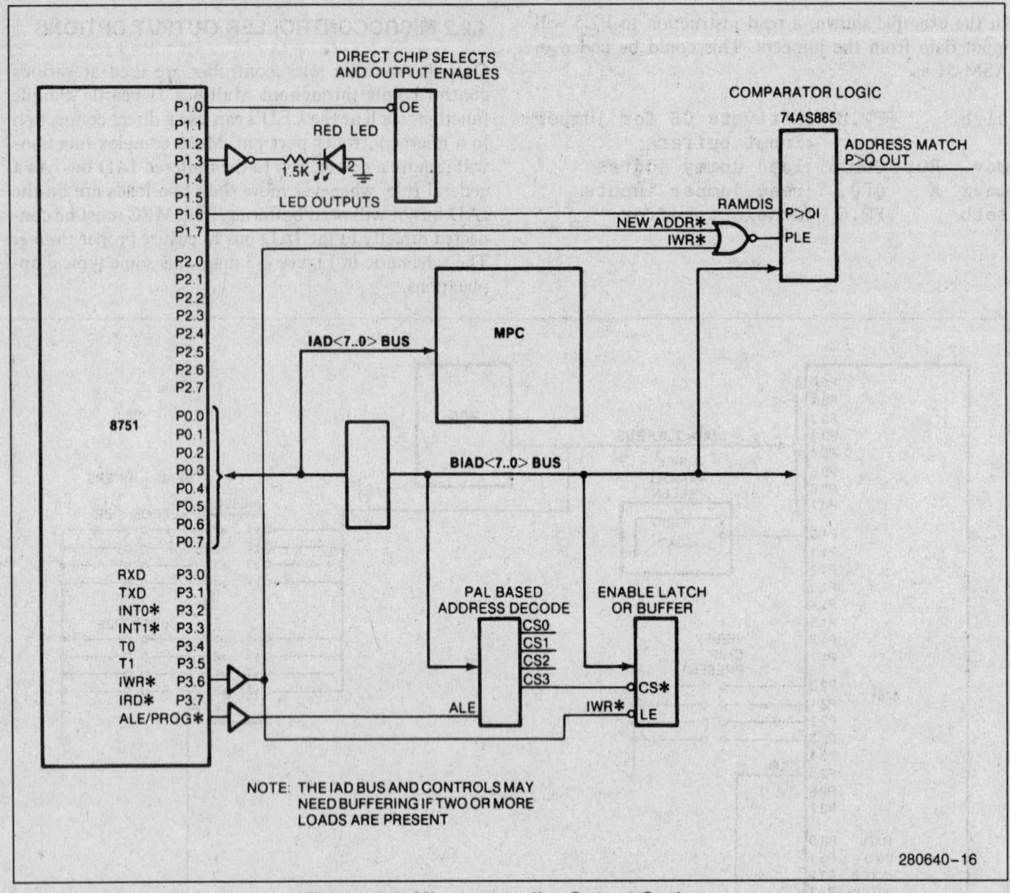

Figure 4-3. Microcontroller Output Options

4.2.3 LED OUTPUTS

Nearly all Multibus II boards contain one or more LED indicators on the front panel. These provide a visual indication of board activity and status. Typically, the red LED is provided as a user programmable indicator and is illuminated by the setting or clearing of a bit in a control register. A green LED is often used to indicate CPU activity. If the green LED is present, drive it with an Address Latch Enable (**ALE**) signal or equivalent. The yellow LED, if present, is lit during diagnostic testing and represents the ORed condition of the following bits in the BIST Slave Status Register:

BIST running + BIST failed + RSTNC timeout.

4.2.4 OUTPUT ENABLES AND CHIP SELECTS

A microcontroller port pin can be used for a bus transceiver, **ALE**, or a direct chip enable. When used as a direct chip select, care must be taken to guarantee proper timing and maintaining the state relationships with the other board occupants. A common application of this technique is a memory enable and disable signal. Direct chip selection is also used to enable the iPSB bus transceivers (via signal **BTROE***) in the core interconnect design.

4.2.5 ADDRESS DECODE ON THE IAD BUS

The IAD bus address can be mapped to generate chip selects using simple "1 of n" decoders gated by a **ALE** signal. As an alternative, a PAL-based decoder can be used. A variety of chip select signals can be generated using this technique. Some designs use the chip selects to enable secondary latches and buffers.

The ASM-51 coding for the circuit shown in Figure 4-3 could look something like this:

```
mov A,  ICDATA      ;Get value being written
mov R0, Latch_addr  ;Load the address of the
                    ;latch
movx@R0,A           ;Generate chip select and
                    ;write data
```

4.2.6 COMPARATORS

Comparators are often used for address boundary checks in association with Local Bus Extension (iLBX™) or local memory. A comparator logic example is shown in Figure 4-3. A select term can be generated on greater than, less than, or equal to the data placed on the IAD bus. The set point for the comparison is latched-in during the data phase of the microcontroller's P0 bus. In this way, a port pin (the **NEW ADDR*** signal) can combine with the microcontroller's **IWR*** to control when the address comparison is enabled. The ASM-51 code to load a new address into the comparator could look like this:

```
mov   A,    ICDATA    ;Get the new setpoint
clrb        NEW_ADDR  ;This is the PLE signal
mov   R0,   00h       ;Dummy address
movx  @R0,  A         ;Output, the new address
setb        NEW_ADDR  ;Latch it in
```

4.3 Bidirectional I/O on the IAD Bus

Even a modest implementation of interconnect can easily exceed the available port resources of the microcontroller, especially when a byte wide data path is required. For these applications, numerous port expansion techniques exist. Your choice of which technique is best in your particular design will be based on such factors as on board space requirements, cost, bidirectionality, and ease of programming. An example of interfacing a complex peripheral to the IAD bus is shown in Figure 4-4. The ASM-51 coding for this circuit is very straightforward since device selection is based on an IAD bus address.

```
mov R0,      IO_ADDR ;This is the address of
                     ;the device
movxA,       @R0     ;Input from the device
mov ICDATA,A         ;Save the data

mov R0,      IO_ADDR ;This is the address of
                     ;the device
mov A,       ICCNTR  ;Load a control value for
                     ;output
movx@R0,     A       ;Output to the device
```

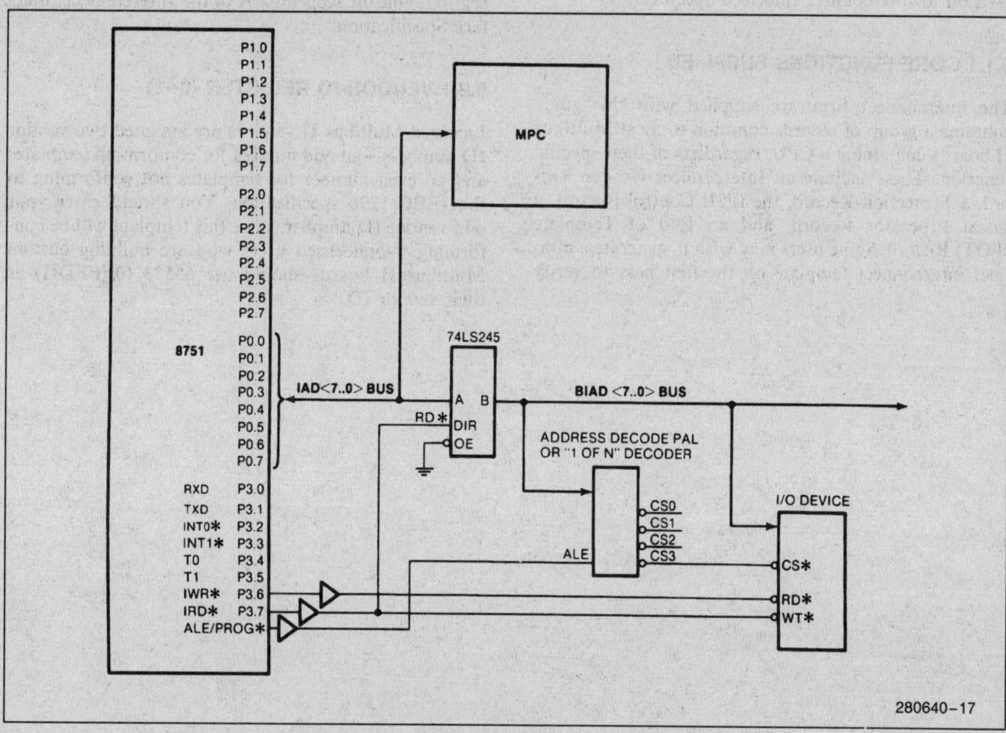

Figure 4-4. Bidirectional I/O on the IAD Bus

5.0 DEFINING THE INTERCONNECT TEMPLATE

5.1 What Goes into Interconnect?

The design implementation phase of your interconnect subsystem begins with a careful evaluation of what functions to include. Common core functions are supplied on the accompanying diskette and you can add supplemental records to the interconnect template for board-level features you intend to support. Many frequently used function records are already defined in the Interconnect Interface Specification and the reader is requested to review this document before proceeding. If none of the furnished function records meet your needs, you can create your own function record using one of the record types available for vendor definition or board specific functions.

If your function record is likely to have broad industry appeal and could be used by other vendors to support similar functions, you may wish to fill out the petition application included with the reader comment sheet at rear of this guide. Your petition will be evaluated based on suitability for a general class of hardware, industry standardization, and feedback from the Multibus II user community, and if accepted, published in the next revision to Interconnect Interface Specification.

5.1.1 CORE FUNCTIONS SUPPLIED

The interconnect firmware supplied with this guide contains a group of records common to most Multibus II boards containing a CPU, regardless of their specific function. These include an Interconnect Header Record, a Protection Record, the iPSB Control Record, a Local Processor Record, and an End of Template (EOT) Record. Some users may wish to generate a minimal interconnect template on the first pass to verify the operation of their base har are before adding their own advanced functions. This approach simplifies debugging and allows new features to be added incrementally.

5.1.2 GETTING STARTED: THE INTERCONNECT WORKSHEET

Unless you are using the supplied interconnect template without modification, it is a two-step process to complete the configuration tables. In the first step, you will fill-in a worksheet with information about default values, RAM usage, read/write and edit routine numbers, and other details. Figure 5-1 is an example of such a worksheet. While completing these tables, you might notice opportunities to reduce code size by making use of generic read, write, and edit routines. In the second step, the information in the worksheet is copied into a series of tables used by the configuration macros.

5.2 The Interconnect Header Record

The interconnect template begins with a standard Interconnect Header Record. This record contains fields that require specific values supplied by the user. You should fill-in this information in as we proceed through this chapter. For a detailed discussion concerning each register, consult Appendix A of the Interconnect Interface Specification.

5.2.1 VENDOR ID REGISTER (0–1)

Licensed Multibus II vendors are assigned two vendor ID numbers—an odd number for conforming templates and an even number for templates not conforming to the IEEE 1296 specification. You should enter your odd vendor ID number, since this template will be conforming. Nonlicensed users who are building custom Multibus II boards should use 65533 (0FFFDH) as their vendor ID.

REGISTER NAME	GAR	RAM	DFT	RRT	ERT	WRT	CONST	EET	VAR
HEADER RECORD									
VENDOR ID, LOW BYTE	0	0	____	000H	000H	?	?	000H	?
VENDOR ID, HIGH BYTE	0	0	____	000H	000H	?	?	000H	?
BOARD ID, CHARACTER 1	0	0	____	000H	000H	?	?	000H	?
BOARD ID, CHARACTER 2	0	0	____	000H	000H	?	?	000H	?
BOARD ID, CHARACTER 3	0	0	____	000H	000H	?	?	000H	?
BOARD ID, CHARACTER 4	0	0	____	000H	000H	?	?	000H	?
BOARD ID, CHARACTER 5	0	0	____	000H	000H	?	?	000H	?
BOARD ID, CHARACTER 6	0	0	____	000H	000H	?	?	000H	?
BOARD ID, CHARACTER 7	0	0	____	000H	000H	?	?	000H	?
BOARD ID, CHARACTER 8	0	0	____	000H	000H	?	?	000H	?
BOARD ID, CHARACTER 9	0	0	____	000H	000H	?	?	000H	?
BOARD ID, CHARACTER 10	0	0	____	000H	000H	?	?	000H	?
INTEL RESERVED	0	0	000H	000H	000H	?	?	000H	?
INTEL RESERVED	0	0	000H	000H	000H	?	?	000H	?
INTEL RESERVED	0	0	000H	000H	000H	?	?	000H	?
INTEL RESERVED	0	0	000H	000H	000H	?	?	000H	?
HARDWARE TEST REV NO.	0	0	____	000H	000H	?	?	000H	?
CLASS ID	0	0	____	000H	000H	?	?	000H	?
RFU	0	0	000H	000H	000H	?	?	000H	?
RFU	0	0	000H	000H	000H	?	?	000H	?
RFU	0	0	000H	000H	000H	?	?	000H	?
RESET STATUS RGTR	0	1	003H	001H	000H	?	?	000H	RST
PROGRAM TABLE INDEX	1	1	000H	001H	001H	000H	00H	001H	PTI
NMI ENABLE RGTR	1	1	000H	001H	001H	000H	38H	002H	NMI_EN
GENERAL STATUS	0	1	000H	003H	000H	?	?	000H	GEN_STS
GENERAL CONTROL	1	1	000H	001H	001H	002H	78H	003H	GEN_CTL
BIST-SUPPORT-LEVEL	0	1	000H	001H	005H	000H	18H,07H,04H	004H	BIST_SL
BIST-DATA-IN	1	1	000H	001H	001H	000H	00H	001H	BIST_DI
BIST-DATA-OUT	0	1	000H	001H	001H	000H	00H	001H	BIST_DO
BIST-SLAVE-STATUS	0	1	010H	001H	001H	000H	00H	001H	BIST_SS
BIST-MASTER-STATUS	1	1	020H	001H	001H	000H	50H	005H	BIST_MS
BIST-TEST-ID	0	1	000H	001H	002H	000H	01H,0FEH	006H	BIST_TID
PROTECTION RECORD									
PROTECTION RECORD TYPE	0	0	00BH	000H	000H	?	?	000H	PROT_OFF
RECORD LENGTH	0	0	002H	000H	000H	?	?	000H	?
PROTECTION LEVEL RGTR	0	2	000H	004H	001H	003H	0FEH	007H	UACRS
RFU	0	0	000H	000H	000H	?	?	000H	?
PSB CONTROL RECORD									
PSB CONTROL RECORD TYPE	0	0	006H	000H	000H	?	?	000H	PSB_CTL_OFF
RECORD LENGTH	0	0	006H	000H	000H	?	?	000H	?
PSB SLOT ID NO.	0	0	000H	002H	000H	?	?	000H	?
PSB ARBITRATION ID NO.	1	0	000H	002H	003H	?	?	008H	?
PSB ERROR RGTR	1	0	000H	002H	001H	001H	0FFH	009H	?
PSB CONTROL/STATUS RGTR	1	1	01FH	005H	001H	004H	63H	00AH	PSB_CS
PSB DIAGNOSTICS RGTR	1	1	000H	002H	004H	?	?	00BH	PSB_DIAG
RFU	0	0	000H	000H	000H	?	?	000H	?

280640–18

Figure 5-1. Interconnect Configuration Worksheet (Sheet 1 of 2)

REGISTER NAME	GAR	RAM	DFT	RRT	ERT	WRT	CONST	EET	VAR
----LOCAL PROC RECORD----									
LOCAL PROC RECORD TYPE	0	0	013H	000H	000H	?	?	000H	?
RECORD LENGTH	0	0	003H	000H	000H	?	?	000H	?
LOCAL PROC CONTROL	0	0	000H	006H	001H	006H	0FEH	00CH	?
LOCAL PROC STATUS	0	0	000H	007H	000H	?	?	000H	?
RFU	0	0	000H	000H	000H	?	?	000H	?
---- END OF TEMPLATE RECORD ----									
EOT RECORD TYPE	0	0	0FFH	000H	000H	?	?	000H	EOT_OFF

280640-19

Figure 5-1. Interconnect Configuration Worksheet (Sheet 2 of 2)

5.2.2 BOARD ID REGISTERS (2–11)

These 10 registers contain the ASCII product code as described in your user's manual. You should avoid the use of nonprinting ASCII characters so the system software can display the product code verbatim on a CRT screen. If the product code is less than 10 characters, pad the remaining register fields with ASCII null characters (zeros).

5.2.3 HARDWARE TEST REVISION NUMBER REGISTER (16)

This register is part of a system of control for matching the firmware revision to the automatic test equipment used with that board. The master or local test handler software uses this as a mechanism for revision control of diagnostics.

5.2.4 CLASS ID REGISTER (17)

Determine your calss ID from the list supplied in the Interconnect Interface Specification. The class ID occupies the most significant nibble (4 bits) of the register and the subclass ID occupies the least significant nibble.

5.2.5 BIST SUPPORT LEVEL REGISTER (26)

The BIST Support Level Register defines the support level of the diagnostics on-board. This will determine which commands can be issued to your board via the BIST Data Input Register.

5.3 OPTIONAL USER FUNCTIONS

There is virtually no limit to the number and variety of function records that users can add to the core firmware—provided the following common sense guidelines are met:

a. A maximum of 256 interconnect registers are allowed due to the page limit length of the configuration tables. Most boards will need fewer than 100 registers.

b. The microcontroller you are using has certain resource limitations—the most pressing of which is on-chip RAM. Nested stack operations also require RAM, so you must avoid recursive procedures and nesting of calls beyond four levels in any of the USER code modules. Normally, it is preferable to pass parameters in registers rather than on the stack.

c. An interconnect request must complete operations within 1 ms to avoid an iPSB timeout. The actual time available to complete a USER routine is less than 0.5 ms because interconnect is dual ported and a local access can temporarily lockout an iPSB request. A timing analysis of your design will be done prior to PROMming the code (refer to paragraph 5.8.2). (Sheet 1 of 2)

d. Caution must be exercised whenever the potential for deadlock of a resource exists. Solutions to this problem include prioritization, reporting of error status, or timeout to guarantee that system hand does not occur.

e. User read, write and edit routines must follow the naming convention described in this chapter to guarantee that the macro expansion works properly. Any global variable names used within existing core modules are considered reserved and should not be used in your own procedures (ASM-51 and/or RL51 will report duplicate symbol errors). A list of existing public variables may be found in program file ICFW\SRC\USER.M (Sheet 2 of 2)OD.

5.4 Completing the Interconnect Configuration Worksheet

If you decided that a user-defined function record is to be incorporated in the interconnect template, then you must define the access rights, default values, and complete the remaining worksheet entries needed by the microcontroller firmware to support those features. You then write the functional read, write, and edit routines and tag them with appropriate labels. The new function record(s) must be inserted ahead of the EOT record of the core interconnect template.

As discussed in Chapter 3, the interconnect firmware uses a series of tables to associate a register with the correct read, write, and edit routine numbers. The information you supply here will be loaded into those tables during the code assembly process. In Figure 5-2, an example of a completed interconnect configuration worksheet for the core firmware is shown. The parameters that must be supplied for each interconnect register identified on the configuration worksheet are described below.

5.4.1 GLOBAL ACCESS RIGHTS

All interconnect registers are readable from both the local and the iPSB bus. The state of the Global Access Rights (GAR) bit determines whether the register can be written to by another iPSB agent. If this bit is 0, then the register is read only on the iPSB bus and edit routine ED00H is used. A register will be locally read/writable only if an edit routine other than ED00H is supplied for this entry. If the GAR bit is 1, then this register is read/writable on both interfaces and an edit routine must be supplied.

5.4.2 RAM USAGE

The microcontroller RAM is a precious resource and must be managed as efficiently as possible. Some registers in interconnect may contain static values that never change. These values should be stored in microcontroller ROM. In cases where the contents of an inteconnect register are variable, either a byte or a bit of RAM must be allocated to store data, unless the data can be read directly from a port. The microcontroller's bit manipulation features can be used when a full 8-bit register is not required. The RAM entry in the worksheet must specify whether to reserve a bit location (RAM = 2), a byte location (RAM = 1), or no memory at all (RAM = 0). If RAM memory is requested, then a name for the public variable for that location must be supplied (refer to paragraph 5.4.9).

5.4.3 DEFAULT VALUE

The Default Value (DFT) is a hex number placed in this register during a cold or recovery reset. If this is a static register, then the default value represents the permanent contents of that register. The default value is also placed into dynamic registers following a cold reset; however, the register contents may subsequently change due to reprogramming or environmental changes (e.g., reading a value from a port).

5.4.4 READ ROUTINE ENTRY

Read routines contain the code that actually perform the work in satisfying an interconnect read request. Eight read routines are used in the interconnect core firmware. These are listed below and all are user callable. Read routines are sequentially numbered from 00H to nnH and contain no numbering gaps. A single read routine may be referenced by several different interconnect registers. If you are adding a new read routine, the first available Read Routine (RRT) number would be RD08H. The value supplied for the RRT is the two digit hex portion of the read routine number.

RD00h	Load Default Value into ICDATA	Generic
RD01h	Get RAM Access Rights	Generic
RD02h	PSB Control/Status Register	Specific
RD03h	General Status Register	Specific
RD04h	Protection Level Register	Specific
RD05h	MPC General Parameter Register	Specific
RD06h	Local Processor Control Register	Specific
RD07h	Local Processor Status Register	Specific

5

```
;*****************************************************************
;
;  NAME:          TABGEN  (TABLE GENERATION)
;
;  DESCRIPTION:   USES ENTAB MACRO TO ASSOCIATE EACH IC
;                 REGISTER WITH:
;                         GAR - GLOBAL ACCESS RIGHTS
;                         RAM - RAM USEAGE (WHETHER OR
;                               NOT UC RAM IS NEEDED)
;                         DFT - DEFAULT VALUE
;                         RRT - READ ROUINTE NUMBER
;                         EET - EDIT ENTRY NUMBER
;                         VAR - SYMBOL FOR RAM/BIT
;                               VARIABLE
;
; UPDATE HISTORY: 5-14-87 JR UPDATE FOR IDX
;
;*****************************************************************
;       G R
;       A A
;       R M  DFT  RRT  EET  VAR
;------------- HEADER RECORD ------------------------
%ENTAB(0,0,001H,000H,000H,?)        ;VENDOR ID, LOW BYTE
%ENTAB(0,0,000H,000H,000H,?)       ;VENDOR ID, HIGH BYTE
%ENTAB(0,0,000H,000H,000H,?)      ;BOARD ID, CHARACTER 1
%ENTAB(0,0,000H,000H,000H,?)      ;BOARD ID, CHARACTER 2
%ENTAB(0,0,000H,000H,000H,?)      ;BOARD ID, CHARACTER 3
%ENTAB(0,0,000H,000H,000H,?)      ;BOARD ID, CHARACTER 4
%ENTAB(0,0,000H,000H,000H,?)      ;BOARD ID, CHARACTER 5
%ENTAB(0,0,000H,000H,000H,?)      ;BOARD ID, CHARACTER 6
%ENTAB(0,0,000H,000H,000H,?)      ;BOARD ID, CHARACTER 7
%ENTAB(0,0,000H,000H,000H,?)      ;BOARD ID, CHARACTER 8
%ENTAB(0,0,000H,000H,000H,?)      ;BOARD ID, CHARACTER 9
%ENTAB(0,0,000H,000H,000H,?)     ;BOARD ID, CHARACTER 10
%ENTAB(0,0,000H,000H,000H,?)              ;INTEL RESERVED
%ENTAB(0,0,000H,000H,000H,?)              ;INTEL RESERVED
%ENTAB(0,0,000H,000H,000H,?)              ;INTEL RESERVED
%ENTAB(0,0,000H,000H,000H,?)              ;INTEL RESERVED
%ENTAB(0,0,001H,000H,000H,?)      ;HARDWARE TEST REV NO.
%ENTAB(0,0,000H,000H,000H,?)                    ;CLASS ID
%ENTAB(0,0,000H,000H,000H,?)                         ;RFU
%ENTAB(0,0,000H,000H,000H,?)                         ;RFU
%ENTAB(0,0,000H,000H,000H,?)                         ;RFU
;       G R  DFT  RRT  EET  VAR
%ENTAB(0,1,003H,001H,000H,RST_STS)  ;RESET STATUS RGTR
%ENTAB(1,1,000H,001H,001H,PTI)     ;PROGRAM TABLE INDEX
%ENTAB(1,1,000H,001H,002H,NMI_EN)     ;NMI ENABLE RGTR
%ENTAB(0,1,000H,003H,000H,GEN_STS)     ;GENERAL STATUS
%ENTAB(1,1,000H,001H,003H,GEN_CTL)    ;GENERAL CONTROL
%ENTAB(0,1,000H,001H,004H,BIST_SL) ;BIST-SUPPORT-LEVEL
%ENTAB(1,1,000H,001H,001H,BIST_DI)      ;BIST-DATA-IN
```

280640-20

Figure 5-2. ENTAB Macro Source Code Listing (Sheet 1 of 2)

```
%ENTAB(0,1,000H,001H,001H,BIST_DO)      ;BIST-DATA-OUT
%ENTAB(0,1,010H,001H,001H,BIST_SS)  ;BIST-SLAVE-STATUS
%ENTAB(1,1,020H,001H,005H,BIST_MS) ;BIST-MASTER-STATUS
%ENTAB(0,1,000H,001H,006H,BIST_TID)      ;BIST-TEST-ID
;----------- PROTECTION RECORD ---------------------
;       G R  DFT  RRT  EET  VAR
%ENTAB(0,0,00BH,000H,000H,PROT_OFF)  ;PROTECT REC TYPE
%ENTAB(0,0,002H,000H,000H,?)           ;RECORD LENGTH
%ENTAB(0,2,000H,004H,007H,UACRS)  ;PROTECT LEVEL RGTR
%ENTAB(0,0,000H,000H,000H,?)                     ;RFU
;----------- PSB CONTROL RECORD --------------------
;       G R  DFT  RRT  EET  VAR
%ENTAB(0,0,006H,000H,000H,PSB_CTL_OFF)    ;PSB CR TYPE
%ENTAB(0,0,006H,000H,000H,?)           ;RECORD LENGTH
%ENTAB(0,0,000H,002H,000H,?)         ;PSB SLOT ID NO.
%ENTAB(1,0,000H,002H,008H,?)          ;PSB ARB ID NO.
%ENTAB(1,0,000H,002H,009H,?)          ;PSB ERROR RGTR
%ENTAB(1,1,01FH,005H,00AH,PSB_CS)  ;PSB CONT/STAT RGTR
%ENTAB(1,1,000H,002H,00BH,PSB_DIAG)     ;PSB DIAG RGTR
%ENTAB(0,0,000H,000H,000H,?)                     ;RFU
;----------- LOCAL PROC RECORD --------------------
;       G R  DFT  RRT  EET  VAR
%ENTAB(0,0,013H,000H,000H,?)    ;LOCAL PROC RECORD TYPE
%ENTAB(0,0,003H,000H,000H,?)           ;RECORD LENCTH
%ENTAB(0,0,000H,006H,00CH,?)      ;LOCAL PROC CONTROL
%ENTAB(0,0,000H,007H,000H,?)       ;LOCAL PROC STATUS
%ENTAB(0,0,000H,000H,000H,?)                     ;RFU
;--------- END OF TEMPLATE RECORD -----------------
;       G R  DFT  RRT  EET  VAR
%ENTAB(0,0,0FFH,000H,000H,EOT_OFF)   ;EOT RECORD TYPE
$EJECT
```

280640-21

Figure 5-2. ENTAB Macro Source Code Listing (Sheet 2 of 2) (Continued)

5.4.5 EDIT ROUTING TABLE

The purpose of the Edit Routine Table (ERT) parameter in the worksheet is to associate each register with the correct edit routine number. There are six edit routines supplied within this firmware:

ED00h	Used for Read-Only Registers	Generic
ED01h	Check that RFU Bits Match a Mask	Generic
ED02h	Range Checking Between Two Constants	Generic
ED03h	PSB ARB ID Register	Specific
ED04h	PSB Diagnostic Register	Specific
ED05h	Greater Than Check (>)	Generic

5.4.6 WRITE ROUTINE NUMBER

The Write Routine (WRT) parameter specifies which write routine number to jump to once access rights and value checking are complete. A given edit routine can jump to any write routine (there is no requirement for the edit routine number to match the write routine number). In the generic routines, several edit routines can reference the same write routine using different constant lists based on register number. In the specific routines, it is sometimes more expedient to jump directly to the edit routine rather than going through the write jump table. In this case, a "?" should be entered for the WRT. Seven write routines are supplied, therefore, the first available number assignment for user code is WR07H.

WR00h	Write to a RAM Based Register	Generic
WR01h	Write to a MPC Based Register	Generic
WR02h	Write to PSB Control Register	Specific
WR03h	Write to Protection Level Register	Specific
WR04h	Write to PSB Control/Status Register	Specific
WR05h	Write to PSB Diagnostic Control	Specific
WR06h	Write to Local Processor Control	Specific

5.4.7 CONSTANTS FOR VALUE CHECKING

This column contains a list of constants (CONST) used by the edit routines in value checking register contents. During an edit routine, illegal values cause error reports to the General Status Register and the IC handler will exit without performing the write operation. The advantage of using the CONST is that edit routines can be made "sharable" because a different list of constants is used for each register. If no constants are required, a "?" should be entered. This implies that your value checking algorithm will use constants supplied by the edit routine (i.e., specific to that register).

5.4.8 THE EDIT ENTRY TABLE

The Edit Entry Table (EET) number is a value used as the index into the edit entry table during table look up operations. The order of how EET numbers get assigned is not important, however, numbering must start at 0H and run in sequence until every register has an assigned EET number. Two or more registers having the same attributes share the same EET number. This is true if (and only if) all of the columns match for the ERT, WRT, and CONST values. When this occurs, there is an opportunity for code compaction and the same EET number will be assigned to two or more registers.

5.4.9 SYMBOLIC REFERENCE TO RAM LOCATIONS

Whenever a dynamic register is defined (RAM = 1 or 2), an on-chip RAM bit or memory location is reserved. Entries in the Symbolic Reference to RAM (VAR) column represent the symbolic name to be used for references to that RAM bit or memory location. The VAR entry serves an important purpose—it reserves a location in on-chip memory and declares a public symbol under the name of that variable. Read, write and edit routines can now reference that variable directly without needing to know its exact location.

One word of caution with respect to bit variable declarations. If the RAM parameter in the worksheet is a byte location (RAM = 1), then the value listed as default will be loaded into the location reserved for that symbolic name at initialization time as expected (VAR = DFT). But if a bit location was reserved (RAM = 2), the current software has no provision to load the reserved bit location with its default value. Users are therefore advised to initialize all reserved bit locations explicitly in their INIT_USER routines. The public variable specified by the VAR parameter will be in effect and can be used as a symbolic reference for direct addressing (e.g., setb/clrb var). An example of the use of bit variables can be found in the RD04 and WR03 routines contained in Appendix C.

5.5 Loading the Macro Tables

The interconnect worksheet was used as an intermediate step to allow the user to identify opportunities for code reduction through the use of generic read, write, and edit routines. Now that the worksheet is complete, you must enter this data into table generating macro files on your IBM PC. The macro assembler will use these tables to generate the final interconnect firmware code.

5.5.1 THE ENTAB TABLE

The program file \ICFW\SRC\TABGEN.A51 contains a list of calls to the ENTAB configuration macro (Figure 5-2). This list determines the register order in the interconnect template. Enter the values for GAR, RAM, DFT, RRT, EET, and VAR from the worksheet into this table.

5.5.2 THE EETGEN TABLE

The program file \ICFW\SCR\EETGEN.A51 contains a list of calls to the EETGEN configuration macro (Figure 5-3). This list is used to build the edit entry table. Enter the values for ERT, CONST, and WRT from the worksheet into this table.

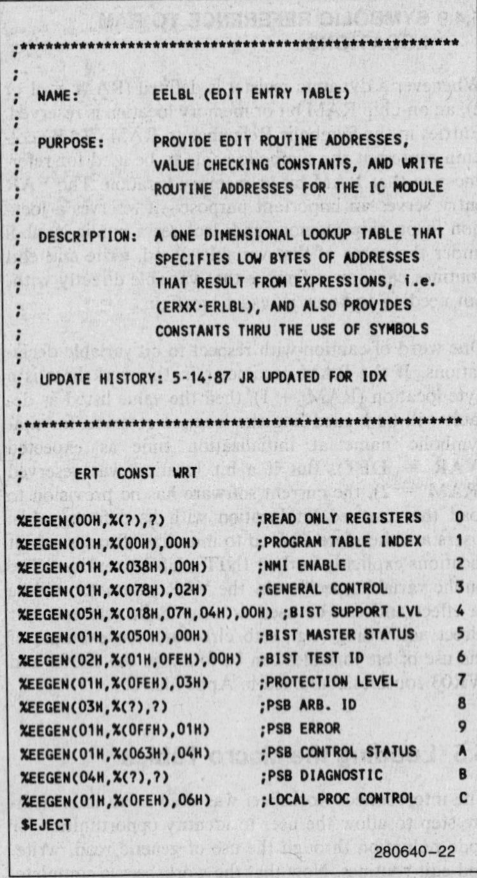

```
;*****************************************************
;
; NAME:           EELBL (EDIT ENTRY TABLE)
;
; PURPOSE:        PROVIDE EDIT ROUTINE ADDRESSES,
;                 VALUE CHECKING CONSTANTS, AND WRITE
;                 ROUTINE ADDRESSES FOR THE IC MODULE
;
; DESCRIPTION:    A ONE DIMENSIONAL LOOKUP TABLE THAT
;                 SPECIFIES LOW BYTES OF ADDRESSES
;                 THAT RESULT FROM EXPRESSIONS, i.e.
;                 (ERXX-ERLBL), AND ALSO PROVIDES
;                 CONSTANTS THRU THE USE OF SYMBOLS
;
; UPDATE HISTORY: 5-14-87 JR UPDATED FOR IDX
;
;*****************************************************
;
;     ERT  CONST  WRT
%EEGEN(00H,%(?),?)                ;READ ONLY REGISTERS    0
%EEGEN(01H,%(00H),00H)            ;PROGRAM TABLE INDEX    1
%EEGEN(01H,%(038H),00H)           ;NMI ENABLE             2
%EEGEN(01H,%(078H),02H)           ;GENERAL CONTROL        3
%EEGEN(05H,%(018H,07H,04H),00H)   ;BIST SUPPORT LVL       4
%EEGEN(01H,%(050H),00H)           ;BIST MASTER STATUS     5
%EEGEN(02H,%(01H,0FEH),00H)       ;BIST TEST ID           6
%EEGEN(01H,%(0FEH),03H)           ;PROTECTION LEVEL       7
%EEGEN(03H,%(?),?)                ;PSB ARB. ID            8
%EEGEN(01H,%(0FFH),01H)           ;PSB ERROR              9
%EEGEN(01H,%(063H),04H)           ;PSB CONTROL STATUS     A
%EEGEN(04H,%(?),?)                ;PSB DIAGNOSTIC         B
%EEGEN(01H,%(0FEH),06H)           ;LOCAL PROC CONTROL     C
$EJECT
```

280640–22

Figure 5-3. EEGEN Macro Source Code Listing

5.5.3 THE EXTERNS MACRO: GENERATING EXTERNAL LABELS

After completing the entries in the ENTAB and EETGEN tables, the final step before code generation is to supply values to the EXTERNS macro so that the correct number of external labels are generated for your user routines. The EXTERNS macro is used in the file \ICFW\SRC\TABLE.MOD. Here you will find the call to EXTGEN, where you must supply the highest number of your edit, write, and read routines as parameters in that order.

```
%EXTERNS(06,07,08)          ;Six edit routines
                            ;Seven write routines
                            ;Eight read routines
```

5.6 Programming Techniques for Read, Write, and Edit Routines

There are a group of user callable macro functions supplied with the interconnect firmware in the file \ICFW\SRC\GLOBAL.MAC. These are called by entering a "%" symbol in front of the name and supplying a list of parameters. This results in code expansion, which supplies the requested function. The following macros are callable by users.

```
RD_MPC (dest,src)      Read MPC Register
WRT_MPC(dest,src)      Write MPC Register
LOOKUP(table,offset)Retrieve parameter from
                         table
SUB (opr)              Subtract operand from
                         accumulator
MOVBIT
  (dest_bit,src_bit)Perform bit move
                         operation
GET_EEC                Get Edit Table Constant
                         (Data pointer must be
                         pointing to EETABLE.
                         Byte is returned in
                         Accumulator. You must
                         perform one LOOKUP be-
                         fore making this call.)
```

All user routines should be declared PUBLIC so that the table generating macros can locate the routines entry point. Place the user routines you write in the file ICFW\SRC\USER.MOD.

5.6.1 RETRIEVING THE CONSTANT LIST FROM THE EETABLE

While in a read, write, or edit routine, one or more constants can be retrieved by using the global symbol EET_OFF as the offset into the EETABLE for this register.

For example, consider this range checking algorithm in an edit routine:

```
ER05H: INC   EET_OFF              ;Point to RFU Mask
                                  ;in EETABLE
       %LOOKUP
        (#EETABLE,EET_OFF)        ;Get It
       ANL   A,ICDATA             ;Check all RFUs=0
       JNZ   ERR_5                ;JMP if illegal
       %GET_EEC                   ;Get Don't Care Mask
                                  ;From EETABLE
       ANL   A,ICDATA             ;Mask off Don't Care
                                  ;Bits from ICDATA
       MOV   TEMP,A               ;Save Result
       %GET_EEC                   ;Get Max Allowable
                                  ;Write Value
       %SUB(TEMP)                 ;SUB Value Being
                                  ;Written
       JC    ERR_5                ;If ICDATA > Max
                                  ;Allowable, ERR
       %GET_EEC                   ;Else Get Write
                                  ;Routine Offset
       MOV   DPTR,#WRLBL          ;Point to WR
       JMP   @A+DPTR              ;GOTO WR
ERR_5  AJMP  VALERR               ;Report Value ERR
```

5.6.2 HANDLING OF VALUE ERRORS

If a value error is detected in an edit routine, then the write operation will not be performed and instead, a jump to a public routine VALERR should be executed. This routine updates the General Status Register with the appropriate Value Error and returns to the IC handler to complete the interconnect operation.

5.7 Hooks for User Supplied Routines

Every board design is just a little bit different and recognizing this fact, calls to user supplied routines are provided at certain critical locations in the code. These include initialization, polling, and reset routines and timer based functions. As delivered, these routines are nothing more than program stubs. You can find them in the \ICFW\SRC\USER.MOD file. The following discussion suggests some ideas for what you might do with the user routine calls in your interconnect design.

5.7.1 INIT USER: CUSTOM INITIALIZATION CODE

The INIT__USER routine is only called on a cold reset. It gives the user an opportunity to initialize their I/O and modify defaults before entering the mainline code. This routine also gives the user a chance to modify the MPC register defaults after the call to MPC__INIT. If you are using any bit segments (RAM = 2), they must be explicitly initialized at this time. A special feature has been added to the INIT__USER routine which disables the RSTNC timeout function based on a jumper input. This helps out ICE™ users since these emulators have difficulty dealing with external resets.

5.7.2 RST USER: SPECIAL HANDLING UPON WARM RESET

When RST__USER is called, you should reset any I/O devices connected to the microcontroller. If dual-port memory is present, rewrite the upper and lower address boundaries to the MPC because the internal MPC registers are all cleared after an iPSB reset. In most cases, the contents of interconnect registers will remain unchanged.

5.7.3 POLL USER: POLLED USER FUNCTIONS

The POLL__USER routine is called from the mainline code. It polls user functions on each loop through the mainline code (approximtely 39 μs). Typical uses are to scan for on-board errors and to set the general error status bit in the General Status Register when errors are found.

5.7.4 USER TIMER: TIMER BASED FUNCTIONS

The USER__TIMER routine is called every 1 ms as part of timer 0 interrupt routine. USER__TIMER is similar to the POLL__USER, except that the granularity of the timer is predictable since the timer 0 interrupt has the highest priority (other than reset). The USER__TIMER routine is used for self-toggling resets and other time based functions. A software prescale counter can be maintained for timing longer intervals.

5.8 GENERATING THE OBJECT MODULE

The final step in code preparation is to assemble all of your new user routines with ASM-51 and then link to the core module using the RL51 linker. Two batch files are supplied to automate the firmware generation process. To use these files, the current directory must be the \ICFW\SRC subdirectory. Here you will find three files with a .MOD file extension. These are the default module, the tables, and your user code. To assemble these modules enter:

ASMMOD dft
ASMMOD table
ASMMOD user

The list files will be placed in the \ICFW\SRC\LST subdirectory and the object files are placed in the \ICFW\SRC\OBJ subdirectory. Next, the object modules will be linked with the core library to produce a PROM image. Select a name for the output file (e.g., TEST), and invoke the linker by entering:

LNKUSR file name Link Map for test. LNK (Main)

TYPE	BASE	LENGTH	RELOCATION	SEGMENT NAME
REG	0000H	0008H		"REG BANK 0"
DATA	0008H	000DH	UNIT	RW_SEG
DATA	0015H	0008H	UNIT	DATA_SEG
	001DH	0003H		*** GAP ***
DATA	0020H	0002H	BIT_ADDR	BIT_ADDR_BYTE_SEG
BIT	0022H	0000H.2	UNIT	BIT_SEG
	0022H.2	0000H.6		*** GAP ***
IDATA	0023H	0008H	UNIT	STACK_SEG
CODE	0000H	004EH	ABSOLUTE	
CODE	004EH	0433H	UNIT	CODE_SEG
CODE	0481H	00BFH	UNIT	EDIT_SEG
CODE	0540H	0067H	UNIT	WRITE_SEG
CODE	05A7H	005AH	UNIT	READ_SEG
CODE	0601H	000AH	UNIT	USER_CSEG
	060BH	09F3H		*** GAP ***
CODE	0FFEH	0002H	ABSOLUTE	

You will now find a PROMmable file with a .LNK extension in the \ICFW\SRC\OBJ subdirectory. There will also be a file in this subdirectory with a .MAP extension. This file (a link map) will be used in the next step to verify microcontroller resources.

5.8.1 CHECKING MICROCONTROLLER RESOURCE UTILIZATION

The link map file contains information about how much code and register space was requested by the core and user routines and where symbolic variables are located. Examine the link map to check that the limits on RAM and ROM usage have not been exceeded. A gap will be reported whenever additional free space is available. The core firmware will create the following segments:

5.8.2 CHECKING CRITICAL TIMING PATHS

Figure 5-4 shows a state diagram of the microcontroller core firmware and includes the instruction cycle counts for each of the major functions. In this step, you will evaluate the impact user code has on interconnect subsystem timing. All timing calculations are based on counting microcontroller machine cycles to compensate for the different crystal frequencies that may be used. To calculate the elapsed time, multiply the cycle count by 1/xtal frequency (i.e., 0.909 μs at 11 MHz). Some microprocessors have specific timing requirements for the pulse width of reset and interrupt signals. These should be checked against the timing values given below:

Reset Timing:

Max RES Latency from UCINT = 41 Cycles

Min RES Inactive after UCINT Inactive = 38 Cycles + RST_USER

NMI Timing:

Max Interrupt Latency = Mainline + IC Handler = 39 + 136 Cycles

Min Interrupt Latency = Mainline = 39 Cycles

The timer 0 interrupt occurs every 1 ms when using the recommended 11 MHz crystal oscillator. However, the time 0 interrupt is masked in both the IC handler and the mainline code. Therefore, the worst case timer 0 latency is calculated:

Max Timer 0 Latency = IC Handler + Mainline = 136 + 49 Cycles

An iPSB timeout will occur if an incoming interconnect request is not completed within 1 ms after **SC0*** becomes active. Consider the case where a local interconnect request is received just a moment before the iPSB request. The microcontroller might be in a timer 0 interrupt routine and would have to pass again through mainline code before servicing the local request. Thus, the worst case iPSB response can be calculated:

Worst Case iPSB Response = Mainline + Timer_0 + Mainline + Local IC Access + Mainlino + PSB Access

For the core firmware without user code, the worst case local firmware response is approximately 485 μs at 11 MHz. This leaves a total of 515 μs for the iPSB interconnect cycle to complete (including MPC and write data delays) before a timeout occurs.

5

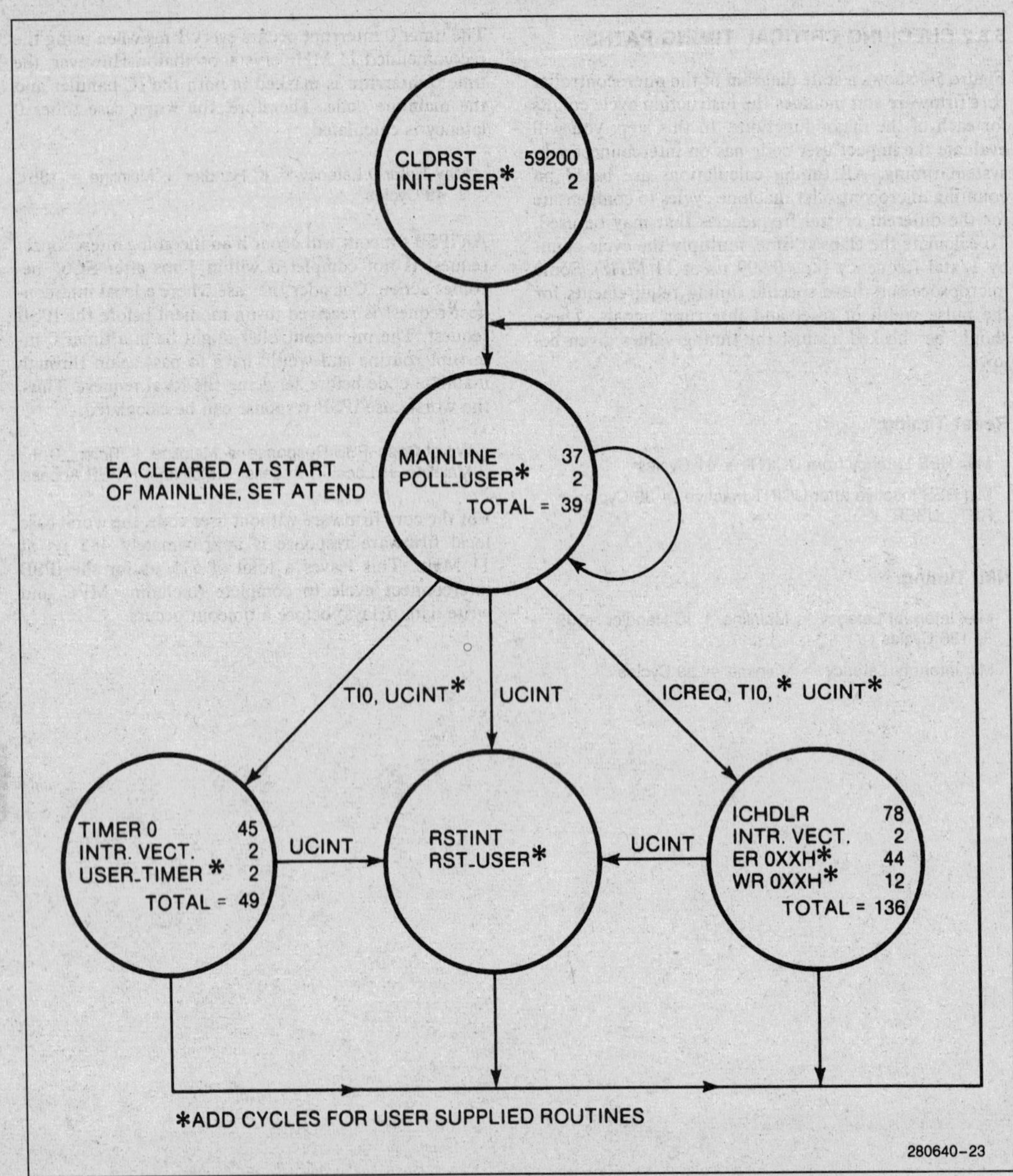

Figure 5-4. Microcontroller Cycle Count of Major Firmware Functions

5.8.3 PROGRAMMING THE 8751

One of the three initialization self-checks that the microcontroller performs following a reset is the PROM check sum test. The firmware computes a 16-bit sum of all code bytes from 0 through (top of the PROM memory-2). The actual check sum is the two's complement of the sum. This value is programmed into the last two bytes of PROM space and given the label CHECKSUM. The check sum label is assigned in the default program file \ICFW\SRC\DFT.MOD and is originally set to address 0FFEH. The address of this label can be modified to accommodate other microcontrollers with larger EPROM size (e.g., an 8752 Microcontroller), as long as the check sum always occupies the last two bytes of code space.

The check sum is initially assembled with a data value of 0000H. After assembling and linking the interconnect firmware, the actual check sum value will be programmed into the PROM in a separate step. The following procedure assumes that an Intel iUP 201 PROM Programmer and iPPS software used. If you are using another brand of PROM programmer, you must guarantee that their check sum algorithm matches the method used here.

Step 1. Invoke iPPS.

Step 2. Initialize default base to hex and the file format to 80.

I 80

Step 3. Set PROM type to 8751.

T 8751

Step 4. Load data buffer with 0FFH.

L B W 0FFH

Step 5. Copy object file to buffer.iPPS will display a check sum.

C<file name>T B

Step 6. Copy check sum displayed by iPPS into address 0FFEH. The low byte of the 16-bit check sum loads to address 0FFEH and the high byte to address 0FFFH.

S 0FFEH
0FFE:(low byte) (high byte)

Step 7. Save a copy of the complete object file on your hard disk

C B T<file name>

Step 8. Install a blank 8751 in the programmer and copy the buffer to PROM.

C B T P

At this point you will have a programmed microcontroller, which is ready to install on the prototype board for functional testing. As an alterntive, you can load the file created in step 7 above into an ICE 51 In-Circuit Emulator and test the firmware directly without programming the 8751. This method gives you access to internal variables and tables in addition to hardware control of the microcontroller.

6.0 FUNCTIONAL TESTING OF THE INTERCONNECT SUBSYSTEMS

6.1 Testing the Interconnect Subsystem

Assuming you were successful in Sections 4 and 5, you now have a functional prototype of your interconnect subsystem ready for testing. Proper interconnect operation depends on complex interrelationships between the 8751 Microcontroller, CPU, Message Passing Coprocessor (MPC), and various TTL circuits. Since interconnect forms the basis of higher level diagnostic services, we must have complete confidence that the interconnect subsystem is functioning properly before implementing the design. Evaluation of the interconnect subsystem is facilitated through the use of an interconnect utility program and a systematic approach to design testing.

6.2 Power-On and Initialization Functions

When a prototype board is inserted into the backplane for the first time, there is a distinct possibility that a design error in the reset initialization sequence could cause a bus error or Reset-Not-Complete (RSTNC) condition. Either of these conditions prevents other boards from coming on-line. Fortunately, these events can usually be detected by watching the front panel LEDs cycle through the power-on sequence.

Under normal reset conditions, the majority of Multibus II boards first illuminate their yellow BIST LED, progress on to illuminate the green LED (run indicator) and leave no other LEDs lit. If the Central Services Module (CSM) has a BUSERR indicator, it will be lit to indicate a bus error due to RSTNC condition. If the bus error persists for more than a few seconds, then a strong likelihood exists that your board has failed to clear the RSTNC* bit. This is confirmed if, after 30 seconds, the CSM BUSERR condition disappears due to the microcontroller clamping reset active and forcing a reset complete indication to the iPSB (unless disabled using the ICE compatibility jumper).

6.3 The Interconnect Configuration Utility

In the \ICFW\ICU subdirectory is an interconnect (IC.P28) written in PL/M source code to run on the iRMX™ 86/286 Operating Systems. The executable object file for this utility may be obtained from the iRMX Users Group (iRUG), 5200 N.E. Elam Young Parkway, Hillsboro, OR 97124-9987. If you are not working in one of these programming environments, you will need to adapt this code to your own environment by substituting the appropriate I/O and interconnect system calls.

Before invoking the IC utility on your prototype, you must create the subdirectory /USER/BOARDS and enter into that directory a file for the board. The file name you assign must correspond with the ASCII description contained in the 10 character board ID field of the Interconnect Header Record. Slashes (/) present in the description must be converted to ASCII periods. For example, iSBC386/100 is converted to iSBC386.100. The actual values for each interconnect register are entered into the template plus any user comments you may wish to add for that board. A typical configuration file listing is shown in Figure 6-1. The control characters that appear in the file listing are used by the utility to mark the display area and field boundaries.

- The @ symbol is the screen delimiter. As the user pages through the file and encounters this symbol, the utility will prompt the user for input.
- The ; symbol is the register field delimiter. The utility scans for an opening semicolon; then fetches a register value for each character found until encountering the closing semicolon. Legal character type descriptors are:

  b (binary)

  d (decimal)

  h (hexadecimal)

  a (ASCII)

The IC utility enables you to identify, examine, and modify the configuration of a system board from the comfort of your console (no jumpers to move!). The utility locates the board ID character fields in the Interconnect Header Record of the board in the cardslot you select to configure. It then searches the subdirectory /USER/BOARDS for the file having a file name that matches the board ID. Speciic interconnect registers may be modified (provided access rights and value checking are valid), however, an attempt to enter illegal values into an interconnect register are ignored and the existing register content is unaffected. Entries are displayed as they are made. Once invoked, the IC utility prompts the user for input and you will find it very easy to use. A sample screen output from this utility is shown in Figure 6-2.

6.4 A Test Methodology for Interconnect Functions

Given a functional prototype board and an interconnect utility such as the one described above, we now use these tools to verify correct operation of the interconnect subsystem. One might assume that this process would be quite simple and straightforward—and usually, it is. But we are now looking for more subtle conditions such as timing related problems and secondary affects on interconnect register content. While every board is different, a test methodology that looks for all possible contingencies is an important step in design verification. The following checklist is an example of what to look for during evaluation testing of interconnect using a prototype board:

Look for initialization conditions:

Do the correct default register values appear after cold-start?

Do the front panel LEDs work properly?

Is RSTNC handled correctly? (also test RSTNC recovery by disabling the CPU).

Look for dual-port operation on both local and system buses:

Can the registers be accessed from off-board as well as on-board?

Do the function records all have correct record type values and byte counts?

Are the read/write privileges working for both on-board and off-board references?

Is the protection record function working properly?

Look for proper register content and function:

Do all the bit level functions in control registers work as expected?

Are all the status registers reporting correctly?

Look for secondary effects:

Changes to memory addressing registers are only allowed when memory is disabled.

Look for iPSB timeout conditions:

Saturate the local bus with interconnect I/O commands in a tight loop; then attempt an interconnect operation from off-board.

Once you have accomplished this type of testing methodology for each register on the prototype board, you can have reasonable confidence that all is well with the interconnect subsystem. Now you can proceed forward with the development of device drivers and extended diagnostics. If any changes are made to the microcontroller after its initial release, be sure to update the revision control field in the header record so users can identify which version of the firmware they hold.

6.5 Summary and Conclusion

Multibus II is a system architecture composed of standarized hardware and software modules. Having successfully implemented the interconnect subsystem on your board, you are ensured of the functional compatibility and interoperability of that board with other industry-standard Multibus II products that use interconnect.

If you found this guide useful, you may also be interested in other design guides available from Intel. A list of documents available at the time of this guide's publication are listed in Appendix A. As the Multibus II system architecture matures and proliferates, we look forward to supplying additional design guides that encourage the production of compatible hardware and software products.

```
Function                        Value     RW   Comments
Vendor ID Number               ;h h ;     ro
Board ID Number            ;aaaaaaaaaa;   ro
PBA Number, Rev            ;d d d d ;     ro
Hardware Test Rev #              ;d ;     ro
Class ID                         ;b ;     ro
Reserved                   ;b b b b ;     ro
Program Table Index              ;b ;     rw
NMI Enable Register              ;b ;     rw
General Status                   ;b ;     ro
General Control                  ;b ;     rw
BIST Support Level               ;b ;     rw
BIST Data In                     ;b ;     rw
BIST Data Out                    ;b ;     rw
BIST Slave Status                ;b ;     rw
BIST Master Status               ;b ;     rw
BIST Test ID                     ;b ;     rw

Protection Record               Value     RW   Comments
Protection Record Type           ;b ;     ro
Record Length                    ;b ;     ro
Protection Level Reg             ;b ;     rw
Reserved                         ;b ;     ro

Memory Record Type              Value     RW   Comments
Memory Record Type               ;b ;     ro
Record Length                    ;b ;     ro
Memory Size (bits 7..0)          ;b ;     ro
Memory Size (bits 15..8)         ;b ;     ro
Memory Control                   ;b ;     rw
Memory Status                    ;b ;     ro
MM2 ID                           ;b ;     ro

iPSB Control Record             Value     RW   Comments
iPSB Control Record Type         ;b ;     ro
Record Length                    ;b ;     ro
iPSB Slot ID Number              ;b ;     ro
iPSB Arbitration ID Number       ;b ;     rw
iPSB Error Register              ;b ;     rw
iPSB Control/Status Register     ;b ;     rw
iPSB Diagnostic Register         ;b ;     rw
Reserved                         ;b ;     ro
```

280640-24

Figure 6-1. Configuration File Format for the IC Utility (Sheet 1 of 3)

```
Reg   iPSB Memory Record Type         Value    RW   Comments
33    iPSB Memory Record Type          ;b ;    ro
34    Record Length                    ;b ;    ro
35    iPSB Start Address (23..16)      ;b ;    rw
36    iPSB Start Address (31..24)      ;b ;    rw
37    iPSB End Address (23..16)        ;b ;    rw
38    iPSB End Address (31..24)        ;b ;    rw
39    iPSB Memory Control              ;b ;    rw
@
Reg   Local Memory Record Type        Value    RW   Comments
3A    Local Memory Record Type         ;b ;    ro
3B    Record Length                    ;b ;    ro
3C    Local Start Address (23..16)     ;b ;    ro
3D    Local Start Address (31..24)     ;b ;    ro
3E    Local End Address (23..16)       ;b ;    rw
3F    Local End Address (31..24)       ;b ;    ro
40    Local Control Register           ;b ;    rw
@
Reg   Memory Parity Record Type       Value    RW   Comments
41    Memory Parity Record Type        ;b ;    ro
42    Record Length                    ;b ;    ro
43    Parity Control Register          ;b ;    rw
44    Parity Status Register           ;b ;    ro
45    Bank Status Register             ;b ;    ro
46    Error Offset               ;b b b b ;    ro
4A    Reserved                         ;b;     ro
@
Reg   Cache Memory Record             Value    RW   Comments
4B    Cache Memory Record Type         ;b ;    ro
4C    Record Length                    ;b ;    ro
4D    Cache Size (bits 7..0)           ;b ;    ro
4E    Cache Size (bits 15..8)          ;b ;    ro
4F    Cache Entry Size                 ;b ;    ro
50    Cache Control                    ;b ;    rw
51    Reserved                         ;b ;    ro
@
```

280640-25

Figure 6-1. Configuration File Format for the IC Utility (Sheet 2 of 3)

```
Reg   Firmware Comm Record Type    Value  RW   Comments
52    Firmware Comm Record Type     ;b ; ro
53    Record Length                 ;b ; ro
54    Communications Byte 1         ;b ; rw
55    Communications Byte 2         ;b ; rw
56    Communications Byte 3         ;b ; rw
57    Communications Byte 4         ;b ; rw
58    Communications Byte 5         ;b ; rw
59    Communications Byte 6         ;b ; rw
5A    Communications Byte 7         ;b ; rw
5B    Communications Byte 8         ;b ; rw
5C    Communications Byte 9         ;b ; rw
5D    Communications Byte 10        ;b ; rw
5E    Communications Byte 11        ;b ; rw
5F    Communications Byte 12        ;b ; rw
60    Communications Byte 13        ;b ; rw
61    Communications Byte 14        ;b ; rw
62    Communications Byte 15        ;b ; rw
63    Communications Byte 16        ;b ; rw
@
Reg   Host ID Record Type           Value  RW   Comments
64    Host ID Record Type           ;b ; ro
65    Record Length                 ;b ; ro
66    Host ID (bits 7..0)           ;b ; rw
67    Host ID (bits 15..8)          ;b ; rw
68    Message Address               ;b ; rw
69    Reserved                      ;b ; ro
@
Reg   Serial Comm Record Type       Value  RW   Comments
6A    Serial Comm Record Type       ;b ; ro
6B    Record Length                 ;b ; ro
6C    Serial Data In                ;b ; ro
6D    Serial Data Out               ;b ; rw
6E    Serial Port Status            ;b ; ro
6F    Serial Interrupt Enable       ;b ; rw
70    Serial Port Options           ;b ; rw
71    Reserved                      ;b ; ro
@
Reg   386/100 Specific Record       Value  RW   Comments
72    386/100 Spec Record Type      ;b ; ro
73    Record Length                 ;b ; ro
74    On-board Control Register     ;b ; rw
@
Reg   End Of Template Record        Value  RW   Comments
75    EOT Record Type               ;b ; ro
@
```

280640-26

Figure 6-1. Configuration File Format for the IC Utility (Sheet 3 of 3)

```
          INTERCONNECT CONFIGURATION UTILITY

Commencing Board Search Routine:  .........
Board Search Complete.  The following boards were found:

Slot#  Vendor ID          Board ID   PBA #        Class
00     Intel Corporation  CSM/001    147304-0003  Central Services Module
01     Intel Corporation  186/410    000000-0002  16-bit Communications Board
02*    Intel Corporation  386/100    000000-0002  32-bit Processor Board
03
04     Intel Corporation  MEM/310    000000-0001  Memory Board
05     Intel Corporation  286/100A   000000-0001  16-bit Processor Board
06
07     Intel Corporation  186/224A   000000-0001  16-bit Peripheral Controller
08

Options: <Configure,Slot#>, <Memory> or <Quit> Type First Letter):c2

Configuration File Attached - File: /user/boards/386.100

Reg   Function                 Value  RW   Comments
00    Vendor ID Number          0100; ro
02    Board ID Number        386/100; ro
0C    PBA Number, Rev       00000000; ro
10    Hardware Test Rev #         02; ro
11    Class ID                    F1; ro
12    Reserved              00000080; ro
16    Program Table Index         00; rw
17    NMI Enable Register         04; rw
18    General Status              80; ro
19    General Control             00; rw
1A    BIST Support Level          00; rw
1B    BIST Data In                00; rw
1C    BIST Data Out               00; rw
1D    BIST Slave Status           10; rw
1E    BIST Master Status          30; rw
1F    BIST Test ID                10; rw

Would you like to make any changes?

Enter <reg_num,new_value_in_hex>,<Quit>,<CR> or <Up>:
```

280640-27

Figure 6-2. Interconnect Utility Screens (Sheet 1 of 2)

5

```
Reg   Protection Record              Value  RW     Comments
20    Protection Record Type           0B;  ro
21    Record Length                    02;  ro
22    Protection Level Reg             00;  rw
23    Reserved                         00;  ro

Reg   Memory Record Type             Value  RW     Comments
24    Memory Record Type               01;  ro
25    Record Length                    05;  ro
26    Memory Size (bits 7..0)          3F;  ro
27    Memory Size (bits 15..8)         00;  ro
28    Memory Control                   01;  rw
29    Memory Status                    A1;  ro
2A    MM2 ID                           22;  ro

Would you like to make any changes?

Enter <reg_num,new_value_in_hex>,<Quit>,<CR> or <Up>:

Reg   iPSB Control Record            Value  RW     Comments
2B    iPSB Control Record Type         06;  ro
2C    Record Length                    06;  ro
2D    iPSB Slot ID Number              10;  ro
2E    iPSB Arbitration ID Number       E8;  rw
2F    iPSB Error Register              88;  rw
30    iPSB Control/Status Register     18;  rw
31    iPSB Diagnostic Register         00;  rw
32    Reserved                         00;  ro

Would you like to make any changes?

Enter <reg_num,new_value_in_hex>,<Quit>,<CR> or <Up>:q
```

280640-28

Figure 6-2. Interconnect Utility Screens (Sheet 2 of 2) (Continued)

APPENDIX A
BIBLIOGRAPHY OF RELATED READING

Interconnect Architecture Specification—Intel Order Number 149299-002.

MPC User's Guide—Intel Order Number 176525-001.

IEEE 1296 Specification (High Performance Synchronous 32-Bit Bus Standard)

iSBC™ 386/116 Hardware Reference Manual—Intel Order Number 451833-001.

BUSCON Paper: An Architecture for Initializing Multibus II Multiprocessor Systems. Stephen Rogers, October 1987.

Computer Technology Review Quarterly: Interconnect Simplifies Configuration. Roger Finger, September 1987.

Intel Application Note AP-70, Using the Intel MCS® 51 Boolean Processing Capabilities. John Wharton, 1980.

Embedded Controller Handbook 8751 Data Sheet—Intel Order Number 210918-005.

iUP 200/201A Programmer User's Guide—Intel Order Number 166608-001.

MCS™ Macro Assembler User's Guide for DOS Systems—Intel Order Number 122752-001.

MCS™ 51 Utilities User's Guide for DOS Systems—Intel Order Number 122747-001.

Intel Application Note AP-422, Designing a Central Services Module for Multibus II. Jory Radke, 1987.

APPENDIX B
FLOWCHARTS FOR IC CORE FIRMWARE

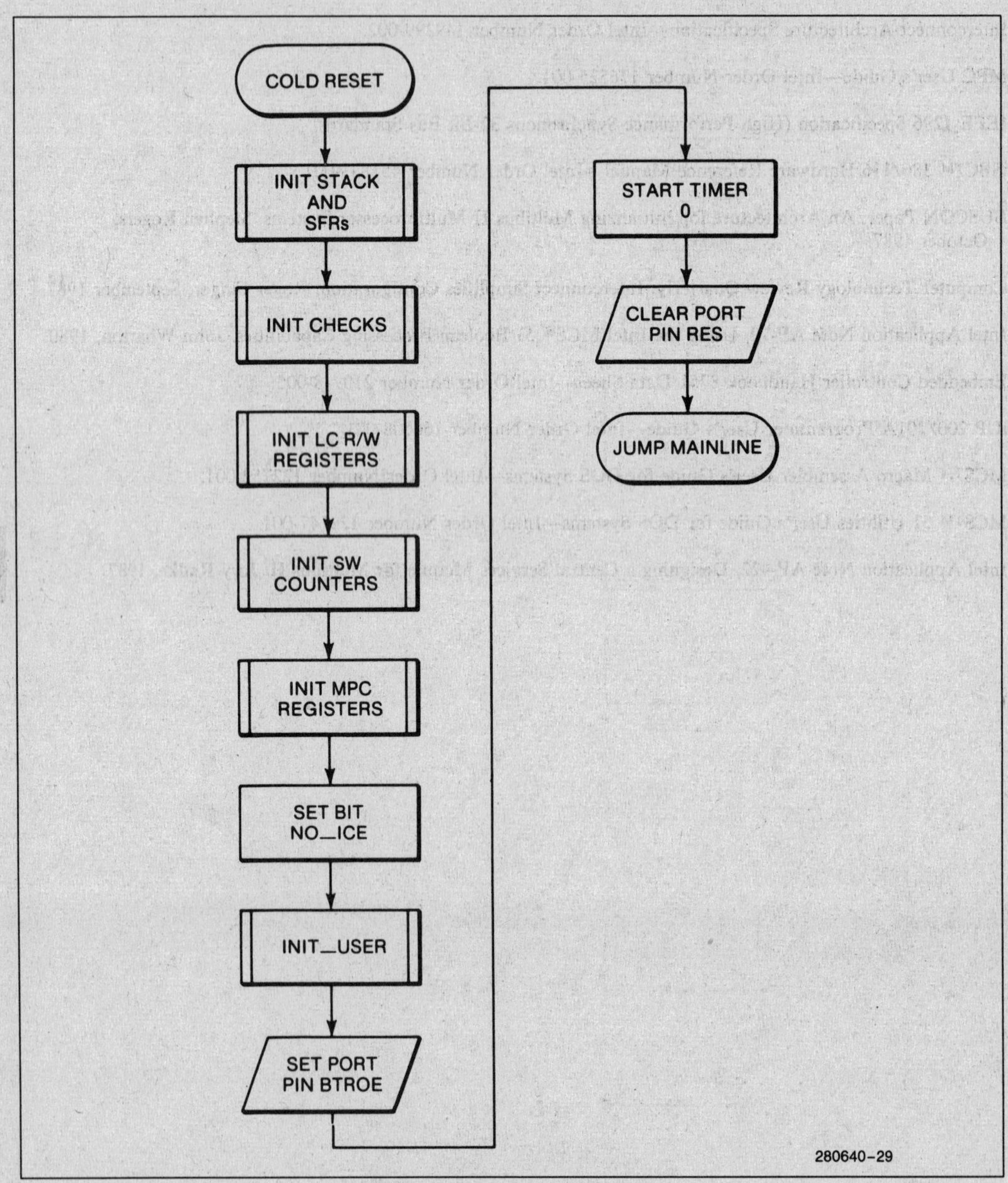

Figure B-1. Cold Reset Routine

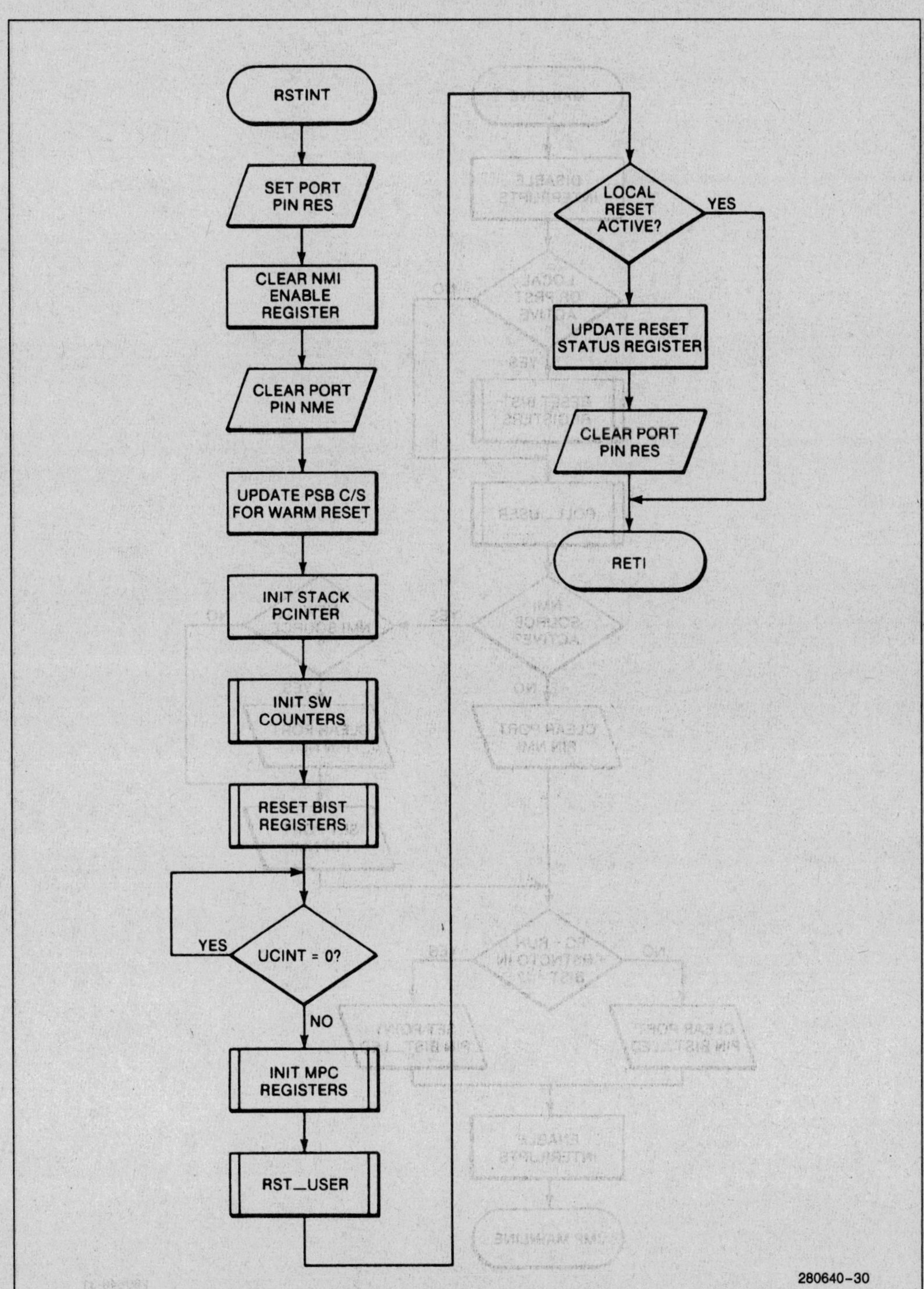

Figure B-2. Reset Interrupt Routine

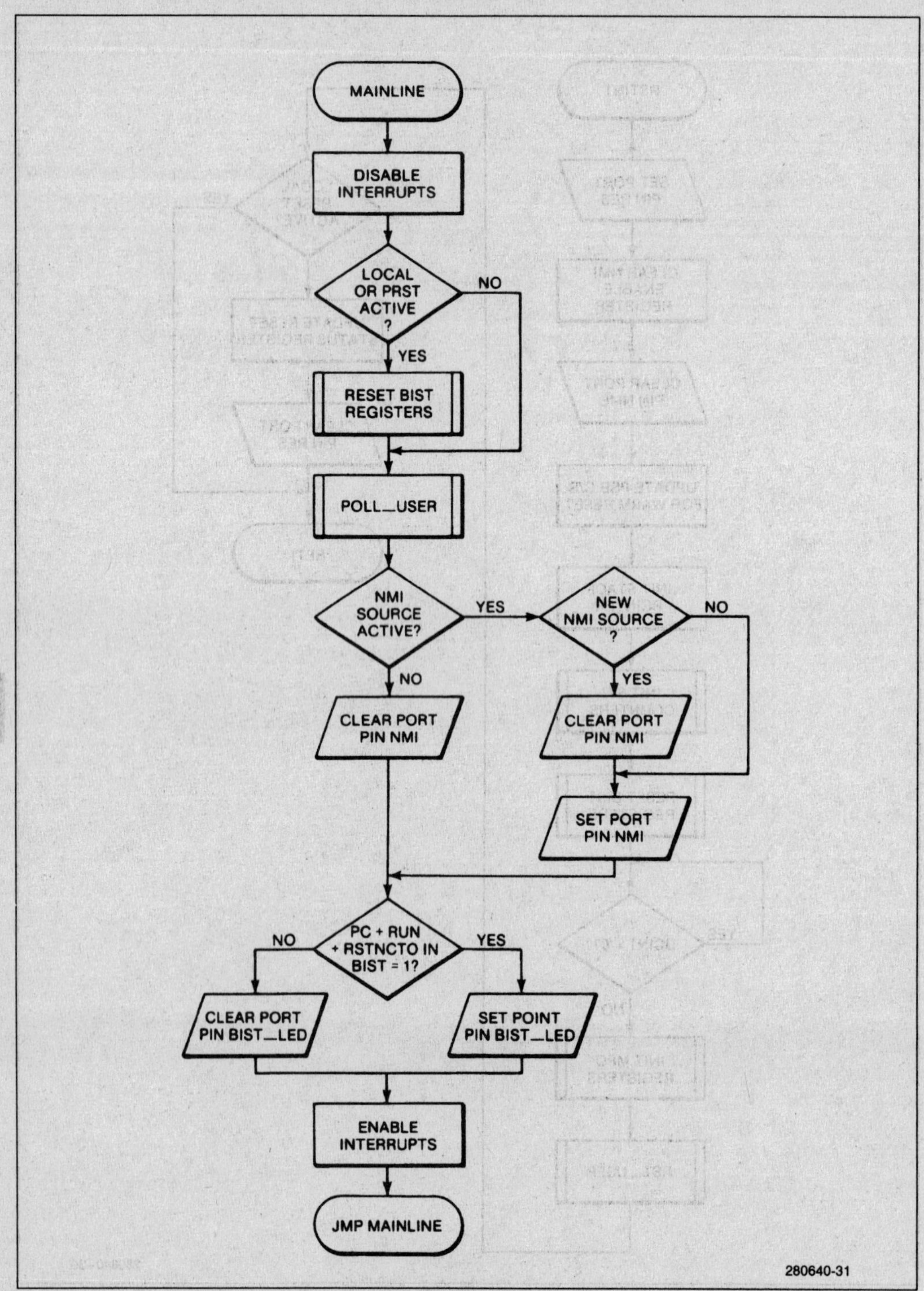

Figure B-3. Mainline Program Flow

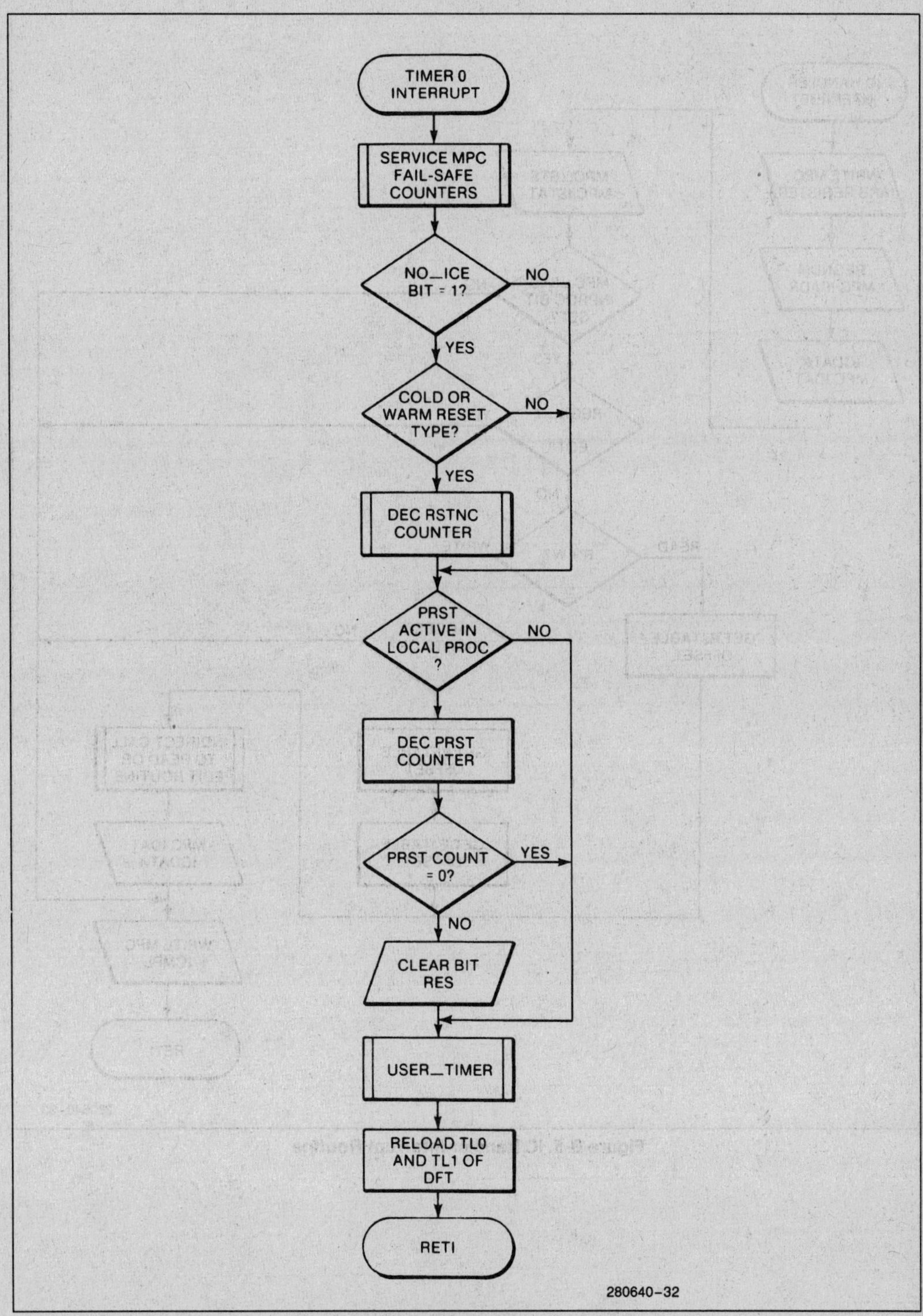

Figure B-4. Timer 0 Interrupt Routine

5

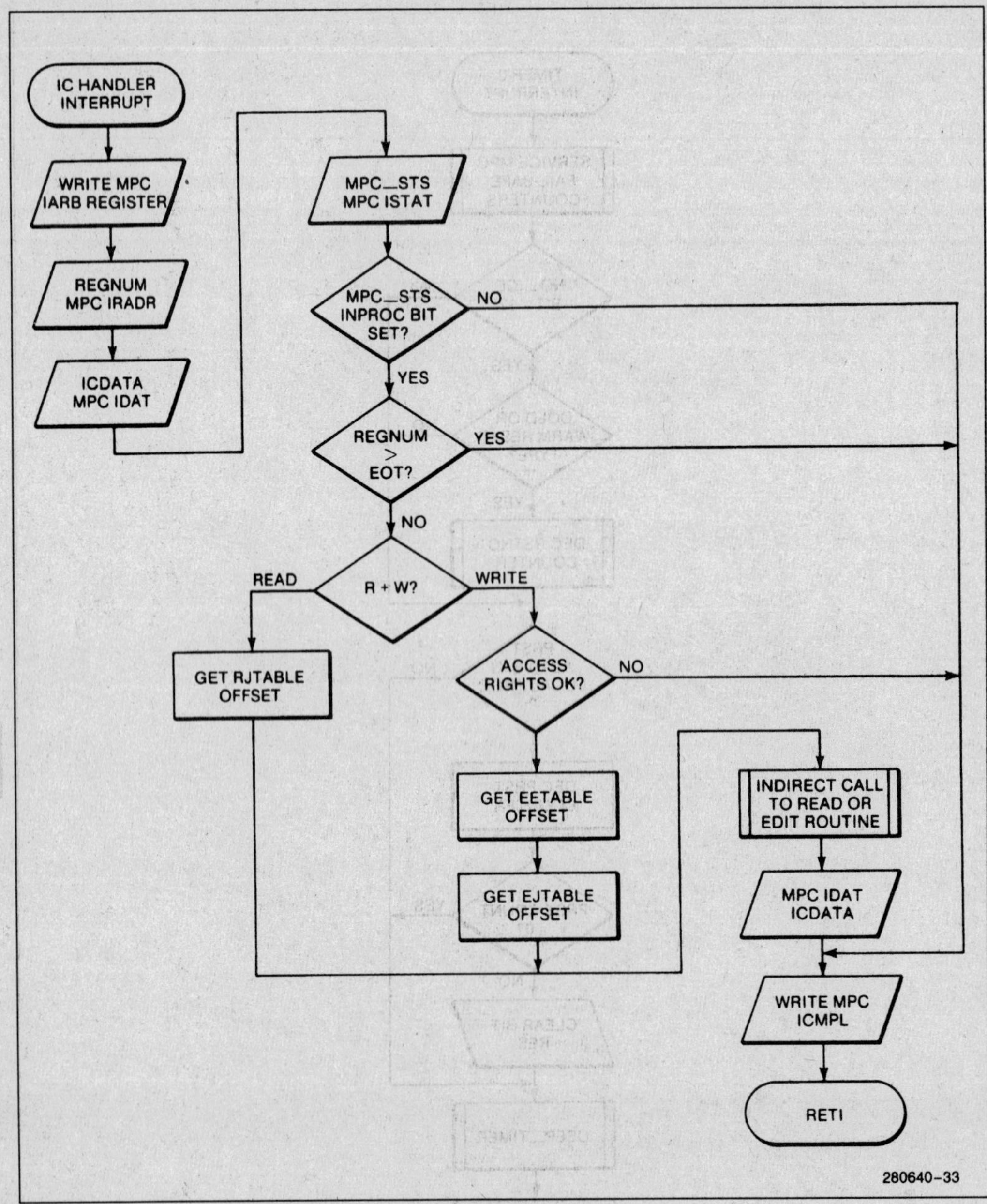

Figure B-5. IC Handler Interrupt Routine

APPENDIX C
READ, WRITE, AND EDIT ROUTINES

```
;*************************************************************
;
; NAME:          IC_TO_MPC
;
; PURPOSE:       CORRELATE IC REGISTER NUMBER TO MPC
;                REGISTER NUMBER
;
; DESCRIPTION:   CORRELATES IC PSB C/S REGISTERS WITH
;                THE PROPER MPC REGISTER NUMBER,
;                STARTING WITH THE PSB SLOT ID
;                REGISTER.
;
; UPDATE HISTORY:
;
;*************************************************************
;
IC_TO_MPC:  DB      SID         ;PSB SLOT ID
            DB      AID         ;PSB ARB ID
            DB      RERR        ;PSB ERROR
            DB      00H         ;DUMMY
            DB      DIAG        ;PSB DIAGNOSTIC
$EJECT
```

280640-34

Figure C-1. IC_TO_MPC Corrrelation

5

```
;************************************************************
;
; NAME:         RD00H
;
; PURPOSE:      READ DEFAULT VALUE FROM DFTABLE
;
; CALLED BY:    JUMPED TO FROM SERVICE
;
; CALLS:        NONE
;
; NEST LEVEL:   ??
;
; DESCRIPTION:  USES REGNUM TO INDEX INTO DFTABLE.
;
; REG BANK:     ASSUMES IC_BANK, SELECTS NONE
;
; INPUTS:       REGNUM
;
; DESTROYS:     ACC, DPTR
;
; RETURNS:      ICDATA
;
; UPDATE HISTORY:
;
;************************************************************

RD00H:  %LOOKUP(#DFTABLE,REGNUM) ;GET DEFAULT FM TABLE
        MOV    ICDATA,A         ;RET DEFAULT IN ICDATA
        RET                     ;RETURN TO IC HANDLER
$EJECT
```

280640-35

Figure C-2. RD00H Read DFTABLE

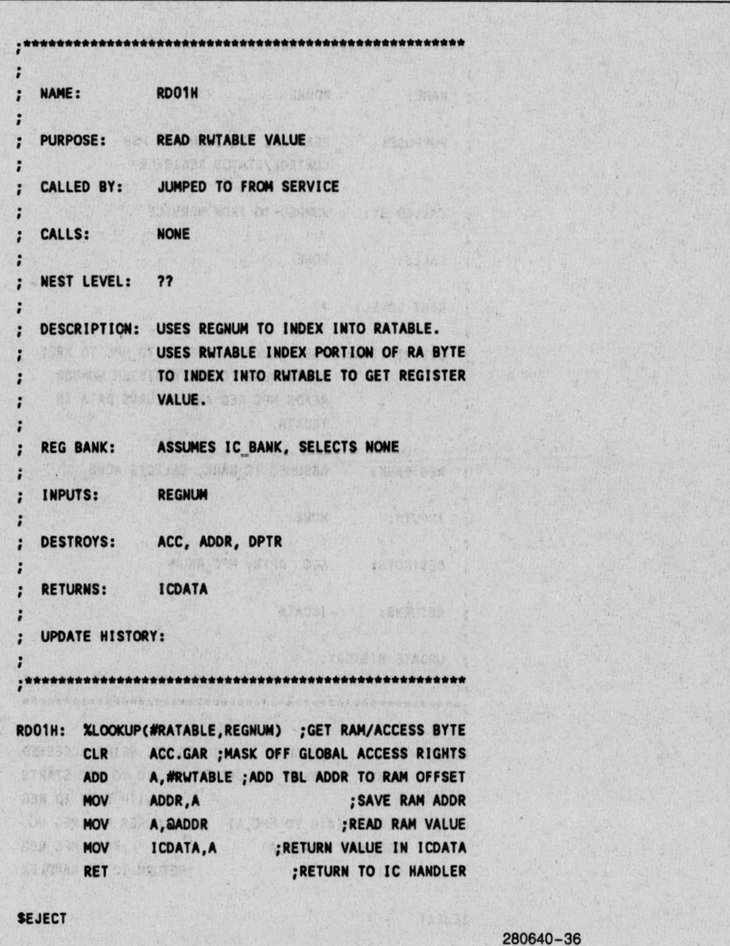

```
;*********************************************************
;
; NAME:         RD01H
;
; PURPOSE:      READ RWTABLE VALUE
;
; CALLED BY:    JUMPED TO FROM SERVICE
;
; CALLS:        NONE
;
; NEST LEVEL:   ??
;
; DESCRIPTION:  USES REGNUM TO INDEX INTO RATABLE.
;               USES RWTABLE INDEX PORTION OF RA BYTE
;               TO INDEX INTO RWTABLE TO GET REGISTER
;               VALUE.
;
; REG BANK:     ASSUMES IC_BANK, SELECTS NONE
;
; INPUTS:       REGNUM
;
; DESTROYS:     ACC, ADDR, DPTR
;
; RETURNS:      ICDATA
;
; UPDATE HISTORY:
;
;*********************************************************

RD01H:  %LOOKUP(#RATABLE,REGNUM)  ;GET RAM/ACCESS BYTE
        CLR    ACC.GAR ;MASK OFF GLOBAL ACCESS RIGHTS
        ADD    A,#RWTABLE ;ADD TBL ADDR TO RAM OFFSET
        MOV    ADDR,A                  ;SAVE RAM ADDR
        MOV    A,@ADDR                 ;READ RAM VALUE
        MOV    ICDATA,A        ;RETURN VALUE IN ICDATA
        RET                        ;RETURN TO IC HANDLER

$EJECT
```

280640-36

Figure C-3. RD01H Read RWTABLE

5

```
;************************************************************
;
; NAME:         RD02H
;
; PURPOSE:      READ MPC REGISTER FOR PSB
;               CONTROL/STATUS REGISTER
;
; CALLED BY:    JUMPED TO FROM SERVICE
;
; CALLS:        NONE
;
; NEST LEVEL:   ??
;
; DESCRIPTION:  USES LOOKUP TABLE IC_TO_MPC TO XREF
;               IC ADDRESS TO MPC REGISTER NUMBER,
;               READS MPC REG AND RETURNS DATA IN
;               ICDATA.
;
; REG BANK:     ASSUMES IC_BANK, SELECTS NONE
;
; INPUTS:       NONE
;
; DESTROYS:     ACC, DPTR, MPC_RNUM
;
; RETURNS:      ICDATA
;
; UPDATE HISTORY:
;
;************************************************************

RD02H:  MOV     A,REGNUM   ;GET REG NO. BEING ACCESSED
        SUBB    A,#PSB_CTL_OFF+5   ;IC_TO_MPC STARTS
                                   ;WITH SLOT ID REG
        %LOOKUP(#IC_TO_MPC,A)  ;GET CORRES MPC REG NO.
        %RD_MPC(ICDATA,A)          ;READ MPC REG
        RET                    ;RETURN TO IC HANDLER

$EJECT
```

280640-37

Figure C-4. RD02H Read MPC Register

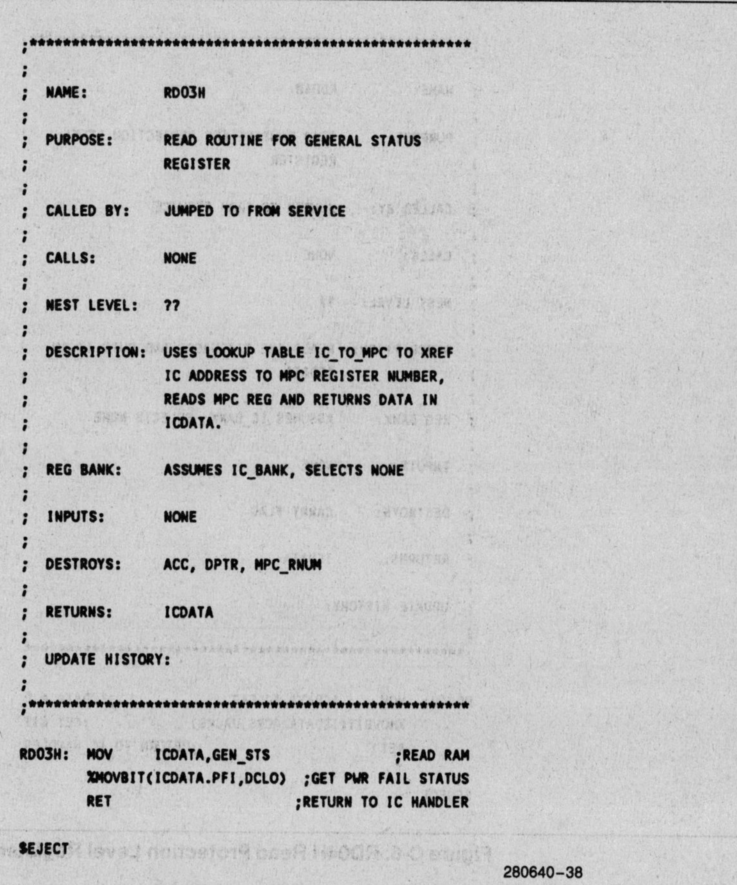

```
;*********************************************************
;
;  NAME:          RD03H
;
;  PURPOSE:       READ ROUTINE FOR GENERAL STATUS
;                 REGISTER
;
;  CALLED BY:     JUMPED TO FROM SERVICE
;
;  CALLS:         NONE
;
;  NEST LEVEL:    ??
;
;  DESCRIPTION:   USES LOOKUP TABLE IC_TO_MPC TO XREF
;                 IC ADDRESS TO MPC REGISTER NUMBER,
;                 READS MPC REG AND RETURNS DATA IN
;                 ICDATA.
;
;  REG BANK:      ASSUMES IC_BANK, SELECTS NONE
;
;  INPUTS:        NONE
;
;  DESTROYS:      ACC, DPTR, MPC_RNUM
;
;  RETURNS:       ICDATA
;
;  UPDATE HISTORY:
;
;*********************************************************

RD03H:  MOV     ICDATA,GEN_STS              ;READ RAM
        %MOVBIT(ICDATA.PFI,DCLO)  ;GET PWR FAIL STATUS
        RET                       ;RETURN TO IC HANDLER

$EJECT
```

280640-38

Figure C-5. RD03H Read General Status Register

```
;*************************************************************

; NAME:          RD04H
;
; PURPOSE:       READ ROUTINE FOR PROTECTION LEVEL
;                REGISTER
;
; CALLED BY:     JUMPED TO FROM SERVICE
;
; CALLS:         NONE
;
; NEST LEVEL:    ??
;
; DESCRIPTION:   READS THE BIT UACRS AND PUTS IT IN
;                ICDATA
;
; REG BANK:      ASSUMES IC_BANK, SELECTS NONE
;
; INPUTS:        NONE
;
; DESTROYS:      CARRY FLAG
;
; RETURNS:       ICDATA
;
; UPDATE HISTORY:
;
;*************************************************************

RD04H:  MOV     ICDATA,#CLEAR                   ;ICDATA = 0
        %MOVBIT(ICDATA.ACRS,UACRS)              ;GET BIT
        RET                             ;RETURN TO IC_HANDLER

$EJECT
```

280640-39

Figure C-6. RD04H Read Protection Level Register

```
;***********************************************************
;
;  NAME:          RD05H
;
;  PURPOSE:       READ ROUTINE FOR PSB CONTROL/STATUS
;                 REGISTER
;
;  CALLED BY:     JUMPED TO FROM SERVICE
;
;  CALLS:         NONE
;
;  NEST LEVEL:    ??
;
;  DESCRIPTION:   COMBINES VALUES OF MPC GENERAL
;                 PARAMETER REGISTER WITH VALUE
;                 FROM RWTABLE FOR PSB_CS TO GET
;                 COMPLETE REGISTER VALUE.
;
;  REG BANK:      ASSUMES IC_BANK, SELECTS NONE
;
;  INPUTS:        NONE
;
;  DESTROYS:      ACC, MPC_RNUM, CARRY FLAG
;
;  RETURNS:       ICDATA
;
;  UPDATE HISTORY:
;
;***********************************************************

RD05H:  %RD_MPC(A,#GEN_PAR)    ;READ MPC GENL PARAM REG
        MOV     ICDATA,PSB_CS         ;READ RAM
        %MOVBIT(ICDATA.HPRO,ACC.PRY)  ;MOV MPC BITS TO
                                      ;ICDATA
        %MOVBIT(ICDATA.RSTNC,ACC.RSTNCIN)
        RET                   ;RETURN TO IC_HANDLER

$EJECT
```

280640-40

Figure C-7. RD05H Read Control/Status Register

5

```
;*********************************************************
;
; NAME:         RD06H
;
; PURPOSE:      READ ROUTINE FOR LOCAL PROC CONTROL
;               REGISTER
;
; CALLED BY:    JUMPED TO FROM SERVICE
;
; CALLS:        NONE
;
; NEST LEVEL:   ??
;
; DESCRIPTION:  IF PROC RESET AND RESET STATUS =
;               PRST, THEN SETS PRST = TRUE, ELSE
;               PRST = FALSE.
;
; REG BANK:     ASSUMES IC_BANK, SELECTS NONE
;
; INPUTS:       NONE
;
; DESTROYS:     CARRY FLAG
;
; RETURNS:      ICDATA
;
; UPDATE HISTORY:  5-14-87 JR UPDATED FOR IDX
;
;*********************************************************

RD06H:  MOV   ICDATA,#CLEAR             ;ICDATA = 0
        JNB   RES,END_R6  ;IF NOT PROC RESET THEN DONE
        MOV   A,RST_STS     ;ELSE GET LAST RESET TYPE
        CJNE  A,#PRST_TYPE,END_R6   ;IF NOT PRST THEN
                                                ;DONE
        SETB  PRST                      ;ELSE SET PRST = TRUE
END_R6: RET                             ;RETURN TO IC HANDLER

$EJECT
```

280640-41

Figure C-8. RD06H Read Local Processor Control Register

```
;***********************************************************
;
; NAME:          RD07H
;
; PURPOSE:       READ ROUTINE FOR LOCAL STATUS
;                REGISTER
;
; CALLED BY:     JUMPED TO FROM SERVICE
;
; CALLS:         NONE
;
; NEST LEVEL:    ??
;
; DESCRIPTION:   IF RESET STATUS = PRST TYPE, THEN
;                PRST STATUS = TRUE, ELSE PRST
;                STATUS = FALSE.
;
; REG BANK:      ASSUMES IC_BANK, SELECTS NONE
;
; INPUTS:        NONE
;
; DESTROYS:      CARRY FLAG
;
; RETURNS:       ICDATA
;
; UPDATE HISTORY:  5-14-87 JR ADDED FOR IDX
;
;***********************************************************

RD07H:  MOV     ICDATA,#CLEAR              ;ICDATA = 0.
        MOV     A,RST_STS           ;GET LAST RESET TYPE
        CJNE    A,#PRST_TYPE,END_R7  ;IF NOT PRST THEN
                                             ;DONE
        SETB    ICDATA.PRST_STS   ;ELSE PRST_STS = TRUE
END_R7: RET                       ;RETURN TO IC HANDLER
$EJECT
```

280640–42

Figure C-9. RD07H Read Local Status Register

5

```
;***********************************************************
;
; NAME:          WR00H
;
; PURPOSE:       WRITE TO A RAM BASED IC REGISTER
;
; CALLED BY:     JUMPED TO FROM EDIT ROUTINES
;
; CALLS:         NONE
;
; NEST LEVEL:    ??
;
; DESCRIPTION:   USES REGNUM TO INDEX INTO RATABLE.
;                USES RWTABLE INDEX PORTION OF RA BYTE
;                TO INDEX INTO RWTABLE, WHERE ICDATA
;                IS THEN WRITTEN TO.
;
; REG BANK:      ASSUMES IC_BANK, SELECTS NONE
;
; INPUTS:        REGNUM
;
; DESTROYS:      ACC, DPTR, ADDR
;
; RETURNS:       NOTHING, RETURNS TO ICHANDLER
;
; UPDATE HISTORY:
;
;***********************************************************

WR00H:  %LOOKUP(#RATABLE,REGNUM)          ;GET RAM/ACCESS
                                          ;BYTE FOR REG
        CLR     ACC.GAR           ;EXTRACT RWTABLE INDEX
        ADD     A,#RWTABLE  ;ADD TABLE ADDR TO GET RAM
                                          ;ADDR
        MOV     ADDR,A  ;PUT ADDR IN INDIRECT ADDR REG
        MOV     @ADDR,ICDATA              ;WR RWTABLE REG
        RET                         ;RETURN TO IC HANDLER

$EJECT
```

280640-43

Figure C-10. WR00H Write RAM Based IC Register

```
;*********************************************************
;
; NAME:          WR01H
;
; PURPOSE:       WRITE ROUTINE FOR MPC BASED IC
;                REGISTERS
;
; CALLED BY:     JUMPED TO FROM EDIT ROUTINES
;
; CALLS:         NONE
;
; NEST LEVEL:    ??
;
; DESCRIPTION:   USES LOOKUP TABLE IC_TO_MPC TO XREF
;                IC ADDRESS TO MPC REGISTER NUMBER,
;                WRITES MPC REG WITH DATA IN ICDATA.
;
; REG BANK:      ASSUMES IC_BANK, SELECTS NONE
;
; INPUTS:        ICDATA
;
; DESTROYS:      DPTR, MPC_RNUM
;
; RETURNS:       NOTHING, RETURNS TO ICHDLR
;
; UPDATE HISTORY:
;
;*********************************************************

WR01H:  MOV     A,REGNUM            ;GET REQUESTED REG NO.
        SUBB    A,#PSB_CTL_OFF+5    ;IC_TO_MPC STARTS
                                    ;WITH PSB SLOT ID REG
        %LOOKUP(#IC_TO_MPC,A)  ;GET CORRES MPC REG NO.
        %WRT_MPC(A,ICDATA)                 ;WR MPC REG
        RET                         ;RETURN TO IC HANDLER

$EJECT
```

280640-44

Figure C-11. WR01H Write MPC Based IC Register

```
;************************************************************
;
;  NAME:          WR02H
;
;  PURPOSE:       WRITE ROUTINE FOR GENERAL CONTROL
;                 REGISTER
;
;  CALLED BY:     JUMPED TO FROM EDIT ROUTINE
;
;  CALLS:         NONE
;
;  NEST LEVEL:    ??
;
;  DESCRIPTION:   PROC RESET = LOCAL RESET.  IF LOCAL
;                 RESET, THEN UPDATE RESET STATUS REG.
;                 UPDATES GEN_CTRL IN RWTABLE BY
;                 JUMPING TO WR00H.
;
;  REG BANK:      ASSUMES IC_BANK, SELECTS NONE
;
;  INPUTS:        ICDATA
;
;  DESTROYS:      NOTHING
;
;  RETURNS:       NOTHING, JUMPS TO WR00H
;
;  UPDATE HISTORY:  5-14-87 JR UPDATED FOR IDX
;
;************************************************************

WR02H:  %MOVBIT(RES,ICDATA.LRST)  ;UPDATE RST PORT PIN
        JNC     END_W2     ;IF NO LOCAL RESET THEN DONE
        MOV     RST_STS,#LRST_TYPE  ;ELSE UPDATE RESET
                                    ;STATUS
END_W2: SJMP    WR00H

$EJECT
```

280640-45

Figure C-12. WR02H Write General Control Register

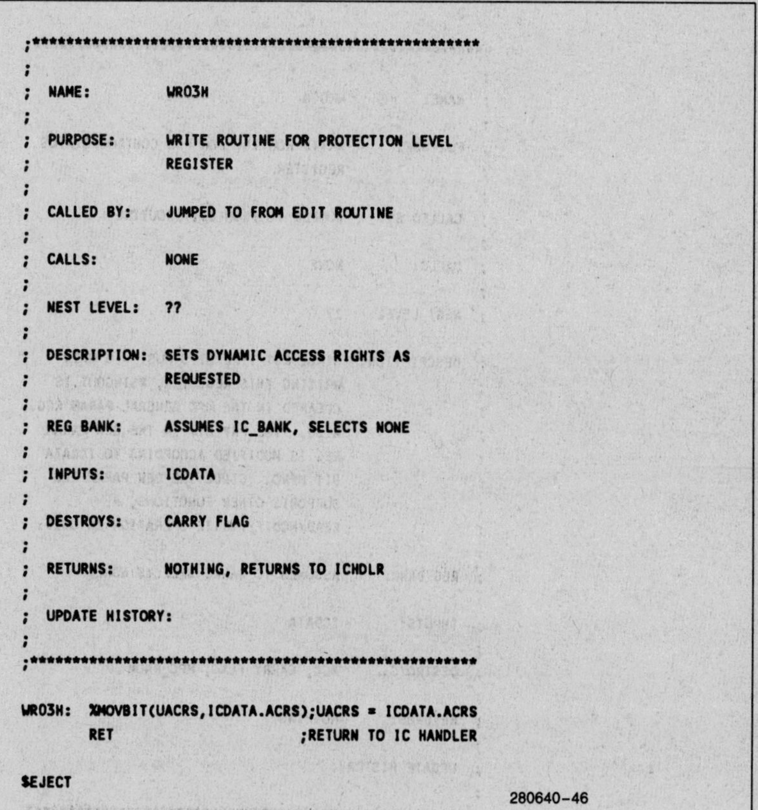

```
;*********************************************************
;
; NAME:         WR03H
;
; PURPOSE:      WRITE ROUTINE FOR PROTECTION LEVEL
;               REGISTER
;
; CALLED BY:    JUMPED TO FROM EDIT ROUTINE
;
; CALLS:        NONE
;
; NEST LEVEL:   ??
;
; DESCRIPTION:  SETS DYNAMIC ACCESS RIGHTS AS
;               REQUESTED
;
; REG BANK:     ASSUMES IC_BANK, SELECTS NONE
;
; INPUTS:       ICDATA
;
; DESTROYS:     CARRY FLAG
;
; RETURNS:      NOTHING, RETURNS TO ICHDLR
;
; UPDATE HISTORY:
;
;*********************************************************

WR03H:  %MOVBIT(UACRS,ICDATA.ACRS);UACRS = ICDATA.ACRS
        RET                      ;RETURN TO IC HANDLER

$EJECT
```

280640-46

Figure C-13. WR03H Write Protection Level Register

```
;***********************************************************
;
; NAME:          WR04H
;
; PURPOSE:       WRITE ROUTINE FOR PSB CONTROL/STATUS
;                REGISTER
;
; CALLED BY:     JUMPED TO FROM EDIT ROUTINE
;
; CALLS:         NONE
;
; NEST LEVEL:    ??
;
; DESCRIPTION:   SINCE RST TYPE BITS MUST = 0 WHEN
;                WRITING THIS REGISTER, RSTNCOUT IS
;                CLEARED IN THE MPC GENERAL PARAM REG.
;                ALSO,  THE PRY BIT IN THE GEN PARAM
;                REG IS MODIFIED ACCORDING TO ICDATA
;                BIT HPRO.  SINCE THE GEN PARAM REG
;                SUPPORTS OTHER FUNCTIONS, A
;                READ/MODIFY/WRITE OPERATION IS USED.
;
; REG BANK:      ASSUMES IC_BANK, SELECTS NONE
;
; INPUTS:        ICDATA
;
; DESTROYS:      ACC, CARRY FLAG, MPC_RNUM
;
; RETURNS:       NOTHING
;
; UPDATE HISTORY:
;
;***********************************************************

WR04H:  MOV   A,PSB_CS ;GET VALUE OF PSB CONT/STAT REG
        %MOVBIT(ICDATA.RSTH0,ACC.RSTH0)     ;SAVE RESET
                                         ;TYPE HISTORY BITS
        %MOVBIT(ICDATA.RSTH1,ACC.RSTH1)
        MOV   PSB_CS,ICDATA              ;UPDATE RWTABLE
        %RD_MPC(A,#GEN_PAR)            ;READ MPC GEN_PAR
        CLR   ACC.RSTNCOUT      ;QUIT DRVG RSTNC TO BUS
        %MOVBIT(ACC.PRY,ICDATA.HPRO)   ;UPDATE PRY BIT
        %WRT_MPC(#GEN_PAR,A)          ;WR MODIFIED DATA
                                         ;BACK TO GEN_PAR
        RET                        ;RETURN TO IC HANDLER

$EJECT
```

280640-47

Figure C-14. WR04H Write PSB Control/Status Register

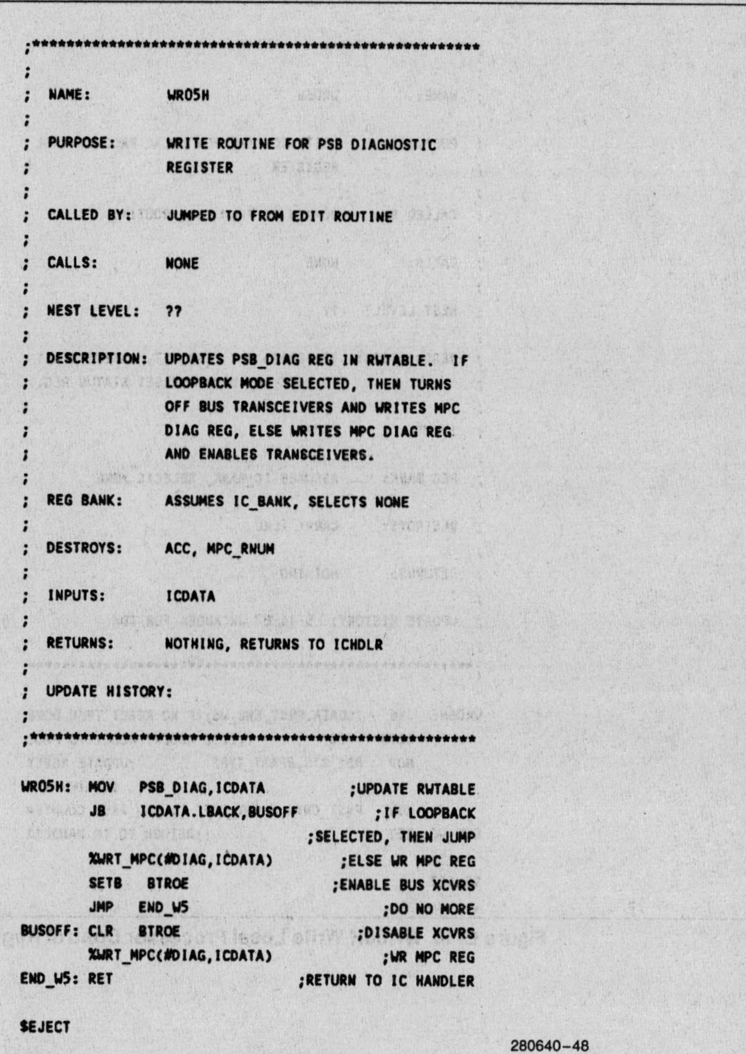

```
;*********************************************************
;
; NAME:          WR05H
;
; PURPOSE:       WRITE ROUTINE FOR PSB DIAGNOSTIC
;                REGISTER
;
; CALLED BY:     JUMPED TO FROM EDIT ROUTINE
;
; CALLS:         NONE
;
; NEST LEVEL:    ??
;
; DESCRIPTION:   UPDATES PSB_DIAG REG IN RWTABLE.  IF
;                LOOPBACK MODE SELECTED, THEN TURNS
;                OFF BUS TRANSCEIVERS AND WRITES MPC
;                DIAG REG, ELSE WRITES MPC DIAG REG
;                AND ENABLES TRANSCEIVERS.
;
; REG BANK:      ASSUMES IC_BANK, SELECTS NONE
;
; DESTROYS:      ACC, MPC_RNUM
;
; INPUTS:        ICDATA
;
; RETURNS:       NOTHING, RETURNS TO ICHDLR
;
; UPDATE HISTORY:
;
;*********************************************************

WR05H:  MOV   PSB_DIAG,ICDATA            ;UPDATE RWTABLE
        JB    ICDATA.LBACK,BUSOFF        ;IF LOOPBACK
                                         ;SELECTED, THEN JUMP
        %WRT_MPC(#DIAG,ICDATA)           ;ELSE WR MPC REG
        SETB  BTROE                      ;ENABLE BUS XCVRS
        JMP   END_W5                     ;DO NO MORE
BUSOFF: CLR   BTROE                      ;DISABLE XCVRS
        %WRT_MPC(#DIAG,ICDATA)           ;WR MPC REG
END_W5: RET                              ;RETURN TO IC HANDLER

$EJECT
```

280640-48

Figure C-15. WR05H Write PSB Diagnostic Register

```
;*********************************************************
;
; NAME:          WR06H
;
; PURPOSE:       WRITE ROUTINE FOR LOCAL PROC CONTROL
;                REGISTER
;
; CALLED BY:     JUMPED TO FROM EDIT ROUTINE
;
; CALLS:         NONE
;
; NEST LEVEL:    ??
;
; DESCRIPTION:   IF ICDATA BIT PRST SET, ASSERT RESET
;                TO PROC AND UPDATE RESET STATUS REG.
;
; INPUTS:        ICDATA
;
; REG BANK:      ASSUMES IC_BANK, SELECTS NONE
;
; DESTROYS:      CARRY FLAG
;
; RETURNS:       NOTHING
;
; UPDATE HISTORY:  5-14-87 JR ADDED FOR IDX
;
;*********************************************************

WR06H:  JNB   ICDATA.PRST,END_W6;IF NO RESET THEN DONE
        SETB  RES               ;ELSE ASSERT RESET TO PROC
        MOV   RST_STS,#PRST_TYPE          ;UPDATE RESET
                                          ;STATUS REG
        MOV   PRST_CNTR,#PRST_CNT  ;LOAD PRST COUNTER
END_W6: RET                     ;RETURN TO IC HANDLER

$EJECT
```

280640-49

Figure C-16. WR06H Write Local Processor Control Register

```
;***********************************************************
;
; MACRO NAME:   GET_EEC (GET EDIT ENTRY CONSTANT)
;
; SYNTAX:       GET_EEC
;
; PURPOSE:      INDEX INTO EETABLE TO GET NEXT EDIT
;               ENTRY CONSTANT
;
; DESCRIPTION:  EET_OFF IS INCREMENTED AND THE CODE
;               BYTE AT EET_OFF FROM DPTR (ASSUMED TO
;               BE POINTING TO EETABLE) IS MOVED TO
;               THE ACCUMULATOR.
;
; INPUTS:       NONE, HOWEVER DPTR ASSUMED = EETABLE
;               (INTR ROUTINES USING DPTR SHOULD
;               PUSH/POP).
;
; DESTROYS:     ACC
;
; RETURNS:      NEXT EET CONSTANT FROM LIST IN ACC
;
; UPDATE HISTORY:
;
;***********************************************************

%*DEFINE(GET_EEC)(
$SAVE NOGEN
        INC     EET_OFF
        MOV     A,EET_OFF
        MOVC    A,@A+DPTR
$RESTORE
)
$EJECT
```

280640-50

Figure C-17. Macro GET_EEC

```
;************************************************************
;
; NAME:           VALERR
;
; PURPOSE:        ROUTINE FOR REPORTING IC WRITE VALUE
;                 ERRORS
;
; CALLED BY:      JUMPED TO FROM EDIT ROUTINES UPON
;                 VALUE ERROR DETECTION
;
; CALLS:          NONE
;
; NEST LEVEL:     ??
;
; DESCRIPTION:    CHECKS FOR LOCAL OR GLOBAL ACCESS AND
;                 UPDATES GENERAL STATUS REGISTER
;                 ACCORDINGLY WITH VALUE ERROR STATUS.
;                 RETURNS TO ICHDLR.
;
; REG BANK:       ASSUMES 0, SELECTS NONE
;
; INPUTS:         MPC_STS
;
; DESTROYS:       NOTHING
;
; RETURNS:        GENERAL STATUS REG, UPDATED FOR VALUE
;                 ERROR, TO ICHDLR
;
; UPDATE HISTORY:
;
;************************************************************

VALERR: JB      MPC_STS.PORT,LCVLER     ;IF LOCAL ACCESS
                                        ;THEN JUMP, ELSE
        ORL     GEN_STS,#GBL_VL_ERR     ;SET GENERAL STATUS
                                       ;= GLOBAL VALUE ERROR
        SJMP    ENDVAL                  ;RESTORE AND RETURN
LCVLER: ORL     GEN_STS,#LCL_VL_ERR     ;SET GENERAL STATUS
                                        ;= LOCAL VALUE ERROR
ENDVAL: RET                            ;RETURN TO IC HANDLER

$EJECT
```

280640-51

Figure C-18. Report IC Write Value Error

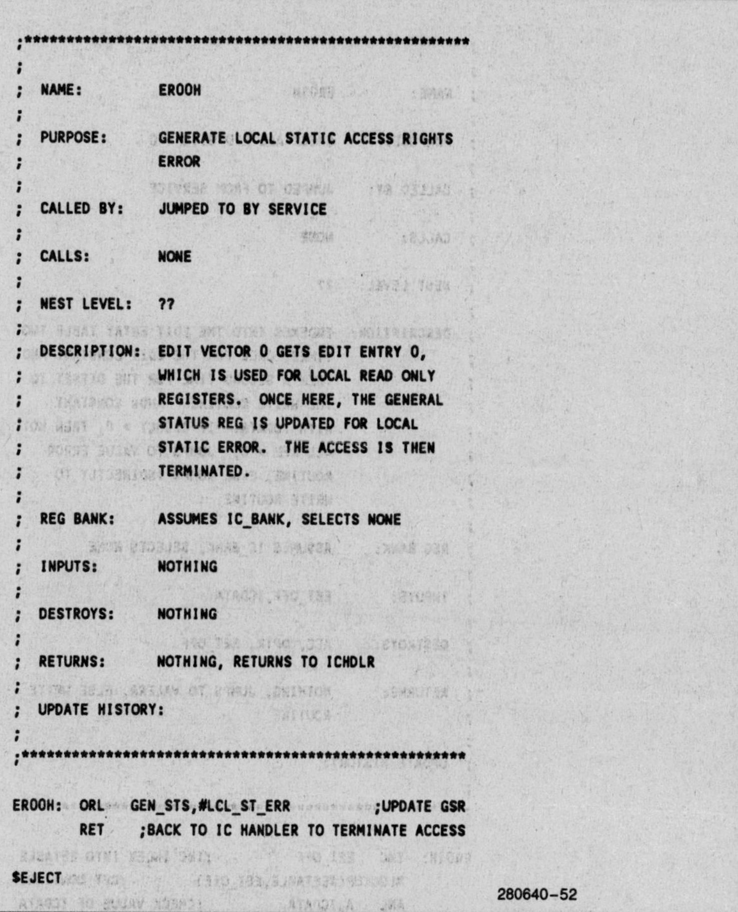

```
;*************************************************************
;
; NAME:          EROOH
;
; PURPOSE:       GENERATE LOCAL STATIC ACCESS RIGHTS
;                ERROR
;
; CALLED BY:     JUMPED TO BY SERVICE
;
; CALLS:         NONE
;
; NEST LEVEL:    ??
;
; DESCRIPTION:   EDIT VECTOR 0 GETS EDIT ENTRY 0,
;                WHICH IS USED FOR LOCAL READ ONLY
;                REGISTERS.  ONCE HERE, THE GENERAL
;                STATUS REG IS UPDATED FOR LOCAL
;                STATIC ERROR.  THE ACCESS IS THEN
;                TERMINATED.
;
; REG BANK:      ASSUMES IC_BANK, SELECTS NONE
;
; INPUTS:        NOTHING
;
; DESTROYS:      NOTHING
;
; RETURNS:       NOTHING, RETURNS TO ICHDLR
;
; UPDATE HISTORY:
;
;*************************************************************

EROOH:  ORL    GEN_STS,#LCL_ST_ERR          ;UPDATE GSR
        RET    ;BACK TO IC HANDLER TO TERMINATE ACCESS

$EJECT
```

280640-52

Figure C-19. ER00H Generate Local Static Access Rights Error

```
;*************************************************************
;
;  NAME:          ER01H
;
;  PURPOSE:       CHECK ALL RFU BITS = 0
;
;  CALLED BY:     JUMPED TO FROM SERVICE
;
;  CALLS:         NONE
;
;  NEST LEVEL:    ??
;
;  DESCRIPTION:   INDEXES INTO THE EDIT ENTRY TABLE TWO
;                 TIMES, ONCE FOR THE EDIT CONSTANT AND
;                 THEN A SECOND TIME FOR THE OFFSET TO
;                 THE WRITE ROUTINE.  ANDs CONSTANT
;                 WITH ICDATA.  IF RESULT > 0, THEN NOT
;                 ALL RFU = 0,  JUMPS TO VALUE ERROR
;                 ROUTINE, ELSE JUMPS INDIRECTLY TO
;                 WRITE ROUTINE.
;
;  REG BANK:      ASSUMES IC_BANK, SELECTS NONE
;
;  INPUTS:        EET_OFF,ICDATA
;
;  DESTROYS:      ACC, DPTR, EET_OFF
;
;  RETURNS:       NOTHING, JUMPS TO VALERR, ELSE WRITE
;                 ROUTINE
;
;  UPDATE HISTORY:
;
;*************************************************************

ER01H:  INC    EET_OFF          ;INC INDEX INTO EETABLE
        %LOOKUP(#EETABLE,EET_OFF)       ;GET CONSTANT
        ANL    A,ICDATA           ;CHECK VALUE OF ICDATA
        JNZ    ERR_1                ;JMP IF ILLEGAL VALUE
        %GET_EEC         ;GET WR ROUTINE OFFSET FM EET
        MOV    DPTR,#WRLBL    ;GET WR ROUTINE LABEL ADDR
        JMP    @A+DPTR                  ;JMP TO WR ROUTINE
ERR_1:  AJMP   VALERR                     ;REPORT VALUE ERR
                                  ;(TOO FAR FOR REL JMP)

$EJECT
```

280640-53

Figure C-20. ER01H Check for RFU Bits = 0

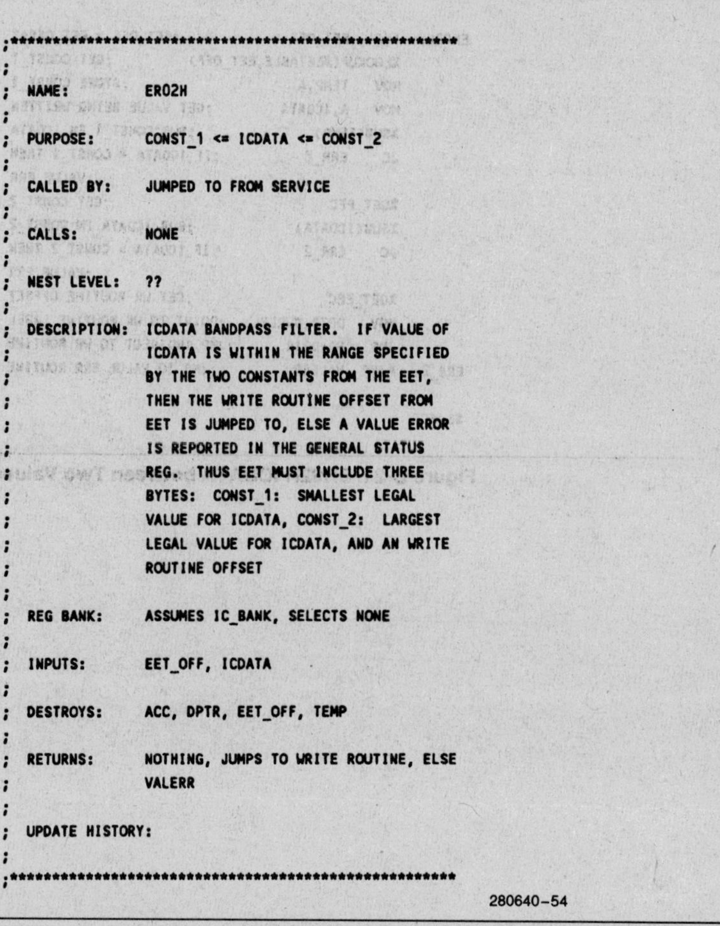

```
;************************************************************
;
;  NAME:          ER02H
;
;  PURPOSE:       CONST_1 <= ICDATA <= CONST_2
;
;  CALLED BY:     JUMPED TO FROM SERVICE
;
;  CALLS:         NONE
;
;  NEST LEVEL:    ??
;
;  DESCRIPTION:   ICDATA BANDPASS FILTER.  IF VALUE OF
;                 ICDATA IS WITHIN THE RANGE SPECIFIED
;                 BY THE TWO CONSTANTS FROM THE EET,
;                 THEN THE WRITE ROUTINE OFFSET FROM
;                 EET IS JUMPED TO, ELSE A VALUE ERROR
;                 IS REPORTED IN THE GENERAL STATUS
;                 REG.  THUS EET MUST INCLUDE THREE
;                 BYTES:  CONST_1:  SMALLEST LEGAL
;                 VALUE FOR ICDATA, CONST_2:  LARGEST
;                 LEGAL VALUE FOR ICDATA, AND AN WRITE
;                 ROUTINE OFFSET
;
;  REG BANK:      ASSUMES IC_BANK, SELECTS NONE
;
;  INPUTS:        EET_OFF, ICDATA
;
;  DESTROYS:      ACC, DPTR, EET_OFF, TEMP
;
;  RETURNS:       NOTHING, JUMPS TO WRITE ROUTINE, ELSE
;                 VALERR
;
;
;  UPDATE HISTORY:
;
;************************************************************
```

280640-54

Figure C-21. ER02H ICDATA between Two Values

5

```
ER02H:  INC   EET_OFF                 ;EET_OFF = EET_OFF+1
        %LOOKUP(#EETABLE,EET_OFF)            ;GET CONST_1
        MOV   TEMP,A                       ;STORE CONST_1
        MOV   A,ICDATA           ;GET VALUE BEING WRITTEN
        %SUB(TEMP)                ;SUB CONST_1 FM ICDATA
        JC    ERR_2             ;IF ICDATA < CONST_1 THEN
                                               ;VALUE ERR
        %GET_EEC                             ;GET CONST_2
        %SUB(ICDATA)              ;SUB ICDATA FM CONST_2
        JC    ERR_2             ;IF ICDATA > CONST_2 THEN
                                               ;VALUE ERR
        %GET_EEC                  ;GET WR ROUTINE OFFSET
        MOV   DPTR,#WRLBL     ;POINT TO WR ROUTINE LABEL
        JMP   @A+DPTR       ;JMP INDIRECT TO WR ROUTINE
ERR_2:  AJMP  VALERR            ;JMP TO VALUE ERR ROUTINE

$EJECT
```

280640-55

Figure C-21. ER02H ICDATA between Two Values

```
;*****************************************************
;
; NAME:          ER03H
;
; PURPOSE:       EDIT ROUTINE FOR PSB ARB ID REGISTER
;
; CALLED BY:     JUMPED TO FROM SERVICE
;
; CALLS:         NONE
;
; NEST LEVEL:    ??
;
; DESCRIPTION:   CHECKS ALL RFUs = 0, THEN CHECKS FOR
;                LEGAL ARB ID BY COUNTING THE BIT
;                TRANSITIONS IN ICDATA.
;
; REG BANK:      ASSUMES IC_BANK, SELECTS NONE
;
; INPUTS:        NONE
;
; DESTROYS:      ACC, TEMP
;
; RETURNS:       JUMPS DIRECTLY TO WR01H, ELSE VALERR
;
; UPDATE HISTORY:
;
;*****************************************************

ER03H:  MOV   A,#PSB_ARB_MSK          ;GET RFU MASK
        ANL   A,ICDATA             ;MASK ALL BUT RFUs
        JNZ   ERR_3    ;IF NOT ALL RFUs = 0 THEN ERROR
        MOV   TEMP,#TRANS_CNT         ;LOAD TRANS CNTR
        MOV   A,ICDATA        ;GET VALUE BEING WRITTEN
        CLR   C
        RLC   A                       ;SEE IF MSB SET
        JNC   ID_TR               ;IF NO CARRY, THEN OK
        SETB  ACC.3                   ;ELSE SET BIT 3
                              ;(ARB ID IS ONLY 5 BITS)
ID_TR:  XRL   A,ICDATA            ;ID BIT TRANSITIONS
ROT_A:  CLR   C                 ;ROTATE ZEROS INTO ACC
        RLC   A                  ;LOOK FOR TRANSITIONS
        JNC   CHK_ACC         ;IF CARRY BIT IS NOT SET
                                           ;THEN JMP
        DJNZ  TEMP,ROT_A ;ELSE TALLY UP ONE TRANSITION
ERR_3:  AJMP  VALERR        ;IF TRANS_CNTR REACHES ZERO
                                         ;THEN ERROR
CHK_ACC:JNZ   ROT_A                   ;IF ACC NOT ZERO
                                ;THEN CONTINUE LOOKING
        AJMP  WR01H           ;ELSE JUMP TO WR ROUTINE

$EJECT
```

280640–56

Figure C-22. ER03H Edit PSB ARB ID Register

```
;*********************************************************
;
; NAME:         ER04H
;
; PURPOSE:      EDIT ROUTINE FOR PSB DIAG REGISTER
;
; CALLED BY:    JUMPED TO FROM SERVICE
;
; CALLS:        NONE
;
; NEST LEVEL:   ??
;
; DESCRIPTION:  CHECKS ALL RFUs = 0, THEN IF
;               LOOPBACK MODE BEING SELECTED,
;               CHECKS FOR RSTNC* ASSERTED.
;
; REG BANK:     ASSUMES IC_BANK, SELECTS NONE
;
; INPUTS:       NONE
;
; DESTROYS:     ACC, DPTR
;
; RETURNS:      JUMPS DIRECTLY TO WR06H, ELSE VALERR
;
; UPDATE HISTORY:
;
;*********************************************************

ER04H:  MOV   A,#PSB_DIAG_MSK     ;GET PSB DIAG RFU MASK
        ANL   A,ICDATA            ;MASK ALL BUT RFUs
        JNZ   ERR_4               ;IF ALL RFUs NOT = 0
                                  ;THEN VALUE ERROR
        JNB   ICDATA.LBACK,END_E4 ;IF LOOPBACK NOT
                            ;SELECTED, SET THE WR REG
        MOV   A,#RST_TYPE_MSK     ;GET MASK FOR RESET
                                  ;TYPE BITS
        ANL   A,PSB_CS            ;MASK ALL BUT RESET
                                  ;TYPE FROM PSB C/S
        JZ    ERR_4         ;IF RSTNC HAS BEEN CLEARED
                                  ;THEN VALUE ERR
END_E4: AJMP  WR05H               ;WR REG
ERR_4:  AJMP  VALERR              ;REPORT VALUE ERROR

$EJECT
```

280640-57

Figure C-23. ER04H Edit PSB Diagnostic Register

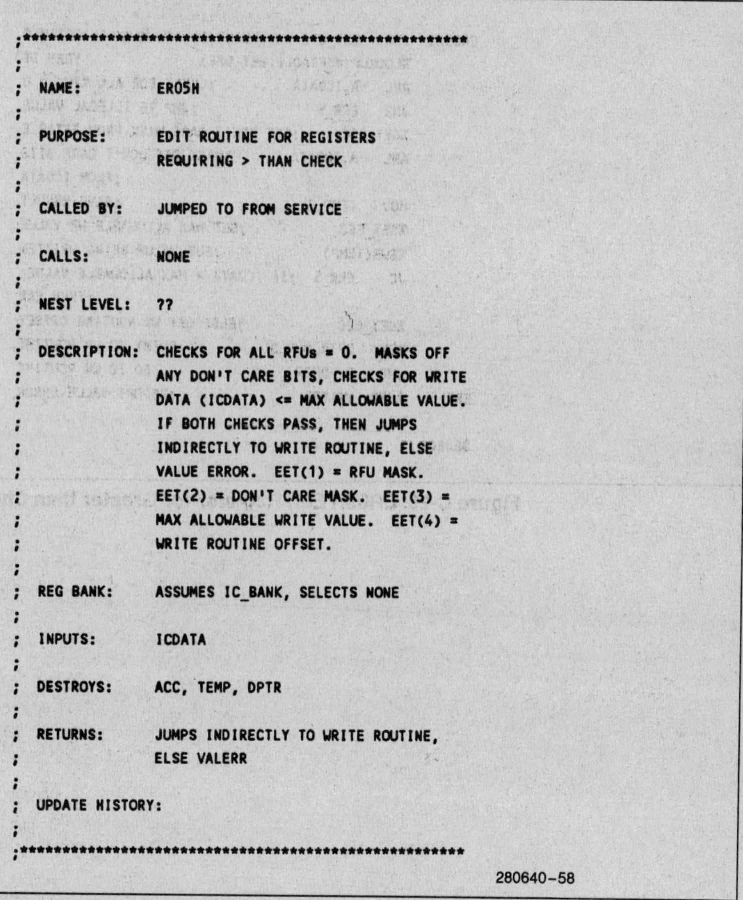

```
;*******************************************************
;
; NAME:          ER05H
;
; PURPOSE:       EDIT ROUTINE FOR REGISTERS
;                REQUIRING > THAN CHECK
;
; CALLED BY:     JUMPED TO FROM SERVICE
;
; CALLS:         NONE
;
; NEST LEVEL:    ??
;
; DESCRIPTION:   CHECKS FOR ALL RFUs = 0.  MASKS OFF
;                ANY DON'T CARE BITS, CHECKS FOR WRITE
;                DATA (ICDATA) <= MAX ALLOWABLE VALUE.
;                IF BOTH CHECKS PASS, THEN JUMPS
;                INDIRECTLY TO WRITE ROUTINE, ELSE
;                VALUE ERROR.  EET(1) = RFU MASK.
;                EET(2) = DON'T CARE MASK.  EET(3) =
;                MAX ALLOWABLE WRITE VALUE.  EET(4) =
;                WRITE ROUTINE OFFSET.
;
; REG BANK:      ASSUMES IC_BANK, SELECTS NONE
;
; INPUTS:        ICDATA
;
; DESTROYS:      ACC, TEMP, DPTR
;
; RETURNS:       JUMPS INDIRECTLY TO WRITE ROUTINE,
;                ELSE VALERR
;
; UPDATE HISTORY:
;
;*******************************************************
```

280640–58

Figure C-24. ER05H Edit Register for Greater than Check

5

```
ER05H: INC    EET_OFF      ;POINT TO RFU MASK IN EETABLE
       %LOOKUP(#EETABLE,EET_OFF)           ;GET IT
       ANL    A,ICDATA        ;CHECK FOR ALL RFUs = 0
       JNZ    ERR_5              ;JMP IF ILLEGAL VALUE
       %GET_EEC     ;GET DON'T CARE MASK FROM EETABLE
       ANL    A,ICDATA       ;MASK OFF DON'T CARE BITS
                                         ;FROM ICDATA
       MOV    TEMP,A                     ;SAVE RESULT
       %GET_EEC            ;GET MAX ALLOWABLE WR VALUE
       %SUB(TEMP)            ;SUB VALUE BEING WRITTEN
       JC     ERR_5  ;IF ICDATA > MAX ALLOWABLE VALUE,
                                           ;THEN ERR
       %GET_EEC            ;ELSE GET WR ROUTINE OFFSET
       MOV    DPTR,#WRLBL         ;POINT TO WR ROUTINE
       JMP    @A+DPTR               ;GO TO WR ROUTINE
ERR_5: AJMP   VALERR               ;REPORT VALUE ERROR

$EJECT
```

280640-59

Figure C-25. ER05H Edit Register for Greater than Check

APPENDIX D
USER CALLABLE MACRO ROUTINES

```
;***********************************************************
;
; MACRO NAME:   RD_MPC  (READ MPC)
;
; SYNTAX:       RD_MPC(DEST,SRC)
;
; PURPOSE:      READ REGISTER FROM MPC IC REGISTER
;               SET
;
; DESCRIPTION:  THE VALUE CONTAINED IN OR BY SRC (MAY
;               BE CONSTANT OR DIRECT ADDRESS) MUST
;               BE A LEGAL MPC REGISTER ADDRESS.  THE
;               REGISTER DATA IS RETURNED IN THE
;               LOCATION SPECIFIED IN DEST.
;
; INPUTS:       DEST, SRC
;
; DESTROYS:     MPC_RNUM, ACC
;
; RETURNS:      MPC REGISTER DATA IN DEST
;
; UPDATE HISTORY:
;
;***********************************************************

%*DEFINE(RD_MPC(DEST,SRC))(
$SAVE nogen
      MOV     MPC_RNUM,%SRC
      MOVX    A,@MPC_RNUM
      %IF(%NES(A,%DEST)) THEN (
      MOV     %DEST,A
      )FI
$RESTORE
)

$EJECT
```

280640-60

Figure D-1. Macro RD_MPC

```
;*************************************************************
;
; MACRO NAME:   WRT_MPC  (WRITE MPC)
;
; SYNTAX:       WRT_MPC(DEST,SRC)
;
; PURPOSE:      WRITE DATA TO MPC IC REGISTER
;
; DESCRIPTION:  THE VALUE CONTAINED IN OR BY SRC (MAY
;               BE CONSTANT OR DIRECT ADDRESS) IS
;               WRITTEN TO THE MPC REGISTER SPECIFIED
;               BY DEST, WHICH MAY ALSO BE A CONSTANT
;               OR DIRECT ADDRESS.
;
; INPUTS:       DEST, SRC
;
; DESTROYS:     MPC_RNUM, ACC
;
; RETURNS:      NOTHING
;
; UPDATE HISTORY:
;
;*************************************************************

%*DEFINE(WRT_MPC(DEST,SRC))(
$SAVE nogen
        MOV     MPC_RNUM,%DEST
        %IF(%NES(A,%SRC)) THEN (
        MOV     A,%SRC
        )FI
        MOVX    @MPC_RNUM,A
$RESTORE
)

$EJECT
```

280640–61

Figure D-2. Macro WRT_MPC

```
;*******************************************************
;
; MACRO NAME:   LOOKUP
;
; SYNTAX:       LOOKUP(TABLE,OFFSET)
;
; PURPOSE:      RETRIEVE BYTE FROM TABLE.
;
; DESCRIPTION:  THE SPECIFIED TABLE IS INDEXED BY THE
;               VALUE OF OFFSET AND RESULTING ADDRESS
;               IS READ INTO THE ACCUMULATOR.
;
; INPUTS:       TABLE, OFFSET
;
; DESTROYS:     DPTR, ACC
;
; RETURNS:      DESIRED BYTE IN ACC
;
; UPDATE HISTORY:
;
;*******************************************************

%*DEFINE(LOOKUP(TABLE,OFFSET))(
$SAVE nogen
        %IF(%NES(A,%OFFSET)) THEN (
        MOV     A,%OFFSET
        )FI
        MOV     DPTR,%TABLE
        MOVC    A,@A+DPTR
$RESTORE
)

$EJECT
```

280640-62

Figure D-3. Macro LOOKUP

5

```
;*****************************************************************
;
; MACRO NAME:   SUB     (SUBTRACT)
;
; SYNTAX:       SUB(OPR)
;
; PURPOSE:      SUBTRACT OPERAND FROM ACC
;
; DESCRIPTION:  THE CARRY FLAG IS CLEARD AND THE
;               VALUE SPECIFIED IN OR BY OPR IS
;               SUBTRACTED FROM THE ACCUMULATOR.
;
; INPUTS:       OPR
;
; DESTROYS:     ACC, CARRY FLAG
;
; RETURNS:      RESULT IN C AND ACC
;
; UPDATE HISTORY:
;
;*****************************************************************

%*DEFINE(SUB(OPR))(
$SAVE nogen
        CLR     C
        SUBB    A,%OPR
$RESTORE
)

$EJECT
```

280640-63

Figure D-4. Macro SUB (Subtract)

```
;*****************************************************************
;
; MACRO NAME:   MOVBIT  (MOVE BIT)
;
; SYNTAX:       MOVBIT(DEST_BIT,SRC_BIT)
;
; PURPOSE:      PERFORM A BIT MOVE OPERATION
;
; DESCRIPTION:  THE SOURCE BIT IS MOVED TO THE CARRY
;               FLAG.  THE CARRY FLAG IS MOVED TO THE
;               DESTINATION BIT.
;
; INPUTS:       DEST_BIT, SRC_BIT
;
; DESTROYS:     CARRY FLAG
;
; RETURNS:      DEST_BIT = SRC_BIT
;
; UPDATE HISTORY:
;
;*****************************************************************

%*DEFINE(MOVBIT(DEST_BIT,SRC_BIT))(
$SAVE nogen
        MOV     C,%SRC_BIT
        MOV     %DEST_BIT,C
$RESTORE
)

$EJECT
```

280640-64

Figure D-5. Macro MOVBIT

```
;**********************************************************
;
; MACRO NAME:   GET_EEC (GET EDIT ENTRY CONSTANT)
;
; SYNTAX:       GET_EEC
;
; PURPOSE:      INDEX INTO EETABLE TO GET NEXT EDIT
;               ENTRY CONSTANT
;
; DESCRIPTION:  EET_OFF IS INCREMENTED AND THE CODE
;               BYTE AT EET_OFF FROM DPTR (ASSUMED TO
;               BE POINTING TO EETABLE) IS MOVED TO
;               THE ACCUMULATOR.
;
; INPUTS:       NONE, HOWEVER DPTR ASSUMED = EETABLE
;               (INTR ROUTINES USING DPTR SHOULD
;               PUSH/POP).
;
; DESTROYS:     ACC
;
; RETURNS:      NEXT EET CONSTANT FROM LIST IN ACC
;
; UPDATE HISTORY:
;
;**********************************************************

%*DEFINE(GET_EEC)(
$SAVE NOGEN
        INC     EET_OFF
        MOV     A,EET_OFF
        MOVC    A,@A+DPTR
$RESTORE
)
$EJECT
```

280640-65

Figure D-6. Macro GET_EEC

November 1990

Multibus II Simplifies Partitioning of a Complex Design

FRANCOIS HUGUENIN
SENIOR FIELD APPLICATION ENGINEER
INTEL SWITZERLAND

Order Number: 280691-001

5

Multibus II Simplifies Partitioning of a Complex Design

CONTENTS PAGE

CONTENTS PAGE

PREFACE

Several years ago, prior to joining Intel, I worked at the Swiss Federal Institute of Technology in the Group for Automatic Control. As part of my job responsibilities there, we made some real-time simulation studies in the field of aircraft performance computers. The engine model was implemented on an 8086-based single board computer. It also had special custom-made hardware for displaying the instruments similar to those in the original aircraft cockpit. During the course of this work, we were able to demonstrate the feasibility of using microcomputers in this application field. A paper describing this work was then presented at the AIAA Flight Simulation Technologies Conference, Long Beach, California in June 1980.[1] While the use of microcomputers in aircraft simulation has become quite common in recent years, this work anticipated the impact of major cost reductions and performance improvements which were to follow in the flight simulation industry.

In more recent years, I have served as an Application Engineer for Intel Corporation in the Swiss District. In this role I am often confronted with the problem of how to demonstrate the capabilities of a product in a way which engineers can easily relate to and understand. This was the case with Multibus II—an industry standard bus, specially designed for the more rigorous demands of multiprocessing. Since few applications today are partitioned to take advantage of parallel computing, my goal was to demonstrate how functional partitioning could be applied to a computationally intensive application with relative ease. The goal of breaking the "Von Neuman bottleneck" would be to increase the aggregate computing power without a substantial increase in overhead.

For assistance on this project, I called upon the Furrer & Gloor Company, a Multibus manufacturer with broad experience in industrial automation. With their assistance I was able to modify the work done seven years ago on aircraft simulation and convert it to Multibus II to demonstrate multiprocessing. This application provides a good example of the typical Multibus II design cycle. We begin with the basic architectural decisions, define the message contents between processors, show the use of software development and debug tools, and then finally test for performance tuning on the final system once it is up and running. As you read through this document you will learn about the process of application development in addition to the special demands of the aircraft simulation experiment.

I would like to thank Markus Schoenbucher and Christoph Graf of the Furrer & Gloor Company for their great support during the weeks of implementation in the labs. George Walker of WeDV deserves special thanks for designing and debugging the iRMX®II part of the application. I wish also to thank P. Marti, H. -R. Aeschilmann, K. Krizaj and B. Leiser of the Simulator Maintenance Group at Swissair in Zurich who gave me access in the early phase to all the important engine data and most valuable inputs on the flight simulation technology in general back in the late 70's. Finally I especially want to thank Roger Finger from Multibus II Application Engineering at the Intel factory in Hillsboro, Oregon for his guidance in helping me get this Ap Note done and for his corrections to my "Swiss English".

—Francois Huguenin

1.0 INTRODUCTION

Aircraft simulation trains pilots at a substantial savings. Flight crews can train around the clock, without regard to weather conditions and airport congestion. This important simulation model is a complex technical system which includes several high-performance digital computers. One key part of the simulator is the engine model: it is vital to the functioning of the entire machine:

— For the flight model equations (thrust and torque)

— For the "man in the loop" process with the important flight deck instruments (the pilot reacts on the settings and feedback from the engine instruments)

— For the flight engineer with all subsystems which are fed by the engines (hydraulics, electrical power supply, air conditioning, anti-icing, etc.)

The basic problem for good simulation is computing speed, because the quality of the pilot's training is a direct function of the flight simulator's update speed. Previously most simulators were using more than one processor based on a shared memory architecture. The trend today is dictated by the ever-increasing complexity of modern aircraft which are using more and more electronics on board. The new generation of flight simulators has a collection of black boxes (navigation computer, display units, engine control) used directly as in the original aircraft. In this complex environment, the engine is a closed subsystem which can be modeled without having to build a whole flight simulator. This part of the machine has well-known interaction points to the rest of the simulator. The work which was done at the Swiss Federal Institute of Technology some years ago was to be part of an on-board performance computer to calculate fuel optimal flight trajectories.[2] The following implementation of the engine model with Multibus II is based on these results.

2.0 DESIGN PROBLEM OF THE SIMULATION OF THE JET ENGINE

The General Electric CF6-50C Fan Jet Engine which is installed on all of Swissair's DC-10 aircraft provides our study model. This engine of the now "older" generation delivers up to 75% of the thrust power through the fan. The model designed during the years 1978 to 1980 is based on data made available by the engine manufacturer General Electric, McDonnell Douglas for the installed data (measurements made during the certification of the DC-10) and finally from CAE, the flight simulator manufacturer, with the actual programs written in assembler for the SIGMA computer.

2.1 The Engine Model

In order to be as realistic as possible, the engine model is very complex and has the following main characteristics:

— It is multivariable, with secondary interdependencies.

— It has basically two states: the transient state when coming up after ignition, and steady state when being held at a stable working point.

— It is a function of many parameters which directly influence the engine.

A cross section of the CF6-50C engine is shown in Figure 2-1.

Undoubtedly, the main problem of the model is the fuel control unit, which controls the whole engine. This unit also defines the transient behavior of the engine startup and excursions of the working point in the steady state mode. Of course, some simplifications are necessary for simulation. It was necessary to concentrate on the steady state model to reduce the modeling problem to a manageable task.[1] No startup sequence of the engine was to be modeled, but this approach has the great advantage of allowing the direct use of the previously mentioned data tables from the engine manufacturer. The model was exact in the range for which the data tables were originally measured. This reduced and more manageable model is shown in Figure 2-2.

A collection of modules are building the model with some interactions between them. These subsystems are:

— INLET:	Reduction of mach, temperature and pressure to standard values sea level, standard day and temperature
— POWER LEVEL:	Model of the power lever in the cockpit. From these, the pilot sets the throttles
— N2 TRANSIENT:	Simplified model of the fuel control unit (basically a fourth order digital filter)
— N1:	Model of the FAN as function of mach and N2
— THRUST:	Model of the thrust as function of N1 and N2
— FUEL FLOW:	Model of the fuel flow inside the engine in tons per hour as function of N2, altitude and mach
— EGT:	Model of the engine temperature as function of N2 and mach
— EPR:	Model of the engine pressure ration as function of mach and N2

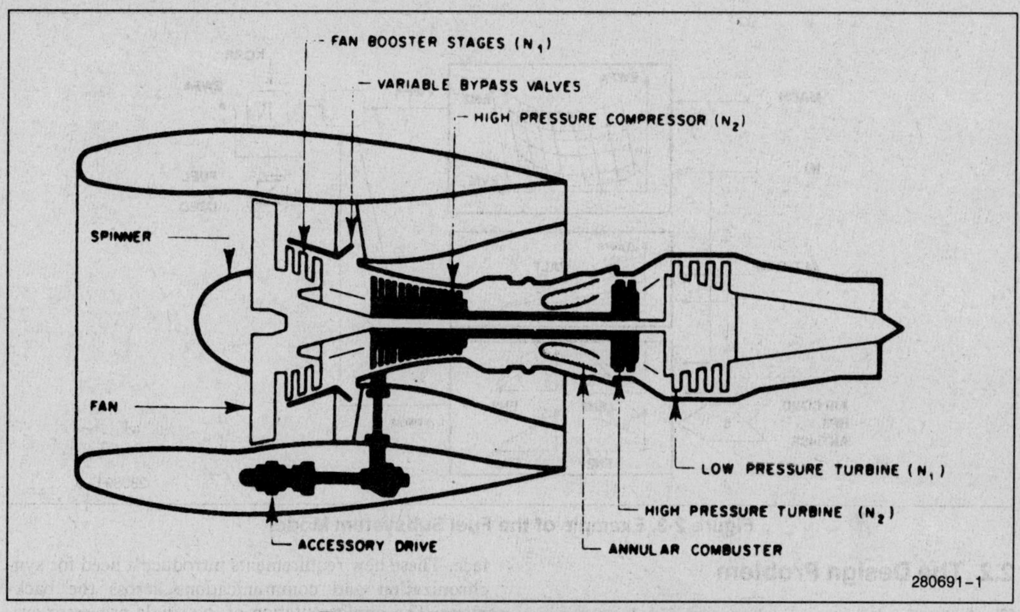

Figure 2-1. The CF6-50C Engine Layout

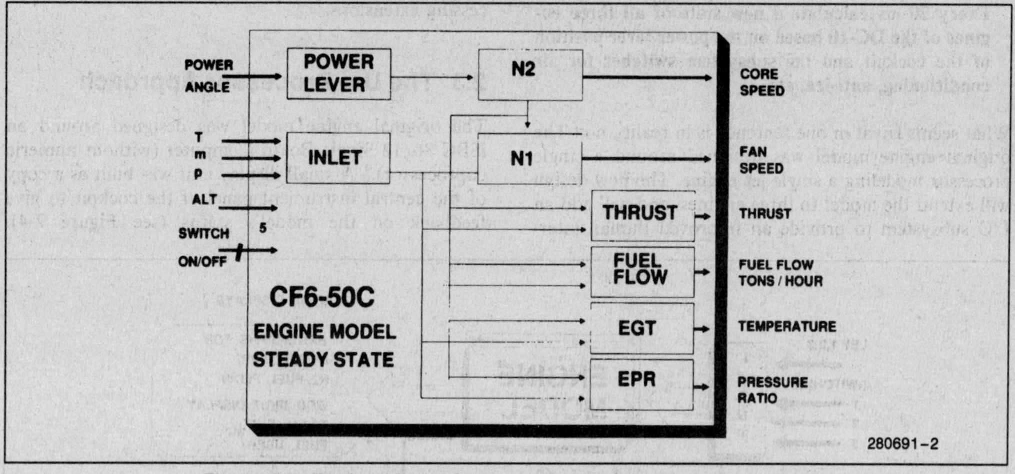

Figure 2-2. Engine Model Structure for Steady State Operation

The power plant of an aircraft is, as mentioned before, a closed system and provides additional tasks besides thrust for motion. The engine must provide fresh air for the cabin, and electric power for the cockpit, kitchen, cockpit electronics, etc. It must also activate and sustain the hydraulic subsystem for the control surfaces of the wings, and feed the anti-icing system for the wing tips, etc. The model, to be realistic, must take into account that these additional tasks will also have an appreciable influence on the state of the engine.

This can be demonstrated best with the fuel model as shown in Figure 2-3. The fuel model is basically a function of mach and N2 (referred core speed). This gives the main data curve and the basic fuel flow in tons per hour and will be interpolated through a high-speed algorithm. When the aircraft is climbing, the fuel flow will change according to a second data curve for correction with the value DELTA EWFA1. The correction, due to the on or off switching of air conditioning, etc., will also be taken into account with other data tables. The total fuel flow, as well as the fuel used by the engine, finally can be calculated with all the deltas. This model was validated with actual data taken from the Aircraft Data System of the DC-10.[1]

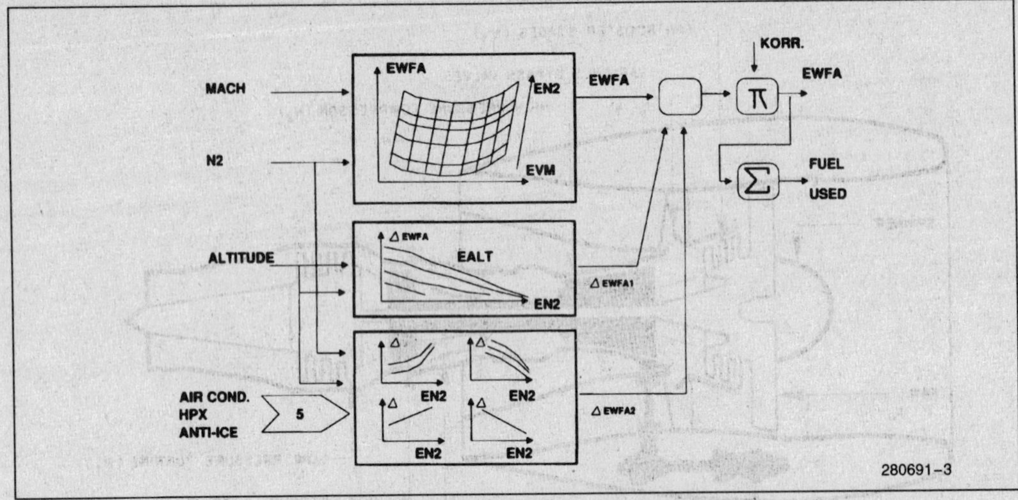

Figure 2-3. Example of the Fuel Subsystem Model

2.2 The Design Problem

The task to be done now can be summarized as follows:

Every 20 ms calculate a new state of all three engines of the DC-10 based on the power lever position of the cockpit and the subsystem switches for air conditioning, anti-ice, etc.

What seems trival in one sentence is in reality not! The original engine model was designed around a single processor modeling a single jet engine. The new design will extend the model to three engines, and will add an I/O subsystem to provide an improved human interface. These new requirements introduce a need for synchronization and communications across the backplane. The implementation of the single processor system will be discussed first, followed by the multiprocessing extensions.

2.3 The Uni-Processor Approach

The original engine model was designed around an iSBC 86/12 Single Board Computer (without numeric coprocessor).[1] A small display unit was built as a copy of the central instrument panel of the cockpit to give feedback on the model's status (see Figure 2-4).

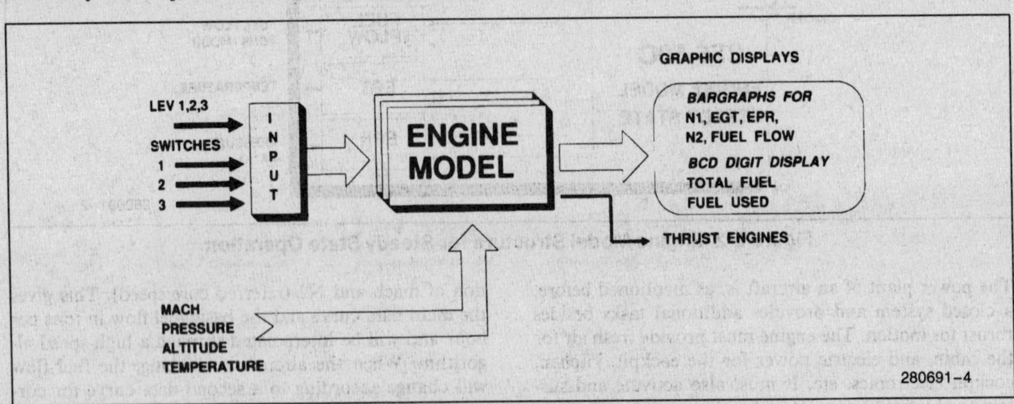

Figure 2-4. The Engine Model Architecture for the DC-10

With a single processor, the software architecture is relatively simple: on every clock interrupt, the I/O unit was activated to read input data (power level position, on/off switches, etc.) and the engine model called three times in sequence with the appropriate parameters. Afterwards, some scaling took place to display the bar graphs and fuel used digits (see Figure 2-4). Using this approach, the compute time depended on programming quality in the loop and therefore was optimized using assembler coded routines. The complete computing cycle consists of: read the inputs, calculate the engine model three times with the new state due to input parameters, scale the results and output them to the I/O unit.

2.4 The Multiprocessor Approach

To relieve the computational bottleneck and further reduce the update time, additional processors are needed. The basic question when using multiple processors is how to partition the application (in this case the modeling of all three DC-10 engines). For this application, one processor for each engine is appropriate because each engine model can be considered as a closed system with well-known interaction points. This results in a four-computer system: one processor must be a kind of "master" to coordinate the I/O and simulate the flight simulator; the remaining three are each modeling one engine of the DC-10.

The data flow changes slightly compared to the one processor approach. Because each processor is independent, each must be synchronized in some way.

Using the Multibus II technology[4] overcomes the hurdles of designing a multiprocessing hardware and is available off the shelf. The synchronization uses messages, exchanged between the host and its partners allowing a data exchange. This results in the architecture shown in Figure 2-5 where CPU #2, #3, #4 all have a local implementation of the engine model. The host or CPU #1 will handle all the coordination work and some key functions for the transient model and display scaling. The coupler board MBII/LNK-1 will handle the input-output processing.

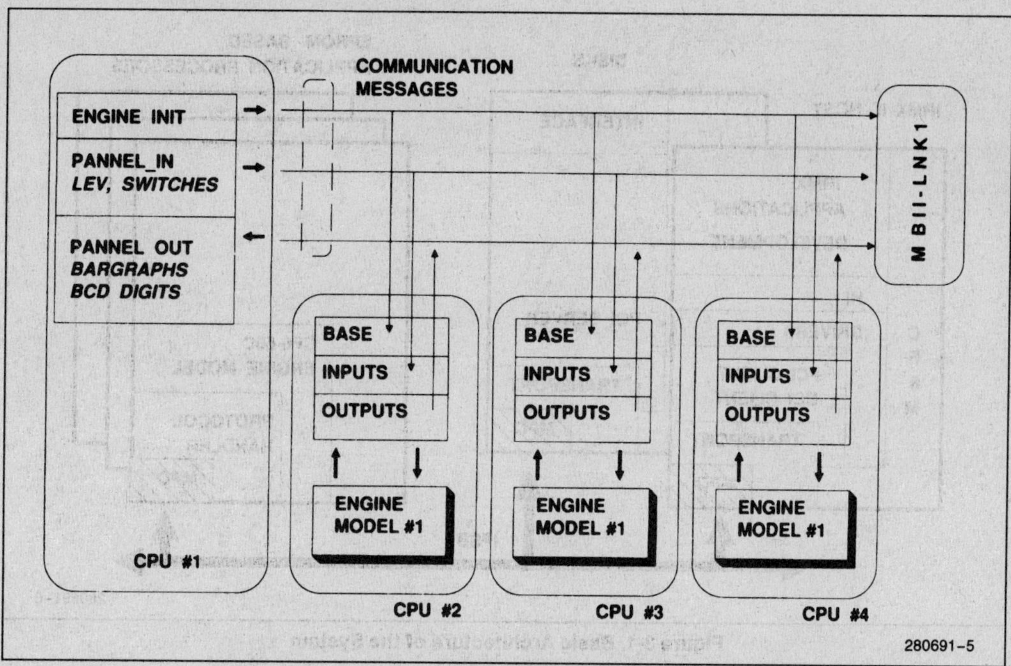

Figure 2-5. Functional Partitioning Using Four Processors

3.0 MULTIPROCESSOR SOFTWARE DESIGN WITH iRMX® II

The architecture chosen for the application is based on a fully-configured iRMX II system as a host, complemented with three "EPROM"-based application processors, one for each engine of the DC-10. This decision was made to minimize the amount of recoding which would be necessary for the original engine model. Software which was written a couple of years ago can be reused without change. In the process, the older iSBC 86/12 hardware will be upgraded to iSBC 286/100A boards for faster execution speed and Multibus II compatibility. Figure 3-1 shows the system architecture of the new multiprocessing system.

Each of the four processors in this system has some primary task to fulfill:

Host:

This is the central control processor which runs a complete real-time operating system. The iRMX II operating system was configured with a human interface, disk I/O subsystem (PCI—Peripheral Communications Interface), and a message passing communications layer. The iRMX II console will also be used as an on-target host for software development.

Applications Processors:

Each of the applications processors runs an EPROM based program which contains the engine model software. The only change which was required to the original software was the addition of a message passing communications interface. Since there is no operating system on these boards, a low-level MPC protocol handler is responsible for this function.

LNK-1:

This board serves as a bridge to the low-cost I/O subsystem and the master clock during simulation time.

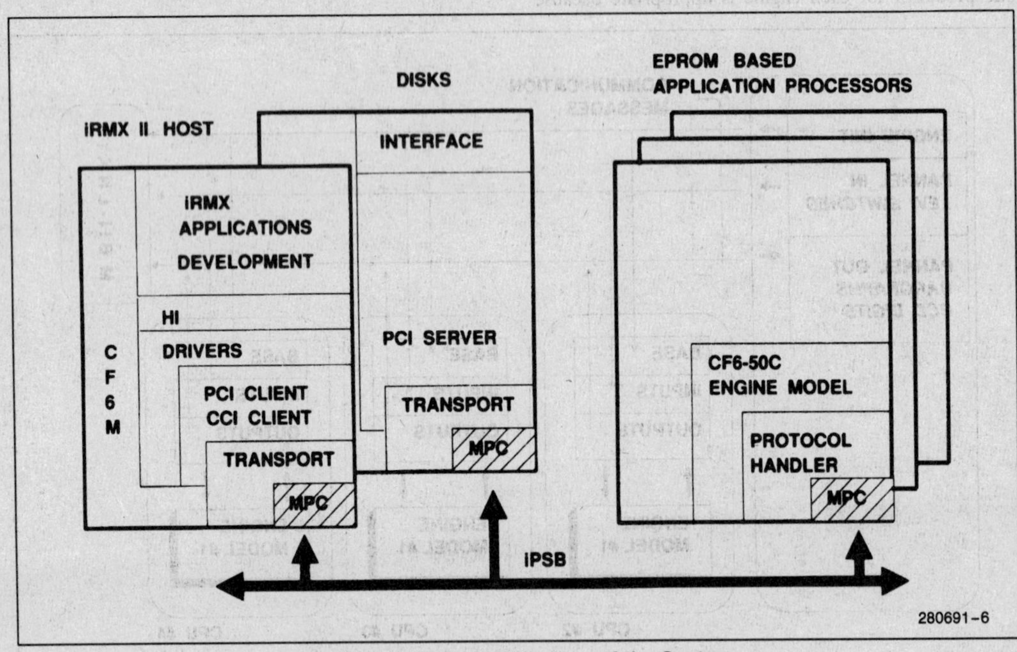

Figure 3-1. Basic Architecture of the System

3.1 The I/O Subsystem

As previously mentioned, the engine model also contains a display unit for control of the model. In order to add this important function, a coupler board manufactured by an independent MMG vendor (Multibus Manufacturers Group) was used as a bridge to the I/O subsystem, as shown in Figure 3-2. The I/O system interfaces to:

— A panel with the "on/off" switches for each engine (anti-ice subsystem, etc.), as mentioned in Section 2.1.

— An A/D converter to read and convert the position of the throttles to a binary value.

— A video controller to display the state of the engine as on the cockpit instruments.

In the following sections we will discuss in detail the various steps necessary to initegrate the above design into a real Multibus II system:

— Choice of the messages and their structure

— HOST startup sequence, iRMX II related topics

— Use of the iRMX II communications layer

— "Application Processor" design

3.2 Choosing a Communications Protocol

The Multibus II architecture defines several types of processor access to the parallel system bus:[4.1] solicited message transfer, unsolicited message transfer, dual port memory access and interconnect address access. Interconnect address space will be used for configuration and initialization of the Multibus II system and will not be accessed following system start-up. Dual-port memory as implemented on the MBII/LNK-1 board is used in the design[3] and allows use of unsolicited messages and memory transfer. The transfer of information between the host and the application processors is expected to require high speed transfers of numerous small blocks of data. For this, message passing is ideal.

The decision as to what type of message transfer will be used (solicited or unsolicited) will be based on how much data has to be transferred among the processors. As shown in Figure 2-5, there are basically three types of messages to be transferred:

—BASE: This message contains the base information, such as mach, pressure and altitude for the INLET portion of the engine model (Figure 2-2). This message is outbound from the host only.

—INPUTS: This message contains the N2 variable (core speed) of the engine, as calculated from the preprocessing in the Host. It also contains the decoded switch information from the panel of the model "cockpit" for the "on/off" switches of the subsystems, i.e., anti-ice, etc.

—OUTPUTS: This message has much more data to transfer back to the host for the final processing: all main computed data from the model must be sent back to the host.

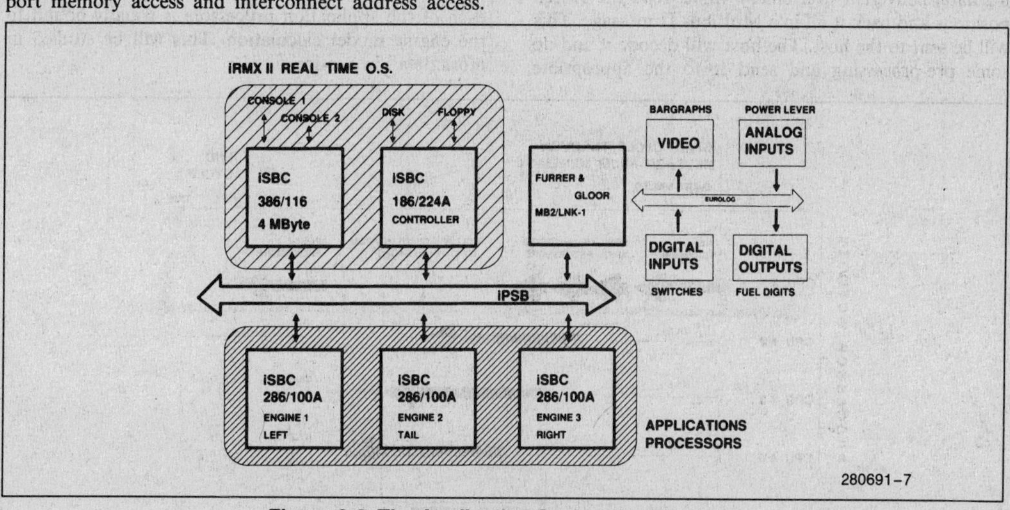

Figure 3-2. The Application System Architecture

Once the structure of "what has to be transferred" is defined, detailed analysis begins on the amount of data to be transferred. In this application the number of bytes to be transferred is relatively small, as follows: BASE—3 words; INPUTS—7 words; OUTPUTS—9 words. During the implementation phase it was quickly realized that it would be wise to define a flag word to ease the debugging task. This flag word is an overhead, but it allows identification of messages being received for debugging.

The next choice to make is what kind of message: unsolicited or solicited? Using solicited messages means that a certain amount of data has to be sent between the processors in order to be useful. In this design, the use of a solicited message will mean only overhead and complexity in the software. Only a few words need to be transferred. Therefore the choice is to simplify and use unsolicited messages only. In a case where a data transfer with more than 20 bytes is needed, an unsolicited message may be sent twice. This is faster than setting up an entire solicited transaction.[4.3] The big advantage is simplification of application software and of the debugging task.

3.3 The Final Configuration and State Cycle

Looking at the final configuration of the system as shown in Figure 3-2, there will be a number of transfers through the PSB for each simulation cycle. Each of them will be started by the local processor sitting on the EUROLOG local bus. This processor will read the analog data, convert it to a binary value, read the switch positions and pack it all in a Multibus II message. This will be sent to the host. The host will decode it and do some pre-processing and send it to the appropriate application processor (or engine). After a simulation step has been done locally, each of the application processors will send the result back to the host for encoding the display and some post-processing. Afterwards, the results will be sent back to the MBII/LNK-1 board using two unsolicited messages for the display process because there are more than 20 bytes needed for this task. Therefore, a complete simulation cycle will involve nine unsolicited transfers among the various processors.

3.4 The Cycle Time Analysis

The next task is to look at the activities of all processors with respect to time. For this purpose, a "processor activity timing" diagram, as shown in Figure 3-3, is set up. The horizontal axis is time; the vertical has one entry for each processor. During the work cycle, in this case one simulation step based on the incoming unsolicited message from the MBII/LNK-1 coupler board, the main tasks of each of the processors is estimated and shown with an arrow. Each outgoing or incoming message is a transition vertical arrow to the next processor and means the start or the end of an activity.

Using this diagram, it is now possible to make a quantitative analysis about the workload of each of the processors. In this case we see that the CPU #2, #3, and #4 are usually sitting idle waiting for messages. This simply means that there is a lot of spare processing time available. The diagram also shows that during some time in the cycle there is true parallel processing happening, which confirms the design goal of shortening the simulation calculation cycle. The compute time of each of the application processors is usually bound to the engine model calculation. This will be studied in more detail in Section 5.

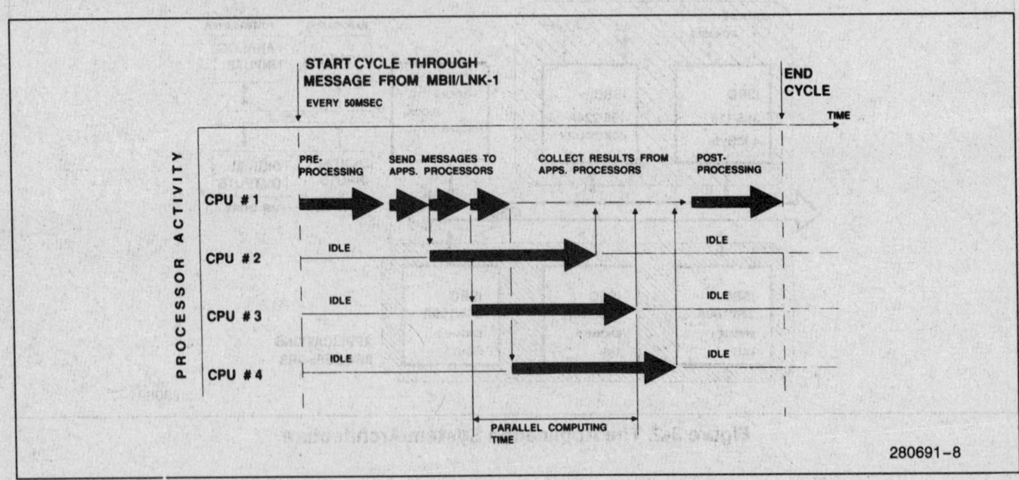

Figure 3-3. The Processor Activity Timing Diagram

3.5 The iRMX® II Host

As earlier mentioned, there will be a human interface (HI) job running under iRMX II which will monitor all the simulation activities. This monitor program will use the comm layer of iRMX II and be responsible for the startup of the system.

One part of the monitor program will also be the pre- and post-processing for the engine model as mentioned before. The startup sequence will include a board scan in order to be able to locate the application processors and define the necessary communications ports. The monitor program will function as follows:

— Create the connections to the terminal

— Scan the backplane and check the BIST (Built-In Self Test) status of each board

— If okay, then define the ports and sockets for the iRMX communications layer

— Create a buffer pool to preallocate free memory segments

— Create the iRMX memory segments and release them to the buffer pool

— Attach pool to port

— Ask for an amount of fuel in tons at the console

— Send the startup synchronization message to CPU #2, #3, #4 and to the MBII/LNK-1 board

— Send the start command to the MBII/LNK-1 board and give it control

— Do every 50 ms until no fuel available.

— Receive the message from the MBII/LNK-1 board with the decoded power lever angle and switches

— Make the preprocessing

— Send to each application processor the incoming data for a simulation step

— Collect the resulting messages asynchronously (there might be a slower board . . . !)

— After having received all the results, make the post-processing

— Send the two result messages back to the MBII/LNK-1 board. This finishes the "new state calculation" cycle.

— When no more fuel, stop everything and ask again at the console for more fuel

The coding of this monitor program is done in PL/M 286 using the iRMX II system calls. All the features of the PL/M 286 are used, especially the STRUCTURE DEFINITIONS which are very useful in this kind of application programming. Portions of the code are shown in Appendix B. Note that the transport system calls are very easy to use.

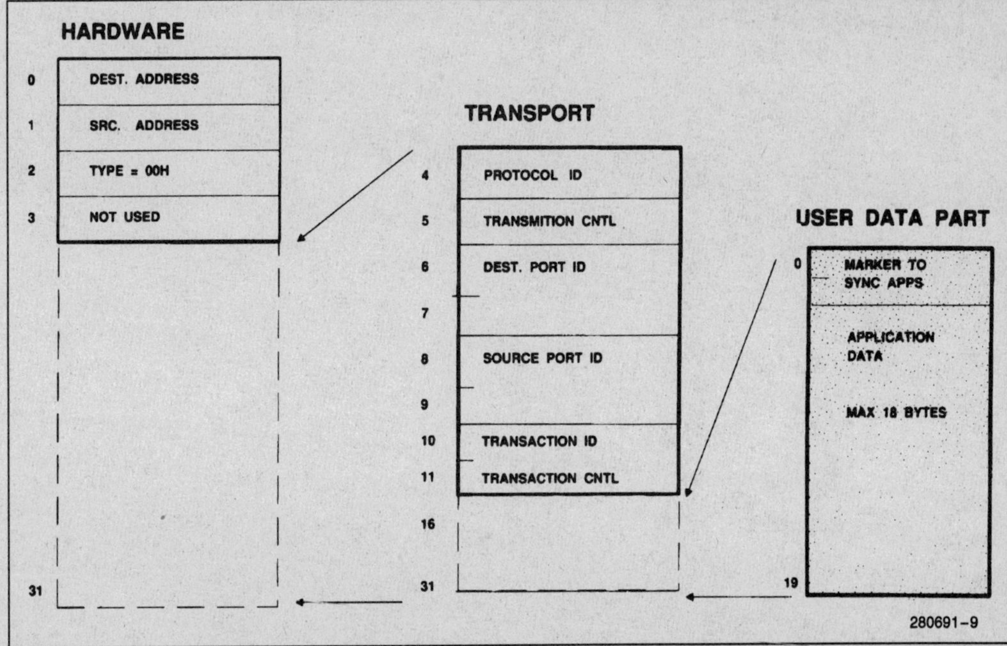

Figure 3-4. The iRMX II Comm-Layer Unsolicited Message Format

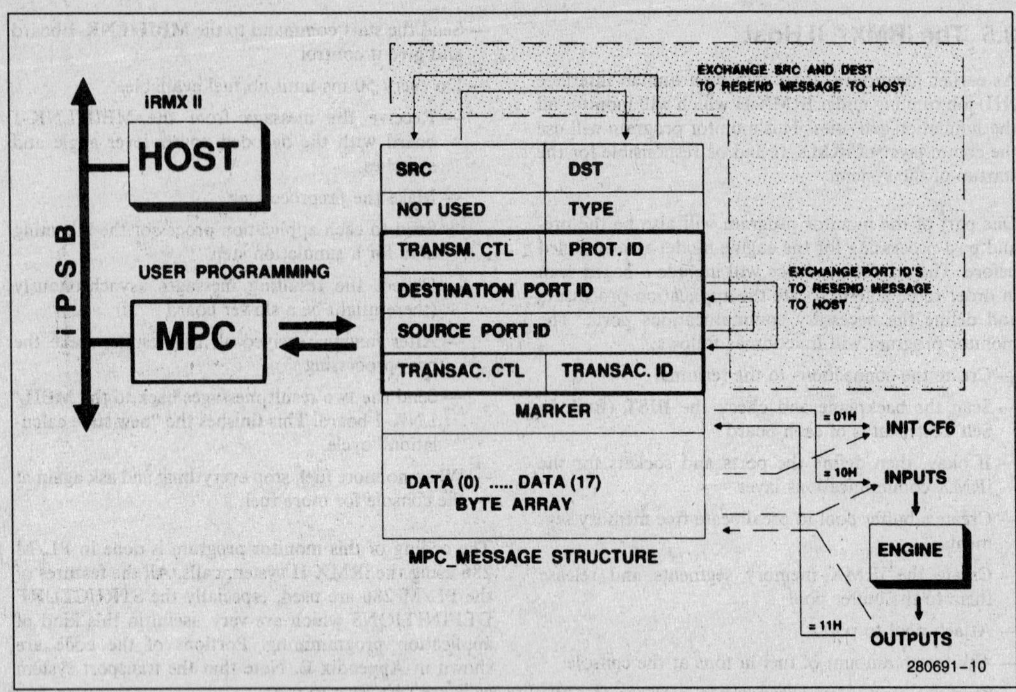

Figure 3-5. Data Processing on the MPC__DATA Structure

4.0 THE APPLICATION PROCESSOR DESIGN

The structure of the local software is, in principle, simple, due to the task which must be performed and can be split in two portions:

— A main program which will initialize the board and the whole local software, and

— An interrupt handler to handle the incoming messages accordingly. In addition, the interrupt handler calculates the new state of the engine and contains the engine model which needs no modification.

This leads to the design of several separate modules with well-known tasks:

—MAIN: Init of the board upon cold reset, (int. controller, MPC)

—INTERRUPT HANDLER: Activated on an MPC hardware interrupt. Will initialize the engine model or calculate the next state of the engine (so-called simulation step).

—MPC-LOW LEVEL DRIVER: Receive a message, transmit a message, init the MPC, error case.

The MPC low level driver routines can be directly taken from the MPC User's Manual.[4.2] The programming was done using 32 byte messages since the structure of the application fits exactly in the unsolicited message format. However there are some implications when receiving an iRMX II message sent under the comm layer. The general format of the message is shown in Figure 3.4. This explains that not all available bytes can be used in the unsolicited message transfer since eight of them are used for the transport protocol overhead, making the logical task binding over the bus possible.[4.3] Therefore, the user has to be careful when using the message formatted under iRMX II and received locally without any operating system software. Since only one single task runs on the board (our interrupt handler), no port and sockets are needed locally, but the host has a port and a socket defined for accessing the application processor. To transmit the data back as described in the design section above, the comm layer must "understand" what is coming back. The following operations ensure this:

1. The source and destination fields of the message structure will have to be exchanged before returning the message with the engine simulation results. That is for the low-level hardware and is absolutely logical.
2. Exactly the same has to be done for the transport part of the message structure. The DESTINATION_PORT_ID and the SOURCE_PORT_ID have to be exchanged to allow the comm layer software to receive the results correctly.

The second step seems trivial, but it took several hours in front of the emulator to understand why the engine variable N1, a result of the simulation step, was always the same value. We had not taken into account the unsolicited message set up under iRMX II which has the whole TRANSPORT PROTOCOL integrated. Once this was discovered, we had no problems at all. Therefore, all applications using no operating system, kernel or executive locally, must have an "own" protocol handler implemented. Main portions of the documented code listings for total implementation of the application processor can be found in Appendix C.

The "data processing" done flag in the MPC_MESSAGE data structure is shown in Figure 3-5. The previously mentioned marker differentiates the kind of message and is, in some sense, part of a "user application protocol". In this case it allows initialization of the engine software or to make a simulation step.

5.0 DEBUGGING AND PERFORMANCE ANALYSIS

The debugging of the application for the local processor was done using the I2ICE 286 emulator. This instrument allows a very efficient debugging, especially when using the macro facility to display data. Therefore a small library of macros was written to display the incoming and outgoing messages. With this it was possible to quickly locate the above mentioned problem of the missing TRANSPORT adaptation. The whole applicaton was debugged in the high speed RAM of the emulator and afterwards relocated to be EPROM resident. However, debugging a multiprocessor system is, by definition, not simple because of all the coordination involved. The debug session around the application processor was based on the following methodology:

— Send a known message from the host

— Debug the MPC_RECEIVE_MESSAGE routine step by step and get the known message to local RAM

— Loopback with same message to check the MPC_TRANSMIT_MESSAGE routine

— When the loopback is okay, then add the full engine calculation and . . . it runs!

A small log of a debug session with I2ICE 286 and the use of the predefined macros can be found in Appendix D. It shows the big advantage of using symbolic debugging.

Afterwards, an analysis with the iPAT Performance Analyzer was done to get more confidence about the timing situation. Most impressive was the terrific speed of the whole thing.

The iPAT performance analyzer offers may features such as profile, coverage, usage, linkage mode, etc.[5] In this kind of environment, the objective was to measure how long the various elements of the cycle are, so only the duration mode was of read use. Of first interest was to check how much time is spent in a routine and the latency from the MPC Interrupt Hardware signal to the start of a particular routine. Initially the cycle time of 50 ms was chosen to have enough spare time due to the use of the relatively slow 5 MHz iSBC 86/12A. A time of about 15.5 ms could be achieved with the Multibus I system.

Porting to the much faster iSBC 286/100A with 8 MHz speeds up the whole design. Depending on the switch position for the engine subsystems (see Figures 2-3 and 2-4) the total cycle time is in the range of 1380 ms to 1490 ms. Figure 5-1 shows in detail the timing situation of one cycle and how much time was spent in each of the routines. Note the overhead due to the Multibus II transport, and that the message passing handling is not very large. The MPC handling (receive and transmit the message) takes 180 ms, and the swap for the transport adaptation takes 17 ms, which means a total of around 200 ms for the "overhead". Therefore, the bottom line message is very clear: There is enough spare time to add more functions to the engine model. During the timing analysis, 15 tons of "software fuel" was burned!

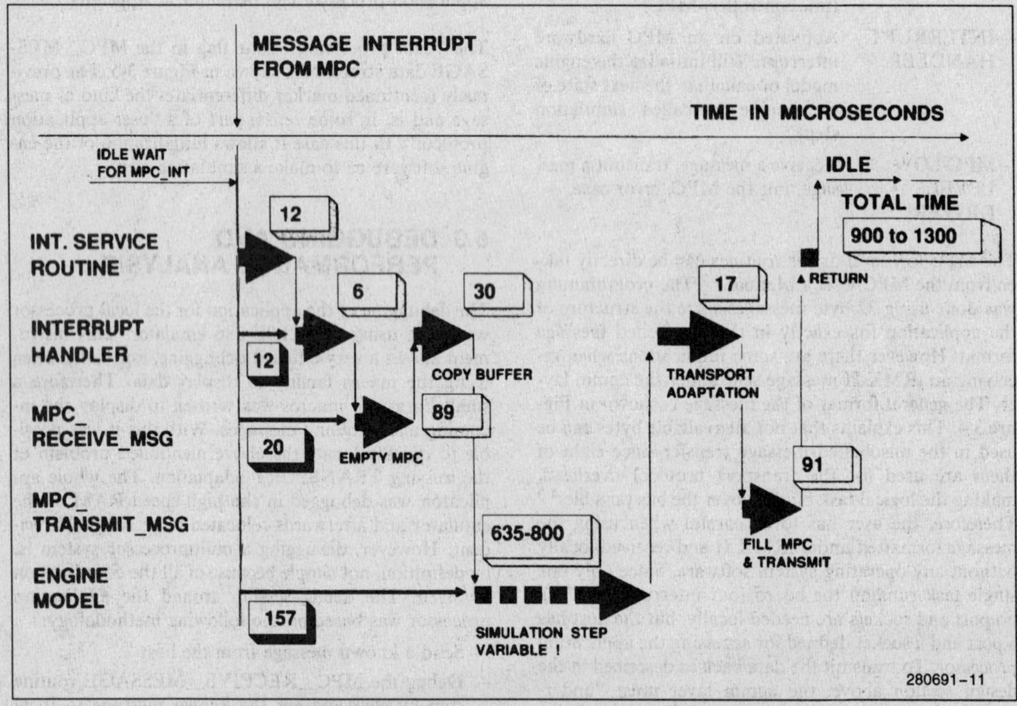

Figure 5-1. The Application Processor Timing Analysis

6.0 SUMMARY AND CONCLUSIONS

The design and implementation of the engine simulation model has given the opportunity to discuss and study a couple of interesting problems around a Multibus II application:

— Given a task, how to partition an application to use more than one processor and assess the problems around it.

— To demonstrate that the port of an existing software written a couple of years ago can still be integrated and ported to the latest hardware technology.

— To adapt an existing Multibus I system to use the benefits of the Multibus II technology.

— To demonstrate the use of the iRMX II operating system together with custom-made software and study its implications when the comm layer is used.

In addition, this application allowed discussion of actual implementation starting from the given problem statement and ending with the final integration in a real system using single board computers. The results show the feasibility, including the important performance analysis.

APPENDIX A

Bibliography and Related Readings

1. Francois Huguenin, "Microcomputer Based Engine Model Used in Flight Simulation Applications", *AIAA Paper 81-0973*, AIAA Flight Simulation Technologies Conference, June 16-18, 1981, Long Beach, CA.

2. F. Huguenin, P. Grepper, "Four-Dimensional Helical Approach of Aircraft in an Air Traffic Control Environment", *AIAA Paper 79-1776R, Journal of Guidance and Control,* June 1981.

3. Furrer + Gloor AG Multibus II MMG
   Furrer + Gloor Silbernstrasse 10
   CH 8953 Dietikon ZH Switzerland
   MBII/LNK-1 Coupler Board User's Guide

4. Intel Multibus II Documentation:
   4.1 Multibus II Specifications, Order #146077C
   4.2 MPC User's Manual, Order #176526-001
   4.3 Multibus II Transport Specs, Order #453508-001
   4.4 iSBC 286/100A User's Manual Order #149093-001
   4.5 iRMX II Nucleus User's Guide, Order #461845-001
   Nucleus Commmuncation Services, Section 12

5. iPAT Analyst User's Guide, Order #450583-002

APPENDIX B

Glossary of Terms

Application Terms:

T	Temperature
p	Pressure
m	Mach
HPX	Horse Power Extraction
EN2	Engine Variable N2 Calibrated
EALT	Engine Variable Altitude Calibrated
EWFA	Engine Variable Fuel Flow Calibrated
EVM	Engine Variable Mach Calibrated

Multibus II Terms:

MPC	Message Passing Co-Processor (VLSI Multibus II Interface)
Solicited Message Transfer	A data transfer through Multibus II message space that requires buffer negotiation. May be up to 16 Mbytes long.
Unsolicited Message Transfer	Unsolicited messages arrive at a host unpredictably and can have the effect of an interrupt. Message can have up to 20 bytes of user data.
Dual Port Memory Access	A means of accessing shared memory between two processors. Hardware arbitration is required.
Interconnect Address Access	Access to the Multibus II interconnect address space for test and/or configuration purposes.
Buffer Pool	A collection of memory buffers which are managed by the iRMX II Operating System.
Transport Protocol	This is a generic term describing the function of the software layer that implements the Multibus II Transport Protocol as defined in the IEEE 1296 Specification.

APPENDIX C

Documented Portions of the iRMX II Host Monitor Program

Note that all comments written in bold are added to the original listing portions.

The following code listing contains the most important parts of the iRMX II Host Monitor Program. Since this is a quite large lisiting, it was choosen only to take out which is really important.

B1. Declarations

These word declarations make the interface to the exisiting assembly coded routines.

```
840   1  =   declare std_conditions word external;
841   1  =   declare state_1 word external;
842   1  =   declare state_2 word external;
843   1  =   declare state_3 word external;
844   1  =   declare result_1 word external;
845   1  =   declare result_2 word external;
846   1  =   declare result_3 word external;
```

The following is an abstract of the definition for the messages which are used between the processors in the system.

```
         =
         =   /*
         =   ; 1. standard conditions message from main to all
             slaves
         =   */
```

This is the general unsolicited message structure to be used.

```
847   1  =   declare mpc_message structure
         =   ( dest byte,
         =   src byte,
         =   type byte, not_used byte, message_data (28) byte)
             public;
```

This message will be used for synchronizing all processors together.

```
848   1  =   declare std_conditions_msg  structure
         =          ( header_std_conditions (4) byte,
         =              transport(4) word,
         =              std_marker word,
         =              evm word,
         =              ealt word,
         =              ep0 word,
         =              et0 word,
         =              dummy_std_conditions (10) word) at
                        (@std_conditions);
```

280691-12

```
These messages are to be used for  the information transfer
between the application processors.

Note that the structures are overlayed to the word defined a lines
840 to 846 !

            =   ; 2.1 Engine #1
            =   */

 849   1    =   declare state_1_msg  structure
            =            ( header_state_1 (4) byte,
            =              transport (4) word,
            =              message_data (10) word) at (@state_1);

            =   ; 3.1 Engine #1
            =   */

 852   1    =   declare result_1_msg  structure
            =            ( header_result_1 (4) byte,
            =              transport (4) word,
            =              message_data (10) word) at (@result_1);
```

280691-13

```
The following three procedures are used for creating a port, and
to send and receive the messages under iRMX II control.
See also iRMX II System documentation.

        NEW$PORT: PROCEDURE (port$token$ptr,id,type);
        /**********************************************/
        /*
        this procedure creates a port for access by iRMX II
        */

           DECLARE port$token$ptr POINTER;
           DECLARE id word;
           DECLARE type byte;
           DECLARE port$token based port$token$ptr token;

           /*
           **  Create a new port: port$token$ptr is pointer
           **  to port$token to be returned
           **     id is:  for data transport: port ID
           **             for signal service: message ID
           **    type is:  port type
           */

           if type = data_port then do;
              port$info.port$id = id;
              port$info.type = type;
              port$info.flags = 0;
              port$token = rq$create$port
                             (queue$size,@port$info,@status);
           end;

           if type = signal_port then do;
              msg$info.msg$id = id;
              msg$info.type = type;
              msg$info.flags = 0;
              port$token = rq$create$port
                             (queue$size,@msg$info,@status);
           end;

           return;
        end NEW$PORT;
```

280691-14

send a message to the MPC

```
1095    1    FORWARD$MSG: PROCEDURE (message$pointer,port$id);
1096    2        DECLARE message$pointer POINTER;
1097    2        DECLARE port$id BYTE;

1098    2    DECLARE
                 transaction$id          WORD,
                 status                  WORD;

1099    2        call no$exc$mode;       /*  Set Exception Mode
                                              to 0 (No RMX Action) */

1100    2        transaction$id = rq$send(
                              own$port$tok,sockets(port$id),
                              message$pointer, NIL, 0, 0,
                                          @status);

1101    2        call full$exc$mode;          /*  Reset Exception
                                                  Handling */
1102    2        count$out = count$out+1;     /*  Update Counter for
                                                  messages sent */

1103    2        RETURN;
1104    2    END FORWARD$MSG;
```

280691-15

5

receive a message from the MPC

```
1105   1      WAIT$FOR$MSG: PROCEDURE (buffer$ptr) WORD;

1106   2         DECLARE buffer$ptr pointer;

1107   2         DECLARE buffer$ptr_origin POINTER;

1108   2         DECLARE
                 info_buf                 STRUCTURE(
                                          flags             WORD,
                                          status            WORD,
                                          transaction$id    WORD,
                                          length            DWORD,
                                          forward$port      TOKEN,
                                          socket            DWORD,
                                          message(20)       BYTE,
                                          reserve(4)        BYTE),

                 status                   WORD;

1109   2         call no$exc$mode;    /*  Set Exception Mode to 0
                                          (No RMX Action) */

1110   2         buffer$ptr_origin = rq$receive(
                                         own$port$tok, notimeout,
                                         @info_buf, @status);

1111   2         call full$exc$mode;  /* Reset Exception
                                         Handling*/
                                      /*  Update Counter for
                                          Messages sent */
1112   2         count$in = count$in + 1;
1113   2         socket = info_buf.socket;
                 /*
                 ** We expect just a Control Message ==>
                 ** Copy contents of control message to buffer
                 ** provided by paramter buffer$ptr and return
                 ** sending host ID.
                 */

1114   2         call movb(@info_buf.message,buffer$ptr,20);
1115   2         return socket$def.host$id;

1116   2      END WAIT$FOR$MSG;
```

280691-16

The following code section is the DO UNTIL NO_FUEL loop with the iRMX II System calls used to transfer the data to and receive them back from the Appliaction processors.

```
/**********************************************************************/
/*                                                                    */
/*  Wait for state_in Message from LINK                               */
/*  Copy MSG to Buffer =>                                             */
/*                     SWITCH_DECODE,LEVER_TO_2,N2_TRANSIENT          */
/*  Send State_i Message to Engine-Simulators                         */
/*  Wait for Simulators having calculated  ==>                        */
/*           EGT_FILTER, SKAL_BARGRAPHS,SKAL_DIGITS                   */
/*  Send display  Message to Link                                     */
/*                                                                    */

/**********************************************************************/


1366   2          DO WHILE nofuel=0;
```

The state_message contains the data from the I/O subsystem. When received, one simulation step can be processed.

```
                   /* Wait for STATE_IN Message, then Copy */

1367   3           id = WAIT$FOR$MSG(@state_in_msg.state_in);
```

Make the preprocessing.

```
1368   3           CALL SWITCH_DECODE;
1369   3           CALL LEVER_TO_N2;
1370   3           CALL N2_TRANSIENT;
```

Set the marker word to 10H prior to send the data.

```
1371   3           call movb
                        (@(10H),@state_1_msg.message_data,1);
1372   3           call movb
                        (@(10H),@state_2_msg.message_data, 1);
1373   3           call movb
                        (@(10H),@state_3_msg.message_data, 1);

1373   3           call movb (@(10H), @state_3_msg.message_data,
1);
```

280691–17

5

```
1374   3      call forward$msg(
                         @state_1_msg.message_data,engine_1);
1375   3      call forward$msg(
                         @state_2_msg.message_data,engine_2);
1376   3      call forward$msg(
                         @state_3_msg.message_data,engine_3);

              /*
              ** Wait for all three having terminated:
              ** Use logical variables all$done,done$1
              **    ,done$2,done$3.
              **
              ** When a Message arrives, copy it to local
              ** buffers.
              */

1377   3      all$done,done$1,done$2,done$3 = FALSE;

1378   3      DO WHILE NOT all$done;

1379   4         id = WAIT$FOR$MSG(@intermediate);
                 /*
                 ** Message arrived: set corresponnding done
                 ** flag and copy buffer
                 */
1380   4         if id = host$ids(engine_1) then do;
1382   5            done$1 = true;
1383   5            call movb(@intermediate,
                              @result_1_msg.message_data,28);
1384   5         end;
1385   4         if id = host$ids(engine_2) then do;
1387   5            done$2 = true;
1388   5            call movb(@intermediate,
                              @result_2_msg.message_data,28);
1389   5         end;

1390   4         if id = host$ids(engine_3) then do;
1392   5            done$3 = true;
1393   5            call movb(@intermediate,
                              @result_3_msg.message_data,28);
1394   5         end;

1395   4         all$done = done$1 AND done$2 AND done$3;
1396   4      END;
```

Make the postprocessing.

```
1397   3      CALL EGT_FILTER;
1398   3      CALL SKAL_BARGRAPHS;
1399   3      CALL SKAL_DIGITS;
```

280691–18

```
            /*    send results to MBII/LNK-1 Board with two
                  consecutive unsolicited messages
            */

Set the marker word to 44H and 45H for identification
inside the MBII/LNK-1 Baord.

1400   3          call movb (@(44H),
                     @display_on_line_msg_1.display_on_line,1);
1401   3          call movb (@(45H),
                     @display_on_line_msg_2.display_on_line,1);

Send the two conscutive messages to the MBII/LNK-1 board.

1402   3          CALL FORWARD$MSG(
                       @display_on_line_msg_1.display_on_line,
                                                        link_1);
1403   3          CALL FORWARD$MSG(
                       @display_on_line_msg_2.display_on_line,
                                                        link_1);

                  /*
                  **  Update Message Counter for display on the
                  **  console
                  */

1404   3          status = put$char(@pos$in,fb);
1405   3          status = put$ddec(count$in,fb);
1406   3          status = put$char(@(alloff,0),fb);
1407   3          call put$line(nolf);

1408   3          status = put$char(@pos$out,fb);
1409   3          status = put$ddec(count$out,fb);
1410   3          status = put$char(@(alloff,0),fb);
1411   3          call put$line(nolf);

1412   3          ttime.systime=0;
1413   3          call dq$decode$time(@ttime,@status);
1414   3          if last$sec <> ttime.time(7) then do;
1416   4             call movb(@pos$time,@outbuff,12);
1417   4             call movb(@ttime.time,@outbuff(12),8);
1418   4             call movb(@(alloff),@outbuff(20),4);
1419   4             out$buff(24)=0;
1420   4             call disp(@out$buff);
1421   4             last$sec = ttime.time(7);
1422   4          end;
1423   3       END;
```

280691-19

5

APPENDIX D

Documented Code Listing of the Application Software Based in EPROM

This appendix contains most of the listings generated for the application processor EPROM resident software:

— MAIN05 : Main Module for Cold Start
— MPCDR3 : Low-Level MPC Driver
— C28I6 : Interrupt Handling Routine
— CF650L : Engine Model Module

Note also the last page of the LOCATE MAP which gives an idea on how much memory was needed for this application.

```
iRMX 86 8086/87/88/186 MACRO ASSEMBLER V2.0 ASSEMBLY OF MODULE MAIN_MODULE_286
OBJECT MODULE PLACED IN MAIN05.OBJ
ASSEMBLER INVOKED BY:  :LANG:asm86 MAIN05.A86 DEBUG SYMBOLS TYPE


LOC  OBJ                 SOURCE

                         name    main_module_286

                         ;              PROJECT        CF6-50C Multicomputer

                         ;              08.10.87   v1.0 fh add reset not complete on entry point
                         ;              03.10.87   v1.0 fh add in it of ewfaold, efuelused
                         ;              21.08.87   v2.1 CG/Scm OCW2 has address pic_cntl0
                         ;              04.08.87   v2.0fh  change interrupt structure
                         ;              03.08.87   v1.1fh  change external segments

                         ;              03.08.87   v1.0fh  initial start up module


                         ; This module contains the cold reset start up of the sbc286/100A
                         ; and the interrupt processing routine.



                         ; note that all written in CAPITAL is original software written
                         ; end of 1979, early 1980 '
                         ; all other is modification done to port the original application
                         ; to Multibus II





                      +1 $nogen

                         ; interrupt controller PIC

  00C0                   pic_cntl0          equ     0c0h   ; command port 1
  00C2                   pic_cntl1          equ     0c2h   ; command port 2


----                     int_pointers       segment at 0

0000                                        org     0h
0000 (32                 type_x             dd      32     dup(?)  ; discard all system interrupts
    ????????
    )
                                                                   ; which are not used here

                                        ; master pic of iSBC 286/100A

0080 00000000            type_32            dd      0       ; ir 0
0084 00000000            type_33            dd      0       ; ir 1
0088 00000000            type_34            dd      0       ; ir 2 message interrupt
008C 00000000            type_35            dd      0       ; ir 3 iPSB message error
0090 00000000            type_36            dd      0       ;
0094 00000000            type_37            dd      0       ;
0098 00000000            type_38            dd      0       ;
009C 00000000            type_39            dd      0       ;


----                     int_pointers       ends

                         ; external variables needed for initialization
                         ; first time after reset

```

280691-20

```
LOC  OBJ                          SOURCE

----                              EFGIO   SEGMENT COMMON
                                  extrn   ewfaold:word
                                  extrn   efuelused:word
                                  extrn   deltat:word

----                              EFGIO   ENDS

                                  $eject


----                              STACKSEG              SEGMENT STACK
0000 (100                                       DW      100 DUP(?)      ;ALLOCATE 100 WORDS FOR STACK
     ????
     )
00C8                              STACKTOP      LABEL   WORD            ;OFFSET ADDRESS OF THE TOS
----                              STACKSEG              ENDS

----                              iodatseg              SEGMENT public

----                              iodatseg              ENDS


                                  ; two external routines

                                  extrn   mpc_init:far             ; initialization of the mpc
                                  extrn   mpc_interrupt:far        ; mpc interrupt routine
                                                                   ; for handling I/O and engine

----                              EFGCOD          SEGMENT PUBLIC

                                          ;GIVE ASSEMBLER INITIAL REGISTER TO SEGMENT CORRESPONDENCE

                                  ASSUME  CS: EFGCOD,     DS: IODATSEG,    ES: EFGIO,      SS: STACKSEG



0000                              interrupt_routine        proc


                                  ; This Interrupt routine will be activated by the MINT line
                                  ; of the MPC when the MPC has received a message
                                  ; This routine call the interrupt handler written in PLM86
                                  ; which will calculate a new state of the engine based on the
                                  ; incoming message. Afterwards the result message will be formed
                                  ; and send back to the host.

0000 50                                   push    ax
0001 9A0000----         E                 call    mpc_interrupt

                                  ; EOI handling for the 8259A Controller

0006 B020                                 mov     al,20h           ; non specific eoi
0008 E6C0                                 out     pic_cnt10,al     ; write to ocw2
000A 58                                   pop     ax
000B FB                                   sti                      ; enable interrupts
000C CF                                   iret                     ; return from interrupt


                                  interrupt_routine       endp



000D                              start:

                                          %reset_interconnect      ; RSTNC# Bit reset inside 8751
                                                                   ; Microcontroller


                                          %set_int_vector(08h,08h,interrupt_routine)

                                  ; set up segment registers of cpu

0032 B8----             R                 mov     AX,IODATSEG      ;LOAD SEGMENT REG
0035 8ED8                                 mov     DS,AX            ;CS IS LOADED AUTOMATICALY BY RESET
0037 B8----             R                 MOV     AX,EFGIO
003A 8EC0                                 MOV     ES,AX
003C B8----             R                 MOV     AX,STACKSEG
003F 8ED0                                 MOV     SS,AX
0041 BCC800             R                 MOV     SP,OFFSET STACKTOP  ;SET SP  TO TOS

                                          ; cpu now ready for work for the engine model

                                          ; but first initialize the mpc


0044 9A0000----         E                 call    mpc_init

                                          ; then set to zero fuel variables

0049 26C70600000000 E                     mov     es:ewfaold,0
0050 26C70600000000 E                     mov     es:efuelused,0
0057 26C70600005046 E                     mov     es:deltat,18000


                                          ; then initialize master PIC of iSBC 286/100A

005E BAC000                               mov     dx,pic_cnt10     ; icw1
0061 B017                                 mov     al,00010111b     ; edge triggered, single mode, call
```

280691-21

5

```
LOC  OBJ              SOURCE

                                                 ; address
0063 EE                         out    dx,al
0064 BAC200                     mov    dx,pic_cntl1   ; icw2
0067 B020                       mov    al,00100000b   ; base=type 32 (80h)
0069 EE                         out    dx,al
006A B01D                       mov    al,00011101b   ; special fully nested mode, buffered
                                                      ; master, normal eoi, 86 mode
006C EE                         out    dx,al
006D B0FB                       mov    al,0fbh        ; enable only ir2 message interrupts
006F EE                         out    dx,al

                        ; and finally enable cpu interrupts

0070 FB                         sti


0071 90                 idle:   nop
0072 90                         nop
0073 90                         nop                   ; do nothing but wait for message
```

280691-22

```
iRMX 86 PL/M-86 V2.7 COMPILATION OF MODULE C286_INT_HANDLER
OBJECT MODULE PLACED IN C286I6.OBJ
COMPILER INVOKED BY:  :LANG:plm86 C286I6.P86 DEBUG SYMBOLS LARGE TYPE


   1          c286_int_handler:   do;

              /*
              main control interrupt handler for the local engine
              control. Will check for type of message, start up the model
              and carry out one simulation step at a time based on
              incomming messages.
              */

              /*
              history

              c286i6  v1.1    08.10.87    remoce error for std conditions
              c286i6  v1.0    03.10.87    clear mpc_message structure after transmit
                                          and after receiving for next time
              c286i5  v1.0    03.10.87    remove error in adressing mpc_messsage struc
              c286i4  v1.3    03.10.87    normal mode of ops for i2ice test
              c286i4  v1.22   21.08.87    engine and movb removed for test
              c286i4  v1.2    11.08.87    exchange source/dest for retransmit
              c286i4  v1.1    06.08.87    change data strutures
              c286i4  v1.0    06.08.87    change for std_conditions message
              c286i3  v1.1    04.08.87    add source id for the main processor
              c286i3  v1.0    04.08.87    add destination id
              c286i2  v1.0    04.08.87    remove types
              c286i1  v1.0    03.08.87    initial version

              */


   2   1      declare std_conditions word external;
   3   1      declare inputs word external;
   4   1      declare outputs word external;
   5   1      declare byte_dummy   byte;
   6   1      declare word_dummy   word;


   7   1      declare mpc_message structure
              ( dest           byte,              /* 4 Byte Hardware-Header */
                src            byte,
                type           byte,
                not_used       byte,
                prot_id        byte,              /* 8 Byte RMX-Header */
                transm_ctr     byte,
                dest_port_id   word,
                source_port_id word,
                transact_id    byte,
                transact_ctr   byte,
                message_data  (20)  byte) public; /* 20 Byte User-Data */


   8   1      declare index byte;

              /* Declaration of external procedures ******************/

   9   1      engine: procedure external;
  10   2      end engine;

  11   1      mpc_receive_message: procedure external;
  12   2      end mpc_receive_message;

  13   1      mpc_transmit_message: procedure external;
  14   2      end mpc_transmit_message;

              /* Start MPC-Interrupt-Procedure (MINT-Signal) **********/

  15   1      mpc_interrupt: procedure  public;

              /*

              first empty the MPC FIFO into mpc_message structure

              */

  16   2      call mpc_receive_message;


  17   2      if mpc_message.message_data(0)= 01h

                  then                /* we had a engine init message */
  18   2      do;
  19   3              call movb(@mpc_message.message_data(0),@std_conditions,20);

                    /* clear the mpc_message data structure after receive  */
  20   3              do index = 0 to 19;
  21   4              mpc_message.message_data(index)= 00h;
  22   4              end;
  23   3          end;
```

280691-23

```
24   2          else                /* normal message for one simulation step */

            if mpc_message.message_data(0) = 10h then
25   2          do;
26   3             call movb (@mpc_message.message_data(0),@inputs,20);

27   3             call engine;     /* one simulation step */

28   3             call movb (@outputs, @mpc_message.message_data(0),20);


29   3           mpc_message.message_data(0) = 11h;     /*Set marker for result */

             /* Transport Protocol adjustment to be
                conforming to the Comm Layer of iRMX II*/

30   3           byte_dummy          = mpc_message.dest;
31   3           mpc_message.dest = mpc_message.src;
32   3           mpc_message.src  = byte_dummy;

33   3           word_dummy                  = mpc_message.dest_port_id;
34   3           mpc_message.dest_port_id  = mpc_message.source_port_id;
35   3           mpc_message.source_port_id = word_dummy;

            /* transmit results back to host */

36   3           call mpc_transmit_message;

             /* clear the mpc_message data structure after transmit */
37   3             do index = 0 to 19;
38   4             mpc_message.message_data(index)= 00h;
39   4             end;
40   3          end;



41   2                                                          else
            do;
            /* Error-processing: Error in message_data(0)
               error case not implemented in this version */
42   3          end;



43   2      end mpc_interrupt;


44   1      end;
```

280691-24

```
iRMX 86 8086/87/88/186 MACRO ASSEMBLER V2.0 ASSEMBLY OF MODULE MPC_HANDLER_MODULE
OBJECT MODULE PLACED IN MPCDR3.OBJ
ASSEMBLER INVOKED BY:  :LANG:asm86 MPCDR3.A86 DEBUG SYMBOLS TYPE

LOC  OBJ                  LINE     SOURCE

                                   name     mpc_handler_module

                                   ;        mpcdr3  v1.5 CG/Scm 21.8.87     reference to mpc_message via 'seg'
                                   ;        mpcdr3  v1.4 fh 07.08.87        change ds register for far call
                                   ;        mpcdr3  v1.3 fh 06.08.87        change cl to cx for loop
                                   ;        mpcdr3  v1.1 fh 06.08.87        rotate message id
                                   ;        mpcdr3  v1.0 fh 05.08.87        add mctl register
                                   ;        mpcdr2  v1.1 fh 04.08.87        make procedures far type
                                   ;        mpcdr2  v1.0 fh 03.08.87        add mpc_init
                                   ;        mpcdr1  v1.0 fh 22.06.87        add mpc control
                                   ;        mpcdr0  v1.0 fh 19.06.86        original version


                                   ; This module contains the low level MPC handling routines needed
                                   ; for this application. Several simplifications are assumed:
                                   ; the receive and transmit message routines are working on 32 byte
                                   ; messages only. No length programming assumed. Further, the error
                                   ; handling is not implemented in this first release of the low level
                                   ; driver.
                                   ; all three routines are a direct implementation of the work
                                   ; flow described in the mpc user's guide and are coded in the large
                                   ; model for compatibility with the engine model and the plm86
                                   ; interrupt processing.
                                   ;
                                   ;


                              +1   $include(mpca86.def)
                     =1            ; i/o port addresses of MPC
                     =1
                     =1
0010                 =1            mdata    equ     10h      ; message data port
001C                 =1            mcmd     equ     1ch      ; message command port
0000                 =1            mstat    equ     00h      ; message status register
0000                 =1            mrst     equ     00h      ; message reset register
000C                 =1            mctl     equ     0ch      ; message control register
0014                 =1            merr     equ     14h      ; message error port
0008                 =1            mcon     equ     08h      ; message configuration register
                     =1
0020                 =1            msocmp   equ     20h      ; sol message completion port
0024                 =1            msicmp   equ     24h      ; sol message input completion port
0020                 =1            msocan   equ     20h      ; sol message output cancel port
0024                 =1            msican   equ     24h      ; sol message input cancel port
                     =1
0004                 =1            mid      equ     04h      ; message id register
                     =1
0030                 =1            icadrl   equ     30h      ; interconnect address low
0034                 =1            icadrh1  equ     34h      ; interconnect address high1
0031                 =1            icadrh2  equ     31h      ; interconnect address high2
003C                 =1            icdata   equ     3ch      ; interconnect data register
                     =1
                     =1            ; bit definitions
                     =1
0001                 =1            xmtnf    equ     1                ; transmit FIFO not full
0004                 =1            xmterr   equ     4                ; transmit error on PSB
0083                 =1            rcvne    equ     10000011b        ; receive FIFO not empty
                     =1
0080                 =1            init_done        equ     80h      ; filter for bit 7
0000                 =1            zero             equ     00h
0085                 =1            width_config     equ     10000101b        ; set 16 bit fifo and dma
                     =1                                                      ; full message passing
                     =1
0002                 =1            mpc_control      equ     00000010b        ; receive interrupt enable

                                   extrn    mpc_message:word


----                               code     segment
                                   assume   cs:code
                                   assume   ds:seg mpc_message

                                   public   mpc_receive_message,mpc_transmit_message,mpc_init


0000                               mpc_transmit_message     proc far

                                   ; v1.1 mpc_write_message                add transmit FIFO control
                                   ; v1.0 mpc_write_message                basic priciple written

                                   ; mpc_transmit message will copy the data from the mpc_message
                                   ; structure to the fifo of the mpc and send it out to the iPSB.
                                   ; 32 byte length assumed.

0000 1E                                     push    ds
0001 B8----          E                      mov     ax,seg mpc_message
0004 8ED8                                   mov     ds,ax

0006 B91000                                 mov     cx,16           ; 32 byte message
                                                                    ; 16 words
0009 BA1000                                 mov     dx,mdata        ; data port of mpc
000C BE0000          E                      mov     si, offset mpc_message

```

280691-25

```
LOC  OBJ               SOURCE

000F 8B04              write_1: mov   ax, [si]              ; load data to ax
0011 EF                         out   dx,ax                 ; store to mpc
0012 46                         inc   si
0013 46                         inc   si                    ; double to next word
0014 E2F9                       loop  write_1               ; continue till all 32 byte
                                                            ; writte to MPC FIFO

0016 32C0                       xor   al,al                 ;
0018 E61C                       out   mcmd,al               ; write 00 to MPC CMD Register

001A                   continue:

001A E400                       in    al,mstat              ; read MPC status_register
001C 2401                       and   al,xmtnf              ; mask transmit fifo bit
001E 3C01                       cmp   al,1
0020 7409                       je    transmit_complete     ; message transmitted '
0022 2404                       and   al,xmterr             ; mask transmit error bit
0024 3C00                       cmp   al,0
0026 74F2                       jz    continue              ; message transmition still in progress

0028 E85600                     call  transmit_error  ; error handling

002B                   transmit_complete:

002B 1F                         pop   ds
002C CB                         ret

                       mpc_transmit_message    endp

                +1     $eject



002D                   mpc_receive_message     proc far

                       ; v1.1 mpc_read_message            add receive FIFO control
                       ; v1.0 mpc_read_message            basic priciple written

                       ; mpc_receive_message will copy the data to the mpc_message
                       ; structure from the fifo of the mpc.
                       ; 32 byte length assumed.

002D 1E                         push  ds
002E B8----        E            mov   ax,seg mpc_message
0031 8ED8                       mov   ds,ax

0033                   not_ready_1:

0033 E400                       in    al,mstat              ; 8 bit read of MPC_status_register
0035 3C83                       cmp   al,rcvne
0037 75FA                       jne   not_ready_1           ; wait until flag set

0039 E410                       in    al,mdata              ; read one byte for length

                       ; read mpc_fifo  assuming 32 byte valid data and 16 bit transfers
                       ; initialized inside the MPC

003B B91000                     mov   cx,16                 ; 32 byte message
                                                            ; 16 words
003E BA1000                     mov   dx,mdata              ; data port of mpc
0041 BF0000        E            mov   di, offset mpc_message
0044 ED                read_2:  in    ax,dx                 ; read from mpc
0045 8905                       mov   [di],ax               ; store data to message buffer
0047 47                         inc   di
0048 47                         inc   di                    ; double to next word
0049 E2F9                       loop  read_2                ; continue till all 32 byte
                                                            ; read

004B E41C                       in    al,mcmd               ; read MPC_command port for resync

                                                            ; service of message read now complete


004D 1F                         pop   ds
                                                            ; continue with processing of data
004E CB                         ret

                       mpc_receive_message     endp


                +1     $eject


004F                   mpc_init         proc far


                       ; this routine will initialize the MPC for use in this application.

004F 1E                         push  ds
0050 B8----        E            mov   ax,seg mpc_message
0053 8ED8                       mov   ds,ax

```

280691-26

```
LOC  OBJ         SOURCE

0055 B000                  mov     al,zero
0057 E600                  out     mrst,al             ; reset the mpc

0059             chck_reset:
0059 E400                  in      al,mstat
005B 2480                  and     al,init_done
005D 3C00                  cmp     al,zero
005F 75F8                  jne     chck_reset          ; do whil not reset

0061 B085                  mov     al,width_config
0063 E608                  out     mcon,al             ; set to 16 bit
0065 B002                  mov     al,mpc_control      ; interrupt control
0067 E60C                  out     mctl,al
0069 E408                  in      al,mcon             ; no check for error case this time
006B B0FA                  mov     al,0fAh
006D E634                  out     icadrh1,al          ; interconnect address high
006F E631                  out     icadrh2,al          ; interconnect address high
0071 B098                  mov     al,098h
0073 E630                  out     icadrl ,al          ; interconnect address low
0075 E43C                  in      al,3ch              ; read interconnect register slot_id
0077 D0E8                  shr     al,1
0079 D0E8                  shr     al,1
007B D0E8                  shr     al,1
007D E604                  out     mid,al              ; set the message id to slot_id

007F 1F                    pop     ds
0080 CB                    ret



                 mpc_init          endp


0081             transmit_error  proc

                 ; this routine is  n o t  implemented in this release of
                 ; this handler
                 transmit_error  endp


----             code    ends
```

280691-28

5

```
iRMX 86 8086/87/88/186 MACRO ASSEMBLER V2.0 ASSEMBLY OF MODULE CF6_ENGINE_LOCAL
OBJECT MODULE PLACED IN CF650L.OBJ
ASSEMBLER INVOKED BY:  :LANG:asm86 CF650L.A86 DEBUG SYMBOLS TYPE

LOC  OBJ            LINE     SOURCE

                             NAME CF6_engine_local


                             ;                  ****************************************
                             ;                  ****************************************
                             ;                  **                                    **
                             ;                  **       ENGINE    MAIN-PROGRAM       **
                             ;                  **                                    **
                             ;                  ****************************************
                             ;                  ****************************************

                             ;                  PROJECT      CF6-50C Multicomputer

                             ;                  03.10.87    v1.0    put n2lim as a constant inside routine
                             ;                  11.08.87    v2.2cg  correct flags
                             ;                  04.08.87    v2.1fh  make engine procedure far
                             ;                  03.08.87    v2.0fh  remove local start
                             ;                  21.07.87    v1.7fh  add for main module test version
                             ;                  19.06.87    v1.1fh  adapt to local processor architecture
                             ;                  19.06.87    v1.0fh  add message structure


                             ;        PROGRAM FOR THE SIMULATION OF THE CF6-50C ENGINE. FOLLOWING
                             ;        SURSYTEM MODULES ARE USED:
                             ;                                  EPR-SYSTEM
                             ;                                  EGT-SYSTEM
                             ;                                  FUEL-FLOW-SYSTEM
                             ;                                  THRUST-SYSTEM
                             ;                                  N1-SYSTEM
                             ;                                  INLET SYSTEM

                             ;        SEE ALSO ADDITIONAL DOCUMENTATION IN THE WRITTEN DOCUMENTS
                             ;        SIMULATION OF A JET ENGINE USING A MICROCOMPUTER
                             ;        DIPLOMA WORK            WS 1979/80

                             ;*****************************************************************************
                             ;
                             ;      THIS PROGAM USES FOLLOWING EXTERNAL MODULE: CF6LIB.LIB(SYSTEM-MODULE).
                             ;        1.CF6LIB.LIB (SYSTEM-MODULE)
                             ;        2.TABLIB.LIB (DATA FUNCTIONS-TABLES )
                             ;****************************************************************************



                             ; note that all written in CAPITAL is original software written
                             ; end of 1979, early 1980 '
                             ; all other is modification done to port the original application
                             ; to Multibus II

                             public std_conditions

                             PUBLIC EVM,EVML,EVMH,EALT,EALTL,EALTH,EP0,ET0,ENGN,INPUTS
                             PUBLIC ET2,ED2,ETHE,EDAM,ERTHE,DEPR,DEGT,DEWFA,DN1,DFNA

                             PUBLIC EN2,EN2L,EN2H,OUTPUTS,EN1,EN1L,EN1H,EN1A
                             PUBLIC EPR,EGT,EWFA,EFUELUSED,EFNA
                             PUBLIC EACPSW,EHPXSW,CFAISW,ECAISW,EBLESW,EREVSW
                             PUBLIC EWFAOLD,DELTAT

                             ;               ****************************
                             ;               *                          *
                             ;               *   DATA VARIABLES         *
                             ;               *                          *
                             ;               ****************************

----                         EFGIO   SEGMENT COMMON

                             ;            ****************************************
                             ;            *  WORK DATA OF ENGINE MODEL           *
                             ;            ****************************************

                             ; global engine input variables

                             ; NOTE THE USE OF ACCESS BOTH AS BYTE AND WORD !

  0000                       std_conditions  equu    this word
0000 (1                                      dw      1        dup(0)              ; Flag-Word only used to sync
                             hronize
     0000
     )
                                                                                  ; sim step from initi
                             alization

  0002                       EVM      EQU     THIS WORD           ;MACH              (INPUT)
0002 00                      EVML     DB      0                   ;                     "
0003 00                      EVMH     DB      0                   ;                     "
  0004                       EALT     EQU     THIS WORD           ;ALTITUDE             "
0004 00                      EALTL    DB      0                   ;                     "
0005 00                      EALTH    DB      0                   ;                     "
0006 0000                    EP0      DW      0                   ;AMBIENT PRESSURE     "
0008 0000                    ET0      DW      0                   ;AMBIENT  TEMPERATURE "
000A (10                     reserved         DW  10 dup(0)          ;10 byte reserved (multibus II
     0000
     )
```

280691-29

```
LOC  OBJ          SOURCE

                        ; the message !                                   ; data strucutre o

                        ; local engine variables

001E 0000               ET2             DW      0
0020 0000               ED2             DW      0
0022 0000               ETHE    DW      0
0024 0000               EDAM    DW      0
0026 0000               ERTHE   DW      0

                        ;TEMP VARIABLES
0028 0000               DEFR    DW      0
002A 0000               DEGT    DW      0
002C 0000               DEWFA   DW      0
002E 0000               DN1             DW      0
0030 0000               DFNA    DW      0

                        ;N2 LOW LIMIT CONSTANT = 80

0032 FF0F               EN2LIM  DW      4095    ;SCALED VALUE FOR LOWER LIMIT N2
                        ;
                        ;


                        $eject

                        ; message data buffers for MPC communication

 0034                   INPUTS EQU      THIS WORD               ;                       "
0034 (1                                 dw              1 dup(0)        ; Flag-Word only
     0000
     )

 0036                   EN2     EQU     THIS WORD               ;REFERRED CORE SPEED     "
0036 00                 EN2L    DB      0                       ;                        "
0037 00                 EN2H    DB      0                       ;                        "
0038 0000               EACPSW  DW      0                       ;AIR COND. SWITCH        "
003A 0000               EHPXSW  DW      0                       ;HORSE POWER EX. SWITCH  "
003C 0000               EFAISW  DW      0                       ;FULL ANTI ICE SWITCH    "
003E 0000               ECAISW  DW      0                       ;COWL ANTI ICE SWITCH    "
0040 0000               EBLESW  DW      0                       ;BLEED SWITCH            "
0042 0000               EREVSW  DW      0                       ;REVERSER SWITCH         "
0044 (2                 in_reserved     dw   2 dup(0)           ; reserved for future use
     0000
     )




0048 0000               ENGN    DW      0                       ;TRIEBWERKNUMMER         "




 004A                   OUTPUTS EQU     THIS WORD
004A (1                                 dw      1 dup(0)                ; Flag-word only
     0000
     )

004C 0000               EWFAOLD DW      0                       ;"OLD VALUE FUEL FLOW           OUTPUT
004E 0000               DELTAT  DW      0                       ; SAMPLING TIME                  "
0050 0000               EFUELUSED       DW      0               ; FUEL USED                      "
 0052                   EN1     EQU     THIS WORD               ; REFERD FAN SPEEDD              "
0052 00                 EN1L    DB      0
0053 00                 EN1H    DB      0
0054 0000               EN1A    DW      0                       ; N1 DIGITAL DSIPLAY             "
0056 0000               EPR     DW      0                       ; ENG.PRESSURE RATIO             "
0058 0000               EGT     DW      0                       ; EXHAUST GAS TEMP.              "
005A 0000               EWFA    DW      0                       ; FUEL-FLOW                      "
005C 0000               EFNA    DW      0                       ; THRUST                         "


005E 0000               EFUELUSED1      dw      0
0060 0000               EFUELUSED2      dw      0
0062 0000               EFUELUSED3      dw      0

----                    EFGIO   ENDS

                        $eject


----                    STACKSEG                SEGMENT STACK
0000 (100                               DW      100 DUP(?)      ;ALLOCATE 100 WORDS FOR STACK
     ????
     )
00C8                    STACKTOP        LABEL   WORD            ;OFFSET ADDRESS OF THE TOS
----                    STACKSEG                ENDS

----                    iodatseg                SEGMENT public

0000 0000               TIME50  dw      0
0002 00                 NOFUEL  db      0

----                    iodatseg                ENDS
```

280691-30

5

```
LOC  OBJ                SOURCE

----                    EFGCOD          SEGMENT PUBLIC

                                ;GIVE ASSEMBLER INITIAL REGISTER TO SEGMENT CORRESPONDENCE

                        ASSUME  CS: EFGCOD,     DS: IODATSEG,    ES: EFGIO,      SS: STACKSEG

                        public  engine





                        EXTRN INLETSYS:NEAR,EPRSYS:NEAR,EGTSYS:NEAR,N1SYS:NEAR,EWFASYS:NEAR
                        EXTRN FNASYS:NEAR

                                ASSUME ES:EFGIO,CS:EFGCOD

                        ;                       ******************************
                        ;                       *                            *
                        ;                       *  ENGINE MODEL ROUTINE      *
                        ;                       *                            *
                        ;                       ******************************


0000                    ENGINE          PROC    far

                        START_engine:
0000                                            PUSH    ES
0000 06                                 PUSH    DS      ;ES,DS SAVE ONTO STACK
0001 1E                                 MOV     AX,EFGIO  ; REORGANIZE SEGEMENTS FOR THE
0002 B8----        R                                                     ; OPTIMAL USE OF THE CPU ;
                        SPEED AND
                                                                         ; AGAIN SPEED....
0005 8EC0                               MOV     ES,AX
0007 E80000        E                    CALL    INLETSYS  ;CALCULATE THE INLET VALUES




                        ;       *****************
                        ;       *   ENGINE     *
                        ;       *****************


000A 26A13600                           MOV     AX,EN2
000E 3DFF0F                             CMP     AX,4095         ; >>> put absolute value here
                                                                        ; due to EPROM version
0011 7706                               JA      NORMAL2
0013 E81500                             CALL    IDLEBYPASS      ; IN IDLE BYPASS MODEL CALCULATION
                                                                        ; BASED ON A SIMPLIFICATION A
                        SSUPTION
0016 EB1090                             JMP     idle_state

                                        ; NORMAL NON IDLE MODE : CALCULATE A NEW STATE OF THE ENGINE
                                        ; SUBSYSTEMS

0019 E80000        E    NORMAL2:        CALL    EPRSYS          ; EPR
001C E80000        E                    CALL    N1SYS           ; N1
001F E80000        E                    CALL    EWFASYS         ; FUEL FLOW
0022 E80000        E                    CALL    EGTSYS          ; EGT
0025 E80000        E                    CALL    FNASYS          ; THRUST

0028                    idle_state :

0028 1F                                 POP     DS
0029 07                                 POP     ES
002A CB                                 RET
                        ENGINE  ENDP

                        ;                       *****************
                        ;                       *  END ENGINE  *
                        ;                                               *****************

002B                    IDLEBYPASS      PROC

002B 50                         PUSH    AX              ;SAVE EN2
002C 26C70636000010             MOV     EN2,4096

0033 E80000        E            CALL    EPRSYS          ;N1SYS SIMPLIFICATION ASSUMPTION
0036 E80000        E            CALL    EWFASYS
0039 E80000        E            CALL    EGTSYS
003C E80000        E            CALL    FNASYS

003F 268F063600                 POP     EN2             ;RECALL EN2
0044 C3                         RET

                        IDLEBYPASS      ENDP



----                    EFGCOD  ENDS
                                END
```

280691-31

```
MODULE = FUELFLOW_SYSTEM

BASE    OFFSET TYPE SYMBOL          BASE    OFFSET TYPE SYMBOL          BASE    OFFSET TYPE SYMBOL

0041H   0A10H  SYM  CONT1           0041H   0A33H  SYM  CONT2           0041H   0C0BH  SYM  ENDE
0041H   0B25H  SYM  EWFAC           0041H   09C0H  SYM  EWFASYS         0041H   0A06H  SYM  NEG1
0041H   0A29H  SYM  NEG2            0041H   09C0H  SYM  START           0041H   0AABH  SYM  TACP
0041H   0ACEH  SYM  TCAI            0041H   0A6CH  SYM  TFAI            0041H   0A8DH  SYM  THPX

MEMORY MAP OF MODULE MAIN_MODULE_286

MODULE START ADDRESS  PARAGRAPH = 0041H  OFFSET = 000DH
SEGMENT MAP

START     STOP      LENGTH ALIGN NAME              CLASS          OVERLAY

00000H    0009FH    00A0H   A    INT_POINTERS
00200H    00200H    0000H   G    ??SEG
00200H    00263H    0064H   G    EFGIO
00270H    003FFH    0190H   G    STACKSEG
00400H    00402H    0003H   G    IODATSEG
00410H    01021H    0C12H   G    EFGCOD
01030H    010B0H    0081H   G    CODE
010C0H    0243FH    1380H   G    EFGDAT
02440H    0251EH    00DFH   W    C286_INT_HANDL    CODE
                                 -ER_CODE
02520H    02543H    0024H   W    C286_INT_HANDL    DATA
                                 -ER_DATA
02544H    0254BH    0008H   W    STACK             STACK
0254CH    0254CH    0000H   W    MEMORY            MEMORY
```

280691-32

APPENDIX E

I2ICE Debug Session Sample

This shows a sample debug session using symbolic debugging with I2ICE 286.

```
First include all user pre-defined macros for this application
*
*
*include cf6.mac

std_def is a macro for setting the standard values for local
engine test

*define proc std_def = do
.*evm=0t
.*ep0=20783t
.*et0=303t
.*deltat=18000t
.*end
*
mpc_msg is a macro for displaying the content of the MPC_MESSAGE
STRUCTURE

*define  proc mpc_msg = do
.*write ' '
.*write ' dest     = ', mpc_message.dest
.*write ' src      = ', mpc_message.src
.*write ' type     = ', mpc_message.type
.*write ' not_used = ', mpc_message.not_used
.*write ' transport message passing part '
.*write ' protocol_id        = ', byte .mpc_message.prot_id
.*write ' transmition _cntl  = ', byte .mpc_message.transm_ctr
.*write ' dest port_id       = ', word .mpc_message.dest_port_id
.*write ' src_port_id        = ', word .mpc_message.sourc_port_id
.*write ' transaction_id     = ', byte .mpc_message.transact_id
.*write ' transaction_cntl   = ', byte .mpc_message.transact_ctr
.*write ' data field = '
.*word .mpc_message+12t length 10t
.*end

macro s makes a single step

*define proc s = do
.*istep
.*ASM $
.*end
*

macro input_cf6 displays the inputs data structure
before and engine simulation step
```

280691-33

```
*define proc input_cf6 = do
.*write 'flag_word =',:cf6_engine_local.inputs
.*write 'EN2 =',:cf6_engine_local.EN2
.*write 'EN2L =',:cf6_engine_local.EN2L
.*write 'EN2H =',:cf6_engine_local.EN2H
.*write 'EACPSW =',:cf6_engine_local.EACPSW
.*write 'EHPXSW =',:cf6_engine_local.EHPXSW
.*write 'EFAISW =',:cf6_engine_local.EFAISW
.*write 'ECAISW =',:cf6_engine_local.ECAISW
.*write 'EBLESW =',:cf6_engine_local.EBLESW
.*write 'EREVSW =',:cf6_engine_local.EREVSW
.*end

*

macro output_cf6 displays the outputs data structure
as a result of a simulation step

*
*define proc output_cf6 = do
.*write 'flag_word =',:cf6_engine_local.outputs
.*write 'EWFAOLD =',:cf6_engine_local.EWFAOLD
.*write 'DELTAT =',:cf6_engine_local.DELTAT
.*write 'EFUELUSED =',:cf6_engine_local.EFUELUSED
.*write 'EN1  =',:cf6_engine_local.EN1
.*write 'EN1L  =',:cf6_engine_local.EN1L
.*write 'EN1H  =',:cf6_engine_local.EN1H
.*write 'EN1A  =',:cf6_engine_local.EN1A
.*write 'EPR =',:cf6_engine_local.EPR
.*write 'EGT =',:cf6_engine_local.EGT
.*write 'EWFA =',:cf6_engine_local.EWFA
.*write 'EFNA =',:cf6_engine_local.EFNA
.*end
*

enginestate decode the full state of variables of the
engine model at any time

*DEFINE proc ENGINESTATE = do
.*BASE=decimal
.*WRITE 'N1 =  ',EN1, '  non scaled :',(en1a/1696t)*20t
.*WRITE 'EGT = ',EGT, '  non scaled :',egt
.*WRITE 'EPR = ',EPR, '  non scaled :',epr/3200t
.*WRITE 'N2 =  ',EN2, '  non scaled :',(en2/256t)*5t
.*WRITE 'FF =  ',EWFA,'  non scaled :',ewfa
.*WRITE 'FNA = ',EFNA,'  non scaled :',(efna/378t)*1000t
.*WRITE 'INLET ::::   EP0=',EP0,' ET0= ',ET0,' MACH = ',EVM
.*write ' '
.*write ' switch status '
.*write 'acp =',EACPSW,' hpx =',EHPXSW,' fai =',EFAISW
.*write 'cai =',ECAISW,' ble =',EBLESW,' reverse = ',EREVSW
.*write ' fuel used for this step = ',efuelused
.*BASE=Hex
.*end
```

280691-34

```
macro setn2 sets the en2 variable for a local test
*
*DEFINE proc SETN2 = do
.*word .mpc_message+14t = %0
.*end
*

macro rst allows the reset not complete sequence to take place
see also main text

*define proc rst = do
.*reset regs
.*unithold
.*port(34h)=0f8h
.*port(31h)=0f8h
.*port(30h)=0a4h
.*port(3ch)=000h
.*go from 0ffff:0 forever
.*end
*


make a break at the end of the simulation step

*go til :c286_int_handler#43
*Probe 0 stopped at :C286_INT_HANDLER#41 + 1H because of execute
break
  Clips= F3  Trace Buffer Overflow

see what data are around after a full engine simulation step
using i2ice macros

incoming data packed in mpc_message structure as before
engine simulation step done

message strucuture as received by the MPC

*mpc_msg

 dest       =  01
 src        =  05
 type       =  00
 not_used =  00
 transport message passing part
 protocol_id         = 02
 transmition _cntl = 00
 dest port_id       =  0010
 src_port_id        =  0800
 transaction_id     =  00
 transaction_cntl   =  00
 data field =
0256:000EH  0010 14E0 0000 0001 0001 0000 0000 0000 0000 0000
```

280691-35

```
input data

*input_cf6
flag_word = 0010
EN2 = 14E0
EN2L = E0
EN2H = 14
EACPSW = 0000
EHPXSW = 0001
EFAISW = 0001
ECAISW = 0000
EBLESW = 0000
EREVSW = 0000

output data

*
*output_cf6
flag_word = 0000
EWFAOLD = 1411
DELTAT = 29C7
EFUELUSED = 001B
EN1  = 2CDB
EN1L  = DB
EN1H  = 2C
EN1A  = 2605
EPR = 5346
EGT = 035B
EWFA = 5047
EFNA = 4B0A

full engine state

*
*enginestate
N1 =   11483   non scaled : 100
EGT =  859   non scaled : 859
EPR =  21318   non scaled : 6
N2 =   5344   non scaled : 100
FF =   20551   non scaled : 20551
FNA =  19210   non scaled : 50000
INLET ::::   EP0= 20783  ET0=  303  MACH =  0

 switch status
acp = 0  hpx = 1  fai = 1
cai = 0  ble = 0  reverse =  0
 fuel used for this step =  27
*
```

280691-36

5

```
continue the simulation
*
*go forever
?
?
?
/* end of this debug session */
```

280691-37

iPAT Analysis Protocol

This shows the sample iPAT analysis session done to assess the performance of the application processor design.

```
*
*/* -------ipat analysis   -------*/
*
set the time base to 200 nsec in general
note that we are online with the simulation running

*go
?ptimebase = 200ns

define a macro for analysing

?
?define proc measure = do
.?pat init duration %0
.?histo=false
.?pat display
.?end
?

measure the time spendt in the mpc_receive_message routine

?measure (:mpc_handler_module.mpc_receive_message)

Mode: DURATION
Event: :MPC_HA.MPC_RECEIVE_MESSAGE
Time Range: 200ns TO 1sec
PTIMEBASE = 200 ns
Status: OK

    Time Interval :  Bin Sum : Time    ]
------------------+----------+--------]
        <  200 ns :        0:     0 ns]
  200 ns- 1200 ns+:        0:     0 ns]
 1400 ns- 9200 ns+:        0:     0 ns]
 9400 ns-   65 us+:        0:     0 ns]
   65 us-  447 us+:       58:  5165 us]
------------------+----------+--------]
Time Min:   89.0 us
Time Max:   89.2 us
?
```

280691-38

5

measure the time spent in the mpc_transmit_message routine

```
?measure (:mpc_handler_module.mpc_transmit_message)

Mode: DURATION
Event: :MPC_HA.MPC_TRANSMIT_MESSAGE
Time Range: 200ns TO 1sec
PTIMEBASE = 200 ns
Status: OK

    Time Interval :  Bin Sum : Time    ]
------------------+----------+--------]
        <  200 ns :        0:     0 ns]
  200 ns- 1200 ns+:        0:     0 ns]
 1400 ns- 9200 ns+:        0:     0 ns]
 9400 ns-   65 us+:        0:     0 ns]
   65 us-  447 us+:       58:  5316 us]
------------------+----------+--------]
Time Min:   91.6 us
Time Max:   91.8 us
?
```

measure the time spent in the whole interrupt routine

```
?
?measure (:c286_int_handler)

Mode: DURATION
Event: :C286_INT_HANDLER
Time Range: 200ns TO 1sec
PTIMEBASE = 200 ns
Status: OK

    Time Interval :  Bin Sum : Time    ]
------------------+----------+--------]
        <  200 ns :        0:     0 ns]
  200 ns- 1200 ns+:        0:     0 ns]
 1400 ns- 9200 ns+:        0:     0 ns]
 9400 ns-   65 us+:        0:     0 ns]
   65 us-  447 us+:        0:     0 ns]
------------------+----------+--------]
Time Min: 1409.2 us
Time Max: 1412.8 us
?
```

measure the time spent in the engine model routine
note that the engine model calculation time is variable depending on the switch position of the subsystems

```
?measure (:cf6_engine_local.engine)
```

280691–39

```
Mode: DURATION
Event: :CF6_EN.ENGINE
Time Range: 200ns TO 1sec
PTIMEBASE = 200 ns
Status: OK

   Time Interval :  Bin Sum : Time    ]
------------------+----------+--------]
        <  200 ns :         0:    0 ns]
  200 ns- 1200 ns+:         0:    0 ns]
 1400 ns- 9200 ns+:         0:    0 ns]
 9400 ns-   65 us+:         0:    0 ns]
   65 us-  447 us+:         0:    0 ns]
------------------+----------+--------]
Time Min:  633.0 us
Time Max:  636.6 us
?
```

measure the time spent for copying the data from the mpc_message_structure to the inputs buffer

```
?
?pat init duration :c286_int_handler#26 to :c286_int_handler#27
?pat display

Mode: DURATION
Event: :C286_INT_HAN#26-#27
Time Range: 200ns TO 1sec
PTIMEBASE = 200 ns
Status: OK

   Time Interval :  Bin Sum : Time    ]
------------------+----------+--------]
        <  200 ns :         0:    0 ns]
  200 ns- 1200 ns+:         0:    0 ns]
 1400 ns- 9200 ns+:         0:    0 ns]
 9400 ns-   65 us+:        62: 1895 us]
   65 us-  447 us+:         0:    0 ns]
------------------+----------+--------]
Time Min:    30.4 us
Time Max:    30.6 us

?
```

measure the time spent for the transport protocol adaptation

```
?pat init duration :c286_int_handler#30 to :c286_int_handler#35
?pat display

Mode: DURATION
Event: :C286_INT_HAN#30-#35
Time Range: 200ns TO 1sec
PTIMEBASE = 200 ns
Status: OK
```

280691-40

5

```
   Time Interval :  Bin Sum : Time    ]
-----------------+----------+--------]
         <  200 ns :          0:    0 ns]
  200 ns- 1200 ns+:          0:    0 ns]
 1400 ns- 9200 ns+:          0:    0 ns]
 9400 ns-   65 us+:         50:  873 us]
   65 us-  447 us+:          0:    0 ns]
-----------------+----------+--------]
Time Min:   17.4 us
Time Max:   17.6 us
?
```

measure the total time used for the mpc interrupt processing from hardware interrupt on.

```
Mode: DURATION
Event: :MAIN_M.INTERRUPT_ROUTINE
Time Range: 200ns TO 1sec
PTIMEBASE = 200 ns
Status: OK

   Time Interval :  Bin Sum : Time    ]
-----------------+----------+--------]
         <  200 ns :          0:    0 ns]
  200 ns- 1200 ns+:          0:    0 ns]
 1400 ns- 9200 ns+:          0:    0 ns]
 9400 ns-   65 us+:          0:    0 ns]
   65 us-  447 us+:          0:    0 ns]
-----------------+----------+--------]
Time Min: 1450.0 us
Time Max: 1453.6 us
```

profile the relative time spend by the three main routines

```
?
?pat init profile :mpc_handler_module.mpc_receive_message,&
??:mpc_handler_module.mpc_transmit_message,&
??:cf6_engine_local.engine
?pat display

Mode: PROFILE
PTIMEBASE =  10 us
Include calls
Status: OK
```

280691-41

```
Event              :  Count  0%        10        20
-----------------------------+---------+---------+-------
ENGINE             :      61:xxxxxxxxxxxxxxxxx
MPC_TRANSMIT_ME    :      61:xxxxxxxxxxxxxxxxx
MPC_RECEIVE_MES    :      61:xxxxxxxxxxxxxxxxx
*Background*       :     182:xxxxxxxxxxxxxxxxxxxxxxxxxxxx
-----------------------------+---------+---------+-------
      Total      :       365 0%        10        20
?histo=false
?pat display

Mode: PROFILE
PTIMEBASE =  10 us
Include calls
Status: OK

Event                    : Count :  Time:Time Min:Time Avg:Time Max
-----------------------------+-------------+--------+--------+--
:CF6_EN.ENGINE           : 444 :  318 ms:  710 us:  710 us:  720 us
:MPC_HA.MPC_TRANSMIT     : 444 :   41 ms:   90 us:   90 us:  100 us
MPC_RECEIVE_MESSAGE      : 444 :   39 ms:   80 us:   80 us:   90 us
*Background*             : 1331:   22sec:   40 us:   16 ms:   50 ms
---------------------------------+----------+--------+--------+--
      Total                      :       2663:   22sec
?
?
```

make the interrupt to routine activation measurents

mpc interrupt to start of the interrupt routine

```
?pat init duration interrupt to :c286_int_handler.mpc_interrupt
?histo = false
?pat display

Mode: DURATION
Event: *INT*-:C286_INT_HANDLER#15
Time Range: 10us TO 1sec

PTIMEBASE = 200 ns
Status: OK

    Time Interval :  Bin Sum : Time   ]
------------------+----------+--------]
        <   10 us :        0:    0 ns]
   10 us-   11 us+:        0:    0 ns]
   11 us-   19 us+:       70:  919 us]
   19 us-   75 us+:        0:    0 ns]
   75 us-  457 us+:        0:    0 ns]
------------------+----------+--------]
Time Min:   12.8 us
Time Max:   13.6 us
```

280691-42

5

```
mpc interrupt to start of mpc_receive_message

?pat init duration interrupt to
:mpc_handler_module.mpc_receive_message
?pat display

Mode: DURATION
Event: *INT*-00109DH
Time Range: 200ns TO 1sec
PTIMEBASE = 200 ns
Status: OK

    Time Interval :  Bin Sum : Time    ]
------------------+----------+--------]
        <  200 ns :        0:     0 ns]
  200 ns- 1200 ns+:        0:     0 ns]
 1400 ns- 9200 ns+:        0:     0 ns]
 9400 ns-   65 us+:       71:  1523 us]
   65 us-  447 us+:        0:     0 ns]
------------------+----------+--------]
Time Min:   21.0 us
Time Max:   22.0 us
?
?
?
?/* end of test session */
?
?halt
*Probe 0 stopped at :MAIN_MODULE_286 + 74H because of halt
  Clips= F6  Trace Buffer Overflow
*exit
 I2ICE terminated
```

280691-43

December 1990

Simple I/O Design Example using the Multibus II Modular Interface eXtension (MIX) Architecture

ERIK A. STEEB
OMSO TECHNICAL MARKETING ENGINEER

Order Number: 281004-001

Simple I/O Design Example using the Multibus II Modular Interface Extension (MIX) Architecture

CONTENTS

1.0 INTRODUCTION

Since its introduction, Multibus II has proven to be a very good solution for high performance computing. The bus is well suited high performance applications due to its ability to support multiple CPUs in a loosely coupled environment. This capability is not only bourne in hardware but in the firmware and software as well.

In this loosely coupled multiprocessing environment, many CPUs are able to interoperate on a common backplane. With this ability comes the need for a system design which is separated along functional boundaries. This means particular I/O needs of the system are handled in a client/server fashion instead of the traditional master/slave method. The difference in the two approaches lies in the ability of the I/O server to support more than one host processor while the slave cannot.

The use of a functionally partitioned system allows for better structured programming and ease of upgrading system resources. However, the designers of special I/O are faced with the challenge of more complex board designs. For Multibus II this means not only designing a board which supports message passing and the multiple address spaces defined for the bus, but also one with an intelligent CPU core and a high speed memory subsystem. These added requirements not only increase the design complexity but can also greatly affect the time to market of a product.

Intel has developed an I/O strategy which eliminates the burden of developing the compute engine and PSB interface of the I/O server, therefore easing the problems associated with designing special I/O for Multibus II. This is done by decoupling the specific I/O technology from the CPU technology in a baseboard/module fashion as shown in Figure 1. With this design, an Intel baseboard is coupled with an I/O module supplied by Intel, the customer, or a third party. Although the baseboard and module are separate boards, the combination forms a single slot I/O server Multibus II.

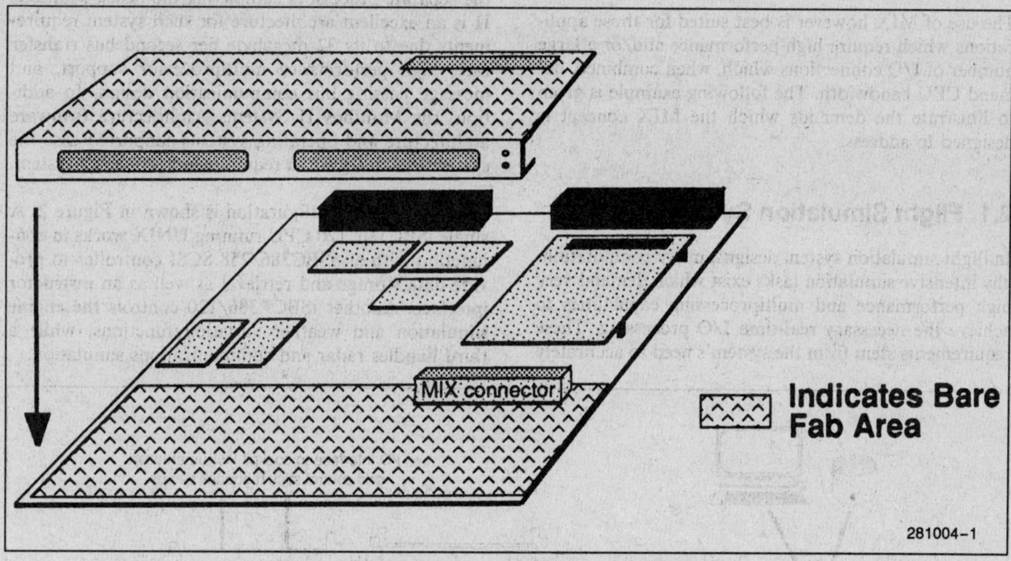

Figure 1. MIX Baseboard/Module Combination

MIS is an acronym for Modular Interface eXtension. MIX® is a trademark of MIX Software, Inc.
MULTIBUS is a registered trademark of Intel Corporation.
UNIX is a trademark of AT&T, Inc.
OrCAD is a trademark of OrCAD SYSTEMS CORPORATION.
PALASM is a trademark of Monolithic Memories, Inc.

The modular design allows an engineer to focus his efforts on the I/O needs of a product by integrating his special I/O design with an intelligent Multibus II I/O platform supplied by Intel. This platform provides the necessary computational power required of an I/O server but leaves the special I/O module design to the customer.

The strategy outlined above is known as the Modular Interface eXtension (MIX) architecture. This document gives an application example and illustrates a simple I/O design which utilizes the Multibus II MIX architecture.

2.0 MIX APPLICATION EXAMPLE

Because the MIX architecture allows stacking of up to three MIX modules on a high performance baseboard, price/performance scalability is offered along with ease of design for Multibus II, ease of upgrade potential, and support for Intel operating systems. Therefore, a MIX design fits well in virtually any Multibus II application.

The use of MIX however is best suited for those applications which require high performance and/or a large number of I/O connections which, when combined, demand CPU bandwidth. The following example is given to illustrate the demands which the MIX concept is designed to address.

2.1 Flight Simulation System

In flight simulation system designs, many computationally intensive simulation tasks exist which demand very high performance and multiprocessing capabilities to achieve the necessary real-time I/O processing. These requirements stem from the system's need to accurately and quickly convert pilot and aircraft action into control and instrumentation reaction.

This application requires plenty of computational muscle, a fast real-time kernel to handle the simulation tasks, and lots of I/O bandwidth. In addition, a custom interface for cockpit controls and instrumentation is required to handle all aspects of the simulation process.

Consider simulating airflow over a wing. A processor must not only compute the forces on the wing which result from the fluid motion of air over its surface, but also determine and apply (in real-time) the proper amount of feedback pressure to the pilot's control stick.

In addition to the simulation requirements of the system, a flight data collection and storage mechanism, and possibly an instructor interface, will be needed to handle on line customization of the flight variables and post-flight critiques.

These tasks demand multiprocessing capabilities in an environment which allows constant interaction among the separate processors completing the tasks. Multibus II is an excellent architecture for such system requirements due to its 32 megabyte per second bus transfer rate, high performance multiprocessor support, and message passing bus communication design. In addition, the Multibus II Systems Architecture firmware architecture and operating systems supported ease the system level integration requirements for such a system.

A rough system configuration is shown in Figure 2. A single iSBC386/120 CPU running UNIX works in conjunction with an iSBC386/258 SCSI controller to provide data storage and retrieval as well as an instructor interface. Another iSBC®386/120 controls the engine simulation and weather variation functions, while a third handles radar and communications simulation.

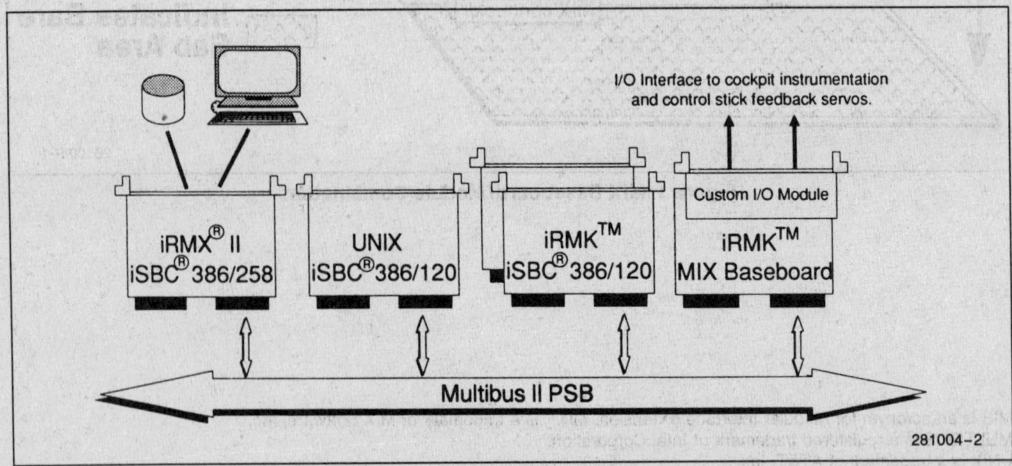

Figure 2. Flight Simulator Example

The MIX baseboard in this example controls the airflow simulation as well as the instrumentation output and control stick feedback I/O. The I/O interface to the actual simulator instruments and control stick is accomplished via a slave MIX module which utilizes a high speed digital I/O link. This module is the only hardware which must be designed by the systems integrator.

In addition to the high performance hardware functions this solution provides, it also offers support for current Intel system firmware and operating systems.

From a firmware point of view, all boards discussed ship with Intel MSA compatible firmware. This allows ease of integration into a system environment in terms of board and system level diagnostics, boot mechanisms, and board-to-board communication support.

Ease of integrating the custom MIX module into this firmware architecture is also provided. Functions in the MIX baseboard firmware allow the I/O module firmware to interact with the baseboard firmware for diagnostics. boot, and operating requirements without the need for modifying the baseboard EPROM contents. This enables any standard or special I/O modules to participate in BIST testing and boot procedures.

The demand for high performance software capabilities can be easily realized with the use of the iRMK® real-time kernel. This 32-bit kernel includes the transport and message passing support necessary for the intra-system communication used in completing the system level task. In this example, the MIX baseboard and each iSBC 386/120 performing simulation tasks runs the iRMK kernel.

UNIX System V/3.2 is run on the host iSBC 386/120 to provide the operator interface and flight record databasing functions of the system. These functions are typical of the capabilities of standard UNIX and exist as software packages supported by the UNIX operating system.

With the host running UNIX System V/3.2, the 386/120 boards running the iRMK kernel can take advantage of the capabilities of Intel's System V/iRMK. This version of iRMK is designed to operate in a UNIX hosted environment and provides a UNIX hosted development environment as well as a tested transport package for UNIX/iRMK communications. These capabilities greatly simplify the data collection and storage requirements of the system.

The remaining pieces of the system which must be developed by the system integrator are the custom MIX module, the iRMK tasks to perform the simulation, and the instructor interface routines for the UNIX subsystem. This document will discuss the MIX module portion of the design.

3.0 MODULE DEFINITION

3.1 Module Purpose

The MIX module to be designed must be capable of supplying many external digital I/O connections which can be quickly accessed and latched for reliable digital I/O performance. The module will also contain a serial interface to the MIX baseboard for debug purposes. These functional goals of the module can be realized in a simple 8-bit slave I/O MIX module design. To improve the aggregate I/O throughput of the design, the module architecture will be extended to support 32-bit accesses to the digital I/O channels.

This module design does not demonstrate the full capabilities of the MIX architecture as the module does not have MIX master capabilities. It does however, function as a useful example to demonstrate the considerations and issues involved in the design of a simple MIX module.

3.2 I/O Component Definition

In this module design example, a simple slave I/O device is used for digital I/O control. The 8255A Programmable Peripheral Interface component provides all of the I/O capabilities required of the external interface. The device provides three 8-bit parallel I/O ports programmable in three modes. The speed requirements of the digital I/O interface are met by utilizing the 82C55A CHMOS version of the chip. This version offers much better timing specifications for command widths and command recovery times as compared to the NMOS 8255A. In addition, the CHMOS device consumes much less power than its NMOS relative.

For the serial interface, the module will utilize the 82510 Asynchronous Serial Controller. This chip is chosen over the more common 82530 due to its proven high performance and its low power, CHMOS characteristics. In addition, this chip is being used on other Intel MIX modules such as the MIX 450 Terminal Concentrator and the MIX 560 Ethernet Controller.

3.3 Module Functional Blocks

The I/O chips chosen above have signal sets based on the 8086 architecture. Because the MIX interface supports an i386™ signal set, the module design must supply a signal conversion function for these components. Furthermore, the module must supply data transceivers, an I/O address decode scheme, and an interconnect EEPROM interface.

5

By separating the design into functional partitions, the task of transforming MIX signals into signals compatible with the I/O devices becomes a straight forward process.

The features described above are easily separated into five main functional blocks as shown in Figure 3. They are the MIX interface, the data transceivers, the control logic block, the I/O block, and the configuration data block.

The MIX interface block simply consists of the MIX connector and the terminating resistors required for the data bus and control signals. The data buffer block contains the data drivers which provide bidirectional data transfers and support the MIX interface TTL drive requirements. These devices will be set up in a byte swap configuration which allows BYTE, WORD, or DWORD accesses to the I/O devices.

The control logic block is made up of PALs which perform the I/O address decode and convert the MIX bus i386 family signals into read and write commands useable by the parallel and serial components. It also handles the READY logic for the module and generates the proper gate and direction signals for the data drivers. This block is by far the most complex portion of the module. The I/O block contains the parallel and serial chips as well as the drivers and connectors required to interface with external devices. The final block is the configuration data block. This block contains a serial EEPROM device which provides dynamic configurability of the baseboard's interconnect space during power up.

4.0 DESIGN TOOLS USED

Several engineering tools are used in this project to shorten the design cycle, simplify logic design requirements, and provide a means of simulation before the module is prototyped. Because this is a relatively simple design, engineered by a single person, it is desirable to find engineering tools which can run on a common desktop PC. Many PC/AT compatible design tools exist which offer the capabilities needed for this type of board design.

The tools purchased from third parties for this project include a schematic capture package and a PAL design and simulation utility.

4.1 OrCAD Schematic Capture Package

OrCAD Systems Corporation provides a CAE package which includes a schematic capture design tool and a PCB layout utility. The schematic capture tool is used in this module design.

The OrCAD schematic package offers hierarchical or flat file schematic design, common component libraries, annotation, back annotation, cleanup, cross referencing, error checking, netlist, and parts list utilities. The completeness of this package allows the entire module design to be completed on a simple PC/AT computer.

4.2 PALSAM 2 PAL Specification Utility

The control portion of this MIX module must perform address decode functions as well as generate chip selects, provide transceiver gate signals, and handle the READY circuitry. While these functions can be designed using discrete logic, they are more appropriately and efficiently handled using a PAL or EPLD device.

A PAL programming utility is required to input PAL logic equations and convert those equations into fusemaps which a PAL programmer understands. Such a utility is provided by Monolithic Memories, Inc. This utility is called PALASM 2. It is a follow on to MMI's PALASM software which assembles PAL design specification code, generates PAL device fuse patterns in JEDEC format, checks for syntax and assembly errors, and provides a means for simulating the PALs operation based upon given input states.

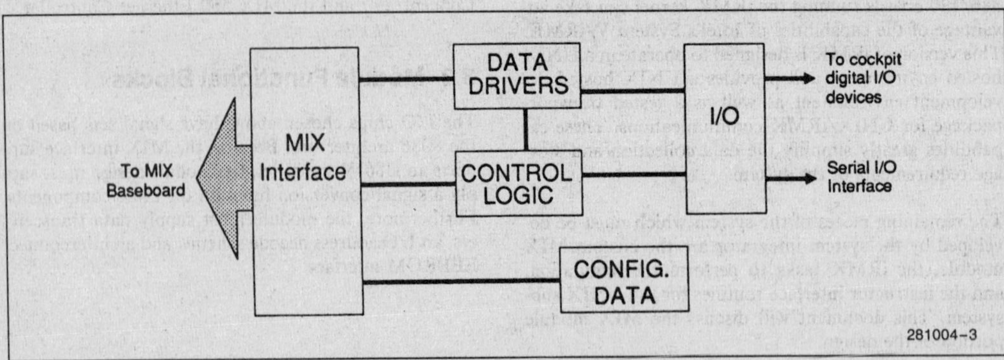

Figure 3. MIX Module Block Diagram

5.0 MODULE LOGIC DESIGN

To complete the logic design for this MIX module, the hierarchical capabilities of the schematic capture package are used in conjunction with the preliminary block diagram shown previously in Figure 3. This procedure allows the design to be broken down into simpler functional design tasks. As shown on sheet 1 of the module schematic (Appendix A), the five functional blocks of Figure 3 have been expanded to eight. A capacitor block has been added to provide the decoupling needed in any TTL design. The MIX block has been broken into the MIX interface block and termination block, and the I/O block has been divided into the Programmable Peripheral Interface (PPI) block and the Serial Interface block.

To start the design with the MIX interface block would not be productive as we have not yet defined the MIX signals which must be supported. Because this design is a MIX slave, the module need only support the MIX signals required to complete its I/O function. To understand which signals are required for this module, the module is designed from the I/O devices back to the MIX interface.

As mentioned earlier, the I/O block defined in Chapter 3 has been divided into two blocks. This is done because the module utilizes two distinctly different I/O devices. We therefore divide the I/O block into a parallel I/O block and a serial I/O block.

5.1 Parallel I/O Block

The 82C55A PPI will serve as the central I/O device for this block. This 8-bit device provides 24 programmable I/O pins which may be individually programmed in 2 groups of 12. It allows direct bit set/reset capabilities and is fully TTL compatible.

As shown in Figure 4, the 82C55A requires 8086 compatible signals for read and write control. The conversion from 386 to 8086 compatible signals as well as the chip select generation will be handled in the Control Block of the design. Aside from RESET, the two remaining chip control signals are A0 and A1. These will be obtained from the MIX interface signals MXA2* and MXA3* respectively. This addressing scheme will have the effect of separating the internal chip registers by 4 bytes.

As stated in section 3.1, the MIX module is to provide a 32-bit data path to the parallel I/O interface. To accomplish this, four 82C55A components operate in parallel. Except for the select lines, the control signals for each chip may be wire ORed together. This is shown on sheets 8 and 9 of the module schematic (Appendix A). To facilitate BYTE, WORD, and DWORD accesses to the digital I/O interface, the data drivers in the Data Buffer Block are designed in a byte swap configuration.

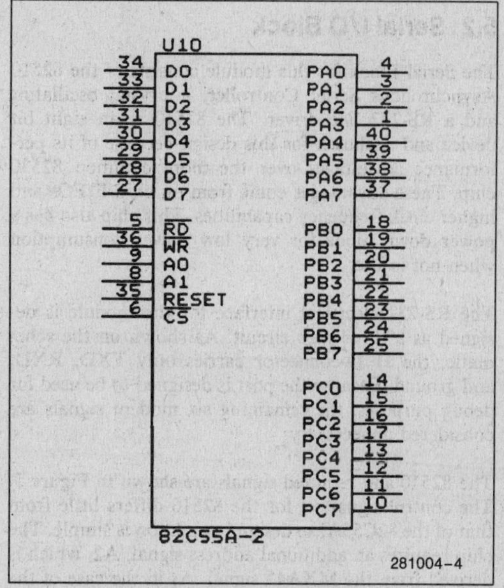

Figure 4. 82C55A PPI

Finally, the Control Block decodes the type of access being made and generates the proper chip select(s) to the peripheral chips.

Because the PPI is capable of only 2.5 mA of DC drive, the parallel I/O block also incorporates line drivers between the PPI and the target I/O devices. In this design, only ports A and C of the PPI are used. This gives 64 bits of digital I/O and uses up to 16 line driver components.

As shown on the module schematic, four 74F245 Octal Transceivers drive the port A signals. Two signals from port B enable and configure the drive direction for the transceivers. These fast devices provide 64 mA of low level output current on the "B" side of the driver. This level is sufficient to drive most digital I/O needs.

Eight 14 pin DIP sockets are used for installation of the port C signal drivers. This allows the user to configure port C with a variety of Quad Two-Input drivers or terminators. This design also uses a 64 pin DIN connector to provide external connection to the 32 port A signals and their associated ground lines. Eight 74ALS00 devices drive the port C outputs to illuminate four banks of eight LEDs. This is shown on the module schematic.

Although Port C of the parallel I/O block in this design is set up for display (LEDs), the block can be easily modified to provide 64 or 96 (using port B) lines of external I/O.

5.2 Serial I/O Block

The Serial Block for this module consists of the 82510 Asynchronous Serial Controller, a crystal oscillator, and a RS-232 line driver. The 82510 is an eight bit device and is chosen for this design because of its performance advantages over the more common 82530 chip. These advantages come from on chip FIFOs and higher clock frequency capabilities. This chip also has a power down mode for very low power consumption when not in use.

The RS-232 electrical interface for the module is designed as a three wire circuit. As shown on the schematic, the J1 D-connector carries only TXD, RXD, and ground. Because the port is designed to be used for debug purposes, the remaining six modem signals are considered unnecessary.

The 82510 and required signals are shown in Figure 5. The control signal set for the 82510 differs little from that of the 82C55A, so design integration is simple. The chip requires an additional address signal, A2, which is derived from the MXA4* signal. As in the case of the 82C55A, the address line connections cause the internal registers of the component to be DWORD aligned.

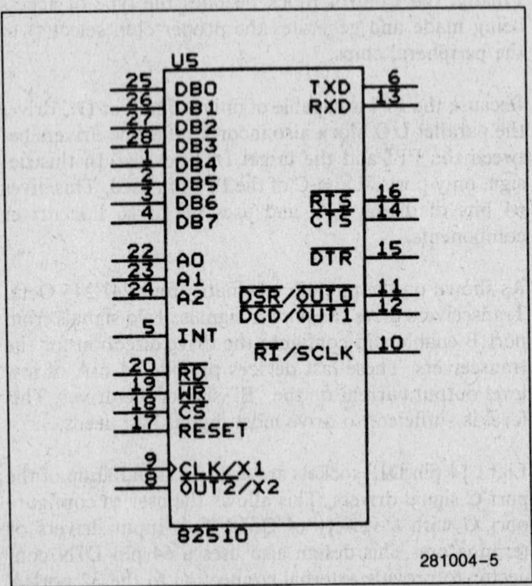

One interrupt line also comes from the 82510 to signal FIFO conditions, errors, etc. This interrupt line is routed through an inverter and a series terminating resister to the LCLINT* pin of the MIX interface since this is the only interrupt on the module. The MIX interface termination requirements are found in the *MIX Module Design Specification* (Intel p/n 500729-001).

The chip also requires a clock source for baud rate generation. The 82510 allows two modes of operation for the clock source. The first mode uses an external oscillator to internally generate its system clock while the second uses an externally generated clock. This module design opts for the former for several reasons. First, an internally generated clock has lower cost and is electrically "cleaner" than using an external clock. Furthermore, the low power sleep mode of the chip is easily utilized with an internally generated clock. This mode requires the RTS pin to be driven low during a reset. This is provided by the CLKMOD signal shown on the schematic. In this mode, we will use an external 18.432 MHz crystal which results in a 9.216 MHz internal clock (/2). This crystal frequency provides a 0% error baud rate generation for standard baud rate values.

The serial driver used is an MC145406 component. This device is RS-232 compatible and supports both transmit and receive signal voltage conversions on a single chip. Because only the Transmit Data and Receive Data signals are driven, a single MC145406 is sufficient for this application.

Now that the I/O blocks have been specified and the data line requirements known, we may proceed to design the data driver block of the MIX module.

5.3 Data Driver Block

As stated in the design requirements, the module must support 32-bit accesses to the four PPI devices as well as eight bit accesses to the serial device. Restricting parallel port accesses to only 32 bits would limit the baseboard software to 32-bit code or limit the number of PPI devices accessible with BYTE or WORD transfers. To solve this problem, each PPI will be accessible as a separate I/O device or all PPIs will be accessible as a single 32-bit I/O device.

This structure requires a byte swap mechanism in the data driver design. The design allows each PPI and the 82510 ASC to be accessed on the data signals MXD0–MXD7. Furthermore, to obtain a "32-bit" parallel port, one PPI (PPI1) is accessible on MXD8–MXD15, one (PPI2) on MXD16–MXD23, and one (PPI3) on MXD24–MXD31. This configuration requires 7 data transceivers as shown on the schematic.

When accessing the four PPIs as a single 32-bit device, data transceivers U7, U9, U19, and U29 must be enabled at the same time. When accessing the PPIs as separate 8-bit devices, the U7, U8, U18, or U28 transceiver is individually enabled to provide a connection between the PPI being accessed and data signals MXD0–MXD7.

The "G" pin of the transceiver stands for "gate" and is used to enable the driver. The data driver setup requires 5 gate signals to enable the proper transceivers for a PPI transfer cycle. The signal GAT32* is activated during a 32-bit parallel port access. GATB0* transfers data between the U10 PPI and the low data byte on the MIX interface, GATB1* does the same for the U20 PPI, and so on. These signals, along with the data direction signal, are generated by the Control Logic Block of the module design.

5.4 MIX Interface Block

As stated previously, a MIX slave module need only support those MIX interface signals which allow it to complete its I/O function and remain MIX compatible.

Now that the I/O device and data drivers blocks have been defined, we can determine the MIX interface signals needed to support this simple slave design.

The 130 signals on the MIX interface can be broken up and viewed as 11 functional groups. This eases the task of selecting the necessary signals. Aside from the Spares group, the MIX slave module signal groups are listed in Table 1. Notice that a slave module does not utilize any of the signals of the Arbitration Group as it will never need control of the interface.

The address group consists of 30 address lines, four byte enables, and three select lines. Because the module is a simple slave without memory mapped devices, only I/O address space need be considered. A MIX module is allotted 1 Kbytes of I/O address space in either the

Table 1. MIX Slave Module Signal Set

Function	Signal Name	Signal Type	Used
Address	MXA[31:28]*	Pass-through	N
	MXA[27:7]*	Bussed	N
	MXA[6:2]*	Bussed	Y
	MXBE[3:0]*	Bussed	Y
	LCLSEL*	Owned	Y
	MXSEL[2:1]*	Pass-through	N
Data	MXD[31:0]	Bussed	Y
Status	MXMIO	Bussed	Y
	MXWR	Bussed	Y
	MXDC	Bussed	Y
Control	MXCYC*	Bussed	Y
	MXCMD*	Bussed	Y
	MXBS16*	Bussed	N
	MXWAIT*	Bussed	Y
Configuration	LCLID*	Owned	Y
	MXID[2:1]*	Pass-through	N
	SCLK	Bussed	Y
	SDIN	Bussed	Y
	SDOUT	Bussed	Y
	MXRST*	Bussed	Y
Interrupt	LCLINT*	Owned	Y
	MXINT[2:1]*	Pass-through	N
DMA	LCLDRQ*	Owned	N
	MXDRQ[2:1]*	Pass-through	N
	LCLDACK*	Owned	N
	MXDACK[2:1]*	Pass-through	N
Option	LCLOP*	Owned	N
	MXOP[2:1]*	Pass-through	N
Spares	Reserved	Bussed	N
Power	+5 VDC	Bussed	Y
	GND	Bussed	Y
	+12 VDC	Bussed	Y
	−12 VDC	Bussed	Y

5

second, third, or fourth Kbyte in the baseboard's I/O space, depending on the stack position of the MIX module. Luckily, the baseboard's decode logic determines which module is selected and signals that module with a MXSELx* signal, seen as LCLSEL* on the module. This way, the baseboard assigns a module's base I/O address at 400H, 800H, or 0C00H and a module is designed based only on address offsets within that 1 Kbytes of space. In this scheme however, the module must use the LCLSEL* signal as a qualifier in the address decode scheme to assure it is the module being accessed. To support 1 Kbytes of address space, we need only support MXA2* through MXA9* and the byte enable signals. The module must also input its LCLSEL* signal to aid in the decode scheme. Furthermore, although the module does not act on the remaining address and MXSELx* signals, it must route the signals from the primary to secondary sides of the module. This is true for all signals of the MIX interface.

Because this module has been defined to support 32-bit accesses to the parallel I/O devices, all 32 data lines must be supported. All signals in the status group must also be supported to determine the type of access being made to the module.

In the Control group, the signals MXCYC* and MXCMD* are used to determine the state of a MIX transfer cycle. These two signals must be supported by even the simplest of modules. These signals are very useful in generating I/O commands to devices as well as chip select signals. The other signals in the Control group, MXBS16* and MXWAIT*, need only be used by modules which cannot support all 32-bit byte enable combinations or cannot accommodate full speed MIX transfers.

The MXBS16* is used to inform the baseboard that the 32-bit access being made is not supported by the module. This is the same as the BS16* signal for the i386 processor. This MIX module will support 32-bit access to the four PPI device group but not the individual PPIs or 82510 ASC. Therefore, the MXBS16* signal is generated for any access made on the module except an access to the PPI0 address since this is the address we use to enable all four PPIs during a 32-bit access.

To determine the need for the MXWAIT* signal, we must investigate the requirements of the I/O devices being used on the module and understand the result of using the MXWAIT* signal. The MXWAIT* signal can only be used on the MIX interface to extend the cycle time of the MIX transfer being made (i.e., extend the length of the MXCMD* and MXCYC* active time). This signal is very similar to the iSBXMWAIT* signal. Because of the effect of this signal, we need only consider the command duration time requirements of the device. Timing needs for parameters such as address or data setup, hold, and command recovery timings are not affected by simply activating the MXWAIT* signal. Meeting these requirements will necessitate additional control circuitry between the MIX interface and the I/O device.

Timing requirements for TTL components, of course, vary with the device. Typically, as is the case in this module design example, it is the peripheral devices which have the longest timing requirements. A full speed MIX transfer cycle is specified as 175 ns which corresponds to a 73 ns MXCMD* pulse width. If we use the MXCMD* signal to generate our RD* and WT* commands, we would have a minimum command pulse of 73 ns. Although the current MIX baseboard does not support a full speed MIX transfer, it is desir-

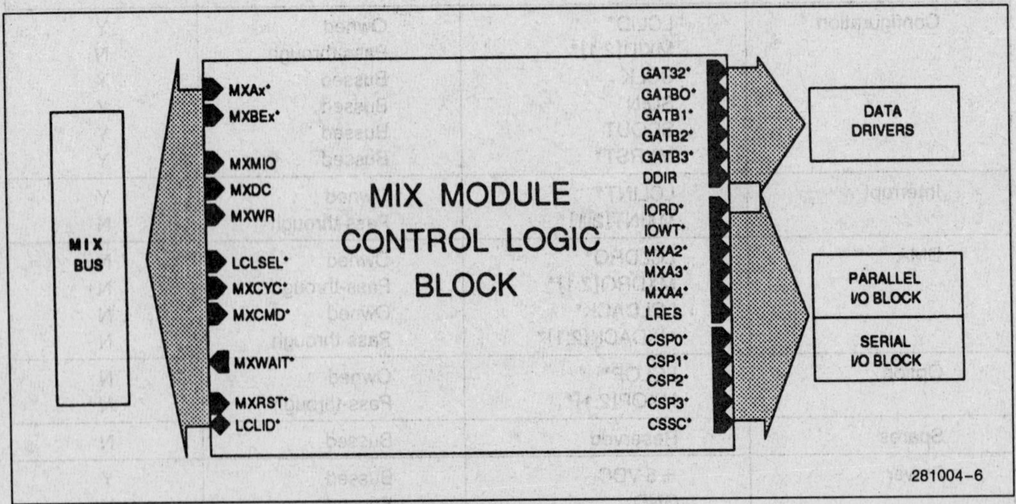

Figure 6. Mix Module Control Block

able to design the MIX module to the capabilities of the MIX specification (not the baseboard spec) so that the module will be compatible with future MIX baseboards. For this reason, the decision to support MXWAIT* is based upon a 73 ns command pulse time.

In the case of the PPI and the 82510 ASC, the parameters we are concerned with are the I/O Read and Write command hold times. The 82510 requires a minimum RD* active width of 2 T_{CY} + 65 ns which is 282 ns. Already we see we cannot support a full speed MIX transfer and will therefore need to use the MXWAIT* signal.

Support of all signals in the configuration group is a requirement of the MIX specification. These signals allow the baseboard and other PSB agents to determine the types of MIX modules present in any given MIX stack.

The Interrupt group of the MIX interface consists only of a single interrupt line per module. This interrupt line supports cascading which facilitates the use of a slave interrupt controller on a MIX module. Because this module has only one interrupt signal source (the serial controller), the cascading option is not needed. The remaining signal groups include the DMA and Option lines. This module does not utilize baseboard DMA resources nor does it require an additional interrupt signal, so these signals need not be supported. As spares go, MIX modules are required to bus the signals for future use but may not drive the signals.

It is a requirement of the MIX specification to connect to all power pins of any voltage which is used on the module. Because this module supports RS-232 communications, all available voltage levels are utilized. The module must therefore connect to all +5V, +12V, −12V, and GND pins.

As shown in Table 1, the final summary of supported signals for this module is designated with a "Y" in the "Used" column. Now that the MIX interface signal support and I/O blocks are defined, the next task is to design the block which converts the MIX compatible signals to commands understood by the I/O devices being used. This is accomplished in the Control Logic Block of the Module.

5.5 Module Control Logic Block

As shown in Figure 6, the MIX module control logic block resides between the MIX interface and the module's I/O and data driver devices. Because this block is similar to that which may be utilized on other MIX slave modules, detailed attention will be given to its design.

The control block has three basic functions; translating MIX signals into commands and timings understood by the I/O devices, performing address decode operations, and handling the module reset functions. The reset function is the simplest of the two, so it will be designed first. The reset function on the MIX interface is driven by the baseboard's microcontroller and, as stated in the module design specification, is guaranteed to be a minimum of 10 μs in duration. The requirements of all devices used in this module design are at least an order of magnitude less than this. For this reason, we need only invert the MXRST* signal to supply the active high RESET required by the peripheral devices.

Another requirement of MIX modules is the support of the MXIDx*/MXEECSx* signal. During reset, the module must drive its LCLID* signal to inform the baseboard it is present. We can generate this signal by simply inverting the inverted MXRST* signal during a reset (this is accomplished with a tri-state inverter which drives the signal only during reset). Note that we could not simply connect the MXRST* to the LCLID* signal, or simply invert the MXRST* signal at all times since LCLID* takes on the function of LCLEECS* after reset. If we had simply tied MXRST* to LCLID*, an access to the serial EEPROM would result in a MXRST* being active on the MIX bus. If we did not tri-state the LCLID* driver, the baseboard MXEECSx* driver and our LCLID* driver would attempt to drive the same signal to opposite polarities. Also note that this design meets all reset timing requirements as listed in the *MIX Module Design Specification.*

The address decode functions and command conversion logic are the next portions of the control block which must be designed. Because of the relative isolation between these two functions, they can be partitioned into two designs, however, proper timing between the two functions must be ensured.

Typical operation for a peripheral chip is to set up address and chip select signals to the device, set up the data (for a write), and then pulse the read or write command. To do this, we can construct two logic subblocks we will call the I/O control and I/O decode blocks.

The I/O control block will be responsible for generating the RD* and WT* pulses to the chips, and controlling the MXWAIT* and MXBS16* functions.

The I/O decode block therefore has the responsibility of performing all the address decode operations and generation of the chip selects and data driver gate signals. These functions are derived from the states of the address and byte enable signals during a valid transfer cycle. The functions in both blocks are best handled by PAL or PLD logic design due to the device's logic flexibility and the number of input signals required of the functions.

5

5.5.1 I/O DECODE PAL

The main function of this block is the generation of the peripheral device chip select signals. Each addressable device on the module is assigned a unique I/O offset address by this PAL. A device's chip select is only activated when the MIX baseboard accesses the chip's assigned I/O address via the MXA[6:2]* and LCLSEL* signals.

In addition to a valid address, it is wise to ensure the proper byte enable combination exists to provide valid data to the chip being selected. Therefore, our chip selects will be qualified by three things; one, a valid MIX transfer cycle is present; two, the proper I/O address is selected; and three, a valid byte enable combination exists. Because each of the peripheral devices require MXA3* and MXA2* for internal register access, we need not use these in qualifying accesses to a specific chip. This will force our address decode to place the peripheral devices on DWORD boundaries.

The addresses for each chip may be arbitrarily chosen between I/O offsets 0 and 3F0H. Note that as specified in the *MIX Module Design Specification*, I/O address offsets 3F0H through 3FEH are reserved. This module utilizes address lines MXA[6:2]* for its decode function. Because this module does not decode address lines nine through seven, the I/O chips are mirrored in the address map every 128 bytes. The first occurance of the chips I/O addresses are shown in Table 2.

Table 2. I/O Addresses

I/O Offset	Device
0xH	Byte PPI (PPI0) Word PPI (PPIs 0,1) Dword PPI (PPI 0–3)
1xH	Byte PPI (PPI1)
2xH	Byte PPI (PPI2)
3xH	Byte PPI (PPI3)
4xH 5xH	Byte 82510 ASC

A secondary function of this block is the control of the data transceiver gate signals.

There are seven data transceivers in the Data Driver Block of the module which have enable pins ("G") which must be driven during peripheral accesses.

Of the seven data drivers three are only used for 32-bit transfers. These may be hard wired together and enabled as a group during a 32-bit access (This signal will be called GAT32*). The four remaining gate signals are used during byte wide accesses to the PPIs (We will call these GATB[3:0]* based on which byte of the module data bus the driver controls).

The data driver gate signal /GATB0 enables the data driver which transfers data from the low byte of the MIX data bus to the low byte of the module's data bus. PPI0 and the 82510 reside on this bus. This driver should be enabled on four access occasions. Three involve byte, word, or dword accesses to PPI0 and the fourth is for a byte access to the serial chip. The /GAT32 signal enables three data drivers which transfer data from the upper three bytes of the MIX data bus to the corresponding upper three bytes of the module's data bus. This signal should be activated only during word or dword accesses to PPI0. By providing simultaneous chip selects to the other PPIs, we can make the baseboard believe it is making an access to a single word or dword device when in actuality, two or four PPIs are being utilized.

The remaining gate signals (GATB[3:1]*) allow the upper three PPI devices to be accessed via the low byte of the MIX data bus. These three signals drive data between the low byte of the MIX data bus and one of the upper MIX module data bus bytes (1, 2 or 3). The signals are only activated during byte accesses to PPIs 1, 2 or 3.

Because the data timing for our devices must conform to the MIX interface timing requirements as well as the timing requirements of the peripheral chips, we must activate these drivers in a manner which meets the minimum data turn-on and minimum data hold time requirements. This can be accomplished by dividing the enable function between read and write accesses to the module. During a read operation, the module must tri-state its data drivers within 40 ns of the MXCMD* signal being deactivated. During write accesses, the 82C55A requires data be held at least 30 ns after the RD* or WT* signal is removed. Both needs are met by varying the gate parameters based on whether a read or write access is occurring.

From these definitions we find the total number of signals used by the decode logic is 12 inputs and 10 outputs. A common 22V10 PAL facilitates this logic design perfectly.

The PAL signal definitions are shown in Table 3. Note that the chip select generation scheme for the PPI devices will also allow us to make 16-bit accesses to the two PPIs which occupy the low word of the data bus (U10 and U20) without modification to the data driver scheme.

The actual PAL source code for this block is listed in Appendix B under the title "IODCD PAL".

Table 3. I/O Decode PAL Signals

Signal	Description
/A6-/A4	Inputs from MXA9*-MXA4*
/BE3-/BE0	Inputs from MXBE3*-MXBE0*
/LCLSEL	MIX i/f input
/MXCMD	MIX i/f input
/MXCYC	MIX i/f input
MXWR	MIX i/f input
/GATB0	Byte 0 data driver gate signal
/GATB1	Byte 1 data driver gate signal
/GATB2	Byte 2 data driver gate signal
/GATB3	Byte 3 data driver gate signal
/GAT32	Bytes 1, 2 and 3 drivers gate
/CSP3	PPI3 chip select
/CSP2	PPI2 chip select
/CSP1	PPI1 chip select
/CSP0	PPI0 chip select
/CSSC	82510 chip select

5.5.2 I/O CONTROL PAL

As discussed earlier, the I/O control portion of the design is responsible for translating MIX compatible signals into commands recognized by the peripheral devices. It must also provide the MXWAIT* support for proper command timing and MXBS16* support for proper data accesses to the peripherals.

Since the devices supported on this module will act only on I/O read and I/O write commands, this PAL must translate the MIX Status group signal states into either IORD* or IOWT* commands to the 82510 and PPI devices. This is accomplished by decoding the states of MXMIO, MXDC, MXWR, LCLSEL*, MXCYC*, and MXCMD*. As an added check, we will qualify our decodes with the state of the MXRST* signal to ensure chip selects are not generated from the arbitrary signal states present during reset.

Because of the pulse width and command recovery timing requirements of the 82510 and the 82C55A we must support the MXWAIT* signal of the MIX interface. This signal will directly fulfill our pulse width needs and indirectly provide the command recovery time needed by the peripheral devices. As stated in the *MIX Module Design Specification,* the MXWAIT* signal must be asserted within 40 ns of the MXCYC* signal being activated. This requirement will require asynchronous and synchronous state machines to be linked in the PAL logic.

The I/O Control Block will also drive the MXBS16* signal on the MIX interface. A MIX module must drive this signal when it cannot support 32-bit accesses to its devices. This module design will activate this signal on all accesses except for those to the PPI0 address since this address is the one used for our 32-bit PPI access. To distinguish a PPI0 access, the control PAL will input several of the address lines.

An additional function not yet mentioned is the direction signal generation required by the data transceivers. Because these transceivers are only enabled during valid command cycles, we simply drive the direction pins with the MXWR signal. Note that the stub length requirements of the MIX interface and the drive requirements of the transceivers necessitate the use of a driver to produce the direction signal. This driver is a simple hex noninverter and may be implemented external to the PAL design.

As specified, our PAL design will require twelve inputs (including a clock signal for the MXWAIT* machine) and four outputs. From these requirements a 22V10PAL device may again be used. This device allows twelve input and ten output pins. Although we have only defined four outputs, additional output pins will be consumed by the WAIT state machine design. A particularly nice feature of the 22V10 device is the ability to configure the outputs as either registered or simple combinatorial output pins. This is useful since we have both asynchronous and synchronous needs for this PAL design.

The first consideration in our PAL design is the tristate needs of the MIX bus signals. The MIX specification dictates that the MXWAIT* and MXBS16* signals be tri-stated while a MIX cycle is not occurring. Furthermore, these signals must be in their logical false state before they are tri-stated. To facilitate this, we define a signal called IOCYC.* This signal is a combination of inputs which represent a valid I/O cycle (read or write) is occurring. The actual input signals can then be used to activate and deactivate the MXWAIT* and MXBS16* signals, while the IOCYC output is used to tri-state them. This provides 15 ns (the prop delay of the PAL) between the signals being deactivated and being tri-stated.

5

The IORD* and IOWT* signals can build upon the IOCYC* signal by using IOCYC* as a qualifier. Once IOCYC* is valid, the MXWR signal is used to distinguish between read and write accesses, and the MXCMD* signal is used to allow address and chip select setup times to the peripheral devices. The read and write commands will require one additional qualifier to provide the command recovery timing needs for the PPI chips. This addition will be discussed during the WAIT state machine design.

The MXBS16* function is a fairly simple signal to generate for this design. The module will only allow 32-bit accesses to the address specified for PPI0. This address, along with the Byte Enable signals, is used in the decode logic to enable all PPIs simultaneously when a 32-bit access is made to PPI0. Therefore, this PAL will not drive the MXBS16* signal during an access to PPI0. This is assured by verifying an access to PPI0 is not occurring.

Because of the propagation delays involved in PAL decode, we are not able to use the chip selects generated by the I/O Decode PAL for the generation of MXBS16*. The 15 ns delay of the chip select would result in a MXBS16* glitch during a PPI0 access. We can however, use the address lines MXA[6:4]* as signal qualifiers. These signals are specified to be glitch free during valid transer cycles and will indicate which device is selected when MXCYC* is activated. We therefore use the address lines with MXCYC* line in generating MXBS16*. Note that if the PAL offered more inputs, the signals MXA[9:7]* could also be used which would cover the full 1 kilobyte address range of the module.

The last requirement placed on the MXBS16* signal is that it be tri-stated within 46 ns of MXCYC* going inactive. This is so because the MXBS16* signal is bussed on the MIX interface. Since our 22V10 PAL device allows us to individually assign tri-state conditions to outputs, we can use IOCYC* to tri-state the MXBS16* output. This allows us to force MXBS16* inactive (high) with the removal of the MXCYC* signal and tri-state the line 15 ns (the propagation delay of the device) later when IOCYC* is deactivated.

The final function provided by this PAL is the MXWAIT* support. As discussed previously, the 82510 device requires a command pulse width of 282 ns for a read operation and 232 ns for a write. The 82C55A PPI device requires pulse widths of only 150 ns for a RD and 100 ns for a WR. Although we could include logic to distinguish PPI accesses from 82510 accesses, a generic MXWAIT* which supports the worst case time is much simpler to design. Therefore, a state machine must be designed which will produce a pulse greater than or equal to our maximum pulse width constraint of 282 ns.

Our peripheral devices also specify command recovery requirements which are not met by a full speed MIX cycle. The command recovery is the amount of inactive time between RD* or WT* pulses to single chip. For the 82510 this value is 120 ns. The PPI requires 200 ns. As stated in the *MIX Module Design Specification,* all modules MUST provide hardware support for command recovery needs. This support can be rolled into the MXWAIT* state machine by designing in a number of inactive states in which the RD* or WT* signals cannot be activated. To assure these times are met and to assure we meet the MXWAIT* activation time requirements, we will utilize an asynchronous state machine to generate the actual MXWAIT* signal, coupled with a synchronous state machine which "turns off" the asynchronous machine. We will also use the output of our synchronous machine as a qualifier in the IORD* and IOWT* signal generation. This will give us the command recovery time needed for proper operation of the 82510 and 82C55A chips.

The asynchronous machine will define the conditions which must be present for the MXWAIT* signal to be asserted. In the synchronous state machine design, we must define three things; the clock frequency for the PAL device, the number of states in which SWAIT (synchronous WAIT) is active, and the number of states SWAIT is inactive. By qualifying IORD* and IOWT* with an active SWAIT, the added inactive SWAIT states provide our recovery time.

For the asynchronous machine, we define an idle state for a reset state or otherwise idle module (no transfer occurring) condition. Once the module is accessed and MXCYC* is asserted, we must provide MXWAIT* within 40 ns. A second state is therefore defined with MXWAIT* active. This state is entered when IOCYC* is active. With the PAL device used, we know MXWAIT* will be activated a maximum of 30 ns after MXCYC* is activated (15 ns from MXCYC* to IOCYC* and 15 ns from IOCYC* to MXWAIT* coming out of tri-state). This second state is held until the synchronous machine sets SWAIT active. Once this occurs, the machine moves into a third state which also has MXWAIT* active. This state is held until the synchronous machine indicates the delay time has expired (falling edge of SWAIT). The asynchronous machine then deactivates MXWAIT* and enters its final state until the cycle has completed. This state exists so that the loop is not repeated during the same MIX transfer cycle. Once IOCYC* goes inactive, the idle state is reentered.

To design the synchronous machine, we need to know the requirements for pulse widths and recovery times. As stated previously, our longest pulse width requirement comes from an 82510 read cycle (282 ns) and our worst case recovery time requirement comes from back to back 82C55A accesses (200 ns). With these in mind, the equation $n/f = T_{WAIT}$ is used to determine the number of active and inactive WAIT cycles, "n", used in our synchronous state machine. The value "n" will vary based on the clock frequency, "f", of the PAL, and the required cycle time, "T_{WAIT}".

For the active cycles, T_{WAIT} represents the maximum command pulse width. For the inactive cycles, T_{WAIT} is the maximum command recovery time. Since both of these values are divisible by 40 ns we will use an "f" of 25 MHz (1/25 MHz = 40 ns). For this frequency we need 7 active states and 5 inactive states. Remember these active and inactive states represent states where MXCMD* is active or inactive respectively. We must therefore add an additional state for both the active and inactive transitions which waits for MXCMD* to transition to its desired state.

Two state diagrams are shown in Figure 7. The top represents the synchronous machine while the bottom represents the asynchronous machine. For the synchronous machine, four state variables are defined: S0, S1, S2, and SWAIT. The "0000" state is the machine's idle state. Once a cycle is initiated on the module and the asynchronous machine asserts MXWAIT*, the synchronous machine moves through its states as shown in the diagram. Notice that the 0000, 0001, and 1000 states require MXWAIT* or MXCMD* to transition before the next state is entered. The MXWAIT* requirement ensures the cycle is only entered once per valid module transfer cycle. This is accomplished without requiring the synchronous machine to be in a specific state when a MIX cycle starts. Note that a new transfer cycle could start anywhere between the 1100 and 0000 states of the synchronous machine. The MXCMD* loops exist to ensure the command widths and recovery timing needs are met. Note that SWAIT is asserted with MXWAIT* active but the clocked cycle is not executed until MXCMD* is activated. This is desirable since MXCMD* is the signal we need to extend by our T_{WAIT} value. Similarly, once SWAIT is deactivated, the machine will wait for MXCMD* to be deactivated before continuing with its cycle. By only allowing the IORD* and IOWT* commands to be activated while SWAIT is active, we satisfy our recovery time requirements by assuring SWAIT is inactive for our second (recovery time) T_{WAIT} value after MXCMD* is released.

SWAIT is the synchronous variable which is linked with the asynchronous machine. Regardless of the state of SWAIT, MXWAIT* will be activated with the onset of a valid MIX cycle (IOCYC* active). Once activated however, MXWAIT* will remain active until the falling edge of SWAIT. Once deactivated, MXWAIT* will not be reactivated until the falling edge of IOCYC* is detected.

With this machine, MXWAIT* will always be activated within 40 ns of MXCYC* being activated, however, the IORD* or IOWT* command will not be activated until recovery requirements from the previous access are met (SWAIT goes active).

Remember that the MXWAIT* signal is tri-stated when IOCYC* is inactive. This is necessary because of the bussed nature of the MXWAIT* signal and is accomplished in the PAL specification with the IOCYC* signal. The requirement that MXWAIT* be in its inactive (HIGH) state before it is tri-stated is also met with this design because MXWAIT* will go inactive while both MXCMD* and MXCYC* are asserted. MXWAIT* is then tri-stated by the IOCYC* signal going inactive.

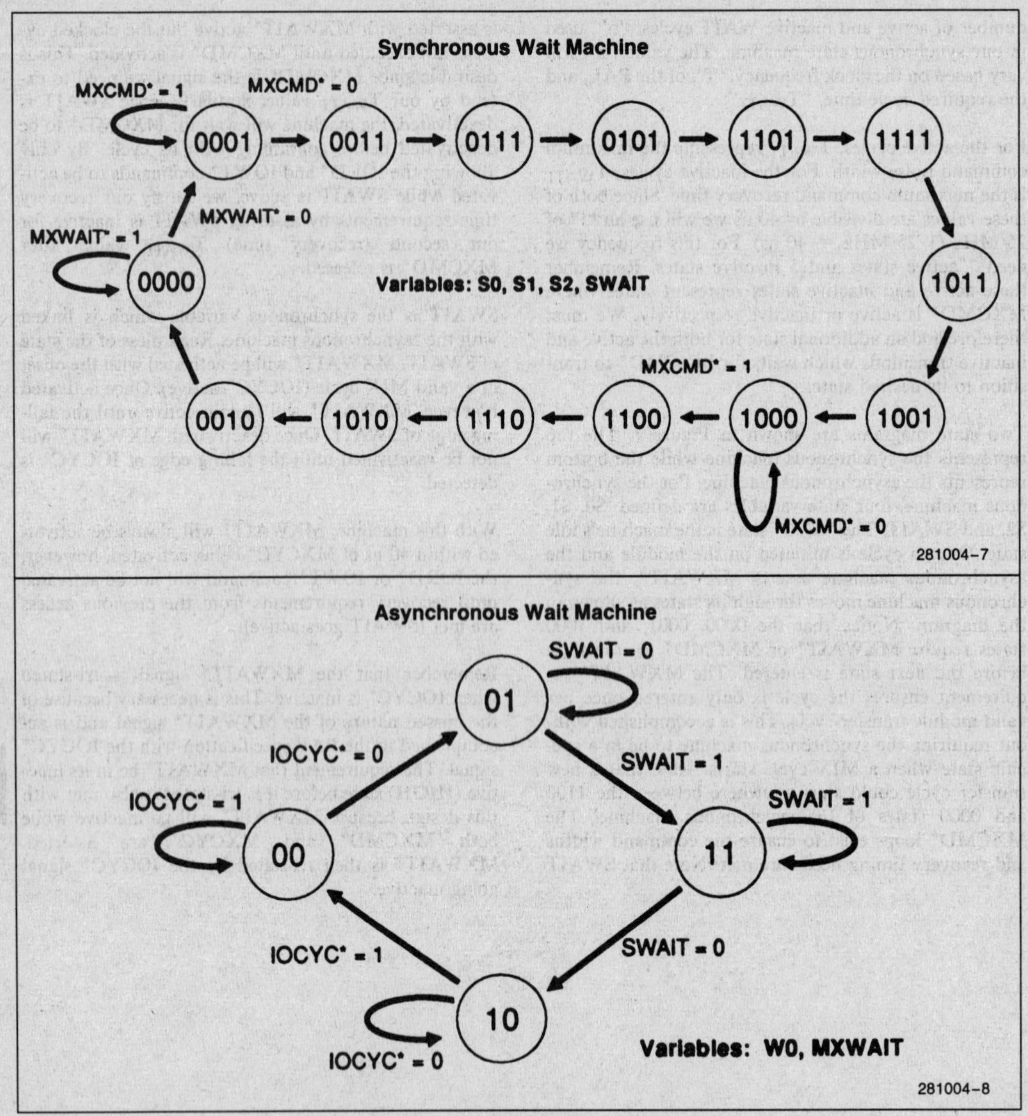

Figure 7. MXWAIT Machine State Diagram

Although the W0 and Sx variables are only used as internal variables to the PAL device, they must be assigned to actual pins on the 22V10PAL device, bringing the number of output pins on the device to ten. Furthermore, the Sx and SWAIT variables are defined in the PAL source as registered (synchronous) outputs via the " := " syntax.

From the asynchronous machine states, we can assign a truth table as shown in Table 4. Note that Table 4 gives values for CYC which is the logical state of the IOCYC* signal (IOCYC* = 0–CYC = 1). Also "SW" represents the state of SWAIT and WAIT represents the logical value of MXWAIT (i.e. WAIT = 1–MXWAIT* = 0). This leads to the equations for W0 and MXWAIT as listed in the PAL source code in Appendix B.

The synchronous machine follows a similar design, although in the synchronous case there are six variables instead of four. The PAL source for the synchronous machine is also listed in Appendix B.

Table 4. WAIT State Machine Truth Tables

Current State				Next State	
W0	WAIT	CYC	SW	W0	WAIT
0	0	0	0	0	0
0	0	1	0	0	1
0	0	1	1	0	1
0	1	1	0	0	1
0	1	1	1	1	1
1	1	1	1	1	1
1	1	1	0	1	0
1	0	1	0	1	0
1	0	0	0	0	0

For the I/O Control PAL's 25 MHz clock source, a 50 MHz crystal oscillator is routed through a D flip-flop which provides a divide by 2 function. The output of the flip-flop is then tied to the clock input pin of the PAL.

The final piece of the I/O control block which must be designed is the logic which supplies the address lines to the peripheral devices. Because the devices require active high address lines, we need only invert the MXA4* through MXA2* signals and route them appropriately. Note that the 82510 is the only device which requires the MXA4* signal.

5.6 Configuration Data Block

The serial EEPROM on the MIX module provides a means with which the baseboard microcontroller may download configuration data during power up. This allows the baseboard's interconnect space to reflect specific configuration data of the MIX modules present on the stack, while allowing the microcontroller firmware to remain standard.

The hardware requirements of the module's serial EEPROM block consist of a single device, a 128 byte 93C46 serial EEPROM. This device is available in an eight pin skinny dip package which may be connected directly to the MIX interface signals. Of the 8 pins, 2 are N/C ("no-connect") pins.

The filmware portions of the serial EEPROM are discussed in Chapter 6 of this document.

5.7 Simulation

Because this module is an extremely simple design and is being prototyped in a wire wrap version, hardware simulation is considered superfluous. In this case, a trace routing or device interaction problem will not cost additional fab production cycles or considerable CAD problems.

The PAL devices however, are easily simulated using the PALASM2 software. This software includes a state simulator which allows the designer to set the trace mode for various PAL signal outputs and encode various input signal states into a line equation. By changing the input states, the designer can examine the output conditions generated. This is true for both the asynchronous and synchronous PALs designed for this module.

In the simulation for the IODCD PAL, we should investigate both valid and invalid accesses to the peripheral chips. In the PALASM source file for the I/O decode PAL (IODCD) in Appendix B, there is a section marked SIMULATION. The TRACE ON statement lists the signals which are to be examined and the SETF statements are used to change the states of the input signals.

The first SETF statement sets up an address to the PAL of 1xH, which corresponds to PPI1. The next statement specifies a word access is occurring, and finally an indication of a valid I/O cycle is given. Finally, the IOCMD signal is activated to indicate either an IORD* or IOWT* command is active. As shown in the selective trace listing, these inputs result in no chip selects since PPI1 may only be accessed as a byte wide device or in combination with PPI0.

The next group of statements changes the byte enables to a byte access which results in the /CSP1 signal being activated. The next changes the address to 0xH which is the address of PPI0. This leads to /CSP0 and /GATB0 being activated. Note the widths of the gate signals during both read and write accesses. They are longer during writes to provide the data hold requirements of the peripheral devices. The remaining portion of the simulation sets up the byte enables to represent WORD and DWORD transfers to the PPIs. The word transfer results in the /CSP0, /CSP1, /GATB0, and /GAT32 signals being activated, while the DWORD transfer also activates the /CSP2 and /CSP3 signals. These accesses are therefore equivalent to having 16- or 32-bit PPIs.

The simulation for the I/O control PAL follows a similar process. This simulation however, allows the designer to simulate clock ticks as well as input signal state changes. The simulation is set up by placing the PAL in a reset state. The clock is cycled, then the reset is removed and an I/O read status is set. The LCLSEL*, MXCYC*, and MXCMD* signals are then set to simulate the states the PAL would normally encounter. To check the MXBS16* function, the PPI0 address is simulated on address lines /A6* through /A4*. The PAL is clocked several times to examine the operation of the MXWAIT* and MXBS16* outputs. As shown in the selective trace listing, the WAIT state machines step through their states as designed (MXWAIT* =0 correspond to MXWAIT = 1), with the MXWAIT* signal active for four clock pulses. Furthermore, the listing shows MXBS16* inactive throughout the cycle. This is desirable since 32-bit accesses are allowed for PPI0. Also we see IOCYC* go active with the MXCYC* signal and the IORD* signal go active when MXCMD* is activated. This occurs because the SWAIT signal is already active when MXCMD* is activated.

A second MIX transfer cycle is simulated to represent a full speed transfer cycle. In this cycle, we want to assure the proper WAIT machine function for command recovery and further examine the MXBS16* function. To do this, the address of PPI1 is presented to the PAL which should force MXBS16* to activate. We desire this since 32-bit cycles are only allowed for the PPI0 address offset. We also present active MXCYC* and MXCMD* signals to the PAL very soon after the end of the previous transfer cycle. This means MXCYC* has a short inactive time between cycles 1 and 2. This second simulation changes the polarity of the MXWR signal to represent a write request.

Once MXCYC* is activated we see both MXBS16* and MXWAIT* immediately activated. This ensures us we provide MXBS16* and MXWAIT* within the allotted 40 ns. In this cycle, when the command signal (MXCMD*) is activated the IOWT* signal does not come on. This occurs because the synchronous machine has not yet cycled through all of its inactive states. In the selective trace listing we see the synchronous machine continue through its inactive states even though there is a valid transfer cycle occurring. Once the machine reaches the 0001 state, IOWT* is activated. This has the effect of holding off the write command until the synchronous machine is ready to acknowledge it. Therefore, this is the command recovery mechanism built into the WAIT machine.

With acceptable PAL code simulations completed we can turn our attention to firmware requirements and module prototyping.

6.0 MODULE FIRMWARE

The MIX architecture has several firmware requirements for modules to assure proper interaction with MIX compatible baseboards and other modules. These requirements place the responsibility of supplying necessary configuration data and BIST tests on the module. While the module is responsible for supplying it, configuration data for the MIX modules is treated as an extension of the baseboard's interconnect space. This allows a MIX baseboard to use standard microcontroller code while allowing PSB agents to determine the type of MIX modules present via the baseboard's interconnect space. This structure allows dissimilar MIX modules to stack together without the need for modifying the baseboard's interconnect configuration data. Module resident BIST code allows the baseboard to test the hardware on the modules without the need for custom firmware on the baseboard. This allows different modules to stack together without the necessity of custom BIST code on the baseboard.

6.1 Serial EEPROM

The requirement placed on modules for interconnect space is the support of the National Microwire™ standard serial EEPROM. This is a 128 byte device which is arranged in a 64 x 16-bit configuration which allows random access of 64 word registers over four signal lines. It is programmed to contain two interconnect records which describe the configuration of the MIX module. Each interconnect register is a two byte value. The MSB contains the register protection information and the LSB contains the function's value. The baseboard's 8751 microcontroller downloads this information during power up and appends it to its own interconnect data. The *MIX Module Design Specification* describes the format which the EEPROM firmware must follow in order to function with the baseboard's 8751.

The standard format has two interconnect records, the Hardware Extension Record and the Module Specific Record as shown in Table 5. A custom module uses the standard template as a guide to defining the module's interconnect data. Required values for the registers are included in Table 5. Those registers listed as TBS in the value column have register values "To Be Specified" by the module designer.

This module defines its registers as shown in the "EX" column of Table 5. The vendor ID, 0001 (0900, 0901), represents the Intel vendor number for MULTIBUS II. Intel administers the assignment of specific vendor numbers to MULTIBUS II board manufacturers.

This Module's ID has been defined to be "TM_MIX_MOD", with the "T" occupying register 6 and the "D" occupying register 0FH. Note that the ASCII equivalent of the string is placed in the Module ID registers.

Because this module is a wire wrap prototype, all revision level registers are given the value of 0. Finally, since this module was not designed with EPROM devices or self test capabilities, its BIST support level is defined as 0. This level means either the module hardware is not tested during power up or the baseboard firmware is responsible for supplying the module BIST code. In the case of this module, the former is true. A BIST support level of 0 implies that the Jump Table Pointer registers are assigned a value of 0.

Now that the register values are defined, the EEPROM device must simply be programmed and installed on the module. All download functions are handled by the baseboard microcontroller and do not concern the module designer.

Table 5. MIX Module Interconnect Template

Register Offset	Description	Access Local	Rights Global	Value	Ex
HARDWARE EXTENSION RECORD					
0	H/W Ext. Record Type	R/O	R/O	0914H	0914H
1	Record Length	R/O	R/O	0913H	0913H
2	H/W Ext. Type (LSB)	R/O	R/O	0910H	0910H
3	H/W Ext. Type (MSB)	R/O	R/O	0900H	0900H
4	Vendor ID, Low	R/O	R/O	TBS	0901H
5	Vendor ID, High	R/O	R/O	TBS	0900H
6-0FH	Module ID, Char 1–10	R/O	R/O	TBS	*
10H	H/W Test Rev Level	R/O	R/W1	TBS	2900H
11H	Number of Records	R/O	R/O	0901H	0901H
12H	RFU	R/O	R/O	0900H	0900H
13H	RFU	R/O	R/O	0900H	0900H
14H	RFU	R/O	R/O	0900H	0900H
MODULE SPECIFIC RECORD					
15H	Mod. Specific Record Type	R/O	R/O	09F0H	09F0H
16H	Record Length	R/O	R/O	TBS	0909H
17H	EPROM Entry Table Ptr., MSB	R/O	R/O	TBS	0900H
18H	EPROM Entry Table Ptr., Byte 3	R/O	R/O	TBS	0900H
19H	EPROM Entry Table Ptr., Byte 2	R/O	R/O	TBS	0900H
1AH	EPROM Entry Table Ptr., LSB	R/O	R/O	TBS	0900H
1BH	RFU	R/O	R/O	0900H	0900H
1CH	H/W Rev Level	R/O	R/W1	TBS	2900H
1DH	BIST Test Support Level	R/O	R/W1	TBS	2900H
1EH	RFU	R/O	R/O	0900H	0900H
1EF	RFU	R/O	R/O	0900H	0900H
20H	RFU	R/O	R/O	0900H	0900H
21H–3FH	Module Specific Info	Module Defined			

The 93C64 device can be programmed using a standard EEPROM programmer which supports the device. Because the device is electrically erasable, it is possible for the EEPROM to be programmed by the baseboard's microcontroller. At the time of this module design, this support was not included in the baseboard 8751 firmware.

6.2 BIST Support Levels

The MIX architecture provides several BIST support levels as described in the *Mix Module Design Specification*. Inclusion of EPROMS and BIST firmware on modules allows power up verification of the module hardware problems are encountered.

This module does not incorporate EPROM or BIST support in its design. This is defined as BIST support level 0. Although level 0 allows the stipulation that the MIX baseboard carry the module BIST code in its EPROM, this module design assumes no power up testing is performed on the module hardware. This option was chosen because of the simplicity of the module hardware used in the design. Furthermore, addition of module EPROMs would have further complicated the I/O control block portion of the design, which would have lessened the simple example intentions of this module design.

7.0 MODULE PROTOTYPING

Once the module is fully defined and its schematic has been completed, a final check of the modules electrical characteristics can be made. The main concern here is the power requirements of the module. We should ensure the devices used in this design meet the power consumption requirements listed for the MIX interface. Once we have assured these characteristics, layout and actual wire wrapping and debug can be done.

7.1 Electrical Considerations

Before the actual module assembly begins, we must check the module design against the electrical specifications for the MIX interface. The two major issues here involve the drive characteristics of the devices which connect to the MIX signals and the total maximum power consumption of the module. Both of these parameters may affect how the module operates with the MIX baseboard or other modules.

The drive characteristic check deals with the type of driver used on the MIX bus. The MIX specification states that no module may use open collector devices to drive the MIX bus signals. A quick check of the module device specifications assure us that the module meets this requirement.

The second area of concern is the power consumption of the module. The *MIX Module Design Specification* states that each module may consume up to 3 Amps of +5 VDC. Again, by going through each device's spec sheet we can compute the maximum and typical power consumption of the module.

In reviewing the components used for this module, we find the maximum current draw on the +5V power is just under 2.5 Amps for the entire module, including the LEDs. Although we find this simple module is surprisingly near the 3 Amp limit, a typical module design would not implement 32 LEDs which draw about 25 mA each.

7.2 Wire Wrap Layout

Now that the electrical requirements of the MIX module are verified, actual prototyping will be done. The layout portion of the prototyping requires knowledge of the signal paths and component interconnection. The schematic capture program used in this design contains a program which generates a netlist from the schematic output. With this netlist and the MIX MOD2 Breadboard Module, we are ready to begin the layout.

In laying out components for the MIX design, careful attention should be given to the trace length requirements given in the *MIX Module Design Specification*. Although this is merely a wire wrap version of the final product, adhering to the trace length rules may save some debugging headaches later. The Breadboard module offers the standard MIX module width and MIX interface footprint, however, the board length is much longer than a standard module. This added length is provided to allow an engineer to prototype surface mount designs using DIP components which require more design area.

The module layout follows the signal paths between the MIX interface and I/O devices. The termination resistors and data transceivers are placed nearest the MIX connector. The two PAL devices and EEPROM also reside adjacent to the connector due to their direct connection to interface signals. The PPI devices and 82510 are placed next, and the output drivers, LEDs, and connectors are placed at the edges of the board. This layout structure provides a natural signal propagation from the MIX interface out to the edges of the module and ensures the trace lengths are kept to a minimum. Once the components are placed, they may be connected via wire wrap.

7.3 Module Debug

Once the module has been completely wired up, it is ready for verification and debug. Although most designers are confident to immediately initiate a "smoke test", it is wise to verify the device connections with the netlist provided by the schematic capture package. This is time consuming but is easily done using a simple ohmmeter. Once this has been checked out, the module may be installed on the baseboard for final debug.

The final validation for this module was performed on a MIX 386/M0xPP Pre-production baseboard with a MIX MOD1 Test Module in module slot 0 and the wire wrap module in slot 1. In this stacking configuration, the wire wrap module's I/O address space ranges from 0800H to 0C00H. This means the I/O address offsets encoded in the IODCD PAL are added to the base address of 0800H to obtain the actual addresses for the module's devices. For example, the baseboard 386 microprocessor would access PPI0 at 098xH.

To facilitate ease of baseboard I/O access, firmware was placed on the MIX baseboard which contained a DMON 386 monitor configured (with the proper 82510 port address) to run with MIX MOD1 in module slot 0. This provides a serial interface for the baseboard and removes the need for additional system boards (except the CSM/001) for the module debug.

In debugging the board, we must check out several things, access to the boards serial EEPROM, parallel port functionality, and 82510 functionality. The serial EEPROM interface is verified by reading the baseboards interconnect space. DMON 386 provides an input interconnect (ii) function which aids in this task. The *MIX 386/M0xPP Baseboard User's Guide* shows the first H/W Extension Record should begin at interconnect offset 65H. This register can be checked for a value of 14H. If the 14H is found, the module ID registers (6BH–74H) can be read. If the module's ID is present (in ASCII), the serial interface is functioning.

Parallel ports may be verified by using the LEDs designed on the module's PPI port C or by using a logic analyzer. Using the LEDs requires setting up port C of the PPI as a simple output port and then making output accesses to port C to toggle the LEDs. To use a logic analyzer, direct accesses to the PPIs may be checked, or the port outputs may be checked. To verify the port A connector, ports A and B must be configured as an output port since bits 0 and 1 of port B control the direction and enable pin of the port A drivers.

The addressing scheme used in this module places the port A data bus at x0H, the port B data bus at x4H, port C's data at x8H, and the PPI's control port at xCH. For the PPI verification, all PPI ports are set up as simple output channels. This is done by writing 80H to ports 098CH, 099CH, 09ACH, and 09BCH. As shown on sheet 10 of the schematic, port B bits 0 and 1 affect the function of the port A driver chip. Therefore, a 3 is output to 0984H to enable the port A drivers and set their direction as outputs. Data is then output to both ports A and C to verify the module operation.

The 82510 device may be similarly checked out. With the module in slot 1, the 82510 internal registers begin at I/O address 09C0H. The chip can be verified by setting its 35 internal registers to configure a loopback mode to verify data transmit and receive data consistency.

Once the 82510, PPIs, and EEPROM operation have been verified, a high level of design confidence is achieved, and production cycles may proceed as needed.

8.0 CONCLUSIONS

Although this module design is a simple one and has been done simply for display and example purposes, it conveys the considerations required in a MIX module design effort. Furthermore, the control and data drivers blocks of the module may be used as a design guide in many simple slave I/O module designs.

The module schematics and PAL source codes have been included in Appendices A and B as an aid to designing simple I/O modules and as a basis for more complex module designs.

APPENDIX A
MIX MODULE SCHEMATICS

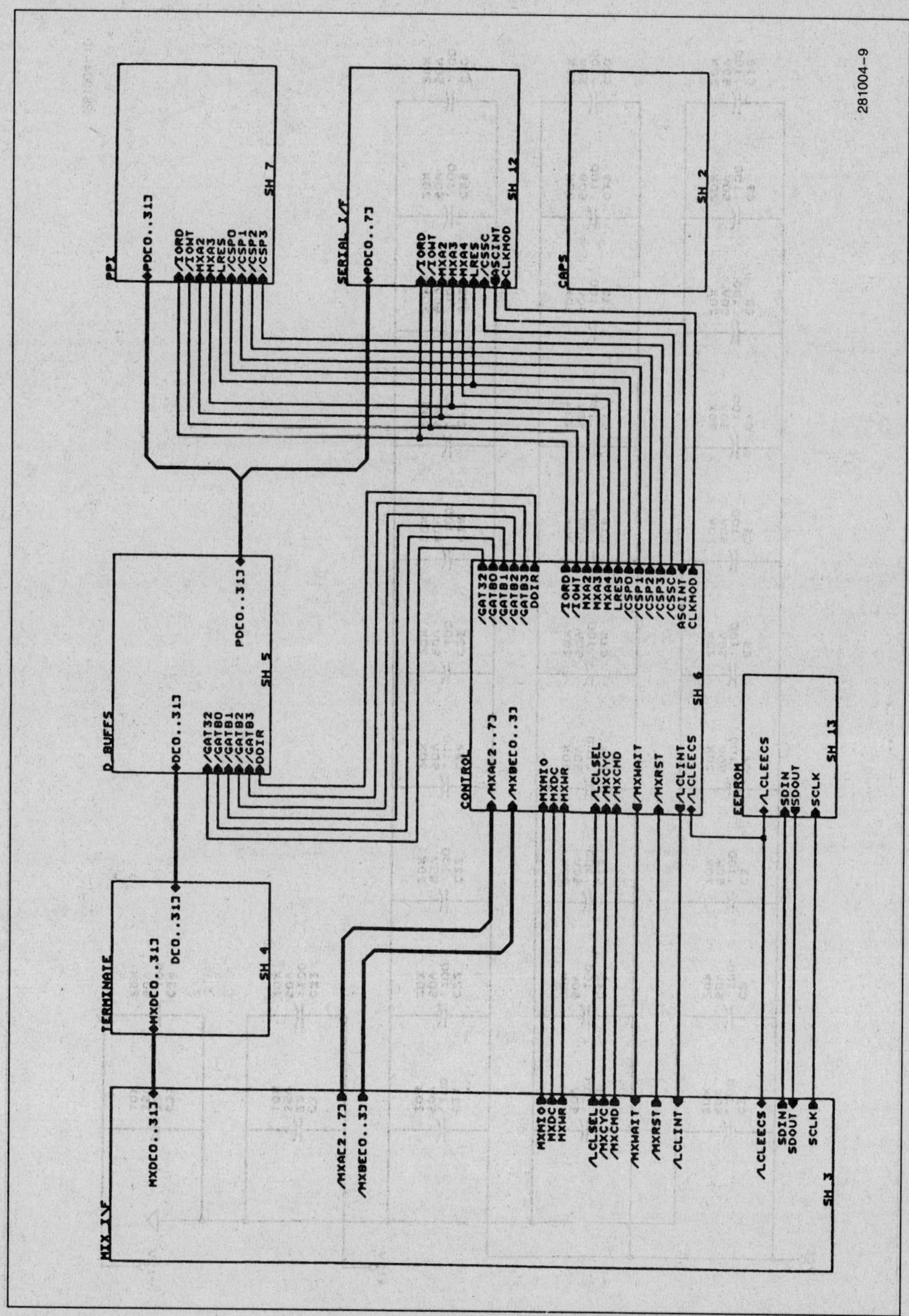
PPI
PD[0..31]
/IORD
/IOWT
MXA2
MXA3
LRES
/CSP0
/CSP1
/CSP2
/CSP3
SH 7
SERIAL I/F
PD[0..7]
/IORD
/IOWT
MXA2
MXA3
MXA4
LRES
/CSSC
ASCINT
CLKMOD
SH 12
CAPS
SH 2
D BUFFS
PD[0..31]
D[0..31]
/GAT32
/GATB0
/GATB1
/GATB2
/GATB3
DDIR
SH 5
CONTROL
/MXA[2..7]
/MXBE[0..3]
MXMIO
MXDC
MXWR
/LCLSEL
/MXCYC
/MXCMD
/MXWAIT
/MXRST
/LCLINT
/LCLEECS
SH 6
EEPROM
/LCLEECS
SDIN
SDOUT
SCLK
SH 13
TERMINATE
MXD[0..31]
D[0..31]
SH 4
MX I/F
MXD[0..31]
/MXA[2..7]
/MXBE[0..3]
MXMIO
MXDC
MXWR
/LCLSEL
/MXCYC
/MXCMD
/MXWAIT
/MXRST
/LCLINT
/LCLEECS
SDIN
SDOUT
SCLK
SH 3
281004-9

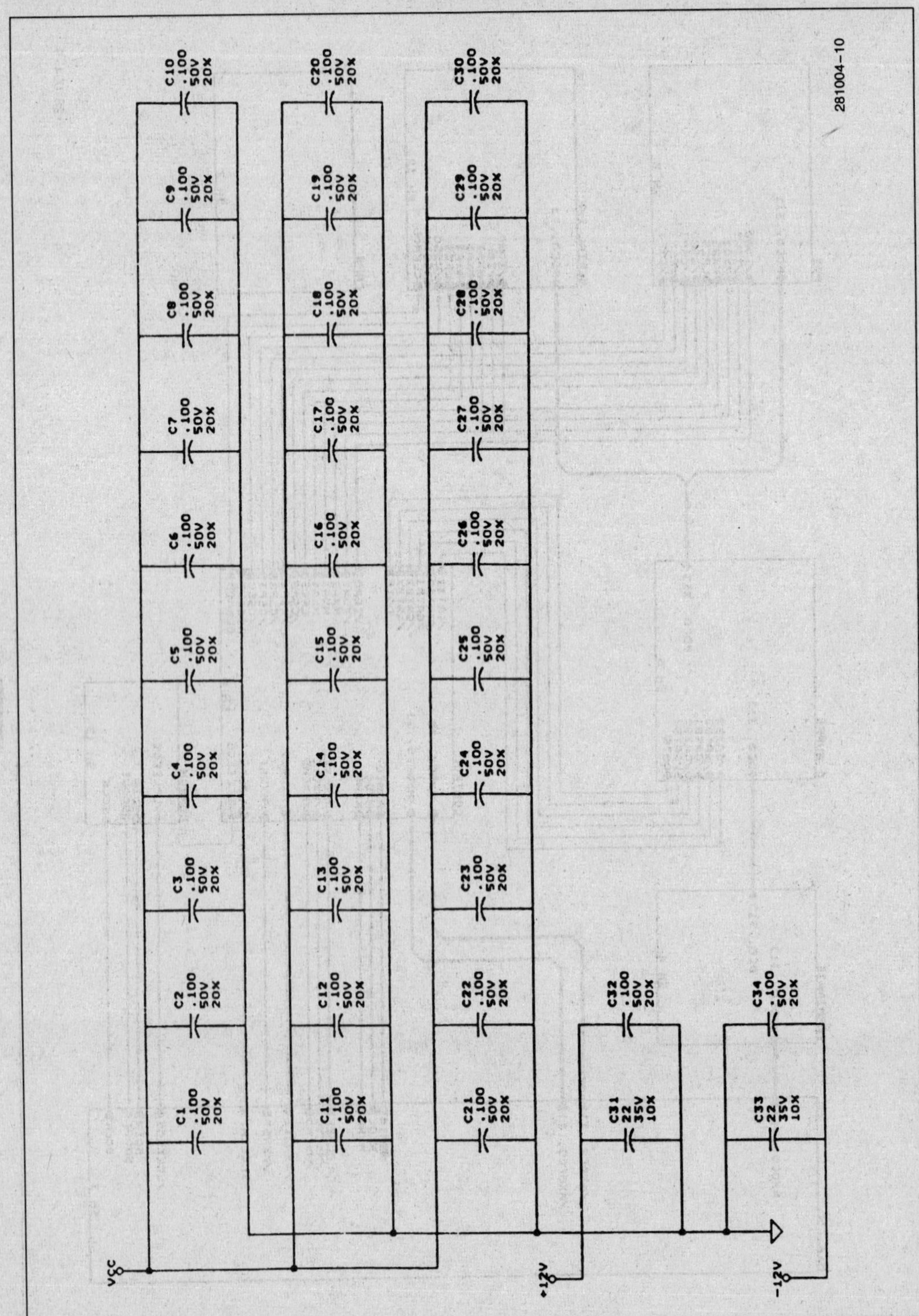
C1 .100 50V 20X
C2 .100 50V 20X
C3 .100 50V 20X
C4 .100 50V 20X
C5 .100 50V 20X
C6 .100 50V 20X
C7 .100 50V 20X
C8 .100 50V 20X
C9 .100 50V 20X
C10 .100 50V 20X
C11 .100 50V 20X
C12 .100 50V 20X
C13 .100 50V 20X
C14 .100 50V 20X
C15 .100 50V 20X
C16 .100 50V 20X
C17 .100 50V 20X
C18 .100 50V 20X
C19 .100 50V 20X
C20 .100 50V 20X
C21 .100 50V 20X
C22 .100 50V 20X
C23 .100 50V 20X
C24 .100 50V 20X
C25 .100 50V 20X
C26 .100 50V 20X
C27 .100 50V 20X
C28 .100 50V 20X
C29 .100 50V 20X
C30 .100 50V 20X
C31 22 35V 10X
C32 .100 50V 20X
C33 22 35V 10X
C34 .100 50V 20X
VCC
+12V
-12V
281004-10

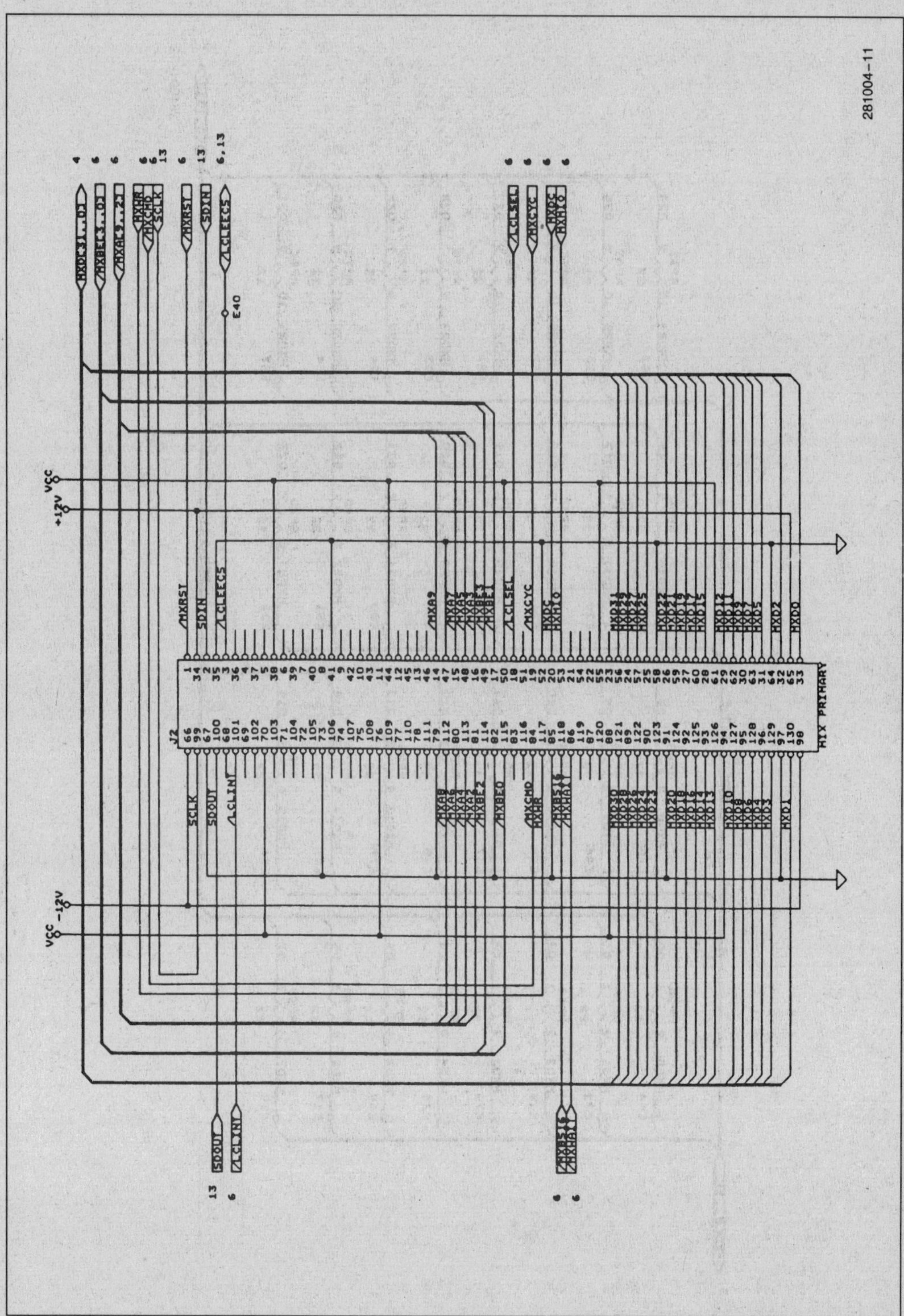

281004-11

5

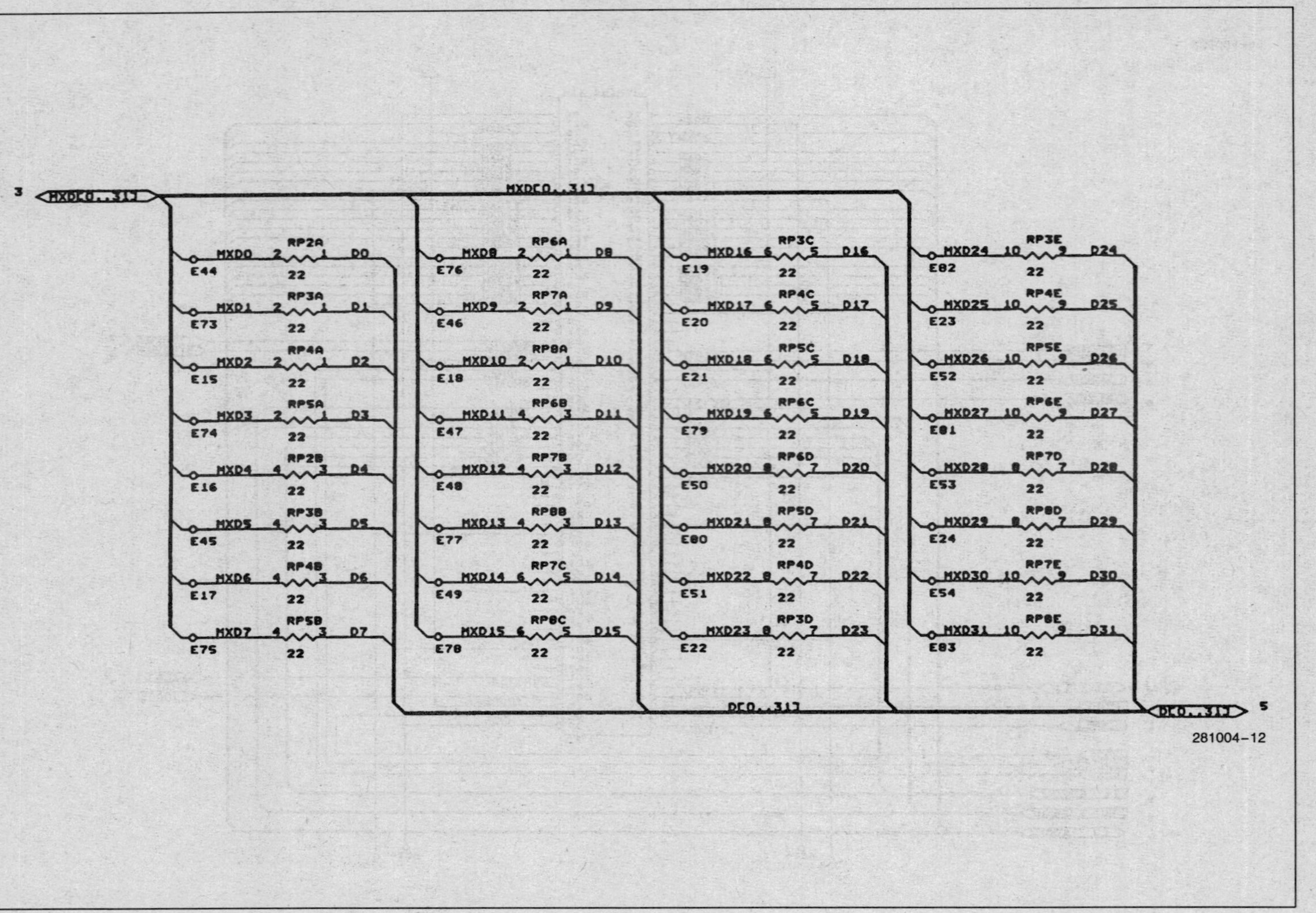
3
MXD[0..31]
MXD[0..31]
E44 MXD0 2 RP2A 1 D0 22
E73 MXD1 2 RP3A 1 D1 22
E15 MXD2 2 RP4A 1 D2 22
E74 MXD3 2 RP5A 1 D3 22
E16 MXD4 4 RP2B 3 D4 22
E45 MXD5 4 RP3B 3 D5 22
E17 MXD6 4 RP4B 3 D6 22
E75 MXD7 4 RP5B 3 D7 22
E76 MXD8 2 RP6A 1 D8 22
E46 MXD9 2 RP7A 1 D9 22
E18 MXD10 2 RP8A 1 D10 22
E47 MXD11 4 RP6B 3 D11 22
E48 MXD12 4 RP7B 3 D12 22
E77 MXD13 4 RP8B 3 D13 22
E49 MXD14 6 RP7C 5 D14 22
E78 MXD15 6 RP8C 5 D15 22
E19 MXD16 6 RP3C 5 D16 22
E20 MXD17 6 RP4C 5 D17 22
E21 MXD18 6 RP5C 5 D18 22
E79 MXD19 6 RP6C 5 D19 22
E50 MXD20 8 RP6D 7 D20 22
E80 MXD21 8 RP5D 7 D21 22
E51 MXD22 8 RP4D 7 D22 22
E22 MXD23 8 RP3D 7 D23 22
E82 MXD24 10 RP3E 9 D24 22
E23 MXD25 10 RP4E 9 D25 22
E52 MXD26 10 RP5E 9 D26 22
E81 MXD27 10 RP6E 9 D27 22
E53 MXD28 8 RP7D 7 D28 22
E24 MXD29 8 RP8D 7 D29 22
E54 MXD30 10 RP7E 9 D30 22
E83 MXD31 10 RP8E 9 D31 22
D[0..31]
D[0..31]
5

281004-12

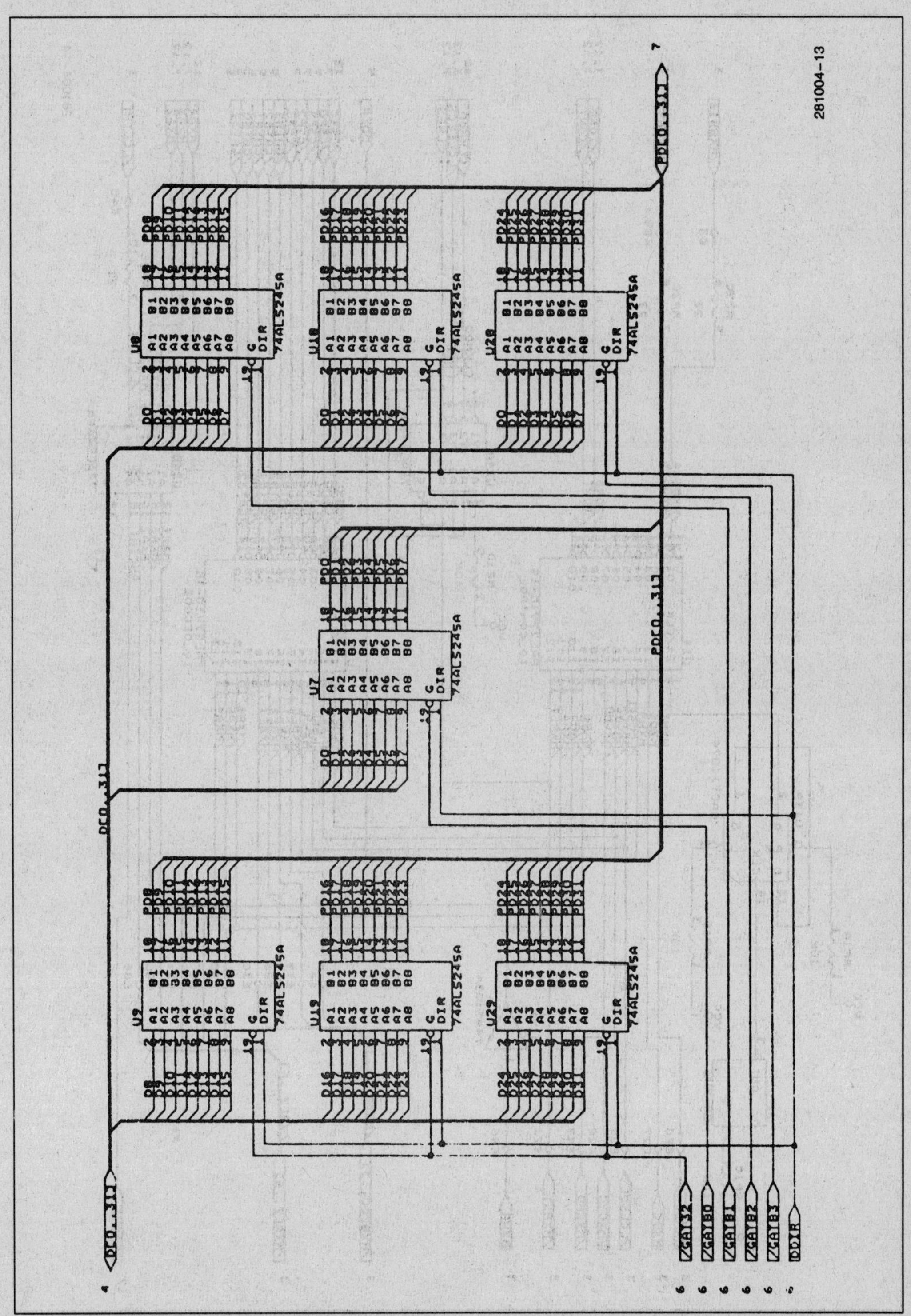

281004-13

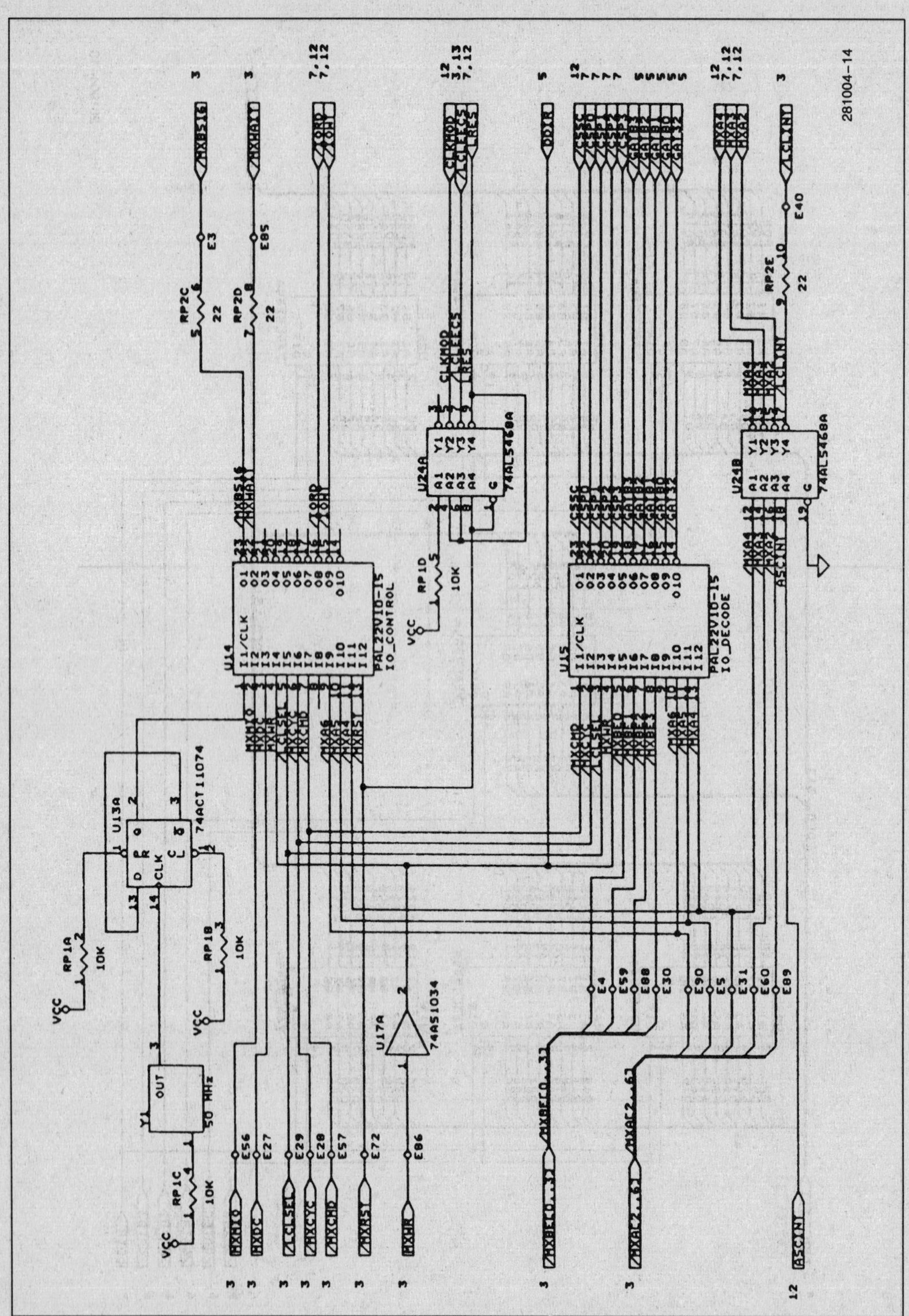

281004-14

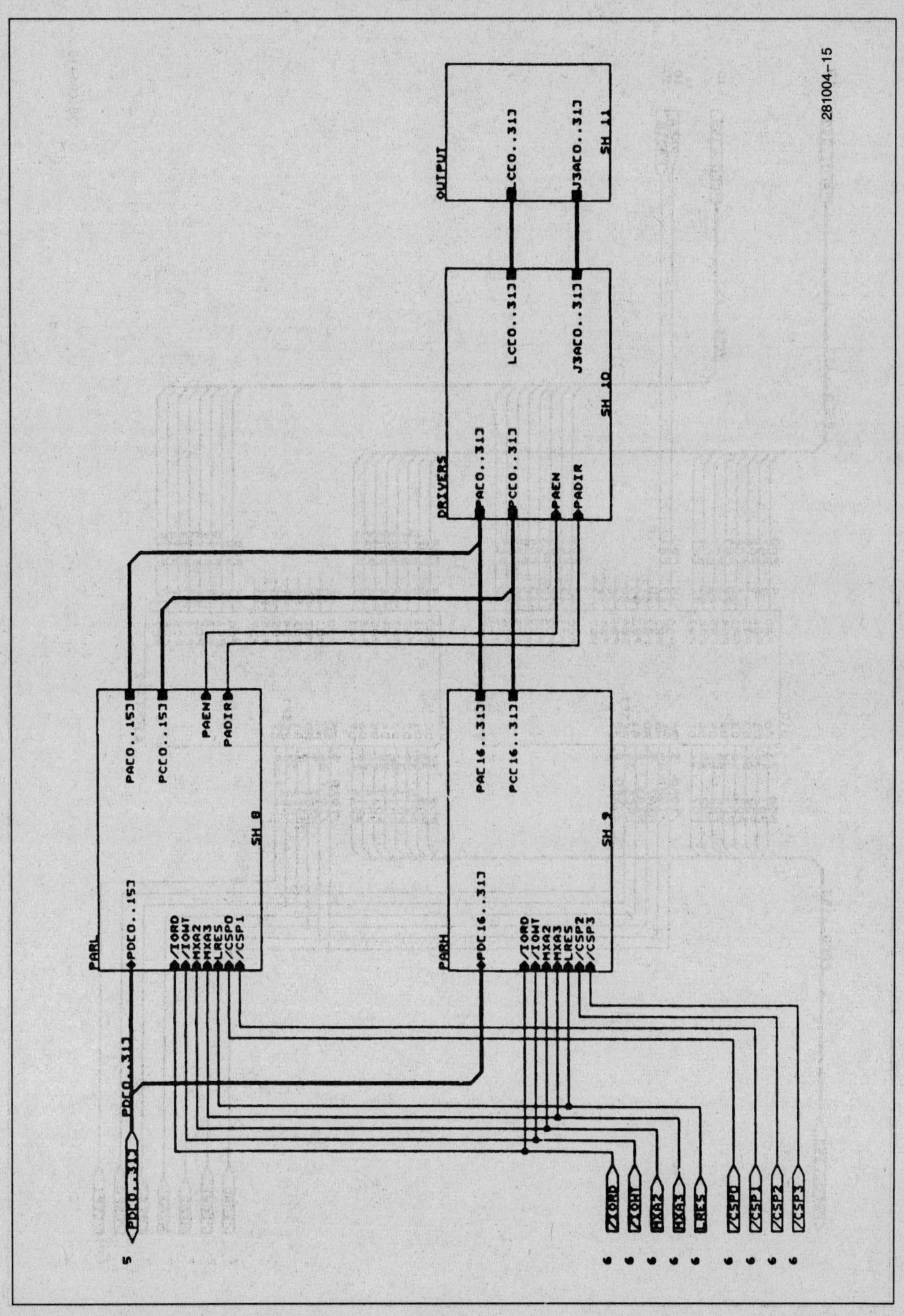

OUTPUT
LC[0..31]
J3A[0..31]
SH 11
DRIVERS
PA[0..31]
PC[0..31]
PAEN
PADIR
LC[0..31]
J3A[0..31]
SH 10
PARL
PD[0..15]
/IORD
/IOWT
MXA2
MXA3
LRES
/CSP0
/CSP1
PA[0..15]
PC[0..15]
PAEN
PADIR
SH 8
PARH
PD[16..31]
/IORD
/IOWT
MXA2
MXA3
LRES
/CSP2
/CSP3
PA[16..31]
PC[16..31]
SH 9
PD[0..31]
/IORD
/IOWT
MXA2
MXA3
LRES
/CSP0
/CSP1
/CSP2
/CSP3

281004-15

5

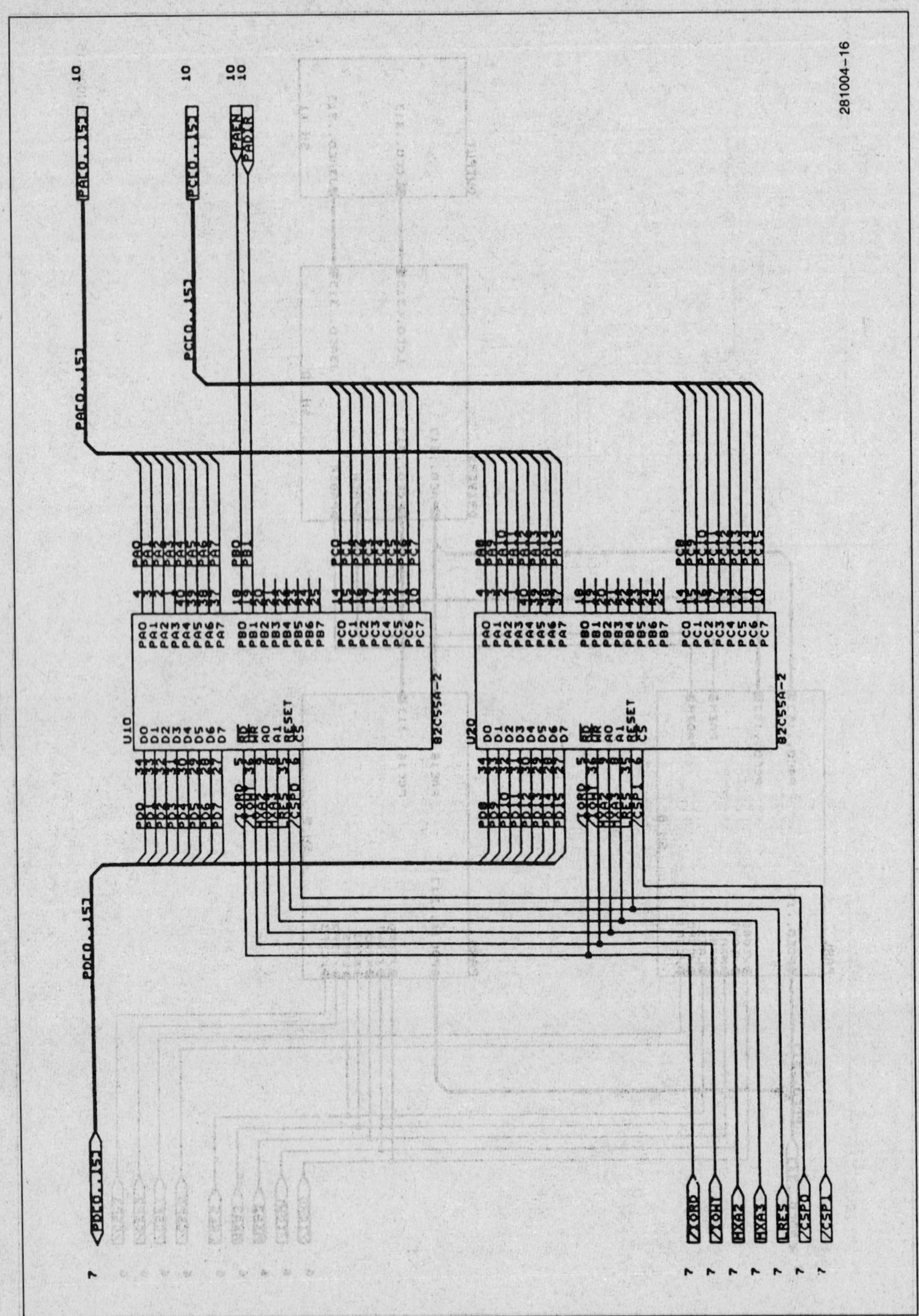
U10
82C55A-2
U20
82C55A-2
281004-16

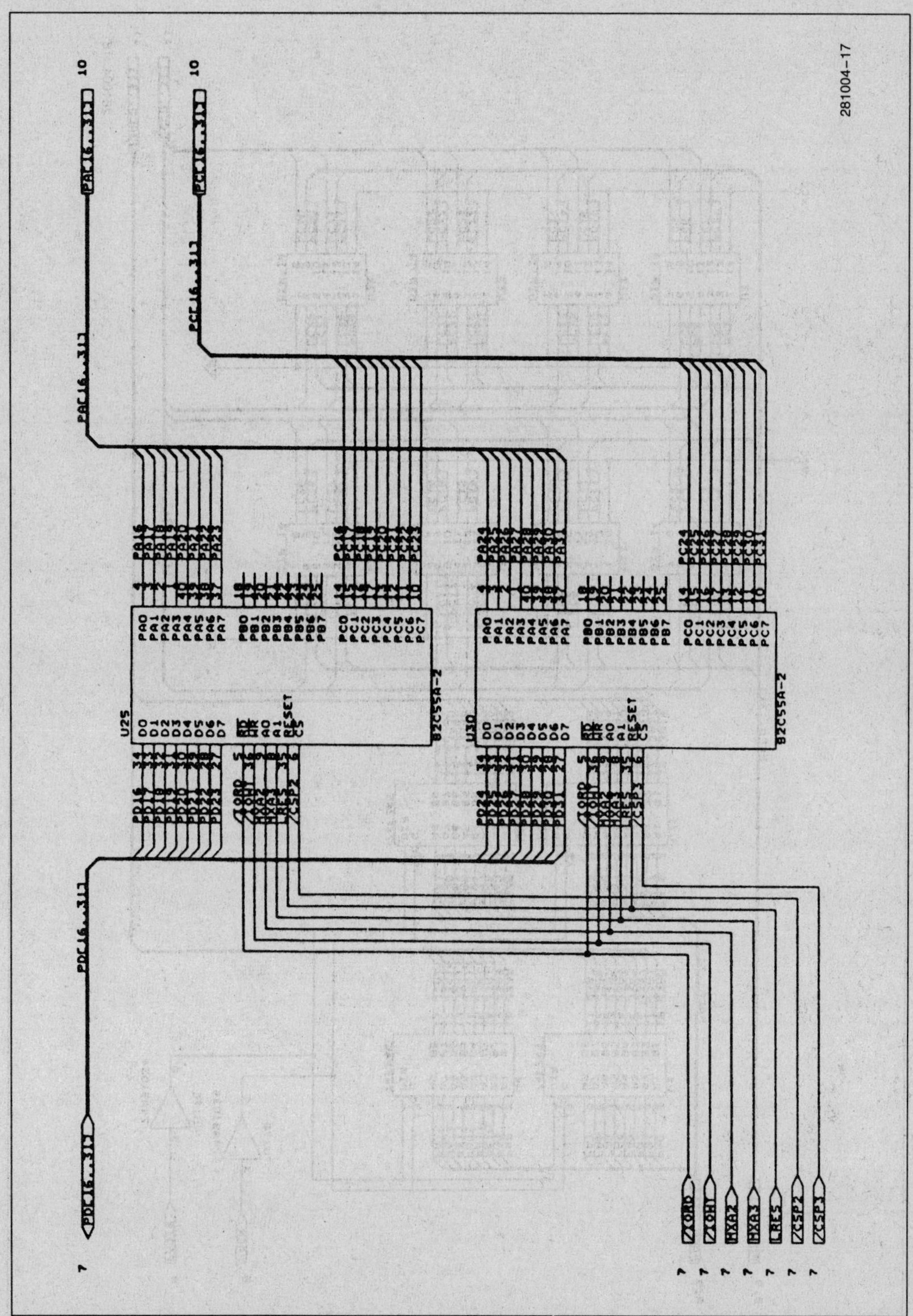
U25
82C55A-2
U30
82C55A-2
PAC[16..31]
PCC[16..31]
PDC[16..31]
/IORD
/IOWT
MXA2
MXA3
LRES
/CSP2
/CSP3

281004-17

5

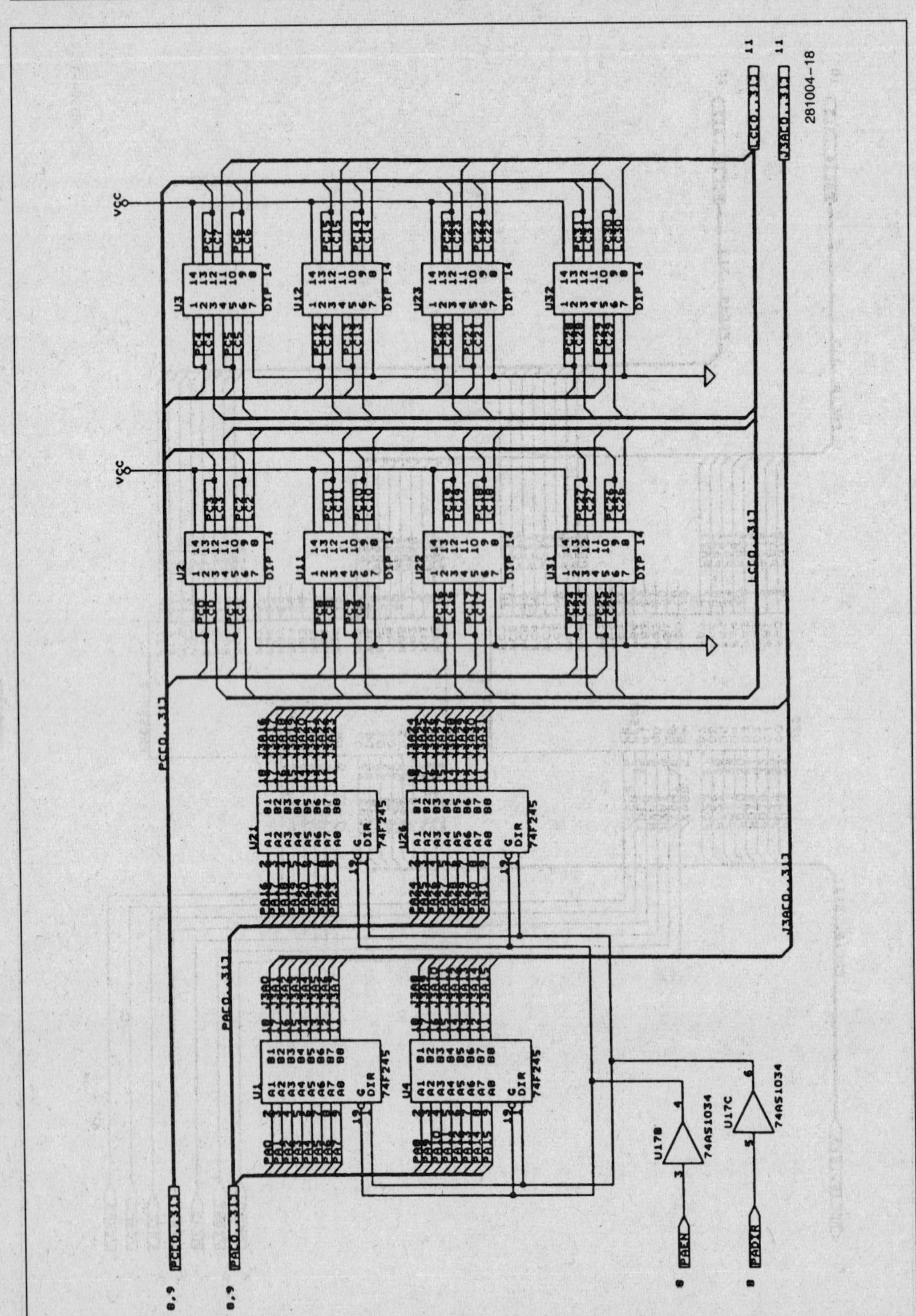
281004-18

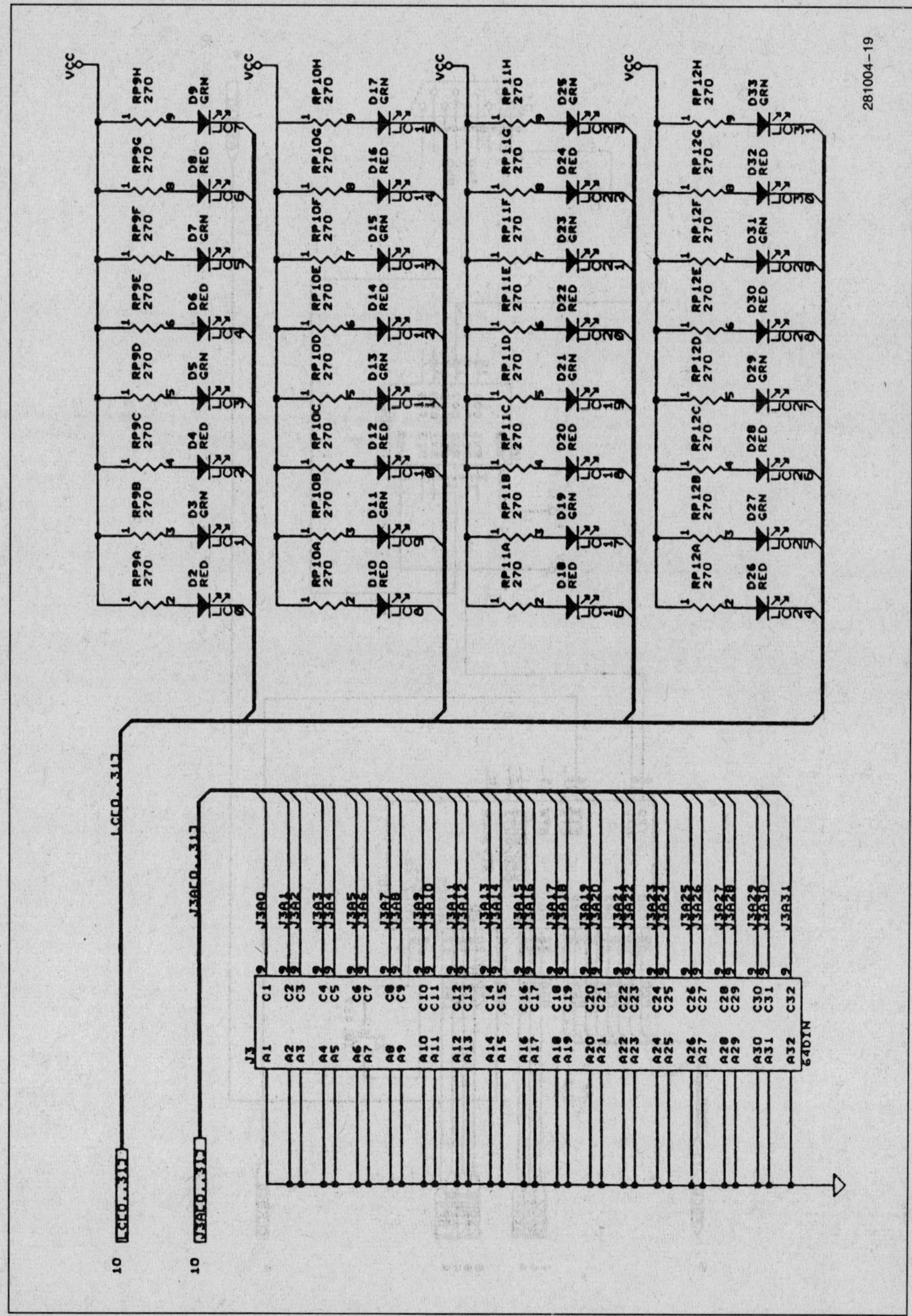

281004-19

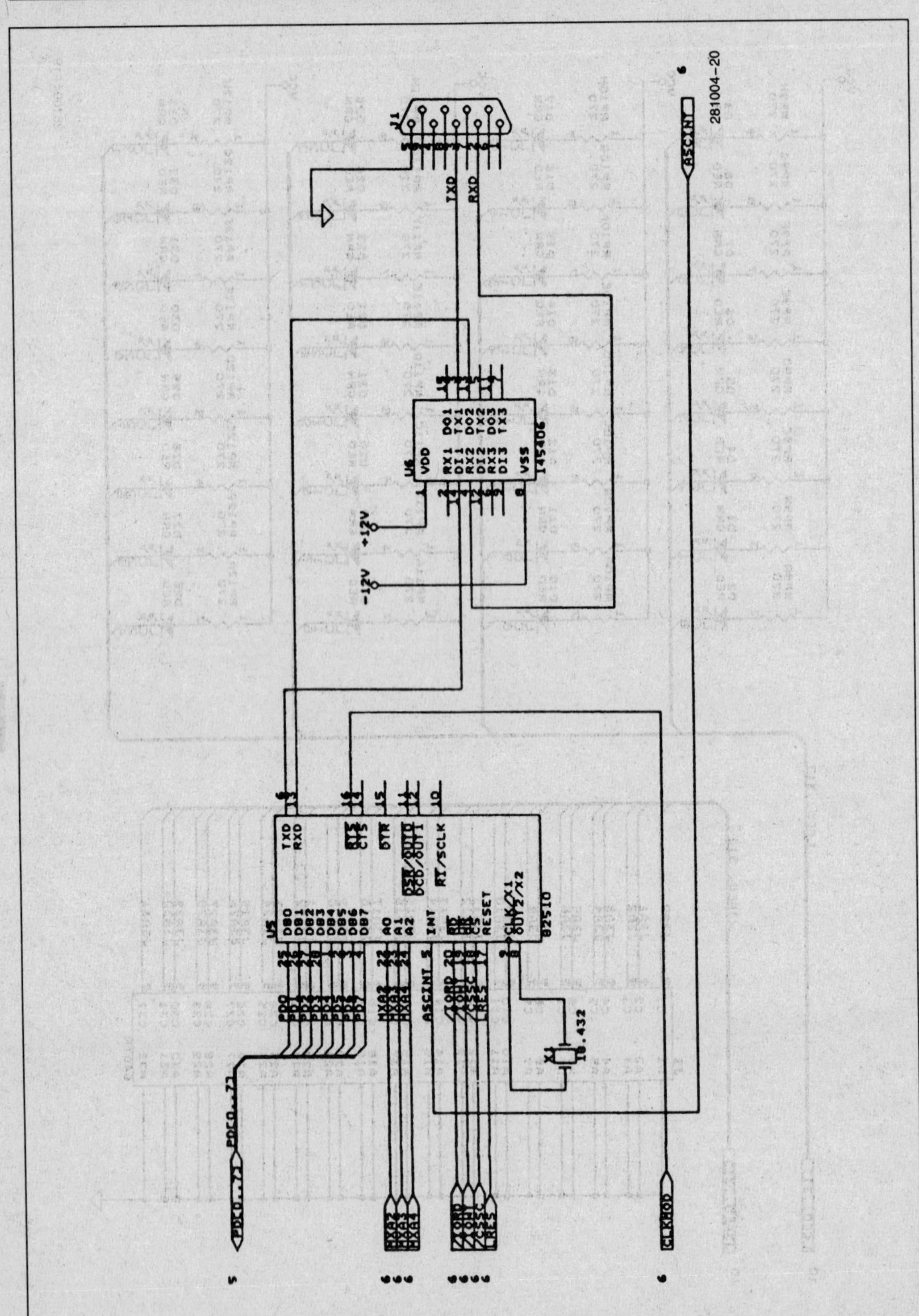
J1
TXD
RXD
U6
VDD
RX1 DI1 RX2 DI2 RX3 DI3
DO1 TX1 DO2 TX2 DO3 TX3
VSS
145406
+12V
-12V
U5
DB0 DB1 DB2 DB3 DB4 DB5 DB6 DB7
A0 A1 A2
INT
RESET
CLK/X1
OUT2/X2
82510
TXD
RXD
RTS
CTS
DTR
DCD/OUT1
RT/SCLK
X1
18.432
ASCINT
CLKMOD
PD[0..7]
281004-20

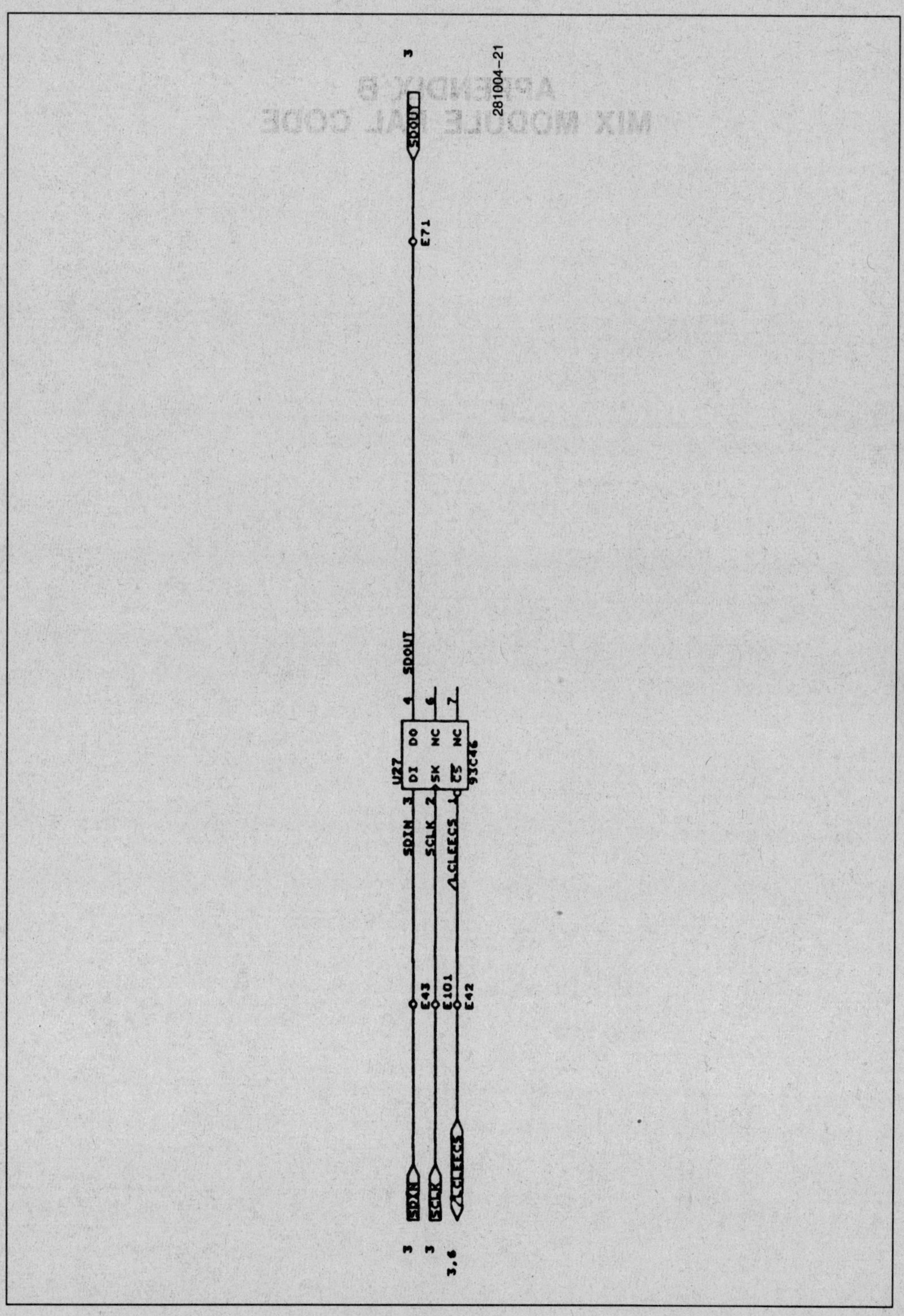
SDOUT
3
E71
SDOUT
U27
DI
DO
SK
NC
CS
NC
93C46
SDIN
SCLK
CLEECS
E43
E101
E42
SDIN
SCLK
CLEECS
3
3
3,6

281004-21

APPENDIX B
MIX MODULE PAL CODE

Title	: IOCTL PAL
Pattern	: U14
Rev	: 1.02
Author	: Erik A. Steeb
Company	: INTel Corporation
Date	: 10/2/89

Monolithic Memories PAL22V10-15

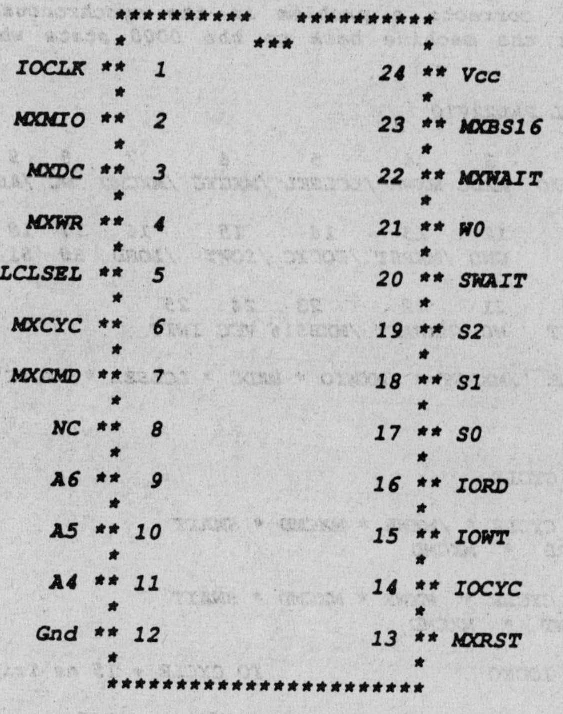

281004–22

5

```
; created by eas
; (C) - COPYRIGHT INTeL Corporation, 1989
 TITLE IOCTL PAL
 PATTERN U14
 REVISION 1.02
 AUTHOR ERIK A STEEB
 COMPANY INTeL Corporation
 DATE 10/2/89

;Revision 1.02 corrects a problem in the synchronous wait machine
;which brought the machine back to the 0000 state when IOCYC went
;inactive.

CHIP IO_CONTROL PAL22V10

;PINS  1     2      3    4     5       6      7      8    9
      IOCLK MXMIO  MXDC MXWR /LCLSEL /MXCYC /MXCMD  NC  /A6

;PINS 10    11     12    13     14     15      16    17   18
      /A5   /A4    GND /MXRST /IOCYC /IOWT   /IORD  S0   S1

;PINS 19    20     21    22      23     24    25
       S2  SWAIT   W0  /MXWAIT /MXBS16 VCC  INIT

STRING IO_CYCLE '/MXRST * /MXMIO * MXDC * LCLSEL * MXCYC'

EQUATIONS

IOCYC   =  IO_CYCLE

IORD    =  IO_CYCLE * /MXWR * MXCMD * SWAIT
        +  IORD   *  MXCMD

IOWT    =  IO_CYCLE *  MXWR * MXCMD * SWAIT
        +  IOWT   *  MXCMD

MXBS16.TRST = IOCYC                     ; IO_CYCLE + 15 ns Tri-State

MXBS16  =  IO_CYCLE *  A6               ; BS16* asserted any access
        +  IO_CYCLE *  A5               ; except to PPI 0.
        +  IO_CYCLE *  A4
```

281004-24

```
;  *** SYNCHRONOUS PORTION OF WAIT MACHINE ***

INIT.RSTF = MXRST                    ; Global reset of register outputs

S0     :=  S0 *  S1
        +  S0 * /S2
        +  S0 *  SWAIT
        +  S1 * /S2 * SWAIT

S1     := /MXCMD *  S0 * /S2 * /SWAIT
        +  S0 *  S1 * /S2
        + /S0 *  S1 *  S2
        + /S0 *  S2 *  SWAIT
        +  S1 * /S2 *  SWAIT

S2     :=  S0 *  S1
        +  S0 *  S2 * /SWAIT
        + /S0 * /S1 *  S2 *  SWAIT
        + /S0 * /S1 *  SWAIT *  MXCMD

SWAIT  := /S0 *  SWAIT
        +  S0 *  S1 *  SWAIT
        +  S0 * /S1 *  S2 *  SWAIT
        +  IO_CYCLE *  MXWAIT * /S0 * /S1 * /S2 * /SWAIT

;  *** ASYNCHRONOUS PORTION OF WAIT MACHINE ***

W0      =  IO_CYCLE * /SWAIT * W0
        +  IO_CYCLE *  SWAIT * MXWAIT

MXWAIT.TRST = IOCYC             ;( IO_CYCLE + 15 ns TRI-STATE )

MXWAIT  =  IO_CYCLE *  SWAIT * MXWAIT
        +  IO_CYCLE * /W0

;
;  DESCRIPTION
;
;  The IOCYC variable is used by the tri-state outputs for MXBS16* and
;  MXWAIT* to facilitate the "logical false before tri-state" rule.
;
```

281004-25

5

```
SIMULATION

TRACE_ON  /IORD /IOWT /IOCYC /MXCYC /MXCMD S0 S1 S2 SWAIT W0 /MXWAIT
/MXBS16
SETF /IOCLK MXRST /MXCMD /LCLSEL /MXCYC
CLOCKF
CLOCKF
SETF /MXRST /MXMIO MXDC /MXWR       ; set I/O read status
SETF /A6 /A5 /A4                    ; set PPI0 address
CLOCKF
CLOCKF
SETF LCLSEL                         ; select the module
CLOCKF
CLOCKF
SETF MXCYC                          ; start a valid cycle
CLOCKF                              ; provide plenty of clocks
CLOCKF
CLOCKF
CLOCKF
CLOCKF
CLOCKF
CLOCKF
CLOCKF
CLOCKF
CLOCKF
CLOCKF
CLOCKF
CLOCKF
SETF MXCMD                          ; issue the command
CLOCKF
CLOCKF
CLOCKF
CLOCKF
CLOCKF
CLOCKF
CLOCKF
CLOCKF
CLOCKF
CLOCKF
CLOCKF
SETF /MXCMD                         ; release the command
CLOCKF
SETF /MXCYC                         ; end transfer cycle
SETF /MXRST /MXMIO MXDC MXWR        ; set I/O write status
SETF /A6 /A5 A4                     ; set PPI1 address
CLOCKF
SETF MXCYC                          ; begin transfer cycle
CLOCKF
SETF MXCMD                          ; issue command
```

281004-26

```
CLOCKF
CLOCKF
CLOCKF
CLOCKF
CLOCKF
CLOCKF
CLOCKF
CLOCKF
CLOCKF
CLOCKF
CLOCKF
CLOCKF
CLOCKF
CLOCKF
CLOCKF
CLOCKF
CLOCKF
CLOCKF
CLOCKF
CLOCKF
CLOCKF
CLOCKF
SETF /MXCMD                     ; release command
CLOCKF
CLOCKF
CLOCKF
CLOCKF
CLOCKF
CLOCKF
CLOCKF
SETF /MXCYC                     ; end cycle
CLOCKF
CLOCKF
CLOCKF
CLOCKF
CLOCKF
CLOCKF
CLOCKF
CLOCKF
SETF /LCLSEL                    ; deselect module
CLOCKF
CLOCKF
TRACE_OFF
```

281004-27

5

```
PALASM SIMULATION, V2.23 - MARKET RELEASE (2-1-88)
(C) - COPYRIGHT MONOLITHIC MEMORIES INC, 1988
PALASM SIMULATION SELECTIVE TRACE LISTING

Title    : IOCTL PAL                    Author   : ERIK A STEEB
Pattern  : U14                          Company  : INTeL Corporation
Revision : 1.02                         Date     : 10/2/89

PAL22V10
Page :  1
        g c cgg  c   cg  c  c g  c  c  c   c  c  c
/IORD   HHHHHHHHHH HHHHHHHHHH HHHHHHHHHH HHHHHHHHHH
/IOWT   HHHHHHHHHH HHHHHHHHHH HHHHHHHHHH HHHHHHHHHH
/IOCYC  HHHHHHHHHH HHHHHHHHHH LLLLLLLLLL LLLLLLLLLL
/MXCYC  HHHHHHHHHH HHHHHHHHHH LLLLLLLLLL LLLLLLLLLL
/MXCMD  HHHHHHHHHH HHHHHHHHHH HHHHHHHHHH HHHHHHHHHH
 S0     LLLLLLLLLL LLLLLLLLLL LLLLLLLLLL LLLLLLLLLL
 S1     LLLLLLLLLL LLLLLLLLLL LLLLLLLLLL LLLLLLLLLL
 S2     LLLLLLLLLL LLLLLLLLLL LLLLLLLLLL LLLLLLLLLL
 SWAIT  LLLLLLLLLL LLLLLLLLLL LLHHHHHHHH HHHHHHHHHH
 W0     LLLLLLLLLL LLLLLLLLLL LLHHHHHHHH HHHHHHHHHH
/MXWAIT HHHHHHHHHH HHHHHHHHHH LLLLLLLLLL LLLLLLLLLL
/MXBS16 HHHHHHHHHH HHHHHHHHHH HHHHHHHHHH HHHHHHHHHH

Page :  2
         c  c  c   c  c  c  c g  c  c  c   c  c  c
/IORD   HHHHHHHHHH HHHHHHHHHH LLLLLLLLLL LLLLLLLLLL
/IOWT   HHHHHHHHHH HHHHHHHHHH HHHHHHHHHH HHHHHHHHHH
/IOCYC  LLLLLLLLLL LLLLLLLLLL LLLLLLLLLL LLLLLLLLLL
/MXCYC  LLLLLLLLLL LLLLLLLLLL LLLLLLLLLL LLLLLLLLLL
/MXCMD  HHHHHHHHHH HHHHHHHHHH LLLLLLLLLL LLLLLLLLLL
 S0     LLLLLLLLLL LLLLLLLLLL LLLLLLLLLL LHHHHHHHHH
 S1     LLLLLLLLLL LLLLLLLLLL LLLLLHHHHH HHHHHHHLLL
 S2     LLLLLLLLLL LLLLLLLLLL LLHHHHHHLL LLLLHHHHHH
 SWAIT  HHHHHHHHHH HHHHHHHHHH HHHHHHHHHH HHHHHHHHHH
 W0     HHHHHHHHHH HHHHHHHHHH HHHHHHHHHH HHHHHHHHHH
/MXWAIT LLLLLLLLLL LLLLLLLLLL LLLLLLLLLL LLLLLLLLLL
/MXBS16 HHHHHHHHHH HHHHHHHHHH HHHHHHHHHH HHHHHHHHHH

Page :  3
         c  c  c   c  cg  cg  gg  cg   c g  c  c  c
/IORD   LLLLLLLLLL LLLLHHHHHH HHHHHHHHHH HHHHHHHHHH
/IOWT   HHHHHHHHHH HHHHHHHHHH HHHHHHHHHH HHHHHHHHLL
/IOCYC  LLLLLLLLLL LLLLLLLLHH HHHHHLLLLL LLLLLLLLLL
/MXCYC  LLLLLLLLLL LLLLLLLLHH HHHHHLLLLL LLLLLLLLLL
/MXCMD  LLLLLLLLLL LLLLHHHHHH HHHHHHHHHH LLLLLLLLLL
 S0     HHHHHHHHHH HHHHHHHHHH HHHHHHHHHH HHLLLLLLLL
 S1     LLLLLLLLLL LLLLLLHHHH HHHHHHHHLL LLLLLLLLLL
 S2     LLLLLLLLLL LLLLLLLLLL LLLHHHHHHH HHHHHLLLLL
 SWAIT  HHHLLLLLLL LLLLLLLLLL LLLLLLLLLL LLLLLLLLHH
 W0     HHHHHHHHHH HHHHHHHHLL LLLLLLLLLL LLLLLLLLHH
/MXWAIT LLLHHHHHHH HHHHHHHHHZ ZZZZZZLLLL LLLLLLLLLL
/MXBS16 HHHHHHHHHH HHHHHHHHHZ ZZZZZZLLLL LLLLLLLLLL
```

281004-28

```
Page :   4
              c   c   c    c   c   c    c   c   c   c    c   c   c
/IORD    HHHHHHHHHH HHHHHHHHHH HHHHHHHHHH HHHHHHHHHH
/IOWT    LLLLLLLLLL LLLLLLLLLL LLLLLLLLLL LLLLLLLLLL
/IOCYC   LLLLLLLLLL LLLLLLLLLL LLLLLLLLLL LLLLLLLLLL
/MXCYC   LLLLLLLLLL LLLLLLLLLL LLLLLLLLLL LLLLLLLLLL
/MXCMD   LLLLLLLLLL LLLLLLLLLL LLLLLLLLLL LLLLLLLLLL
 S0      LLLLLLLLLL HHHHHHHHHH HHHHHHHHHH HHHHHHHHHH
 S1      LLLLHHHHHH HHHHHHLLLL LLLLLLLLLL LLLLLLLLLL
 S2      LHHHHHHLLL LLLHHHHHHL LLLLLLLLLL LLLLLLLLLL
 SWAIT   HHHHHHHHHH HHHHHHHHHH HHLLLLLLLL LLLLLLLLLL
 W0      HHHHHHHHHH HHHHHHHHHH HHHHHHHHHH HHHHHHHHHH
/MXWAIT  LLLLLLLLLL LLLLLLLLLL LLHHHHHHHH HHHHHHHHHH
/MXBS16  LLLLLLLLLL LLLLLLLLLL LLLLLLLLLL LLLLLLLLLL

Page :   5
            c   c   c    c   c   cg   c   c   c   c    c   c   cg
/IORD    HHHHHHHHHH HHHHHHHHHH HHHHHHHHHH HHHHHHHHHH
/IOWT    LLLLLLLLLL LLLLLLLHHH HHHHHHHHHH HHHHHHHHHH
/IOCYC   LLLLLLLLLL LLLLLLLLLL LLLLLLLLLL LLLLLLLLLH
/MXCYC   LLLLLLLLLL LLLLLLLLLL LLLLLLLLLL LLLLLLLLLH
/MXCMD   LLLLLLLLLL LLLLLLLHHH HHHHHHHHHH HHHHHHHHHH
 S0      HHHHHHHHHH HHHHHHHHHH HHHHHHHHLL LLLLLLLLLL
 S1      LLLLLLLLLL LLLLLLLLLH HHHHHLLLLL LLLLLLLLLL
 S2      LLLLLLLLLL LLLLLLLLLL LLHHHHHHHH HLLLLLLLLL
 SWAIT   LLLLLLLLLL LLLLLLLLLL LLLLLLLLLL LLLLLLLLLL
 W0      HHHHHHHHHH HHHHHHHHHH HHHHHHHHHH HHHHHHHHHL
/MXWAIT  HHHHHHHHHH HHHHHHHHHH HHHHHHHHHH HHHHHHHHHH
/MXBS16  LLLLLLLLLL LLLLLLLLLL LLLLLLLLLL LLLLLLLLLH

Page :   6
              c   c   c    c   c   c    c  cg   c    c
/IORD    HHHHHHHHHH HHHHHHHHHH HHHHHHHHHH HH
/IOWT    HHHHHHHHHH HHHHHHHHHH HHHHHHHHHH HH
/IOCYC   HHHHHHHHHH HHHHHHHHHH HHHHHHHHHH HH
/MXCYC   HHHHHHHHHH HHHHHHHHHH HHHHHHHHHH HH
/MXCMD   HHHHHHHHHH HHHHHHHHHH HHHHHHHHHH HH
 S0      LLLLLLLLLL LLLLLLLLLL LLLLLLLLLL LL
 S1      LLLLLLLLLL LLLLLLLLLL LLLLLLLLLL LL
 S2      LLLLLLLLLL LLLLLLLLLL LLLLLLLLLL LL
 SWAIT   LLLLLLLLLL LLLLLLLLLL LLLLLLLLLL LL
 W0      LLLLLLLLLL LLLLLLLLLL LLLLLLLLLL LL
/MXWAIT  ZZZZZZZZZZ ZZZZZZZZZZ ZZZZZZZZZZ ZZ
/MXBS16  ZZZZZZZZZZ ZZZZZZZZZZ ZZZZZZZZZZ ZZ
```

281004-29

5

Title : IODCD PAL
Pattern : U15
Rev : 1.01
Author : Erik A. Steeb
Company : INTel Corporation
Date : 5/24/89

Monolithic Memories PAL22V10-15

```
           ***********     **********
           *          ***          *
     WR ** 1                    24 ** Vcc
           *                       *
    SEL ** 2                    23 ** CSSC
           *                       *
    CYC ** 3                    22 ** CSP0
           *                       *
    CMD ** 4                    21 ** CSP1
           *                       *
    BE0 ** 5                    20 ** CSP2
           *                       *
    BE1 ** 6                    19 ** CSP3
           *                       *
    BE2 ** 7                    18 ** GATB3
           *                       *
    BE3 ** 8                    17 ** GATB2
           *                       *
     A7 ** 9                    16 ** GATB1
           *                       *
     A6 ** 10                   15 ** GATB0
           *                       *
     A5 ** 11                   14 ** GAT32
           *                       *
    Gnd ** 12                   13 ** A4
           *                       *
           *************************
```

281004-23

```
; created by eas
; (C) - COPYRIGHT INTeL Corporation, 1989
 TITLE IODCD PAL
 PATTERN U15
 REVISION 1.01
 AUTHOR ERIK STEEB
 COMPANY INTeL Corporation
 DATE 5/24/89

CHIP IO_DECODE PAL22V10

;PINS    1    2    3    4    5    6    7    8    9   10   11
         WR /SEL /CYC /CMD /BE0 /BE1 /BE2 /BE3  NC /A6 /A5

;PINS  12    13   14     15     16     17
       GND  /A4 /GAT32 /GATB0 /GATB1 /GATB2

;PINS   18     19     20     21     22     23   24   25
      /GATB3 /CSP3 /CSP2 /CSP1 /CSP0 /CSSC VCC INIT

STRING  CYCLE    'SEL * CYC'
STRING  GATE_RD  'SEL * CYC * /WR * CMD'
STRING  GATE_WT  'SEL * CYC *  WR'

EQUATIONS

GATB0  = GATE_RD * /A6 * /A5 * /A4
       + GATE_WT * /A6 * /A5 * /A4
       + GATE_RD *  A6 * /A5
       + GATE_WT *  A6 * /A5

GATB1  = GATE_RD * /A6 * /A5 *  A4 * /BE1 *  BE0
       + GATE_WT * /A6 * /A5 *  A4 * /BE1 *  BE0

GATB2  = GATE_RD * /A6 *  A5 * /A4 * /BE1 *  BE0
       + GATE_WT * /A6 *  A5 * /A4 * /BE1 *  BE0

GATB3  = GATE_RD * /A6 *  A5 *  A4 * /BE1 *  BE0
       + GATE_WT * /A6 *  A5 *  A4 * /BE1 *  BE0

GAT32  = GATE_RD * /A6 * /A5 * /A4 *  BE3 *  BE2 *  BE1 * BE0
       + GATE_WT * /A6 * /A5 * /A4 *  BE3 *  BE2 *  BE1 * BE0
       + GATE_RD * /A6 * /A5 * /A4 * /BE3 * /BE2 *  BE1 * BE0
       + GATE_WT * /A6 * /A5 * /A4 * /BE3 * /BE2 *  BE1 * BE0
```

281004-30

5

```
CSP0   = CYCLE   * /A6 * /A5 * /A4 *  BE3 *  BE2 *  BE1 * BE0
       + CYCLE   * /A6 * /A5 * /A4 * /BE3 * /BE2 *  BE1 * BE0
       + CYCLE   * /A6 * /A5 * /A4 * /BE3 * /BE2 * /BE1 * BE0

CSP1   = CYCLE   * /A6 * /A5 * /A4 *  BE3 *  BE2 *  BE1 * BE0
       + CYCLE   * /A6 * /A5 * /A4 * /BE3 * /BE2 *  BE1 * BE0
       + CYCLE   * /A6 * /A5 *  A4 * /BE3 * /BE2 * /BE1 * BE0

CSP2   = CYCLE   * /A6 * /A5 * /A4 *  BE3 *  BE2 *  BE1 * BE0
       + CYCLE   * /A6 *  A5 * /A4 * /BE3 * /BE2 * /BE1 * BE0

CSP3   = CYCLE   * /A6 * /A5 * /A4 *  BE3 *  BE2 *  BE1 * BE0
       + CYCLE   * /A6 *  A5 *  A4 * /BE3 * /BE2 * /BE1 * BE0

CSSC   = CYCLE   *  A6 * /A5 * /BE3 * /BE2 * /BE1 * BE0


 ; DESCRIPTION;:
 ;
 ; NAME CHANGES       SCHEMATIC  to  PIN LIST
 ;
 ;                       /LCLSEL           /SEL
 ;                       /MXCYC            /CYC
 ;                       /MXCMD            /CMD
 ;                        MXWR              WR
 ;                       /MXBEx            /BEx
 ;                       /MXAx             /Ax
 ;
 ;  Read and write accesses distinquished in "GAT" equations to meet
 ;  82C55A-2 data hold times for writes and MIX spec data off times
 ;  for reads.
 ;
 ; I/O DECODE SCHEME AS FOLLOWS:
 ;
 ;  Byte  Parallel Port @ offset xxx000xxxx binary (first = 0xH)
 ;  Byte  Parallel Port @ offset xxx001xxxx binary (first = 1xH)
 ;  Byte  Parallel Port @ offset xxx010xxxx binary (first = 2xH)
 ;  Byte  Parallel Port @ offset xxx011xxxx binary (first = 3xH)
 ;  Word  Parallel Port @ offset xxx000xxxx (Combo of two byte ports)
 ;  DWord Parallel Port @ offset xxx000xxxx (Combo of four byte ports)
 ;  Serial Port         @ offset xxx10xxxxx  (first = 4xH & 5xH)
 ;
 ;  NOTE: Address lines /MXA9, /MXA8, and /MXA7 not used so decode
 ;        is mirrored every 128 bytes.
```

281004-31

```
SIMULATION

TRACE_ON  /SEL /CYC /CMD WR /CSP0 /CSP1 /CSP2 /CSP3 /CSSC
          /GATB0 /GATB1 /GATB2 /GATB3 /GAT32
SETF      SEL
SETF      /WR /A6 /A5 A4                ; Set PPI1 address read
SETF      /BE3 /BE2 BE1 BE0             ; Word access
SETF      CYC                           ; Begin valid cycle
SETF      CMD
SETF      /CMD
SETF      /CYC                          ; end cycle
SETF      /BE1                          ; Byte access
SETF      CYC                           ; Begin cycle
SETF      CMD
SETF      /CMD
SETF      /CYC                          ; end cycle
SETF      WR                            ; Write access
SETF      CYC                           ; Begin cycle
SETF      CMD
SETF      /CMD
SETF      /CYC                          ; end cycle
SETF      /A4                           ; Set PPI0 address
SETF      CYC                           ; Begin cycle
SETF      CMD
SETF      /CMD
SETF      /CYC                          ; end cycle
SETF      BE1                           ; Word access
SETF      CYC                           ; Begin valid cycle
SETF      CMD
SETF      /CMD
SETF      /CYC                          ; end cycle
SETF      /WR BE3 BE2                   ; Dword access read
SETF      CYC                           ; Begin valid cycle
SETF      CMD
SETF      /CMD
SETF      /CYC                          ; end cycle
SETF      A6 A5                         ; Set invalid address read
SETF      CYC                           ; Begin valid cycle
SETF      CMD
SETF      /CMD
SETF      /CYC                          ; end cycle
SETF      /BE3 BE2 BE1 /BE0             ; Set invalid byte enable
SETF      CYC                           ; Begin valid cycle
SETF      CMD
SETF      /CMD
SETF      /CYC                          ; end cycle
TRACE_OFF
```

281004-32

5

```
PALASM SIMULATION, V2.23 - MARKET RELEASE (2-1-88)
(C) - COPYRIGHT MONOLITHIC MEMORIES INC, 1988
PALASM SIMULATION SELECTIVE TRACE LISTING

Title      : IODCD PAL                   Author     : ERIK STEEB
Pattern    : U15                         Company    : INTeL Corporation
Revision   : 1.01                        Date       : 5/24/89

PAL22V10
        gggggggggg gggggggggg gggggggggg gggggggggg
/SEL    LLLLLLLLLL LLLLLLLLLL LLLLLLLLLL LLLLLLLLLL
/CYC    XXXLLLHHLL LHHLLLHHLL LHHLLLHHLL LHHLLLHHLL
/CMD    XXXXLHHHHL HHHHLHHHHL HHHHLHHHHL HHHHLHHHHL
 WR     XLLLLLLLLL LLHHHHHHHH HHHHHHHLLL LLLLLLLLLL
/CSP0   XHHHHHHHHH HHHHHHHHLL LHHLLLHHLL LHHHHHHHHH
/CSP1   XXHHHHHHLL LHHLLLHHHH HHHLLLHHLL LHHHHHHHHH
/CSP2   XHHHHHHHHH HHHHHHHHHH HHHHHHHHLL LHHHHHHHHH
/CSP3   XHHHHHHHHH HHHHHHHHHH HHHHHHHHLL LHHHHHHHHH
/CSSC   XHHHHHHHHH HHHHHHHHHH HHHHHHHHHH HHHHHHHHHH
/GATB0 XHHHHHHHHH HHHHHHHHLL LHHLLLHHHL HHHHHHHHHH
/GATB1 XXHHHHHHHL HHHLLLHHHH HHHHHHHHHH HHHHHHHHHH
/GATB2 XHHHHHHHHH HHHHHHHHHH HHHHHHHHHH HHHHHHHHHH
/GATB3 XHHHHHHHHH HHHHHHHHHH HHHHHHHHHH HHHHHHHHHH
/GAT32 XHHHHHHHHH HHHHHHHHHH HHHLLLHHHL HHHHHHHHHH

Page :  2
        gg
/SEL    LL
/CYC    LH
/CMD    HH
 WR     LL
/CSP0   HH
/CSP1   HH
/CSP2   HH
/CSP3   HH
/CSSC   HH
/GATB0 HH
/GATB1 HH
/GATB2 HH
/GATB3 HH
/GAT32 HH
```

281004-33

April 1990

Designing a MULTIBUS® II CPU Board with the Message Passing Coprocessor (MPC)—82389

JOE BECKER
TECHNICAL MARKETING ENGINEER

TIM MOSTAD
TECHNICAL MARKETING MANAGER

Order Number: 281022-001

5

Designing a MULTIBUS® II CPU Board with the Message Passing Coprocessor (MPC)—82389

CONTENTS

PAGE

CONTENTS

PAGE

CHAPTER 1: INTRODUCTION

1.0 WHO SHOULD READ THIS DOCUMENT?

Readers of this document may be considering the design of an intelligent MULTIBUS II board. Concise descriptions of the various possibilities of a board's design are presented in this document, in particular, a focus on the use of the MPC (Message Passing Coprocessor or 82389), which provides a majority of the interface logic. Descriptions here represent summaries of other documentation available, and experience with the design of Intel's MULTIBUS II product line.

After reading this document, one will feel confident that the design of a MULTIBUS II CPU board is no more complex than the design of another bus system. Actually, it is much easier because of the use of the MPC; almost all of the necessary interface logic is buried in it. All that is needed is a little glue logic and buffering.

1.1 Overview

Before reading this document, the reader should have some exposure to the MULTIBUS II architecture, IEEE/ANSI 1296. Possibly this information has been gathered at a seminar or by looking at the bus specifications. Through either of these two means one might be aware of the parity bits that protect each of the various signal sets, arbitration logic, interconnect space, error indicators, etc. All of these features add up to a great deal of logic. If the control signals are fully understood, a fundamental read/write I/O board can be designed with an interface consisting of basic TTL and programmable logic devices. Since the signals are all synchronous to the bus clock and can easily be decoded it makes the design easy. However, designing a board with a microprocessor takes advantage of more advanced bus features and requires a little more work. The cost and real estate necessary to implement these features quickly make custom interface design prohibitive. The design of the MULTIBUS II Parallel System Bus, PSB, make it very reasonable to fabricate all bus functions in one VLSI device. The multiplexed signals, parity circuitry, arbitration logic, etc. are all interesting but unnecessary to deal with each time a board is being designed.

This application note will look at the various interfacing concerns of a CPU board's design and describe what the MPC provides and what the board designer needs to add.

1.2 Objectives

This application note is not intended to displace other documentation on the actual PSB bus operation or cover the internal operation of the MPC itself. The MPC interfacing required to connect to the PSB, the local CPU and the interconnect space capabilities of MULTIBUS II will be explained. The MPC is packaged in a 149-pin PGA (Pin Grid Array) package. In partitioning the pin functions of the MPC there are three major interfaces; the PSB interface, the local bus, and interconnect space (Figure 1). These are the activities to which most of the pins are allocated. The PSB interface is very straight-forward; there are few options for the designer. This makes that part of the board design simple. It also helps enforce compatibility with other boards. One has little latitude to make a mistake and develop an incompatibility problem.

The local bus interface of the MPC does offer the board designer a number of options. For instance, the local CPU might be 8-, 16-, or 32-bits. There are also DMA control lines and lines to assist in dual-port memory operation. Since the bus's design has its basis at Intel we would expect that the interface of the MPC to an Intel processor would be pretty well thought out, but what if a board design dictates a non-Intel processor? There are many boards being designed with other manufacturers' processors. For example, Huerikon Corp., Microbar Systems Inc., and Tadpole Technology all have developed CPU boards using the Motorola 68K microprocessor family.

The interconnect interface is intended to mate with the local bus of an 8051 series of microcontrollers. The 8051 coordinates the reset, configuration and diagnostics of the board. The design of interconnect space allows for some very powerful features to be designed into a board. With the capabilities of interconnect space it is possible to configure resources with software, enable or disable the board, provide imbedded diagnostics in the board, and at the very basic level provide machine readable information on the board's manufacturer, its part number and revision level. There is a companion application note (the MULTIBUS II Interconnect Design Guide, AP-423) that explores this subject in a lot of detail, so only the fundamentals of this MPC interconnect space interface will be described here.

After reading this application note, one should have a good basis for starting the detailed design of a unique board. Good Luck!

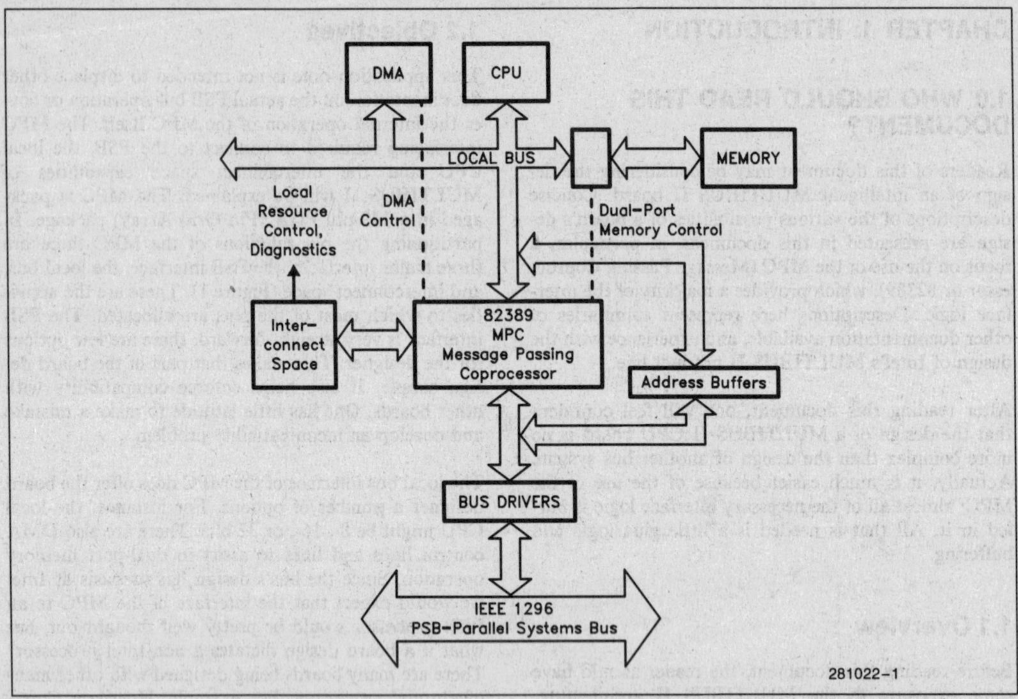

Figure 1. MPC Interfaces and Control Lines

CHAPTER 2: PSB INTERFACING

2.0 INTERFACING TO THE IEEE/ANSI 1296 PARALLEL SYSTEM BUS

All of the complex timing and control logic necessary to connect to the PSB are contained within the MPC. For the actual definition and operation of these control signals, refer to the IEEE/ANSI 1296 Specification. For the purposes of this application note, it is not necessary to understand all the signals, except in the case of reset and power fail situations, explained in section 2.2.2. There are a few mechanical orientation issues to be considered when laying out a board. These will be covered also.

2.1 IEEE/ANSI 1296 Fundamentals which must be Understood to Design a Board

The IEEE/ANSI 1296 description of MULTIBUS II defines very distinctly all the aspects of the PSB: the mechanical layout, the signal timings, signal drive capability, the bus protocol to other boards within the backplane, the backplane layout, etc. All boards are required to address the full 32-bit capability of the bus. Everything is well defined so that board designers will have few, if any, opportunities to develop incompatibilities between their boards and boards available from other vendors.

At a very fundamental level, the first thing that will impact design is the board size. The boards are based on the Eurocard format; the conventional size is 233.35mm (two connectors) x 220 mm deep. This is commonly referred to as a 6U board in the Eurocard style. This board format has two connectors, but all of the PSB requirements are satisified by one 96-pin DIN connector, referred to as P1 in Figure 2. P2 is uncommitted and allows flexibility for a unique design. This could include additional power requirements, specialized I/O, a subsystem interconnect bus, or whatever a unique design might require. For our purposes, P1 is the connector that we are interested in, so we will focus on the circuitry necessary to interface the MPC to the P1 connector.

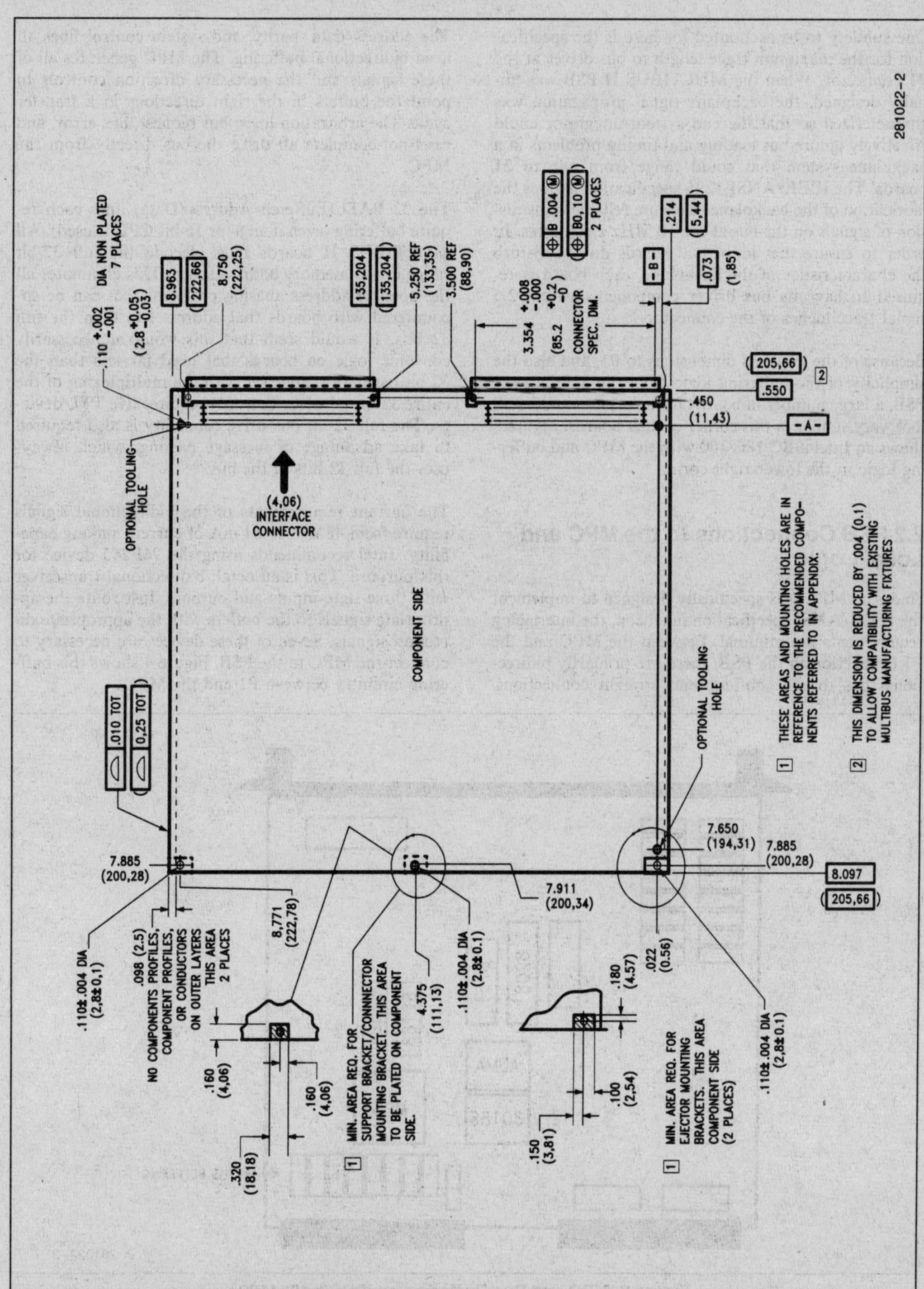

Figure 2. MULTIBUS®II Board Dimensions

One subtlety to be accounted for here is the specification for the maximum trace length to bus driver at the P1 connector. When the MULTIBUS II PSB was initially designed, the backplane signal propagation was characterized so that the end system integrator could effectively ignore bus loading and timing problems in a backplane system that could range from two to 21 boards. The IEEE/ANSI 1296 specification defines the fabrication of the backplane to ensure reliable transmission of signals on the bus at the 10 MHz clock rates. In order to ensure that individual boards do not disturb the characteristics of the backplane, each board is required to have its bus driver components within 2.5 signal trace inches of the connector.

Because of the required dimensions to P1, and also the simplicity of the buffering logic from the MPC to the PSB, a large number of boards from various vendors all look very similar in this corner of their boards. Figure 3 shows an Intel iSBC 186/100 with the MPC and buffering logic in the lower right corner.

2.2 PSB Connections to the MPC and Local Logic

Since the MPC was specifically designed to implement the IEEE/ANSI specification in silicon, the interfacing requirements are minimal. Between the MPC and the P1 connection to the PSB, there are primarily bidirectional bus drivers, buffers, and straight connections. The address/data, parity, and system control lines all need bidirectional buffering. The MPC generates all of these signals and the necessary direction controls to point the buffers in the right directions in a transfer cycle. The arbitration lines, bus request, bus error, and reset-not-complete all drive the bus directly from the MPC.

The 32 BAD (Buffered Address/Data) lines each require buffering (even if an 8- or 16-bit CPU is used). All MULTIBUS II boards must decode the full 32-bit range of the memory address space. This eliminates all the possible address aliasing problems that can be encountered with boards that address less than the full 32 bits. It would seem that this would unnecessarily consume logic on boards that need far less than the 32-bit capability, however with the multiplexing of the entire 32-bit interface this only requires five TTL devices. The full 32-bit bus drive capability is also required to take advantage of message passing, which always uses the full 32 bits of the bus.

The current requirements of the bidirectional signals require from 48 mA to 64 mA of current sinking capability. Intel recommends using the 74F245 device for this purpose. This is an octal, bidirectional transceiver with three-state inputs and outputs. Just route the appropriate signals to the buffers with the appropriate direction signals. Seven of these devices are necessary to connect the MPC to the PSB. Figure 4 shows this buffering circuitry between P1 and the MPC.

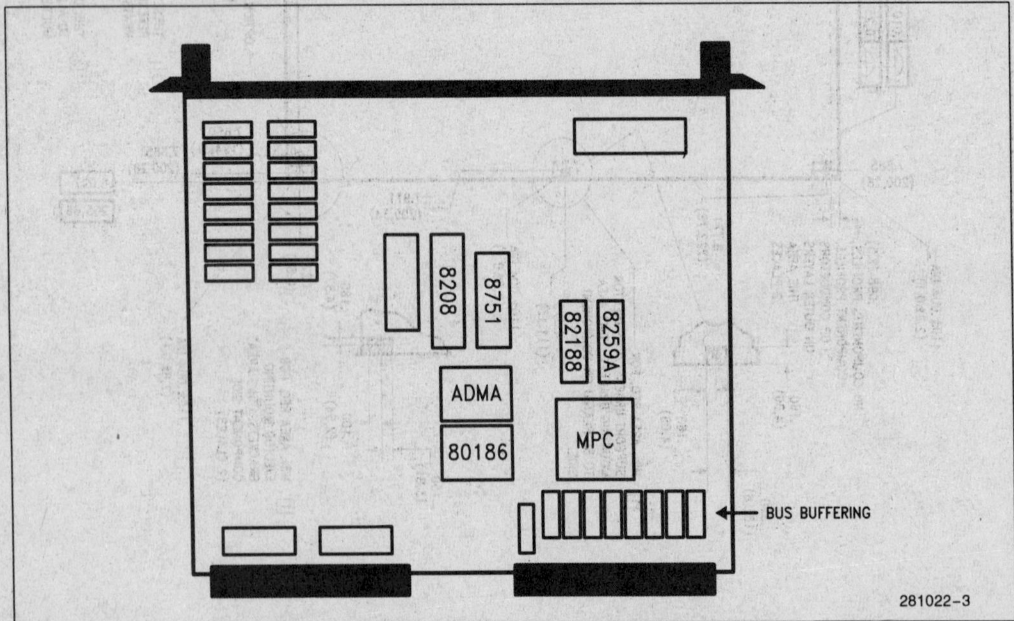

Figure 3. MPC and Bus Buffering on iSBC® 186/100

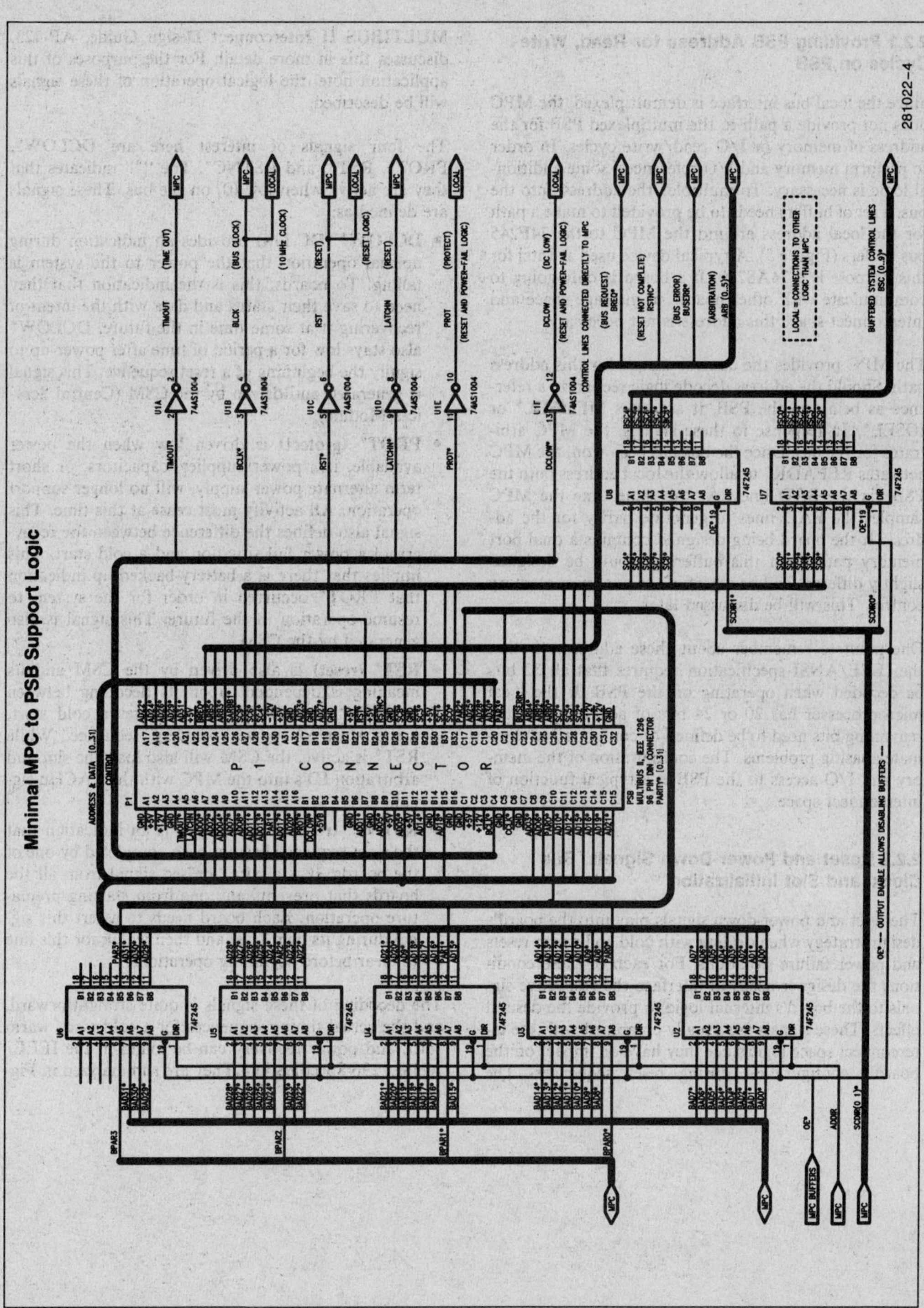

Figure 4. Circuitry between MPC and PSB

2.2.1 Providing PSB Address for Read, Write Cycles on PSB

Since the local bus interface is demultiplexed, the MPC does not provide a path to the multiplexed PSB for the address of memory or I/O read/write cycles. In order to perform memory and I/O references, some additional logic is necessary. To multiplex the address onto the bus, a set of buffers needs to be provided to make a path for the local address around the MPC to the 74F245 bus buffers (Figure 5). A typical device used at Intel for this purpose is a 74AS240. If a board is only going to communicate with other boards in message space and interconnect space this address is not necessary.

The MPC provides the control signals for this address path. Should the address decode logic recognize a reference as being on the PSB, it activates MEMSEL* or IOSEL*. In response to these signals, the MPC arbitrates for the bus. Once the bus has been won, the MPC activates REFADR* to allow the local address onto the PSB via the BAD lines. At the same time the MPC samples the BAD lines to generate parity for the address. If the board being designed contains a dual port memory path, then this buffering would be designed slightly different and be a part of the dual port memory control. This will be discussed later.

One point to remember about these addresses is that the IEEE/ANSI specification requires that all 32 bits be decoded when operating on the PSB. If the local microprocessor has 20 or 24 bits of address, then the remaining bits need to be defined or configured to eliminate aliasing problems. The configuration of the memory and I/O access to the PSB is a typical function of interconnect space.

2.2.2 Reset and Power-Down Signals, Bus Clock, and Slot Initialization

The reset and power-down signals play into the board's design strategy when dealing with cold and warm resets and power failure situations. For each of these conditions the designer needs to interface the respective signals to the board's internal logic to provide the desired effects. These signals are usually combined with the interconnect space logic since they have an impact on the board's configuration during reset sequences. The MULTIBUS II Interconnect Design Guide, AP-423, discusses this in more detail. For the purposes of this application note, the logical operation of these signals will be described.

The four signals of interest here are DCLOW*, PROT*, RST*, and RSTNC*. The "*" indicates that they are active when low (0) on the bus. These signals are defined as:

- **DCLOW* (DC low)** provides an indication during normal operation that the power to the system is falling. To boards, this is the indication that they need to save their status and data with the intent of recovering it at some time in the future. DCLOW* also stays low for a period of time after power-up to signify the beginning of a reset sequence. This signal is generated and driven by the CSM (Central Services Module).
- **PROT* (protect)** is driven low when the power available, i.e., power supplies, capacitors, or short term alternate power supply, will no longer support operation. All activity must cease at this time. This signal also defines the difference between the recovery of a power fail situation and a cold start. This implies that there is a battery-backed-up indication that PROT* occurred in order for the system to resume operation in the future. This signal is also generated by the CSM.
- **RST* (reset)** is also driven by the CSM and its meaning is dependent upon its decoding between DCLOW* and PROT*. It indicates a cold start, warm start, or power recovery sequence. While RST* is active, the CSM will also load the slot and arbitration ID's into the MPC with the LACHn signal.
- **RSTNC* (reset not complete)** is an indication that the reset sequence has not been completed by one of the boards. It is a wire "or"-ed signal from all the boards that prevents any one from starting premature operation. Each board needs to assert this signal during its own reset and then watch for this line to clear before beginning operations.

The decoding of these signals is quite straightforward, and the actual timing sequences for a cold start, warm start, and power recovery can be found in the IEEE/ANSI 1296 Specification. They are summarized in Figure 6.

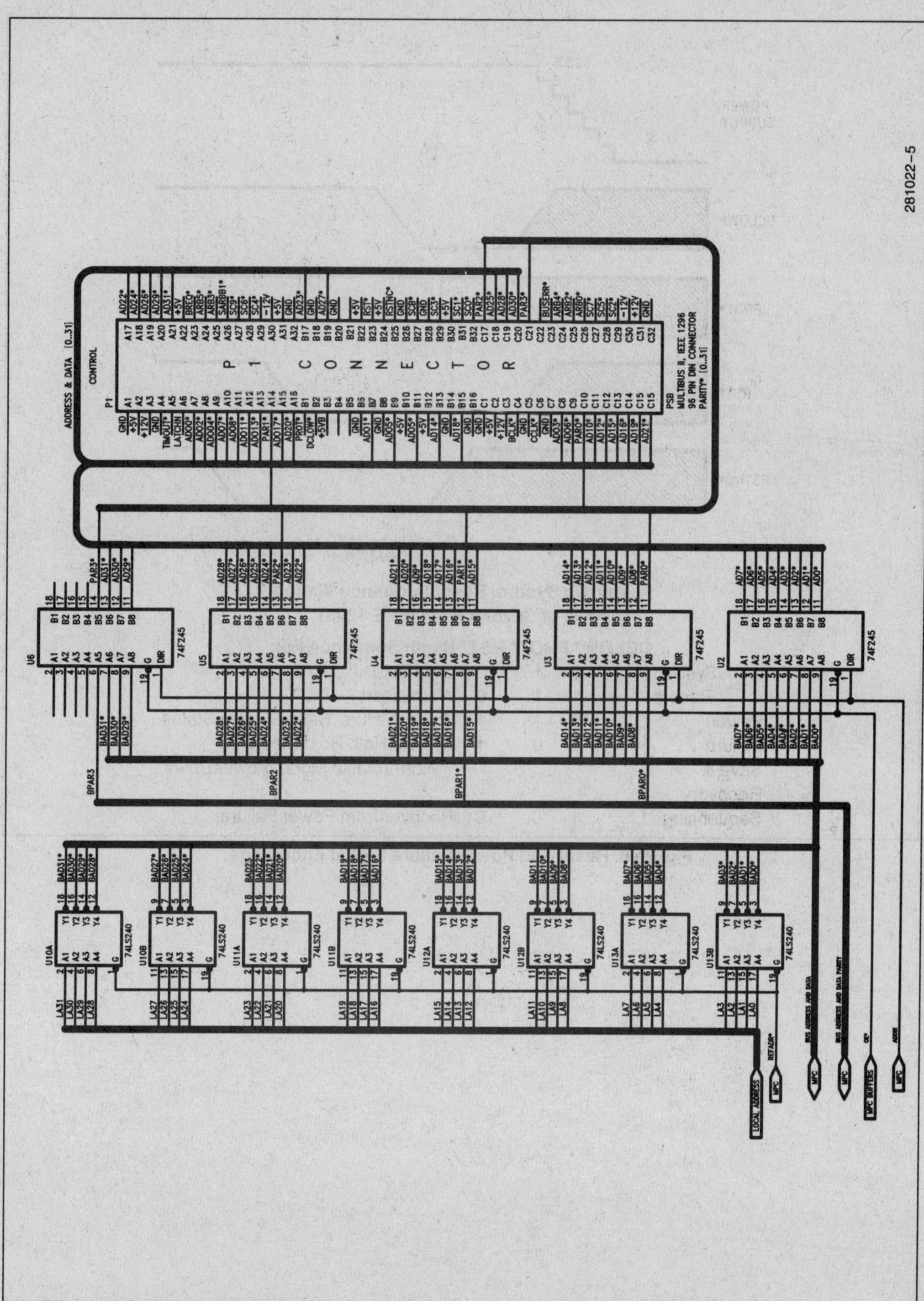

Figure 5. Providing PSB Address for Read/Write Cycles on the PSB

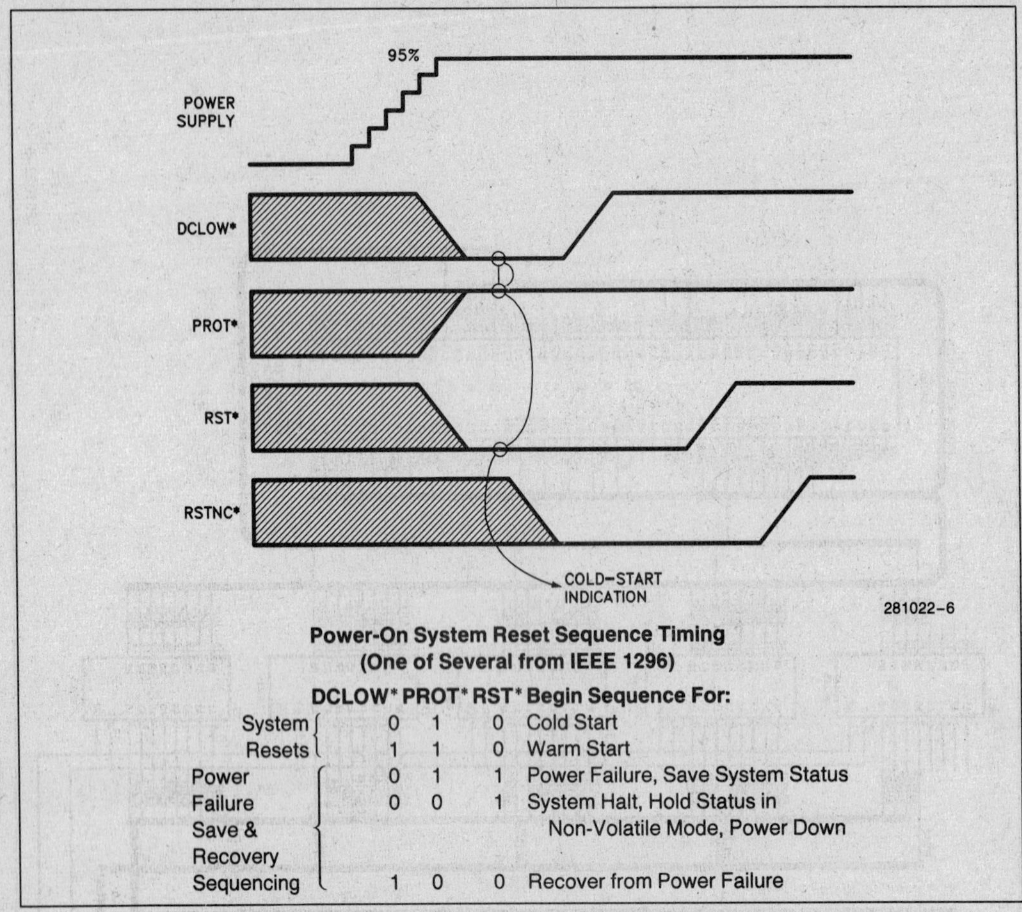

Power-On System Reset Sequence Timing
(One of Several from IEEE 1296)

	DCLOW*	PROT*	RST*	Begin Sequence For:
System Resets	0	1	0	Cold Start
	1	1	0	Warm Start
Power Failure Save & Recovery Sequencing	0	1	1	Power Failure, Save System Status
	0	0	1	System Halt, Hold Status in Non-Volatile Mode, Power Down
	1	0	0	Recover from Power Failure

Figure 6. Reset and Power Failure Signal Encodings

The RST*, DCLOW*, and PROT* signals typically are buffered by a 74AS1004 device. The RSTNC* signal is connected directly from the MPC to the PSB. RESET is carried from the RST* buffer directly to the MPC, then the three of these signals combined drive the reset control logic of the board.

There is another signal, LACHn*, which is driven by the CSM during the reset sequence. During the time that the RST* time is held low, the CSM is going through the backplane, loading the card slot and arbitration ID's into each MPC.

This LACHn line is also buffered by the same 74AS1004 device as the reset of the reset signals, and it is simply connected to the MPC. With this signal, the CSM is presenting the arbitration and card slot ID's to the MPC over the arbitration lines during the reset sequence. Within the backplane, each slot has its LACHn line connected to the unique AD (address data) line that is equal to the slot number in the backplane. The CMS pulls the appropriate AD line low and the LACHn line in that slot will go low, loading the ID's on the ARB lines. This is handled automatically by the MPC. You can refer to the IEEE/ANSI 1296 Specification for more details.

There are only two other signals which need buffering to the MPC. The first is TIMOUT*, which provides an indication to the MPC that a bus timeout has occurred. It is buffered by the 74AS1004 and it connects directly to the MPC. BCLK* is the second signal and it is also buffered by the same 74AS1004 and passed on to the MPC. This clock is used for all synchronous internal MPC timing.

At this point we have added one 74AS1004 to the seven 74F245 bidirectional buffers, to complete the connection of the MPC to the PSB. These buffering devices need to be connected as closely as possible to the PSB and MPC, so that the bus timing is not disturbed. Intel boards provide good examples of the layouts of these components.

Chapter 3: INTERCONNECT SPACE IMPLEMENTATION CIRCUITRY

3.0 THE CONCEPT OF INTERCONNECT SPACE

The incorporation of the interconnect space circuitry (also referred to as geographical addressing in some buses) makes it easier for a systems integrator to configure a board into a system. Jumpers which might typically be used to configure board resources can be placed under software control. By configuring with software, errors in jumpers are eliminated during manufacturing and field modifications are simplified. Also within the concept of interconnect space is the ability to enable or disable boards in fault situations. Board diagnostics can also be enhanced since more options can be tested without hardware configuration. For the purposes of this application note, the hardware employed in interconnect space will be described in an example. For more information on interconnect space, Intel Application Note AP-423 describes in more detail the hardware and software associated with this concept. This is an area where tremendous value can be added to a board's design that will greatly benefit its users.

3.1.1 INTERFACING BETWEEN THE MPC AND 8751 MICROCONTROLLER

A typical first question of a new MULTIBUS II board designer is "Why is there a microcontroller on each board in addition to the microprocessor?" As it turns out, using a microcontroller to implement interconnect space becomes very efficient from a real estate point of view and adds to the capability that can be included in interconnect space. This microcontroller will reset the microprocessor, configure resources on the board, and run board diagnostics in conjunction with the microprocessor. The microcontroller actually translates many complex functions into what appears to be a uniform set of registers. Other boards can then access these standardized registers to learn its configuration or request it to execute diagnostics. In addition, the microcontroller simplifies system configuration and diagnostics software.

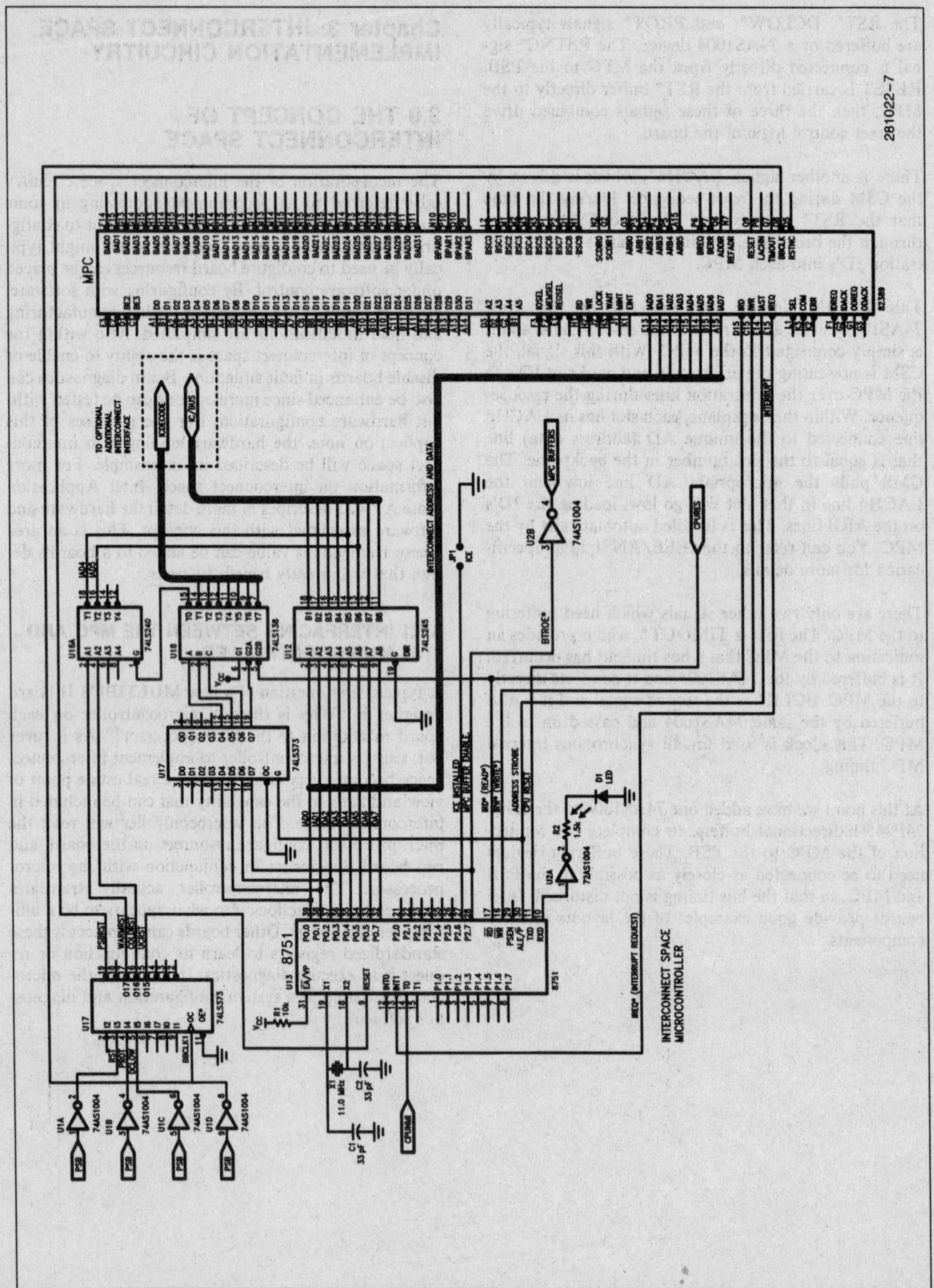

Figure 7. 8751—MPC Interconnect Space Circuitry Example

The MPC is designed to connect directly to the data bus of an 8751. Figure 7 shows typical 8751-MPC interconnect circuitry. The address/data bus, labeled IAD <0...7>, is used to transfer data and addresses between the 8751 and the MPC. The data and address transfer operations are controlled by the control lines labeled read, write, strobe, and interrupt. A typical interconnect operation is triggered by the MPC recognizing an interconnect space address from the local CPU or the PSB. The MPC then sends an interrupt request to the microcontroller telling it that an interconnect access needs to take place. After the interrupt request, the microcontroller reads the address and data off the address/data bus, then executes the appropriate interconnect service routine.

Figure 8 shows a diagram for interconnect bus timing. Both a read and a write diagram are presented. In both the read and write operations the microcontroller sends the IAST (strobe) signal to the MPC telling it that there is a valid address on the bus. The MPC will then latch the address into its buffer. At this point, when a read operation needs to occur, the microcontroller will send an IRD* (read) signal to the MPC, signalling that it wants to read data from the address specified. The MPC will then supply data to the microcontroller from the specified address. Conversely, if a write operation needs to occur, the IWR* (write) signal is sent to the MPC indicating that the microcontroller wants to send information to the specified address via the MPC. The MPC will then proceed to receive data from the microcontroller and send it to the specified address.

3.1.2 CONTROLLING BOARD RESOURCE CONFIGURATIONS THROUGH INTERCONNECT SPACE

Board designers will configure local board resources through interconnect space. Figure 7 indicates an additional branch off the address/data bus. This branch is the address/data bus to other configuration devices, or status indicators on the board. In addition, LIAD0.2 of the bus branches to a decoder which will coordinate selection of the particular device. The one path shown to U16A allows the 8751 to read whether a warm or cold reset is occurring. More details of these operations can be found in the MPC User's Manual, 286/100A User's Guide, and Application Note AP-423.

3.1.3 RESET OPERATIONS

The reset PAL is used to coordinate the reset operations. Figure 7 displays the control signals for the reset PAL and the associated output of the PAL. Reset signals are received over the PSB and decoded through the reset PAL. The reset PAL is able to generate a cold-reset or a warm-reset. The reset PAL also resets the 8751, which starts it through its reset sequence. One of the first things it determines is what type of reset is occurring. When address/data lines <0–2> are all low, it causes a 3 x 8 decoder to enable the U16A buffer, putting the cold or warm reset signal on the bus of the 8751. Once on the address/data bus, the microcontroller and MPC read this signal and execute the appropriate reset sequence.

The condition of a cold start reset causes all functions of the system to act as an original power-on condition. Furthermore, the MPC and interconnect registers are set to their default values, and any initialization checks will occur. A warm start is usually caused by the human operator pressing the reset button while there is power to the system. The sequence of events are the same for a warm and cold start, however, a warm start will not modify interconnect registers or memory, and initialization checks are not executed.

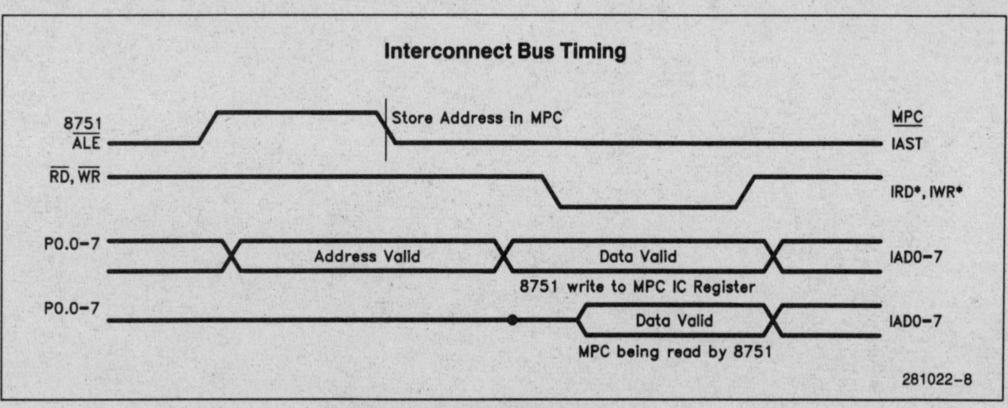

Figure 8. Interconnect Bus Timing

CHAPTER 4: INTEL® MICROPROCESSOR INTERFACING EXAMPLES

Interfacing a microprocessor to the MPC is very similar to the interface that occurs typically between a microprocessor and a peripheral device. The notable differences, in addition to the fact that it has a lot of registers, are that the MPC:

- Supports a 32-bit data path,
- Provides support for generic microprocessor signals, lock, mem, and I/O sel, etc. to pass through to the PSB,
- Has byte-enable lines allowing 8-, 16-, or 32-bit microprocessors of different architectures to interface to the MPC and the PSB.

Examples of some interface possibilities are described for various Intel microprocessors in the subsequent sections.

4.1 80186 Interface Example

The signals required to interface the 80186 to the MPC are all shown in Figure 9.

Starting at the top of the MPC, the byte-enable lines (BE) are set for a 16-bit microprocessor; BE2 and BE3 are tied high to allow the microprocessor to address the MPC registers or the PSB via the two lower bytes, D0–D15, of the data lines. A0, *BHE, allow the 80186 to transfer 8 or 16 bits of data appropriately across D0–D15. Both the 80186 Hardware Reference Guide and the MPC User's Manual describe these signals in more detail.

The data lines AD <0...15> map from the 80186 to the MPC. The data on these lines is appropriately timed with the read and write lines of the 80186, however the 80186 multiplexes address and data and the appropriate address for the MPC register needs to be picked off these lines with the ALE signal. The 74L573 is recommended for this function.

The function of the Decode Logic element is to capture the address coming out of the 80186 and, using the 80186 status signals, decide if the address is a PSB I/O (IOSEL), PSB Memory (MEMSEL), or MPC Register (REGSEL). The read and write signals would drive the data to its appropriate destination.

The signal (LOCK*) locks the bus from other microprocessors during semaphore operations and (WAIT*) holds off the 80186, until the MPC and the addressed resource on the bus are ready to be read or written.

Two interrupts can be generated by the MPC: MINT will go active to the CPU if there is an outstanding message operation. EINT is asserted if there are errors which occurred in memory, I/O, or Interconnect space. Both of these would require software routines to appropriately handle the situation.

The 80186 possesses the ability to perform DMA operations. If cost must be kept to a minimum and/or real estate is very limited, the use of a separate DMA controller, therefore, is not necessary if the 80186 is implemented. In order for the 80186 to accomplish DMA, DRQ0 and DRQ1 of the 80186 must be tied directly to the DMA request lines of the MPC. Each request line of the 80186 controls a DMA channel. In Figure 9, channel 0 of the 80186 is used for DMA input to the MPC and channel 1 is used for the output to the 80186.

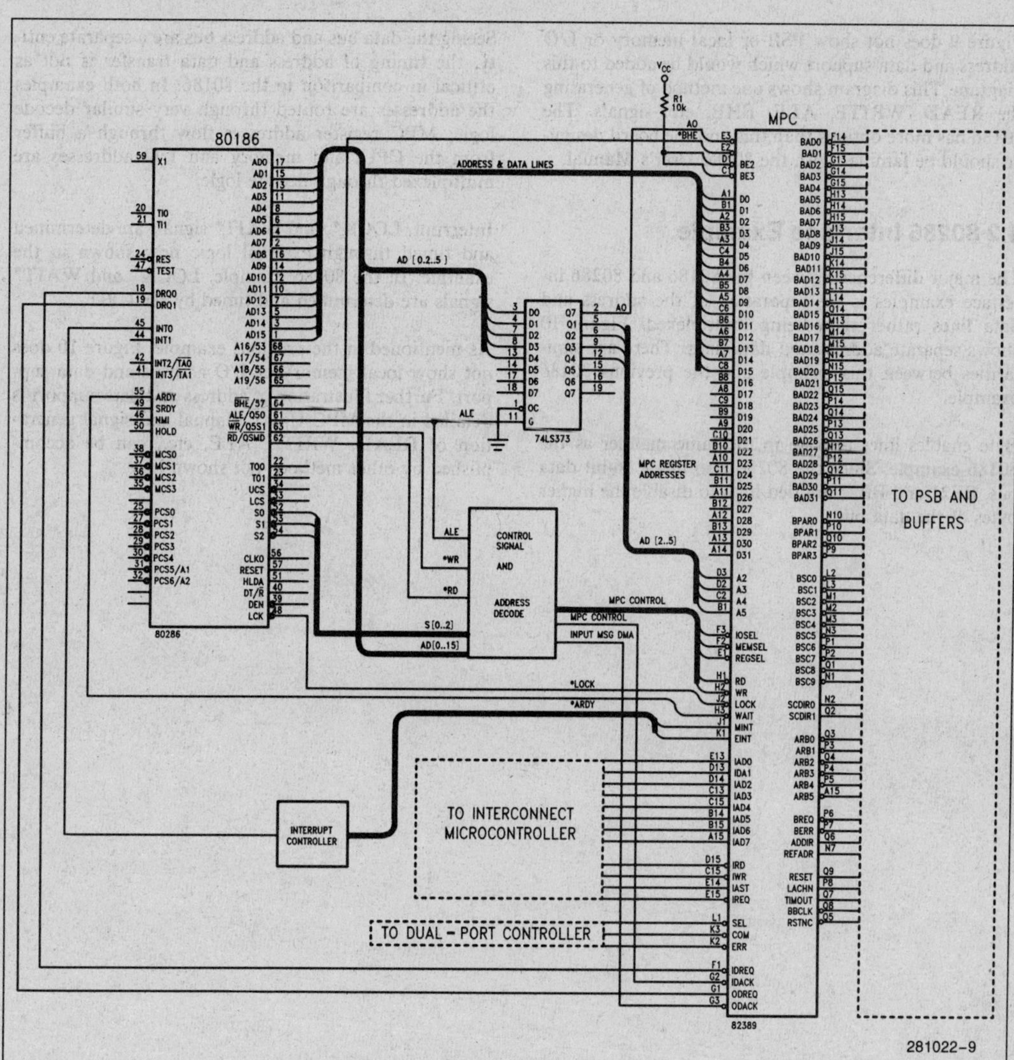

Figure 9. 80186—MPC Interface Example

5

Figure 9 does not show PSB or local memory or I/O address and data support which would be added to this diagram. This diagram shows one method of generating the READ, WRITE, ALE, BHE, etc. signals. The 80186 has more options than this and the board designer should be familiar with the 80186 User's Manual.

4.2 80286 Interface Example

The major difference between the 80186 and 80286 interface examples is the separation of the address and data lines rather than being multiplexed. Figure 10 shows separate address and data lines. There are similarities between this example and the previous 80186 example.

Byte enables lines operate in the same manner as the 80186 example. Since the 80286 also has a 16-bit data bus, BE2* and BE3* are tied high to disable the higher bytes of the data bus.

Seeing the data bus and address bus are a separate entity, the timing of address and data transfer is not as critical in comparison to the 80186. In both examples the addresses are routed through very similar decode logic; MPC register addresses flow through a buffer from the CPU, and memory and I/O addresses are multiplexed through decode logic.

Interrupt, LOCK*, and WAIT* signals are determined and timed through external logic now shown in the example. In the 80186 example, LOCK* and WAIT* signals are determined and timed by the CPU.

As mentioned in the previous example, Figure 10 does not show local memory or I/O address and data support. Further illustration of address and data support is detailed in the MPC User's Manual and signal generation of READ, WRITE, ALE, etc., can be accomplished by other methods not shown here.

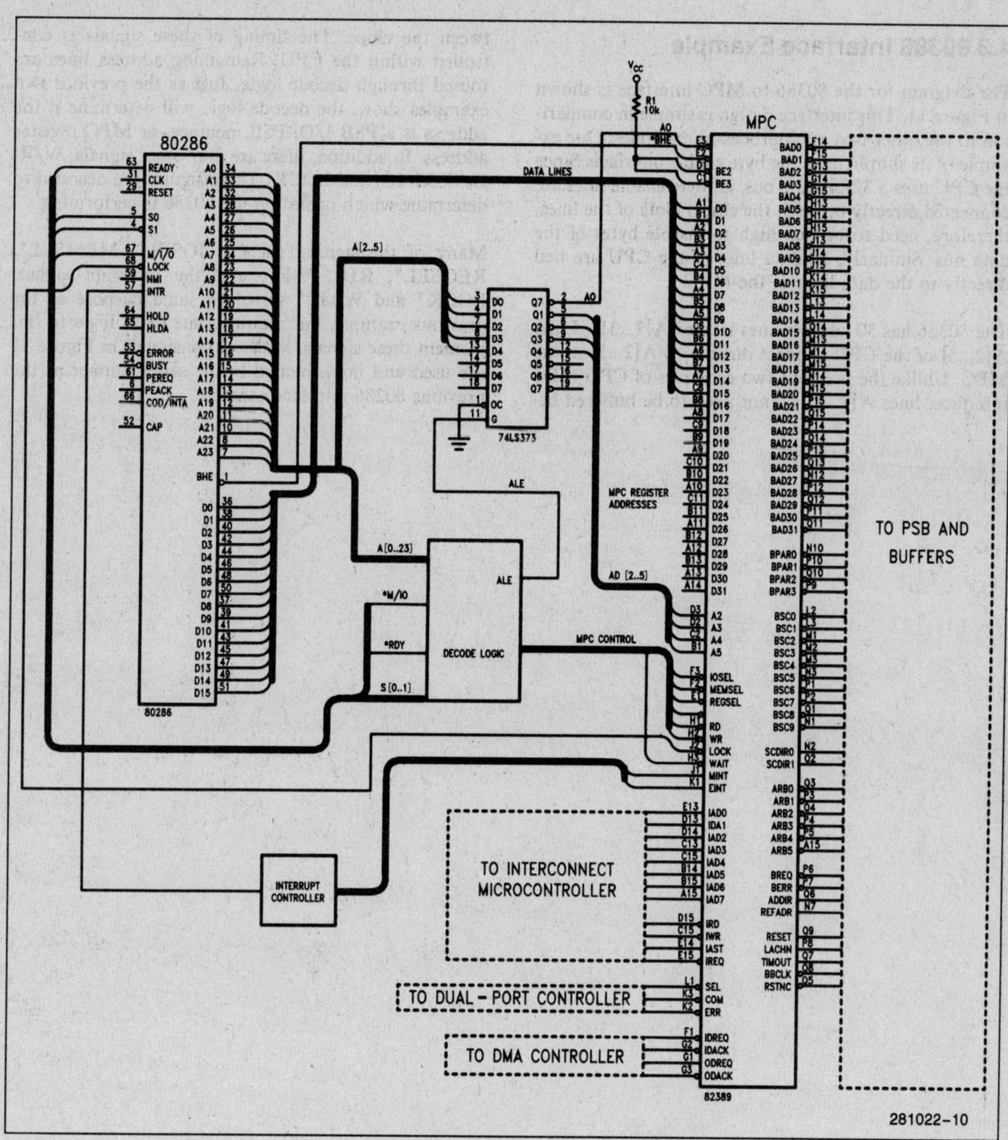

Figure 10. 80286— MPC Interface Example

4.3 80386 Interface Example

The diagram for the 80386 to MPC interface is shown in Figure 11. This interface design is simple in comparison to the other two microprocessor examples. One example of its simplicity is the byte enable interface. Since the CPU uses a 32-bit data bus, all byte enable lines are connected directly between the chips. Note of the lines, therefore, need to be tied high to disable bytes of the data bus. Similarly, all data lines of the CPU are tied directly to the data lines of the MPC.

The 80386 has 30 address lines labeled A[2...31]. Lines A[2...5] of the CPU connect directly to A[2...5] of the MPC. Unlike the previous two examples of CPU MPC interface, lines A[2...5] do not need to be buffered between the chips. The timing of these signals is controlled within the CPU. Remaining address lines are routed through decode logic. Just as the previous two examples show, the decode logic will determine if the address is a PSB I/O, PSB memory, or MPC register address. In addition, there are four other signals: W/R, D/C, M/IO, and LOCK. These signals are decoded to determine which operation the 80386 is performing.

Many of the signals, such as IOSEL*, MEMSEL*, REGSEL*, RD*, WR*, and the interrupt signals LOCK* and WAIT* serve the same purpose as the previous example, but require some extra logic to implement these signals. Many of the signals in Figure 11 are used and implemented in the same manner as the previous 80286 interface example.

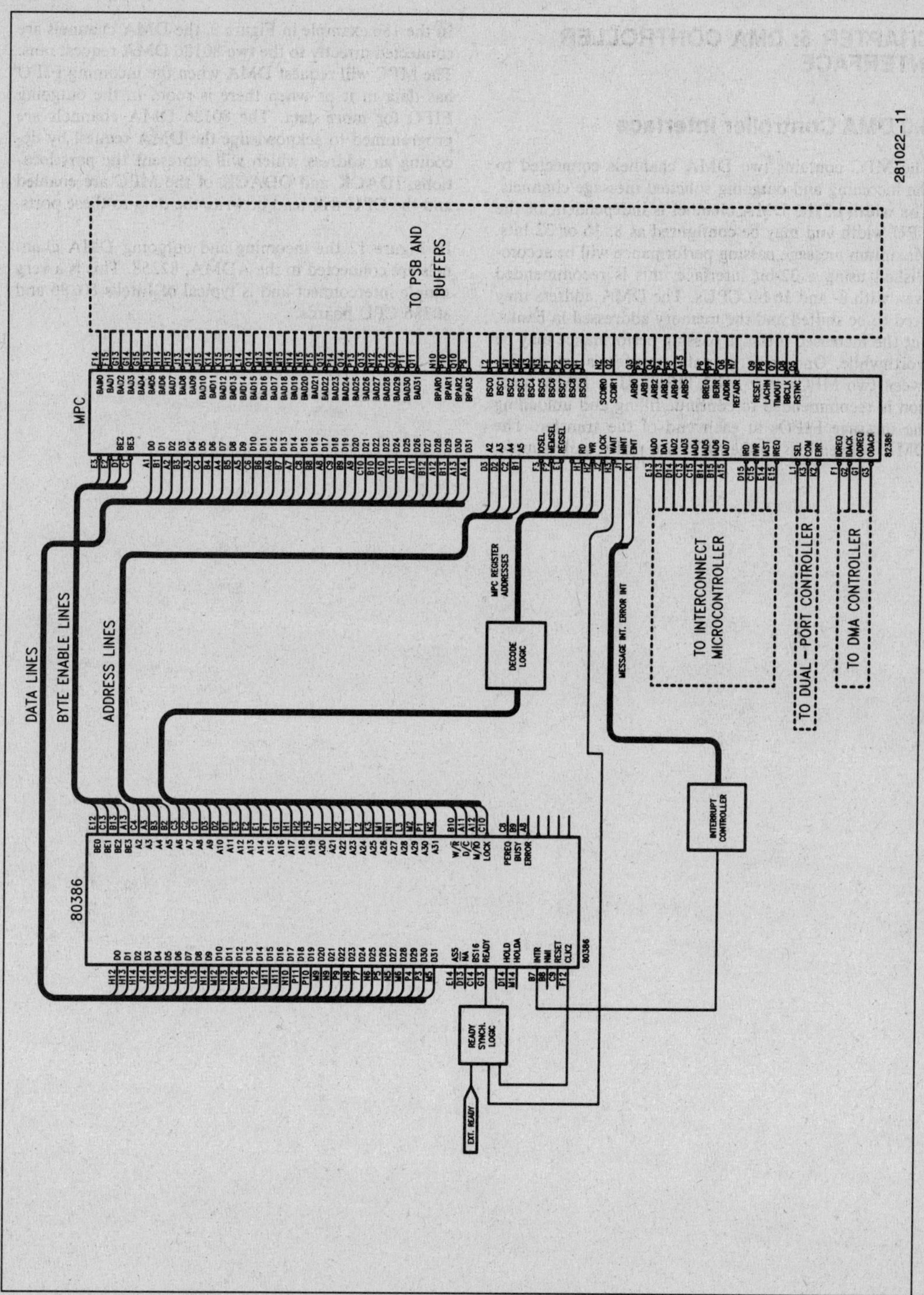

Figure 11. 80386—MPC Interface Example

CHAPTER 5: DMA CONTROLLER INTERFACE

5.0 DMA Controller Interface

The MPC contains two DMA channels connected to the incoming and outgoing solicited message channels. The width of the DMA channel is independent of the CPU width and may be configured as 8, 16 or 32 bits. Maximum message passing performance will be accomplished using a 32-bit interface; this is recommended even with 8- and 16-bit CPUs. The DMA address may need to be shifted and the memory addressed in banks, but the increased message passing performance may be worthwhile. Once a large data transfer is set up between two MPCs over MULTIBUS II, a DMA function is recommended to continue filling and unloading the message FIFOs at each end of the transfer. The DMA connections to the MPC are really quite simple.

In the 186 example in Figure 9, the DMA channels are connected directly to the two 80186 DMA request pins. The MPC will request DMA when the incoming FIFO has data in it or when there is room in the outgoing FIFO for more data. The 80186 DMA channels are programmed to acknowledge the DMA request by decoding an address which will represent the port locations. IDACK and ODACK of the MPC are enabled and the CPU will read or write the data to these ports.

In Figure 12 the incoming and outgoing DMA channels are connected to the ADMA, 82258. This is a very simple interconnect and is typical of Intel's 80286 and 80386 CPU boards.

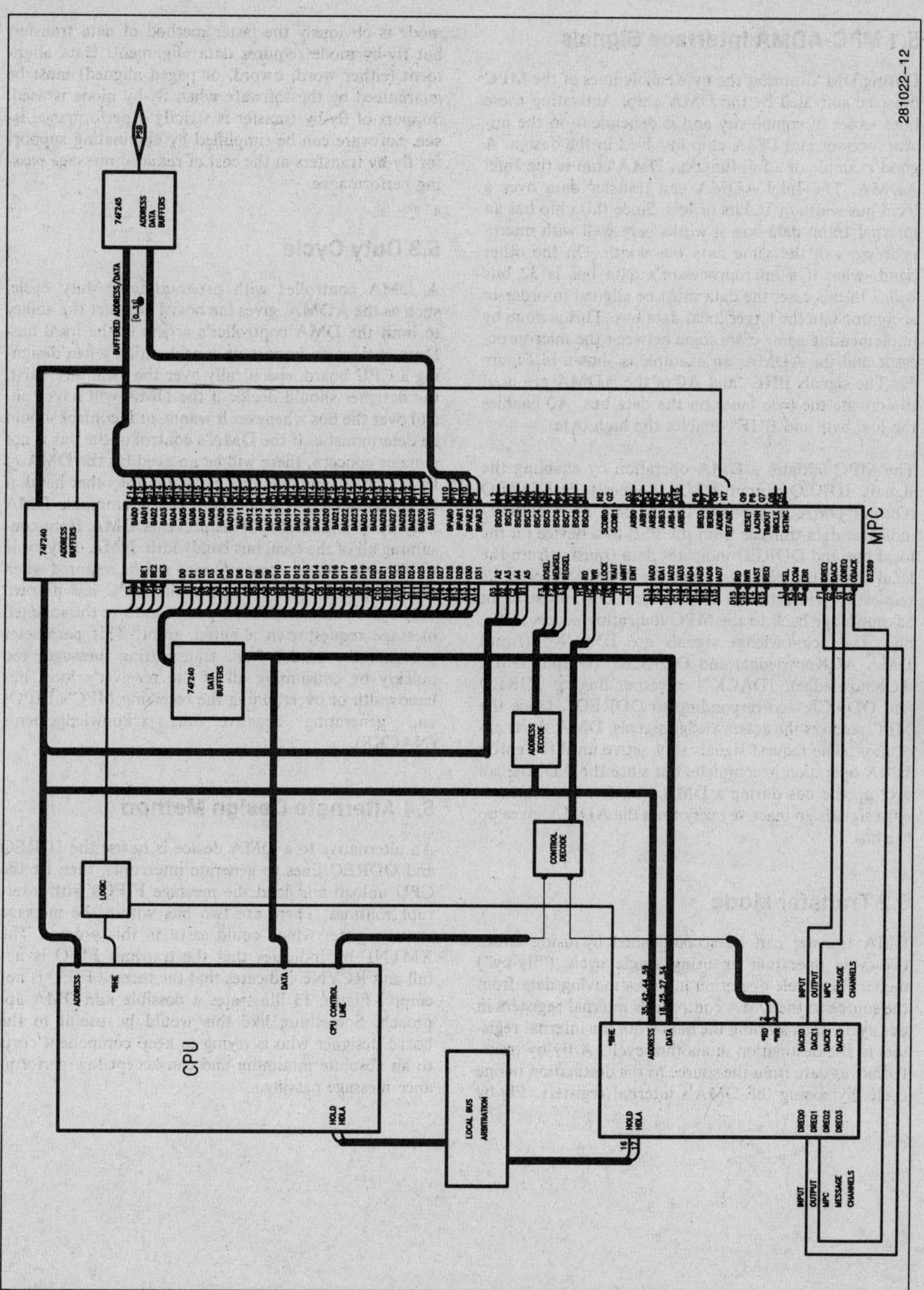

Figure 12. ADMA—MPC DMA Interface

5.1 MPC-ADMA Interface Signals

During DMA transfer the byte enable lines of the MPC must be activated by the DMA chip. Activating these lines varies in complexity and is dependent on the microprocessor and DMA chip involved in the design. A good example of a full-function DMA chip is the Intel ADMA. The Intel ADMA can transfer data over a local bus width of 16 bits or less. Since this chip has an internal 16-bit data bus, it works very well with microprocessors of the same data bus width. On the other hand, what if a microprocessor's data bus is 32 bits wide? In this case, the data must be aligned in order to accommodate the larger local data bus. This is done by implementing some extra logic between the microprocessor and the ADMA; an example is shown in Figure 12. The signals BHE* and A0 of the ADMA are used to activate the byte lanes on the data bus. A0 enables the low byte and BHE* enables the high byte.

The MPC initiates a DMA operation by enabling the signals IDREQ (Input DMA Request) or ODREQ (Output DMA Request) to the ADMA chip. IDREQ indicates data transfer from the PSB to a device on the local bus and ODREQ indicates data transfer from the local bus to the PSB bus. Once the ADMA receives its request, it will arbitrate for the local bus and send an acknowledge back to the MPC indicating access to the bus. The acknowledge signals are IDACK* (Input DMA ACKnowledge) and ODACK* (Output DMA ACKnowledge), IDACK* corresponding to IDREQ and ODACK* corresponding to ODREQ*. Once the MPC receives the acknowledge signals, DMA starts execution. The request signals stay active until the entire DMA operation is complete, but since the ADMA can give up the bus during a DMA transfer, the acknowledge signals go inactive every time the ADMA gives up the bus.

5.2 Transfer Mode

DMA transfer can be accomplished by using either two-cycle operation or using single cycle ("fly-by") mode. Two-cycle operation involves moving data from the source to the DMA controller's internal registers in one cycle, then sending the data from the internal registers to the destination in another cycle. A fly-by transfer moves data from the source to the destination in one cycle, bypassing the DMA's internal registers. Fly-by mode is obviously the faster method of data transfer, but fly-by mode requires data alignment. Data alignment (either word, dword, or paged aligned) must be guaranteed by the software when fly-by mode is used. Support of fly-by transfer is strictly a performance issue. Software can be simplified by eliminating support for fly-by transfers at the cost of reduced message passing performance.

5.3 Duty Cycle

A DMA controller with programmable duty cycle, such as the ADMA, gives the board designer the ability to limit the DMA controller's access to the local bus. Duty cycle is an important consideration when designing a CPU board, specifically over the local bus. First, the designer should decide if the DMA will have control over the bus whenever it wants, or if control should be deterministic. If the DMA's control of the bus is not a major concern, there will be no need for the DMA to have a programmable duty cycle. On the other hand, if local bus latency is a concern, a programmable DMA duty cycle is desirable. This prevents DMA from consuming all of the local bus bandwidth. DMA duty cycle (to throttle message passing) may not be required when designing with the MPC since the MPC has its own duty cycle parameter that is passed back to the solicited message requestor in a buffer grant. This parameter prevents the sender from transmitting messages too quickly by consuming all of the receiver's local bus bandwidth or overrunning the receiving MPC's FIFOs and generating negative bus acknowledgements (NACKS).

5.4 Alternate Design Method

An alternative to a DMA device is to use the IDREQ and ODREQ lines to generate interrupts, then let the CPU unload and load the message FIFOs with interrupt routines. There are two bits within the message status register which could assist in this process. The XMTNF bit indicates that the transmit FIFO is not full and RCVNE indicates that the receive FIFO is not empty. Figure 13 illustrates a possible non-DMA approach. Something like this would be useful to the board designer who is trying to keep component costs to an absolute minimum and can accept low performance message passing.

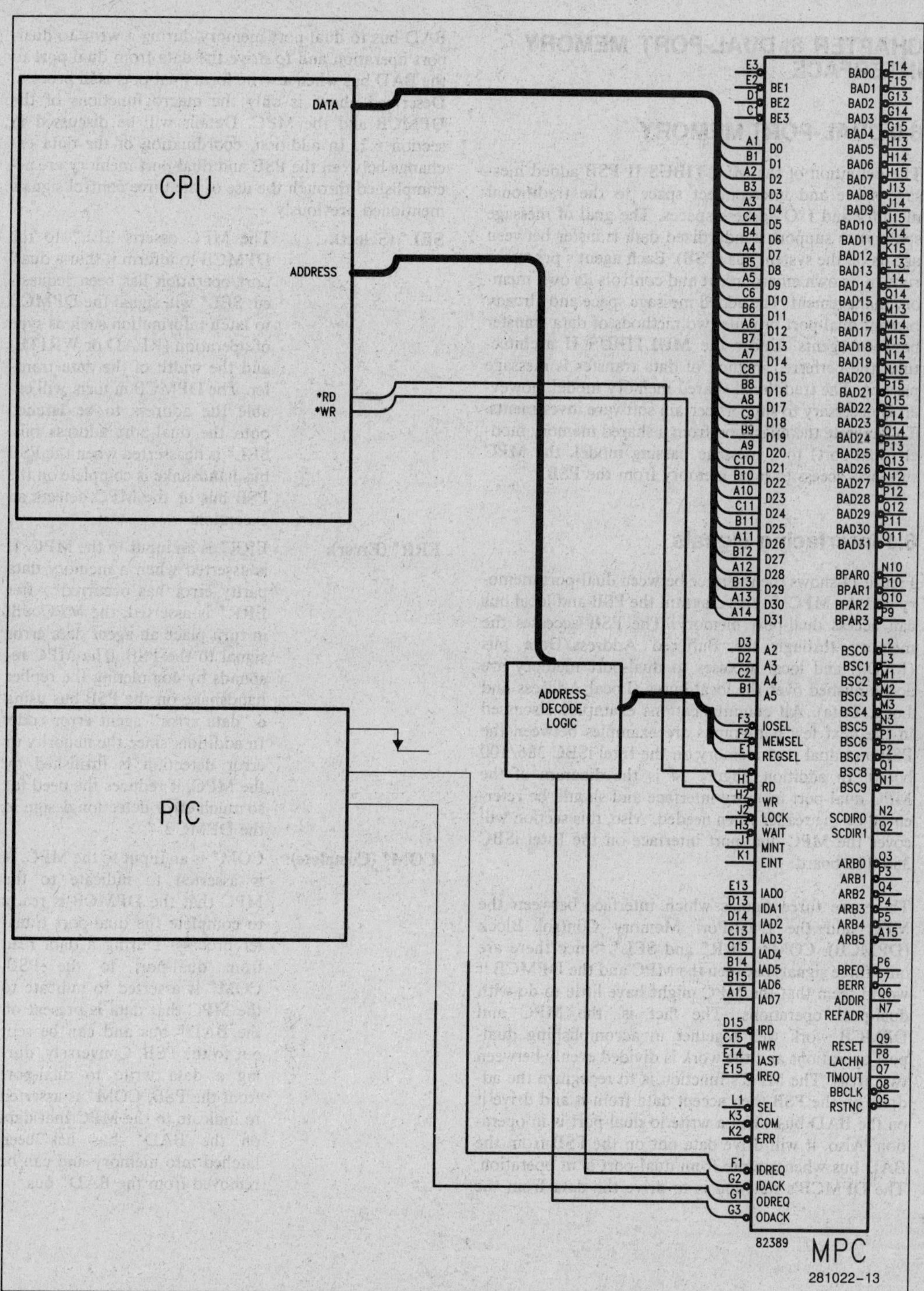

Figure 13. Servicing Message FIFOs without a DMA Controller

CHAPTER 6: DUAL-PORT MEMORY INTERFACE

6.0 DUAL-PORT MEMORY

The definition of the MULTIBUS II PSB added message space and interconnect space to the traditional memory and I/O address spaces. The goal of message space is to support standardized data transfer between agents on the system bus (PSB). Each agent's processor runs in its own environment and controls its own memory management. The added message space and already present dual-port provide two methods of data transfer between agents. Under the MULTIBUS II architecture, the perferred method of data transfer is message passing. The traditional shared memory model, however, is necessary to support certain software investments. To facilitate the migration from a shared memory model (dual-port) to a message passing model, the MPC supports access to local memory from the PSB.

6.1 Interfacing Signals

Figure 14 shows the interface between dual-port memory and the MPC. In this diagram the PSB and local bus can access dual-port memory. The PSB accesses the memory through the Buffered Address/Data bus (BAD*) and local accesses to dual-port memory are accomplished over the local buses (Local Address and Local Data). All communications examples discussed in the next few paragraphs are examples between the PSB and dual-port memory on the Intel iSBC 386/100 board. In addition, Figure 14 is the diagram of the MPC dual-port memory interface and should be referenced by the reader when needed. Also, this section will cover the MPC dual-port interface on the Intel iSBC 386/116 board.

There are three signals which interface between the MPC and the Dual-Port Memory Control Block (DPMCB): COM*, ERR* and SEL*. Since there are only three signals between the MPC and the DPMCB it would seem that the MPC might have little to do with dual-port operations. The fact is, the MPC and DPMCB work well together in accomplishing dual-port operations and the work is divided evenly between two areas. The MPC's function is to recognize the address on the PSB then accept data from it and drive it on the BAD bus when a write to dual-port is in operation. Also, it will drive data out on the PSB from the BAD bus when a write from dual-port is in operation. The DPMCB's function is to drive the data from the BAD bus to dual-port memory during a write to dual-port operation and to drive the data from dual-port to the BAD bus when a write form dual-port is in process. Described above is only the macro functions of the DPMCB and the MPC. Details will be discussed in section 6.2. In addition, coordination of the data exchange between the PSB and dual-port memory are accomplished through the use of the three control signals mentioned previously.

SEL* (Select): The MPC asserts SEL* to the DPMCB to inform it that a dual-port operation has been requested. SEL* will signal the DPMCB to latch information such as type of operation (READ or WRITE) and the width of the data transfer. The DPMCB in turn, will enable the address to be latched onto the dual-port address bus. SEL* is deasserted when the PSB bus handshake is complete on the PSB bus or the MPC detects an exception.

ERR* (Error): ERR* is an input to the MPC. It is asserted when a memory data parity error has occurred. After ERR* is asserted, the MPC will in turn place an agent data error signal to the PSB. The MPC responds by completing the replier handshake on the PSB bus using a "data error" agent error code. In addition, since the majority or error detection is furnished by the MPC, it reduces the need for so much error detection design in the DPMCB.

COM* (Complete): COM* is an input to the MPC. It is asserted to indicate to the MPC that the DPMCB is ready to complete the dual-port transfer process. During a data read from dual-port to the PSB, COM* is asserted to indicate to the MPC that data is present on the BAD* bus and can be sent out to the PSB. Conversely, during a data write to dual-port from the PSB, COM* is asserted to indicate to the MPC that data on the BAD* bus has been latched into memory and can be removed from the BAD* bus.

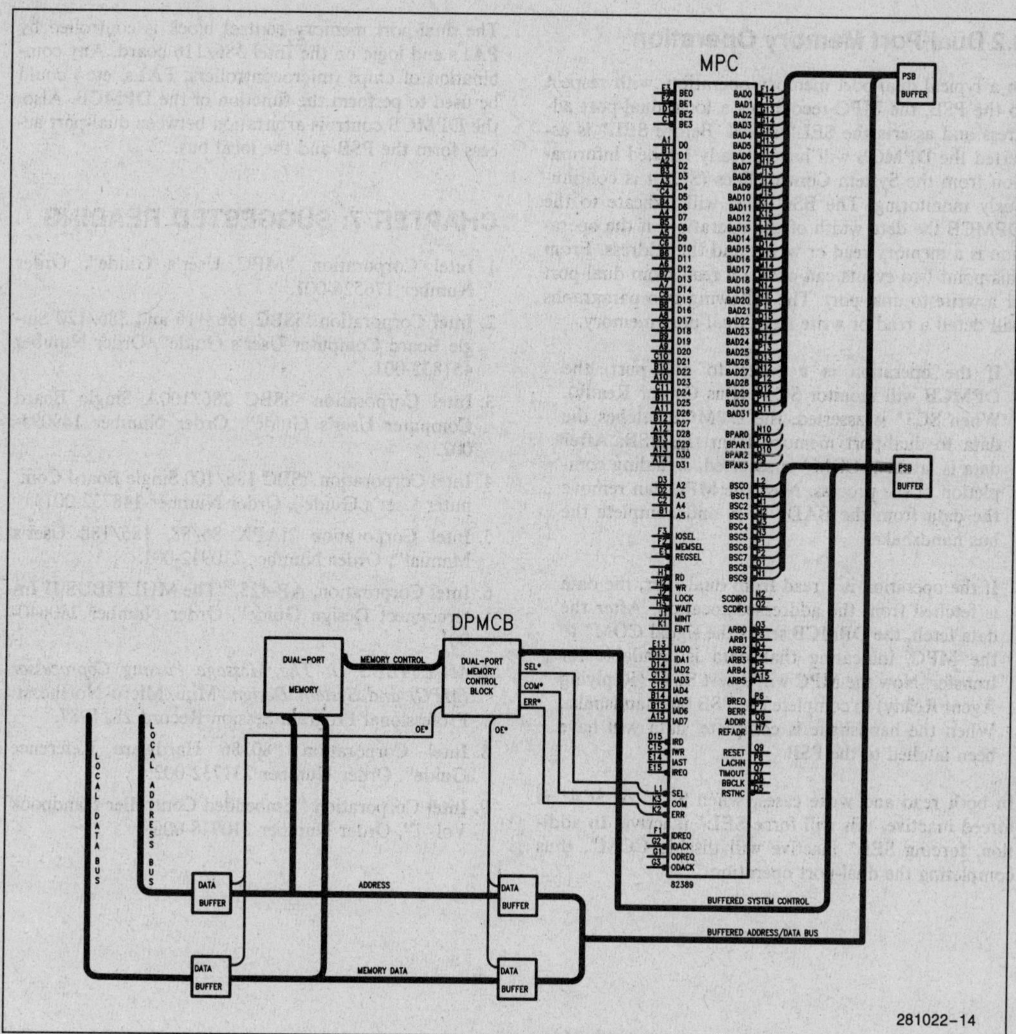

Figure 14. MPC Dual-Port Interface

6.2 Dual-Port Memory Operation

In a typical dual-port memory operation, with respect to the PSB, the MPC recognizes a local dual-port address and asserts the SEL* signal. Before SEL* is asserted the DPMCB will have already latched information from the System Control lines (SC) it is continuously monitoring. The BSC lines will indicate to the DPMCB the data width of the operation, if the operation is a memory read or write, and the address. From this point two events can occur: a read from dual-port or a write to dual-port. The following two paragraphs will detail a read or write from dual-port memory.

If the operation is a write to dual-port, the DPMCB will monitor SC3* (Bus Owner Ready). When SC3* is asserted, the DPMCB latches the data to dual-port memory from the PSB. After data is latched, COM* is asserted, signaling completion of the process. Now the MPC can remove the data from the BAD* lines and complete the bus handshake.

If the operation is a read from dual-port, the data is fetched from the addressed location. After the data fetch, the DPMCB sends the signal COM* to the MPC, indicating that data is available for transfer. Now the MPC will assert SC4* (Replying Agent Ready) to complete the PSB bus handshake. When the handshake is complete, data will have been latched to the PSB.

In both read and write cases, when SC3* or SC4* is forced inactive, this will force SEL* inactive. In addition, forcing SEL* inactive will disable COM*, thus completing the dual-port operation.

The dual-port memory control block is controlled by PALs and logic on the Intel 386/116 board. Any combination of chips (microcontrollers, PALs, etc.) could be used to perform the function of the DPMCB. Also, the DPMCB controls arbitration between dual-port access form the PSB and the local bus.

CHAPTER 7: SUGGESTED READING

1. Intel Corporation "MPC User's Guide", Order Number 176526-001.

2. Intel Corporation "iSBC 386/116 and 386/120 Single Board Computer User's Guide", Order Number 451833-001.

3. Intel Corporation "iSBC 286/100A Single Board Computer User's Guide", Order Number 149093-002.

4. Intel Corporation 'iSBC 186/100 Single Board Computer User's Guide", Order Number 148732-001.

5. Intel Corporation "iAPX 86/88, 186/188 User's Manual", Order Number 210912-001.

6. Intel Corporation, AP-423, "The MULTIBUS II Interconnect Design Guide", Order Number 280640-001.

7. *MULTIBUS II: The Message Passing Coprocessor (MPC) and Systèm Design,* Mini/Micro Northeast: Professional Program Session Record 28, 1987.

8. Intel Corporation "80386 Hardware Reference Guide", Order Number 231732-002.

9. Intel Corporation "Embedded Controller Handbook Vol. 1", Order Number 210918-006.

iSBX™ Expansion Modules 6

6

intel®

iSBX™ 279A DISPLAY SUBSYSTEM

280667-1

HIGH-SPEED GRAPHICS/WINDOWING FOR iRMX®II SYSTEMS

The iSBX™ 279A is a complete graphics subsystem designed to provide users of Intel's iRMX® II, and RMX® III real-time systems with advanced interactive graphics functions. Based on Intel's 82786 Display Processor, the iSBX 279A efficiently off-loads bitmap and window manipulation from the application CPU, preserving real-time system performance. High-speed windowing, ASCII terminal emulation with system console support, and powerful drawing commands are provided in a convenient system expansion package. Complete software support, including iRMX Device Drivers, Application Interface Libraries for C-286, 386 and PL/M 286, 386 and loadable fonts, provides a high-level, network transparent interface, allowing application portability across Intel's real-time platforms and shortening application development time.

FEATURES

- Intel 82786 Display Processor
- iRMX Operating System Device Drivers
- High-Level Language Interface
- System Console Support Kits
- Windowed User Interface
- Terminal Emulator
- Standard Graphics Command Interpreter
- Network Transparent Graphics Protocol

September 1991
Order Number: 280667-001

FEATURES

INTEL 82786 DISPLAY PROCESSOR

The Intel 82786 Display Processor is used to provide nearly instantaneous window manipulation. Together with the iSBX 279A firmware and iRMX software, this allows multiple overlapping windows displaying graphical information or terminal sessions to be presented simultaneously.

iRMX® OPERATING SYSTEM DEVICE DRIVER

The iRMX Interactive Configuration Utility provides the screens needed to configure the iSBX 279. The device driver manages the device interface and performs I/O on behalf of application requests through device/file connections in the iRMX IOS. The device driver is compatible with iRMX Terminal Support. This speeds development by allowing the programmer to remain unaware of the device interface, instead concentrating on the application code needed for the target system.

HIGH-LEVEL LANGUAGE INTERFACE

Application interface libraries are provided for C-286, C-386 and PL/M 286, 386. The application interface is a rich set of graphics and windowing primitives that provide standard drawing functions with complete control of bitmaps and windows. This allows the application programmer to quickly begin writing sophisticated real-time graphics applications using a portable interface for iRMX systems.

WINDOWED USER INTERFACE

The user may interactively MOVE, RESIZE, PUSH, POP, and SELECT windows using the mouse and an easy-to-use menu provided for this purpose. Several terminal sessions and interactive graphics applications can be managed from a single console. Window and bitmap manipulation is performed locally by the iSBX 279A, allowing complex user-interface operations to proceed in parallel with time-critical real-time tasks on the host-CPU.

TERMINAL EMULATOR

The terminal emulator allows existing applications to run in a window without modification. The terminal emulator is compatible with the iRMX Human Interface, the AEDIT text editor, iRMX Virtual Terminal software, and other terminal oriented programs that can be configured to operate with a smart CRT. By using the virtual terminal capability, it is possible to access any host on an OpenNET™ network from a single display.

STANDARD GRAPHICS COMMAND INTERPRETER

The graphics command interpreter is an implementation of the Computer Graphics Interface (CGI), providing an interface that is consistent with current ISO-CGM and ANSI-CGI standardization efforts, while extending this interface to include window and bitmap manipulation functions. The interface is fully compatible with Intel's existing iVDI 720 R1.8 interface providing a direct upgrade for iSBC 186/78A applications.

NETWORK TRANSPARENT GRAPHICS PROTOCOL

Using OpenNET it is possible to display images stored on remote nodes, run interactive applications from any node on the network, allow multiple applications on several processors to share a single display, and access other displays from a local application processor. Network transparency allows distributed applications to be controlled from a single console.

INTEL QUALITY AND RELIABILITY

The components of the iSBX 279A subsystem are designed and manufactured in accordance with Intel's high quality standards. Quality is assured through rigorous testing in our state-of-the-art Environmental Testing Laboratory.

intel®

SPECIFICATIONS

REAL-TIME GRAPHICS INTERFACE COMMAND SUMMARY

Graphics Server Commands			
gqbeginmetafile	gqendmetafile	gqbeginpicture	gqendpicture
gqsetbackgroundcolor	gqsetvdcextent	gqsetcliprectangle	gqsetclipindicator
gqclearviewsurface	gqresetdefaults	gqsetdeviceviewport	gqopencgi
gqclosecgi	gqsetscalingmode	gqpolyline	gqline
gqpolymarker	gqmarker	gqpolygon	gqrectangle
gqcircle	gqarc	gqarcclose	gqcellarray
gqtext	gqappendtext	gqarccenter	gqarccenterclose
gqsetasfs	gqsetpolylinebundleindex	gqsetpolylinebundlerep	gqsetlinetype
gqsetlinewidth	gqsetlinecolor	gqsetpolymarkerbundleindex	gqsetpolymarkerbundlerep
gqsetmarkertype	gqsetmarkersize	gqsetmarkercolor	gqsetfillareabundleindex
gqsetfillareabundlerep	gqsetinteriorstyle	gqsetfillcolor	gqsethatchindex
gqsetpatternindex	gqsetpatterntable	gqsetpatternreferencepoint	gqsetpatternsize
gqsetperimetertype	gqsetperimeterwidth	gqsetperimetercolor	gqsettextfontindex
gqsettextfontlist	gqsettextbundleindex	gqsettextbundlerep	gqsettextprecision
gqsetcharacterexpansionfactor	gqsetcharacterspacing	gqsettextcolor	gqsetcharacterheight
gqsetcharacterorientation	gqsetcharacterpath	gqsettextalignment	gqsetcolortable
gqsettransparency	gqsetdisplaycorner	gqsetblinkmode	gqsetblinkcolor
gqsetblinkinterval	gqsetimagebounds	gqdisplayimage	gqsetcursorcolor
gqsetwritemask	gqsetcursorsize	gqcreatewindow	gqdeletewindow
gqdeleteallwindows	gqcreatebitmap	gqdeletebitmap	gqdeleteallbitmaps
gqsetwindowpriority	gqpopwindow	gqpushwindow	gqchangebitmap
gqselectdrawingbitmap	gqmovewindow	gqpanbitmap	gqpanwindow
gqresizewindow	gqsetwindowvisi	gqsetbordervisi	gqsetfieldcolor
gqsetbordercolor	gqset1bppcolorpad	gqset2bppcolorpad	gqset4bppcolorpad
gqsetsyscursorcolor	gqsetcursorvisi	gqloadfont	gqdeletefont
gqsetdrawingmode	gqbitblt	gqloadbitmap	gqloadcursor
gqdeletecursor	gqassigncursor	gqloadmenu	gqdeletemenu
gqselectmenu	gqenablesystemmenu	gqdisablesystemmenu	gqinqerrorinfo
gqinqwindowinfo	gqreqwindowinfo	gqinqbitmapinfo	gqinqcursorinfo
gqinqfontinfo	gqinitializelocator	gqinitializestring	gqreleaseinputdevice
gqsetinputdevicemode	gqsamplelocator	gqsamplestring	gqrequestlocator
gqrequeststring	gqsetpromptstate	gqsetechostate	gqstartinput
gqendinput	gqrequestinput		

Terminal Server Commands		
LINE FEED	BACKSPACE	RETURN
CURSOR UP	CURSOR RIGHT	CURSOR HOME
MOVE CURSOR	INSERT LINE	DELETE LINE
CLEAR SCREEN	CLEAR TO END OF SCREEN	CLEAR TO END OF LINE
VISUAL BELL	DISABLE VISUAL BELL	ENABLE VISUAL BELL
INVERT SCREEN	SET BACKGROUND COLOR	SET FOREGROUND COLOR
RESET TO DEFAULTS	SELECT PRIMARY CHARACTER SET	SELECT SECONDARY CHARACTER SET
SELECT PRIMARY FONT INDEX	SELECT SECONDARY FONT INDEX	USE PRIMARY FONT
USE SECONDARY FONT	START REVERSE VIDEO	END REVERSE VIDEO

Buffered Operating System Interface		
cgi_initialize	cgi_terminate	cgi_send_cmd
cgi_send	cgi_sendreply	cgi_flush

6

SPECIFICATIONS

- 640 by 480 Pixel Display, 25MHZ Pixel Clock
- 60 HZ Non-interlaced Frame Rate, 31.5Khz Horizontal Rate
- 1 Megabyte of Bitmap Memory
- Bitmap Depths of 1, 2, 4, or 8 bits
- Up to 256 Displayed Colors from a Palette of 16.7 Million[1]
- On-board Self-Test and Diagnostics

Interfaces Supported
IBM[2] PC/AT[3] Keyboard (or compatible)
PC-MOUSE (or compatible) locator device
NEC MultiSync[4] Analog-RGB Monitor (or compatible)
8-bit iSBX Bus Interface (all signals TTL compatible)

Physical Characteristics			
Width:	7.5 in.	≅ 19.05 cm.	
Length:	3.15 in.	≅ 8.00 cm.	
Height:	0.80″ 1.14 in.	≅ 2.03 cm. ≅ 2.89 cm.	iSBX 279 Only With iSBC Host
Weight:	6.0 oz.	≅ 170.1 gm.	iSBX 279 Only

Electrical Requirements
+5 VDC ±5% @ ≈ 3.0 A
+12 VDC ±5% @ ≈ 0.025 A
−12 VDC ±5% @ ≈ 0.025 A

Environmental Requirements	
Operating Temperature:	0°C to 55°C@200 LFPM minimum air flow
Storage Temperature:	−40°C to +70°C
Humidity:	0% to 95%, non-condensing

[1] See the RGI279 Product Release Notes for restrictions on window size/placement when displaying 256 colors.
[2] IBM is a registered trademark of International Business Machines, Inc.
[3] PC/AT is a trademark of International Business Machines, Inc.
[4] MultiSync is a trademark of NEC.

ORDERING INFORMATION

Order Code	*Description*
SBX279A	Display Subsystem (Board Only)
SXM279I286K	Complete iSBC 286/1X System Upgrade (Includes SBX279)
SXM279I386K	Complete iSBC 386/XX System Upgrade (Includes SBX279)

Note: iRMX must be purchased separately. Kits include all software, firmware, and hardware needed to begin using the iSBX 279A Display Subsystem immediately. Software Royalty included in each iSBX 279A.

iSBX™ 218A* FLEXIBLE DISK CONTROLLER

- IEEE 959 iSBX™ Bus Compatible 8″ or 5.25″ Floppy Diskette Controller Module
- Hardware and Software Compatible with iSBX 218 Module
- Controls Most Single/Double Density and Single/Double Sided Floppy Drives
- User Programmable Drive Parameters Allow Wide Choice of Drives
- Motor On/Off Latch Under Program Control
- Drive-Ready Timeout Circuit for 5.25 Inch Floppy Drives
- Phase Lock Loop Data Separator Assures Data Integrity
- Read and Write on Single or Multiple Sectors
- Single +5 Volt Supply Required

The Intel iSBX™ 218A Flexible Disk Controller module is a software and hardware compatible replacement for the iSBX 218 module and provides additional features. The iSBX 218A module is a double-wide iSBX module floppy disk controller capable of supporting virtually any soft-sectored, single/double density and single/double sided floppy drives. The controller can control up to four drives. In addition to the standard IBM 3740 and IBM system 34 formats, the controller supports sector lengths up to 8192 bytes. The iSBX 218A module's wide range of drive compatibility is achieved without compromising performance. The operating characteristics are specified under user control. The controller can read and write either single or multiple sectors.

503810–1

*The iSBX™ 218A is also manufactured under product code pSBX 218A by Intel Puerto Rico, Inc.

August 1990
Order Number: 503810-003

BLOCK DIAGRAM

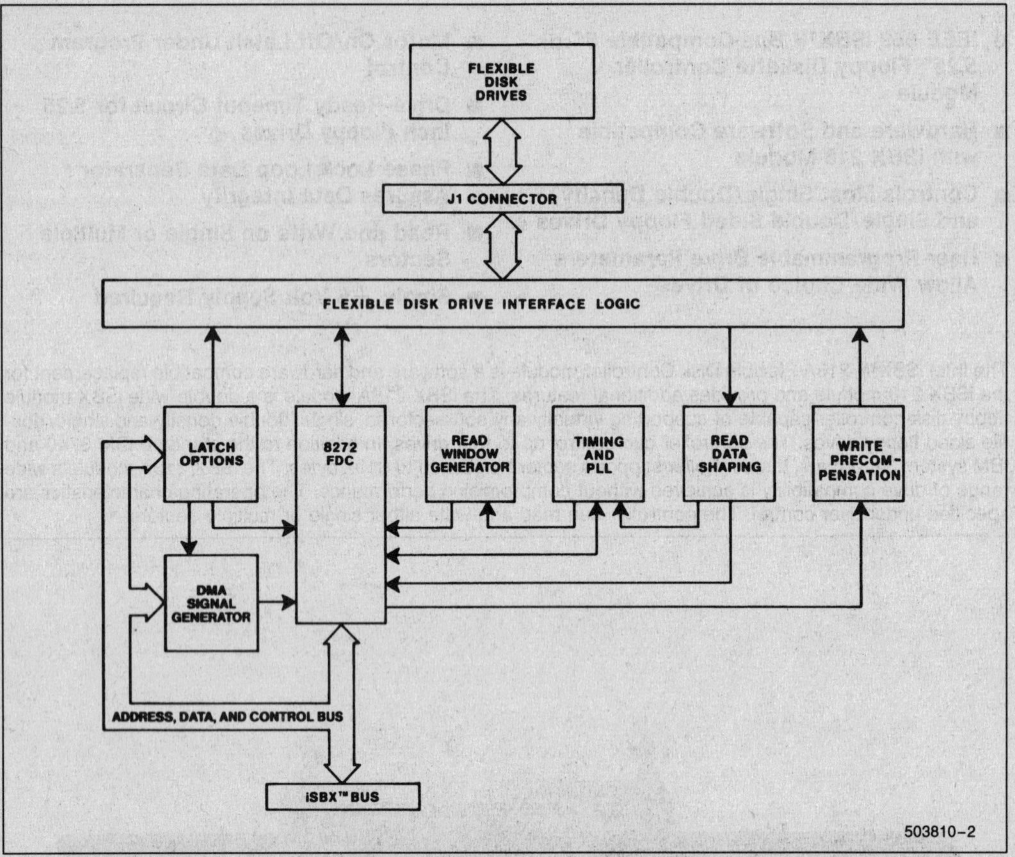

Block Diagram of iSBX™ 218A Board

SPECIFICATIONS

Compatibility

CPU—Any single board computer or I/O board implementing the iSBX bus interface and connector.

Devices—Double or single density standard (8″) and mini (5¼″) flexible disk drives. The drives may be single or double sided. Drives known to be compatible are indicated in the table to the right.

Standard (8″)		Mini (5¼″)	
Caldisk	**143M**	**Shugart**	**450/400**
Remex	**RFD 4000**	**Shugart**	**460/410**
Memorex	**550**	**Micropolis**	**1015-IV**
MFE	**700**	**Pertec**	**250**
Siemens	**FDD 200-8**	**Siemens**	**200-5**
Shugart	**SA 850/800**	**Tandon**	**TM-100**
Shugart	**SA 860/810**	**CDC**	**9409**
Pertec	**FD650**	**MPI**	**51/52/91/92**
CDC	**9406-3**		

Diskette—Unformatted IBM Diskette 1 (or equivalent single-sided media); unformatted IBM Diskette 2D (or equivalent double-sided).

Equipment Supplied

iSBX 218A Controller

Reference Schematic

Controller-to-drive cabling and connectors are not supplied with the controller. Cables can be fabricated with flat cable and commercially-available connectors as described in the iSBX 218A Hardware Reference Manual.

Nylon Mounting Screws and Spacers

Physical Characteristics

Width: 3.15 inches (8.0 cm)

Height: 0.83 inches (2.1 cm)

Length: 7.5 ounces (19.1 cm)

Weight: 4.5 ounces (126 gm)

Mounting: Occupies one double-wide iSBX MULTIMODULE™ position on boards; increases board height (host plus iSBX board) to 1.13 inches (2.87 cm).

Data Organization and Capacity

Standard Size Drives

	Double Density						Single Density					
	IBM System 34			Non-IBM			IBM System 3740			Non-IBM		
Bytes per Sector	256	512	1024	2048	4096	8192	128	256	512	1024	2048	4096
Sectors per Track	26	15	8	4	2	1	26	15	8	4	2	1
Tracks per Diskette	77			77			77			77		
Bytes per Diskette (Formatted, per diskette surface)	512,512 (256 bytes/sector) 591,360 (512 bytes/sector) 630, 784 (1024 bytes/sector)			630,784			256,256 (128 byte/sector) 295,680 (256 bytes/sector) 315, 392 (512 bytes/sector)			315,392		

Electrical Characteristics

Power Requirements: +5VDC @ 1.7A max.

Environmental Characteristics

Temperature: 0°C to +55° (operating); −55°C to +85°C (non-operating).

Humidity: Up to 90% Relative Humidity without condensation (operating); all conditions without condensation or frost (non-operating).

Reference Manual

145911— iSBX 218A Flexible Disk Controller Hardware Reference Manual (NOT SUPPLIED).

Reference manuals may be ordered from any Intel sales representative, distributor office, or from Intel Literature Department, 3065 Bowers Avenue, Santa Clara, California 95051.

Drive Characteristics

	Standard Size	**Mini Size**
	Double/Single Density	**Double/Single Density**
Transfer Rate (K bytes/sec)	62.5/31.25	31.25/15.63
Disk Speed (RPM)	360	300
Step Rate Time (Programmable)	1 to 16 ms/track in 1 ms increments	2 to 32 ms/track in 2 ms increments
Head Load Time (Programmable)	2 to 254 ms in 2 ms increments	4 to 508 ms in 4 ms increments
Head Unload Time (Programmable)	16 to 240 ms in 16 ms increments	32 to 480 ms in 32 ms increments

ORDERING INFORMATION

Order Code	Description
SBX218A	Flexible Disk Controller

intel®

iSBX™ 311* ANALOG INPUT MULTIMODULE™ BOARD

- Low Cost Analog Input Via iSBX™ Bus Connector
- 8 Differential/16 Single-Ended, Fault Protected Inputs
- 20 mV to 5V Full Scale Input Range, Resistor Gain Selectable
- Unipolar (0 to +5V) or Bipolar (−5V to +5V) Input, Jumper Selectable
- 12-Bit Resolution Analog-To-Digital Converter
- 18 KHz Samples Per Second Throughput to Memory

The Intel iSBX 311 Analog Input MULTIMODULE board provides simple interfacing of non-isolated analog signals to any iSBC board having an IEEE 959 iSBX I/O Expansion Bus connector. The single-wide iSBX 311 plugs directly onto the iSBC board, providing data acquisition of analog signals from eight differential or sixteen single-ended voltage inputs, jumper selectable. Resistor gain selection is provided for both low level (20 mV full scale range) and high level (5 volt FSR) signals. Incorporating the latest high quality IC components, the iSBX 311 MULTIMODULE board provides 12 bit resolution, 11 bit accuracy, and a simple programming interface, all on a low cost SBX board.

280233–1

*The iSBX™ 311 is also manufactured under product code pSBX 311 by Intel Puerto Rico, Inc.

6

BLOCK DIAGRAM

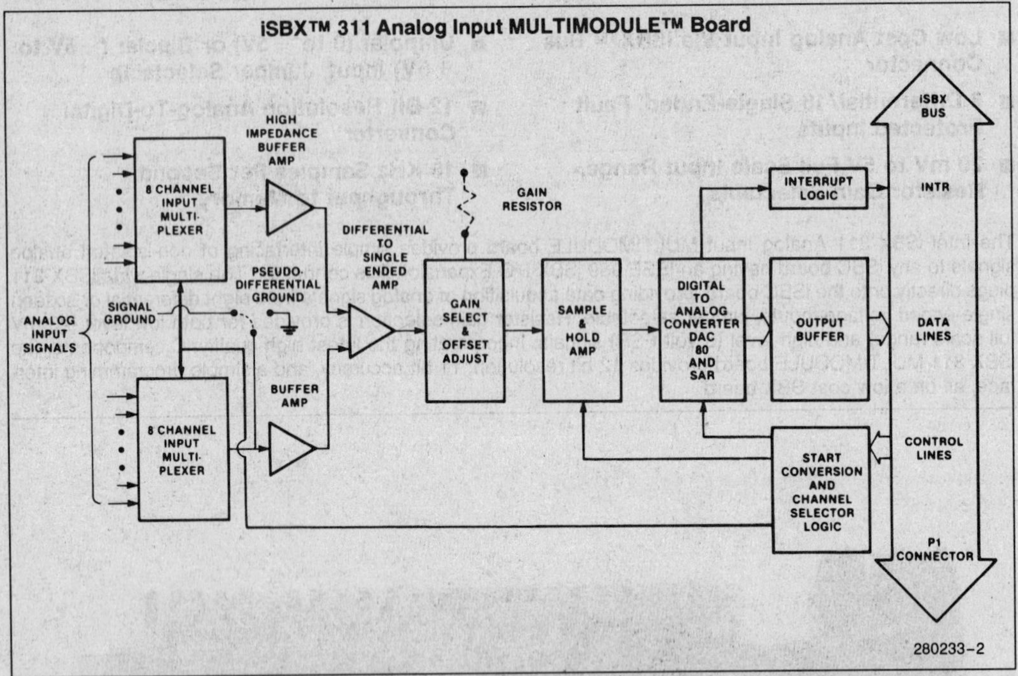

SPECIFICATIONS

Inputs—8 differential. 16 single-ended. Jumper selectable.

Voltage Range—−5 to +5 volts (bipolar). 0 to +5 volts (unipolar). Jumper selectable.

Gain—User-configurable through installation of two resistors. Factory-configured for gain of X1.

Resolution—12 bits over full scale range (1.22 mV at 0–5V, 5 μV at 0–20 mV).

Accuracy—

Gain	Accuracy at 25°C
1	±0.035% ± ½ LSB
5	±0.035% ± ½ LSB
50	±0.035% ± ½ LSB
250	±0.035% ± ½ LSB

NOTE:
Figures are in percent of full scale reading. At any fixed temperature between 0° and 60°C, the accuracy is adjustable to ±0.035% of full scale.

Dynamic Error—±0.015% FSR for transitions.

Gain TC (at Gain = 1): 30 PPM per degree centigrade (typical); 56 PPM per degree centigrade (max).

Offset TC (in percent of FSR/°C):

Gain	Offset
1	0.0018
5	0.0036
50	0.024
250	0.116

Offset is measured with user-supplied 10 PPM/°C gain resistors installed.

Input Protection—±30 volts.

Input Impedance—20 MΩ (minimum).

Conversion Speed—50 ms (nominal).

Common Mode Rejection Ratio—60 db (minimum).

Sample and hold—sample time 15 ms.

Aperture—hold aperture time: 120 ns.

Connectors—

Interface	Pins (Qty)	Centers		Mating Connectors
		in	cm	
J1 8/16 Channels Analog	50	0.1	0.254	3m 3415-000

Physical Characteristics

Width: 9.40 cm (3.7 inches)

Length: 6.35 cm (2.5 inches)

Height: 2.03 cm (0.80 inch) MULTIMODULE board only

2.82 cm (1.13 inches) MULTIMODULE and iSBC board

Weight: 68.05 gm (2.4 ounces)

Electrical Characteristics (from iSBX connector)

V_{CC} = ±5 volts (±0.25V), I_{CC} = 250 mAmax
V_{dd} = +12 volts (±0.6V), I_{dd} = 50 mAmax
V_{ss} = −12 volts (±0.6V), I_{ss} = 55 mAmax

Environmental Characteristics

Operating Temperature: 0° to 60°C (32° to 140°C)

Relative Humidity: to 90% (without condensation)

Reference Manuals

142913— iSBX 311 Analog Input MULTIMODULE Board Hardware Reference Manual (order separately)

ORDERING INFORMATION

Order Code	Description
SBX311	Analog Input MULTIMODULE Board

6

iSBX™ 328* ANALOG OUTPUT MULTIMODULE™ BOARD

- Low Cost Analog Output Via iSBX™ Bus Connector
- 8 Channel Output, Current Loop or Voltage in any Mix
- 4–20 mA Current Loop; 5V Unipolar or Bipolar Voltage Output
- 12-Bit Resolution
- 0.035% Full Scale Voltage Accuracy @ 25°C
- Programmable Offset Adjust in Current Loop Mode

The Intel iSBX 328 MULTIMODULE board provides analog signal output for any intelligent board having an IEEE 959 iSBX I/O Expansion bus connector. The single-wide iSBX 328 plugs directly onto the host board, providing eight independent output channels of analog voltage for meters, programmable power supplies, etc. Voltage output can be mixed with current loop output for control of popular 4–20 mA industrial control elements. By using an Intel single chip computer (8041) for refreshing separate sample-hold amplifiers through a single 12 bit DAC, eight channels are contained on a single SBX board for high density and low cost per channel. High quality analog components provide 12 bit resolution, and slew rates per channel of 0.1V per microsecond. Maximum channel update rates are 5 KHz on a single channel to 1 KHz on all eight channels.

280234–1

*The iSBX™ 328 is also manufactured under product code pSBX 328 by Intel Puerto Rico, Inc.

August 1990
Order Number: 280234-002

BLOCK DIAGRAM

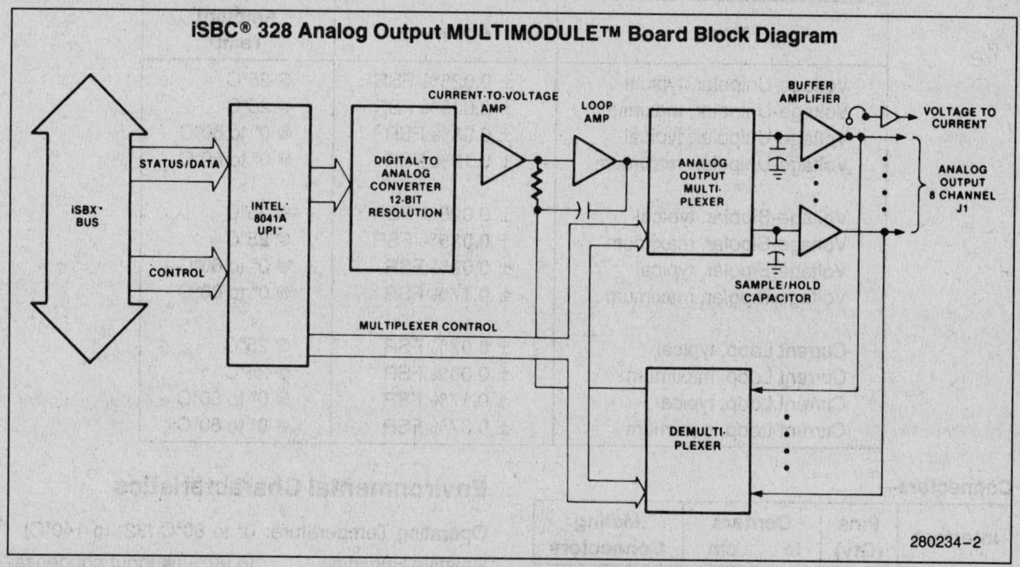

SPECIFICATIONS

Outputs — 8 non-isolated channels, each independently jumpered for voltage output or current loop output mode.

Voltage Ranges — 0 to +5V (unipolar operation) −5 to +5V (bipolar operation)

Current Loop Range — 4 to 20 mA (unipolar operation only)

Output Current — ±5 mA maximum (voltage mode-bipolar operation)

Load Resistance — 0 to 250Ω with on-board iSBX power. 1000Ω minimum with 30 VDC max. external supply

Compliance Voltage — 12V using on-board iSBX power. If supplied by user, up to 30 VDC max

Resolution — 12 bits bipolar or unipolar

Slew Rate — 0.1V per microsecond minimum

Single Channel Update Rate — 5 KHz

Eight Channel Update Rate — 1 KHz

Output Impedance— 0.1Ω. Drives capacitive loads up to 0.05 microfarads. (approx. 1000 foot cable)

Temperature Coefficient — 0.005%/°C

Refresh and Throughput Rates**	
Refresh 1 channel (no new data):	80 μs
Refresh all 8 channels (no new data):	650 μs
Update and refresh 1 channel with new data: firmware program 2	150 μs
for each additional channel	130 μs
Update and refresh 1 channel with new data: firmware program 1 or 3	200 μs
for each additional channel	155 μs
Update and refresh all 8 channels (all new data): firmware program 2	1,050 ms
per channel of new data	50 μs
Update and refresh all 8 channels (all new data): firmware program 1or 3	1,280 ms
per channel of new data	80 μs

**All times nominal

6

Accuracy—

Mode	Accuracy	Ambient Temp
Voltage-Unipolar, typical	± 0.025% FSR	@ 25°C
Voltage-Unipolar, maximum	± 0.035% FSR	@ 25°C
Voltage-Unipolar, typical	± 0.08% FSR	@ 0° to 60°C
Voltage-Unipolar, maximum	± 0.19% FSR	@ 0° to 60°C
Voltage-Bipolar, typical	± 0.025% FSR	@ 25°C
Voltage-Bipolar, maximum	± 0.035% FSR	@ 25°C
Voltage-Bipolar, typical	± 0.09% FSR	@ 0° to 60°C
Voltage-Bipolar, maximum	± 0.17% FSR	@ 0° to 60°C
Current Loop, typical	± 0.07% FSR	@ 25°C
Current Loop, maximum	± 0.08% FSR	@ 25°C
Current Loop, typical	± 0.17% FSR	@ 0° to 60°C
Current Loop, maximum	± 0.37% FSR	@ 0° to 60°C

Connectors—

Interface	Pins (Qty)	Centers in	Centers cm	Mating Connectors
J1 8/16 channels analog	50	0.1	0.254	3m 3415-000

Physical Characteristics

Width: 9.40 cm (3.7 inches)

Length: 6.35 cm (2.5 inches)

Height: 1.4 cm (0.56 inch) MULTIMODULE board only

2.82 cm (1.13 inches) MULTIMODULE and iSBC board.

Weight: 85.06 gm (3.0 ounces)

Electrical Characteristics

$V_{CC} = \pm 5V$ (0.25V), $I_{CC} = 140$ mA max

$V_{DD} = \pm 12V$ ($\pm 0.6V$), $I_{DD} = 45$ mA max (voltage mode)

= 200 mA max (current loop mode

$V_{SS} = -12V$ ($\pm 0.6V$), $I_{SS} = 55$ mA max

Environmental Characteristics

Operating Temperature: 0° to 60°C (32° to 140°C)

Relative Humidity: to 90% (without condensation)

Reference Manuals

142914— iSBX 328 Analog Output MULTI-MODULE Board Hardware Reference Manual (Order Separately)

Manuals may be ordered from any Intel sales representative, distributor office or from Intel Literature Department, 3065 Bowers Avenue, Santa Clara, California 95051.

ORDERING INFORMATION

Order Code	Description
SBX328	Analog Output MULTIMODULE Board

iSBX™ 350* PARALLEL I/O MULTIMODULE™ BOARD

- IEEE 959 SBX Bus Compatible I/O Expansion
- 24 Programmable I/O Lines with Sockets for Interchangeable Line Drivers and Terminators
- Three Jumper Selectable Interrupt Request Sources
- Accessed as I/O Port Locations
- Single +5V Low Power Requirement
- SBX Bus On-Board Expansion Eliminates Multibus System Bus Latency and Increases System Throughput

The Intel iSBX 350 Parallel I/O MULTIMODULE Board is a member of Intel's line of IEEE 959 SBX I/O Expansion Bus products. The iSBX 350 module provides 24 programmable I/O lines with sockets for interchangeable line drivers and terminators. The board is closely coupled to the host board through the SBX bus, and as such, offers maximum on-board performance and frees Multibus system traffic for other system resources. In addition, incremental power dissipation is minimal at only 1.6 watts (not including optional driver/terminators).

280235–1

*The iSBX™ 350 is manufactured under product code pSBX 350 by Intel Puerto Rico, Inc.

SPECIFICATIONS

I/O Capacity

24 programmable lines

Parallel I/O Port Operation Modes

Port	Lines (qty)	Mode of Operation					
		Unidirectional				Bidirectional	Control
		Input		Output			
		Unlatched	Latched & Strobed	Latched	Latched & Strobed		
A	8	X	X	X	X	X	
B	8	X	X	X	X		
C	4	X		X			X(1)
	4	X		X			X(1)

NOTE:
1. Part of Port C must be used as a control port when either Port A or Port B are used as a latched and strobed input or a latched and strobed output port or Port A is used as a bidirectional port.

Word Size

Data: 8 Bits

I/O Addressing

82C55A-5 Ports	iSBX 350 Address
Port A	X0 or X4
Port B	X1 or X5
Port C	X2 or X6
Control	X3 or X7
Reserved	X8 to XF

NOTE:
The first digit of each port I/O address is listed as "X" since it will change dependent on the type of host single board computer used. Refer to the Hardware Reference Manual for your host single board computer to determine the first digit of the port address.

Interrupts

Interrupt requests may originate from the programmable peripheral interface (2) or the user specified I/O (1).

Transfer Rates

Maximum rates are 2.8 MBytes/sec.

NOTE:
Actual transfer speed is dependent upon the cycle time of the host microcomputer.

Parallel Interface Connectors

Interface	No. of Pairs/ Pins	Centers (in.)	Connector Type	Vendor	Vendor Part No.
Parallel I/O Connector	25/50	0.1	Female	3M	3415-0001 with Ears
Parallel I/O Connector	25/50	0.1	Female Soldered	GTE Sylvania	6AD01251A1DD

NOTE:
Connector compatible with those listed may also be used.

Line Drivers and Teminators

I/O Drivers—The following line drivers and terminators are all compatible with the I/O driver sockets on the iSBX 350.

Driver	Characteristic	Sink Current (mA)
7438	I, OC	48
7437	I	48
7432	NI	16
7426	I, OC	16
7409	NI, OC	16
7408	NI	16
7403	I, OC	16
7400	I	16

NOTE:
I = Inverting, NI = Non-Inverting, OC = Open Collector

Port 1 has 25 mA totem pole drivers and 1 kΩ terminators.

I/O Terminators—220Ω/330Ω divider or 1 kΩ pull up - user supplied.

Physical Characteristics

Width: 7.24 cm (2.85 in.)

Length: 9.40 cm (3.70 in.)

Height*: 2.04 cm (0.80 in.) iSBX 350 Board

2.86 cm (1.13 in.) iSBX 350 Board + Host Board

Weight: 51 gm (1.79 oz)

*See Figure 2

Electrical Characteristics

DC Power Requirements

Power Requirements	Configuration
+5 @ 320 mA	Sockets XU3, XU4, XU5, and XU6 empty (as shipped).
+5V @ 500 mA	Sockets XU3, XU4, XU5, and XU6 contain 7438 buffers.
+5V @ 620 mA	Sockets XU3, XU4, XU5, and XU6 contain iSBC 901 termination devices.

Environmental

Operating Temperature: 0°C to +55°C

Reference Manual

9803191—iSBX 350 Parallel I/O MULTIMODULE Manual (NOT SUPPLIED)

Reference Manuals may be ordered from any Intel sales representative, distributor office or from Intel Literature Department, 3065 Bowers Ave., Santa Clara, California 95051.

ORDERING INFORMATION

Order Code	Description
pSBX350	Parallel I/O MULTIMODULE Board

6

iSBX™ 700* PARALLEL I/O MULTIMODULE™ BOARD

- **IEEE 959 SBX Bus Compatible I/O Expansion**
- **48 Programmable I/O Lines with Sockets for Interchangeable Line Drivers and Terminators**
- **Three Jumper Selectable Interrupt Request Sources**
- **Accessed as I/O Port Locations**
- **Single +5V Low Power Requirement**
- **SBX Bus On-Board Expansion Eliminates Multibus System Bus Latency and Increases System Throughput**

The Intel iSBX 700 Parallel I/O MULTIMODULE Board is a member of Intel's line of IEEE 959 SBX I/O Expansion Bus products. The iSBX 350 module provides 48 programmable I/O lines with sockets for interchangeable line drivers and terminators. The board is closely coupled to the host board through the SBX bus, and as such, offers maximum on-board performance and frees Multibus system traffic for other system resources. In addition, incremental power dissipation is minimal at only 0.18 BTU/minute (not including optional driver/terminators).

281112-1

*The iSBX™ 700 is manufactured under product code pSBXC700 by Intel Corporation.

December 1990
Order Number: 281112-001

SPECIFICATIONS

I/O Capacity

48 programmable lines (via two 82C55As)

Parallel I/O Port Operation Modes

Port	Lines (qty)	Mode of Operation					
		Unidirectional				Bidirectional	Control
		Input		Output			
		Unlatched	Latched & Strobed	Latched	Latched & Strobed		
A	8	X	X	X	X	X	
B	8	X	X	X	X		
C	4	X		X			X(1)
	4	X		X			X(1)

NOTE:
1. Part of Port C must be used as a control port when either Port A or Port B are used as a latched and strobed input or a latched and strobed output port or Port A is used as a bidirectional port.

Word Size

Data: 8 Bits

Interrupts

Interrupt requests may originate from the programmable peripheral interface (2) or the user specified I/O (1).

I/O Addressing

82C55A Ports	iSBX 700 Address
Port A	X0 or X4
Port B	X1 or X5
Port C	X2 or X6
Control Word	X3 or X7
Reserved	X8 to XF

NOTE:
The first digit of each port I/O address is listed as "X" since it will change dependent on the type of host single board computer used. Refer to the Hardware Reference Manual for your host single board computer to determine the first digit of the port address.

Parallel Interface Connectors

Interface	No. of Pairs/ Pins	Centers (in.)	Mating Connector Type	Vendor	Vendor Part No.
J1	50/100	0.100	Female	3M	3M-82100-6000

NOTE:
Connector compatible with that listed may also be used.

6

Line Drivers and Terminators

I/O Drivers—The following line drivers and terminators are all compatible with the I/O driver sockets on the iSBX 700.

Driver	Characteristic	I_{OL} (ma)²	I_{OH} (ma)²
7438	I, OC	48	—
7437	I	48	−1.2
7432	NI	16	−0.8
7426	I, OC	16	—
7409	NI, OC	16	—
7408	NI	16	−0.8
7403	I, OC	16	—
7400	I	16	−0.4

NOTE:
I = Inverting, NI = Non-Inverting, OC = Open Collector
I_{OL} specified for V_{OL} = 0.4V.
I_{OH} specified for V_{OH} = 2.4V.

Port 1 has 25 mA totem pole drivers and 1 kΩ terminators.

I/O Terminators—220Ω/330Ω divider or 1 kΩ pull up - user supplied.

Physical Characteristics

Width: 7.62 cm (3.0 in.)

Length: 9.40 cm (3.70 in.)

Height*: 2.03 cm (0.80 in.) iSBX 700 Board
2.87 cm (1.13 in.) iSBX 700 Board + Host Board

Weight: 51 gm (1.79 oz)

Electrical Characteristics

DC Power Requirements

Power Requirements	Configuration
+5 @ 22 mA	Sockets XU3, XU4, XU5, and XU6 empty (as shipped).
+5V @ 382 mA	Sockets XU3, XU4, XU5, and XU6 contain 7438 buffers.
+5V @ 622 mA	Sockets XU3, XU4, XU5, and XU6 contain iSBC 901 termination devices.

Environmental

Operating Temperature: 0°C to +55°C

Reference Manual

500581— iSBX 700 Parallel I/O MULTIMODULE Hardware Reference Manual (NOT SUPPLIED)

Reference Manuals may be ordered from any Intel sales representative, distributor office or from Intel Literature Department, 3065 Bowers Ave., Santa Clara, California 95051.

ORDERING INFORMATION

Order Code	Description
pSBX700	Parallel I/O MULTIMODULE Board

intel®

iSBX™ 488*
GPIB MULTIMODULE™ BOARD

- **Complete IEEE 488-1978 Talker/Listener Functions Including:**
  — Addressing, Handshake Protocol, Service Request, Serial and Parallel Polling Schemes
- **Complete IEEE 488-1978 Controller Functions Including:**
  — Transfer Control, Service Requests and Remote Enable
- **Simple Read/Write Programming**
- **Software Functions Built into VLSI Hardware for High Performance, Low Cost and Small Size**
- **Standard iSBX Bus Interface for Easy Connection to Intel iSBC™ Boards**
- **IEEE 488-1978 Standard Electrical Interface Transceivers**
- **Five Volt Only Operation**

The Intel iSBX 488 GPIB Talker/Listener/Controller MULTIMODULE board provides a standard interface from any Intel iSBC board equipped with an IEEE 959 iSBX I/O Expansion Bus connector to over 600 instruments and computer peripherals that use the IEEE 488-1978 General Purpose Interface Bus. By taking full advantage of Intel's VLSI technology the single-wide iSBX 488 MULTIMODULE board implements the complete IEEE 488-1978 Standard Digital Interface for Programmable Instrumentation on a single low cost board. The iSBX 488 MULTIMODULE board includes the 8291A GPIB Talker/Listener, 8292 GPIB Controller and two 8293 GPIB Transceiver devices. This board represents a significant step forward in joining microcomputers and instrumentation using industry standards such as the MULTIBUS® system bus, iSBX bus and IEEE 488-1978. The high performance iSBX 488 MULTIMODULE board mounts easily on Intel iSBX bus compatible single board computers.

A simple user programming interface for easy reading, writing and monitoring of all GPIB functions is provided. This intelligent interface minimizes the impact on host processor bandwidth.

143580-1

*The iSBX™ 488 is also manufactured under product code pSBX 488 by Intel Puerto Rico, Inc.

August 1990
Order Number: 143580-002

BLOCK DIAGRAM

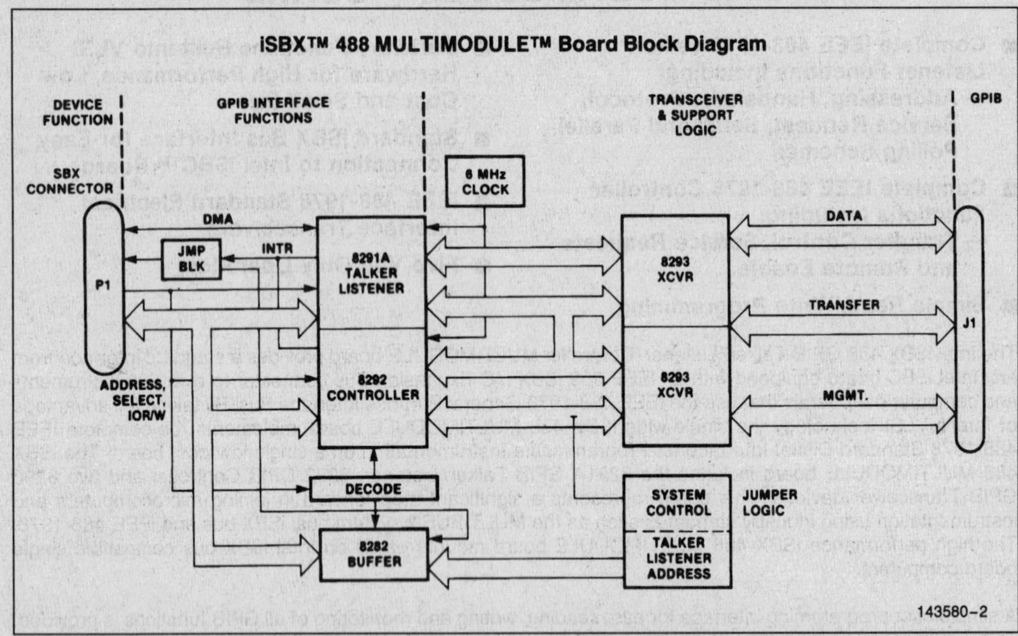

Installation

The iSBX 488 MULTIMODULE board plugs directly onto the female iSBX connector available on many Intel iSBC boards. The MULTIMODULE board is then secured at one additional point with nylon hardware (supplied) to insure the mechanical security of the assembly.

SPECIFICATIONS

Physical Characteristics

Width: 3.70 in (0.94 cm)

Length: 2.85 in (7.24 cm)

Height: 0.8 in (2.04 cm)

Weight: 3.1 oz (87.8 gm)

GPIB Data Rate*

300K bytes/sec transfer rate with DMA host iSBC board

GPIB Functions Supported

IEEE 488-1978 Functions(1)

Function	iSBX™ 488 Supported IEEE Subsets
Source Handshake (SH)	SH0, SH1
Acceptor Handshake (AH)	AH0, AH1
Talker (T)	T0 through T8
Extended Talker (TE)	TE0 through TE8
Listener (L)	L0 through L4
Extended Listener (LE)	LE0 through LE9
Service Request (SR)	SR0, SR1
Remote Local (RL)	RL0, RL1
Parallel Poll (PP)	PP0, PP1, PP2
Device Clear (DC)	DC0 through DC2
Device Trigger (DT)	DT0, DT1
Controller (C)	C0 through C28

NOTE:
1. For detailed information refer to IEEE Standard Digital Interface for Programmable Instrumentation published by The Institute of Electrical and Electronics Engineers, Inc. 1978.

50K bytes/s transfer rate using programmed I/O
730 ns Data Accept Time

*Data rates are iSBX board maximum. Data rates will vary and can be slower depending on host iSBC board and user software driver.

Electrical Characteristics

DC Power Requirements: $V_{CC} = +5$ VDC ±5%

$I_{CC} = 600$ milliamps maximum

GPIB Electrical and Mechanical Specifications

Conforms to IEEE 488-1978 standard electrical levels and mechanical connector standard when purchased with the iSBC 988 GPIB cable.

Environmental Characteristics

Operating Temperature: 0° to 60°C (32° to 140°F)

Relative Humidity: Up to 90% R.H. without condensation.

Reference Manual

143154— iSBX 488 GPIB MULTIMODULE Board Hardware Reference Manual (not supplied).

ORDERING INFORMATION

Order Code	Description
SBX488	GPIB MULTIMODULE

iSBX™ 351* SERIAL I/O MULTIMODULE™ BOARD

- IEEE959 iSBX™ Bus Compatible I/O Expansion
- Programmable Synchronous/Asynchronous Communications Channel with RS232C or RS449/422 Interface
- Software Programmable Baud Rate Generator
- Two Programmable 16-Bit BCD or Binary Timer/Event Counters
- Four Jumper Selectable Interrupt Request Sources
- Accessed as I/O Port Locations
- Low Power Requirements
- Single +5V when Configured for RS449/422 Interface
- iSBX Bus On-Board Expansion Eliminates MULTIBUS® System Bus Latency and Increases System Throughput

The Intel iSBX 351 Serial I/O MULTIMODULE board is a member of Intel's line of IEEE 959 iSBX I/O Expansion Bus compatible products. The iSBX 351 module provides one RS232C or RS449/422 programmable synchronous/asynchronous communications channel with software selectable baud rates. Two general purpose programmable 16-bit BCD or binary timers/event counters are available to the host board to generate accurate time intervals under software control. The iSBX board is closely coupled to the host board through the SBX bus, and as such, offers maximum on-board performance and frees MULTIBUS system traffic for other system resources. In addition, incremental power dissipation is minimal requiring only 3.0 watts (assumes RS232C interface).

280236–1

*The iSBX™ 351 is also manufactured under product code pSBX 351 by Intel Puerto Rico, Inc.

December 1990
Order Number: 280236-002

SPECIFICATIONS

I/O Addressing

I/O Address for an 8-Bit Host	I/O Address for a 16-Bit Host	Chip Select	Function
X0, X2, X4 or X6	Y0, Y4, Y8 or YC	8251A USART	Write: Data Read: Data
X1, X3, X5 or X7	Y2, Y6, YA or YE	MCS0/ Activated (True)	Write: Mode or Command Read: Status
X8 or XC	Z0 or Z8	8253 PIT	Write: Counter 0 Load: Count (N) Read: Counter 0
X9 or XD	Z2 or ZA	MSC1/Activated (True)	Write: Counter 1 Load: Count N Read: Counter 1
XA or XE	Z4 or ZC		Write: Counter 2 Load: Count (N) Read: Counter 2
XB or XF	Z6 or ZE		Write: Control Read: None

NOTE:
X = The iSBX base address that activates MCS0 & MSC1 for an 8-bit host.
Y = The iSBX base address that activates MCS0 for a 16-bit host.
Z = The iSBX base address that activates MCS1 for a 16-bit host.
The first digit, X, Y or Z, is always a variable, since it will depend on the type of host microcomputer used. Refer to the Hardware Reference Manual for your host microcomputer to determine the first digit of the I/O base address.
The first digit of each port I/O address is listed as "X" since it will change depending on the type of host iSBC microcomputer used. Refer to the Hardware Reference Manual for your host iSBC microcomputer to determine the first digit of the I/O address.

Word Size

Data—8 bits

Access Time

Read—250 ns max
Write—300 ns max

NOTE:
Actual transfer speed is dependent upon the cycle time of the host microcomputer.

Serial Communications

Synchronous—5–8-bit characters; internal character synchronization; automatic sync insertion; even, odd or no parity generation/detection.

Asynchronous—5–8-bit characters; break character generation and detection; 1, 1½, or 2 stop bits; false start bit detection; even, odd or no parity generation/detection.

Interval Timer and Baud Rate Generator

Input Frequency (selectable):

1.23 MHz ±0.1% (0.813 μs period nominal)
153.6 kHz ±0.1% (6.5 μs period nominal)

Sample Baud Rate

8253 PIT(1) Frequency (kHZ, Software Selectable)	8251 USART Baud Rate (Hz)(2)		
	Synchronous	Asynchronous	
		÷16	÷64
307.2	—	19200	4800
153.6	—	9600	2400
76.8	—	4800	1200
38.4	38400	2400	600
19.2	19200	1200	300
9.6	9600	600	150
4.8	4800	300	75
2.4	2400	150	—
1.76	1760	110	—

NOTES:
1. Frequency selected by I/O writes of appropriate 16-bit frequency factor to Baud Rate Register.
2. Baud rates shown here are only a sample subset of possible software-programmable rates available. Any frequency from 18.75 Hz to 614.4 kHz may be generated utilizing on-board crystal oscillator and 16-bit Programmable Interval Timer (used here as frequency divider).

Output Frequency

	Rate Generator (Frequency)		Real-Time Interrupt (Interval)	
	Min	Max	Min	Max
Single Timer(1)	18.75 Hz	614.4 kHz	1.63 μs	53.3 ms
Single Timer(2)	2.34 Hz	76.8 kHz	13.0 μs	426.7 ms
Dual Timer(3) (Counters 0 and 1 in Series)	0.000286 Hz	307.2 kHz	3.26 μs	58.25 min
Dual Timer(4) (Counters 0 and 1 in Series)	0.0000358 Hz	38.4 kHz	26.0 μs	7.77 hrs

NOTES:
1. Assuming 1.23 MHz clock input.
2. Assuming 153.6 kHz clock input.
3. Assuming Counter 0 has 1.23 MHz clock input.
4. Assuming Counter 0 has 153.6 kHz clock input.

Interrupts

Interrupt requests may originate from the USART (2) or the programmable timer (2).

Interfaces

IEEE959 iSBX I/O Expansion Bus

Serial—configurable of EIA Standards RS232C or RS449/422

EIA Standard RS232C signals provided and supported.

Clear to Send (CTS)
Data Set Ready (DSR)
Data Terminal Ready (DTR)
Request to Send (RTS)
Receive Clock (RXC)
Receive Data (RXD)
Transmit Clock (DTE TXC)
Transmit Data (TXD)

EIA Standard RS449/422 signals provided and supported.

Clear to Send (CS)
Data Mode (DM)
Terminal Ready (TR)
Request to Send (RS)
Receive Timing (RT)
Receive Data (RD)
Terminal Timing (TT)
Send Data (SD)

Physical Characteristics

Width: 7.24 cm (2.85 inches)

Length: 9.40 cm (3.70 inches)

Height*: 2.04 cm (0.80 inches)
iSBX 351 Board
2.86 cm (1.13 inches)
iSBX 351 Board and Host Board

Weight: 51 grams (1.79 ounces)

Electrical Characteristics

DC Power Requirements

Mode	Voltage	Amps (Max)
RS232C	+5V ±0.25V	460 mA
	+12V ±0.6V	30 mA
	−12V ±0.6V	30 mA
RS449/422	+5V ±0.25V	530 mA

Environmental Characteristics

Temperature: 0°C–55°C, free moving air across the base board and MULTIMODULE board.

Reference Manual

9803190— iSBX 351 Serial I/O MULTIMODULE Manual (NOT SUPPLIED)

Reference Manuals may be ordered from any Intel sales representative, distributor office or from Intel Literature Department, 3065 Bowers Ave., Santa Clara, California, 95051.

ORDERING INFORMATION

Order Code	Description
SBX351	Serial I/O MULTIMODULE Board

6

iSBX™ 354* DUAL CHANNEL SERIAL I/O MULTIMODULE™ BOARD

- Two RS232C or RS422A/449 Programmable Synchronous/ Asynchronous Communications Channels
- Programmable Baud Rate Generation for Each Channel
- Full Duplex Operation
- IEEE 959 SBX Bus Compatible I/O Expansion
- Supports HDLC/SDLC, NRZ, NRZI or FM Encoding/Decoding
- Three Interrupt Options for Each Channel
- Low Power Requirements

The Intel iSBX™ 354 Serial I/O MULTIMODULE board is a member of Intel's line of IEEE 959 iSBX I/O Expansion Bus products. Utilizing Intel's 82530 Serial Communications Controller component, the iSBX 354 module provides two RS232C or RS422A/449 programmable synchronous/asynchronous communications channels. The 82530 component provides two independent full duplex serial channels, on chip crystal oscillator, baud-rate generator and digital phase locked loop capability for each channel. The iSBX board connects to the host board through the iSBX bus. This offers maximum on-board performance and frees the MULTIBUS® System bus for use by other system resources.

280045–1

*The iSBX™ 354 is also manufactured under product code pSBX 354 by Intel Puerto Rico, Inc.

August 1990
Order Number: 280045-004

SPECIFICATIONS

Word Size

Data—8 bits

Clock Frequency

4.9152 MHz

Serial Communications

Synchronous—Internal or external character synchronization on one or two synchronous characters

Asynchronous—5–8 bits and 1, 1½ or 2 stop bits per character; programmable clock factor; break detection and generation; parity, overrun, and framing error detection

Sample Baud Rate:

Synchronous X1 Clock	
Baud Rate	**82530 Count Value (Decimal)**
64000	36
48000	49
19200	126
9600	254
4800	510
2400	1022
1800	1363
1200	2046
300	8190
Asynchronous X16 Clock	
Baud Rate	**82530 Count Value (Decimal)**
19200	6
9600	14
4800	30
2400	62
1800	83
1200	126
300	510
110	1394

INTERFACES

SBX Bus: Meets the IEEE 959 Specification, Compliance Level: D8 F

Serial: Meets the EIA RS232C standard on Channels A and B. Meets the EIA RS422A/449 standard on Channels A and B, Multi-drop capability on Channel A only.

Signals Provided

RS232C DTE

-Transmit Data
-Receive Data
-Request to Send
-Clear to Send
-Data Set Ready
-Signal Ground
-Carrier Detect
-Transmit Clock (2)
-Receive Clock
-Data Terminal Ready
-Ring Indicator

RS232C DCE

-Transmit Data
-Receive Data
-Clear to Send
-Data Set Ready
-Signal Ground
-Carrier Detect
-Transmit Clock (2)
-Receive Clock
-Ring Indicator

RS422A/449

-Send Data
-Receive Timing
-Receive Data
-Terminal Timing
-Receive Common

I/O Port Addresses

Port Address 8-Bit	Port Address 16-Bit	Function
X0		Read Status Channel B Write Command Channel B
X2		Read Data Channel B Write Data Channel B
X4		Read Status Channel A Write Command Channel A
X6		Read Data Channel A Write Data Channel A
Y0		Read Disable RS422A/449 Buffer Write Enable RS422A/449 Buffer

NOTES:
1. The "X" and "Y" values depend on the address of the iSBX interface as viewed by the base board.
2. "X" corresponds with Activation of the MCS0/interface signal; "Y" corresponds with Activation of the MCS1/interface signal.

Power Requirements

+5V at 0.5A
+12V at 50 mA
−12V at 50 mA

Physical Characteristics

Width: 2.85 inches

Length: 3.70 inches

Height: 0.8 inches

Weight: 85 grams

ENVIRONMENTAL CHARACTERISTICS

Temperature: 0°C to 55°C operating at 200 linear feet per minute across baseboard and MULTIMODULE board

Humidity: To 90%, without condensation

ORDERING INFORMATION

Order Code	Description
SBX354	Dual Channel I/O MULTIMODULE

REFERENCE MANUAL

146531—iSBX 354 Channel Serial I/O Board Hardware Reference Manual

Reference manuals may be ordered from any Intel sales representative, distributor office, or from Intel Literature Department, 3065 Bowers Avenue, Santa Clara, CA 95051.

Real-Time Systems and Software

7

intel®

iRMX® SYSTEM 120

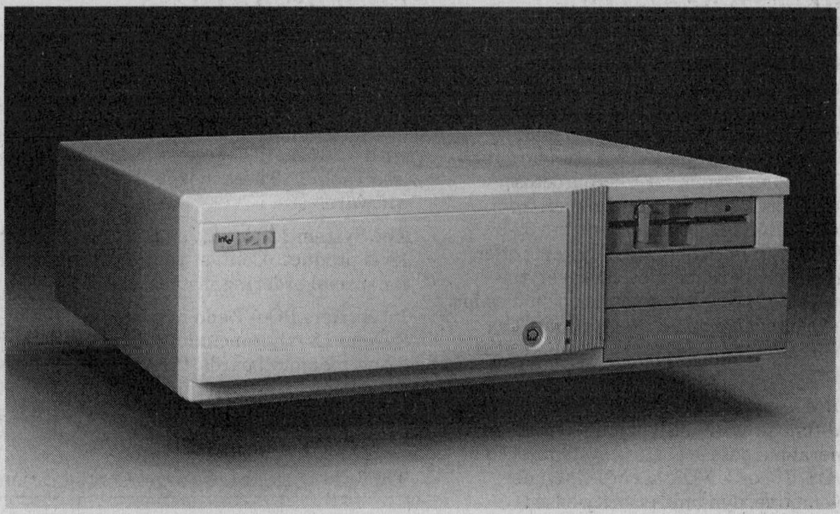

280649–1

LOW-COST REAL-TIME 386™ SYSTEMS FROM INTEL

The Intel System 120 delivers real-time capability to users demanding a low-cost system for running time-critical applications, such as high-speed switching, process control, and data acquisition. The System 120 combines the rich functionality of the world's most popular Real-Time Operating System with the power and speed of the 386™ 32-bit microprocessor.

The System 120 makes available the ability to host, on a standard computing platform, real-time applications that have previously been impractical with other AT-Bus systems.

Applications developed for the System 120 can be moved easily to Intel's complete line of Multibus I and Multibus II products, giving the user a broad spectrum of price, performance, and functions from which to choose.

FEATURES

- iRMX® II: a complete real-time operating system; more than a kernel
- Intel 386 25 MHz AT-Bus systems
- Development platform for iRMX applications
- Easy migration of applications to and from Multibus systems
- I/O expansion for PC-AT* and PC boards
- iRMX O/S to DOS file exchange
- OpenNET™ networking support
- 387™ numeric coprocessor support

The 25-MHz System 120 is shown at the top of the page.

386™ and 387™ are trademarks of Intel Corporation.
*PC-AT is a trademark of International Business Machines Corporation.

7

September 1991
Order Number: 280649-004

FEATURES

iRMX® II AND iRMX® III: COMPLETE REAL-TIME OPERATING SYSTEMS

iRMX system software is used in more real-time designs than any other operating system (O/S). There are over 500,000 CPUs worldwide running iRMX operating systems, making them the most widely accepted standard real-time operating system for microprocessor-based designs. The designer can pick from either the iRMX II, 16-bit O/S or the 32-bit iRMX III O/S. Both operating systems offer true real-time performance; however, the iRMX III O/S provides faster performance for numeric-intensive 32-bit applications. The iRMX III O/S can also run 16-bit application software.

The iRMX operating systems provide a rich set of real-time programming facilities not found in general-purpose operating systems such as DOS, OS/2** or UNIX**. These include:

- Pre-emptive, dynamic priority-based scheduling of application tasks
- Bounded interrupt latency
- Multitasking support for real-time applications
- Inter-task communications through priority-based mailboxes, semaphores, and regions
- Interrupt management with exception handling
- Cross or on-target development

The iRMX operating systems also offer high performance and code integrity. iRMX software typically responds 100 times faster than general-purpose operating systems, enabling real-time applications to keep up with the rapid data and control flow of machine and communications interfaces. Code integrity is ensured through sophisticated memory protection schemes.

Finally, the iRMX operating systems are highly configurable. Their modular design allows you to select only those functions and device drivers that are required. This keeps memory requirements to a minimum. Guided by the many examples in the System 120 Development Toolkit documentation, you can add custom device drivers and applications to the iRMX operating systems.

LOW COST PC-AT BASED CONFIGURATIONS

The System 120 target models are available with a number of processor speed, memory, and mass storage options to fit a range of applications. These include a basic system with 8 open slots, and a 40M-byte hard disk system with a 387 math coprocessor and floppy disk (see Table 1). These models do not include software.

The System 120 is also available as a board-level product. (Contact your local Intel office for special ordering instructions.)

Intel offers PC-AT add-in boards for the System 120 that include: 2M-byte and 8M-byte 32-bit memory boards, the OpenNet PCLINK2 networking board and the iPCX 344A BITBUS™ board. A standard keyboard is also available.

Table 1: System 120 Target Configurations

Product Code	CPU		RAM*	Floppy Disk	Hard Disk
	386	387	Mbytes	1.2 Mbytes	40 Mbytes
SYP120Z5X0	25 MHz		4		
SYP120Z5M40	25 MHz	25 MHz	4	✓	✓

*Subtract 384 Kbytes of RAM which is unavailable to iRMX® Operating System.

The iRMX software supports a range of popular display adapters, disk and tape controllers, and a four/eight-channel I/O controller. Additional drivers are available from third parties and from Intel's field systems engineers.

FEATURES

EASY APPLICATION DEVELOPMENT

You can develop applications for AT bus, Multibus I and Multibus II directly on the system using the System 120. To help designers get started with their real-time application, the System 120 is also available with development software. The System 120 Development Toolkits include the iRMX II configurable O/S software, the PL/M 286 compiler, the ASM 86/286 assemblers, the AEDIT text editor and a source level debugger, the Soft-Scope* II and an interface manager (JAM) that can be used as a front end to applications. Intel also offers a number of compilers (C, Fortran, Pascal), performance and debug tools for iRMX applications.

For iRMX II-based applications, designers should purchase one of the 4 M- byte System 120 target models, the iRMX III O/S, and the soft-scope III debugger (see Table 3).

INTEL QUALITY AND RELIABILITY

The System 120 is designed to meet the high standards of quality and reliability that users have come to expect from Intel products. The iRMX operating system software has undergone thousands of hours of testing and evaluation and is one of the most stable operating systems in the industry today.

FEATURES

Table 2: System 120 Development Toolkits

Product Code	Software		CPU	RAM	Disk	
	iRMX® II	PL/M 286 ASM AEDIT SOFTSCOPE JAM	386 & 387	Mbytes	Floppy	Hard
					1.2 Mbytes	40 Mbytes
SYS120KITM40	✓	✓	25 MHz	4	✓	✓
SYS120RMXM40	✓		25 MHz	4	✓	✓

Product Code	Host	Target	Description
SYRIIIATKIT	SYSTEM 120 iRMX® III O/S	AT-BUS System 120 Multibus I Multibus II	iRMX® III O/S with ASM 86/286/386 and utils, AEDIT, PL/M 386, and SDM III assembly-level debugger
RMXIIISFSCP	Same as above		Soft-Scope III source-level debugger

APPLICATION MIGRATION TO HIGHER PERFORMANCE SYSTEMS

Applications written for the System 120 can be easily moved to the higher performance and functionality of Multibus I and Multibus II designs. That's because the System 120 iRMX operating systems are binary compatible with the Multibus implementation of the O/S software.

The iRMX operating systems span the entire Intel systems product line, from the low-cost System 120 through the Multibus I System 320, to the high-end, multi-processing Multibus II System 520. Applications can easily be re-hosted on different bus architectures, allowing you to create a group of products satisfying a wide range of customer performance requirements.

DOS APPLICATION COMPATIBILITY

The System 120 supports the DOS 3.X operating system as well as the iRMX software, enabling you to use popular DOS applications to process data collected in real time. Some common applications are already available from software vendors. The applications include data bases, menu systems, and device drivers. The System 120 hard disk can be divided into iRMX and DOS partitions, allowing users to boot from either partition. A System 120 utility allows transfer of iRMX files into a DOS environment. DOS execution requires a customer-supplied version of DOS, a video adapter, a monitor, and a keyboard.

WORLDWIDE SERVICE AND SUPPORT

The System 120 is fully supported by Intel's worldwide staff of trained hardware and software support engineers. Intel also provides field application assistance, extensive iRMX Operating System classes, maintenance services, and a help hotline.

Among many services, Intel's systems engineers can implement special user needs, such as new device drivers.

The System 120 Development Toolkit comes with a 90-day software warranty and a one-year hardware warranty. System 120 target units come with a one year hardware warranty. Other support packages are optionally available; for more information please contact your local Intel Sales Office.

SPECIFICATIONS

SYSTEM 120 25-MHz BASE SYSTEM

Central Processor	Intel 386, 25 MHz
Floating-Point Coprocessor	Intel 387, 25 MHz**
Main Memory	4 Mbytes on CPU Board
Maximum RAM	40 Mbytes
Cycle Time	120 ns
Data Bus Width	32-bits
Error Detection	Byte Parity
I/O	2 serial ports (asynchronous, RS232C, 9-pin connector) 1 parallel port (Centronics compatible, 25-pin connector)
8 expansion slots	Two 32-, 16- or 8-bit slots Five 16- or 8-bit slots One 8-bit slot

**See tables 1 and 2 for configurations that apply

ELECTRICAL

AC Voltage/Frequency	Switching power supply, 115 V/60Hz or 230 V/50 Hz
DC Power	220 Watts
+5V	23.0 A maximum continuous
+12V	8.0 A maximum continuous; 12.0 A maximum for 12 seconds
−12V	0.5 A maximum continuous
−5V	0.5 A maximum continuous

DIMENSIONS

Length	47.5 cm (18.7 inches)
Width	54.1 cm (21.3 inches)
Height	16.5 cm (6.5 inches)

WEIGHT

Base System:	20 kilograms (44 lbs)

ORDERING INFORMATION

For more information or the number of your nearest Intel sales office, call 800-548-4725 (good in the U.S. and Canada).

SYSTEM 310* AP

280129-1

SYSTEM 310 AP

The System 310 AP is faster than many minicomputers. Powerful dedicated processors for communications and mass storage input/output control allow the 8 MHz 80286 CPU to concentrate on application software. The System 310 AP is open, which means you can upgrade performance and/or functionality in the future without purchasing a new system. The open system design protects your investment from becoming obsolete. Open systems design also means easy system customization with Intel and third-party add-in Multibus boards.

FEATURES

- 80286 Based System
- Open System Multibus architecture for upgradeability and growth
- iRMX® Operating System
- OpenNET™ Local Area Networking
- Total hardware and software support from Intel's worldwide customer support organization

*MSNET is a trademark of Microsoft Corporation.
*VAX/VMS is a trademark of Digital Equipment Corporation.
*The System 310 AP is also manufactured under product code pSYS310 by Intel Puerto Rico, Inc.

September 1991
Order Number: 280129-005

FEATURES

SYSTEM 310 AP—AN OPEN SYSTEM

The Intel System 310 AP is based on the Multibus architecture, (IEEE 796) industry standard system bus supported by over 200 vendors providing over 2000 compatible products.

The System 310 AP is an 80286 based open system designed with expansion in mind. The system can be expanded to accommodate up to 9MB of parity-checked RAM, all accessible with no wait states across the Local Bus Extension (LBX). For terminal communications, the systems can be expanded to a total of 18 RS232 serial ports.

The System 310 AP supports 40MB-140MB of Winchester disk storage. The 310 AP also supports a 320KB 5″ floppy drive and a 45/60MB streaming tape cartridge drive.

iRMX® OPERATING SYSTEM

The iRMX operating system delivers real-time performance. Designed to manage and extend the resources of the System 310 AP, this multitasking operating system provides configurable resources ranging from interrupt management and standard device drivers to data file maintenance commands for human interface and program development.

A wide range of popular industry standard high-level languages are supported for application development. The operating system includes powerful utilities for easy, interactive configuration and debugging.

OpenNET™—NETWORKING CAPABILITY

Intel's OpenNET product family provides a complete set of networking software and hardware that follows the International Standards Organization (ISO) Open Systems Interconnect (OSI) model.

OpenNET Network File Access Protocol adheres to the IBM/Microsoft/Intel Core File Sharing Protocol specification, providing transparent local/remote file access and file transfer capability between Intel's complete line of systems products, as well as with MSNET* and VAX/VMS* # based systems.

The System 310 AP distributes the transport protocol processing to intelligent Ethernet controllers that host Intel's OSI-compliant iNA 960 Class 4 Transport software, thereby unburdening the system CPU for greater performance.

INTEL SERVICE AND SUPPORT

The System 310 AP is backed by Intel's worldwide service and support organization. Total hardware and software support is available, including a hotline number for when you need help fast.

SPECIFICATIONS

SYSTEM/MODELS	310 AP-40B	310 AP-42A	310 AP-142A
Microprocessor	80286 8 MHz	80286 8 MHz	80286 8 MHz
Numeric Coprocessor	80287	80287	80287
RAM Memory	1MB	1MB	2MB
Floppy	360KB	360KB	360KB
Mass Storage	40MB	40MB	140MB
Tape Backup	NA	45/60MB	45/60MB
Serial I/O Ports	2	10	10
Parallel Ports	1	1	1
OpenNET			

SPECIFICATIONS

ENVIRONMENT

Operating Temperature	10°C to 35°C
Wet Bulb Temperature	26°C maximum
Relative Humidity	20% to 70% noncondensing
Altitude	Sea level to 8,000 feet

REGULATIONS

Meets or exceeds the following requirements:

Safety

US	UL114
Canada	CSA C22.2
Europe	TUV ICE 435

EMI/RFI

US and Canada	FCC Docket 20780—Class A
Europe	VDE 0871 Class A

ELECTRICAL

DC Power Output	360 watt maximum
AC Power Input	88-132 VAC or 180-264 VAC, 47-63 Hz (user selectable)

DIMENSIONS

Height	6½″
Width	17″
Depth	22″
Weight	Approx. 55 lbs

intel®

SYSTEM 320*

280502-1

SYSTEM 320

The System 320 gives you the performance and capabilities of a minicomputer at less than half the cost. When combined with Intel's iRMX® Real-time Multitasking Operating System, the System 320 is especially suited for applications requiring real-time response and resource control typically found in financial transaction, industrial automation, medical and communications markets. The System 320 is also appropriate as the development environment for module-based design.

SYSTEM 320 FEATURES

- 386™ Based System
- Open System Architecture
- OpenNET™ Local Area Networking
- Variety of Peripherals Available
- Range of Configurations Available
- Complete Installation, Service and Support Available

7

*MSNET is a trademark of Microsoft Corporation.
**VAX/VMS is a trademark of Digital Equipment Corporation.
*The System 320 is also manufactured under product code pSYS320 by Intel Puerto Rico, Inc.

October 1990
Order Number: 280502-002

FEATURES

SYSTEM 320—AN OPEN SYSTEM

The System 320 is based on the IEEE 796 Multibus architecture, an industry standard system bus supported by over 200 vendors providing over 2000 compatible products. Special configurations can be tailored by the user, by Intel's Custom System Integration group or by Intel's authorized Value Added Distribution Centers.

OpenNET™ NETWORKING CAPABILITY

Intel's OpenNET product family provides a complete set of networking software and hardware that follows the International Standards Organization (ISO) Open Systems Interconnect (OSI) model.

OpenNET Network File Access Protocol adheres to the IBM/Microsoft/Intel Core File Sharing Protocol specification, providing transparent local/remote file access and file transfer capability between Intel's complete line of systems products, as well as with MSNET* and VAX/VMS* based systems.

The System 320 distributes the transport protocol processing to intelligent Ethernet controllers that host Intel's OSI-compliant iNA 960 Class 4 Transport software, thereby unburdening the system CPU for greater performance.

INSTALLATION SERVICE & SUPPORT

The System 320 is backed by Intel's worldwide service and support organization. Installation is available to quickly get the system up and running. Total hardware and software support is available, including a hotline number for when the user needs help fast. Intel also provides hands-on training workshops to give the user a thorough understanding of the System 320. These workshops are conducted at Intel training centers or customer sites worldwide.

RANGE OF CONFIGURATIONS

Intel offers a wide range of configurations for the System 320. Contact your local Intel representative for further information.

SPECIFICATIONS

ENVIRONMENT

Operating Temperature	10°C to 40°C
Wet Bulb Temperature	26°C maximum
Relative Humidity	85% at 40°C
Altitude	Sea level to 10,000 feet

REGULATIONS

Meets or exceeds the following requirements:

Safety	
US	UL 478
Canada	CSA C22.2
Europe	IEC 435
EMI/RFI	
US and Canada	FCC Class B Computing Device
Europe	VDE Limit Class B

ELECTRICAL

DC Power Output	435 watt maximum
AC Power Input	88-132 VAC or 176-264 VAC, 47 Hz-63 Hz, single phase

DIMENSIONS

Height	8″
Width	17.5″
Depth	22.25″
Weight	Approx. 55 lbs

ORDERING INFORMATION

For more information or the number of your nearest Intel sales office, call 800-548-4725 (good in the U.S. and Canada).

iRMX® FOR WINDOWS*

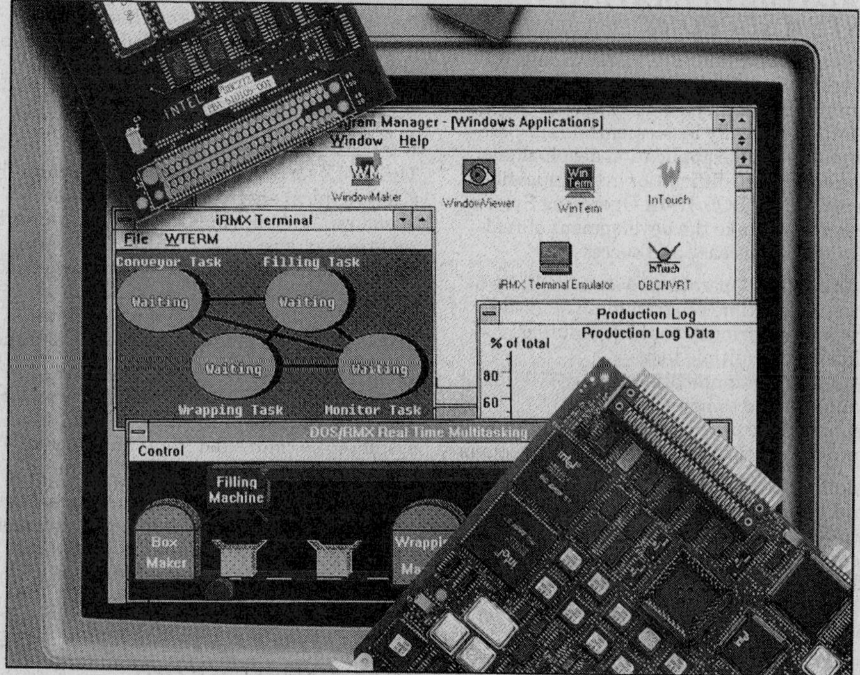

281116–1

REAL-TIME OPERATING SYSTEM FOR WINDOWS AND DOS APPLICATIONS*

The DOS/RMX Operating System provides system designers of Intel386™ or i486™ microprocessor-based ISA, EISA, and Multibus AT products the ability to take advantage of the features and capabilities of two standard operating systems. One is DOS, the standard OS for the PC architecture, with billions of dollars of application software and a rich graphical Microsoft Windows* 3 environment. The other is the iRMX® Operating System, the standard real-time software for the x86 architecture, used in over 7500 different real-time designs. These operating systems, running concurrently on a single microprocessor, can provide the systems designer a powerful set of capabilities to tackle the most difficult and demanding application. When time-to-market is important and your customer is demanding a solution that DOS and Windows alone cannot meet, then iRMX for Windows is your answer.

FEATURES

- iRMX Operating System: a full 32-bit multitasking, multiuser, OS with a preemptive real-time scheduler
- Supports standard MS-DOS* or PC-DOS and Windows 3
- Networking Support
  - — LAN manager-compatible
- Provides Real-Time extensions to DOS and MS-Windows:
  - — Data sharing between DOS or Windows and iRMX tasks
  - — Inter-task communications and synchronization
  - — DOS applications have access up to 4 Gbytes of extended memory

7

FEATURES

REAL-TIME OPERATING SYSTEM SUPPORT

Real-time applications are easier to develop with real-time software. Operating systems designed for general business use (like DOS and UNIX) typically lack essential real-time features. Real-time application development can be expensive, difficult or even impossible. In contrast, the DOS/RMX Operating System is designed to make the development of real-time applications easy and successful.

The DOS/RMX Operating System includes a rich set of real-time programming facilities:

- Preemptive, priority based scheduling
- Support for multiple tasks
- Inter-task communication through mailboxes and semaphores
- Deterministic program execution
- Control of critical resources through regions

In addition, the DOS/RMX Operating System provides a memory protection scheme that detects coding errors. When iRMX software allocates memory, it assigns a combination read, write and execute-only status to the allocated code and data segments. If code attempts to execute outside this range or write to a data segment marked read-only, the operating system issues a protection error.

If the DOS operating system hangs or crashes, the real-time iRMX operating system will continue to function correctly and allow DOS to be reloaded and restarted.

STANDARD SOFTWARE SUPPORT

iRMX for Windows software supports MS-DOS or PC-DOS versions 3.3 and 4.01; no emulations or changes to standard DOS are required.

After the DOS operating system is loaded, it only takes a few keystrokes to load the iRMX operating system and the real-time extensions. When the iRMX operating system is initializing, it suspends DOS, switches the microprocessor into full 32-bit mode and encapsulates DOS as a VM86 task. DOS then runs as a task under the iRMX operating system.

A hot key allows the user to switch the console display between the DOS prompt and the iRMX command line interpreter.

Application software such as databases, word processors, graphical drawing tools, industrial packages and custom DOS programs can be run under DOS without any changes. Applications that use expanded memory are also supported.

YOUR WINDOW INTO REAL-TIME

The iRMX for Windows software supports the rich graphical environment of Microsoft Windows. Windows applications can access the real-time extensions of the iRMX operating system to pass data and/or synchronize tasks. Applications using the Dynamic Data Exchange Interface (DDE) can pass data between other Windows applications and the real-time iRMX task.

Included with DOS/RMX is a Windows source program that allows the iRMX operating system to be controlled from the Windows environment.

Third-party applications like the Marketfield WinTerm terminal emulator, that implement the DDE interface and the iRMX real-time DOS extensions, can directly interface with iRMX and Windows applications.

REAL-TIME EXTENSIONS FOR DOS AND WINDOWS

The DOS/RMX Operating System provides a set of 30 system calls to the DOS application programmer. These allow DOS tasks to create and manipulate inter-task communications mechanisms and extended memory segments. These iRMX objects can be cataloged and made available to the 32-bit iRMX tasks so that DOS and iRMX tasks can share data and synchronize activities.

An example is an application that provides fast response times to a number of external events and displays the results on a high-resolution VGA screen. The event-handler is controlled by the multitasking iRMX OS, while the graphics run under DOS. The real-time data is passed to the DOS graphics environment by way of the real-time DOS extension.

CONFIGURED iRMX® SOFTWARE

The DOS/RMX Operating System is based on the iRMX III Operating System and is configured especially for the PC-AT architecture. Support for a range of iRMX device drivers is available through the loadable device driver feature. This means that users

FEATURES

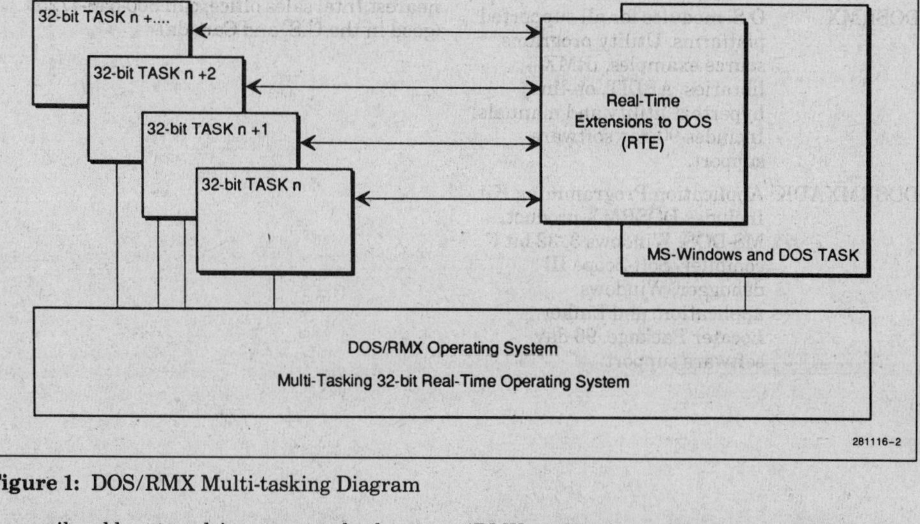

Figure 1: DOS/RMX Multi-tasking Diagram

can easily add custom drivers or standard drivers like the RAM driver or the multi-channel I/O driver. Configurations for the following are included in the product:

- Intel System 3xx, 4xx platforms and boards
- Multibus I iSBC 386SX single board PC
- Multibus II iSBC 386PC-16 PC system
- Intel System 120

Each configuration also includes a networking version with support for the SPCL2ANIA, iSBX 586 and iSBC 186/530. This allows both standard MS-NET and the native iRMX-NET support. Novell networking and Microsoft LAN Manager are supported through transparent file access from both the iRMX operating system and DOS.

APPLICATION DEVELOPMENT

iRMX designers can choose from these Intel programming languages: C, PL/M and assembler (iC386, PL/M386 and ASM386). The DOS/RMX manual also includes a DOS hypertext program along with detailed system call and operating system concepts text files. Using the hypertext utility, the developer can cut and paste system call details or example code from the on-line documentation and incorporate it directly into application source modules.

iRMX applications written for the DOS/RMX Operating System run under the iRMX Human Interface layer either in foreground or background mode. The addition of a new system call allows any type of iRMX application—to run under the DOS/RMX Operating System.

Use the Soft-Scope III source level debugger to complement the development environment.

SERVICE AND SUPPORT

With the DOS/RMX Operating System, you're not alone when extending your DOS application into a real-time application. Intel has the best technical sales support in the real-time business. The iRMX for Windows software includes a 90-day software support contract that includes:

- product updates
- technical information phone service
- subscription service and technical information via
  - monthly issues of *Comments* newsletter
  - quarterly Troubleshooting Guide
  - software problem report service

The software support contract can be extended to a full one-year contract after the first 90 days.

ORDERING INFORMATION

Order Code	Description
DOSRMX	O.S. modules for all supported platforms. Utility programs, source examples, iRMX libraries, AEDIT, on-line hypertext utility and manuals. Includes 90-day software support.
DOSRMXADK	Application Programming Kit. Includes DOSRMX product, MS-DOS, Windows 3, 32-bit C compiler, Soft-Scope III debugger, Windows application, and Linker Locater Package. 90-day software support.

For further information or the number of your nearest Intel sales office, call 800-548-4725 (good in the U.S. and Canada).

iRMK™ VERSION I.3 REAL-TIME KERNEL

280613-1

A 32-BIT REAL-TIME KERNEL

The iRMK™ Version I.3 Real-time Kernel is the 32-bit real-time executive developed, sold and supported by Intel. It reduces the cost and risk of designing and maintaining software for numerous real-time applications such as embedded control systems and dedicated real-time subsystems in multiple-processor systems.

KEY FEATURES

- 32-bit, real-time multitasking kernel
- Rich set of real-time services
- Designed and optimized for the 386™ and 376™ microprocessor families
- Comprehensive development tool support
- Integrated with the Phar Lap 386|DOS-Extender* to allow the kernel and its application to run as a DOS application
- Extremely fast execution with predictable response times for time-critical applications
- Optional Multibus II multiprocessing support
- Requires only the 386DX, 386SX, i486™, or 376 microprocessor; optional support for 387™ and 387SX numeric coprocessors and other peripheral devices
- Easy customized and enhanced
- Supported by Intel

December 1990
Order Number: 280613-003

FEATURES

REAL-TIME SOFTWARE FROM THE INDUSTRY LEADER

Intel has been the industry leader in microprocessor-based real-time computing since it invented the microprocessor. No other company supplies a comparable range of real-time solutions. Since 1977, thousands of customers have used Intel's iRMX® real-time operating systems and the iRMK real-time kernels.

Now Intel has put its real-time expertise into a 32-bit kernel that supports the i486, 386, and 376 families of microprocessors. The iRMK Version I.3 Kernel saves you the cost of designing, debugging and maintaining your own executive for real-time systems. You can concentrate on writing your application rather than a kernel.

THE QUICKEST PATH FOR A WIDE RANGE OF REAL-TIME APPLICATIONS

The iRMK Kernel's high performance and rich set of real-time services make it ideal for a wide range of real-time applications, including:

Data acquisition and analysis
Continuous process control
Discrete process control
Simulation
Medical instrumentation
Test instrumentation
Image processing
Automated test
Avionics and navigation
Field command control
Energy control
Environmental control
Radio control
Satellite communications
Terminals
Graphics work stations
Robots
Signal processing
Laser printing
Front-end concentrators
Host communications

A RICH SET OF REAL-TIME SERVICES

The iRMK Version I.3 Kernel provides a rich set of services for real-time applications, including:

- Task management with system calls to create, manage, and schedule tasks in a multitasking environment. The Kernel offers preemptive priority scheduling combined with optional time-slice (round robin) scheduling.
  The scheduling algorithm used by the iRMK Kernel allows it to reschedule tasks in a fixed amount of time, regardless of the number of tasks.
  An application can provide optional task handlers to customize task management. These handlers can execute on task creation, task switch, task deletion and task priority change. You can use task handlers for a wide range of functions, including saving and restoring the state of coprocessor registers on task switch, masking interrupts based on task priority or implementing diagnostic monitors.
- Interrupt management by immediately switching control to user-written interrupt handlers when an interrupt occurs. Response to interrupts is both fast and predictable. Most of the Kernel's system calls can be executed directly from interrupt handlers.
- Time management, providing single-shot alarms, repetitive alarms and a real-time clock. Alarms can be reset to implement watchdog, also known as deadman, timers.
- Semaphores, regions, and mailboxes for intertask synchronization and communication. Semaphores are used for intertask signalling and synchronization. Regions are binary semaphores used to ensure mutual exclusion and prevent priority inversion when tasks contend for control of system resources. A task holding a region's unit runs at the priority of the highest priority task waiting for the region's unit.

FEATURES

Mailboxes are queues that can hold any number of messages and are used to exchange data between tasks. Either data or pointers can be sent using mailboxes. The kernel allows mailbox messages to be of any length. High-priority messages may be placed (jammed) at the front of the message queue to ensure that they are received before other messages queued at the mailbox.

To ensure that high-priority tasks are not blocked by lower priority tasks, the kernel allows tasks to queue at semaphores and mailboxes in priority order. The kernel also supports first-in, first-out task queuing.

- Memory pool manager that provides fixed and variable block allocation. Memory can be divided into any number of pools. Multiple memory pools might be created for different speed memories or for allocating different size blocks. Access to a memory pool for fixed-sized allocation is always deterministic. The kernel-supplied memory manager works with flat, segmented and paged addressing. Users can write their own memory managers to provide different memory management policies or to support virtual memory.

SUPPORT FOR MULTIPROCESSING VIA THE MULTIBUS II ARCHITECTURE

The Multibus II architecture is designed to optimize multiple-processor designs. This bus:

- Implements a loosely coupled architecture in which inter-processor interrupts and data are exchanged via messages transmitted as packets over the bus;
- Provides fast bus access;
- Allows inter processor signalling at interrupt speeds from as many as 255 sources;
- Provides data transfer rates of up to 32 megabytes per second;
- Allows multiple communication sessions to occur simultaneously between processors;
- Supports up to 21 CPU boards per chassis with each board providing the processor, memory, and I/O needed for its portion of the application; and
- Provides registers—called Interconnect Space—on each board, that can be used for dynamic system configuration.

Two optional modules allow iRMK Kernel applications to make full use of the Multibus II architecture. The first module implements message passing, allowing the application to have direct access to the message-passing hardware or to use Intel's Multibus II transport protocol. The second module implements interconnect space access to support dynamic system configuration.

These modules can be used to implement high performance multiple-processor designs that:

- Break a highly complex real-time application into multiple lower-complexity applications distributed across multiple processors
- Distribute an application that's too CPU-intensive for a single processor between several processors
- Provide redundancy
- Dedicate processors to specific tasks
- Provide inter-operation with any operating system or controller board that uses Intel's Multibus II transport protocol, including the iRMX III, iRMX II, iRMK I, and Intel System V/386 operating systems.

INTEGRATED ONTO PC/AT-COMPATIBLE PLATFORMS

The iRMK Kernel and its real-time application can run as a 32-bit DOS application on 386 CPU-based PC AT compatible systems. Phar Lap Software's 386|DOS-Extender marries the worlds of DOS and the 386 processor's protected mode. As Figure 1 shows, the real-time application can take full advantage of the services of both the iRMK Kernel and of DOS. For example, the application can use the Kernel's multitasking and interrupt-handling features. At the same time, it can make calls to DOS to access the disk or network.

The 386 CPU-based, PC/AT-compatible platform can be used as either the target for the application or as a convenient development platform.

The 386|DOS-Extender allows the iRMK Kernel application to take full advantage of all DOS services while still running in the 386 CPU's protected mode. For example, the application can use MetaWare's C libraries to make calls to DOS BIOS and to access the DOS file system. A sample program showing use of the DOS-Extender with the iRMK Kernel is provided.

FEATURES

HARDWARE REQUIREMENTS AND SUPPORT

The iRMK Kernel requires only a 386 or 376 family microprocessor and sufficient memory for itself and its application. Its design, however, recognizes that many systems use additional programmable peripheral devices and coprocessors. The Kernel provides optional device managers for the:

- 387 and 387SX Numeric Coprocessors
- 82380 and 82370 Integrated System Peripherals
- 8254 Programmable Interval Timer
- 8259A Programmable Interrupt Controller
- 82530 Serial Communication Controller

An application can supply managers for other devices and coprocessors in addition to or in replacement of the devices listed above.

The iRMK Kernel was designed to be programmed into PROM or EPROM, making it easy to use in embedded designs.

The iRMK Kernel can be used with any system bus including the Multibus I and Multibus II buses. The optional Multibus II message-passing and Interconnect Space access modules use the Message Passing Coprocessor (MPC). The Kernel provides managers to use the 82380/82370 Integrated System Peripherals or the 82258 Advanced DMA controller with an MPC for message passing.

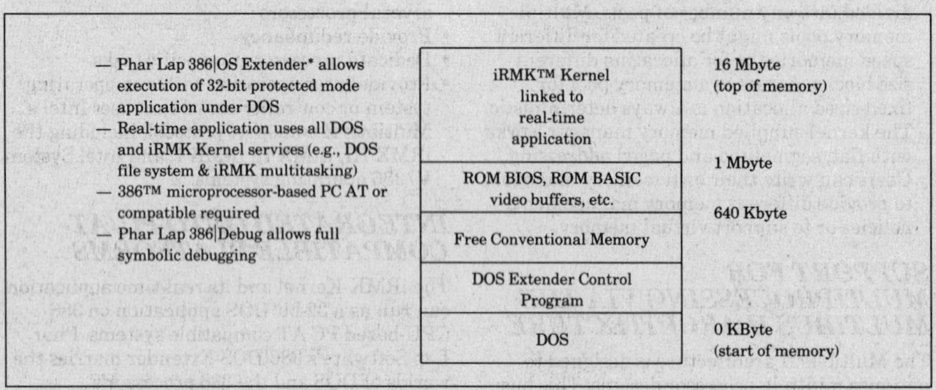

Figure 1: iRMKTM Kernel and real-time application as DOS application.

FEATURES

SUPPORT FOR THE INTEL 386™ AND INTEL 376™ ARCHITECTURES

The iRMK Kernel provides 32-bit, protected-mode 386 and 376 CPU operation. By default, the kernel and its application execute in a flat memory space of up to 4 gigabytes in a single privilege level. Applications can add support for any mixture of additional protected mode features including:

- Any model of segmentation
- Memory paging
- Virtual memory
- Multiple privilege levels
- Call and trap gates

These protected mode features can be used to increase the reliability of the application by using the processor's hardware to:

- Protect against attempts to write beyond segment bounds (to catch situations like stack overflow or underflow)
- Allow only privileged or trusted code to access key routines and data
- Isolate bugs to single modules so that the rest of the application and the kernel are not corrupted
- Assign access rights to code and data
- Isolate address spaces

To use these features, the application manipulates the processor's descriptor tables. Because the kernel was implemented specifically to support 386 and 376 microprocessor-based applications, it provides an optional descriptor table manager that simplifies protected mode programming. This manager provides system calls to read and write descriptor table entries, to convert addresses from linear to physical and vice versa, and to get a segment's selector.

A MODULAR ARCHITECTURE FOR EASY CUSTOMIZING

The iRMK Kernel offers maximum flexibility so that it can be customized for each application. Each major function such as mailboxes is implemented as a separate module. The kernel's modules are linked together and supplied individually. Simply link the modules you need for your application. An unused module does not need to be linked in and does not increase the size of the kernel in your application. You can also replace any optional kernel module with one that implements specific features required by your application. For example, you might want to replace the kernel's memory manager with one that supports virtual memory.

Core Modules
— Task Manager
— Interrupt Manager
— Time Manager

Optional Modules
— Mailbox Manager
— Semaphore Manager
— Memory Manager
— Descriptor Manager
— Multibus II Message Passing
— Multibus II Interconnect Space Access

Optional Device Managers
— 387 and 387SX Numeric Coprocessors
— 8259A PIC
— 8254 PIT
— 82380/82370 Integrated System Peripheral PIT and PIC functions

Figure 2 shows the Kernel's modules.

FEATURES

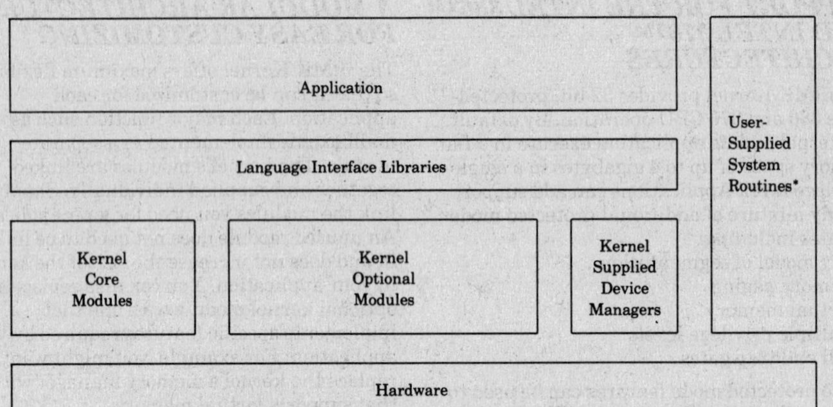

Figure 2: iRMK™ Real-Time Kernel Architecture

*User-supplied system routines would include interrupt handlers, user-written device managers, and similar routines.

FEATURES

DEVELOPING WITH THE iRMK™ REAL-TIME KERNEL

As Figure 3 shows, Intel supports a complete line of development tools for writing and debugging iRMK Kernel applications. The kernel comes with interface libraries for the compilers shown in Figure 3. The source code for these libraries is provided, so you can modify them to support other compilers and languages.

THE SOFT-SCOPE III/386™ AND iM III DEBUGGING TEAM

The Soft-Scope III Debugger and iM III Monitor provide a complete cross-debugging environment for iRMK Kernel applications. The Debugger resides on a PC/AT-compatible system and provides high-level debugging capabilities. The monitor resides on the target with the kernel and its real-time application and provides low-level, processor-oriented debug capabilities. Together, the two provide:

- Complete support for the 386DX, 386SX, i486, and 376 processor protected-mode architectures
- Access to the processor's system data structures such as the GDT, IDT, and LDT
- Breakpoints set on instructions or data-read or-write
- Full display of symbolic information and the application source code
- Full display of key kernel data such as the state of tasks, the ready-task queue, mailboxes, semaphores, memory pools, ports, and Multibus II message queues and messages
- Powerful macros and C expression evaluation
- 100 kilobytes per minute download between the SoftScope III debugger and the iM III Monitor target

The SoftScope III Debugger runs on PC/AT-compatible systems. It requires a minimum of 512 kilobytes of memory and a serial port. You can configure the iM III Monitor for any target system that contains a 386 family processor, a minimum of 16 kilobytes of memory, and a serial port. The monitor's native command set provides low-level, hardware-oriented debugging capabilities. These basic capabilities can be augmented by extending the monitor itself, using the Soft-Scope III Debugger or writing your own high-level debugger.

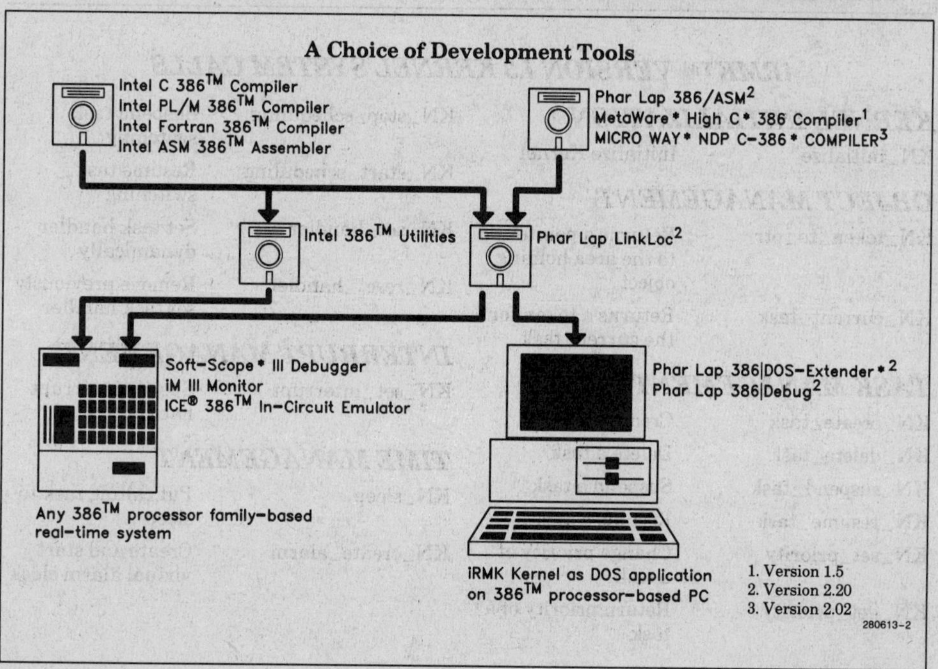

FEATURES

CONTENTS OF THE iRMK™ KERNEL DEVELOPMENT PACKAGE

The iRMK Kernel comes in a comprehensive package that includes:

- Kernel object modules
- Source for the kernel-supplied 82380 and 82370 Integrated System Peripherals; 8259A PIC; 8254 PIT; 387 and 387SX Numeric Coprocessor; and 82530 Serial Communication Controller device managers.

Source also is provided for the 82258 and 82380 DMA managers for Multibus II message passing.

- Source for language interface libraries
- Source for the call gate interface
- Source for examples showing:
  - — Structure of kernel applications
  - — Use of the kernel with applications written with Intel's PL/M 386, C 386, and FORTRAN 386 compilers and MetaWare's High C 386 compilers
  - — Execution of the kernel as a DOS application using the Phar Lap 386|DOS-Extender
  - — Compile, bind, and build sequences
  - — Sample initialization code for the 386 and 376 microprocessors
  - — Multibus II message passing
  - — Applications written to execute in a flat memory space and in a segmented memory space
- User Reference guide
- 90 days of Customer Support

INTEL SUPPORT, CONSULTING, AND TRAINING

With the iRMK Kernel you get the 386 architecture and real-time software expertise of the Intel's customer support engineers. Intel provides phone support, on- or off-site consulting, troubleshooting guides and updates. The kernel includes 90 days of Intel's Technical Information Phone Service (TIPS). Extended support and consulting are also available.

SYSTEM CALLS

iRMK™ VERSION I.3 KERNEL SYSTEM CALLS

KERNEL INITIALIZATION

KN_initialize	Initialize Kernel

OBJECT MANAGEMENT

KN_token_to_ptr	Returns a pointer to the area holding object
KN_current_task	Returns a token for the current task

TASK MANAGEMENT

KN_create_task	Create a task
KN_delete_task	Delete a task
KN_suspend_task	Suspend a task
KN_resume_task	Resume a task
KN_set_priority	Change priority of a task
KN_get_priority	Return priority of a task
KN_stop_scheduling	Suspend task switching
KN_start_scheduling	Resume task switching
KN_set_handler	Set task handler dynamically
KN_reset_handler	Remove previously set task handler

INTERRUPT MANAGEMENT

KN_set_interrupt	Specify interrupt handler

TIME MANAGEMENT

KN_sleep	Put calling task to sleep
KN_create_alarm	Create and start virtual alarm clock

SYSTEM CALLS

KN_reset_alarm	Reset an existing alarm
KN_delete_alarm	Delete alarm
KN_get_time	Get time
KN_set_time	Set time
KN_tick	Notify Kernel that clock tick has occurred

INTER-TASK COMMUNICATION AND SYNCHRONIZATION

KN_create_semaphore	Create a semaphore
KN_delete_semaphore	Delete a semaphore
KN_send_unit	Add a unit to a semaphore
KN_receive_unit	Receive a unit from a semaphore
KN_create_mailbox	Create a mailbox
KN_delete_mailbox	Delete a mailbox
KN_send_data	Send data to a mailbox
KN_send_priority_data	Place (jam) priority message at head of message queue
KN_receive_data	Request a message from a mailbox

MEMORY MANAGEMENT

KN_create_pool	Create a memory pool
KN_delete_pool	Delete a memory pool
KN_create_area	Create a memory area from a pool
KN_delete_area	Return a memory area to a memory pool
KN_get_pool_attributes	Get a memory pool's attributes

DESCRIPTOR TABLE MANAGEMENT

KN_get_descriptor_attributes	Get a descriptor's attributes
KN_set_descriptor_attributes	Set a descriptor's attributes
KN_initialize_LDT	Initialize local descriptor table (LDT)
KN_null_descriptor	Overwrite a descriptor with the null descriptor
KN_initialize_subsystem	Allows application to be divided into multiple subsystems when application interfaces to Kernel through a call gate
KN_linear_to_ptr	Convert a linear address to a pointer
KN_ptr_to_linear	Convert a pointer to a linear address
KN_get_data_selector	Get the selector for the data segment
KN_get_code_selector	Get the selector for the code segment
KN_translate_ptr	Converts a pointer that will be based on a user-specified selector

82380, 82370, AND 8259A PIC MANAGEMENT

KN_initialize_PICs	Initialize the PICs
KN_mask_slot	Mask out interrupts on a specified slot
KN_unmask_slot	Unmask interrupts on a specified slot
KN_send_EOI	Signal the PIC that the interrupt on a specified slot has been serviced
KN_new_masks	Change interrupt masks
KN_get_slot	Return the most important active interrupt slot

7

SYSTEM CALLS

82380, 82370, AND 8254 PIT MANAGEMENT

KN_initialize_PIT	Initialize an 8254 PIT
KN_start_PIT	Start PIT counting
KN_get_PIT_interval	Return PIT interval

387™ AND 387SX NUMERIC COPROCESSOR MANAGEMENT

KN_initialize_NDP	Initialize a 387 or 387SX Numeric Coprocessor

CHARACTER I/O DEVICE SUPPORT

KN_initialize_console	Initialize the console device
KN_ci	Read ASCII character from console input device
KN_co	Transfer a character to console output device
KN_csts	Read immediate character, if any, from console input device
KN_initialize_stdio	Initialize stdio library functions
putchar, getchar, printf, scanf	stdio functions for console I/O

MULTIBUS II MESSAGE PASSING MANAGEMENT

KN_initialize_message_passing	Initialize the message passing module
KN_mp_working_storage_size	Compute size of work space needed for message passing
KN_send_tp	Send a transport message
KN_attach_receive_mailbox	Attach a receive mailbox
KN_cancel_tp	Cancel a solicited message or request-response transaction
KN_send_dl	Send a data link message
KN_attach_protocol_handler	Attach a protocol handler
KN_cancel_dl	Cancel a data link buffer request

MULTIBUS II INTERCONNECT SPACE MANAGEMENT

KN_initialize_interconnect	Initialize the interconnect module
KN_get_interconnect	Get the value of an interconnect register
KN_set_interconnect	Set the value of an interconnect register
KN_local_host_ID	Get the host ID of the local host

ORDERING INFORMATION

Order Code	Product
RMK	iRMK Version I.3 development software
RMKIRFX/RMKCRFX	iRMK Kernel incorporation license fees. A separate incorporation license must be signed prior to making incorporations.
IMMIII	iM III Monitor development software
IMIIIRFX	iM III Monitor incorporation license fees. A separate incorporation license must be signed prior to making incorporations.
SFTSCPIIID	Soft-Scope III debugger.
SSC-430	Technical Information Support including Phone support, *;Comments* Magazine, and Troubleshooting Guides
	On- or off-site consulting on iRMK I.3 Kernel or other Intel systems engineer. Available on a daily or long term basis.
USER WORKSHOPS	iRMK Real-time Kernel 80386 Programming Using ASM386 Customer Training Workshop 80386 System Software Customer Training Workshop 80386 System Hardware Design Overview Customer Training Workshop 80376/80386 Embedded Processor System Design Customer Training Workshop 80486 for 80386 Designers Customer Training Workshop

intel®

iRMX® OPERATING SYSTEM FAMILY

281019–1

The iRMX® family of operating systems provides designers with the world's most advanced real-time software for designs based on the Intel 8086/88, 80186/88, 80286, 386™, and i486™ family microprocessors. The product of twelve years of real-time expertise by Intel, iRMX software provides high-performance response to external events, excellent support of special-purpose hardware, and sophisticated real-time programming facilities.

A COMPLETE FAMILY OF REAL-TIME OPERATING SYSTEMS

- Multiprocessing support
- Multiple tasks and multiple jobs
- Multiple users
- On-target development
- Priority based and/or round robin scheduling
- User-extendable object oriented architecture

iRMX® and iSBC® are registered trademarks of Intel Corporation.
386™, 387™, i486™, Insite™, iSBX™, iSDM™, OpenNET™, and TIPS™ are trademarks of Intel Corporation.
*MS-DOS and XENIX are registered trademarks of Microsoft Corporation.
PC-AT is a registered trademark of International Business Machines Corporation.
Soft-Scope is a registered trademark of Concurrent Sciences, Inc.
UNIX is a registered trademark of AT&T in the U.S.A. and other countries.
VAX/VMS is a registered trademark of Digital Equipment Corporation.
Ethernet is a registered trademark of Xerox Corporation.

November 1990
Order Number: 281019-003

intel.

iRMX® OPERATING SYSTEMS

SOFTWARE WITH A FUTURE

- Leading real-time microprocessor software with over 6000 licenses sold
- Active iRMX Users Group (iRUG) with worldwide chapters, a regular newsletter, and an annual technical convention
- Applications easily migrated from iRMX I to iRMX II to iRMX III
- Application software from third-party sources
- Fully supported on the Intel x86 processor family
- Runs on Multibus I, Multibus II, and AT-bus Systems
- Optional networking to systems running the MS-DOS*, VAX/VMS*, UNIX*, XENIX*, iRMX I, iRMX II, and iRMX III operating systems

7

iRMX® OPERATING SYSTEMS

SUPPORT FOR THE FULL RANGE OF REAL-TIME APPLICATIONS

The iRMX operating systems support the full range of real-time applications, from embedded control designs to reprogrammable systems which require dynamic creation, deletion, and priority arbitration of tasks. This flexibility makes it possible to save substantial staff retraining and software maintenance costs by using a single operating system for many different real-time systems and subsystems. Users have shown that the iRMX operating systems are ideal for such applications as:

avionics	manufacturing test
communications	medical instruments
data acquisition and analysis	process control
	railroad control
energy management	missile controls
factory automation	satellite communications
financial trader workstations	simulation
image processing	transaction processing
machine control	

REAL-TIME SOFTWARE FOR REAL-TIME APPLICATIONS

Real-time applications are easier to develop with real-time software. Operating systems designed for general business use typically lack essential real-time features, so real-time application development is often expensive, difficult, or even impossible. In contrast, iRMX software is real-time software designed to make the development of real-time applications easy and successful. Attributes offered by the iRMX software include:

High performance

For real-time applications, iRMX software is many times faster than general purpose operating systems. This high performance enables applications based on the iRMX operating systems to keep up with the rapid data and control flow of machine and communication interfaces.

A rich set of real-time programming facilities

The iRMX software includes a rich set of real-time programming facilities that are usually missing in whole or in part from non-real-time operating systems. These facilities include:

- preemptive, priority-based scheduling with round robin (time slice) scheduling within a priority level
- interrupt management with standard or user-defined exception handlers
- support for multiple tasks
- inter-task communication through mailboxes and semaphores
- deterministic program execution
- control of critical resources through regions

Support for designs based on Intel systems, single board computers, and components

Excellent support for special purpose hardware

Most real-time applications involve some special purpose hardware, and general purpose operating systems are often relatively monolithic and difficult to interface to this hardware. The iRMX operating systems are highly configurable, modular software systems which easily support custom hardware.
Support for special purpose hardware includes:

- the ability to configure the operating system by layer
- hooks for user-written handlers at key points
- the ability to add operating system extensions
- standard device driver interfaces

More reliable code through iRMX® II and iRMX® III memory protection

When the iRMX II or iRMX III software allocates memory to a task, it assigns a combination of read, write, and execute-only status to the allocated code and data segments. If the code attempts to execute outside of this range (e.g., stack overflow) or write to a data segment marked read-only, the operating system will issue a "protection" error. This flag can be used to notify an operator of the exact location in the code where the problem occurred. Bounds and access rights checking, which is enforced by the hardware, can catch up to 90% of common coding errors.

COMPLETE REAL-TIME OPERATING SYSTEMS, NOT JUST A KERNEL

With comparable performance, the iRMX operating systems provide many features that are extra-cost items, or simply unavailable, in real-time kernels. These features make the development of real-time applications much easier and faster, but do not add unnecessary overhead. In fact, all functional layers above the nucleus are optional in the iRMX operating systems. This flexibility allows you to include only those features that your application requires.

The following is a brief description of the major functional groups within the iRMX operating systems.

Nucleus

The Nucleus is the heart of the operating system and controls all resources available to the system. The nucleus provides key real-time features including:

- Support of multiple tasks
- Priority based and time slice scheduling
- Dynamic priority adjustment
- Memory management
- Inter-task communication and synchronization using mailboxes and semaphores
- Interrupt management with custom exception handlers
- Time management
- Object management
- Addition of custom operating system extensions
- Inter-processor communication for multi-processor systems

iRMX® OPERATING SYSTEMS

Basic I/O System (BIOS)

The Basic I/O System (BIOS) provides primitives to read from and write to peripherals. The BIOS also sets up the file structures used by the system and provides access to all required peripherals through a standard device driver interface. Both synchronous and asynchronous system calls are supported. Many device drivers are provided with the iRMX operating systems, and custom device drivers and file drivers may be added by the user.

Extended I/O System (EIOS)

The Extended I/O System (EIOS) provides similar services to the BIOS, with simplified calls that give less explicit control of device behavior and performance. The software supports synchronous system calls and provides automatic buffering of I/O operations. The EIOS also provides a logical-to-physical device connection, and allows a program to specify a logical address for output.

Application Loader

The Application Loader is used to load programs from mass storage into memory, where they execute. Programs may be loaded under program or operator control.

Bootstrap Loader

The Bootstrap Loader is used to load the operating system or an iRMX application from mass storage into memory, and then to begin the system's execution.

Universal Development Interface (UDI)

The Universal Development Interface provides an easy-to-use interface with a standard set of system calls to allow programs and languages to be easily transported to or from the iRMX operating systems to other operating systems which support the UDI standard. For example, UDI lets iRMX host many Intel DOS-based tools.

System Debugger

The System Debugger or SDB is a static-level debugger that can be used to debug applications or to view operating system objects. The iRMX I operating system also includes a dynamic debugger. Source-level debuggers are separately available.

Human Interface

The Human Interface allows multiple users to effectively develop applications, maintain files, run programs, and communicate with the operating system. It consists of a set of system calls, a set of commands, and a Command Line Interpreter. Commands are available for file management, device management, and system status. Features include password protected log-on, full line editing, user extensions, and support for background jobs. In addition, the Command Line Interpreter may be replaced for special applications. For example, a Computer Aided Tomography (CAT) scanner controlled by an iRMX operating system could use a custom Command Line Interpreter to allow the operator to direct the movement of the scanner.

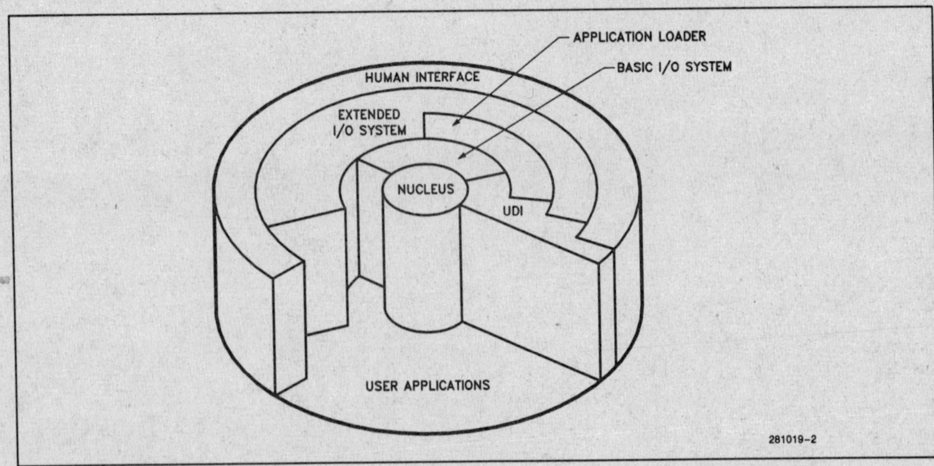

Figure 1: iRMX® Operating System Functional Elements

iRMX® I OPERATING SYSTEM

The iRMX I Operating System is the system first developed for real-time operating system support of the 8088 and 8086 microprocessors. It has become today's most widely accepted real-time operating system for microcomputers. Its features include:

- 16-bit operating system; uses 8086 instruction set and 8086 compilers
- Microprocessors: 8088, 8086, 80186, 80188; 80286, 386, i486 (Real address mode)
- Math co-processors: 8087, 80287, 387™
- Memory management: up to 1 MB, real address mode
- Applications can be written using C, FORTRAN, Pascal, and PL/M compilers and assembler available from Intel.
- Ideal for embedded, nucleus-only applications, optimized for speed and compactness
- Applications can be easily upgraded to iRMX II- and iRMX III-based designs
- For Multibus I and custom designs
- iRMX-hosted development

iRMX® II OPERATING SYSTEM

The iRMX II operating system features include:

- 16-bit operating system; uses 80286 instruction set and 80286 compilers
- Microprocessors: 80286, 386, i486
- Math co-processors: 80287, 387
- Dynamic memory management: up to 16 MB, 16-bit Protected address mode
- Applications can be written using C, FORTRAN, Pascal, and PL/M compilers and assembler available from Intel.
- Applications can be easily upgraded to iRMX III-based designs.
- For Multibus I, Multibus II, AT-bus, and custom designs
- iRMX-hosted development

iRMX® III OPERATING SYSTEM

The iRMX III operating system is a compatible derivative of the iRMX II operating system. The 32-bit functions let users gain the 32-bit power of the Intel 386 and i486 microprocessors. The iRMX III operating system handles 32-bit math and segments up to 4 gigabytes, retaining protection.

Binary compatibility with 16-bit iRMX II software lets iRMX II users easily move their applications to 32-bits on the iRMX III O/S with the 386 and 387 or i486 processors. Most 16-bit applications run without change. Selected parts of an application can be moved to 32-bits while others remain unchanged.

The iRMX III Operating System is available in two versions, DOS/iRMX III, which is preconfigured for AT-BUS and DOS-compatible Multibus boards, and the fully configurable iRMX III operating system.

Both versions feature:

- 32-bit operating system; uses full 386/387 instruction set
- Microprocessors: 386, i486
- Dynamic memory management: up to 4 GB, segmented or flat, 32-bit Protected mode
- 32- and 16-bit tasks can run concurrently with full inter-task communication
- Applications can be written using C, FORTRAN, and PL/M compilers and assembler available from Intel
- Only device drivers and interrupt and exception handlers need to be 32 bits

DOS/iRMX® III O/S

The DOS/iRMX III (pre-configured) operating system is designed to run DOS as a task under the iRMX III O/S. Both DOS and the iRMX III run concurrently with DOS executing in VM86 mode. This capability provides a true real-time extension for DOS applications and an enhanced DOS graphics interface to real- time applications.

- DOS application can pass data to/from iRMX application via memory or files
- 30 real-time calls available to DOS applications
- Provides multi-tasking capability and extended memory (up to 4 GB) to PC applications
- iRMX tasks can make direct DOS or ROM BIOS calls
- iRMX apps can access VGA graphics via DOS applications
- Supports DOS-only or DOS and iRMX partitioned file systems with full file transparency
- Preconfigured for Intel AT-platforms, and Intel PC-compatible Multibus boards: iSBX™ 386/PC/6 (Multibus II); and iSBC® 386SX (Multibus I)

CONFIGURABLE iRMX® III O/S

This software can be easily configured to a wide variety of Multibus and AT-bus platforms (see following table). This version of the software does not support DOS-under-iRMX operation.

- For 386- and 486-based Multibus I, Multibus II, AT-BUS and custom design
- Software includes drivers for over 40 boards and peripheral devices and can be easily reconfigured to meet specific application needs

iRMX® FAMILY COMPATIBILITY

iRMX® I	iRMX® II	iRMX® III

INTEL SYSTEMS

iRMX® I	iRMX® II	iRMX® III
System 310 Family System 320 Family	System 120 Family System 320 Family System 520 Family	System 120 Family System 320 Family System 520 Family Systems 301, 302, 300SX, 303, 401

MULTIBUS I SINGLE BOARD COMPUTERS

iRMX® I	iRMX® II	iRMX® III
iSBC 86/C38 iSBC 86/05A iSBC 86/12A iSBC 86/30 iSBC 86/35 iSBC 186/03A iSBC 186/51 iSBC 188/56 iSBC 286/10A* iSBC 286/12* iSBC 286/14* iSBC 286/16* iSBC 386/12* iSBC 386/12S* iSBC 386/2X* iSBC 386/3X*	iSBC 286/10A iSBC 286/12 iSBC 286/14 iSBC 286/16 iSBC 386/12† iSBC 386/12S† iSBC 386/2X† iSBC 386/3X† iSBC 486/12S†	iSBC 386/12 iSBC 386/12S iSBC 386/2X iSBC 386/3X iSBC 386SX iSBC 486/12S

MULTIBUS II SINGLE BOARD COMPUTERS

iRMX® I	iRMX® II	iRMX® III
	iSBC 286/100A iSBC 386/116† iSBC 386/120† iSBC 386/258† iSBC 386/133†	iSBC 386/116 iSBC 386/120 iSBC 386/258 iSBC 386/133 iSBC 486/125 iSBC 386/PC16 iSBC 486/133

INTEL MICROPROCESSOR DESIGNS

iRMX® I	iRMX® II	iRMX® III
8086, 8088, 80186, 80188, 80286*, 386*, i486*	80286, 386†, i486†	386, i486
8259A Programmable Interrupt Controller 8254 or 8253 Programmable Interval Timer 8274, 8251A, and 82530 serial controllers 8255 parallel interface Necessary memory		

COPROCESSOR SUPPORT

iRMX® I	iRMX® II	iRMX® III
8087, 80287*, 387*	80287, 387†	387

*Real address mode with 8086/8087 instruction set
†16-bit mode, 80286/80287 instruction set

iRMX® AND MULTIBUS II SYSTEMS

MULTIBUS II HARDWARE AND iRMX® SOFTWARE BUILD HIGH-PERFORMANCE SYSTEMS

Multibus II systems, which pass data over the bus using high-speed messages, enable engineers to easily assemble high-performance multiprocessor systems. Bus arbitration problems are virtually eliminated and slower speed I/O boards cannot slow down data transfer across the bus since all data is passed at the full bus bandwidth of 40 MBytes/second.

Nucleus Communications Service

The Nucleus Communications Service, a part of the iRMX II and iRMX III operating systems, provides the software interface between application code and the Multibus II message-passing coprocessor. This software simplifies the job of sending messages between tasks on different boards and provides a standard software interface to any other Multibus II board in the system.

Multiprocessor iRMX® Systems

With iRMX II and iRMX III software and other software from Intel's family of real-time software products, engineers can design complex, high-capability systems with a minimum of custom code. An example is the system shown in Figure 2. This system has a single iSBC 386/258 peripheral controller board that functions as both a boot server and file server to multiple CPU boards in the system. File transfers are handled via the iSBC 186/530 Network Interface Adapter, which also provides an Ethernet network connection. The iSBC 186/410 terminal controller board uses communication software that is downloaded from the system disk. The iSBX 279 Display Subsystem, together with iRMX Virtual Terminal software, provides access to any processor in the system via a single console displaying multiple windows.

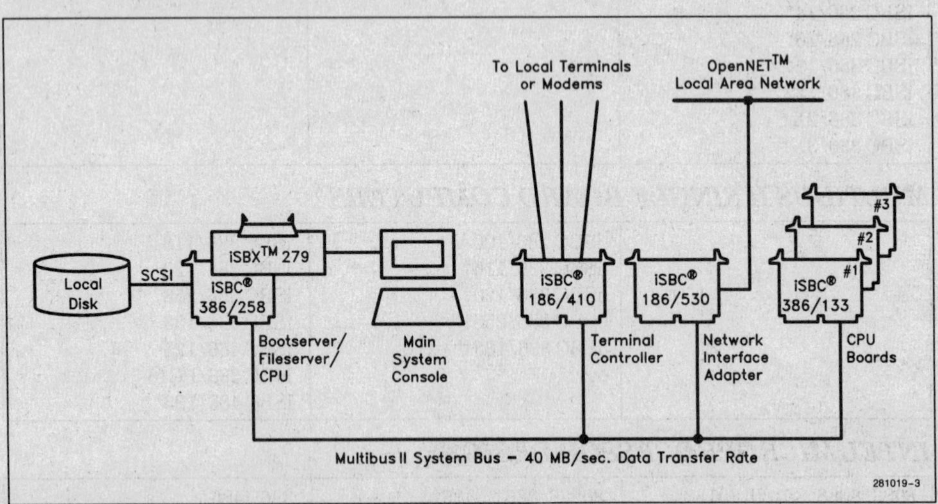

Figure 2: Multibus II iRMX® II Multiprocessor System

ON-TARGET DEVELOPMENT

A CONVENIENT WAY TO DEVELOP REAL-TIME APPLICATIONS

Designers familiar with both cross development and on-target development agree that on-target development is an easy, reliable method for developing applications. Testing is greatly simplified, and you need to become comfortable with only one operating system.

The iRMX operating systems provide solid on-target development capability—a capability entirely missing from other real-time software for microprocessors.

Developers can use the full, rich feature set of the iRMX operating systems for development, and then include only a minimum set of iRMX functions in their final applications. As a result, your final application receives the benefits of on-target development without the overhead that general purpose operating systems incur.

Included with the iRMX operating systems

- Interactive Configuration Utility (ICU)—a tool that can be used to generate a custom version of the operating system to match exact system requirements. The ICU automates the otherwise time consuming and error prone configuration of the system. The ICU accepts the user's system parameters and requirements, then builds a command file to compile, assemble, link, and locate necessary files. The ICU is not provided with the pre-configured DOS/iRMX III O/S.
- A Human Interface supporting multiple users
- Over 50 Human Interface commands for system status, device management, and file management
- A Command Line Interpreter supporting background jobs and full line editing
- Hardware traps to catch up to 90% of typical programming errors for iRMX II or iRMX III applications
- System Debugger
- PROMmable bootstrap loader for Multibus CPU boards
- Parameter and data validation of operating system calls
- Numerous device drivers for Intel boards

Other development facilities are available separately for use with the iRMX® operating systems

- Re-entrant languages
- Assembly- and source-level debuggers
- Development utilities
- Graphics software for the iSBX 279 subsystem graphics controller (iRMX II and iRMX III systems) for Multibus-hosted applications
- iPAT Performance Analysis Tool
- In Circuit Emulators, hosted on an IBM PC-AT or equivalent, to aid in hardware debugging and software tracing
- A variety of user-supplied utilities and special software available from the iRMX Users Group (iRUG)

iRMX® LANGUAGES

FULL LANGUAGE SUPPORT FOR iRMX® SYSTEMS

Intel has the languages you will need to develop a wide range of high-performance applications. iRMX-hosted languages include C, PL/M, FORTRAN, Pascal, and Assembler. iRMX language compilers run on an Intel 120, 300, or 500 series microcomputer systems as well as DOS-compatible Multibus boards and can be used for Multibus I, Multibus II, or AT-bus target systems or embedded applications.

In addition to the wealth of languages available, iRMX-based systems are complemented by utilities with which to create and manage object modules. For the iRMX II and iRMX III operating systems, utilities are provided that allow system programmers to initialize and manage the memory protection features of the 80286, 386, and i486 microprocessors transparently to the applications programmer. This latitude in configurability allows programmers to team their efforts in order to achieve a shorter development time than would otherwise be possible.

Because the high-level languages are actually resident on the iRMX-based system and can be licensed on a development license or pass-through license, OEMs can pass application software directly on to end users. End users may then tailor the OEM's system to better meet application needs by writing programs using the same languages.

iRMX® LANGUAGES

Language-Independent Application Development

Intel's Object Module Format (OMF) enables several users to write different modules of an application in different languages, then link them together. Users can choose exactly the right language tools for specific pieces of the application, rather than compromising specialized tasks for the sake of one project-wide language.

Fast, Lean Programs for Rapid Processing

iRMX operating system calls are made directly from C, FORTRAN, Pascal (iRMX I and II), and PL/M. This means that application developers can take full advantage of the iRMX multi-tasking capability, whereby multiple applications execute concurrently on the operating system.

Application code can be easily transported across processor architectures to yield increased performance. For example, 8086 object code will run on the 80286, 386, and i486 processors.

Standardized Math Support

All iRMX languages support floating point operations. This ensures universal consistency in numeric computation results and enables the user to take advantage of the Intel 8087, 80287, and 387 Numeric Data Processors.

C LANGUAGE

The C programming language is known for its flexibility and portability. It is a block-structured, high-level language that is ideal for developing real-time, multitasking applications.

Intel C compilers provide many substantial benefits to software developers, including:

- **Built-in functions.** Allow highly optimized code and eliminate the need for in-line assembly code. With built-in functions, you can enable interrupts or directly control hardware I/O from the high level language.
- **Symbolic debug information.** Intel C compilers provide extensive symbolic debug information to speed development with an ICE or Soft-Scope* debugger.

In addition, runtime libraries include the STDIO library, conversion routines, string manipulation routines, routines for performing 32-bit arithmetic and floating-point operations, and routines that provide an interface to the operating system.

The iC 86 compiler is a new generation C compiler providing high performance for embedded microprocessor designs. In addition to the features above, this compiler has the ability to mix memory models with "near" and "far" pointers. iC 86 is compatible with other ANSI C standard compilers and PL/M providing both standard C and PL/M calling conventions and has four optimization levels.

iC 286 supports the 16 MB physical address space of the 80286 and enables programs to use 80286 features such as protection and virtual memory. It is upward compatible with iC 86.

iC 386 supports the full 4 Gigabyte physical address space of the 386 and enables programs to use new 80386 features, such as memory paging. It manipulates bit fields, pointers, addresses, and registers, enabling programs to take full advantage of the fundamental concepts of the 386 and i486 microprocessors. It is upward compatible from iC 86 and iC 286.

FORTRAN LANGUAGE

FORTRAN has long been the industry-standard programming language for numerical processing applications. FORTRAN meets the ANSI FORTRAN 77 Language Subset Specification and includes many features of the full standard. It supports single-precision (32-bit), double-precision (64-bit), double-extended-precision (80-bit), complex (two 32-bit), and double-complex (two 64-bit) floating-point data types. Floating-point operations can be performed with software or with numeric coprocessors, such as the 8087, 80287, and 387. In addition, FORTRAN has microprocessor extensions for performing direct byte- or word-oriented port I/O, developing reentrant procedures, and creating interrupt procedures.

- Available in three versions: FORTRAN 86, FORTRAN 286, and FORTRAN 386, fully supporting the 80×86 family microprocessors
- Features high-level support for floating-point calculations, transcendentals, interrupt procedures, and run-time exception handling
- Meets ANSI FORTRAN 77 subset language specifications
- Produces Intel OMF object modules that can be compiled separately and linked to programs written in any corresponding Intel OMF language

- Supports the IEEE floating-point math standard with 8087, 80287, and 387 coprocessors
- Supports arrays larger than 64K bytes

PASCAL LANGUAGE

The Pascal compilers provide a complete implementation of the ISO proposed standard for Pascal for 8086, 80186, 80286, 386, and i486 microprocessors. In addition, the Intel Pascal compilers contain extensions to standard Pascal that tailor the resulting code to fit microcomputer applications. There are extensions for interrupt handling and port I/O. Predefined type extensions also allow you to specify the precision of real, integer, and unsigned calculations; check errors on 8087 or 80287 operations; and circumvent the type checking on calls to non-Pascal routines.

- Available in two versions, Pascal 86 and Pascal 286
- Offers strict implementation of ISO standard Pascal
- Contains extensions to the ISO standard that are essential for microcomputer applications
- Allows separate compilation with type-checking enforced between modules
- Has compiler option to support full run-time range-checking
- Supports large array operation

PL/M LANGUAGE

The PL/M language is a structured language created specifically as a system development language for Intel microprocessor-based applications. It provides the advantages of a high-level language with the power of assembly language. PL/M is an excellent alternative to C in, for example, I/O-intensive applications. PL/M does not require a run-time environment and thus can produce highly optimized code. In 80286, 386, and i486 systems, PL/M is ideal for developing multi-user, multitasking, virtual-memory operation systems to run in protected mode. It is easy to learn and use, yet it allows complete access to the processor and it produces code whose efficiency rivals that of assembly language.

- Has a block-structured syntax that encourages program modularity
- Has built-in syntax checker
- Allows foreign character sets in comments and strings

Three PL/M compilers are available: PL/M 86 for 16-bit real address mode applications; PL/M 286 for 16-bit protected mode applications; and PL/M 386 for 32-bit applications. The compilers are upwardly compatible with each other. As a result, applications can be easily upgraded from PL/M 86 to PL/M 286 to PL/M 386 with only minor changes to the source code.

iRMX® LANGUAGES

ASSEMBLERS

The Assemblers and Relocation/Linkage packages provide the tools that assembly-language programmers need to maintain complete control over the 8086, 80186, 80286, 386, and i486 microprocessors. The assembly languages are strongly typed, providing extensive checks on variables and labels. This helps catch many programming errors long before the debugging cycle. Macro facilities are also available to speed and simplify your work.

The relocation and linkage packages make your programs ready to run. They link programs together, assign absolute addresses, gather modules into libraries, and perform other system functions.

Assembler 86, 286 and 386:

- Are highly mnemonic and compact, and are strongly typed to detect errors at assembly time
- Place high-level symbolic information in object modules to enable symbolic debugging
- Have powerful text macro facility with three macro listing options, including string functions, and can expand conditional assembly pseudo-ops

The Relocation/Linkage Packages:

- Resolve PUBLIC/EXTERNAL references and perform intermodule type checking
- Select required modules from libraries to satisfy symbolic references and provide fast, easy management of object module libraries
- Simplify debugging by producing detailed maps that show references between program modules

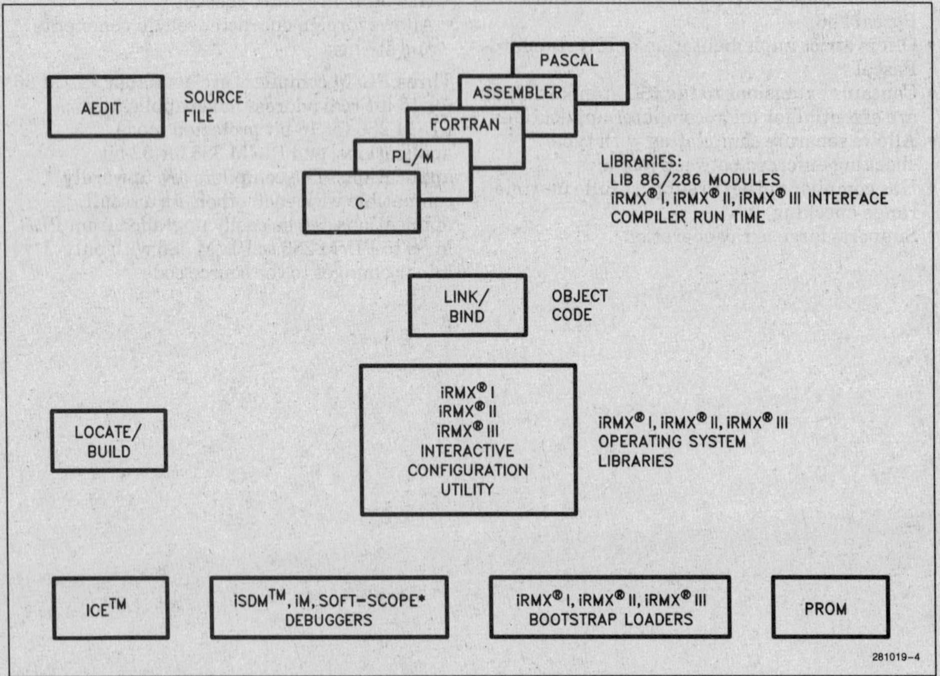

Figure 3: iRMX® Operating Systems Development Environment

SOFT-SCOPE* HIGH-LEVEL DEBUGGER

COMPLETE HIGH-LEVEL DEBUGGING

The Soft-Scope debuggers focus on original source code for most debugging operations. All breakpoint prompts and high-level stepping operations prompt with original source code rather than reporting what line number the program has reached or what assembly instruction is next.

Source Code Interface and On-Line Listings

The source code interface frees the programmer from having to divide attention between the console and program listings, eliminates the need to get a fresh program listing each time a small change is made, and reduces the time needed to make software modifications.

Automatic Expansion of Data Types

Symbols declared in the program are accessible by name for display and modification of contents. These symbols include arrays, structures, static variables, based variables, and stack-based variables (including local variables, re-entrant variables, and passed parameters). Memory can also be displayed with absolute references or with register-relative references.

Symbolic Display of All iRMX® System Objects

The VIEW command allows viewing the status of any iRMX object including tasks, jobs, mailboxes, semaphores, regions, and segments. With VIEW, the stack of a task can be examined to determine which iRMX call the task has made most recently. Any job's object directory and the list of ready and sleeping tasks can be examined.

Second Terminal Option

Because so many applications are screen-intensive, the Soft-Scope Debuggers allow the option of using a second terminal for all debugger I/O, freeing the main console for exclusive use by the application for application output.

Multi-Tasking Support

The Soft-Scope debuggers support simultaneous debugging of concurrent tasks when they are all linked together as a Human Interface command and each concurrent task is coded in a separate module. The debugger loads and then allows the user to suspend and resume execution of the tasks from the command line with the SUSPEND and RESUME commands. In this way the developer can observe the effect of dynamic changes on the software under test.

Handling of 80286, 386™, and i486™ Protection Traps and Software Exceptions

Exception Handling: The exact source line which causes an exception can easily be reached and displayed. All environmental and programmer exceptions are trapped and reported, without causing a Soft-Scope debugger exit.

Most of the 80286/386/i486 hardware traps are handled by the Soft-Scope debuggers, including Bounds Check (INT 5), Invalid Opcode (INT 6), Double Fault (INT 8), Stack Fault (INT 12), and General Protection (INT 13). Upon encountering one of these interrupts, the debugger breaks execution with a message similar to the following:

```
< General Protection fault (INT 13) >
[ Break near line #145 in TEST (:TESTMOD) ]
145: ARRAY(INDEX)=XYZ;
```

In the above example, the General Protection trap could have been caused by the variable INDEX being too large for the segment which contained ARRAYX, or by ARRAYX being based on an undefined pointer. Because the debugger handles these traps directly, other users in a multi-user system won't even be aware in most cases that there was a hardware fault.

Soft-Scope debuggers are available for iRMX I, iRMX II, and iRMX III designs. The Soft-Scope II and Soft-Scope III debuggers are available directly from Intel. The Soft-Scope debugger for iRMX I applications is available from Concurrent Sciences, inc.

iSDM™ MONITOR

ASSEMBLY-LEVEL DEBUGGING

The user can use the iSDM monitor package to load programs into the target system from the development system, execute programs in an instruction-by-instruction manner, and add custom commands through the command extension interface.

Powerful Debugging Commands

The iSDM Monitor contains a powerful set of commands to support the debugging process on Intel 16- and 32-bit microprocessors. Some of the features included are: bootstrap of application software; selective execution of program modules based on breakpoints or single stepping requests; examination, modification, and movement of memory contents; examination and modification of CPU registers, including NPX registers; and disassembly of object code. All results are displayed in clearly understandable formats.

Two versions of iSDM are available. iSDM II supports 16-bit code debug on 8086/186, 8088/188, 80286, and 386 processors. iSDM III supports 16- and 32-bit code debug on the 386 and i486 processors for iRMX III applications.

Numeric Data Processor Support

Arithmetic applications utilizing the 8087, 80287, or 387 Numeric Processor Extension (NPX) are fully supported by the iSDM Monitor. In addition to executing applications with the full NPX performance, users may examine and modify the NPX's registers using decimal and real number format.

This feature allows the user to feel confident that correct and meaningful numbers are entered for the application without having to encode and decode complex real, integer, and BCD hexadecimal formats.

Command Extension Interface

The Command Extension Interface (CEI) allows the addition of custom commands to the iSDM Monitor commands. The CEI consists of various procedures that can be used to generate custom commands. Up to three custom commands (or sets of commands) can be added to the monitor without programming new EPROMs or changing the monitor's source code.

Program Load Capability

The iSDM loader allows the loading of 8086, 8088, 80186, 80188, 80286, 386, or i486 CPU-based programs into the target system. It executes on an iRMX development system and communicates with the target system through a serial link, a parallel link, or a fast parallel link.

Configuration Facility

The monitor contains a full set of configuration facilities which allows it to be carefully tailored to the requirements of the target system. Pre-configured EPROM-resident monitors are supplied by Intel for most Multibus I and Multibus II CPU boards. iRMX I and iRMX II system users may use the configuration facilities to include the Bootstrap Loader (V5.0 or newer) in the monitor. iSDM can be easily configured for custom hardware.

The iSDM III monitor is preconfigured to be loaded with the iRMX III operating system. The user can configure I/O devices to be used by the monitor. The iSDM III monitor runs on any hardware iRMX III software runs on.

The iSDM Monitor does not require the use of a development system. The monitor can be used by simply attaching a stand-alone terminal to the target system. iSDM II is available as a separate product. The iSDM III monitor is included with the iRMX III operating system.

AEDIT EDITOR

AEDIT is a full-screen editor designed specifically for software engineers and writers. It has many features that make it ideal for program editing. For example, it lets you switch between files instantly, and its split-screen windowing capability enables you to view two files at once. It has a macro facility that you can use to combine multiple functions into a single command. These macros can be created in two ways: by using AEDIT's "learning" mode to store your keystrokes or by using the powerful macro language. You can also use and modify the extensive library of macros provided with the editor.

With these and other features, such as context-sensitive command menus and shell escape to the operating system, AEDIT is the complete program-editing tool.

- Allows full screen editing of source code and documentation
- Provides a full range of editing support, from document processing to hexadecimal code entry
- Supports macros for repetitive or complex editing tasks
- Provides a powerful macro language for developing "smart" macros
- Supports dual-file editing with optional split-screen windowing
- Allows unlimited file size and line length
- Offers quick response with easy-to-use, context-sensitive command menus
- Is configurable and extensible for complete control of the editing process, yet remains easy to learn and use
- Supports documentation preparation with paragraph filling and justification options
- Provides shell escape function for access to operating system commands

iPAT™ PERFORMANCE ANALYSIS TOOLS

iPAT™, Intel's Performance Analysis Tool, helps engineers control the performance and reliability of a software-driven system by showing, via histograms and tables, the real-time execution activity of software in terms of range names or addresses.

- Provides real-time performance and code coverage analysis non-intrusively with 100% sampling
- Displays information using histograms or analysis tables
- Accepts specification of ranges with addresses, program symbolic names, or user-defined symbolic names
- Performs disarm/arm analysis on called subroutines, external interrupts, interrupt routines, operating system functions, or any execution address or range
- Hosted on PC/XT and PC/AT systems, using a serial link for target communications
- Presents an easy-to-use human interface, including function keys and color/monochrome graphics
- Available for 8086/88, 80286, and 386 microprocessors.

The iPAT products consist of DOS-hosted control and display software, plus appropriate microprocessor probes which replace the microprocessor in the target system.

The iPAT 386 also can be operated in piggy-back fashion with the Intel ICE-386/25 in-circuit emulator in prototype systems at speeds up to 20 MHz. All iPAT products use an iPAT core base system, which also can be attached to ICE-186 or ICE-286 in-circuit emulators.

intel.

iRMX® TOOLBOX

ASSISTANCE FOR iRMX® PROJECT DOCUMENTS

The iRMX toolbox is a set of utilities to provide assistance to the software developer in text processing and document preparation.

Text Formatting (SCRIPT)

The SCRIPT utility is a text formatting program that streamlines document formatting and preparation. Commands include facilities to do paging, centering, left and right margins, justification, subscripts, superscripts, page headers and footers, underlines, boldface type, upper and lower case, etc.

Input text which has been prepared using the AEDIT text editor can be formatted using the SCRIPT utility.

Spelling Verification (SPELL, WSORT)

The SPELL utility finds misspelled words in a text file. The included dictionary can be expanded by the user for specialized vocabularies. This utility can be used interactively or in a batch mode.

File Comparisons (COMP)

The COMP utility performs line oriented text file comparisons showing changes between text, source, or object files.

Sort (ESORT, HSORT)

Files can be sorted on multiple keys (or fields) in ascending or descending order and the resultant sorted files stored.

iRMX® SOURCE CONTROL SYSTEM

SOFTWARE VERSION MANAGEMENT

The iRMX Source Control System (SCS) provides an integrated version control and generation management system for users in an iRMX software development cycle. This facility is useful for large and small software projects to assist in bringing more control, order and methodology to the software development process. SCS can be effectively used on a single iRMX System or across the OpenNET™ network. It can be utilized by developers using any of the popular iRMX languages—PL/M, Assembler, FORTRAN, C, Pascal or other special language requirements.

Controls Access to Source Files

With iRMX Source Control System the system manager has certain privileged commands. These commands can be useful to designate those team members who can access the source files only for object generation and those who can access the source files for updating or changing. Other such privileged commands include the ability to archive a specific version of source and combine several versions of a source file.

Tracks Changes to Source Files

The iRMX Source Control System keeps track of changes made to any source files. These changes are stored as backward deltas for disk economy and fast access to the latest version. The project team can now better interact and synchronize using the latest updated version for integration and testing. The specific versions of tools used to produce the source code is also tracked.

Approachable and Efficient

The iRMX Source Control System has a tutorial, a menu interface, and on-line help facility that help make it very approachable by the user.

iRMX® DEVELOPMENT PLATFORMS

ONE OPERATING SYSTEM FAMILY; A CHOICE OF BUS ARCHITECTURES

Intel has integrated iRMX development software into systems based on the PC AT bus, Multibus I, and Multibus II, all using the power of the Intel 386 32-bit microprocessor. These systems are available in configurations suited for software development and target systems.

Compatibility of iRMX-based software across buses makes it easy to move applications among Intel AT-bus systems and the Multibus I and Multibus II-based System 320 and System 520. This flexibility lets the user select from systems that range from AT-bus price to minicomputer performance and functions.

SYSTEM 120

The iRMX II and iRMX III operating systems are designed to run on the System 120, which is available in two different versions for 16 MHz and 25 MHz operation. The 16 MHz system features 2 MB of memory, a 387 Math Coprocessor, a 40 MB hard disk drive and a 1.2 MB floppy disk drive. The 25 MHz system is similar, but includes 4 MB of system memory.

The System 120 is available with or without software. Developer kits are available that include the iRMX II O/S, compilers, and other tools. See the System 120 fact sheet for a detailed description and product order codes.

300SX, 310Z, 302, 303, and 401 MICROCOMPUTERS

The models 300SX, 301Z and 303 are all AT-bus platforms that use a 386 processor running at 16-33 MHz depending on the model. The model 401 is an AT- bus platform with a 25 MHz i486 microprocessor. The systems are available with a range of system memory and peripherals and optional math coprocessors.

Easy Application Development

Using the System 120 or the 300SX, 301Z, 302, 303, and 401 microcomputers, you can develop applications for AT bus, Multibus I, or Multibus II-based designs as well as embedded applications.

Intel offers PC/AT add-in boards including: 2 MB and 8 MB 32-bit memory boards, the OpenNET PCLINK2 networking board and the iPCX 344A BITBUS™ board. A standard keyboard is also available.

DOS Application Compatibility

The AT-BUS systems support the DOS 3.X and later operating systems enabling you to use popular DOS applications to process data collected in real time. Many common applications are already available from software vendors. The applications include data bases, menu systems, and device drivers. The system hard disk can be divided into iRMX and DOS partitions, allowing users to boot from either partition. A utility allows transfer of iRMX files to a DOS disk. With DOS/iRMX III software, a separate iRMX partition is not required. DOS execution requires a customer-supplied version of DOS, a video adapter, a monitor, and a keyboard.

SYSTEM 320

The System 320 is based on the Multibus I architecture (IEEE 796) industry standard system bus and the iRMX® operating systems, highly configurable for tailoring to target applications. Special hardware configurations can be tailored for the user, by Intel's Custom System Integration group or by Intel's authorized Value Added Distribution Centers.

The System 320 consists of a system package which contains a seven slot Multibus cardcage, a power supply, and three 5¼″ full-height peripheral bays. Available options include CPU, memory, peripheral controller, operating systems, storage devices, channel communications, host communications, networks, productivity software and accessories.

The System 320 is available in a wide range of configurations based on the 386 microprocessor. All 386 based models include the 387 numeric processor.

SYSTEM 520

The System 520 is built around Intel's Multibus II System Architecture (MSA) to ease the development and integration work of Multibus II OEM system designers. MSA delivers open system interface and protocol standards that build on and extend the basic Multibus (IEEE/ANSI 1296) bus standard. The MSA specifications define diagnostics, built-in self test, system initialization and boot loading, board configuration, and message passing. The user benefits from MSA because the level of vendor and board compatibility has been raised above basic electrical bus specifications to a set of powerful programmatic interfaces

iRMX® DEVELOPMENT PLATFORMS

that handle all of the details of bus specifics with software. This provides OEMs quicker time to market with faster system integration and shorter design cycles.

Easy User Expansion and Re-Composable Systems

The Multibus II System Architecture is used as the foundation for integrating Intel's full line of Single Board Computer (iSBC®) modules and iRMX II or iRMX III system software into the System 520. OEMs have the option to buy the contents of the system (i.e., the boards, the firmware, the software, etc.) separately, and re-compose all or part of the system's pieces into a different configuration or enclosure.

The System 520 is available with or without the iRMX II/III Operating System.

Easy user expansion and recomposability of the System 520 is supported by a line of System Integration Toolkits (SIT kits) that contain all the firmware necessary to allow standard, off-the-shelf Multibus II boards to integrate cleanly into the System 520. With these toolkit products, the OEM can purchase the pieces needed and profit from greater ease of use, ease of integration, and higher levels of open standards.

A Network IN the System

With Multibus II-based applications, engineers can design systems using multiple processor boards each running a different operating system. For example, a single system with three CPU boards can run iRMX II, iRMX III, and the UNIX* operating systems all at the same time. Boards communicate with each other and other I/O boards using OpenNET software, a local networking controller card, and the Multibus II backplane. Since the Multibus II bus can transfer data up to 40 MB/sec., data transfer between boards is much faster than a normal Ethernet connection. With this capability, systems can be easily optimized for the application. For example, iRMX software can be used for the control of a real-time process and the UNIX operating system used for the operator interface.

The major advantage to the OEM is total network extensibility inside and outside the system, using the same OpenNET software. The key benefits are: reduced cost through the "replacement" of multiple uni-processor networked systems and servers, drastically reduced physical space requirements, increased overall network throughput and performance, and preserved software investment.

The customer can choose the combination of packaging, CPU/system performance, and communications bandwidth suited for the application.

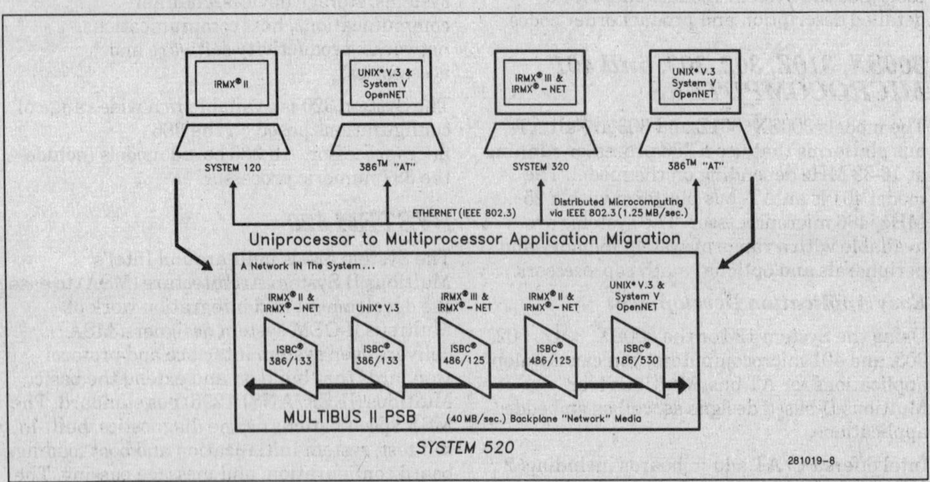

Figure 4: A Network **IN** the System with an iSBC 386 and i486 board cluster; also shows iRMX and UNIX application migration from networked AT-bus platforms to a System 520 running OpenNET **IN** the System

OpenNET™ NETWORKING

COMPLETE OpenNET™ SOLUTION FOR REAL-TIME SYSTEMS

Many real-time applications require network communication. Intel's iRMX-NET Release 3.0 delivers a rich set of networking capabilities and a full range of iRMX platform support for Intel AT-bus systems, the system 320, and the system 520.

Transparent Network File Access

iRMX-NET implements the NFA protocol to provide transparent file access capabilities among iRMX, DOS, VAX/VMS*, UNIX*, XENIX* and iNDX systems on the OpenNET network. Remote files are accessed as if they resided on the local iRMX system. iRMX-NET can be configured as a network file consumer, file server, or both, depending on the application's requirements.

With the addition of iRMX-NET, the iRMX Human Interface commands and system calls are transparently extended to remote access as well. Transparency means that applications using the iRMX Human Interface commands or BIOS system calls do not need to know whether the files they access reside locally or on some remote system.

OSI Transport and Distributed Name Server with Programmatic Interface

The iRMX-NET R3.0 product includes iNA 960 R3 OSI Transparent and Network software preconfigured for a variety of Intel Network Interface Adapters.

iRMX-NET R3.0 also includes the iRMX-NET Distributed Name Server software. The Distributed Name Server software maintains and provides access to a network directory database. The database is distributed across the network with each system maintaining its own logical piece of the directory. The Distributed Name Server software provides a full set of network directory services and is used to perform such tasks as logical name to network address mapping for establishing network connections between systems.

The combination of transparent network file access with iRMX commands and system calls, plus direct programmatic access to the iNA 960 Transport and iRMX-NET Distributed Name Server software gives the programmer a powerful set of capabilities for developing real-time network applications.

Remote Boot for Diskless Systems

iRMX-NET R3.0 supports networked diskless systems by providing network Boot Consumer, Boot Server and File Server capabilities.

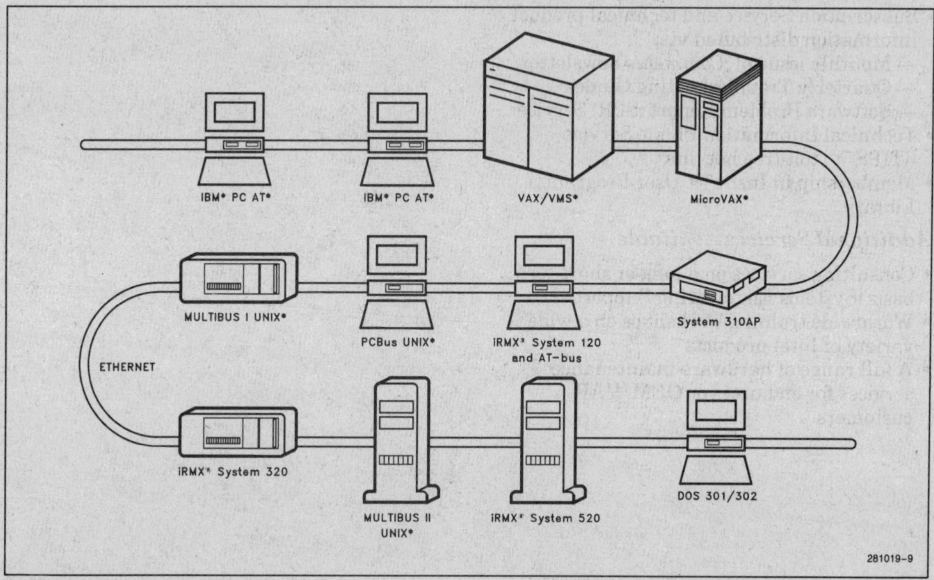

Figure 5: OpenNET™ local area network connections to iRMX® systems.

iRMX® VIRTUAL TERMINAL

Virtual Terminal allows local iRMX users to "Logon" to a remote Intel iRMX node within an OpenNET network or across the Multibus II system bus. This capability enables users to access all the available resources on the remote system. In addition the iRMX Virtual Terminal is fully interoperable with other OpenNET Virtual Terminal products. Now a PC, VAX, or UNIX user can "connect" to a remote iRMX system without the need to use a locally connected iRMX terminal.

The iRMX Virtual Terminal server can be configured to support from 1 to 32 virtual terminal connections per system.

The administration utility allows the system manager to disable, terminate or start the iRMX Virtual Terminal server. The capability to report on the status of all the virtual terminal connections to the local server is also supported.

SOFTWARE SERVICES

A FULL RANGE OF TECHNICAL SUPPORT

With the iRMX operating systems you're not alone when you're developing a real-time application. Intel has the best technical sales support in the real-time business. If you need help, training, consulting, and design advice are readily available.

Standard Software Support

All Intel software products include Intel's Software Support for a 90 day period immediately following the licensing and receipt of the product. Standard Support includes:

- Product updates
- Subscription Service and technical product information distributed via:
  - — Monthly issue of *;Comments* newsletter
  - — Quarterly Troubleshooting Guides
  - — Software Problem Report (SPR) Service
- Technical Information Phone Service (iTIPS™) toll-free hot line
- Membership in Insite™ User Program Library

Additional Services Available

- Consulting services on a long or short-term basis (Systems Engineering Support)
- Worldwide training workshops on a wide variety of Intel products
- A full range of hardware maintenance services for end users or OEM/VAR customers

iRMX® FAMILY PRODUCT SUMMARY

Ordering Codes	Product

iRMX® OPERATING SYSTEMS

Ordering Codes	Product
RMXI(J,E)KIT	iRMX I operating system (specify J = 5¼″ media, E = 8″ media)
RMXI(J,E)KITS	iRMX I operating system with one-year software support
SYRI(J,E)KIT	iRMX I operating system with AEDIT, ASM 86, and PL/M 86
SYRI(J,E)KITS	iRMX I operating system with AEDIT, ASM 86, and PL/M 86 and one-year software support
RMXIDC	iRMX I manual set
RMXIIKIT	iRMX I operating system
RMXIIKITS	iRMX II operating system with one-year software support
SYRIIKIT	iRMX II operating system with AEDIT, ASM 86, ASM 286, PL/M 286
SYRIIKITS	iRMX II operating system with AEDIT, ASM 86, ASM 286, PL/M 286 and one-year software support
RMXIIDC	iRMX II manual set
SYRIIIATKIT	iRMX III (configurable) operating system for AT-bus host systems (Target develop on all buses). Includes AEDIT, ASM 86/286/386, RLL 386 (relocation and linkage tools), and PL/M 386, and SDM III. 3½″ and 5¼″ media.
SYRIIIATKITS	Same as above with one-year software support.
SYRIIIMBKIT	Same as SYRIIIATKIT except designed for Multibus I (System 320) and Multibus II (System 520) host systems. 5-¼″ media.
SYRIIIMBKITS	Same as above with one-year software support
RMXIIIMNL	iRMX II manual set
DOSRMXIIIPC	Preconfigured DOS/iRMX III Operating System. Hosted on AT-bus systems and DOS-compatible Multibus boards. Includes 3½″ and 5¼″ media.

iRMX® FAMILY PRODUCT SUMMARY

Ordering Codes	Product

DEVELOPMENT TOOLS

Ordering Codes	Product
iRMX864 **R286EDI286**	AEDIT text editor for iRMX I operating system AEDIT text editor for iRMX II and iRMX III operating systems
R86ASM86SU **R286ASM86SU** **R286ASM286SU** **ASM386, RLL386**	ASM/R&L 86 package for iRMX I operating system ASM/R&L 86 package for iRMX II and iRMX III operating systems ASM/R&L 286 package for iRMX II and iRMX III operating systems ASM 386 package for iRMX III operating system (included with iRMX III O/S)
R86C86SU **R286C286SU** **R386C386SU**	iC 86 package for iRMX I operating system iC 286 package for iRMX II and iRMX III operating systems iC 386 package for iRMX III operating system
R86FOR86SU **R286FOR286SU** **R386FOR386SU**	FORTRAN 86 package for iRMX I operating system FORTRAN 286 package for iRMX II and iRMX III operating systems FORTRAN 386 package for iRMX III operating systems
R86PLM86SU **R286PLM86SU** **R286PLM286SU** **PLM386**	PL/M 86 package for iRMX I operating system PL/M 86 package for iRMX II and iRMX III operating systems PL/M 286 package for iRMX II and iRMX III operating systems PL/M 386 package for iRMX III operating system (included with iRMX III O/S)
R86PAS86SU **R286PAS286SU**	Pascal 86 package for iRMX I operating system Pascal 286 package for iRMX II and iRMX III operating systems
RMXIISFTSCP **RMXIIISFSCP**	Soft-Scope II source-level debugger for iRMX II-based applications Soft-Scope III source-level debugger for iRMX III-based applications
SDMSC **SYRIIPATKIT**	Assembly-level System Debug Monitor II for iRMX I and iRMX II-based systems iRMX II O/S (SYRIIKIT) and iPAT 286 performance analysis tool
RMX286TLB	iRMX II Toolbox
RMXSCSKITSU	Source Control

iRMX® FAMILY PRODUCT SUMMARY

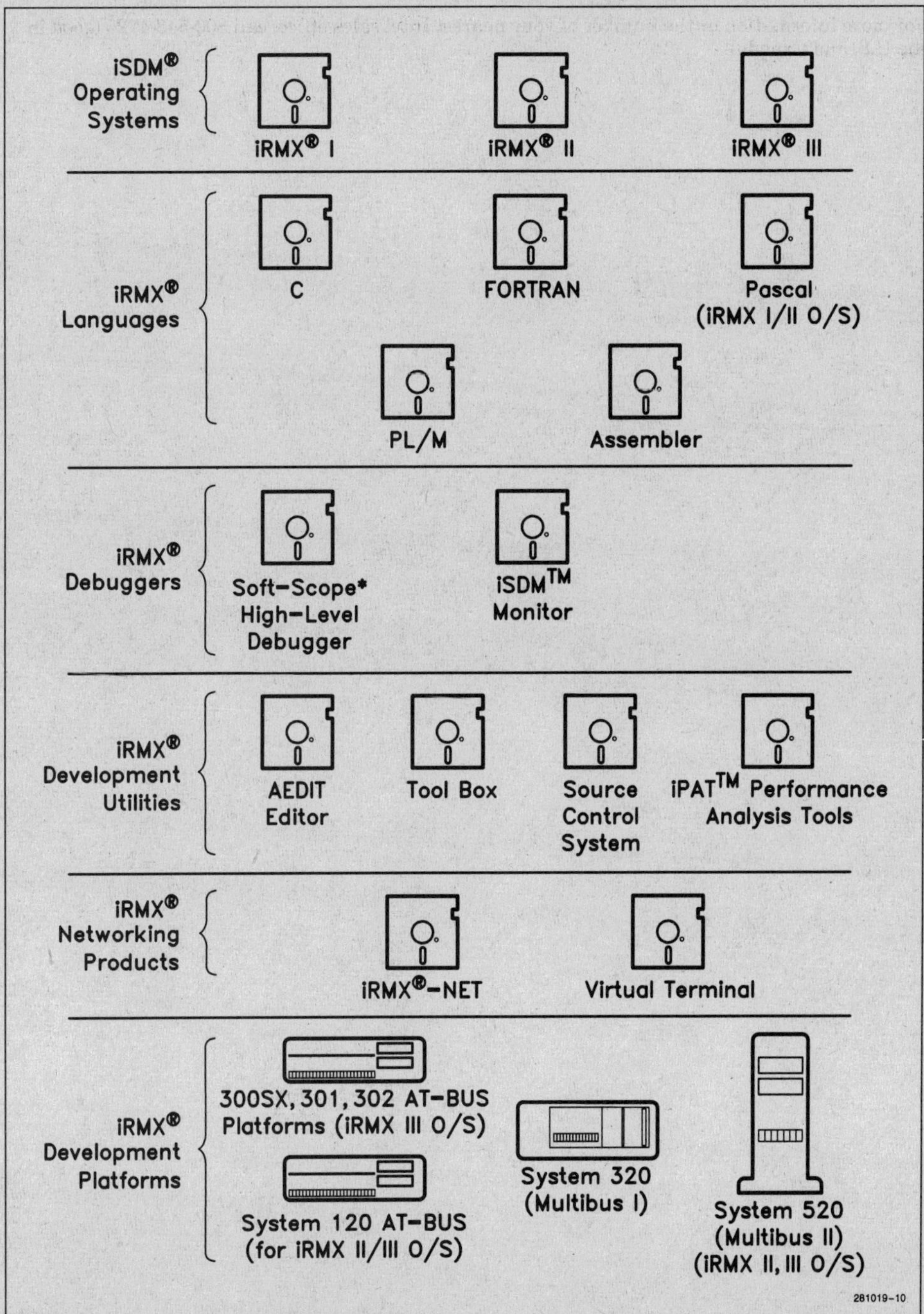

Figure 6: iRMX® Family Product Chart

ORDERING INFORMATION

For more information or the number of your nearest Intel sales office, call 800-548-4725 (good in the U.S. and Canada).

INTEL SYSTEM V/386 PRODUCT FAMILY

280692-1

STANDARD UNIX SUPPORTS MULTIBUS SYSTEM ARCHITECTURES*

The UNIX System V/386 operating system now delivers full support for Intel's Multibus II System Architecture. Intel has built a complete System V/386 product family providing OEMs, System Integrators and Computing Manufacturers with industry standard UNIX, OpenNET™ networking, system hardware, and Ada development tools for the Multibus II System Architecture. Together, these elements deliver a rich, complete UNIX development environment. System V/386 family products are also available for Multibus I system architectures.

The UNIX System V operating system is the core of the family. It provides portability of applications and systems programs from one hardware architecture to another, and robust development support. Integrated with Intel's System 520 Multibus II system, the UNIX operating system provides a powerful open system platform. The System V/386 product family is ideal as a base for developing custom multi-user systems, applications and multi-purpose network servers requiring open system configurability and flexible packaging.

UNIX® is a registered trademark of AT&T in the U.S.A. and other countries.
ADA® is a registered trademark of the U.S. Government (ADA Joint Program Office).
MUTIBUS® is a registered trademark of Intel Corporation.
OpenNET™, 386™, and 387™ are trademarks of Intel Corporation.
VMS® is a registered trademark of Digital Equipment Corporation.
XENIX™ is a trademark of Microsoft Corporation.

November 1990
Order Number: 280692-002

SYSTEM V/386 OPERATING SYSTEM

FEATURES

- Standard UNIX System V/386, Release 3.2
- System V Interface Definition, Issue 2 (SVID2) certified; de facto 386™ Application Binary Interface conformant
- Native 32-bit, 386 and i486™ UNIX port
- 80287 and 387™ numeric coprocessor support
- Integrated support for Multibus II System Architecture (MSA) Standards
- UNIX System V STREAMS & TLI-based System V/OpenNET™ networking
- UNIX hosted and targeted Ada-386 compilation system support
- Complete documentation
- Worldwide service and support

STANDARD UNIX OPERATING SYSTEM AND TOOLS

Intel has worked with AT&T and others to produce a powerful UNIX System V technology base for the 386 microprocessor and Multibus systems. The System V/386 package contains the complete, standard UNIX operating system and development environment. The C Programming Language Utilities, System Generation Utilities, the Advanced Programming Utilities, and Productivity tools are included in the product, in addition to all basic, runtime facilities.

STANDARD UNIX SYSTEM V FEATURES

Ongoing enhancements and improvements to System V/386 releases included are executable shared libraries, demand paging/virtual memory, reliable signals, the 2KB file system, file and record locking, media independent UUCP, extensive terminal support utilities, the terminfo database and tools, and multiple installation and system administration tools. Support for international environments, including full support for 8-bit code sets, alternate date and time formats, and alternate character and conversion sets is also provided. In addition, Multibus II MSA support has been integrated into AT&T's UNIX System V/386 source code package as a standard feature, available from both AT&T and Intel. Conformance to final IEEE POSIX standards will be provided in future releases.

MULTIBUS II SYSTEM ARCHITECTURE SUPPORT

Intel's System V/386 product comes with complete support for the Multibus II System Architecture (MSA) in the UNIX kernel. MSA delivers open system interface and protocol standards that build on and extend the basic Multibus II (IEEE/ANSI 1296) bus standard. MSA specifications define diagnostics control, built-in self-test, system initialization and boot loading, board configuration, transport message passing, and an OSI Transport Service. The UNIX system developer has available an application level interface and a kernel driver level interface to Multibus II transport message passing and interconnect space. Use of these MSA interfaces masks the system bus specifics from the system and application developer, facilitating system integration.

OSI TRANSPORT FOR LOOSELY-COUPLED SYMMETRICAL MULTIPROCESSING

OSI transport services support the use of the Multibus II backplane as an ultra-fast network. Multiple peer-to-peer 386 application processors can operate as independent networked UNIX "systems" over a single Multibus II Parallel System Bus (PSB). Two UNIX application processors, each with its own hard disk, can be installed in a UNIX System 520, and each processor provides a TLI-based application interface for complete, transparent, inter-CPU and application communications. Larger system configurations with more processor boards can also be built using these standard interfaces. System V/ OpenNET utilizes TLI to provide transparent, distributed file sharing, file transfer and Virtual Terminal facilities for networked UNIX systems.

SYSTEM V/386 OPERATING SYSTEM

SYSTEM V/386 "ABI" FOR UNIX BINARY APPLICATION PORTABILITY

The creation of a defacto standard ABI (Application Binary Interface) for the Intel 386 architecture makes machine-independent execution of UNIX/386 binary applications a reality. This opens up the System V/386 operating system, so application developers no longer have to port applications and test them on different System V/386 machines. It makes possible a world of off-the-shelf, shrink-wrapped, UNIX binary applications for 386 and i486 machines supporting the ABI standard.

SOURCE RELEASES

The complete Multibus I and II source base is available to AT&T and Intel-licensed customer sites. Device driver source licenses and code are also available independent of the complete UNIX source base products.

SYSTEM V/OpenNET™

COMPLETE OpenNET™ LAN SOLUTION FOR UNIX SYSTEM V/386

UNIX STREAMS and TLI (Transport Level Interface) facilities are a standard part of Intel System V/386. Intel has developed and is delivering a STREAMS/TLI-based version of OpenNET for Multibus UNIX systems, called System V/OpenNET. It provides interoperation and communication with all OpenNET family products, including iRMX-NET, MSNET(PCLINK2), VMS*NET, XNXNET and iNDX OpenNET. The product comes packaged as a complete software solution including mail, virtual terminal, print spooler, nameserver interface library (NSI), and network management facilities. Support for TCP/IP and NFS networking is also available. System V/OpenNET is available for Multibus I, Multibus II and PC/AT architectures.

THE UNIX SYSTEM 520

AN OEM MULTIBUS II DISTRIBUTED SYSTEM

The Intel System 520 is a series of customizable Multibus II platforms designed for OEMs demanding the highest levels of flexibility, configurability and compatibility. The UNIX System 520 combines MSA (Multibus II System Architecture), the Intel 386 and i486 microprocessors and the UNIX System V standard to offer a complete System V/386 Multibus II development system. Moreover, various hardware configurations are available to serve as the basis for an OEM target system or server. The System 520 users may add to these basic configurations or purchase and integrate specific system contents separately to meet their system configuration needs.

STANDARD FEATURES

- High performance Intel 386 Multibus II OEM system
- System V/386, Release 3.2 multi-user operating system
- Complete UNIX (SVID2) Software Development Extension
- One 386 application processor
- 386 microprocessor-based SCSI disk controller
- 186/410 six-channel serial I/O controller
- 186/530 Ethernet controller
- iSBX™ 279 Hardware Window console controller (no graphics)
- Easy system expansion via Intel's Multibus II System Architecture (MSA) & iSBC® board family
- OpenNET transparent remote file sharing & virtual terminal
- NFS and TCP support

SYSTEM V/386 SELF-TARGETED ADA*-386 COMPILATION SYSTEM

UNIX HOSTED ADA-386 DEVELOPMENT

Intel's System V/386 Self-Targeted Ada-386 Compilation System comprises a rich set of Ada language tools for the programmer wanting to develop Ada applications for the Intel System 520. This UNIX hosted, self-targeted and validated Ada toolset contains the Compiler & Library Tools, the Global Optimizer, the COFF Linker, an Ada Execution Environment, an Ada Symbolic Debugger, as well as other development environment tools for handling cross-referencing, source dependency, and source formatting. The compiler and its tools create a flexible, project-oriented development environment for commercial, industrial, and military applications.

INTEL SUPPORT AND LICENSING INFORMATION

BACKED BY INTEL MANUFACTURING AND CUSTOMER SUPPORT

All Intel software and hardware products are fully supported by Intel's worldwide staff of trained service and support engineers. Intel also provides system engineering and field applications consulting services, worldwide training workshops, a full range of maintenance services, and a software support hotline. Custom board and system configurations, as well as custom manufacturing, can also be provided by Intel. Every product includes a standard 90-day warranty replacement guarantee. Selected products include an extended warranty package. The complete UNIX System 520 development package (SYS520R1DKITSV) is backed by a full, one-year service and support package. See specific product literature for more details.

LICENSING

Each copy of UNIX is licensed for use on a single system regardless of the number of CPUs or users. Intel also provides licenses for copying and distributing Multibus I/II versions of System V/386. Licensing for the use of source code and distribution of binary, derived works is also available.

7

SYSTEM V/386 FEATURES

- Editing Package
- C Software Development Set
- Extended Terminal Interface Package
- Remote Terminal Package Capability for unlimited number of users—there is no multi-user upgrade license
- Network Support Utilities Package
- Remote File Sharing Package
- 2 Kilobyte File System Utility Package
- XENIX File System Package
- System Administration Software Package
- Kernel Debugger Package
- DiskUtils Package (DOS and RMX diskette utilities)
- i350 Parallel Port Printer Driver Package
- Ethernet Streams Driver Package. Includes *edlina* driver and a device driver for either the iSBC552A or the iSBC186/530. Permits the user to install and use TCP/IP on these boards.
- Multibus II Streams Transport Application Interface (TAI) Package
- Multibus II Bootserver Package
- Multibus II SV-oti Driver Package (OTS driver)

ORDERING INFORMATION

SYSTEM V/386™ FAMILY ORDER CODES

SYSTEMV386I	SVR3.2 multiuser, base UNIX Operating System software for Multibus I, tape installation, development package and all documentation
SYSTEMV386II	SVR3.2 multiuser, base UNIX Operating System software for Multibus II, tape installation, development package and all documentation
SVNET	SVR3.2 OpenNET, on 3½, 5¼ and tape installation. Includes drivers and iNA961 (Ethernet board image to support ISO/OSI Transport and DataLink for TCP/IP) for iSBC552A (Multibus I), iSBC186/530 (Multibus II) and PCLINK2 (PC-BUS)
SYSTEMV386SRC	UNIX V.3.2 Source (common tape for all buses).
NFS32	NFS, Network File System for SVR3.2, includes both 3½ and 5¼ floppy installation
TCP32	TCP/IP for SVR3.2, includes both 3½ and 5¼ floppy installation
U386ADA386SW	UNIX hosted, Self-Targeted Ada-386 Compilation System for System 520 Multibus II OEM Systems
U386ADA386SS	UNIX hosted, Self-Targeted Ada-386 Software

Product Literature

Multibus UNIX System V/386 Product Family Factsheet	280692-001
Multibus I and II Product Family Poster	281008-001
Multibus II 386 CPU Boards Factsheet	280620-001
iSBC486/125 & iSBC386/133 CPU Boards Factsheet	281007-001
Multibus I/O Products	281009-001
Multibus II PC Subsystem (PC/16) Factsheet	280673-001
iSBC386/258 Peripheral Controller	280670-001
Multibus UNIX Documentation (Transport Application I/F Guide, Device Driver Guide and Reference Manual)	UNX386LITII
Prentice Hall UNIX System V/386 Documentation Library	UNX386DOC

Networking Literature

OpenNET Family Factsheet	280669-002
NFS Software For Release 3.2 Factsheet	281032-001
TCP/IP Software For Release 3.2 Factsheet	281034-001
X WINDOW Software For Release 3.2 Factsheet	281031-001

intel®

APPLICATION NOTE

AP-446

November 1990

Porting Applications from the iRMX®II to the iRMX®III Operating System (16 Bits to 32 Bits)

RABINDRA P. KAR
SENIOR TECHNICAL MARKETING ENGINEER

Order Number: 281103-001

7

PORTING APPLICATIONS FROM THE iRMX®II TO THE iRMX®III OPERATING SYSTEM (16 BITS TO 32 BITS)

CONTENTS PAGE

APPENDICES

1.0 INTRODUCTION

When a user wishes to move from the iRMX® II Operating System (OS) to the iRMX III (OS) there are two portation choices. He/she may choose to keep most or all of the application in 16-bit compatibility mode, porting only 16-bit device drivers, interrupt handlers and OS extensions, if any. Or he may recompile the entire application with 32-bit compilers and linkage tools and reap the performance benefits.

This document explains the software development steps and the trade-offs involved in either choice, in theory, and by means of actual programming examples.

Before describing the mechanics of HOW applications must be modified to run under iRMX III, we will examine WHY one might want to undertake 16- to 32-bit portation. The following issues will be considered:

a. In what situations is it advantageous to move from iRXM II to III? In what circumstances is it not worthwhile?

b. What 16-bit applications are most likely to benefit performance-wise when ported to 32 bits, and why.

The following sections will answer the above questions and then describe, with examples how application code can be moved from an iRMX II to iRMX III execution environment. Issues pertaining to 16- and 32-bit development and debug tools for the iRMX III OS will also be discussed.

2.0 REASONS FOR AND AGAINST MOVING TO iRMX® III

It is very important to keep in mind that a change of execution environment from iRMX II to iRMX III does not necessarily entail portation of application code to 32 bits. A special 16-bit compatibility interface was built into iRMX III so that many existing iRMX II programs will continue to run unchanged (binary compatibility); case I provides more details about compatibility-mode execution. There is a slight performance penalty when 16-bit programs are run under iRMX III, but there are good reasons why one may want to upgrade to iRMX III even though the application continues to run in 16-bit mode.

a. With the constantly falling cost of RAM, it is now reasonably economical to build computer systems containing 16 Mbytes of RAM or more. iRMX III can use upto 4 Gbytes of physical memory (even when running several 16-bit programs), while iRMX II is restricted to 16 Mbytes.

b. It is possible to run 16-bit and 32-bit tasks concurrently under iRMX III. Existing 16-bit programs can be used without modification while new programs run concurrently in 32-bit mode. Under certain circumstances, a single application can consist of a mix of 16- and 32-bit code modules.

c. OEM users of iRMX are exposed to less project risk when making the transition from 16 bits to 32 bits, because they can do it in two steps—first upgrade to iRMX III, then port the application code to 32 bits after they are comfortable with the upgraded Operating System.

Upgrading from iRMX II to iRMX III is not recommended in certain circumstances. These include:

a. If the CPU being used is an 80286 and there is no performance or other need to move to an 386™ or i486™ CPU (the iRMX II OS requires an 386™ microprocessor).

b. If all computations only involve integers smaller than 64K (65,536) AND there is no present or forseeable need to use contiguous memory areas larger than 64 Kbytes.

c. Intel's 386™ microprocessor object module format (OMF386) does not support memory overlays, so iRMX III cannot support overlay-loading in 32-bit applications. iRMX II applications that use overlays can still be executed in 16-bit compatibility mode.

d. In general, applications require more code and data space when ported to 32 bits (a rule of thumb is about 30% more memory space). iRMX III also requires that more memory be set aside for the operating system itself. If there are severe constraints on memory in the system, it may not be advisable to switch to 32 bits.

e. In a few cases, the application may be written in a language for which a 32-bit compiler is not yet available. Porting of the application may have to be postponed until one is.

What kinds of applications are likely to benefit by moving from 16 bits to 32 bits? The following is a short, and by no means exhaustive, list:

- Applications that involve intensive computations with unsigned integers larger than 64K (65,536) or signed integers larger than 32K (32,768). Case III illustrates this situation with a matrix multiplication example.
- Applications where more than 64 Kbytes of contiguous code or data space are needed. Large databases, high-resolution graphics and fluid dynamics analysis are some examples.
- The 386™ microprocessor offers several bit and bit-string manipulation instructions. Applications that do bit-field manipulation in software could see a performance gain. Applications that previously used bytes to store binary flags could be rewritten much more compactly.
- Applications where the processor might access memory across a 32-bit bus, like MULTIBUS II.
- When there is a 32-bit interface between the CPU, the numeric coprocessor (e.g., 80387) and memory, floating-point applications will see a moderate performance boost, because operands can be transferred in 32-bit blocks to and from the coprocessor. The speed of the floating-point operation itself depends on the coprocessor. The 387™ coprocessor adds support for some functions like sine/cosine, not available in the 287; this could result in a performance gain for applications that use transcendental functions.

3.0 16- AND 32-BIT PROGRAMMING CASE STUDIES

The rest of this document presents several typical "cases" that illustrate the changes required in an iRMX II application when the base operating system is upgraded to iRMX III. 16- and 32-bit program listings are included, along with some performance comparisons made while running the programs on a SYSTEM 120B (16 MHz 80386 and 80387, 512K base + 2048K extended memory). The application examples are in PL/M, assembler and iC286, since these are by far the most commonly used languages (with iRMX).

3.1 Case I: 16-Bit Applications without Custom Interrupt-Handlers, Device Drivers

iRMX II applications (either run-time loadable or configured as first-level jobs) will run under iRMX III without modification, as long as they do not include 16-bit interrupt-handlers, device-drivers, and OS extensions. Such applications are said to execute in "16-bit compatibility mode".

"twsit.p28", a PLM-286 benchmark program is shown in Listing 1. It measures the time it takes to switch between two iRMX tasks of equal priority; all task switches take place during rq$sleep calls. Listing 1a lists the commands used to compile and bind this program under iRMX II. The very same executable file will run under iRMX III in 16-bit mode exhibiting full binary compatibility. However, some performance degradation will be seen; the reasons are explained later.

16-bit C programs (complied with iC-286 V4.1+) are also fully binary compatible when run under iRMX III. The same caveats apply as for PLM applications-namely, that the C application involve no 16-bit device drivers, interrupt handlers or OS extensions. C applications tend to be more stack-intensive than PLM ones though. They may run out of stack space under iRMX III unless they were allocated liberal amounts of stack using the SEGSIZE control in BND286.

Though the 16-bit "twsit" program can be run without changes, the user has the option of using a 32-bit compiler, making only one small change in the source code (see listing 2). To compile it with PL/M386 under iRMX III, the $WORD16 compiler control was added, at the start of the code, for the following reasons:

- The USE OF THE $WORD16 CONTROL IS HIGHLY RECOMMENDED WHEN PLM-286 PROGRAMS ARE PORTED TO PLM-386. When this control is in effect, PLM-386 treats a WORD as a 16-bit variable (and a DWORD as a 32-bit variable), the same as PLM-286. Since most WORDs and DWORDs in the program do not really need to be doubled in size (unless 32-bit integer math or 64K + data arrays are involved), $WORD16 provides a painless method of saving data and code space.
- Even though iRMX III is a 32-bit OS, the parameters of most operating system calls still contain only 16 bits or 8 bits of SIGNIFICANT data; which is why many of the program's variables can remain as 16-bit WORDs. However, when a CALL instruction is executed, PLM-386 (or any other 32-bit compiler) always PUSH 32 bits on the stack at a time, after zero-extending the 16- or 8-bit parameters in the call. The $WORD16 control does NOT affect stack operations. As a general rule iRMX III programs require at least twice the stack size of an equivalent iRMX II program. That is why the stack size for twsit.p38 was increased by 2000 hex bytes, using the SEGSIZE control in BND386 (see listing 2a).

A comparison of Listings 1a and 2a illustrate the differences in the generation process between 16- and 32-bit iRMX executables. The most salient are:

a. The logical pathname (:rmxinc:) is changed to point to the "/rmx386/inc" directory instead of "/rmx286/inc". These directories contain files with "EXTERNAL" declarations for the iRMX and UDI calls in the source.

b. The 32-bit iRMX III code must be bound with 32-bit iRMX and UDI interface libraries (rmxifc32.lib, udiifc32.lib, in this example).

c. When binding "compact" model object files, a RENAMESEG control must be used to rename the code segment (output by PLM-386) from "CODE32" to "CODE". The code segments of the rmxifc and udiifc libraries are already named "CODE". In the "compact" model only one code segment is allowed and BND386 can only combine segments that have the same name.

NOTE:

When a 386™ microprocessor runs 32-bit code each segment can be as large as 4 GB. Hence even the largest programs will fit in PLM-386 COMPACT model; so there are no size advantages to using LARGE model. If a LARGE model PLM-286 program is being ported, it should be re-compiled in PLM-386 compact model.

3.1.1 Performance and Compatibility Mechanism

The "tswit" task switching program was run on iRMX II and iRMX III in 16- and 32-bit modes,using the same hardware (16 MHz SYSTEM 120B). The task switch times it measured were as follows:

iRMX II: 99 ms

iRMX III:16-bit mode — 134 ms, 32-bit mode — 111 ms

The task switch times may surprise those who believe that a 32-bit Operating System must do everything faster than a 16-bit one. However, task switching essentially involves the saving and re-loading of a task's context—CPU registers and "task-state" areas in RAM. While iRMX III does save and load 32 bits at a time, versus 16 bits for iRMX II, the width of iRMX III's registers and task-state variables is twice that of iRMX II, so context switching is no faster under iRMX III.

Why is there a significant performance degradation in 16-bit task switch time under iRMX III? When a 16-bit program makes a system call, the 16-bit binary compatibility interface within iRMX III builds a 32-bit copy of the 16-bit stack frame (16-bit parameters are zero-extended to 32 bits). Then the call is executed like a 32-bit call. However, the building of a second (32-bit) stack frame (and stack unwinding after a call) does impose a performance penalty. That is why, given the same hardware environment, 16-bit applications run faster on iRMX II than iRMX III.

3.1.2 iRMX® II Cross-Development Under iRMX® III

A very useful aspect of 16-bit binary compatibility mode is that it allows iRMX II cross-development under iRMX III. The iRMX II ICU as well as the 16-bit compilers and linkage tools (ASM286, PLM286, iC286, BND286, BLD286) run under iRMX III without modification. Since the two operating systems also have the same disk and file formats, the development libraries for both can be installed on the same hard disk (need a 40 MB or larger disk); then application development for either one can be done after booting iRMX III.

3.2 Case II: 16-Bit Applications with Custom Device Drivers, Interrupt Handlers, or Operating System (OS) Extensions

If an iRMX II application includes a user-written device driver or interrupt handler or OS extension, iRMX III does not offer 100% binary compatibility. Device drivers, handlers etc. are too closely bound to the Operating System to provide a 16- or 32-bit conversion interface for them. These pieces of the application software must be ported to 32 bits when moving to iRMX III, even though the rest of the application may remain 16-bit.

Listings 3a and 3b show an iRMX II benchmark application consisting of a PL/M main program (ltncy.p28) and a dynamically loaded interrupt handler in assembler (latch.a28). This application measures interrupt latency—the number of clock ticks between the CPU's receipt of an interrupt request and the execution of the first instruction in the interrupt handler routine (after the CPU's context has been saved on the stack).

To run the interrupt latency benchmark program under iRMX III, the interrupt handler must be ported to 32 bits. The ASM-386 version of latch.a28 is latch.a38 (see listing 3c). It is a simple example illustrating what needs to be changed when porting from 16 bits to 32 bits. Note how latch.a38's instructions manipulate 32-bit registers and a 32-bit stack (PUSHAD, POPAD). The IRETD instruction replaces IRET because the handler is entered via a 386 interrupt gate, which pushes 32-bit EIP and EFLAGS registers on the stack.

3.2.1 MIXING 16-BIT AND 32-BIT MODULES

Referring again to the previous example even though the interrupt handler ("latch module) was ported to 32 bits, the PL/M module ("ltncy") did not have to be ported. But care has to be taken when combining the two modules to form a single executable using BND386 (see listing 3d). First, the PL/M module must be compiled with the LARGE memory model, since its code segment must remain separate from latch's assembler code. Second, the iRMX II interface libraries must be linked-in because ltncy.p28 makes 16-bit iRMX calls.

It is possible to create mixed 16 and 32-bit executables (as described above) because Intel's 386 Relocation and linkage tools (BND386, BLD386 . . .) will accept both 16-bit and 32-bit modules as valid input. But it is the software developer's responsibility to make sure that if 16 and 32-bit code functions call each other, the size of parameters on the stack is adjusted properly before the call, and cleaned up after the call.

The 80386 microprocessor recognizes and handles either 16 or 32-bit code by examing the descriptor of each code segment just before execution. iRMX III figures out whether a 16 or 32-bit program is making a system call by looking at the parameter stack of the call itself. Hence, the system is very flexible in multi-tasking any combination of 16 and 32-bit tasks running in the foreground or background.

3.3 Case III: Speeding Up an Application by Porting to 32 Bits

In cases I and II, the possibilities and limitations of running existing 16-bit iRMX II applications (or mixed 16/32 bit applications) under iRMX III, were examined. But the main purpose of moving to a 32-bit operating system is to run 32-bit applications that enjoy higher performance and a larger memory size. The following case illustrates how minor source modifications can turn a 16-bit computational application into a 32-bit one with a greater than 2x performance boost AND INCREASED ACCURACY too.

The multiplication of integer matrices is a very common computational task and source code for this function already exists in most computer languages. Listings 4a and 4b are 16 and 32-bit versions of a PL/M program that multiples two square matrices with integer elements.

The two programs are extremely similar except for the declarations of the input matrices (A, B) and the result matrix (C). In the 16-bit version all three matrices consist of DWORD elements. Using WORD-sized elements would mean restricting all input elements to less than 65,536 which is too small to be useful in many practical applications. In the 32-bit version the elements of A & B are WORDs. Since the $WORD16 control is NOT used here, these are 32-bit WORDs (max value up to 4 billion), which is large enough for most applications.

When the 32-bit integer matrix multiplication was benchmarked, the iRMX III version ran nearly twice as fast as the iRMX II version. This is a direct consequence of the 386's ability to multiply 32-bit integers with a single "IMUL" (integer multiply) instruction. Under iRMX II, the 32-bit multiplication was actually emulated by a software routine (LQ_DWORD_MULTIPLY in plm286.lib) which is much slower.

An added advantage of matrix multiplication under iRMX III is that the result of each multiplication can be accommodated in a 64-bit variable, which means that there is no chance of an overflow. Under iRMX II both the result matrix and the input matrix have 32-bit elements, so the computation of any element in the C matrix may result in an overflow, thus decreasing computational accuracy.

When porting a program to 32 bits, look for the following situations (in the 16-bit source), to exploit the larger machine word size for higher accuracy and performance:

1. Any arithmetic operation involving DWORDs (in PLM-286) or "long/double" declarations in C-286.
2. String searching/copying operations (CMPB/CMPW/MOVB/MOVW in PL/M) are limited to 64K segments with a 16-bit OS. All of physical memory can be covered by a one 32-bit operation.
3. Look carefully at the variable declarations at the start of each source module and procedure/function, specially at the size of arrays. Any arrays of close to 64K byte size, or 32K 16-bit WORD size, will probably benefit from being extended.

4. The 80386 CPU has special bit manipulation instructions in hardware. Programs written for the 80286 may perform these functions in software, or may (wastefully) use a byte to store binary flags etc. for performance reasons. These program sections can be recoded to enhance performance and compactness, though it may be necessary to call assembler routines to take advantage of the bit manipulation instructions.

OTHER PORTATION ISSUES

4.0 OVERLAY SUPPORT

Some large (and easily partitioned) iRMX II applications utilize its overlay support to execute in a relatively small amount of RAM. The OVL286 utility is used to create separate overlay sections in an OMF286 executable file. iRMX II's application loader provides runtime support for overlay loading.

OMF386 (the output of BND386 and BLD386) completely drops overlay support, since disk-swapping ("virtual-memory") can be implemented using the 386's paging functionality. Consequently iRMX III is unable to support (or even recognize) overlays in 32-bit (OMF386) executable code. Overlays are still supported in 16-bit compatibility mode.

Since RAM chips are much cheaper and more compact today, compared to when the 80286 was introduced, the easiest solution is to use more RAM and avoid overlays entirely. A long-term solution might be to implement paging and disk-swapping in iRMX III. But this solution would definitely impact the "real time", determinate nature of iRMX, and its response-time to critical events.

4.1 iRMX® Reconfiguration

Many iRMX II users have reconfigured it to suit their application. This may have involved adding custom device drivers, integration of application code as a first-level job, or the stripping away of the operating system's outer layers. Reconfiguration is usually achieved using iRMX's Interactive Configuraion Utility (ICU).

iRMX III's ICU is extremely similar in appearance and operation to iRMX II release 4's ICU. Users will have to go through essentially the same steps to reconfigure iRMX III as they did iRMX II. Of course, the 32-bit language and linkage tooks (ASM386, BND386 and BLD386) must be present on the development system to regenerate a new iRMX III boot file.

4.2 Debug Environment

Superficially, the application debug environments of iRMX II and III seem quite similar. This is convenient for the iRMX II user who will not have to learn new debuggers when moving to iRMX III. However, there are some important underlying differences that the user needs to be aware of. These are described below.

a. Self-Hosted Debug:

At the assembler/machine-instruction level, iRMX II offers the iSDM™ II and sdb debugger. iSDM II is burnt into PROM on the target CPU board and sdb establishes links to it when iRMX II is booted on the board. iSDM II is available as a separate, configurable product.

iRMX III's assembler-level debugger, iSDM III, has the same human interface as iSDM II, but it actually consists of an iSDM interface layered on top of Intel's 32-bit iM-III monitor. Moreover, iSDM III and iM-III are part of the iRMX III boot file that is loaded and activated when iRMX III is booted. The debuggers are not burnt separately into PROM. At present, iSDM III is not a separate product, nor can it be configured for CPU boards that iRMX does not know about.

For source-level debugging in iRMX II the recommended debugger is Soft-Scope* II. Soft-Scope II does not support multi-user or multi-tasking debug adequately (in cases where more than one task hit a breakpoint/exception simultaneously). iRMX III-hosted Soft-Scope III allows the user to set breakpoints in multiple tasks simultaneously, even if the tasks are using the same code segment in a reentrant manner.

b. DOS-Hosted Debug:

Cross debugging (from a PC host to iRMX target) is NOT an Intel-supported environment at present. However, DOS-hosted Soft-Scope III/286 can be used to debug a target running iRMX II. An RS-232 cable connecting the serial ports on the host PC and the target CPU board is the physical link. Soft-Scope III talks to iSDM II (in PROM on the target) and downloads/debugs iRMX II through iSDM.

DOS-hosted Softscope III/386 talks to an iM-III monitor. Downloading iRMX III using Soft-Scope is not feasible in this scenario, because the iM-III monitor is present only after iRMX III (along with iSDM III and iM-III) is booted on the target. If the bootloading can be done independently, a debug connection may be established, over a serial cable, between iM and Soft-Scope. Note that this scenario has not been evaluated or tested by Intel.

5.0 SUMMARY

This document covers the following major points:

- Why an iRMX II user might want to upgrade to the iRMX III OS and keep the existing application in 16-bit compatibility mode.
- The kinds of applications that will gain the most if ported from 16- to 32-bit code under iRMX.
- The special circumstances under which moving to iRMX III may not be recommended for the iRMX II user.

Three case studies are presented along with programming examples. They cover the portation of 16-bit applications that do or do not include custom device drivers/interrupt handlers/OS extensions. The final section deals with miscellaneous issues like overlay support and the debug environment for the two operating systems.

*Soft-Scope is a trademark of Concurrent Sciences.

APPENDIX A

SOURCE AND GENERATION FILE OF 16-BIT iRMX® II PROGRAM

```
$title(tswit)
/***************************************************************************\
 *  Task-switch time benchmarking program, on iRMX II.
 *    Compiler: PL/M-286 V2.7
 *                Q1 1988, by R. P. Kar
 *    Last modified:  Oct 1989
\***************************************************************************/

tswit: DO;

DECLARE
    TOKEN LITERALLY 'SELECTOR',
    BOOLEAN LITERALLY 'BYTE';

$include(:rmxinc:nuclus.ext)
$include(:rmxinc:bios.ext)
$include(:rmxinc:udi.ext)

DECLARE
    MAX_LOOPS LITERALLY '500000',
    CR         LITERALLY '0DH',     LF         LITERALLY '0AH',
    WRITE_ONLY LITERALLY '2',       READ_ONLY LITERALLY '1',
    ONE_BUFFER LITERALLY '0',

    (el_time, status)            WORD,
    (task1_t, task2_t, co_conn) TOKEN,
    pri                          BYTE,
    (count1, count2, spare_d)   DWORD,
    (start_time, end_time, tswit_time) DWORD;


/*
 * Utility procedure to display a number in decimal or hex ASCII
 */
$include(utils.inc)


$subtitle(task)
/* Tasks 1 and 2 merely increment a counter everytime they complete a loop
 * and call rq$sleep so iRMX will switch execution from one to another.
 */

task1: PROCEDURE PUBLIC;

  DO WHILE 1;
    IF count1 = MAX_LOOPS THEN
      CALL RQ$DELETE$TASK( SELECTOR$OF(NIL), @status ); /* delete self */
    CALL RQ$SLEEP(0, @status);              /* Task switch happens here */
    count1 = count1 + 1;
  END;

END task1;
```

281103-1

Listing 1: Task Switch Measurement Program (tswit.p28) (Continued)

```
$subtitle(task2)
task2: PROCEDURE PUBLIC;

  DO WHILE 1;
    IF count2 = MAX_LOOPS THEN
      CALL RQ$DELETE$TASK( SELECTOR$OF(NIL), @status ); /* delete self */
    CALL RQ$SLEEP(0, @status);                /* Task switch happens here */
    count2 = count2 + 1;
  END;

END task2;


/***************************  MAIN PROGRAM  ****************************/

co_conn = DQ$ATTACH (@(4,':CO:'), @status);
CALL DQ$OPEN (co_conn, WRITE_ONLY, ONE_BUFFER, @status);

CALL DQ$WRITE (co_conn, @(LF,'Task Switch measurement: '), 26, @status);
CALL disp_num (MAX_LOOPS, 2, 0);
CALL DQ$WRITE (co_conn, @(' task loops..',CR,LF,LF), 16, @status);

/*
 * Measure the time to execute the task code (2 * MAX_LOOPS) times
 * WITHOUT task switching.
 */
spare_d = 2 * MAX_LOOPS;
/* Start of timing loop */
start_time = RQ$GET$TIME (@status);

  count1 = 0;
  DO WHILE 1;
    IF count1 >= spare_d THEN
      GOTO label1;
    /* CALL RQ$SLEEP(0, @status); */ /* Task switch would happen here */
    count1 = count1 + 1;
  END;

label1:
/* End of timing loop */
end_time = RQ$GET$TIME (@status);

el_time = end_time - start_time;


/* Get main program's priority */
pri = RQ$GET$PRIORITY (SELECTOR$OF(NIL), @status);

count1, count2 = 0;

task1_t = RQ$CREATE$TASK (pri+1, @task1, SELECTOR$OF(@count1),
                                        NIL, 512, 0, @status);
IF status <> 0 THEN
  CALL DQ$WRITE (co_conn, @('RQ$CREATE$TASK error',CR,LF), 22, @status);

task2_t = RQ$CREATE$TASK (pri+1, @task2, SELECTOR$OF(@count1),
                /* SELECTOR$OF(NIL), */ NIL, 512, 0, @status);

/* Start of timing loop */
start_time = RQ$GET$TIME (@status);
```

281103-2

Listing 1: Task Switch Measurement Program (tswit.p28) (Continued)

```
/*
 * Set main program's priority lower than tasks 1 & 2.
 * Then the tasks will keep switching between themselves until
 * (2 * MAX_LOOPS) task switches have occurred. Then they will delete
 * themselves and control will return to main program.
 */
CALL RQ$SET$PRIORITY( SELECTOR$OF(NIL), pri+2, @status );

/* End of timing loop */
end_time = RQ$GET$TIME (@status);

/* Restore main program's original priority */
CALL RQ$SET$PRIORITY( SELECTOR$OF(NIL), pri, @status );

/*
 * Subtract the time to execute tasks without task switching from the time
 * to execute while switching.
 */
el_time = (end_time - start_time) - DOUBLE(el_time);


/* Display the results on the screen */

CALL DQ$WRITE (co_conn, @('        '), 8, @status);
CALL disp_num (DOUBLE(el_time), 2, 0);
CALL DQ$WRITE (co_conn, @(' secs = time for '), 17, @status);
CALL disp_num ((MAX_LOOPS * 2), 2, 0);
CALL DQ$WRITE (co_conn, @(' task switches',CR,LF), 16, @status);

/* Calculate task switch time in microseconds */
tswit_time = ( DOUBLE(el_time) * 1000000 ) / (MAX_LOOPS * 2);

CALL DQ$WRITE (co_conn, @('        i.e. '), 13, @status);
CALL disp_num (tswit_time, 2, 0);
CALL DQ$WRITE (co_conn, @(' microsecs per task switch',CR,LF), 28, @status);

CALL DQ$EXIT(0);

END tswit;


        LISTING 1a:  COMPILING AND LINKING TSWIT.P28


af /rmx286/inc as :rmxinc:

PLM286 tswit.p28 COMPACT

BND286 tswit.obj, :lang:plm286.lib, &
   /rmx286/lib/rmxifc.lib, &
   /rmx286/lib/udiifc.lib &
   RC(DM(1000H,2000H)) SEGSIZE(stack(2000H)) &
   OBJECT(%0_pc)
```

281103-3

Listing 1: Task Switch Measurement Program (tswit.p28) (Continued)

APPENDIX B

iRMX® II PROGRAM (WITHOUT DEVICE DRIVERS, INTERRUPT HANDLERS) PORTED TO IRMX® III

```
$TITLE(tswit)

$WORD16

/*****************************************************************************\
 *  Task-switch time benchmarking program, on iRMX III.
 *        Oct 1989, by R.P.Kar
\*****************************************************************************/

tswit: DO;

DECLARE
    TOKEN LITERALLY 'SELECTOR',
    BOOLEAN LITERALLY 'BYTE';

$include(:rmxinc:nuclus.ext)
$include(:rmxinc:bios.ext)
$include(:rmxinc:udi.ext)

                                  :
                                  :
                                  :
                                  :

          LISTING 2a:  32-BIT COMPILE AND LINK UNDER iRMX III

af /rmx386/inc as :rmxinc:

PLM386 tswit.p38 COMPACT

BND386 tswit.obj, & :lang:plm386.lib,
   /rmx386/lib/rmxifc32.lib, &
   /rmx386/lib/udiifc32.lib &
   RENAMESEG(CODE32 TO CODE) &
   RC(DM(1000H,20000H))  SEGSIZE(stack(+2000H)) &
   OBJECT(%0_3pc)
```

281103-4

Listing 2: Use of $WORD16 Control when Porting to PLM-386 (File: tswit.p38)

APPENDIX C

PORTING AN iRMX® II PROGRAM (WITH CUSTOM INTERRUPT HANDLER) to iRMX® III

```
$title(ltncy)
/*****************************************************************************\
 *  iRMX II interrupt latency benchmarking program.
 *
 *  Method:  This program first sets up an interrupt handler for an unused
 *           interrupt level. It then reads the count in the system timer
 *           (timer 0 on the 8254 chip) and simulates an external interrupt
 *           to the CPU by a cause$interrupt instruction. The interrupt
 *           handler latches timer 0, so this program can read it again
 *           after the handler returns control. The difference in the
 *           two timer-count values is the interrupt latency.
 *
 *                       Q1 1988, by R. P. Kar
 *    Last Modified:  Oct 1989
\*****************************************************************************/
ltncy: DO;

DECLARE
    TOKEN LITERALLY 'SELECTOR',
    BOOLEAN LITERALLY 'BYTE';

$include(:rmxinc:udi.ext)
$include(:rmxinc:nuclus.ext)

DECLARE
    PIT_ADDR   LITERALLY '40H',
    CR         LITERALLY '0DH',      LF         LITERALLY '0AH',
    WRITE_ONLY LITERALLY '2',        READ_ONLY  LITERALLY '1',
    single_buffer LITERALLY '0',
    el_time WORD,
    dummy_w WORD,
    co_conn TOKEN,
    pri     BYTE,
    (lo_cnt1, hi_cnt1, lo_cnt2) BYTE,
    (timer_cnt1, timer_cnt2)    WORD,
    status  WORD;


/*
 * To display a number in decimal or hex ASCII
 */
$include(utils.inc)

/**********************************
 *  Interrupt handler
 **********************************/
int_hndlr: PROCEDURE EXTERNAL;
END int_hndlr;
```

281103-5

Listing 3a: Interrupt Latency Benchmark (ltncy.p28)

```
/******************************   MAIN PROGRAM   *****************************/

co_conn = DQ$ATTACH (@(4,':CO:'), @status);
CALL DQ$OPEN (co_conn, WRITE_ONLY, single_buffer, @status);

CALL DQ$WRITE (co_conn,
@('                    ***  WARNING ***',CR,LF,LF),38,@status);
CALL DQ$WRITE (co_conn,
@('  This program assumes strict PC/AT compatible hardware',CR,LF),57,@status);

/* Set up local handler for IRQ3 on master 8259 */
CALL RQ$SET$INTERRUPT (38H, 0, @int_hndlr, SELECTOR$OF(NIL), @status);

DISABLE;

/* Latch and read timer value. Interrupt handler will latch it again */
OUTPUT (PIT_ADDR + 3) = 0;  /* Latch counter 0 */

/* The following two instructions read the value latched in counter 0. They
    are unavoidable measurement overhead and inflate the interrupt latency
    by a few clock cycles.
 */
lo_cntl = INPUT(PIT_ADDR);
hi_cntl = INPUT(PIT_ADDR);

/* Activate the interrupt handler. It will latch timer 0 and return.
 */
CAUSE$INTERRUPT(59);

/* The interrupt handler has latched the timer 0 count. Now read it
 */
lo_cnt2 = INPUT(PIT_ADDR);
dummy_w = DOUBLE(INPUT(PIT_ADDR));
timer_cnt2 = DOUBLE(lo_cnt2) + SHL(dummy_w,8);

ENABLE;

dummy_w = DOUBLE(hi_cntl);
timer_cntl = DOUBLE(lo_cntl) + SHL(dummy_w,8);
/*
CALL disp_num (timer_cntl, 1, 'H');
CALL DQ$WRITE (co_conn, @(' = countl  '), 11, @status);
CALL disp_num (timer_cnt2, 1, 'H');
CALL DQ$WRITE (co_conn, @(' = count2',CR,LF), 11, @status);
 */

/* Calculate difference in timer counts (timer counts DOWN to 0) */
IF timer_cntl > timer_cnt2
THEN el_time = timer_cntl - timer_cnt2;
ELSE  /* Rare case when timer has wrapped around */
     el_time = timer_cntl + (OFFFFH - timer_cnt2 + 1);
```

281103–6

Listing 3a: Interrupt Latency Benchmark (ltncy.p28) (Continued)

7

```
/* Display results */

CALL DQ$WRITE (co_conn,
@(LF,'   Interrupt latency = '), 24, @status);
CALL disp_num (el_time, 1, 0);
CALL DQ$WRITE (co_conn, @(' timer ticks',CR,LF), 16, @status);
CALL DQ$WRITE (co_conn,
@('   Latency in microsecs = timer ticks / 1.19 Mhz',CR,LF,LF), 51,
                @status);

CALL RQ$RESET$INTERRUPT (38H, @status);

CALL DQ$EXIT(0);

END ltncy;


LISTING 3b: INTERRUPT HANDLER FOR INTERRUPT LATENCY BENCHMARK (LATCH.A28)

; Interrupt handler. Merely latches timer 0 in a PC/AT (or hardware
; compatible computer).

        NAME latch

latch SEGMENT PUBLIC

int_hndlr PROC FAR
PUBLIC int_hndlr

    PUSHA
    PUSH DS
    PUSH ES
    XOR  AX,AX
    OUT  43H, AL     ; Latch 8254 counter 0
    POP  ES
    POP  DS
    POPA
    IRET

int_hndlr ENDP

latch ENDS

        END
```

281103–7

Listing 3a: Interrupt Latency Benchmark (ltncy.p28) (Continued)

```
; Interrupt handler. Merely latches timer 0 in a PC/AT (or hardware
; compatible computer).
;

      NAME latch

code SEGMENT PUBLIC

int_hndlr PROC
PUBLIC int_hndlr

  PUSHAD            ; push 32-bit registers
  PUSH DS
  PUSH ES
  PUSH FS
  PUSH GS

  XOR  EAX,EAX
  OUT  43H, AL      ; Latch 8254 counter 0

  POP  GS
  POP  FS
  POP  ES
  POP  DS
  POPAD
  IRETD

int_hndlr ENDP

code ENDS

      END
```

LISTING 3d: GENERATING AN iRMX III PROGRAM WITH BOTH 16 AND 32-bit MODULES

```
af /rmx286/inc as :rmxinc:

PLM286 ltncy.p28 LARGE

ASM386 latch.a38

BND386 ltncy.obj, latch.obj, &
       /lang286/plm286.lib, &
       /rmx286/lib/rmxifl.lib, &
       /rmx286/lib/udiifl.lib &
       RC(DM(1000H,20000H))  SEGSIZE(stack(+2000H))
```

281103-8

Listing 3c: 32-Bit Version of Interrupt Handler (LATCH.A38)

APPENDIX D

SPEEDING UP INTEGER MATH USING iRMX® III

```
/*  Matrix multiply: A * B = C */
mtrx_mlt: DO;

DECLARE
    TOKEN LITERALLY 'SELECTOR',
    BOOLEAN LITERALLY 'BYTE';
$INCLUDE(:rmxinc:bios.ext)
$INCLUDE(:rmxinc:udi.ext)

DECLARE
    MAXROWS LITERALLY '64',
    CR         LITERALLY '0DH',    LF        LITERALLY '0AH',
    WRITE_ONLY LITERALLY '2',     READ_ONLY LITERALLY '1',
    ONE_BUFFER LITERALLY '0',

    co_conn TOKEN,
    (status, i, j, k, rows, last, m, el_time) WORD,
    (start_time, end_time, temp_d) DWORD,
    spare_b BYTE, in_buf(80) BYTE ,
    A(MAXROWS) STRUCTURE (col(MAXROWS) DWORD),
    B(MAXROWS) STRUCTURE (col(MAXROWS) DWORD),
    C(MAXROWS) STRUCTURE (col(MAXROWS) DWORD);

$INCLUDE(utils.inc)


co_conn = DQ$ATTACH (@(4,':CO:'), @status);
CALL DQ$OPEN (co_conn, WRITE_ONLY, ONE_BUFFER, @status);

rows = 9;
last = rows - 1;

CALL DQ$WRITE (co_conn, @('Multiplying matrices...',CR,LF), 25, @status);

start_time = RQ$GET$TIME( @status );         /* Start of timed period */

    DO i = 0 TO last;
      DO j = 0 TO last;
        temp_d = 0;
        DO k = 0 TO last;
          temp_d = temp_d + ( A(i).col(k) * B(k).col(j) );
        END;
        C(i).col(j) = temp_d;
      END;
    END;


end_time = RQ$GET$TIME( @status );          /* End of timed period */
                                  :
                         /* Print results */
                                  :
el_time = LOW( end_time - start_time );
CALL disp_num( el_time, 1, 0 );
CALL DQ$WRITE( co_conn, @(' secs = elapsed time',CR,LF,LF), 23, @status);

CALL DQ$EXIT(0);

END mtrx_mlt;
```

281103-9

Listing 4a: Matrix Multiplication Under iRMX® II (MTRX_MLT.P28)

7

```
/*  Matrix multiply: A * B = C */
mtrx_mlt: DO;

DECLARE
    TOKEN LITERALLY 'SELECTOR',
    BOOLEAN LITERALLY 'BYTE';
$INCLUDE(:rmxinc:bios.ext)
$INCLUDE(:rmxinc:udi.ext)

DECLARE
    MAXROWS LITERALLY '64',
    CR         LITERALLY 'ODH',     LF        LITERALLY 'OAH',
    WRITE_ONLY LITERALLY '2',       READ_ONLY LITERALLY '1',
    ONE_BUFFER LITERALLY '0',

    co_conn TOKEN,
    (status, i, j, k, rows, last, m, el_time) WORD,
    (start_time, end_time, temp_d) DWORD,
    spare_b BYTE, in_buf(80) BYTE ,
    A(MAXROWS) STRUCTURE (col(MAXROWS) WORD),
    B(MAXROWS) STRUCTURE (col(MAXROWS) WORD),
    C(MAXROWS) STRUCTURE (col(MAXROWS) DWORD);

$INCLUDE(SRC/utils.inc)


co_conn = DQ$ATTACH (@(4,':CO:'), @status);
CALL DQ$OPEN (co_conn, WRITE_ONLY, ONE_BUFFER, @status);

rows = 9;
last = rows - 1;

CALL DQ$WRITE (co_conn, @('Multiplying matrices...',CR,LF), 25, @status);

start_time = RQ$GET$TIME( @status );         /* Start of timed period */


    DO i = 0 TO last;
      DO j = 0 TO last;
        temp_d = 0;
        DO k = 0 TO last;
          temp_d = temp_d + ( A(i).col(k) * B(k).col(j) );
        END;
        C(i).col(j) = temp_d;
      END;
    END;


end_time = RQ$GET$TIME( @status );          /* End of timed period */
                                :
                         /* Print results */
                                :
el_time = LOW( end_time - start_time );
CALL disp_num( el_time, 1, 0 );
CALL DQ$WRITE( co_conn, @(' secs = elapsed time',CR,LF,LF), 23, @status);

CALL DQ$EXIT(0);

END mtrx_mlt;
```

281103-10

Listing 4b: Matrix Multiplication under iRMX® III (MTRX_MLT.P38)

intel®

iRMX® TOOLBOX

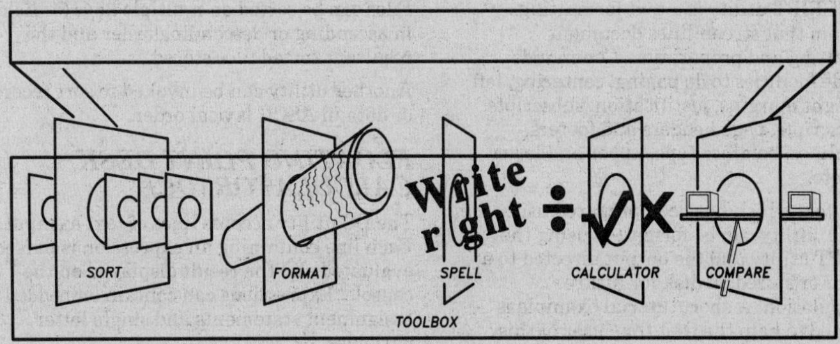

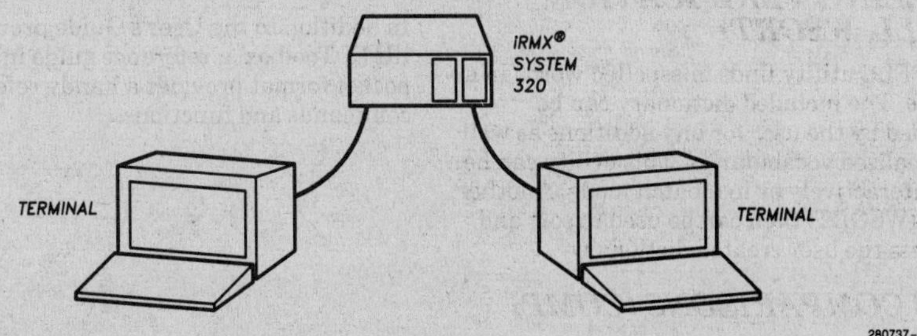

280737-1

The iRMX® toolbox is a set of utilities to provide assistance to the software developer in the housekeeping aspects of program development. These utilities offer facilities for text processing and document preparation.

Sort facilities and a desk calculator are also included.

FEATURES

- Text formatting
- Spelling verification
- File comparisons
- Sort
- Floating point desk calculator
- Pocket reference guide

7

intel

FEATURES

TEXT FORMATTING (SCRIPT)

The SCRIPT utility is a text formatting program that streamlines document formatting and preparation. Commands include facilities to do paging, centering, left and right margins, justification, subscripts, superscripts, page headers and footers, underlines, boldface type, upper and lower case, etc.

Input text which has been prepared using the AEDIT utility can be formatted using the SCRIPT utility and the output directed to a printer or stored on disk for future manipulation. A short tutorial example is provided to help the first time user of this formatter.

SPELLING VERIFICATION (SPELL, WSORT)

The SPELL utility finds misspelled words in a text file. The included dictionary can be expanded by the user for any additions as well as specialized vocabularies. This utility can be used interactively or in a batch mode. Another utility (WSORT) then can be used to sort and compress the user created dictionary.

FILE COMPARISONS (COMP)

The COMP utility performs line oriented text file comparisons showing changes between text or source files. This utility can also compare object files.

SORT (ESORT, HSORT)

Files can be sorted on multiple keys (or fields) in ascending or descending order and the resultant sorted files stored.

Another utility can be invoked to sort records or data in ASCII lexical order.

FLOATING POINT DESK CALCULATOR (DC)

The DC utility accepts lines of text as input. Each line containing an expression is parsed, evaluated and the result displayed on the console. Expressions can contain embedded assignment statements and single letter variables.

POCKET REFERENCE GUIDE

In addition to the User's Guide provided with iRMX Toolbox, a reference guide in small pocket format provides a handy reference to commands and functions.

SPECIFICATIONS

OPERATING ENVIRONMENT

iRMX 286 Operating System Release 2.0 or later running on an Intel Series 300 System or equivalent hardware with Numeric Data Processor (NDP) support and at least 1MB of memory. The AEDIT utility is required for use of the SCRIPT text formatting program.

DOCUMENTATION

An iRMX 286 Toolbox User's Guide and Pocket Reference Guide are shipped with the product.

ORDERING INFORMATION

Product Code: RMX286TLB

The product is shipped on a 5¼″ iRMX formatted floppy diskette.

iRMX® VIRTUAL TERMINAL

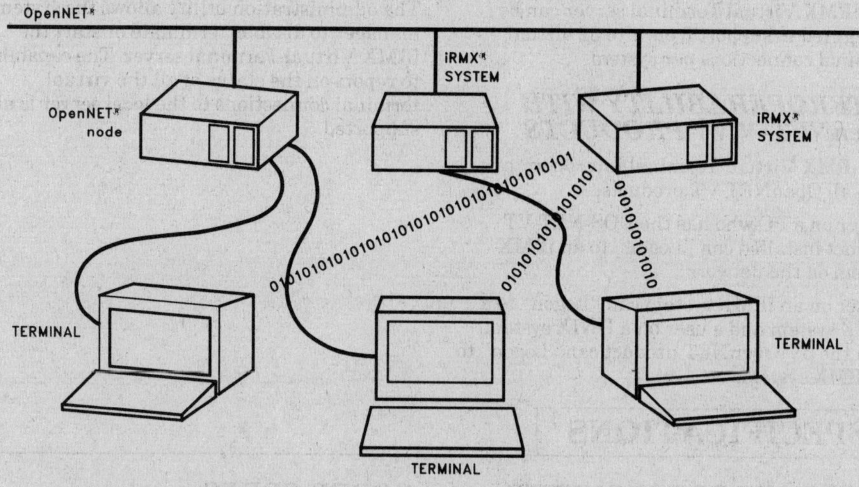

Virtual Terminal capability allows local iRMX® I, II, or III users to "logon" to the following remote hosts running the OpenNET™ networking software:

- iRMX II & III
- UNIX* System V
- VAX/VMS*
- XENIX*

Additionally, you can access an iRMX II or iRMX III system from the following remote systems running the OpenNET networking software:

- iRMX I, II, III
- MS/DOS*
- UNIX System V
- VAX/VMS*
- XENIX*

The Virtual Terminal capability enables users to access all the available resources on the remote host. Now an iRMX, PC, XENIX, UNIX or VMS can connect to a remote iRMX II or III system without the need to use a locally connected iRMX terminal.

FEATURES

- User configurable
- Interoperable with Intel's OpenNET VT products

*XENIX is a trademark of Microsoft Corporation.
*UNIX is a registered trademark of AT&T.
*VAX and VMS are registered trademarks of Digital Equipment Corporation.
*MS-DOS is a registered trademark of Microsoft Corporation.

November 1990
Order Number: 280741-002

iRMX® VIRTUAL TERMINAL

USER CONFIGURABLE

The iRMX Virtual Terminal server can be configured to support from 1 to 32 virtual terminal connections per system.

INTEROPERABILITY WITH OpenNET™ VT PRODUCTS

The iRMX Virtual Terminal interoperates with all OpenNET VT products.

A user on a PC who has the DOS-NET VT product installed can "Logon" to an iRMX system on the network.

A user on an iRMX system can "Logon" to a UNIX system and a user on a UNIX system with the SV-OpenNET product can "Logon" to an iRMX system.

ADMINISTRATION UTILITY

The administration utility allows the system manager to disable, terminate or start the iRMX Virtual Terminal server. The capability to report on the status of all the virtual terminal connections to the local server is also supported.

SPECIFICATIONS

SOFTWARE PREREQUISITE

iRMX II or iRMX III
iRMX-NET for iRMX II or iRMX III

HARDWARE PREREQUISITE

Hardware configuration should include appropriate Ethernet Controller.

ORDER CODES

RMXIINETSW
RMXIIINETSW

ORDERING INFORMATION

For more information or the number of your nearest sales office call 800-548-4725 (good in

intel®

iSDM™ II SYSTEM DEBUG MONITOR

- **Supports Target System Debugging for iSBC® 8086, 8088, 80186, 80188, 80286 and 386™ CPU-Based Applications**
- **Provides Interactive Debugging Commands Including Single-Step Code Execution and Symbolic Displays of Results**
- **Supports 8087, 80287, and 387™ Numeric Processor Extensions (NPX) for High-Speed Math Applications**
- **Allows Building of Custom Commands Through the Command Extension Interface (CEI)**
- **Supports Application Access to ISIS-II Files**
- **Provides Program Load Capability from iSBC 8086, 80286 and 386 CPU-Based iRMX® I and II Development Systems and from an Intellec® Development System**
- **Contains Configuration Facilities which Allow an Applications Bootstrap from iRMX® File Compatible Peripherals**
- **Modular to Allow Use from an Intellec® Development System, from a Stand-Alone Terminal or from iRMX I or iRMX II Based Systems**

The Intel iSDM™ II System Debug Monitor package contains the necessary hardware, software, cables, EPROMs and documentation required to interface, through a serial or parallel connection, an iSBC 86/05A, 86/12A, 86/14, 86/30, 86/35, 88/25, 88/40A, 88/45, 186/03A, 186/51, 188/48, 188/56, 286/10A, 286/12/14/16, 386/2X, 386/3X, 386/1XX or 8086, 8088, 80186 or 80188, 80286 and 386 CPU-based target system to a Series III, or Series IV Intellec® Microcomputer Development System or iRMX I or II Based System for execution and interactive debugging of applications software on the target system. The Monitor can: load programs into the target system; execute the programs instruction by instruction or at full speed; set breakpoints; and examine/modify CPU registers, memory content, and other crucial environmental details. Additional custom commands can be built using the Command Extension Interface (CEI). The Monitor supports the OEM's choice of the iRMX I Operating System, the iRMX II Operating System, or a custom system for the target application system. OEM's may utilize any iRMX supported target system peripheral for a bootstrap of the application system or have full access to the ISIS-II files of the Intellec System or the iRMX file system.

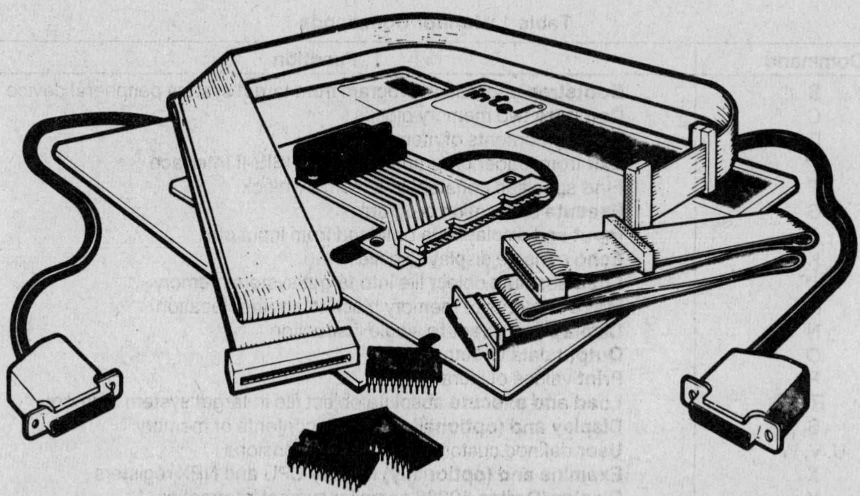

230882–1

7

FUNCTIONAL DESCRIPTION

Overview

The iSDM II Monitor extends the software development capabilities of an iRMX or Intellec system so the user can effectively develop applications to ensure timely product availability.

The iSDM II package consists of four parts:

- The loader program
- The iSDM II Monitor
- The Command Extension Interface (CEI)
- The UDI Library Interface

The user can use the iSDM II package to load programs into the target system from the development system, execute programs in an instruction-by-instruction manner, and add custom commands through the command extension interface. The user also has the option of using just the iSDM II Monitor and the CEI in a stand-alone application, without the use of a development system.

Powerful Debugging Commands

The iSDM II Monitor contains a powerful set of commands to support the debugging process. Some of the features included are: bootstrap of application software; selective execution of program modules based on breakpoints or single stepping requests; examination, modification and movement of memory contents; examination and modification of CPU registers, including NPX registers. All results are displayed in clearly understandable formats. Refer to Table 1 for a more detailed list of the iSDM II monitor commands.

Numeric Data Processor Support

Arithmetic applications utilizing the 8087, 80287 or 387™ Numeric Processor Extension (NPX) are fully supported by the iSDM II Monitor. In addition to executing applications with the full NPX performance, users may examine and modify the NPX's registers using decimal and real number format.

This feature allows the user to feel confident that correct and meaningful numbers are entered for the application without having to encode and decode complex real, integer, and BCD hexadecimal formats.

Command Extension Interface (CEI)

The Command Extension Interface (CEI) allows the addition of custom commands to the iSDM Monitor commands. The CEI consists of various procedures that can be used to generate custom commands. Up to three custom commands (or sets of commands) can be added to the monitor without programming new EPROMs or changing the monitor's source code.

Table 1. Monitor Commands

Command	Function
B	**Bootstrap** application program from target system peripheral device
C	**Compare** two memory blocks
D	**Display** contents of memory block
E*	**Exit** from loader program to iRMX or ISIS-II Interface
F	**Find** specified constant in a memory block
G	**Execute** application program
I	**Input** and display data obtained from input port
K	**Echo** console display to a file
L*	**Load** absolute object file into target system memory
M	**Move** contents of memory block to another location
N	**Display and execute** single instruction
O	**Output** data to output port
P	**Print** values of literals
R*	**Load and execute** absolute object file in target system memory
S	**Display and (optionally) modify** contents of memory
U, V, W	**User** defined custom commands extensions
X	**Examine and (optionally) modify** CPU and NPX registers
Y	**Display/Define** 80286 compiler symbol information

*Commands require an attached development system.

Universal Development Interface

The Universal Development interface (UDI) consists of libraries that contain interfaces to iRMX and ISIS II I/O calls. A program running on an 8086, 8088, 80186, 80188, 80286, or 386 CPU-based system can use UDI and access iRMX and ISIS II I/O calls. The interface allows the inclusion of these calls into the program; however, most of the calls require an iRMX or Intellec host system. Table 2 contains a summary of the major I/O calls.

Program Load Capability

The iSDM loader allows the loading of 8086, 8088, 80186, 80188, 80286 or 386 CPU-based programs into the target system. It executes on a development system and communicates with the target system through a serial or a parallel load interface.

Configuration Facility

The monitor contains a full set of configuration facilities which allows it to be carefully tailored to the requirements of the target system. Pre-configured EPROM-resident monitors are supplied by Intel for the iSBC 86/05A, 86/12A, 86/14, 86/30, 86/35, 88/25, 88/10A, 88/45, 186/03A, 186/51, 188/48, 188/56, 286/10A, 286/12/14/16, 386/2X/3X, and 386/1XX boards. The monitor must be configured by the user for other 8086, 8088, 80186, or 80188 applications. iRMX I and iRMX II system users may use the configuration facilities to include the Bootstrap Loader (V5.0 or newer) in the monitor.

Variety of Connections Available

The physical interface between the development system and the target system can be established in one of three ways. The systems can be connected via a serial link, a parallel link or a fast parallel link. The cabling arrangement is different depending upon the development system being used.

The iSDM II Monitor does not require the use of a development system. The monitor can be used by simply attaching a stand-alone terminal to the target system.

Table 2. Routines for Services Available to Target System Applications

Routine	Target System Function
DQ$ATTACH	Creates a connection to a specified file.
DQ$CLOSE	Closes the specified file connection.
DQ$CREATE	Creates a file for use by the application.
DQ$DELETE	Deletes a file.
DQ$DETACH	Closes a file and deletes its connection.
DQGETCON-NECTION$STATUS	Returns status of a file connection.
DQ$OPEN	Opens a file for a particular type of access.
DQ$READ	Reads the next sequence of bytes from a file.
DQ$RENAME	Renames the specified file.
DQ$SEEK	Moves the current position pointer of a file.
DQ$SPECIAL	Defines options and actions for the program execution environment.
DQ$TRUNCATE	Truncates a file to the specified length.
DQ$WRITE	Writes a sequence of bytes to a file.

SPECIFICATIONS

Hardware

- Supported iSBC Microcomputers:

iSBC 86/05A	Single Board Computer
iSBC 86/30	Single Board Computer
iSBC 86/35	Single Board Computer
iSBC 88/25	Single Board Computer
iSBC 88/45	Single Board Computer
iSBC 186/03A	Single Board Computer
iSBC 186/51	Single Board Computer
iSBC 188/56	Single Board Computer
iSBC 286/10A	Single Board Computer
iSBC 286/12/14/16	Single Board Computer
iSBC 386/2X/3X	Single Board Computer
iSBC 386/1XX	Single Board Computer

- Supported iSBX™ MULTIMODULE Boards:
  iSBX 351 Serial I/O MULTIMODULE Board
  iSBX 354 Serial I/O MULTIMODULE Board
- Supported Microcomputer Systems 8086/8088/80186/80188/80286/386/CPU 8087/80287/80387 NPX with Serial Controller: 8274 Serial Controller and 8253/8254 timer, or 8251A Serial Controller and 8253/8254 timer, or 82530 Serial Controller 4 KB RAM, and 32 KB EPROM

iSDM™ II Package Contents

Cables:

4—RS232 Cable Assemblies (for iRMX/Intellec host system and standard terminals)
Hardware package for the cable assemblies

Interface and Execution Software Diskettes:

2—DS/DD, iRMX-Format 5¼″
2—SS/DD, iRMX—Format 8″
2—SS/DD, ISIS II-Format 8″

System Monitor EPROMs:

Intel Board	EPROM Description
iSBC 86/05A iSBC 86/14 iSBC 86/30 iSBC 86/35	Two 27128 EPROMs
iSBC 86/12A	SUBMIT Files on the Release Diskette

System Monitor EPROMs: (Continued)

Intel Board	EPROM Description
iSBC 88/25	Two 27128 EPROMs
iSBC 88/45	Two 27128 EPROMs
iSBC 186/03A	Two 27128 EPROMs
iSBC 186/51	Two 27128 EPROMs
iSBC 188/56	Two 27128 EPROMs
iSBC 286/10A iSBC 286/12/14/16	Two 27128 EPROMs
iSBC 386/2X/3X	Two 27256 EPROMs
iSBC 386/1XX	Two 27256 EPROMs

Reference Manual (Supplied):

iSDM II System Debug Monitor Installation and Configuration

iSDM II System Debug Monitor User's Guide

ORDERING INFORMATION

Part Number	Description
SDMSC	Object Software iRMX and Intellec host to target system interface and target system monitor, suitable for use on iSBC 86, 88, 186, 188, 286, 386 computers, or other 8086, 8088, 80186, 80188, 80286, 386 microcomputers. Package includes cables, EPROMs, software and reference manual. The OEM license option listed here allows use on a single host/target system and incorporation into their applications. Each incorporation requires payment of an Incorporation Fee. The iSDM package also includes 90 days of support services that include Software Program Report Services. As with all Intel Software, purchase of any of these options requires execution of a standard Intel Software License Agreement.
SDMRFX	Incorporation fee. Permits incorporation of a configured iSDM II monitor into a target system.

SOFT-SCOPE * II SOURCE-LEVEL DEBUGGER

280637-1

SOURCE-LEVEL ON-TARGET DEBUGGER FOR iRMX® II APPLICATIONS

The SOFT-SCOPE II Debugger is an interactive debugging tool specifically designed for software developed to execute with the iRMX II Operating Systems on Intel's broad set of system and board-level products. It reduces the time required to debug real-time software and allows the developer to degug at the most effective level, in the original source code itself.

FEATURES:

- Complete High-Level Debugging Functionality
- Source Code Interface and On-line Listings
- Automatic Expansion of Data Types
- Symbolic Display of iRMX II Objects
- Second Terminal Option for "Remote" Debugging
- Multitasking Support
- Handling of 80286/386™ Protection Traps and Software Exceptions

*SOFT-SCOPE is a registered trademark of Concurrent Sciences, Inc.

7

December 1990
Order Number: 280637-002

FEATURES

COMPLETE HIGH-LEVEL DEBUGGING

For real-time applications running with iRMX II Operating Systems on Intel 80286/386 CPU boards, software professionals want to focus on original source code for most debugging operations. SOFT-SCOPE II does just that. It integrates the original source code into the debugging process directly. All breakpoint prompts and high-level stepping operations prompt with original source code rather than reporting what line number the program has reached or what assembly instruction is next.

SOURCE CODE INTERFACE AND ON-LINE LISTINGS

The source code interface frees the programmer from having to divide attention between the console and program listings, eliminates the need to get a fresh program listing each time a small change is made, and reduces the time needed to make software modifications.

AUTOMATIC EXPANSION OF DATA TYPES

Symbols declared in the program are accessible by name for display and modification of contents. These symbols include arrays, structures, static variables, based variables, and stack-based variables (including local variables, re-entrant variables, and passed parameters). Memory can also be displayed with absolute references or with register-relative references.

SYMBOLIC DISPLAY OF ALL iRMX II SYSTEM OBJECTS

The VIEW command allows viewing the status of any iRMX II object including tasks, jobs, mailboxes, semaphores, regions, and segments. With VIEW, the stack of a task can be examined to determine which iRMX II call the task has made most recently. Any job's object directory and the list of ready and sleeping tasks can be examined.

SECOND TERMINAL OPTION

Because so many applications today are screen-intensive, the SOFT-SCOPE Debugger allows the option of using a second terminal for all debugger I/O, freeing the main console for exclusive use by the application for application output.

MULTI-TASKING SUPPORT

The SOFT-SCOPE II Debugger supports simultaneous debugging of concurrent tasks when they are all linked together as a Human Interface command and each concurrent task is coded in a separate module. SOFT-SCOPE loads and then allows the user to suspend and resume execution of the tasks from the command line with the SUSPEND and RESUME commands. In this way the developer can observe the effect of dynamic changes on the software under test.

HANDLING OF 80286/386 PROTECTION TRAPS AND SOFTWARE EXCEPTIONS

Exception Handling: The exact source line which causes an exception can easily be reached and displayed. All environmental and programmer exceptions are trapped and reported, without causing a SOFT-SCOPE debugger exit.

Most of the 80286/386 hardware traps are handled by the SOFT-SCOPE II Debugger, including Bounds Check (INT 5), Invalid Opcode (INT 6), Double Fault (INT 8), Stack Fault (INT 12), and General Protection (INT 13). Upon encountering one of these interrupts, the SOFT-SCOPE II Debugger breaks execution with a message similar to the following:

```
< General Protection fault (INT 13) >?
[ Break near line #145 in TESTPROC
(:TESTMODULE) ]
145: ARRAYX(INDEX) = XYZ;
```

In the above example, the General Protection trap could have been caused by the variable INDEX being too large for the segment which contained ARRAYX, or by ARRAYX being based on an undefined pointer. Because the debugger handles these traps directly, other users in a multi-user system won't even be aware in most cases that there was a hardware fault.

INTEL QUALITY—YOUR GUARANTEE

The SOFT-SCOPE Debugger is built to the same exacting standards as Intel's component and board products. This product's reliability

FEATURES

has been proven in many real-time product settings over the past several years.

WORLDWIDE SUPPORT AND SERVICE—AN INTEL STANDARD

Standard support products for the SOFT-SCOPE Debugger are available through Intel's support organization.

SOFT-SCOPE II COMMANDS

Function	Commands
Invoking the Debugger	SSCOPE
Viewing the Source Code	LIST, LINE, FINE
Opening a Module	LINE, OPEN, MODULES, ASSIGN, DETACH
Controlling Execution	GO, STEP, ASTEP
Setting Breakpoints	GO, STEP, BREAKPOINT, RANGE
Examine Data/ Descriptor	.variable, TYPE, EVAL, DUMP, STACK, ADDR
Examining Code	LINE, ASM
Port I/O	IN, OUT
Debugger I/O	CONSOLE, ECHO
Examining Registers	REG, NPXREG
Requesting Help	HELP
Setting Options	OPTIONS
View iRMX II Objects	VIEW
Start/Stop Tasks	SUSPEND, RESUME
Execute a Submit File	SUBMIT
Run an RMX Program	RUN
Stack Trace	NEST
Initialize Stack	STACKINIT

SPECIFICATIONS

The SOFT-SCOPE II Debugger supports the following languages:

Intel PL/M 286
Intel C 286
Intel Pascal 286
Intel ASM 286
Intel FORTRAN 286

The SOFT-SCOPE Debugger requires a full configuration of the iRMX II Operating System, including the Human Interface and UDI. Either the iSDM System Debug Monitor or the D-MON monitor must be included in the firmware of the CPU board to use the VIEW command. The debugger utilizes approximately 130k bytes of memory beyond the load size of the program being debugged.

ORDERING INFORMATION

Product Code	Product Contents
RMXIISFTSCP	SOFT-SCOPE II Debugger for iRMX II Operating Systems of $5\frac{1}{4}$″ iRMX media diskettes

Multibus I Single Board Computers

8

iSBC® 486/12* AND iSBC® 386/12* SINGLE BOARD COMPUTERS

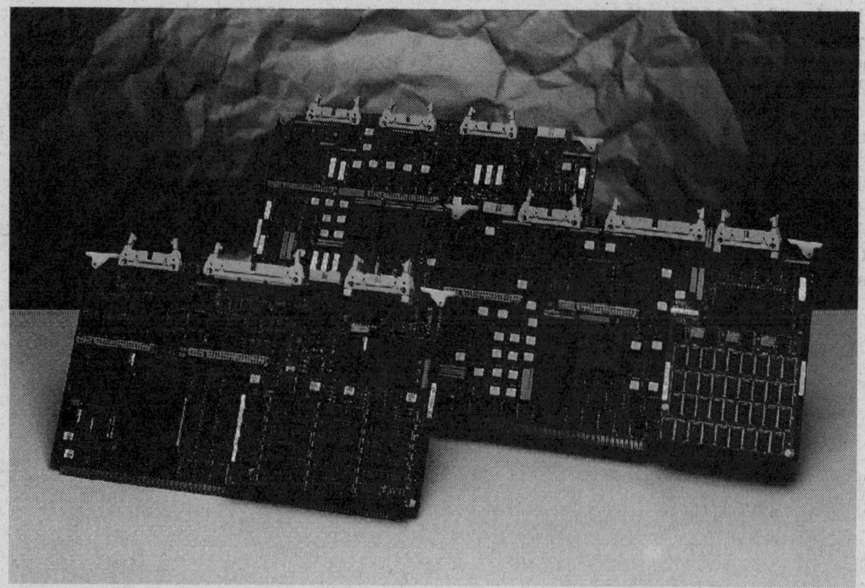

281110-1

HIGH INTEGRATION 486™ and 386™ MICROPROCESSOR-BASED MULTIBUS I SINGLE BOARD COMPUTERS

The iSBC® 486/12 and iSBC 386/12 products are high performance, high integration Multibus I single board computers. These boards share a common core design that provides functional compatibility with the iSBC 286/12 single board computer with a 2X to 5X performance improvement.

The iSBC 486/12 single board computer combines 486™ microprocessor performance and the iSBC 286/12 I/O functionality. The iSBC 386/12 single board computer does the same with 386™ microprocessor performance. The iSBC 486/12S and 386/12S boards provide the CPU performance and I/O functionality supplied on the iSBC 486/12 and 386/12 boards plus support for the industry standard, high-speed SCSI bus (Small Computer System Interface) on a single Multibus I CPU board. SCSI data transfers to local DRAM are DMA supported and FIFO buffered enabling sustained synchronous SCSI data rates up to 5 MBytes/sec.

8

*The iSBC 486/12 and iSBC 386/12 are also manufactured under product codes pSBC48612 and pSBC38612 by Intel Puerto Rico, Inc.

November 1990
Order Number: 281110-001

iSBC® 486/12* AND iSBC® 386/12* SINGLE BOARD COMPUTERS

FEATURES

- 33 MHz 486 or 20 MHz 386 Microprocessors
- Optional 387™ Numeric Coprocessor on 386 products
- 82258 Advanced DMA Controller
- Dual Bus Architecture—Dedicated 32-bit processor execution bus
- 1-16 MB on-board 32-bit dual-port parity DRAM on 386 boards
- 2-64 MB on-board 32-bit dual-port parity DRAM on 486 boards
- SCSI Interface—5 MBytes/sec synchronous data rate
- Two 32-pin JEDEC EPROM sites
- Two serial ports via 8274
- 82C55A parallel port
- Three on-board timers via 82C54
- Two IEEE 959 SBX Bus interface connectors
- iLBX™ Bus support on 386 boards (no iLBX bus support on 486 boards)
- Multiprocessor support, including memory aliasing
- Functional superset of iSBC® 86/xx and 286/1x single board computers

iSBC® 486/12S SINGLE BOARD COMPUTER

MICROPROCESSOR PERFORMANCE

486™ CPU Boards

The iSBC 486/12 and 486/12S CPU boards feature a 486 microprocessor running at 33 MHz. A 32-bit on-board system bus optimizes the compute performance of the 486 microprocessor. The same bus also provides support for up to 64 MB of zero wait-state parity DRAM.

Numeric processing applications are easily handled by the 486 on-chip floating point unit (FPU). The 486 FPU conforms fully to the ANSI/IEEE 754-1985 standard for floating point arithmetic and it provides full-compatibility for applications written to the 387™ Numeric Coprocessor.

386™ CPU Boards

The iSBC 386/12 and 386/12S CPU boards feature a 386 microprocessor running at 20 MHz. The on-board processor execution bus optimizes the compute performance of the 386 microprocessor. The on-board 32-bit memory bus provides support for up to 16 MB of zero wait-states (pipelined read hit) parity DRAM.

Numeric processing on the 386 CPU boards may be enhanced with the 32-bit 387 floating point math coprocessor. The 387 provides 80-bit precision, accelerating floating point calculations through hardware execution.

DUAL-BUS ARCHITECTURE

The iSBC 486/12 and 386/12 CPU boards use multiple on-board busses, a design technique that increases overall system performance. The boards utilize both a high speed 32-bit execution bus for optimized CPU, memory, and math operations, and a dedicated I/O bus for on-board I/O, SBX bus I/O, and EPROM operations.

FEATURES

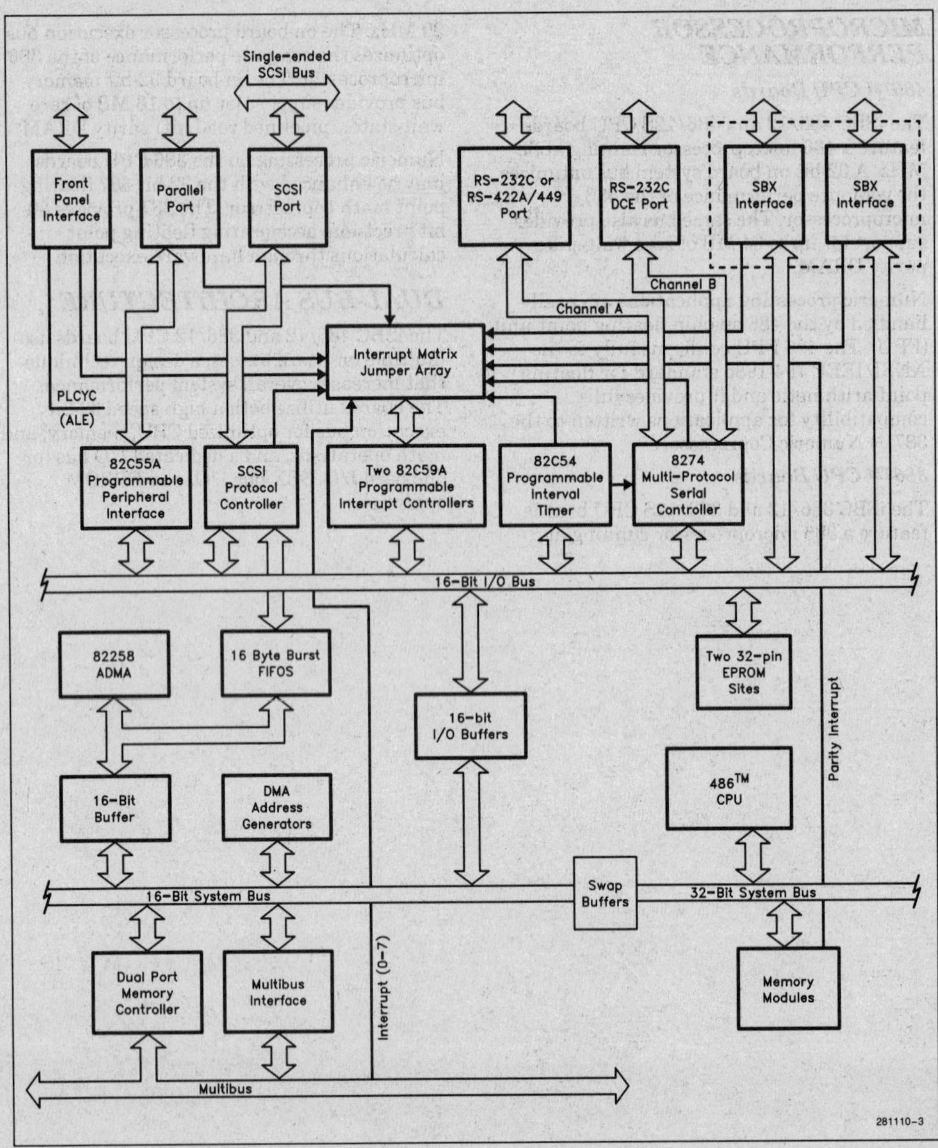

Figure 1: iSBC® 486/12S Block Diagram

iSBC® 386/12S SINGLE BOARD COMPUTER

HIGH-SPEED DMA

486™ CPU Boards

2-64 MB of DRAM is supported via modules attached to the CPU baseboard. DRAM module access is optimized by a high-speed DMA controller and the latest fast-page DRAM technology. A DMA address generator (DAG) provides addressing for the full 4 gigabyte 486 memory address range. DRAM is dual-ported and addressable from the on-board 32-bit system bus or from the Multibus I bus.

386™ CPU Boards

1-16 MB of DRAM is supported via modules attached to the CPU baseboard, DRAM module access is optimized by a high-speed DMA controller and the latest fast page DRAM technology. DRAM is dual-ported and fully addressable from the on-board 32-bit bus or from the Multibus I bus.

SCSI BUS INTERFACE

The iSBC 486/12S and 386/12S boards integrate a 10 MHz Fujitsu 87033B SCSI Protocol Controller (SPC). The 87033B SPC device supports a synchronous data rate of 5 MBytes/sec and an asynchronous rate of 2 MBytes/sec. SCSI data transfers are buffered into 16-bit wide, 512-bit deep bi-directional FIFOs and DMA transferred into (or from) local RAM at rates above the maximum incoming synchronous data rate. A 16-byte burst mode via a separate 16-byte burst FIFO is supported on the iSBC 486/12S. The SCSI implementation is ideal for applications requiring sustained high-speed SCSI data transfers.

The 87033B SPC device has integrated single-ended driver/receiver circuitry. These SCSI bus drivers support host to target connections of up to 6 meters.

The 87033B SPC device supports both SCSI bus initiator and target modes. In addition, the SPC device supports selection/reselection commands for optimum SCSI bus utilization.

An iRMX® Operating System driver for the SCSI interface is available from Intel. This driver supports only the SCSI bus initiator mode.

FEATURES

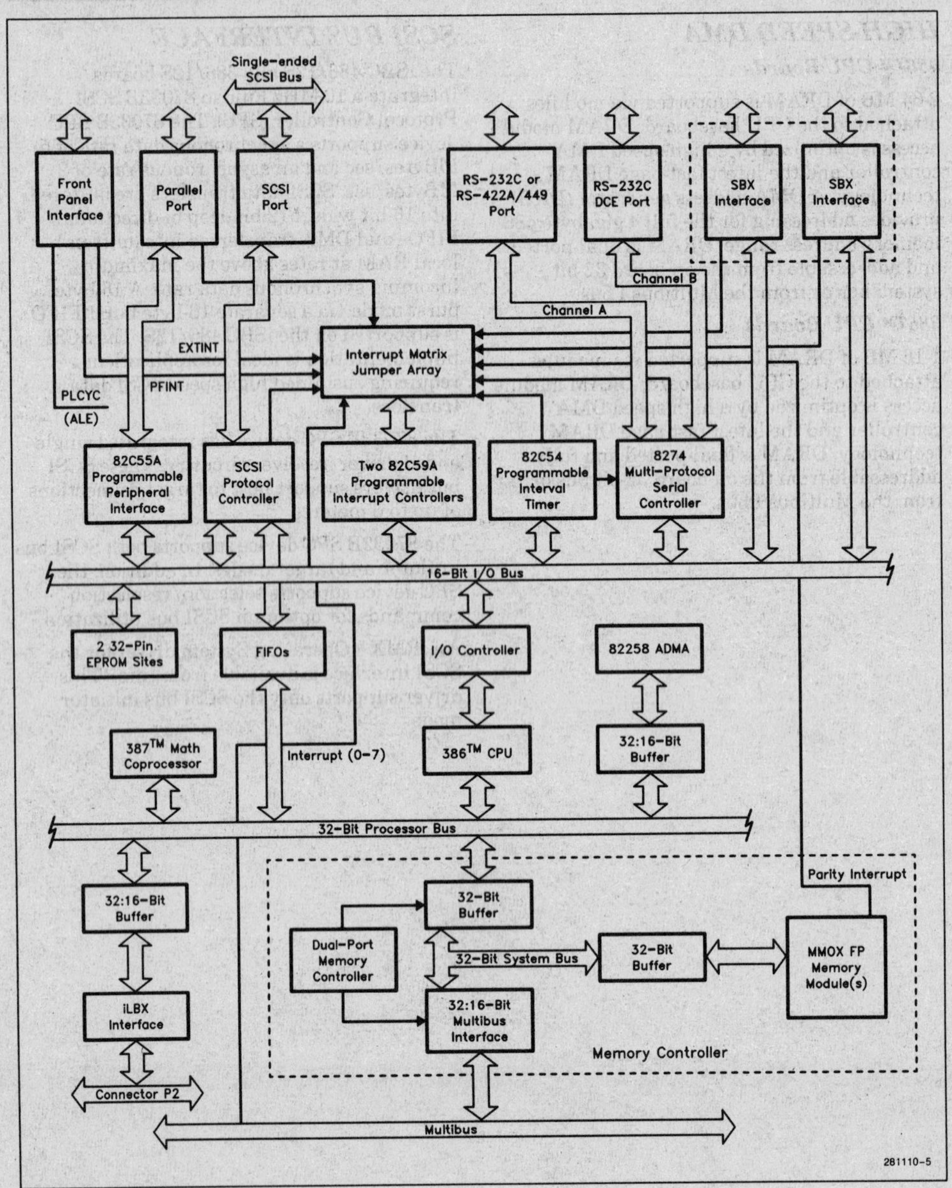

Figure 2: iSBC® 386/12S Block Diagram

FEATURES

COMPLETE ON-BOARD I/O FEATURE SET

The iSBC 486/12 and 386/12 boards provide fully integrated on-board I/O functionality. Two serial ports are provided via Intel's 8274 Multi-Protocol Serial Controller. An 82C55A Programmable Peripheral Interface provides support for the parallel line printer interface. These boards also provide interrupt support based on two 82C59A Programmable Interrupt Controllers and the microprocessor's own non-maskable interrupt (NMI) line. Programmable timer/counter functions are provided by an 82C54 Programmable Interval Timer.

Direct memory access transfers are provided by the 82258 advanced DMA (ADMA) controller. The DMA support is enhanced to increase flexibility and support synchronous transfers over the SCSI interface (486/12S and 386/12S), serial ports (386/12 and 386/12S only) and SBX Bus for high speed I/O data transfers.

SBX BUS FOR I/O EXPANSION

Two IEEE 959 SBX Bus interface connectors are provided for I/O expansion. Functions such as additional serial/parallel ports, graphics, BITBUS™, LAN interface, or analog to digital modules can be added onto the CPU boards via this industry standard I/O expansion interface. The SBX Bus interface is also ideal for integration of custom-built modules. These CPU boards support either two single-wide modules or one double-wide module.

FEATURES

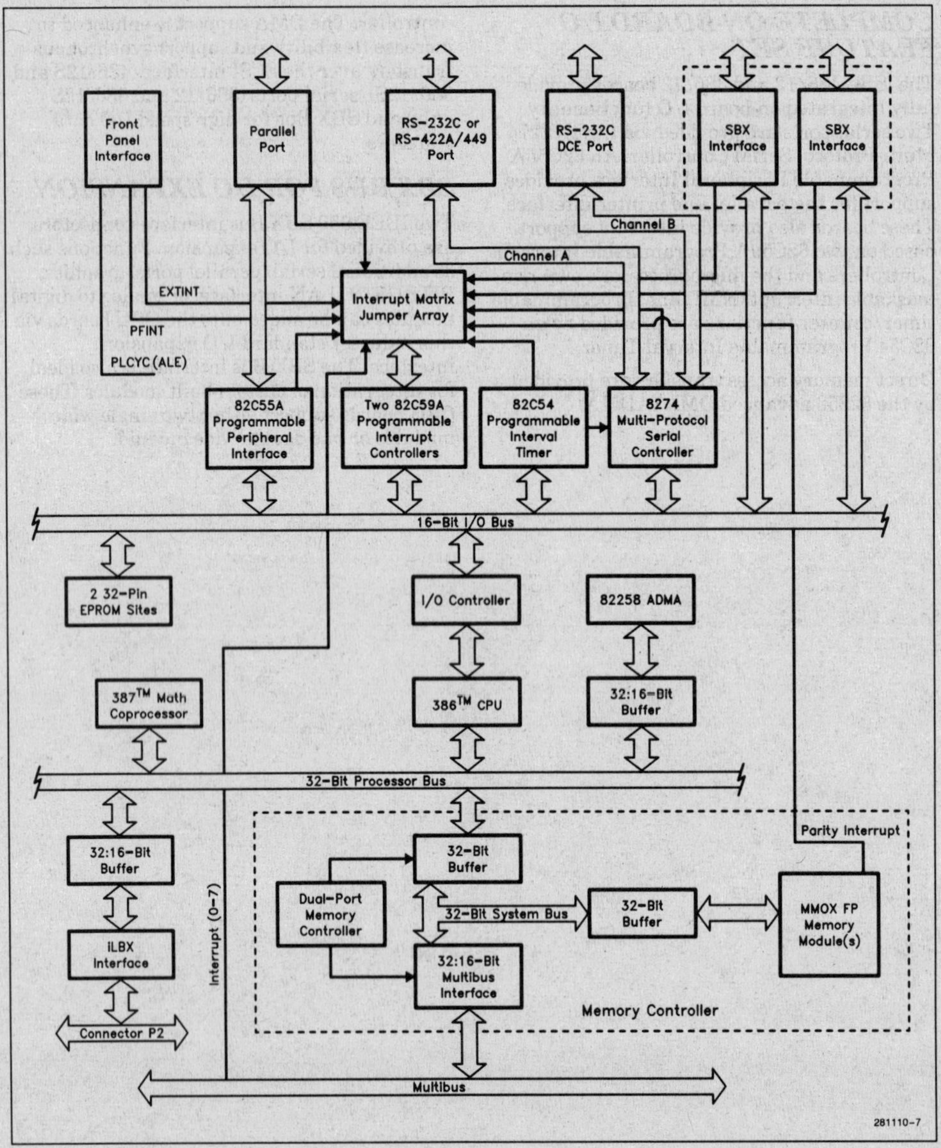

Figure 3: iSBC® 386/12 Block Diagram

FEATURES

MULTIBUS I, SBX, and iLBX™ COMPLIANCE

The iSBC 486/12 and 386/12 boards comply with the published IEEE 796 Multibus specification (including full Multimaster) and the published IEEE 959 SBX specification.

The iSBC 386/12 and 386/12S boards support Multibus bus vectored interrupts and Intel's iLBX P2 bus. The iSBC 486/12 and 486/12S do not support these two capabilities.

Please see the specifications for more detail on Multibus, SBX, and iLBX bus compliance.

MULTI-PROCESSING SUPPORT

Multiprocessor support is enhanced through high performance dual-port arbitration control logic and features such as memory aliasing over Multibus and real mode page registers. In addition, the addressing approach used for the iSBC 386/2X/3X series of boards is also supported.

MEMORY MAPS

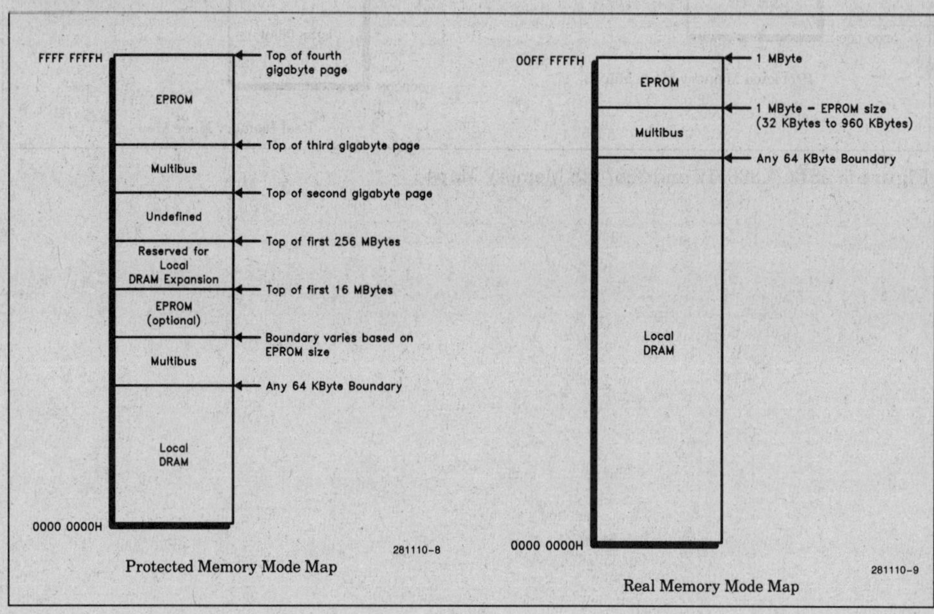

Protected Memory Mode Map

Real Memory Mode Map

Figure 4: iSBC® 486/12 and 486/12S Memory Map

8

FEATURES

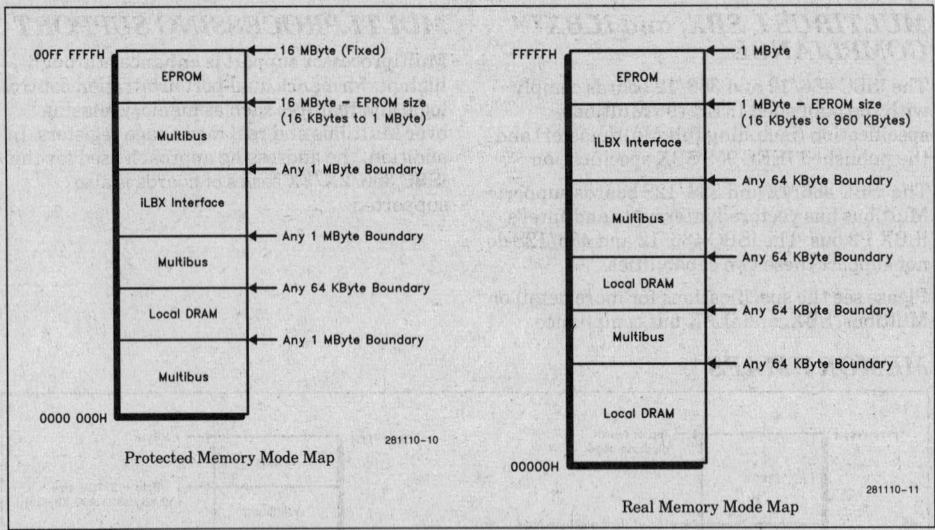

Figure 5: iSBC® 386/12 and 386/12S Memory Maps

SPECIFICATIONS

WORD SIZE

Instruction: 8, 16, 24, 32 or 40 bits

Data: 8, 16, or 32 bits

SYSTEM CLOCK

486 Microprocessor @ 33 MHz
386 Microprocessor @ 20 MHz
387 Numeric Coprocessor @ 20 MHz

DRAM ACCESS

	PageHit"	PageMiss"
READ	7 wait-states	9 wait-states
WRITE	0 wait-states	0 wait-states
BURST READ	7 wait-states	9 wait-states

INTERRUPT CAPACITY

Interrupt sources: 26 total: On iSBC 486/12 and 486/12S all 26 are jumper selectable; On iSBC 386/12 and 386/12S 5 are hard-wired to the 8259A PIC and 21 are jumper selectable

Interrupt levels: 16 vectored requests using two 8259A devices and the CPU's NMI line.

Bus-vectored interrupts are supported only on the iSBC 386/12 and 386/12S boards

I/O CAPABILITY

Expansion: Two 8/16-bit SBX connectors, supporting up to two single-wide boards or one double-wide board.

Parallel: Line printer interface, on-board functions, and 3-bit board installed options code.

Serial: Two programmable channels using one 8274 device

SCSI: Single-ended, synchronous/asynchronous

Timers: Three programmable times using one 82C54 device

DMA: 10 MHz 82258 advanced DMA (ADMA) controller. Supports DMA block transfers between on-board memory over the Multibus I interface, SCSI interface (486/12S and 386/12S), iLBX interface (386/12 and 386/12S only), both SBX interfaces, and both serial channels (386/12 and 386/12S only).

SERIAL COMMUNICATIONS CHARACTERISTICS

Synchronous: 5-8 bit characters; internal or HDLC/SDLC character synchronization; automatic sync insertion; even or odd parity, baud rates from 600 baud to 615 KB.

Asynchronous: 5-8 bit characters; break character generation; 1, 1½, or 2 stop bits; false start bit detection; even or odd parity; baud rates from 75 baud to 19.2 KB.

INTERFACES

Multibus IEEE 796 Compliance Level

iSBC 486/12 and 486/12S
Master D16/M24/I16/V0 EL

iSBC 386/12 and 386/12S
Master D16/M24/I16/V02 EL

Which translates to:

Master	A system master
D16	8-, 16-bit data transfers
M24	24-bit memory addressing
I16	8-, 16-bit I/O transfers
V0	Non-vectored interrupts
V02	Non- or two-cycle bus-vectored interrupts
EL	Level or edge-triggered interrupts

SBX IEEE 959 Compliance Level

iSBC 486/12S and 386/12S
D16/D16/DMA

Which translates to:

D16	16-bit board addresses
D16	8-bit or 16-bit expansion modules
DMA	DMA transfers

SCSI Interface: ANSI X3.131—1986

Serial I/O: Channel A: RS232C/RS422/RS449 compatible, DCE or DTE

Channel B: RS232C compatible, DCE

NOTE: For RS422/RS449 operation, line drivers and resistor terminators must be supplied.

SPECIFICATIONS

PHYSICAL CHARACTERISTICS

Width: 12.00 in. (30.48 cm)
Height: 7.05 in. (18.00 cm)
Depth: 0.86 in. (2.18 cm), 1.62 in. (4.11 cm) with added memory module

Recommended slot spacing: 1.2 in. (3.0 cm), 1.8 in. (4.6 cm) for double-stacked memory modules.

ELECTRICAL CHARACTERISTICS

iSBC 486/12 and 486/12S DC Power Requirements (Maximum):

	Volts	Current
Baseboard	+ 5.25	TBD
Baseboard	± 12	TBD
2 MByte DRAM Module	+ 5.25	TBD
4 MByte DRAM Module	+ 5.25	TBD
8 MByte DRAM Module	+ 5.25	TBD

iSBC 386/12 and 386/12S DC Power Requirements (Maximum):

	Volts	Current
Baseboard	+ 5.25	14.5A
Baseboard	± 12	50mA
1 MByte Memory Module	+ 5.25	0.89A
2 MByte Memory Module	+ 5.25	1.2A
4 MByte Memory Module	+ 5.25	0.89A
8 MByte Memory Module	+ 5.25	1.2A
387™ Math Coprocessor	+ 5.25	0.31A

ENVIRONMENTAL CHARACTERISTICS

Operating Temperature: 0° to 55°C at 200 LFM airflow across board (default configuration)
Relative Humidity: 0% to 90% (without condensation)
Storage Temperature: −40° to + 70°C

REFERENCE MANUALS

507914-001 *iSBC 486/12S Single Board Computer Hardware Reference Manual* (order separately). Provides complete information on hardware features, installation, jumpering, memory maps, and addressing.

455528-001 *iSBC 386/12 Series Hardware Reference Manual* (order separately). Provides complete information on hardware features, installation, jumpering, memory maps, addressing, and schematics.

459913-001 *iSBC 386/12S Series Hardware Reference Manual* (order separately).

462435-001 *iSBC 386/12 Series Software Upgrade Guide* (order separately). Provides complete information on upgrading existing applications (hardware and software), from an iSBC 286/10A/12/14/ 16, iSBC 86/30/35, or iSBC 386/2X/3X to an iSBC 386/12 board.

ORDERING INFORMATION

486™ SINGLE BOARD COMPUTERS

Part Number	Description
SBC48612SF4A3	33 MHz with SCSI, DMA, and 4 MB DRAM
SBC48612SF8A3	33 MHz with SCSI, DMA, and 8 MB DRAM
SBC48612F2A33	33 MHz with 2 MB DRAM
SBC48612F4A33	33 MHz with 4 MB DRAM
SBC48612F8A33	33 MHz with 8 MB DRAM

386™ SINGLE BOARD COMPUTERS

Part Number	Description
pSBC38612SF01	20 MHz with SCSI and 1 MB DRAM
pSBC38612SF02	20 MHz with SCSI and 2 MB DRAM
pSBC38612SF04	20 MHz with SCSI and 4 MB DRAM
pSBC38612SF08	20 MHz with SCSI and 8 MB DRAM
pSBC3861220F01	20 MHz with 1 MB DRAM
pSBC3861220F02	20 MHz with 2 MB DRAM
pSBC3861220F04	20 MHz with 4 MB DRAM
pSBC3861220F08	20 MHz with 8 MB DRAM

iSBC 386/12S models with an installed 387 coprocessor may be ordered by adding an M suffix to the above order codes. For example, pSBC3861220F08M is the order code for 20 MHz with 8 MB DRAM memory and the 387 math coprocessor installed.

MEMORY MODULES

486™ Single Board Computers

Part Number	Description
SBCMM308	8 MB, 85ns fast page parity DRAM module

386™ Single Board Computers

Part Number	Description
pSBCMM01FP	1 MB, 85ns fast page parity DRAM module
pSBCMM02FP	2 MB, 85ns fast page parity DRAM module
pSBCMM04FP	4 MB, 85ns fast page parity DRAM module
pSBCMM08FP	8 MB, 85ns fast page parity DRAM module

For more information or the number of your nearest Intel sales office, call 800-548-4725 (good in the U.S. and Canada.)

iSBC® 386 SX* SINGLE BOARD COMPUTER AND iSBC® 272* VGA GRAPHICS MODULE

281111–1

PC AT AND MULTIBUS I-COMPATIBLE 386™ SX™ CPU-BASED SINGLE BOARD COMPUTER*

The iSBC® 386 SX single board computer is a cost-effective way to add 32-bit performance and DOS software compatibility to a Multibus I application. Based on the high-performance 386™ SX™ microprocessor and optional 387™ SX™ Math Coprocessor, the iSBC 386 SX provides a 4X increase in compute power over most 8086 and 80186-based single board computers.

The iSBC 386 SX has the complete set of on-board I/O, real-time, and peripheral control resources found on a PC AT* motherboard and a Multibus I CPU board. Included are an on-board floppy controller, Winchester hard disk controller, two serial ports, parallel port, interrupt controllers, real-time clock, DMA and two full iSBX connectors. The optional iSBC 272 graphics module completes these capabilities by providing full VGA graphics.

*PC AT® and EGA® are registered trademarks of International Business Machines Corporation.
*The iSBC 386 SX and iSBC 272 are manufactured under product code pSBC 386 SX and pSBC 272 in Intel Puerto Rico II, Inc.
*Soft-Scope™ is a trademark of Concurrent Sciences, Inc.

November 1990
Order Number: 281111-001

FEATURES

FEATURES

- 16 MHz 386 SX CPU
- PC AT and DOS software compatibility
- Supports iRMX® III 32-bit real time operating system with DOS at the same time
- 387 SX Math Coprocessor socket
- 512K or 2 MB on-board DRAM, expandable to 8 MB
- Two 32-pin EPROM sockets plus two universal sockets for EPROM, SRAM, or FLASH
- On-board IDE hard disk and floppy controllers
- Two serial and one parallel ports
- Two 8/16-bit iSBX connectors
- Graphics add-on module supporting VGA, EGA*, CGA, Hercules Mono formats
- Complete on-board BIOS in EPROM

FEATURES

HIGH-PERFORMANCE, COST-EFFECTIVE 386™ SX™ CPU PROVIDES EXCELLENT UPGRADE PATH

The iSBC 386 SX uses the powerful, cost-effective 386 SX microprocessor. The iSBC 386 SX supports an optional 387 SX Math Coprocessor for improved floating point calculations. To optimize compute performance, an on-board bus connects the 386 SX CPU, 387 SX Math Coprocessor, and local fast-page, 100ns, parity DRAM SIMM memory. A modular design helps reduce cost by providing sockets for the 387 SX and expandable DRAM memory so they may be selected to fit the needs of the design. The iSBC 386 SX is provided with 512K or 2 MB of local DRAM which may be expanded to 8 MB using plug-on SIMM packages.

iSBC® 386 SX PROVIDES DOS PLUS REAL-TIME TO MICROCOMPUTER APPLICATIONS

The iSBC 386 SX is software compatible with the PC-AT motherboard, enabling users access to the large installed base of DOS software. The iSBC 386 SX comes ready to run, with an on-board BIOS that supports loading DOS from either the locally supported hard disk or floppy disks. The iSBC 386 SX can also run other 386-based software such as the iRMX III real-time operating system (O/S). This 32-bit operating system is ideal for controlling real-time processes common in industrial, communication, and other time-critical applications. The iRMX III software also enables DOS and the iRMX O/S to run concurrently on the board with full data exchange between the DOS and real-time applications. Using this software, engineers can design high performance real-time systems with easy-to-use DOS user interfaces.

HIGH INTEGRATION BOARD PROVIDES COMPLETE I/O FEATURE SET

First, the iSBC 386 SX includes the full set of I/O resources found on high-integration Multibus I single board computers, including two RS232 asynchronous serial ports, a Centronics-compatible parallel port, two integrated 8259 interrupt controllers, two 8/16 bit iSBX connectors, DMA and the Multibus interface. It also includes the full set of PC AT motherboard I/O resources, including an IDE interface to Winchester hard disks, interface to floppy drives, a real-time clock, and a keyboard and mouse interface. Traditional Multibus resources are shared with the AT features to provide interrupt and DMA services for the on-board I/O. Finally, the optional iSBC 272 VGA graphics module allows you to easily add VGA and extended VGA graphics to the iSBC 386 SX board.

ON-BOARD FEATURES HELP IN FITTING THE iSBC® 386 SX INTO EXISTING MULTIBUS I DESIGNS

On-board features help you fit the iSBC 386 SX into existing Multibus I designs. The memory map includes access to the Multibus interface in memory space and I/O space. In memory space the board provides a 1 MB window, located at on-board address 13 MB and relocatable in your Multibus system memory space through use of a programmable register. Multibus I/O space is located at 8000H. If the board needs access to other intelligent boards through dual-ported memory, jumpers allow you to map SRAM or FLASH memory in the universal sites into the appropriate memory space required by your Multibus I system memory map (on one megabyte boundaries).

FEATURES

Address	Local On-board Memory	Off board Access
16 MB – 15 MB	BIOS (64K) **EPROM sites**	Not available over ISA
15 MB – 14 MB	**Dual-ported Universal sites**	
14 MB – 13 MB	**Multibus window:** Access to Multibus System memory	
13 MB – 8 MB	Not Available	Extended memory over ISA
8 MB – 1 MB	**Extended memory** local DRAM	If DRAM not installed goes to ISA
1 MB – 0	Local DRAM SIMM	video BIOS video RAM ISA

Figure 1: Multibus I Memory Map

ON-BOARD EPROM AND COMPLETE FEATURE SET INCREASE FLEXIBILITY

The iSBC 386 SX includes two 32-pin EPROM sockets for the BIOS and for addition of user-embedded code. Two additional 32-pin, universal JEDEC sites are provided for on-board, dual-ported memory. The sites support use of SRAM, FLASH or additional EPROM memory.

HIGH-INTEGRATION CUTS BOARD COUNT AND COSTS

The iSBC 386 SX board's complete set of I/O resources makes it possible to eliminate several boards from your design. For example, the iSBC 386 SX/iSBC 272 combination can take the place of the CPU board, peripheral controller board, graphics board, and any add-on modules for local memory or access to local printers, keyboard or console. Designs are simplified and cost-reduced, and performance is improved through a reduction in system bus traffic.

SOFTWARE AND DEVELOPMENT SUPPORT

To help complete system designs, Intel offers operating systems, compilers, debuggers, and other software development tools. Applications may be written in C, PL/M, FORTRAN, or assembler to run on DOS and/or the iRMX III operating system. Source-level debuggers include DB86 and Soft-Scope* III. In-circuit emulators and performance analysis tools are also available. To help develop your first system, Intel also offers a cable kit, converting the board's pin connectors to the appropriate industry-standard I/O connector.

ONE YEAR WARRANTY

All Intel board level products have a one year mail-in warranty on both parts and labor.

WORLD WIDE SERVICE AND SUPPORT

Should any Intel board ever need service, Intel maintains a world wide network of service and repair facilities to keep you and your customers up and running.

INTEL QUALITY — YOUR GUARANTEE

The iSBC 386 SX and iSBC 272 boards are designed and manufactured to meet Intel's strict standards, assuring their reliability and high quality.

SPECIFICATIONS

iSBC® 386 SX SPECIFICATIONS

Computing and Memory Resources

- CPU: 386 SX microprocessor at 16 MHz
- Floating point math: 387™ SX Numerics Coprocessor socket

DRAM Memory

- DRAM memory is fast page, 100 ns memory with parity
- DRAM Supplied:
  — iSBC386SX00 includes 512K using two 256 × 9 SIMM packages
  — iSBC386SX02 includes 2 MB using two 1Meg × 9 SIMM packages

Memory Performance

	Page "Hit"	Page "Miss"
READ	0 wait states	2 wait states
WRITE	1 wait state	1 wait state

Memory Expansion

- Sockets are provided for eight SIMM modules.
- Max DRAM available: 8 MB using 1Meg × 1 Meg SIMMs

EPROM and Other Local Memory

- Two 32-pin sites containing 128 Kbytes of EPROM memory with Phoenix BIOS. Sites will support 512 KB using 27020 EPROMs.
- Two additional 32-pin universal JEDEC sockets for additional EPROM, or for dual-ported SRAM or FLASH memory. Supports additional 512 KB using 27020 EPROMs.
- 114 bytes CMOS RAM for saving BIOS configurations, with provisions for off-board battery backup

I/O Resources

Hard Disk Controller

- Provides IDE interface to fixed disk drives.

Floppy Disk Controller

- Provides interface to the following floppy drives:
  1.44 MB or 720K 3.5″ floppy disk drive
  1.2 MB or 360K 5.25″ floppy disk drive

Serial Communications

- Two asynchronous serial ports, COM1 and COM2: RS232C DTE asynchronous

Parallel Port

- Centronics compatible port, configurable as a printer port LPT1 or LPT2.

DMA

- Two integrated 8237 DMA controllers providing seven DMA channels.
- Supports DMA between on-board floppy, memory, and iSBX connectors.

Other I/O

Timers/Counters:	integrated 8254 programmable interval timer/counter used for PC-compatibility
Real-time clock:	complete time-of-day clock with alarm, 100-year calendar, programmable periodic interrupt, 50 bytes SRAM.
Watchdog Timer:	Dallas semiconductor DS1232S watchdog timer. Resets CPU on timeout (every 600ms) once activated. Jumper-selectable.
Battery back-up connectors:	connectors are provided to off-board battery back-up via the P2 connector or via an on-board connector.

Interrupt Capacity

- Two integrated 8259 PICs
- 15 interrupts, 8 for Multibus interface

SPECIFICATIONS

Interfaces/Connectors

Hard disk:	40-pin header
Floppy Disk:	connector (J4), 34-pin header
Serial port COM1:	10-pin, two row header
Serial port COM2:	10-pin, two row header
Parallel port:	26-pin, two row header
Keyboard/Mouse share same connector	10-pin, two row header
Battery back-up:	using either P2, or using four on-board stake pins
Speaker:	two stake pins for connecting a piezo speaker
Multibus I (IEEE796) Bus Compliance:	Master D16 M24 I16 VOL SLAVE D16 M24
iSBX Bus Compliance:	D16/16 DMA I

iSBC® 272 SPECIFICATIONS

Graphics Protocols Supported

- Software protocols: VGA, extended VGA, EGA, CGA, Hercules monochrome

Resolution

- Standard VGA modes: 640×480, 16 colors, graphics; 720×400, text
- Extended VGA modes: 800×600, 16 colors, graphics; 1024×768, 4 colors, graphics

Memory

- 256K DRAM

Connectors

- Ten-pin header to analog cable for VGA monitors

iSBC® 386 SX AND iSBC® 272 SPECIFICATIONS

Software Support

- Operating systems: DOS, MS-DOS, iRMXIII, and DOS/iRMX operating systems

PHYSICAL CHARACTERISTICS

Physical Dimensions

Width and length conform to Multibus I specifications.
Depth: 1.00", 1.62" with iSBC272 module.

ELECTRICAL CHARACTERISTICS

DC Power Requirements (Typical):

	Current
iSBC 386 SX	6A
iSBC 272	1A

ENVIRONMENTAL CHARACTERISTICS

Operating Temperature: 0°C to 55°C at 200 LFM airflow

Relative Humidity: 0% to 90% (without condensation)

Storage Temperature: −40°C to +70°C

REFERENCE MANUALS

iSBC® 386 SX Hardware User's Manual, Order Number: 507913-001

ORDERING INFORMATION

Part Number	Description
SBC386SX00	386 SX microprocessor-based, PC AT compatible single board computer with 512 Kbytes on-board DRAM.
SBC386SX02	Same as iSBC386SX00 with 2 MB on-board DRAM.
SBC272	VGA graphics module for use with iSBC386SX boards.
CABLESBC386SX	Complete set of cables for hard disk, floppy, two serial ports, parallel port, keyboard/mouse, and VGA analog interfaces. Cables convert pin header connectors to industry-standard, PC-compatible connectors.

For more information or the number of your nearest Intel sales office, call 800-548-4725 (good in the U.S. and Canada.)

iSBC® 386/21/22/24/28 AND 386/31/32/34/38* SINGLE BOARD COMPUTERS

- **Choice of 16 MHz or 20 MHz 386™ Microprocessor**
- **Available with 1, 2, 4, or 8 Megabytes of On-Board 32-Bit Memory, expandable to 16 Megabytes**
- **High Speed 80387 Floating Point Math Coprocessor**
- **Two 32-Bit JEDEC Sites for up to 512 Kilobytes of EPROM Memory**
- **RS232C Interface for Local/Remote Control and Diagnostics**
- **iSBX® Interface for Low Cost I/O Expansion**
- **16 Levels of Direct Vectored Interrupt Control**
- **64 Kilobyte 0 Wait-State Cache Memory**

The iSBC® 386/2x and 3x series boards (iSBC 386/21/22/24/28 and iSBC 386/31/32/34/38) are Intel's highest performance Multibus I CPU boards. These boards feature either a 16 MHz or 20 MHz 386 CPU, an 80387 math coprocessor, a 64k byte, 0 wait-state cache memory to support the CPU, and a 32-bit interface to 1, 2, 4, or 8 megabytes of dual-port parity DRAM memory. An additional 1, 2, 4, or 8 MB iSBC MM0x series memory module may be installed to provide up to 16 MB of on-board DRAM memory. The iSBC 386/2x and 3x boards also feature an 8/16-bit iSBX MULTIMODULE interface for low-cost I/O expansion, an asynchronous RS232C interface to support a local terminal or modem, two 16-bit programmable timer/counters, a 16-level direct-vectored interrupt controller, two 32-pin JEDEC sites and multimaster Multibus arbitration logic.

280602–1

*The iSBC® 386/21/22/24/28 and iSBC® 386/31/32/34/38 Boards are manufactured under product code pSBC 386/21/22/24/28 and pSBC 386/31/32/34/38 by Intel Puerto Rico, Inc.

*XENIX is a registered trademark of Microsoft Corp.
*UNIX is a trademark of AT&T.

OVERVIEW—iSBC 386/2x AND 3x SERIES CPU BOARDS

The iSBC 386/21/22/24/28 and iSBC 386/31/32/34/38 boards (iSBC 386/2x and 3x series) are 16 MHz and 20 MHz versions of Intel's first Multibus I 386™ microprocessor CPU boards. The boards employ a dual-bus structure, a 32-bit CPU bus for data transfers between the CPU and memory, and a 16-bit bus for data transfers over the MULTIBUS interface, iSBX interface, EPROM local memory, and I/O interfaces. The boards take advantage of the 386 CPU's 32-bit performance while maintaining compatibility with the Multibus I interface.

The DRAM memory, which is on a module that is secured to the baseboard, may be expanded by installing a second 1, 2, 4, or 8M byte memory module.

16 MHz or 20 MHz Central Processor Unit

The heart of the iSBC 386/2x and 3x CPU board is the 386 microprocessor. The complete series includes two lines, with a choice of CPU speed. The iSBC 386/21/22/24/28 boards use the 16 MHz 386 microprocessor and the iSBC 386/31/32/34/38 boards use the 20 MHz 386 microprocessor. The 386 CPU utilizes address pipelining, a high speed execution unit, and on-chip memory management/protection to provide the highest level of system performance. The 386 microprocessor also features an Address Translation Unit that supports up to 64 terabytes of virtual memory.

The 386 CPU is upward compatible from Intel's 8088, 8086, 80186, and 80286 CPUs. Application software written for these other 8- and 16-bit microprocessor families can be recompiled to run on the 80386 microprocessor. Some changes to the software such as adjustment of software timing loops and changing I/O address references may be required. The 386 microprocessor resides on the 32-bit wide CPU bus which interconnects the CPU with the math coprocessor and dual-port memory.

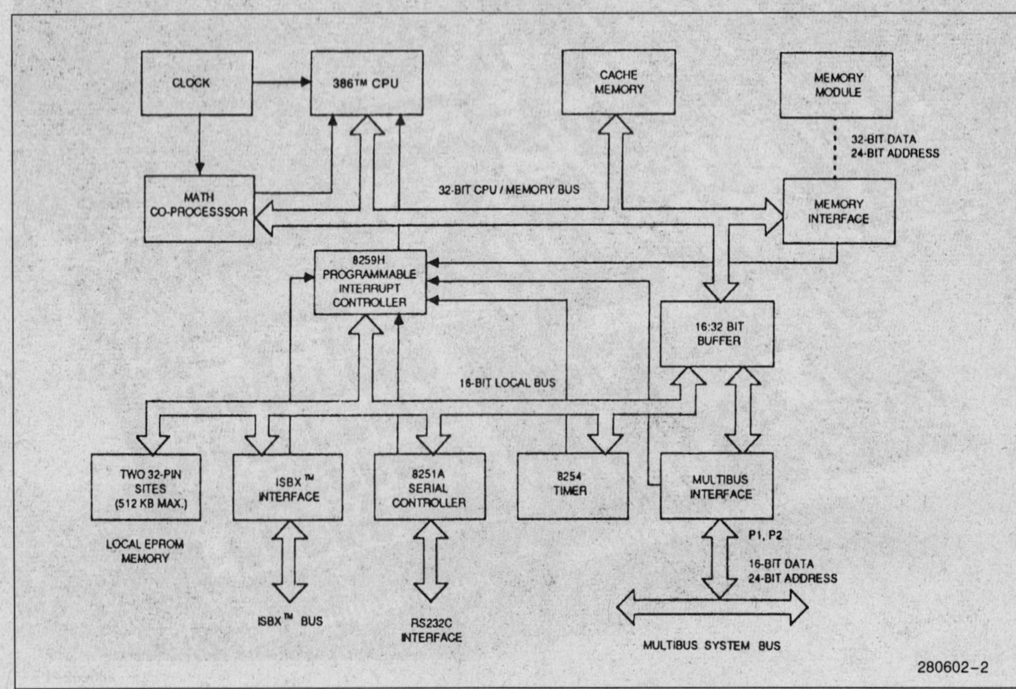

Figure 1. iSBC® 386/2x and 3x CPU Board Block Diagram

Instruction Set

The 386 CPU instruction set includes: variable length instruction format (including double operand instructions; 8-, 16-, and 32-bit signed and unsigned arithmetic operators for binary, BCD and unpacked ASCII data; and iterative word and byte string manipulation functions. All existing instructions have been extended to support 32-bit addresses and operands. New bit manipulation and other instructions have been added for extra flexibility in designing complex software.

Numeric Data Processor

For enhanced numerics processing compatibility, the iSBC 386/2x and 3x boards include an 80387 numeric coprocessor. Over 60 numeric instructions offer arithmetic, trigonometric, transcendental, logarithmic and exponential instructions. Supported data types include 16-, 32-, and 64-bit integer, 32- and 64-bit floating point, 18-digit packed BCD and 80-bit temporary. Data transfers to and from the CPU are 32-bits wide.

Architectural Features

The 8086, 8088, 80188, 80286, and 386 microprocessor family contain the same basic sets of registers, instructions, and addressing modes. The 80386 processor is upward compatible with the 8086, 8088, 80186, 80188, and 80286 CPU's.

Architectural Features

The 386 CPU operates in two modes: protected virtual address mode; and 8086 real address mode. In protected virtual address mode (also called protected mode), programs use virtual addresses. In this mode, the 386 CPU automatically translates logical addresses to physical addresses. This mode also provides memory protection to isolate the operating system and ensure privacy of each task's programs and data. In 8086 real address mode, programs use real addresses with up to one megabyte of address space. Both modes provide the same base instruction set and registers.

Interrupt Control

Incoming interrupts are handled by two cascaded on-board 8259A programmable interrupt controllers and by the 386's NMI line. Twenty interrupt sources are routed to the programmable controllers and the interrupt jumper matrix. Using this jumper matrix, the user can connect the desired interrupt sources to specific interrupt levels. The interrupt controllers prioritize interrupts originating from up to 15 sources and send them to the CPU. The user can connect a sixteenth interrupt to the 386 NMI line. Table 1 includes a list of devices and functions suported by interrupts. Bus vectored interrupts are not supported.

Table 1. Interrupt Request Sources

Source	Function	Number of Interrupts
Multibus Interface	Requests from Multibus resident peripherals or other CPU boards	8
8251A Serial Controller	Indicates status of transmit and receive buffers and RI lead of the RS232C interface	3
8254 Timers	Timer 0, 1 outputs; function determined by timer mode (hardwired to interrupt controller)	2
iSBX™ Connector	Function determined by iSBX™ MULTIMODULE™ board	4
Bus Timeout	Indicates addressed Multibus or iSBX™ resident device has not responded to a command within 10 ms	1
Power Fail Interrupt	Indicates AC power is not within tolerance (signal generated by system power supply)	1
Parity Interrupt	Indicates on-board parity error	1
Programmable Register	Generate interrupt under program control	1

8

Memory Capabilities

The iSBC 386/2x and 3x boards support both EPROM local memory and dynamic RAM (DRAM), which is located on-board. The DRAM is supported by a high speed on-board cache memory.

DRAM Memory

The iSBC 386/2x and 3x series CPU boards come with 1, 2, 4, or 8M bytes of DRAM memory. This memory is on a low profile module that is installed on the baseboard. The module measures approximately 4″ x 4″ and uses surface mount DRAM devices. The DRAM memory supports byte-parity error detection and has a 32-bit wide data path to the 80386 CPU and 16-bit wide data path to the Multibus interface.

The memory may be expanded by installing an additional iSBC MM0x series memory module, which is available in 1, 2, 4, or 8M byte sizes. All mounting hardware is included. Maximum DRAM memory is 16M bytes using an iSBC 386/28 or 386/38 CPU board and an 8M byte iSBC MM08 memory module. This combination requires 1.8 inches of cardcage space.

Cache Memory

A 64K byte cache memory on the iSBC 386/2x and 3x boards supports the 386 CPU and provides 0 wait-state reads for data and program code resident in the cache memory. The cache memory is updated whenever data is written into the dual-port memory or when the CPU executes a read cycle and the data or program code is not present in cache memory. This process is controlled by the cache replacement algorithm. Cache "misses" require additional wait-states to retrieve data from the DRAM memory. If the processor is in pipelined mode, 2 wait-states (4 clock cycles) are required to retrieve data. If the processor is in non-pipelined mode, 3 wait-states are required. All writes to DRAM memory require 2 (pipelined) or 3 (non-pipelined) wait-states.

The cache memory supports 16K entries, with each entry comprised of a 32-bit data field and an 8-bit tag field. The tag field is used to determine which actual memory word currently resides in a cache entry. The cache memory size and effective replacement algorithm are designed to optimize both the probability of cache "hits" and local bus utilization.

EPROM Memory

The EPROM memory consists of two 32-pin JEDEC sites that are intended for boot-up and system diagnostic/monitor routines, application code, and ROM-able operating system software. Maximum local memory capacity is 512K bytes using Intel 27020 (256k x 8) 2 megabit EPROM devices. The EPROM memory resides at the upper end of the 386 device's memory space for both real address mode and PVAM operation.

Memory Map

In real address mode, the maximum amount of addressable physical memory is 1 Mbyte. In protected virtual address mode (PVAM), the maximum amount of addressable physical memory is 16 Mbytes. The system designer can easily change the CPU memory map to adapt the CPU board to the required overall system memory map. Reconfiguration is usually necessary for multiple processor-based systems with more than two CPU boards and/or intelligent I/O boards. By changing PAL devices and/or by moving jumpers, the designer can set:

- EPROM memory space
- Starting address of DRAM memory
- Amount of DRAM memory that is dual-ported to the CPU and Multibus interface or single-ported to the CPU
- Access to off-board Multibus address space

EPROM Memory

The EPROM memory space is set using four jumpers to accommodate 27256 (256 kb), 27512 (512 kb), 27010 (1 Mb), or 27020 (2 Mb) byte-wide devices. Smaller EPROM devices may be used, however the EPROM will appear more than once within the EPROM address space. Using a pair of 27020 EPROMs will provide 512k bytes of memory. The iSBC 386/2x and 3x series boards are designed to accommodate EPROM devices with access times ranging from 130 ns–320 ns. In real address mode, the ending address of EPROM memory is always 1M byte (FFFFFH). In PVAM, the ending address of EPROM memory is always 4G bytes (FFFF FFFFH), which is the top of the 386 CPU address space.

DRAM Memory Size/Location

The iSBC 386/2x and 3x boards allow the user to control the location and size of the DRAM memory (on the iSBC 386/2x and 3x boards) available for use by the CPU and other boards in the system. In PVAM, the starting address of DRAM can be set to start on any 1M byte boundary up through 15M bytes by setting jumpers and by installing a custom-programmed PAL device. In real address mode, the DRAM memory always starts at 0H (hex).

The ending address can be set on 64k byte boundaries using jumpers in both PVAM and real address mode. Setting the ending address at lower than the actual amount of installed memory effectively deselects a portion of DRAM and creates additional Multibus address space.

Multibus Address Space

Any address space not set aside as EPROM or DRAM memory automatically becomes address space the CPU can use to access other boards in the system. For example, Figure 2A shows a real address mode CPU memory map for a 1M byte iSBC 386/21 board. With the DRAM ending address set at 512k bytes and 128k bytes of installed EPROM, 384k bytes of Multibus address space is accessable by the CPU. Figure 2B shows a typical PVAM configuration where the 4 Mbytes of DRAM has been set to start at 1M byte and end at 4.5M bytes. The address space from 0 to 1M byte and 4.5 to 16M bytes is the Multibus address space accessable by the CPU.

Figure 2C illustrates another way the board can establish additional Multibus address space. If the DRAM memory starts at 0, a jumper on the board can be used to create additional Multibus address space between 512k bytes and 1M byte. This feature is available both in real address mode and PVAM.

Dual-Port/Local Memory

A portion or all of the DRAM memory can be selected to be dual-port (shared) memory. Both the starting and ending addresses are set on 256k byte boundaries using jumpers on the board. Any DRAM memory that is not configured as dual-port memory is local (single-port) memory available only to the CPU.

Programmable Timer

Three 16-bit, programmable interval timer/counters are provided using an 8254 device, with one timer dedicated to the serial port for use as a baud rate generator. The other two timers can be used to generate accurate time intervals under software control. The timers are not cascadable. Four timer/counter modes are available as listed in Table 2. Each counter is capable of operating in either BCD or binary modes. The contents of each counter may be read at any time during system operation.

Table 2. Programmable Timer Functions

Function	Operation
Interrupt on terminal count	When terminal count is reached, an interrupt request is generated. This function is extremely useful for generation of real-time clocks.
Rate generator	Divide by N counter. The output will go low for one input clock cycle, and the period from one low going pulse to the next is N times the input clock period.
Square-wave rate generator	Output will remain high until one-half the count has been completed, and go low for the other half of the count.
Software triggered strobe	Output remains high until software loads count (N). N counts after count is loaded, output goes low for one input clock period.

Serial I/O

The iSBC 386/2x and 3x boards include one RS232C serial channel, which is configured as an

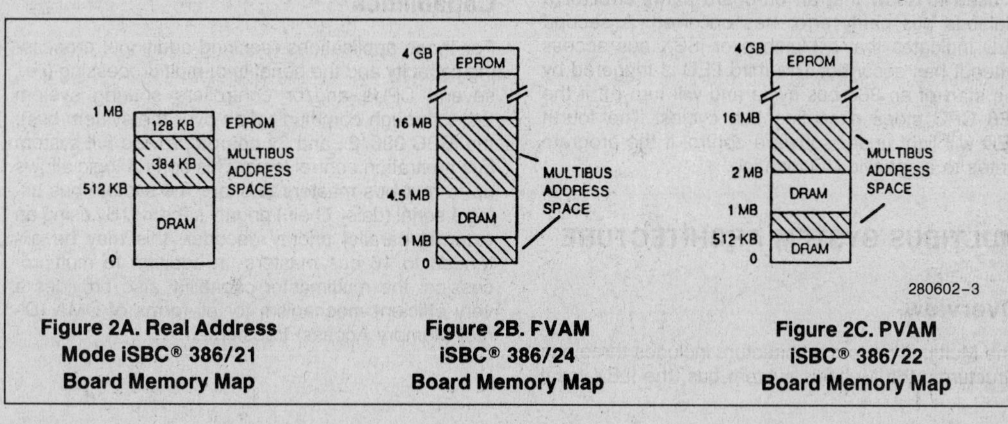

Figure 2A. Real Address Mode iSBC® 386/21 Board Memory Map

Figure 2B. FVAM iSBC® 386/24 Board Memory Map

Figure 2C. PVAM iSBC® 386/22 Board Memory Map

asynchronous, DTE interface. Data rates up to 19.2k baud may be selected. The serial channel can connect either to a host system for software development or to a stand alone terminal for field diagnostic support. For stand alone use, unhosted monitor software needs to be programmed by the user into the local EPROM memory. The serial channel may also be connected to a modem to provide remote diagnostic support or to download program codes. The physical interface is a 10-pin ribbon-style connector located on the front edge of the board.

iSBX™ Interface

For iSBX MULTIMODULE support, the iSBC 386/2x and 3x CPU boards provide an 8/16-bit iSBX connector that may be configured for use with either 8- or 16-bit, single or double-wide iSBX MULTIMODULE boards. Using the iSBX interface, a wide variety of specialized I/O functions can be added easily and inexpensively to the iSBC 386/2x and 3x boards.

Reset Functions

The iSBC 386/2x and 3x boards are designed to accept an Auxilliary Reset signal via the boards' P2 interface. In this way, system designs that require front panel reset switches are supported. The iSBC 386/2x and 3x boards use the AUX reset signal to reset all on-board logic (excluding DRAM refresh circuitry) and other boards in the Multibus system. The iSBC 386/2x and 3x boards will also respond to an INIT reset signal generated by another board in the system.

LED Status Indicators

Mounted on the front edge of the iSBC 386/2x and 3x boards are four LED indicators that indicate the operating status of the board and system. One LED is used to show that an on-board parity error or a Multibus bus parity error has occurred. A second LED indicates that a Multibus or iSBX bus access timeout has occurred. The third LED is triggered by the start of an 386 bus cycle and will turn off if the 386 CPU stops executing bus cycles. The fourth LED will light under software control if the program writes to a specific I/O location.

MULTIBUS SYSTEM ARCHITECTURE

Overview

The Multibus system architecture includes three bus structures: the Multibus system bus, the iLBX local bus extension and the iSBX MULTIMODULE expansion bus. Each bus structure is optimized to satisfy particular system requirements. The system bus provides a basis for general system design including memory and I/O expansion as well as multiprocessing support. The iLBX bus, which is usually used for memory expansion, is not supported by the iSBC 386/2x and 3x boards since all DRAM memory is located on-board. The iSBX bus povides a low cost way to add I/O to the board.

System Bus—IEEE 796

The Multibus system bus is an industry standard, IEEE 796, microcomputer bus structure. Both 8- and 16-bit single board computers are supported on the IEEE 796 structure with 24 address and 16 data lines. In its simplest application, the system bus allows expansion of functions already contained on a single board computer (e.g., memory and digital I/O). However, the IEEE 796 bus also allows very powerful distributed processing configurations using multiple processors, I/O boards, and peripheral boards. The Multibus system bus is supported with a broad array of board level products, VLSI interface components, detailed published specifications and application notes.

System Bus—Expansion Capabilities

The user can easily expand or add features to his system by adding various Multibus boards to his system. Products available from Intel and others include: video controllers; D/A and A/D converter boards; peripheral controller cards; communications/networking boards; voice synthesis and recognition boards; and EPROM memory expansion boards.

System Bus—Multimaster Capabilities

For those applications requiring additional processing capacity and the benefits of multiprocessing (i.e., several CPUs and/or controllers sharing system tasks through communication over the system bus), the iSBC 386/2x and 3x boards provide full system bus arbitration control logic. This control logic allows up to four bus masters to share the system bus using a serial (daisy chain) priority scheme. By using an external parallel priority decoder, this may be extended to 16 bus masters. In addition to multiprocessing, the multimaster capability also provides a very efficient mechanism for all forms of DMA (Direct Memory Access) transfers.

iSBX™ Bus MULTIMODULE™ On-Board Expansion

Through this interface, additional on-board I/O functions may be added, such as parallel and serial I/C, analog I/O, small mass storage device controllers (e.g., floppy disks), BITBUS Control, and other custom interfaces to meet specific needs. Compared to other alternatives such as Multibus I boards, iSBX modules need less interface logic and power, and offer simpler packaging and lower cost. The iSBX interface connector on the iSBC 386/2x and 3x boards provides all the signals necessary to interface to the local on-board bus, and is compatible with both 8-bit and 16-bit MULTIMODULES.

SOFTWARE SUPPORT

Operating Systems

The iSBC 386/2x and 3x boards are supported by a variety of operating systems, including the iRMX I, iRMX II, iRMX III, XENIX (from Intel) and System V/386 operating systems (third party vendors).

See the datasheets on these software products for further details.

BOARD SPECIFICATIONS

Word Size

Instruction—8, 16, 24, 32 or 40 bits
Data—8, 16, 32 bits

System Clock

386 CPU—16 MHz or 20 MHz
Numeric Processor—80387 module—16 MHz or 20 MHz

DRAM Memory

On-board parity memory
- iSBC 386/21/31 board—1M byte
- iSBC 386/22/32 board—2M bytes
- iSBC 386/24/34 board—4M bytes
- iSBC 386/28/38 board—8M bytes

Memory expansion—One additonal plug-in module:
- iSBC MM01—1M byte
- iSBC MM02—2M bytes
- iSBC MM04—4M bytes
- iSBC MM08—8M bytes

Maximum Addressable Physical Memory—16 Megabytes (protected virtual address mode) 1 Megabyte (real address mode)

EPROM Memory

Number of sockets—Two 32-pin JEDEC Sites (compatible with 28-pin and 32-pin devices)

Sizes accommodated—64 kb (8k x 8), 128 kb (16k x 8), 256 kb (32k x 8), 512 kb (64k x 8), 1 Mb (128k x 8), 2 Mb (256k x 8)

Device access speeds—130 ns to 320 ns
Maximum memory—512k bytes with 27020 (2M bit) EPROMs

I/O Capability

Serial Channel

Type—One RS232C DTE asynchronous channel using an 8251A device

Data Characteristics—5-8 bit characters; break character generation; 1, 1½, or 2 stop bits; false start bit detection; automatic break detect and handling; even/odd parity error generation and detection

Speed—110, 150, 300, 600, 1.2 kb, 2.4 kb, 4.8 kb, 9.6 kb, 19.2 kb

Leads supported—TD, RD, RTS, CTS DSR, RI, CD, SG

Connector Type—10 pin ribbon

Expansion—One 8/16-bit iSBX interface connector for single or double wide iSBX MULTIMODULE board.

Interrupt Capacity

Potential Interrupt Sources—21 (2 fixed, 19 jumper selectable)

Interrupt Levels—16 using two 8259A devices and the 80386 NMI line

Timers

Two programmable timers using one 8274 device.

8

Output Frequencies/Timing Intervals

Function	Single Counter	
	Min	Max
Real-time interrupt	1.63 µs	53.3 ms
Rate Generator	18.8 Hz	615 kHz
Square-wave rate generator	18.8 Hz	615 kHz
Software triggered strobe	1.63 µs	53.3 ms

Interfaces

Multibus Bus—All signals TTL compatible
iSBX Bus—All signals TTL compatible
Serial I/O—RS 232C, DTE

MULTIBUS® DRIVERS

Function	Type	Sink Current (mA)
Data	Tri-State	64
Address	Tri-State	24
Commands	Tri-State	32
Bus Control	Open Collector	16/32

Power Requirements

iSBC 386/2x and 3x boards
Maximum: +5V, 12.5A
±12V, 35 mA
Typical: +5V, 9A
±12V, 20 mA

NOTE:
Does not include power for iSBX module, EPROM memory, or added iSBCMM0x memory modules.

Add the following power when adding iSBC MM0X memory modules:

iSBC MM01 +5V, 0.71A
MM02 +5V, 0.96A
MM04 +5V, 0.71A
MM08 +5V, 0.96A

Environmental Requirements

Operating Temperature—0°C to 60°C at 300 LFM
Relative Humidity—0% to 85% noncondensing
Storage Temperature—−40°C to +70°C

Physical Characteristics

Dimensions
Width—12.00 in. (30.48 cm)
Height—7.05 in. (17.91 cm)
Depth—0.86 in. (2.18 cm), 1.62 in. (4.11 cm) with added memory module

Recommended Minimum Cardcage Slot Spacing
1.2 in. (3.0 cm), with or without iSBX MULTIMODULE
1.8 in. (4.6 cm), with addded iSBC MM0x memory module

Approximate Weight
26 oz. (738 gm)

Reference Manual

149094—iSBC 386/21/22/24/28 Hardware Reference Manual (order separately)

453652—iSBC 386/31/32/34/38 Single Board Computer Hardware Reference Manual

Ordering Information

Part Number	Description
CPU Boards	
SBC38621	16 MHz 386 Multibus I CPU Board with 1 MB DRAM Memory
SBC38622	16 MHz 386 Multibus I CPU Board with 2 MB DRAM Memory
SBC38624	16 MHz 386 Multibus I CPU Board with 4 MB DRAM Memory
SBC38628	16 MHz 386 Multibus I CPU Board with 8 MB DRAM Memory
SBC38631	20 MHz 386 Multibus I CPU Board with 1 MB DRAM Memory
SBC38632	20 MHz 386 Multibus I CPU Board with 2 MB DRAM Memory
SBC38634	20 MHz 386 Multibus I CPU Board with 4 MB DRAM Memory
SBC38638	20 MHz 386 Multibus I CPU Board with 8 MB DRAM Memory
Memory Modules	
SBCMM01	1 MB Parity DRAM Memory Expansion Module
SBCMM02	2 MB Parity DRAM Memory Expansion Module
SBCMM04	4 MB Parity DRAM Memory Expansion Module
SBCMM08	8 MB Parity DRAM Memory Expansion Module

intel®

iSBC® 286/12, 286/14, 286/16* SINGLE BOARD COMPUTERS

- **8 MHz 80286 Microprocessor**
- **Two JEDEC 28-Pin Sites for up to 128K Bytes of Local EPROM Memory, Expandable to 256K Bytes Using an iSBC® 341 Expansion Module**
- **1, 2, or 4 Megabyte, 0 Wait-State, Dual-Port, Parity Memory**
- **Supports User Installed 80287 Numeric Data Processor and 82258 Advanced DMA Controller Devices**
- **Two iSBX™ Bus Interface Connectors for I/O Expansion**
- **Synchronous High-Speed Interface for 0 Wait-State Read/Write to EX Memory Expansion Boards**
- **iLBX™ Interface for iLBX Memory Board Expansion**
- **16 Levels of Vectored Interrupt Control**
- **Centronics-Compatible Parallel I/O Printer Interface**
- **Two Programmable Multiprotocol Synchronous/Asynchronous Serial Interfaces; One RS232C, the Other RS232C or RS422/449 Compatible**

The iSBC 286/12, iSBC 286/14, and iSBC 286/16 Single Board Computers are members of Intel's family of 16-bit microcomputers. The boards feature an 80286 microprocessor running at 8 MHz together with 1, 2, or 4 megabytes of dual-ported, 0 wait-state, parity memory. These features make the iSBC 286/12/14/16 boards the ideal single board solution for applications requiring high performance and up to 1, 2, or 4 megabytes of memory. For those applications needing more memory, up to four memory expansion boards may be connected to the iSBC 286/12/14/16 boards over its P2 interface. The P2 interface supports both standard iLBX memory boards and Intel's EX series of synchronous, 0 wait-state, memory boards that provide up to 16 megabytes of system memory. The iSBC 286/12/14/16 boards also feature two sockets for user installed 80287 Numeric Data Processor and 82258 Advanced Direct Memory Access Controller devices. These components further increase board performance by off-loading time intensive tasks from the 80286 microprocessor. The iSBC 286/12/14/16 CPU boards are true single-board solutions that also include two serial I/O channels, one parallel line printer channel, local memory, interrupt controllers and programmable timers all on one board.

*The iSBC® 286/12; iSBC 286/14 and iSBC 286/16 are also manufactured under product code pSBC28612; pSBC28614 and pSBC28616 by Intel Puerto Rico, Inc.

280147–1

*XENIX is a registered trademark of Microsoft Corp.
**UNIX is a trademark of Bell Laboratories.

October 1990
Order Number: 280147-004

FUNCTIONAL DESCRIPTION

Overview

The iSBC 286/12/14/16 boards utilizes the 80286 CPU within the Multibus system architecture, enhanced by the industry standard iLBX bus and a new, 0 wait-state, synchronous memory interface, to provide a high-performance 16-bit solution. This board features 1, 2, or 4 megabytes of dual-port, 0 wait-state, parity memory, plus interrupt, memory and I/O features facilitating a complete single-board computer system. The iSBC 286/12/14/16 boards can be used in many applications originally designed for Intel's other 16-bit microcomputers.

Central Processing Unit

The central processor for the iSBC 286/12/14/16 board is the 80286 CPU operating at an 8.0 MHz clock rate. The 80286 CPU is upwardly compatible with Intel's 8088 and 8086 CPUs. The 80286 CPU runs 8088 and 8086 code at substantially higher speeds due to its parallel architecture. In addition, the 80286 CPU provides on-chip memory management and protection and virtual memory addressing of up to 1 gigabyte per task. Processing speed and efficiency may be further enhanced by installing an 80287 numerics coprocessor and an 82258 ADMA controller. The clock rates for the 80286 and the 80287 are independent with the 80287 rate jumper selectable at either 5.3 MHz or 8.0 MHz.

Instruction Set

The 80286 instruction repertoire includes variable length instruction format (including double operand instructions), 8-bit and 16-bit signed and unsigned arithmetic operators for binary, BCD and unpacked ASCII data, and iterative word and byte string manipulation functions.

Numeric Data Processor

For enhanced numerics processing capability, the 80287 Numeric Data Processor extends the 80286 architecture and data set. Over 60 numeric instructions offer arithmetic, trigonometric, transcendental, logarithmic and exponential instructions. Supported data types include 16-, 32-, and 64-bit integer, 32- and 64-bit floating point, 18-digit packed BCD and 80-bit temporary.

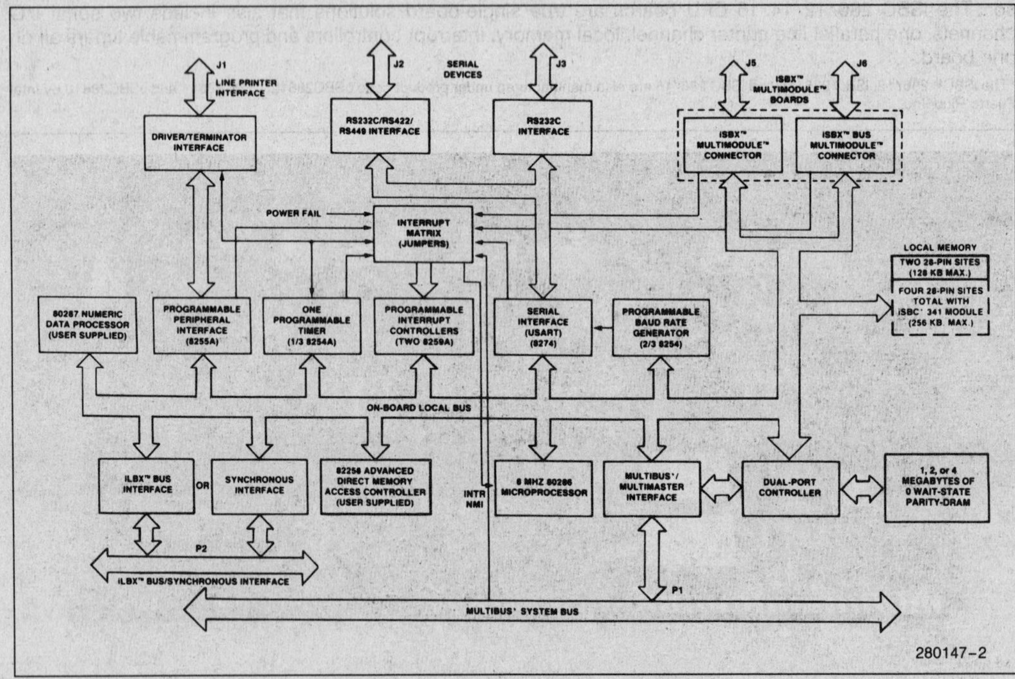

Figure 1. iSBC® 286/12 Block Diagram

Advanced DMA Controller

For those applications that require frequent moving of large blocks of data, the user may install an Intel 82258, 4 channel, advanced DMA (ADMA) controller to further increase system performance. The ADMA Controller supports DMA requests from the 8274 USART (2 channels) and the iSBX interfaces on the board (1 per interface). The ADMA can also perform data transfers over the on-board CPU bus, the MULTIBUS (P1) interface, and the iLBX/synchronous (P2) interface.

ARCHITECTURAL FEATURES

The 8086, 8088, 80186 and 80286 microprocessor family contains the same basic set of registers, instructions, and addressing modes. The 80286 processor is upward compatible with the 8086, 8088, and 80186 CPUs.

The 80286 operates in two modes: 8086 real address mode, and protected virtual address mode. In 8086 real address mode, programs use real address with up to one megabyte of address space. Programs use virtual addresses in protected virtual address mode, also called protected mode. In protected mode, the 80286 CPU automatically maps 1 gigabyte of virtual addresses per task into a 16 megabyte real address space. This mode also provides memory protection to isolate the operating system and ensure privacy of each task's programs and data. Both modes provide the same base instruction set and registers.

Vectored Interrupt Control

Incoming interrupts are handled by two on-board 8259A programmable interrupt controllers (PIC) and by the 80286's NMI line. Interrupts originating from up to 15 sources are prioritized and then sent to the CPU. The 8259A devices support both polled and vectored mode of operation. Further interrupt capability is available through bus vectored interrupts where slave 8259A interrupt controllers resident on separate iSBC Boards supply an interrupt vector to the on-board CPU.

Interrupt Sources

Twenty-six potential interrupt sources are routed to the slave PIC device and to the interrupt jumper matrix where the user can connect the desired interrupt sources to specific interrupt levels.

Memory Capabilities

DUAL-PORT MEMORY

The iSBC 286/12/14/16 boards feature 1, 2, or 4 megabytes of 0 wait-state, parity memory installed on the board. This memory, which is implemented using 256 Kb or 1 Mb DRAMs installed on a daughter board, is dual-ported to the on-board CPU bus and the Multibus (P1) interface. For those applications requiring more memory, the iSBC 286/12/14/16 boards also feature an iLBX and synchronous memory interface to increase physical memory capacity to 16 megabytes.

The iSBC 322/324 memory upgrade modules allow for expansion of on-board dual-port DRAM. The iSBC 322 upgrades an iSBC 286/12 to 2 MBytes. The iSBC 324 upgrades an iSBC 286/12 or iSBC 286/14 to 4 MBytes.

LOCAL MEMORY

Two, 28-pin sites are provided for installing up to 128 KB of EPROM firmware.

By installing an iSBC 341 EPROM expansion module, local memory can be increased to four sites to support up to 256 KB of EPROM. Local memory access time is selectable at one, two, or three wait-states and is a function of the device speed.

Serial I/O

A two-channel serial communications interface using Intel's 8274 Multi-Protocol Serial Controller (MPSC) is contained on the iSBC 286/12/14/16 boards. Two independent software selectable baud rate generators provide the MPSC with all common communication frequencies. The protocol (i.e. asynchronous, bisync, or SDLC/HDLC), data format, control character format, parity and baud rate are all under program control. Software interfacing to the MPSC can be via either a polled or interrupt driven routine. Channel A may be configured for an RS232C or RS422/RS449 interface; channel B is set for RS232C operation only. DMA operation for channel A is available if the optional 82258 (ADMA) is installed.

Programmable Timers

The iSBC 286/12/14/16 boards provide three independent, fully programmable 16-bit interval timers/event counters utilizing the Intel 8254 Programmable Interval Timer. Each counter is capable of operating in either BCD or binary modes. Two of these timers/counters are available to the systems designer to generate accurate time intervals under software control. Routing for the outputs of these counters is jumper selectable. The outputs may be independently routed to the 8259A Programmable Interrupt Controller or to the 8274 MPSC to count external events or provide baud rate generation. The third interval timer in the 8254 is dedicated to providing a clock for the programmable baud rate generator in the iSBC 286/12/14/16 boards' MPSC serial controller.

Line Printer Interface/Board ID

An 8255A Programmable Peripheral Interface (PPI) provides a Centronics compatible line printer interface, several on-board functions, and four non-dedicated input bits. Drivers are provided for a complete Centronics compatible line printer interface.

Software Reset

The software reset feature allows the 80286 microprocessor to return to Real Address mode operation from PVAM under software control. The system reset line (INIT*) and the dual-port memory are not affected, and all I/O context is preserved. The software reset is activated by a byte write to I/O location 00E0H. To distinguish the software reset from a true system initialization reset, a flag is provided. Another flag is provided that indicates whether the iSBC 286/12/14/16 board hardware (not the 80286 device) is currently configured for PVAM or Real Address Mode.

Front Panel Connector

A 14-pin connector (J4) is mounted on the top edge of the board and is designed to connect to the front panel and power supply of the system enclosure. Leads supported include Reset and Interrupt input lines from (conditioned) front panel switches, a Run signal to drive a front panel LED, a Power Fail Interrupt line that connects to the power supply, and extra power and ground leads to support miscellaneous front panel circuitry.

Multimaster Capabilities

The iSBC 286/12/14/16 boards provide full system bus arbitration control logic. This control logic allows up to three iSBC 286/12/14/16 boards or other bus masters to share the system bus using a serial (daisy chain) priority scheme and allows up to 16 masters to share the Multibus system bus with an external parallel priority decoder.

Memory Map

The memory map of the iSBC 286/12/14/16 board is shown in Figure 1. The memory maps for the iSBC 286/14 and iSBC 286/16 boards are similar, except the total amount of on-board DRAM memory is 2 or 4 MB, and the dual-port memory space is larger. The memory map, which shows the default configuration of the board, may be easily changed by the user to meet the needs of almost any system design. As a result, the iSBC 286/12/14/16 boards are particularly suited for complex multiple processor and/or multiple intelligent I/O board-based systems.

The memory map can be changed by moving on-board jumpers or by installing user-programmed PALs (programmable array logic devices).

Using only the jumpers on the iSBC 286/12/14/16 board, the Multibus window size can be set at 0 (no window), 64 KB, 128 KB, 256 KB, or 1 MB in real address mode. The Multibus window is normally not available in PVAM, however, a PAL may be programmed to provide this feature. Jumpers are also used to set aside a portion of the dual-port memory so that it may only be accessed by the CPU (single-ported memory). Block sizes of 64 KB, 128 KB, 256 KB, 512 KB or 1 MB may be selected. Finally, jumpers are used to select any of 6 EPROM memory

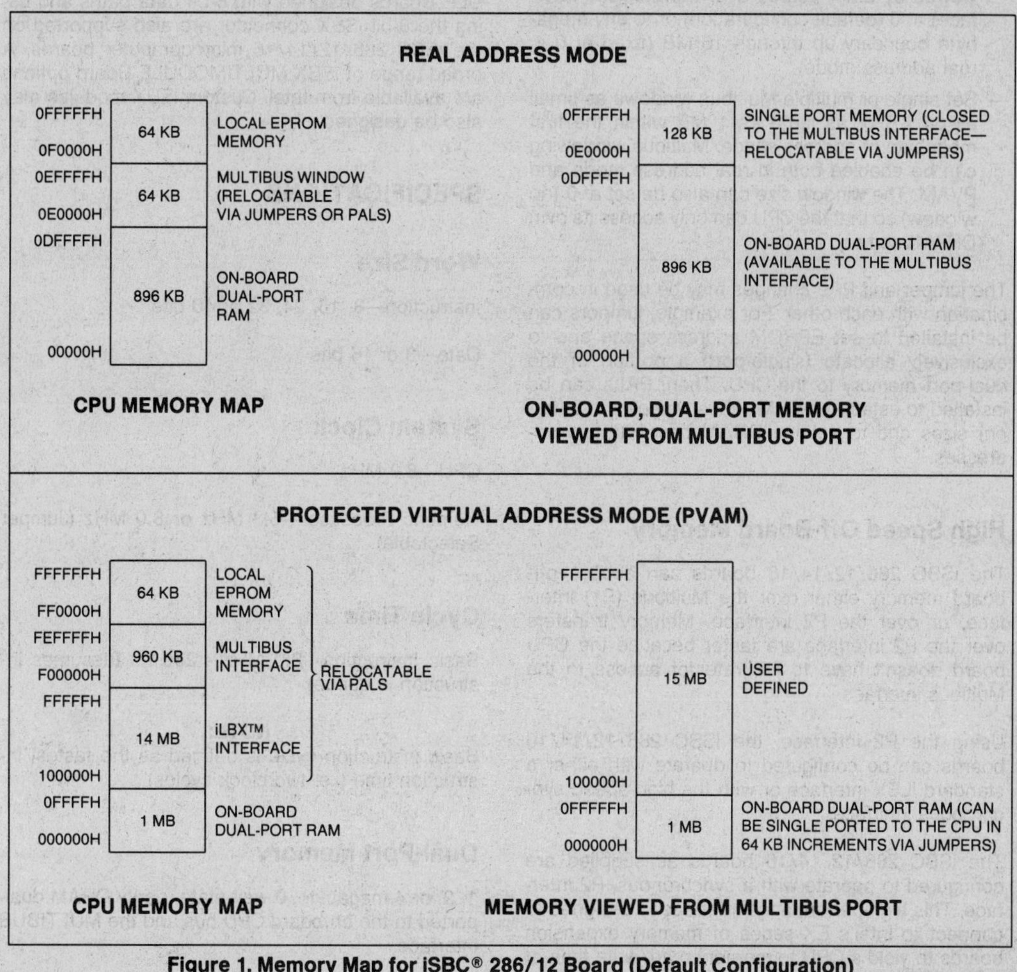

Figure 1. Memory Map for iSBC® 286/12 Board (Default Configuration)

8

sizes ranging from 4 KB (using 2716 devices) up to 256 KB (using 27512 devices and an iSBC 341 module).

If the user needs to alter the memory map further, five PALs on the baseboard are socketed and may be replaced by custom designed devices. Using programmed PALs, the designer can:

- Set the base DRAM memory starting address (as viewed by the 80286 microprocessor) at 0 (default configuration) or to any ½ megabyte boundary up through 16 MB (0 or 512 KB in real address mode).
- Set the base DRAM memory starting address (as viewed by other boards over the Multibus interface) at 0 (default configuration) or to any megabyte boundary up through 16 MB (fixed at 0 in real address mode).
- Set single or multiple Multibus windows as small as 64 KB or as large as 1 MB within the first megabyte of address space. Multibus windowing can be enabled both in real address mode and PVAM. The window size can also be set at 0 (no window) so that the CPU can only access its own DRAM memory.

The jumper and PAL changes may be used in combination with each other. For example, jumpers can be installed to set EPROM address space and to exclusively allocate (single-port) a portion of the dual-port memory to the CPU. Then, PALs can be installed to establish two Multibus windows of different sizes and to set the DRAM base starting addresses.

High Speed Off-Board Memory

The iSBC 286/12/14/16 boards can access off-board memory either over the Multibus (P1) interface, or over the P2 interface. Memory transfers over the P2 interface are faster because the CPU board doesn't have to arbitrate for access to the Multibus interface.

Using the P2 interface, the iSBC 286/12/14/16 boards can be configured to operate with either a standard iLBX interface or with the high-speed synchronous interface.

The iSBC 286/12/14/16 boards as supplied are configured to operate with a synchronous, P2 interface. This high-performance interface is designed to connect to Intel's EX series of memory expansion boards to yield a CPU to memory read/write time of 0 wait-states. The EX memory expansion boards are available in sizes ranging from 512K bytes up to 4M bytes.

A total of four memory boards can be placed on the iLBX or synchronous interface bus. With 4M byte memory boards, this results in a total of 16M bytes on the memory expansion bus.

iSBX™ Bus MULTIMODULE™ On-Board Expansion

Two 8-, 16-bit iSBX MULTIMODULE connectors are provided on the iSBC 286/12/14/16 boards. The iSBX interface connectors on the iSBC 286/12/14/16 boards provide all signals necessary to interface to the local on-board bus, including 16 data lines for maximum data transfer rates. The iSBX MULTIMODULE Boards designed with 8-bit data paths and using the 8-bit iSBX connector are also supported on the iSBC 286/12/14/16 microcomputer boards. A broad range of iSBX MULTIMODULE Board options are available from Intel. Custom iSBX modules may also be designed.

SPECIFICATIONS

Word Size

Instruction—8, 16, 24, 32 or 40 bits

Data—8 or 16 bits

System Clock

CPU—8.0 MHz

Numeric Processor—5.3 MHz or 8.0 MHz (Jumper Selectable)

Cycle Time

Basic Instruction—8.0 MHz - 250 ns (assumes instruction in queue)

NOTE:
Basic instruction cycle is defined as the fastest instruction time (i.e. two clock cycles)

Dual-Port Memory

1, 2, or 4 megabyte, 0 wait-state, parity DRAM dual-ported to the on-board CPU bus and the MULTIBUS interface.

Local Memory

Number of sockets—two 28-pin JEDEC sites, expandable to 4 sites using iSBC 341 JEDEC Expansion Module

Maximum Size—128 KB expandable to 256 KB by installing an iSBC 341 EPROM Expansion Module. Memory size is set by jumpers on the iSBC 286/12/14/16 board.

Compatible Devices—EPROM, up to 64K x 8 (Intel 27512)

Interrupt Capacity

26 interrupt sources (total); 5 hard-wired to the 8259A PIC; 21 jumper selectable

Interrupt Levels—16 vectored requests using two 8259A devices and the 80286 microprocessor's NMI line

I/O Capability

Parallel — Line printer interface, on-board functions, and 3-bit board installed options code

Serial — Two programmable channels using one 8274 device

Timers — Three programmable timers using one 8254 device

Expansion— Two 8/16-bit iSBX MULTIMODULE connectors

Interfaces

MULTIBUS Bus—All signals TTL compatible

iSBX Bus—All signals TTL compatible

iLBX Bus—All signals TTL compatible

Synchronous Interface—All signals TTL compatible

Serial I/O— Channel A: RS232C/RS422/RS449 compatible, DCE or DTE

Channel B: RS232C compatible, DCE

Timer—All signals TTL compatible

Interrupt Requests—All TTL compatible

Serial Communications Characteristics

Synchronous—5–8 bit characters; internal or HDLC/SDLC character synchronization; automatic sync insertion; even or odd parity

Asynchronous—5–8 bit characters; break character generation; 1, 1½, or 2 stop bits; false start bit detection; even or odd parity

Physical Characteristics

Width: 12.00 in. (30.48 cm)

Height: 7.05 in. (18.00 cm)

Depth: 0.88 in. (2.24 cm)
1.16 in. (2.95 cm) with iSBX MULTIMODULE board installed

Recommended Slot spacing (without iSBX MULTIMODULE): 1.2 in. (3.0 cm)

Weight: 26 oz. (731 gm)

Electrical Characteristics

DC Power Requirements:

Maximum: +5V, 8.7A; ±12V, 35 mA (for serial I/O)

Typical: +5V, 5.7A; ±12V, 20 mA

NOTE:
Power requirements are for the default configuration. Does not include power for optional EPROM, 80287 or 82258 devices, or installed iSBX MULTIMODULE boards.

Environmental Characteristics

Operating Temperature: 0°C to 60°C with 8 CFM airflow across board (default configuration)

Relative Humidity: to 90% (without condensation)

Reference Manual

147533— iSBC 286/12/14/16 Hardware Reference Manual (order separately)

ORDERING INFORMATION

Part Number	Description
SBC 286/12	Single Board Computer with 1 MB of Memory
SBC 286/14	Single Board Computer with 2 MB of Memory
SBC 286/16	Single Board Computer with 4 MB of Memory
SBC 322	2 MB DRAM Module
SBC 324	4 MB DRAM Module

iSBC® 286/10A*
SINGLE BOARD COMPUTER

- 8 MHz 80286 Microprocessor
- Supports User Installed 80287 Numeric Data Processor
- iLBX™ Interface for iLBX Memory Board Expansion
- 0 Wait-State Synchronous Interface to EX Memory Expansion Boards
- Eight JEDEC 28-Pin Sites for Optional SRAM/iRAM/EPROM/E²PROM Components
- Optional Expansion to Sixteen JEDEC 28-Pin Sites with Two iSBC® 341 Boards
- Maximum On-Board Memory Capacity 384 KB
- Two iSBX™ Bus Interface Connectors for I/O Expansion
- 16 Levels of Vectored Interrupt Control
- Centronics-Compatible Parallel I/O Printer Interface
- Two Programmable Multiprotocol Synchronous/Asynchronous Serial Interfaces; One RS232C, the Other RS232C or RS422/449 Compatible

The iSBC® 286/10A Single Board Computer is a member of Intel's complete line of microcomputer modules and systems which take advantage of Intel's VLSI technology to provide economical, off-the-shelf, computer-based solutions for OEM applications. The CPU, system clock, memory sockets, I/O ports and drivers, serial communications interface, priority interrupt logic and programmable timers all reside on the board. The iSBC 286/10A supports both the standard iLBX interface and the synchronous high speed interface (EX-series memory boards).

280079–1

*The iSBC® 286/10A is also manufactured under product code pSBC28610A by Intel Puerto Rico, Inc.

September 1991
Order Number: 280079-006

FUNCTIONAL DESCRIPTION

Overview

The iSBC 286/10A board utilizes the 80286 CPU within the Multibus system architecture, enhanced by the industry standard iLBX bus and a new, 0 wait-state, synchronous memory interface, to provide a high performance 16-bit solution. This board also includes on-board interrupt, memory and I/O features facilitating a complete signal board computer system.

Central Processing Unit

The central processor for the iSBC 286/10A board is the 80286 CPU operating at a 8.0 MHz clock rate. The 80286 CPU runs 8088 and 86 code at substantially higher speeds due to it's parallel chip architecture. In addition, the 80286 CPU provides on chip memory management and protection and virtual memory addressing of up to 1 gigabyte per task. Numeric processing power may be enhanced with the user installed 80287 numerics processor. The clock rates for the 80286 and the 80287 are independent with the 80287 rate jumper selectable at either 5.3 or 8.0 MHz.

Instruction Set

The 80286 instruction repertoire includes variable length instruction format (including double operand instructions), 8-bit and 16-bit signed and unsigned arithmetic operators for binary, BCD and unpacked ASCII data, and iterative word and byte string manipulation functions.

For enhanced numerics processing capability, the 80287 Numeric Data Processor extends the 80286 architecture and data set. Over 60 numeric instructions offer arithmetic, trigonometric, transcendental, logarithmic and exponential instructions. Supported data types include 16-, 32-, and 64-bit integer, 32- and 64-bit floating point, 18-digit packed BCD and 80-bit temporary.

Architectural Features

The 8086, 8088, 80186 and the 80286 microprocessor family contains the same basic set of registers, instructions, and addressing modes. The 80286 processor is upward compatible with the 8086, 8088, and 80186 CPUs.

The 80286 operates in two modes: 8086 real address mode, and protected virtual address mode. In 8086 real address mode, programs use real address with up to one megabyte of address space. Programs use virtual addresses in protected virtual address mode, also called protected mode. In protected mode, the 80286 CPU automatically maps 1 gigabyte of virtual addresses per task into a 16 megabyte real address space. This mode also provides memory protection to isolate the operating system and ensure privacy of each task's programs and data. Both modes provide the same base instruction set, registers, and addressing modes.

VECTORED INTERRUPT CONTROL

Incoming interrupts are handled by two on-board 8259A programmable interrupt controllers and by the 80286's NMI line. Interrupts originating from up to 16 sources are prioritized and then sent to the CPU as a vector address. Further interrupt capability is available through bus vectored interrupts where slave 8259A interrupt controllers are resident on separate iSBC boards and are then cascaded into the on-board interrupt control.

INTERRUPT SOURCES

Twenty-three potential interrupt sources are routed to the interrupt jumper matrix where the user can connect the desired interrupt sources to specific interrupt levels.

MEMORY CAPABILITIES

There are a total of eight 28-pin JEDEC sites on board. Four sites are for local memory and can contain up to 256K bytes of EPROM devices. The four other sites are known as the dual-port memory and may be addressed by the Multibus interface and the on-board CPU bus. Up to 128K bytes of either iRAM, SRAM, EPROM, or E^{2}PROM can reside in these sites. Both the local and dual-port memory can be expanded to eight sites each by using two iSBC 341 JEDEC expansion modules. In this way, smaller size memory devices can be used up to the 256KB (local) and 128KB (dual-port) memory capacities.

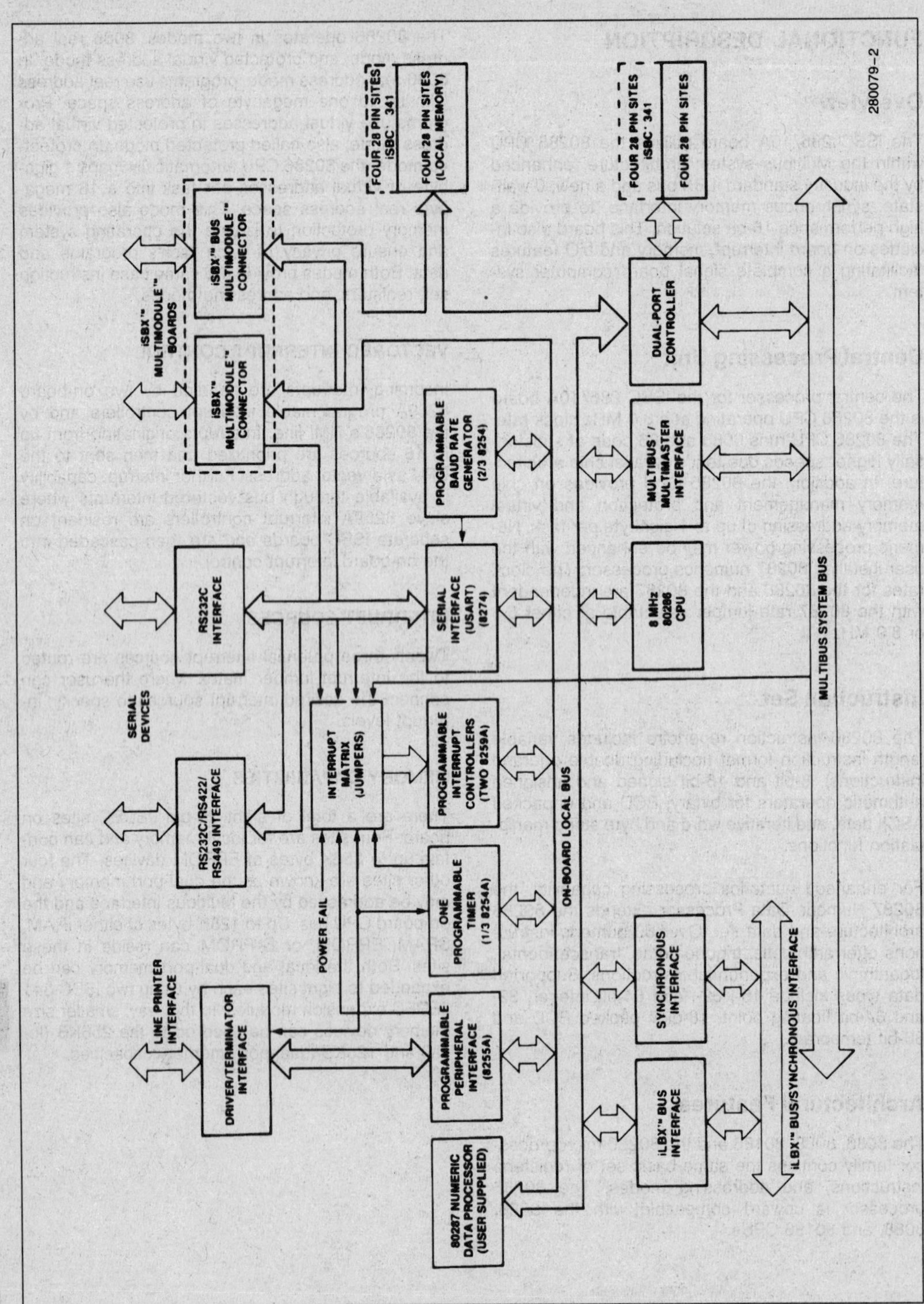

Figure 1. iSBC® 286/10A Block Diagram

SERIAL I/O

A two channel serial communications interface using Intel's 8274 Multi-Protocol Serial Controller (MPSC) is contained on the iSBC 286/10 board. Two independent software selectable baud rate generators provide the MPSC with all common communication frequencies. The protocol (i.e., asynchronous, IBM* bisync, or SDLC/HDLC), data format, control character format, parity and baud rate are all under program control. Software interfacing to the MPSC can be via either a polled or interrupt driven routine. One channel may be configured for an RS232C or RS422/RS449 interface with the other channel RS232C only.

PROGRAMMABLE TIMERS

The iSBC 286/10A board provides three independent, fully programmable 16-bit interval timers/event counters utilizing the Intel 8254 Programmable Interval Timer. Each counter is capable of operating in either BCD or binary modes. Two of these timers/counters are available to the systems designer to generate accurate time intervals under software control. Routing for the outputs of these counters is jumper selectable. The outputs may be independently routed to the 8259A Programmable Interrupt Controller or to the 8274 MPSC to count external events or provide baud rate generation. The third interval timer in the 8254 is dedicated to providing a clock for the programmable baud rate generator in the iSBC 286/10A board's MPSC serial controller.

LINE PRINTER INTERFACE

An 8255A Programmable Peripheral Interface (PPI) provides a line printer interface, several on-board functions, and four non-dedicated input bits. Drivers are provided for a complete Centronics compatible line printer interface.

MULTIMASTER CAPABILITIES

The iSBC 286/10A board provides full system bus arbitration control logic. This control logic allows up to three iSBC 286/10A boards or other bus masters, to share the system bus using a serial (daisy chain) priority scheme and allows up to 16 masters to share the Multibus system bus with an external parallel priority decoder.

HIGH SPEED OFF-BOARD MEMORY

The iSBC 286/10A board can access off-board memory either over the Multibus (P1) interface, or over the P2 interface. Memory transfers over the P2 interface are faster because the CPU board doesn't have to arbitrate for access to the Multibus interface Using the P2 interface, the iSBC 286/10A Board can be configured to operate with either a standard iLBX interface or with a high-performance, synchronous interface.

The iSBC 286/10A Board as supplied is configured to operate with a synchronous, P2 interface. This high-performance interface is designed to connect to Intel's new EX series of memory expansion boards to yield a CPU to memory read/write time of 0 wait-states. The EX memory expansion boards are available in sizes ranging from 512K bytes up to 4M bytes and available in sizes ranging from 512K bytes up to 2M bytes. Memory expansion boards from other manufacturers that meet the iLBX standard may also be used. CPU to memory access time is usually 1 or more wait-states depending on the speed of the memory used.

A total of four memory boards can be placed on the iLBX or synchronous interface bus. With 4M byte memory boards, this results in a total of 16M bytes on the memory expansion bus.

iSBX™ BUS MULTIMODULE™ ON-BOARD EXPANSION

Two 8/16-bit iSBX MULTIMODULE connectors are provided on the iSBC 286/10A microcomputer board. The iSBX interface connectors on the iSBC 286/10A provide all signals necessary to interface to the local on-board bus, including 16 data lines for maximum data transfer rates. iSBX MULTIMODULE boards designed with 8-bit data paths and using the 8-bit iSBX connector are also supported on the iSBC 286/10A microcomputer board. A broad range of iSBX MULTIMODULE options are available from Intel. Custom iSBX modules may also be designed.

SPECIFICATIONS

Word Size

Instruction—8, 16, 24, 32 or 40 bits
Data—8 or 16 bits

System Clock

CPU—8.0 MHz
Numeric Processor—5.3 or 8.0 MHz (Jumper Selectable)

Cycle Time

Basic Instruction—8.0 MHz—375 ns; 250 ns (assumes instruction in queue)

8

NOTE:
Basic instruction cycle is defined as the fastest instruction time (i.e., two clock cycles)

Local Memory

Number of sockets—Four 28-pin JEDEC sites, expandable to 8 sites using iSBC 341 JEDEC Expansion Module

Maximum Size—256 KB

Compatible Devices—EPROM, up to 64K x 8 (Intel 27512)

Dual-Port Memory

Number of sockets—Four 28-pin JEDEC sites, expandable to 8 sites using iSBC 341 JEDEC Expansion Module

Maximum Size—128 KB

Compatible Devices—EPROM, up to 32K x 8 (Intel 27256)

SRAM
iRAM, up to 8K x 8 (Intel 2186)
E²PROM, up to 2K x 8 (Intel 2817A)

I/O Capability

Parallel—Line printer interface, on-board functions, and four non-dedicated input bits

Serial—Two programmable channels using one 8274 device

Timers—Three programmable timers using one 8254 device

Expansion—Two 8/16-bit iSBX MULTIMODULE connectors

Serial Communications Characteristics

Synchronous—5–8 bit characters; internal or HDLC/SDLC character synchronization; automatic sync insertion; even or odd parity

Asynchronous—5–8 bit characters; break character generation; 1, 1½, or 2 stop bits; false start bit detection; even or odd parity

Interrupt Capacity

Potential Interrupt Sources—25, 5 fixed, 20 jumper selectable

Interrupt Levels—16 vectored requests using two 8259As and the 80286's NMI line.

INTERFACES

MULTIBUS Bus—All signals TTL compatible

iSBX Bus—All signals TTL compatible

iLBX Bus—All signals TTL compatible

Synchronous Interface—All signals TTL compatible

Serial I/O—Channel A: RS232C/RS422/RS449 compatible, DCE or DTE; Channel B; RS232C compatible, DCE only

Timer—All signals TTL compatible

Interrupt Requests—All TTL compatible

Physical Characteristics

Width: 12.00 in. (30.48 cm)
Height: 6.75 in. (17.15 cm)
Depth: 0.4 in. (1.0 cm)
Minimum Slot Spacing: 0.6 in. (1.5 cm)
Weight: 14 oz. (397 gm)

Electrical Characteristics

DC Power Requirements: +5V, 7.0A; ±12V, 50 mA (serial I/O)

NOTE:
Does not include power for optional EPROM, E²PROM, or RAM memory devices, or installed MULTIMODULE boards

Environmental Characteristics

Operating Temperature: 0°C to 60°C with 7 CFM airflow across board

Relative Humidity: to 90% (without condensation)

Reference Manual

147532—iSBC® 286/10A Hardware Reference Manual (order separately)

ORDERING INFORMATION

Order Code	Description
SBC 286/10A	Single Board Computer

intel®

iSBC® 186/03A* SINGLE BOARD COMPUTER

- 8.0 MHz 80186 Microprocessor with Optional 8087 Numeric Data Processor
- Eight (Expandable to 12) JEDEC 28-Pin Sites
- Six Programmable Timers and 27 Levels of Vectored Interrupt Control
- Multibus Interface for System Expansion and Multimaster Configuration
- 24 Programmable I/O Lines Configurable as a SCSI Interface, Centronics Interface or General Purpose I/O
- Two iSBX™ Bus Interface Connectors for Low Cost I/O Expansion
- iLBX™ (Local Bus Extension) Interface for High-Speed Memory Expansion
- Two Programmable Serial Interfaces; One RS 232C, the Other RS 232C or RS 422 Compatible

The iSBC 186/03A Single Board Computer is a member of Intel's complete line of microcomputer modules and systems that take advantage of Intel's VLSI technology to provide economical, off-the-shelf, computer-based solutions for OEM applications. The board is a complete microcomputer system on a 7.05 x 12.0 inch printed circuit card. The CPU, system clock, memory, sockets, I/O ports and drivers, serial communications interface, priority interrupt logic and programmable timers, all reside on the board.

The iSBC 186/03A board incorporates the 80186 CPU and SCSI interface on one board. The extensive use of high integration VLSI has produced a high-performance single-board system. For large memory applications, the iLBX local bus expansion maintains this high performance.

230988–1

*The iSBC® 186/03A board is also manufactured under product code pSBC 186/03A by Intel Puerto Rico, Inc.

September 1991
Order Number: 230988-006

OVERVIEW

Operating Environment

The iSBC 186/03A single board computer features have been designed to meet the needs of numerous microcomputer applications. Typical applications include:

- Multiprocessing single board computer
- BITBUS master controller
- Stand-alone singel board system

MULTIPROCESSING SINGLE BOARD COMPUTER

High-performance systems often need to divide system functions among multiple processors. A multiprocessing single board computer distributes an applications processing load over multiple processors that communicate over a system bus. Since these applications use the system bus for inter-processor communication, it is required that each processor has local execution memory.

The iSBC 186/03A board supports loosely coupled multiprocessing (where each processor performs a specific function) through its Multibus compatible architecture. The IEEE 796 system bus facilitates processor to processor communication, while the iLBX bus makes high-speed data and execution memory available to each CPU as shown in Figure 1. This architecture allows multiple processors to run in parallel enabling very high-performance applications.

BITBUS™ MASTER CONTROLLER

The BITBUS interconnect environment is a high performance low-cost microcontroller interconnect technology for distributed control of intelligent industrial machines such as robots and process controllers. The BITBUS interconnect is a special purpose serial bus which is ideally suited for the fast transmission of short messages between the microcontroller nodes in a modularly distributed system.

The iSBC 186/03A board can be implemented as the Multibus-based master controller CPU which monitors, processes and updates the control status of the distributed system. The iSBX 344 board is used to interface the iSBC 186/03A board to the BITBUS interconnect. Actual message transfer over the iSBX bus can be accomplished by either software polling by the CPU or by using the on-chip 80186 DMA hardware instead of the CPU. Using DMA, the CPU is only required to start the DMA process and then poll for the completion of the message transfer, thus dramatically improving the data transmission rate and master control processor efficiency. The maximum transfer rates over the iSBX bus for the iSBC 186/03A board are about 900 messages/second in polled mode and 2500 messages/second in DMA mode. An 8 MHz iSBC 186/03A board in DMA mode is 3 times as fast as a typical 5 MHz iSBC 86/30 board running in polled mode. The iSBC 186/03A board in DMA mode provides the highest performance/price solution for BITBUS message transmission out of all of Intel's complete line of 16-bit CPU modules.

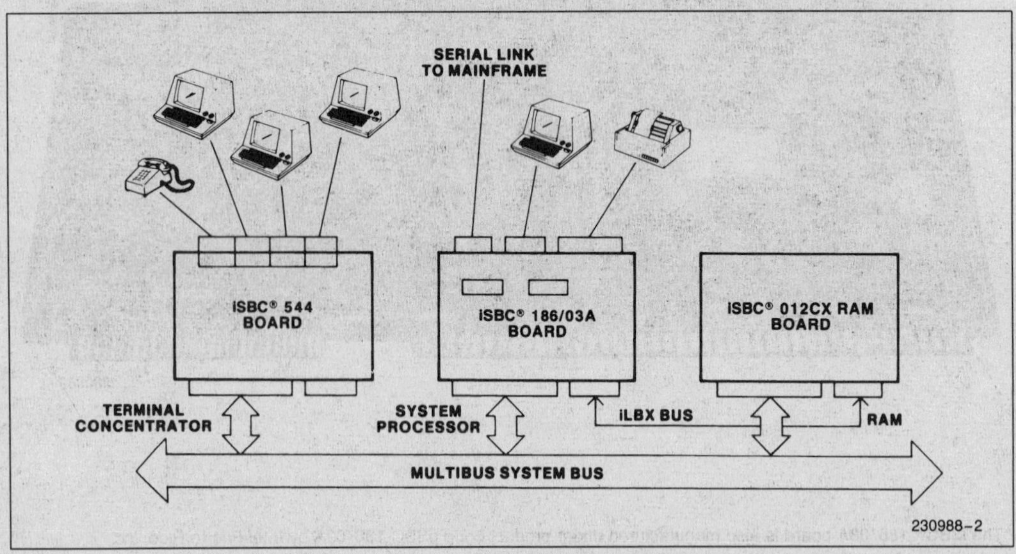

Figure 1. A Multiprocessing Single Board Computer Application

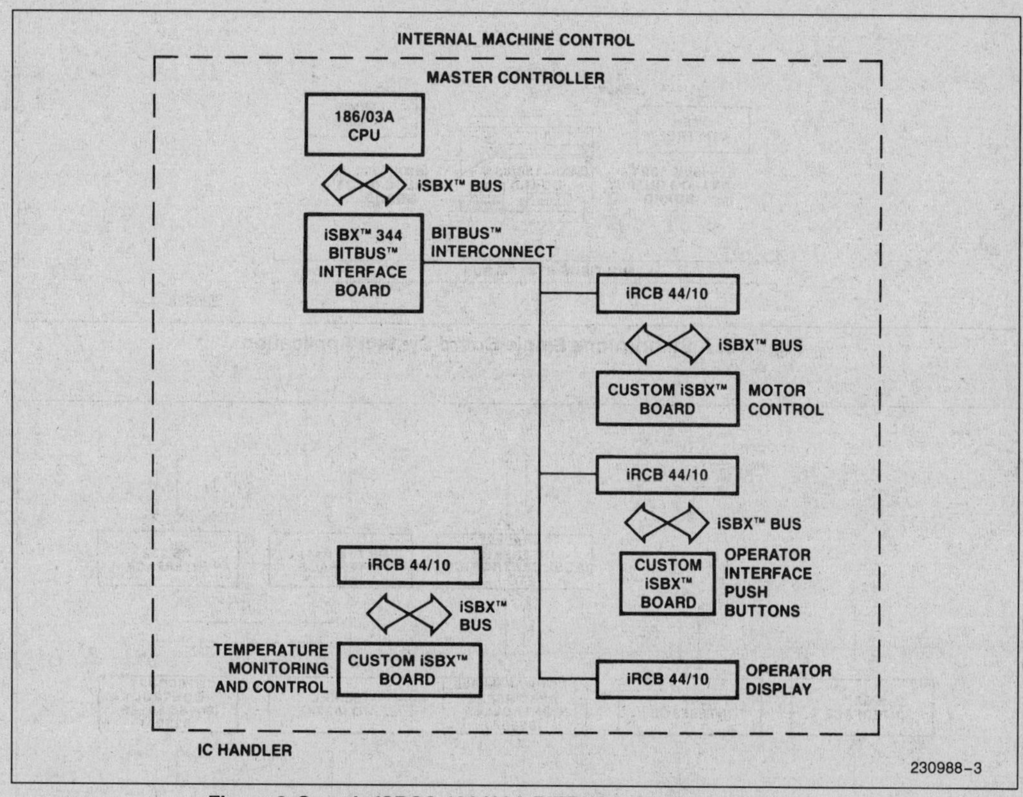

Figure 2. Sample iSBC® 186/03A BITBUS™ Master Application

STAND-ALONE SINGLE BOARD SYSTEM

A stand-alone single board system is a complete computer system on one board. By reducing the system's board count, the single board system saves space, power, and ultimately, costs. The on-board resources need to be capable of performing all of the basic system functions. These applications typically require terminal support, peripheral control, local RAM and program execution. In previous generations of single board computers, these functions could only be obtained with multiple board solutions.

The iSBC 186/03A board integrates all the functions of a general purpose system (CPU, memory, I/O and peripheral control) onto one board. The iSBC 186/03A board can also be customized as a single board system by the selection of memory and iSBX I/O options. The board's 8 JEDEC 28-pin sockets can accommodate a wide variety of byte-wide memory devices.

If more memory is needed, an optional iSBC 341 memory site expansion board can be added to provide an additional four JEDEC sites. Two iSBX MULTIMODULE™ boards can be added to the iSBC 186/03A board to customize the board's I/O capabilities. As shown in Figure 3, the iSBX connectors can support a single-board system with the analog input and output modules needed by machine or process control systems.

FUNCTIONAL DESCRIPTION

Architecture

The iSBC 186/03A board is functionally partitioned into six major sections: central processor, memory, SCSI compatible parallel interface, serial I/O, interrupt control and Multibus bus expansion. These areas are illustrated in Figure 4.

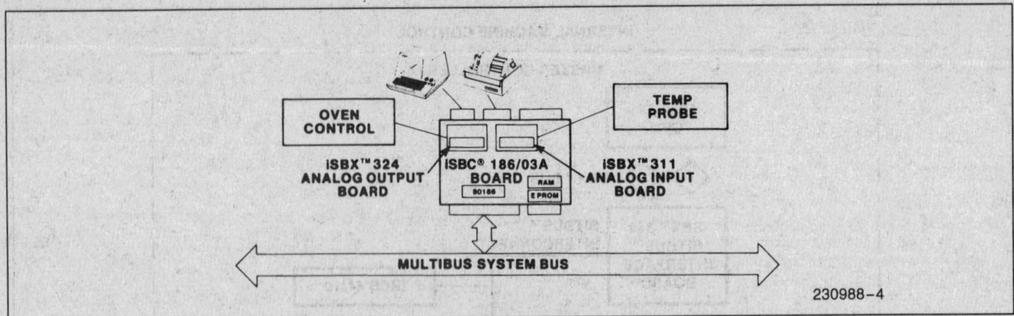

Figure 3. A Stand-Alone Single Board System Application

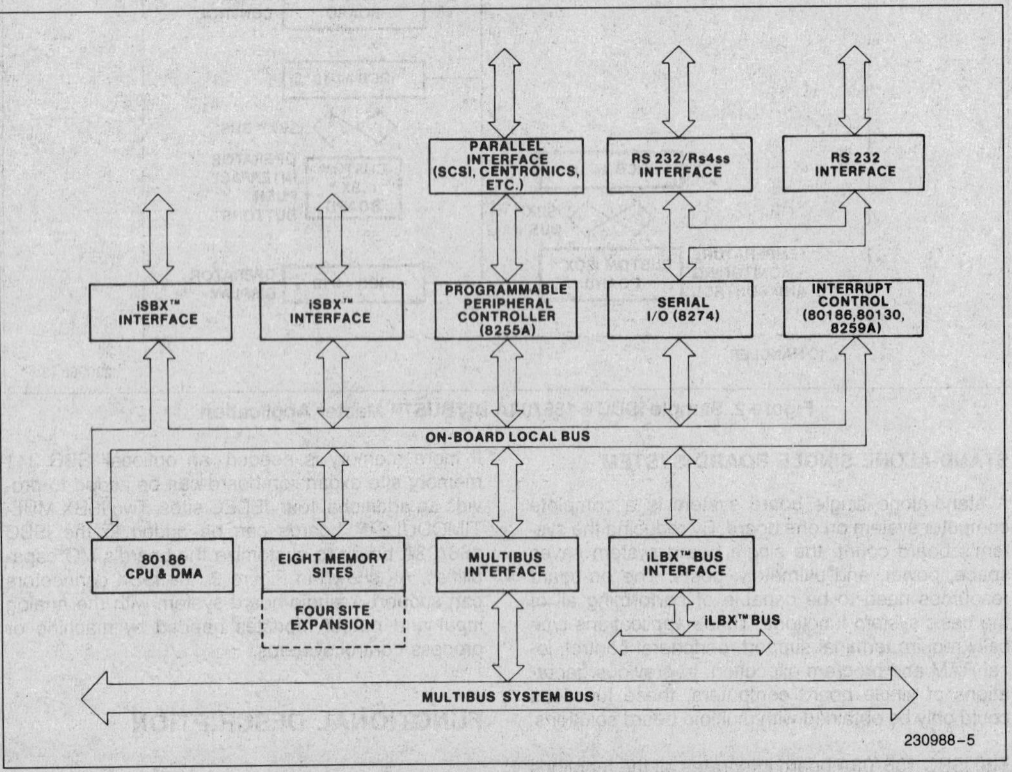

Figure 4. iSBC® 186/03A Board Block Diagram

CENTRAL PROCESSOR

The 80186 component is a high-integration 16-bit microprocessor. It combines several of the most common system components onto a single chip (i.e. Direct Memory Access, Interval Timers, Clock Generator and Programmable Interrupt Controller). The 80186 instruction set is a superset of the 8086. It maintains object code compatability while adding ten new instructions. Added instructions include: Block I/O, Enter and Leave subroutines, Push Immediate, Multiply Quick, Array Bounds Checking, Shift and Rotate by Immediate, and Pop and Push All.

Use of the 80130 component is limited to the 3 timers and 8 levels of interrupts available. Direct processor execution of the 16K bytes of iRMX I Operating System nucleus primitives is not supported.

An optional 8087 Numeric Data Processor may be installed by the user to dramatically improve the 186/03A board's numerical processing power. The interface between the 8087 and 80186 is provided by the factory-installed 82188 Integrated Bus Controller which completes the 80186 numeric data processing system. The 8087 Numeric Data Processor option adds 68 floating-point instructions and eight 80-bit floating point registers to the basic iSBC 186/03A board's programming capabilities. Depending on the application, the 8087 will increase the performance of floating point calculations by 50 to 100 times.

TIMERS

The 80186 provides three internal 16-bit programmable timers. Two of these are highly flexible and are connected to four external pins (two per timer). They can be used to count external events, time external events, generate nonrepetitive waveforms, etc. As shipped on the iSBC 186/03A board, these two timers are connected to the serial interface, and provide baud rate generation. The third timer is not connected to any external pins, and is useful for real-time coding and time-delay applications. In addition, this third timer can be used as a prescaler to the other two, or as a DMA request source. The 80130 provides three more programmable timers. One is a factory default baud rate generator and outputs an 8254 compatible square wave that can be used as an alternate baud rate source to either serial channel. The 80130's second timer is used as a system timer. The third timer is reserved for use by the iRMX Operating System. The system software configures each timer independently to select the desired function. Available functions include: interrupt on terminal count, programmable one-shot, rate generator, square-wave generator, software triggered strobe, hardware triggered strobe and event counter. The contents of each counter may be read at any time during system operation.

MEMORY

There are eight JEDEC 28-pin memory sites on the iSBC 186/03A board providing flexible memory expansion. Four of these sites (EPROM sites) may be used for EPROM or E^{2}PROM program storage, while the other four (RAM sites) may be used for static RAM or iRAM data storage or used as additional program storage. The eight sites can be extended to twelve by the addition of an iSBC 341 MULTIMODULE board. These additional sites will provide up to 64K bytes of RAM using 8K x 8 SRAM or iRAM devices. The EPROM sites (Bank B) are compatible with 8K x 8 (2764), 16K x 8 (27128A), 32K x 8 (27256), 64K x 8 (27512) as well as 2K x 8 (2817A) and 8K x 8 (2864) E^{2}PROMs. The RAM sites (Bank A) are compatible with all bytewide SRAM, iRAM or NVRAM devices. NVRAM usage requires additional circuitry in order to guarantee data retention. Bank A can be reassigned to upper memory just below the assigned memory space for Bank B to support additional EPROM or E^{2}PROMs.

Memory addressing for the JEDEC sites depends on the device type selected. The four EPROM sites are top justified in the 1 MB address space and must contain the power-on instructions. The device size determines the starting address of these devices. The four RAM sites are, by default, located starting at address 0. The addressing of these sites may be relocated to upper memory (immediately below the EPROM site addresses) in applications where these sites will contain additional program storage. The optional iSBC 341 MULTIMODULE sites are addressable immediately above the RAM site addresses.

Power-fail control and auxiliary power are provided for protection of the RAM sites when used with static RAM devices. A memory protect signal is provided through an auxiliary connector (J4) which, when asserted, disables read/write access to RAM memory on the board. This input is provided for the protection of RAM contents during system power-down sequences. An auxiliary power bus is also provided to allow separate power to RAM for systems requiring battery back-up of read/write memory. Selection of this auxiliary RAM power bus is made via jumpers on the board.

SCSI PERIPHERAL INTERFACE

The iSBC 186/03A board includes a parallel peripheral interface that consists of three 8-bit parallel ports. As shipped, these ports are configured for general purpose I/O. The parallel interface may be reconfigured to be compatible with the SCSI disk interface by adding two user-supplied and programmed Programmable Array Logic (PAL) devices, moving jumpers and installing a user-supplied 74LS640-1 device. Alternatively, the parallel interface may be reconfigured as a DMA controlled Centronics compatible line printer interface by adding one PAL and changing jumpers. Refer to the iSBC 186/03A Hardware Reference Manual for PAL equations and a detailed implementation procedure.

The SCSI (Small Computer Systems Interface) interface allows up to 8 mass storage peripherals such as Winchester disk drives, floppy disk drives and tape drives to be connected directly to the iSBC 186/03A board. Intel's iSBC 186/03A board utilizes a single initiator, single target implementation of the SCSI bus specification. Bus arbitration and deselect/reselect SCSI features are not supported. Single host, multiple target configurations can be used. However, the iSBC 186/03A board will stay connected to one target until the transaction is completed before switching to the second target. The iSBC 186/03A board's SCSI interface implements a 5 megabit/second transfer rate. A sample SCSI application is shown in Figure 5.

The Centronics interface requires very little software overhead since a PAL device is used to provide necessary handshake timing. Interrupts are generated for printer fault conditions and a DMA request is issued for every character. The interface supports Centronics type printers compatible with models 702 and 737.

SERIAL I/O

The iSBC 186/03A Single Board Computer contains two programmable communications interfaces using the Intel 8274 Multi-Protocol Serial Controller (MPSC).

Two 80186 timer outputs are used as software selectable baud rate generators capable of supplying the serial channels with common communications frequencies. An 80130 baud rate timer may be jumpered to either serial port to provide higher frequency baud rates. The mode of operation (i.e., asynchronous, byte synchronous or bisynchronous protocols), data format, control character format, parity, and baud rate are all under program control. The 8274 provides full duplex, double buffered transmit and receive capability. Parity, overrun, and framing error detection are all incorporated in the MPSC. The iSBC 186/03A board supports operation in the polled, interrupt and DMA driven interfaces through jumper options. The default configuration is with channel A as RS422A/RS449, channel B as RS232C. Channel A can optionally be configured to support RS232C. Both channels are default configured as data set (DCE). Channel A can be reconfigured as data terminal (DTE) for connection to a modem-type device.

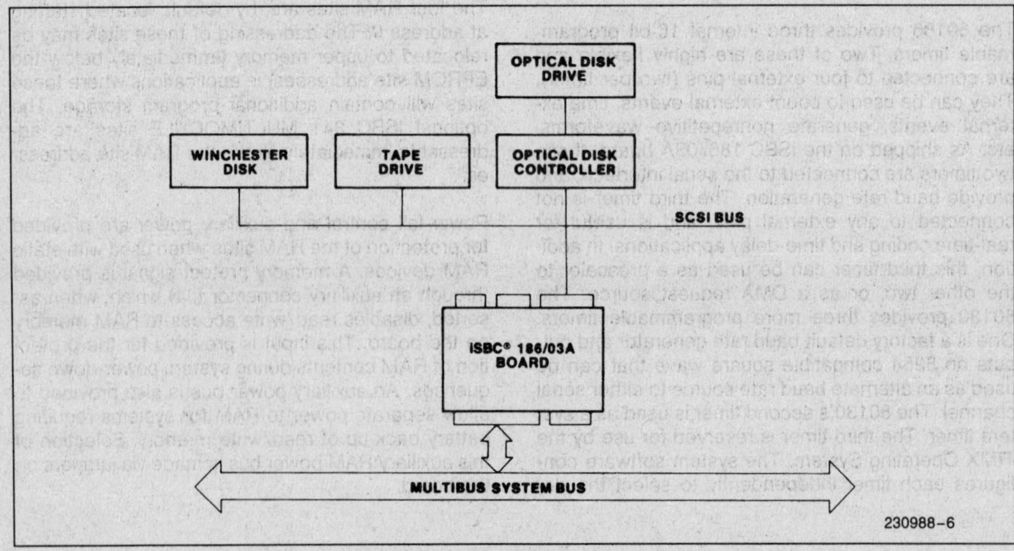

Figure 5. Sample SCSI Application

INTERRUPT CONTROL

The iSBC 186/03A board provides 27 on-board vectored interrupt levels to service interrupts generated from 33 possible sources.

The interrupts are serviced by four programmable interrupt controllers (PICs): one in the 80186 component, one in the 80130 component, one in the 8259A component and one in the 8274 component. The 80186, 8259A and 8274 PICs act as slaves to the 80130 master PIC. The highest priority interrupt is the Non-Maskable Interrupt (NMI) line which is tied directly to the 80186 CPU. This interrupt is typically used to signal catastrophic events (e.g. power failure). The PICs provide prioritization and vectoring for the other 26 interrupt requests from on-board I/O resources and from the Multibus system bus. The PICs then resolve the requests according to the programmable priority resolution mode, and if appropriate, issue an interrupt to the CPU.

MULTIBUS SYSTEM BUS—IEEE 796

The Multibus system bus is an industry standard (IEEE 796) microcomputer bus structure. Both 8- and 16-bit single board computers are supported on the IEEE 796 structure with 20 or 24 address and 16 data lines. In its simplest application, the system bus allows expansion of functions already contained on a single board computer (e.g., memory and I/O). However, the IEEE 796 bus also allows very powerful distributed processing configurations with multiple processors and intelligent slave, I/O and peripheral boards capable of solving the most demanding microcomputer applications. The Multibus system bus is supported with a broad array of board-level products, LSI interface components, detailed published specifications and application notes.

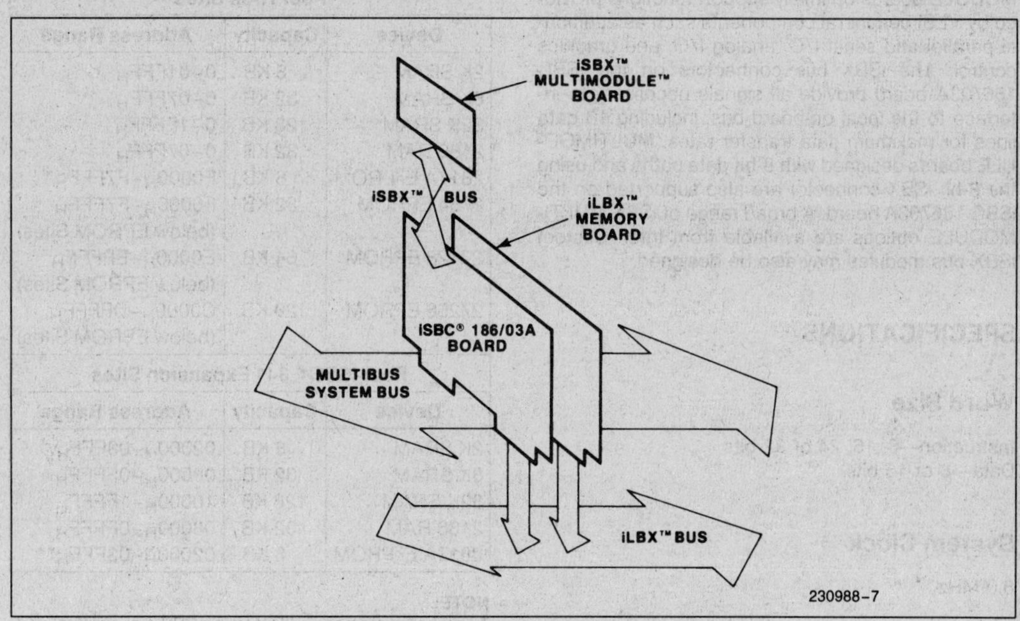

Figure 6. iSBC® 186/03A Board System Architecture

iLBX™ BUS—LOCAL BUS EXTENSION

The iSBC 186/03A board provides a local bus extension (iLBX) interface. This standard extension allows on-board memory performance with physically off-board memory. The combination of a CPU board and iLBX memory boards is architecturally equivalent to a single board computer and thus can be called a "virtual single board computer". The iLBX bus is implemented over the P2 connector and requires independent cabling or backplane connection.

iSBX™ BUS MULTIMODULE™ ON-BOARD EXPANSION

Two iSBX MULTIMODULE board connectors are provided on the iSBC 186/03A microcomputer board. Through these connectors, additional on-board I/O functions may be added. iSBX MULTIMODULE boards optimally support functions provided by VLSI peripheral components such as additional parallel and serial I/O, analog I/O, and graphics control. The iSBX bus connectors on the iSBC 186/03A board provide all signals necessary to interface to the local on-board bus, including 16 data lines for maximum data transfer rates. MULTIMODULE boards designed with 8-bit data paths and using the 8-bit iSBX connector are also supported on the iSBC 186/03A board. A broad range of iSBX MULTIMODULE options are available from Intel. Custom iSBX bus modules may also be designed.

SPECIFICATIONS

Word Size

Instruction—8, 16, 24 or 32 bits
Data—8 or 16 bits

System Clock

8.0 MHz

Numeric Data Processor (Optional)

8087-1

Basic Instruction Cycle Time

750 ns
250 ns (assumes instruction in the queue)

NOTE:
Basic instruction cycle is defined as the fastest instruction time (i.e. two clock cycles plus instruction fetch). Zero wait-state memory is assumed.

MEMORY CAPACITY/ADDRESSING

Four EPROM Sites		
Device	**Capacity**	**Address Range**
2764 EPROM	32 KB	$F8000_H$–$FFFFF_H$
27128 EPROM	64 KB	$F0000_H$–$FFFFF_H$
27256 EPROM	128 KB	$E0000_H$–$FFFFF_H$
27512 EPROM	256 KB	$C0000_H$–$FFFFF_H$
Four RAM Sites		
Device	**Capacity**	**Address Range**
2K SRAM	8 KB	0–$01FFF_H$
8K SRAM	32 KB	0–$07FFF_H$
32K SRAM	128 KB	0–$1FFFF_H$
2186 RAM	32 KB	0–$07FFF_H$
2817A E^2PROM	8 KB	$F0000_H$–$F7FFF_H$*
2764 EPROM	32 KB	$F0000_H$–$F7FFF_H$ (below EPROM Sites)
27128 EPROM	64 KB	$E0000_H$–$EFFFF_H$ (below EPROM Sites)
27256 EPROM	128 KB	$C0000_H$–$DFFFF_H$ (below EPROM Sites)
Four iSBC® 341 Expansion Sites		
Device	**Capacity**	**Address Range**
2K SRAM	8 KB	02000_H–$03FFF_H$
8K SRAM	32 KB	08000_H–$0FFFF_H$
32K SRAM	128 KB	10000_H–$1FFFF_H$
2186 RAM	32 KB	08000_H–$0FFFF_H$
2817A E^2PROM	8 KB	02000_H–$03FFF_H$**

NOTE:
All on board memory is local to the CPU (i.e. not dual-ported).

*Must use 8k x 8 decode option, there are four copies of the E^2PROM in the 8K x 8 address area.

**(May be mixed with 2K x 8 SRAM)

Serial Communications Characteristics

Synchronous— 5–8 bit characters, internal or external character synchronization; automatic sync insertion; break character generation

Asynchronous— 5–8 bit characters; 1, ½, or 2 stop bit; false start bit detection.

Interface Compliance

MULTIBUS— IEEE 796 compliance: Master D16 M24 116 VO EL

iSBX Bus— Two 8/16 bit iSBX bus connectors allow use of up to 2 single-wide modules or 1 single-wide and 1 double-wide module. Intel iSBX bus compliance: D16/16 DMA

iLBX— Intel iLBX bus compliance: PM D16

Serial— Channel A: Configurable as RS 422A or RS 232C compatible, configurable as a data set or data terminal

Channel B: RS 232C compatible, configured as data set

Parallel I/O— SCSI (ANSI—X3T9, 2/82-s) compatible or Centronics 702 or 737 compatible (requires user supplied PALs and 74LS640-1)

ORDERING INFORMATION

Part Number	Description
SBC 186/03A	186-based Single Board Computer

REFERENCE MANUAL

iSBC® 186/03A Single Board Computer Hardware Reference Manual—Order Number 148060

PHYSICAL CHARACTERISTICS

Width: 12.00 in. (30.48 cm)

Length: 7.05 in (17.90 cm)

Height: 0.50 in. (1.78 cm)

Weight: 13 ounces

ENVIRONMENTAL CHARACTERISTICS

Operating Temperature: 0°C to 60°C at 6 CFM airflow over the board.

Relative Humidity: to 90% (without condensation)

ELECTRICAL CHARACTERISTICS

The maximum power required per voltage is shown below. These numbers do not include the power required by the optional memory devices, SCSI PALs, battery back-up or expansion modules.

Voltage (volts)	Max. Current (amps)	Max Power (watts)
+5	5.4	27
+12	0.04	0.48
−12	0.04	0.48

iSBC® 86C/38* SINGLE BOARD COMPUTER

280630-1

CMOS 80C86-BASED MULTIBUS I SINGLE-BOARD COMPUTER

The iSBC® 86C/38 Single-Board Computer is a high-performance, low-power Multibus I CPU board based on advanced CMOS (complementary metal oxide semiconductor) technology. The board features Intel's 8 MHz 80C86 microprocessor—which provides the highest performance possible with static CMOS devices—a full megabyte of zero wait state DRAM memory, and power consumption of typically less than 8 watts when operating at full speed. The board's high performance, low power consumption, low heat generation and high reliability make it ideal for embedded real-time applications in harsh industrial environments.

STANDARD FEATURES

- Advanced CMOS 8 MHz 80C86 microprocessor
- 1 Mbyte of dual-port, zero wait state DRAM with parity
- Sockets for up to 512 Kbytes of standard 32-pin JEDEC EPROM devices
- Real-time clock/calendar with on-board battery backup
- Temperature-sensing device socket
- Optional 8087 numeric data processor with iSBC 337A MULTIMODULE™
- Upward-compatible with iSBC 86/35
- iRMX® I Real-Time Operating System support

*The iSBC® 86C/38 Board is also manufactured under product code pSBC86C38 by Intel Puerto Rico, Inc.

November 1990
Order Number: 280630-002

FEATURES

CMOS TECHNOLOGY FOR LOW POWER, LOW HEAT

The Intel iSBC 86C/38 has been implemented entirely in CMOS, from the 80C86 CPU and EPLDs to the discrete logic and peripheral components. CMOS means low power consumption and low heat generation.

When running at full speed (8 MHz), the iSBC 86C/38 typically requires less than 8 watts of power. However, a power-saving Slow Mode further reduces power consumption to about 4 watts when operating speed is reduced to 1 MHz.

Slow Mode operation is especially useful during temporary or emergency conditions when battery power is called into use. In a power-fail situation, for instance, Slow Mode operation allows the uninterrupted processing of an application on battery power.

The iSBC 86C/38 generates so little heat that it can operate without any air flow. This allows elimination of fans and other expensive cooling equipment and operation of the iSBC 86C/38 in a sealed enclosure, protected from harsh environments.

HIGH RELIABILITY

The iSBC 86C/38 features improved reliability on several levels. First, CMOS technology is inherently more reliable than NMOS technology: because devices run at lower junction temperatures, they last longer.

Parity error checking in the DRAM circuitry improves system integrity by detecting memory errors.

Finally, improved pin and socket I/O connectors with locking tabs assure secure connections of cables to the board.

MORE MEMORY

The amount of on-board memory has been doubled in the iSBC 86C/38 from earlier iSBC 86/35 board models. The iSBC 86C/38 comes with a full megabyte of zero wait state dynamic RAM, supporting the full 8086 address space. A full megabyte of on-board memory also eliminates the need to add DRAM modules, preserving the economy of a single-slot solution.

UPWARD-COMPATIBILITY WITH iSBC® 86/35 DESIGNS

The iSBC 86C/38 provides complete hardware and software compatibility with Intel iSBC 86/35 designs. All features supported on the iSBC 86/35 board run on the iSBC 86C/38 board with no changes. This includes full access to the Multibus I 16 Mbyte memory address range and support for Multibus I multimaster, 8087 math coprocessor, iSBC 86/35 I/O devices, iSBX connectors and interrupt capability.

PERFECT FOR REAL-TIME EMBEDDED APPLICATIONS

Real-time process control and industrial automation applications frequently require the CPU and control system to be physically located on the factory floor or in the field. These environments are typically harsh, full of dust, dirt, electrical noise and widely fluctuating temperatures.

Because the iSBC 86C/38 generates so little heat and can operate without cooling, it can be placed in a sealed enclosure, protected from harsh factory environments. It also offers excellent noise immunity and tolerance to extreme temperatures.

FEATURES

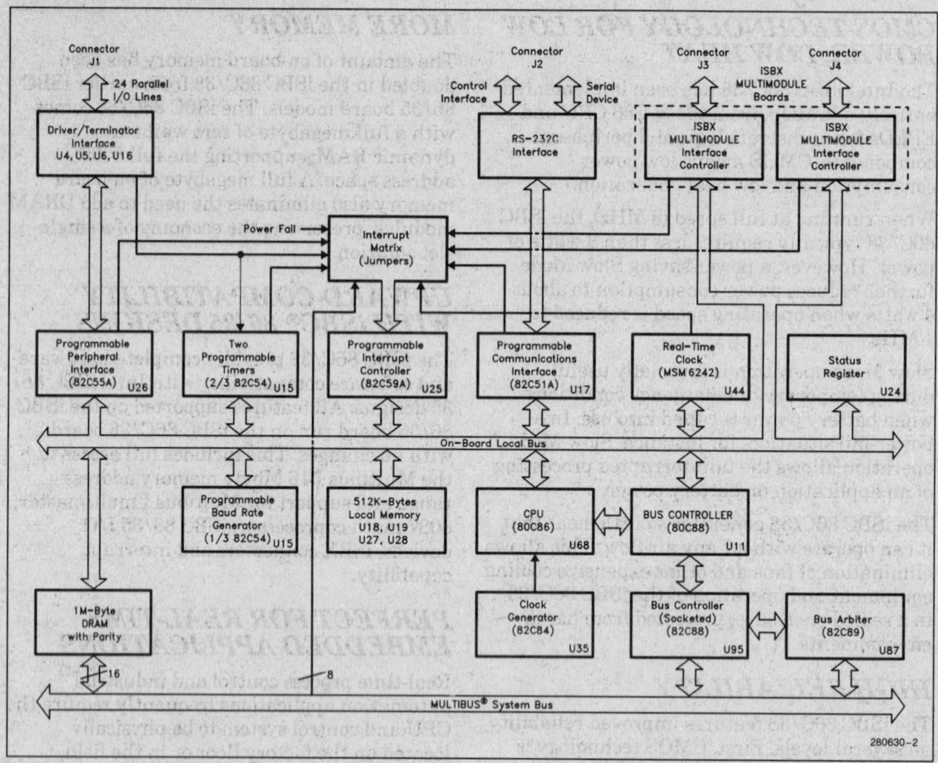

Figure 1: iSBC® 86C/38 Block Diagram

SPECIFICATIONS

Central Processor

80C86 CPU	8 MHz
Numeric Processor iSBC 337A MULTIMODULE	8 MHz

Cycle Time

Basic Instruction	8 MHz 500 ns (assumes instruction in queue)

Note: Basic instruction cycle is defined as the fastest instruction time (i.e. four clock cycles)

DRAM Memory

On-board parity memory	1 Mbyte, 0 Wait States at 8 MHz

Note: Power fail battery backup capability via P2 connector.

EPROM Memory

Number of sockets	Four 32-pin JEDEC Sites (compatible with 28-pin and 32-pin devices)
Device access speeds	265ns (minimum) to 640ns (maximum)
Maximum memory	512 Kb with 27010 (1 M-bit) EPROMS

Note: EPROM. E^2PROM (read only), and Static RAM devices are supported.

I/O CAPABILITY

Parallel Channel	Three 8-bit parallel ports (50 pin socket connectors) using an 82C55A
Serial Channel	One RS-232-C channel using an 82C51 device with speeds from 110 Kb to 19.2 Kb
iSBX Expansion	Two 8/16-bit iSBX interface connectors for single or double wide iSBX MULTIMODULE boards

Real Time Clock/Calendar

An OKI MSM6242 provides real time clock/calendar capability with clock operation in either 12 or 24 hour format. The clock/calendar is sustained up to 10,000 hours by an on-board BR2325 lithium battery.

Temperature Sensing

Temperature sensing is an optional capability, allowing system designers to choose the appropriate level of temperature sensing for their application. A socket is on-board which supports four-pin temperature sensor devices.

Interrupt Capacity

Potential Interrupt Sources	37 jumper selectable
Interrupt Levels	9 using the 82C59A device and the 80C86 NMI line

Note: Bus Vectored Interrupt capability is supported.

Timers	Three programmable timer/counters using one 82C54 device

Interfaces

Multibus Bus	All signals TTL compatible
iSBX Bus	All signals TTL compatible
Parallel I/O	All signals TTL compatible
Serial I/O	RS-232-C

POWER REQUIREMENTS/ CONSUMPTION

	8 MHz	1 MHz
Maximum:		
+5V	1.56 A, 7.8 Watts	0.8 A, 4.0 Watts
+12V	0.06 A, 0.72 Watts	0.06 A, 0.72 Watts
−12V	0.08 A, 0.96 Watts	0.08 A, 0.96 Watts
Typical:		
+5V	0.82 A, 4.1 Watts	0.7 A, 3.5 Watts
+12V	0.04 A, 0.48 Watts	0.04 A, 0.48 Watts
−12V	0.06 A, 0.72 Watts	0.06 A, 0.72 Watts

Note: Does not include power for iSBC modules, iSBX modules or EPROM memory.

ENVIRONMENTAL REQUIREMENTS

Operating Temperature	0°C to +60°C at zero LFM air flow
Relative Humidity	0% to 95% noncondensing
Storage Temperature	−40°C to +70°C

SPECIFICATIONS

PHYSICAL CHARACTERISTICS

Dimensions

Width:	12.00 in (30.48 cm)
Depth:	7.05 in. (17.91 cm)
Height:	.375 in. (.96 cm)

Recommended Minimum Cardcage Slot Spacing

0.6 in (1.5 cm) without iSBC 337A or iSBX MULTIMODULE

1.2 in (3.0 cm) with iSBC 337A or iSBX MULTIMODULE

Approximate Weight 21.5 oz (609.5 gm)

REFERENCE MANUAL

454554— iSBC 86C/38 Single Board Computer User's Guide

ORDERING INFORMATION

iSBC 86C38	Single Board Computer

iSBC® 86/35* SINGLE BOARD COMPUTER

- 8086 (8086-2) Microprocessor with 5 or 8 MHz CPU Clock
- Optional Numeric Data Processor with iSBC® 337A MULTIMODULE™
- Upward Compatible with iSBC 86/30 Single Board Computer
- 512K Bytes of Dual-Port Read/Write Memory Expandable On-Board to 640K or 1M Bytes
- Sockets for up to 128K Bytes of JEDEC 24/28-Pin Standard Memory Devices
- Two iSBX™ Bus Connectors
- 24 Programmable Parallel I/O Lines
- Programmable Synchronous/ Asynchronous RS232C Compatible Serial Interface with Software Selectable Baud Rates
- Three Programmable 16-Bit BCD or Binary Timers/Event Counters
- 9 Levels of Vectored Interrupt Control, Expandable Off Board to 65 Levels

The iSBC 86/35 Single Board Computer is a member of Intel's complete line of OEM microcomputer systems that take full advantage of Intel's technology to provide economical, self-contained, computer-based solutions for OEM applications. The board is a complete computer system containing the CPU, system clock, dual port read/write memory, nonvolatile read only memory, I/O ports and drivers, serial communications interface, priority interrupt logic and programmable timers.

210219–1

*The iSBC® 86/35 is also manufactured under product code pSBC 86/35 by Intel Puerto Rico, Inc.

September 1991
Order Number: 210219-005

FUNCTIONAL DESCRIPTION

Overview

The iSBC 86/35 board combines the industry standard 8086 CPU with up to a megabyte page of board resident, dual ported system memory. By placing the direct memory addressing capability of the 8086 CPU on board, MULTIBUS® access to system memory can be eliminated, significantly improving system throughput.

Central Processing Unit

The central processor for the iSBC 86/35 board is Intel's 8086-2 CPU. A clock rate of 8 MHz is supported with a jumper selectable option for 5 MHz. The CPU architecture includes four 16-bit byte addressable data registers, two 16-bit index registers, all accessed by a total of 24 operand addressing modes for comprehensive memory addressing and for support of the data structures required for today's structured, high level languages as well as assembly language.

Instruction Set

The 8086 instruction repertoire includes variable length instruction format (including double operand instructions), 8-bit and 16-bit signed and unsigned arithmetic operators for binary, BCD and unpacked ASCII data, and iterative word and byte string manipulation functions.

For enhanced 5 or 8 MHz numerics processing capability, the iSBC 337A MULTIMODULE Numeric Data Processor extends the architecture and data set. Over 60 numeric instructions offer arithmetic, trigonometric, transcendental, logarithmic and exponential instructions. Supported data types include 16-, 32-, and 64-bit integer, and 32- and 64-bit floating point, 18-digit packed BCD and 80-bit temporary.

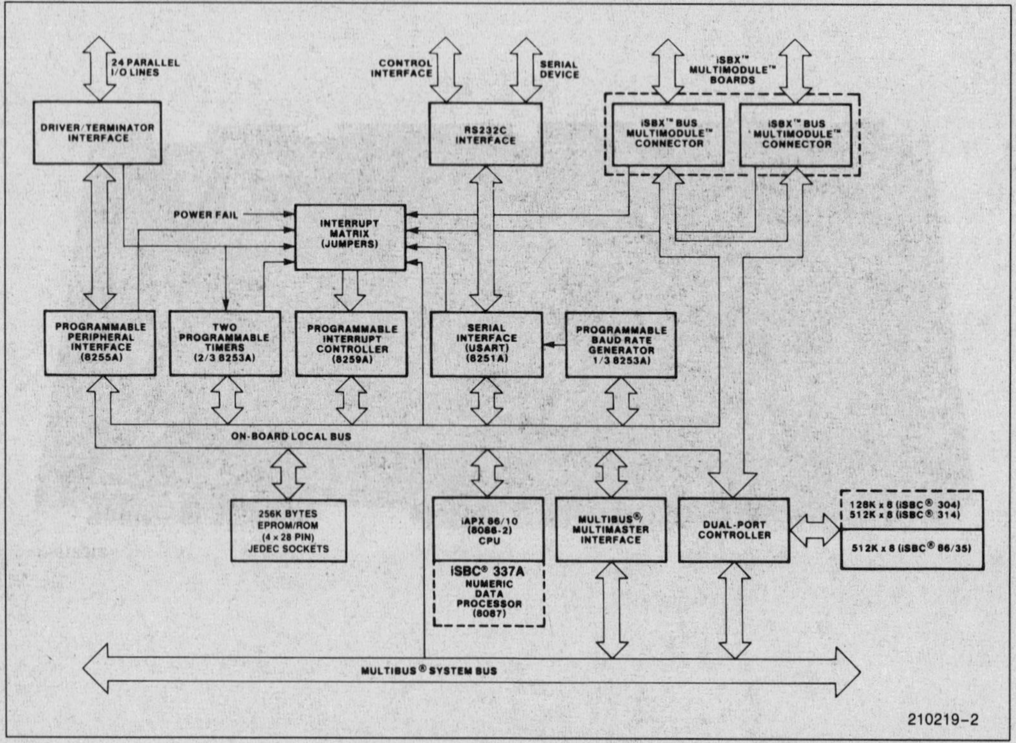

Figure 1. iSBC® 86/35 Block Diagram

Architectural Features

A 6-byte instruction queue provides pre-fetching of sequential instructions and can reduce the 750 ns minimum instruction cycle to 250 ns for queued instructions. The stack-oriented architecture readily supports modular programming by facilitating fast, simple, inter-modular communication, and other programming constructs needed for asynchronous real-time systems. The memory expansion capabilities offer a 1 megabyte addressing range. The dynamic relocation scheme allows ease in segmentation of pure procedure and data for efficient memory utilization. Four segment registers (code, stack, data, extra) contain program loaded offset values which are used to map 16-bit addresses to 20-bit addresses. Each register maps 64K bytes at a time and activation of a specific register is controlled explicitly by program control and is also selected implicitly by specific functions and instructions.

RAM Capabilities

The iSBC 86/35 microcomputer contains 512K bytes of dual-port dynamic RAM which may be expanded on-board by adding a RAM Multimodule board as an option. The on-board RAM may be expanded to 640K bytes with the iSBC 304 MULTIMODULE board mounted onto the iSBC 85/35 board. Likewise, the iSBC 86/35 microcomputer may be expanded to 1 Megabyte with the iSBC 314 MULTIMODULE board option.

The dual-port controller allows access to the on-board RAM (including RAM MULTIMODULE board options) from the iSBC 86/35 board and from any other MULTIBUS master via the system bus. Segments of on-board RAM may be configured as a private resource, protected from MULTIBUS system access.

EPROM Capabilities

Four 28-pin JEDEC sockets are provided for the use of Intel 2764, 27128, 27256, 27512, EPROMs and their respective ROMs. When using 27512, the on-board EPROM capacity is 256K bytes. Other JEDEC standard pinout devices are also supported, including byte-wide static RAMs.

Parallel I/O Interface

The iSBC 86/35 Single Board Computer contains 24 programmable parallel I/O lines implemented using the Intel 8255A Programmable Peripheral Interface. The system software is used to configure the I/O lines in any combination of unidirectional input/output and bidirectional ports indicated in Table 1. In order to take advantage of the large number of possible I/O configurations, sockets are provided for interchangeable I/O line drivers and terminators, allowing the selection of the appropriate combination of optional line drivers and terminators with the required drive/termination characteristics. The 24 programmable I/O lines and signal ground lines are brought out to a 50-pin edge connector.

Serial I/O

A programmable communications interface using the Intel 8251A Universal Synchronous/Asynchronous Receiver/Transmitter (USART) is contained on the iSBC 86/35 board. A software selectable baud rate generator provides the USART with all common communication frequencies. The mode of operation (i.e., synchronous or asynchronous), data format, control character format, parity, and baud rate are all under program control. The 8251A provides full duplex, double buffered transmit and receive capability. Parity, overrun, and framing error detection are all incorporated in the USART. The RS232C command lines, serial data lines and signal ground line are brought out to a 26-pin edge connector.

Programmable Timers

The iSBC 86/35 board provides three independent, fully programmable 16-bit interval timers/event counters utilizing the Intel 8253 Programmable Interval Timer. Each counter is capable of operating in either BCD or binary modes. Two of these timers/counters are available to the systems designer to generate accurate timer intervals under software control. Routing for the outputs and gate/trigger inputs of two of these counters is jumper selectable. The outputs may be independently routed to the 8259A Programmable Interrupt Controller and to the I/O terminators associated with the 8255A to allow external devices or an 8255A port to gate the timer or to count external events. The third interval timer in the 8253 provides the programmable baud rate generator for the iSBC 86/35 board's RS232C USART serial port. The system software configures each timer independently to select the desired function. The contents of each counter may be read at any time during system operation.

iSBX™ MULTIMODULE™ On-Board Expansion

Two 8/16-bit iSBX MULTIMODULE connectors are provided on the iSBC 86/35 microcomputer. Through these connectors, additional on-board I/O functions may be added. The iSBX connectors on the iSBC 86/35 board provides all signals necessary to interface to the local on-board bus, including 16 data lines for maximum data transfer rates. iSBX

MULTIMODULE boards designed with 8-bit data paths and using the 8-bit iSBX connector are also supported on the iSBC 86/35 microcomputer. A broad range of iSBX MULTIMODULE options are available from Intel. Custom iSBX modules may also be designed for use on the iSBC 86/35 board.

Multimaster Capabilities

The iSBC 86/35 board provides full MULTIBUS arbitration control logic. This control logic allows both serial (daisy chain) and parallel priority schemes. The serial scheme allows up to three iSBC 86/35 boards/bus masters to share the MULTIBUS system bus; while up to 16 masters may be connected using the parallel scheme and external decode logic.

Interrupt Capability

The iSBC 86/35 board provides 9 vectored interrupt levels. The highest level is the NMI (Non-Maskable Interrupt) line which is directly tied to the 8086-2 CPU. This interrupt is typically used for signaling catastrophic events (e.g., power failure). The Intel 8259A Programmable Interrupt Controller (PIC) provides control and vectoring for the next eight interrupt levels. A selection of four priority processing modes is available for use in designing request processing configurations to match system requirements for efficient interrupt servicing with minimal latencies. Operating mode and priority assignments may be reconfigured dynamically via software at any time during system operation. The PIC accepts interrupt requests from all on-board I/O resources and from the MULTIBUS system bus. The PIC then resolves requests according to the selected mode and, if appropriate, issues an interrupt to the CPU. Any combination of interrupt levels may be masked via software, by storing a single byte in the interrupt mask register of the PIC. In systems requiring additional interrupt levels, slave 8259A PICs may be interfaced via the MULTIBUS system bus, to generate additional vector addresses, yielding a total of 65 unique interrupt levels.

Interrupt requests to be serviced by the iSBC 86/35 board may originate from 28 sources. All interrupt signals are brought to the interrupt jumper matrix where any combination of interrupt sources may be strapped to the desired interrupt request level on the 8259A PIC or the NMI input to the CPU directly.

Power-Fail Control and Auxiliary Power

Control logic is included to accept a power-fail interrupt in conjunction with the AC-low signal from the Power Supply to initiate an orderly shut down of the system in the event of a power failure. Additionally, an active-low TTL compatible memory protect signal is brought out on the auxiliary connector which when asserted, disables read/write access to RAM memory on the board. This input is provided for the protection of RAM contents during system powerdown sequences. An auxiliary power bus is also provided to allow separate power to RAM for systems requiring battery backup of read/write memory. Selection of this auxiliary RAM power bus is made via jumpers on the board.

SPECIFICATIONS

Word Size

INSTRUCTION — 8, 16, 24, or 32 bits

DATA — 8, 16 bits

System Clock

5 MHz or 8 MHz ±0.1% (jumper selectable)

Cycle Time

BASIC INSTRUCTION CYCLE

8 MHz — 250 ns (assumes instruction in the queue)

5 MHz — 400 ns (assumes instruction in the queue)

NOTE:
Basic instruction cycle is defined as the fastest instruction time (i.e., two clock cycles). Jumper selectable for 1 wait-state on-board memory access.

Memory Capacity/Addressing

ON-BOARD EPROM

Device	Total Capacity	Address Range
2764	32K bytes	$F8000–FFFFF_H$
27128	64K bytes	$F0000–FFFFF_H$
27256	128K bytes	$E0000–FFFFF_H$
27512	256K bytes	$D0000–FFFFF_H$

ON-BOARD RAM

Board	Total Capacity	Address Range
iSBC 86/35	512K bytes	$0–7FFFF_H$

WITH MULTIMODULE™ RAM

Board	Total Capacity	Address Range
iSBC 304	640K bytes	$8–9\ FFFF_H$
iSBC 314	1M bytes	$8–FFFFF_H$

Serial Communications Characteristics

SYNCHRONOUS—5-8 bit characters; internal or external character synchronization; automatic sync insertion

ASYNCHRONOUS—5-8 bit characters; break character generation; 1, 1½, or 2 stop bits; false start bit detection

Interfaces

MULTIBUS®—All signals TTL compatible

iSBX™ BUS—All signals TTL compatible

PARALLEL I/O—All signals TTL compatible

SERIAL I/O—RS232C compatible, configurable as a data set or data terminal

TIMER—All signals TTL compatible

INTERRUPT REQUESTS—All TTL compatible

Physical Characteristics

Width: 12.00 in. (30.48 cm)
Height: 6.75 in. (17.15 cm)
Depth: 0.70 in. (1.78 cm)
Weight: 14 oz. (388 gm)

Electrical Characteristics

DC POWER REQUIREMENTS

Configuration	Current Requirements (All Voltages ±5%)		
	+5V	+12V	−12V
Without EPROM(1)	5.1A	25 mA	23 mA
RAM only(2)	660 mA	—	—
With 32K EPROM(3) (using 2764)	5.6A	25 mA	23 mA
With 64K EPROM (using 27128)	5.7A	25 mA	23 mA
With 128K EPROM (using 27256)	5.8A	25 mA	23 mA

NOTES:
1. Does not include power for optional ROM/EPROM, I/O drivers, and I/O terminators.
2. RAM chips powered via auxiliary power bus in power-down mode.
3. Includes power required for 4 ROM/EPROM chips, and I/O terminators installed for 16 I/O lines; all terminator inputs low.

Environmental Characteristics

OPERATING TEMPERATURE — 0°C to 55°C @ 200 linear feet per minute (LFM) air velocity

RELATIVE HUMIDITY — to 90% (without condensation)

Reference Manual

146245-002 — iSBC 86/35 Hardware Reference Manual (NOT SUPPLIED)

ORDERING INFORMATION

Part Number	Description
SBC 86/35	Single Board Computer

iSBC® 86/30* SINGLE BOARD COMPUTER

- 8086 Microprocessor with 5 or 8 MHz CPU Clock
- Fully Software Compatible with iSBC® 86/12A Single Board Computer
- Optional Numeric Data Processor with iSBC® 337A MULTIMODULE™
- 32K/128K bytes of Dual-Port Read/Write Memory Expandable On-Board to 256K bytes with On-Board Refresh
- Sockets for up to 64K bytes of JEDEC 24/28-pin Standard Memory Devices
- Two iSBX™ Bus Connectors
- 24 Programmable Parallel I/O Lines
- Programmable Synchronous/Asynchronous RS232C Compatible Serial Interface with Software Selectable Baud Rates
- Two Programmable 16-Bit BCD or Binary Timers/Event Counters
- 9 Levels of Vectored Interrupt Control, Expandable to 65 Levels
- Multibus Interface for Multimaster Configurations and System Expansion

The iSBC 86/30 Single Board Computer is a member of Intel's complete line of OEM microcomputer systems which take full advantage of Intel's technology to provide economical, self-contained, computer-based solutions for OEM applications. The CPU, system clock, read/write memory, nonvolatile read only memory, I/O ports and drivers, serial communications interface, priority interrupt logic and programmable timers, all reside on the boards.

280007–1

*The iSBC® 86/14 and iSBC® 86/30 are also manufactured under product code pSBC8614 and pSBC8630 by Intel Puerto Rico, Inc.

September 1991
Order Number: 280007-006

FUNCTIONAL DESCRIPTION

Central Processing Unit

The central processor for the iSBC 86/30* boards is Intel's 8086-2 CPU. A clock rate of 8 MHz is supported with a jumper selectable option of 5 MHz. The CPU architecture includes four 16-bit byte addressable data registers, two 16-bit memory base pointer registers and two 16-bit index registers, all accessed by a total of 24 operand addressing modes for comprehensive memory addressing and for support of the data structures required for today's structured, high level languages as well as assembly language.

Instruction Set

The 8086 instruction repertoire includes variable length instruction format (including double operand instructions), 8-bit and 16-bit signed and unsigned arithmetic operators for binary, BCD and unpacked ASCII data, and iterative word and byte string manipulation functions.

For enhanced numerics processing capability, the iSBC 337A MULTIMODULE Numeric Data Processor extends the architecture and data set. Over 60 numeric instructions offer arithmetic, trigonometric, transcendental, logarithmic and exponential instructions. Supported data types include 16-, 32, and 64-bit integer, and 32- and 64-bit floating point, 18-digit packed BCD and 80-bit temporary.

Architectural Features

A 6-byte instruction queue provides pre-fetching of sequential instructions and can reduce the 750 nsec minimum instruction cycle to 250 nsec for queued instructions. The stack-oriented architecture readily supports modular programming by facilitating fast, simple, inter-module communication, and other programming constructs needed for asynchronous real-time systems. The memory expansion capabilities offer a 1 megabyte addressing range. The dynamic relocation scheme allows ease in segmentation of pure procedure and data for efficient memory utilization. Four segment registers (code, stack, data, extra) contain program loaded offset values which are used to map 16-bit addresses to 20-bit addresses. Each register maps 64K bytes at a time and activation of a specific register is controlled explicitly by program control and is also selected implicitly by specific functions and instructions.

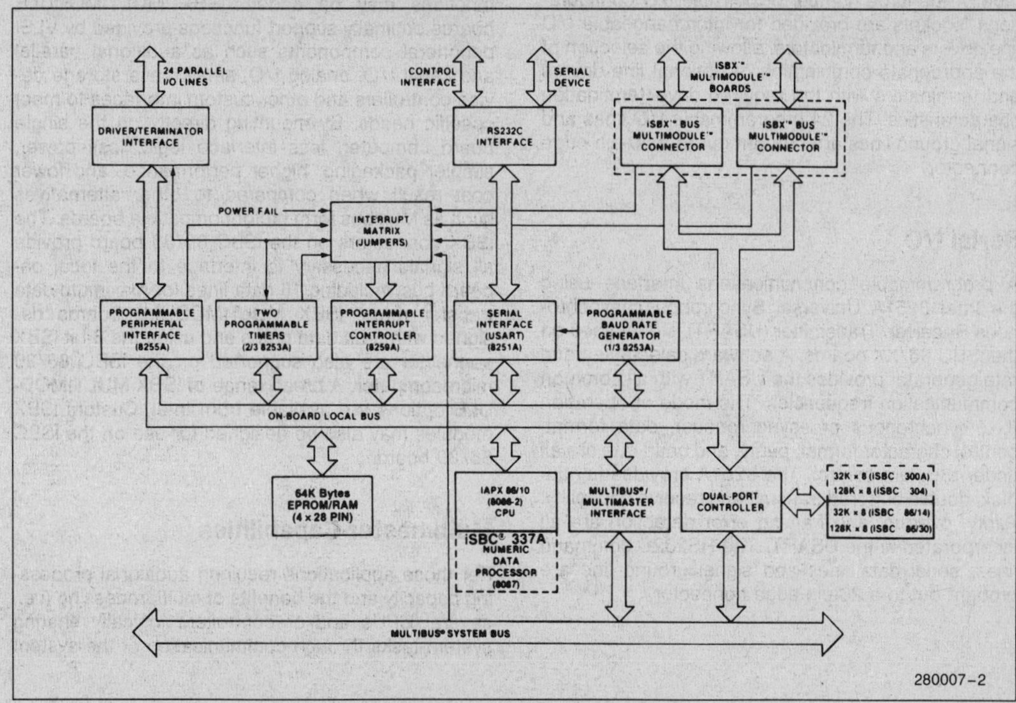

Figure 1. iSBC® 86/30 Block Diagram

8

RAM Capabilities

The iSBC 86/30 microcomputer contains 128K bytes of dual-port dynamic RAM. In addition, on-board RAM may be doubled by optionally adding RAM MULTIMODULE boards. The dual-port controller allows access to the on-board RAM (including RAM MULTIMODULE options) from the iSBC 86/30 boards and from any other Multibus master via the system bus. Segments of on-board RAM may be configured as a private resource, protected from Multibus system access.

EPROM Capabilities

Four 28-pin sockets are provided for a maximum on-board EPROM capacity of 64K bytes. Other JEDEC standard pinout devices are also supported, including byte-wide static RAMs.

Parallel I/O Interface

The iSBC 86/30 Single Board Computers contain 24 programmable parallel I/O lines implemented using the Intel 8255A Programmable Peripheral Interface. The system software is used to configure the I/O lines in any combination of unidirectional input/output and bidirectional ports. In order to take advantage of the large number of possible I/O configurations, sockets are provided for interchangeable I/O line drivers and terminators, allowing the selection of the appropriate combination of optional line drivers and terminators with the required drive/termination characteristics. The 24 programmable I/O lines and signal ground lines are brought out to a 50-pin edge connector.

Serial I/O

A programmable communications interface using the Intel 8251A Universal Synchronous/Asynchronous Receiver/Transmitter (USART) is contained on the iSBC 86/XX boards. A software selectable baud rate generator provides the USART with all common communication frequencies. The mode of operation (i.e., synchronous or asynchronous), data format, control character format, parity, and baud rate are all under program control. The 8251A provides full duplex, double buffered transmit and receive capability. Parity, overrun, and framing error detection are all incorporated in the USART. The RS232C command lines, serial data lines and signal ground line are brought out to a 26-pin edge connector.

Programmable Timers

The iSBC 86/30 board provides three independent, fully programmable 16-bit interval timers/event counters utilizing the Intel 8253 Programmable Interval Timer. Each counter is capable of operating in either BCD or binary modes. Two of these timers/counters are available to the systems designer to generate accurate time intervals under software control. Routing for the outputs and gate/trigger inputs of two of these counters is jumper selectable. The outputs may be independently routed to the 8259A Programmable Interrupt Controller and to the I/O terminators associated with the 8255A to allow external devices or an 8255A port to gate the timer or to count external events. The third interval timer in the 8253 provides the programmable baud rate generator for the iSBC 86/30 board's RS232C USART serial port. The system software configures each timer independently to select the desired function. The contents of each counter may be read at any time during system operation.

iSBX™ MULTIMODULE™ On-Board Expansion

Two 8/16-bit iSBX MULTIMODULE connectors are provided on the iSBC 86/30 microcomputer. Through these connectors, additional on-board I/O functions may be added. iSBX MULTIMODULE boards optimally support functions provided by VLSI peripheral components such as additional parallel and serial I/O, analog I/O, small mass storage device controllers and other custom interfaces to meet specific needs. By mounting directly on the single board computer, less interface logic, less power, simpler packaging, higher performance, and lower cost result when compared to other alternatives such as Multibus form factor compatible boards. The iSBX connectors on the iSBC 86/30 board provide all signals necessary to interface to the local on-board bus, including 16 data lines for maximum data transfer rates. iSBX MULTIMODULE boards designed with 8-bit data paths and using the 8-bit iSBX connector are also supported on the iSBC 86/30 microcomputer. A broad range of iSBX MULTIMODULE options are available from Intel. Custom iSBX modules may also be designed for use on the iSBC 86/30 board.

Multimaster Capabilities

For those applications requiring additional processing capacity and the benefits of multiprocessing (i.e., several CPUs and/or controllers logically sharing system tasks through communication of the system bus), the iSBC 86/XX boards provide full Multibus arbitration control logic. This control logic allows up to three iSBC 86/XX boards or other bus masters, including iSBC 80 family Multibus compatible 8-bit single board computers to share the system bus using a serial (daisy chain) priority scheme and allows up to 16 masters to share the Multibus system bus with an external parallel priority decoder. In addition to the multiprocessing configurations made possible with multimaster capability, it also provides a very efficient mechanism for all forms of DMA (Direct Memory Access) transfers.

Interrupt Capability

The iSBC 86/XX boards provide 9 vectored interrupt levels. The highest level is the NMI (Non-Maskable Interrupt) line which is directly tied to the 8086 CPU. This interrupt is typically used for signaling catastrophic events (e.g., power failure). The Intel 8259A Programmable Interrupt Controller (PIC) provides control and vectoring for the next eight interrupt levels. A selection of four priority processing modes is available for use in designing request processing configurations to match system requirements for efficient interrupt servicing with minimal latencies. Operating mode and priority assignments may be reconfigured dynamically via software at any time during system operation. The PIC accepts interrupt requests from all on-board I/O resources and from the Multibus system bus. The PIC then resolves requests according to the selected mode and, if appropriate, issues an interrupt to the CPU. Any combination of interrupt levels may be masked via software, by storing a single byte in the interrupt mask register of the PIC. In systems requiring additional interrupt levels, slave 8259A PICs may be interfaced via the Multibus system bus, to generate additional vector addresses, yielding a total of 65 unique interrupt levels.

Interrupt requests to be serviced by the iSBC 86/XX boards may originate from 28 sources. All interrupt signals are brought to the interrupt jumper matrix where any combination of interrupt sources may be strapped to the desired interrupt request level on the 8259A PIC or the NMI input to the CPU directly.

Power-Fail Control and Auxiliary Power

Control logic is also included to accept a power-fail interrupt in conjunction with the AC-low signal generation capabilities to initiate an orderly shut down of the system in the event of a power failure. Additionally, an active-low TTL compatible memory protect signal is brought out on the auxiliary connector which, when asserted, disables read/write access to RAM memory on the board. This input is provided for the protection of RAM contents during system power-down sequences. An auxiliary power bus is also provided to allow separate power to RAM for systems requiring battery back-up of read/write memory. Selection of this auxiliary RAM power bus is made via jumpers on the board.

SPECIFICATIONS

Word Size

Instruction: 8, 16, 24, or 32 bits

Data: 8, 16 bits

System Clock

5.00 MHz or 8.00 MHz ±0.1% (jumper selectable)

Cycle Time

BASIC INSTRUCTION CYCLE

8 MHz: 750 ns
250 ns (assumes instruction in the queue)

5 MHz: 1.2 μs
400 ns (assumes instruction in the queue)

NOTE:
Basic instruction cycle is defined as the fastest instruction time (i.e., two clock cycles).

Memory Cycle Time

RAM: 750 ns

EPROM: Jumper selectable from 500 ns to 875 ns

Memory Capacity/Addressing

ON-BOARD EPROM

Device	Total Capacity	Address Range
2716	8K bytes	$FE000-FFFFF_H$
2732A	16K bytes	$FC000-FFFFF_H$
2764	32K bytes	$F8000-FFFFF_H$
27128	64K bytes	$F0000-FFFFF_H$

ON-BOARD RAM

Board	Total Capacity	Address Range
iSBC 86/14	32K bytes	$0-07FFF_H$
iSBC 86/30	128K bytes	$0-1FFFF_H$

8

I/O Capacity

Parallel: 24 programmable lines using one 8255A
Serial: 1 programmable line using one 8251A
iSBX MULTIMODULE: 2 iSBX boards

Serial Communications Characteristics

Synchronous: 5–8 bits characters; internal or external character synchronization; automatic sync insertion

Asynchronous: 5–8 bit characters; break character generation; 1, 1½, or 2 stop bits; false start bit direction

Interfaces

MULTIBUS: All signals TTL compatible

iSBX Bus: All signals TTL compatible

Parallel I/O: All signals TTL compatible

Serial I/O: RS232C compatible, configurable as a data set or data terminal

Timer: All signals TTL compatible

Interrupt Requests: All TTL compatible

Physical Characteristics

Width: 12.00 in. (30.48 cm)
Height: 6.75 in. (17.15 cm)
Depth: 0.70 in. (1.78 cm)
Weight: 14 oz (388 gm)

Environmental Characteristics

Operating Temperature: 0°C to 55°C

Relative Humidity: to 90% (without condensation)

Electrical Characteristics

DC POWER REQUIREMENTS

Configuration	Current Requirements (All Voltages ±5%)		
	+5V	+12V	−12V
Without EPROM[1]	5.1A	25 mA	23 mA
RAM only[2]	600 mA	—	—
With 16K EPROM[3] (using 2732A)	5.5A	25 mA	23 mA
With 32K EPROM[3] (using 2764)	5.6A	25 mA	23 mA

NOTES:
1. Does not include power for optional ROM/EPROM, I/O drivers, and I/O terminators.
2. RAM chips powered via auxiliary power bus in power-down mode.
3. Includes power required for 4 ROM/EPROM chips, and I/O terminators installed for 16 I/O lines; all terminator inputs low.

Environmental Characteristics

Operating Temperature: 0°C to 55°C
Relative Humidity: to 90% (without condensation)

Reference Manual

144044-002: iSBC 86/14 and iSBC 86/30 Hardware Reference Manual (NOT SUPPLIED)

ORDERING INFORMATION

Part Number	Description
SBC 86/14	Single Board Computer
SBC 86/30	Single Board Computer

intel®

iSBC® 86/05A* SINGLE BOARD COMPUTER

- 8086/10 (8086-2) Microprocessor with 5 or 8 MHz CPU Clock
- Software Compatible with 8086, 8088, 80186, 80286 Based 16-bit Single Board Computers
- Optional Numeric Data Processor with iSBC® 337 A MULTIMODULE™
- 8K bytes of Static RAM; Expandable On-Board to 16K Bytes
- Sockets for up to 256K Bytes of JEDEC 24/28-Pin Standard Memory Devices; Expandable On-Board to 512K Bytes
- Two iSBX™ Bus Connectors
- Programmable Synchronous/Asynchronous RS232C Compatible Serial Interface with Software Selectable Baud Rate
- 24 Programmable Parallel I/O Lines
- Two Programmable 16-Bit BCD or Binary Timers/Event Counters
- 9 Levels of Vectored Interrupt Control, Expandable to 65 Levels
- MULTIBUS® Bus Interface for Multimaster Configurations and System Expansion

The iSBC 86/05A Single Board Computer is a member of Intel's complete line of OEM microcomputer systems which take full advantage of Intel's technology to provide economical, self-contained, computer-based solutions for OEM applications. The CPU, system clock, read/write memory, nonvolatile read only memory, I/O ports and drivers, serial communications interface, priority interrupt logic and programmable timers, all reside on the board. The large control storage capacity makes the iSBC 86/05A board ideally suited for control-oriented applications such as process control, instrumentation and industrial automation.

143325–1

*The iSBC® 86/05A is also manufactured under product code pSBC 86/05A by Intel Puerto Rico, Inc.

September 1991
Order Number: 143325-004

FUNCTIONAL DESCRIPTION

Central Processing Unit

The central processor for the iSBC 86/05A board is Intel's 8086-2 CPU. A clock rate of 8 MHz is supported with a jumper selectable option of 5 MHz. The CPU architecture includes four 16-bit byte addressable data registers, two 16-bit memory base pointer registers and two 16-bit index registers. All are accessed by a total of 24 operand addressing modes for comprehensive memory addressing and for support of the data structures required for today's structured, high level languages as well as assembly language.

Instruction Set

The 8086 instruction repertoire includes variable length instruction format (including double operand instructions), 8- and 16-bit signed and unsigned arithmetic operators for binary, BCD and unpacked ASCII data, and iterative word and byte string manipulation functions.

For enhanced numerics processing capability, the iSBC 337A MULTIMODULE Numeric Data Processor extends the architecture and data set. Over 60 numeric instructions offer arithmetic, trigonometric, transcendental, logarithmic and exponential instructions. Supported data types include 16-, 32-, and 64-bit integer, and 32- and 64-bit floating point, 18-digit packed BCD and 80-bit temporary.

Architectural Features

A 6-byte instruction queue provides pre-fetching of sequential instructions and can reduce the 740 ns minimum instruction cycle to 250 ns for queued instructions. The stack-oriented architecture readily supports modular programming by facilitating fast, simple, inter-module communication, and other programming constructs needed for asynchronous realtime systems. The memory expansion capabilities offer a 1 megabyte addressing range. The dynamic relocation scheme allows ease in segmentation of pure procedure and data for efficient memory utilization. Four segment registers (code, stack, data, extra) contain program loaded offset values which are used to map 16-bit addresses to 20-bit addresses. Each register maps 64K bytes at a time with activation of a specific register controlled explicity by program control and selected implicity by specific functions and instructions. All Intel languages support the extended memory capability, relieving the programmer of managing the megabyte memory space yet allowing explicit control when necessary.

Memory Configuration

The iSBC 86/05A microcomputer contains 8K bytes of high-speed 8K x 4 bit static RAM on-board. In addition, the above on-board RAM may be expanded to 16K bytes with the iSBC 302 MULTIMODULE RAM option which mounts on the iSBC 86/05A board. All on-board RAM is accessed by the 8086-2 CPU with no wait states, yielding a memory cycle time of 500 ns.

The iSBC 86/05A board also has four 28-pin, 8-bit wide (byte-wide) sockets, configured to accept JEDEC 24/28-pin standard memory devices. Up to 256K bytes of EPROM are supported in 64K byte increments with Intel 27512 EPROMs. The iSBC 86/05A board also supports 2K x 8, 4K x 8, 8K x 8, 16K x 8 and 32K x 8 EPROM memory devices. These sites also support 2K x 8 and 8K x 8 byte-wide static RAM (SRAM) devices and iRAM devices, yielding up to 32K bytes of SRAM in 8K byte increments on the baseboard.

When the addition of the iSBC 341 MULTIMODULE EPROM option, the on-board capacity for these devices is doubled, providing up to 512K bytes of EPROM and 64K bytes of byte-wide SRAM capacity on-board.

Parallel I/O Interface

The iSBC 86/05A Single Board Computer contains 24 programmable parallel I/O lines implemented using the Intel 8255A Programmable Peripheral Interface. The system software is used to configure the I/O lines in any combination of unidirectional input/output and bidirectional ports indicated in Table 1. In order to take advantage of the large number of possible I/O configurations, sockets are provided for interchangeable I/O line drivers and terminators, allowing the selection of the appropriate combination of optional line drivers and terminators with the required drive/termination characteristics. The 24 programmable I/O lines and signal ground lines are brought out to a 50-pin edge connector.

Serial I/O

A programmable communications interface using the Intel 8251A Universal Synchronous/Asynchronous Receiver/Transmitter (USART) is contained on the iSBC 86/05A board. A software selectable baud rate generator provides the USART with all common communication frequencies. The mode of operation (i.e., synchronous or asynchronous), data format, control character format, parity, and baud rate are all under program control. The 8251A provides full duplex, double buffered transmit and receive capability. Parity, overrun, and framing error detection are all

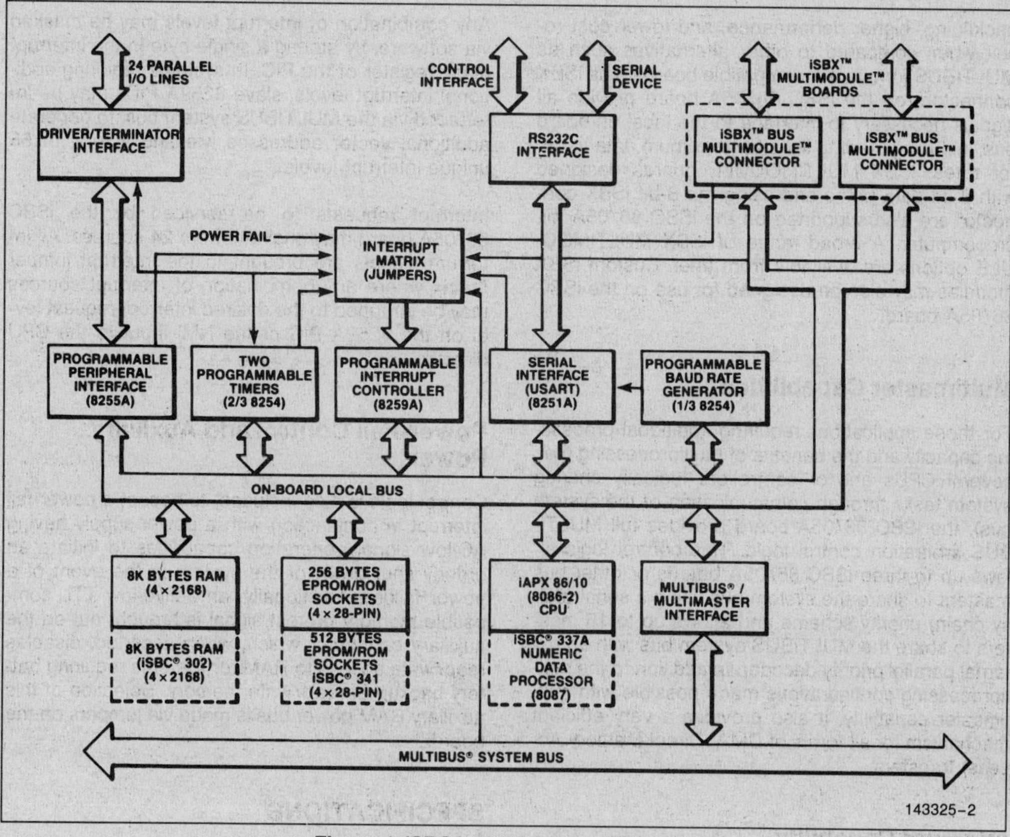

Figure 1. iSBC® 86/05A Block Diagram

incorporated in the USART. The RS232C compatible interface in conjunction with the USART, provides a direct interface to RS232C compatible terminals, cassettes, and asynchronous/synchronous modems. The RS232C command lines, serial data lines and signal ground line are brought out to a 26-pin edge connector.

Programmable Timers

The iSBC 86/05A board provides three independent, fully programmable 16-bit interval timers/event counters utilizing the Intel 8254 Programmable Interval Timer. Each counter is capable of operating in either BCD or binary modes. Two of these timers/counters are available to the systems designer to generate accurate time intervals under software control. Routing for the outputs and gate/trigger inputs of two of these counters is jumper selectable. The outputs may be independently routed to the 8259A Programmable Interrupt Controller and to the I/O terminators associated with the 8255A to allow external devices or an 8255A port to gate the timer or to count external events. The third interval timer in the 8254 provides the programmable baud rate generator for the iSBC 86/05A board RS232C USART serial port. The system software configures each timer independently to select the desired function. The contents of each counter may be read at any time during system operation.

iSBX™ MULTIMODULE™ On-Board Expansion

Two 8/16-bit iSBX MULTIMODULE connectors are provided on the iSBC 86/05A microcomputer. Through these connectors, additional on-board I/O and memory functions may be added. iSBX MULTIMODULE boards support functions such as additional parallel and serial I/O, analog I/O, mass storage device controllers BITBUS™ controllers, bubble memory, and other custom interfaces to meet specific needs. By mounting directly on the single board computer, less interface logic, less power, simpler packaging, higher performance, and lower cost result when compared to other alternatives such as MULTIBUS form factor compatible boards. The iSBX connectors on the iSBC 86/05A board provide all signals necessary to interface to the local on-board bus, including 16 data lines for maximum data transfer rates. iSBX MULTIMODULE boards designed with 8-bit data paths and using the 8-bit iSBX connector are also supported on the iSBC 86/05A microcomputer. A broad range of iSBX MULTIMODULE options are available from Intel. Custom iSBX modules may also be designed for use on the iSBC 86/05A board.

Multimaster Capabilities

For those applications requiring additional processing capacity and the benefits of multiprocessing (i.e., several CPUs and/or controllers logically sharing system tasks through communication of the system bus), the iSBC 86/05A board provides full MULTIBUS arbitration control logic. This control logic allows up to three iSBC 86/05A boards or other bus masters to share the system bus using a serial (daisy chain) priority scheme and allows up to 16 masters to share the MULTIBUS system bus with an external parallel priority decoder. In addition to the multiprocessing configurations made possible with multimaster capability, it also provides a very efficient mechanism for all forms of DMA (Direct Memory Access) transfers.

Interrupt Capability

The iSBC 86/05A board provides 9 vectored interrupt levels. The highest level is the NMI (Non-Maskable Interrupt) line which is directly tied to the 8086 CPU. This interrupt is typically used for signaling catastrophic events (e.g., power failure). The Intel 8259A Programmable Interrupt Controller (PIC) provides control and vectoring for the next eight interrupt levels. A selection of four priority processing modes is available for use in designing request processing configurations to match system requirements for efficient interrupt servicing with minimal latencies. Operating mode and priority assignments may be reconfigured dynamically via software at any time during system operation. The PIC accepts interrupt requests from all on-board I/O resources and from the MULTIBUS system bus. The PIC then resolves requests according to the selected mode and, if appropriate, issues an interrupt to the CPU.

Any combination of interrupt levels may be masked via software, by storing a single byte in the interrupt mask register of the PIC. In systems requiring additional interrupt levels, slave 8259A PICs may be interfaced via the MULTIBUS system bus, to generate additional vector addresses, yielding a total of 65 unique interrupt levels.

Interrupt requests to be serviced by the iSBC 86/05A board may originate from 24 sources. All interrupt signals are brought to the interrupt jumper matrix where any combination of interrupt sources may be strapped to the desired interrupt request level on the 8259A PIC or the NMI input to the CPU directly.

Power-Fail Control and Auxiliary Power

Control logic is also included, to accept a power-fail interrupt in conjunction with a power-supply having AC-low signal generation capabilities to initiate an orderly shut down of the system in the event of a power failure. Additionally, an active-low TTL compatible memory protect signal is brought out on the auxiliary connector which, when asserted, disables read/write access to RAM for systems requiring battery backup of read/write memory. Selection of this auxiliary RAM power bus is made via jumpers on the board.

SPECIFICATIONS

Word Size

Instruction: 8, 16, 24, or 32 bits
Data: 8, 16 bits

System Clock

5.00 MHz or 8.00 MHz ± 0.1% (jumper selectable)

Basic Instruction Cycle

At 8 MHz: 750 ns
250 ns (assumes instruction in the queue)
At 5 MHz: 1.2 sec.
400 ns (assumes instruction in the queue)

NOTE:
Basic instruction cycle is defined as the fastest instruction time (i.e., two clock cycles).

Memory Cycle Time

500 ns cycle time (no wait states requires a memory component access time of 250 ns or less)
RAM: 500 ns
EPROM: Jumper selectable from 500 ns to 875 ns

Memory Capacity/Addressing

JEDEC 24/28 Pin Sites		
Device	**Total Capacity**	**Address Range**
2K × 8	8K bytes	FE000-FFFFF$_H$
4K × 8	16K bytes	FC000-FFFFF$_H$
8K × 8	32K bytes	F8000-FFFFF$_H$
16K × 8	64K bytes	F0000-FFFFF$_H$
32K × 8	128K bytes	E0000-FFFFF$_H$
64K × 8	256K bytes	C0000-FFFFF$_H$
With iSBC® 341 MULTIMODULE™ EPROM/SRAM		
Device	**Total Capacity**	**Address Range**
2K × 8	16K bytes	FC000-FFFFF$_H$
4K × 8	32K bytes	F8000-FFFFF$_H$
8K × 8	64K bytes	F0000-FFFFF$_H$
16K × 8	128K bytes	E0000-FFFFF$_H$
32K × 8	256K bytes	C0000-FFFFF$_H$
64K × 8	512K bytes	80000-FFFFF$_H$

ON-BOARD STATIC RAM

8K bytes — 0–1FFF$_H$

16K bytes— 0–3FFF$_H$ (with iSBC 302 MULTIMODULE Board)

I/O CAPACITY

PARALLEL — 24 programmable lines using one 8255A.

SERIAL — 1 programmable line using one 8251A.

iSBX MULTIMODULE— 2 iSBX single wide MULTIMODULE board or 1 iSBX double-width MULTIMODULE board.

SERIAL COMMUNICATIONS CHARACTERISTICS

SYNCHRONOUS — 5–8 bit characters; internal or external character synchronization; automatic sync insertion.

ASYNCHRONOUS— 5–8 bit characters; break character generation; 1, 1½, or 2 stop bits; false start bit direction.

INTERFACES

MULTIBUS Bus: All signals TTL compatible

iSBX BUS Bus: All signals TTL compatible

PARALLEL I/O: All signals TTL compatible

SERIAL I/O: RS232C compatible, configurable as a data set or data terminal

TIMER: All signals TTL compatible

INTERRUPT REQUESTS: All TTL compatible

Physical Characteristics

Width: 12.00 in. (30.48 cm)

Height: 6.75 in. (17.15 cm)

Depth: 0.70 in. (1.78 cm)

Weight: 14 oz (388 gm)

8

ELECTRICAL CHARACTERISTICS

DC Power Requirements

Configuration	Current Requirements (All Voltages ±5%)		
	+5V	+12V	−12V
Without EPROM(1) RAM only(2)	4.7A 120 mA	25 mA	23 mA
With 8K EPROM(3) (using 2716)	5.0A	25 mA	23 mA
With 16K EPROM(3) (using 2732)	4.9A	25 mA	23 mA
With 32K EPROM(3) (using 2764)	4.9A	25 mA	23 mA

NOTES:
1. Does not include power for optional ROM/EPROM, I/O drivers, and I/O terminators.
2. RAM chips powered via auxiliary power bus in power-down mode.
3. Includes power required for 4 ROM/EPROM chips, and I/O terminators installed for 16 I/O lines; all terminator inputs low.

ENVIRONMENTAL CHARACTERISTICS

Operating Temperature: 0°C to 55°C

Relative Humidity: to 90% (without condensation)

REFERENCE MANUAL

Order no. 147162-002—*iSBC 86/05A Hardware Reference Manual* (NOT SUPPLIED)

ORDER INFORMATION

Part Number	Description
SBC 86/05A	16-bit Single Board Computer with 8K bytes RAM

iSBC® 88/25* SINGLE BOARD COMPUTER

- 8-Bit 8088 Microprocessor Operating at 5 MHz
- One Megabyte Addressing Range
- Two iSBX™ Bus Connectors
- Optional Numeric Data Processor with iSBC® 337A MULTIMODULE™
- 4K Bytes of Static RAM; Expandable On-Board to 16K Bytes
- Sockets for up to 64K Bytes of JEDEC 24/28-Pin Standard Memory Devices; Expandable On-Board to 128K Bytes
- Programmable Synchronous/Asynchronous RS232C Compatible Serial Interface with Software Selectable Baud Rates
- 24 Programmable Parallel I/O Lines
- Two Programmable 16-Bit BCD or Binary Timers/Event Counters
- 9 Levels of Vectored Interrupt Control, Expandable to 65 Levels
- MULTIBUS® Interface for Multimaster Configurations and System Expansion

The iSBC 88/25 Single Board Computer is a member of Intel's complete line of OEM microcomputer systems which take full advantage of Intel's technology to provide economical, self-contained, computer-based solutions for OEM applications. The CPU, system clock, read/write memory, nonvolatile read only memory, I/O ports and drivers, serial communications interface, priority interrupt logic and programmable timers, all reside on the board. The large control storage capacity makes the iSBC 88/25 board ideally suited for control-oriented applications such as process control, instrumentation and industrial automation.

143847–1

The iSBC® 88/25 is also manufactured under product code pSBC 88/25 by Intel Puerto Rico, Inc.

September 1991
Order Number: 143847-004

FUNCTIONAL DESCRIPTION

Central Processing Unit

The central processor for the iSBC 88/25 board is Intel's 8088 CPU operating at 5 MHz. The CPU architecture includes four 16-bit byte addressable data registers, two 16-bit memory base pointer registers and two 16-bit index registers, all accessed by a total of 24 operand addressing modes for comprehensive memory addressing and for support of the data structures required for today's structured, high level languages, as well as assembly language.

Instruction Set

The 8088 instruction repertoire includes variable length instruction format (including double operand instructions), 8-bit and 16-bit signed and unsigned arithmetic operators for binary, BCD and unpacked ASCII data, and iterative word and byte string manipulation functions.

For enhanced numerics processing capability, the iSBC 337A MULTIMODULE Numeric Data Processor extends the architecture and data set. Over 60 numeric instructions offer arithmetic, trigonometric, transcendental, logarithmic and exponential instructions. Supported data types include 16, 32, and 64-bit integer, and 32 and 64-bit floating point, 18-digit packed BCD and 80-bit temporary.

Architectural Features

A 4-byte instruction queue provides pre-fetching of sequential instructions and can reduce the 750 ns minimum instruction cycle to 250 ns for queued instructions. The stack-oriented architecture readily supports modular programming by facilitating fast, simple, inter-module communication, and other programming constructs needed for asynchronous real-time systems. The memory expansion capabilities

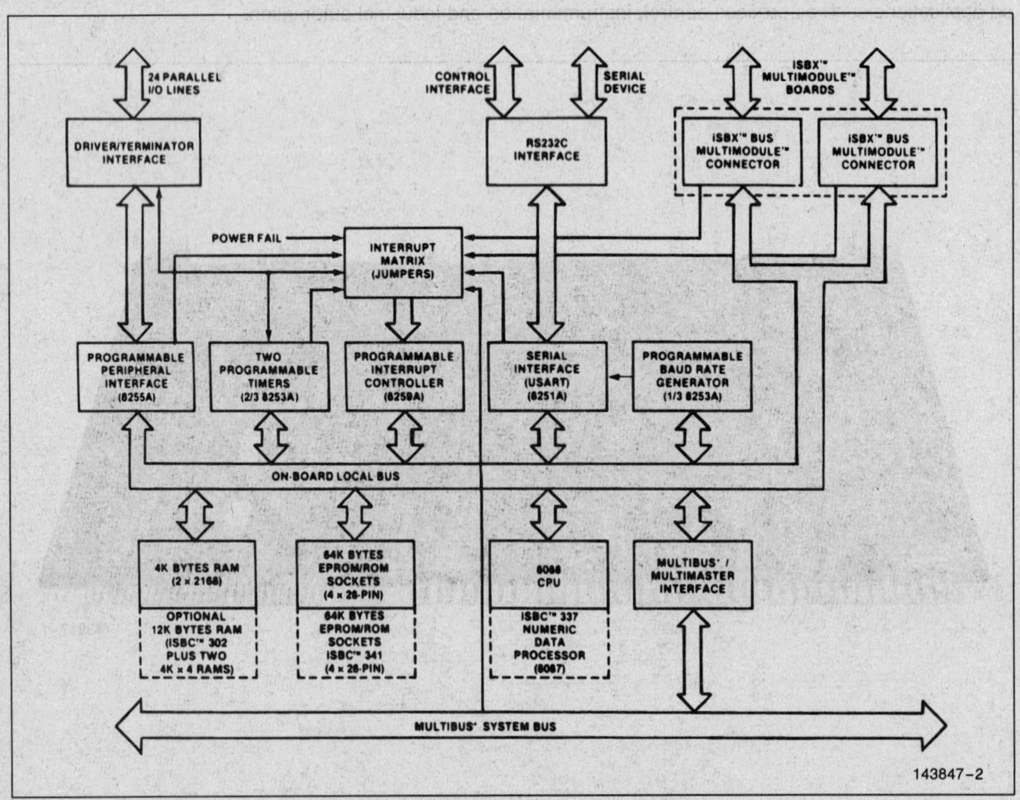

143847–2

Figure 1. iSBC® 88/25 Block Diagram

offer a 1 megabyte addressing range. The dynamic relocation scheme allows ease in segmentation of pure procedure and data for efficient memory utilization. Four segment registers (code, stack, data, extra) contain program loaded offset values which are used to map 16-bit addresses to 20-bit addresses. Each register maps 64 Kbytes at a time and activation of a specific register is controlled explicitly by program control and is also selected implicitly by specific functions and instructions.

Memory Configuration

The iSBC 88/25 microcomputer contains 4 Kbytes of high-speed static RAM on-board. In addition, the on-board RAM may be expanded to 12 Kbytes via the iSBC 302 8 Kbyte RAM module which mounts on the iSBC 88/25 board and then to 16 Kbytes by adding two 4K × 4 RAM devices in sockets on the iSBC 302 module. All on-board RAM is accessed by the 8088 CPU with no wait states, yielding a memory cycle time of 800 ns.

In addition to the on-board RAM, the iSBC 88/25 board has four 28-pin sockets, configured to accept JEDEC 24/28-pin standard memory devices. Up to 64 Kbytes of EPROM are supported in 16 Kbyte increments with Intel 27128 EPROMs. The iSBC 88/25 board is also compatible with the 2716, 2732 and 2764 EPROMs.

With the addition of the iSBC 341 MULTIMODULE EPROM option, the on-board capacity for these devices is doubled, providing up to 128 Kbytes of EPROM capacity on-board.

Parallel I/O Interface

The iSBC 88/25 Single Board Computer contains 24 programmable parallel I/O lines implemented using the Intel 8255A Programmable Peripheral interface. The system software is used to configure the I/O lines in any combination of unidirectional input/output and bidirectional ports indicated in Table 1. In order to take advantage of the large number of possible I/O configurations, sockets are provided for interchangeable I/O line drivers and terminators, allowing the selection of the appropriate combination of optional line drivers and terminators with the required drive/termination characteristics.

The 24 programmable I/O lines and signal ground lines are brought out to a 50-pin edge connector.

Serial I/O

A programmable communications interface using the Intel 8251A Universal Synchronous/Asynchronous Receiver/Transmitter (USART) is contained on the iSBC 88/25 board. A software selectable baud rate generator provides the USART with all common communication frequencies. The mode of operation (i.e., synchronous or asynchronous), data format, control character format, parity and baud rate are all under program control. The 8251A provides full duplex, double buffered transmit and receive capability. Parity, overrun and framing error detection are all incorporated in the USART. The RS232C compatible interface on each board, in conjunction with the USART, provides a direct interface to RS232C compatible terminals, cassettes and asynchronous and synchronous modems. The RS232C command lines, serial data lines and signal ground line are brought out to a 26-pin edge connector.

Table 1. Input/Output Port Modes of Operation

Port	Lines (qty)	Mode of Operation					
		Unidirectional				Bidirectional	Control
		Input		Output			
		Latched	Latched & Strobed	Latched	Latched & Strobed		
1	8	X	X	X	X	X	
2	8	X	X	X	X		
3	4	X		X			X(1)
	4	X		X			X(1)

NOTE:
1. Part of port 3 must be used as a control port when either port 1 or port 2 are used as a latched and strobed input or a latched and strobed output port or port 1 is used as a bidirectional port.

Programmable Timers

The iSBC 88/25 board provides three independent, fully programmable 16-bit interval timers/event counters utilizing the Intel 8253 Programmable Interval Timer. Each counter is capable of operating in either BCD or binary modes. Two of these timers/counters are available to the systems designer to generate accurate time intervals under software control. Routing for the outputs and gate/trigger inputs of two of these counters is jumper selectable.

The outputs may be independently routed to the 8259A Programmable Interrupt Controller and to the I/O terminators associated with the 8255A to allow external devices or an 8255A port to gate the timer or to count external events. The third interval timer in the 8253 provides the programmable baud rate generator for the iSBC 88/25 board RS232C USART serial port. The system software configures each timer independently to select the desired function.

ISBX™ MULTIMODULE™ On-Board Expansion

Two 8-bit iSBX MULTIMODULE connectors are provided on the iSBC 88/25 microcomputer. Through these connectors, additional on-board I/O functions such as additional parallel and serial I/O, analog I/O, mass storage device controllers and other custom interfaces may be added. By mounting directly on the single board computer, less interface logic, less power, simpler packaging, higher performance, and lower cost result when compared to other alternatives such as MULTIBUS form factor compatible boards. The iSBX connectors on the iSBC 88/25 provide all signals necessary to interface to the local on-board bus. A broad range of iSBX MULTIMODULE options are available from Intel. Custom iSBX modules may also be designed for use on the iSBC 88/25 board.

Multimaster Capabilities

For those applications requiring additional processing capacity and the benefits of multiprocessing (i.e., several CPUs and/or controllers logically sharing system tasks through communication of the system bus), the iSBC 88/25 board provides full MULTIBUS arbitration control logic. This control logic allows up to three iSBC 88/25 boards or other bus masters, including iSBC 80 and iSBC 86 family MULTIBUS compatible single board computers to share the system bus using a serial (daisy chain) priority scheme and allows up to 16 masters to share the MULTIBUS system bus with an external parallel priority decoder. In addition to the multiprocessing configurations made possible with multimaster capability, it also provides a very efficient mechanism for all forms of DMA (Direct Memory Access) transfers.

Interrupt Capability

The iSBC 88/25 board provides 9 vectored interrupt levels. The highest level is the NMI (Non-Maskable Interrupt) line which is directly tied to the 8088 CPU. This interrupt is typically used for signaling catastrophic events (e.g., power failure). The Intel 8259A Programmable Interrupt Controller (PIC) provides control and vectoring for the next eight interrupt levels. A selection of four priority processing modes is available for use in designing request processing configurations to match system requirements for efficient interrupt servicing with minimal latencies. Operating mode and priority assignments may be reconfigured dynamically via software at any time during system operation. The PIC accepts interrupt requests from all on-board I/O resources and from the MULTIBUS system bus. The PIC then resolves requests according to the selected mode and, if appropriate, issues an interrupt to the CPU.

Interrupt requests to be serviced by the iSBC 88/25 board may originate from 24 sources. All interrupt signals are brought to the interrupt jumper matrix where any combination of interrupt sources may be strapped to the desired interrupt request level on the 8259A PIC or the NMI input to the CPU directly.

Power-Fail Control and Auxiliary Power

Control logic is also included to accept a power-fail interrupt to initiate an orderly shut down of the system in the event of a power failure. Additionally, an active-low TTL compatible memory protect signal is brought out of the auxiliary connector which, when asserted, disables read/write access to RAM memory on the board. This input is provided for the protection of RAM contents during system power-down sequences. An auxiliary power bus is also provided to allow separate power to RAM for systems requiring battery backup of read/write memory. Selection of this auxiliary RAM power bus is made via jumpers on the board.

SPECIFICATIONS

Word Size

Instruction—8, 16, 24, or 32 bits
Data—8 bits

System Clock

5.00 MHz or 4.17 MHz ±0.1% (jumper selectable)

NOTE:
4.17 MHz required with the optional iSBC 337 module.

Cycle Time

BASIC INSTRUCTION CYCLE

At 5 MHz—1.2 μs
—400 ns (assumes instruction in the queue)

NOTES:
Basic instruction cycle is defined as the fastest instruction time (i.e., two clock cycles).

Memory Cycle Time

RAM—800 ns (no wait states)
EPROM—Jumper selectable from 800 ns to 1400 ns

Memory Capacity/Addressing

ON-BOARD EPROM

Device	Total Capacity	Address Range
2716	8 Kbytes	$FE000\text{-}FFFFF_H$
2732	16 Kbytes	$FC000\text{-}FFFFF_H$
2764	32 Kbytes	$F8000\text{-}FFFFF_H$
27128	64 Kbytes	$F0000\text{-}FFFFF_H$

WITH iSBC 341 MULTIMODULE EPROM

Device	Total Capacity	Address Range
2716	16 Kbytes	$FC000\text{-}FFFFF_H$
2732	32 Kbytes	$F8000\text{-}FFFFF_H$
2764	64 Kbytes	$F0000\text{-}FFFFF_H$
27128	128 Kbytes	$E0000\text{-}FFFFF_H$

ON-BOARD RAM

4 Kbytes—$0\text{-}0FFF_H$

WITH iSBC 302 MULTIMODULE RAM

12 Kbytes—$0\text{-}2FFF_H$

WITH iSBC 302 MULTIMODULE BOARD AND TWO 4K x 4 RAM CHIPS

16 Kbytes—$0\text{-}3FFF_H$

I/O Capacity

Parallel—24 programmable lines using one 8255A
Serial—1 programmable line using one 8251A
iSBX Multimodule—2 iSBX MULTIMODULE boards

Serial Communications Characteristics

Synchronous—5 8-bit characters; internal or external character synchronization; automatic sync insertion
Asynchronous—5 8-bit characters; break character generation; 1, 1½, or 2 stop bits; false start bit detection

Interfaces

Multibus: All signals TTL compatible

iSBX Bus: All signals TTL compatible

Parallel I/O: All signals TTL compatible

Serial I/O: RS232C compatible, configurable as a data set or data terminal

Timer: All signals TTL compatible

Interrupt Requests: All TTL compatible

Physical Characteristics

Width: 12.00 in. (30.48 cm)

Height: 6.75 in. (17.15 cm)

Depth: 0.70 in. (1.78 cm)

Weight: 14 oz. (388 gm)

Electrical Characteristics

DC POWER REQUIREMENTS

Configuration	Current Requirements (All Voltages ±5%)		
	+5V	+12V	−12V
Without EPROM(1)	3.8A	25 mA	23 mA
RAM only(2)	104 mA		
With 8K EPROM(3) (using 2716)	4.3A	25 mA	23 mA
With 16K EPROM(3) (using 2732)	4.4A	25 mA	23 mA
With 32K EPROM(3) (using 2764)	4.4A	25 mA	23 mA

NOTES:
1. Does not include power for optional ROM/EPROM, I/O drivers and I/O terminators.
2. RAM chips powered via auxiliary power bus in power-down mode. Does not include power for optional RAM.
3. Includes power required for 4 ROM/EPROM chips, and I/O terminators installed for 16 I/O lines; all terminator inputs low.

Environmental Characteristics

Operating Temperature: 0°C to 55°C

Relative Humidity: to 90% (without condensation)

Reference Manual

143825-001—iSBC 88/25 Hardware Reference Manual (NOT SUPPLIED)

ORDERING INFORMATION

Part Number	Description
SBC 88/25	8-bit Single Board Computer with 4 Kbytes RAM

iSBC® 80/24A* SINGLE BOARD COMPUTER

- Upward Compatible Replacement for iSBC 80/20-4 Single Board Computer
- 8085A-2 CPU Operating at 4.8 or 2.4 MHz
- Two iSBX™ Bus Connectors for iSBX MULTIMODULE™ Board Expansion
- 8K Bytes of Static Read/Write Memory
- Sockets for Up to 32K Bytes of Read Only Memory
- 48 Programmable Parallel I/O Lines with Sockets for Interchangeable Line Drivers and Terminators
- Programmable Synchronous/Asynchronous RS232C Compatible Serial Interface with Software Selectable Baud Rates
- Full Multibus Control Logic for Multimaster Configurations and System Expansion
- Two Programmable 16-Bit BCD or Binary Timers/Event Counters
- 12 Levels of Programmable Interrupt Control
- Auxiliary Power Bus, Memory Protect, and Power-Fail Interrupt Control Logic Provided for Battery Backup RAM Requirements

The Intel 80/24A Single Board Computer is a member of Intel's complete line of OEM microcomputer systems which take full advantage of Intel's LSI technology to provide economical, self-contained computer-based solutions for OEM applications. The CPU, system clock, iSBX bus interface, read/write memory, read only memory sockets, I/O ports and drivers, serial communications interface, priority interrupt logic, and programmable timers all reside on the board. Full Multibus interface logic is included to offer compatibility with the Intel OEM Microcomputer Systems family of Single Board Computers, expansion memory options, digital and analog I/O expansion boards, and peripheral and communications controllers.

142927–1

*The iSBC® 80/24A Board is also manufactured under product code pSBC 80/24A by Intel Puerto Rico, Inc.

September 1991
Order Number: 142927-005

FUNCTIONAL DESCRIPTION

Central Processing Unit

Intel's 8-bit 8085A-2 CPU is the central processor for the iSBC 80/24A board operating at either 4.8 or 2.4 MHz. The 8085A-2 CPU is directly software compatible with the Intel 8080A CPU. The 8085A-2 contains six 8-bit general purpose registers and an accumulator. The six general purpose registers may be addressed individually or in pairs, providing single and double precision operators. Minimum instruction execution time is 826 nanoseconds.

iSBX™ MULTIMODULE™ On-Board Expansion

Two 8-bit iSBX bus MULTIMODULE connectors are provided for plug-in expansion of iSBX MULTIMODULE boards.

Memory Addressing

The 8085A-2 has a 16-bit program counter which allows direct addressing of up to 64K bytes of memory. An external stack, located within any portion of read/write memory, may be used as a last-in/first-out storage area for the contents of the program counter, flags, accumulator, and all of the six general purpose registers. A 16-bit stack pointer controls the addressing of this external stack. This stack provides subroutine nesting bounded only by memory size.

Memory Capacity

The iSBC 80/24A board contains 8K bytes of static read/write memory using an 8K × 8 SRAMs. All RAM read and write operations are performed at maximum processor speed. Power for the on-board RAM may be provided on an auxiliary power bus, and memory protect logic is included for RAM battery backup requirements.

Four sockets are provided for up to 32K bytes of nonvolatile read only memory on the iSBC 80/24A board.

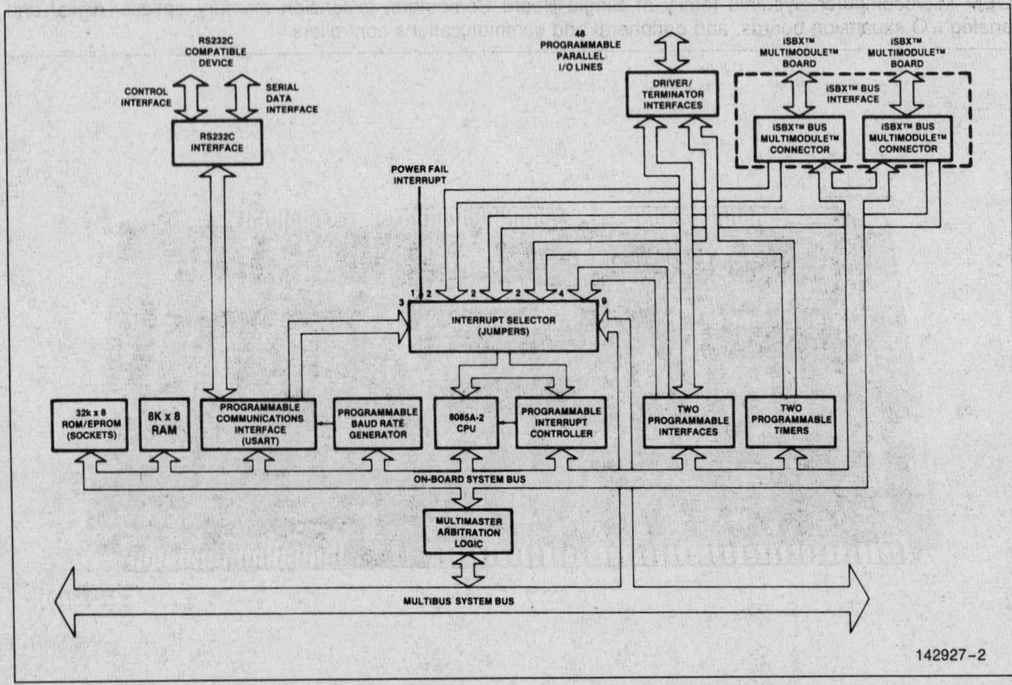

Figure 1. iSBC® 80/24A Single Board Computer Block Diagram

Parallel I/O Interface

The iSBC 80/24A board contains 48 programmable parallel I/O lines implemented using two Intel 8255A Programmable Peripheral Interfaces. The system software is used to configure the I/O lines in any combination of unidirectional input/output and bidirectional ports. Therefore, the I/O interface may be customized to meet specific peripheral requirements. In order to take full advantage of the large number of possible I/O configurations, sockets are provided for interchangeable I/O line drivers and terminators. Hence, the flexibility of the I/O interface is further enhanced by the capability of selecting the appropriate combination of optional line drivers and terminators to provide the required sink current, polarity, and drive/termination characteristics for each application. The 48 programmable I/O lines and signal ground lines are brought out to two 50-pin edge connectors that mate with flat, woven, or round cables.

Serial I/O Interface

A programmable communications interface using the Intel 8251A Universal Synchronous/Asynchronous Receiver/Transmitter (USART) is contained on the iSBC 80/24A board. A software selectable baud rate generator provides the USART with all common communication frequencies. The USART can be programmed by the system software to select the desired asynchronous or synchronous serial data transmission technique (including IBM Bi-Sync). The mode of operation (i.e. synchronous or asynchronous), data format, control character format, parity, and baud rate are all under program control. The 8251A provides full duplex, double buffered transmit and receive capability. Parity, overrun, and framing error detection are all incorporated in the USART. The RS232C compatible interface, in conjunction with the USART, provides a direct interface to RS232C compatible terminals, cassettes, and asynchronous and synchronous modems. The RS232C command lines serial data lines, and signal ground line are brought out to a 26-pin edge connector that mates with RS232C compatible flat or round cable.

Multimaster Capability

For those applications requiring additional processing capacity and the benefits of multiprocessing, the iSBC 80/24A board provides full Multibus arbitration control logic. This control logic allows up to three iSBC 80/24A boards or other bus masters to share the system bus in serial (daisy chain) priority fashion, and up to 16 masters to share the Multibus system bus with the addition of an external priority network. The Multibus arbitration logic operates synchronously with a Multibus clock (provided by the iSBC 80/24A board or optionally connected directly to the Multibus clock) while data is transferred via a handshake between the master and slave modules. This allows different speed controllers to share resources on the same bus since transfers via the bus proceed asynchronously. Thus, transfer speed is dependent on transmitting and receiving devices only. This design provides slow master modules from being handicapped in their attempts to gain control of the bus, but does not restrict the speed at which faster modules can transfer data via the same bus. The most obvious applications for the master-slave capabilities of the bus are multiprocessor configurations, high speed direct memory access (DMA) operations, and high speed peripheral control, but are by no means limited to these three.

Programmable Timers

The iSBC 80/24A board provides three independent, fully programmable 16-bit interval timers/event counters utilizing the Intel 8254 Programmable Interval Timer. Each counter is capable of operating in either BCD or binary modes. Two of these timers/counters are available to the systems designer to generate accurate time intervals under software control. Routing for the outputs and gate/trigger inputs of two of these counters is jumper selectable. The outputs may be independently routed to the 8259A Programmable Interrupt Controller, to the I/O line drivers associated with the 8255A Programmable Peripheral Interface, or may be routed as inputs to the 8255A chip. The gate/trigger inputs may be routed to I/O terminators associated with the 8255A or as output connections from the 8255A. The third interval timer in the 8254 provides the programmable baud rate generator for the RS232C USART serial port. In utilizing the iSBC 80/24A board, the systems designer simply configures, via software, each timer independently to meet system requirements. Whenever a given time delay or count is needed, software commands to the programmable timers/event counters select the desired function. The contents of each counter may be read at any time during system operation with simple read operations for event counting applications, and special commands are included so that the contents of each counter can be read "on the fly".

Interrupt Capability

The iSBC 80/24A board provides vectoring for 12 interrupt levels. Four of these levels are handled directly by the interrupt processing capability of the 8085A-2 CPU and represent the four highest priority interrupts of the iSBC 80/24A board. Requests are routed to the 8085A-2 interrupt inputs—TRAP, RST 7.5, RST 6.5, and RST 5.5 (in decreasing order of priority), each of which generates a call instruction to a unique address (TRAP: 24H; RST 7.5: 3CH; RST 6.5: 34H; and RST 5.5: 2CH). An 8085A-2 JMP instruction at each of these addresses then provides linkage to interrupt service routines located independently anywhere in memory. All interrupt inputs with the exception of the trap interrupt may be masked via software. The trap interrupt should be used for conditions such as power-down sequences which require immediate attention by the 8085A-2 CPU. The Intel 8259A Programmable Interrupt Controller (PIC) provides vectoring for the next eight interrupt levels. As shown in Table 3, a selection of four priority processing modes is available to the systems designer for use in designing request processing configurations to match system requirements. Operating mode and priority assignments may be reconfigured dynamically via software at any time during system operation. The PIC accepts interrupt requests from the programmable parallel and serial I/O interfaces, the programmable timers, the system bus, iSBX bus, or directly from peripheral equipment. The PIC then determines which of the incoming requests is of the highest priority, determines whether this request is of higher priority than the level currently being serviced, and, if appropriate, issues an interrupt to the CPU. Any combination of interrupt levels may be masked, via software, by storing a single byte in the interrupt mask register of the PIC. The PIC generates a unique memory address for each interrupt level. These addresses are equally spaced at intervals of 4 or 8 (software selectable) bytes. This 32 or 64-byte block may be located to begin at any 32 or 64-byte boundary in the 65,536-byte memory space. A single 8085A-2 JMP instruction at each of these addresses then provides linkage to locate each interrupt service routine independently anywhere in memory.

Programmable Interrupt Modes

Mode	Operation
Fully nested	Interrupt request line priorities fixed at 0 as highest, 7 as lowest.
Autorotating	Equal priority. Each level, after receiving service, becomes the lowest priority level until next interrupt occurs.
Specific priority	System software assigns lowest priority level. Priority of all other levels based in sequence numerically on this assignment.
Polled	System software examines priority-encoded system interrupt status via interrupt status register.

Interrupt Request Generation

Interrupt requests may originiate from 23 sources. Two jumper selectable interrupt requests can be generated by each iSBX MULTIMODULE board. Two jumper selectable interrupt requests can be automatically generated by each programmable peripheral interface when a byte of information is ready to be transferred to the CPU (i.e., input buffer is full) or a byte of information has been transferred to a peripheral device (i.e., output buffer is empty). Three jumper selectable interrupt requests can be automatically generated by the USART when a character is ready to be transferred to the CPU (i.e., receiver channel buffer is full), a character is ready to be transmitted (i.e., the USART is ready to accept a character from the CPU), or when the transmitter is empty (i.e., the USART has no character to transmit). A jumper selectable request can be generated by each of the programmable timers. Nine interrupt request lines are available to the user for direct interface to user designated peripheral devices via the MULTIBUS system bus. A power-fail signal can also be selected as an interrupt source.

Power-Fail Control

A power-fail interrupt may be detected through the AC-low signal generated by the power supply. This signal may be configured to interrupt the 8085A-2 CPU to initiate an orderly power down instruction sequence.

SPECIFICATIONS

Word Size

Instruction— 8, 16 or 24 bits
Data — 8 bits

Cycle Time

BASIC INSTRUCTION CYCLE

826 ns (4.84 MHz operating frequency)
1.65 μs (2.42 MHz operating frequency)

NOTE:
Basic instruction cycle is defined as the fastest instruction (i.e., four clock cycles).

Memory Addressing

ON-BOARD EPROM

0-0FFF using 2708, 2758 (1 wait state)
0-1FFF using 2716 (1 wait state)
0-3FFF using 2732 (1 wait state)
using 2732A (no wait states)
0-7FFF using 2764A (no wait states)

ON-BOARD RAM

E000-FFFF

NOTE:
Default configuration—may be reconfigured to top end of any 16K boundary.

Memory Capacity

ON-BOARD EPROM

32K bytes (sockets only)

ON-BOARD RAM

8K bytes

Serial Communications Characteristics

Synchronous — 5–8 bit characters; internal or external character synchronization; automatic sync insertion

Asynchronous— 5–8 bit characters; break character generation; 1, 1½, or 2 stop bits; false start bit detectors

Interfaces

MULTIBUS — All signals TTL compatible
iSBX Bus — All signals TTL compatible
Parallel I/O — All signals TTL compatible
Serial I/O — RS232C compatible, configurable as a data set or data terminal
Timer — All signals TTL compatible
Interrupt Requests— All TTL compatible

System Clock (8085A-2 CPU)

4.84 or 2.42 MHz ±0.1% (jumper selectable)

Auxiliary Power

An auxiliary power bus is provided to allow separate power to RAM for systems requiring battery backup of read/write memory. Selection of this auxiliary RAM power bus is made via jumpers on the board.

Memory Protect

An active-low TTL compatible memory protect signal is brought out on the auxiliary connector which, when asserted, disables read/write access to RAM memory on the board. This input is provided for the protection of RAM contents during system power-down sequences.

Physical Characteristics

Width: 12.00 in. (30.48 cm)
Height: 6.75 in. (17.15 cm)
Depth: 0.50 in. (1.27 cm)
Weight: 12.64 oz. (354 gm)

Electrical Characteristics

DC POWER REQUIREMENTS

Configuration	Current Requirements			
	V_{CC} = +5V ±5% (max)	V_{DD} = +12V ±5% (max)	V_{BB} = −5V ±5% (max)	V_{AA} = −12V ±5% (max)
Without EPROM(1)	2.66A	40 mA	—	20 mA
RAM Only(2)	0.01A	—	—	—
With iSBC 530(3)	2.66A	140 mA	—	120 mA
With 4K EPROM(4) (using 2708)	3.28A	300 mA	180 mA	20 mA
With 4K EPROM(4) (using 2758)	3.44A	40 mA	—	20 mA
With 8K EPROM(4) (using 2716)	3.44A	40 mA	—	20 mA
With 16K EPROM(4) (using 2732A)	3.46A	40 mA	—	20 mA
With 32K EPROM(4) (using 2764A)	3.42A	40 mA	—	20 mA

NOTES:
1. Does not include power for optional EPROM, I/O drivers, and I/O terminators.
2. RAM chips powered via auxiliary power bus.
3. Does not include power for optional EPROM, I/O drivers, I/O terminators. Power for iSBC 530 Adapter is supplied via serial port connector.
4. Includes power required for four EPROM chips, and I/O terminators installed for 16 I/O lines; all terminators inputs low.

Environmental Characteristics

Operating Temperature: 0°C to 55°C

Reference Manual

148437-001— iSBC 80/24A Single Board Computer Hardware Reference Manual (NOT SUPPLIED)

ORDERING INFORMATION

Part Number	Description
SBC 80/24A	Single Board Computer

iSBC® 80/10B* SINGLE BOARD COMPUTER

- 8080A Central Processing Unit
- One iSBX™ Bus Connector for iSBX™ MULTIMODULE™ Board Expansion
- 1K Byte of Read/Write Memory with Sockets for Expansion up to 4K Bytes
- Sockets for up to 16K Bytes of Read Only Memory
- 48 Programmable Parallel I/O Lines with Sockets for Interchangeable Line Drivers and Terminators
- Programmable Synchronous/ Asynchronous Communications Interface with Selectable RS232C or Teletypewriter Compatiblity
- Single Level Interrupt with 11 Interrupt Sources
- Auxiliary Power Bus and Power-Fail Interrupt Control Logic for RAM Battery Backup
- 1.04 Millisecond Interval Timer
- Limited Master MULTIBUS® Interface

The Intel iSBC 80/10B board is a member of Intel's complete line of OEM microcomputer systems which take full advantage of Intel's LSI technology to provide economical, self-contained computer-based solutions for OEM applications. The CPU, system clock, iSBX bus interface, read/write memory, read only memory sockets, I/O ports and drivers, serial communications interface, bus control logic, and drivers all reside on the board.

280217-1

*The iSBC® 80/10B is also manufactured under product code pSBC 80/10B by Intel Puerto Rico, Inc.

August 1990
Order Number: 280217-003

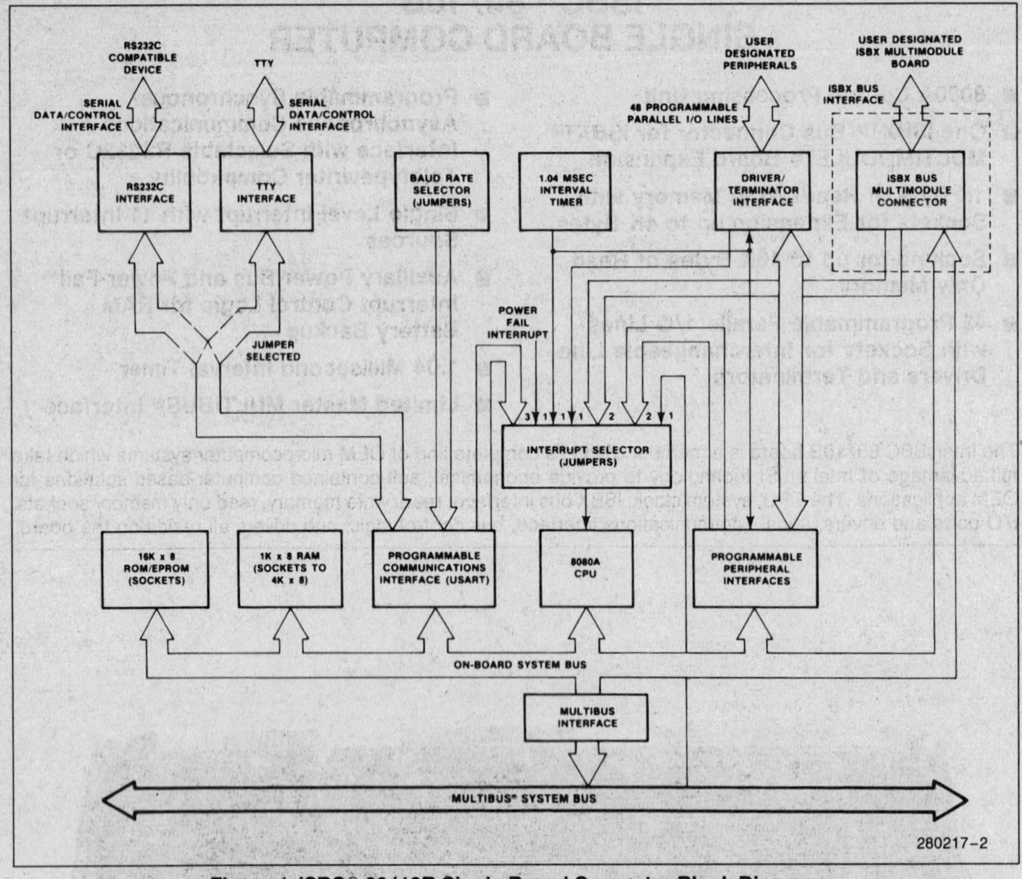

Figure 1. iSBC® 80/10B Single Board Computer Block Diagram

FUNCTIONAL DESCRIPTION

Intel's 8-bit n-channel MOS 8080A CPU, fabricated on a single LSI chip, is the central processor for the iSBC 80/10B board. The 8080A contains six 8-bit general purpose registers and an accumulator. The six general purpose registers may be addressed individually or in pairs, providing both single and double precision operators. A block diagram of iSBC 80/10B board functional components is shown in Figure 1.

iSBX™ Bus MULTIMODULE™ Board Expansion

One iSBX bus connector interface is provided to accomplish plug-in expansion with any iSBX MULTIMODULE board.

Memory Addressing

The 8080A has a 16-bit program counter which allows direct addressing of up to 64K bytes of memory. An external stack, located within any portion of read/write memory, may be used as a last-in/first-out storage area for the contents of the program counter, flags, accumulator, and all of the six general purpose registers. A 16-bit stack pointer controls the addressing of this external stack. This stack provides subroutine nesting bounded only by memory size.

Memory Capacity

The iSBC 80/10B board contains 1K bytes of read/write static memory. In addition, sockets for up to 4K bytes of RAM memory are provided on board. Read/write memory may be added in 1K byte increments. Sockets for up to 16K bytes of nonvolatile read-only-memory are provided on the board. All on-board RAM, ROM or EPROM read operations are performed at maximum processor speed.

Parallel I/O Interface

The iSBC 80/10B board contains 48 programmable parallel I/O lines implemented using two Intel 8255A programmable peripheral interfaces. The system software is used to configure the I/O lines in any combination of unidirectional input/output, and bidirectional ports. In order to take full advantage of the large number of possible I/O configurations, sockets are provided for interchangeable I/O line drivers and terminators. The flexibility of the I/O interface is further enhanced by the capability of selecting the appropriate combination of optional line drivers and terminators to provide the required sink current, polarity, and drive/termination characteristics for each application. The 48 programmable I/O lines and signal ground lines are brought out to two 50-pin edge connectors that mate with flat cable or round cable.

Serial I/O Interface

A programmable communications interface using the Intel 8251A Universal Synchronous/Asynchronous Receiver/Transmitter (USART) is contained on the board. A jumper selectable baud rate generator provides the USART with all common communications frequencies. The USART can be programmed by the system software to select the desired synchronous or asynchronous serial data transmission technique (including IBM Bi-Sync). The mode of operation (i.e., synchronous or asynchronous), data format, control character format and parity are all under program control. The 8251A provides full duplex, double-buffered transmit and receive capability. Parity, overrun, and framing error detection are all incorporated in the USART. The inclusion of jumper selectable TTY or RS232C compatible interfaces on the board, in conjunction with the USART, provides a direct interface to teletypes, CRTs, RS232C compatible cassettes, and asynchronous and synchronous modems. The RS232C or TTY command lines, serial data lines, and signal ground lines are brought out to a 26-pin edge connector that mates with RS232C compatible flat or round cable.

Interrupt Capability

Interrupt requests may originate from 11 sources. Two jumper selectable interrupt requests can be automatically generated by the programmable peripheral interface when a byte of information is ready to be transferred to the CPU (i.e., input buffer is full) or a byte of information has been transferred to a peripheral device (i.e., output buffer is empty). Three jumper selectable interrupt requests can be automatically generated by the USART when a character is ready to be transferred to the CPU (i.e., receive channel buffer is full), a character is ready to be transmitted (i.e., the USART is ready to accept a character from the CPU), or when the transmitter is empty (i.e., the USART has no character to transmit). These five interrupt request lines are all maskable under program control. Two interrupt request lines may be interfaced directly to user designated peripheral devices; one via the MULTIBUS system bus and the other via the I/O edge connector. One jumper selectable interrupt request may be interfaced to the power-fail interrupt control logic. One jumper selectable interrupt request may originate from the interval timer. Two general purpose interrupt requests are jumper selectable from the iSBX interface. These two signals permit a user installed MULTIMODULE board to interrupt to 8080A CPU. The eleven interrupt request lines share a single CPU interrupt level. When an interrupt request is recognized, a restart instruction (RESTART 7) is generated. The processor responds by suspending program execution and executing a user defined interrupt service routine.

Power-Fail Control

A power-fail interrupt may be detected through the AC-low signal generated by the power supply. This signal may be configured to interrupt the 8080A CPU to initiate an orderly power down instruction sequence.

Interval Timer

A 1.04 millisecond timer is available for interval interrupts or as a clock output to the parallel I/O connector. The timer output is jumper selectable to the programmable parallel interface, the parallel I/O connector (J1), or directly to the 8080A CPU.

SPECIFICATIONS

Word Size

Instruction: 8, 16, or 24 bits
Data: 8 bits

Cycle Time

Basic Instruction Cycle: 1.95 μs

NOTE:
Basic instruction cycle is defined as the fastest instruction (i.e., four clock cycles).

Memory Addressing

On-Board ROM/EPROM
0–0FFF using 2708, 2758
0–1FFF using 2716
0–3FFF using 2732

On-Board RAM
3C00–3FFF with no RAM expansion
3000–3FFF with 2114A-5 expansion

Memory Capacity

On-Board ROM/EPROM
16K bytes (sockets only)

On-Board RAM
1K byte with user expansion in 1K increments to 4K byte using Intel 2114A-5 RAMs.

Off-Board Expansion
Up to 64K bytes using user specified combinations of RAM, ROM, and EPROM.

I/O Capacity

Parallel:	48 programmable lines
Serial:	1 transmit, 1 receive
MULTIMODULE:	1 iSBX Bus MULTIMODULE Board

Serial Communications Characteristics

Synchronous:	5–8 bit characters; internal or external character synchronization; automatic sync insertion
Asynchronous:	5–8 bit characters; break character generation; 1, 1½, or 2 stop bits; false start bit detectors

Interrupts

Single-level with on-board logic that automatically vectors the processor to location 38H using a restart instruction (RESTART 7). Interrupt requests may originate from user specified I/O (2); the programmable peripheral interface (2); the iSBX MULTIMODULE board (2); the programmable communications interface (3); the power fail interrupt (1); or the interval timer (1).

Interfaces

MULTIBUS:	All signals TTL compatible
iSBX Bus:	All signals TTL compatible
Parallel I/O:	All signals TTL compatible
Serial I/O:	RS232C or a 20 mil current loop TTY interface (jumper selectable)
Interrupt Requests:	All TTL compatible (active-low)

Clocks

System Clock: 2.048 MHz ±0.1%
Interval Timer: 1.042 ms ±0.1% (959.5 Hz)

Physical Characteristics

Width:	12.00 in (30.48 cm)
Height:	6.75 in. (17.15 cm)
Depth:	0.05 in. (1.27 cm)
Weight:	14 oz. (397.3 gm)

Electrical Characteristics

DC Power Requirements

Voltage	Without EPROM(1)	With 2708 EPROM(2)	With 2758, 2716, or 2732 EPROM(3)	Power Down Requirements (RAM and Support Circuit)
V_{CC} = +5V ±5%	I_{CC} = 2.0A(4)	3.1A	3.46A	84 mA + 140 mA/K (2114A-5)
V_{DD} = +12V ±5%	I_{DD} = 150 mA	400 mA	150 mA	Not Required
V_{BB} = −5V ±5%	I_{BB} = 2 mA	200 mA	2 mA	Not Required
V_{AA} = −12V ±5%	I_{AA} = 175 mA	175 mA	175 mA	Not Required

NOTES:
1. Does not include power required for optional ROM/EPROM, I/O drivers, or I/O terminators.
2. With four Intel 2708 EPROMS and 220Ω/330Ω for terminators, installed for 48 input lines. All terminator inputs low.
3. Same as #2 except with four 2758s, 2716s, or 2732s installed.
4. I_{CC} shown without RAM supply current. For 2114-5 add 140 mA per K byte to a maximum of 560 mA.

Environmental Characteristics

Operating Temperature: 0°C to 55°C

Reference Manual

9803119-01— iSBC 80/10B Single Board Computer Hardware Reference Manual (NOT SUPPLIED).

ORDERING INFORMATION

Part Number	Description
iSBC80/10B	Single Board Computer

8

iSBC® 337A MULTIMODULE™ NUMERIC DATA PROCESSOR

- **High Speed Fixed and Floating Point Functions for iSBC® Boards**
- **Extends Host CPU Instruction Set with Arithmetic, Logarithmic, Transcendental and Trigonometric Instructions**
- **MULTIMODULE™ Option Containing 8087 Numeric Data Processor**
- **Supports Seven Data Types Including Single and Double Precision Integer and Floating Point**
- **Fully Supported in the Multi-Tasking Environment of the iRMX™ I Operating System**

The Intel iSBC® 337A MULTIMODULE™ Numeric Data Processor offers high performance numerics support for iSBC 86 and iSBC 88 Single Board Computer users, for applications including simulation, instrument automation, graphics, signal processing and business systems. The coprocessor interface between the 8087 and the host CPU provides a simple means of extending the instruction set with over 60 additional numeric instructions supporting seven additional data types.

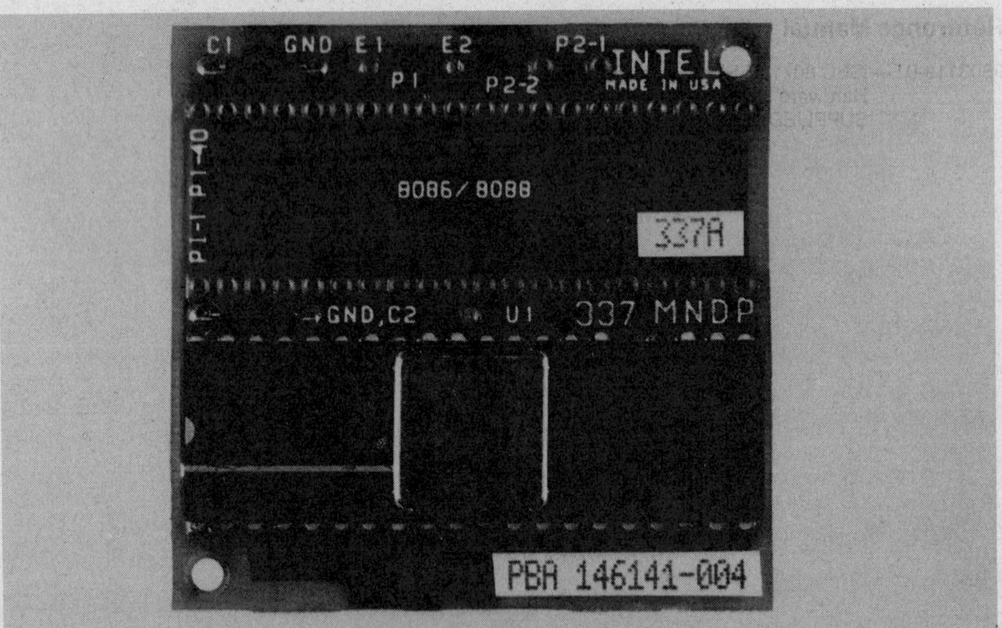

280077-1

September 1989
Order Number: 280077-002

OVERVIEW

The iSBC 337A MULTIMODULE Numeric Data Processor (NDP) provides arithmetic and logical instruction extensions to the 86/88 families. The instruction set consists of arithmetic, transcendental, logical, trigonometric and exponential instructions which can all operate on seven different data types. The data types are 16-, 32-, and 64-bit integer, 32- and 64-bit floating point, 18 digit packed BCD and 80-bit temporary.

Coprocessor Interface

The coprocessor interface between the host CPU and the iSBC 337A MULTIMODULE provides easy to use and high performance math processing. Installation of the iSBC 337A is simply a matter of removing the host CPU from its socket, installing the iSBC 337A MULTIMODULE into the host's CPU socket, and reinstalling the host CPU chip into the socket provided for it on the iSBC 337A MULTIMODULE (see Figure 1).

All synchronization and timing signals are provided via the coprocessor interface with the host CPU. The two processors also share a common address/data bus. The NDP component is capable of recognizing and executing NDP numeric instructions as they are fetched by the host CPU. This interface allows concurrent processing by the host CPU and the NDP. It also allows NDP and host CPU instructions to be intermixed in any fashion to provide the maximum overlapped operation and the highest aggregate performance.

High Performance and Accuracy

The 80-bit wide internal registers and data paths contribute significantly to high performance and minimize the execution time difference between single and double precision floating point formats. This 80-bit architecture provides very high resolution and accuracy.

This precision is complemented by extensive exception detection and handling. Six different types of exceptions can be reported and handled by the NDP. The user also has control over internal precision, infinity control and rounding control.

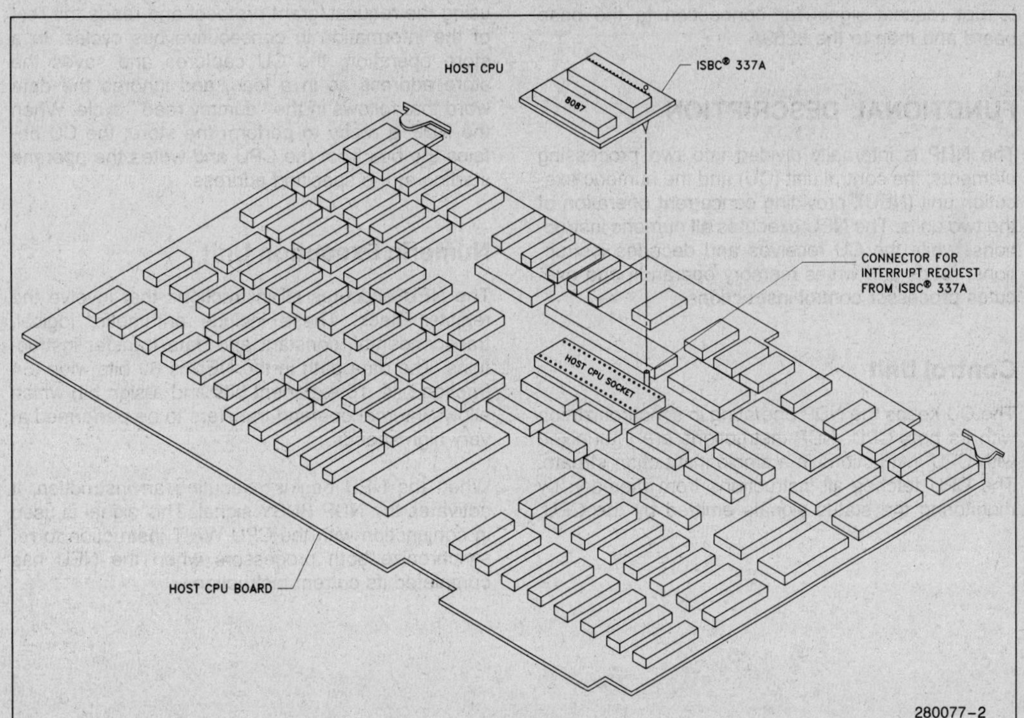

Figure 1. iSBC® 337A MULTIMODULE Installation

SYSTEM CONFIGURATION

As a coprocessor to the Host CPU, the NDP is wired in parallel with the CPU. The CPU's status and queue status lines enable the NDP to monitor and decode instructions in synchronization with the CPU and without any CPU overhead. Once started, the NDP can process in parallel with and independent of the host CPU. For resynchronization, the NDP's BUSY signal informs the CPU that the NDP is executing an instruction and the CPU WAIT instruction tests this signal to insure that the NDP is ready to execute subsequent instructions.

The NDP can interrupt the CPU when it detects an error or exception. The interrupt request line is routed to the CPU through an 8259A Programmable Interrupt Controller. This interrupt request signal is brought down from the iSBC 337A MULTIMODULE to the single board computer through a single pin connector (see Figure 1). The signal is then routed to the interrupt matrix for jumper connection to the 8259A Interrupt Controller. Other iAPX designs may use a similar arrangement, or by masking off the CPU "READ" pin from the iSBC 337A socket, provisions are made to allow the now vacated pin of the host's CPU socket to be used to bring down the interrupt request signal for connection to the base board and then to the 8259A.

FUNCTIONAL DESCRIPTION

The NDP is internally divided into two processing elements, the control unit (CU) and the numeric execution unit (NEU), providing concurrent operation of the two units. The NEU executes all numeric instructions, while the CU receives and decodes instructions, reads and writes memory operands and executes processor control instructions.

Control Unit

The CU keeps the NDP operating in synchronization with its host CPU. NDP instructions are intermixed with CPU instructions in a single instruction stream. The CPU fetches all instructions from memory; by monitoring the status signals emitted by the CPU, the NDP control unit determines when a 8086-2 instruction is being fetched. The CU taps the bus in parallel with the CPU and obtains that portion of the data stream.

After decoding the instruction, the host executes all opcodes but ESCAPE (ESC), while the NDP executes only the ESCAPE class instructions. (The first five bits of all ESCAPE instructions are identical). The CPU does provide addressing for ESC instructions however.

An NDP instruction either will not reference memory, will require loading one or more operands from memory into the NDP, or will require storing one or more operands from the NDP into memory. In the first case, a non-memory reference escape is used to start NDP operation. In the last two cases, the CU makes use of a "dummy read" cycle initiated by the CPU, in which the CPU calculates the operand address and initiates a bus cycle, but does not capture the data. Instead, the CPU captures and saves the address which the CPU places on the bus. If the instruction is a load, the CU additionally captures the data word when it becomes available on the local data bus. If data required is longer than one word, the CU immediately obtains the bus from the CPU using the request/grant protocol and reads the rest of the information in consecutive bus cycles. In a store operation, the CU captures and saves the store address as in a load, and ignores the data word that follows in the "dummy read" cycle. When the NDP is ready to perform the store, the CU obtains the bus from the CPU and writes the operand starting at the specified address.

Numeric Execution Unit

The NEU executes all instructions that involve the register stack. These include arithmetic, logical, transcendental, constant and data transfer instructions. The data path in the NEU is 80 bits wide (64 fraction bits, 15 exponent bits and a sign bit) which allows internal operand transfers to be performed at very high speeds.

When the NEU begins executing an instruction, it activates the NDP BUSY signal. This signal is used in conjunction with the CPU WAIT instruction to resynchronize both processors when the NEU has completed its current instruction.

SPECIFICATIONS

Physical Characteristics

Width— 5.33 cm (2.100")
Length— 5.08 cm (2.000")
Height— 1.82 cm (0.718")
iSBC 337A board + host board
Weight— 17.33 grams (0.576 oz.)

Electrical Characteristics

DC Power Requirements

V_{CC} = 5V ±5%
I_{CC} = 475 mA max.
I_{CC} = 350 mA typ.

Environmental Characteristics

Operating Temperature—0°C to 55°C with 200 linear feet/minute airflow

Relative Humidity—Up to 90% R.H. without condensation.

Reference Manual

147163-001—iSBC 337A MULTIMODULE Numeric Data Processor Hardware Reference Manual (NOT SUPPLIED WITH MULTIMODULE BOARD).

ORDERING INFORMATION

Part Number	Description
SBC 337A	MULTIMODLE Numeric Data Processor

8

Multibus I Memory Expansion Boards

9

intel®

iSBC® 010EX, 020EX, and 040EX* HIGH PERFORMANCE RAM BOARDS

- 0 Wait States at 8 MHz Performance with the iSBC® 286/10A, iSBC 286/12 Board
- Dual Port Capability Via Multibus and High Speed Synchronous Interface
- Configurable to Function Over iLBX™ Bus
- On-Board Parity Generator/Checker
- Independently Selectable Starting and Ending Addresses
- 16 Megabyte Addressing Capability
- 1024K Byte, 2048K Byte, and 4096K Byte Densities Available

The iSBC 010EX, iSBC 020EX, and iSBC 040EX RAM memory boards are members of Intel's complete line of iSBC memory and I/O expansion boards. The EX boards are dual ported between the Multibus interface and one of two types of dedicated memory buses. The dedicated buses are the iLBX bus and a high speed interface. The EX series of RAM-boards can be configured to be accessed over the iLBX bus, as well as Multibus bus, to provide memory support for the iSBC 286/10 board, iSBC 186/03A, or iSBC 386/12. The EX boards are default configured to run over the Multibus interface and the high speed interface. This provides 0 wait state 8 MHz memory support for the iSBC 286/10A and iSBC 286/12 boards.

The EX RAM-boards generate byte oriented parity during all write operations and perform parity checking during all read operations. An on-board LED provides a visual indication that a parity error has occurred.

The iSBC 010EX, iSBC 020EX, and iSBC 040EX boards contain 1M byte, 2M bytes, and 4M bytes of read/write memory using 256K dynamic RAM components.

280142–1

*The iSBC® 010EX, 020EX and 040EX Boards are also manufactured under product code pSBC 010EX, 020EX and 040EX by Intel Puerto Rico, Inc.

September 1991
Order Number: 280142-003

FUNCTIONAL DESCRIPTION

General

The iSBC 010EX, 020EX, and 040EX RAM boards are physically and electrically compatible with the Multibus interface standard, IEEE-796, as outlined in the Intel Multibus architecture specification.

Dual Port Capabilities

The "EX" series of RAM-Boards can be accessed by the Multibus interface, and either the iLBX Bus, or the high speed synchronous interface (see Figures 1 and 2). The EX series require jumper and PAL configuration to be accessed over iLBX Bus.

Intel's iLBX interface is an unarbitrated bus architecture which allows direct transfer of data between the CPU and the memory boards without accessing the Multibus bus. Due to the unarbitrated nature of the iLBX interface, significant improvements in memory access times compared to the Multibus bus accesses result. The EX Boards provide 1 wait state performance at 6 MHz and 2 wait states at 8 MHz over the iLBX board. The EX Memory Board Hardware Reference Manual should be consulted for details.

The high speed synchronous interface, like the iLBX Bus, is a bus architecture which allows direct transfer of data between the CPU and the memory boards without accessing the Multibus bus. This high speed interface runs synchronously with the iSBC 286/10A and iSBC 286/12 to provide 0 wait state performance at 8 MHz.

System Memory Size

Maximum system memory size with this series of boards is 16 megabytes. Memory partitioning is independent for the Multibus interface and the iLBX interface.

Address Selection/Memory

SELECTABLE STARTING ADDRESS

A 512K boundary select is implemented on the iSBC 010EX board. A 1M boundary is implemented on the iSBC 020EX and iSBC 040EX boards.

SELECTABLE ENDING ADDRESS

The ending address is selectable as memory size minus select options of 0, 128K, 256K, or 512K on all of the EX boards.

PARITY INTERRUPT CLEAR

The I/O address of the Parity Interrupt Clear circuitry is jumperable to any one of 256 addresses.

SPECIFICATIONS

Word Size Supported

8- or 16-bits.

Memory Size

1,048,576 bytes (iSBC 010EX board)

2,097,152 bytes (iSBC 020EX board)

4,194,304 bytes (iSBC 040EX board)

Access Times (All densities)

MULTIBUS SYSTEM BUS

Read/Full Write— 375 ns (max)

Write Byte— 375 ns (max)

HIGH SPEED SYNCHRONOUS INTERFACE

Read/Full Write— 167 ns (max)

Write Byte— 132 ns (max)

iLBX™ BUS

Read/Full Write— 295 ns (max)

Write Byte— 116 ns (max)

Cycle Times (All densities)

MULTIBUS SYSTEM BUS

Read/Full Write— 625 ns (max)

Write Byte— 625 ns (max)

HIGH SPEED SYNCHRONOUS INTERFACE

Read/Full Write— 250 ns (max)
Write Byte — 250 ns (max)

iLBX™ BUS

Read/Full Write— 437.5 ns (max)
Write Byte — 437.5 ns (max)

Memory Partitioning

Maximum System memory size is 16M Bytes for the Multibus, iLBX bus and the high speed interface.

BASE ADDRESS

Board	Base Address
iSBC 010EX Board	any 512K boundary in first 8 megabytes
iSBC 020EX Board	any 1M boundary
iSBC 040EX Board	any 1M boundary

Power Requirements

Voltage—5 VDC ±5%

Product	Current
iSBC 010EX Board	3.4A (typ) 5.0A (max)
iSBC 020EX Board	3.7A (typ) 5.2A (max)
iSBC 040EX Board	3.9A (typ) 5.5A (max)

ENVIRONMENTAL REQUIREMENTS

Operating Temperature: 0°C to 60°C airflow of 5 cubic feet per minute

Storage Temperature: −40°C to +75°C

Operating Humidity: To 90% without condensation

PHYSICAL DIMENSIONS

Width: 12 inches (30.48 cm)
Height: 6.75 inches (17.15 cm)
Thickness: 0.50 inches (1.27 cm)
Weight: iSBC 010EX board: 9.0 ounces (2550 gm)
iSBC 020EX board: 13.5 ounces (3830 gm)
iSBC 040EX board: 18.0 ounces (5100 gm)

REFERENCE MANUALS

144456-001— Intel iLBX Specification

ORDERING INFORMATION

Part Number	Description
SBC010EX	1M byte RAM board with parity
SBC020EX	2M byte RAM board with parity
SBC040EX	4M byte RAM board with parity
EXASYNCX86	PALs and jumper configuration for iLBX mode

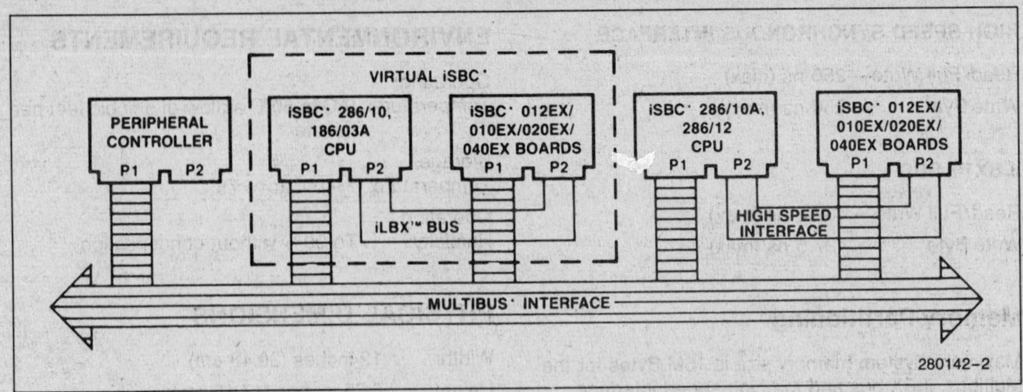

Figure 1. Typical iLBX™ System Configuration

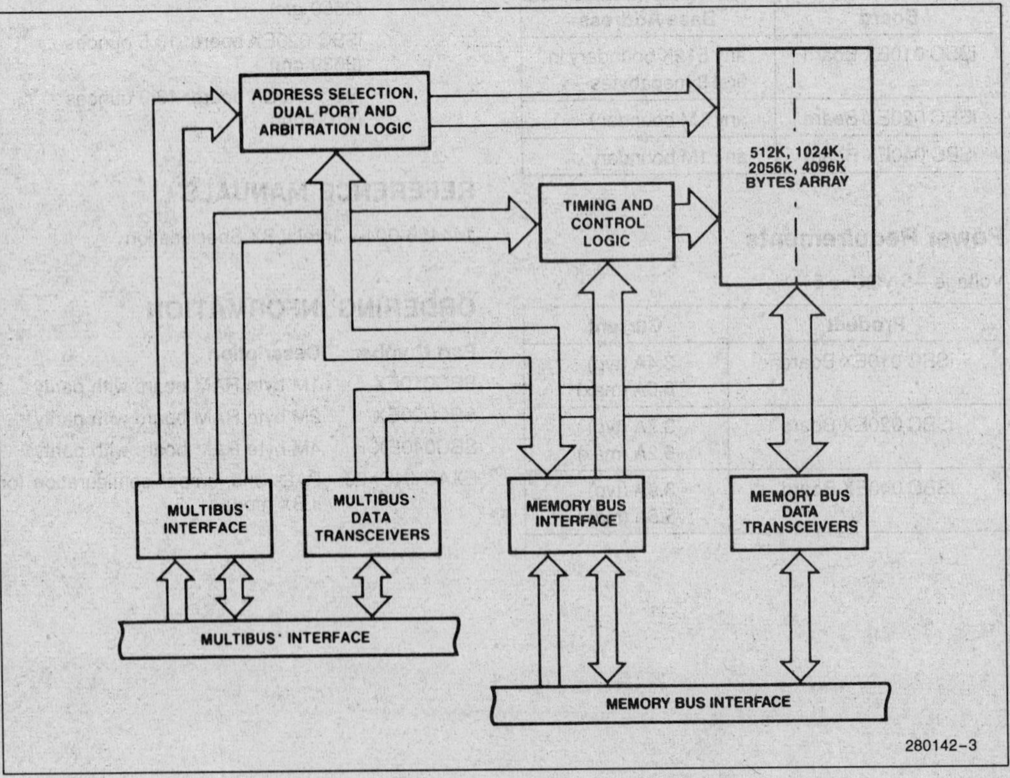

Figure 2. iSBC® EX Memory Board Block Diagram

iSBC® 012CX, 010CX, AND 020CX* iLBX™ RAM BOARDS

- Dual Port Capability via Multibus and iLBX Interfaces
- Single Bit Error Correction and Double Bit Error Detection Utilizing Intel 8206 ECC Device
- 512K Byte, 1024K Byte, and 2048K Byte Versions Available
- Control Status Register Supports Multiple ECC Operating Modes
- Error Status Register Provides Error Logging by Host CPU Board
- 16 Megabyte Addressing Capability
- Supports 8- or 16-bit Data Transfer and 24-bit Addressing
- Auxiliary Power Bus and Memory Protect Logic for Battery Back-Up RAM Requirements

The iSBC 012CX, iSBC 010CX and iSBC 020CX RAM memory boards are members of Intel's complete line of iSBC memory and I/O expansion boards. The dual port feature of the CX series of RAM-boards allow access to the memory of both the Multibus and iLBX bus interfaces.

In addition to the dual port features the "CX" series of RAM-boards provide Error Checking and Corrections Circuitry (ECC) which can detect and correct single bit errors and detect, but not correct, double and most multiple bit errors.

The iSBC 012CX board contains 512K bytes of read/write memory using 64K dynamic RAM components. The iSBC 010 CX and iSBC 020 CX boards contain 1024K and 2048K bytes of read/write memory using 256K dynamic RAM components.

231023-1

*The iSBC® 012CX, 010CX, and 020CX Boards are also manufactured under product code pSBC 012CX, 010CX, and 020CX by Intel Puerto Rico, Inc.

September 1991
Order Number: 231023-003

FUNCTIONAL DESCRIPTION

General

The iSBC 012CX, 010CX, and 020CX RAM boards are physically and electrically compatible with the Multibus interface standard, IEEE-796, as outlined in the Intel Multibus specification. In addition the CX series of RAM-boards are physically and electrically compatible with the iLBX bus (Local Bus Extension) interface as outlined in the Intel iLBX Specification (see Figure 1).

Dual Port Capabilities

The "CX" series of RAM-boards can be accessed by either the Multibus interface or the iLBX interface (see Figure 2). Intel's iLBX interface is an unarbitrated bus architecture which allows direct transfer of data between the CPU and the memory boards

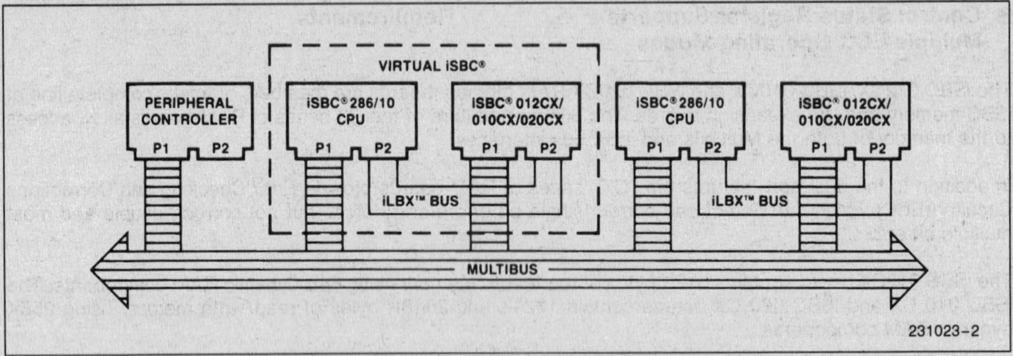

Figure 1. Typical iLBX™ System Configuration

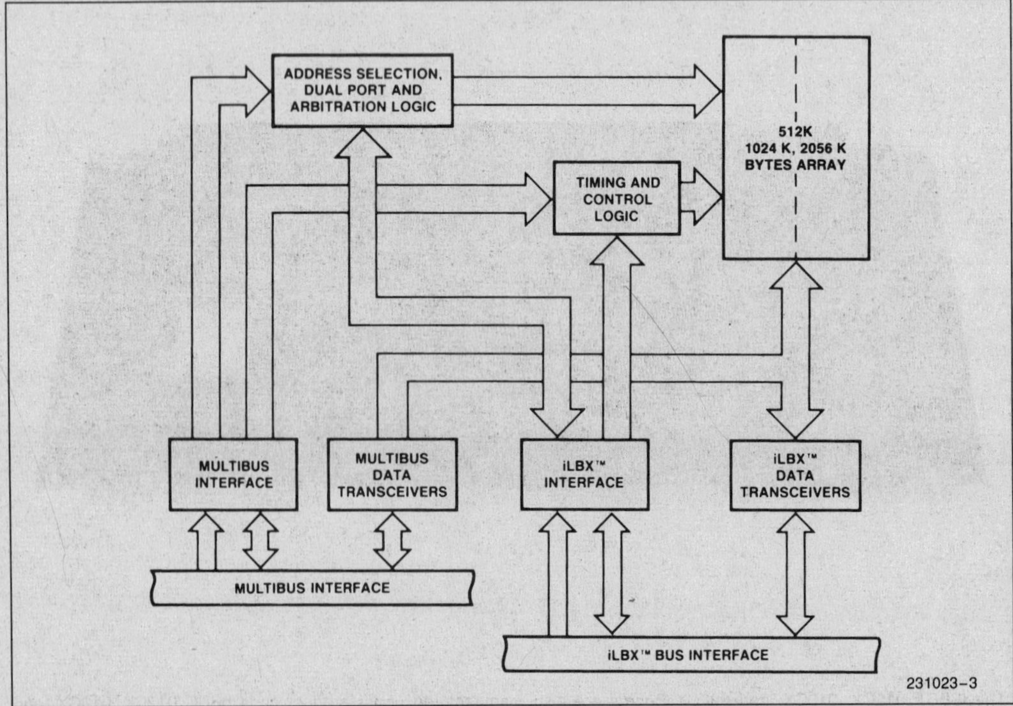

Figure 2. iSBC® 012CX/010CX/020CX Block Diagram

without accessing the Multibus bus. Due to the unarbitrated nature of the iLBX interface significant improvements in memory access times result, typically a 2-6 Wait State improvement over Multibus memory access.

System Memory Size

Maximum system memory size with this series of boards is 16 megabytes. Memory partitioning is independent for the Multibus interface and the iLBX interface.

For Multibus operations, on-board jumpers assign the board to one of four 4-megabyte pages. Each page is partitioned into 256 blocks of 16K bytes each. The smallest partition on any board in this series is 8K bytes. Jumpers assign the base address (lowest 16K block) within the selected 4-megabyte page.

The iLBX bus memory partitioning differs from the Multibus bus partitioning in that the iLBX bus address space consists of 256 contiguous blocks of 64K bytes totaling 16 megabytes. As with the Multibus bus partitioning, the base addresses are set with on-board jumpers.

Error Checking and Correcting (ECC)

Error checking and correction is accomplished with the Intel 8206 Error Checking and Correcting device. This ECC component, in conjunction with the ECC check bit RAM array, provides error detection and correction of single bit errors and detection only of double bit and most multiple bit errors. The ECC circuitry can be programmed via the Control Status Register (CSR) to various modes while error logging is supported by the Error Status Register (ESR). Both CSR and ESR communicate with the master CPU board through a single I/O port.

Battery Back-Up/Memory Protect

An auxiliary power bus is provided to allow separate power to the RAM array for systems requiring back-up of read/write memory. An active low TTL compatible memory protect signal is brought out on the auxiliary bus connector which, when asserted, disables read/write access to the RAM board. This input is provided for the protection of RAM contents during system power-down sequences.

SPECIFICATIONS

Word Size Supported

8- or 16-bits

Memory Size

524,288 bytes (iSBC 012CX board)

1,048,576 bytes (iSBC 010CX board)

2,097,152 bytes (iSBC 020CX board)

Access Times (All densities)

Multibus System Bus

Read/Full Write— 380 ns (max)

Write Byte — 530 ns (max)

iLBX™ Local Bus

Read/Full Write— 340 ns (max)

Write Byte — 440 ns (max)

Cycle Times (All densities)

Multibus System Bus

Read/Full Write— 490 ns (max)

Write Byte — 885 ns (max)

iLBX™ Local Bus

Read/Full Write— 375 ns

Write Byte — 740 ns

NOTE:

If an error is detected, read access time and cycle times are extended to 255 ns (max)

9

Memory Partitioning

Maximum System memory size is 16M Bytes for both Multibus and iLBX BUS. Multibus partitioning is by Page, Block and Base, while the iLBX BUS is by Block and Base only.

Page Address

Multibus— 0–4 megabytes; 4–8 megabytes, 8–12 megabytes; 12–16 megabytes

iLBX™ BUS —N/A

Base Address

Multibus System Bus—Any 16K byte boundary within the 4M-byte page.

iLBX™ Local Bus — Any 64K byte boundary selectable on board boundaries to 8M-bytes and some 64K-byte boundaries in the first megabyte. Others available if PAL programming is changed.

Power Requirements

Voltage—5 VDC ±5%

Product	Current	Standby (Battery Back-Up)
iSBC® 012CX Board	4.4A (typ.) 6.8A (max.)	2.2A (typ.) 2.4A (max.)
iSBC® 010CX Board	4.8A (typ.) 7.0A (max.)	2.1A (typ.) 2.3A (max.)
iSBC® 020CX Board	5.3A (typ.) 7.5A (max.)	2.2A (typ.) 2.4A (max.)

Environmental Requirements

Operating Temperature: 0°C to 55°C airflow of 200 linear feet per minute

Operating Humidity: To 90% without condensation

Physical Dimensions

Width: 30.48 cm (12 inches)

Height: 17.15 cm (6.75 inches)

Thickness: 1.27 cm (0.50 inches)

Weight: iSBC 012CX board: 6589 gm (23.5 ounces); iSBC 010CX board: 5329 gm (19.0 ounces); iSBC 020CX board: 6589 gm (23.5 ounces)

Reference Manuals

145158-003—iSBC® 028CX/iSBC® 056CX/iSBC® 012CX Hardware Reference Manual

144456-001—Intel iLBX™ 010CX, 020CX Specification

ORDERING INFORMATION

Part Number	Description
iSBC 012CX	512K byte RAM board with ECC
iSBC 010CX	1M byte RAM board with ECC
iSBC 020CX	2M byte RAM board with ECC

intel®

iSBC® 314*
512K BYTE RAM MULTIMODULE™ BOARD

- On-Board Memory Expansion for the iSBC® 86/35 Single Board Computer
- iSBC 314 Module Provides 512K Bytes of Dual Port RAM Expansion for the iSBC 86/35 Board
- Reliable Mechanical and Electrical Interconnection
- Completes iSBC 86/35 Memory Array Providing a Full Megabyte Page of System Memory
- Increases System Throughput by Reducing Accesses to MULTIBUS® Global Memory
- Low Power Requirements
- Battery Backup Capability

The iSBC® 314 512K byte RAM MULTIMODULE board provides simple, low cost expansion to double the on-board RAM capacity of the iSBC 86/35 Single Board Computer host to one megabyte. This RAM MULTIMODULE option offers system designers a simple, practical solution to expanding and improving the memory capability and performance of the iSBC 86/35 board. The iSBC 314 memory is configured on-board and can be accessed as quickly as the standard iSBC 86/35 memory, eliminating the need for accessing additional memory via the MULTIBUS system bus.

280000–1

9

*The iSBC® 314 Board is also manufactured under product code pSBC 314 by Intel Puerto Rico, Inc.

August 1990
Order Number: 280000-003

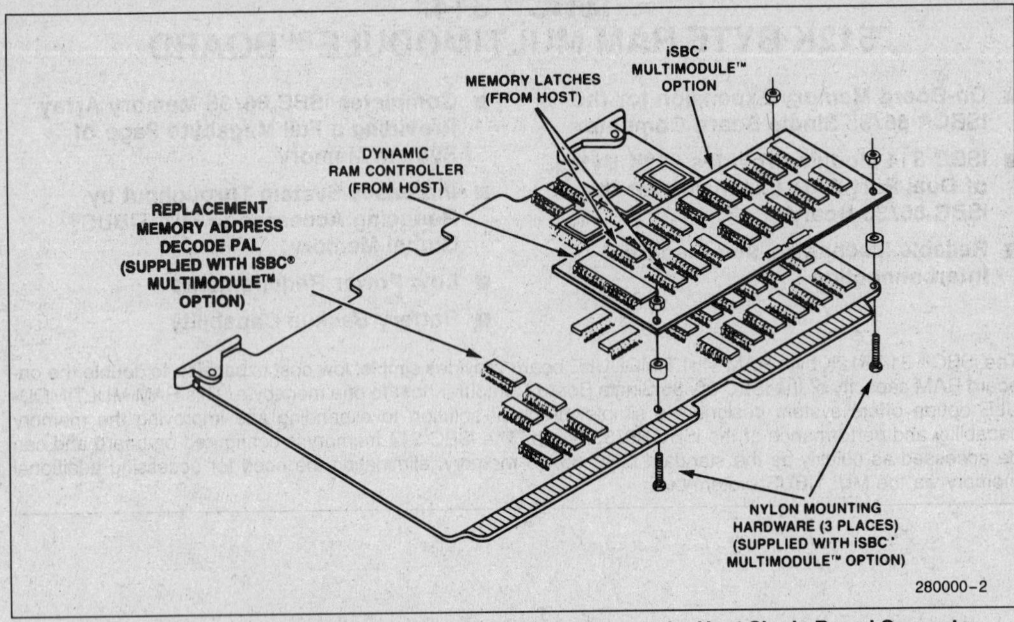

Figure 1. Installation of the MULTIMODULE™ RAM Module on the Host Single Board Computer

FUNCTIONAL DESCRIPTION

The iSBC 314 MULTIMODULE board measures 2.40″ by 5.75″ and mounts above the RAM array on the iSBC 86/35 Single Board Computer. The iSBC 314 board contains sixteen 256 Kbit x 1 dynamic RAM devices and three sockets; two for the memory latches and one for the Intel 8203 dynamic RAM controller. The addition of the iSBC 314 memory MULTIMODULE board to the iSBC 86/35 board makes possible a one megabyte single board solution.

To install the module, the latches and controller from the host iSBC 86/35 board, are removed and inserted into sockets on the iSBC 314 board. The module is then mounted onto the host board. Pins extending from the controller and latch sockets mate with device sockets underneath (see Figure 1). Additional pins mate to supply other signals to complete the electrical interface. The module is then secured at three additional points with nylon hardware to ensure the mechanical security of the assembly.

To complete the installation, one socketed PAL is replaced on the iSBC 86/35 board with the one supplied with the MULTIMODULE kit. This is the PAL which allows the host board logic to recognize its expanded on-board memory compliment.

SPECIFICATIONS

Word Size

8 or 16 bits (16-bit data paths)

Memory Size

512K bytes RAM

System Cycle Time (8 MHz, 2 Wait States)

750 ns (read); 750 ns (write)

NOTE:
1 wait state achieved with jumper change on iSBC 86/35 board.

Memory Addressing

iSBC 314 module with iSBC 86/35 board — 1M byte (total capacity); 0–FFFFFH. (See Figure 2, Memory Allocation)

Interface

The interface for the iSBC 314 MULTIMODULE board option is designed only for the iSBC 86/35 host board.

Wait-State Performance

A significant performance advantage of 2 wait-states is achieved when accessing memory on-board the iSBC 86/35 versus the performance of 6 wait-states when accessing memory off-board over the MULTIBUS. The iSBC 314 puts an additional 512K bytes of system memory on-board the iSBC 86/35 reducing the execution time by as much as 70%.

Memory Allocation

Segments of the combined host/MULTIMODULE RAM may be configured to be accessed either from off-board or on-board resources. The amount of memory allocated as either public or private resource may be configured in a variety of sizes. The address range boundaries for the 1 megabyte of RAM array of the iSBC 314 and iSBC 86/35 board combination are shown in Figure 2 for accesses from both on-board and off-board resources.

Auxiliary Power

The low power memory protection option included on the iSBC 86/35 board supports the iSBC 314 module.

Physical Characteristics

Width: 2.4 in. (6.10 cm)
Length: 5.75 in. (14.61 cm)
Depth*: 0.72 in. (1.83 cm)
Weight: 0.13 oz. (59g)

NOTE:
*Combined depth including host board.

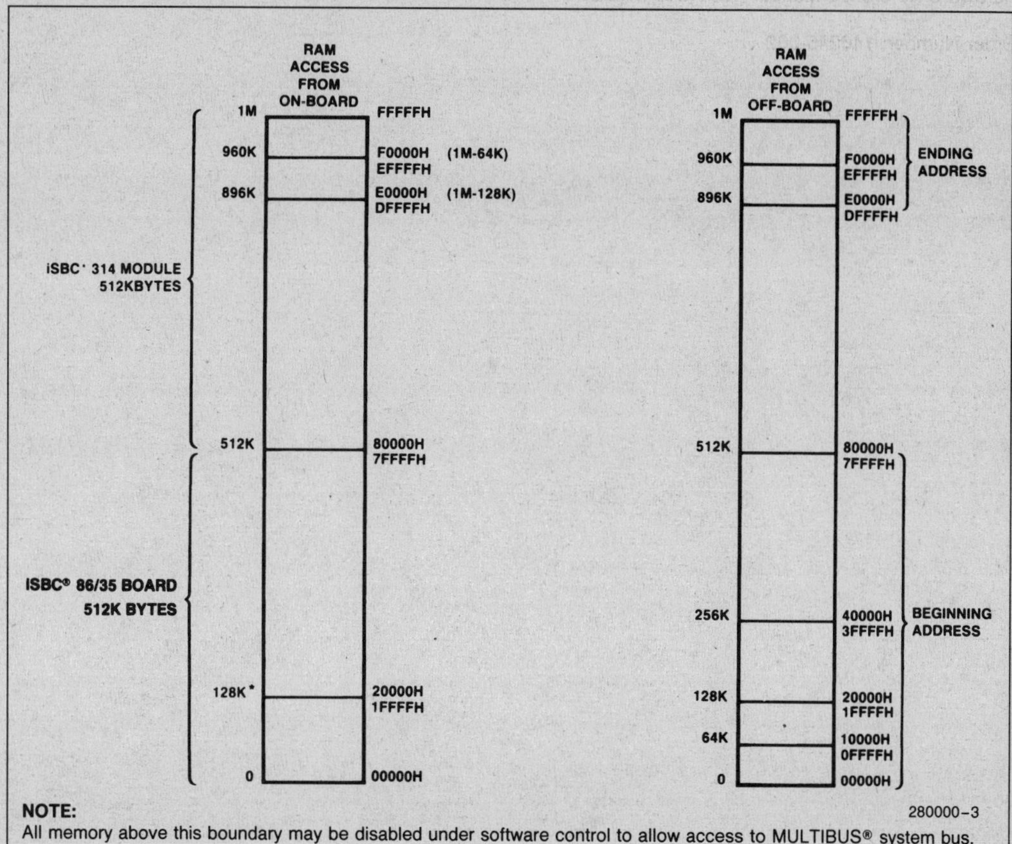

Figure 2. Address Range Selection

Electrical Characteristics

DC Power Requirements*

*Additional power required by the iSBC 314 MULTIMODULE is:

Typical: 60 mA @ +5V

Maximum: 140 mA @ +5V

Environmental Characteristics

Operating Temperature: 0°C to +55°C

Relative Humidity: to 90% (without condensation)

Reference Manual

All necessary documentation for the iSBC 314 MULTIMODULE board is included in the iSBC 86/35 Hardware Reference Manual (NOT SUPPLIED).

Order Number: 146245-002

ORDERING INFORMATION

Part Number	Description
SBC 314	512K byte Memory MULTIMODULE option for iSBC 86/35 board

iSBC® 304*
128K BYTE RAM MULTIMODULE™ BOARD

- **iSBC® 304 Module Provides 128K Bytes of Dual Port RAM Expansion for the iSBC 86/30 or iSBC 86/35 Board**
- **On-board Memory Expansion Eliminates MULTIBUS® System Bus Latency and Increases System Throughput**

The iSBC® 304 module provides simple, low cost memory expansion for the iSBC 86/30 and iSBC 86/35 Single Board Computers. The iSBC 304 provides 128K bytes RAM expansion to the iSBC 86/35 giving a total capacity of 640K bytes RAM memory. The RAM MULTIMODULE option offers flexibility in defining and implementing Intel single board computer systems. RAM MULTIMODULES expand the memory configuration on-board, eliminating the need for accessing the additional memory via the MULTIBUS system bus.

210329–1

*The iSBC® 304 Board is also manufactured under product code pSBC 304 by Intel Puerto Rico, Inc.

August 1990
Order Number: 210329-003

FUNCTIONAL DESCRIPTION

Each MULTIMODULE contains dynamic RAM devices and sockets for the dynamic RAM controller. To install the module, the latches and controller from the host CPU board are removed and inserted into sockets on the RAM MULTIMODULE. The module is then mounted onto the host board. Pins extending from the controller and latch sockets mate with device sockets underneath (see Figure 1). Additional pins mate to supply other signals to complete the electrical interface.

The module is then secured at three additional points with nylon hardware to ensure the mechanical security of the assembly.

To complete the installation, one socketed PROM is replaced on the host CPU board with the one supplied with the MULTIMODULE kit. This is the MULTIBUS address decode PROM which allows the host board logic to recognize its expanded on-board memory compliment.

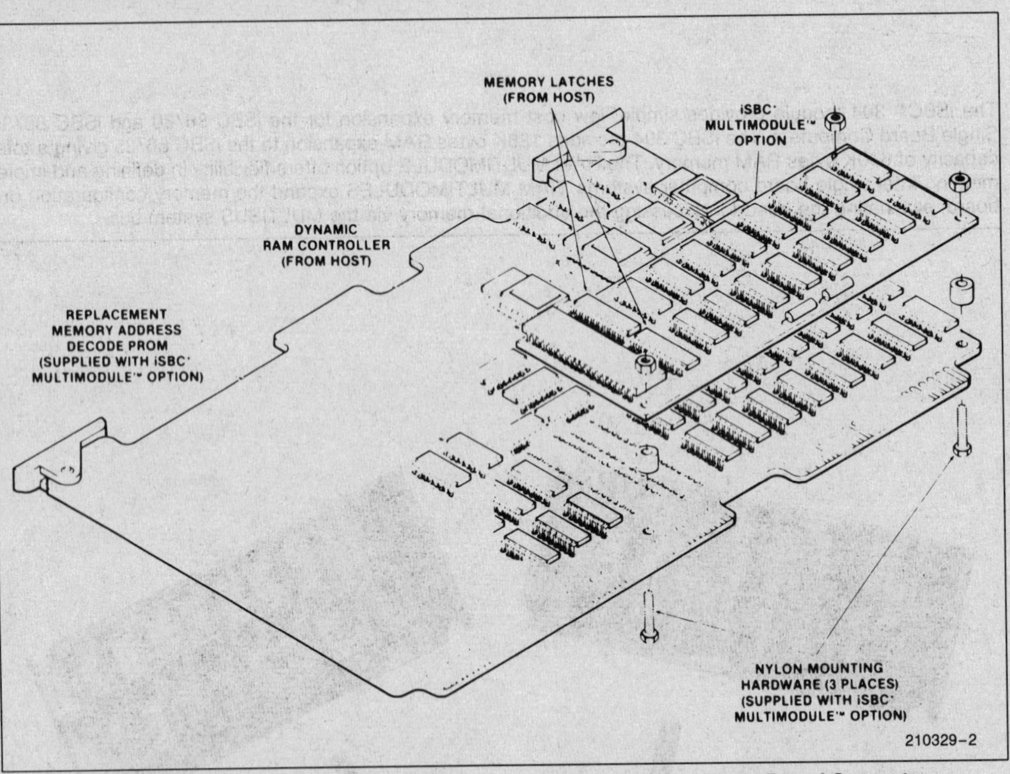

Figure 1. Installation of the MULTIMODULE™ RAM on the Host Single Board Computer

SPECIFICATIONS

Word Size

8 or 16 bits (16-bit data paths)

Memory Size

iSBC 304 Module—128K bytes RAM

Cycle Time

iSBC 304—700 ns (read); 700 ns (write)

Memory Addressing

CPU ACCESS

iSBC 304 (with iSBC 86/35)—640K bytes (total capacity); 0–9FFFFH (address range)

iSBC 304 (with iSBC 86/30)—256K bytes (total capacity); 0–3FFFFH (address range)

MULTIBUS® Access

Jumper selectable for any 32K byte boundary, but not crossing a 256K byte boundary.

Private Memory Allocation

Segments of the combined host/MULTIMODULE RAM memory may be configured as a private resource, protected from MULTIBUS system access. The amount of memory allocated as a private resource may be configured in increments of 25% of the total on-board memory ranging from 0% to 100%.

Auxiliary Power

The low power memory protection option included on the CPU host boards supports the RAM modules.

Physical Characteristics

Width: 2.4 in. (6.10 cm)
Height: 5.75 in. (14.61 cm)
Depth*: 0.72 in. (1.83 cm)
Weight: 0.13 oz. (59 g)

***NOTE:**
Combined depth including host board.

Electrical Characteristics

DC POWER REQUIREMENTS

iSBC 304: 640 mA at +15V incremental power

Environmental Characteristics

Operating Temperature: 0°C to 55°C

Relative Humidity: to 90% (without condensation)

ORDERING INFORMATION

Order Code	Description
SBC304	128K MULTIMODULE option for iSBC 86/30 or iSBC 86/35 CPU boards

iSBC® 302*
8K BYTE RAM MULTIMODULE™

- **Expands On-Board Memory of the iSBC 86/05A and iSBC 88/25 Signal Board Computers**

The Intel iSBC 302 8K byte MULTIMODULE RAM provides simple, low cost expansion to double the RAM capacity on the iSBC 86/05A Single Board Computer to 16K bytes or increase RAM capacity on the iSBC 88/25 Single Board Computer to 12K bytes. Because the MULTIMODULE memory is configured on-board, it can be accessed as quickly as the standard on-board iSBC 86/05A or iSBC 88/25 memory, eliminating the need for accessing the additional memory via the MULTIBUS system bus.

280225-1

*The iSBC® 302 is also manufactured under product code pSBC 302 by Intel Puerto Rico, Inc.

FUNCTIONAL DESCRIPTION

The iSBC 302 MULTIMODULE and mounts above the RAM area on the iSBC 86/05A or iSBC 88/25 Single Board Computer. The iSBC 302 MULTIMODULE board contains four 4K x 4 static RAM devices and sockets for two of the RAM devices on the iSBC 80/05A board. With the iSBC 302 MULTIMODULE mounted on the iSBC 88/25 board, the two sockets on the iSBC 302 MULTIMODULE may be filled with 4K x 4 static RAMs. The two sockets on the iSBC 302 module have extended pins which mate with two sockets on the base board. Additional pins mate to the power supply and chip select lines to complete the electrical interface. The mechanical integrity of the assembly is assured with nylon hardware securing the module in two places.

SPECIFICATIONS

Word Size

8/16 bits

Memory Size

16,384 bytes of RAM

Cycle Time

Provides "no wait state"memory operations on the iSBC 86/05A board at 5 MHz or 8 MHz or the iSBC 88/25 at 5 MHz.

5 MHz cycle time — 800 ns

8 MHz cycle time — 500 ns

Memory Addressing

Memory addressing for the iSBC 302 MULTIMODULE board is controlled by the host board via the address and chip select signal lines.

Physical Characteristics

Width: 2.6 in. (6.60 cm)

Length: 2.3 in. (5.84 cm)

Height: 0.56 in. (1.42 cm) iSBC 302 board + Baseboard

Weight: 1.25 oz. (35 gm)

Electrical Characteristics

DC Power Requirements: 720 mA at +5V incremental power

Environmental Characteristics

Operating Temperature: 0°C to +55°C

Relative Humidity: to 90% (without condensation)

Reference Manuals

All necessary documentation for the iSBC 302 MULTIMODULE board is included in the CPU board Hardware Reference Manuals (NOT SUPPLIED).

iSBC 86/05A —Order No. 147162-002

iSBC 88/25 —Order No. 143825-002

ORDERING INFORMATION

Part Number	Description
SBC 302	8K byte RAM MULTIMODULE

intel®

iSBC® 429 UNIVERSAL SITE MEMORY EXPANSION BOARD

280668-1

CMOS MULTIBUS I MEMORY EXPANSION BOARD SUPPORTS LATEST MEMORY TECHNOLOGY

The iSBC® 429 board provides a wide range of memory expansion capabilities for Multibus designs. Up to 4 MBytes of memory can be installed using EPROM, Flash memory, SRAM, E^2PROM or Static NVRAM.

The CMOS implementation of the iSBC 429 makes it ideal for low power applications.

All of Intel's Single Board Computers can communicate with the iSBC 429 using the Multibus System bus. Alternatively, the iSBC 429 may be optionally configured to use the iLBX™ bus for faster access to the iSBC 186/03A, 286/10A, 286/12 series or 386/12 series of Single Board Computers.

FEATURES

- Supports EPROM, Page Mode EPROM, E^2PROM, Flash Memory, SRAM and Static NVRAM
- Thirty-two standard 32-pin JEDEC sites (supports both 28-pin and 32-pin devices) up to 4 MByte capacity
- iLBX Bus or Multibus Configurability
- Low power CMOS design
- Battery Backup/Memory Protect support
- Assignable anywhere within a 16 Megabyte address space on 4 Kbyte boundaries

November 1990
Order Number: 280668-001

FEATURES

iLBX™ BUS

The iSBC 429 board can be configured via jumpers to communicate with either the Multibus interface or the iLBX Bus interface. Significant memory access time improvements can be realized using the iLBX Bus interface versus the Multibus interface, due to its dedicated, unarbitrated architecture. Additional information on the iLBX Bus is available in the iLBX Specification, order number 145695-Rev. A.

CMOS DESIGN

For embedded control applications which are sensitive to power consumption, the iSBC 429 was designed with CMOS components and it will support many CMOS memory devices. Unpopulated, the iSBC 429 requires 5.25 watts at 5 volts.

FLASH MEMORY SUPPORT

The iSBC 429 board supports Intel's new CMOS Flash Memory devices. These new memory devices offer the most cost-effective and reliable alternative for updatable non-volatile memory. Memory contents can be erased and reprogrammed on-board during subassembly test, in-system during final test, and in-system after sale.

MEMORY BANKS

The thirty-two sites on the iSBC 429 board are partitioned into two banks of 16 sites each. Both banks are independently configurable to any of the device types supported on the board. Each bank can support up to 2 Megabytes using 27010 devices.

MEMORY ADDRESSING

The address space of each bank can be independently configured for starting address and size. The starting address can be on any 4 KByte boundary within the 16 MByte Multibus address space. The size of each bank is a multiple of 64 KBytes.

MODE OF OPERATION

The iSBC 429 board can operate in one of two modes: the 8 bit only mode or the 8/16 bit mode. The 8 bit mode provides the most efficient memory configuration for systems handling 8 bit data only. The 8/16 bit mode allows the iSBC 429 board to be compatible with systems employing 8 bit and 16 bit masters. The mode of operation is selected by on-board jumpers and is available for both Multibus and iLBX Bus configurations.

MEMORY ACCESS

The iSBC 429 board has jumper-selectable access times for each bank which allows the board to be tailored to the performance of the particular devices which are installed in the iSBC 429 board. The iSBC 429 accepts devices with an access time ranging from 150 ns with a minimum granularity of 99 ns and results in a board access time from 182 ns to 1667 ns. Each bank can be configured for access time.

INHIBITS

Inhibit signals are provided on the iSBC 429 board to allow ROM to overlay RAM for bootstrapping or diagnostic operations. Each bank of the iSBC 429 board can be overlayed with the system RAM by jumpers provided on the board. (i.e. If banks are overlapped, inhibits can be used to select the appropriate bank.)

BATTERY BACKUP

The iSBC 429 board supports battery backup operation via a connector on the board. An auxiliary power bus is provided to allow separate power to the memory array for systems requiring battery backup. Selection of this auxiliary power bus is made via jumpers on the board.

An active-low TTL compatible Memory Protect signal is brought out on the auxiliary connector which, when asserted, disables access to the memory array. This input is provided for the protection of Memory contents during system power-down sequences.

intel.

SPECIFICATIONS

Type	Size							
	8K×8	16K×8	32K×8	64K×8	128K×8	256K×8	4×16K×8	8×16×8
EPROM	2764	27128	27256	27512	27010	27020	—	—
ROM	✓[1]	✓	✓	✓	✓	✓	—	—
Page Mode EPROM	—	—	—	—	—	—	27513	27011
E²PROM[2]	2864A	—	—	—	—	—	—	—
Flash27F64 Memory[3]		—	27F256 28F256	—	—	—	—	—
Static NVRAM[4]	✓	—	✓	—	—	—	—	—
SRAM	✓	—	✓	—	—	—	—	—

MEMORY DEVICES SUPPORTED BY THE iSBC® 429

1 "✓" denotes that the iSBC 429 board will support the device indicated, but that it is not currently available from Intel.
2 Five Volt only, Enhanced
3 12 Volt V_{pp} only
4 Static NVRAM devices exceed the height specification for Multibus. The iSBC 429 will occupy more than one slot with these devices installed.

WORD SIZE

8 or 8/16 bits

MEMORY SIZE

Sockets are provided for up to thirty-two 32-pin or 28-pin devices which can provide up to 4 Megabytes of EPROM/ROM/SRAM/Flash Memory.

ACCESS TIME

Access time is jumperable from 182 ns to 1667 ns with a granularity of 99 ns to optimize performance for the devices which are installed and is equivalent for Multibus and iLBX Bus.

POWER REQUIREMENTS

V_{cc} = 5 volts ±5%
V_{pp} = 12 volts ±5%
I_{cc} = 1.2 amps, maximum, without any memory devices in the board.

PHYSICAL CHARACTERISTICS

Width - 12.00 inches (30.48 cm)
Depth - 7.05 inches (17.91 cm)
Height - .5 inches (1.27 cm)

ENVIRONMENT

Operating Temperature - 0° C to +60° C (Convection cooling)
Relative Humidity - 90% non-condensing

ORDERING INFORMATION

PART NUMBER	DESCRIPTION
SBC 429	Universal Site Memory Expansion Board

REFERENCE MANUAL

457317-001 - iSBC 429 Hardware Reference Manual (NOT SUPPLIED)

iSBC® 428 UNIVERSAL SITE MEMORY EXPANSION BOARD

- **Supports EPROM, ROM, E²PROM, SRAM, IRAM and NVRAM**
- **iLBX™ BUS or MULTIBUS® Selectable**
- **Provides Support for Battery Backup/ Memory Protect**
- **Sixteen 28-Pin Universal Sites**
- **Assignable Anywhere within a 16 Mbyte Address Space on 256K Byte Boundries**
- **Jumper Selectable Base Address on 4K Byte Boundaries**

The iSBC® 428 Universal Site Board is a member of Intel's complete line of Memory and I/O Expansion boards. The iSBC 428 Universal Site Memory Expansion Board interfaces directly to the iSBC 80, iSBC 88, or iSBC 86 Single Boad Computers via the MULTIBUS® System Bus to expand system memory requirements, while system memory requirements for iSBC 286 Single Board Computer can interface via either the MULTIBUS or the high speed iLBX™ Bus.

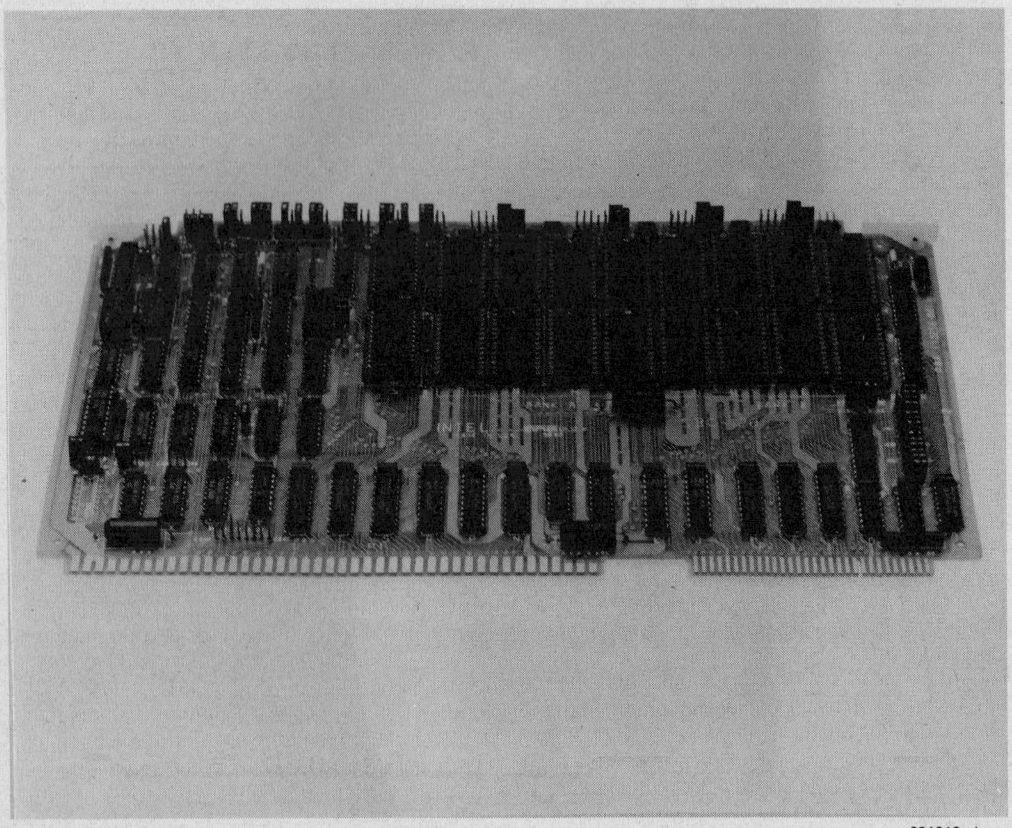

281013–1

October 1989
Order Number: 281013-001

FUNCTIONAL DESCRIPTION

General

The iSBC 428 board contains sixteen 28 pin sockets. The actual capacity of the board is determined by the type and quantity of components installed by the user. The iSBC 428 board is compatible with five different types and densities of devices: the 2K by 8 thru 64K by 8 EPROM/ROM devices, 2K by 8 thru 8K by 8 "Five Volt Only, Enhanced" E^{2}PROM devices, 512 by 8 thru 16K by 8 NVRAM (Non-Volatile RAM) devices, 2K by 8 thru 32K by 8 SRAM devices, and 8K by 8 IRAM (Integrated RAM) devices. In addition the board can be accessed by either the MUTIBUS System Bus or Intel's new high speed iLBX Bus.

iLBX™ Bus

The iSBC 428 board can be configured via jumpers to communicate with either the MULTIBUS interface or the iLBX Bus interface. Significant memory access time improvements can be realized over the iLBX Bus interface (versus the MULTIBUS interface) due to its dedicated, unarbitrated architecture. Additional information on the iLBX Bus is available in the iLBX Specification #144456.

Memory Banks

The sixteen sites on the iSBC 428 board are partitioned into two banks of 8 sites each. Within each bank the 8 sites are futher partitioned into 2 groups of 4 sites each. Each group of 4 sites is configurable to each of the six device types described above via a "Configurator". The "Configurator" is an arrangement of push-on jumpers which configures each of the four groups of 4 sites. Within each bank devices of the same density must reside and within each group devices of the same type must reside (i.e., SRAM or EPROM).

Memory Addressing

Addressing of the iSBC 428 board is by pages. There are 64–256K pages which are jumpers selectable. Each of the two banks are independently addressable and can reside in any page. Actual beginning and ending addresses within a page are a function of the actual device size and, as with the pages, are determined by jumpers. Because of the paging based memory addressing architecture more than one iSBC 428 board can be placed in a system.

Mode of Operation

The iSBC 428 board can operate in one of two modes: the 8 bit only mode or the 8/16 bit mode. The 8 bit mode provides the most efficient memory configuration for systems handling 8 bit data only. The 8/16 bit mode allows the iSBC 428 board to be compatible with systems employing 8 bit and 16 bit masters. The mode of operation is selected by on board jumpers and is available for both MULTIBUS and iLBX Bus configurations.

Memory Access

The iSBC 428 board has jumper selectable access time, which allows the board to be tailored to the performance of the particular devices which are installed in the iSBC 428 board. The board can be configured via jumpers to accept devices with an access time range of 50 ns to 500 ns with a granularity of 50 ns and results in a board access time from 225 ns to 775 ns.

Interrupt

The iSBC 428 board has the capability of generating an interrupt for the write and erase operations of E^{2}PROMs. The interrupt can be configured in two ways: one, to signal completion of the E^{2}PROM write cycle, or two, allow polling by the system to determine the status of the E^{2}PROM during the write programming time.

Inhibits

Inhibits are provided on the iSBC 428 board to allow ROM to overlay RAM for bootstrapping or diagnostic operations. Each bank of the iSBC 428 board can be overlayed with the system RAM by jumpers provided on the board.

Battery Backup

The iSBC 428 board supports battery backup operation via a connector on the board. An auxiliary power bus is provided to allow separate power to the memory array for systems requiring battery backup. Selection of this auxiliary power bus is made via jumpers on the board.

An active-low TTL compatible Memory Protect signal is brought out on the auxiliary connector which, when asserted, disables access to the memory array. This input is provided for the protection of Memory contents during system power-down sequences.

Devices Supported

Listed below are the current and future devices supported by the iSBC 428 board.

	Size							
Type	**512 x 8**	**2K x 8**	**4K x 8**	**8K x 8**	**16K x 8**	**32K x 8**	**64K x 8**	**Comments**
EPROM	—	2716	2732A	2764	27128	27256	27512	—
ROM	—	X	X	X	X	X	X	—
EEPROM	—	2817A	X	X	X	X	—	5V, Enhanced
SRAM	—	X	X	X	X	X	—	NMOS & CMOS
NVRAM	—	X	X	X	—	—	—	—
IRAM	—	—	—	2186	—	X	—	—

X—Denotes that the iSBC 428 board will support the device indicated but that it is not currently available from Intel.

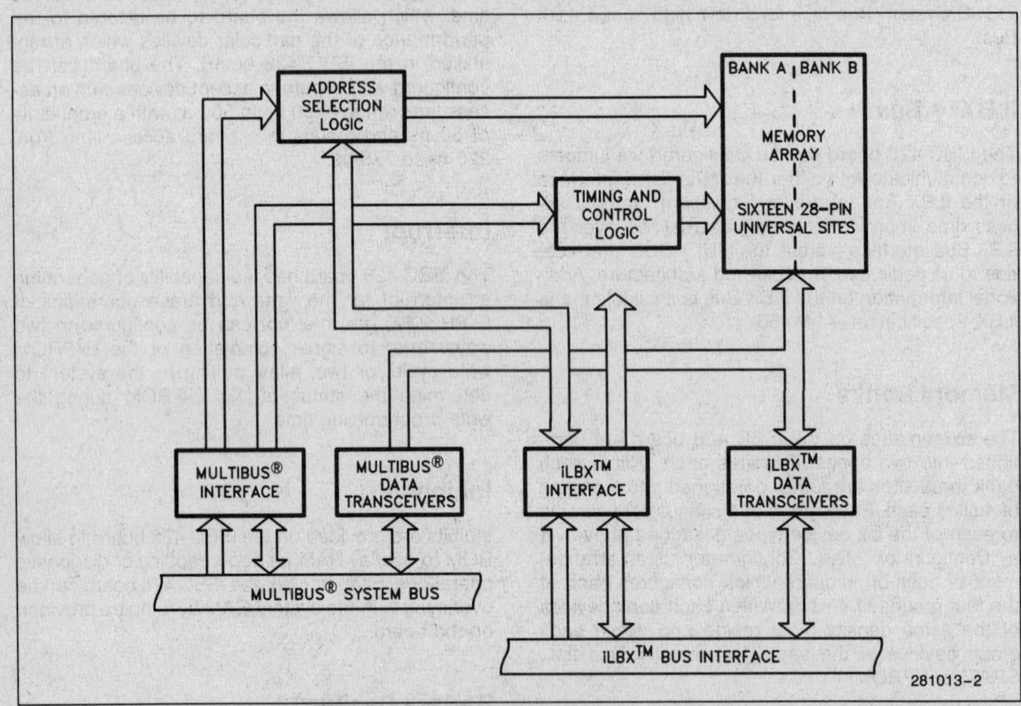

iSBC® 428 Block Diagram

SPECIFICATIONS

Word Size

8 or 8/16 bits

Memory Size

Sockets are provided for up to sixteen 28 pin devices which can provide up to 512K bytes of EPROM/ROM/SRAM.

Access Time

Jumperable from 225 ns to 775 ns with a granularity of 50 ns and is equivalent for both MULTIBUS and the iLBX Bus.

Power Requirements

V_{CC} = 5 volts ±5%

I_{CC} = 2.0 amps, maximum, without any memory devices in the board.

Physical Characteristics

Length: 30.48 cm (12 inches)
Width: 17.15 cm (7.05 inches)
Depth: 1.27 cm (0.5 inches)

Environment

Operating Temperature: 0°C to +55°C
Relative Humidity: 90% non-condensing

ORDERING INFORMATION

Order Code	Description
SBC428	Universal Site Memory Expansion Board

iSBC® 341
28-PIN MULTIMODULE™ EPROM

- **On-board Memory Expansion for iSBC® 86/05A, iSBC 88/25, iSBC 186/03A, iSBC 286/10A, iSBC 286/12 Series, and iSBC 88/40A Microcomputers**
- **Supports JEDEC 24/28-Pin Standard Memory Devices, Including EPROMs, Byte-Wide RAMs, and E²PROMs**
- **Sockets for Up to 256K Bytes of Expansion with Intel 27512 EPROMs**
- **On-Board Expansion Provides "No Wait State" Memory Access with Selected Devices**
- **Simple, Reliable Mechanical and Electrical Interface**

The iSBC 341 28-pin MULTIMODULE EPROM board provides simple, low-cost expansion of the on-board EPROM capacity of the iSBC 86/05A, the iSBC 88/25, iSBC 186/03A, iSBC 286/10A, iSBC 286/12 Series Single Board Computers and the iSBC 88/40A Measurement and Control Computer. Four additional 28-pin sockets support JEDEC 24/28-pin standard devices, including EPROMs, byte-wide static and psuedo-static RAMs.

The MULTIMODULE expansion concept provides the optimum mechanism for incremental memory expansion. Mounting directly on the microcomputer, the benefits include low cost, no additional power requirements beyond the memory devices, and higher performance than MULTIBUS-based memory expansion.

280214-1

FUNCTIONAL DESCRIPTION

The iSBC 341 28-pin MULTIMODULE EPROM option effectively doubles the number of sockets available for EPROM on the base microcomputer board on which it is mounted. The iSBC 341 board contains six 28-pin sockets. Two of the sockets have extended pins which mate with two of the sockets on the base board. Two of the EPROMs which would have been inserted in the base board are then reinserted in the iSBC 341 sockets. Additional interface pins also connect chip select lines and power. The mechanical integrity of the assembly is assured with nylon hardware securing the unit in two places.

Through its unique interface, the iSBC 341 board can support 8- or 16-bit data paths. The data path width is determined by the base board—being 8 bits for the iSBC 88/40A and iSBC 88/25 microcomputers, and 8/16 bits for the iSBC 86/05A, iSBC 186/03A, iSBC 286/10A, and iSBC 286/12 Series Single Board Computers.

SPECIFICATIONS

Word Size

8 or 8/16 bits (determined by data path width of base board).

Memory Size

256K bytes with available technology (JEDEC standard defines device pin-out to 512-bit devices).

Device Size (Bytes)	EPROM Type	Max iSBC® 341 Capacity (Bytes)
2K x 8	2716	8K
4K x 8	2732A	16K
8K x 8	2764	32K
16K x 8	27128	64K
32K x 8	27256	128K
64K x 8	27512	256K

Access Time

Varies according to base board and memory device access time. Consult data sheet of base board for details.

Memory Addressing

Consult data sheet of base board for addressing data.

POWER REQUIREMENTS

Devices[1]	Max Current @ 5V ±5%
2716	420 mA
2732A	600 mA
2764	600 mA

NOTE:
1. Incremental power drawn from host board for four additional devices.

Auxiliary Power

There are no provisions for auxiliary power (battery backup) on the iSBC 341 option.

Physical Characteristics

Width: 3.4 in. (8.64 cm)

Length: 2.7 in. (6.86 cm)

Height: 0.78 in. (1.98 cm)*

Weight: 5 oz. (141.5 gm)

*Includes height of mounted memory devices and base board.

All necessary mounting hardware (nylon screws, spacers, nuts) is supplied with each kit.

Environmental Characteristics

Operating Temperature: 0°C to +55°C

Relative Humidity: to 90% (without condensation)

Reference Manuals

All necessary documentation for the iSBC 341 module is included in the CPU board Hardware Reference Manuals (NOT SUPPLIED)

iSBC 186/03A — Order No. 148060-001
iSBC 86/05A — Order No. 147162-002
iSBC 88/25 — Order No. 143825-002
iSBC 88/40A — Order No. 147049-001
iSBC 286/10A — Order No. 147532-001
iSBC 286/12 — Order No. 147533-001

Manuals may be ordered from any Intel sales representative, distributor office, or from Intel Literature Department, 3065 Bowers Avenue, Santa Clara, California 95051.

ORDERING INFORMATION

Part Number	Description
SBC 341	28-Pin MULTIMODULE EPROM

Multibus I Peripheral Controllers

10

iSBC® 221* PERIPHERAL CONTROLLER

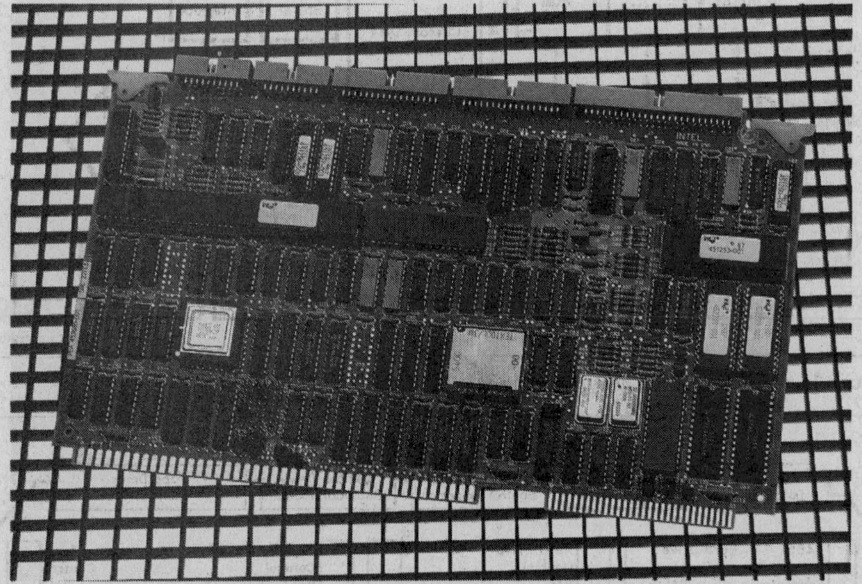

280410-1

10

MULTIBUS I CONTROLLER FOR HIGH PERFORMANCE, HIGH CAPACITY PERIPHERALS

The iSBC® 221 is a multifunction peripheral controller that provides access to high-performance, high-capacity disk drives (hard, flexible, and streaming tape). I/O bound applications and/or those requiring high disk capacity will especially benefit from this fast, reliable controller. The iSBC 221 can replace the Intel iSBC 214 without changing the operating system device driver or the disk drives.

FEATURES

- Support for ESDI and ST506/412 hard disk drives, SA 45X/46X/475 flexible disk drives, and QIC-02 streaming tape drives
- Multiple track caching via 128K on-board data buffer
- Dual bus structure
- 10 MHz 80186 Microprocessor
- Mirror backup/restore between tape and hard drive
- On-board self-test diagnostics
- Error-checking and correcting code logic
- Support for 4,096 cylinders and 16 heads

*The iSBC® 221 is also manufactured under product code pSBC 221 by Intel Puerto Rico, Inc.
*XENIX is a trademark of Microsoft, Inc.
UNIX is a trademark of American Telephone and Telegraph, Inc.

September 1991
Order Number: 280410-002

FEATURES

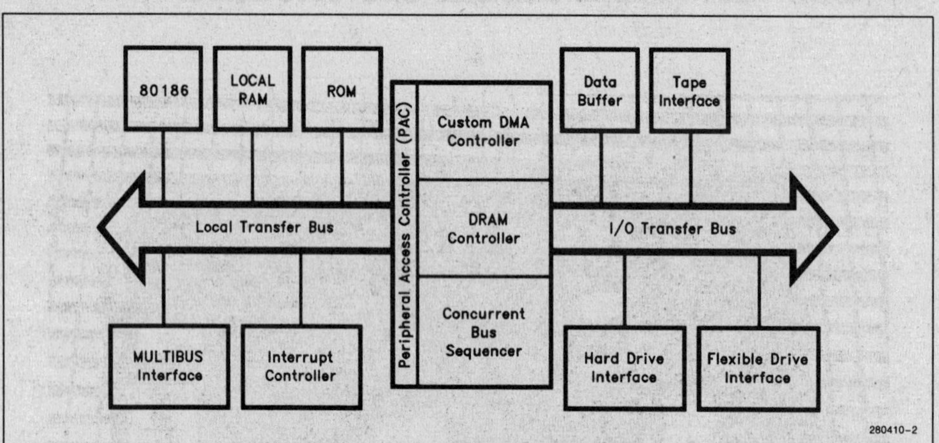

Figure 1: Simplified Block Diagram of iSBC® 221 Peripheral Controller

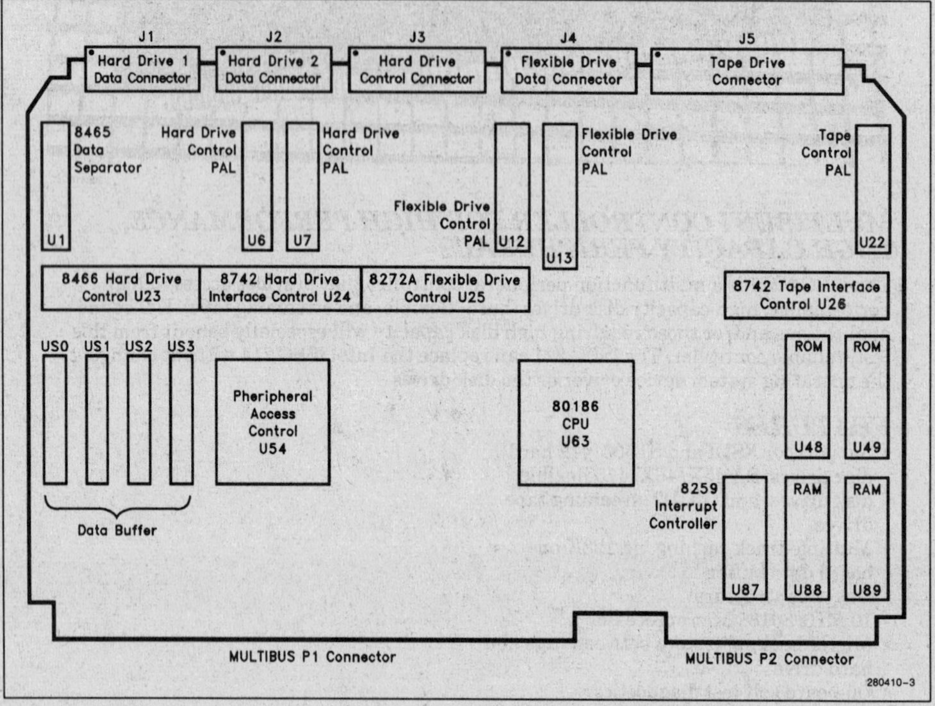

Figure 2: Connectors and Major Components of iSBC 221 Peripheral Controller

FEATURES

INTERFACE SUPPORT

	Interface	Transfer Rate
Hard Disk (up to 2)	ESDI	up to 15 Mbit/sec
	ST506/412	5 Mbit/sec
Flexible Disk (up to 4)	SA 475	250/500 Kbit/sec
	SA 460/465	125/250 Kbit/sec
	SA 450/455	125/250 Kbit/sec
Streaming Tape (up to 4)	QIC-02	90/112.5 Kbit/sec (typical)

HIGH PERFORMANCE

I/O-bound applications are accelerated by the combination of the ESDI standard, a 128K data buffer, a 10 MHz 80 186 microprocessor, and a dual bus structure. The dual bus structure allows the iSBC 221 to concurrently transfer data between the controller and the peripheral devices and between the controller and the host.

WORLDWIDE SERVICE AND SUPPORT

Intel provides support for board repair or on-site service. Development support options include phone support, subscription service, on-site consulting and customer training.

QUALITY AND RELIABILITY TESTING

The iSBC 221 is designed and manufactured in accordance with Intel's high quality standards. We then verify quality through rigorous testing in our state-of-the-art Environmental Test Laboratory.

10

SPECIFICATIONS

PHYSICAL CHARACTERISTICS

Length: 12.0 in. (304.8 mm)
Width: 6.75 in. (171.5 mm)
Approximate Weight: 24 oz. (680 g)

POWER REQUIREMENTS

+5 VDC @ 4.5A maximum
±12V @ 0.5A

ENVIRONMENTAL REQUIREMENTS

Operating Temperature: 0°C to +55°C @ 200 LFM
Non-Operating: −55°C to +85°C
Humidity: 0% to 90% non-condensing

REFERENCE MANUAL

iSBC 221 Peripheral Controller User's Guide
Order Number 451210

DEVICE DRIVERS

Check the latest release of the following operating systems for details:

iRMX I	XENIX*
iRMX II	UNIX*
iRMX III	

ORDERING INFORMATION

Order Code	Description
SBC221	Peripheral Controller

iSBC® 208*
FLEXIBLE DISKETTE CONTROLLER

- Compatible with All iSBC® 80, iSBC 86, and iSBC 88 Single Board Computers
- Controls Most Single and Double Density Diskette Drives
- On-Board SBX Bus for Additional Functions
- User-Programmable Drive Parameters allow Wide Choice of Drives
- Phase Lock Loop Data Separator Assures Maximum Data Integrity
- Read and Write on Single or Multiple Sectors
- Single +5V Supply
- Capable of Addressing 16M Bytes of System Memory

The Intel iSBC 208 Flexible Disk Controller is a diskette controller capable of supporting virtually any soft-sectored, double density or single density diskette drive. The standard controller can control up to four drives with up to eight surfaces. In addition to the standard IBM 3740 formats and IBM System 34 formats, the controller supports sector lengths of up to 8192 bytes. The iSBC 208 board's wide range of drive compatiblity is achieved without compromising performance. The operating characteristics are specified under user program control. The controller can read, write, verify, and search either single or multiple sectors. Additional parallel or serial I/O capability can be added to the iSBC 208 board via the SBX bus (IEEE 959) connector.

280228–1

*The iSBC® 208 is also manufactured under product code pSBC 208 by Intel Puerto Rico, Inc.

September 1991
Order Number: 280228-002

10

BLOCK DIAGRAM

iSBC® 208 Flexible Disk Controller Block Diagram

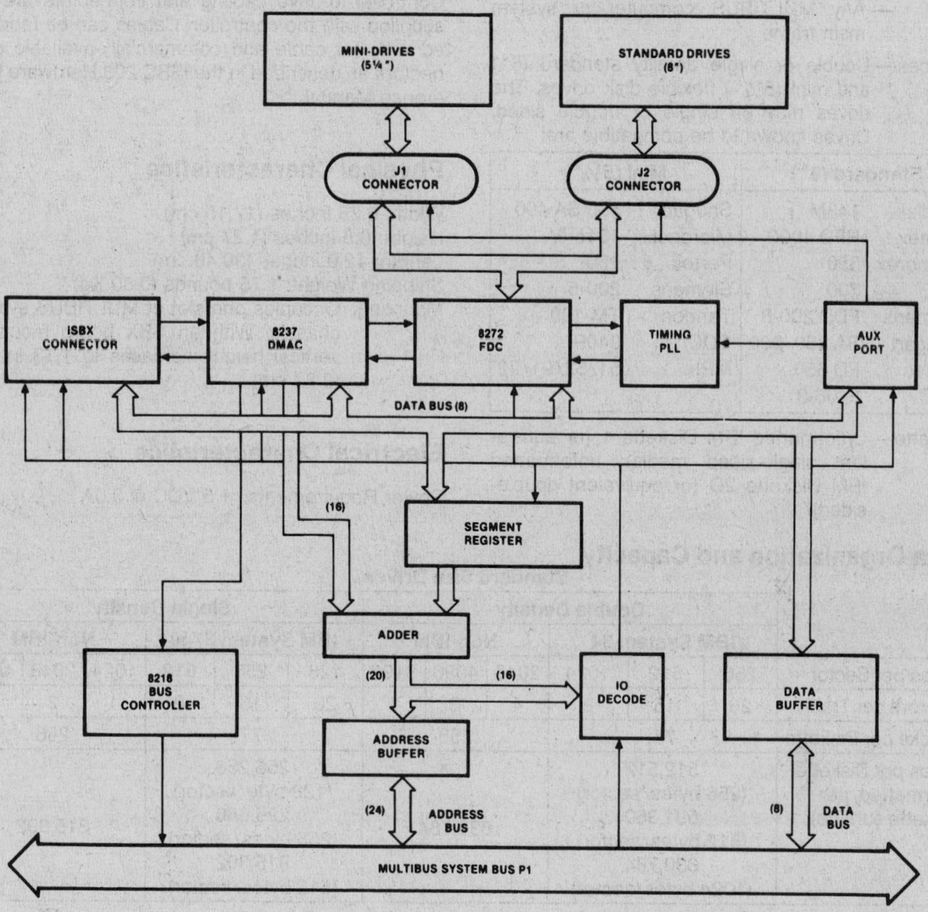

MINI-DRIVES (5¼")
STANDARD DRIVES (8")
J1 CONNECTOR
J2 CONNECTOR
ISBX CONNECTOR
8237 DMAC
8272 FDC
TIMING PLL
AUX PORT
DATA BUS (8)
(16)
SEGMENT REGISTER
ADDER
(20)
(16)
IO DECODE
DATA BUFFER
8218 BUS CONTROLLER
ADDRESS BUFFER
(24)
ADDRESS BUS
(8)
DATA BUS
MULTIBUS SYSTEM BUS P1
280228–2

SPECIFICATIONS

Compatibility

CPU — Any MULTIBUS computer or system main frame

Devices— Double or single density standard (8") and mini (5¼") flexible disk drives. The drives may be single or double sided. Drives known to be compatible are:

Standard (8")		Mini (5¼")	
Caldisk	143M	Shugart	450 SA 400
Remex	RFD 4000	Micropolis	1015-IV
Memorex	550	Pertec	250
MFE	700	Siemens	200-5
Siemens	FDD 200-8	Tandon	TM-100
Shugart	SA 850/800	CDC	9409
Pertec	FD 650	MPI	51/52/91/92
CDC	9406-3		

Diskette— Unformatted IBM Diskette 1 (or equivalent single-sided media); unformatted IBM Diskette 2D (or equivalent double-sided)

Equipment Supplied

iSBC 208 Controller
Reference Schematic
Controller-to-drive cabling and connectors are not supplied with the controller. Cables can be fabricated with flat cable and commercially-available connectors as described in the iSBC 208 Hardware Reference Manual

Physical Characteristics

Width: 6.75 inches (17.15 cm)
Height: 0.5 inches (1.27 cm)
Length: 12.0 inches (30.48 cm)
Shipping Weight: 1.75 pounds (0.80 Kg)
Mounting: Occupies one slot of MULTIBUS system chassis. With an SBX board mounted, vertical height increases to 1.13 inches (2.87 cm).

Electrical Characteristics

Power Requirements: +5 VDC @ 3.0A

Data Organization and Capacity

Standard Size Drives

	Double Density						Single Density					
	IBM System 34			Non-IBM			IBM System 3740			Non-IBM		
Bytes per Sector	256	512	1024	2048	4096	8192	128	256	512	1024	2048	4096
Sectors per Track	26	15	8	4	2	1	26	15	8	4	2	1
Tracks per Diskette	77			256			77			256		
Bytes per Diskette (Formatted, per diskette surface)	512,512 (256 bytes/sector) 591,360 (512 bytes/sector) 630,784 (1024 bytes/sector)			630,784			256,256 (128 byte/sector) 295,680 (256 bytes/sector) 315,392 (512 bytes/sector)			315,392		

Drive Characteristics

Drive Characteristics	Standard Size	Mini Size
	Double/Single Density	Double/Single Density
Transfer Rate (K bytes/s)	62.5/31.25	31.25/15.63
Disk Speed (RPM)	360	300
Step Rate Time (Programmable)	1 to 16 ms/track in 1 ms increments	2 to 32 ms/track in 2 ms increments
Head Load Time (Programmable)	2 to 254 ms in 2 ms increments	4 to 508 ms in 4 ms increments
Head Unload Time (Programmable)	16 to 240 ms in 16 ms increments	32 to 480 ms in 32 ms increments

Environmental Characteristics

Temperature: 0°C to 55°C (operating); −55°C to +85°C (non-operating)

Humidity: Up to 90% Relative Humidity without condensation (operating); all conditions without condensation or frost (non-operating)

Reference Manual

143078— iSBC 208 Flexible Disk Controller Hardware Reference Manual (NOT SUPPLIED).

Reference manuals may be ordered from any Intel sales representative, distributor office, or from Intel Literature Department, 3065 Bowers Avenue, Santa, Clara, CA 95051.

ORDERING INFORMATION

Order Code	Description
SBC208	Flexible Disk Controller

Multibus I Serial Communication Boards

11

iSBC® 548/549 TERMINAL CONTROLLERS

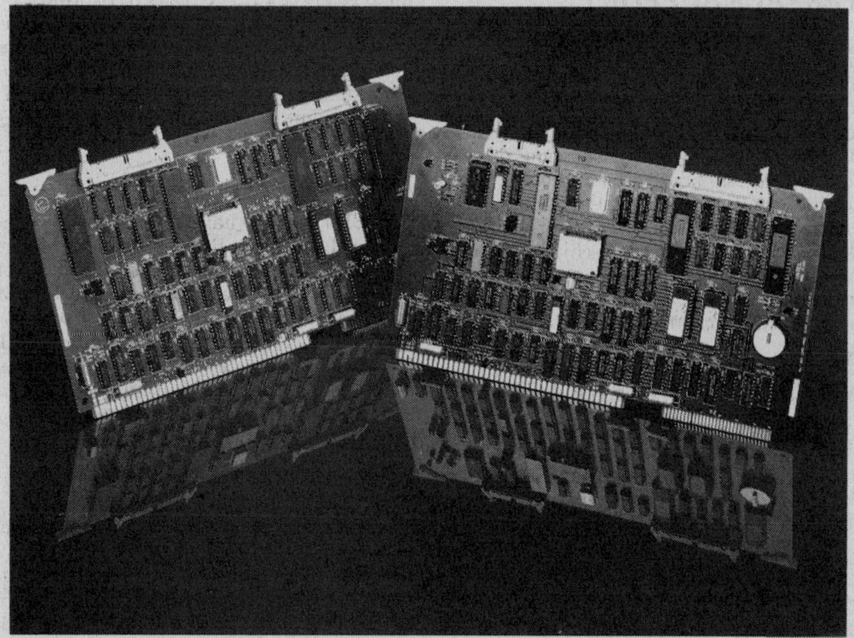

280674-1

11

HIGH PERFORMANCE TERMINAL CONTROLLER BOARDS FOR MULTIBUS I

The iSBC® 548 and iSBC 549 are intelligent terminal controllers for Multibus I applications. The iSBC 548 provides basic multiuser support with 8 channels of RS 232 Asynchronous interface. The iSBC 549 combines 4 serial channels with a real-time clock and a line printer interface. Acting as intelligent slaves for communication expansion, these boards provide high performance, low cost solutions for multi-user systems.

FEATURES

iSBC® 548 Features

- Supports eight channels asynchronous RS232 interface

iSBC® 549 Features

- Supports four channels asynchronous RS232 interface
- Line printer interface
- Real-time clock/calendar with battery backup

Standard iSBC® 548/549 Features

- 8 MHz 80186 Microprocessor
- Supports transfer rates up to 19.2K Baud
- 128 Kbytes Zero Wait State DRAM (32K Dual Port)
- Supports Full Duplex Asynchronous Transmissions
- Jumper selectable memory mapping, I/O mapping and Multibus Interrupts

*IBM is a trademark of International Business Machines.
*Centronics is a registered trademark of Centronics, Inc.

November 1990
Order Number: 280674-002

FEATURES

ASYNCHRONOUS RS232 INTERFACE SUPPORT

The iSBC 548/549 Asynchronous RS232 Internal support is presented in DTE Configuration. 82530 Serial Communications Controllers (SCCs) provide channels of half/full duplex serial I/O. Configurability of the 82530 allows handling all asynchronous data formats regardless of data size, number of start or stop bits, or parity requirements. The synchronous transmission features of the 82530 are not supported. An on-chip baud rate generator allows independent baud rates on each channel. The serial lines can be brought to the back-panel via 40-pin connectors and ribbon cable.

LINE PRINTER INTERFACE

The iSBC 549 incorporates a standard line printer interface compatible with IBM* or Centronics* line printers. Intelligent buffering on the iSBC 549 allows the CPU to offload printing tasks and return to higher priority jobs.

REAL-TIME CLOCK/CALENDAR

Multibus systems will benefit from the real-time clock present on the iSBC 549 in applications requiring time stamp operations, unattended boots and other calendar requirements. The clock/calendar circuit is backed up by a non-rechargeable battery which keeps the clock/calendar operating for six months with all other power off.

8 MHZ 80186 MICROPROCESSOR

The 80186 central processor component provides high- performance, flexibility, and powerful processing. The 80186/82530 combination with on-board PROM/EPROM sites, and dual-port RAM provides the intelligence and speed to manage multi-user communications.

TRANSFER RATES UP TO 19.2K BAUD

Collectively, each board has dual-port RAM providing an on-board buffer to handle incoming and outgoing messages at data rates up to 19.2K baud. The resident firmware supports asynchronous RS232 serial channels, provides modem control and performs power-up diagnostics. Each serial channel can be individually programmed to different baud rates to allow system configurations with differing terminal types.

MEMORY

The iSBC 548/549 have three areas of memory on-board: dual-port RAM, private RAM, and EPROM. Each board contains 128K bytes of on-board RAM, 32K bytes of dual-port RAM can be addressed by other Multibus boards. The dual port memory is configurable in a 16 Mbyte address space on 32 Kbyte boundaries as addressed from the Multibus port. The starting address is jumper selectable.

The second area of memory is 96 Kbytes of private RAM which is addressable by the 80186 on-board.

The third area of memory is EPROM memory expansion. Two 28-pin JEDEC sockets are provided. These sockets come populated with two EPROMs which contain the controller firmware. The boards can support 2764, 27128 and 27256 EPROMs, giving a total capacity of 64 Kbytes. The EPROM runs with zero wait states if EPROMs of access times 250ns or less are used. No jumper changes are needed to access different size EPROMs.

WORLDWIDE SERVICE AND SUPPORT

Intel provides support for board repair or on-site service. Development options include phone support, subscription service, on-site consulting, and customer training.

QUALITY AND RELIABILITY

The iSBC 548 and iSBC 549 are designed and manufactured in accordance with Intel's high quality standards. We then verify quality through rigorous testing in our state-of-the-art Environmental Test Laboratory.

FEATURES

80186
FIRM-WARE
iSBC® 548 CONTROLLER
iSBC® 386/12 HOST
80186
FIRM-WARE
iSBC® 549 CONTROLLER
CLUSTER CONTROLLER
SYSTEM PROCESSOR
CLUSTER CONTROLLER
MULTIBUS SYSTEM BUS
MULTIBUS SYSTEM BUS
280674-2

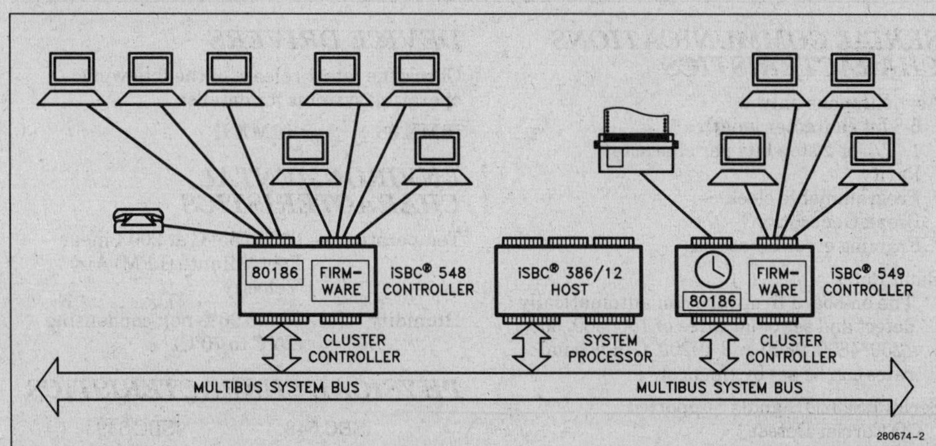

Figure 1: Terminal/Cluster Controller Application

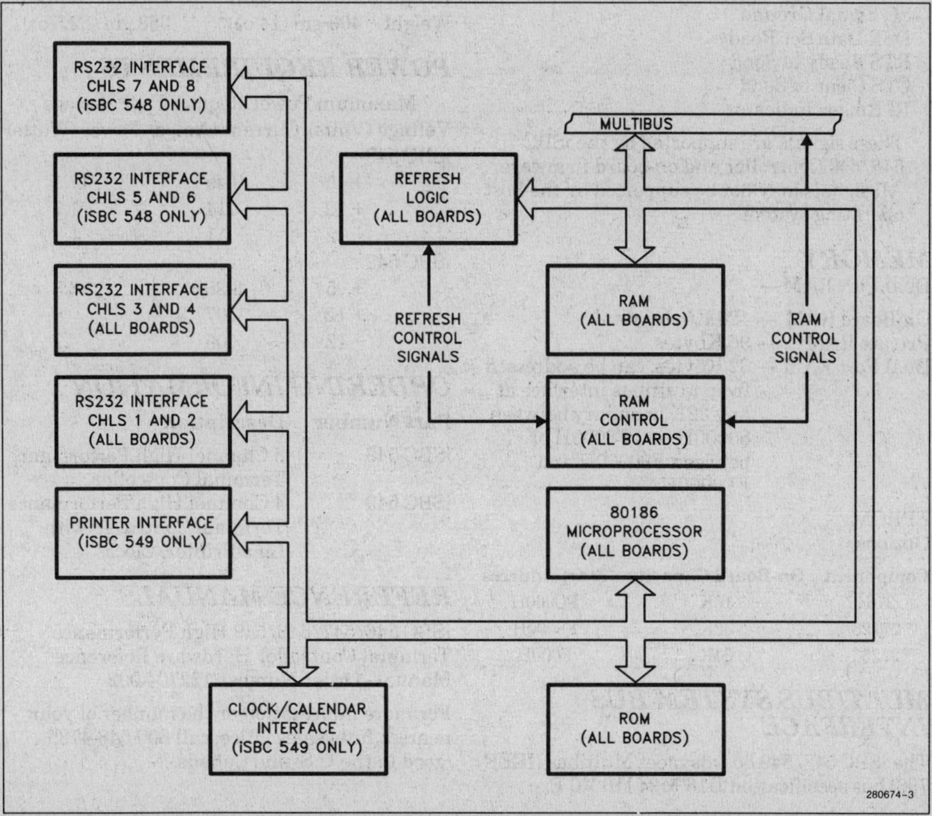

RS232 INTERFACE CHLS 7 AND 8 (iSBC 548 ONLY)
RS232 INTERFACE CHLS 5 AND 6 (iSBC 548 ONLY)
RS232 INTERFACE CHLS 3 AND 4 (ALL BOARDS)
RS232 INTERFACE CHLS 1 AND 2 (ALL BOARDS)
PRINTER INTERFACE (iSBC 549 ONLY)
MULTIBUS
REFRESH LOGIC (ALL BOARDS)
REFRESH CONTROL SIGNALS
RAM (ALL BOARDS)
RAM CONTROL SIGNALS
RAM CONTROL (ALL BOARDS)
80186 MICROPROCESSOR (ALL BOARDS)
CLOCK/CALENDAR INTERFACE (iSBC 549 ONLY)
ROM (ALL BOARDS)
280674-3

Figure 2: iSBC® 548/549 Boards Block Diagram

SPECIFICATIONS

SERIAL COMMUNICATIONS CHARACTERISTICS

Asynchronous only
- 6-8 bit character length
- 1, 1½, or 2 stop bits per character
- Parity
- Programmable clock
- Break Generation
- Framing error detection

Baud Rates

The on-board firmware can automatically detect and set baud rates of 150, 300, 600, 1200, 4800, 9600 and 19200. Other baud rates can be set by the host.

Serial RS232C Signals Supported
- CD Carrier Detect
- RXD Receive Data
- TXD Transmit Data
- DTR Data Terminal Ready
- SG Signal Ground
- DSR Data Set Ready
- RTS Ready to Send
- CTS Clear to Send
- RI Ringer Indicator

These signals are supported by the iSBC 548/549 Controller and on-board firmware. All signals may not be supported by the host operating system.

MEMORY

Dual Port RAM —

On-Board RAM — 128 Kbytes total
Private RAM — 96 Kbytes
Dual Port RAM — 32 Kbytes, can be addressed from Multibus interface at any 32K boundary between 80000H and F8000H or between F80000H and FF8000H.

EPROM Options —

Component	On-Board Capacity	Start Address
2764	16K	FC000H
27128	32K	F8000H
27256	64K	F000H

MULTIBUS SYSTEM BUS INTERFACE

The iSBC 548/549 boards meet Multibus (IEEE 796) bus specification D16 M24 I16 V0 E.

DEVICE DRIVERS

Check the latest release of the following operating systems for details:

iRMX 86   iRMX II

ENVIRONMENTAL CHARACTERISTICS

Temperature — 0°C to 55° C at 200 Linear Feet/Minute (LFM) Air Velocity

Humidity — 5% to 90% non-condensing (25°C to 70°C)

PHYSICAL CHARACTERISTICS

	iSBC 548	iSBC 549
Width	30.34cm (12.00 in)	30.34cm (12.00 in)
Length	16.87cm (6.75 in)	16.87cm (6.75 in)
Height	1.27 cm (.5 in)	1.27 cm (.5 in)
Weight	400 gm (14 oz)	358 gm (12.5 oz)

POWER REQUIREMENTS

Maximum Power Required per Voltage

Voltage (Volts)	Current (Amps)	Power (Watts)
iSBC 548		
+ 5	3.49	17.5
+12	.14	1.7
−12	.11	1.3
iSBC 549		
+ 5	3.26	16.3
+12	.07	.8
−12	.06	.7

ORDERING INFORMATION

Part Number	Description
iSBC 548	8 Channel High Performance Terminal Controller
iSBC 549	4 Channel High Performance Terminal Controller with Line Printer/Clock

REFERENCE MANUALS

iSBC 546/547/548/549 High Performance Terminal Controller Hardware Reference Manual - Order Number 122704-002

For more information or the number of your nearest Intel sales office, call 800-548-4725 (good in the U.S. and Canada).

iSBC® 188/56* ADVANCED COMMUNICATING COMPUTER

- iSBC® Single Board Computer or Intelligent Slave Communication Board
- 8 Serial Communications Channels, Expandable to 12 Channels on a Single Multibus Board
- 8 MHz 80188 Microprocessor
- Supports RS232C Interface on 6 Channels, RS422A/449 or RS232C Interface Configurable on 2 Channels
- Supports Async, Bisync HDLC/SDLC, On-Chip Baud Rate Generation, Half/Full-Duplex, NRZ, NRZI or FM Encoding/Decoding
- 7 On-Board DMA Channels for Serial I/O, 2 80188 DMA Channels for the iSBX Bus Interface
- Multibus Interface for System Expansion and Multimaster Configuration
- Two iSBX Connectors for Low Cost I/O Expansion
- 256K Bytes Dual-Ported RAM On-Board
- Two 28-pin JEDEC PROM Sites Expandable to 6 Sites with the iSBC 341 MULTIMODULE Board for a Maximum of 192K Bytes EPROM
- Resident Firmware to Handle up to 12 RS232C Async Lines

11

The iSBC 188/56 Advanced Communicating Computer is an intelligent 8-channel single board computer. This iSBC board adds the 8 MHz 80188 microprocessor-based communications flexibility to the Intel line of Multibus OEM microcomputer systems. Acting as a stand-alone CPU or intelligent slave for communication expansion, this board provides a high performance, low-cost solution for multi-user systems. The features of the iSBC 188/56 board are uniquely suited to manage higher-layer protocol requirements needed in today's data communications applications. This single board computer takes full advantage of Intel's VLSI technology to provide state-of-the-art, economic, computer based solutions for OEM communications-oriented applications.

*The iSBC® 188/56 is also manufactured under product code pSBC 188/56 by Intel Puerto Rico, Inc.

280715–1

*IBM is a registered trademark of International Business Machines
*UNIX is a trademark of Bell Laboratories
*XENIX is a trademark of Microsoft Corporation

September 1991
Order Number: 280715-003

OPERATING ENVIRONMENT

The iSBC 188/56 board features have been designed to meet the needs of numerous communications applications. Typical applications include:

1. Terminal/cluster controller
2. Front-end processor
3. Stand-alone communicating computer

Terminal/Cluster Controller

A terminal/cluster controller concentrates communications in a central area of a system. Efficient handling of messages coming in or going out of the system requires sufficient buffer space to store messages and high speed I/O channels to transmit messages. More sophisticated applications, such as cluster controllers, also require character and format conversion capabilities to allow different types of terminals to be attached.

The iSBC 188/56 Advanced Communicating Computer is well suited for multi-terminal systems (see Figure 1). Up to 12 serial channels can be serviced in multi-user or cluster applications by adding two iSBX 354 MULTIMODULE boards. The dual-port RAM provides a large on-board buffer to handle incoming and outgoing messages at data rates up to 19.2K baud. Two channels are supported for continuous data rates greater than 19.2K baud. Each serial channel can be individually programmed for different baud rates to allow system configurations with differing terminal types. The firmware supplied on the iSBC 188/56 board supports up to 12 asynchronous RS232C serial channels, provides modem control and performs power-up diagnostics. The high performance of the on-board CPU provides intelligence to handle protocols and character handling typically assigned to the system CPU. The distribution of intelligence results in optimizing system performance by releasing the system CPU of routine tasks.

Front-End Processor

A front-end processor off-loads a system's central processor of tasks such as data manipulation and text editing of characters collected from the attached terminals. A variety of terminals require flexible terminal interfaces. Program code is often dynamically downloaded to the front-end processor from the system CPU. Downloading code requires sufficient memory space for protocol handling and program code. Flow control and efficient handling of interrupts require an efficient operating system to manage the hardware and software resources.

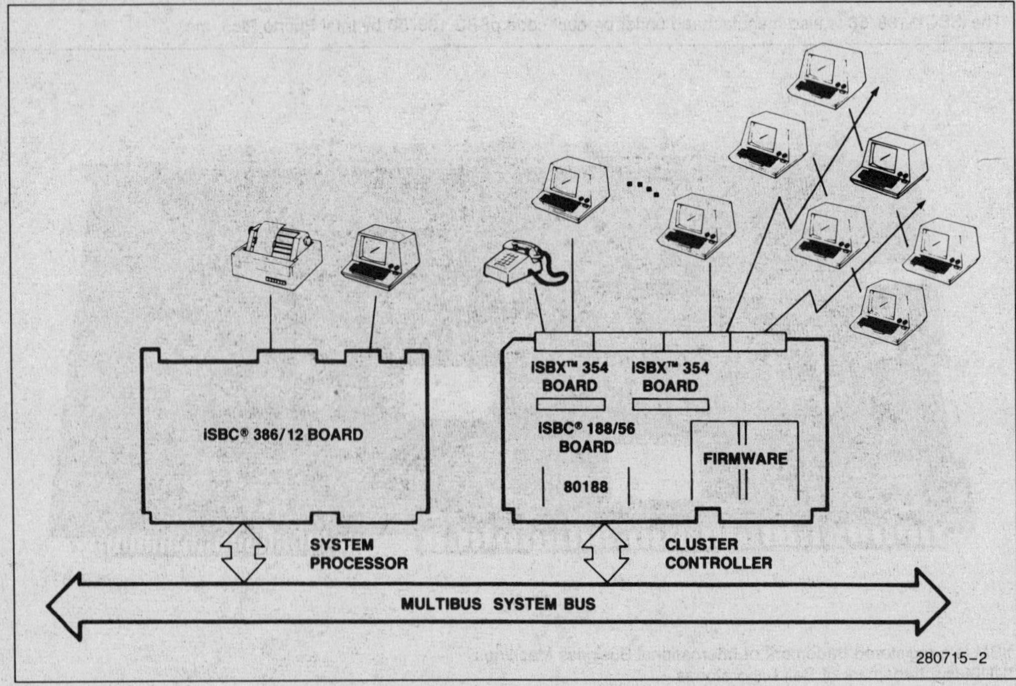

Figure 1. Terminal/Cluster Controller Application

The iSBC 188/56 board features are designed to provide a high performance solution for front-end processor applications (see Figure 2). A large amount of random access memory is provided for dynamic storage of program code. In addition, local memory sites are available for storing routine programs such as X.25, SNA or bisync protocol software. The serial channels can be configured for links to mainframe systems, point-to-point terminals, modems or multidrop configurations.

Stand-Alone Application

A stand-alone communication computer is a complete computer system. The CPU is capable of managing the resources required to meet the needs of multi-terminal, multi-protocol applications. These applications typically require multi-terminal support, floppy disk control, local memory allocation, and program execution and storage.

To support stand-alone applications, the iSBC 188/56 board uses the computational capabilities of an on-board CPU to provide a high-speed system solution controlling 8 to 12 channels of serial I/O (see Figure 3). The local memory available is large enough to handle special purpose code, execution code and routine protocol software. The Multibus interface can be used to access additional system functions. Floppy disk control and graphics capability can be added to the iSBC stand-alone computer through the iSBX connectors.

ARCHITECTURE

The four major functional areas are Serial I/O, CPU, Memory and DMA. These areas are illustrated in Figure 4.

Serial I/O

Eight HDLC/SDLC serial interfaces are provided on the iSBC 188/56 board. The serial interface can be expanded to 12 channels by adding 2 iSBX 354 MULTIMODULE boards. The HDLC/SDLC interface is compatible with IBM* system and terminal equipment and with CCITT's X.25 packet switching interface.

11

Four 82530 Serial Communications Controllers (SCC) provide eight channels of half/full duplex serial I/O. Six channels support RS232C interfaces. Two channels are RS232C/422/449 configurable and can be tri-stated to allow multidrop networks. The 82530 component is designed to satisfy several serial communications requirements; asynchronous,

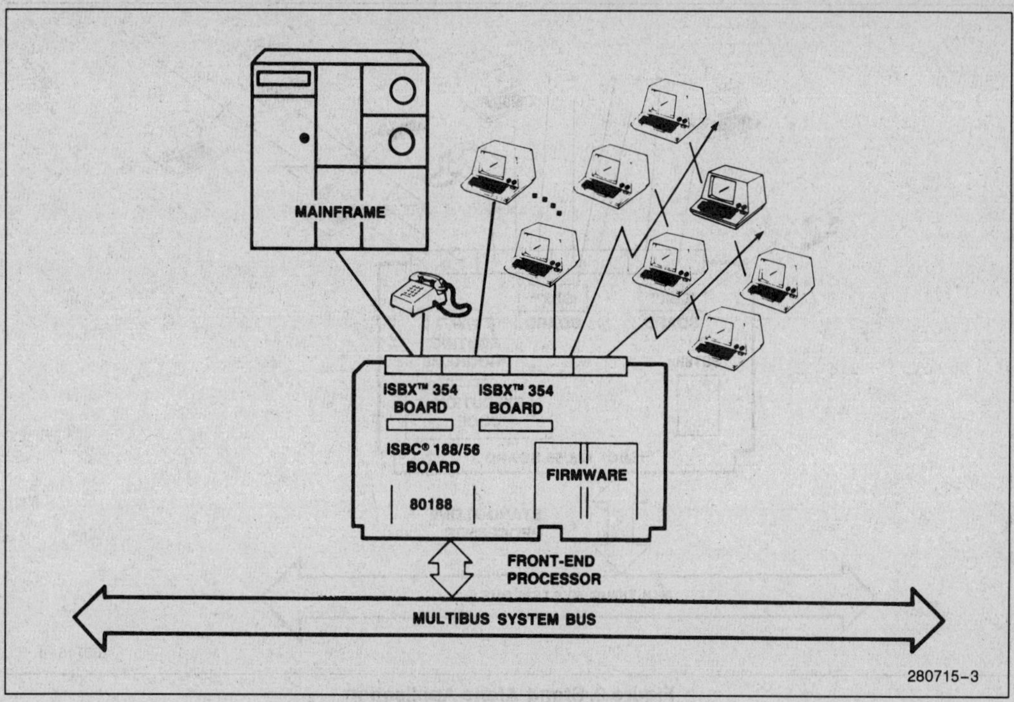

Figure 2. Front-End Processor Application

byte-oriented synchronous (HDLC/SDLC) modes. The increased capability at the serial controller point results in off-loading the CPU of tasks formerly assigned to the CPU or its associated hardware. Configurability of the 82530 allows the user to configure it to handle all asynchronous data formats regardless of data size, number of start or stop bits, or parity requirements. An on-chip baud rate generator allows independent baud rates on each channel.

The clock can be generated either internally with the SCC chip, with an external clock or via the NRZ1 clock encoding mechanism.

All eight channels can be configured as Data Terminal Equipment (DTE) or Data Communications Equipment (DCE). Table 1 lists the interfaces supported.

Table 1. iSBC® 188/56 Interface Support

Connection	Synchronous	Asynchronous
	Modem to Direct	Modem to Direct
Point-to-Point	X**	X
	Channels	Channels
Multidrop	0 and 1	0 and 1
Loop	X	N/A

**All 8 channels are denoted by X.

Central CPU

The 80188 central processor component provides high performance, flexibility and powerful processing. The 80188 component is a highly integrated microprocessor with an 8-bit data bus interface and a 16-bit internal architecture to give high performance. The 80188 is upward compatible with 86 and 186 software.

The 80188/82530 combination with on-board PROM/EPROM sites, and dual-port RAM provide the intelligence and speed to manage multi-user, multi-protocol communication operations.

Memory

There are two areas of memory on-board: dual-port RAM and universal site memory. The iSBC 188/56 board contains 256K bytes of dual-port RAM that is addressable by the 80188 on-board. The dual-port memory is configurable anywhere in a 16M byte address space on 64K byte boundaries as addressed from the Multibus port. Not all of the 256K bytes are visible from the Multibus bus side. The amount of dual-port memory visible to the Multibus side can

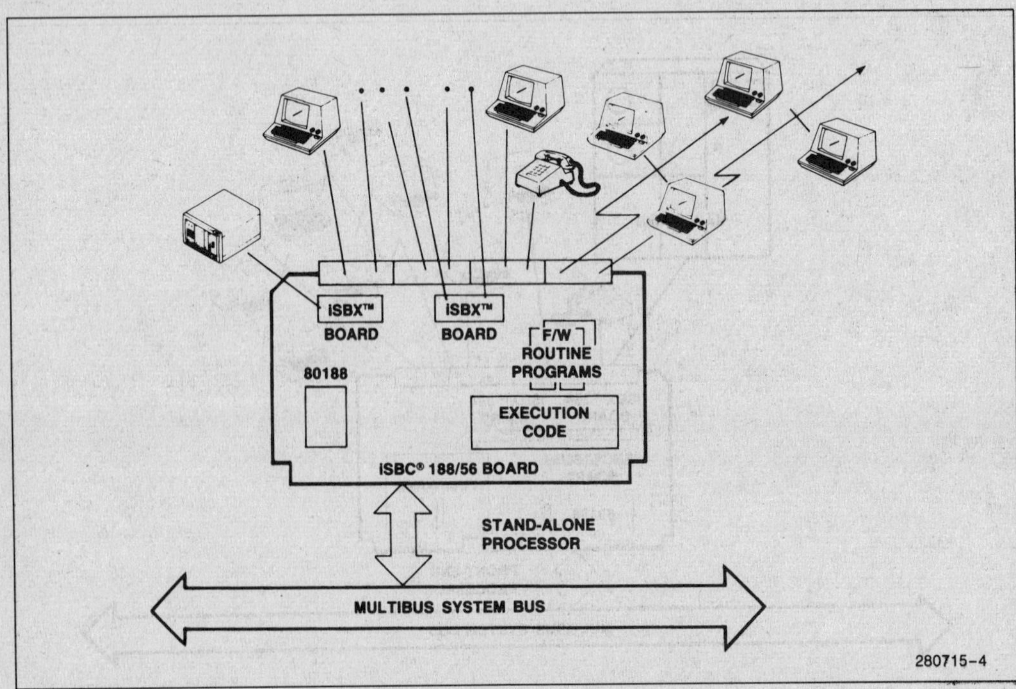

Figure 3. Stand-Alone Application

be set (with jumpers) to none, 16K bytes, or 48K bytes. In a multiprocessor system these features provide local memory for each processor and shared system memory configurations where the total system memory size can exceed one megabyte without addressing conflicts.

The second area of memory is universal site memory providing flexible memory expansion. Two 28-pin JEDEC sockets are provided. One of these sockets is used for the resident firmware as described in the FIRMWARE section.

The default configuration of the boards supports 16K byte EPROM devices such as the Intel 27128 component. However, these sockets can contain ROM, EPROM, Static RAM, or EEPROM. Both sockets must contain the same type of component (i.e. as the first socket contains an EPROM for the resident firmware, the second must also contain an EPROM with the same pinout). Up to 32K bytes can be addressed per socket giving a maximum universal site memory size of 64K bytes. By using the iSBC 341 MULTIMODULE board, a maximum of 192K bytes of universal site memory is available. This provides sufficient memory space for on-board network or resource management software.

On-Board DMA

Seven channels of Direct Memory Access (DMA) are provided between serial I/O and on-board dual port RAM by two 8237-5 components. Each of channels 0, 1, 2, 3, 5, 6, and 7 is supported by their own DMA line. Serial channels 0 and 1 are configurable for full duplex DMA. Configuring the full duplex DMA option for Channels 0 and 1 would require Channels 2 and 3 to be interrupt driven or polled. Channel 4 is interrupt driven or polled only.

Two DMA channels are integrated in the 80188 processor. These additional channels can be connected to the iSBX interfaces to provide DMA capability to iSBX MULTIMODULE boards such as the iSBX 218A Floppy Disk Controller MULTIMODULE board.

11

OPERATING SYSTEM SUPPORT

Intel offers run-time foundation software to support applications that range from general purpose to high-performance solutions.

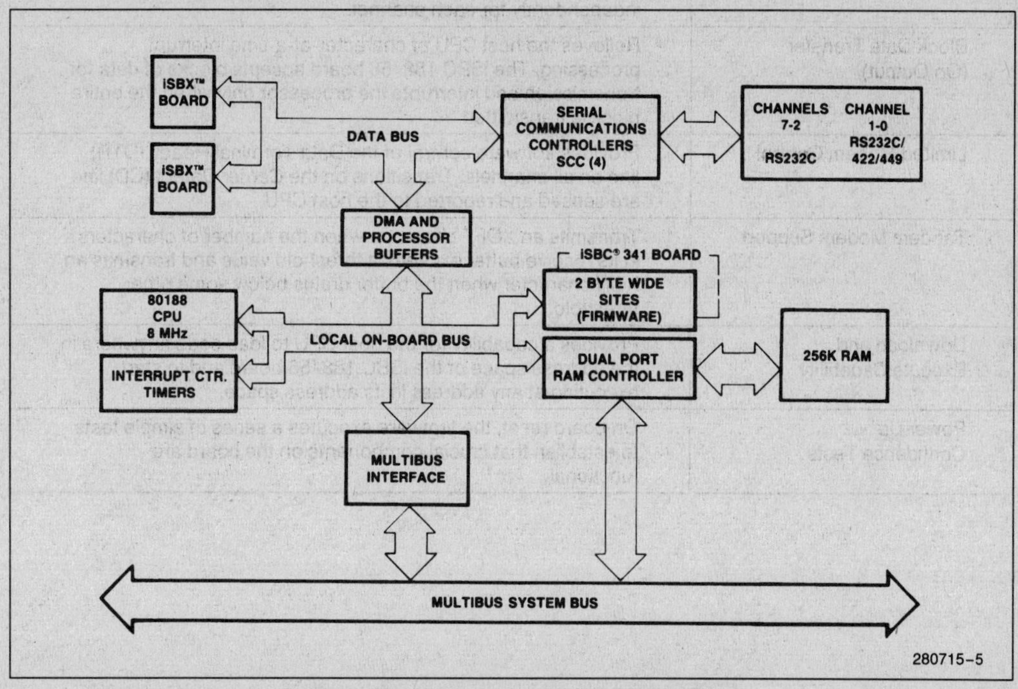

Figure 4. Block Diagram of iSBC® 188/56 Board

The iRMX Operating System provides a rich set of features and options to support sophisticated standalone communications applications on the iSBC 188/56 Advanced Communicating Computer. If the iSBC 188/56 board is acting as an intelligent slave in a system environment, an iRMX driver resident in the host CPU is available.

The System Debug Monitor (SDM) supports target system debugging for the iSBC 188/56 Advanced Communicating COMMputer board. The monitor contains the necessary hardware, software and documentation required to interface the iSBC 188/56 target system to an Intel microcomputer development system for debugging application software.

The XENIX* Operating System includes a software driver for the iSBC 188/56 board (and up to two iSBX 354 MULTIMODULE Boards) acting as an intelligent slave for multi-user applications requiring multiple persons running independent, terminal-oriented jobs.

FIRMWARE

The iSBC 188/56 Communicating COMMputer board is supplied with resident firmware that supports up to 12 RS232C asynchronous serial channels. In addition, the firmware provides a facility for a host CPU to download and execute code on the iSBC 188/56 board. Simple power-up confidence tests are also included to provide a quick diagnostic service. The firmware converts the iSBC 188/56 COMMputer board to a slave communications controller. As a slave communications controller, it requires a separate Multibus host CPU board and requires the use of Multibus interrupt line to signal the host processor. Table 2 summarizes the features of the firmware.

Table 2. Features of the iSBC® 188/56 Firmware

Feature	Description
Asynchronous Serial Channel Support	Supports the serial channels in asynchronous ASCII mode. Parameters such as baud rate, parity generation, parity checking and character length can be programmed independently for each channel.
Block Data Transfer (On Output)	Relieves the host CPU of character-at-a-time interrupt processing. The iSBC 188/56 board accepts blocks of data for transmission and interrupts the processor only when the entire block is transmitted.
Limited Modem Control	Provides software control of the Data Terminal Ready (DTR) line on all channels. Transitions on the Carrier Detect (CD) line are sensed and reported to the host CPU.
Tandem Modem Support	Transmits an XOFF character when the number of characters in its receive buffer exceeds a threshold value and transmits an XON character when the buffer drains below some other threshold.
Download and Execute Capability	Provides a capability for the host CPU to load code anywhere in the address space of the iSBC 188/56 board and to start executing at any address in its address space.
Power Up Confidence Tests	On board reset, the firmware executes a series of simple tests to establish that crucial components on the board are functional.

INTERRUPT CAPABILITY

The iSBC 188/56 board has two programmable interrupt controllers (PICs). One is integrated into the 80188 processor and the other in the 80130 component. The two controllers are configured with the 80130 controller as the master and the 80188 controller as the slave. Two of the 80130 interrupt inputs are connected to the 82530 serial controller components to provide vector interrupt capabilities by the serial controllers. The iSBC 188/56 board provides 22 interrupt levels. The highest level is the NMI (Non-Maskable Interrupt) line which is directly tied to the 80188 CPU. This interrupt is typically used for signaling catastrophic events (e.g. power failure).

There are 5 levels of interrupts internal to the 80188 processor. Another 8 levels of interrupts are available from the 80130 component. Of these 8, one is tied to the programmable interrupt controller (PIC) of the 80188 CPU. An additional 8 levels of interrupts are available at the Multibus interface. The iSBC 188/56 board does not support bus vectored interrupts. Table 3 lists the possible interrupt sources.

SUPPORT FOR THE 80130 COMPONENT

Intel does not support the direct processor execution of the iRMX nucleus primitives from the 80130 component. The 80130 component provides timers and interrupt controllers.

Table 3. Interrupt Request Sources

Device	Function	Number of Interrupts
Multibus Interface INT0–INT7	Requests from Multibus resident peripherals or other CPU boards.	8
82530 Serial Controllers	Transmit buffer empty, receive buffer full and channel errors 1 and external status.	8 per 82530 Total = 32
Internal 80188 Timer and DMA	Timer 0, 1, 2 outputs and 2 DMA channel interrupts.	5
80130 Timer Outputs	Timer 0, 1, 2 outputs of 80130.	3
Interrupt from Flag Byte Logic	Flag byte interrupt set by Multibus master (through Multibus I/O Write).	1
Bus Flag Interrupt	Interrupt to Multibus (Selectable for INT0 to INT7) generated from on-board 80188 I/O Write.	1
SBX Connectors SBX DMA	Function determined by iSBX board. DMA interrupt from iSBX (TDMA).	4 (Two per Connector) 2
Bus Fail-Safe Timeout Interrupt.	Indicates iSBC 188/48 board timed out either waiting for Multibus access or timed out from no acknowledge while on Multibus System Bus.	1
Latched Interrupt	Converts pulsed event to a level interrupt. Example: 8237A-5 EOP.	1
OR-Gate Matrix	Concentrates up to 4 interrupts to 1 interrupt (selectable by stake pins).	1
Ring Indicator Interrupt	Latches a ring indicator event from serial channels 4, 5, 6, or 7.	1
NOR-Gate Matrix	Inverts up to 2 interrupts into 1 (selectable by stake pins).	1

EXPANSION

EPROM Expansion

Memory may be expanded by adding Intel compatible memory expansion boards. The universal site memory can be expanded to six sockets by adding the iSBC 341 MULTIMODULE board for a maximum total of 192K bytes of universal site memory.

iSBX™ I/O Expansion Bus (IEEE 959)

Two 8-bit iSBX bus connectors are provided on the iSBC 188/56 board. Using iSBX modules additional functions can be added to extend the I/O capability of the board. In addition to specialized or custom designed iSBX boards, there is a broad range of iSBX boards from Intel including serial and parallel I/O, analog I/O, and IEEE 488 GPIB, boards.

The serial I/O SBX boards available include the iSBX 354 Dual Channel Expansion MULTIMODULE board. Each iSBX 354 MULTIMODULE board adds two channels of serial I/O to the iSBC 188/56 board for a maximum of twelve serial channels. The 82530 serial communications controller on the MULTIMODULE board handles a large variety of serial communications protocols. This is the same serial controller as is used on the iSBC 188/56 board to offer directly compatible expansion capability for the iSBC 188/56 board.

MULTIBUS INTERFACE

The iSBC 188/56 board can be a Multibus master or intelligent slave in a multimaster system. The iSBC 188/56 board incorporates a flag byte signalling mechanism for use in multiprocessor environments where the iSBC 188/56 board is acting as an intelligent slave. The mechanism provides an interrupt handshake from the Multibus System Bus to the onboard-processor and vice-versa.

The Multimaster capabilities of the iSBC 188/56 board offers easy expansion of processing capacity and the benefits of multiprocessing. Memory and I/O capacity may be expanded and additional functions added using Intel Multibus compatible expansion boards.

SPECIFICATIONS

Word Size

Instruction—8, 16, 24 or 32 bits
Data Path—8 bits

Processor Clock	82530 Clock	DMA Clock
8 MHz	4.9152 MHz	4 MHz

Dual Port RAM

iSBC 188/56 Board—256 bytes

As viewed from the 80188—64K bytes

As viewed from the Multibus System Bus—Choice: 0, 16K or 48K

EPROM

iSBC® 188/56 Board Using:	Size	On Board Capacity	Address Range
2732	4K	8K bytes	FE000–FFFFF$_H$
2764	8K	16K bytes	FC000–FFFFF$_H$
27128	16K	32K bytes	F8000–FFFFF$_H$
27256	32K	64K bytes	F0000–FFFFF$_H$
27512	64K	128K bytes	E0000–FFFFF$_H$

Memory Expansion

EPROM with iSBC® 341 Board Using:	Capacity	Address Range
2732	24K bytes	F8000–FFFFF$_H$
2764	48K bytes	F0000–FFFFF$_H$
27128	96K bytes	E0000–FFFFF$_H$
27256	192K bytes	C0000–FFFFF$_H$

I/O Capacity

Serial—8 programmable lines using four 82530 components

SBX Bus—2 SBX single-wide boards

Serial Communications Characteristics

Synchronous—Internal or external character synchronization on one or two synchronous characters

Asynchronous—5–8 bits and 1, 1½, or 2 stop bits per character; programmable clock factor; break detection and generation; parity, overrun, and framing error detection.

Baud Rates

Synchronous X1 Clock	
Baud Rate	**82530 Count Value (Decimal)**
64000	36
48000	49
19200	126
9600	254
4800	510
2400	1022
1800	1363
1200	2046
300	8190
Asynchronous X16 Clock	
Baud Rate	**82530 Count Value (Decimal)**
19200	6
9600	14
4800	30
2400	62
1800	83
1200	126
300	510
110	1394

Interfaces

iSBX™ BUS

The iSBC 188/56 board meets IEEE 959 compliance level D8/8 DMA

MULTIBUS® SYSTEM BUS

The iSBC 188/56 board meets IEEE 796 compliance level Master/Slave D8 M24 I16 VO EL.

SERIAL RS232C SIGNALS

CD	Carrier
CTS	Clear to Send
DSR	Data Set Ready
DTE TXC	Transmit Clock
DTR	Data Terminal Ready
RTS	Request to Send
RXC	Receive Clock
RXD	Receive Data
SG	Signal Ground
TXD	Transmit Data
RI	Ring Indicator

RS422A/449 SIGNALS

RC	Receive Common
RD	Receive Data
RT	Receive Timing
SD	Send Data
TT	Terminal Timing

Environmental Characteristics

Temperature: 0 to 55°C at 200 Linear Feet/Min. (LFM) Air Velocity

Humidity: to 90%, non-condensing (25°C to 70°C)

Physical Characteristics

Width: 30.48 cm (12.00 in)
Length: 17.15 cm (6.75 in)
Height: 1.04 cm (0.41 in)
Weight: 595 gm (21 oz)

Electrical Characteristics

The power required per voltage for the iSBC 188/56 board is shown below. These numbers do not include the current required by universal memory sites or expansion modules.

Voltage (Volts)	Current (Amps) typ.	Power (Watts) typ.
+5	4.56A	22.8W
+12	0.12A	1.5W
−12	0.11A	1.3W

Reference Manual

iSBC 188/56 Advanced Data Communications Computer Reference Manual Order Number 148209.

ORDERING INFORMATION

Order Code	Description
SBC188/56	8-Serial Channel Advanced Communicating Computer

iSBC® 544A* INTELLIGENT COMMUNICATIONS CONTROLLER

- iSBC® Communications Controller Acting as a Single Board Communications Computer or an Intelligent Slave for Communications Expansion
- On-Board Dedicated 8085A Microprocessor Providing Communications Control and Buffer Management for Four Programmable Synchronous/Asynchronous Channels
- Sockets for Up To 8K Bytes of EPROM
- 16K Bytes of Dual Port Dynamic Read/Write Memory with On-Board Refresh
- Extended Multibus Addressing Permits Board Partitioning into 16K-Byte Segments in a 1-Megabyte Address Space
- Ten Programmable Parallel I/O Lines Compatible with Bell 801 Automatic Calling Unit
- Twelve Levels of Programmable Interrupt Control
- Individual Software Programmable Baud Rate Generation for Each Serial I/O Channel
- Three Independent Programmable Interval Timer/Counters
- Interface Control for Auto Answer and Auto Originate Modem

The iSBC 544A Intelligent Communications Controller is a member of Intel's family of Multibus single-board computers, memory, I/O, and peripheral controller boards. The iSBC 544A board is a complete communications controller on a single 6.75 x 12.00 inch printed circuit card. The on-board 8085A CPU may perform local communications processing by directly interfacing with on-board read/write memory, nonvolatile read only memory, four synchronous/asynchronous serial I/O ports, RS232/RS366 compatible parallel I/O, programmable timers, and programmable interrupts.

280239–1

*The iSBC® 544A is also manufactured under product code pSBC 544A by Intel Puerto Rico, Inc.

September 1991
Order Number: 280239-002

BLOCK DIAGRAM

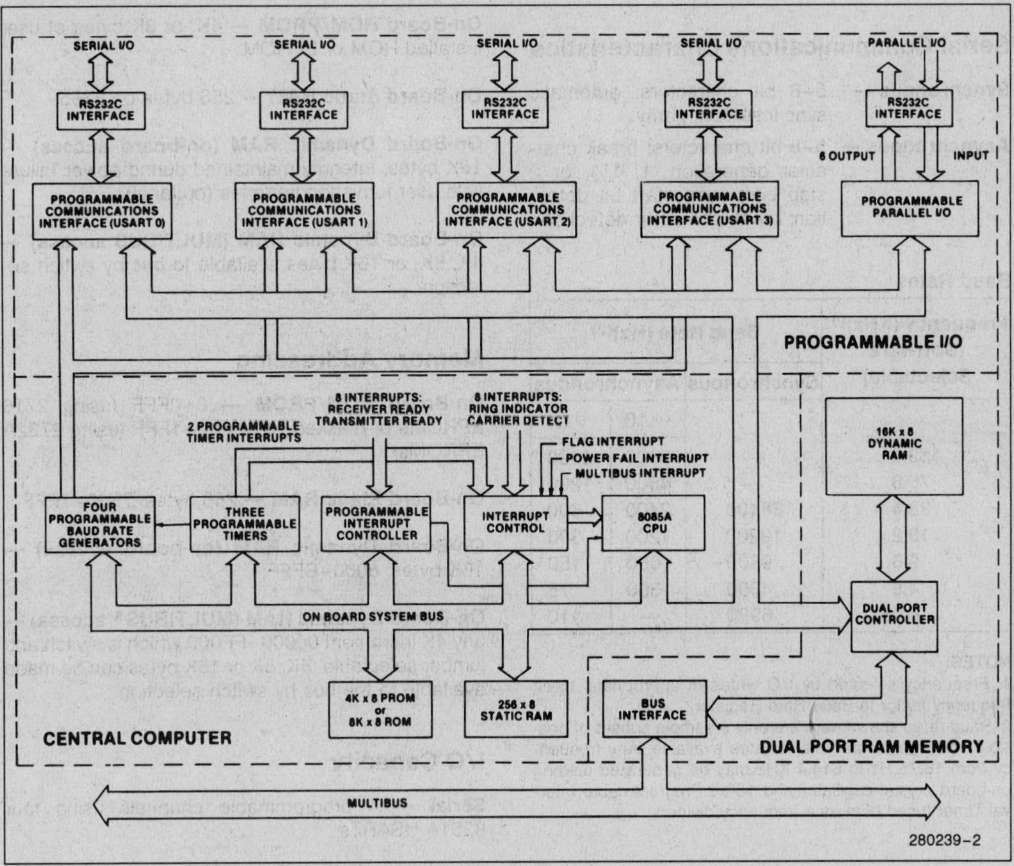

iSBC® 544A Intelligent Communications Controller Block Diagram

SPECIFICATIONS

Serial Communications Characteristics

Synchronous — 5–8 bit characters; automatic sync insertion; parity.

Asynchronous — 5–8 bit characters; break character generation; 1, 1½, or 2 stop bits; false start bit detection; break character detection.

Baud Rates

Frequency (KHz)(1) (Software Selectable)	Baud Rate (Hz)(2)		
	Synchronous	Asynchronous	
		÷16	÷64
153.6	—	9600	2400
76.8	—	4800	1200
38.4	38400	2400	600
19.2	19200	1200	300
9.6	9600	600	150
4.8	4800	300	75
6.98	6980	—	110

NOTES:
1. Frequency selected by I/O writes of appropriate 16-bit frequency factor to Baud Rate Register.
2. Baud rates shown here are only a sample subset of possible software programmable rates available. Any frequency from 18.75 Hz to 614.4 KHz may be generated utilizing on-board crystal oscillator and 16-bit Programmable Interval Timer (used here as a frequency divider).

8085A CPU

Word Size — 8, 16 or 24 bits/instruction; 8 bits of data

Cycle Time — 1.45/μs ±0.01% for fastest executable instruction; i.e., four clock cycles.

Clock Rate — 2.76 MHz ± 0.1%

System Access Time

Dual port memory — 740 ns

NOTE:
Assumes no refresh contention.

Memory Capacity

On-Board ROM/PROM — 4K, or 8K bytes of user installed ROM or EPROM

On-Board Static RAM — 256 bytes on 8155

On-Board Dynamic RAM (on-board access) — 16K bytes. Integrity maintained during power failure with user-furnished batteries (optional)

On-Board Dynamic RAM (MULTIBUS access) — 4K, 8K, or 16K bytes available to bus by swtich selection

Memory Addressing

On-Board ROM/PROM — 0–0FFF (using 2716 EPROMs or masked ROMs); 0–1FFF (using 2732A EPROMs)

On-Board Static RAM — 256 bytes: 7F00–7FFF

On-Board Dynamic RAM (on-board access) — 16K bytes: 8000–BFFF.

On-Board Dynamic RAM (MULTIBUS® access) — any 4K increment 00000–FF000 which is switch and jumper selectable. 4K, 8K or 16K bytes can be made available to the bus by switch selection.

I/O Capacity

Serial — 4 programmable channels using four 8251A USARTs

Parallel — 10 programmable lines available for Bell 801 ACU, or equivalent use. Two auxiliary jumper selectable signals

I/O Addressing

On-Board Programmable I/O

Port	Data	Control
USART 0	D0	D1
USART 1	D2	D3
USART 2	D4	D5
USART 3	D6	D7
8155 PPI	E9 (Port A)	E8
	EA (Port B)	
	EB (Port C)	

Interrupts

Address for 8259A Registers (Hex notation, I/O address space)

E6 Interrupt request register
E6 In-service register
E7 Mask register
E6 Command register
E7 Block address register
E6 Status (polling register)

NOTE:
Several registers have the same physical address: Sequence of access and one data bit of the control word determines which register will respond.

Interrupt levels routed to the 8085 CPU automatically vector the processor to unique memory locations:

24 TRAP
3C RST 7.5
34 RST 6.5
2C RST 5.5

Timers

Addresses for 8253 Registers (Hex notation, I/O address space)

Programmable Interrupt Timer One

D8	Timer 0	BDG0
D9	Timer 1	BDG1
DA	Timer 2	BDG2
DB	Control register	

Programmable Interrupt Timer Two

DC	Timer 0	BDG3
DD	Timer 1	BDG4
DE	Timer 2	TINT1
DF	Control register	

Address for 8155 Programmable Timer

E8	Control	
	Timer (LSB)	TINT0
ED	Timer (MSB)	TINT0

Input Frequencies — Jumper selectable reference 1.2288 MHz ± 0.1% (0.814 μs period nominal) or 1.843 MHz ±0.1% crystal (0.542 μs period, nominal)

Output Frequencies (at 1.2288 MHz)

Function	Single Timer/Counter		Dual Timer/Counter (two timers cascaded)	
	Min	Max	Min	Max
Real-Time Interrupt Interval	1.63 μs	53.3 μs	3.26 μs	58.25 min
Rate Generator (frequency)	18.75 Hz	614.4 KHz	0.00029 Hz	307.2 KHz

Interfaces

Serial I/O — EIA Standard RS232C signals provided and supported:

Carrier Detect	Receiver Data
Clear to Send	Ring Indicator
Data Set Ready	Secondary Receive Data*
Data Terminal Ready	Secondary Transmit Data *
Request to Send	Transmit Clock
Receive Clock	Transmit Data
	DTE Transmit clock

* Optional if parallel I/O port is not used as Automatic Calling Unit.

Parallel I/O — Four inputs and eight outputs (includes two jumper selectable auxiliary outputs). All signals compatible with EIA Standard RS232C. Directly compatible with Bell Model 801 Automatic Calling Unit, or equivalent.

On-Board Addressing

All communications to the parallel and serial I/O ports, to the timers, and to the interrupt controller, are via read and write commands from the on-board 8085A CPU.

Auxiliary Power

An auxiliary power bus is provided to allow separate power to RAM for systems requiring battery backup of read/write memory. Selection of this auxiliary RAM power bus is made via jumpers on the board.

Memory Protect

An active-low TTL compatible memory protect signal is brought out on the auxiliary connector which, when asserted, disables read/write access to RAM memory on the board. This input is provided for the protection of RAM contents during the system power-down sequences.

Bus Drivers

Function	Characteristic	Sink Current (mA)
Data	Tri-state	50
Address	Tri-state	15
Commands	Tri-state	32

NOTE:
Used as a master in the single board communications computer mode.

Physical Characteristics

Width:	30.48 cm (12.00 inches)
Depth:	17.15 cm (6.75 inches)
Thickness:	1.27 cm (0.50 inch)
Weight:	3.97 gm (14 ounces)

Electrical Characteristics

DC Power Requirements

Configuration	Current Requirements			
	V_{CC} = +5V ±5% (max)	V_{DD} = ±12V ±5% (max)	V_{BB} = −5V(3) ±5% (max)	V_{AA} = −12V ±5% (max)
With 4K EPROM (using 2716)	I_{CC} = 3.4A max	I_{DD} = 350 mA max	I_{BB} = 5 mA max	I_{AA} = 200 mA max
Without EPROM	3.3A max	350 mA max	5 mA max	200 mA max
RAM only(1)	390 mA max	176 mA max	5 mA max	—
RAM(2) refresh only	390 mA max	20 mA max	5 mA max	

NOTES:
1. For operational RAM only, for AUX power supply rating.
2. For RAM refresh only. Used for battery backup requirements. No RAM accessed.
3. V_{BB} is normally derived on-board from V_{AA}, eliminating the need for a V_{BB} supply. If it is desired to supply V_{BB} from the bus, the current requirement is as shown.

Environmental Characteristics

Operating Temperature: 0°C to 55°C (32°F to 131°F)

Relative Humidity: To 90% without condensation

Reference Manual

502160 — iSBC 544 Intelligent Communications Controller Board Hardware Reference Manual (NOT SUPPLIED)

Reference manuals are shipped with each product only if designated SUPPLIED (see above). Manuals may be ordered from any Intel sales representative, distributor office or from Intel Literature Department, 3065 Bowers Avenue, Santa Clara, California 95051.

ORDERING INFORMATION

Order Code	Description
SBC 544A	Intelligent Communications Controller

iSBC® 534*
FOUR CHANNEL COMMUNICATION EXPANSION BOARD

- **Serial I/O Expansion Through Four Programmable Synchronous and Asynchronous Communications Channels**
- **Individual Software Programmable Baud Rate Generation for Each Serial I/O Channel**
- **Two Independent Progammable 16-Bit Interval Timers**
- **Sixteen Maskable Interrupt Request Lines with Priority Encoded and Programmable Interrupt Algorithms**
- **Jumper Selectable Interface Register Addresses**
- **16-Bit Parallel I/O Interface Compatible with Bell 801 Automatic Calling Unit**
- **RS232C/CCITT V.24 Interfaces Plus 20 mA Optically Isolated Current Loop Interfaces (Sockets)**
- **Programmable Digital Loopback for Diagnostics**
- **Interface Control for Auto Answer and Auto Originate Modems**

The iSBC 534 Four Channel Communication Expansion Board is a member of Intel's complete line of memory and I/O expansion boards. The iSBC 534 interfaces directly to any single board computer via the Multibus to provide expansion of system serial communications capability. Four fully programmable synchronous and asynchronous serial channels with RS232C buffering and provision for 20 mA optically isolated current loop buffering are provided. Baud rates, data formats, and interrupt priorities for each channel are individually software selectable. In addition to the extensive complement of EIA Standard RS232C signals provided, the iSBC 534 provides 16 lines of RS232C buffered programmable parallel I/O. This interface is configured to be directly compatible with the Bell Model 801 automatic calling unit. These capabilities provide a flexible and easy means for interfacing Intel iSBC based systems to RS232C and optically isolated current loop compatible terminals, cassettes, asynchronous and synchronous modems, and distributed processing networks.

280238–1

*The iSBC® 534 is also manufactured under product code pSBC 534 by Intel Puerto Rico, Inc.

September 1991
Order Number: 280238-002

BLOCK DIAGRAM

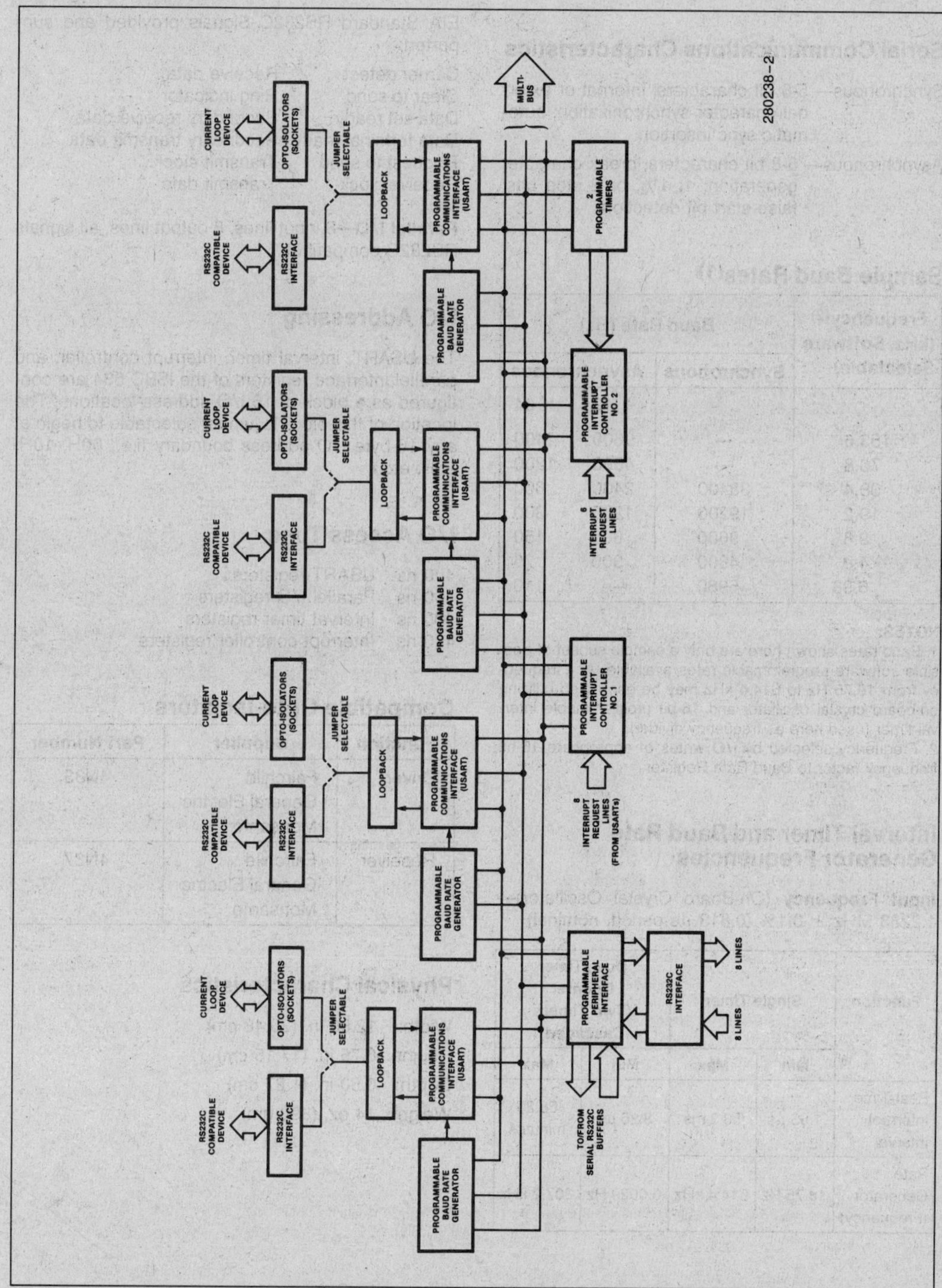

iSBC® 534 Four Channel Communications Expansion Board Block Diagram

SPECIFICATIONS

Serial Communications Characteristics

Synchronous— 5-8 bit characters; internal or external character synchronization; automatic sync insertion.

Asynchronous— 5-8 bit characters; break character generation; 1, 1½, or 2 stop bits; false start bit detection.

Sample Baud Rates[1]

Frequency[2] (kHz, Software Selectable)	Baud Rate (Hz)		
	Synchronous	Asynchronous	
		÷ 16	÷ 64
153.6	—	9600	2400
76.8	—	4800	1200
38.4	38400	2400	600
19.2	19200	1200	300
9.6	9600	600	150
4.8	4800	300	75
6.98	6980	—	110

NOTES:
1. Baud rates shown here are only a sample subset of possible software programmable rates available. Any frequency from 18.75 Hz to 614.4 kHz may be generated utilizing on-board crystal oscillator and 16-bit programmable interval timer (used here as frequency divider).
2. Frequency selected by I/O writes of appropriate 16-bit frequency factor to Baud Rate Register.

Interval Timer and Baud Rate Generator Frequencies

Input Frequency (On-Board Crystal Oscillator)— 1.2288 MHz ± 0.1% (0.813 μs period, nominal)

Function	Single Timer		Dual/Timer Counter (Two Timers Cascaded)	
	Min	Max	Min	Max
Real-Time Interrupt Interval	1.63 μs	53.3 ms	3.26 μs	58.25 minutes
Rate Generator (Frequency)	18.75 Hz	614.4 kHz	0.0029 Hz	307.2 kHz

Interfaces—RS232C Interfaces

EIA Standard RS232C Signals provided and supported:

Carrier detect	Receive data
Clear to send	Ring indicator
Data set ready	Secondary receive data
Data terminal ready	Secondary transmit data
Request to send	Transmit clock
Receive clock	Transmit data

Parallel I/O—8 input lines, 8 output lines, all signals RS232C compatible

I/O Addressing

The USART, interval timer, interrupt controller, and parallel interface registers of the iSBC 534 are configured as a block of 16 I/O address locations. The location of this block is jumper selectable to begin at any 16-byte I/O address boundary (i.e., 00H, 10H, 20H, etc.).

I/O Access Time

400 ns USART registers
400 ns Parallel I/O registers
400 ns Interval timer registers
400 ns Interrupt controller registers

Compatible Opto-Isolators

Function	Supplier	Part Number
Driver	Fairchild General Electric Monsanto	4N33
Receiver	Fairchild General Electric Monsanto	4N37

Physical Characteristics

Width: 12.00 in. (30.48 cm)
Height: 6.75 in. (17.15 cm)
Depth: 0.50 in. (1.27 cm)
Weight: 14 oz. (398 gm)

Electrical Characteristics

Average DC Current

Voltage	Without Opto-Isolators	With Opto-Isolators(1)
V_{CC} = +5V	1.9 A, max	1.9 A, max
V_{DD} = +12V	275 mA, max	420 mA, max
V_{AA} = −12V	250 mA, max	400 mA, max

NOTE:
1. With four 4N33 and four 4N37 opto-isolator packages installed in sockets provided to implement four 20 mA current loop interfaces.

Environmental Characteristics

Operating Temperature: 0°C to +55°C

Reference Manual

502140—iSBC 534 Hardware Reference Manual (NOT SUPPLIED)

Reference manuals are shipped with each product only if designated SUPPLIED (see above). Manuals may be ordered from any Intel sales representative, distributor office or from Intel Literature Department, 3065 Bowers Avenue, Santa Clara, California 95051.

ORDERING INFORMATION

Order Code	Description
SBC534	Four Channel Communication Expansion Board

11

iSBC® 88/45*
ADVANCED DATA COMMUNICATIONS PROCESSOR BOARD

- **Three HDLC/SDLC Half/Full-Duplex Communication Channels—Optional ASYNC/SYNC on Two Channels**
- **Supports RS232C (Including Modem Support), CCITT V.24, or RS422A/449 Interfaces**
- **On-Board DMA Supports 800K Baud Operation**
- **Self-Clocking NRZI SDLC Loop Data Link Interface**
  - **Point-to-Point**
  - **Multidrop**
- **Software Programmable Baud Rate Generation**
- **8088 (8088-2) Microprocessor Operates at 8 MHz**
- **iSBC® 337A Numeric Data Processor Option Supported**
- **16K Bytes Static RAM (12K Bytes Dual-Ported)**
- **Four 28-Pin JEDEC Sites for EPROM/RAM Expansion; Four Additional 28-Pin JEDEC Sites Added with iSBC® 341 Board**
- **Two SBX Bus (IEEE 959) Connectors**
- **Multibus Interface Supports Multimaster Configuration**

The iSBC 88/45 Advanced Data Communications Processor (ADCP) Board adds 8 MHz, 8088 (8088-2) 8-bit microprocessor-based communications flexibility to the Intel line of Multibus OEM microcomputer systems. The iSBC 88/45 ADCP board offers asynchronous, synchronous, SDLC, and HDLC serial interfaces for gateway networking or general purpose solutions. The iSBC 88/45 ADCP board provides the CPU, system clock, EPROM/RAM, serial I/O ports, priority interrupt logic, and programmable timers to facilitate higher-level application solutions.

210372–1

*The iSBC® 88/45 is also manufactured under product code pSBC 88/45 by Intel Puerto Rico, Inc.

September 1991
Order Number: 210372-003

BLOCK DIAGRAM

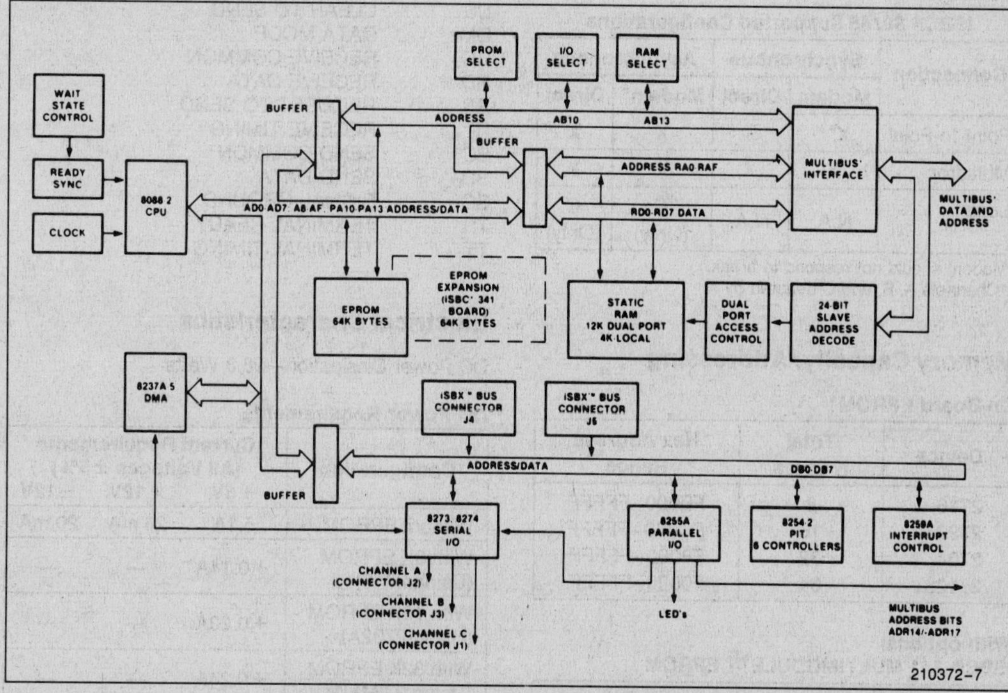

Block Diagram of the iSBC® 88/45 ADCP Board

SPECIFICATIONS

Word Size

Instruction: 8, 16, 24, or 32 bits
Data: 8 or 16 bits

System Clock

8 MHz: ±0.1%

NOTE:
Jumper selectable for 4 MHz operation with iSBC 337 Numeric Data Processor module or ICE-88 product.

Cycle Time

Basic Instruction Cycle at 8.00 MHz: 1.25 μs, 250 ns (assumes instruction in the queue)

NOTE:
Basic instruction cycle is defined as the fastest instruction time (i.e., two clock cycles).

Memory Cycle Time

RAM: 500 ns (no wait states)
EPROM: jumper selectable from 500 ns to 625 ns.

On-Board RAM*

K Bytes	Hex Address Range
16 (total)	0000–3FFF
12 (dual-ported)	1000–3FFF

*Four iSBC 88/45 EPROM sockets support JEDEC 24/28-pin standard EPROMs and RAMs (3 sockets); iSBC 341 (4 sockets)

Environmental Characteristics

Temperature: 0°C to +55°C, free moving air across the base board and MULTIMODULE board

Humidity: 90%, non-condensing

Physical Characteristics

Width: 30.48 cm (12.00 in)
Length: 17.15 cm (6.75 in)
Height: 1.50 cm (0.59 in)
Weight: 6.20 gm (22 oz)

Configurations

iSBC® 88/45 Supported Configurations

Connection	Synchronous		Asynchronous	
	Modem	Direct	Modem*	Direct
Point-to-Point	X**	X	X	X
Multidrop	X	X	X	X
Loop	N.A.	N.A.	C (Only)	C (Only)

*Modem should not respond to break.
**Channels A, B, and C denoted by X.

Memory Capacity/Addressing

On-Board EPROM*

Device	Total K Bytes	Hex Address Range
2716	8	FE000–FFFFF
2732A	16	FC000–FFFFF
2764	32	F8000–FFFFF
27128	64	F0000–FFFFF

With optional iSBC® 341 MULTIMODULE™ EPROM

Device	Total K Bytes	Hex Address Range
2716	16	FC000–FFFFF
2732A	32	F8000–FFFFF
2764	64	F0000–FFFFF
27128	128	E0000–FFFFF

*Four iSBC 88/45 EPROM sockets support JEDEC 24/28-pin standard EPROMs and RAMs (static and iRAM, 3 sockets); iSBC 341 sockets also support EPROMs and RAMs.

Timer Input Frequency—8.00 MHz ±0.1%

Interfaces

IEEE 959 SBX I/O Bus Expansion

Serial RS232C Signals—

CTS	CLEAR TO SEND
DSR	DATA SET READY
DTE TXC	TRANSMIT CLOCK
DTR	DATA TERMINAL READY
FG	FRAME GROUND
RTS	REQUEST TO SEND
RXC	RECEIVE CLOCK
RXD	RECEIVE DATA
SG	SIGNAL GROUND
TXD	TRANSMIT DATA

Serial RS422A/449 Signals—

CS	CLEAR TO SEND
DM	DATA MODE
RC	RECEIVE COMMON
RD	RECEIVE DATA
RS	REQUEST TO SEND
RT	RECEIVE TIMING
SC	SEND COMMON
SD	SEND DATA
SG	SIGNAL GROUND
TR	TERMINAL READY
TT	TERMINAL TIMING

Electrical Characteristics

DC Power Dissipation—28.3 Watts

DC Power Requirements

Configuration	Current Requirements (All Voltages ±5%)		
	+5V	+12V	−12V
Without EPROM(1)	5.1A	20 mA	20 mA
With 8K EPROM (Using 2716)	+0.14A	—	—
With 16K EPROM (Using 2732A)	+0.20A	—	—
With 32K EPROM (Using 2764)	+0.24A	—	—
With 64K EPROM (Using 27128)	+0.24A	—	—

NOTE:
1. AS SHIPPED—no EPROMs in sockets, no iSBC 341 module. Configuration includes terminators for two RS422A/449 and one RS232C channels.

Serial Communication Characteristics

Channel	Device	Supported Interface	Max. Baud Rate
A	8274(1)	RS442A/449 RS232C CCITT V.24	800K SDLC/HDLC 125K Synchronous 50K Asynchronous
B	8274	RS232C CCITT V.24	125K Synchronous(2) 50K Asynchronous
C	8273(3)	RS442A/449 RS232C CCITT V.24	64K SDLC/HDLC(3) 9.6K SELF CLOCKING

NOTES:
1. 8274 supports HDLC/SDLC/SYNC/ASYNC multiprotocol
2. Exceed RS232C/CCITT V.24 rating of 20K baud
3. 8273 supports HDLC/SDLC

BAUD RATE EXAMPLES (Hz)

8254 Timer Divide Count N	Synchronous K Baud	Asynchronous ÷16 K Baud	÷32	÷64
10	800	50.0	25.0	12.5
26	300	19.2	9.6	4.8
31	256	16.1	8.06	4.03
52	154	9.6	4.8	2.4
104	76.8	4.8	2.4	1.2
125	64	4.0	2.0	1.0
143	56	3.5	1.7	0.87
167	48	3.0	1.5	0.75
417	19.2	—	—	—
833	9.6	—	—	—
EQUATION	$\frac{8,000,000}{N}$	$\frac{500K}{N}$	$\frac{250K}{N}$	$\frac{125K}{N}$

Line Drivers (Supplied)

Device	Characteristic	Qty	Installed
1488	RS232C	3	1
1489	RS232C	3	1
3486	RS422A	2	2
3487	RS422A	2	2

Reference Manual

143824—iSBC 88/45 Advanced Data Communications Processor Board Hardware Reference Manual (not supplied).

Reference manuals may be ordered from any Intel sales representative, distributor office or from Intel Literature Department, 3065 Bowers Avenue, Santa Clara, CA 95051.

ORDERING INFORMATION

Order Code	Description
SBC88/45	iSBC 88/45 Advanced Data Communications Processor Board

Multibus I Digital and Analog I/O Boards

12

iSBC® 519A PROGRAMMABLE I/O EXPANSION BOARD

- **I/O Expansion via Direct MULTIBUS® Interface**
- **72 Programmable I/O Lines with Sockets for Interchangeable Line Drivers and Terminators**
- **Provides Full 16-Bit I/O Addressability**
- **Provides 3 iSBX Multimodule Connectors**
- **Provides 16 Maskable Interrupt Request Lines**
- **Jumper Selectable 0.5, 1.0, 2.0, or 4.0 ms Interval Timer**
- **Provides Eight Maskable Interrupt Request Lines with Priority Encoded and Programmable Interrupt Algorithms**

The iSBC 519A Programmable I/O Expansion Board is a member of Intel's complete line of iSBC memory and I/O expansion boards. The iSBC 519A interfaces directly to any iSBC single board computer via the system bus to expand input and output port capacity. The iSBC 519A provides 72 programmable I/O lines. The system software is used to configure the I/O lines to meet a wide variety of peripheral requirements. The flexibility of the I/O interface is further enhanced by the capability of selecting the appropriate combination of optional line drivers and terminators to provide the required sink current, polarity, and drive/termination characteristics for each application. Address selection is accomplished by using wire-wrap jumpers. The board operates with a single +5V power supply.

12

280230–1

October 1989
Order Number: 280230-002

FUNCTIONAL DESCRIPTION

The 72 programmable I/O lines on the iSBC 519A are implemented utilizing three Intel 82C55A programmable peripheral interfaces. The system software is used to configure the I/O lines in combinations of undirectional input/output and bidirectional ports. In order to take full advantage of the large number of possible I/O configurations, sockets are provided for interchangeable I/O line drivers and terminators. The 72 programmable I/O lines and signal ground lines are brought out to three 50-pin edge connectors that mate with flat, round, or woven cable.

Interval Timer

Typical I/O read access time is 350 nanoseconds.

Typical I/O read/write cycle time is 450 nanoseconds. The interval timer provided on the iSBC 519A may be used to generate real time clocking in systems requiring the periodic monitoring of I/O functions. The time interval is derived from the constant clock (BUS CCLK) and the timing interval is jumper selectable. Intervals of 0.5, 1.0, 2.0, and 4.0 milliseconds may be selected when an iSBC single board computer is used to generate the clock. Other timing intervals may be generated if the user provides a separate constant clock reference in the system.

Eight-Level Vectored Interrupt

Two Intel 82C59A programmable interrupt controllers (PIC) provide vectoring for interrupt levels. As shown in Table 1, a selection of three priority processing algorithms is available to the system designer so that the manner in which requests are serviced may be configured to match system requirements. Priority assignments may be reconfigured dynamically via software at any time during system operation.

Table 1. Interrupt Priority Options

Algorithm	Operation
Fully nested	Interrupt request line priorities fixed.
Auto-rotating	Equal priority. Each level, after receiving service, becomes the lowest priority level until next interrupt occurs.
Specific priority	System software assigns lowest priority level. Priority of all other levels are based in sequence numerically on this assignment.

SBX Expansion Bus (IEEE 959) Capabilities

Three SBX bus connectors are provided on the iSBC 519A board. Up to three single-wide or one double-wide and one single-wide IEEE 959 SBX board can be added to the iSBC 519A board. A wide variety of expansion options are available.

Physical Characteristics

Width: 12.00 in. (30.48 cm)
Height: 6.75 in. (17.15 cm)
Depth: 0.50 in. (1.27 cm),
1.16 in. (2.95 cm) with iSBX modules
Weight: 14 oz. (397.3 gm)

Electrical Characteristics

Average DC Current

Voltage	Without Termination(1)	With Termination(2)
V_{CC} = +5V ±5%	I_{CC} = 1.5A max	3.5A max

NOTES:
1. Does not include power required for operational I/O drivers and I/O terminators.
2. With 18 220Ω/330Ω input terminators installed, all terminator inputs low.

Environmental Characteristics

Operating Temperature: 0°C to +55°C

Reference Manual

9800385B—iSBC iSBC 519A Hardware Reference manual (NOT SUPPLIED)

Manuals may be ordered from any Intel sales representative, distributor office or from Intel Literature Department, 3065 Bowers Avenue, Santa Clara, California 95051.

ORDERING INFORMATION

Order Code	Description
SBC519A	Programmable I/O Expansion Board

iSBC® 556*
OPTICALLY ISOLATED I/O BOARD

- **Up to 48 Digital Optically Isolated Input/Output Data Lines for MULTIBUS® Systems**
- **Choice of**
  - **—24 Fixed Input Lines**
  - **—16 Fixed Output Lines**
  - **—8 Programmable Lines**
- **Provisions for Plug-In, Optically Isolated Receivers, Drivers, and Terminators**
- **Voltage/Current Levels**
  - **—Input up to 48V**
  - **—Output up to 30V, 60 mA**
- **Common Interrupt for up to 8 Sources**
- **+5V Supply Only**

The iSBC 556 Optically Isolated I/O Board provides 48 digital input/output lines with isolation between process application or peripheral device and the system CPU board(s). The iSBC 556 contains two 8255A programmable interface devices, and sockets for user supplied optically isolated drivers, receivers, and input resistor terminators, together with common interrupt logic and interface circuitry for the system bus. Input signals can be single-ended or differential types with user defined input range (resistor terminator and opto-isolated receiver selection), allowing flexibility in design of voltage and threshold levels. The output allows user selection of Opto-Isolated Darlington Pair which can be used as an output driver either as an open collector or current switch.

280231–1

*The iSBC® 556 is also manufactured under product code piSBC® 556 by Intel Puerto Rico, Inc.

October 1989
Order Number: 280231-002

Table 1. I/O Ports Opto-Isolator Receivers, Drivers, and Terminators

Port No. X = I/O Base Address	Type of I/O	Lines (qty)	Resistor Terminator Pac-Rp 16-Pin DIP Bourns 4116R-00 or Equivalent	Dual Opto-Isolator 8-Pin DIP Monsanto MC T66 or Equivalent	Driver 7438 or Equivalent	Pull-Up iSBC® 902
X + 0	Input	8	1	4	—	
X + 1	Output	8	—		—	
X + 2	Input/ Control	8	1		—	
X + 4	Input	8	1	4	—	
X + 5	Output	8			—	
X + 6 X + 7	Input/ Output Control	8	1 if input		2 if input	2 if input

SPECIFICATIONS

Number of Lines

24 input lines

16 output lines

8 programmable lines: 4 input — 4 output

I/O Interface Characteristics

Line-to-Line Isolation: 235V DC or peak AC

Input/Output Isolation: 500V DC or peak AC

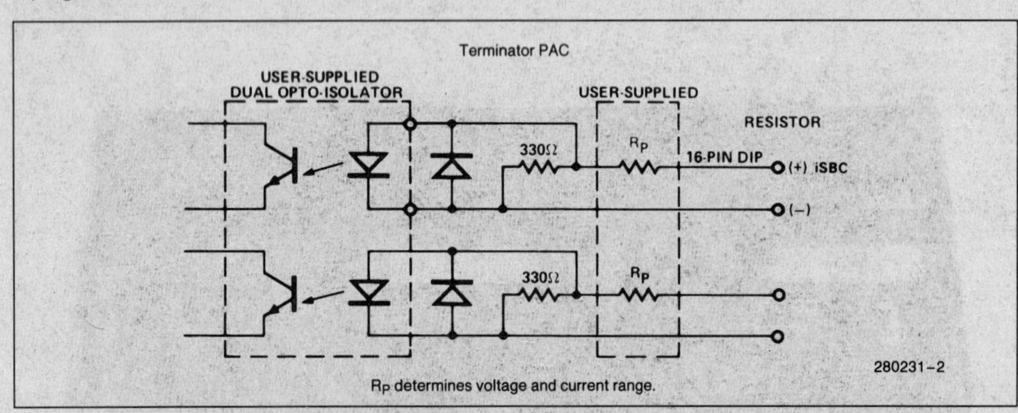

RP determines voltage and current range.

I/O Addressing

Port	8255 #1			Con-trol	8255 #2			Con-trol
	A	B	C		A	B	C	
Address	X+0	X+1	X+2	X+3	X+4	X+5	X+6	X+7

Where: base address is from 00H to 1FH (jumper selectable)

Physical Characteristics

Width: 12.00 in. (30.48 cm)

Height: 6.75 in. (17.15 cm)

Depth: 0.50 in. (1.27 cm)

Weight: 12 oz. (397.3 gm)

Electrical Characteristics

Average DC Current

V_{CC} = +5V ±5%, 1.0A without user supplied isolated receiver/driver

I_{CC} = 1.6A max with user supplied isolator receiver/driver

Environmental Characteristics

Temperature: 0°C to 55°C

Relative Humidity: 0% to 90%, non-condensing

Reference Manual

502170— iSBC 556 Hardware Reference Manual (Order Separately)

Reference manuals are shipped with each product only if designated SUPPLIED (see above). Manuals may be ordered from any Intel sales representative, distributor office or from Intel Literature Department, 3065 Bowers Avenue, Santa Clara, California 95051.

12

ORDERING INFORMATION

Order Code	Description
SBC556	Optically Isolated I/O Board

iSBC® 569* INTELLIGENT DIGITAL CONTROLLER

- Single Board Digital I/O Controller with up to Four Microprocessors to Share the Digital Input/Output Signal Processing
- 3 MHz 8085A Central Control Processor
- Three Sockets for 8041/8741A Universal Peripheral Interface (UPI-41A) for Distributed Digital I/O Processing
- Three Operational Modes
  - Stand-Alone Digital Controller
  - MULTIBUS® Master
  - Intelligent Slave (Slave to MULTIBUS Master)
- 2K Bytes of Dual Port Static Read/Write Memory
- Sockets for up to 8K Bytes of Intel 2758, 2716, 2732 Erasable Programmable Read Only Memory
- 48 Programmable Parallel I/O Lines with Sockets for Interchangeable Line Drivers or Terminators
- Three Programmable Counters
- 12 Levels of Programmable Interrupt Control
- Single +5V Supply
- MULTIBUS Standard Control Logic Compatible with Optional iSBC 80 and iSBC® 86 CPU, Memory, and I/O Expansion Boards

The Intel iSBC® 569 Intelligent Digital Controller is a single board computer (8085A based) with sockets for three 8041A/8741A Universal Peripherals Interface chips (UPI-41A). These devices, which are programmed by the user, may be used to offload the 8085A processor from time consuming tasks such as pulse counting, event sensing and parallel or serial digital I/O data formatting with error checking and handshaking. The iSBC 569 board is a complete digital controller with up to four processors on a single 6.75 inches x 12.00 inches (17.15 cm x 30.48 cm) printed circuit board. The 8085A CPU, system clock, read/write memory, non-volatile memory, priority interrupt logic, programmed timers, MULTIBUS control and interface logic, optional UPI processors and optional line driver and terminators all reside on one board.

280232-1

*The iSBC® 569 is also manufactured under product code piSBC® 569 by Intel Puerto Rico, Inc.

October 1989
Order Number: 280232-002

BLOCK DIAGRAM

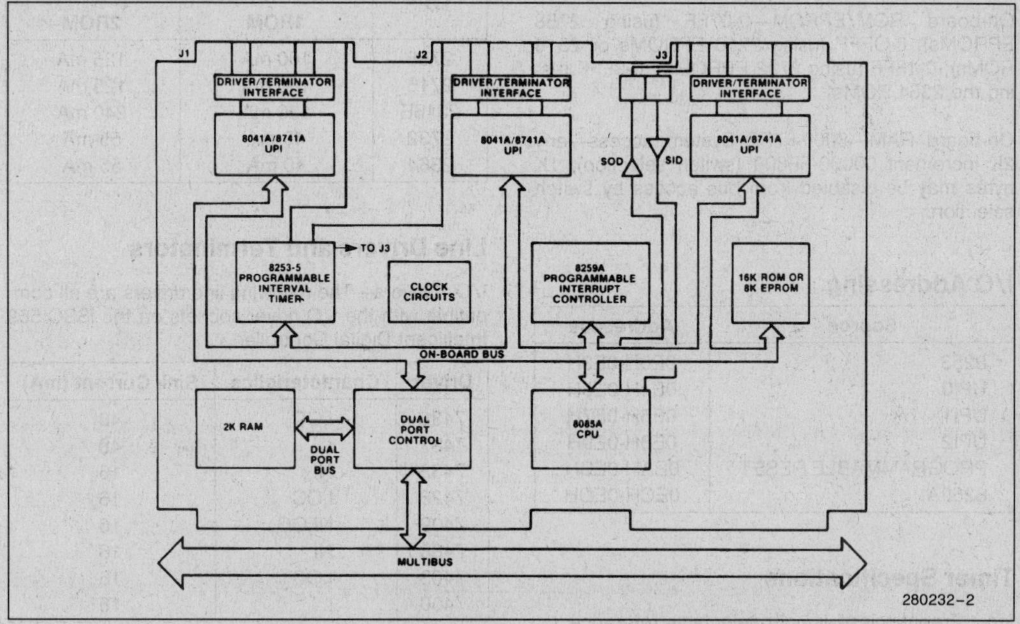

iSBC® 569 Intelligent Digital Controller Block Diagram

SPECIFICATIONS

8085A CPU

Word Size: 8, 16 or 24 bits

Cycle Time: 1.30 µs ±0.1% for fastest executable instruction; i.e., four clock cycles.

Clock Rate: 3.07 MHz ±0.1%

System Access Time

Dual port memory—725 ns

Memory Capacity

On-board ROM/EPROM—2K, 4K, 8K, or 16K bytes of user installed ROM or EPROM.

On-board RAM—2K bytes of static RAM. Fully accessible from on-board 8085A. Separately addressable from system bus.

Off-board expansion—up to 64K bytes of EPROM/ROM or RAM capacity.

I/O Capacity

Parallel-Timers—Three timers, with independent gate input, clock input, and timer output user-accessible. Clock inputs can be strapped to an external source or to an on-board 1.3824 MHz reference. Each timer is connected to a 8259A Programmable Interrupt Controller and may also be optionally connected to UPI processors.

UPI-I/O—Three UPI-41A interfaces, each with two 8-bit I/O ports plus the two UPI Test Inputs. The 8-bit ports are user-configurable (as inputs or outputs) in groups of four.

Serial—1 TTL compatible serial channel utilizing SID and SOD lines of on-board 8085A CPU.

On-Board Addressing

All communications to the UPI-41A processors, to the programmable reset latch, to the timers, and to the interrupt controller are via read and write commands from the on-board 8085A CPU.

12

Memory Addressing

On-board ROM/EPROM—0-07FF (using 2758 EPROMs); 0-OFFF (using 2716 EPROMs or 2316 ROMs); 0-1FFF (using 2732 EPROMs); 0-3FFF (using the 2364 ROMs)

On-board RAM—8000-87FF System access—any 2K increment 00000-FF800 (switch selection); 1K bytes may be disabled from bus access by switch selection.

I/O Addressing

Source	Addresses
8253	0E0H-0E3H
UPI0	0E4H-0E5H
UPI1	0E6H-0E7H
UPI2	0E8H-0E9H
PROGRAMMABLE RESET	0EAH-0EBH
8259A	0ECH-0EDH

Timer Specifications

Input Frequencies—jumper selectable reference

Internal: 1.3824 MHz ±0.1% (0.723 μs, nominal)
External: User supplied (2 MHz maximum)

Output Frequencies (at 1.3824 MHz)

Function	Min[1]	Max[1]
Real-time interrupt interval	1.45 μsec	47.4 msec
Rate Generator (frequency)	21.09 Hz	691.2 KHz
1. Single 16-bit binary count		

Physical Characteristics

Width: 30.48 cm (12.00 inches)

Depth: 17.15 cm (6.75 inches)

Thickness: 1.27 cm (0.50 inch)

Weight: 3.97 gm (14 ounces)

Electrical Characteristics

DC Power Requirements—+5V @ 2.58A with no optional devices installed. For each 8741A add 135 mA. For each 220/330 resistor network, add 60 mA. Add the following for each EPROM/ROM installed.

Type	+5.0V Current Requirement	
	1ROM	2ROM
2758	100 mA	125 mA
2716	100 mA	125 mA
2316E	120 mA	240 mA
2732	40 mA	55 mA
2364	40 mA	55 mA

Line Drivers and Terminators

I/O /Drivers—The following line drivers are all compatible with the I/O driver sockets on the iSBC 569 Intelligent Digital Controller.

Driver	Characteristics	Sink Current (mA)
7438	I,OC	48
7437	I	48
7432	NI	16
7426	I,OC	16
7409	NI,OC	16
7408	NI	16
7403	I,OC	16
7400	I	16

NOTE:
I = inverting; NI = non-inverting; OC = open collector.

I/O Terminators— 220Ω/330Ω divider or 1 kΩ pull-up (DIP) - user supplied

Environmental Characteristics

Operating Temperature: 0° C to 55° C (32° F to 131 °F)
Relative Humidity: To 90% without condensation

Reference Manual

502180— iSBC 569 Intelligent Digital Controller Board Hardware Reference Manual (NOT SUPPLIED)

Reference manuals are shipped with each product only if designated SUPPLIED (see above). Manuals may be ordered from any Intel sales representative, distributor office or from Intel Literature Department, 3065 Bowers Avenue, Santa Clara, California 95051.

ORDERING INFORMATION

Order Code	Description
SBC569	Intelligent Digital Controller

Multibus I System Packaging and Power Supplies

13

SYP341 CARD CAGE MODULE

280641–1

13

A 16-SLOT Multibus I CARD CAGE MODULE FOR FLEXIBLE, EXPANDABLE SYSTEMS CONFIGURATIONS

Intel's SYP341 Card Cage is a standard module designed to provide, along with the companion SYP342 Peripheral Module, a basic platform for the integration of large capacity systems. Intel's modular packaging scheme allows for integration into standard 19 inch rack-mount cabinets or NEMA-type enclosures.

FEATURES

- 16-slot Multibus I backplane with integrated priority and interrupt circuitry.
- Accepts standard 7 x 12 inch Multibus I boards and up to seven 10 x 12 inch boards.
- Meets EIA, 19 inch rack standard.
- 4-layer backplane construction. Interleaved bus signal traces. Dedicated power and ground layers.
- 24-bit addressing supported on all slots.
- Extended gold pins for all P2 signals. Supports iLBX bus cables.
- Backplane generated bus clock.
- Multibus reset and interrupt switches with power-on and status indicators.
- 750 watt multiple output switching power supply. Switch selectable 110/220 VAC.
- Forced air cooling. Provides 300 lfm across boards.

December 1990
Order Number: 280641-002

SPECIFICATIONS

ENVIRONMENTALS

Ambient Temperature	
Operating	0 to 55°C
Non-Operating	−40 to 80°C
Relative Humidity	
Operating	80% at 40°C
Non-Operating	95% at 55°C
Altitude	
Operating	Sea Level to 10,000 feet
Non-Operating	Sea Level to 40,000 feet

ELECTRICAL

DC Power Output	750 watt maximum
+5V	100.0 A maximum
+12V	10.0 A maximum
−12V	10.0 A maximum
AC Power Input	90–132 VAC or 180–264 VAC 47–63 Hz

REGULATIONS

Meets the following safety requirements:

US	UL478 5th Edition recognized
Canada	CSA C22.2 No. 220 certified
Europe	IEC 380 and IEC 950

Power Supply meets the following EMI/RFI requirements:

US	FCC Class B Conducted emissions
Europe	VDE Limit Class B Conducted emissions

PHYSICAL CHARACTERISTICS

Dimensions

Standard Rear Mount Power Supply

Height	488.1 mm (19.22 in)
Width	482.7 mm (19.00 in)
Depth	501.6 mm (19.75 in)
Weight	23.9 kilograms (53 lbs)

Optional Mounting;
Side Mounted Power Supply

Width	597.0 mm (23.50 in)
Depth	355.7 mm (14.00 in)

Backplane Slot Spacing

Slots 5, 13 — 1.8″
Slot 1 — 1.4″
Slots 2–4, 6–12, 14–16 — 0.8″
Slots 6–12 accommodate 10 x 12 inch boards

ORDER CODES

SYP341V1—Configured 110 VAC
SPY341V2—Configured 220 VAC

WORLDWIDE SERVICE AND SUPPORT

Intel provides support for Intel and non-Intel boards and peripherals as well as on-site service.

Development support options include phone support, subscription service, on-site consulting, and customer training.

QUALITY AND RELIABILITY

The SYP341 is designed, tested and manufactured in accordance with Intel's industry leading quality and reliability standards.

iSBC® 604/614 MODULAR CARDCAGE ASSEMBLIES

- Interconnects and Houses up to Four MULTIBUS® Boards per Cardcage
- Connectors Allow Interconnection of up to Four Cardcage Assemblies for 16 Board Systems
- Strong Cardcage Structure Helps Protect Installed Boards from Warping and Physical Damage
- Cardcage Mounting Holes Facilitate Interconnection of Units
- Compatible with 3.5-Inch RETMA Rack Mount Increments
- Interleaved Grounds on Backplane Minimize Noise and Crosstalk
- Up to 3 CPU Boards per System for Multiprocessing Applications

The iSBC 604 and iSBC 614 Modular Cardcage Assemblies units provide low-cost, off-the-shelf housing for OEM products using two or more MULTIBUS boards. Each unit inerconnects and houses up to four boards. The base unit, the iSBC 604 Cardcage Assembly, contains a male backplane PC edge connector and bus signal termination circuits, plus power supply connectors. It is suitable for applications requiring a single unit, or may be interconnected with up to three iSBC 614 cardcage assemblies for a four cardcage (16 board) system. The iSBC 614 contains both male and female backplane connectors, and may be interconnected with iSBC 604/614 units. Both units are identical, with the exception of the bus signal terminator feature. A single unit may be packaged in a 3.5 inch RETMA rack enclosure, and two interconnected units may be packaged in a 7 inch enclosure. The units are mountable in any of three planes.

13

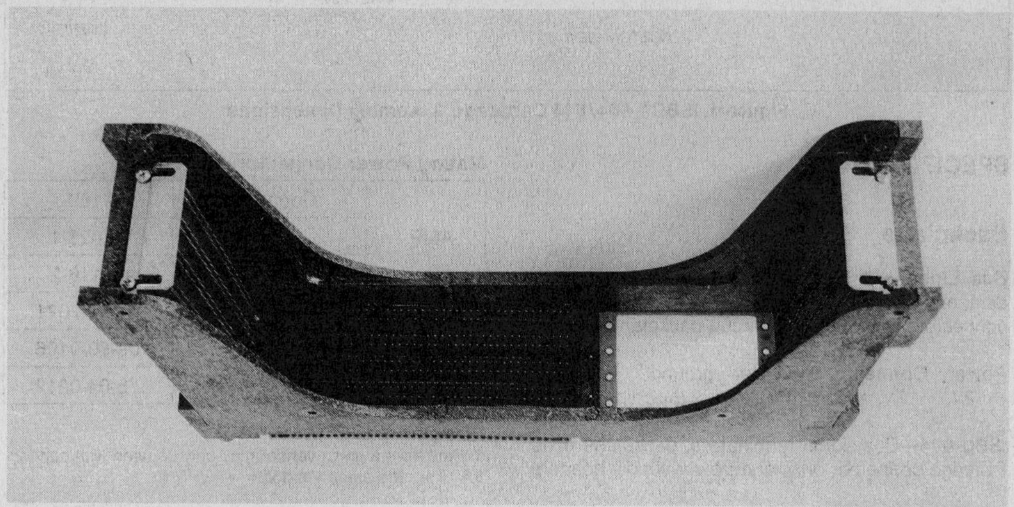

280205–1

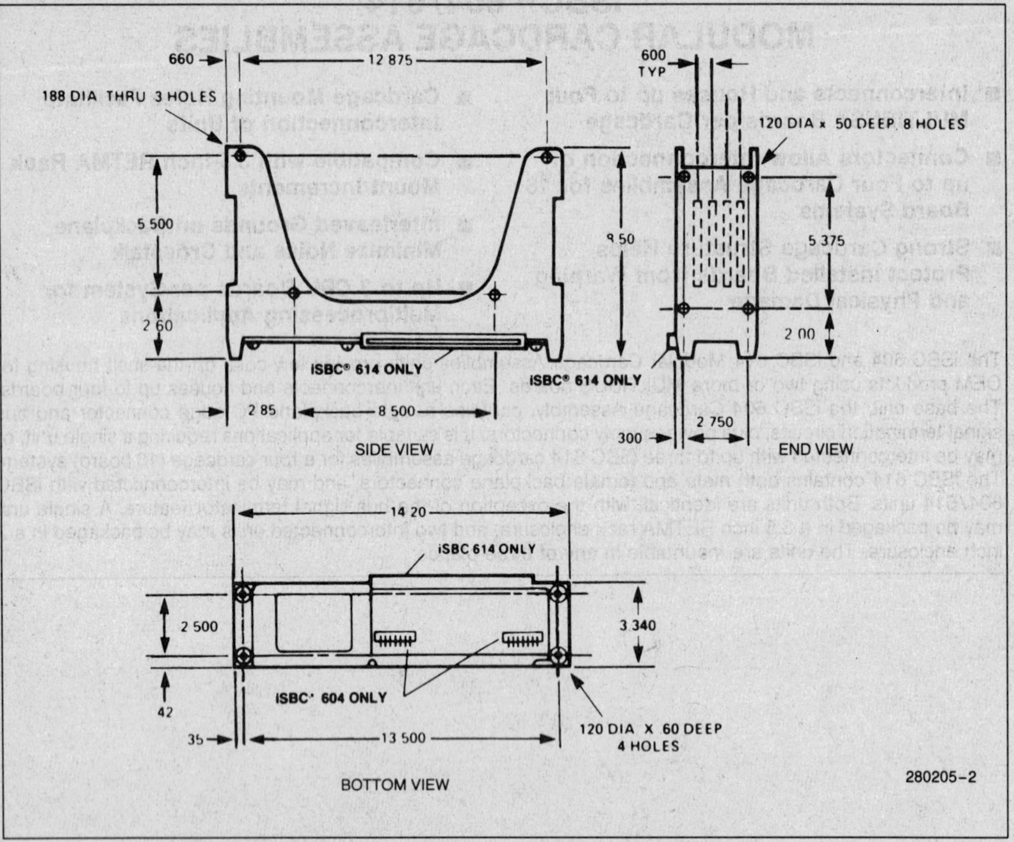

Figure 1. iSBC® 604/614 Cardcage Assembly Dimensions

SPECIFICATIONS

Backplane

Bus Lines—All MULTIBUS system bus address, data, and command bus lines are bussed to all four connectors on the printed circuit backplane

Power Connectors—G for ground, +5, −5, +12V, −12V, and −10V power supply lines

iSBC 604—Bus signal terminators, backplane male PC edge connector only, and power supply headers

iSBC 614—Backplane male and female connectors and power supply headers

Mating Power Connectors

AMP	Connector	87159-7
	Pin	87023-1
	Polarizing Key	87116-2
Molex	Connector	09-50-7071
	Pin	08-50-0106
	Polarizing Key	15-04-0219

NOTE:
1. Pins from a given vendor may only be used with connectors from the same vendor.

ORDERING INFORMATION

Part Number	Description
SBC 604	Modular Cardcage Assembly (Base Unit)

Bus Arbitration: Serial; up to 3 CPU masters

Equipment Supplied: iSBC 604 or iSBC 614 Cardcage Schematic

Physical Dimensions

Height: 8.5 in. (21.59 cm)

Width: 14.2 in. (36.07 cm)

Depth: 3.34 in. (8.48 cm)

Weight: 35 oz. (992.23 gm)

Card Slot Spacing: 0.6 in.

Environmental Characteristics

Operating Temperature: 0°C to 55°C

Reference Manual

9800708—iSBC 604/614 Cardcage Hardware Reference Manual (ORDER SEPARATELY)

Part Number	Description
SBC 614	Modular Cardcage Assembly (Expansion Unit)

iSBC® 608/618 CARDCAGES

- **Houses Eight MULTIBUS® iSBC® Boards in an Aluminum Package**
- **Board-to-Board Clearance for iSBC® MULTIMODULE™ Boards on All Slots**
- **Board-to-Board Clearance for iSBX™ MULTIMODULE™ Boards on Two Slots**
- **Parallel Priority Circuitry for up to Eight Multimaster iSBC® Boards**
- **Enhanced Bus Noise Immunity for High Speed Systems**
- **Plug on iSBC 618 Unit for up to Sixteen Board Systems**
- **NEMA-Type Backwall or 19-Inch Rack Mount Hardware Included**
- **Signal Line Termination Circuitry on iSBC® 608 Cardcage**

Intel's iSBC 608/618 Cardcages are matched to the latest generation of iSBC/iSBX boards which mount in the MULTIBUS system bus. These products provide several features which make them the industry's leading price/performance cardcage product. MULTIMODULE board clearance, parallel priority circuitry, enhanced backplane noise immunity, and precision fit card guides are a few of the distinctions which make this the industry's better product.

The iSBC 608 Cardcage is the base unit, housing up to eight iSBC boards and their MULTIMODULE boards. Additionally, this base unit includes mounting hardware and fan mounting bracketry. The iSBC 618 is the expansion unit, providing eight additional iSBC board slots to the iSBC 608 Cardcage for a total of sixteen board slots which can be NEMA-type backwall or 19-inch rack mounted. This is accomplished with the mounting hardware of the iSBC 608 Cardcage. The iSBC 618 expansion unit also includes fan mounting bracketry.

210373-1

November 1986
Order Number: 210373-001

FUNCTIONAL DESCRIPTION

Mechanical Aspects

The iSBC 608/618 Cardcages provide housing and a MULTIBUS system bus for up to sixteen single board computers and their MULTIMODULE boards. The iSBC 608 unit and iSBC 618 unit offer board-to-board clearance (0.8 inches or greater) on all eight slots for iSBC MULTIMODULE boards. Two slots provide clearance (1.2 inches or greater) for iSBX MULTIMODULE boards as shown in Figure 1. Each cardcage includes precision fitted nylon cardguides for secure board fit and accurate MULTIBUS board pin alignment. Fan mounting bracketry is also included with each cardcage. This bracketry allows the mounting of several industry standard fans. The iSBC 608 Cardcage base unit includes aluminum mounting hardware for NEMA-type backwall mounting, or anchoring a sixteen slot iSBC 608/618 combination in a standard 19-inch rack.

Electrical Aspects

The iSBC 608/618 Cardcages implement a parallel priority resolution scheme by using plug-in jumper connections. There are six different priority schemes allowed, each requiring a different jumper configuration. In systems where an iSBC 618 Cardcage is attached to the base unit, the base unit will have lower priority overall. That is, master boards in the iSBC 608 base unit bay gain control of the MULTIBUS lines only when no boards in the iSBC 618 expansion unit are asserting the bus request (BREQ/) signal.

Noise-minimizing ground traces are strategically interleaved between signal and address lines on these backplanes. This provides the enhanced noise immunity and minimized signal-to-signal coupling which is important in high speed, high board count microcomputer systems.

The iSBC 608/618 Cardcages provide power connector lug bolts for +5 VDC and ground. The lug bolts, compared to other power connection methods, help transfer higher amounts of current. Other voltages (±12 VDC, −5 VDC) are connected via a mating power connector plug as shown in Figure 2.

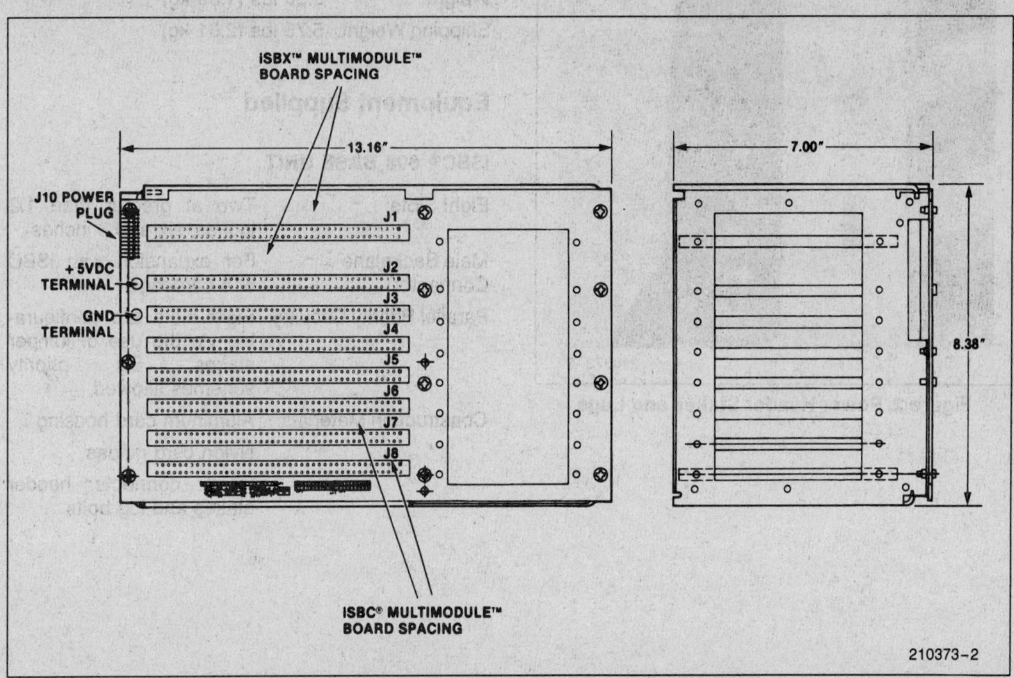

Figure 1. iSBC® 608/618 Cardcages Dimensions

SPECIFICATIONS

Bus Lines

All MULTIBUS (IEEE 796) system bus address and command lines are bussed to each of the eight MULTIBUS connectors on the backplane. Ground traces are interleaved among these signal lines and bussed to the backplane edge connector for interconnection of the iSBC 608 and iSBC 618 backplane.

Power Connectors

Ground (0V), +5V, −5V, +12V, −12V power supply header stakes and power lug bolts are provided on the iSBC 608/618 Cardcages as shown in Figure 2.

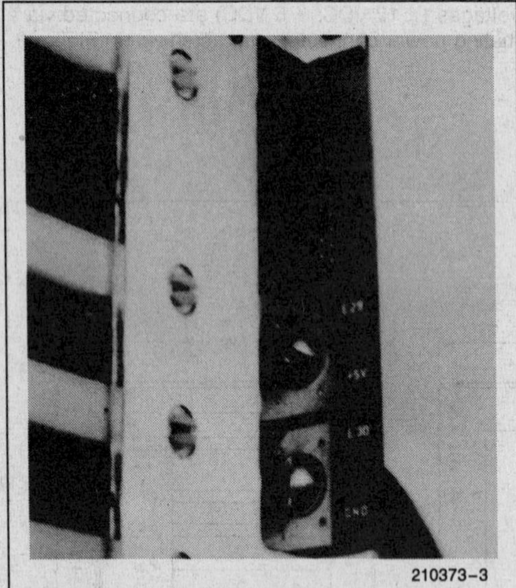

210373-3

Figure 2. Power Header Stakes and Lugs

Environmental Characteristics

Operating Temperature: 0°C to 55°C

Storage Temperature: −40°C to +85°C

Humidity: 50% to 95% non-condensing at 25°C to 40°C.

Vibration and Shock: 2G max. through 50 Hz

Physical Characteristics

SLOT-TO-SLOT DIMENSIONS (See Figure 1)

Top-J1: 1.200 in. (to center)

J1-J2: 1.300 in. (center to center)

J8-Bottom: 0.700 in. (to center)

All Others: 0.800 (center to center)

Physical Dimensions

Height: 8.38 in. (21.29 cm)

Length: 13.16 in. (33.43 cm)

Width: 7.50 in. (19.05 cm)

Weight: 3.50 lbs (1.59 kg)

Shipping Weight: 5.75 lbs (2.61 kg)

Equipment Supplied

iSBC® 608 BASE UNIT

Eight Slots: Two at greater than 1.2 inches; six at 0.8 inches

Male Backplane Connector: For expansion with iSBC 618 cardcage

Parallel Priority Circuitry: Eight slots are configurable via the use of jumper stakes. Six priority schemes allowed

Construction Materials: Aluminum card housing

Nylon card guides

Power connector header stakes and lug bolts

Accessories

iSBC® 618 EXPANSION UNIT

Eight-Slots:	Two at greater than 1.2 inches; six at 0.8 inches
Female Backplane Connector:	For expansion to iSBC 608 base unit
Parallel Priority Circuitry:	Eight slots are configurable via the use of jumper stakes. Six priority schemes allowed.
Construction Materials:	Aluminum card housing
	Nylon card guides
	Power connector header stakes and lug bolts
	Fan Mounting Hardware
	Schematic

User-Supplied Equipment

MATING POWER CONNECTORS

Vendor	Part Number
3M	3399-6026
Ansley	609-2600M
Berg	65485-009

MOUNTABLE FANS

Vendor	Part Number
Rotron	SU2A1-028267
Torin	TA300-A30473-10
Pamotor	8506D

iSBC® 661 SYSTEM CHASSIS

- Eight-Slot MULTIBUS® Chassis with Parallel Priority Circuitry
- UL, FCC and CSA Approved for Data Processing Equipment
- 230 Watt Power Supply with Power Fail Warning
- Designed for Slide Rack Mounting or Table-Top Use
- Extra-Wide Cardcage Slot Spacing for iSBX™ MULTIMODULE™ Board Clearance
- Configurable for Front or Rear Access to MULTIBUS® Circuit Boards
- Five Connector Ports for I/O Cabling
- Operational from 47 Hz to 63 Hz, 100/120/220/240 VAC ±10%

The iSBC 661 System Chassis is an advanced MULTIBUS (IEEE) 796 chassis which incorporates unique usability and service features not found on competitive products. This chassis is designed or rack-mount or table-top applications and reliably operates up to an ambient temperature of 50°C. Additionally, this sytem chassis is certified by UL, CSA and FCC for data processing equipment.

An application requiring multiprocessing will find this eight-slot MULTIBUS chassis particularly well suited to its needs. Parallel priority bus arbitration circuiry has been integrated into the backplane. This permits a bus master to reside in each slot. Extra-wide inter-slot spacing on the cardcage allows the use of plug-on MULTIMODULE boards without blocking adjacent slots. For this reason, the iSBC 661 System Chassis provides the slot-functionality of most 16-slot chassis. Standard logic recognizes a system AC power failure and generates a TTL signal for use in powerdown control. Additionally, current limiting and over-voltage protection are provided at all outputs.

210866-1

October 1986
Order Number: 210866-002

FUNCTIONAL DESCRIPTION

Mechanical Features

The iSBC 661 System Chassis houses, cools, powers, and interconnects up to eight iSBC single board computers and their MULTIMODULE boards for the MULTIBUS System Bus. Based on Intel's iSBC 608 Cardcage, the chassis provides 0.8 inches of board center-to-center clearance on six slots, and 1.2 inches or more of center-to-center clearance on two slots. This permits the users of standard MULTIMODULE boards and custom wire-wrap boards to plug into the MULTIBUS System Bus without blocking adjacent slots. All slots provide enough clearance for iSBC MULTIMODULE boards, and two slots can accommodate iSBX MULTIMODULE boards.

High-technology MULTIBUS applications requiring rack-mount, or laboratory table-top use will find the iSBC 661 System Chassis ideal. Standard 19″ slid-rack mounting is possible with user-provided slides attached to the side panels. Slide mounting holes are provided in the chassis for the slide-rails listed under User Supplied Options. Rubber feet are included on the chassis for convenient table-top use.

The chassis is constructed of burnished aluminum which has been coated with corrosion-resistant chromate. It contains a system control module which presents the front panel control switches to the user, and holds the I/O cabling bulkhead to the rear. The chassis has the unique feature of being configurable for either front or rear access to MULTIBUS circuit boards.

This is accomplished by a simple procedure involving removal of the system control module, reversing it end-for-end, and re-securing it to the chassis. The system chassis is shipped in a configuration such that the MULTIBUS boards are installed from the front.

Electrical Features

The iSBC 661 System Chassis is powered by the iSBC 640 power supply. This is a standard Intel power supply which has been adopted by several MULTIBUS vendors throughout the industry. It sup-

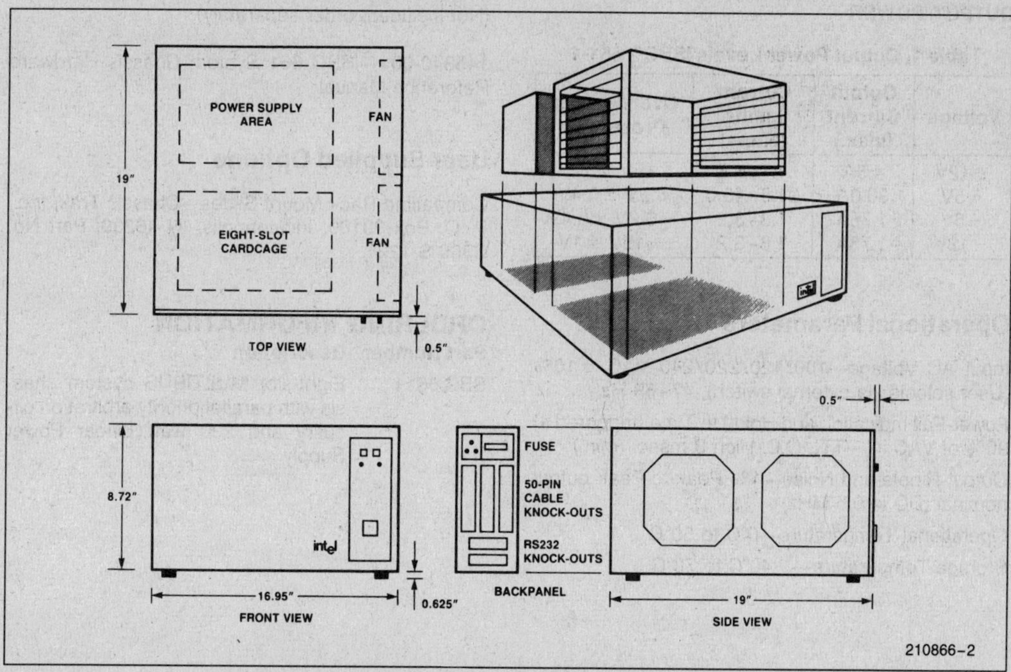

Figure 1. iSBC® 661 System Chassis Dimensions

plies 230 watts of power, power fail warning, and remote sensing of +5 volts. Its electrical and operational parameters are listed under Specifications.

The cardcage of the iSBC 661 System Chassis implements a user-changeable parallel priority bus arbitration scheme by using plug-in jumper connections. Six different priority schemes are allowed, each scheme fixing the priority to the eight MULTIBUS board slots. Bus contention among eight busmasters in a multiprocessing environment can be managed using this approach.

Noise minimizing ground traces are strategically interleaved between signal and address lines on the system bus. This provides the enhanced noise immunity and minimized signal-to-signal coupling which is particularly important in high speed, high board count microcomputer systems.

SPECIFICATIONS

Electrical Parameters

OUTPUT POWER

Table 1. Output Power Levels iSBC® 661-1

Voltage	Output Current (max.)	Current Limits (amps)	Over-Voltage Protection
+12V	4.5A	4.7–6.8	15V ±1V
+5V	30.0A	31.5–45.0	6.2V ±0.4V
−5V	1.75A	1.8–3.2	−6.2V ±0.4V
−12V	1.75A	1.8–3.2	−15V ±1V

Operational Parameters

Input AC Voltage—100/120/220/240 VAC ±10% (User selects via external switch), 47–63 Hz

Power-Fail Indication and Hold-Up Time (triggered at 90% of VAC in)—TTL O.C. High 3 msec. (min.)

Output Ripple and Noise—1% Peak-to-Peak output nominal (DC to 0.5 MHz)

Operational Temperature—0°C to 50°C

Storage Temperature— −40°C to 70°C

Operational Humidity—10% to 85% relative, non-condensing

Remote Sensing—Provided for +5 VCD

Output Transient Response—50 μs or less for ±50% load change

Physical Characteristics

Width: 16.95 inches (43.05 cm)

Height: 8.72 inches (22.2 cm)

Depth: 19.00 inches (48.3 cm)

Weight: 41 pounds (21 kg)

Shipping Weight (approx.): 50 pounds (25 Kg)

Equipment Supplied

iSBC® 661-1—Eight-slot MULTIBUS system chassis with parallel priority arbitration circuitry and 230 watt linear power supply

Reference Manual

(Not included: order separately)

145340-001—iSBC 661 System Chassis Hardware Reference Manual

User Supplied Options

Compatible Rack-Mount Slides—Chassis Trak, Inc., P. O. Box 39100, Indianapolis, IN 46239; Part No. C300 S 122

ORDERING INFORMATION

Part Number	Description
SBC 6611	Eight-slot MULTIBUS system chassis with parallel priority arbitration circuitry and 230 watt Linear Power Supply

Microcomputer Platforms 14

INTEL MICROCOMPUTER MODEL 386/33H

281360-1

ADVANCED DESIGN IN AN EXPANDABLE DESKTOP

14

Outstanding SVGA graphics coupled with the Intel386 DX 33 MHz microprocessor provide exceptional performance. And the six *open* ISA slots, four peripheral bays, and 32 MB of maximum on-board SIMM memory offer expandability to meet even the most demanding desktop applications. The chassis is designed to make integration and servicing easy. No tools are required to get into the system and all upgradeable features are easily accessible.

BOARD-LEVEL FEATURES

- i386™ DX microprocessor running at 33 MHz
- Intel 82395 Smartcache
- i387™ DX/Weitek math coprocessor socket
- 4 MB on-board SIMM memory (expandable to 32 MB)
- Integrated Super VGA graphics (with patent-pending accelerator)
- Integrated floppy disk and hard disk controllers
- Integrated serial ports (2), parallel port, PS/2 style mouse port
- Six ISA slots
- Phoenix BIOS, FLASH upgradeable with floppy

SYSTEM-LEVEL FEATURES

- Compact 17.3″ wide chassis
- Four Peripheral Bays (2 half height 5.25″, 2 3.5″ bays)
- Optional 1.44 MB 3.5″ floppy
- Optional 52 MB and 105 MB IDE hard disks
- Full FCC Class B emission compliance

OPTIONS

- 101-key enhanced keyboard
- Worldwide Intel service/maintenance/network support
- DOS, OS/2* and Windows*

i486™, i386™, and IntelTechDIRECT™ are trademarks of Intel Corporation.
IBM™, OS/2™, and PS/2™ are trademarks of International Business Machines Corporation.
MS-DOS™ and MS OS/2™ are trademarks of Microsoft Corporation.
VAX™ is a trademark of Digital Equipment Corporation.
Unix™ is a trademark of AT&T Bell Laboratories.
Banyan™ is a trademark of Banyan Systems, Inc.

October 1991
Order Number: 281360-002

INTEL MICROCOMPUTER MODEL 386/33H

STELLAR GRAPHICS PERFORMANCE

The on-board graphics are so good that we applied for a patent. A full 16-bit Paradise graphics controller coupled with 512K of video RAM (DRAM) and Intel's proprietary graphics accelerator produce high performance graphics at resolutions from standard VGA, all the way up to 1024 × 768.

EXPANDABLE

Although the Model 386/33H is packaged in a small footprint chassis, you will find all the expandability you need for even the most demanding desktop applications. The six ISA expansion slots and four peripheral bays provide the basic expandability of the system. And the system's capacity of 32 MB of on-board RAM can even meet the demands of a desktop fileserver.

EASY TO CONFIGURE

No tools are necessary to remove the cover: simply turn the two captured "thumbscrews." Once inside the system, you will find all areas of baseboard directly accessible. So, adding additional RAM, a math coprocessor or an expansion card is easy. The Model 386/33H even has a configuration label to help guide system expansion.

Updating BIOS has never been easier. Simply use the FLASH diskette utility to upgrade the BIOS. You never have to go into the system and swap EPROMs.

HIGH INTEGRATION MEANS HIGH RELIABILITY

Take a look at the 386/33H. With the integration of video, floppy disk and hard disk controller, and the essential I/O functions, there are fewer parts than the typical PC. This increases reliability and reduces your costs of configuring, maintaining and servicing the system.

QUALITY THAT YOU CAN SEE

We've also incorporated several other features which go the extra mile for you: like metal tab SIMM connectors which reduce the number of memory failures due to socket cracking. And the on-board floppy and IDE hard disk connectors are shrouded/locking so you can get a good, solid connection. We've even added transorbs to the serial port lines which absorb incoming voltage spikes which may damage your system.

COMPATIBILITY YOU CAN DEPEND ON

281360-2

Of course the Model 386/33H is compatible with MS-DOS*, Windows, MS OS/2 and UNIX* operating systems, giving you access to thousands of applications. Rigorous compatibility testing ensures that the Model 386/33H is also compatible with the vast array of industry standard software, expansion boards and peripheral devices. Extensive in-house and third party compatibility testing has been performed to ensure that compatibility has been designed-in from the ground up. The Model 386/33H is also Novell, Banyan*, DEC PCSA and DVI certified.

FLEXIBLE SERVICE AND SUPPORT

Intel offers service and support "building blocks" which can be mixed, matched, and customized to meet your specific needs.

All Intel platforms come with a free 12 month parts and labor warranty. Customers can choose carry-in to local depot repair or mail-in to factory repair. Intel offers an express parts service to eligible customers.

On-site service is available either by contract or on a time and material basis. We also offer spare kits for volume OEMs and VARs who want to provide immediate service to their customers.

IntelTechDirect™ technical support gives you fast answers to both technical questions about Intel platforms. It includes monthly Product Update Bulletins, a 24-hour-a-day electronic bulletin board, and telephone hot line support. Ask your local Intel representative for more details on any of Intel's building block services.

SPECIFICATIONS

BOARD

CPU	386 DX microprocessor; 33 MHz
Cache	16K Intel SmartCache
Math Coprocessor	i387 DX and Weitel 3167 socket; 33 MHz
On-Board Memory	8 SIMM sockets
Standard RAM	4 MB (4 1M×9 fast page mode SIMMs)
Maximum RAM	32 MB
Upgrade RAM	4-256K×9, 4-1 MB×9 or 4-4 M×9
Speed	80 ns or faster
Error Detection	Byte Parity

INTEGRATED GRAPHICS

Controller	Western Digital WD90C11
Video Memory	512K (70 ns DRAM)
Maximum Resolution	1024×768, 16 colors 800×600, 256 colors
Compatible with	VGA, EGA, CGA, HGC, MDA
Output Port	15 pin connector; analog
Video Drivers	Included with system

I/O

2 serial ports	Async, RS 232 C, 9 pin
1 parallel port	Centronics-compatible, 25 pin
1 mouse port	PS/2* compatible
1 keyboard port	PS/2 compatible
Floppy disk controller	82077AA
IDE hard disk connector	
6 available ISA slots	

SYSTEM

Height	6.2″ (15.8 cm)
Width	17.3″ (43.9 cm)
Depth	17.1″ (43.4 cm)
Weight	35lbs (15.9 kg.)
Expansion Bays	2 5.25″ half height external 1 3.5″ half height (1.625″) external 1 3.5″ half height (1.625″) internal
Floppy Disk Option	
Footprint	3.5″
Capacity	1.44 MB high density
Hard Disk Options	
Model	Quantum LPS52AT/105AT
Footprint	3.5″
Capacities	52 MB or 105 MB formatted
Average access	17 ms, (<12 ms with 64K DisCache)
Interface	IDE
Accessories	
User's manual	
Peripherals expansion kit	
Video driver diskette	

ELECTRICAL

Input: AC Voltage	115V/60Hz, 230V/50Hz Auto switching (autoranging)	
Output DC Voltage:	Board	Max
+5V	3.6A continuous	23
+12V	.02A continuous	5.2
−5V	0A continuous	0.5
−12V	.02A continuous	0.2
Total Power output	200 Watts	

ENVIRONMENT

Ambient Temperature Board	
Operating	0°C to 55°C
Non Operating	−40°C to 70°C
System	
Operating	15°C to 40°C
Non Operating	−40°C to 70°C
Relative Humidity	
Operating	20% to 80% at 36°C
Non Operating	20% to 92% at 36°C
Altitude	
Operating	to 10,000 ft.
Non Operating	to 50,000 ft.
Noise (typical)	40dB (peripherals idle, at 1 meter)
Static Discharge	7.5kV Max

ORDERING INFORMATION

REGULATIONS

Meets or exceeds the following requirements

Safety	
US	UL 478 5th Edition
Canada	CSA C22.2 No. 154
Europe	IEC 435 & VDE 0806
EMI/RFI	
US	FCC 47 CFR Part 15 Subpart J.
Canada	DOC CRR B74 Class B
Europe	VDE 0871 1 Level B

Certifications
- Banyan Certified
- DEC Pathworks for DOS qualified
- Novell Certified

DT38633H4B0	33 MHz 386 DX Microcomputer system, 4 MB RAM
DT38633H4I1	33 MHz 386 DX Microcomputer system, 4 MB RAM, 3.5″ floppy, 52MB IDE Hard Disk
DT38633H4I2	33 MHz 386 DX Microcomputer system, 4 MB RAM, 3.5″ floppy, 105MB IDE Hard Disk
DT38633H8I1	33 MHz 386 DX Microcomputer system, 8 MB RAM, 3.5″ floppy, 52MB IDE Hard Disk
B38633H0	33 MHz 386 DX motherboard, 0MB RAM
B38633H4	33 MHz 386 DX motherboard, 4MB RAM

For more information or the number of your nearest Intel sales office, call 800-548-4725 (good in the U.S. and Canada).

INTEL386™ MICROCOMPUTER MODEL LP386SX20

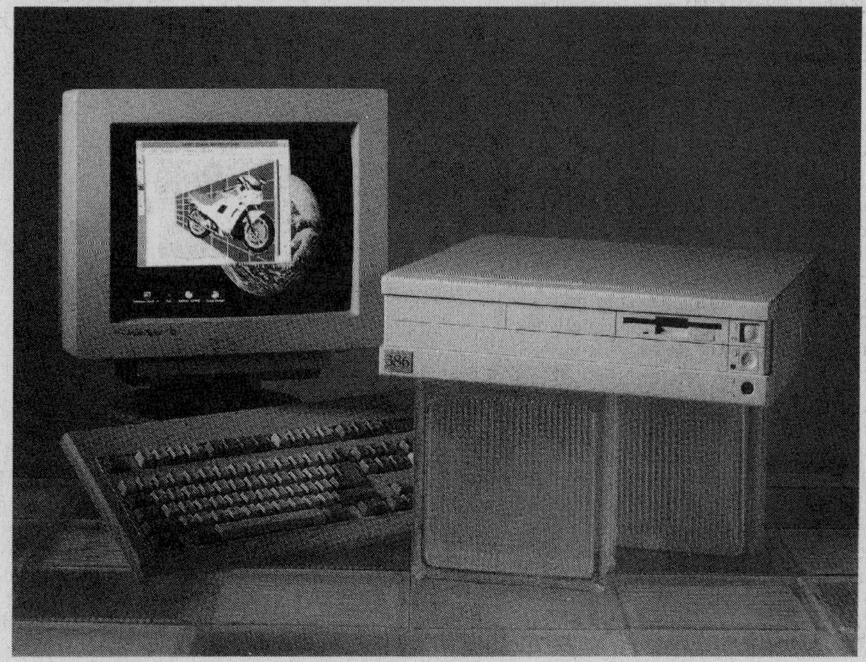

281361–1

LOW-PROFILE i386™SX PACKED WITH VALUE

The Intel386™ MicroComputer Model LP386SX20 packs the 32-bit power of the 20MHz i386™SX microprocessor, Super VGA graphics, and IDE hard disk interface into a compact 3.9″ high chassis. This small, low-profile package takes up less desk space, making the Model LP386SX20 an ideal foundation for a personal workstation—standalone or networked. With a wealth of integrated features, the Model LP386SX20 minimizes your investment in procurement, system integration and installation.

FEATURES

- 20 MHz i386 SX microprocessor
- i387™SX math coprocessor socket
- 2 MB on-board SIMM memory, expandable to 32 MB
- Integrated Super VGA with 512 KB of video RAM (up to 1024 × 768, 16 colors)
- Integrated IDE hard disk connector
- Integrated floppy controller
- One serial port
- One parallel port
- PS/2* Style mouse port
- Three available 16-bit ISA slots
- Optional 1.44 MB floppy
- Optional 52 MB hard disk
- FCC Class B Certification/VDE Class B Compliance
- Novell certified, DEC qualified, Banyan compatible

i486™, i386™, and TechDIRECT™ are trademarks of Intel Corporation.
IBM™, OS/2™, and PS/2™ are trademarks of International Business Machines Corporation.
MS-DOS™, MS OS/2™, and Windows™ are trademarks of Microsoft Corporation.
DEC™, PATHWORKS™, and VAX™ are trademarks of Digital Equipment Corporation.
Unix™ is a trademark of AT&T Bell Laboratories.
Banyan™ is a trademark of Banyan Systems, Inc.

October 1991
Order Number: 281361-001

FEATURES

ALL THE FEATURES YOU NEED IN A SMALL PACKAGE

The Model LP386SX-20 integrates all the essential PC features onto the baseboard: up to 32 MB of RAM, Super VGA graphics, a serial port, a parallel port, a mouse port and an IDE hard disk interface. The Model LP386SX-20 also comes with three 16-bit expansion slots and three drive bays for customization.

The Model LP386SX-20 is only 3.9″ high, 15.4″ wide and 15.8″ deep. This size is ideal for a standalone PC, a network client, or a front-end for an embedded application. The Model LP386SX-20 is available in a diskless configuration, providing a cost-effective platform on which you can build network clients or embedded systems.

UP TO 32 MB OF ON-BOARD MEMORY

The Model LP386SX-20 can accommodate up to 32 MB of on-board memory: 16 MB extended and 16 MB expanded. Expanded memory can serve as a fast RAM disk, providing a big performance boost in a disk-intensive environment such as Microsoft* Windows*.

GRAPHICS AND HARD DISK INTERFACE . . . ON-BOARD

The Model LP386SX-20 integrates graphics and IDE hard disk interface directly onto the motherboard. This eliminates the need for a separate video card and a disk controller, saving you time and expense in purchasing, integrating, and maintaining your system, while ensuring optimal reliability and performance.

The graphics subsystem on-board the Model LP386SX-20 provides resolutions ranging from standard VGA all the way up to 1024×768 with 16 colors (interlaced). It also provides emulation for older video standards such as EGA, CGA, MDA, and Hercules.

The on-board IDE hard disk connector offers a direct connection to fast, reliable hard disk drives. IDE provides the best price/performance disk capability for single-user environment.

i386™ PERFORMANCE AT AN AFFORDABLE PRICE

Powered by the 20 MHz i386 SX microprocessor, the Model LP386SX-20 offers the 32-bit i386 speed and software compatibility at an entry-level price. This economical system contains plenty of power for today's popular applications and allows you to run all future 32-bit software.

COMPATIBILITY YOU CAN DEPEND ON

281361-2

The Model LP386SX-20 is compatible with MS-DOS*, Windows, MS OS/2* and UNIX* operating systems, giving you access to thousands of popular applications. Rigorous compatibility testing ensures that the Model LP386SX-20 is also compatible with the vast array of industry standard software, expansion boards and peripheral devices. Extensive in-house and third-party compatibility testing by companies such as Veritest has been performed throughout the design stage to ensure that compatibility has been designed-in from the ground up. The Model LP386SX-20 has been tested to be compatible with Banyan VINES and is Novell certified and DEC qualified.

FLEXIBLE SERVICE AND SUPPORT

Intel offers service and support "building blocks" which can be mixed, matched, and customized to meet your specific needs.

All Intel platforms come with a free 12 month parts and labor warranty. Customers can choose from carry-in to local depot repair, mail-in factory repair, or express parts services.

On-site service is available either by contract or by time and material. We also offer spares kits for volume OEMs and VARs who want to provide immediate service to their customers.

SPECIFICATIONS

IntelTechDirect™ technical support gives you fast answers to both technical and business questions about Intel products. It includes monthly Product Update Bulletins, a 24-hour-a-day electronic bulletin board, and hot-line support. Ask your local Intel representative for more details on any of Intel's building block services.

BOARD

CPU	i386 SX microprocessor; 20 MHz
Math Coprocessor	i387 SX socket; 20 MHz
On-board Memory	8 SIMM sockets
Standard RAM	2 MB (2-1 M × 9 fast page mode SIMMs)
Maximum RAM	32 MB
Upgrade RAM	2-256K × 9, 2-1M × 9 or 2-4M × 9 SIMMs at a time
Access time	80 ns or faster
Error Detection	Byte Parity
Integrated Graphics	
Controller	Western Digital WD90C11
Video Memory	512K (70 ns DRAM)
Maximum Resolution	800 × 600, 256 colors 1024 × 768, 16 colors
Compatible with	VGA, EGA, CGA, HGC, MDA
Video Port	15 pin connector; analog
Video Drivers	Included with system
I/O	
1 serial port	Async, RS 232 C, 9-pin
1 parallel port	Centronics-compatible, 25 pin
1 mouse port	PS/2 compatible
1 keyboard port	PS/2 compatible
Floppy disk controller	87310
IDE hard disk connector	
3 available slots	16-bit ISA compatible

SYSTEM

System Dimensions	
Height	3.9× (9.9 cm)
Width	15.4× (39.1 cm)
Depth	15.8× (40.1 cm)
Weight	17 lbs (7.7kg) without peripherals
Drive Bays	
External	2 3.5″ ⅓ height (1.0″)
Internal	1 3.5″ ½ height (1.625″)
Floppy Disk Option	
Footprint	T 3.5″, ⅓ Height
Capacity	1.44 MB high density
Hard Disk Option	
Model	Quantum LPS52AT
Footprint	3.5″, ½ Height
Capacity	52 MB
Average access	17 msec
Interface	IDE

Accessories
- User's manual
- Second floppy drive accessory kit
- Video driver diskette

ELECTRICAL

AC Voltage/Frequency	115V/60Hz or 230V/50Hz (externally switchable)
DC Power	115W
+5V	13.5 A maximum continuous
+12V	3.5 A maximum continuous
−12V	0.3 A maximum continuous
−5V	0.3 A maximum continuous
Available Power	11.06A @ +5V (2I configuration with coprocessor)

ENVIRONMENT

Ambient Temperature	
Operating	10°C to 35°C
Non-operating	−40° to 70°C
Relative Humidity	
Operating	20% - 80% at 35°C
Non-operating	92% at 55°C
Altitude	
Operating	To 10,000 feet
Non-operating	To 50,000 feet
Noise	37 dB max (peripherals idle, at 1 m.)
Static Discharge	7.5 kV max

SPECIFICATIONS

REGULATIONS

Meets or exceeds the following requirements:

Safety	
U.S.	UL 1950
Canada	CSA C22.2 No. 950
Europe	TUV EN 60950 with ZH1/618 Ergonomics
EMI/RFI	
U.S.	FCC CFR 47 Part 15, level B
Canada	DOC CRC c.1374 Class B
Europe	VDE 0871 Class B

NETWORK CERTIFICATIONS

Banyan Compatible

DEC PATHWORKS* for DOS Qualified

Novell Certified #5-619

ORDERING INFORMATION

LP386SX20I2N	20 MHz i386 SX computer with 2 MB of memory; diskless
LP386SX20I2F	20 MHz i386 SX computer with 2 MB, and a 1.44 MB 3.5" floppy disk drive
LP386SX20I2I	20 MHz i386 SX computer with 2 MB, floppy and a 52 MB IDE hard disk drive

For more information or the number of your nearest Intel sales office, call 800-548-4725 (good in the U.S. and Canada).

INTEL386™ MICROCOMPUTER MODEL 300LPSX-16

281329–1

14

WINDOWS CLIENT FOR COST-SENSITIVE USERS*

The Intel386™ MicroComputer Model 300LPSX-16 harnesses the power of the i386™ microprocessor, VGA graphics and IDE hard disk technology in a compact 3.9″ high chassis. Packed with all these features, the Model 300LPSX-16 minimizes your investment in procurement, system integration and installation. After your systems are installed, Intel backs you with a worldwide, world-class service and support organization.

BOARD-LEVEL FEATURES

- i386™ SX microprocessor running at 16 MHz
- 387™ SX math coprocessor socket
- 1 or 2 MB on-board memory (expandable to 8 MB)
- Integrated VGA graphics
- IDE disk connector
- One serial port, one parallel port
- One PS/2* Style mouse port
- Three ISA expansion slots
- Phoenix Technologies ROM BIOS

SYSTEM-LEVEL FEATURES

- Low-profile chassis (3.9″ high)
- 1.44 MB 3.5″ floppy
- Optional 40 MB hard disk
- Full FCC Class B emission compliance

OPTIONS

- 101-key enhanced keyboard
- Intel worldwide service/maintenance/ network support
- MS DOS*, MS OS/2* (and Intel UNIX* System V 3.2 software)

i486™ and 386™ are trademarks of Intel Corporation.
PS/2™ and OS/2™ are trademarks of International Business Machines Corporation.
MS-DOS™ and MS OS/2 Windows™ are trademarks of Microsoft Corporation.
UNIX™ is a trademark of AT&T Bell Laboratories.

October 1991
Order Number: 281329-002

INTEL386™ MICROCOMPUTER MODEL 300LPSX-16

ALL THE FEATURES YOU NEED IN A LOW-PROFILE PACKAGE

The MicroComputer Model 300LPSX integrates all the essential features onto the motherboard. This includes up to 8 MB RAM, VGA graphics, a serial port, a parallel port, a mouse port and an IDE hard disk connector.

Yet the Model 300LPSX-16 is only 3.9″ high, 15.4″ wide and 15.4″ deep. The system size is ideal for a personal workstation or a front-end industrial application.

STATE-OF-THE-ART GRAPHICS AND HARD DISK TECHNOLOGY ... ON-BOARD

The MicroComputer Model 300LPSX-16's on-board graphics is capable of providing up to 800×600 Super VGA resolution; it is also compatible with standard VGA, EGA, CGA, Hercules and monochrome standards. And the IDE hard disk connects directly to the motherboard, offering a direct connection to fast, reliable hard disk drives.

The Model 300LPSX-16's on-board graphics and IDE hard disk connector eliminate the need for a separate video card and a disk controller. This saves you time and expense in purchasing, integrating and maintaining your system.

THE PERFORMANCE OF THE i386™ AT AN AFFORDABLE PRICE

The MicroComputer Model 300LPSX-16 is powered by a 16 MHz i386 SX microprocessor. And of course this allows you to run all of today's software, and all future 32-bit software that can only be run on i386 or i486™ microcomputers like the Model 300LPSX-16.

INDUSTRY STANDARD SOFTWARE

The Model 300LPSX-16 microcomputer runs the industry standard MS-DOS, MS OS/2, and UNIX* operating systems, plus the Windows operating environment, to give you access to thousands of popular applications and preserve your existing software investment. Intel further reduces your software development and support costs with thorough hardware and software compatibility testing.

The MS-DOS and MS OS/2 operating systems and other system software are available from Intel as options with the Model 300 LPSX-16. Intel software ensures that you get a product with thorough testing and evaluation on the hardware platform.

COMPATIBILITY YOU CAN DEPEND ON

Of course the MicroComputer Model 300LPSX-16 is compatible with DOS, Windows, OS/2 and UNIX operating systems. Rigorous compatibility testing ensures that the Model 300LPSX-16 is also compatible with the vast array of industry standard software and expansion boards. Extensive in-house and third party compatibility testing has been performed to ensure that compatibility has been designed-in from the ground up.

ONE-STOP SOLUTIONS SERVICE AND SUPPORT

At Intel, we service our own systems. That means that you do not have to deal with a third party that may not be familiar with your computer (or may not have spares). Our Customer Engineers are factory-trained on all Intel computers. These technicians are also experienced on other manufacturers' computers. This can provide you with a single-contact solution for all your networked equipment, both Intel and non-Intel. The following programs can be mixed, matched, and customized to meet your specific needs:

STANDARD WARRANTY

All Intel platforms come with a 12-month warranty. Resolve any service-related problem by calling 1-800-INTEL-4-U (1-800-468-3548).

EXTENDED ON-SITE WARRANTY

Our standard warranty program can be enhanced to provide one year on-site service and expanded to cover non-Intel products. Ask your Intel representative.

IntelTECHDIRECT™ TECHNICAL SUPPORT

This comprehensive program gives you fast answers to both technical and business questions about Intel products. It also includes monthly Product Update Bulletins and a 24-hour-a-day electronic bulletin board which allows you to access our product database, enter questions and examine past and present Product Update Bulletins. Call 1-503-696-7257 to learn more.

INTEL386™ MICROCOMPUTER MODEL 300LPSX-16

NETWORK CONSULTING

Our customer engineers have designed, managed and serviced more than 1,500 local area networks, including connections to DEC, VAX, and IBM hosts. Plus we're certified by both Novell and Banyan. We'll handle all the details and get you up and running in no time. For further details contact your Intel representative or distributor.

SPECIFICATIONS

I/O

1 serial port	Async, RS 232 C, 9 pin
1 parallel port	centronics-compatible, 25 pin
1 mouse port	PS/2* compatible
1 keyboard port	PS/2 compatible
3 expansion slots	2 16-bit, 1 8-bit
1 floppy disk controller	
1 IDE hard disk connector	

SYSTEM

Height	3.9″ (9.9 cm)
Width	15.4″ (39.1 cm)
Depth	15.4″ (39.1 cm)
Weight	22 lbs (10 kg) without peripherals

Expansion Bays
- 2 3.5″ third-height (1″) external
- 1 3.5″ half-height (1.625″) internal

Floppy Disk

Footprint	3.5″
Capacity	1.44 MB high density

Hard Disk option

Footprint	3.5″
Capacity	40 MB formatted
Average Access	25 ms

BOARD

CPU	i386SX microprocessor running at 16 MHz
Math Coprocessor	387SX socket

On-Board Memory

Standard RAM	1 or 2 MB SIMM
Maximum RAM	8 MB SIMM
Speed	100 ns, interleaved

Integrated Graphics

Controller	Western Digital WD90C00
Video Memory	256 Kbytes
Maximum resolution	800 × 600 16 colors
Compatible resolution	VGA, EGA, CGA, Hercules, and Monochrome
Output port	15 pin analog

SPECIFICATIONS

ELECTRICAL

Input AC Voltage: 115V/60 Hz 230V/50 Hz (externally configurable)

Output DC Voltage:

+5V	13.5 A maximum continuous
+12V	3.5 A maximum continuous
−12V	0.3 A maximum continuous
−5V	0.3 A maximum continuous

Total Power Output 115 Watts (switching)

ENVIRONMENT

Ambient Temperature:
Operating 15°C to 30°C

Relative Humidity:
Operating 20% – 80%

Altitude:
Operating To 10,000 feet

Static Discharge: 7.5 Kv max

REGULATIONS

Meets or exceeds the following requirements:

Safety

USA	UL 478, Edition 5
Canada	CSA C22.2 No. 220
Europe	IEC 950 & IEC 380

EMI/RFI

USA	FCC Class B; CFR 47 Part 15
Europe	VDE 0871 Level B
Canada	DOC; CRC c, 1374

ORDERING INFORMATION

S300LPSX161F	16 MHz i386 SX MicroComputer system with 1 MB on-board memory and a 3.5″ floppy drive
S300LPSX161I	16 MHz i386 SX MicroComputer system with 1 MB on-board memory, a 3.5″ floppy drive and a 40MB IDE hard disk drive
S300LPSX162F	16 MHz i386 SX MicroComputer system with 2 MB on-board memory and a 3.5″ floppy drive
S300LPSX162I	16 MHz i386 SX MicroComputer system with 2 MB on-board memory, a 3.5″ floppy drive and a 40MB IDE hard disk drive

INTEL386™ MICROCOMPUTER MODEL 300SX-20

281330–1

LOW-COST, HIGH INTEGRATION 386SX COMPUTE PLATFORM

The Intel386™ MicroComputer Model 300SX-20 maximizes the price/performance for 32-bit computing by utilizing the low-cost 20 MHz 386™ SX microprocessor. Available in various configurations, the Model 300SX-20 provides excellent integration flexibility for OEMs building custom 20 MHz 386 SX systems. The Model 300SX-20 features four slots for OEM customization, on-board memory expansion up to 16 MB, and integrated graphics and disk control to maximize expansion slots.

FEATURES

- 20 MHz 386 SX CPU
- 16K cache with 385 SX cache controller
- 2 MB on-board memory, expandable to 16 MB
- Four 16-bit ISA slots
- Integrated VGA and Super VGA with 512K video memory
- Video pass-through connector
- On-board floppy controller (82077)
- 82340 AT chip set
- Complete 32-bit software compatibility
- 387 SX socket for math-intensive operations
- 2 serial ports with FIFO
- 1 parallel port
- PS/2*-style Mouse and keyboard connectors
- Small footprint chassis
- Worldwide Intel service and support

October 1991
Order Number: 281330-001

INTEL386™ MICROCOMPUTER MODEL 300SX-20

HIGHLY INTEGRATED MOTHERBOARD

The Model 300SX-20 offers the highest possible level of integration, resulting in lower cost, higher reliability and maximum performance.The 300SX-20 single-board computer contains the following standard features:

- 2 MB SIMM memory (standard)
- 8 standard SIMM sockets
- Capability to mix and match various SIMM sizes, including 4 MB SIMMS
- Industry-standard Western Digital VGA and Super VGA graphics
- 387SX socket for math-intensive operations
- PS/2 mouse port and keyboard connector
- Two 9-pin serial ports
- 25-Pin Centronics compatible parallel port
- Analog video connectors
- 82077 floppy disk controller

LOW-COST 386™ SX TECHNOLOGY IN A HIGH-PERFORMANCE SYSTEM

The Intel386 MicroComputer Model 300SX-20 provides multiple configuration options and high-performance system features. All configurations feature four 16-bit slots available for OEM customization, 2 MB of on-board RAM, a high-performance disk subsystem, built-in graphics support, and a small footprint chassis.

HIGH-PERFORMANCE DISK SUBSYSTEM

The Model 300SX-20 frees an expansion slot by providing an on-board floppy controller and an embedded IDE Winchester controller interface right on the motherboard. A look-ahead cache boosts hard disk access times to 12 msec. Optional peripherals include a 3.5″ 1.44 MB floppy and either a 40 MB or 80 MB 3.5″ Winchester disk.

INTEGRATED GRAPHICS

The Model 300SX-20 offers high performance 16-bit VGA graphics integrated directly onto the motherboard. This graphics subsystem, utilizing the industry standard Western Digital WD90C11, provides resolutions ranging from standard VGA all the way up to $1024 \times 768 \times 16$ (interlaced). The Model 300SX-20 also supports older video standards such as EGA, CGA, MDA, and Hercules. If your application requires even higher performance graphics, such as 8514/A, the Model 300SX-20 has a feature connector to pass through the video control.

WORLDWIDE SERVICE AND SUPPORT

Multiply your sales potential in new markets throughout the world using Intel's worldwide service organization to install and maintain your system at your customer's site.

Field services include product installation, on-site maintenance, (including third party peripherals, and other vendors systems) per-call services are also available.

Factory services include system-level, board or peripheral repair or exchange. Spare part sales and advance service diagnostics are also available.

IntelTechDirect™ is an exclusive service from Intel which provides direct access to design engineers. This service offers the highest level of support for OEMs.

SPECIFICATIONS

BOARD

CPU	386SX microprocessor at 20 MHz
Floating point math	387SX socket
Memory	
Standard RAM	2 MB SIMM
Maximum RAM	16 MB SIMM
Access Time	80 ns
Error Detection	Byte Parity
Integrated Graphics	
Controller	Western Digital WD90CII
Video memory	512 Kb DRAM (70 ns)
Maximum Resolutions	640 × 480, × 256 colors 800 × 600, × 16 colors 1024 × 768, × 16 colors
Output port	15 pin port

I/O

2 serial ports	Async, RS 232 C, 9-pin
1 parallel port	Centronics compatible, 25-pin
1 mouse port	PS/2 compatible
4 slots	16-bit ISA compatible
1 keyboard port	PS/2 compatible

BOARD DIMENSIONS

Width	12″ (30 cm)
Depth	10″ (25 cm)
Weight	3.3 lbs (1.5 kg)

SYSTEM

Floppy Disk Option	
Footprint	3.5″, ⅓ Height
Capacity	1.44 MB
Winchester Disk Option	
Footprint	3.5″, ⅓ Height
Capacity	40 MB or 80 MB
Average access	19 msec
Effective access with cache	12 msec
Interface	IDE
Drive Bays	
External	5¼″ width, ½ height (1.625″)
External	3½″ width, ⅓ height (1.0″)
Internal	3½″ width, ½ height (1.625″)
System Dimensions	
Height	6.2″ (15 cm)
Width	14.0″ (36 cm)
Depth	15.7″ (40 cm)
Weight	27 lbs (12.3 kg)

ELECTRICAL

AC Voltage/Frequency	Switching power supply, 115V/60 Hz or 230V/50 Hz; convenience outlet
DC Power	145 W
+5 V	18.0 A maximum continuous
+12 V	4.2 A maximum continuous 6.0A maximum continuous for 15 seconds
−12 V	0.3 A maximum continuous
−5 V	0.3 A maximum continuous

SPECIFICATIONS

REGULATIONS

Meets or exceeds the following requirements:

Safety	
U.S.	UL 478 5th edition
Canada	CSA C22.2 No. 220
Europe	IEC 435 and VDE 0806
EMI/RFI	
U.S. and Canada	FCC47 CFR Part 15 Subpart J Class B
Europe	VDE 0871 Level B

ENVIRONMENTALS

Temperature	Operating: 0°C to +55°C ambient Nonoperating: −40°C to +70°C ambient
Humidity	Operating: 85% RH at +55°C Nonoperating: 95% RH at +55°C
Altitude	Operating: 10,000 ft. Nonoperating: 50,000 ft
ESD	Tested to 25 kV

PRODUCT DESCRIPTIONS

S300SX202BO	20 MHz 386 SX computer system with 2 MB on board memory
S300SX202F	20 MHz 386 SX computer system with 2 MB on board memory and a 3.5″ 1.44 MB floppy disk drive
S300SX202I4	20 MHz 386 SX computer system with 2 MB on board memory and a 3.5″ floppy disk drive, and a 40 MB IDE-interface hard disk drive
S300SX202I8	20 MHz 386 SX computer system with 2 MB on board memory, a 3.5″ 1.44 floppy disk drive, and an 80 MB IDE-interface hard disk drive

INTEL386™ MICROCOMPUTER MODEL 302

280984–1

14

INTEL 25 MHZ 386™ PERFORMANCE, ISA COMPATIBILITY

Running at 25 MHz, the Intel386™ MicroComputer Model 302 offers OEMs state-of-the-art 386™ microprocessor performance and Industry Standard Architecture (ISA) compatibility at either the board or system-level. Eight I/O expansion slots and up to 40 MB of zero wait-state memory allow extensive configuration flexibility. And, the Model 302 complies with all FCC B and VDE B emission levels.

Systems designed around the Model 302 take advantage of the full power of the 386 microprocessor at 25 MHz while maintaining compatibility with the industry-standard 8 MHz ISA bus.

FEATURES

- 25 MHz 386 microprocessor
- Zero wait-state performance provided by a 64 Kbyte cache
- Up to 40 MB memory
- Eight I/O expansion slots
- Phoenix Technologies ROM BIOS
- Two serial ports, one parallel port
- Five half-height 5¼″ peripheral bays (system only)
- FCC class B/VDE level B certification (system only)

*The Model 302 is also manufactured under product code pSYP30225 by Intel Puerto Rico, Inc.
The Model 302 motherboard is also manufactured under product code sSBC386AT25A by Intel Singapore, Ltd.

September 1991
Order Number: 280984-003

SPECIFICATIONS

BOARD

CPU	386™ microprocessor; 25 MHz
Floating point math	387™ socket; 25 MHz
Memory	
Standard RAM	2 or 4 MB
Maximum RAM	40 MB
Cycle time	100 ns
Error detection	Byte parity
Cache	64 Kbytes, direct mapped
I/O	
2 serial ports	Async, RS-232-C, 9-pin, AT-compatible
1 parallel port	Centronics-compatible, 25-pin, AT-compatible
8 expansion slots	2 32-bit, 16-bit or 8-bit 1 8-bit 5 16-bit or 8-bit
Physical Characteristics	
Width	13.8 in.
Depth	12.0 in.
Weight	43 oz.

SYSTEM

Floppy Disk Option	
Footprint	5.25″
Capacity	1.2 MB high density
Step rate	3 milliseconds
Settle time	15 ms max
Hard Disk Option	
Footprint	3.5″ half height
Capacity	52 MB formatted
Average access	19 msec
Physical Characteristics	
Height	6.4″
Width	21.3″
Length	18.7″
Weight	35 lbs

ELECTRICAL

AC Voltage/ Frequency	Switching power supply, 115V/60 Hz or 230V/50 Hz, switchable
DC Power	220W
+5 V	23.0 A maximum continuous
+12 V	8.0 A maximum continuous 12.0 A maximum surge for 15 seconds
−12 V	0.5 A maximum continuous
−5 V	0.5 A maximum continuous

ENVIRONMENT

Ambient Temperature:	
Board	
Operating	0 to 55°C
Non-operating	−40 to 70°C
System	
Operating	15 to 35°C
Non-operating	−34 to 60°C
Relative Humidity:	
Operating	to 85%
Altitude	
Operating	to 10,000 feet
Non-operating	to 50,000 feet

REGULATIONS

Meets or exceeds the following requirements:

Safety	
US	UL 478 5th Edition
Canada	CSA C22.2 No. 154
Europe	IEC 435 & VDE 0806
EMI/RFI	
US and Canada	FCC 47 CFR Part 15 Subpart J, Class B
Europe	VDE 0871 Level B

INTEL386™ MICROCOMPUTER MODEL 303

280976–1

14

33 MHZ AT-BUS PLATFORM FOR BUILDING HIGH-PERFORMANCE 386™ SYSTEMS

Based on the 33 MHz 386™ microprocessor, the Intel386™ MicroComputer Model 303 combines state-of-the-art performance, ISA compatibility, and unparalleled expansion capability to deliver a microcomputer platform ideally suited for file server and other high-performance applications. Available in either board or system configurations, the Model 303 features 33 MHz performance, 10 I/O expansion slots, and full FCC emission compliance.

FEATURES

- 33 MHz i386™ CPU motherboard with 4 MB RAM
- 10 I/O expansion slots
  - — Two 8/16/32 bit
  - — Seven 8/16 bit
  - — One 8-bit
- Full FCC Class B emission compliance
- 33 MHz i387™ math coprocessor socket
- 64 Kbyte cache with 0 wait states

ADDITIONAL SYSTEM-LEVEL FEATURES

- 170 MB SCSI hard drive
- 150 MB SCSI tape drive
- 1.44 MB 3.5″ floppy drive
- 1.2 MB 5.25″ floppy drive
- 4 half-height and 2 full-height peripheral bays
- Power sequencing board

October 1991
Order Number: 280976-003

FEATURES

THE FASTEST i386™ CPU ENGINE AROUND

At 33 MHz, the Intel386 MicroComputer Model 303 is the fastest 386 CPU-based compute platform on the market today. The high-speed 386 CPU can be augmented by an 387 math coprocessor, also running at 33 MHz. Performance is further enhanced by a 64 Kbyte cache memory that provides zero wait state execution without the cost of accessing main memory.

EXPANSION FLEXIBILITY

The Model 303 motherboard was designed from the ground up for OEM customization. Standard features include 4 MB of main memory, ten I/O expansion slots, two serial ports, one parallel port, one AT-style keyboard connector, and one PS/2-style mouse connector.

On-board memory can be expanded to 8 MB using SIMM memory technology. Additional add-in memory—up to 32 MB—is available utilizing Intel's proprietary 32-bit memory bus and Intel add-in memory cards. The maximum memory configuration is 40 MB of high-speed memory.

The high-speed CPU easily supports heavy peripheral I/O traffic. The Model 303 system configuration contains 4 half-height and 2 full-height peripheral bays to support the increased storage demands of high-performance applications such as servers, CAD/CAM, and graphics. A power sequencing board supports smooth simultaneous power-up of multiple peripherals. And, the 303.5 watt power supply powers the loading of all eight peripheral bays, as well as the ten I/O slots on the baseboard.

FULL FCC EMISSION COMPLIANCE

The Model 303 baseboard has been designed for emission suppression and complies fully with FCC Class B emission requirements, a significant accomplishment at 33 MHz. The Model 303 system chassis also helps contain emissions. Emissions reduction facilitates product integration where stringent FCC-B/VDE-B compliance is required.

WORLDWIDE SERVICE AND SUPPORT

Multiply your sales potential in new markets throughout the world using Intel's worldwide service organization to install and maintain your system at your customer's site.

Field services include product installation, on-site maintenance, including third-party peripherals, per-call or carry-in repair. Network installation and configuration services are also available.

Factory services include system-level, board or peripheral repair or exchange. Spare parts sales and advance service diagnostics are also available.

SPECIFICATIONS

BOARD

CPU	386 microprocessor at 33 MHz
Floating point	387 MHz socket
Motherboard Memory	
Standard RAM	4 MB SIMM
Maximum RAM	8 MB SIMM

32-bit Add-in Memory (via 4, 8, 16 MB add-in cards)

Maximum add-in memory	32 MB
Maximum system memory	40 MB
Cycle Time	100 nsec
Error Detection	Byte Parity

64 KByte cache, 0 wait state execution on read hit (direct mapped, posted write through)

I/O EXPANSION SLOTS

- 2 8/16/32 bit slots (AT-32/ISA)
- 7 8/16 bit slots (ISA)
- 1 8 bit slot (ISA)

SPECIFICATIONS

BOARD SPECIFICATIONS (Continued)

I/O

- 2 serial ports (9 pin)
- 1 parallel port (Centronics compatible, 25 pin)
- 1 AT style keyboard connector
- 1 PS/2 style mouse connector

Board Dimensions

13″ × 13.6″

Electrical

Input:

AC Voltage/Frequency	115 V/60 Hz 230 V/50 Hz (externally configurable)

Output DC Voltage:

+5V	35.0 A maximum continuous
+12V	10.0 A maximum continuous (14A peak for 15 seconds)
−12V	0.5 A maximum continuous
−5V	0.5 A maximum continuous
Total Power Output:	303.5 Watts (switching)

SYSTEM

Floppy Disk Options

Footprint	3.5″
Capacity	1.44 MB
Footprint	5.25″
Capacity	1.2 MB

SCSI Winchester Disk Option

Footprint	5.25″
Capacity	170 MB
Average Seek Time	14 ms

SCSI Tape Drive Option

Footprint	5.25″
Capacity	150 MB

4 half-height and 2 full-height peripheral bays

Front mounted recessed reset switch

SYSTEM DIMENSIONS

Height	24.4 inches
Width	6.8 inches
Depth	27.75 inches
Base System Weight	67 pounds (without peripherals)

REGULATIONS

Meets or exceeds the following requirements:

Safety

U.S.	UL 478 5th edition
Canada	CSA C22.2 No. 154
Europe	IEC 435 and VDE 0806

EMI/RFI

U.S. and Canada	FCC47 CFR Part 15 Subpart J Class B
Europe	VDE 0871 Level B

INTEL i486™ MICROCOMPUTER MODEL 403E

281323-1

33 MHz i486™ EISA SYSTEM FOR HIGH-PERFORMANCE APPLICATIONS

Take advantage of the combined performance of a 33 MHz i486™ processor and the 32-bit EISA bus with Intel's MicroComputer Model 403E. The Model 403E system features 10 EISA expansion slots, an external cache option, and a burst mode interface supporting up to 64 MB of onboard RAM. Combine that with Intel's world-class quality, service and support, and you have an ideal platform for today's high-powered server and workstation applications.

BOARD-LEVEL FEATURES

- i486™ microprocessor running at 33 MHz
- 8 Kbytes of 4-way set-associative on-chip cache memory with zero wait- states
- 10 EISA expansion slots (8-slot version available also)
- Up to 64 MB of onboard SIMM memory
- On-board floppy disk controller
- Weitek 4167 socket
- Phoenix Technologies ROM BIOS
- Optional secondary cache

i486™ and 386™ are trademarks of Intel Corporation.
OS/2™ are trademarks of International Business Machines Corporation.
MS-DOS™ and MS OS/2™ are trademarks of Microsoft Corporation.
UNIX™ is a trademark of AT&T Bell Laboratories.

September 1991
Order Number: 281323-002

FEATURES

SYSTEM-LEVEL FEATURES

- Four half-height, two full height bays
- 1.44 MB 3.5″ flexible disk drive
- 1.2 MB 5.25″ flexible disk drive
- 170 MB SCSI hard disk drive with EISA bus master controller
- 150 MB SCSI tape drive
- Full FCC Class B emission certification
- 396W Autoranging Power Supply

OPTIONS

- 101-key enhanced keyboard
- Intel worldwide service/maintenance/network support
- MS-DOS*, MS OS/2* and UNIX* V 3.2 software

MAXIMUM PERFORMANCE AND CONFIGURABILITY

The Model 403E is a high-powered platform that can handle the most demanding application requirements. The 33 MHz i486 CPU is ideal for CAD, desktop publishing, image processing and other compute-intensive applications. The system can be configured with up to 64 MB of 80 ns SIMMs to support large numbers of users and today's memory-hungry software.

The 32-bit EISA bus provides a high-speed datapath that can accommodate the combinations of disk and communications controllers found in large file and network servers. Additionally, full compatibility with ISA (AT) boards is a standard feature of systems based on the EISA bus standard, including the Model 403E. This preserves your investment in the many boards available for ISA systems.

You have complete flexibility in configuring Model 403E-based systems. You can get your product to market quickly by purchasing systems that are completely integrated with peripherals, or in basic configurations with a chassis. Or, if you wish to develop the system packaging yourself, the motherboard is available separately in either an 8- or 10-slot versions.

A configuration utility is provided to identify all EISA boards to the system. When a new EISA board is added into a Model 403E system, the utility ensures that the board is properly configured and places important identification information in a non-volatile RAM store located on the motherboard.

FLOORSTAND CONFIGURATION IDEAL FOR SERVERS

Configured with ten expansion slots, a floorstand chassis with 4 half-height bays, 2 full-height bays, and a 396W autoranging power supply, the Model 403E provides the OEM with an ideal platform for large server and I/O-intensive applications.

The cabinet design allows for hidden peripheral and network cabling connections at the top rear of the chassis with an easy access door. Ease-of-use features include a power switch and reset switches on the front bezel.

281323-2

INDUSTRY-STANDARD SOFTWARE

The Model 403E runs industry-standard operating systems like MS-DOS, MS OS/2 and UNIX, preserving your existing software investment and guaranteeing a smooth growth path from 386™ to i486 architectures. Intel further reduces your software development and support costs through extensive hardware and software compatibility testing.

WORLDWIDE SERVICE AND SUPPORT

Multiply your sales potential in new markets throughout the world using Intel's worldwide service organization to install and maintain your system at your customers' sites. A flexible warranty program provides OEMs with the option of a one-year depot repair warranty or a 90-day onsite service plan.

Support contracts are available for hardware/software engineering assistance; repair and maintenance for Intel and non-Intel systems and peripherals; network design, installation and maintenance; and training.

SPECIFICATIONS

Factory services include system-level, board or peripheral repair or exchange. Spare parts sales and advance service diagnostics are also available.

BOARD

CPU	i486 microprocessor at 33 MHz
Main memory	
Structure	Interleaved, up to eight 2 MB and/or 8 MB SIMMs (may be mixed but must be added in like pairs)
Standard options	4 MB 8 MB
Maximum	64 MB
Cache memory	
Internal	8 Kbytes on-chip 4-way set-associative
Optional External Cache	
On-Board Floppy Controller	
Board dimensions	13.0″ × 13.6″ (33.0 cm × 34.5 cm)

I/O EXPANSION SLOTS

Ten 32-bit EISA slots	Six bus master slots Four bus slave slots
Optional 8-Slot Motherboard:	
Eight 32-bit EISA slots (motherboard only	Six bus master slots Two bus slave slots

I/O

Two serial ports (9-pin)
Two parallel ports (Centronics-compatible, 25-pin)
One PS/2-style keyboard connector
One PS/2-style mouse connector

ELECTRICAL

Input:	
AC Voltage/Frequency	115V/60 Hz 230V/50 Hz (automatically configured)
Total Power Output	
+5V	45A maximum continuous
+12V	13A maximum continuous
−12V	1A maximum continuous
−5V	.5A maximum continuous
Total power output	396 Watts (switching)

SYSTEM ENVIRONMENT

Ambient Temperature	
Operating:	10° to 35°C
Relative Humidity	
Operating:	To 85%
Altitude	
Operating:	To 10,000 feet
Static Discharge:	7.5Kv max

SYSTEM

Floppy Disk Options	
Footprint	3.5″ half-height
Capacity	1.44 MB
Footprint	5.25″ half-height
Capacity	1.2 MB
SCSI Hard Disk Option	
Footprint	5.25″ full-height
Capacity	170 MB
Average Seek Time	14 ms
SCSI Tape Option	
Footprint	5.25″ half-height
Capacity	150 MB

SYSTEM DIMENSIONS

Height	24.4 inches (62.0 cm)
Width	6.8 inches (17.3 cm)
Depth	27.75 inches (70.5 cm)
Base system weight	67 pounds (30.5 kg) without peripherals

REGULATIONS

Meets or exceeds the following requirements:

Safety	
USA	UL 478, Edition 5
Canada	CSA C22.2 No. 220
Europe	IEC 950 & IEC 380
EMI/RFI	
USA	FCC Class B; CFR 47 Part 15 Subpart J
Canada	DOC; CRC c. 1374, Class B
Europe	VDE 087 1 Level B

Intel386™ INDUSTRIAL MICROCOMPUTER: Model 302i

281124–1

A RELIABLE, RACK-MOUNT MICROCOMPUTER

For systems integrators, equipment OEMs, or others needing a highly reliable, ISA-compatible PC, Intel's Industrial Microcomputer provides a 25 MHz Intel386™ performance microprocessor in an easily embeddable 19″ rack-mount package. Multiple fans provide filtered air for cool and reliable operation at temperatures and in harsh environments where ordinary PC's can fail. A steel and plastic door provides environmental protection to the front access peripherals and protects the power and reset switch from accidental operation. Eight I/O expansion slots, 230 watt power supply, and up to 40MB or zero wait-state memory allow extensive configuration flexibility to meet the demands of your product or project.

The system is designed with highly reliabile components that are easy to integrate or replace with few tools. The motherboard is mounted on a slide-in tray, and can be replaced in 6.5 minutes. To customize the system to your exact application need, the door's plastic panel insert is removable.

For any application needing rugged reliability with PC- compatibility, the Intel Model 302i is your solution!

Features

- 25 MHz Intel386™ microprocessor with cache
- ISA (PC-AT) compatibility
- Rugged 19″ rack-mounted chassis
- Shock-mounted 5.25″ peripheral bay
- 3.5″ front-access peripheral bay
- 5.25″ front-access peripheral bay
- Steel and plastic protective door
- Easy front access filter
- Multiple fans provide positive air pressure
- Eight I/O expansion slots
- Two serial ports, one parallel port
- I/O board retention bracket

October 1991
Order Number: 281124-002

FEATURES

The Industrial PC Model 302i is loaded with the features most needed for the factory control environment.

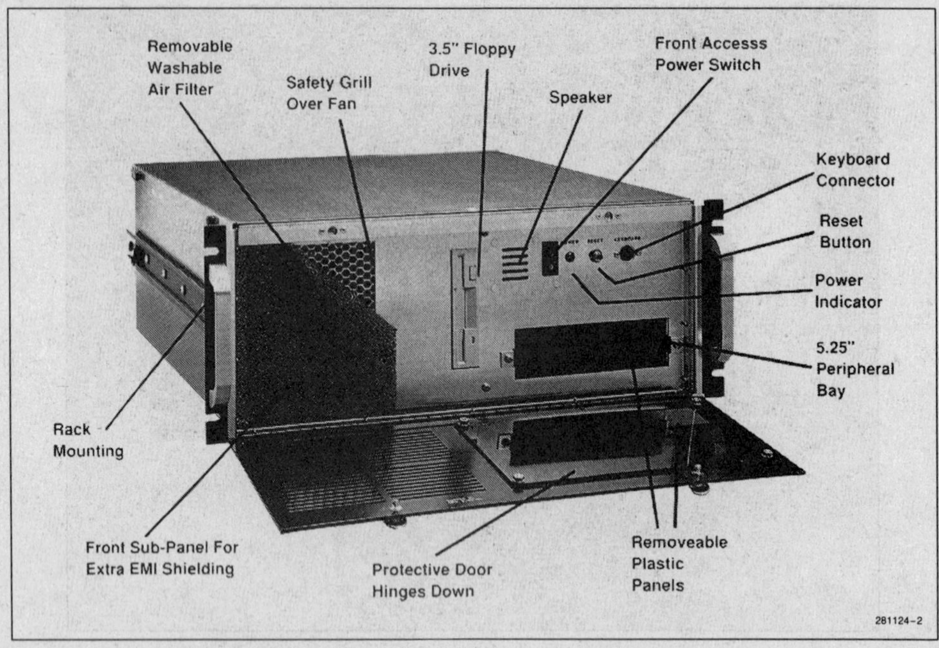

281124-2

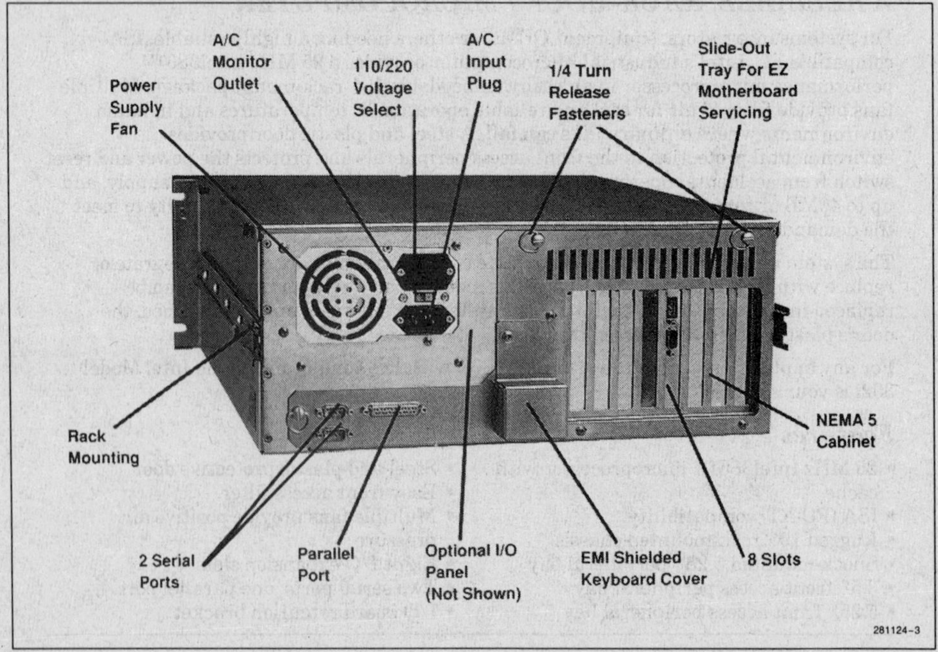

281124-3

FEATURES

One-Year Warranty

Intel microcomputers are backed by a one-year system return warranty. Factory services include system, board or peripheral repair or exchange.

Worldwide Service and Support

Intel maintains a worldwide network of service and repair facilities to keep you and your customers up and running. Should you need design support, our international Systems Engineering orgainzation is available to assist you.

Ease of Serviceability

Elapsed Time: 10 sec.

281124-4

Remove to cover using one $1/4$ turn screw and four thumb screws.

Elapsed Time: 20 sec.

281124-5

Remove controller board cables reset cable and speaker cable.

Elapsed Time: 40 sec.

281124-6

Remove EMI shield, unplug key board, slide tray out and disconnect power cables.

Elapsed Time: 60 sec.

281124-7

Slide motherboard tray out completely*. Remove I/O cards.

Elapsed Time: 2 min.

281124-8

Remove parallel and serial cables. Remove motherboard with 9 philips head screws with captive washers.

Reassembly Time: 4:30 min.

281124-9

Reasseble the 302i in the reverse sequence.

* In critical applications the slide out tray with I/O cards would be the field replaceable unit (FPU).

FEATURES

Easily Removable Hard Disk and Fan Units

Unlike many other industrial PCs the hard disk and fan units of the 302i are removable using simple tools as this sequence shows. (These steps not included in the timed sequence shown above.

Additional Time: 30 sec.

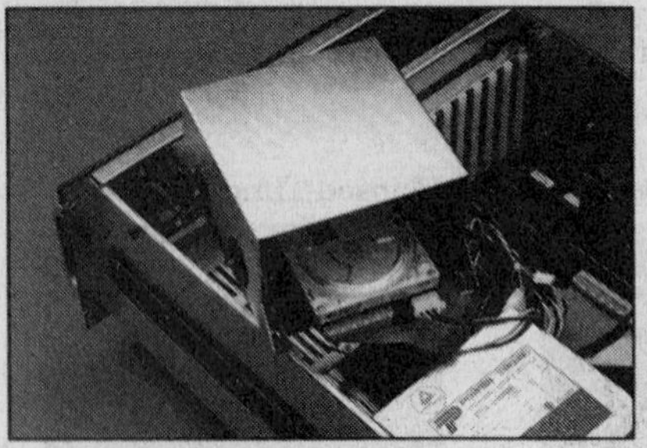

281124–10

The hard disk removes with 4 screws.

Additional Time: 20 sec.

281124–11

The fan lifts out after removing 4 screws.

Drive Positions

Front access	1 3.5″
Peripherals	1 5.25″ half-height
Shock-mounted peripherals	1 5.25″ full-height

Electrical

Power Supply Type	Switching
AC Voltage/ Frequency	115V 60 Hz or 230V 50 Hz switch selectable
DC Power	230W
+5V	23.0A max. continuous
+12V	9.0A max. continuous
−12V	0.5A max. continuous
−5V	0.5A max. continuous

Environment

Ambient Temperature

Operating	
System	0°C to 50°C
Hard Disk	4°C to 50°C
Floppy	4°C to 50°C
Non-operating	
System	−40°C to 70°C
Hard Disk	−40°C to 60°C
Floppy	−22°C to 60°C

Maximum Temperature Gradient

Operating	10°C/hr.
Non-operating	20°C/hr.

SPECIFICATIONS

Relative Humidity (non-condensing)

Operating	
System	0%–85%
Hard Disk	8%–85%
Floppy	20%–80%
Non-Operating	
System	0%–95%
Hard Disk/Floppy	5%–95%

Elevation

Operating	
System	TBD
Hard Disk	−200 ft. (61M)–10,000 ft. (3000M)
Floppy	−1000 ft–16,500 ft.
Non-operating	
System	TBD
Hard Disk	−200 ft.–40,000 ft. (12000M)
Floppy	0–50,000 ft.

Vibration (all three orthrogonal axes)

Operating	
System	TBD
Hard Disk	1.5G 10–100
Floppy	1.0G 100–200 0.5G 200 Hz–600 Hz
Non-operating	
System	TBD
Hard Disk	5 Hz–500 Hz Sine Wave P-P, 2.0G
Floppy	—

Shock

Operating	
System	TBD
Hard Disk	6G ½ Sine, 11 ms
Floppy	5G ½ Sine, 11 ms
Non-Operating	
System	TBD
Hard Disk/Floppy	60G ½ Sine, 11 ms
Floppy	60G ½ Sine, 11 ms

Physical Characteristics

Dimensions	7″ H × 19″ W × 21″ D
Weight	42 lbs. (est.)

Regulations

Safety	
US	UL 1950
Canada	CSA C22.2 No. 154
Europe	IEC 435 & VDE 0806
EMI/RFI	
US and Canada	FCC 47 CFR Part 15 subpart J, Class A
Europe	VDE 0871 Level B

Reliability

CPU w/4 MB RAM	162,597 hrs. @ 25°C
Fan	50,000 hrs. @ 25°C
Power Supply	50,000 hrs. @ 25°C
Hard Disk	50,000 hrs. @ 25°C

PC PLATFORMS SOFTWARE PRODUCTS

280952–1

SOFTWARE PRODUCTS FOR FAST TIME TO MARKET

Intel has a wide range of software products and services to support microcomputer OEMs. These include MS-DOS*, MS* OS/2* and Microsoft Windows*. All have been tested and evaluated to meet Intel's high standard of compatibility and reliability. With Intel's software, you can be assured the highest quality software for Intel386™ and Intel486™ microprocessor-based platforms.

FEATURES

- Industry-standard software
- Proven software reduces risk
- Complete end-user packages with documentation
- Intel-supplied device drivers for integrated systems
- End-user break-the-seal license
- Security-sealed; guaranteed virus-free
- Optimized for Intel386 and Intel486 platforms

November 1991
Order Number: 280952-004

PC PLATFORMS SOFTWARE PRODUCTS

MICROSOFT MS-DOS 5.0 OPERATING SYSTEM*

MS-DOS 5.0 is the most user-friendly and memory efficient DOS ever. On Intel platforms, MS-DOS 5.0 will run in extended memory, and thereby free an average of 45 kbytes of conventional memory for applications. That's why it's the perfect DOS for Windows; there's more room for the Windows program itself and for large spreadsheets, databases, and graphics files.

MS-DOS 5.0 is the easiest-to-use DOS to date, especially when combined with our MS-Mouse. The new shell features drop-down menus. Browse through options or "drag" files with a mouse from one directory to another. An improved on-line help makes DOS easier to use. New commands help users to recover from disasters, including accidentally deleted files and formatted hard disks.

MS-DOS 5.0 features include:

- Advanced memory management, including running DOS in extended memory and TSRs in high memory
- Support for large hard disk partitions
- New shell program for graphical file management
- "DOSKEY" a special program providing keyboard macros capability
- Instant "hot key" switching between applications with MS-DOS 5.0 task switching
- Task swapping the ability to press a "hot key" combination to switch between applications
- Complete on-line help
- Many new or enhanced commands

MICROSOFT MS OS/2 OPERATING SYSTEM*

Microsoft MS OS/2 Release 1.21 is a single-user multitasking operating system for the Intel386 and Intel486 platforms. It gives users preemptive multitasking capabilities, memory protection among applications, a standardized graphical user interface, a high- performance file system (2-10 times the speed of the MS-DOS file system), dynamic data exchange between applications, dynamic data linking and interprocess communication. MS OS/2 also gives you access to the wealth of MS-DOS software using the MS-DOS compatibility mode.

The MS OS/2 operating system has numerous features that make it an excellent choice for large-memory applications. It eliminates the 640 Kbyte memory constraints by allowing you to address up to 16 MB of user memory. MS OS/2 is the host operating system required to run LAN Manager revision 2.0.

MS OS/2 also provides a standard graphical user interface. The MS OS/2 Presentation Manager represents the state of the art in graphical user interfaces for personal workstations.

Intel's adaptation of MS OS/2* contains the following features:

- Preemptive multitasking
- Memory protection
- Presentation Manager
- MS-DOS compatibility
- Optional high-performance file system
- Intel386 and Intel486 architecture support
- Dynamic data exchange
- Memory support up to 16 MB

MICROSOFT WINDOWS OPERATING ENVIRONMENT*

Microsoft Windows is an extension to the MS-DOS operating system which brings an easy graphical interface to users who run DOS applications. A common user interface among Windows specific applications makes programs easier to learn and use and greatly simplifies interaction with the operating system. Multiple on- screen windows allow multitasking with instant switching between applications simply by pointing with the mouse, along with cut-and- paste of data between applications. The Intel MS-Mouse is a perfect companion for the Windows environment.

Some of the key features of Microsoft Windows are:

- Presentation-style graphics interface
- Time-slice multitasking
- Access to extended Intel386 and Intel486 features
- Up to 40 MB of Virtual memory support
- 3D style human interface
- Advanced networking support for files and printers
- Advanced RAM disk and disk cache
- "File Manager" MS-DOS shell
- Complete compatibility with non-Windows specific applications

14

PC PLATFORMS SOFTWARE PRODUCTS

MICROSOFT MOUSE

The Microsoft mouse is the perfect compliment to today's graphical operating systems, including OS/2 Presentation Manager, Windows, and even the MS-DOS shell. It also contains device drivers for use with many industry standard programs containing built-in mouse support.

- 400 dpi resolution tracking
- PS/2 or 9-pin serial connection
- User profile utility and configuration software
- MS-DOS installation utility and mouse driver

SCSI DEVICE DRIVERS FOR DOS, OS/2, AND NETWARE

Intel SCSI device driver packages contain drivers needed to provide hard disk and tape support for Intel system platforms. Our SCSI drivers optimize performance of hard drives using our SCSI hard disk controllers when running DOS. In addition, SCSI driver software is required for users running Novell Netware and MS OS/2.

For Intel platforms with built-in tape drives, special SCSI driver packages include the Sytos tape operating system which gives tape backup and restore capabilities in both interactive and batch modes.

Key features of the SCSI device drivers products include:

- Hard disk drivers for MS OS/2, Novell Netware, and MS-DOS
- Extensive documentation
- Sytos Plus Tape operating system software for MS OS/2 and MS-DOS (in certain packages only)

Separate SCSI driver packages are currently available for Intel EISA bus systems (Model 403) and Intel ISA bus systems (Models 303 and 401). As new Intel system platforms are available, check with Intel to ensure the proper match of driver package with hardware platform.

JAPANESE SOFTWARE SUPPORT

The Japanese AX MS-DOS and Microsoft Windows kit support the Kanji-Katakana character set. The AXDOSKIT includes a Japanese graphics card, Japanese keyboard, localized MS-DOS, Windows and character set conversion software. The AXDOSKIT supports all of the Intel PC platforms hardware. English-language installation instructions are included for non-Japanese OEM installation.

Japanese AX DOS kit includes:

- International break-the-seal licence
- AX MS-DOS 3.21 with 5.25″ and 3.5″ media
- AX Windows 2.11 with 5.25″ and 3.5″ media
- AX-compatible Kanji-Katakana keyboard (105 key)
- AX-compatible graphics card (JEGA style)

Keyboard

Kana-Katakana keyboard support English and Japanese character sets. Supports double-byte character encription and encoding required for AX support. Meets or exceeds Japanese emission standard. FCC Class B equivalent.

JEGA

Japanese Enhanced Graphics Adaptor board. Supports U.S. EGA and double-byte KANJI character set for AX support. Meets or exceeds Japanese emission standard; FCC Class B equivalent.

SPECIFICATIONS

SUPPORTED HARDWARE

All Intel software fully supports the Intel386 and Intel486 platforms and is available in either 5.25″ or 3.5″ media for maximum OEM flexibility.

SERVICE/SUPPORT/TRAINING

Intel provides resellers with complete technical support through its IntelTechDirect™ service program. IntelTechDirect provides access to Intel experts via telephone, on- line bulletin boards, and product bulletins. All software packages are fully warranted for media replacement. IntelTechDirect provides you with your best information and access to software release updates.

ORDERING INFORMATION

If your development schedule is short or your performance criteria high, consider Intel training and consultation services, offered jointly with Microsoft University. Training courses include the MS OS/2 software development kit (SDK) and the device driver development kit (DDDK). Intel also has a staff of experienced software engineers who can be contracted by the hour or month to be a part of your project team. Call your local Intel sales office for more information.

Intel's software products may be ordered with any Intel386 and Intel486 platform. Software has a five-unit minimum purchase, which enables Intel to offer competitive software pricing. Certain products come with five units per carton; others are individual units with a five-unit minimum purchase. Most software purchases require completion of an OEM software distribution agreement. The following product descriptions include order quantities:

MS-DOS

MSDOSF1	MS-DOS R5.0 on 5.25″ media. Single unit; 5-unit/order minimum.
MSDOSM1	MS-DOS R5.0 on 3.5″ media. Single unit; 5- unit/order minimum.

MS OS/2

NOTE: Check price guide for current version

MSOS2F	MS OS/2 1.21 on 5.25″ (1.2MB) diskettes with manuals. Each unit = 5 copies.
MSOS2M	MS OS/2 1.21 on 3.5″ (1.44MB) diskettes with manuals. Each unit = 5 copies.

MICROSOFT WINDOWS

NOTE: Check price guide for most current version

MWIN386F	MS Windows 3.0 and manual (5.25″ media). Each unit = 5 copies.
MWIN386M	MS Windows 3.0 and manual (3.5″ media). Each unit = 5 copies.

DEVICE DRIVER SOFTWARE

NOTE: Be sure device driver is matched to correct system product.

EISAUTIL	DPT device drivers for MS OS/2, MS-DOS and Novell Netware, user documentation and tape driver software. Use for EISA platforms. Single unit.
EISAUTILNT	Same as EISAUTIL, but without tape support.
UTILITIES	Adaptech 1542 device drivers for MS OS/2, MS- DOS, and Novell Netware, user documentation and tape driver software. Use for ISA bus platforms. Single unit.
UTILITIESNT	Same as for UTILITIES but without tape support.

OTHER PRODUCTS

MMOUSES	MS serial-PS/2 400 dpi mouse and manual (both 5.25″ and 3.5″ media). Each unit = 5 mice.
EISACONFIG	EISA Configuration Utility (403E) (both 5.25″ and 3.5″ media). Each unit = 1 copy.
TECHDIRECT	Technical support service. Includes one-year subscription to iPUB, iPAN, and access to iPALS for technical phone support.

JAPANESE SOFTWARE SUPPORT

AXDOSKITR3.21	Contains dual-media software, graphics card, keyboard, and localized language materials. English installation instructions are included.

Local Area Network Boards and Software

15

15

OpenNET™ LOCAL AREA NETWORK FAMILY

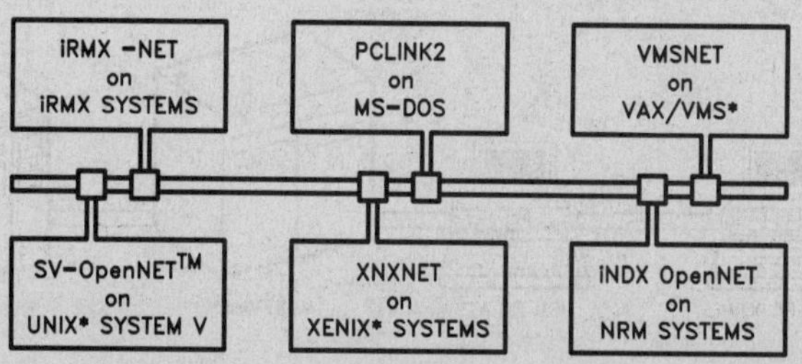

280669-1

OpenNET™: THE COMPLETE OPEN NETWORK SOLUTION

The OpenNET™ family provides the OEM with complete *Open Network* solutions for an enterprise-wide, multi-vendor network based on international standards.

FEATURES

- Interoperability between the factory, office, and engineering environments
- Complete hardware and software network solutions
- Ongoing customer support through extensive training and application development

GUIDE TO THE OpenNET™ PRODUCTS

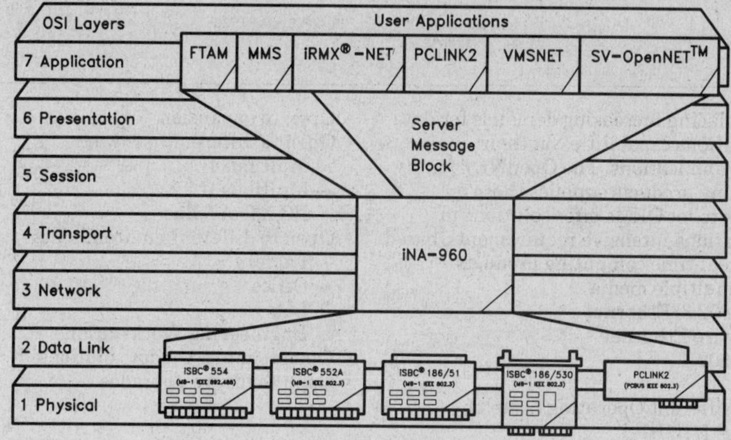

280669-2

15

*UNIX is a registered trademark of AT&T
MS-DOS, XENIX are trademarks of Microsoft Corporation
DECnet, VAX/VMS, MicroVAX, UNIBUS, Q-bus are trademarks of Digital Equipment Corporation
sSXM120NETKIT, sPCLINK2NIA, sPCLINK2, sPCLINKIIBD, sPCLINK2TWKIT, sPCLINK2DEVKIT, sSBC18651, and sSBX586 are manufactured by Intel Singapore, Ltd.
pSVNET552AKIT, pSVNET530KIT, pSBC552A, pSXM552A, pSBC186530, and pDCM9111 are manufactured by Intel Puerto Rico, Inc.

December 1990
Order Number: 280669-002

OpenNET™ OVERVIEW

OpenNET™ MEANS OPEN NETWORKS

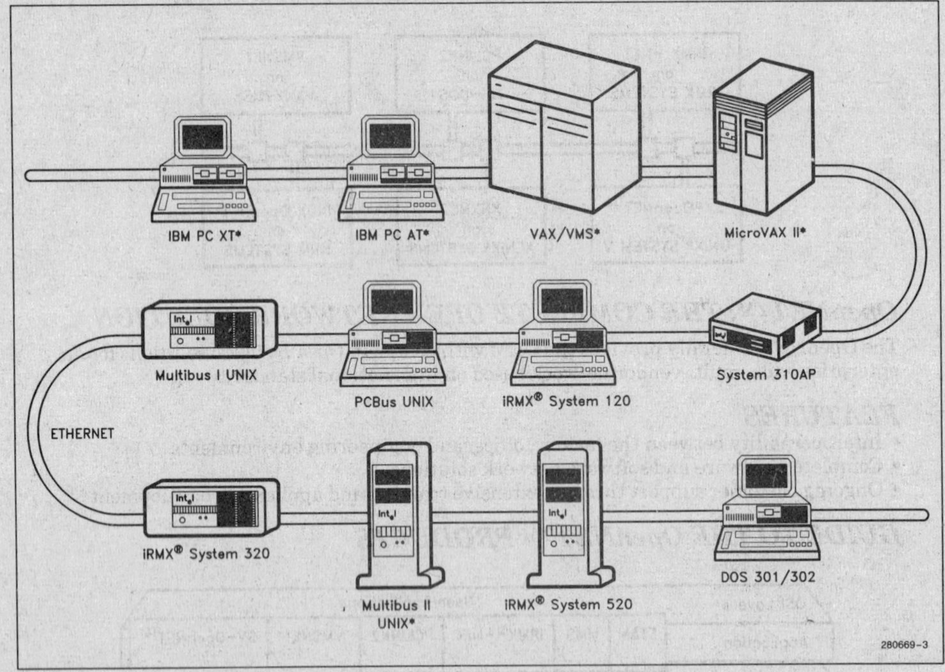

Users are placing increasing demands for data communications capabilities on their computing applications. The OpenNET family of networking products supplies those capabilities to let OEMs offer solutions to communications-intensive requirements, based on Intel's real-time computing products.

- Open to multiple media
  - IEEE 802.3/Ethernet
  - Thin-wire Ethernet
  - IEEE 802.4
  - X.25
- Open to different Operating Systems
  - iRMX® I/II/III
  - MS-DOS*
  - PC-DOS
  - UNIX SYSTEM V*
  - VAX/VMS*
  - XENIX*
  - iNDX
- Open to expansion
- Open to different hardware
  - Multibus I
  - Multibus II
  - PC XT/AT Bus
- Open to different environments
  - Factory
  - Office
  - Lab
  - Engineering Workstation
- Open to multi-vendor solutions
- Open to future upgrades

OpenNET™ OVERVIEW

OpenNET™ ARCHITECTURE

Intel's OpenNET communications architecture applies networking standards to offer an open network. Open connectivity lets Multibus-based systems talk to systems such as IBM PCs and VAX minicomputers.

OpenNET™ DELIVERS INTERNATIONAL STANDARDS

The OpenNET products use ISO and CCITT Data Communications Standards for the Physical, Data Link, Network, and Transport layers of the Open System Interconnection (OSI) model. The Session, Presentation, and Application layers use the Server Message Block (SMB) protocol promulgated by Intel, Microsoft, and IBM. The SMB protocol is used by Microsoft and IBM in their PC networks.

SMB: TRUE TRANSPARENT REMOTE FILE ACCESS

The OpenNET Server Message Block protocol allows applications to access remote files as if they were local. This consistent view of the file system throughout the network allows distributed processing of existing applications without change. The SMB protocol protects the user's data with file security established by either the consumer or server system.

OpenNET™ WILL FOLLOW THE STANDARDS, TRANSPARENTLY

As the OSI standards evolve, Intel will conform to them. The user's application will be protected from the changing protocols because the OpenNET Interface ("\\" on DOS or "//" on XENIX and UNIX) will NOT change. This will allow applications to move to the OSI standards with little or no modification. The OpenNET products will allow the user to run all current applications that use the OpenNET Interface on either the SMB or the OSI protocols.

OpenNET™ SUPPORT FOR DISKLESS WORKSTATION

For certain real-time applications, it is desirable that a networked system not have a local mass storage device such as a hard disk. One example is harsh environments such as factory floor process control, where rotating media can cause system reliability problems. Another example is financial workstations, where stock and market information must be updated in real-time on a centralized file server and accessed by diskless trader workstations.

The Boot Server system responds to network boot requests from diskless Boot Consumer systems and downloads both the appropriate operating system and communications software over the network to boot the diskless system. With the diskless system booted, the File Server system provides the diskless system with network access to mass storage devices. The Boot Server and File Server can reside in separate systems or in the same system on the network.

OpenNET™ VIRTUAL TERMINAL CAPABILITY

The OpenNET product family supports a Virtual Terminal (VT) capability. This feature allows a terminal or PC user to "login", over the network, as an interactive user under the remote node's operating system. VT is purchased separately as an optional application program.

All OpenNET™ PRODUCTS BACKED BY INTEL CUSTOMER SUPPORT

All Intel software products include Intel's Software Support for a 90 day period immediately following the licensing and receipt of the product.

STANDARD SOFTWARE SUPPORT INCLUDES

- Product updates
- Subscription Service and technical product information distributed via:
  - — Monthly issue of *Comments* newsletter
  - — Quarterly Troubleshooting Guides
  - — Software Problem Report (SPR) Service
- Technical Information Phone Service (iTIPS™) toll-free hotline
- Membership in Insite™ User Program Library

ADDITIONAL SERVICES AVAILABLE INCLUDE

- Consulting services on a long or short-term basis (Systems Engineering Support)
- Worldwide training workshops on a wide variety of Intel products
- A full range of hardware maintenance services for end users or OEM/VAR customers

iRMX®-NET OpenNET™ NETWORKING SOFTWARE

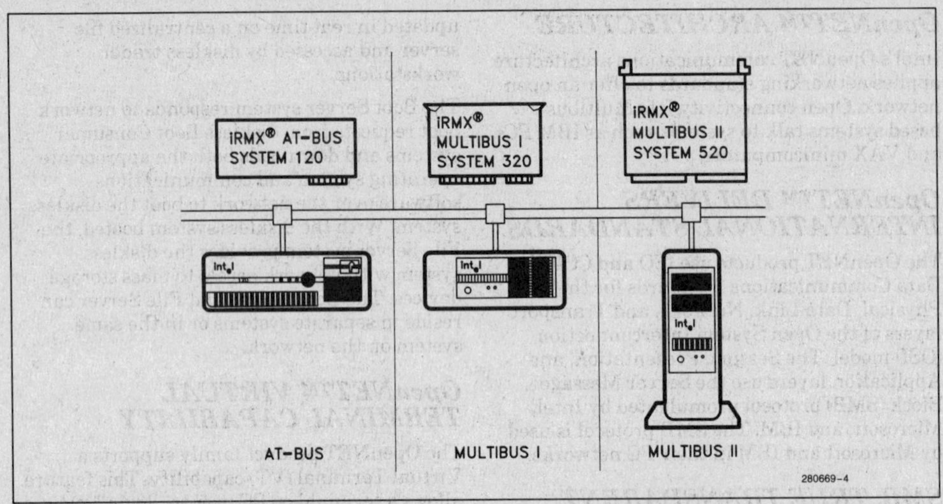

COMPLETE OpenNET™ SOLUTION FOR REAL-TIME SYSTEMS

Real-Time computer systems require a real-time operating system. The family of iRMX operating systems from Intel is the world's most popular operating system software for real-time systems.

Many real-time applications require network communication. Intel's iRMX-NET Release 3.1 delivers a rich set of networking capabilities and a full range of iRMX platform support:

- Transparent Network File Access
- Transport and Distributed Name Server Software with Programmatic Access
- iRMX System 120 (AT-bus), 320 (Multibus I) and 520 (Multibus II) Connections
- Remote Boot for Diskless Systems

Networked iRMX systems serve in a wide range of real-time application areas including data acquisition, factory automation, financial workstations, military, medical instrumentation, simulation and process control.

TRANSPARENT NETWORK FILE ACCESS

iRMX-NET implements the NFA protocol to provide transparent file access capabilities among iRMX, DOS, VAX/VMS, UNIX, XENIX and iNDX systems on the OpenNET network. Remote files are accessed as if they resided on the local iRMX system. iRMX-NET can be configured as a network file consumer, file server, or both, depending on the application's requirements.

The iRMX operating system provides a rich set of human interface commands and system calls for accessing local files. With the addition of iRMX-NET, these commands and system calls are transparently extended to remote access as well. Transparency means that applications using the iRMX Human Interface commands or BIOS system calls do not need to know whether the files they access reside locally or on some remote system.

iRMX®-NET OpenNET™ NETWORKING SOFTWARE

OSI TRANSPORT AND DISTRIBUTED NAME SERVER WITH PROGRAMMMATIC INTERFACE

The iRMX-NET R3.1 product includes iNA 960 R3 OSI Transport and Network software preconfigured for a variety of Intel Network Interface Adapters.

iRMX-NET R3.1 also includes the iRMX-NET Distributed Name Server software. The Distributed Name Server software maintains and provides access to a network directory database. The database is distributed across the network with each system maintaining its own logical piece of the directory. The Distributed Name Server software provides a full set of network directory services and is used to perform such tasks as logical name to network address mapping for establishing network connections between systems.

The combination of transparent network file access with iRMX commands and system calls, plus direct programmatic access to the iNA 960 Transport and iRMX-NET Distributed Name Server software gives the programmer a powerful set of capabilities for developing real-time network applications.

iRMX® SYSTEM 120, 320 AND 520 CONNECTIONS

iRMX-NET R3.1 provides networking support for the full range of Intel real-time Systems, from the low-cost AT-Bus System 120, through the Multibus I System 320, to the high-end multiprocessing Multibus II System 520. iRMX-NET R3.1 also supports iRMX board-level designs built around Intel's family of host CPU boards and Network Interface Adapters. Consistent operating system and networking software interfaces provide for easy development of network applications that span the various iRMX platforms.

REMOTE BOOT FOR DISKLESS SYSTEMS

iRMX-NET R3.1 supports networked diskless systems by providing network Boot Consumer, Boot Server and File Server capabilities.

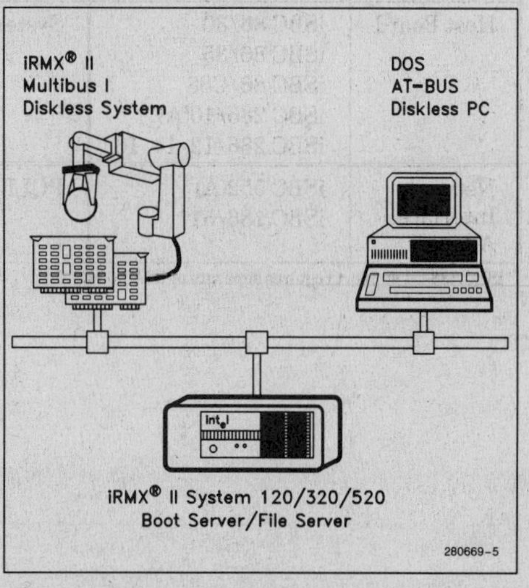

PRODUCT CODES

RMXINETSW	iRMX-NET Networking Software for the iRMX I operating system.
RMXIINETSW	iRMX-NET Networking Software for the iRMX II operating system.
sSXM120NETKIT	Preconfigured iRMX-NET and sPCLINK2 for networking iRMX and DOS on the System 120.
RMXIIINETSW	iRMX-NET Networking Software for the iRMX III operating system.

15

iRMX®-NET OpenNET™ NETWORKING SOFTWARE

REAL-TIME BOARD AND SYSTEM LEVEL SUPPORT

	iRMX® I	iRMX® II/III		
	Multibus I	AT-BUS	Multibus I	Multibus II
System	System 310AP	System 310	System 310AP, 320	System 520
Host Board	iSBC 86/30 iSBC 86/35 iSBC 86/C38 iSBC 286/10(A) iSBC 286/12, 14, 16	System 120	iSBC 286/10A iSBC 286/12, 14, 16 iSBC 386/12 iSBC 386/2X iSBC 386 3X	iSBC 386/116 iSBC 386/120 iSBC 386/258
Network Interface Adapter	iSBC 552(A) iSBC 186/51*	PCLINK2	iSBC 552(A)	iSBC 186/530

*iSBC 186/51 support requires separate of iNA 960 R3.0

PCLINK2, NetBIOS, AND MS-NET ACCESS FOR THE PC

COMPLETE OpenNET™ SOLUTION FOR THE PC

Users of IBM PC AT, PC XT and other compatible computers can access Intel's OpenNET networking family through the OpenNET PCL2 hardware and software products. The hardware connection is provided by an 80186/82586-based intelligent expansion board, the PCL2 Network Interface Adapter (PCL2NIA). The software package incorporates: MS-NET for transparent file access under DOS, iNA 961, NetBIOS interface, dynamic name resolution and user-friendly installation software.

The NetBIOS interface provides the flexibility to use the PCL2NIA with commercially available NetBIOS compatible applications, such as IBM's PC-LAN program. Optionally, MS-NET networking software is available for the upper layers.

TRANSPARENT NETWORKING FILE ACCESS

OpenNET/PCL2 gives users the freedom to network PCs as consumer workstations or as file servers. PCLINK2 with MS-NET implements the SMB Protocol for easy access to files on other operating systems, such as iNDX, XENIX, UNIX, iRMX, or VAX/VMS.

REMOTE BOOT FOR DISKLESS SYSTEM

Diskless workstation support for the PC is provided by on-board firmware, an iRMX-NET Boot Server and any OpenNET File Server on the network.

PRODUCT CODES

sPCL2NIA	PCL2 Network Interface Adapter with 256 Kbyte of memory, hardware only
SPCL2ANIA	PCL2 Network Interface Adapter with 512 Kbyte of memory
sPCLINK2DEVKIT	NetBIOS Developer's Kit with: 2-sPCLINK2TWKITs, NetBIOS and Request Block Developer's Software with iNA 961 for PCLINK2
MSNET	OpenNET for MS-DOS

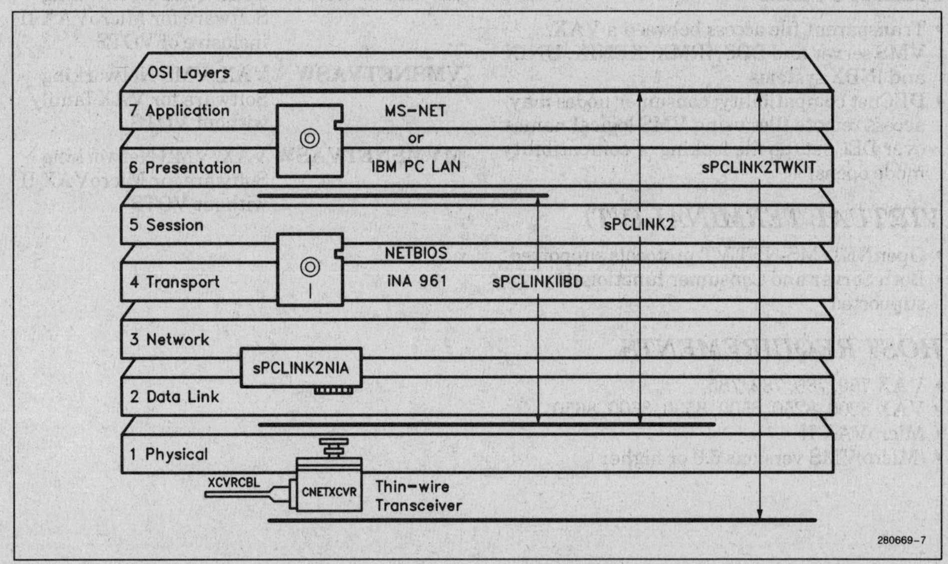

VAX/VMS* OpenNET™ NETWORKING SOFTWARE

COMPLETE OpenNET™ SOLUTION FOR THE VAX

VAX/VMS Networking software (VMSNET) is designed to serve on top of Digital Equipment's VAX OSI Transport Services (VOTS) and provides the OpenNET connection for a VAX* or MicroVAX II* system to iRMX, XENIX, DOS, UNIX System V and iNRM systems.

VMSNET enables a MicroVAX or VAX system to act as an OpenNET file server system allowing any OpenNET consumer node transparent file access to files on the MicroVAX or VAX.

The use of VOTS in the product allows the OpenNET software to run on any VAX running VOTS 5.0+ and having a DEC supplied LAN controller.

VMSNET software performs the OpenNET functions via an implementation of the Network File Access (NFA) file server protocols, VMS consumer bi-directional file transfer utilities, and Intel's iNA 960 transport layer software running on the supplied intelligent LAN controllers.

A set of network management utilities provide (Micro)VAX users with information and statistics about VMSNET activities.

FILE ACCESS

- Transparent file access between a VAX/VMS server and DOS, iRMX, XENIX, UNIX and iNDX systems
- DECnet compatibility: consumer nodes may access remote files using VMS logical names over DECnet (no file locking or compatibility mode opens)

VIRTUAL TERMINAL (VT)

- OpenNET/MS-NET VT protocols supported
- Both Server and Consumer functionality supported

HOST REQUIREMENTS

- VAX 750, 780, 782, 785
- VAX 8200, 8250, 8500, 8530, 8600, 8650
- MicroVAX II
- (Micro)VMS versions 5.0 or higher

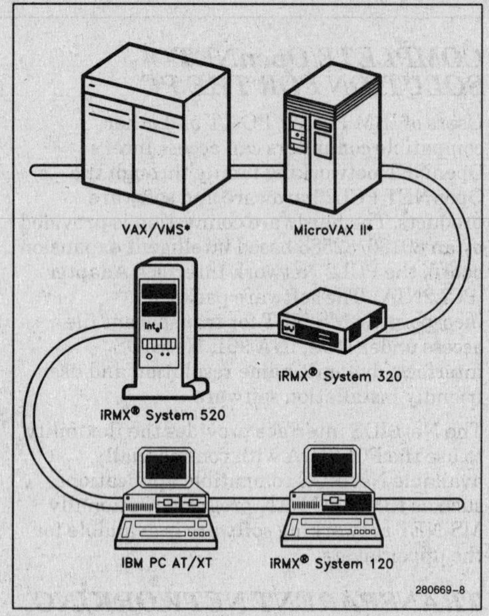

PRODUCT CODES

VMSNETVA	VAX/VMS Networking Software for VAX family inclusive of VOTS
MVMSNETA	VAX/VMS Networking Software for MicroVAX II inclusive of VOTS
VMSNETVASW	VAX/VMS Networking Software for VAX family without VOTS
MVMSNETVASW	VAX/VMS Networking Software for MicroVAX II without VOTS

INTEL SYSTEM V OpenNET™ NETWORKING SOFTWARE

COMPLETE OpenNET™ SOLUTION FOR UNIX SYSTEM V

SV-OpenNET connects Intel SYSTEM V/386 systems with all the OpenNET nodes. SV-OpenNET is available for Multibus I and Multibus II. The product includes a complete solution: communications board, Mail, VT, print spooling, nameserver interface library (NSI), and network management.

SV-OpenNET allows application interfacing through the UNIX TLI library. Applications may also access SV-OpenNET via the higher-level NSI library. SV-OpenNET can also coexist with the UNIX network, RFS.

FEATURES

Server Message Block (SMB) Transparent File Access

- Transparent file access between DOS, iRMX, XENIX, UNIX and iNDX systems.
- Both Server and Consumer functionality supported
- Remote Batch Execution (RBE) through "rexec"

NETWORK ADMINISTRATION AND MANAGEMENT

- Compatible with XENIX-NET
- File-based Nameserver compatible with XENIX-NET/net/data files

MAIL

- Supports MMDF
- Interoperates with XENIX-NET mail

VIRTUAL TERMINAL (VT)

- OpenNET/MS-NET VT protocols supported
- Both Server and Consumer functionality supported

PRINT SPOOLING

- Interface through "rprint"
- Supports Core printer spooling protocol

UNIX STANDARD INTERFACE

- Interface via AT&T supplied TLI (Streams) library, allowing all TLI applications to interoperate with SV-OpenNET
- SV-OpenNET provides a library, NSI, for high-level Virtual Circuit (VC) creation and name to address translation. The NSI then communicates directly with the UNIX TLI

HOST REQUIREMENTS

Intel SYSTEM V.3.1 UNIX Operating System on Multibus I or Multibus II

PRODUCT CODES

SVNET SV-OpenNET for Multibus I, Multibus II and PC AT

iNA 960 OpenNET™ NETWORKING SOFTWARE

FULLY COMPLIANT ISO/OSI TRANSPORT AND NETWORK

iNA 960 is a complete Network and Transport (ISO/OSI Layers 3 and 4) software system plus a comprehensive set of network management functions, Data Link (OSI Layer 2) drivers for IEEE 802.3 Ethernet, and system environment features.

FLEXIBLE AND HIGHLY CONFIGURABLE

iNA 960 is a mature, flexible, and ready-to-use software building block for OEM suppliers of networked systems.

This software is highly configurable for designs based on the 82586 and 82588 LAN controllers, 82501 and 82502 Ethernet serial interface and transceiver, and the 80×86 family of microprocessors.

CONFIGURABLE AT THE OBJECT CODE LEVEL

Consisting of linkable object modules, the iNA 960 software can be configured to implement a range of capabilities and interface protocols. iNA 960 has a large installed base and has been used reliably in a variety of systems from IBM PC XT/ATs to VAX/VMS to IBM mainframes.

BASED ON INTERNATIONAL STANDARDS

Based on the ISO/OSI seven layer model for network communications, iNA 960 implements ISO 8073 Transport Class 4 providing reliable full-duplex message delivery service on top of the internet capabilities offered by the network layer. The iNA 960 network layer is an implementation of the ISO 8473 Network Class 3 Connectionless Network Protocol and supports ISO 9542 End System to Intermediate System Network Dynamic Routing. iNA 960 also supports ISO 8602 Connectionless Transport Protocol (Datagram).

PRECONFIGURED iNA 961

iNA 960 contains the preconfigured iNA 961 which includes support for the iSBC 552A, iSBC 186/530, and the iSBC 554.

REMOTE BOOT SERVER SUPPORT

iNA 960 provides basic boot server capabilities that will transmit predefined images to diskless network nodes that request them.

MULTI-SERVER/CONSUMER SUPPORT

iNA 960 supports the powerful Multibus II feature of multiple host and communications boards. Ideal for LAN load balancing and redundant networks for fault-tolerant systems.

FEATURES

- Certified ISO/OSI Transport and Network Layer Software
- ISO 8072/8073 Transport Class 4
- ISO 8602 Connectionless Transport
- ISO 8348/8473 Connectionless Network
- ISO 9542 End System to Intermediate System Dynamic Routing
- Comprehensive Network Management Functions
- Remote Boot Server for diskless workstations
- Data Link Drivers for iSBC 552A, iSBX 586, iSBC 186/530, iSBC 554, and iSBC 186/51

PRODUCT CODES

INA960JRO Includes iNA 961 on iRMX diskette format

MULTIBUS I OpenNET™ NETWORKING HARDWARE

iSBC® 186/51 MULTIBUS I IEEE 802.3/ETHERNET COMMUNICATION COMPUTER

- 82586 LAN coprocessor for Ethernet/IEEE 802.3 communication
- Two serial interfaces, RS232C and RS422A/RS449 compatible
- 6 MHz 80186 microprocessor
- 128 Kbytes of dual-port RAM expandable on-board to 256 Kbytes
- Sockets for up to 192 Kbytes of JEDEC 28-pin standard memory devices
- Product Code: sSBC18651

CPU	80186 (6 MHz)
RAM (Bytes)	128K/256K dual port
EPROM (Bytes)	192K (27256), 96K (27128), 48K (2764), 4K (2732)
Serial I/O	2 ports, 26-pin 3M connector (RS232C/422A/449)
Ethernet I/O	1 port, 10-pin AMP connector
Baud rates (RS232/422/449)	75–9600 baud (async.) 1.76–38.4K baud (sync.)
Timers	3
Interrupts	9 levels, 28 sources
iSBX™ Connectors	2
Software Support	iRMX I O.S., iNA 960, iRMX-NET
Power Requirements	
+5V	7.45 A
+12V	40 mA
−12V	40 mA

iSBC®/iSXM™ 552A MULTIBUS I IEEE 802.3/ETHERNET NETWORK INTERFACE ADAPTER

- High Performance IEEE 802.3/Ethernet compatible network front-end processor
- Resident network software can be down-loaded over the bus or the LAN
- On-board diagnostic and boot firmware
- iSXM™ 552A version is a preconfigured controller for executing iNA 961 (ISO 8073 Transport and ISO 8473 Network software) in System 310 and 320 family products
- Product Code: pSBC552A, pSXM552A

CPU	80186 (8 MHz)
LAN Coprocessor	82586
RAM (Bytes)	256K
EPROM (Bytes)	128K (27512), 16K (2764)
Multibus Address	Any 64 KB boundary with a 16 MB address space
Software Support	iNA 960/961
Power Requirements	
+5V	6.2 A
+12V	0.5 A

15

MULTIBUS II OpenNET™ NETWORKING HARDWARE

iSBC® 186/530 MULTIBUS II IEEE 802.3/ETHERNET NETWORK INTERFACE ADAPTER

- Provides Ethernet (IEEE 802.3) compatible networking capability for all Multibus II systems
- Multibus II iPSB (Parallel System Bus) interface with full Message Passing capability
- Resident firmware to support Built-in-Self-Test (BIST) power-up diagnostics, and host-to-controller software download
- Four 28-pin JEDEC sites, expandable to 8 sites with iSBC 341 MULTIMODULE™ for a maximum of 512 Kbytes of EPROM
- Provides one RS232C serial port for use in debug and testing
- Product Code: pSBC186530

CPU	80186 (8 MHz)
DRAM	512 KB on-board
EPROM	4 28-pin JEDEC sites, up to 256 KB (max.) using 27512 devices, up to 512 KB (total) using iSBC 341 module
Ethernet I/O	1 channel 15-pin connector
Controller	82586 LAN Coprocessor
Serial I/O	1 channel RS232C, 15-pin connector
Controller	8031
Leads Supported	TD, RD
Timers	3
Interrupts	5 levels with 5 on-board sources and 255 sources from iPSB Bus
Power Requirements	
+5V	8.8 A (excludes power for user-installed memory devices)
+12V	50 mA
−12V	50 mA

PC BUS OpenNET™ NETWORKING HARDWARE

PCL2 AND PCL2A NETWORK INTERFACE ADAPTERS (PCL2NIA, PCL2ANIA)

- Intelligent high performance hardware with on-board microprocessor, 16 Kbytes EPROM and 256 Kbytes RAM
- Full slot PC AT, PC XT (or compatible computer system) board
- 80186 microprocessor, 82586 LAN coprocessor, 8 MHz zero-wait-state memory access
- RAM shared by the PC host and PCL2 board via an 8K memory window
- DRAM 512 KB (dual port), 0 wait-state memory access by the CPU
- Jumper selection for Ethernet or IEEE 802.3
- Effective self diagnostics
- Product Code: sPCL2NIA

CPU	80186 (8 MHz)
LAN Communications Controller	82586
Ethernet Interface	15-pin connector, 82501 serial interface
DRAM	256 KB (dual-port), 0 wait-state memory access by the CPU
EPROM	16 KB
Size	4.15 in H×13.3 in W
Power Requirements	
+5V	2.0 A
+12V	0.5 A

OpenNET™ NETWORKING ACCESSORIES

iSBX™ 586 DATA LINK ENGINE MULTIMODULE™ BOARD

- Provides an IEEE 802.3/Ethernet compatible connection for 8086 and 80186-based host boards over a 16-bit iSBX interface
- Single-wide iSBX MULTIMODULE
- Compatible with iNA 960/961 ISO 8073 Transport and ISO 8473 Network software
- Provides an IEEE 802.3 to IEEE 802.4 Router capability when used with the iSBC® 554 IEEE 802.4 LAN controller
- Product Code: sSBX586

LAN Coprocessor	82586 (8 MHz)
RAM (Bytes)	16K (dual-port)
Software Support	iNA 960/961
Power Requirements	
+5V	2.0 A
+12V	1.0 A

iDCM 911-1 INTELLINK™ FAN-OUT UNIT

- Connects up to nine Ethernet compatible workstations without the need for transceivers or coaxial cable
- Connects directly to the Ethernet coaxial cable through a standard transceiver cable
- Cascadable to support 17–81 workstations
- Product Code: pDCM9111

Size	14 in. W x 7.8 in. H x 5.5 in. D
Power Requirements	10/120/220/240 VAC, 47–64 Hz

ETHERNET/IEEE 802.3 THIN-WIRE TRANSCEIVER

- Die-cast metal case for protection, reduced EMI, and efficient heat dissipation
- Low inrush current at power-up, auto shutdown when low-input voltage occurs, and surge protection
- IEEE 802.3-compliant, Ethernet V1.0/V2.0 compatible
- Three LEDs monitor power status, packet collisions and signal quality
- Removable BNC type cable tap
- User-configurable for use with or without heartbeart
- Product Code: CNETXCVR

Size	2.8 in. x 3.6 in. x 3.8 in.
Power Requirements	+12V 375 mA (from transceiver cable)

15

OpenNET™ NETWORKING ORDERING INFORMATION

Code	Description

iRMX®-NET OpenNET™ PRODUCTS

RMXINETSW	iRMX-NET for iRMX I operating system
RMXIINETSW	iRMX-NET for iRMX II operating system on MB-I, MB-II, and System 120
RMXIIINETSW	iRMX-NET for iRMX III operating system on MB-II and System 120
sSXM120NETKIT	Preconfigured iRMX-NET and sPCLINK2 for networking iRMX and DOS on System 120
RMXIINETVT	Virtual Terminal Support for iRMX II
RMXIIINETVT	Virtual Terminal Support for iRMX III

PCLINK2 OpenNET™ PRODUCTS

sPCL2NIA*	PCLink2 Network Interface Adapter Hardware only (256 KB)
sPCL2ANIA*	PCLink2 Network Interface Adapter Hardware only (512 KB)
sPCLINK2DEVKIT*	NetBIOS Developer's Kit, NetBIOS programmer kit
MSNET	OpenNET for MS-DOS (order with sPCL2NIA or sPCLANIA)
PCLINKSWOPKIT	OpenNET for MS-DOS (stand-alone software order)

VAX/VMS OpenNET™ PRODUCTS

VMSNETVA	VMSNET for 11/78x thru 8700 (includes Digital's VOTS)
VMSNETVB	VMSNET for 6xxx thru 89xx (includes Digital's VOTS)
MVMSNETVA	MVMSNET for uVAX 11 and 2000 (includes Digital's VOTS)
MVMSNETVB	MVMSNET for uVAX 3xxx (includes Digital's VOTS)
VMSNETVASW	VMSNET for 11/78x thru 8700 (does not include Digital's VOTS)
VMSNETVBSW	VMSNET for 6xxx thru 89xx (does not include Digital's VOTS)
MVMSNETVASW	VMSNET for uVAX 11 and 2000 (does not include Digital's VOTS)
MVMSNETVBSW	VMSNET for uVAX 3xxx (includes Digital's VOTS)
VMSNETCLIC	VAX Cluster software license for VMSNETVx products

UNIX SYSTEM V OpenNET™ PRODUCTS

SVNET	SV-OpenNET for UNIX System V Release 3.2 on Multibus I, Multibus II and PC AT

iNA 960 OpenNET™ ISO/OSI PRODUCTS

INA960JRO	ISO/OSI Transport and Network layers, includes iNA961
INA960RF	Royalty fee for INA960

MULTIBUS I AND MULTIBUS II IEEE 802.3/ETHERNET PRODUCTS

sSBC18651*	iSBC 186/51 Multibus I IEEE 802.3/Ethernet Communication Computer
pSBC552A*	iSBC 552A Multibus I IEEE 802.3/Ethernet Network Interface Adapter
pSXM552A*	iSXM 552A preconfigured for Intel System 310 and 320, includes iNA 961 royalty

OpenNET™ NETWORKING ORDERING INFORMATION

Code	Description

OpenNET™ NETWORKING ACCESSORIES

sSBX586*	iSBX 586 MULTIMODULE IEEE 802.3/Ethernet Data Link board

OpenNET™™ NETWORKING LITERATURE

iRMX®-NET OpenNET™ PRODUCTS

Code	Description
462040	iRMX-NET Software Release 3.1 Installation and Configuration Guide
462041	iRMX-NET Software Release 3.1 User's Guide

PCL2 OpenNET™ PRODUCTS

Code	Description
460665	MS-NET User's Guide
450772	PCL2 Hardware Reference Manual
462305	PCL2 NIA Hardware Installation Guide
462311	PCL2 Software Developer's Manual
462308	PCL R3.0 Software For DOS—Installation Guide

VAX/VMS OpenNET™ PRODUCTS

Code	Description
480071	VAX/VMS OpenNET User's Manual

UNIX SYSTEM V OpenNET™ PRODUCTS

Code	Description
462740	SV-OpenNET User's Manual
462741	SV-OpenNET Installation and Administration Guide

iNA 960 OpenNET™ ISO/OSI PRODUCTS

Code	Description
462250	iNA 960 R3 Programmer's Reference Manual
462252	iNA 960 R3 Installation and Configuration Guide

MULTIBUS I AND MULTIBUS II IEEE 802.3/ETHERNET PRODUCTS

Code	Description
122330	iSBC 186/51 COMMputer Board Hardware Reference Manual
149228	iSBC 552A IEEE 802.3 Communications Controller User's Guide
149226	iSBC 186/530 Network Interface Adapter User's Guide

OpenNET™ NETWORKING ACCESSORIES

Code	Description
122290	iSBX 586 MULTIMODULE Ethernet Communication Controller Hardware Reference Manual
122074	iDCM 911-1 Intellink Cluster Module Reference Manual
280665	Ethernet/IEEE 802.3 Thin-wire Transceiver Factsheet

iSBX™ 586 Ethernet Data Link Engine

- Provides an IEEE 802.3 (Ethernet) Data Link Connection for Host Boards with 16-Bit SBX Bus Capability
- Based on Intel's 8 MHz 82586 LAN Coprocessor Chip which Includes the following Features:
  - Automatic Retransmission
  - On-Board Multicast Address Filtering
  - Host Interface via Buffer Chaining
- 16 Kbytes of Local Dual-Ported Buffer RAM
- Single-Wide iSBX™ Board That Conforms to IEEE 959 Specifications
- Compatible with iNA 960 ISO Transport Layer Software
  - Direct Support for iRMX® Operating Systems
  - Source Code Support for Other Operating Systems

The iSBX™ 586 Ethernet Data Link Engine is a single wide iSBX sized card that provides a low cost Ethernet controller for single board computers with 16-bit SBX bus capability. Based on the 82586 Local Area Network Coprocessor, the iSBX 586 implements the data link (Layer 2) and physical (Layer 1) layers of the International Standards Organization (ISO) Open Systems Interconnect (OSI) Reference Model. This allows the iSBX 86 to supply an IEEE 802.3 10 Mbps (Ethernet) connection for a single board computer having a 16-bit SBX bus connector.

The iSBX 586 MULTIMODULE is a low cost building block that can implement an Ethernet connection at various levels of integration. One application for the iSBX 586 is as a "best effort" datagram message delivery engine. In conjunction with the host single board computer running iNA 960 R2.0 ISO Transport Software, the iSBX 586 can allow for a four-layer, OpenNET compatible solution for Ethernet connections.

231668-1

15

November 1989
Order Number: 231668-001

BLOCK DIAGRAM

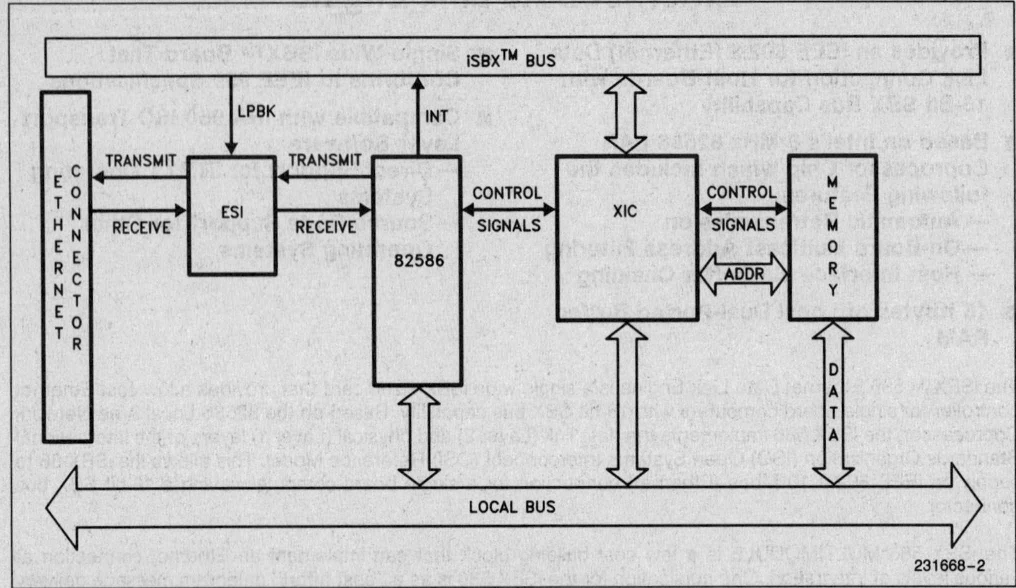

iSBX™ 586 Block Diagram

SPECIFICATIONS

SBX Interface	IEEE 959
Data Transfer	16 bits
Signal Levels	See the iSBX 586 Hardware Reference Manual
Signals Supported	All iSBX bus signals are supported except: MA2 MINTR1 MCLK OPT1 MDACK TDMA MDRQT −12V
Serial Interface	IEEE 802.3 compatible
DC Power Requirements	All voltages supplied by the iSBX interface +5V DC ±5%, 2A max. +12V DC ±5%, 1A max.

ENVIRONMENTAL

Temperature:	0°C to 55°C Operating (Free moving air across the base board and iSBX 586) −40°C to +65°C Non-Operating
Humidity:	5% to 90% Operating 5% to 95% Non-Operating

Refer to the iSBX™ 586 Hardware Reference Manual (not supplied) for details.

ORDERING INFORMATION

Order Code	Description
SBX 586	Ethernet Data Link Engine

iSBC® 552A
IEEE 802.3 COMPATIBLE
NETWORK INTERFACE ADAPTOR

- **Provides High-Performance Network Front-End Processing for All Multibus I Systems Regardless of the Operating System of the Host**
  - **— Intelligent Controller with an 8 MHz 80186 Processor and 256K of DRAM Memory**
  - **— IEEE 802.3 Network Port Driven by the 82586 LAN Coprocessor**
- **Can Execute On-Board the Intel iNA 960/961 Software, an Implementation of Industry Standard ISO 8073 Transport and ISO 8473 Network Protocols**
- **Resident Network Software Can be Down-Loaded over the Bus or LAN**
- **On-Board Diagnositc and Boot Firmware**
- **Supported by XNX-NET and RMX-NET Network File Service Software Products**
- **iSBC 552A is a Flexible, Intelligent Communications Controller for IEEE 802.3 LANs**

The iSBC 552A is designed for communications front end processor applications connecting Multibus I systems onto IEEE 802.3 compatible LANs. This Network Interface Adaptor is dedicated to the network communications tasks within a system allowing the host to spend more time processing user applications. A major advantage of this product is that it can be used to network existing systems and established designs without forcing the redesign of the entire system architecture.

The iSBC board can be used with any operating system because it requires only a high level interface to communicate with the host. The result is a powerful system building block which enables the OEM to network Multibus I based systems with different operating systems. Applications for the 552A products include networked multiuser XENIX based systems for the office and laboratory, iRMX-based systems for real-time applications, or many other system applications.

280385-1

15

October 1990
Order Number: 280385-002

THE iSBC® BOARD

The iSBC 552A version is a board that offers the hardware necessary for the user to construct an IEEE 802.3 front-end processor for custom requirements. The Intel iNA 960 ISO standard transport and network software can be configured and optimized to run on the iSBC 552A board.

Operating Systems Environment

The iSBC 552A board and iNA 960/961 software can function in any Multibus I environment. The communication between the iSBC 552A and the host processor is entirely independent of any host operating systems. iNA 960/961 uses the MIP protocol to interface with the host processor. The MIP is a reliable, host operating system independent, process to process communication scheme between any processors on the Multibus I System Bus. iNA 960/961 can service multiple processes utilizing its services at the same time.

A host processor passes iNA 960/961 commands and buffers in the Multibus I system memory to the iNA 960/961 software. This software is responsible for updating the response fields of these commands. It is responsible for copying the user send buffer in Multibus I system memory into its onboard buffers for transmission and for copying received messages to user buffers in Multibus I system memory.

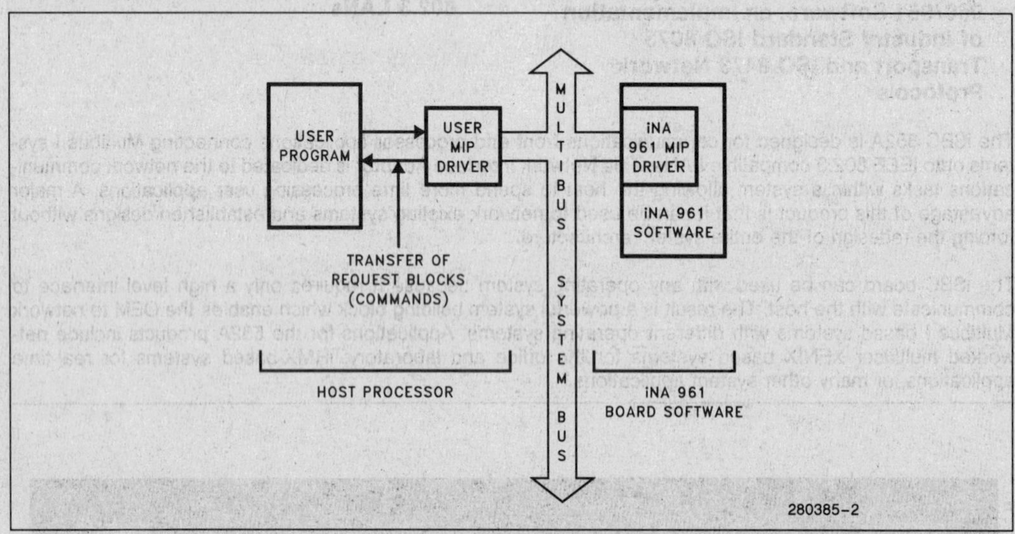

Figure 1. iNA 961 MIP Interface

DEVELOPMENT ENVIRONMENT

The iSBC 552A allows a user to fine tune iNA 960 and to put the software on the board. Both iNA 960 and the iSBC 552A can be flexibly configured to best meet the users' requirements. An Intel development system, together with the Intel I2ICE™ system or equivalent product can be used if the user desires to do extensive development work on the iSBC 552A. Intel also supplies a wide range of host processor boards and systems (such as the iSBC 286/12 and system 310) that will function well with the iSBC 552A.

SPECIFICATIONS

Data Transfer: 8 or 16 bits

Average Raw Multibus I Transfer Rate:

8.7 Mbits/second (450 ns, 16-bit system memory and no Multibus I contention)

Transceiver Interface

Transmit Data Rate: 10 Mbits/second

Signal Levels: Series 10,000 ECL-compatible

Host Interrupts: One Multibus I non-vector interrupt for use in system/host handshaking

Multibus Interface: The iSBC 552A board conforms to all AC and DC requirements outlined in Intel Multibus I Specification. Order Number 142686-022m except for the following signals:

Signal DAT0–DAT7

Signal Specification:

I_{IL} = 180 μA I_{IH} = 125 μA

DC Power Required: All voltages supplied by the Multibus I Interface

+5.0V ±5%, 6.2A maximum

+12.0V ±5%, 0.5 maximum

Environmental

Temperature: 0°C to +55°CC Operating

−40°C to −65°C Non-Operating

Humidity: 5% to 90% Operating

5% to 95% Non-Operating

ORDERING INFORMATION

Order Code	Description
SBC552A	IEEE 802.3 COMMengine
NA960	Configurable transport software usable with the SBC552A
NA961	Preconfigured transport software for the SXM552A

15

iSBC® 186/51 COMMUNICATING COMPUTER

- 6 MHz 80186 Microprocessor
- 128K Bytes of Dual-Ported RAM Expandable On-Board to 256K Bytes
- 82586 Local Area Network Coprocessor for Ethernet/IEEE 802.3 Specifications
- Two Serial Interfaces, RS-232C and RS-422A/RS-449 Compatible
- Supports Transport Layer Software (iNA 960) and Higher Layer Communications Software (such as iRMX®-NET)
- Sockets for up to 192K Bytes of JEDEC 28 Pin Standard Memory Devices
- Two iSBX™ Bus Connectors
- 16M Bytes Address Range of MULTIBUS® Memory
- MULTIBUS Interface for Multimaster Configurations and System Expansion
- Supported by a Complete Family of Single Board Computers, Peripheral Controllers, Digital and Analog I/O, Memory, Packaging and Software

The iSBC® 186/51 COMMUNICATING COMPUTER is a member of Intel's OpenNET™ family of products, and supports Intel's network software. The iSBC 186/51 utilizes Intel's VLSI technology to provide an economical self-contained computer for applications in processing and local area network control. The combination of the 80186 Central Processing Unit and the 82586 Local Area Network Coprocessor makes it ideal for applications which require both communication and processing capabilities such as networked workstations, factory automation, office automation, communications servers, and many others. The CPU, Ethernet interface, serial communications interface, 128K Bytes of RAM, up to 192K Bytes of ROM, I/O ports and drivers and the MULTIBUS interface all reside on a single 6.75″ x 12.00″ printed circuit board.

280207–1

October 1989
Order Number: 280207-001

BLOCK DIAGRAM

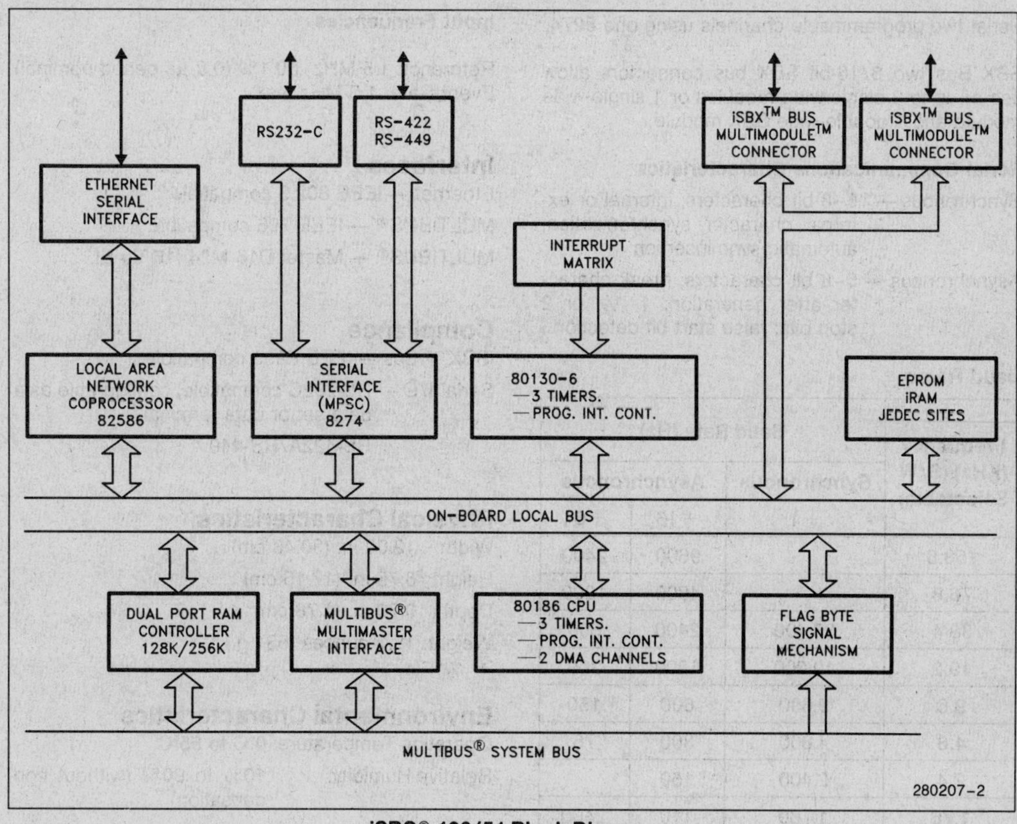

iSBC® 186/51 Block Diagram

SPECIFICATIONS

Word Size

Instruction: 8, 16, 24, or 32 bits
Data: 8, 16 bits

System Clock

6.00 MHz ± 0.1%

Cycle Time

Basic Instruction Cycle

6 MHz— 1000 ns
333 ns (assumes instruction in the queue)

NOTE:
Basic instruction cycle is defined as the fastest instruction time (i.e., two clock cycles).

Memory Capacity/Addressing

Six Universal Memory Sites support JEDEC 24/28 pin EPROM, PROM, iRAM and static RAM.

Example for EPROM:

Device	Total Capacity	Address Range
2732	24K Bytes	F8000–FFFFF$_H$
2764	48K Bytes	F0000–FFFFF$_H$
27128	96K Bytes	E0000–FFFFF$_H$
27256	192K Bytes	C0000–FFFFF$_H$

On-Board RAM

Board	Total Capacity	Address Range
iSBC 186/51	128K Bytes	0–1FFFF$_H$

With MULTIMODULE™ RAM

Board	Total Capacity	Address Range
iSBC 304	256K Bytes	0–3FFFF$_H$

15

I/O Capacity

Serial two programmable channels using one 8274.

SBX Bus two 8/16-bit SBX bus connectors allow use of up to 2 single-wide modules or 1 single-wide module and 1 double-wide SBX module.

Serial Communications Characteristics

Synchronous — 5–8 bit characters; internal or external character synchronization; automatic sync insertion

Asynchronous — 5–8 bit characters; break character after generation; 1, ½, or 2 stop bits; false start bit detection

Baud Rates

Frequency (KHz) (S/W Selectable)	Baud Rate (Hz)		
	Synchronous	Asynchronous	
	÷1	÷16	÷64
153.6		9600	2400
76.8		4800	1200
38.4	38,400	2400	600
19.2	19,200	1200	300
9.6	9,600	600	150
4.8	4,800	300	75
2.4	2,400	150	
1.76	1,760	110	2400

NOTE:
Frequency selected by I/O write of appropriate 16-bit frequency factor to baud rate register (80186 timer 0 and 80130 baud timer).

Timers

Input Frequencies

Reference 1.5 MHz ±0.1% (0.5 μs period nominal)
Event Rate: 1.5 MHz max.

Interfaces

Ethernet — IEEE 802.3 compatible

MULTIBUS® — IEEE 796 compatible

MULTIBUS® — Master D16 M24 I16 V0 EL

Compliance

iSBX™ Bus — IEEE P959 compatible

Serial I/O — RS-232C compatible, configurable as a data set or data terminal, RS-422A/RS-449

Physical Characteristics

Width: 12.00 in. (30.48 cm)

Height: 6.75 in. (17.15 cm)

Depth: 0.70 in. (1.78 cm)

Weight: 18.7 ounces (531 g.)

Environmental Characteristics

Operating Temperature: 0°C to 55°C

Relative Humidity: 10% to 90% (without condensation)

80186 Output Frequencies/Timing Intervals

Function	Single Timer/Counter		Dual (Cascaded) Timer/Counter	
	Min	Max	Min	Max
Real-Time Interrupt	667 ns	43.69 ms	667 ns	47.72 Minutes
Programmable One-Shot	1000 ns	43.69 ms	1000 ns	47.72 Minutes
Rate Generator	22.889 Hz	1.5 MHz	0.0003492 Hz	1.5 MHz
Square-Wave Rate Generator	22.889 Hz	1.5 MHz	0.0003492 Hz	1.5 MHz
Software Triggered Strobe	1000 ns	43.69 ms	1000 ns	47.72 Minutes
Event Counter		1.5 MHz		

Connectors

Interface	Double-Sided Pins	Centers (In.)	Mating Connectors
Ethernet	10	0.1	AMP87531-5
Serial I/O	26	0.1	3M 3452-0001 Flat or AMP88106-1 Flat

Electrical Characteristics

D.C. Power Supply Requirements

Configuration	Maximum Current (All Voltages ± 5%)		
	+5	+12	−12
SBC 186/51 as shipped:			
Board Total	7.45A	40 mA	40 mA
With separate battery back-up	6.30A	40 mA	40 mA
Battery back-up	1.15A	—	—
With SBC-304 Memory Module Installed:			
Board Total	7.55A	40 mA	40 mA
With separate battery back-up	6.30A	40 mA	40 mA
Battery back-up	1.25A	—	—

NOTES:
1. Add 150 mA to 5V current for each device installed in the 6 available Universal Memory Sites.
2. Add 500 mA to 12V current if Ethernet transceiver is connected.
3. Add additional currents for any SBX modules installed.

Reference Manual

122330— iSBC 186/51 Hardware Reference Manual (NOT SUPPLIED)

Manuals may be ordered from any Intel sales representative, distributor office or from Intel Literature Department, 3065 Bowers Avenue, Santa Clara, California 95051.

ORDERING INFORMATION

Order Code	Description
SBC18651	Communicating Computer

Distributed Control Modules 16

BITBUS™ STARTER KIT

280638-1

A COMPLETE BITBUS™ NETWORK YOU CAN HAVE UP AND RUNNING IN TWO HOURS

The BITBUS™ Starter Kit is a complete hardware/software kit containing BITBUS analog and digital boards, tailored application software, and all the accessories (e.g., power supply and cables) required to set up a simple but functional BITBUS network. A first-time user can construct a BITBUS network and execute sample application programs within two hours of opening the box. He can then incorporate this basic network into his own distributed control application.

FEATURES:

- Self-contained BITBUS kit requiring only an IBM PC or compatible host.
- BITBUS analog and digital boards, plus PC Gateway to the BITBUS network.
- Sample application software with built-in installation, configuration, and diagnostic software.
- No BITBUS experience necessary.

November 1990
Order Number: 280638-001

SPECIFICATIONS

REAL-TIME INTERCONNECT FOR DISTRIBUTED CONTROL

The Intel BITBUS network provides the optimal solution for building real-time distributed control systems. The BITBUS serial bus architecture overcomes many of the limitations inherent in traditional industrial connection methods to give you increased performance, reliability, and flexibility and lower implementation costs.

DESIGNED FOR FIRST-TIME BITBUS USERS

The BITBUS Starter Kit is the ideal way for first-time BITBUS users to learn about the BITBUS architecture. Shortly after unpacking this kit, you can be confidently executing your first BITBUS distributed control application.

EVERYTHING YOU NEED

Based on standard Intel products, the BITBUS Starter Kit includes the BITBUS analog board, the BITBUS digital board, the PC Gateway into the BITBUS network, power supply and cables. Supporting the standard product are demonstration boards that the user can manipulate to display analog or digital functionality.

BUILT-IN INSTALLATION AND DIAGNOSTIC SOFTWARE

Application software included with the BITBUS Starter Kit provides network setup information, as well as comprehensive error-checking software to verify that the network is configured correctly. If there is an error, the software directs you to the problem and suggests a correction. Once the network is working properly, the software steps you through optional configurations, from a host-based centralized control system to a node-based distributed control scheme. Each configuration allows you to interact with the network.

SERVICE, SUPPORT AND TRAINING

Intel provides worldwide support for repair, on-site service, network design, and installation. Development support options include phone support, subscription service, on-site consulting, and customer training.

INTEL QUALITY AND RELIABILITY

The BITBUS Starter Kit is designed and manufactured in accordance with Intel's high quality standards. We then verify quality through rigorous testing in our state-of-the-art Environmental Test Laboratory.

SPECIFICATIONS

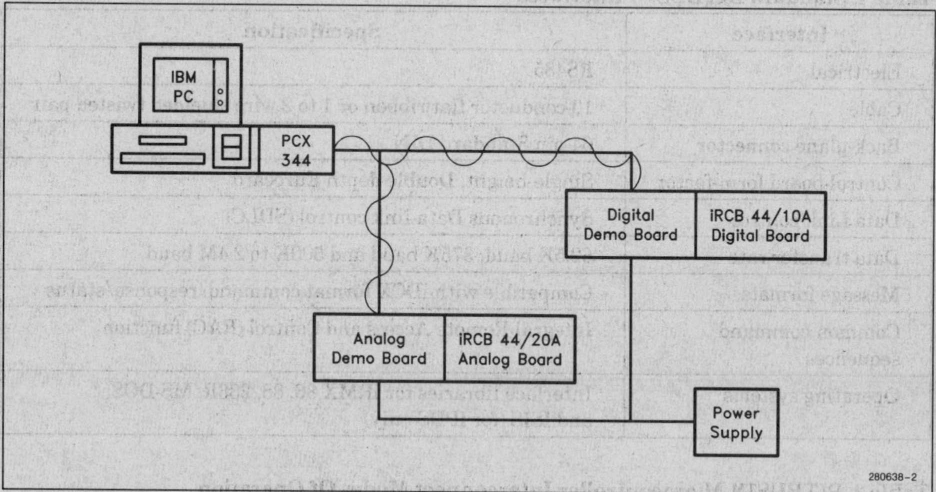

Figure 1: BITBUS Starter Kit

ORDERING INFORMATION

Product Code	Qty	Product Content
BITBUSKIT		Basic Starter Kit which includes the following items:
	1	BITBUS Starter Kit User's Guide
		HARDWARE
	1	iPCX 344A—BITBUS IBM PC Interface Board—PC Gateway to BITBUS Network
	1	iRCB 4410A—BITBUS Digital I/O Remote Controller Board
	1	iRCB 4420A—BITBUS Analog I/O Remote Controller Board
	1	Digital Demonstration Board
	1	Analog Demonstration Board
	1	Power Supply, 25 Watt, UL, VDE, CSA approved
	1	Required Cables, SRAMs, Jumpers, etc.
		SOFTWARE
	1	iDCS100—BITBUS Toolbox—The set of six software utilities that simplify development of host application software
	1	iDCS110—Bitware—iDCX 51 interface library and declaration files
	1	Starter Kit Application Software
BITBUSKITPLUS		Expanded version of the BITBUSKIT providing programming languages used to develop host (8086 environment) and node code (8051 environment) in addition to the basic BITBUS network.

16

SPECIFICATIONS

Table 1. Standard BITBUS™ Interfaces

Interface	Specification
Electrical	RS485
Cable	10-conductor flat ribbon or 1 to 2 wire shielded twisted pair
Back-plane connector	64-pin Standard DIN
Control-board form-factor	Single-height, Double-depth Eurocard
Data Link control	Synchronous Data-link control (SDLC)
Data transfer rate	62.5K baud, 375K baud and 500K to 2.4M baud
Message formats	Compatible with iDCX format command/response/status
Common command sequences	Integral Remote Access and Control (RAC) function
Operating systems	Interface libraries for iRMX 86, 88, 286R, MS-DOS, and ISIS (for iPDS only)

Table 2. BITBUS™ Microcontroller Interconnect Modes Of Operation

	Speed Kb/S	Maximum Distance Between Repeaters M/ft	Maximum # Nodes Per Segment*	Maximum # Repeaters Between A Master And Any Slave
Synchronous	500–2400	30/100	28	0
Self Clocked	375 62.5	300/1000 1200/4000	28 28	2 10

iDCX 51 DISTRIBUTED CONTROL EXECUTIVE

- **Supports MCS®-51 and RUPI™-44 Familes of 8-Bit Microcontrollers**
- **Real-Time, Multitasking Executive — Supports up to 8 Tasks at Four Priority Levels**
- **Local and Remote Task Communication**
- **Small—2.2K Bytes**
- **Reliable**
- **Simple User Interface**
- **Dynamic Reconfiguration Capability**
- **Compatible with BITBUS™/Distributed Control Modules (iDCM) Product Line**

The iDCX 51 Executive is compact, easy to use software for development and implementation of applications using the high performance 8-bit family of 8051 microcontrollers, including the 8051, 8044, and 8052. Like the 8051 family, the iDCX 51 Executive is tuned for real-time control applications requiring manipulation and scheduling of more than one task, and fast response to external stimuli.

The MCS-51 microcontroller family coupled with iDCX 51 is a natural combination for applications such as data acquisition and monitoring, process control, robotics, and machine control. The iDCX 51 Executive can significantly reduce applications development time, particularly BITBUS distributed control environments.

The iDCX 51 Executive is available in two forms, either as configurable software on diskette or as preconfigured firmware within the 8044 BEM BITBUS microcontroller.

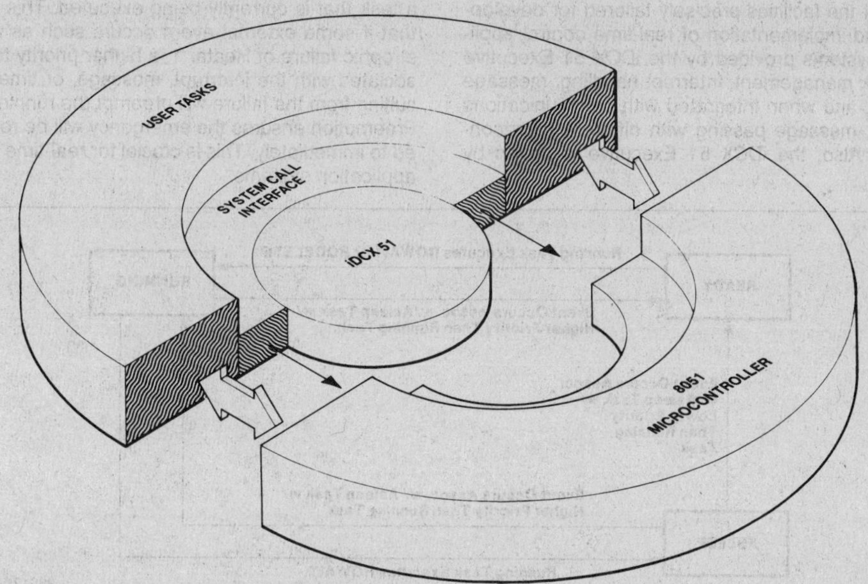

Figure 1. iDCX 51 Distributed Control Executive

*XENIX™ is a trademark of Microsoft Corporation.

October 1987
Order Number: 280176-003

MICROCONTROLLER SUPPORT

The iDCX 51 Executive is designed to support the MCS-51 and RUPI-44 families of 8-bit microcontrollers. MCS-51 microcontrollers that are supported include the 8051, 80C51, 8052, 8031, 8032, and 8751 devices. The RUPI-44 microcontrollers include the 8044, 8344, and 8744 devices. All of these microcontrollers share a common 8051 core.

ARCHITECTURE

Real-time and Multitasking

Real-time control applications must be responsive to the external environment and typically involve the execution of more than one activity (task or set of tasks) in response to different external stimuli. Control of an industrial drying process is an example. This process could require monitoring of multiple temperatures and humidity; control of fans, heaters, and motors that must respond accordingly to a variety of inputs. The iDCX 51 Executive fully supports applications requiring response to stimuli as they occur, i.e., in real-time. This real-time response is supported for multiple tasks often needed to implement a control application.

Some of the facilities precisely tailored for development and implementation of real-time control application systems provided by the iDCX 51 Executive are: task management, interrupt handling, message passing, and when integrated with communications support, message passing with different microcontrollers. Also, the iDCX 51 Executive is driven by events: interrupts, timers, and messages ensuring the application system always responds to the environment appropriately.

Task Management

A task is a program defined by the user to execute a particular control function or functions. Multiple programs or tasks may be required to implement a particular function such as "controlling Heater 1". The iDCX 51 Executive recognizes three different task states as one of the mechanisms to accomplish scheduling of up to eight tasks. Figure 2 illustrates the different task states and their relationship to one another.

The scheduling of tasks is priority based. The user can prioritize tasks to reflect their relative importance within the overall control scheme. For instance, if Heater 1 must go off line prior to Heater 2 then the task associated with Heater 1 shutdown could be assigned a higher priority ensuring the correct shutdown sequence. The RQ WAIT system call is also a scheduling tool. In this example the task implementing Heater 2 shutdown could include an instruction to wait for completion of the task that implements Heater 1 shutdown.

The iDCX 51 Executive allows for PREEMPTION of a task that is currently being executed. This means that if some external event occurs such as a catastrophic failure of Heater 1, a higher priority task associated with the interrupt, message, or timeout resulting from the failure will preempt the running task. Preemption ensures the emergency will be responded to immediately. This is crucial for real-time control application systems.

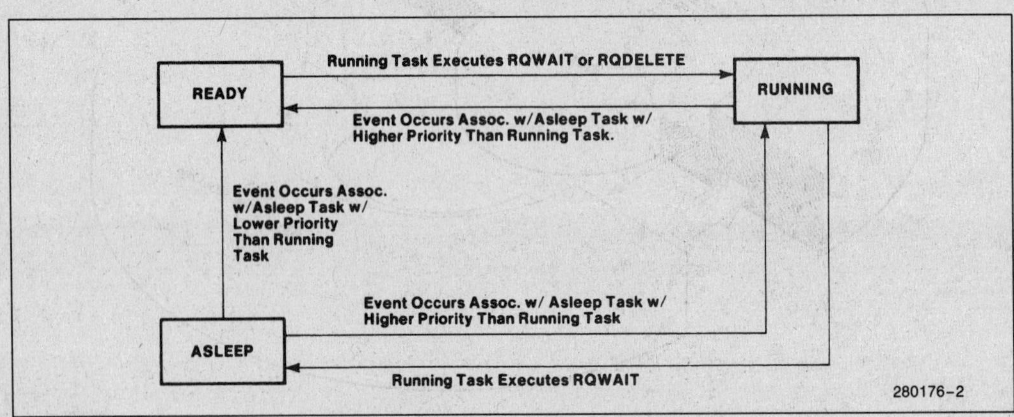

Figure 2. Task State Transition Diagram

Interrupt Handling

The iDCX 51 Executive supports five interrupt sources as shown in Table 1. Four of these interrupt sources, excluding timer 0, can be assigned to a task. When one of the interrupts occurs the task associated with it becomes a running task (if it were the highest priority task in a ready state). In this way, the iDCX 51 Executive responds to a number of internal and external stimuli including time intervals designed by the user.

Table 1. iDCX 51 Interrupt Sources

Interrupt Source	Interrupt Number
External Request 0	00H
Timer 0	01H
External Request 1	02H
Timer 1	03H
Internal Serial Port 1	04H

Message Passing

The iDCX 51 Executive allows tasks to interface with one another via a simple message passing facility. This message passing facility can be extended to different processors when communications support is integrated within a BITBUS/iDCM system, for example. This facility provides the user with the ability to link different functions or tasks. Linkage between tasks/functions is typically required to support development of complex control applications with multiple sensors (input variables) and drivers (output variables). For instance, the industrial drying process might require a dozen temperature inputs, six moisture readings, and control of: three fans, two conveyor motors, a dryer motor, and a pneumatic conveyor. The data gathered from both the temperature and humidity sensors could be processed. Two tasks might be required to gather the data and process it. One task could perform a part of the analysis, then include a pointer to the next task to complete the next part of the analysis. The tasks could continue to move between one another.

REMOTE TASK COMMUNICATION

The iDCX 51 Executive system calls can support communication to tasks on remote controllers. This feature makes the iDCX 51 Executive ideal for applications using distributed architectures. Providing communication support saves significant application development time and allows for more effective use of this time. Intel's iDCM product line combines hardware and software to provide this function.

In an iDCM system, communication between nodes occurs via the BITBUS microcontroller interconnect. The BITBUS microcontroller interconnect is a high performance serial control bus specifically intended for use in applications built on distributed architectures. The iDCX 51 Executive provides BITBUS support.

BITBUS™/iDCM COMPATIBLE

A pre-configured version of the iDCX 51 Executive implements the BITBUS message format and provides all iDCX 51 facilities mentioned previously: task management, interrupt handling, and message passing. This version of the Executive is supplied in firmware on the 8044 BEM with the iDCM hardware products: the iSBX™ 344A BITBUS Controller MULTIMODULE™; the iDCX 344A BITBUS controller board for the PC; and the iRCB boards.

Designers who want to use the iDCX executive on an Intel BITBUS board should purchase either DCS110 or DSC120 BITBUS software. Both of these products include an interface library to iDCX 51 procedures and other development files. It is not necessary to purchase the iDCX 51 Executive.

SIMPLE USER INTERFACE

The iDCX 51 Executive's capabilities are utlilized through system calls. These interfaces have been defined for ease of use and simplicity. Table 2 includes a listing of these calls and their functions. Note that tasks may be created at system initialization or run-time using the CREATE TASK call.

Other Functions such as GET FUNCTION IDS, ALLOCATE/DEALLOCATE BUFFER, and SEND MESSAGE, support communication for distributed architectures.

Table 2. iDCX 51 System Calls

Call Name	Description
TASK MANAGEMENT CALLS	
RQ$CREATE$TASK	Create and schedule a new task.
RQ$DELETE$TASK	Delete specified task from system.
RQGETFUNCTION$IDS	Obtain the function IDs of tasks currently in the system.
RQ$ALLOCATE	Obtain a message buffer from the system buffer pool.
RQ$DEALLOCATE	Return a message buffer to the system buffer pool.
RQ$SEND$MESSAGE	Send a message to specified task.
RQ$WAIT	Wait for a message event.
MEMORY MANAGEMENT CALLS	
RQGETMEM	Get available system memory pool memory.
RQ$RELEASE$MEM	Release system memory pool memory.
INTERRUPT MANAGEMENT CALLS	
RQ$DISABLE$INTERRUPT	Temporarily disable an interrupt.
RQ$ENABLE$INTERRUPT	Re-enable an interrupt.
RQ$WAIT	Wait for an interrupt event.
TIMER MANAGEMENT CALLS	
RQSETINTERVAL	Establish a time interval.
RQ$WAIT	Wait for an interval event.

Another feature that eases application development is automatic register bank allocation. The Executive will assign tasks to register banks automatically unless a specific request is made. The iDCX 51 Executive keeps track of the register assignments allowing the user to concentrate on other activities.

SYSTEM CONFIGURATION

The user configures an iDCX 51 system simply by specifying the initial set of task descriptors and configuration values, and linking the system via the RL 51 Linker and Locator Program with user programs.

Each task that will be running under control of the executive has an Initial Task Description (ITD) that describes it. The ITD specifies to the executive the amount of stack space to reserve, the priority level of the task (1–4), the internal memory register bank to be associated with the task, the internal or external interrupt associated with the task, and a function ID (assigned by the user) that uniquely labels the task. The ITD can also include a pointer to the ITD for the next task. In this way an ITD "chain" can be formed. For example, if four ITD's are chained together, then when the system is initialized, all four tasks will be put into a READY state. Then, the highest priority task will run.

The DCX 51 user can control several system constants during the configuration process (Table 3). Most of these constants are fixed, but by including an Initial Data Descriptor (IDD) in an ITD chain, the system clock priority, clock time unit, and buffer size can be modified at run-time.

This feature is useful for products that use the same software core, but need minor modification of the executive to better match the end application. The initial data descriptor also allows the designer, who is using an 8044 BEM BITBUS Microcontroller, to modify the preconfigured (on-chip) iDCX 51 Executive.

Programs may be written in ASM 51 or PL/M 51. Intel's 8051 Software Development Package contains both ASM 51 and RL 51. Figure 3 shows the software generation process.

Table 3. DCX 51 Configuration Constants

Constant Name	Description
RQ CLOCK PRIORITY	The priority level of the system clock.
RQ CLOCK TICK	The number of time cycles in the system clock basic time unit (a "tick").
RQ FIRST ITD	The absolute address of the first ITD in the ITD chain.
RQ MEM POOL ADR	The start address of the System Memory Pool (SMP) in Internal Data RAM.
RQ MEM POOL LEN	The length of the SMP.
RQ RAM IDD	The absolute RAM address of where iDCX 51 checks for an Initial Data Descriptor (IDD) during initialization.
RQ SYS BUF SIZE	The size, in bytes, of each buffer in the system buffer pool.

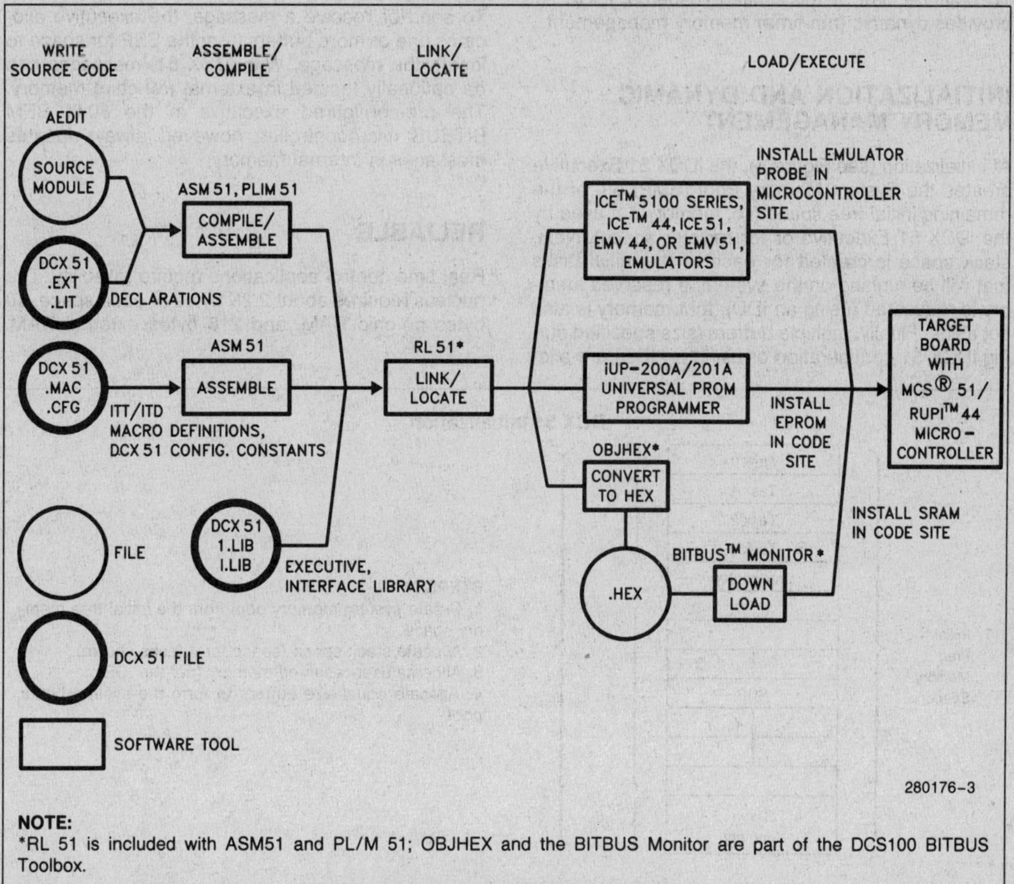

NOTE:
*RL 51 is included with ASM51 and PL/M 51; OBJHEX and the BITBUS Monitor are part of the DCS100 BITBUS Toolbox.

Figure 3. Software Generation Process

16

SOPHISTICATED INTERNAL MEMORY MANAGEMENT

The amount of internal memory available ranges from 128 to 256 bytes depending on the type of microcontroller used.

Internal memory is used for the executive, stack spare for "running" tasks, space for message buffers, and reserved memory for variables storage. Other memory is used for register space. Except for register space, the allocation of internal memory is controlled by the executive, user-specified task/data descriptors and system configuration constants.

To optimize use of this limited resource, iDCX 51 provides dynamic (run-time) memory management.

INITIALIZATION AND DYNAMIC MEMORY MANAGEMENT

At initialization (see Figure 4), the iDCX 51 Executive creates the System Memory Pool (SMP) out of the remaining initial free space (i.e. memory not used by the iDCX 51 Executive or for register space). Next, stack space is created for each of the initial tasks that will be running on the system. If reserved memory is requested (using an IDD), that memory is also set aside. Finally, multiple buffers (size specified during iDCX 51 configuration or using an IDD) are allocated from any remaining memory. These buffers form the System Buffer Pool (SBP) that can be used to create additional stack space or to locate messages sent between tasks.

During run-time, the iDCX 51 Executive dynamically manages this space. If a task is deleted, its stack space is returned to the System Buffer Pool for use by other tasks or as a message buffer.

As new tasks are dynamicallly created, the executive reserves the needed stack space. If no space is available, the executive deallocates a buffer from the System Buffer Pool and then allocates the needed stack space.

To send or receive a message, the executive allocates one or more buffers from the SBP for space to locate the message. With iDCX 51, messages can be optionally located in external (off-chip) memory. The pre-configured executive in the 8044 BEM BITBUS microcontroller, however, always locates messages in internal memory.

RELIABLE

Real-time control applications require reliability. The nucleus requires about 2.2K bytes of code space, 40 bytes on-chip RAM, and 218 bytes external RAM.

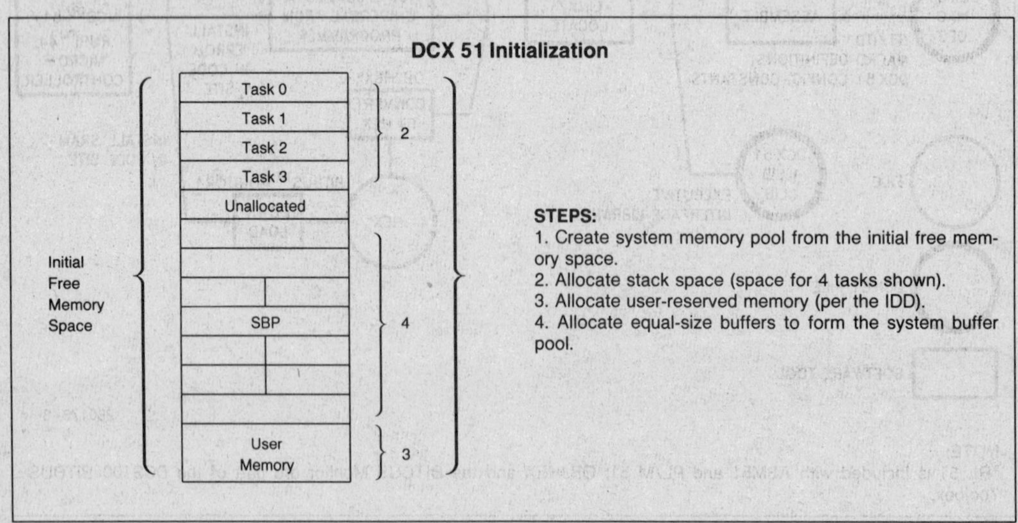

Figure 4. iDCX 51 Initialization of Internal Memory

Streamlined code increases performance and reliability, and flexibility is not sacrificed as code may be added to either on-chip or external memory.

The iDCX 51 architecture and simple user interface further enhance reliability and lower cost. For example, the straightforward structure of the user interfaces, and the transparent nature of the scheduling process contribute to reliability of the overall system by minimizing programming effort. Also, modularity increases reliability of the system and lowers cost by allowing user tasks to be refined independent of the system. In this way, errors are identified earlier and can be easily corrected in each isolated module.

In addition, users can assign tasks a Function ID that allows tracking of the tasks associated with a particular control/monitorig function. This feature reduces maintenance and trouble shooting time thus increasing system run time and decreasing cost.

OPERATING ENVIRONMENT

The iDCX 51 Executive supports applications development based on any member of the high performance 8051 family of microcontrollers. The Executive is available on diskette with user linkable libraries or in the 8044 BITBUS Enhanced Microcontroller preconfigured in on-chip ROM. (The 8044 BEM is an 8044 component that consists of an 8051 microcontroller and SDLC controller on one chip with integral firmware.)

When in the iDCM environment (Figure 5), the preconfigured iDCX 51 Executive can communicate with other BITBUS series controller boards. The BITBUS board at the master node can be associated with either an iRMX™, PC-DOS or XENIX* host system.

DEVELOPMENT ENVIRONMENT

Intel provides a complete development environment for the MCS-51 and RUPI-44 families of microcontrollers. The iDCX 51 Executive is only one of many of the software development products available. The executive is compatible with the following software development utilities available from Intel:

- 8051 Macro Assembler (ASM 51)
- PL/M 51 Compiler
- RL 51 Linker and Relocator Program
- LIB 51

Intel hardware development tools currently available for MCS-51 and RUPI-44 microcontroller development are:

- ICE-5100/252 Emulator for the MCS-51 family of microcontrollers
- ICE-5100/044 Emulator for the RUPI-44 family of microcontrollers (8044, 8344, 8744)
- iUP-200A/201A PROM Programmer, 21X software, and iUP programming modules

The DCX 51 Executive is also compatible with older hardware development tools (no longer available), which include:

- EMV-51/44 Emulation Vehicles
- ICE-51/44 In-Circuit Emulators

Table 4 shows the possible MCS-51 and RUPI-44 families development environments: host systems, operating systems, available software utilities, and hardware debug tools.

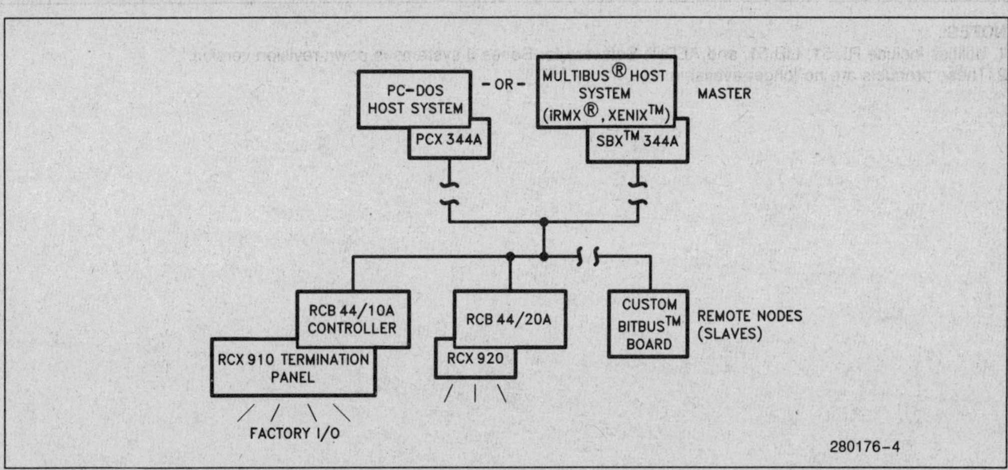

Figure 5. iDCM Operating Environment

SPECIFICATIONS

Supported Microcontrollers

8031	80C31
8051	80C51
8032	8751
8744	8044
8344	8052

Compatible DCM BITBUS™ Software

DCS 100 BITBUS Toolbox Host Software Utilities

DCS 110 BITWARE DCM44 Code for BITBUS emulation

Reference Manual (Supplied)

460367-001— iDCX 51 Distributes Control Executive User's Guide for Release 2.0.

ORDERING INFORMATION

Part Number	Description
DCX51SU	Executive for 8051 Family of Microcontrollers. Single User License, Development Only. Media Supplied for All Host Systems (Table 3).
DCX51RF	Royalty (Incorporation) Fee for iDCX Executive. Set of 50 incorporations. IDCX 51 RF does not ship with software (Order DCX 51SU).

Table 4. MCS®-51/RUPI™-44 Families Development Environments

Development Utilities	Host Systems				
	PC/MS-DOS	iRMX® 86	iPDS™	Intellec®	
				Series II	Series III/IV
SOFTWARE					
ASM 51 + Utilities(1)	✓	✓	✓	✓	✓
PL/M 51 + Utilities(1)	✓	✓	✓	✓	✓
iDCX 51 Executive	✓	✓	✓		✓
HARDWARE					
ICE-5100/044/252	✓				✓
iUP-200A/201A	✓				✓
EMV-51(2), EMV-44(2)				✓	✓
ICE-51(2), ICE-44(2)				✓	✓
iPDS + iUP-F87/44A PROM Programmer			✓		

NOTES:
1. Utilities include RL 51, LIB 51, and AEDIT. Software for Series II systems is down-revision version.
2. These products are no longer available.

ICE™-51/PC IN-CIRCUIT EMULATOR

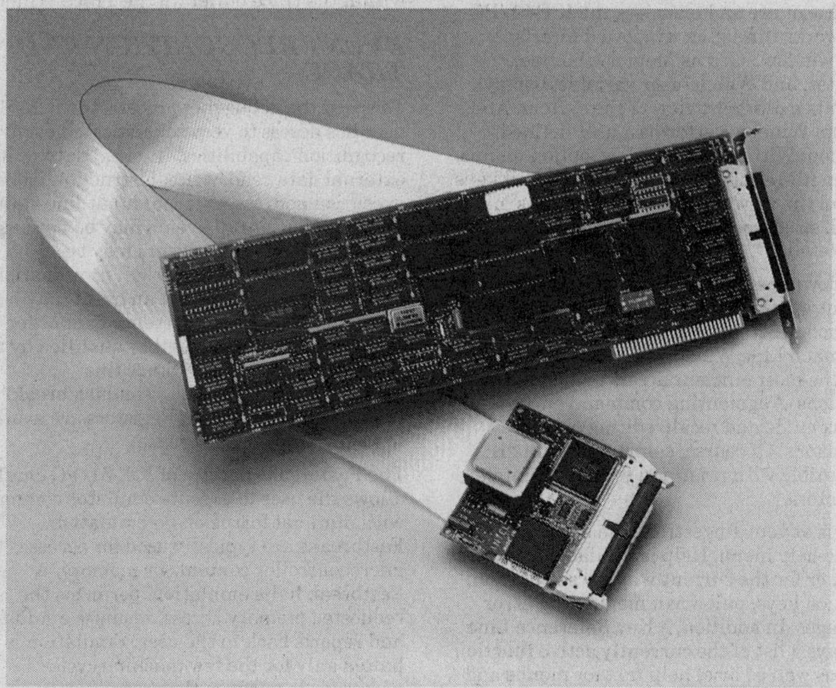

280883-1

CUT COSTS, NOT CORNERS

The ICE™-51/PC family in-circuit emulators for the MCS®-51 family of microcontrollers are easy to use, powerful, and attractive in price. A windowed user interface and source level debugging simplify use. The sophisticated event recognition features, the ability to access debug information during emulation, and performance analysis functions provide debugging power. Intel's long standing expertise in emulator design delivers impressive features for a very respectable price.

ICE™-51/PC FAMILY FEATURES

- Color windowed user interface
- Source level debugging with symbolic referencing and display
- Recognition of internal data write, external data read/write, instruction fetch, execution address, external input line state, and trace buffer full events
- AND/OR combination of events
- Qualification of an event by number of occurrences
- Arming of an event conditional on the occurrence of another event
- Access to microcontroller contents/memory during emulation
- 4096 frame trace buffer accessible during emulation
- Emulation and event timers for performance analysis
- User-definable debug and test procedures with variables and literal definitions
- Mappable emulator memory: 64 Kbytes code plus 64 Kbytes Xdata
- On-circuit emulation of surface mounted components
- Four input logic pins to capture external events

June 1991
Order Number: 280883-002

FEATURES

WINDOWED USER INTERFACE

For ease of use and learning, the ICE-51/PC user works through a windowed interface. Each window, such as Memory, Source, Register, and Watch (user variable display), presents a different view of the system. And a Custom Window performs a user-defined function. Within each window, option menus, pop-up fill-in-the-blank forms, and scroll keys control the view. As expected, windows may be added, sized, zoomed to full screen, or removed completely.

Pull-down menus and function keys streamline emulator use by providing convenient access to common functions. On the other hand, the Command Line Window provides the power user the most efficient access to all emulator functions. Augmenting command entry is a syntax guide and recall/editing of prior commands. Of course, command syntax is compatible with prior non-windowed Intel emulators.

Help is at your fingertips. One keystroke pops up the help menu. Help is available by subject index or for the current window's operation, function keys, pull-down menus, and error messages. In addition, a Key Reference Line displays a list of the currently active function keys as well as brief help text for menus and forms.

SOURCE LEVEL DEBUGGING

Source level debugging features are synergistic with the windowed user interface. For example, simply use a pull-down menu to load the program. Breakpoints are set by pointing to a line of code within the Source Window and pressing a function key. Set trace specifications through the pop-up fill-in-the-blank form in the Trace Window. And with the current execution point and breakpoints highlighted in color, press a function key to begin emulation.

Scroll to another line in the Source Window and press a function key to execute to that point, bypassing yet retaining the previously set breakpoints. From there, use a pull-down menu to add a variable, referenced symbolically, to the Watch Window; with each press of another function key the program is executed one source line at a time and the Watch Window display is updated.

Source statements and symbolic information are also displayed when memory is disassembled (in the Memory Window) or within the trace buffer (in the Trace Window).

EVENT RECOGNITION AND TRACE

To speed the debugging process, the ICE-51/PC user has access to very sophisticated event recognition capabilities. Internal data write, external data read/write, instruction fetch, execution address, external input line state, and trace buffer full events may be used as triggers. Compound triggers may be constructed through AND/OR combinations of events. The recognition of an event may be armed based on the occurrence of another event. Events may be further qualified by a number of occurrences. Since this sophistication may lead to complex break/trace definitions, Break Registers are available to store definitions for reuse.

The Fastbreaks feature of ICE-51/PC emulator allows the user to execute emulator commands with minimal intrusion on emulation. Fastbreaks are typically used for accesses to microcontroller contents or memory. A Fastbreak halts emulation, performs the requested memory access, resumes emulation, and reports back to the user. Emulation is halted only for the few machine cycles necessary to perform the access.

Similarly, the trace buffer is accessible during emulation. The buffer produces 4096 frames of execution address, opcode in hex and mnemonic formats, operands in hex and symbolic formats, bus activity, external line (clips) states, and source code.

To aid performance analysis, an event timer records the time from/to specified events while an emulation timer records the total duration of emulation.

GENUINE INTEL TOOLS

The ICE-51/PC provides the most comprehensive support for Intel's MCS®-51 family of microcontrollers. When you trust your component selection to Intel, why trust its emulation to someone else? And the ICE-51/PC emulators work better because they work together with products, such as C compilers, from leading independent software vendors such as Archimedes, Franklin, and Micro Computer Control as well as Intel's own macro assembler and PL/M compiler.

SPECIFICATIONS

EMULATOR ELECTRICAL CHARACTERISTICS

The AC characteristics for all pins except P0, P2, ALE, and PSEN/ are maintained with a maximum capacitive target load 15pf less than specified in the component data sheet for the 8×C51GB.

The AC timing degradations for P0, P2, ALE, and PSEN/ are maintained with a maximum capacitive target load of 70pf.

The maximum rise and fall times for ALE and PSEN/ with a target load of 20pf are 7ns and 2ns respectively.

The maximum rise and fall times for P0 and P2 with a target load of 50pf are 27ns and 10ns respectively. Rise and fall times are specified at the 10% and 90% points.

The emulation processor requires 2 to 3 clock cycles longer to respond to reset.

For external program memory characteristics involving RD* and WR*, observe the following degradations:

- Setup time to RD* is 11ns longer (max.).
- It takes 30ns longer for data to appear on the bus with respect to WR* (max.).
- The falling edges of RD* and WR* can be delayed by 70ns (max.).

Table C-1 shows the characteristics for external program memory.

Table C-1. External Program Memory Characteristics

Symbol	Parameter	Minimum	Maximum	Units
TAVLL	Address Valid to ALE Low	.85TCLCL-19		ns
TLLAX	Address Hold after ALE Low	10		ns
TLLIV	ALE Low to Valid Instruction In		3.15TCLCL-18	ns
TLLPL	ALE Low to PSEN/Low	.85TCLCL-1		ns
TPLIV	PSEN/Low to Valid Instruction In		2.15TCLCL-18	ns
TPXIZ	Input Instr Float after PSEN/		24	ns
TPXAV	PSEN/ to Address Valid	TCLCL + 20		ns
TAVIV	Address to Valid Instruction In		4.15TCLCL-66	ns
TPLAZ	PSEN/ Low to Address Float		4	ns
TLLDV	ALE Low to Valid Data In		7.15TCLCL-18	ns
TAVDV	Address to Valid Data In		8.15TCLCL-66	ns

SPECIFICATIONS

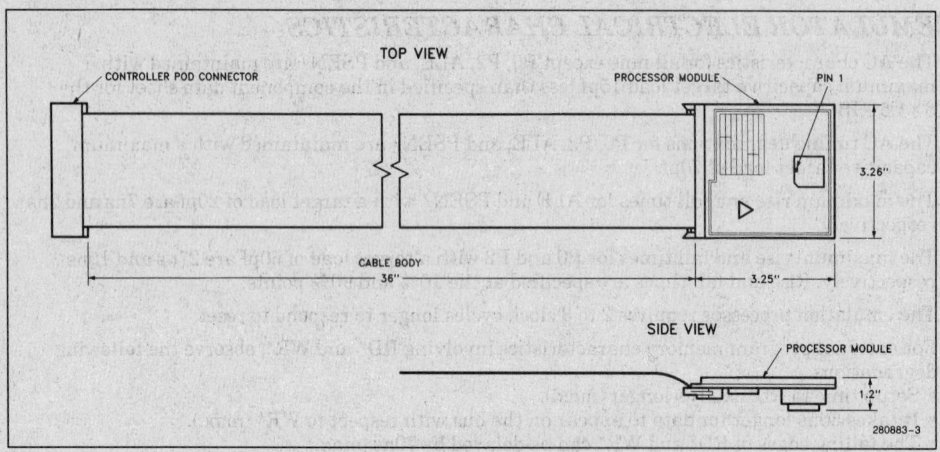

Figure 1: Processor Module Dimensions.
NOTE: Processor module dimensions will vary for the ICE-51FX/PC

WORLDWIDE SERVICE, SUPPORT, AND TRAINING

To augment its development tools, Intel offers a full array of seminars, classes, workshops, field application engineering expertise, hotline technical support, and on-site service.

Intel also offers a Software Support contract which includes technical software information, telephone support, automatic distributions of software and documentation updates, *iCOMMENTS* publication, remote diagnostic software, and a development tools troubleshooting guide.

Intel's 90-day Hardware Support package includes technical hardware information, telephone support, warranty on parts, labor, material, and on-site hardware support.

Intel Development Tools also offers a 30-day, money-back guarantee to customers who are not satisfied after purchasing any Intel development tool.

SPECIFICATIONS

CONFIGURATION AND ORDERING INFORMATION

The ICE-51/PC emulator utilizes an IBM PC XT, PC AT, or compatible personal computer with hard disk drive, 640 Kbytes of memory, and DOS 3.x as the host system. Emulator host software is provided on both 5.25 and 3.5 inch flexible disk media.

An ICE-51/PC emulator utilizes a common emulation controller card with interchangeable target interface boards (TIB). An ICE-51FX/PC may be converted to support the 87C51GB microcontroller by installing a probe kit. Likewise, an ICE-51G/PC may be converted to an ICE-51FX/PC by installing a probe kit.

A Crystal Power Accessory (CPA) is optionally available for testing the TIB to target system connection. Standalone software execution does not require a CPA.

EMULATOR KITS

pICE51FXPC — ICE-51FX/PC emulator kit. Contains all required emulator hardware and software to execute stand-alone or in-target. Kit includes emulation controller board (8-bit, PC-card form factor), 36″ cable (connects controller to probe), target probe fitted with a 40-pin male DIP adapter, and a 44-lead PLCC target adapter. Supports the following components:

1)8031	9)80C31BH-1	16)80C51FA	23)8752BH
2)8031AH	10)80C31BH-2	17)80C52	24)87C51
3)8032AH	11)80C32	18)83C51FA	25)87C51-1
4)8051	12)80C51BH	19)83C51FB	26)87C51-2
5)8051AH	13)80C51BH-1	20)8751BH	27)87C51FA
6)8051AHP	14)80C51BH-2	21)8751H	28)87C51FB
7)8052AH	15)80C51BHP	22)8751H-8	29)87C51FC
8)80C31BH			

pICE51GXPC — ICE-51GX/PC emulator kit. Contains all required emulator hardware and software to execute stand-alone or in-target. Kit includes emulation controller board (8-bit, PC-card form factor), 36″ cable (connects controller to probe), and target probe fitted with a 68-lead male PLCC adapter. Supports 87C51GB components (MCS-51 microcontrollers with on-chip A/D).

Note:
- PC host software is delivered in 5¼″ (360 kB) and 3½″ (720 kB) diskettes
- Emulator kit do NOT include a CPA (Crystal Power Accessory)

pICE51FXCPA — Crystal Power Accessory for ICE-51FX/PC (used to run confidence tests on probe's pin circuitry)

pICE51GXCPA — Crystal Power Accessory for ICE-51GX/PC (used to run confidence tests on probe's pin circuitry)

UPGRADE KITS

pICE51FXPROBE — Upgrade kit for existing ICE-51GX/PC emulators (kit includes FX target probe and PC host software)

pICE51GXPROBE — Upgrade kit for existing ICE-51FX/PC emulators (kit includes GX target probe and PC host software)

TARGET ADAPTERS

HADPTONC44PLCC — Target: 44-lead PLCC components (surface-mounted)

HADPTCA44EIAJ — Target: 44-lead EIAJ QFP components (surface-mounted)

SOFTWARE TOOLS

D86PLM51NL — DOS-hosted PL/M cross-compiler. Language features allow direct architecture access. Optimized for real-time, embedded applications.

D86ASM51NL — DOS-hosted macro assembler. Supports all MCS-51 components.

Note: All software tool packages include a relocator/linker (RL-51), an object-to-hex converter (OH-51), and a librarian (LIB-51).

iSBX™ 344A
BITBUS™ INTELLIGENT MULTIMODULE™ BOARD

- **High Performance 12 MHz 8044 Controller**
- **Integral Firmware Including the iDCX 51 Executive Optimized for Real-Time Control Applications**
- **Full BITBUS™ Support**
- **2 28-Pin JEDEC Memory Sites for User's Control Functions**
- **Low Cost, Double-Wide iSBX™ BITBUS Expansion MULTIMODULE™ Board**
- **Power Up Diagnostics**

The iSBX 344A BITBUS Intelligent MULTIMODULE board is the BITBUS gateway to all Intel products that support the iSBX I/O Expansion Interface. Based on the highly integrated 8044 component (an 8-bit 8051 microcontroller and an SDLC-based controller on one chip) the iSBX 344A MULTIMODULE board extends the capability of other microprocessors via the BITBUS interconnect. With the other members of Intel's Distributed Control Modules (iDCM) family, the iSBX 344A MULTIMODULE board expands Intel's OEM microcomputer system capabilities to include distributed real-time control. Like all members of the iDCM family, the iSBX 344A MULTIMODULE board includes many features that make it well suited for industrial control applications such as: data acquisition and monitoring, process control, robotics, and machine control.

280247–1

March 1988
Order Number: 280247-002

OPERATING ENVIRONMENT

Intel's Distributed Control Modules (iDCM) product family contains the building blocks to implement real-time distributed control applications. The iDCM family incorporates the BITBUS interconnect to provide standard high speed serial communication between microcontrollers. The iDCM hardware products: including the iSBX 344A MULTIMODULE board, iPCX 344A board and all iRCB BITBUS Remote Controller Boards communicate in an iDCM system via the BITBUS interconnect as shown in Figure 1.

As a member of the iDCM product line the iSBX 344A MULTIMODULE board fully supports the BITBUS microcontroller interconnect. Typically, the iSBX 344A MULTIMODULE board would be part of a node (master or slave) on the BITBUS interconnect in an iDCM system. As shown in Figure 2 the iSBX 344A MULTIMODULE board plugs into any iSBC® board with an iSBX connector.

The iSBX 344A MULTIMODULE board is the hardware interface between Intel's MULTIBUS® and the BITBUS environment. With this interface the user can harness the capabilities of other Intel microprocessors e.g. 80386, 80286, 80186, 8086, 80188, 8088 in a iDCM system or extend an existing MULTIBUS system with the iDCM family.

MULTIBUS® Expansion

Typically, MULTIBUS iSBC boards have a maximum of two iSBX I/O expansion connectors. These connectors facilitate addition of one or two iSBX I/O MULTIMODULE boards with varying numbers of I/O lines. The iSBX 344A MULTIMODULE board increases the number of I/O lines that can be accommodated by a MULTIBUS system by at least an order of magnitude.

Extending BITBUS™/iDCM System Processing Capability

The iSBX 344A MULTIMODULE board allows utilization of other processors in a iDCM system to accommodate particular application requirements. The MULTIMODULE board is compatible with any iSBX connector so that any board having a compatible connector can potentially enhance system performance. Intel's DCS100 BITBUS Toolbox Software provides easy to use high performance software interfaces for iSBC boards. The iSBC 86/35, 286/12, and 188/48 boards are a few examples. Custom configurations are also possible with user customized software.

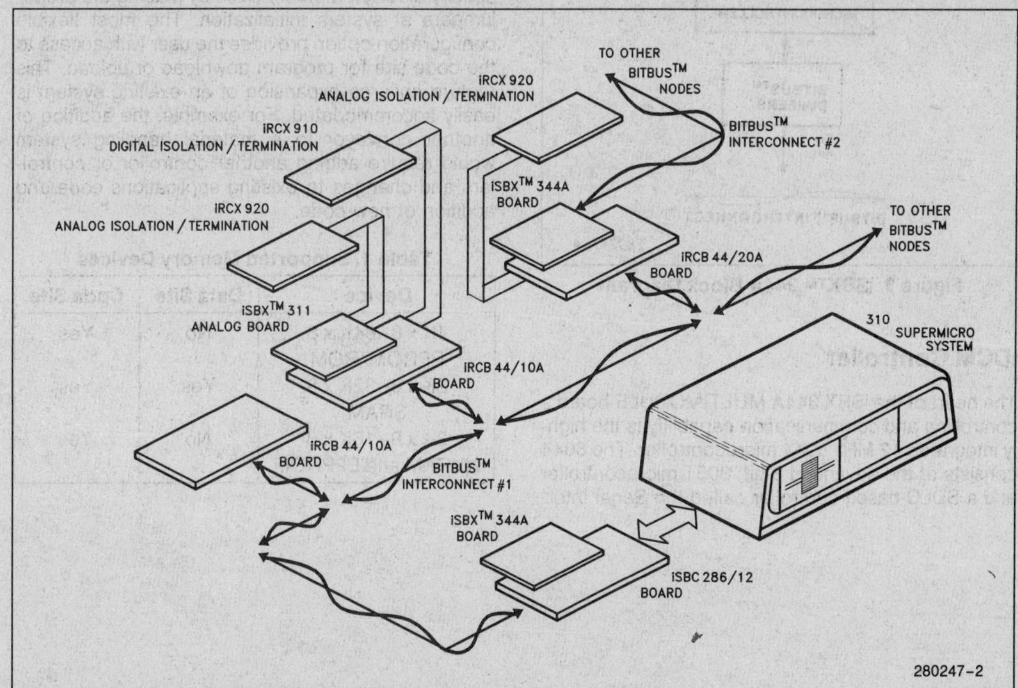

Figure 1. iDCM Operating Environment

ARCHITECTURE

Figure 3 illustrates the major functional blocks of the iSBX 344A board: 8044 BITBUS Enhanced Microcontroller (BEM), memory, BITBUS microcontroller interconnect, Byte FIFO interface, initialization and diagnostic logic.

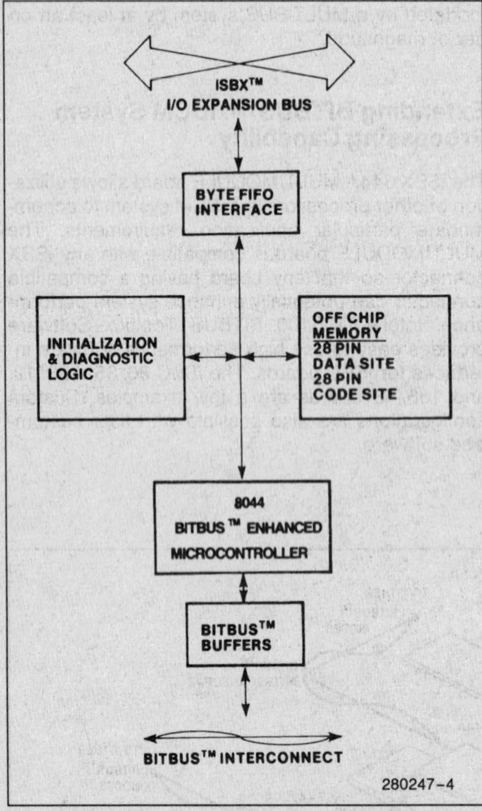

Figure 3. iSBX™ 344A Block Diagram

iDCM Controller

The heart of the iSBX 344A MULTIMODULE board's controlling and communication capability is the highly integrated 12 MHz 8044 microcontroller. The 8044 consists of the advanced 8-bit, 8051 microcontroller and a SDLC-based controller called the Serial Interface Unit (SIU). This dual processor architecture allows complex control and high speed communication to be realized cost effectively.

The 8044 BEM microcontroller also includes built-in firmware known as DCM44. This firmware includes a set of functions called Remote Access and Control (RAC), a preconfigured version of the DCX51 Executive, communications software, and a power-up test procedure.

Memory

The iSBX 344A MULTIMODULE board memory consists of two internal and external memory. Internal memory is located in the on-chip memory of the iDCM controller. The iDCX 51 Executive and the remaining 8044 BEM firmware ration this resource. However, eight bytes of bit addressable internal memory are reserved for the user. Ample space is reserved for user programs and data in the iSBX 344A MULTIMODULE board external memory.

Two 28-pin JEDEC sites comprise the iSBX 344A MULTIMODULE board external memory. One site has been dedicated for data; the other for code. Table 1 lists the supported memory devices for each site. Intel's 2764 and 27128 are examples. The user may choose one of two memory configurations and specify different memory sizes by placing the proper jumpers at system initialization. The most flexible configuration option provides the user with access to the code site for program download or upload. This feature ensures expansion of an existing system is easily accommodated. For example, the addition of another conveyor to a material handling system would require adding another controller or controllers and changes to existing applications code and addition of new code.

Table 1. Supported Memory Devices

Device	Data Site	Code Site
4K x 8–64K x 8 EPROM/ROM	No	Yes
2K x 8–32K x 8 SRAM	Yes	Yes
2K x 8–16K x 8 NVRAM and E2PROM	No	Yes

BITBUS™ Microcontroller Interconnect

The iSBX 344A MULTIMODULE board fully supports the BITBUS microcontroller interconnect. The BITBUS interconnect is a serial bus optimized for control applications. The interconnect supports both synchronous and self-clocked modes of operation. These modes of operation are selectable dependent on application requirements as are the transmission rates. Table 2 shows different combinations of modes of operations, transmission rates, and distances. The SDLC-based protocol, BITBUS message format, and compatibility with Intel's other software and hardware products comprise the remainder of this established architecture. These features contribute to BITBUS reliability and usefulness as a microcontroller interconnect.

The BITBUS connection consists of one or two differential pair(s) of wires. The BITBUS interface of the iSBX 344A MULTIMODULE board consists of a half-duplex RS 485 transceiver and an optional clock source for the synchronous mode of operation.

Byte FIFO Interface

The Byte FIFO Interface on the iSBX 344A MULTIMODULE board implements the required hardware buffering between the 8044 BEM and an extension. An extension is defined as a device attached to the iSBX I/O expansion interface on the iSBX 344A MULTIMODULE board. In an iDCM system, an example of an extension is an iSBC 286/12 board which may be considered the host board in a MULTIBUS system. When used with the software handlers in the BITBUS Toolbox, implementation of this interface is complete.

For particular applications, the user may wish to develop a custom software interface to the extension or host board. On the iSBX 344A MULTIMODULE board side of the interface the iDCM firmware automatically accepts messages for the FIFO. No user code is required, increasing the time available for application system development.

The Byte FIFO supports both byte and message transfer protocol in hardware via three register ports: data, command, and status. The extension side supports polled, interrupt, and limited DMA modes of operation (e.g. 80186 type DMA controllers).

Initialization and Diagnostic Logic

Like the other members of Intel's Distributed Control Modules (iDCM) product line, the iSBX 344A MULTIMODULE board includes many features which make it well suited for industrial control applications. Power up diagnostics is just one of these features. Diagnostics simplify system startup considerably, by immediately indicating an 8044 BEM or external bus failure. The LEDs used for power up diagnostics are available for user diagnostics after power up as well as to further contribute to reliable operation of the system.

Initial iSBX 344A MULTIMODULE board parameters are set by positioning jumpers. The jumpers determine the BITBUS mode of operation: synchronous, self-clocked, transmission rate, and address of the iSBX module in the BITBUS system. This minimizes the number of spare boards to be stocked for multiple nodes, decreasing stocking inventory and cost.

INTEGRAL FIRMWARE

Resident firmware located in the 8044 BEM includes: a pre-configured iDCX 51 Executive for user program development; a Remote Access and Control (RAC) function that enables user communication and control of different microcontrollers and I/O points; a communications gateway to connect the BITBUS interconnect, iSBX bus, and iDCX 51 Executive tasks; and power up diagnostics.

16

Table 2. BITBUS™ Microcontroller Interconnect Modes of Operation

	Speed Kb/s	Maximum Distance Between Repeaters M/ft	Maximum # Nodes Per Segment	Maximum # Repeaters Between a Master and Any Slave
Synchronous	500–2400	30/100	28	0
Self Clocked	375	300/1000	28	2
	62.5	1200/4000	28	10

Segment: Distance between master and repeater or a repeater and a repeater.
Synchronous mode requires user supplied crystal.

The iDCX 51 Executive is an event-driven software manager that can respond to the needs of multiple tasks. This real-time multitasking executive provides: task management, timing, interrupt handling, and message passing services. Table 3 shows the iDCX 51 calls. Both the executive and the communications gateway allow for the addition of up to seven user tasks at each node while making BITBUS operations transparent.

The Remote Access and Control Function is a special purpose task that allows the user to transfer commands and program variables to remote BITBUS controllers, obtain the status of a remote I/O line(s), or reverse the state of a remote I/O line. Table 4 provides a complete listing of the RAC services. No user code need be written to use this function.

The services provided by the iSBX 344A MULTIMODULE board integral firmware simplify the development and implementation of complex real-time control application systems. All iDCM hardware products contain integral firmware thus supplying the user with a total system solution.

DEVELOPMENT ENVIRONMENT

Intel provides a complete development environment for the iSBX 344A MULTIMODULE board. Software development support consists of: the 8051 Software Development Package, the DCS100 BITBUS Toolbox Host Software Utilities, the DSC110 Bitware for ICE™ Support, and the DCS120 Programmer's Support Package. The 8051 Software Development Package provides the RL 51 Linker and Relocator Program, and ASM 51. PL/M 51 is also available. Hardware tools consist of the In-Circuit Emulator (ICE 5100/044).

Table 3. iDCX 51 Calls

Call Name	Description
TASK MANAGEMENT CALLS	
RQ$CREATE$TASK	Create and schedule a new task.
RQ$DELETE$TASK	Delete specified task from system.
RQGETFUNCTION$IDS	Obtain the function IDs of tasks currently in the system.
INTERTASK COMMUNICATION CALLS	
RQ$ALLOCATE	Obtain a message buffer from the system buffer pool.
RQ$DEALLOCATE	Return a message buffer to the system buffer pool.
RQ$SEND$MESSAGE	Send a message to specified task.
RQ$WAIT	Wait for a message event.
MEMORY MANAGEMENT CALLS	
RQGETMEM	Get available SMP memory.
RQ$RELEASE$MEM	Release SMP memory.
INTERRUPT MANAGEMENT CALLS	
RQ$DISABLE$INTERRUPT	Temporarily disable an interrupt.
RQ$ENABLE$INTERRUPT	Re-enable an interrupt.
RQ$WAIT	Wait for an interrupt event.
TIMER MANAGEMENT CALLS	
RQSETINTERVAL	Establish a time interval.
RQ$WAIT	Wait for an interval event.

Table 4. RAC Services

RAC Service	Action Taken by Task 0
RESET__STATION	Perform a software reset.
CREATE__TASK	Perform an RQ$CREATE$TASK system call.
DELETE__TASK	Perform an RQ$DELETE$TASK system call.
GET__FUNCTION__ID	Perform an RQGETFUNCTION$IDS call.
RAC__PROJECT	Suspend or resume RAC services.
READ__I/O	Return values from specified I/O ports.
WRITE__I/O	Write to the specified I/O ports.
UPDATE__I/O	Update the specified I/O ports.
UPLOAD__MEMORY	Return the values in specified memory area.
DOWNLOAD__MEMORY	Write values to specified memory area.
OR__I/O	OR values into specified I/O ports.
AND__I/O	AND values into specified I/O ports.
XOR__I/O	XOR values into specified I/O ports.
READ__INTERNAL	Read values at specified internal RAM areas.
WRITE__INTERNAL	Write values to specified internal RAM areas.
NODE__INFO	Return device related information.
OFFLINE	Set node offline.
UPLOAD__CODE	Read values from code memory space.
DOWNLOAD__CODE	Write values to specified EEPROM memory.

NOTE:
Internal memory locations are included in the 192 bytes of data RAM provided in the microcontroller. External memory refers to memory outside the microcontroller — the 28-pin sockets of the iSBX 344A module and the iRCB 44/10A board. Each RAC Access Function may refer to multiple I/O or memory locations in a single command.

SPECIFICATIONS

CPU

8044 BITBUS Enhanced Microcontroller (BEM)

Word Size

Instruction: 8 bits

Data: 8 bits

Processor Clock 12 MHz

Instruction Execution Times

1 μs 60% instructions

2 μs 40% instructions

4 μs Multiply & Divide

Memory Capacity/Addressing

iDCM Controller: Up to 64 Kbytes code

Address Range

	Option A	Option B
External Data Memory	0000H–7FFFH	0000H–7FFFH
External Code Memory	1000H–0FFFFH	8000H–0FEFFH
Internal Code Memory	0000H–0FFFH	0000H–0FFFH

Option A: Supports maximum amount of external EPROM code memory.
Option B: Supports downloading code into external RAM or EEPROM memory.

Terminations

Sockets provided on board for ¼ Watt 5% Carbon type resistors. Resistor value to match characteristic impedance of cable as closely as possible—120Ω or greater.

Message Size

54 bytes max

8044 BITBUS™ Enhanced Microcontroller (8044 + Firmware) I/O Addressing as Viewed from the 8044

Function	Address	Read	Write	Bit	Comments
Data	FF00H	✓	✓		
Command	FF01H	✓	✓		Write sets command to extension — Read clears command from extension
Status					
-RFNF*	B3H	✓		✓	Also INT1 Input
-TFNE*	B2H	✓		✓	Also INT0 Input
-TCMD*	92H	✓		✓	
LED #1	90H	✓	✓	✓	
LED #2	91H	✓	✓	✓	
RDY/NE*	B4H	✓	✓	✓	
Node Address	FFFFH	✓			
Configuration	FFFEH	✓			

iSBX™ 344A MULTIMODULE™ Board I/O Addressing as Viewed from the iSBX™ 344A MULTIMODULE™ Board

Register Function	Address	Comments
Data	Base′	Read/Write
Command	Base′ + 1	Write sets command from extension Read clears command to extension
Status	Base′ + 2	Read Only

Interrupt/DMA Lines

Signal	Location	Interface Option
RINT	MDRQ/MINT0	INT
TINT	MINT1	INT
RCMI	OPT0	INT or DMA
RDRQ	MDRQ/MINT0	DMA
TDRQ	MINT1	DMA

Status Register Interface

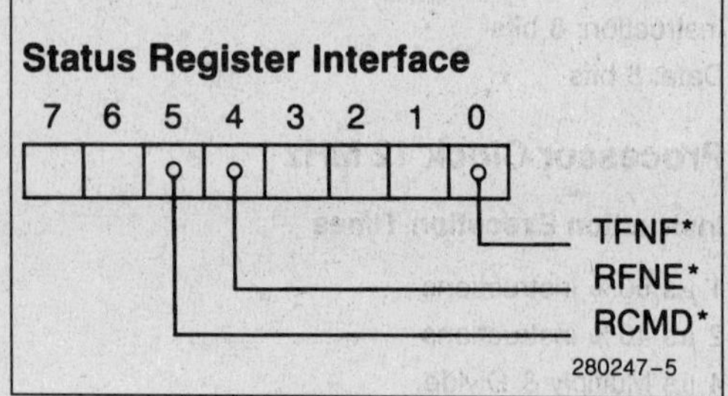

Connector Options

10 Pin Plug

Flat Cable: 3M 3473-6010, TB Ansley 609-1001M, or equal

Discrete Wire: BERG 65846-007, ITT Cannon 121-7326-105, or equal

Pinout

Pin	Signal
1	+12V
2	+12V
3	GND
4	GND
5	DATA*
6	DATA
7	DCLK*/RTS*
8	DCLK/RTS
9	RGND
10	RGND

Electrical Characteristics

Interfaces

iSBX™ I/O Expansion Bus: supports the standard I/O Expansion Bus Specification with compliance level IEEE 959.

Memory Sites: Both code and data sites support the standard 28-pin JEDEC site.

BITBUS™ Interconnect: Fully supported synchronous mode at 2.4 Mbits/sec and self clocked mode for 375 kbits/sec and 62.5 kbits/sec

The iSBX 344A MULTIMODULE board presents one standard load to the BITBUS bus

Power Requirements

0.9A at +5V ±5% (does not include power to the memory devices)

Physical Characteristics

Double-wide iSBX™ MULTIMODULE™ Form Factor

Dimensions

Height: 10.16 mm (0.4 in) maximum component height
Width: 63.5 mm (2.50 in)
Length: 190.5 mm (7.50 in)
Weight: 113 gm (4 ounces)

Environmental Characteristics

Operating Temperature: 0°C to 55°C at 200 Linear Feet/Minute Air Velocity

Humidity: 90% non-condensing

Reference Manual (NOT Supplied)

148099— iSBX 344A Intelligent BITBUS Interface Board User's Guide

Ordering Information

Part Number	Description
iSBX 344A	BITBUS Intelligent MULTIMODULE board

iRCB 44/10A
BITBUS™ DIGITAL I/O REMOTE CONTROLLER BOARD

- High Performance 12 MHz 8044 Controller
- Integral Firmware: iDCX Executive, Optimized for Real-Time Control
- Full BITBUS™ Support
- Standard Industrial Packaging: Eurocard, DIN Connector
- 2 28-Pin JEDEC Memory Sites for User's Control Functions
- I/O Expansion with 8-Bit iSBX™ Connector
- Programmable Control/Monitoring Using 24 Digital I/O Lines
- Power Up Diagnostics
- Compatible with iRCX 910 Digital Signal Isolation and Termination Module

The iRCB 44/10A BITBUS™ Digital I/O Remote Controller Board is an intelligent real-time controller and a remote I/O expansion device. Based on the highly integrated 8044 component (an 8 bit 8051 microcontroller and an intelligent SDLC-based controller on one chip) the iRCB 44/10A board provides high performance control capability at low cost. The iRCB 44/10A board can expand Intel's OEM microcomputer system capabilities to include distributed real-time control. Like all members of the iDCM family, the iRCB 44/10A board is well suited for industrial control applications such as data acquisition and monitoring, process control, robotics, and machine control.

280213–1

September 1990
Order Number: 280213-003

OPERATING ENVIRONMENT

Intel's Distributed Control Modules (iDCM) product family contains the building blocks to implement real-time distributed control applications. The iDCM family incorporates the BITBUS interconnect to provide standard high speed serial communication between microcontrollers. The iDCM hardware products, which include the iPCX 344A board, iSBX 344A MULTIMODULE™ board and the iRCB 44/10A BITBUS Remote Controller Board (and other iRCB boards), communicate in an iDCM system via the BITBUS interconnect as shown in Figure 1.

The iRCB 44/10A board can be used as an intelligent remote controller or an I/O expansion device. When performing as an intelligent controller the iRCB 44/10A board not only monitors the status of multiple process points, but it can execute varied user supplied control algorithms. When functioning as an I/O expansion device, the iRCB 44/10A board simply collects data from multiple I/O ports and transmits this information via the BITBUS or iSBX bus interface to the system controller for analysis or updating purposes.

As a member of the iDCM product line, the iRCB 44/10A board fully supports the BITBUS microcontroller interconnect. Typically, the iRCB 44/10A board would be a node in a BITBUS system. The iRCB 44/10A board could be a master or slave node. (The BITBUS system supports a multidrop configuration: one master, many slaves.)

ARCHITECTURE

Figure 2 illustrates the major functional blocks of the iRCB 44/10A board: 8044 BITBUS Enhanced Microcontroller, memory, BITBUS microcontroller interconnect, parallel I/O, iSBX expansion, initialization and diagnostic logic.

8044 BITBUS™ Enhanced Microcontroller

The heart of the iRCB 44/10A board's controlling and communication capability is the highly integrated 12 MHz 8044 microcontroller. The 8044 consists of the advanced 8-bit 8051 microcontroller and a SDLC controller called the Serial Interface Unit (SIU). This dual processor architecture allows complex control and high speed communication functions to be realized cost effectively. The 8044's SIU acts as a SDLC-based controller which offloads the on-chip 8051 microcontroller of communication tasks; freeing the 8051 to concentrate on real-time control.

The 8044 BEM microcontroller also includes, in firmware, a set of procedures known as Remote Access and Control (RAC), a preconfigured version of the DCX 51 Executive, communications software, and power-up diagnostics.

The BEM (8044 microcontroller and on-chip firmware) provides, in one package, a simple user interface, and high performance communications and control capabilities to efficiently and economically build a complex control system.

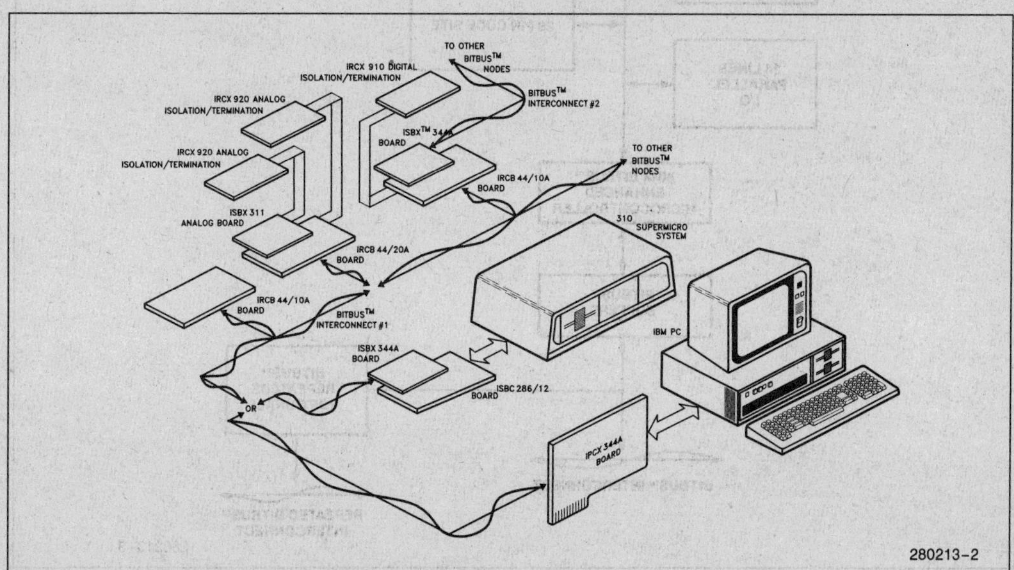

Figure 1. iDCM Operating Environment

Memory

The iRCB 44/10A board memory consists of two sections: internal and external. Internal memory is located in the on-chip memory of the BEM. The iDCX51 Executive and the remaining BEM firmware ration this resource. However, eight bytes of bit addressable internal memory are reserved for the user. Ample space is reserved for user programs and data in the iRCB 44/10A board external memory.

Two 28 pin JEDEC sites comprise the iRCB 44/10A board external memory. One site has been dedicated for data, the other for code. Table 1 lists the supported memory devices for each site. Intel's 2764, and 27128 are examples. The user may choose one of two memory configurations and specify different memory sizes by placing the proper jumpers at system initialization. The most flexible configuration option provides the user with access to the code site for program download or upload. This feature ensures expansion of an existing system is easily accommodated.

Table 1. Supported Memory Devices

Device	Data Site	Code Site
4K × 8-64K × 8 EPROM/ROM	NO	YES
2K × 8-32K × 8 SRAM.	YES	YES
2K × 8-16K × 8 NVRAM and E2PROM	NO	YES

BITBUS™ Microcontroller Interconnect

The iRCB 44/10A board serial interface fully supports the BITBUS microcontroller interconnect. The BITBUS interconnect is a serial bus optimized for

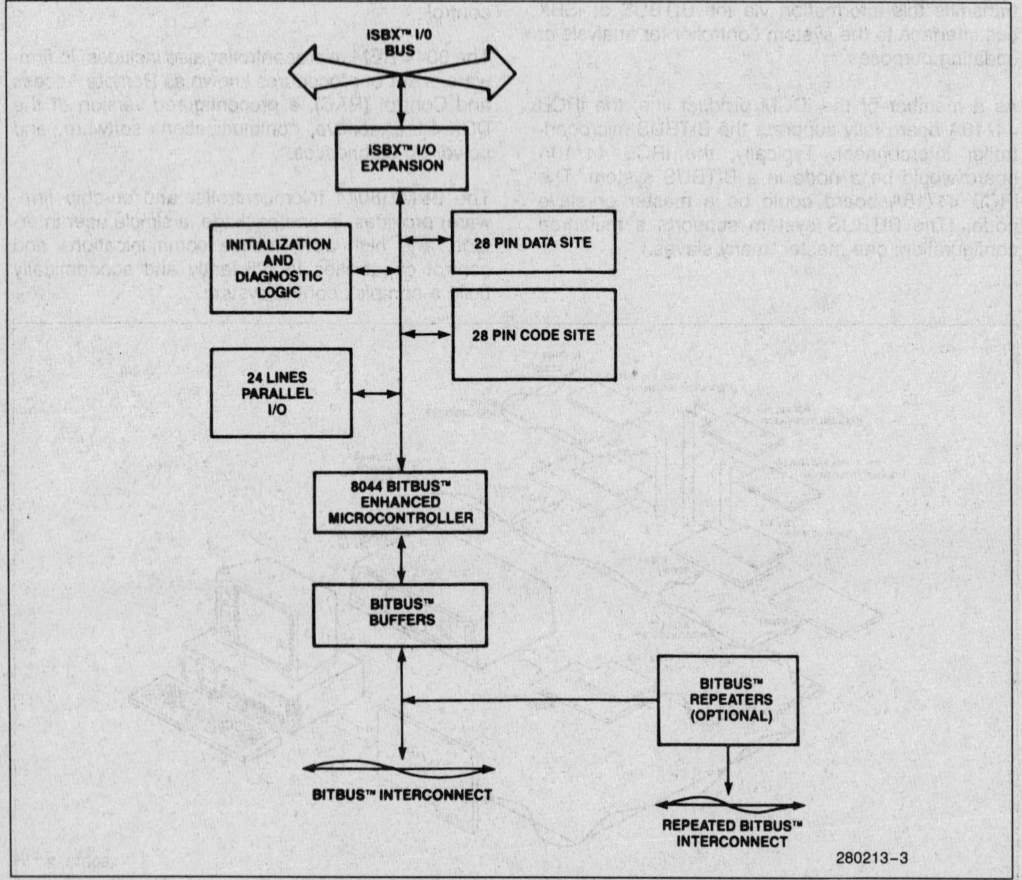

Figure 2. iRCB™ 44/10A Block Diagram

control applications. The bus supports both synchronous and self-clocked modes of operation. These modes of operation are selectable dependent on application requirements as are the transmission speeds. Table 2 shows the different combinations of modes of operation, transmission speeds, and distances. The SDLC-based protocol, BITBUS message format, and compatibility with Intel's other software and hardware products comprise the remainder of the BITBUS architecture. These features contribute to BITBUS system reliability and usefulness as a microcontroller interconnect.

The BITBUS connection consists of one or two differential pair(s) of wires. The serial (BITBUS) interface of the iRCB 44/10A board consists of: a half-duplex RS 485 transceiver, an optional BITBUS repeater and an optional clock source for the synchronous mode of operation.

Digital Parallel I/O

In order to provide an optimal parallel I/O interface for control applications, the iRCB 44/10A board supports 24 software programmable parallel I/O lines. This feature supplies the flexibility and simplicity required for control and data acquisition systems. Sixteen of these lines are fully programmable as inputs or outputs, with loopback, on a bit by bit basis so that bit set, reset, and toggle operations are streamlined. The remaining eight lines are dedicated as inputs. Figure 3 depicts the general I/O port structure.

The parallel I/O lines can be manipulated by using the Remote Access and Control (RAC) function (in BEM firmware) from a supervisory node or locally by a user program. The user program can also access the RAC function or directly operate the I/O lines. Input, output, mixed— input and output, and bit operations are possible simply by reading or writing a particular port.

iSBX™ Expansion

One iSBX I/O expansion connector is provided on the iRCB 44/10A board. This connector can be used to extend the I/O capability of the board. In addition to specialized and custom designed iSBX boards, a full line of compatible high speed, 8-bit expansion MULTIMODULE boards, both single and double wide, are available from Intel. The only incompatible modules are those that require the MWAIT* signal or DMA operation. A few of Intel's iRCB 44/10A board compatible iSBX MULTIMODULE boards include: parallel I/O, serial I/O, BITBUS expansion, IEEE 488 GPIB, analog input and analog output.

With the iSBX 344A BITBUS Controller MULTIMODULE board and user supplied software, the iRCB 44/10A board can act as an intelligent BITBUS repeater facilitating the transition between two BITBUS segments operating at different speeds.

Initialization and Diagnostic Logic

Like the other members of Intel's Distributed Control Modules (iDCM) product line, the iRCB 44/10A board includes many features which make it well suited for industrial control applications. Power up diagnostics is just one of these features. Diagnostics simplify system startup considerably, by immediately indicating an iDCM controller or external bus failure. The LEDs used for power up diagnostics are

Table 2. BITBUS™ Microcontroller Interconnect Modes of Operation

	Speed Kb/s	Maximum Distance Between Repeaters M/ft	Maximum #Nodes Per Segment*	Maximum # Repeaters Between A Master And Any Slave
Synchronous	500–2400	30/100	28	0
Self Clocked	375 62.5	300/1000 1200/4000	28 28	2 10

*Segment: Distance between master and repeater or repeater and repeater. Synchronous mode requires user supplied crystal.

16

available for user diagnostics after power up as well to further contribute to reliable operation of the system.

Initial iRCB 44/10A board parameters are set by positioning jumpers. The jumpers determine the BITBUS mode of operation: synchronous, self clocked, transmission speed, and address of the iRCB 44/10A board in the BITBUS system. This minimizes the number of spare boards to be stocked for multiple nodes, decreasing stocking inventory and cost.

INTEGRAL FIRMWARE

The iRCB 44/10A board contains resident firmware located in the 8044 BEM. The on-chip firmware consists of: a pre-configured iDCX 51 Executive for user program development; a Remote Access and Controller (RAC) function that enables user communication and control of different microcontrollers and I/O points; a communications gateway to connect the BITBUS interconnect, iSBX bus, iPCX bus and iDCX 51 tasks; and power up diagnostics.

Table 3. iDCX 51 Executive Calls

Call Name	Description
TASK MANAGEMENT CALLS	
RQ$CREATE$TASK	Create and schedule a new task.
RQ$DELETE$TASK	Delete specified task from system.
RQGETFUNCTION$IDS	Obtain the function IDs of tasks currently in the system.
INTERTASK COMMUNICATION CALLS	
RQ$ALLOCATE	Obtain a message buffer from the system buffer pool.
RQ$DEALLOCATE	Return a message buffer to the system buffer pool.
RQ$SEND$MESSAGE	Send a message to specified task.
RQ$WAIT	Wait for a message event.
MEMORY MANAGEMENT CALLS	
RQGETMEM	Get available SMP memory.
RQ$RELEASE$MEM	Release SMP memory.
INTERRUPT MANAGEMENT CALLS	
RQ$DISABLE$INTERRUPT	Temporarily disable an interrupt.
RQ$ENABLE$INTERRUPT	Re-enable an interrupt.
RQ$WAIT	Wait for an interrupt event.
TIMER MANAGEMENT CALLS	
RQSETINTERVAL	Establish a time interval.
RQ$WAIT	Wait for an interval event.

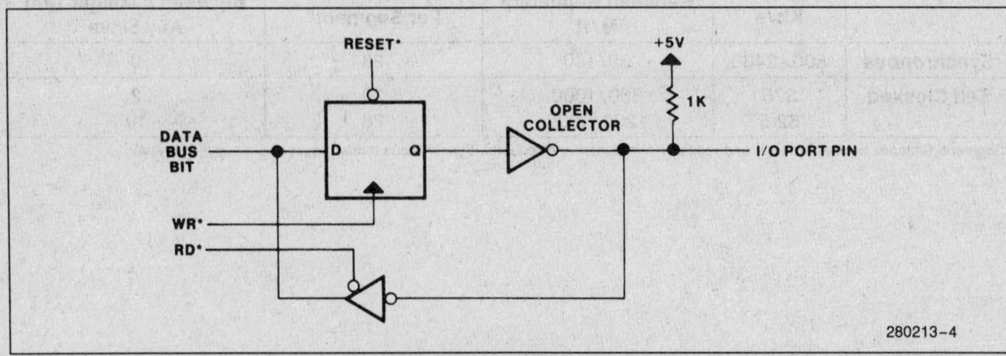

Figure 3. I/O Port Structure

The iDCX 51 Executive is an event-driven software manager that can respond to the needs of multiple tasks. This real-time multitasking executive provides: task management, timing, interrupt handling, and message passing services. Table 3 shows the iDCX 51 calls. Both the Executive and the communications gateway allow for the addition of up to seven user tasks at each node while making BITBUS operation transparent.

The Remote Access and Control Function is a special purpose task that allows the user to transfer commands and program variables to remote BITBUS controllers, obtain the status of a remote I/O line(s), or reverse the state of a remote I/O line. Table 4 provides a complete listing of the RAC services. No user code need be written to use this function. Power up tests provide a quick diagnostic service.

The services provided by the iRCB 44/10A board integral firmware simplify the development and implementation of complex real-time control application systems. All iDCM hardware products contain integral firmware thus supplying the user with a total system solution.

Table 4. RAC Services

RAC Service	Action Taken by Task 0
RESET__STATION	Perform a software reset.
CREATE__TASK	Perform an RQ$CREATE$TASK system call.
DELETE__TASK	Perform an RQ$DELETE$TASK system call.
GET__FUNCTION__ID	Perform an RQGETFUNCTION$IDS call.
RAC__PROTECT	Suspend or resume RAC services.
READ__IO	Return values from specified I/O ports.
WRITE__IO	Write to the specified I/O ports.
UPDATE__IO	Update the specified I/O ports.
UPLOAD__MEMORY	Return the values in specified memory area.
DOWNLOAD__MEMORY	Write values to specified memory area.
OR__I/O	OR values into specified I/O ports.
AND__I/O	AND values into specified I/O ports.
XOR__I/O	XOR values into specified I/O ports.
READ__INTERNAL	Read values at specified internal RAM areas.
WRITE__INTERNAL	Write values at specified internal RAM areas.
NODE__INFO	Return device related information.
OFFLINE	Set node offline.
UPLOAD__CODE	Read values from code memory space.
DOWNLOAD__CODE	Write values to specified EEPROM memory.

INDUSTRIAL PACKAGING

The iRCB 44/10A form factor is a single high, 220 mm deep Eurocard and supports most standard industrial packaging schemes as well as Intel's RCX 910 Digital Signal Conditioning, Isolation and Termination Module (see below). The Eurocard form factor specifies reliable DIN connectors. A standard 64 pin connector is included on the iRCB 44/10A board.

Physical Characteristics

Single high, 220 mm deep Eurocard Form Factor

Dimensions

Width: 13.77 mm (0.542 in) maximum component height

Height: 100 mm (3.93 in.)

Depth: 220 mm (8.65 in.)

Weight: 169 gm (6 ounces)

DIGITAL SIGNAL CONDITIONING, ISOLATION, AND TERMINATION

The RCB 44/10A is fully compatible with the RCX 910 Digital Signal Conditioning, Isolation and Termination Panel. The RCX 910 panel provides integral mounting for one RCB 44/10A, with connectors for power, the BITBUS interconnect signals, and 24 Industry Standard I/O isolation and signal conditioning modules. These modules, available from a number of vendors worldwide, typically provide greater than 1500V isolation and support signal conditioning in a number of voltages including 5–60 VDC, 120 and 240 VAC.

SPECIFICATIONS

Word Size

Instruction: 8 bits

Data: 8 bits

Processor Clock 12 MHz

Instruction Execution Times

1 μsec 60% instructions
2 μsec 40% instructions
4 μsec Multiply & Divide

Memory Capacity/Addressing

iDCM Controller: Up to 64 Kbytes code

DEVELOPMENT ENVIRONMENT

Intel provides a complete development environment for the iRCB 44/10A board.

BITBUS™ Development Environments

	BITBUS™ TOOLS: DCS 100 TOOLBOX						BITBUS™ TOOLS		NODE CODE			ICE™	EPROM PROG.	
	BBM	UBI	BIH	PC Bridge	OBJHEX	UDI2DOS	DCS 110	DCS 120	ASM 51	PL/M 51	RL 51, LIB 51	ICE 5100/044	iUP200A/201A with iUPF87/44A module and iPPS sw	iPDS with iUPF87/44A module and iPPS sw
Series II									C	C	C		X	
III			X				X	X	X	X	X	X	X	
IV							X	X	X	X	X	X	X	
iPDS	A	A	A				X	X	C	C	C			X
iRMX 5¼″	X	X	X	X	X		X	X	D	D	D			
8″	X	X	X	X	X		X	X	D	D	D			
XENIX 5¼″	X	X		B	X									
8″	X	X		B	X									
DOS	X	X	X	X	X	X	X	X	X	X	X	X	X	

NOTES:
A. iPDS uses Release 1 Toolbox.
B. Supports operation with XENIX. XENIX disks not required.
C. Down-revision version.
D. Available for iRMX® 86.

Address Ranges

Memory	Option A	Option B
External —Data —Code	0000H-7FFFH 1000H-0FFFFH	0000H-7FFFH 8000H-0FEFFH
Internal	0000H-0FFFH	0000H-0FFFH

NOTES:
Option A: Supports maximum amount of external EPROM code memory.
Option B: Supports downloading code into RAM or EEPROM memory.

Interrupt Sources

Two external: iSBX I/O Expansion bus sources or other sources.
BITBUS Microcontroller Interconnect.

8044 BITBUS™ Enhanced Microcontroller I/O Addressing

Function	Address	Read	Write	Bit
PORT A	FFC0H	✓	✓	
PORT B	FFC1H	✓		
PORT C	FFC2H	✓	✓	
MCSO	FF80H-FF87H FF00, FF01	✓	✓	
MSC1	FF88H-FF8F	✓	✓	
LED #1	90H	✓	✓	✓
LED #2	91H	✓	✓	✓
RDY/NE*	B4H	✓	✓	✓
NODE ADDRESS	FFFFH	✓		
CONFIGURATION	FFFEH	✓		
OPT0	92H	✓	✓	✓
OPT1	93H	✓	✓	✓
INT0	B2H	✓		✓
INT1	B3H	✓		✓

PARALLEL I/O

Number: 2 8-Bit Bi-directional Ports
1 8-Bit Input Port

Table 5. Parallel I/O Electrical Specification

Parameter	Condition	Min	Max	Units
V_{OL}	$I_{OL} = 16$ mA		0.5	V
V_{OH}	$I_{OH} = -2$ mA	2.4		V
V_{IH}		2.0	7.0	V
V_{IL}		−1.0	0.8	V
I_{IL}	$V_{IL} = 0.5V$		6.0	mA
I_{IH}	V_{IH} = logic high		0.0	mA
I_I	$V_{IH} = 7V$		−2.2	mA

16

Terminations

Sockets provided on board for ¼ Watt 5% Carbon type resistors. Resistor value to match characteristic impedance of cable as closely as possible—120Ω or greater.

Repeaters

Sockets provided on board: Devices 75174 and 75175

Connector Options

10 PIN PLUG

Flat Cable: 3M 3473-6010, TB Ansley 609-1001M, or equal

Discrete Wire: BERG 65846-007, ITT Cannon 121-7326-105, or equal

DIN CONNECTOR PLUG

Flat Cable: GW Elco 00-8259-096-84-124, Robinson Nugent RNE-IDC64C-TG30, or equal

Discrete Wire: ITT Cannon G06 M96 P3 BDBL-004 GW Elco 60 8257 3017, or equal

10 Pin Repeater Connector Pin Out

Pin	Signal
1	+12V
2	+12V
3	GND
4	GND
5	DATA*
6	DATA
7	DCLK*/RTS*
8	DCLK/RTS
9	RGND
10	RGND

Electrical Characteristics

Interfaces

iSBX I/O expansion bus: supports the standard I/O Expansion Bus Specification with compliance level D8/8F

Memory Sites: Both code and data sites support the electrical Universal Memory Site specification

BITBUS™ Interconnect: The iRCB 44/10A Remote Controller Board supports the BITBUS Specification as follows:

Fully supported synchronous mode at 2.4 Mbits/second and self clocked mode for 375 kbits/second and 62.5 kbits/second

The iRCB 44/10A Remote Controller Board presents one standard load to the BITBUS without repeaters, with repeaters two standard loads

Message length up to 54 bytes supported

RAC Function support as shown in Table 4

Parallel I/O: See the Table 5 for Electrical Specifications of the interface.

Power Requirements

0.9A at +5V ±5% iRCB 44/10 board only (power to memory, repeater, or iSBX board NOT included)

Environmental Characteristics

Operating Temperature: 0°C to 55°C at 200 Linear Feet/Minute Air Velocity

Humidity: 90% non-condensing

Reference Manual (NOT Supplied)

iRCB 44/10A Digital I/O Remote 148100-001 Controller Board User's Guide

Ordering Information

Part Number	Description
RCB4410A	BITBUS Digital I/O Remote Controller Board

iRCB 44/20A ANALOG I/O CONTROLLER

- Distributed Intelligence via BITUS™ Serial Bus
- 8044 8-bit Microcontroller at 12 MHz
- 12-bit Analog Resolution
- Up To 20 KHz Aquisition Rate (50 ms)
- Software Programmable Gain: 1, 10, 100, 500
- Two 28-pin JEDEC Memory Sites
- 16 Single-ended or 8 Differential Input Channels
- 2 Outputs Channels
- ±10V Range or 4–20 mA Current Loop
- I/O Expandable via iSBX™ Connector
- Compact Single-Eurocard Packaging
- Low Power Consumption
- Compatible with iRCX 920 Analog Signal Conditioning, Isolation and Termination Panel

The iRCB 44/20A is a fully programmable analog I/O subsystem on a single-Eurocard form-factor board. The resident 8044 microcontroller operating at 12 MHz provides a means of executing data aquisition and control routines remote from the host computer. Real-time capability is made possible by the iDCX 51 Distributed Control Executive, resident in the 8044 microcontroller. Distribution of real-time control is implemented by the BITBUS Serial Bus protocol, which is also managed integrally by the 8044.

Offering high performance, low-cost, and improved system bandwidth via distributed intelligence, the iRCB 44/20A Analog I/O Controller is ideal for data acquisition and control in both laboratory and industrial environments.

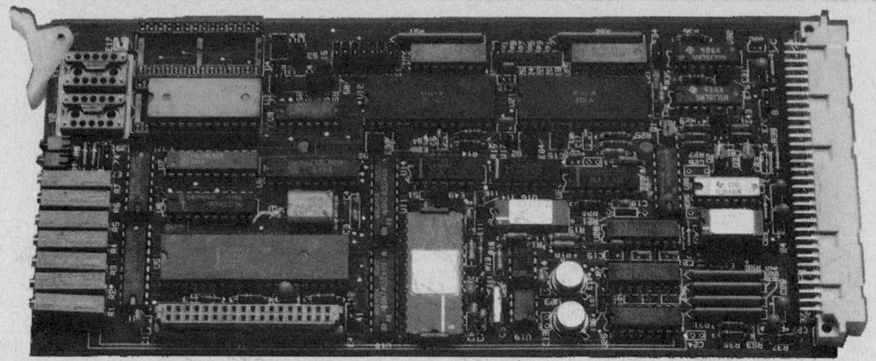

280721–1

16

MULTIMODULE™ is a trademark of Intel Corporation.

IBM® PC is a registered trademark of International Business Machines Corporation.

November 1988
Order Number: 280721-002

APPLICATION ENVIRONMENT

Intel's Distributed Control Modules (iDCM) product family contains the building blocks to implement real-time distributed control applications. The iDCM family incorporates the BITBUS interconnect to provide standard high-speed serial communication between microcontrollers. The iRCB 44/20A may communicate with other nodes in a distributed system via the BITBUS interconnect as shown in Figure 1. Other nodes in the system may be the iSBX 344A BITBUS Controller MULTIMODULE™, the iPCX 344A BITBUS IBM® PC Interface, the iRCB 44/10A BITBUS Digital I/O Controller Board, or other BITBUS compatible products.

The iRCB 44/20A board, can be used as an intelligent remote controller or an I/O expansion device. When performing as an intelligent controller the iRCB 44/20A board not only monitors the status of multiple sensors, it can also locally execute user developed control algorithms. When functioning as an I/O expansion device the iRCB 44/20A board manages the multiple I/O ports, transmitting this information via the BITBUS bus or iSBX interface to the system controller for analysis or data logging purposes.

Typically, the iRCB 44/20A board will operate as a node in a BITBUS system. BITBUS communication supports a multidrop configuration with one master, and multiple subordinate nodes. The iRCB 44/20A board may be either a master or slave node to manage a wide variety of analog input or output tasks.

FUNCTIONAL DESCRIPTION

The major functional blocks of the iRCB 44/20A board, shown in Figure 2, include the 8044 microcontroller and BITBUS interconnect, local memory, Analog I/O, and iSBX expansion.

Distributed Intelligence

The heart of the iRCB 44/20A board's controlling and communication capability is the highly integrated 8044 microcontroller which operates at 12 MHz. The 8044 contains the advanced 8-bit, 8051 microcontroller and a complimentary SDLC controller, called the Serial Interface Unit (SIU). This dual processor architecture provides complex control and high speed communication functions at a low cost.

Another essential part of the 8044 controller is the on-chip firmware that exercises the BITBUS interface. The 8044's SIU acts as an SDLC controller, off loading the on-chip microcontroller of communication tasks so it may concentrate on real-time control.

The 8044 microcontroller simplifies the user interface, and offers high performance communications and control capabilities in a single component package. Many interconnected Distributed Control Modules can form a powerful platform to efficiently and economically administer a complete control system.

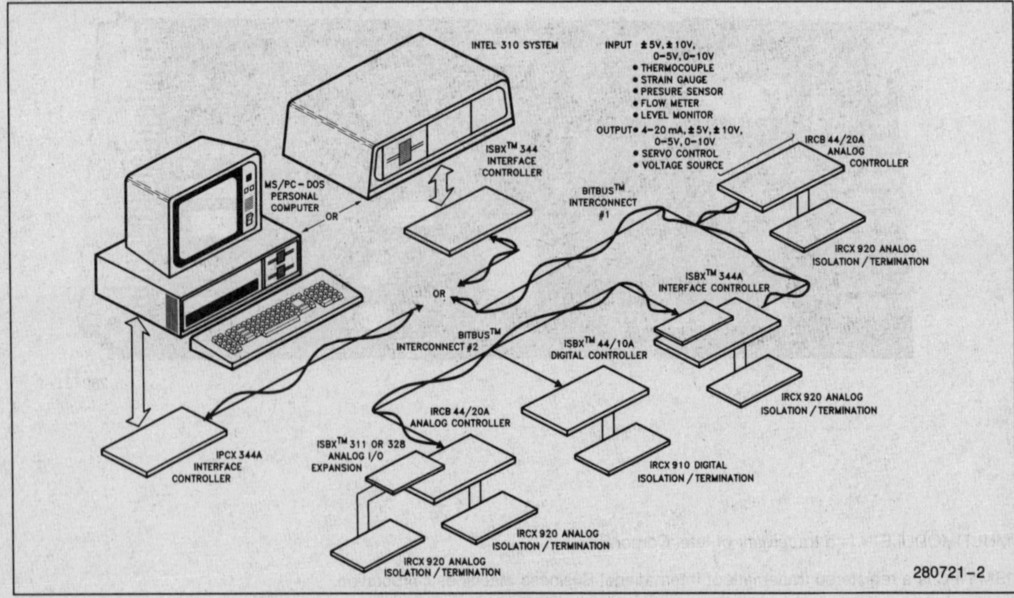

Figure 1. BITBUS Distributed Control Example

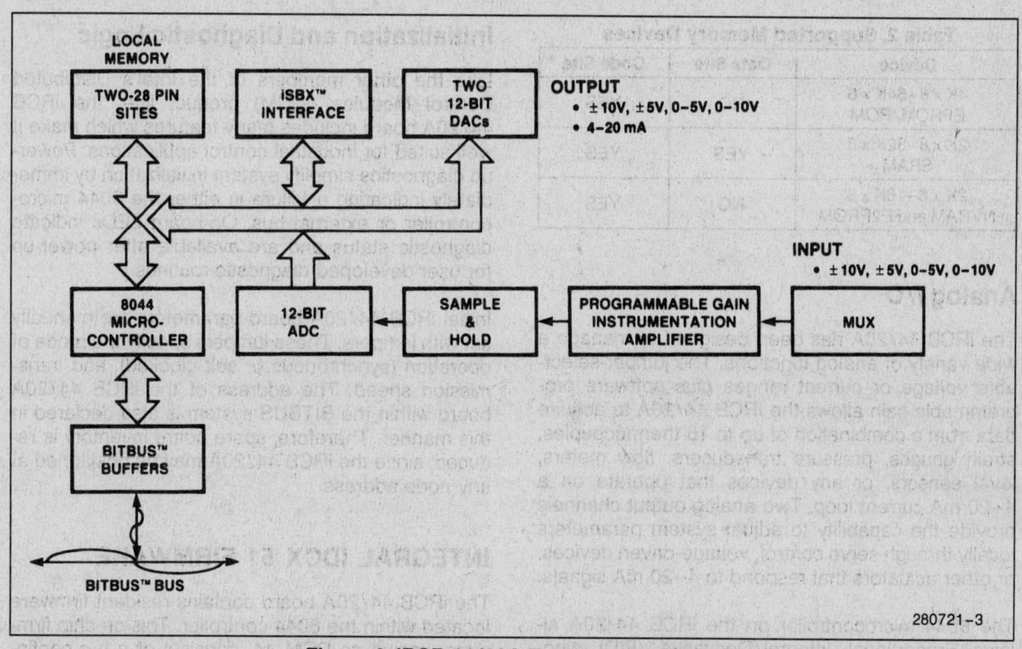

Figure 2. iRCB 44/20A Functional Diagram

BITBUS™ Microcontroller Interconnect

The iRCB 44/20A board fully supports the BITBUS microcontroller interconnect. BITBUS is a serial bus optimized for control applications. Both synchronous and self-clocked modes of operation are supported as well as multiple transmission rates. Table 1 shows the different combinations of modes of operation, transmission speeds, and distances. The SDLC protocol and BITBUS message format comprise the data-link level of the BITBUS architecture. Use of these standards maximizes system reliability and flexibility.

The physical connection to BITBUS uses either one or two pairs of wires across which differential signals travel. The iRCB 44/20A board contains a half-duplex RS 485 tranceiver and an optional clock source for the synchronous mode of operation.

Local Memory

The iRCB 44/20A board contains both internal and external local memory. Internal memory is located within the 8044 controller and is used by the iDCX 51 Executive and the SIU. Eight bytes of bit-addressable internal memory have been reserved for the user.

Two 28-pin JEDEC sites provide the iRCB 44/20A board with memory that is external to the 8044. One site has been dedicated for data, the other for application code. Table 2 lists the supported memory devices for each site. The user may select one of two memory configurations using jumpers. One option provides the user with access to the application code site for uploading or downloading programs, which allows expansion or modification of an existing system from a remote site.

Table 1. BITBUS™ Microcontroller Interconnect Modes Of Operation

	Speed Kb/S	Maximum Distance Between Repeaters M/ft	Maximum # Nodes Per Segment*	Maximum # Repeaters Between A Master And Any Slave
Synchronous	500–2400	30/100	28	0
Self Clocked	375	300/1000	28	2
	62.5	1200/4000	28	10

* Segment: Distance between master and repeater or repeater and repeater. Synchronous Mode requires user supplied crystal.

Table 2. Supported Memory Devices

Device	Data Site	Code Site
4K x 8–64K x 8 EPROM/ROM	NO	YES
2K x 8–32K x 8 SRAM	YES	YES
2K x 8–16K x 8 NVRAM and E2PROM	NO	YES

Analog I/O

The iRCB 44/20A has been designed to manage a wide variety of analog functions. The jumper-selectable voltage or current ranges plus software programmable gain allows the iRCB 44/20A to acquire data from a combination of up to 16 thermocouples, strain gauges, pressure transducers, flow meters, level sensors, or any devices that operate on a 4–20 mA current loop. Two analog output channels provide the capability to adjust system parameters locally through servo control, voltage-driven devices, or other actuators that respond to 4–20 mA signals.

The 8044 microcontroller on the iRCB 44/20A allows Proportional Integral/Derivative (PID) algorithms, event timing, or averaging tasks to operate independent of the host computer or programmable controller. By off-loading the host in this manner, the overall system performance can be improved significantly.

The analog I/O lines can be manipulated from a remote supervisor by communicating with the Remote Access and Control (RAC) functions, which are included in the 8044 controller firmware. The local application program running on the iRCB 44/20A can also access the RAC functions or directly operate the I/O lines.

iSBX™ Expansion

One 8-bit iSBX I/O expansion connector is provided to expand the functionality of the iRCB 44/20A board. A full line of compatible expansion MULTIMODULE boards are available from Intel; both single- and double-wide versions are supported by the iRCB 44/20A. Parallel I/O, serial I/O, IEEE 488, magnetic-bubble memory, or additional analog I/O may be added in this manner.

Also, the iSBX 344A BITBUS Controller MULTIMODULE can be used to implement another BITBUS hierarchy with the iRCB 44/20A functioning as the master. With user supplied software, this product combination can operate as an intelligent BITBUS repeater, facilitating the transmission between two BITBUS segments operating at different speeds.

Initialization and Diagnostic Logic

Like the other members of the Intel's Distributed Control Modules (iDCM) product line, the iRCB 44/20A board includes many features which make it well suited for industrial control applications. Power-up diagnostics simplify system initialization by immediately indicating a failure in either the 8044 microcontroller or external bus. On-board LEDs indicate diagnostic status and are available after power-up for user developed diagnostic routines.

Initial iRCB 44/20A board parameters are manually set with jumpers. These jumpers specify the mode of operation (synchronous or self clocked), and transmission speed. The address of the iRCB 44/20A board within the BITBUS system is also declared in this manner. Therefore, spare board inventory is reduced, since the iRCB 44/20A may be positioned at any node address.

INTEGRAL iDCX 51 FIRMWARE

The iRCB 44/20A board contains resident firmware located within the 8044 controller. This on-chip firmware, known as DCM 44, consists of a pre-configured iDCX 51 Distributed Control Executive for user program development and execution, a library of Remote Access and Control (RAC) functions for internode communications and I/O control, plus an iSBX communications gateway, and power-up diagnostics.

The iDCX 51 Executive is an event-driven software manager that can respond to the needs of multiple tasks. This real-time multitasking executive provides task management and timing, interrupt handling, and message passing services. Table 3 shows the iDCX 51 user command library. Both the executive and the communications gateway allow for the addition of seven user tasks at each node that are independent of BITBUS bus management operations.

Remote Access and Control (RAC) functions are special purpose tasks that allow the host system to transfer commands and program variables to remote BITBUS controllers and read/write to the remote I/O lines. Table 4 provides a complete listing of the RAC commands. No user code need be written to use this function. Power-up tests provide a quick diagnostic service.

The DCM 44 firmware, integral to the iRCB 44/20A board, simplifies the development and implementation of complex real-time control applications. All iDCM hardware products contain this integral firmware, providing the user with application code portability.

Table 3. iDCX 51 Executive Calls

Call Name	Description
TASK MANAGEMENT CALLS	
RQ$CREATE$TASK	Create and schedule a new task.
RQ$DELETE$TASK	Delete specified task from system.
RQGETFUNCTION$IDS	Obtain the function IDs of tasks currently in the system.
INTERTASK COMMUNICATION CALLS	
RQ$ALLOCATE	Obtain a message buffer from the system buffer pool.
RQ$DEALLOCATE	Return a message buffer to the system buffer pool.
RQ$SEND$MESSAGE	Send a message to specified task.
RQ$WAIT	Wait for a message event.
MEMORY MANAGEMENT CALLS	
RQGETMEM	Get available SMP memory.
RQ$RELEASE$MEM	Release SMP memory.
INTERRUPT MANAGEMENT CALLS	
RQ$DISABLE$INTERRUPT	Temporarily disable an interrupt.
RQ$ENABLE$INTERRUPT	Re-enable an interrupt.
RQ$WAIT	Wait for an interrupt event.
TIMER MANAGEMENT CALLS	
RQSETINTERVAL	Establish a time interval.
RQ$WAIT	Wait for an interval event.

Table 4. RAC Services

RAC Service	Action Taken by Task 0
RESET_STATION	Perform a software reset.
CREATE_TASK	Perform an RQ$CREATE$TASK system call.
DELETE_TASK	Perform an RQ$DELETE$TASK system call.
GET_FUNCTION_ID	Perform an RQGETFUNCTION$IDS call.
RAC_PROTECT	Suspend or resume RAC services.
READ_IO	Return values from specified I/O ports.
WRITE_IO	Write to the specified I/O ports.
UPDATE_IO	Update the specified I/O ports.
UPLOAD_MEMORY	Return the values in specified memory area.
DOWNLOAD_MEMORY	Write values to specified memory area.
OR_I/O	OR values into specified I/O ports.
AND_I/O	AND values into specified I/O ports.
XOR_I/O	XOR values into specified I/O ports.
READ_INTERNAL	Read values at specified internal RAM areas.
WRITE_INTERNAL	Write values to specified internal RAM areas.
NODE_INFO	Return device related information.
OFFLINE	Set node offline.
UPLOAD_CODE	Read values from code memory space.
DOWNLOAD_CODE	Write values to specified EEPROM memory.

NOTES:
Internal memory locations are included in the 192 bytes of data RAM provided in the microcontroller. External memory refers memory outside the microcontroller—the 28-pin sockets of iRCB 44/20A board. Each RAC Access Function may refer to 1, 2, 3, 4, 5 or 6 individual I/O or memory locations in a single command.

INDUSTRIAL PACKAGING

The iRCB 44/20A board conforms to a single-wide (3V), 220 mm deep Eurocard form-factor. This allows the iRCB 44/20A to fit within standard industrial racks or chassis as well as Intel's RCX 920 Analog Signal Conditioning, Isolation & Termination Panel (see below). The Eurocard specification references DIN 41612 connectors, which are used on the iRCB 44/20A board.

ANALOG SIGNAL CONDITIONING, ISOLATION AND TERMINATION

The RCB 44/20A is fully compatible with the RCX 920 Analog Signal Conditioning, Isolation and Termination Panel. The RCX 920 panel provides integral mounting for one RCB 44/20A, with connectors for power, the BITBUS interconnect signals, and 18 Analog Devices 5B Series Signal Conditioning and Isolation Modules. These modules provide 240V RMS field wiring protection, and 1500V RMS common mode voltage isolation and support signal conditioning in a wide range of analog voltages and currents including thermocouple and RTD sensors, millivolt and volt inputs and 4–20 mA and 0–20 mA outputs.

SPECIFICATIONS

CPU

8044 BITBUS Enhanced Microcontroller (BEM)

Word Size

Instruction—8 bits
Data—8 bits

Processor Clock

12 MHz

Instruction Execution Times

1 μsec 60% instructions
2 μsec 40% instructions
4 μsec Multiply & Divide

Memory Addressing

iDCM Controller
Up to 64K bytes code

Address Ranges

	Option A	Option B
External Data Memory Site	0000H–7FFFH	0000H–7FFFH
External Code Memory Site	1000H–0FFFFH (0000H–0FFFFH if EA Active)	8000H–0FFEFH
Internal Code Memory	0000H–0FFFH	0000H–0FFFH

NOTES:
Option A: Supports maximum amount of external EPROM code memory
Option B: Supports downloading code into external RAM or EEPROM memory

BITBUS™ Development Environments

HOST SYSTEM	BITBUS™ TOOLS: DCS 100 TOOLBOX								NODE CODE			ICE™	EPROM PROG.	
	BBM	UBI	BIH	PC Bridge	OBJHEX	UDI2DOS	DCS 110	DCS 120	ASM 51	PL/M 51	RL 51, LIB 51	ICE 5100/044	iUP200A/201A with iUPF87/44A module and iPPS sw	iPDS with iUPF87/44A module and iPPS sw
Series II									C	C	C		X	
III			X				X	X	X	X	X	X	X	
IV							X	X	X	X	X	X	X	
iPDS™	A	A	A				X	X	C	C	C			X
iRMX® 5¼″	X	X	X	X	X		X	X	D	D	D			
8″	X	X	X	X	X		X	X	D	D	D			
XENIX 5¼″	X	X		B	X									
8″	X	X		B	X									
DOS	X	X	X	X	X	X	X	X	X	X	X	X	X	

NOTES:
A. iPDS™ uses Release 1 Toolbox.
B. Supports operation with XENIX. XENIX disks not required.
C. Down-revision version.
D. Available for iRMX® 86.

I/O Capability

Analog—16 single-ended or 8 differential channels and 2 outputs channels

Expansion—one single-or double-wide iSBX MULTIMODULE (MWAIT * or DMA not supported by iRCB 44/20)

Interrupt Sources

Two external: iSBX I/O Bus or BITBUS Interconnect sources

Bus Termination

Jumper selectable resistors provide termination capability for cable with an impedance of 120Ω or greater.

Analog Input Specifications

Number of channels—16 single-ended or 8 differential
Input ranges—0 to 5V, 0 to 10V (unipolar) ±5V, ±10V (bipolar)
Gain ranges—1, 10, 100, 500, (software programmable)
Input impedance—100MΩ
Input bias current—±50 nA
Overvoltage protection—±32V power on
±20V power off

Accuracy

Resolution—12 bits
Linearity and Noise—±3/4 LSB (trimmable)
System Accuracy
Gain = 1—±0.035% full-scale range (trimmable)
Gain = 500—±0.15% full-scale range (trimmable)

Stability

Gain tempco—32 ppm/°C (gain = 11)
75 ppm/°C (gain = 500)
Offset tempco—100 microvolts/°C max.

Dynamic Performance

Aggregate throughout—20 KHz (gain = 1, 10)
7.5 KHz (gain = 100, 500)
Common mode rejection—70 dB (gain = 1)
100 dB (gain = 500)
A/D conversion time—30 microseconds

Analog Output Specifications

Number of channels—2
Output ranges—0 to 5V, 0 to 10V (unipolar) ±5V, ±10V (bipolar)
Current-loop range—4 to 20 mA (unipolar mode only)
Output impedance—0.2Ω min. (voltage)
5 MΩ max. (current)
Output current—±5 mA (short-circuit protected)

Accuracy

Resolution—12 bits
Linearity and Noise—±3/4 SB (trimmable)
System Accuracy—
Gain = 1——0.35% full-scale range (trimmable)
Gain = 500—±0.15% full-scale range (trimmable)

Stability

Full-scale temperature coefficient
150 microvolts/°C (unipolar)
300 microvolts/°C (bipolar)
0.6 microamps/°C (current-loop)

Offset temperature coefficient
30 microvolts/°C (unipolar)
180 microvolts/°C (bipolar)
0.3 microamps/°C (current-loop)

Mating Connectors

Function	# of Pins	Type	Vendor	Part Number
BITBUS Connector	64	Flat Cable	GW Elco Robinson Nugent	00-8259-096-84-124 RNE-IDC-64C-TG30
iSBX Connector	36	Wire Wrap	ITT Cannon GW Elco	G06 M96 P3 BDBL-004 60 8257 3017
		Solder	Viking	000292-0001

16

Dynamic Performance

Aggregate throughput—20 KHz (gain = 1, 10)
7.5 KHz (gain = 100, 500)
Settling Time—15 microseconds to ±½ LSB

Electrical Characteristics

Interface Compliance

iSBX BUS (through level D8/8F):
Memory sites—code and data sites are JEDEC compatible

BITBUS:

— Synchronous and self-clocked mode support for 500 Kbps to 2.4 Mbps, 375K and 62.5K bits/sec

NOTE:
On-board ALE clock supports 1 Mbps synchronous operation. All other synchronous mode speeds require user-supplied 2.0–9.6 MHz crystal.

— Equivalent to 1.1 standard (RS 485) loads
— Message length up to 54 bytes maximum

Power Requirement (exclusive of optional memory or iSBX MULTIMODULE)

Voltage	Current (amps)	Max, Power (watts)
+5V ±5%	0.9 max. 0.7 typ	4.5
+12V ±5%	100 mA max.	
−12V ±5%	100 mA max.	

NOTE:
+15V and −15V required for 0 to 10V and ±10V ranges; for ±15V operation, the iRCB 44/20A cannot be used with iSBX MULTIMODULES that use ±12V power sources.

Physical Characteristics

Width: 3.77 mm (0.542 in) maximum component height
Height: 100 mm (3.93 in)
Depth: 220 mm (8.65 in)
Weight: 169 gm (6 ounces)

Environmental Characteristics

Operating Temperature: 0°C to +60°C at 0.8 CFM air volume
Relative Humidity: 90% non-condensing

Reference Manual (Not Supplied)

148816— iRCB 44/20A Hardware Reference Manual

ORDERING INFORMATION

Part Number	Description
iRCB 44/20A	BITBUS Analog I/O Controller Board

iRCX 910/920 DIGITAL/ANALOG SIGNAL CONDITIONING ISOLATION AND TERMINATION PANELS

iRCX 910

- Digital Termination for BITBUS™ iRCB 44/10A Digital Remote Controller Board, iSBX™ 350 Digital MULTIMODULE™ and Multibus Digital I/O Single Board Computers (SBCs)
- Socket for 24 Industry-Standard, Optically Coupled Isolation and Signal Conditioning I/O Modules
- LEDs Indicate Status of Each Module
- Separate Connectors for BITBUS, Power, RCB and Expansion I/O
- Integral Mounting Site for One 24-Channel Digital iRCB 44/10A

iRCX 920

- Analog Termination for iRCB 44/20A, iSBX 311, iSBX 328, and iSBC 88/40
- Sockets Accepting up to 18 Analog Devices Corporation's 5B Series of Isolation and Signal Conditioning Modules
- Separate Connectors for BITBUS, Power, RCB and Expansion I/O
- Integral Mounting Site for One 18-Channel Analog iRCB 44/20A

280443–1

October 1990
Order Number: 280443-001

MORE CONVENIENT BITBUS™ SYSTEM INTEGRATION

Intel now provides one more building block for developing BITBUS™ networks: the iRCX 910/920 Digital/Analog Signal Isolation and Termination Panels. These boards provide remote node termination and isolation in a design that's easy to install and service. They work with Intel's RCB 44/10A and 44/20A, which priovide analog/digital control, and with Intel's BITBUS Monitor, DCX-51 Real-time Multitasking Executive and BITBUS Toolbox, which provide the software support.

Intel makes BITBUS system integration easier and more convenient than ever.

COMPATIBLE WITH A WIDE RANGE OF INTEL MULTIBUS BOARDS

The iRCX 910 and iRCX 920 not only work with the iRCB 44/10A and 44/20A controller boards but also with a wide range of Multibus boards both from Intel and Multibus Manufacturing Group vendors. The 50-pin expansion connection on the iRCX panels makes iSBC and iSBX board connection easy.

Table 1 shows the Intel iSBC and iSBX boards currently compatible with the iRCX products.

[1]Mention of these companies in no way constitutes an endorsement by Intel of their products.

iRCX 910: COMPATIBLE WITH INDUSTRY-STANDARD I/O MODULES

The iRCX 910 provides sockets for 24 channels of user-provided digital I/O to perform AC or DC switching and isolation. The user can configure up to 24 I/O channels, filling only the channels needed for the application. The iRCX 910 accepts a wide range of industry-standard I/O modules, including those from Gordos, Opto 22, Crydom, Potter-Brumfield and others[1]. The input modules convert high-level inputs from such sources as limit or proximity switches to TTL levels. The output modules convert TTL to high-level signals for driving motor starters, solenoids, indicating lights, and the like. Regardless of whether input or output, these modules typically provide greater than 1500V isolation, 2–3 KV of transient noise protection, and signal conditioning in a wide range of voltages. An LED for each channel shows on/off status, and a 5A fuse provides overcurrent protection.

Table 1. Intel Boards Compatible with iRCX 910 and iRCX 920

iRCX 910		iRCX 920	
Intel iSBCs	**iSBX**	**Intel iSBC**	**Intel iSBX**
80/10B	350	88/40A	311
80/20-4			328
80/24A			
80/30			
80/05A			
86/14			
86/30			
86/35			
88/25			
88/40A			
517			
519			

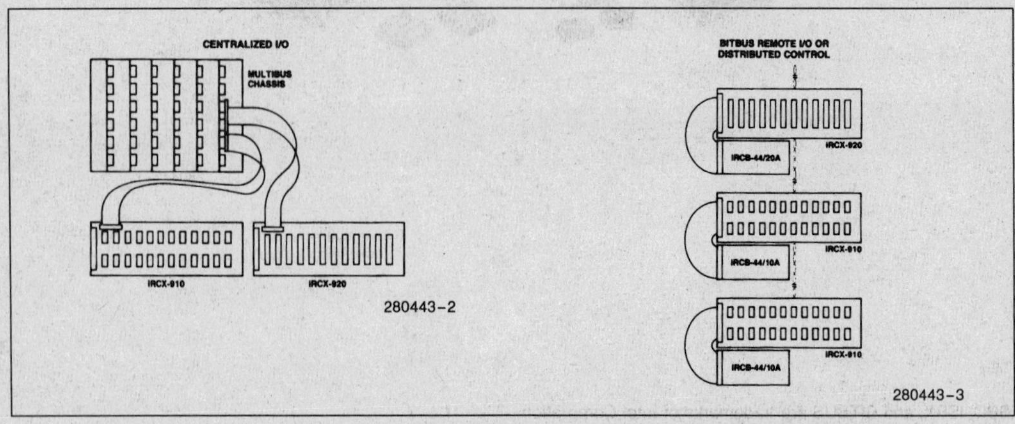

Examples of How iRCX 910 and 920s Can Be Used in Multibus and BITBUS Systems

iRCX 920: USES ANALOG DEVICES CORPORATION MODULES TO PROVIDE STATE-OF-THE-ART SIGNAL CONDITIONING AND ISOLATION

The iRCX 920 terminates 18 analog signals going to and from field wiring and provides signal conditioning and isolation using Analog Devices Corporation's 5B Series of analog isolation and signal conditioning modules (purchased separately). These modules provide 240V RMS field wiring protection, 1500V RMS common mode voltage isolation and signal conditioning in a wide range of analog voltage and currents, including thermocouple and RTD sensors, millivolt and volt inputs, and 0 mA–20 mA and 4 mA–20 mA process current outputs. Possible connections include temperature and pressure sensors, frequency counters and many others. The iRCB 44/20A when used in conjunction with the iRCX 920 provides up to 16 analog inputs and 2 analog outputs.

The iRCX 920 also contains an integral temperature sensor isothermal barrier strip (RTD) to provide a temperature reference for thermocouple modules doing cold junction compensation. Because this compensation is implemented in hardware rather than software, it simplifies the controller software's task, allowing superior software performance.

EASY TO INSTALL, EASY TO USE

The iRCX panels provide a quick and easy, plug-in solution to remote node BITBUS interconnection. They can be mounted to an industrial panel or in a standard RETMA 19″ rack when used with a customer provided 19″ L x 7″ W pan. Quick access to the RCB 44/10A and 44/20A boards is accomplished by loosening six screws and shifting the iRCX slightly. Field wiring connections are made using captive screw terminals, positioned to allow easy wire routing. Installation is quick, service is easy.

The I/O modules on the iRCX 910 are color-coded for easy identification. LEDs provide on/off status, allowing the operator a quick verification of I/O operation, and are also useful for start-up testing, debugging and trouble-shooting a process or machine breakdown.

INCREASED RELIABILITY

The iRCX 910 and 920 feature improved noise immunity through judicious component placement and the inclusion of a ground terminal. Also, they're mounted in front of the iRCB 44/10A and 44/20A boards, protecting the heart of the remote node from accidental damage.

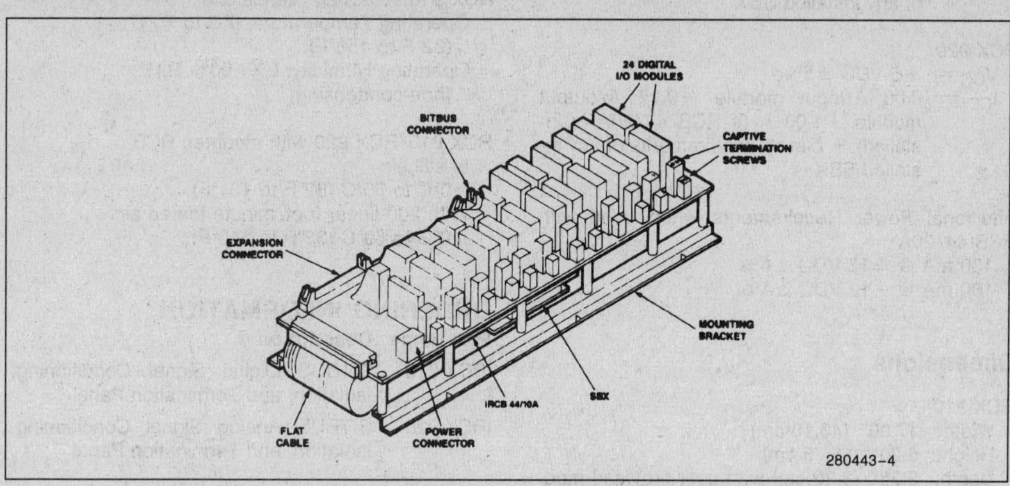

iRCX 910: The Complete Remote Node Solution for Distributed I/O and Control

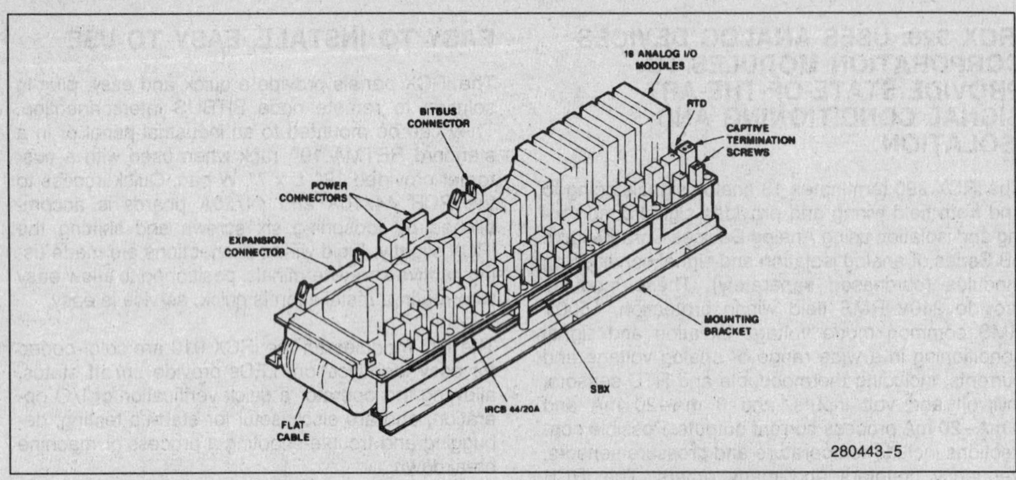

iRCX 920: The Complete Remote Node Solution for Distributed I/O and Control

SPECIFICATIONS

Power Requirements (Typical)

RCX 910

V_{CC} = +5 VDC ±5%

I_{CC} = 0.03 A/module installed +1.00 A (if RCB 44/10A installed) + current requirements of any installed SBX

RCX 920

V_{CC} = +5 VDC ±5%

I_{CC} = 0.03 A/input module +0.17 A/output module +1.00 A (if RCB 44/20A is installed) + current requirements of any installed SBX

Additional Power Requirements when used with RCB 44/20A

100 mA @ +12 VDC ±4%

100 mA @ −12 VDC ±4%

Dimensions

RCX 910

Width: 17.00″ (43.18 cm)

Height: 6.20″ (15.75 cm)

Depth: 3.25″ (8.26 cm) with user-provided modules installed

RCX 920

Width: 17.00″ (43.18 cm)

Height: 6.20″ (15.75 cm)

Depth: 4.25″ (10.80 cm) with user-provided modules installed

Environmental Requirements

RCX 910/RCX 920 Standalone

Operating Temperature: 0°C to 70°C (32°F to 158°F)

Operating Humidity: 0%−90% R.H. (non-condensing)

RCX 910/RCX 920 with mounted RCB

In still air:

0°C to 55°C (32°F to 131°F)

With 200 linear feet/minute forced air:

0°C to 60°C (32°F to 140°F)

ORDERING INFORMATION

Part Name	Description
iRCX 910	BITBUS Digital Signal Conditioning, Isolation, and Termination Panel
iRCX 920	BITBUS Analog Signal Conditioning, Isolation, and Termination Panel

iRCX 900 ISOLATION MODULE

280639–1

ISOLATION AND TRANSIENT PROTECTION FOR BITBUS™ NETWORKS

The Intel iRCX 900 Isolation Module protects against ground loops, voltage differences between nodes, and transient voltage spikes in BITBUS™ networks operating in the 62.5 to 375 Kbps asynchronous (self-clocked) modes. The iRCX 900 also serves as an isolated, standalone repeater, driving up to 28 remote BITBUS nodes.

FEATURES

- Common-mode isolation of 1500 VAC for a working voltage of 480 VAC.
- Transient protection meeting the IEEE 472/ANSI-C37.90a-1974 Surge Withstand Compatibility Test.
- On-board DC-DC switching voltage regulator with 1500 VAC isolation.
- Power-on indicator LEDs.
- Rugged industrial packaging with multiple mounting options.
- Dual termination with 10-pin BITBUS connector and 10-position terminal block.

16

December 1990
Order Number: 280639-001

FEATURES

STANDALONE ISOLATION AND TRANSIENT PROTECTION

The iRCX 900 provides BITBUS network protection against voltage surges and transients in industrial environments. This protection is provided through the use of optocouplers, transient suppressors, and an isolated DC-DC voltage regulator.

DOUBLES AS A NETWORK REPEATER

The iRCX 900 also serves as a network repeater, with each iRCX 900 module capable of driving up to 28 remote BITBUS nodes. The iRCX 900 can be powered either from the 12V BITBUS signal line or a separate 12-24V power source.

EASY TO INSTALL AND UPDATE

Installation and change of configuration are easy, because the iRCX 900 is a standalone module. It can be placed anywhere in the network without piggybacking it to another board. The iRCX 900 can be panel-mounted or placed on a desk or lab benchtop. Wiring instructions are clearly outlined on the module packaging.

SERVICE, SUPPORT AND TRAINING

Intel provides worldwide support for board repair or on-site service.

INTEL QUALITY AND RELIABILITY

The iRCX 900 is designed and manufactured in accordance with Intel's high quality standards. We then verify quality through rigorous testing in our state-of-the-art Environmental Test Laboratory.

SPECIFICATIONS

POWER REQUIREMENTS

Input Voltage: 10.8–26.4 VDC
Input Power: 2.0 watts (typical)

May be powered from a remote BITBUS node or from a user-provided power supply.

DIMENSIONS

Width:	6.48 in. (16.46 cm)
Height:	5.7 in. (14.48 cm)
Depth:	1.78 in. (4.52 cm)

ENVIRONMENTAL REQUIREMENTS

Storage Temperature:	−40°C to 70°C (−40°F to 158°F)
Operating Temperature:	0°C to 55°C (32°F to 131°F)
Storage Humidity:	5%–95% non-condensing at 55°C
Operating Humidity:	8%–90% non-condensing at 55°C

SPECIFICATIONS

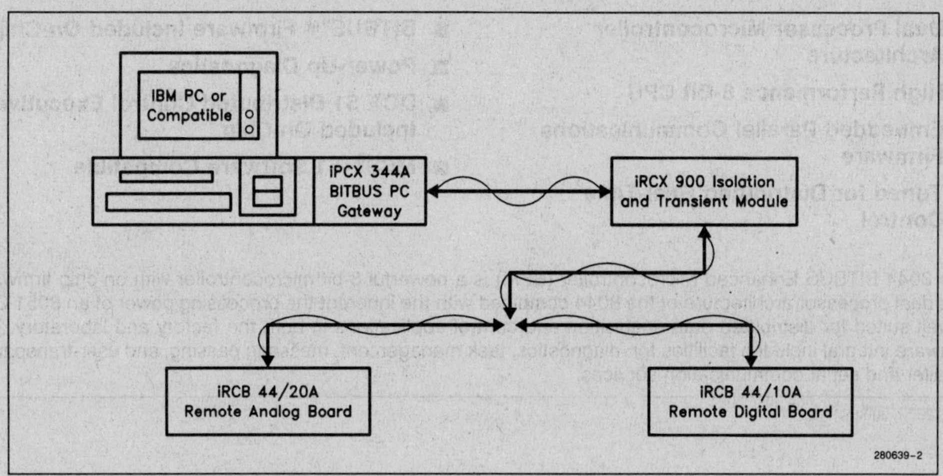

Figure 1: Example Configuration

ORDERING INFORMATION

Order Code

iRCX 900 BITBUS Isolation and Transient Protection Module

For more information or the number of your nearest sales office call 800-548-4725 (good in the U.S. and Canada).

8044 BITBUS™ ENHANCED MICROCONTROLLER

- Dual Processor Microcontroller Architecture
- High Performance 8-Bit CPU
- Embedded Parallel Communications Firmware
- Tuned for Distributed Real-Time Control
- BITBUS™ Firmware Included On-Chip
- Power-Up Diagnostics
- DCX 51 Distributed Control Executive Included On-Chip
- MCS®-51 Software Compatible

The 8044 BITBUS Enhanced Microcontroller (BEM) is a powerful 8-bit microcontroller with on-chip firmware. The dual processor architecture of the 8044 combined with the inherent the processing power of an 8051 CPU is well suited for distributed data acquisition and control applications in both the factory and laboratory. The firmware integral includes facilities for: diagnostics, task management, message passing, and user-transparent parallel and serial communication services.

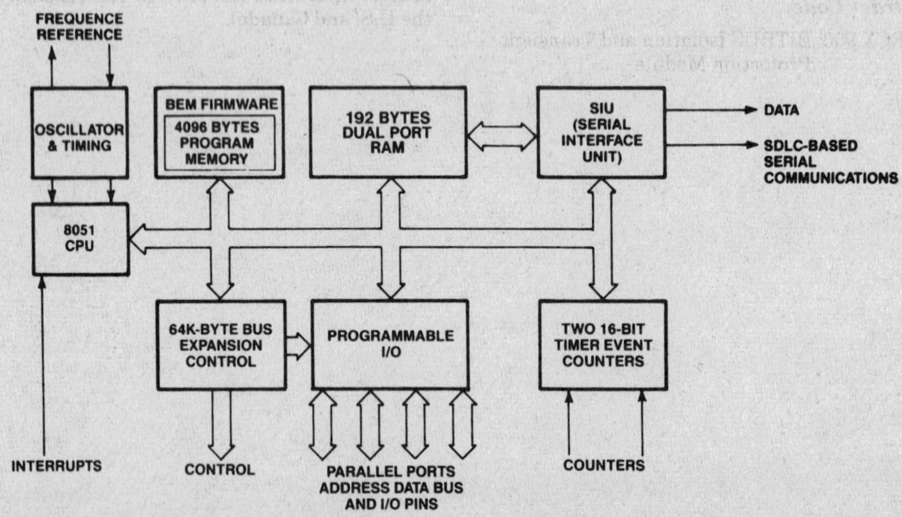

Figure 1. BEM Block Diagram

*IBM is a trademark of International Business Machines Corporation.

September 1990
Order Number: 280129-003

OPERATING ENVIRONMENT

Introduction

The BITBUS Interconnect Serial Control Bus Specification defines an integrated architecture optimized for implementing real-time distributed control systems. The architecture includes a message structure and protocol for multitasking environments, and a predefined interface for I/O access and control. As with traditional bus specifications the mechanical, electrical, and data protocols have been defined. Over a twisted pair of wires the bus can support up to 250 nodes at three different bit rates dependent on application performance requirements. Figure 2 illustrates the BITBUS Interconnect architecture.

The 8044 BITBUS Enhanced Microcontroller (BEM) or DCM Controller provides the user with the smallest BITBUS building block—a BITBUS component solution. With its dual processor architecture, this unique single chip provides both communication and computational engines (Figure 3). Real-time control and computational power are provided by the on-chip 8-bit 8051 CPU. The Serial Interface Unit (SIU) executes a majority of the communications functions in hardware resulting in a high performance solution for distributed control applications where communication and processing power are equally important. The BEM's firmware implements the BITBUS message structure and protocol, and the pre-defined I/O command set.

Firmware

The 8044 microcontroller requires specific hardware to interface to BITBUS. The BEM's firmware also requires a particular hardware environment in order to execute correctly, just as the iDCX 86 Operating System or other operating systems required a specific hardware environment, i.e., interrupt controller, timers, etc. Based upon the hardware provided, Basic or Extended firmware environments result.

The Basic firmware environment supports the minimum configuration for the BEM to execute as a

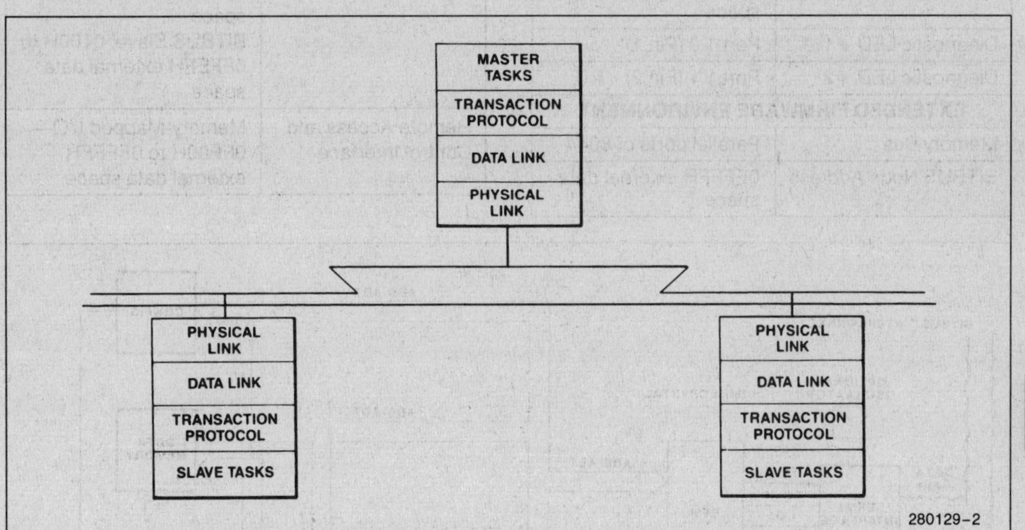

Figure 2. BITBUS™ Architecture

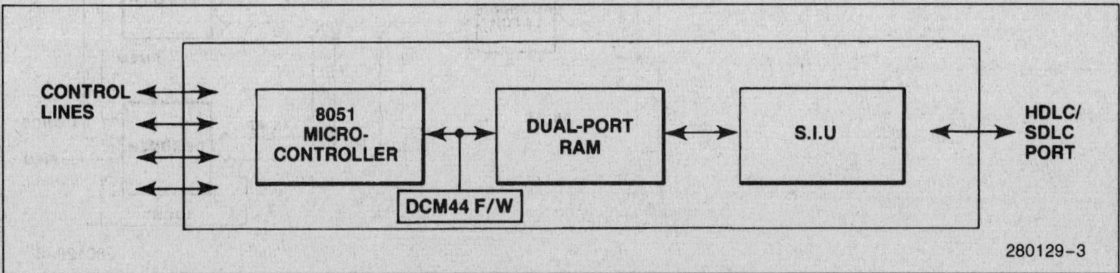

Figure 3. 8044's Dual Processor Architecture

BITBUS device. The Extended firmware environment requires hardware incremental to the Basic environment and allows the user to take full advantage of all the features included in the BEM's firmware. The designer may implement the Basic or Extended firmware environment as desired as long as the programmatic requirements of the firmware are met (see below).

Figure 4 shows one example of an Extended firmware environment. This particular example represents the BITBUS Core as used on Intel's iSBX™ 344A BITBUS Controller MULTIMODULE™ Board and iRCB 44/10A BITBUS Remote Controller Board.

BASIC FIRMWARE ENVIRONMENT	
Memory Bus	Parallel ports of 8044
BITBUS Node Address	0FFFFH external data space
Configuration	0FFFEH external data space
System RAM	0–02FFH external data space
Diagnostic LED #1	Port 1.0 (Pin 1)
Diagnostic LED #2	Port 1.1 (Pin 2)

EXTENDED FIRMWARE ENVIRONMENT	
Memory Bus	Parallel ports of 8044
BITBUS Node Address	0FFFFH external data space
Configuration	0FFFEH external data space
System RAM	0–02FFH external data space
Diagnostic LED #1	Port 1.0 (Pin 1)
Diagnostic LED #2	Port 1.1 (Pin 2)
User Task Interface	First Task Descriptor—0FFF0H to 0FFFFH in External data space Other Task Descriptors and User Code—01000H to 0FFEFH in external code space
User RAM Availability	On-Chip—02AH to 02FH bit space Off-Chip—BITBUS Master: 0400H to 0FFEFH external data space BITBUS Slave: 0100H to 0FFEFH external data space
Remote Access and Control Interface	Memory-Mapped I/O—0FF00H to 0FFFFH external data space

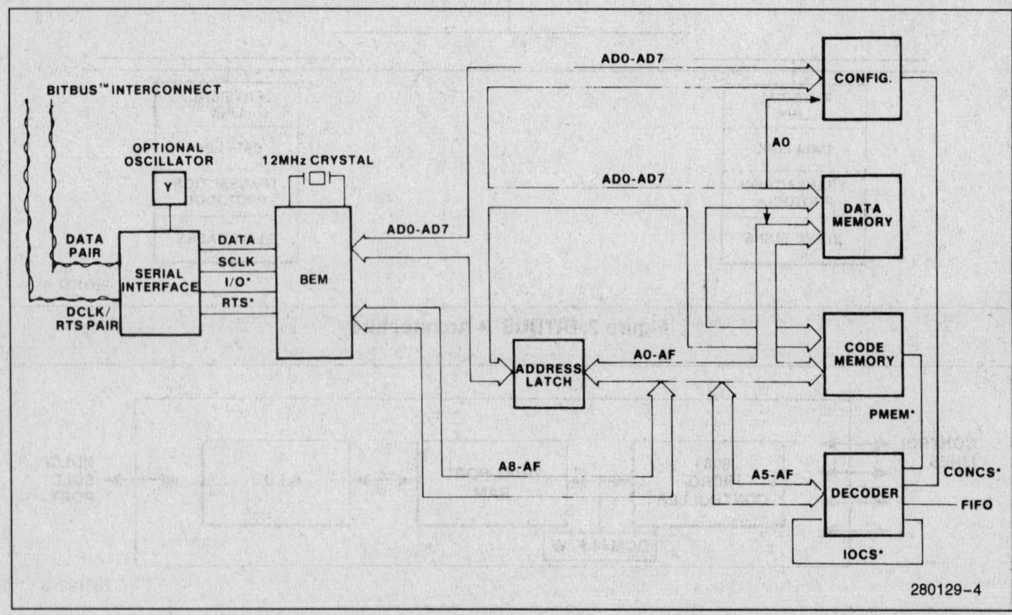

Figure 4. Extended Firmware Environment Example

EXTENDED FIRMWARE ENVIRONMENT (Continued)	
Parallel Interface to Extension Device	FIFO Command Byte—0FF01H external data space FIFO Data Byte—0FF00H external data space Receive Data Intr—INT0 (pin 12) Transmit Data Intr—INT1 (pin 13) Command/Data Bit—P1.2

FUNCTIONAL DESCRIPTION

High Performance 8044 Microcontroller

The 8044 combines the powerful 8051 microcontroller with an intelligent serial communications controller to provide a single-chip solution that efficiently implements distributed processing or distributed control systems. The microcontroller is a self-sufficient unit containing ROM, RAM, ALU, and peripherals. The 8044's architecture and instruction set are identical to the 8051's. The serial interface of the 8051 is replaced with an intelligent communications processor, the Serial Interface Init (SIU), on the 8044. This unique dual processor architecture results in high performance and reliability for distributed control and processing environments. The intelligent SIU offloads the CPU from communication tasks, thus dedicating more of its compute power to external processes.

Major features of the 8051 microcontroller are:

- 8-bit CPU
- On-chip oscillator
- 4K bytes of RAM
- 192 bytes of ROM
- 32 I/O lines
- 64K address space external data memory
- 64K address space external program memory
- Two Programmable 16-bit counters
- Five source interrupt structure with two priority levels
- Bit addressability for Boolean functions
- 1 μs instruction cycle time for 60% instructions
  2 μs instruction cycle time for 40% instructions
- 4 μs cycle time for 8 by 8 unsigned multiple and divide

As noted in the Operating Environment discussion, the BITBUS firmware requires various CPU resources, i.e., memory, timers, and I/O dependent upon the firmware environment selected.

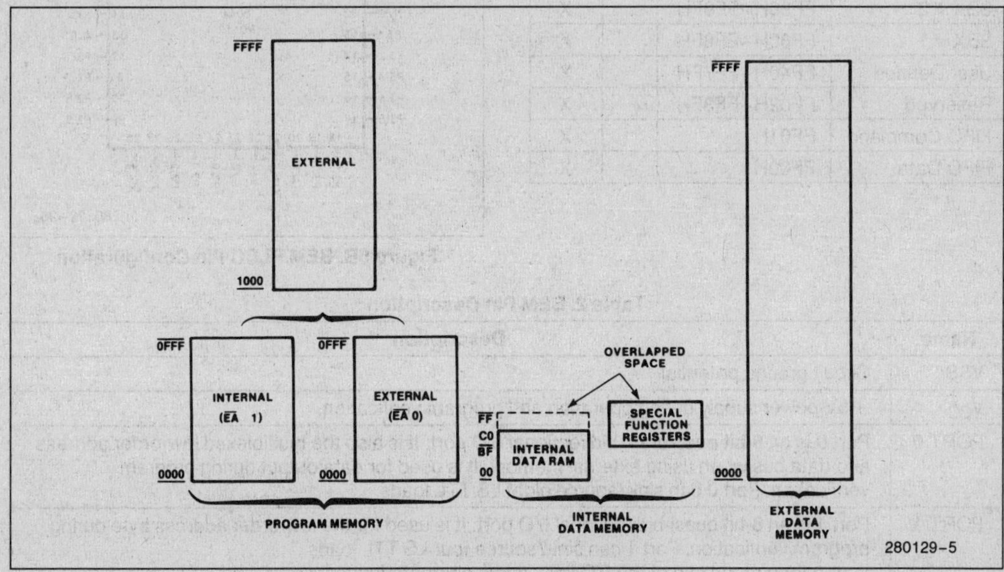

Figure 5. BEM Memory Map

Memory Architecture

The 8044 microcontroller maintains separate data and code memory spaces. Internal data memory and program memory reside on the controller. External memory resides outside the controller. The BEM firmware uses the available internal code memory space and most of the remaining internal data memory with the exception of bit space 02AH to 02FH. Figure 5 shows the BEM's memory map.

I/O ADDRESSING REQUIREMENTS

The table below provides the BEM's I/O port addresses.

Table 1. BEM I/O Addressing

Function	Address	Bit	Byte
Red LED P1.0	90H	X	
Green LED P1.1	91H	X	
TCMD	92H	X	
RFNF#	B3H	X	
TFNF#	B2H	X	
RDY/NE*	B4H	X	
Node Address	FFFFH		X
Configuration	FFFEH		X
Reserved	FFE0H–FFFDH		X
Digital I/O	FFC0H–FFDFH		X
SBX #4	FFB0H–FFBFH		X
SBX #3	FFB0H–FFAFH		X
SBX #2	FF90H–FF9FH		X
SBX #1	FF80H–FF8FH		X
User Defined	FF40H–FF7FH		X
Reserved	FF02H–FF3FH		X
FIFO Command	FF01H		X
FIFO Data	FF00H		X

SIGNAL FUNCTIONS

The 8044 BEM's pin configuration and pin description follow.

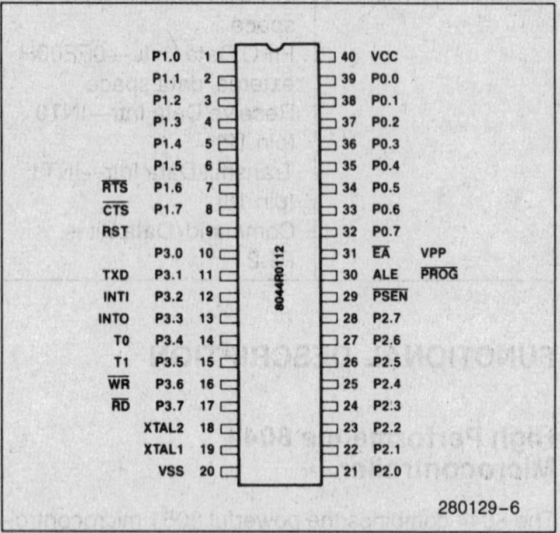

Figure 6A. BEM DIP Pin Configuration

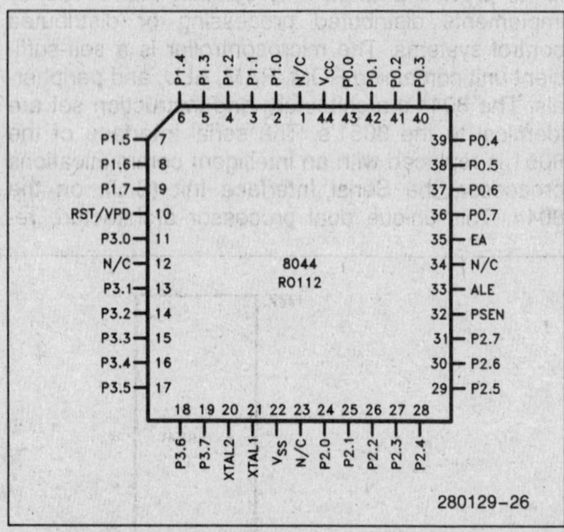

Figure 6B. BEM PLCC Pin Configuration

Table 2. BEM Pin Description

Name	Description
VSS	Circuit ground potential.
V_{CC}	+5V power supply during operation and program verification.
PORT 0	Port 0 is an 8-bit open drain bidirectional I/O port. It is also the multiplexed low-order address and data bus when using external memory. It is used for data output during program verification. Port 0 can sink/source eight LS TTL loads.
PORT 1	Port 1 is an 8-bit quasi-bidirectional I/O port. It is used for the low-order address byte during program verification. Port 1 can sink/source four LS TTL loads. In non-loop mode two of the I/O lines serve alternate functions: —$\overline{RTS}$ (P1.6) Request-to Send output. A low indicates that the 8044 is ready to transmit. —$\overline{CTS}$ (P1.7) Clear-to-Send input. A low indicates that a receiving station is ready to receive.

Table 2. BEM Pin Description (Continued)

Name	Description
PORT 2	Port 2 is an 8-bit quasi-bidirection I/O port. It also emits the high-order address byte when accessing external memory. It is used for the high-order address and the control signals during program verification. Port 2 can sink/source four LS TTL loads.
PORT 3	Port 3 is an 8-bit quasi-bidirectional I/O port. It also contains the interrupt, timer, serial port and RD and WR pins that are used by various options. The output latch corresponding to a secondary function must be programmed to a one (1) for that function to operate. Port 3 can sink/source four LS TTL loads. In addition to I/O some of the pins also serve alternate functions as follows: • I/$\overline{O}$ R x D (P3.0). In point-to-point or multipoint configurations, this pin controls the direction of pin P3.1. Serves as Receive Data input in loop and diagnostic modes. • DATA T x D (P3.1). In point-to-point or multipoint configurations, this pin functions as data input/output. In loop mode, it serves as transmit pin. A '0' written to this pin enables diagnostic mode. • $\overline{\text{INT0}}$ (P3.2). Interrupt 0 input or gate control input for counter 0. • $\overline{\text{INT1}}$ (P3.3). Interrupt 1 input or gate control input for counter 1. • TO (P3.4). Input to counter 0. • SCLK T1 (P3.5). In addition to I/O, this pin provides input to counter 1 or serves as SCLK (serial clock) input. • $\overline{\text{WR}}$ (P3.6). The write control signal latches the data byte from Port 0 into the External Data Memory. • $\overline{\text{RD}}$ (P3.7). The read control signal enables External Data Memory to Port 0.
RST	A high on this pin for two machine cycles while the oscillator is running resets the device. A small external pulldown resistor ($\approx$ 8.2 KΩ) from RST to VSS permits power-on reset when a capacitor ($\approx$ 10 μf) is also connected from this pin to V_{CC}.
ALE/$\overline{\text{PROG}}$	Provides Address Latch Enable output used for latching the address into external memory during normal operation. It is activated every six oscillator periods except during an external data memory access. It also receives the program pulse input for programming the EPROM version.
$\overline{\text{PSEN}}$	The Program Store Enable output is a control signal that enables the external Program Memory to the bus during external fetch operations. It is activated every six oscillator periods, except during external data memory accesses. Remains high during internal program execution.
$\overline{\text{EA}}$/VPP	When held at a TTL high level, the 8044 executes instructions from the internal ROM when the PC is less than 4096. When held at a TTL low level, the 8044 fetches all instructions from external Program Memory. The pin also receives the 21V EPROM programming supply voltage on the 8744.
XTAL 1	Input to the oscillator's high gain amplifier. Required when a crystal is used. Connect to VSS when external source is used on XTAL 2.
XTAL 2	Output from the oscillator's amplifier. Input to the internal timing circuitry. A crystal or external source can be used.

Firmware

The BEM's Basic firmware environment provides two services: BITBUS Communications and Power-Up Diagnostics. The Extended firmware environment provides the Basic firmware services plus Parallel Communications and User Software Services (iDCX 51 Executive, Remote Access and Control functions). A discussion of each service follows.

Basic Firmware Services

POWER-UP DIAGNOSTICS INCREASE RELIABILITY

For added reliability and simplified system start up, the BEM firmware includes power-up diagnostics. At chip reset the BEM diagnostic firmware checks the integrity of the 8044's instruction set, ROM, internal

16

RAM, and external RAM. LED indicator lights may be used to show the progress of the diagnostics. Intel's BITBUS boards use one red LED, and one green LED as indicators for test progress. Since the test halts if a fault is found, the last LED state indicates the trouble area.

No programmatic interface exists for the power-up diagnostics. Only LEDs (or other indicators) connected to the outputs of Port 1 of the 8044 are required. For the test sequence shown in Table 3, the red LED is connected to pin P1.0, and the green LED is connected to pin P1.1.

Table 3. Power-Up Test Sequence

Test Sequence	State of Port* After Test Completion	
	Red LED (Pin 1.0)	Green LED (Pin 1.1)
Power-on	On	On
Prior to Start of Tests	Off	Off
Test 1—Instruction Set	On	On
Test 2—ROM Checksum Test	On	Off
Test 3—Internal RAM	Off	Off
Test 4—External RAM	Off	On

*Ports are Active Low.

BITBUS™ INTERFACE SIMPLIFIES DESIGN OF DISTRIBUTED CONTROL SYSTEMS

The BITBUS Serial Control Bus is a serial bus optimized for high speed transfer of short messages in a hierarchical system. From the perspective of systems using the BITBUS bus there are three external protocols that must be adhered to: physical, data link, and transaction control as shown in Figure 2. The physical interface includes all bus hardware requirements, e.g. cable and connector definition, transceiver specification. The data link interface refers to the device to device transfer of frames on the bus. The transaction control interface indentifies the rules for transmitting messages on the bus as well as the format of the messages passed.

For maximum reliability and to facilitate standardization the following existing standards were chosen as portions of the BITBUS Specification: International Electrotechnical Commission (IEC) mechanical board and connector specifications, the Electronic Industry Association (EIA) RS-485 Electrical Specification and IBM*'s Serial Data Link Control protocol for the physical and data link levels of the BITBUS interface.

BITBUS™ Physical Interface

Implementation of the electrical interface to BITBUS requires external hardware. Specifically, an EIA Standard RS-485 driver and transceiver and an optional clock source for the synchronous mode of operation. A self clocked mode of operation is also available. Different modes of operation facilitate a variety of performance/distance options as noted in Table 4. Figure 7 illustrates the BEM's BITBUS interface hardware requirements.

Table 4. BITBUS™ Interconnect Modes of Operation

	Speed Kb/s	Max. Dist Between Repeaters M/ft	Max # Nodes Between Repeaters	Max # Repeaters
Synchronous	2400	30/100	28	0
Self-Clocked	375	300/1000	28	2
	62.5	1200/4000	28	10

BITBUS™ Data Link Service

The 8044's serial interface unit (SIU) implements a majority of the data link interface, a subset of IBM's Serial Data Link Protocol (SDLC), in hardware resulting in a significant performance advantage compared with multichip solutions. Multichip solutions require both hardware and software glue that degrade performance, decrease reliability, and increase cost. This portion of the BITBUS interface requires no user involvement for execution.

For a detailed discussion of the protocol executed by the BITBUS data link service refer to "The BITBUS Interconnect Serial Control Bus Specification". A basic subset of SDLC with the REJECT option is implemented. The standard frame format transferred across the BITBUS is shown in Figure 8. The information field carries the BITBUS message.

BITBUS™ Transaction Control Service

For added reliability, the BITBUS interface incorporates error checking at the message level in addition to the imbedded error checking provided by SDLC at the data link level. The message control interface defines the format and function of messages transmitted in frames across the BITBUS bus. (Figure 9)

The transaction protocol requires that for every order message transmitted across the bus a reply message must be transmitted in return. Error types and error detection mechanisms are also designated by this interface.

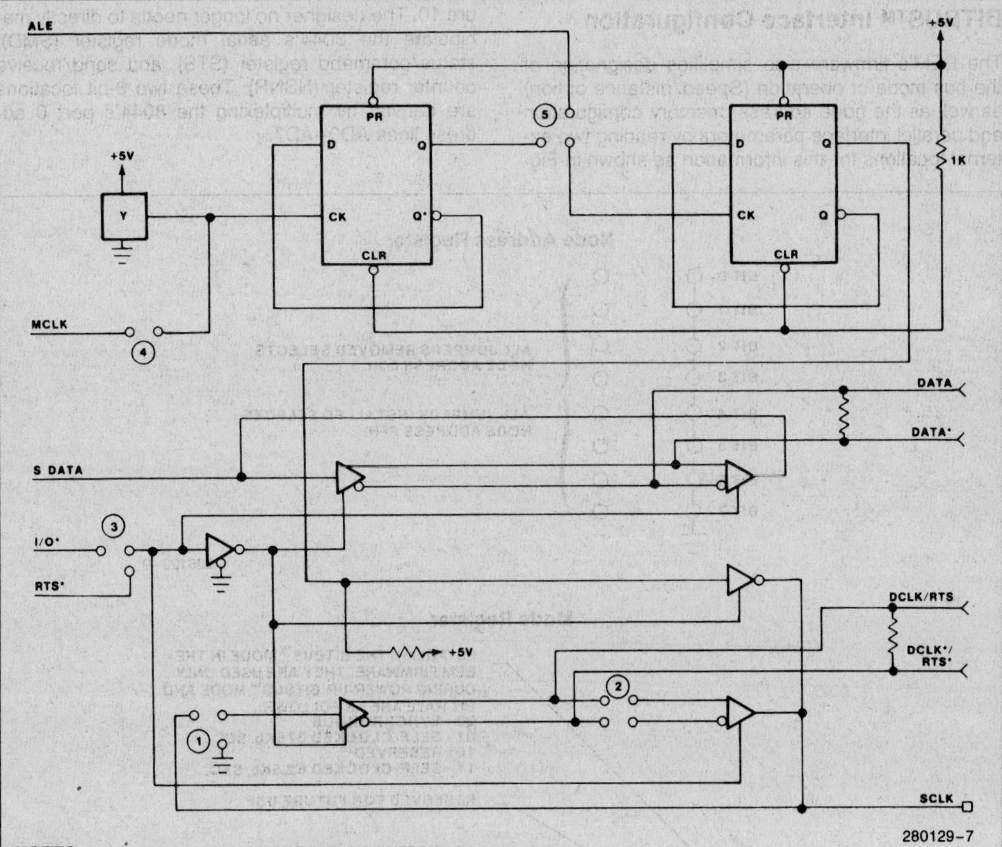

280129-7

NOTES:

1. Connect to ground for self-clocked mode and SCLK for synchronous mode.
2. Remove for self-clocked operation with repeater(s).
3. Connect to RTS* for synchronous mode or I/O* for self-clocked mode.
4. Selects MCLK as serial clock source.
5. Selects ALE or oscillator as serial clock source.

Figure 7. BITBUS™ Interface Hardware Requirements

FLAG	ADDRESS	CONTROL	INFORMATION	FCS	FLAG	
1	1	1	N	2	1	(BYTES)

Figure 8. BITBUS™ Frame Format

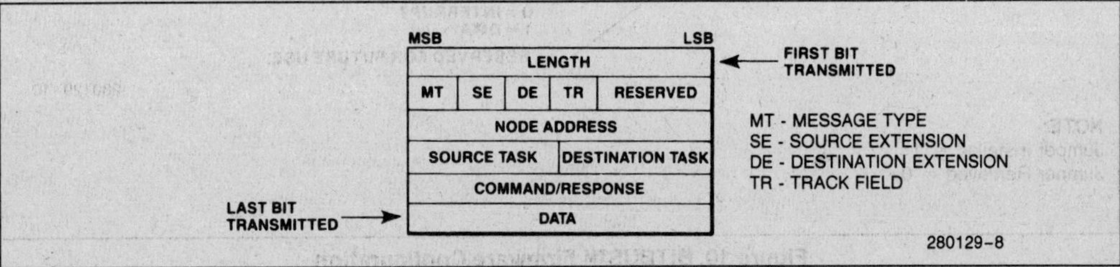

Figure 9. BITBUS™ Message Format

BITBUS™ Interface Configuration

The BEM's firmware also simplifies designation of the bus mode of operation (Speed/distance option) as well as the node address, memory configuration and parallel interface parameters by reading two external locations for this information as shown in Figure 10. The designer no longer needs to directly manipulate the 8044's serial mode register (SMD), status/command register (STS), and send/receive counter register (NSNR). These two 8-bit locations are derived by multiplexing the 8044's port 0 address lines AD0–AD7.

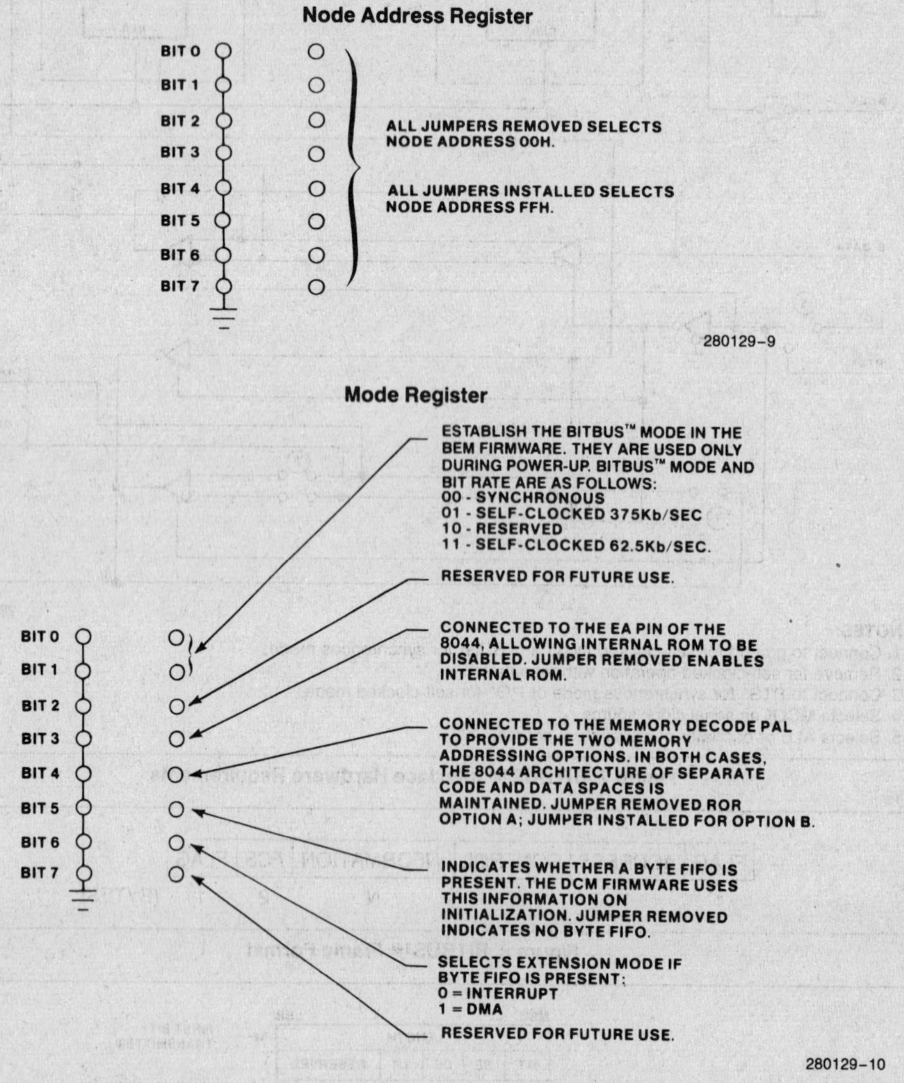

Node Address Register

BIT 0
BIT 1
BIT 2
BIT 3
BIT 4
BIT 5
BIT 6
BIT 7

ALL JUMPERS REMOVED SELECTS NODE ADDRESS 00H.

ALL JUMPERS INSTALLED SELECTS NODE ADDRESS FFH.

280129–9

Mode Register

BIT 0
BIT 1
BIT 2
BIT 3
BIT 4
BIT 5
BIT 6
BIT 7

ESTABLISH THE BITBUS™ MODE IN THE BEM FIRMWARE. THEY ARE USED ONLY DURING POWER-UP. BITBUS™ MODE AND BIT RATE ARE AS FOLLOWS:
00 - SYNCHRONOUS
01 - SELF-CLOCKED 375Kb/SEC
10 - RESERVED
11 - SELF-CLOCKED 62.5Kb/SEC.

RESERVED FOR FUTURE USE.

CONNECTED TO THE EA PIN OF THE 8044, ALLOWING INTERNAL ROM TO BE DISABLED. JUMPER REMOVED ENABLES INTERNAL ROM.

CONNECTED TO THE MEMORY DECODE PAL TO PROVIDE THE TWO MEMORY ADDRESSING OPTIONS. IN BOTH CASES, THE 8044 ARCHITECTURE OF SEPARATE CODE AND DATA SPACES IS MAINTAINED. JUMPER REMOVED ROR OPTION A; JUMPER INSTALLED FOR OPTION B.

INDICATES WHETHER A BYTE FIFO IS PRESENT. THE DCM FIRMWARE USES THIS INFORMATION ON INITIALIZATION. JUMPER REMOVED INDICATES NO BYTE FIFO.

SELECTS EXTENSION MODE IF BYTE FIFO IS PRESENT:
0 = INTERRUPT
1 = DMA

RESERVED FOR FUTURE USE.

280129–10

NOTE:
Jumper Installed = 1
Jumper Removed = 0

Figure 10. BITBUS™ Firmware Configuration

Extended Firmware Services

PARALLEL COMMUNICATION INTERFACE EXTENDS DISTRIBUTED CONTROL CAPABILITY

The BEM's firmware also includes a parallel interface for expanding the capabilities of distributed systems. For example, this interface allows other processors to be employed in BITBUS systems if more processing power is required as shown in Figure 11. This interface provides the means for connection to other buses: iSBX bus, STD bus, IBM's PC bus.

The interface consists of a byte-FIFO queue through which BITBUS messages can be passd via embedded communications firmware. From the BEM's perspective the user simply designates the correct routing information in the BITBUS message header and the message is directed to the communications firmware and passed through the parallel interface. One example of an implementation that uses this interface is the iSBX BITBUS Controller MULTIMODULE Board via the iSBX bus.

Parallel Interface Hardware

To implement the Parallel Interface, the user must provide hardware for two FIFOs (one byte minimum) in external data memory, and control signals to/from the 8044's Pins: INT0 (P3.2), INT1 (P3.3), and P1.2. Key hardware elements required are: decoder for the registers' external addresses, temporary storage for bytes passing through the interface, a way to designate bytes as command or data, and a means to generate the control signals. FIFO's must be used to move the data through the interface although the depth of the FIFO need not exceed one byte.

Interface hardware must also be provided for the "extension" side of the interface. Implementation of this hardware is left to the user with the restriction that the operation of the BEM side remains independent.

Parallel Byte Stream and Message Protocol

The two byte registers (FIFOs) provide the path for bytes to move through the parallel interface. Bytes are read or written from the registers designated: FIFO Data Byte (FF00H) and FIFO Command Byte (FF01H). INT0, INT1 and P1.2 provide control signals to the firmware for moving the bytes through the registers. These signals are referred to as the Parallel Interface Control Bits:

Pin	Function	Internal Bit Address
INT0	RFNF	B3H
INT1	TFNE	B2H
P1.2	TCMD	92H

The hardware uses RFNF to control the output of bytes from the BEM. RFNF is set when the FIFO Data or FIFO Command Byte Registers can receive information. RFNF remains clear when the FIFO Data or Command Bytes are not available. Transmission of a BITBUS message across the parallel interface consists of successively outputing message bytes to the FIFO Data Byte Register until all bytes are sent. The firmware then writes a value of 0 to the Command Byte register indicating all the message bytes have been sent. The first data byte in the message indicates the number of bytes in the message.

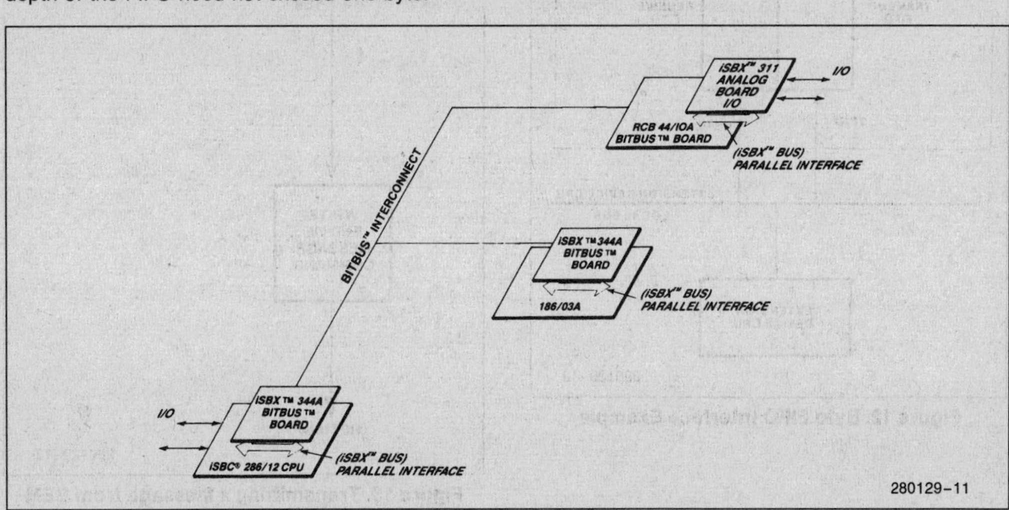

Figure 11. Extending the Capability of BITBUS™ System with the Parallel Communications Interface

TFNE controls the input of data bytes to the BEM. This bit is set when bytes are available for reading. When no bytes are available this bit is clear. TCMD indicates whether the next byte read is a Data Byte or Command Byte. BITBUS messages are received by inputing data bytes until a command byte is received. Data bytes are read from the FIFO Data Byte Register. Command Bytes are read from the FIFO Command Byte Register.

Figure 12 provides one example of a Byte FIFO Interface. This specific example illustrates the interface provided on the iSBX 344A BITBUS Controller MULTIMODULE Board. Figure 13 shows transmission of bytes from the BEM across the parallel interface. Figure 14 shows transmission of bytes to the BEM.

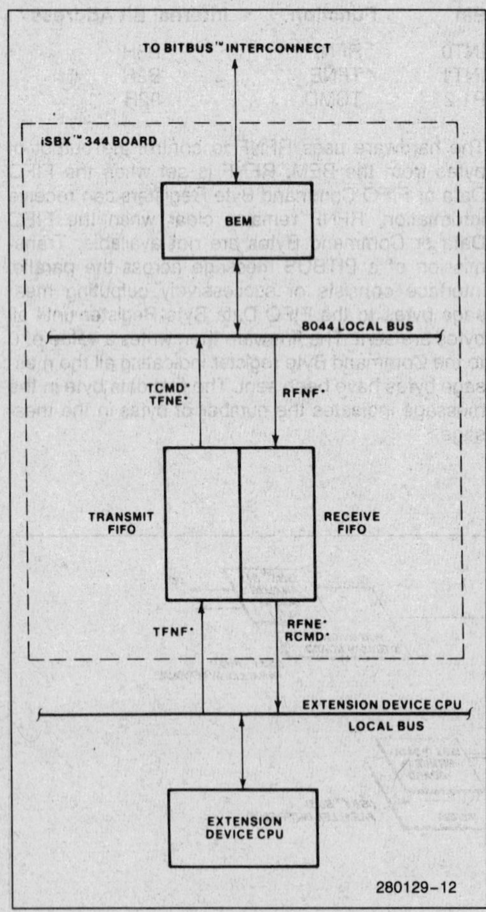

Figure 12. Byte FIFO Interface Example

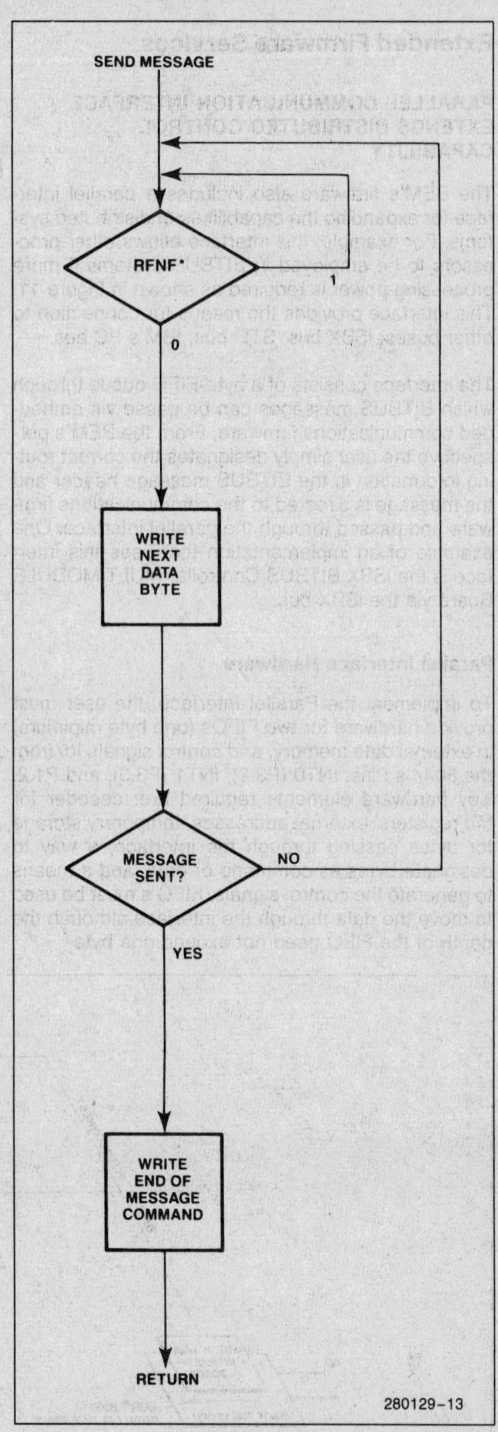

Figure 13. Transmitting a Message from BEM

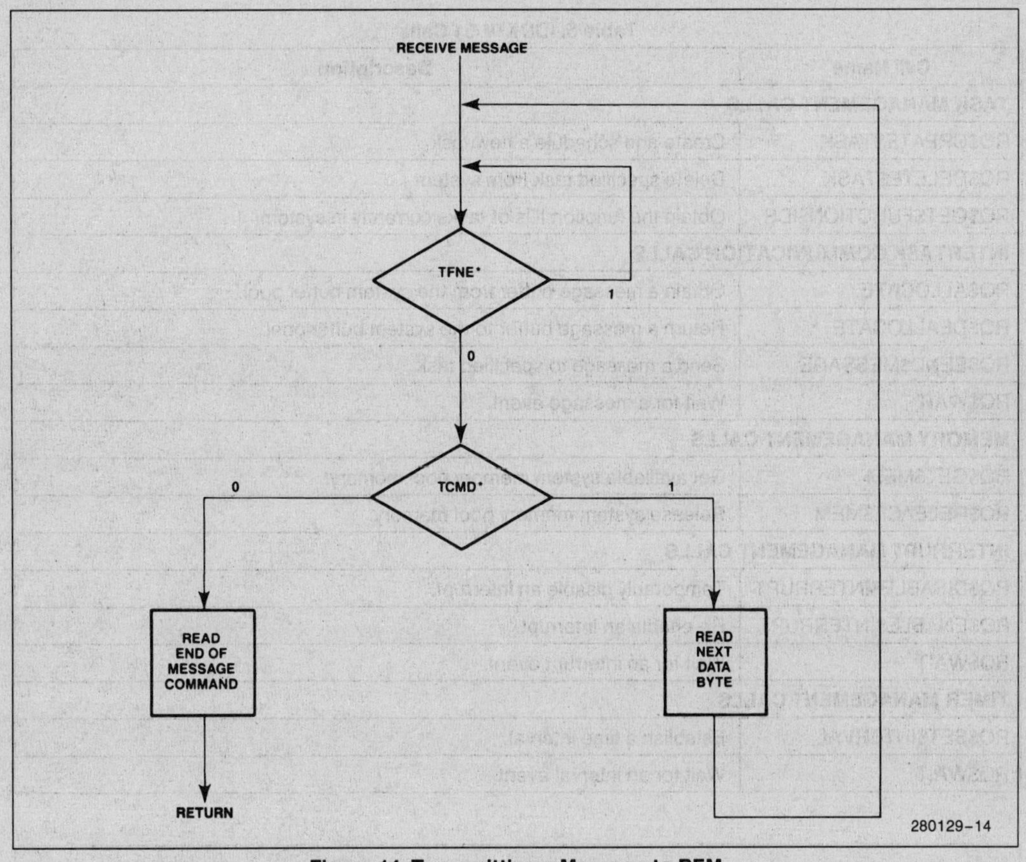

Figure 14. Transmitting a Message to BEM

USER SOFTWARE SERVICES

Multitasking, I/O Access and Control Capabilities

The Extended firmware environment of the BEM provides a multitasking facility via the iDCX 51 Real-time, Multitasking Executive. Operating system calls are listed in Table 5. Other services provided by the Executive: interrupt handling, task scheduling, and intertask communication facilitate smooth development of distributed systems. In addition to the Executive's intertask communication service provided by the RQSENDMESSAGE call, other portions of the firmware extend the communication capability across the parallel and BITBUS interfaces. This embedded communications firmware greatly simplifies and speeds sending messages to different microcontrollers or microprocessors in the system.

To further ease the development of distributed control applications, a pre-defined task (Remote Access and Control Task) provides the means of invoking iDCX 51 Executive services, or accessing I/O and memory from tasks on other devices. The Remote Access and Control functions execute under the iDCX 51 Executive as Task 0. Figure 13 illustrates this concept in a BITBUS system. Table 6 shows the functions provided by the RAC task. All I/O command accesses are memory mapped to locations 0FF00H to 0FFFFH in the BEM's external memory.

Table 5. iDCX™ 51 Calls

Call Name	Description
TASK MANAGEMENT CALLS	
RQ$CREATE$TASK	Create and schedule a new task.
RQ$DELETE$TASK	Delete specified task from system.
RQGETFUNCTION$IDS	Obtain the function IDs of tasks currently in system.
INTERTASK COMMUNICATION CALLS	
RQ$ALLOCATE	Obtain a message buffer from the system buffer pool.
RQ$DEALLOCATE	Return a message buffer to the system buffer pool.
RQ$SEND$MESSAGE	Send a message to specified task.
RQ$WAIT	Wait for a message event.
MEMORY MANAGEMENT CALLS	
RQGETMEM	Get available system memory pool memory.
RQ$RELEASE$MEM	Release system memory pool memory.
INTERRUPT MANAGEMENT CALLS	
RQ$DISABLE$INTERRUPT	Temporarily disable an interrupt.
RQ$ENABLE$INTERRUPT	Re-enable an interrupt.
RQ$WAIT	Wait for an interrupt event.
TIMER MANAGEMENT CALLS	
RQSETINTERVAL	Establish a time interval.
RQ$WAIT	Wait for an interval event.

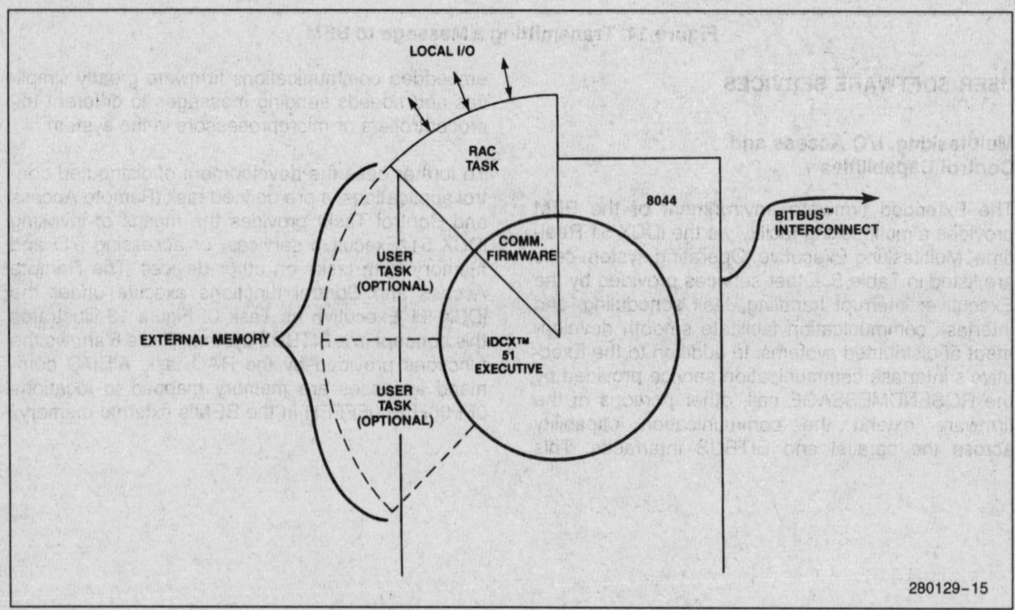

Figure 15. BEM Communication Firmware

Table 6. RAC Functions

Name	Function
RESET_STATION	Perform a software reset.
CREATE_TASK	Perform an RQ$CREATE$TASK system call.
DELETE_TASK	Perform an RQ$DELETE$TASK system call.
GET_FUNCTION_ID	Perform an RQGETFUNCTION$IDS call.
RAC_PROTECT	Suspend or resume RAC services.
READ_IO	Return values from specified I/O ports.
WRITE_IO	Write to the specified I/O ports.
UPDATE_IO	Update the specified I/O ports.
UPLOAD_MEMORY	Return the values in specified memory area.
DOWNLOAD_MEMORY	Write values to specified memory area.
OR_I/O	OR values into specified I/O ports.
AND_I/O	AND values into specified I/O ports.
XOR_I/O	XOR values into specified I/O ports.
READ_INTERNAL	Read values at specified internal RAM areas.
WRITE_INTERNAL	Write values to specified internal RAM areas.
NODE_INFO	Return device related information.
OFFLINE	Set node offline.
UPLOAD_CODE	Read values from code memory space.
DOWNLOAD_CODE	Write values to specified EEPROM memory.

NOTES:
Internal memory locations are included in the 192 bytes of data RAM provided in the microcontroller. External memory refers memory outside the microcontroller—the 28-pin sockets of the iSBX 344A module and the iRCB 44/10A and iRCB 44/20A boards. Each RAC Access Function may refer to 1, 2, 3, 4, 5, or 6 individual I/O or memory locations in a single command.

In addition to allowing creation and deletion of tasks on remote system nodes, the RAC functions allow memory upload and download. This feature eases programming changes in distributed systems and enhances overall system flexibility. Diagnostics can also be downloaded to remote nodes to facilitate system debug.

Another feature optimized for distributed control environments is the GET FUNCTION IDS service. The function ID capability provides the user with the ability to identify specific tasks by function rather than node address and task number. This constant identifier facility remains valid even if functions are moved to different physical locations, eg. another system node.

Aside from the iDCX 51 Executive system calls the user interfaces to the BEM through the task initialization interface; the Initial Task Descriptor. The first user task descriptor must be located at location 0FFF0H in external memory code space so that on power up user code may be automatically detected.

The Initial Task Descriptor (ITD) allows the user to specify the original attributes of a task. Table 7 shows the ITD task structure.

Table 7. ITD Structure

Pattern	Word	value identifying an ITD: "AA55H"
Initial PC	Word	address of first task instruction
Stack-Length	Byte	# bytes of system RAM for tasks stack
Function ID	Byte	value 1–255 associates task w/function
Register Bank	Bit(4)	assigns one register bank to task
Priority	Bit(4)	task priority level
Interrupt Vector	Word	specifies interrupt associated w/task
Next ID	Word	address of the next ITD in linked-list

ABSOLUTE MAXIMUM RATINGS*

Ambient Temperature Under Bias . . . . 0 to 70°C

Storage Temperature . . . . −65°C to +150°C

Voltage on Any Pin with Respect to Ground (V_{SS}) . . . . −0.5V to +7V

Power Dissipation . . . . 2 Watts

NOTICE: This is a production data sheet. The specifications are subject to change without notice.

**WARNING: Stressing the device beyond the "Absolute Maximum Ratings" may cause permanent damage. These are stress ratings only. Operation beyond the "Operating Conditions" is not recommended and extended exposure beyond the "Operating Conditions" may affect device reliability.*

D.C. CHARACTERISTICS T_A = 0°C to 70°C, V_{CC} = 5V ±10%, V_{SS} = 0V

Symbol	Parameter	Min	Max	Units	Test Conditions
VIL	Input Low Voltage	−0.5	0.8	V	
VIH	Input High Voltage (Except RST and XTAL2)	2.0	V_{CC} + 0.5	V	
VIH1	Input High Voltage to PST For Reset, XTAL2	2.5	V_{CC} + 0.5		XTAL1 = V_{SS}
VOL	Output Low Voltage Ports 1, 2, 3 (Note 1)		0.45	V	I_{OL} = 1.6 mA
VOL1	Output Low Voltage Port 0, ALE, \PSEN (Note 1)		0.45	V	I_{OL} = 3.2 mA
VOH	Output High Voltage Ports 1, 2, 3	2.4		V	I_{OH} = −80 μA
VOH1	Output High Voltage Port 0, ALE, \PSEN	2.4		V	I_{OH} = −400 μA
IIL	Logical 0 Input Current Ports 1, 2, 3		−500	μA	XTAL1 at V_{SS} Vin = 0.45V
IIH1	Input High Current to RST/VPD For Reset		500	μA	Vin < V_{CC} − 1.5V
ILI	Input Leakage Current to Port 0, \EA		±10	μA	0.45V < Vin < V_{CC}
ICC	Power Supply Current		170	mA	All Outputs Disconnected, EA = V_{CC}
CIO	Capacitance of $\overline{I/O}$ Buffer		10	pF	fc = 1 MHz
IIL2	Logical 0 Input Current XTAL2		−3.6	mA	XTAL1 at V_{SS} Vin = 0.45V

NOTE:

1. Capacitive loading on Ports 0 and 2 may cause spurious noise pulses to be superimposed on the VOLs of ALE and Ports 1 and 3. The noise is due to external bus capacitance discharging into the Port 0 and Port 2 pins when these pins make 1-to-0 transitions during bus operations. In the worst cases (capacitive loading > 100 pF), the noise pulse on the ALE line may exceed 0.8V. In such cases it may be desirable to qualify ALE with a Schmitt Trigger, or use an address latch with a Schmitt Trigger STROBE input.

A.C. CHARACTERISTICS

T_A to 0°C to 70°C, V_{CC} = 5V ±10%, V_{SS} = 0V, C_L for Port 0, ALE and $\overline{PSEN}$ Outputs = 100 pF; C_L for All Other Outputs = 80 pF

PROGRAM MEMORY

Symbol	Parameter	12 MHz Clock			Variable Clock 1/TCLCL = 3.5 MHz to 12 MHz		
		Min	Max	Units	Min	Max	Units
TLHLL	ALE Pulse Width	127		ns	2TCLCL−40		ns
TAVLL	Address Setup to ALE	43		ns	TCLCL−40		ns
TLLAX(1)	Address Hold after ALE	48		ns	TCLCL−35		ns
TLLIV	ALE to Valid Instr in		233	ns		4TCLCL−100	ns
TLLPL	ALE to $\overline{PSEN}$	58		ns	TCLCL−25		ns
TPLPH	$\overline{PSEN}$ Pulse Width	215		ns	3TCLCL−35		ns
TPLIV	$\overline{PSEN}$ to Valid Instr in		125	ns		3TCLCL−125	ns
TPXIX	Input Instr Hold after $\overline{PSEN}$	0		ns	0		ns
TPXIZ(2)	Input Instr Float after $\overline{PSEN}$		63	ns		TCLCL−20	ns
TPXAV(2)	Address Valid after $\overline{PSEN}$	75		ns	TCLCL−8		ns
TAVIV	Address to Valid Instr in		302	ns		5TCLCL−115	ns
TAZPL	Address Float to $\overline{PSEN}$	−25		ns	−25		ns

NOTES:
1. TLLAX for access to program memory is different from TLLAX for data memory.
2. Interfacing RUPI-44 devices with float times up to 75 ns is permissible. This limited bus contention will not cause any damage to Port 0 drivers.

EXTERNAL DATA MEMORY

Symbol	Parameter	12 MHz Clock			Variable Clock 1/TCLCL = 3.5 MHz to 12 MHz		
		Min	Max	Units	Min	Max	Units
TRLRH	$\overline{RD}$ Pulse Width	400		ns	6TCLCL−100		ns
TWLWH	$\overline{WR}$ Pulse Width	400		ns	6TCLCL−100		ns
TLLAX(1)	Address Hold after ALE	48		ns	TCLCL−35		
TRLDV	$\overline{RD}$ to Valid Data in		252	ns		5TCLCL−165	ns
TRHDX	Data Hold after $\overline{RD}$	0		ns	0		ns
TRHDZ	Data Float after $\overline{RD}$		97	ns		2TCLCL−70	ns
TLLDV	ALE to Valid Data in		517	ns		8TCLCL−150	ns
TAVDV	Address to Valid Data in		585	ns		9TCLCL−165	ns
TLLWL	ALE to $\overline{WR}$ or $\overline{RD}$	200	300	ns	3TCLCL−50	3TCLCL+50	ns
TAVWL	Address to $\overline{WR}$ or $\overline{RD}$	203		ns	4TCLCL−130		ns
TWHLH	$\overline{WR}$ or $\overline{RD}$ High to ALE High	43	123	ns	TCLCL−40	TCLCL+40	ns
TQVWX	Data Valid to $\overline{WR}$ Transition	23		ns	TCLCL−60		ns
TQVWH	Data Setup before $\overline{WR}$	433		ns	7TCLCL−150		ns
TWHQX	Data Hold after $\overline{WR}$	33		ns	TCLCL−50		ns
TRLAZ	RD Low to Address Float		25	ns		25	ns

NOTE:
1. TLLAX for access to program memory is different from TLLAX for access data memory.

SERIAL INTERFACE

Symbol	Parameter	Min	Max	Units
TDCY	Data Clock	420		ns
TDCL	Data Clock Low	180		ns
TDCH	Data Clock High	100		ns
tTD	Transmit Data Delay		140	ns
tDSS	Data Setup Time	40		ns
tDHS	Data Hold Time	40		ns

WAVEFORMS

Memory Access

PROGRAM MEMORY READ CYCLE

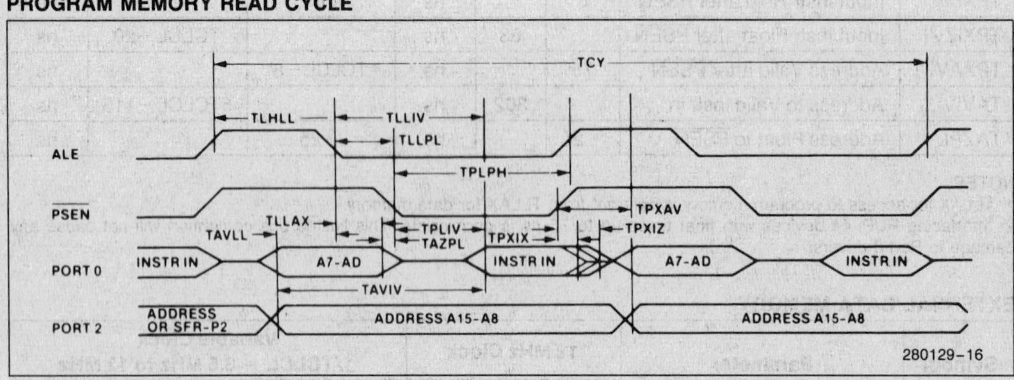

DATA MEMORY READ CYCLE

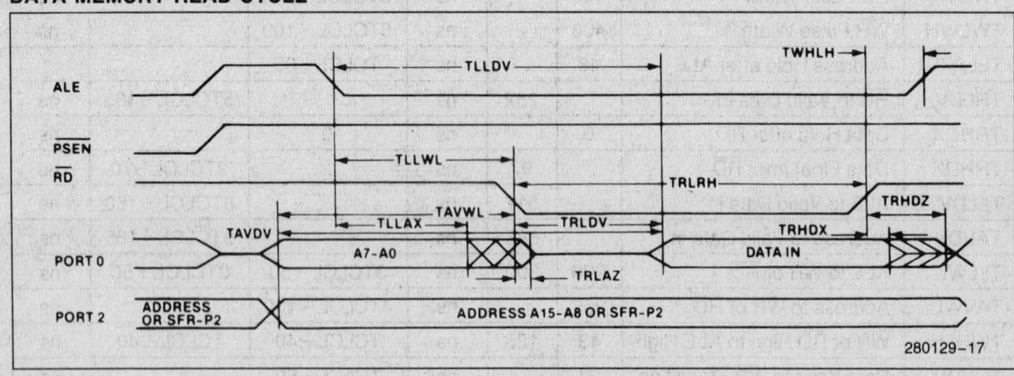

WAVEFORMS (Continued)

DATA MEMORY WRITE CYCLE

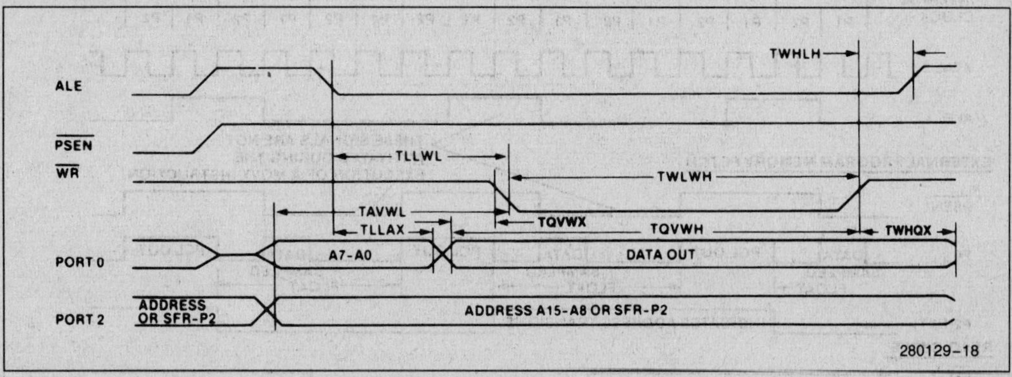

280129-18

SERIAL I/O WAVEFORMS

SYNCHRONOUS DATA TRANSMISSION

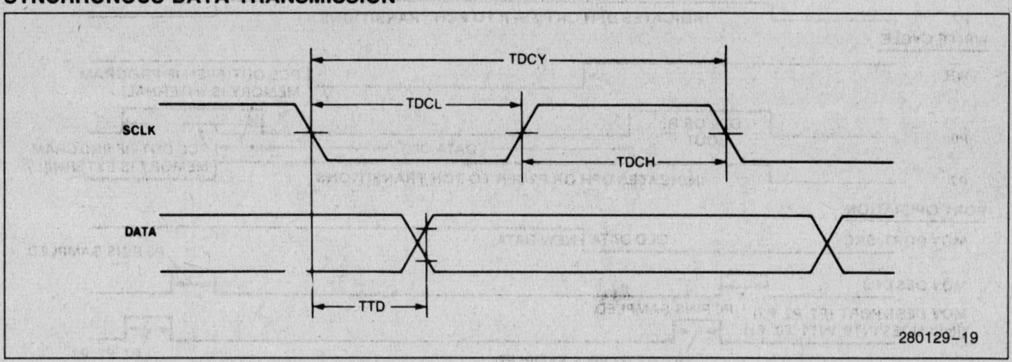

280129-19

SYNCHRONOUS DATA RECEPTION

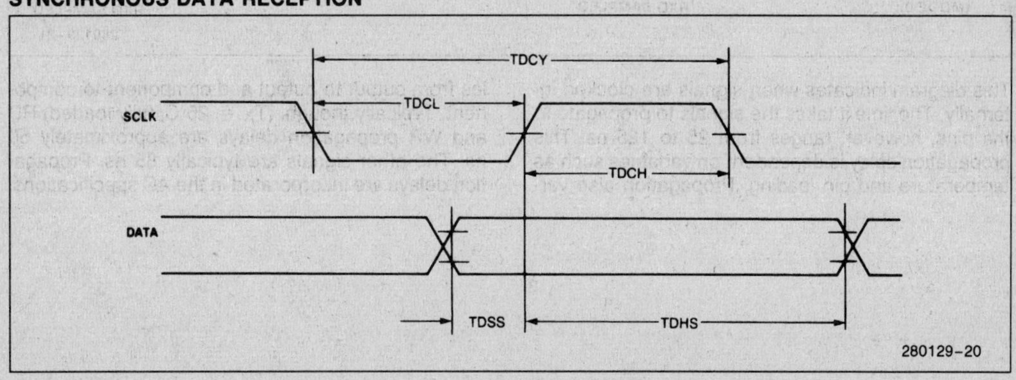

280129-20

CLOCK WAVEFORMS

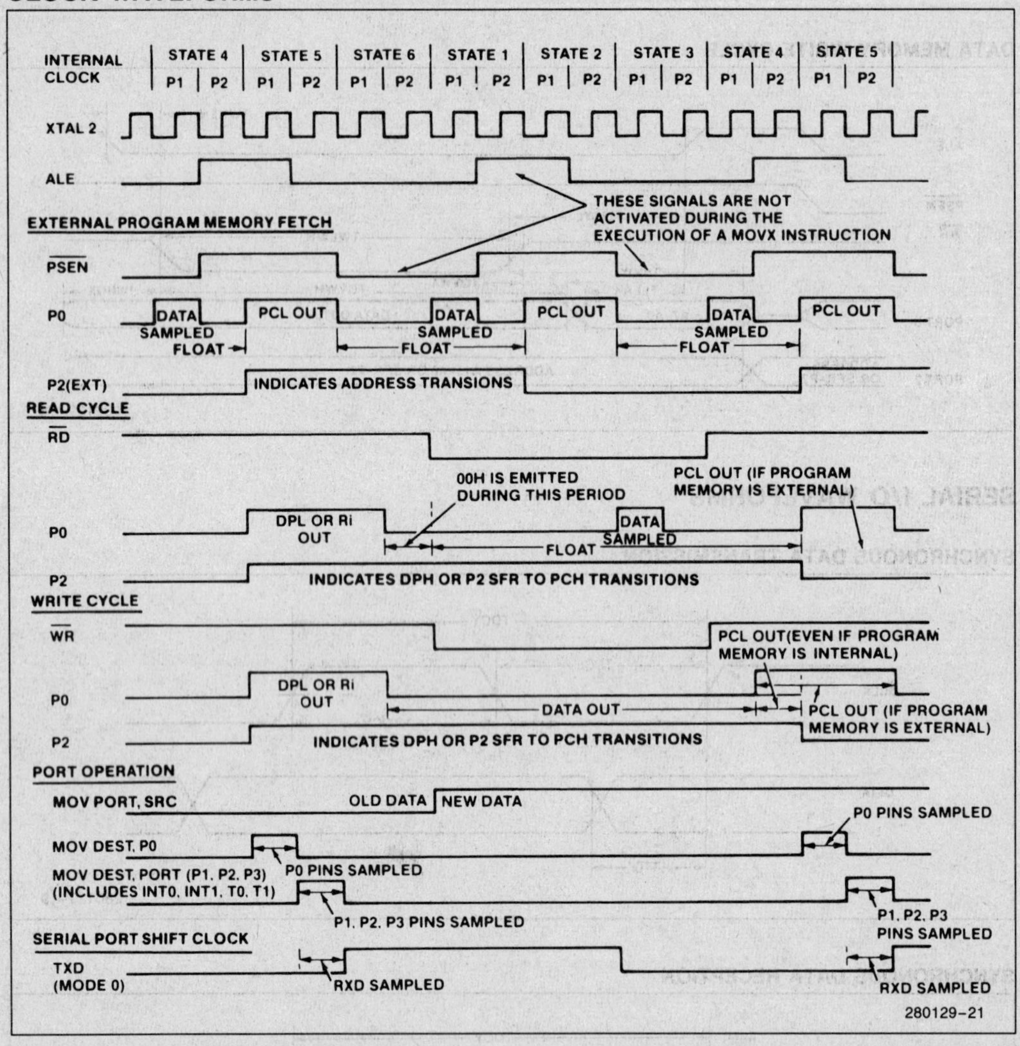

INTERNAL CLOCK
STATE 4 | STATE 5 | STATE 6 | STATE 1 | STATE 2 | STATE 3 | STATE 4 | STATE 5
P1 | P2 | P1 | P2 | P1 | P2 | P1 | P2 | P1 | P2 | P1 | P2 | P1 | P2 | P1 | P2
XTAL 2
ALE
EXTERNAL PROGRAM MEMORY FETCH
THESE SIGNALS ARE NOT ACTIVATED DURING THE EXECUTION OF A MOVX INSTRUCTION
PSEN
P0
DATA SAMPLED
PCL OUT
FLOAT
P2(EXT)
INDICATES ADDRESS TRANSIONS
READ CYCLE
RD
00H IS EMITTED DURING THIS PERIOD
PCL OUT (IF PROGRAM MEMORY IS EXTERNAL)
P0
DPL OR Ri OUT
FLOAT
DATA SAMPLED
P2
INDICATES DPH OR P2 SFR TO PCH TRANSITIONS
WRITE CYCLE
WR
PCL OUT(EVEN IF PROGRAM MEMORY IS INTERNAL)
P0
DPL OR Ri OUT
DATA OUT
PCL OUT (IF PROGRAM MEMORY IS EXTERNAL)
P2
INDICATES DPH OR P2 SFR TO PCH TRANSITIONS
PORT OPERATION
MOV PORT, SRC
OLD DATA
NEW DATA
P0 PINS SAMPLED
MOV DEST, P0
MOV DEST, PORT (P1, P2, P3) (INCLUDES INT0, INT1, T0, T1)
P0 PINS SAMPLED
P1, P2, P3 PINS SAMPLED
P1, P2, P3 PINS SAMPLED
SERIAL PORT SHIFT CLOCK
TXD (MODE 0)
RXD SAMPLED
RXD SAMPLED

280129-21

This diagram indicates when signals are clocked internally. The time it takes the signals to propagate to the pins, however, ranges from 25 to 125 ns. This propagation delay is dependent on variables such as temperature and pin loading. Propagation also varies from output to output and component to component. Typically though, (T_A = 25°C, fully loaded) RD and WR propagation delays are approximately 50 ns. The other signals are typically 85 ns. Propagation delays are incorporated in the AC specifications.

A.C. TESTING INPUT, OUTPUT, FLOAT WAVEFORMS

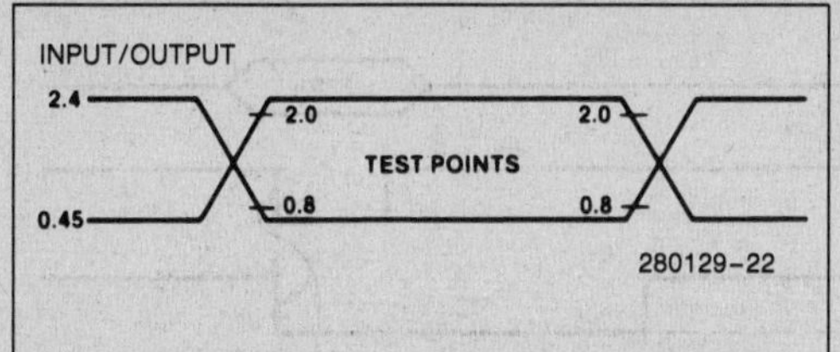

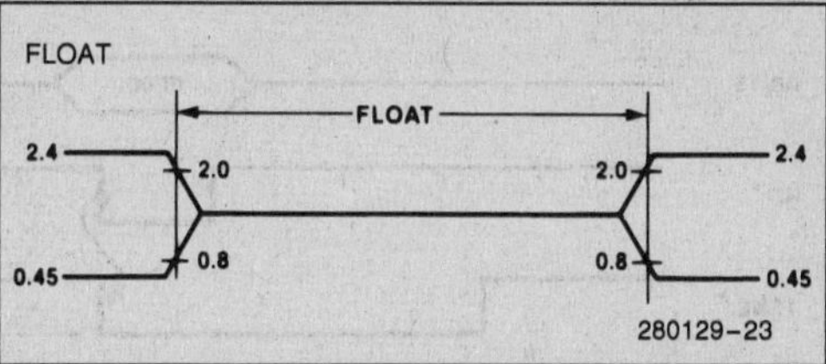

NOTES:
1. A.C. testing inputs are driven at 2.4V for a logic "1" and 0.45V for a logic "0".
2. Timing measurements are made at 2.0V for a logic "1" and 0.8V for a logic "0".

EXTERNAL CLOCK DRIVE XTAL2

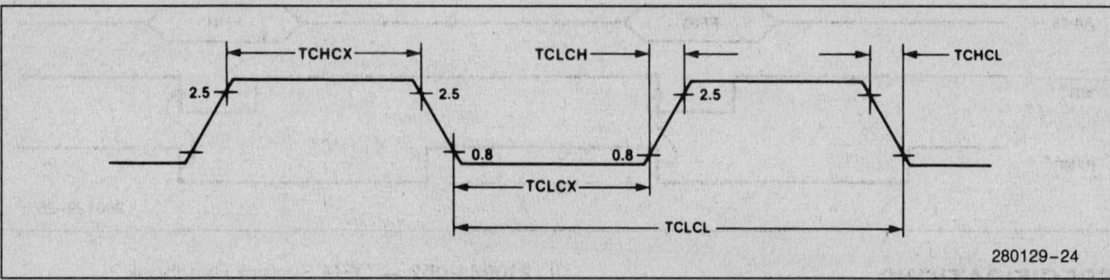

Symbol	Parameter	Variable Clock Freq = 3.5 MHz to 12 MHz		Units
		Min	Max	
TCLCL	Oscillator Period	83.3	285.7	ns
TCHCX	High Time	30	TCLCL − TCLCX	ns
TCLCX	Low Time	20	TCLCL − TCHCX	ns
TCLCH	Rise Time		20	ns
TCHCL	Fall Time		20	ns

16

BEM PARALLEL INTERFACE LOGIC TIMING

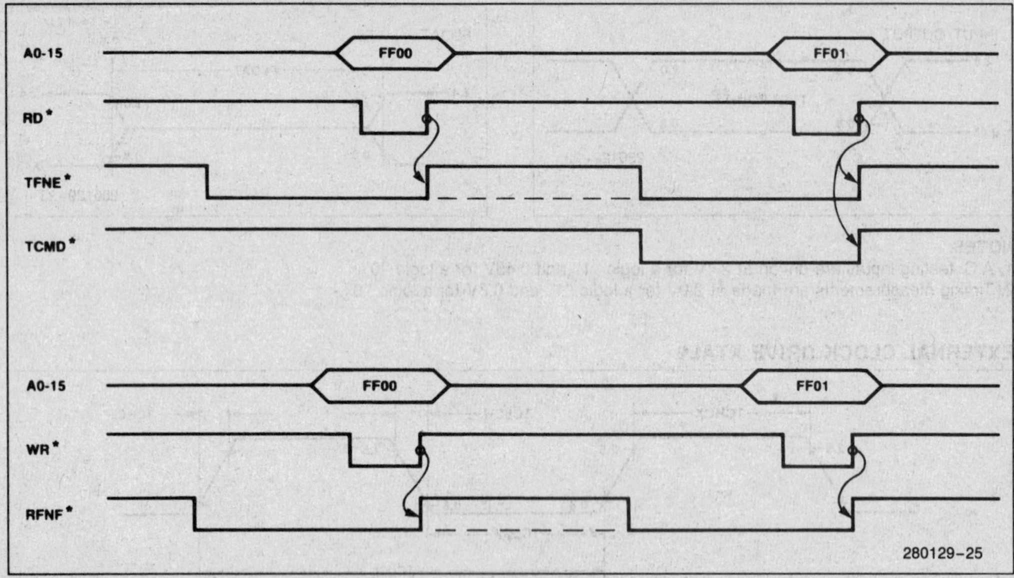

SPECIFICATIONS

Package: 40 pin DIP, 44 pin PLCC
Process: +5V, silicon gate HMOSII

Related Documents (Not Supplied)

Order Number

146312-001— Guide to Using the Distributed Control Modules

231663-002— 8044AH/8344AH/8744H Data Sheet

210941-002 — OEM System Handbook

210918-006 — Embedded Controller Handbook

231166-001 — VLSI Solutions for Distributed Control Applications

ORDERING INFORMATION

Part Number	Description
P,N8044AH,R 0112	BITBUS Enhanced Microcontroller

intel®

8044AH/8344AH/8744H
HIGH PERFORMANCE 8-BIT MICROCONTROLLER WITH ON-CHIP SERIAL COMMUNICATION CONTROLLER

- **8044AH—Includes Factory Mask Programmable ROM**
- **8344AH—For Use with External Program Memory**
- **8744H—Includes User Programmable/Eraseable EPROM**

8051 MICROCONTROLLER CORE

- **Optimized for Real Time Control 12 MHz Clock, Priority Interrupts, 32 Programmable I/O Lines, Two 16-bit Timer/Counters**
- **Boolean Processor**
- **4K × 8 ROM, 192 × 8 RAM**
- **64K Accessible External Program Memory**
- **64K Accessible External Data Memory**
- **4 μs Multiply and Divide**

SERIAL INTERFACE UNIT (SIU)

- **Serial Communication Processor that Operates Concurrently to CPU**
- **2.4 Mbps Maximum Data Rate**
- **375 Kbps using On-Chip Phase Locked Loop**
- **Communication Software in Silicon:**
  - **—Complete Data Link Functions**
  - **—Automatic Station Response**
- **Operates as an SDLC Primary or Secondary Station**

The RUPI-44 family integrates a high performance 8-bit Microcontroller, the Intel 8051 Core, with an Intelligent/high performance HDLC/SDLC serial communication controller, called the Serial Interface Unit (SIU). See Figure 1. This dual architecture allows complex control and high speed data communication functions to be realized cost effectively.

Specifically, the 8044's Microcontroller features: 4K byte On-Chip program memory space; 32 I/O lines; two 16-bit timer/event counters; a 5-source; 2-level interrupt structure; a full duplex serial channel; a Boolean processor; and on-chip oscillator and clock circuitry. Standard TTL and most byte-oriented MCS-80 and MCS-85 peripherals can be used for I/O amd memory expansion.

The Serial Interface Unit (SIU) manages the interface to a high speed serial link. The SIU offloads the On-Chip 8051 Microcontroller of communication tasks, thereby freeing the CPU to concentrate on real time control tasks.

The RUPI-44 family consists of the 8044, 8744, and 8344. All three devices are identical except in respect of on-chip program memory. The 8044 contains 4K bytes of mask-programmable ROM. User programmable EPROM replaces ROM in the 8744. The 8344 addresses all program memory externally.

The RUPI-44 devices are fabricated with Intel's reliable +5 volt, silicon-gate HMOSII technology and packaged in a 40-pin DIP.

The 8744H is available in a hermetically sealed, ceramic, 40-lead dual in-line package which includes a window that allows for EPROM erasure when exposed to ultraviolet light (See Erasure Characteristics). During normal operation, ambient light may adversely affect the functionality of the chip. Therefore applications which expose the 8744H to ambient light may require an opaque label over the window.

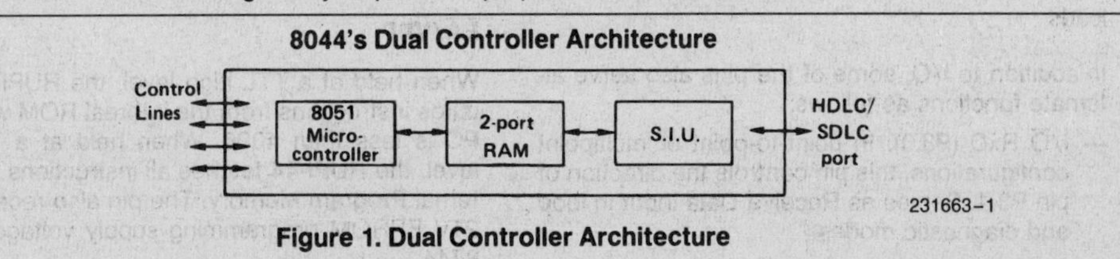

Figure 1. Dual Controller Architecture

16

September 1990
Order Number: 231663-004

Table 1. RUPI™-44 Family Pin Description

VSS

Circuit ground potential.

VCC

+5V power supply during operation and program verification.

PORT 0
Port 0 is an 8-bit open drain bidirectional I/O port. It is also the multiplexed low-order address and data bus when using external memory. It is used for data output during program verification. Port 0 can sink/source eight LS TTL loads (six in 8744).

PORT 1

Port 1 is an 8-bit quasi-bidirectional I/O port. It is used for the low-order address byte during program verification. Port 1 can sink/source four LS TTL loads.

In non-loop mode two of the I/O lines serve alternate functions:

— $\overline{RTS}$ (P1.6). Request-to-Send output. A low indicates that the RUPI-44 is ready to transmit.

— $\overline{CTS}$ (P1.7) Clear-to-Send input. A low indicates that a receiving station is ready to receive.

PORT 2

Port 2 is an 8-bit quasi-bidirection I/O port. It also emits the high-order address byte when accessing external memory. It is used for the high-order address and the control signals during program verification. Port 2 can sink/source four LS TTL loads.

PORT 3

Port 3 is an 8-bit quasi-bidirectional I/O port. It also contains the interrupt, timer, serial port and RD and WR pins that are used by various options. The output latch corresponding to a secondary function must be programmed to a one (1) for that function to operate. Port 3 can sink/source four LS LTT loads.

In addition to I/O, some of the pins also serve alternate functions as follows:

— I/$\overline{O}$ RxD (P3.0). In point-to-point or multipoint configurations, this pin controls the direction of pin P3.1. Serves as Receive Data input in loop and diagnostic modes.

— DATA TxD (P3.1) In point-to-point or multipoint configurations, this pin functions as data input/output. In loop mode, it serves as transmit pin. A '0' written to this pin enables diagnostic mode.

— $\overline{INT0}$ (P3.2). Interrupt 0 input or gate control input for counter 0.

— $\overline{INT1}$ (P3.3). Interrupt 1 input or gate control input for counter 1.

— TO (P3.4). Input to counter 0.

— SCLK T1 (P3.5). In addition to I/O, this pin provides input to counter 1 or serves as SCLK (serial clock) input.

— $\overline{WR}$ (P3.6). The write control signal latches the data byte from Port 0 into the External Data Memory.

— $\overline{RD}$ (P3.7). The read control signal enables External Data Memory to Port 0.

RST

A high on this pin for two machine cycles while the oscillator is running resets the device. A small external pulldown resistor ($\approx$8.2KΩ) from RST to V_{SS} permits power-on reset when a capacitor ($\approx$10μf) is also connected from this pin to V_{CC}.

ALE/$\overline{PROG}$

Provides Address Latch Enable output used for latching the address into external memory during normal operation. It is activated every six oscillator periods except during an external data memory access. It also receives the program pulse input for programming the EPROM version.

$\overline{PSEN}$

The Program Store Enable output is a control signal that enables the external Program Memory to the bus during external fetch operations. It is activated every six oscillator periods, except during external data memory accesses. Remains high during internal program execution.

$\overline{EA}$/VPP

When held at a TTL high level, the RUPI-44 executes instructions from the internal ROM when the PC is less than 4096. When held at a TTL low level, the RUPI-44 fetches all instructions from external Program Memory. The pin also receives the 21V EPROM programming supply voltage on the 8744.

Table 1. RUPI™-44 Family Pin Description (Continued)

XTAL 1	XTAL 2
Input to the oscillator's high gain amplifier. Required when a crystal is used. Connect to VSS when external source is used on XTAL 2.	Output from the oscillator's amplifier. Input to the internal timing circuitry. A crystal or external source can be used.

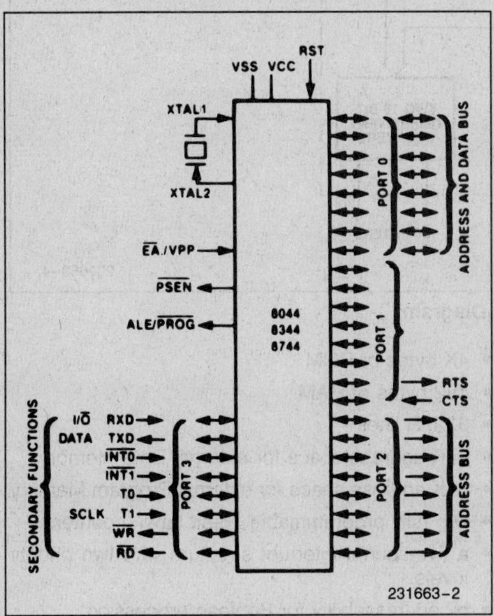

Figure 2. Logic Symbol

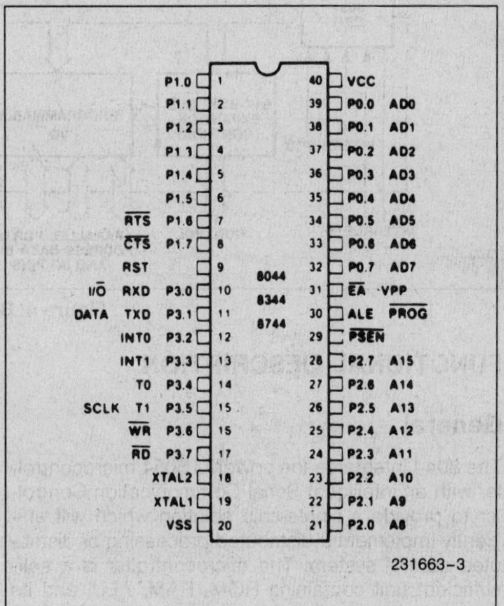

Figure 3A. DIP Pin Configuration

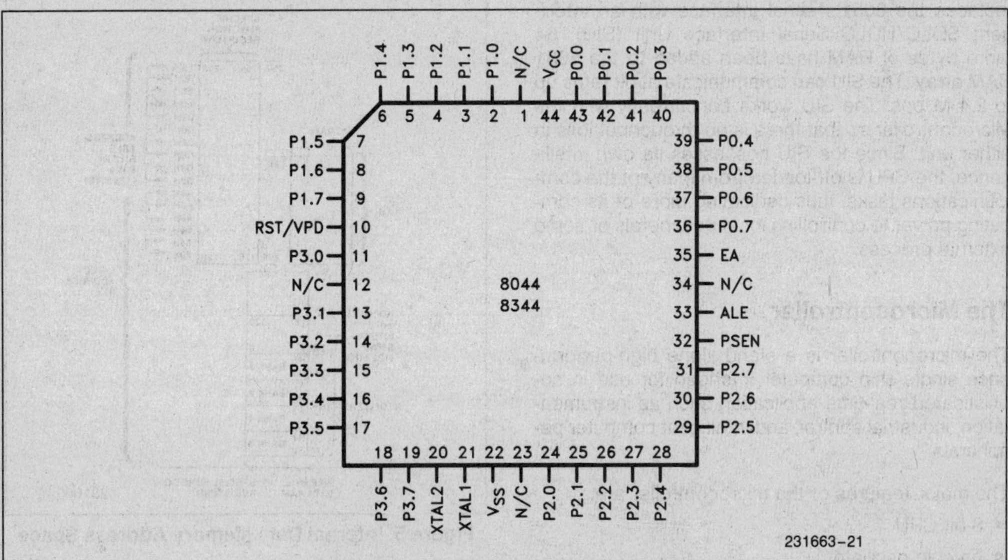

Figure 3B. PLCC Pin Configuration

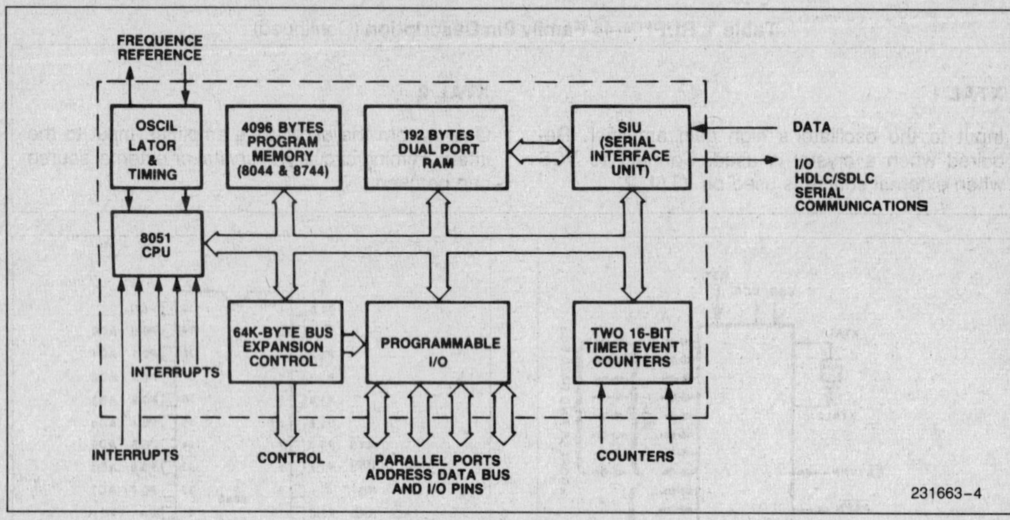

Figure 4. Block Diagram

FUNCTIONAL DESCRIPTION

General

The 8044 integrates the powerful 8051 microcontroller with an intelligent Serial Communication Controller to provide a single-chip solution which will efficiently implement a distributed processing or distributed control system. The microcontroller is a self-sufficient unit containing ROM, RAM, ALU, and its own peripherals. The 8044's architecture and instruction set are identical to the 8051's. The 8044 replaces the 8051's serial interface with an intelligent SDLC/HDLC Serial Interface Unit (SIU). 64 more bytes of RAM have been added to the 8051 RAM array. The SIU can communicate at bit rates up to 2.4 M bps. The SIU works concurrently with the Microcontroller so that there is no throughput loss in either unit. Since the SIU possesses its own intelligence, the CPU is off-loaded from many of the communications tasks, thus dedicating more of its computing power to controlling local peripherals or some external process.

The Microcontroller

The microcontroller is a stand-alone high-performance single-chip computer intended for use in sophisticated real-time application such as instrumentation, industrial control, and intelligent computer peripherals.

The major features of the microcontroller are:

- 8-bit CPU
- on-chip oscillator
- 4K bytes of ROM
- 192 bytes of RAM
- 32 I/O lines
- 64K address space for external Data Memory
- 64K address space for external Program Memory
- two fully programmable 16-bit timer/counters
- a five-source interrupt structure with two priority levels
- bit addressability for Boolean processing

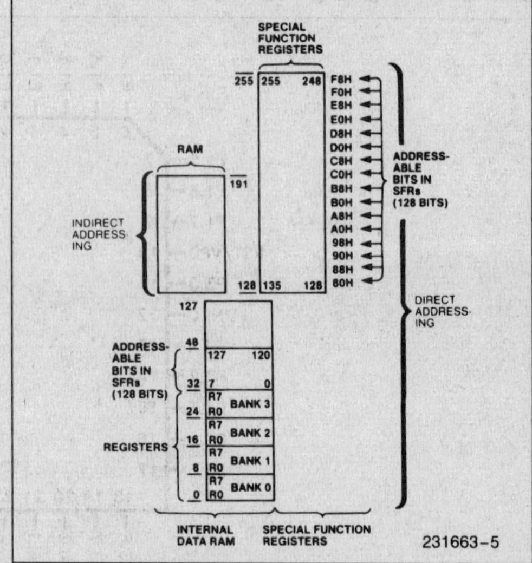

Figure 5. Internal Data Memory Address Space

- 1 μs instruction cycle time for 60% of the instructions 2 μs instruction cycle time for 40% of the instructions
- 4 μs cycle time for 8 by 8 bit unsigned Multiply/Divide

INTERNAL DATA MEMORY

Functionally the Internal Data Memory is the most flexible of the address spaces. The Internal Data Memory space is subdivided into a 256-byte Internal Data RAM address space and a 128-bit Special Function Register address space as shown in Figure 5.

The Internal Data RAM address space is 0 to 255. Four 8-Register Banks occupy locations 0 through 31. The stack can be located anywhere in the Internal Data RAM address space. In addition, 128 bit locations of the on-chip RAM are accessible through Direct Addressing. These bits reside in Internal Data RAM at byte locations 32 through 47. Currently locations 0 through 191 of the Internal Data RAM address space are filled with on-chip RAM.

Parallel I/O

The 8044 has 32 general-purpose I/O lines which are arranged into four groups of eight lines. Each group is called a port. Hence there are four ports; Port 0, Port 1, Port 2, and Port 3. Up to five lines from Port 3 are dedicated to supporting the serial channel when the SIU is invoked. Due to the nature of the serial port, two of Port 3's I/O lines (P3.0 and P3.1) do not have latched outputs. This is true whether or not the serial channel is used.

Port 0 and Port 2 also have an alternate dedicated function. When placed in the external access mode, Port 0 and Port 2 become the means by which the 8044 communicates with external program memory. Port 0 and Port 2 are also the means by which the 8044 communicates with external data memory. Peripherals can be memory mapped into the address space and controlled by the 8044.

Table 2. MCS®-51 Instruction Set Description

Mnemonic		Description	Byte	Cyc
ARITHMETIC OPERATIONS				
ADD	A,Rn	Add register to Accumulator	1	1
ADD	A,direct	Add direct byte to Accumulator	2	1
ADD	A,@Ri	Add indirect RAM to Accumulator	1	1
ADD	A,#data	Add immediate data to Accumulator	2	1
ADDC	A,Rn	Add register to Accumulator with Carry	1	1
ADDC	A,direct	Add direct byte to A with Carry flag	2	1
ADDC	A,@Ri	Add indirect RAM to A with Carry flag	1	1
ADDC	A,#data	Add immediate data to A with Carry flag	2	1
SUBB	A,Rn	Subtract register from A with Borrow	1	1
SUBB	A,direct	Subtract direct byte from A with Borrow	2	1

Mnemonic		Description	Byte	Cyc
ARITHMETIC OPERATIONS (Continued)				
SUBB	A,@Ri	Subtract indirect RAM from A with Borrow	1	1
SUBB	A,#data	Subtract immed data from A with Borrow	2	1
INC	A	Increment Accumulator	1	1
INC	Rn	Increment register	1	1
INC	direct	Increment direct byte	2	1
INC	@Ri	Increment indirect RAM	1	1
INC	DPTR	Increment Data Pointer	1	2
DEC	A	Decrement Accumulator	1	1
DEC	Rn	Decrement register	1	1
DEC	direct	Decrement direct byte	2	1
DEC	@Ri	Decrement indirect RAM	1	1
MUL	AB	Multiply A & B	1	4
DIV	AB	Divide A by B	1	4
DA	A	Decimal Adjust Accumulator	1	1

16

Table 2. MCS®-51 Instruction Set Description (Continued)

Mnemonic		Description	Byte	Cyc
LOGICAL OPERATIONS				
ANL	A,Rn	AND register to Accumulator	1	1
ANL	A,direct	AND direct byte to Accumulator	2	1
ANL	A,@Ri	AND indirect RAM to Accumulator	1	1
ANL	A,#data	AND immediate data to Accumulator	2	1
ANL	direct,A	AND Accumulator to direct byte	2	1
ANL	direct,#data	AND immediate data to direct byte	3	2
ORL	A,Rn	OR register to Accumulator	1	1
ORL	A,direct	OR direct byte to Accumulator	2	1
ORL	A,@Ri	OR indirect RAM to Accumulator	1	1
ORL	A,#data	OR immediate data to Accumulator	2	1
ORL	direct,A	OR Accumulator to direct byte	2	1
ORL	direct,#data	OR immediate data to direct byte	3	2
XRL	A,Rn	Exclusive-OR register to Accumulator	1	1
XRL	A,direct	Exclusive-OR direct byte to Accumulator	2	1
XRL	A,@Ri	Exclusive-OR indirect RAM to A	1	1
XRL	A,#data	Exclusive-OR immediate data to A	2	1
XRL	direct,A	Exclusive-OR Accumulator to direct byte	2	1
XRL	direct,#data	Exclusive-OR immediate data to direct	3	2
CLR	A	Clear Accumulator	1	1
CPL	A	Complement Accumulator	1	1

Mnemonic		Description	Byte	Cyc
LOGICAL OPERATIONS (Continued)				
RL	A	Rotate Accumulator Left	1	1
RLC	A	Rotate A Left through the Carry flag	1	1
RR	A	Rotate Accumulator Right	1	1
RRC	A	Rotate A Right through Carry flag	1	1
SWAP	A	Swap nibbles within the Accumulator	1	1
DATA TRANSFER				
MOV	A,Rn	Move register to Accumulator	1	1
MOV	A,direct	Move direct byte to Accumulator	2	1
MOV	A,@Ri	Move indirect RAM to Accumulator	1	1
MOV	A,#data	Move immediate data to Accumulator	2	1
MOV	Rn,A	Move Accumulator to register	1	1
MOV	Rn,direct	Move direct byte to register	2	2
MOV	Rn,#data	Move immediate data to register	2	1
MOV	direct,A	Move Accumulator to direct byte	2	1
MOV	direct,Rn	Move register to direct byte	2	2
MOV	direct,direct	Move direct byte to direct	3	2
MOV	direct,@Ri	Move indirect RAM to direct byte	2	2
MOV	direct,#data	Move immediate data to direct byte	3	2
MOV	@Ri,A	Move Accumulator to indirect RAM	1	1
MOV	@Ri,direct	Move direct byte to indirect RAM	2	2

Table 2. MCS®-51 Instruction Set Description (Continued)

Mnemonic		Description	Byte	Cyc
DATA TRANSFER (Continued)				
MOV	@Ri,#data	Move immediate data to indirect RAM	2	1
MOV	DPTR,#data16	Load Data Pointer with a 16-bit constant	3	2
MOVC	A,@A+DPTR	Move Code byte relative to DPTR to A	1	2
MOVC	A,@A+PC	Move Code byte relative to PC to A	1	2
MOVX	A,@Ri	Move External RAM (8-bit addr) to A	1	2
MOVX	A,@DPTR	Move External RAM (16-bit addr) to A	1	2
MOVX	@Ri,A	Move A to External RAM (8-bit addr)	1	2
MOVX	@DPTR,A	Move A to External RAM (16-bit) addr	1	2
PUSH	direct	Push direct byte onto stack	2	2
POP	direct	Pop direct byte from stack	2	2
XCH	A,Rn	Exchange register with Accumulator	1	1
XCH	A,direct	Exchange direct byte with Accumulator	2	1
XCH	A,@Ri	Exchange indirect RAM with A	1	1
XCHD	A,@Ri	Exchange low-order Digit ind RAM w A	1	1
BOOLEAN VARIABLE MANIPULATION				
CLR	C	Clear Carry flag	1	1
CLR	bit	Clear direct bit	2	1
SETB	C	Set Carry Flag	1	1
SETB	bit	Set direct Bit	2	1
CPL	C	Complement Carry Flag	1	1
CPL	bit	Complement direct bit	2	1
ANL	C,bit	AND direct bit to Carry flag	2	2

Mnemonic		Description	Byte	Cyc
BOOLEAN VARIABLE MANIPULATION (Continued)				
ANL	C,/bit	AND complement of direct bit to Carry	2	2
ORL	C/bit	OR direct bit to Carry flag	2	2
ORL	C,/bit	OR complement of direct bit to Carry	2	2
MOV	C,/bit	Move direct bit to Carry flag	2	1
MOV	bit,C	Move Carry flag to direct bit	2	2
PROGRAM AND MACHINE CONTROL				
ACALL	addr11	Absolute Subroutine Call	2	2
LCALL	addr16	Long Subroutine Call	3	2
RET		Return from subroutine	1	2
RETI		Return from interrupt	1	2
AJMP	addr11	Absolute Jump	2	2
LJMP	addr16	Long Jump	3	2
SJMP	rel	Short Jump (relative addr)	2	2
JMP	@A+DPTR	Jump indirect relative to the DPTR	1	2
JZ	rel	Jump if Accumulator is Zero	2	2
JNZ	rel	Jump if Accumulator is Not Zero	2	2
JC	rel	Jump if Carry flag is set	2	2
JNC	rel	Jump if No Carry flag	2	2
JB	bit,rel	Jump if direct Bit set	3	2
JNB	bit,rel	Jump if direct Bit Not set	3	2
JBC	bit,rel	Jump if direct Bit is set & Clear bit	3	2
CJNE	A,direct,rel	Compare direct to A & Jump if Not Equal	3	2
CJNE	A,#data,rel	Comp, immed, to A & Jump if Not Equal	3	2

Table 2. MCS®-51 Instruction Set Description (Continued)

Mnemonic	Description	Byte	Cyc
PROGRAM AND MACHINE CONTROL (Continued)			
CJNE Rn,#data,rel	Comp, immed, to reg & Jump if Not Equal	3	2
CJNE @Ri,#data, rel	Comp, immed, to ind. & Jump if Not Equal	3	2
DJNZ Rn,rel	Decrement register & Jump if Not Zero	2	2
DJNZ direct,rel	Decrement direct & Jump if Not Zero	3	2
NOP	No operation	1	1

Notes on data addressing modes:

Rn — Working register R0-R7

direct — 128 internal RAM locations, any I/O port, control or status register

@Ri — Indirect internal RAM location addressed by register R0 or R1

Notes on data addressing modes: (Continued)

#data — 8-bit constant included in instruction

#data16 — 16-bit constant included as bytes 2 & 3 of instruction

bit — 128 software flags, any I/O pin, controll or status bit

Notes on program addressing modes:

addr16 — Destination address for LCALL & LJMP may be anywhere within the 64-K program memory address space

Addr11 — Destination address for ACALL & AJMP will be within the same 2-K page of program memory as the first byte of the following instruction

rel — SJMP and all conditional jumps include an 8-bit offset byte, Range is +127 −128 bytes relative to first byte of the following instruction

Timer/Counters

The 8044 contains two 16-bit counters which can be used for measuring time intervals, measuring pulse widths, counting events, generating precise periodic interrupt requests, and clocking the serial communications. Internally the Timers are clocked at 1/12 of the crystal frequency, which is the instruction cycle time. Externally the counters can run up to 500 KHz.

Interrupt System

External events and the real-time driven on-chip peripherals require service by the CPU asynchronous to the execution of any particular section of code. To tie the asynchronous activities of these functions to normal program execution, a sophisticated multiple-source, two priority level, nested interrupt system is provided. Interrupt response latency ranges from 3 μsec to 7 μsec when using a 12 MHz clock.

All five interrupt sources can be mapped into one of the two priority levels. Each interrupt source can be enabled or disabled individually or the entire interrupt system can be enabled or disabled. The five interrupt sources are: Serial Interface Unit, Timer 1, Timer 2, and two external interrupts. The external interrupts can be either level or edge triggered.

Serial Interface Unit (SIU)

The Serial Interface Unit is used for HDLC/SDLC communications. It handles Zero Bit Insertion/Deletion, Flags automatic access recognization, and a 16-bit cyclic redundancy check. In addition it implements in hardware a subset of the SDLC protocol certain applications it is advantageous to have the CPU control the reception or transmission of every single frame. For this reason the SIU has two modes of operation: "AUTO" and "FLEXIBLE" (or "NON-AUTO"). It is in the AUTO mode that the SIU responds to SDLC frames without CPU intervention; whereas, in the FLEXIBLE mode the reception or transmission of every single frame will be under CPU control.

There are three control registers and eight parameter registers that are used to operate the serial interface. These registers are shown in Figure 5 and Figure 6. The control register set the modes of operation and provide status information. The eight parameter registers buffer the station address, receive and transmit control bytes, and point to the on-chip transmit and receive buffers.

Data to be received or transmitted by the SIU must be buffered anywhere within the 192 bytes of on-chip RAM. Transmit and receive buffers are not allowed to "wrap around" in RAM; a "buffer end" is generated after address 191 is reached.

REGISTER NAMES	SYMBOLIC ADDRESS	BIT ADDRESS	BYTE ADDRESS
B REGISTER	B	247 through 240	240 (F0H)
ACCUMULATOR	ACC	231 through 224	224 (E0H)
*THREE BYTE FIFO	FIFO		223 (DFH)
	FIFO		222 (DEH)
	FIFO		221 (DDH)
TRANSMIT BUFFER START	TBS		220 (DCH)
TRANSMIT BUFFER LENGTH	TBL		219 (DBH)
TRANSMIT CONTROL BYTE	TCB		218 (DAH)
*SIU STATE COUNTER	SIUST		217 (D9H)
SEND COUNT RECEIVE COUNT	NSNR	223 through 216	216 (D8H)
PROGRAM STATUS WORD	PSW	215 through 208	208 (D0H)
*DMA COUNT	DMA CNT		207 (CFH)
STATION ADDRESS	STAD		206 (CEH)
RECEIVE FIELD LENGTH	RFL		205 (CDH)
RECEIVE BUFFER START	RBS		204 (CCH)
RECEIVE BUFFER LENGTH	RBL		203 (CBH)
RECEIVE CONTROL BYTE	RCB		202 (CAH)
SERIAL MODE	SMD		201 (C9H)
STATUS REGISTER	STS	207 through 200	200 (C8H)
INTERRUPT PRIORITY CONTROL	IP	191 through 184	184 (B8H)
PORT 3	P3	183 through 176	176 (B0H)
INTERRUPT ENABLE CONTROL	IE	175 through 168	168 (A8H)
PORT 2	P2	167 through 160	160 (A0H)
PORT 1	P1	151 through 144	144 (90H)
TIMER HIGH 1	TH1		141 (8DH)
TIMER HIGH 0	TH0		140 (8CH)
TIMER LOW 1	TL1		139 (8BH)
TIMER LOW 0	TL0		138 (8AH)
TIMER MODE	TMOD		137 (89H)
TIMER CONTROL	TCON	143 through 136	136 (88H)
DATA POINTER HIGH	DPH		131 (83H)
DATA POINTER LOW	DPL		130 (82H)
STACK POINTER	SP		129 (81H)
PORT 0	P0	135 through 128	128 (80H)

SFR's CONTAINING DIRECT ADDRESSABLE BITS: 240 (F0H), 224 (E0H), 216 (D8H), 208 (D0H), 200 (C8H), 184 (B8H), 176 (B0H), 168 (A8H), 160 (A0H), 144 (90H), 136 (88H), 128 (80H)

231663-6

NOTE:
*ICE Support Hardware registers. Under normal operating conditions there is no need for the CPU to access these registers.

Figure 5. Mapping of Special Function Registers

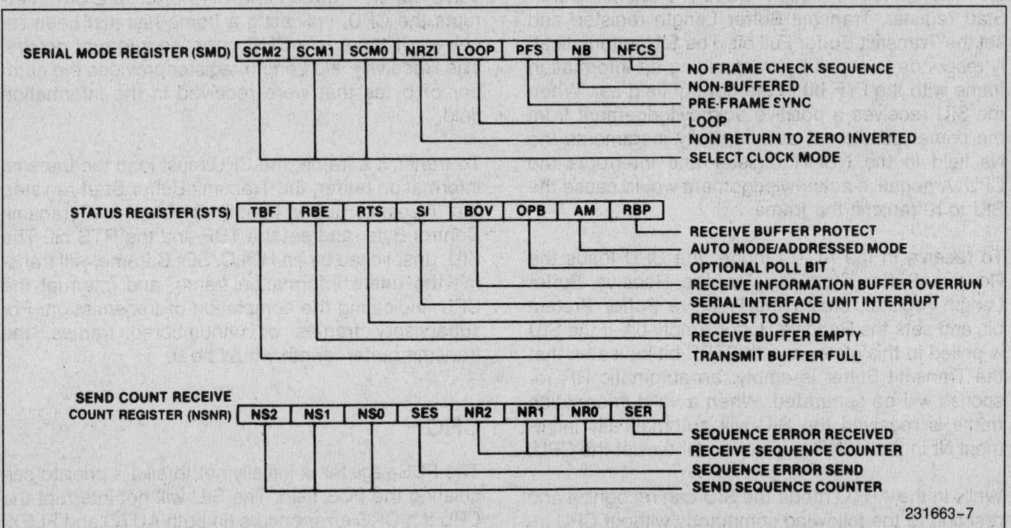

Figure 6. Serial Interface Unit Control Registers

With the addition of only a few bytes of code, the 8044's frame size is not limited to the size of its internal RAM (192 bytes), but rather by the size of external buffer with no degradation of the RUPI's features (e.g. NRZI, zero bit insertion/deletion, address recognition, cyclic redundancy check). There is a special function register called SIUST whose contents dictates the operation of the SIU. At low data rates, one section of the SIU (the Byte Processor) performs no function during known intervals. For a given data rate, these intervals (stand-by mode) are fixed. The above characteristics make it possible to program the CPU to move data to/from external RAM and to force the SIU to perform some desired hardware tasks while transmission or reception is taking place. With these modifications, external RAM can be utilized as a transmit and received buffer instead of the internal RAM.

AUTO Mode

In the AUTO mode the SIU implements in hardware a subset of the SDLC protocol such that it responds to many SDLC frames without CPU intervention. All AUTO mode responses to the primary station will comform to IBM's SDLC definition. The advantages of the AUTO mode are that less software is required to implement a secondary station, and the hardware generated response to polls is much faster than doing it in software. However, the Auto mode can not be used at a primary station.

To transmit in the AUTO mode the CPU must load the Transmit Information Buffer, Transmit Buffer Start register, Transmit Buffer Length register, and set the Transmit Buffer Full bit. The SIU automatically responds to a poll by transmitting an information frame with the P/F bit in the control field set. When the SIU receives a positive acknowledgement from the primary station, it automatically increments the Ns field in the NSNR register and interrupts the CPU. A negative acknowledgement would cause the SIU to retransmit the frame.

To receive in the AUTO mode, the CPU loads the Receive Buffer Start register, the Receive Buffer Length register, clears the Receive Buffer Protect bit, and sets the Receive Buffer Empty bit. If the SIU is polled in this state, and the TBF bit indicates that the Transmit Buffer is empty, an automatic RR response will be generated. When a valid information frame is received the SIU will automatically increment Nr in the NSNR register and interrupt the CPU.

While in the AUTO mode the SIU can recognize and respond to the following commands without CPU intervention: I (Information), RR (Receive Ready), RNR (Receive Not Ready), REJ (Reject), and UP (Unnumbered Poll). The SIU can generate the following responses without CPU intervention: I (Information), RR (Receive Ready), and RNR (Receive Not Ready).

When the Receive Buffer Empty bit (RBE) indicates that the Receive Buffer is empty, the receiver is enabled, and when the RBE bit indicates that the Receive Buffer is full, the receiver is disabled. Assuming that the Receiver Buffer is empty, the SIU will respond to a poll with an I frame if the Transmit Buffer is full. If the Transmit Buffer is empty, the SIU will respond to a poll with a RR command if the Receive Buffer Protect bit (RBP) is cleared, or an RNR command if RBP is set.

FLEXIBLE (or NON-AUTO) Mode

In the FLEXIBLE mode all communications are under control of the CPU. It is the CPU's task to encode and decode control fields, manage acknowledgements, and adhere to the requirements of the HDLC/SDLC protocols. The 8044 can be used as a primary or a secondary station in this mode.

To receive a frame in the FLEXIBLE mode, the CPU must load the Receive Buffer Start register, the Receive Buffer Length register, clear the Receive Buffer Protect bit, and set the Receive Buffer Empty bit. If a valid opening flag is received and the address field matches the byte in the Station Address register or the address field contains a broadcast address, the 8044 loads the control field in the receive control byte register, and loads the I field in the receive buffer. If there is no CRC error, the SIU interrupts the CPU, indicating a frame has just been received. If there is a CRC error, no interrupt occurs. The Receive Field Length register provides the number of bytes that were received in the information field.

To transmit a frame, the CPU must load the transmit information buffer, the Transmit Buffer Start register, the Transmit Buffer Length register, the Transmit Control Byte, and set the TBF and the RTS bit. The SIU, unsolicited by an HDLC/SDLC frame, will transmit the entire information frame, and interrupt the CPU, indicating the completion of transmission. For supervisory frames or unnumbered frames, the transmit buffer length would be 0.

CRC

The FCS register is initially set to all 1's prior to calculating the FCS field. The SIU will not interrupt the CPU if a CRC error occurs (in both AUTO and FLEXIBLE modes). The CRC error is cleared upon receiving of an opening flag.

Frame Format Options

In addition to the standard SDLC frame format, the 8044 will support the frames displayed in Figure 7. The standard SDLC frame is shown at the top of this figure. For the remaining frames the information field will incorporate the control or address bytes and the frame check sequences; therefore these fields will be stored in the Transmit and Receive buffers. For example, in the non-buffered mode the third byte is treated as the beginning of the information field. In the non-addressed mode, the information field begins after the opening flag. The mode bits to set the frame format options are found in the Serial Mode register and the Status register.

FRAME OPTION	NFCS	NB	AM[1]	FRAME FORMAT
Standard SDLC NON-AUTO Mode	0	0	0	F | A | C | I | FCS | F
Standard SDLC AUTO Mode	0	0	1	F | A | C | I | FCS | F
Non-Buffered Mode NON-AUTO Mode	0	1	1	F | A | I | FCS | F
Non-Addressed Mode NON-AUTO Mode	0	1	0	F | I | FCS | F
No FCS Field NON-AUTO Mode	1	0	0	F | A | C | I | F
No FCS Field AUTO Mode	1	0	1	F | A | C | I | F
No FCS Field Non-Buffered Mode NON-AUTO Mode	1	1	1	F | A | I | F
No FCS Field Non-Addressed Mode NON-AUTO Mode	1	1	0	F | I | F

Mode Bits:
AM — "AUTO" Mode/Addressed Mode
NB — Non-Buffered Mode
NFCS — No FCS Field Mode

Key to Abbreviations:
F = Flag (01111110)
A = Address Field
C = Control Field
I = Information Field
FCS = Frame Check Sequence

Note 1:
The AM bit function is controlled by the NB bit. When NB = 0, AM becomes AUTO mode select, when NB = 1, AM becomes Address mode select.

Figure 7. Frame Format Options

16

Extended Addressing

To realize an extended control field or an extended address field using the HDLC protocol, the FLEXIBLE mode must be used. For an extended control field, the SIU is programmed to be in the non-buffered mode. The extended control field will be the first and second bytes in the Receive and Transmit Buffers. For extended addressing the SIU is placed in the non-addressed mode. In this mode the CPU must implement the address recognition for received frames. The addressing field will be the initial bytes in the Transmit and Receive buffers followed by the control field.

The SIU can transmit and receive only frames which are multiples of 8 bits. For frames received with other than 8-bit multiples, a CRC error will cause the SIU to reject the frame.

SDLC Loop Networks

The SIU can be used in an SDLC loop as a secondary or primary station. When the SIU is placed in the Loop mode it receives the data on pin 10 and transmits the data one bit time delayed on pin 11. It can also recognize the Go ahead signal and change it into a flag when it is ready to transmit. As a secondary station the SIU can be used in the AUTO or FLEXIBLE modes. As a primary station the FLEXIBLE mode is used; however, additional hardware is required for generating the Go Ahead bit pattern. In the Loop mode the maximum data rate is 1 Mbps clocked or 375 Kpbs self-clocked.

SDLC Multidrop Networks

The SIU can be used in a SDLC non-loop configuration as a secondary or primary station. When the SIU is placed in the non-loop mode, data is received and transmitted on pin 11, and pin 10 drives a tri-state buffer. In non-loop mode, modem interface pins, RTS and CTS, become available.

Data Clocking Options

The 8044's serial port can operate in an externally clocked or self clocked system. A clocked system provides to the 8044 a clock synchronization to the data. A self-clocked system uses the 8044's on-chip Digital Phase Locked Loop (DPLL) to recover the clock from the data, and clock this data into the Serial Receive Shift Register.

In this mode, a clock synchronized with the data is externally fed into the 8044. This clock may be generated from an External Phase Locked Loop, or possibly supplied along with the data. The 8044 can transmit and receive data in this mode at rates up to 2.4 Mbps.

This self clocked mode allows data transfer without a common system data clock. An on-chip Digital Phase Locked Loop is employed to recover the data clock which is encoded in the data stream. The DPLL will converge to the nominal bit center within eight bit transitions, worst case. The DPLL requires a reference clock of either 16 times (16x) or 32 times (32x) the data rate. This reference clock may be externally applied or internally generated. When internally generated either the 8044's internal logic clock (crystal frequency divided by two) or the timer 1 overflow is used as the reference clock. Using the internal timer 1 clock the data rates can vary from 244 to 62.5 Kbps. Using the internal logic clock at a 16x sampling rate, receive data can either be 187.5 Kbps, or 375 Kbps. When the reference clock for the DPLL is externally applied the data rates can vary from 0 to 375 Kbps at a 16x sampling rate.

To aid in a Phase Locked Loop capture, the SIU has a NRZI (Non Return to Zero Inverted) data encoding and decoding option. Additionally the SIU has a preframe sync option that transmits two bytes of alternating 1's and 0's to ensure that the receive station DPLL will be synchronized with the data by the time it receives the opening flag.

Control and Status Registers

There are three SIU Control and Status Registers:

Serial Mode Register (SMD)

Status/Command Register (STS)

Send/Receive Count Register (NSNR)

The SMD, STS, and NSNR, registers are all cleared by system reset. This assures that the SIU will power up in an idle state (neither receiving nor transmitting).

These registers and their bit assignments are described below.

SMD: Serial Mode Register (byte-addressable)

Bit 7:	6	5	4	3	2	1	0
SCM2	SCM1	SCM0	NRZI	LOOP	PFS	NB	NFCS

The Serial Mode Register (Address C9H) selects the operational modes of the SIU. The 8044 CPU can both read and write SMD. The SIU can read SMD but cannot write to it. To prevent conflict between CPU and SIU access to SMD, the CPU should write SMD only when the Request To Send (RTS) and

Receive Buffer Empty (RBE) bits (in the STS register) are both false (0). Normally, SMD is accessed only during initialization.

The individual bits of the Serial Mode Register are as follows:

Bit #	Name	Description
SMD.0	NFCS	No FCS field in the SDLC frame.
SMD.1	NB	Non-Buffered mode. No control field in the SDLC frame.
SMD.2	PFS	Pre-Frame Sync mode. In this mode, the 8044 transmits two bytes before the first flag of a frame, for DPLL synchronization. If NRZI is enabled, 00H is sent; otherwise, 55H is sent. In either case, 16 preframe transitions are guaranteed.
SMD.3	LOOP	Loop configuration.
SMD.4	NRZI	NRZI coding option. If bit = 1, NRZI coding is used. If bit = 0, then it is straight binary (NRZ).
SMD.5	SCM0	Select Clock Mode—Bit 0
SMD.6	SCM1	Select Clock Mode—Bit 1
SMD.7	SCM2	Select Clock Mode—Bit 2

The SCM bits decode as follows:

SCM				Data Rate
2	1	0	Clock Mode	(Bits/sec)*
0	0	0	Externally clocked	0-2.4M**
0	0	1	Reserved	
0	1	0	Self clocked, timer overflow	244-62.5K
0	1	1	Reserved	
1	0	0	Self clocked, external 16x	0-375K
1	0	1	Self clocked, external 32x	0-187.5K
1	1	0	Self clocked, internal fixed	375K
1	1	1	Self clocked, internal fixed	187.5K

NOTES:
*Based on a 12 Mhz crystal frequency
**0-1 M bps in loop configuration

STS: Status/Command Register (bit-addressable)

Bit:	7	6	5	4	3	2	1	0
	TBF	RBE	RTS	SI	BOV	OPB	AM	RBP

The Status/Command Register (Address C8H) provides operational control of the SIU by the 8044 CPU, and enables the SIU to post status information for the CPU's access. The SIU can read STS, and can alter certain bits, as indicated below. The CPU can both read and write STS asynchronously. However, 2-cycle instructions that access STS during both cycles ('JBC/B, REL' and 'MOV/B, C.') should not be used, since the SIU may write to STS between the two CPU accesses.

The individual bits of the Status/Command Register are as follows:

Bit #	Name	Description
STS.0	RBP	Receive Buffer Protect. Inhibits writing of data into the receive buffer. In AUTO mode, RBP forces an RNR response instead of an RR.
STS.1	AM	AUTO Mode/Addressed Mode. Selects AUTO mode where AUTO mode is allowed. If NB is true, (= 1), the AM bit selects the addressed mode. AM may be cleared by the SIU.
STS.2	OPB	Optional Poll Bit. Determines whether the SIU will generate an AUTO response to an optional poll (UP with P = 0). OPM may be set or cleared by the SIU.
STS.3	BOV	Receive Buffer Overrun. BOV may be set or cleared by the SIU.
STS.4	SI	SIU Interrupt. This is one of the five interrupt sources to the CPU. The vector location = 23H. SI may be set by the SIU. It should be cleared by the CPU before returning from an interrupt routine.
STS.5	RTS	Request To Send. Indicates that the 8044 is ready to transmit or is transmitting. RTS may be read or written by the CPU. RTS may be read by the SIU, and in AUTO mode may be written by the SIU.
STS.6	RBE	Receive Buffer Empty. RBE can be thought of as Receive Enable. RBE is set to one by the CPU when it is ready to receive a frame, or has just read the buffer, and to zero by the SIU when a frame has been received.
STS.7	TBF	Transmit Buffer Full. Written by the CPU to indicate that it has filled the transmit buffer. TBF may be cleared by the SIU.

NSNR: Send/Receive Count Register (bit-addressable)

Bit: 7	6	5	4	3	2	1	0
NS2	NS1	NS0	SES	NR2	NR1	NR0	SER

The Send/Receive Count Register (Address D8H) contains the transmit and receive sequence numbers, plus tally error indications. The SIU can both read and write NSNR. The 8044 CPU can both read and write NSNR asynchronously. However, 2-cycle instructions that access NSNR during both cycles ('JBC /B, REL,' and 'MOV /B,C') should not be used, since the SIU may write to NSMR between the two 8044 CPU accesses.

The individual bits of the Send/Receive Count Register are as follows:

Bit #	Name	Description
NSNR.0	SER	Receive Sequence Error: NS (P) ≠ NR (S)
NSNR.1	NR0	Receive Sequence Counter—Bit 0
NSNR.2	NR1	Receive Sequence Counter—Bit 1
NSNR.3	NR2	Receive Sequence Counter—Bit 2
NSNR.4	SES	Send Sequence Error: NR (P) ≠ NS (S) and NR (P) ≠ NS (S) + 1
NSNR.5	NS0	Send Sequence Counter—Bit 0
NSNR.6	NS1	Send Sequence Counter—Bit 1
NSNR.7	NS2	Send Sequence Counter—Bit 2

Parameter Registers

There are eight parameter registers that are used in connection with SIU operation. All eight registers may be read or written by the 8044 CPU. RFL and RCB are normally loaded by the SIU.

The eight parameter registers are as follows:

STAD: Station Address Register (byte-addressable)

The Station Address register (Address CEH) contains the station address. To prevent acess conflict, the CPU should access STAD only when the SIU is idle (RTS = 0 and RBE = 0). Normally, STAD is accessed only during initialization.

TBS: Transmit Buffer Start Address Register (byte-addressable)

The Transmit Buffer Start address register (Address DCH) points to the location in on-chip RAM for the beginning of the I-field of the frame to be transmitted. The CPU should access TBS only when the SIU is not transmitting a frame (when TBF = 0).

TBL: Transmit Buffer Length Register (byte = addressable)

The Transmit Buffer Length register (Address DBH) contains the length (in bytes) of the I-field to be transmitted. A blank I-field (TBL = 0) is valid. The CPU should access TBL only when the SIU is not transmitting a frame (when TBF = 0).

NOTE:
The transmit and receive buffers are not allowed to "wrap around" in the on-chip RAM. A "buffer end" is automatically generated if address 191 (BFH) is reached.

TCB: Transmit Control Byte Register (byte-addressable)

The Transmit Control Byte register (Address DAH) contains the byte which is to be placed in the control field of the transmitted frame, during NON-AUTO mode transmission. The CPU should access TCB only when the SIU is not transmitting a frame (when TBF = 0). The N_S and N_R counters are not used in the NON-AUTO mode.

RBS: Receive Buffer Start Address Register (byte-addressable)

The Receive Buffer Start address register (Address CCH) points to the location in on-chip RAM where the beginning of the I-field of the frame being received is to be stored. The CPU should write RBS only when the SIU is not receiving a frame (when RBE = 0).

RBL: Receive Buffer Length Register (byte-addressable)

The Receive Buffer Length register (Address CBH) contains the length (in bytes) of the area in on-chip RAM allocated for the received I-field. RBL=0 is valid. The CPU should write RBL only when RBE=0.

RFL: Receive Field Length Register (byte-addressable)

The Receive Field Length register (Address CDH) contains the length (in bytes) of the received I-field that has just been loaded into on-chip RAM. RFL is loaded by the SIU. RFL = 0 is valid. RFL should be accessed by the CPU only when RBE = 0.

RCB: Receive Control Byte Register (byte-addressable)

The Received Control Byte register (Address CAH) contains the control field of the frame that has just been received. RCB is loaded by the SIU. The CPU can only read RCB, and should only access RCB when RBE = 0.

ICE Support

The 8044 In-Circuit Emulator (ICE-44) allows the user to exercise the 8044 application system and monitor the execution of instructions in real time.

The emulator operates with Intel's Intellec™ development system. The development system interfaces with the user's 8044 system through an in-cable buffer box. The cable terminates in a 8044 pin-compatible plug, which fits into the 8044 socket in the user's system. With the emulator plug in place, the user can excercise his system in real time while collecting up to 255 instruction cycles of real-time data. In addition, he can single-step the program.

Static RAM is available (in the in-cable buffer box) to emulate the 8044 internal and external program memory and external data memory. The designer can display and alter the contents of the replacement memory in the buffer box, the internal data memory, and the internal 8044 registers, including the SFR's.

SIUST: SIU State Counter (byte-addressable)

The SIU State Counter (Address D9H) reflects the state of the internal logic which is under SIU control. Therefore, care must be taken not to write into this register. This register provides a useful means for debugging 8044 receiver problem.

ABSOLUTE MAXIMUM RATINGS*

Ambient Temperature Under Bias . . . . . . 0°C to 70°C
Storage Temperature . . . . −65°C to −150°C
Voltage on $\overline{EA}$, VPP Pin to VSS . . . −0.5V to −21.5V
Voltage on Any Other Pin to VSS . . . . −0.5V to −7V
Power Dissipation 2W

NOTICE: This is a production data sheet. The specifications are subject to change without notice.

**WARNING: Stressing the device beyond the "Absolute Maximum Ratings" may cause permanent damage. These are stress ratings only. Operation beyond the "Operating Conditions" is not recommended and extended exposure beyond the "Operating Conditions" may affect device reliability.*

D.C. CHARACTERISTICS T_A = 0°C to 70°C, VCC = 5V = 10%, VSS = 0V

Symbol	Parameter		Min	Max	Unit	Test Conditions
VIL	Input Low Voltage (Except $\overline{EA}$ Pin of 8744H)		−0.5	0.8	V	
VIL1	Input Low Voltage to $\overline{EA}$ Pin of 8744H		0	0.8	V	
VIH	Input High Voltage (Except XTAL2, RST)		2.0	VCC + 0.5	V	
VIH1	Input High Voltage to XTAL2, RST		2.5	VCC + 0.5	V	XTAL1 = VSS
VOL	Output Low Voltage (Ports 1, 2, 3)*			0.45	V	IOL = 1.6mA
VOL1	Output Low Voltage (Port 0,ALE,$\overline{PSEN}$)*	8744H		0.60 0.45	V V	IOL = 3.2 mA IOL = 2.4 mA
		8044AH/8344AH		0.45	V	IOL = 3.2 mA
VOH	Output High Voltage (Ports 1, 2, 3)		2.4		V	IOH = −80 μA
VOH1	Output High Voltage (Port 0 in External Bus Mode, ALE, $\overline{PSEN}$)		2.4		V	IOH = −400 μA
IIL	Logical 0 Input Current (Ports 1, 2, 3)			−500	μA	Vin = 0.45V
IIL1	Logical 0 Input Current to $\overline{EA}$ Pin of 8744H only			−15	mA	
IIL2	Logical 0 Input Current (XTAL2)			−3.6	mA	Vin = 0.45V
ILI	Input Leakage Current (Port 0) 8744H 8044AH/8344AH			 ±100 ±10	 μA μA	 0.45 < Vin < VCC 0.45 < Vin < VCC
IIH	Logical 1 Input Current to $\overline{EA}$ Pin of 8744H			500	μA	
IIH1	Input Current to RST to Activate Reset			500	μA	Vin < (VCC − 1.5V)
ICC	Power Supply Current: 8744H 8044AH/8344AH			 285 170	 mA mA	All Outputs Disconnected: $\overline{EA}$ = VCC
CIO	Pin Capacitance			10	pF	Test Freq. = 1MHz(1)

***NOTES:**

1. Sampled not 100% tested. T_A = 25°C.
2. Capacitive loading on Ports 0 and 2 may cause spurious noise pulses to be superimposed on the VOLs of ALE and Ports 1 and 3. The noise is due to external bus capacitance discharging into the Port 0 and Port 2 pin when these pins make 1-to-0 transitions during bus operations. In the worst cases (capacitive loading > 100 pF), the noise pulse on the ALE line may exceed 0.8V. In such cases it may be desirable to qualify ALE with a Schmitt Trigger, or use an address latch with a Schmitt Trigger STROBE input.

A.C. CHARACTERISTICS

T_A = 0°C to +70°C, VCC = 5V ± 10%, VSS = 0V, Load Capacitance for Port 0, ALE, and PSEN = 100 pF, Load Capacitance for All Other Outputs = 80 pF

EXTERNAL PROGRAM MEMORY CHARACTERISTICS

Symbol	Parameter	12 MHz Osc		Variable Clock 1/TCLCL = 3.5 MHz to 12 MHz		Unit
		Min	Max	Min	Max	
TLHLL	ALE Pulse Width	127		2TCLCL-40		ns
TAVLL	Address Valid to ALE Low	43		TCLCL-40		ns
TLLAX[1]	Address Hold After ALE Low	48		TCLCL-35		ns
TLLIV	ALE Low to Valid Instr in 8744H 8044AH/8344AH		 183 233		 4TCLCL-150 4TCLCL-100	ns
TLLPL	ALE Low to $\overline{\text{PSEN}}$ Low	58		TCLCL-25		ns
TPLPH	$\overline{\text{PSEN}}$ Pulse Width 8744H 8044AH/8344AH	 190 215		 3TCLCL-60 3TCLCL-35		 ns ns
TPLIV	$\overline{\text{PSEN}}$ Low to Valid Instr in 8744H 8044AH/8344AH		 100 125		 3TCLCL-150 3TCLCL-125	 ns ns
TPXIX	Input Instr Hold After $\overline{\text{PSEN}}$	0		0		ns
TPXIZ[2]	Input Instr Float After $\overline{\text{PSEN}}$		63		TCLCL-20	ns
TPXAV[2]	$\overline{\text{PSEN}}$ to Address Valid	75		TCLCL-8		ns
TAVIV	Address to Valid Instr in 8744H 8044AH/8344AH		 267 302		 5TCLCL-150 5TCLCL-115	 ns ns
TAZPL	Address Float to $\overline{\text{PSEN}}$	−25		−25		ns

NOTES:
1. TLLAX for access to program memory is different from TLLAX for data memory.
2. Interfacing RUPI-44 devices with float times up to 75ns is permissible. This limited bus contention will not cause any damage to Port 0 drivers.

EXTERNAL DATA MEMORY CHARACTERISTICS

Symbol	Parameter	12 MHz Osc		Variable Clock 1/TCLCL = 3.5 MHz to 12 MHz		Unit
		Min	Max	Min	Max	
TRLRH	$\overline{RD}$ Pulse Width	400		6TCLCL-100		ns
TWLWH	$\overline{WR}$ Pulse Width	400		6TCLCL-100		ns
TLLAX	Address Hold after ALE	48		TCLCL-35		ns
TRLDV	$\overline{RD}$ Low to Valid Data in		252		5TCLCL-165	ns
TRHDX	Data Hold After $\overline{RD}$	0		0		ns
TRHDZ	Data Float After $\overline{RD}$		97		2TCLCL-70	ns
TLLDV	ALE Low to Valid Data In		517		8TCLCL-150	ns
TAVDV	Address to Valid Data In		585		9TCLCL-165	ns
TLLWL	ALE Low to $\overline{RD}$ or $\overline{WR}$ Low	200	300	3TCLCL-50	3TLCLCL+50	ns
TAVWL	Address to $\overline{RD}$ or $\overline{WR}$ Low	203		4TCLCL-130		ns
TQVWX	Data Valid to $\overline{WR}$ Transition 8744H 8044AH/8344AH	 13 23		 TCLCL-70 TCLCL-60		 ns ns
TQVWH	Data Setup Before $\overline{WR}$ High	433		7TCLCL-150		ns
TWHQX	Data Held After $\overline{WR}$	33		TCLCL-50		ns
TRLAZ	$\overline{RD}$ Low to Address Float		25		25	ns
TWHLH	$\overline{RD}$ or $\overline{WR}$ High to ALE High 8744H 8044AH/8344AH	 33 43	 133 123	 TCLCL-50 TCLCL-40	 TCLCL+50 TCLCL+50	 ns ns

NOTE:
1. TLLAX for access to program memory is different from TLLAX for access data memory.

Serial Interface Characteristics

Symbol	Parameter	Min	Max	Unit
TDCY	Data Clock	420		ns
TDCL	Data Clock Low	180		ns
TDCH	Data Clock High	100		ns
tTD	Transmit Data Delay		140	ns
tDSS	Data Setup Time	40		ns
tDHS	Data Hold Time	40		ns

WAVEFORMS

Memory Access

PROGRAM MEMORY READ CYCLE

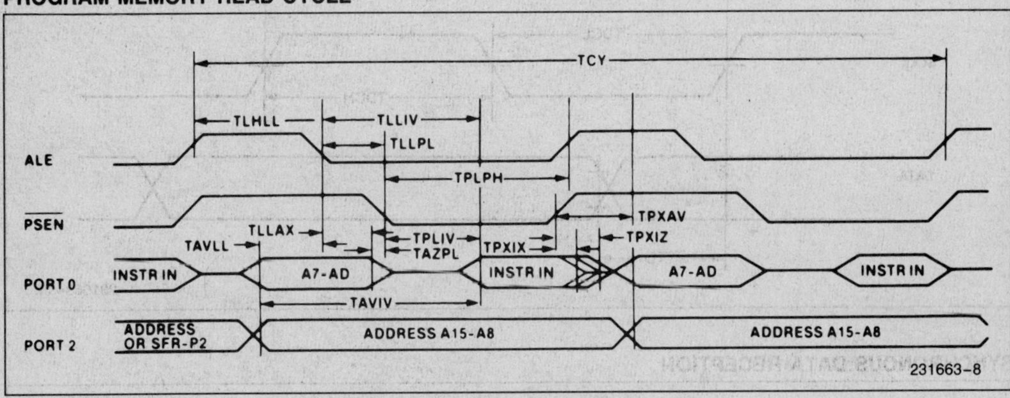

DATA MEMORY READ CYCLE

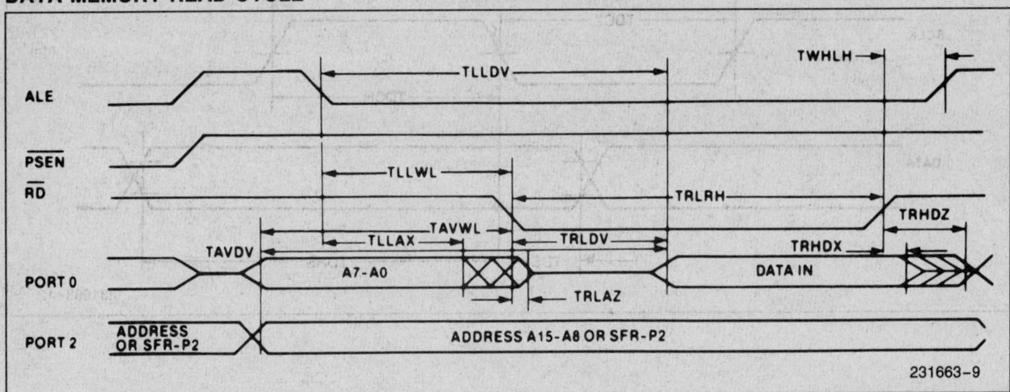

DATA MEMORY WRITE CYCLE

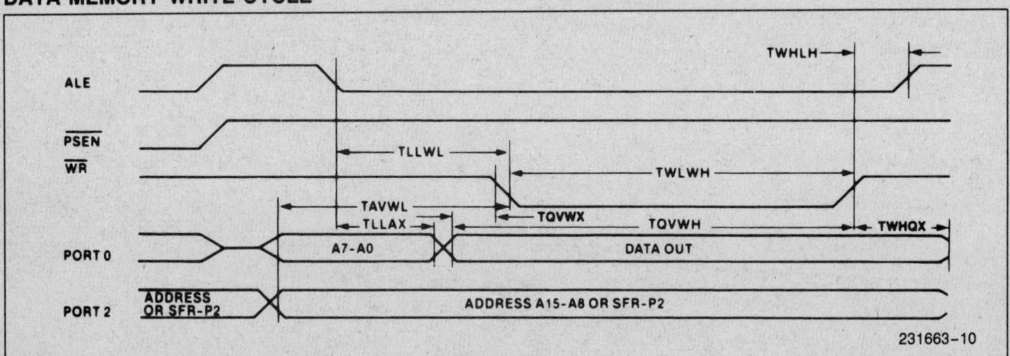

SERIAL I/O WAVEFORMS

SYNCHRONOUS DATA TRANSMISSION

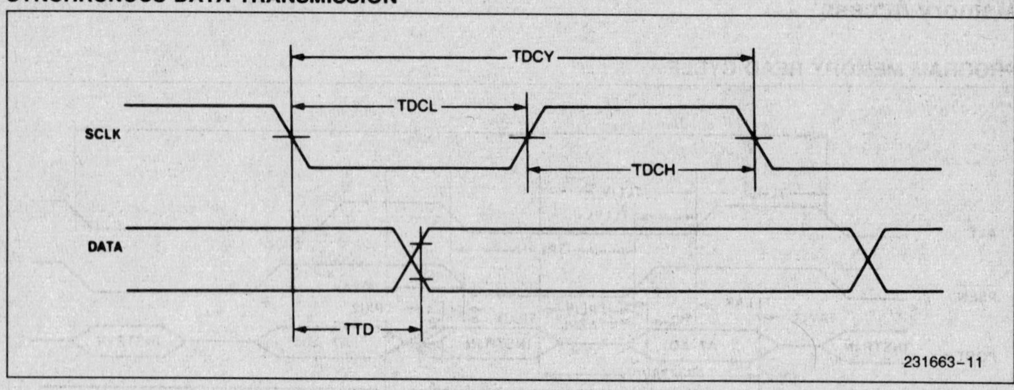

SYNCHRONOUS DATA RECEPTION

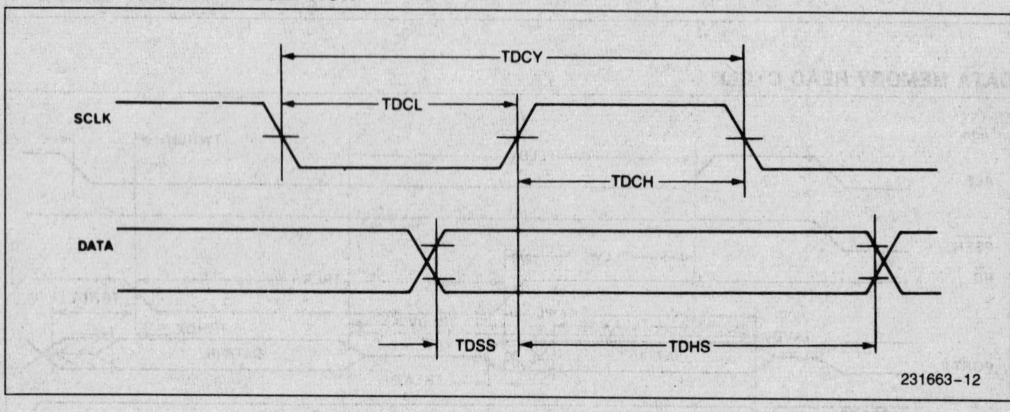

AC TESTING INPUT, OUTPUT, FLOAT WAVEFORMS

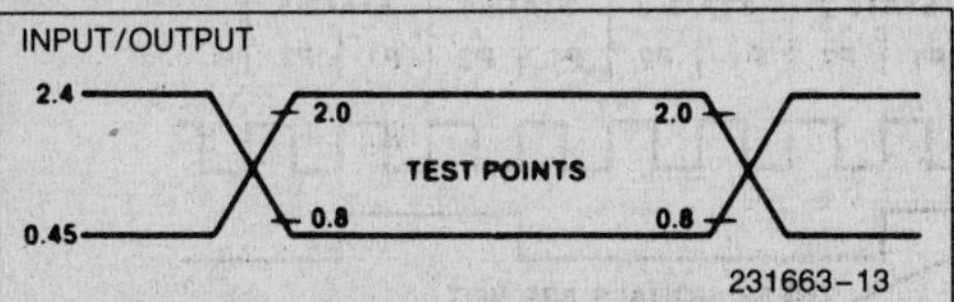

231663-13

AC testing inputs are driven at 2.4V for a Logic "1" and 0.45V for a Logic "0" Timing measurements are made at 2.0V for a Logic "1" and 0.8V for a Logic "0".

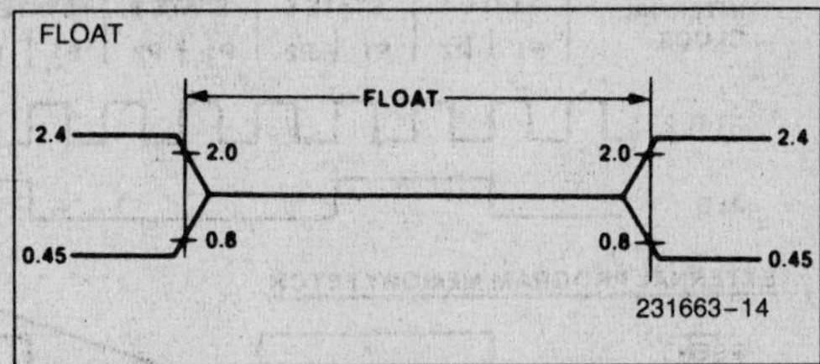

231663-14

EXTERNAL CLOCK DRIVE XTAL2

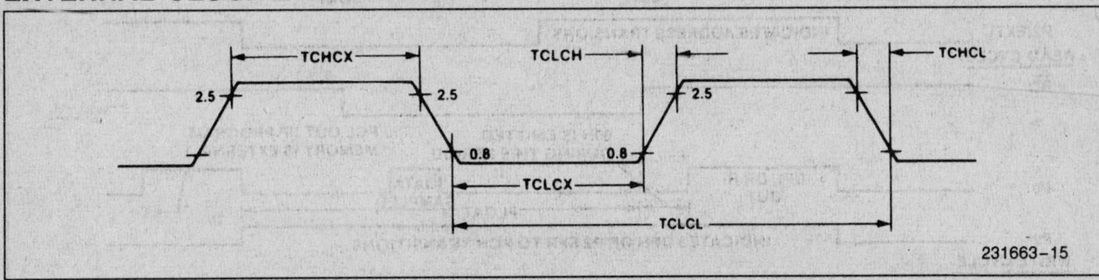

231663-15

Symbol	Parameter	Variable Clock Freq = 3.5 MHz to 12 MHz		Unit
		Min	Max	
TCLCL	Oscillator Period	83.3	285.7	ns
TCHCX	High Time	20	TCLCL-TCLCX	ns
TCLCX	Low Time	20	TCLCL-TCHCX	ns
TCLCH	Rise Time		20	ns
TCHCL	Fall Time		20	ns

16

CLOCK WAVEFORMS

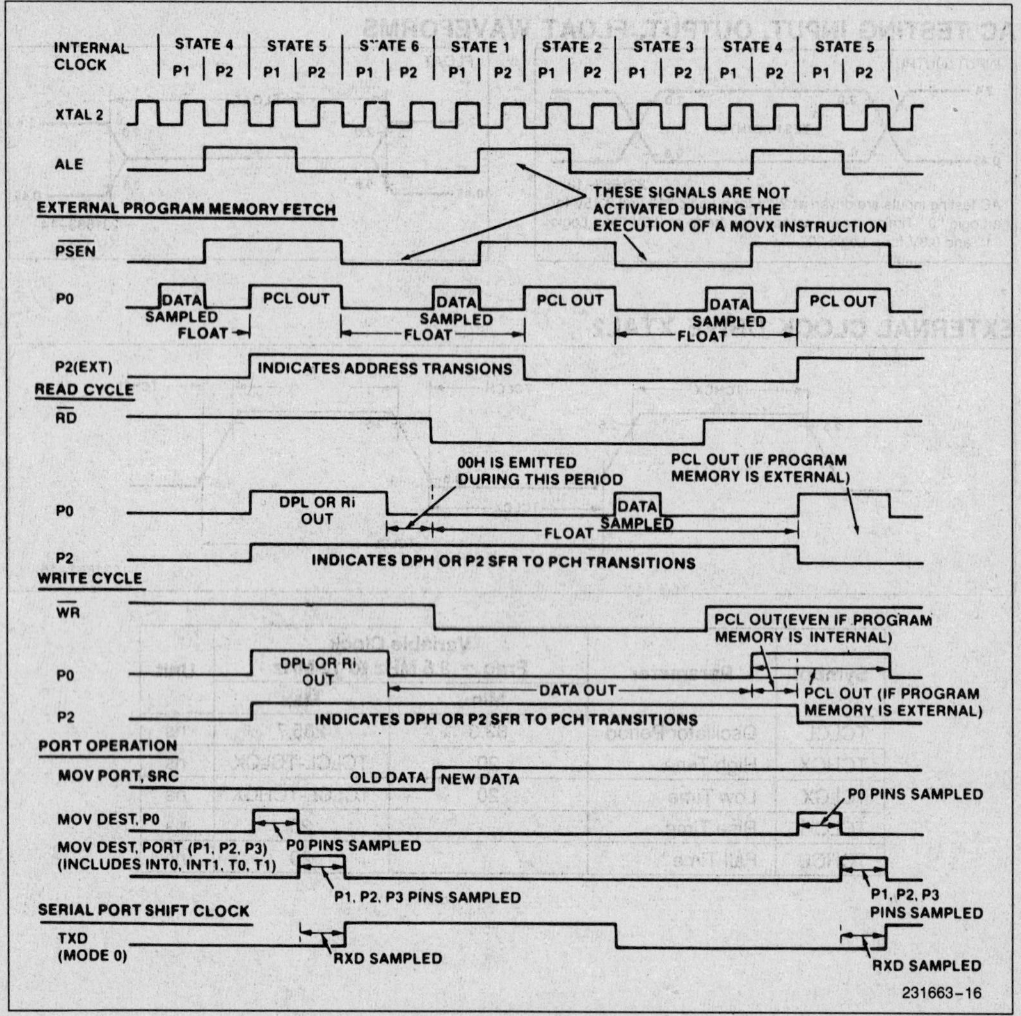

INTERNAL CLOCK
STATE 4 P1 P2 | STATE 5 P1 P2 | STATE 6 P1 P2 | STATE 1 P1 P2 | STATE 2 P1 P2 | STATE 3 P1 P2 | STATE 4 P1 P2 | STATE 5 P1 P2
XTAL 2
ALE
THESE SIGNALS ARE NOT ACTIVATED DURING THE EXECUTION OF A MOVX INSTRUCTION
EXTERNAL PROGRAM MEMORY FETCH
$\overline{PSEN}$
P0
DATA SAMPLED
FLOAT
PCL OUT
DATA SAMPLED
FLOAT
PCL OUT
DATA SAMPLED
FLOAT
PCL OUT
P2(EXT)
INDICATES ADDRESS TRANSIONS
READ CYCLE
$\overline{RD}$
00H IS EMITTED DURING THIS PERIOD
PCL OUT (IF PROGRAM MEMORY IS EXTERNAL)
P0
DPL OR Ri OUT
FLOAT
DATA SAMPLED
P2
INDICATES DPH OR P2 SFR TO PCH TRANSITIONS
WRITE CYCLE
$\overline{WR}$
PCL OUT(EVEN IF PROGRAM MEMORY IS INTERNAL)
P0
DPL OR Ri OUT
DATA OUT
PCL OUT (IF PROGRAM MEMORY IS EXTERNAL)
P2
INDICATES DPH OR P2 SFR TO PCH TRANSITIONS
PORT OPERATION
MOV PORT, SRC
OLD DATA
NEW DATA
P0 PINS SAMPLED
MOV DEST, P0
MOV DEST, PORT (P1, P2, P3) (INCLUDES INT0, INT1, T0, T1)
P0 PINS SAMPLED
P1, P2, P3 PINS SAMPLED
P1, P2, P3 PINS SAMPLED
SERIAL PORT SHIFT CLOCK
TXD (MODE 0)
RXD SAMPLED
RXD SAMPLED
231663-16

This diagram indicates when signals are clocked internally. The time it takes the signals to propagate to the pins, however, ranges from 25 to 125 ns. This propagation delay is dependent on variables such as temperature and pin loading. Propagation also varies from output to output and component to component. Typically though, (T_A = 25°C, fully loaded) RD and WR propagation delays are approximately 50 ns. The other signals are typically 85 ns. Propagation delays are incorporated in the AC specifications.

8744H EPROM CHARACTERISTICS

Erasure Characteristics

Erasure of the 8744H Program Memory begins to occur when the chip is exposed to light with wavelengths shorter than approximately 4,000 Ångstroms. Since sunlight and fluorescent lighting have wavelengths in this range, constant exposure to these light sources over an extended period of time (about 1 week in sunlight, or 3 years in room-level fluorescent lighting) could cause unintentional erasure. If an application subjects the 8744H to this type of exposure, it is suggested that an opaque label be placed over the window.

The recommended erasure procedure is exposure to ultraviolet light (at 2537 Ångstroms) to an integrated dose of at least 15 W-sec/cm^2 rating for 20 to 30 minutes, at a distance of about 1 inch, should be sufficient.

Erasure leaves the array in an all 1s state.

Programming the EPROM

To be programmed, the 8744H must be running with a 4 to 6 MHz oscillator. (The reason the oscillator needs to be running is that the internal bus is being used to transfer address and program data to appropriate registers.) The address of an EPROM location to be programmed is applied to Port 1 and pins P2.0-P2.3 of Port 2, while the data byte is applied to Port 0. Pins P2.4-P2.6 and $\overline{\text{PSEN}}$ should be held low, and P2.7 and RST high. (These are all TTL levels except RST, which requires 2.5V for high.) $\overline{\text{EA}}$/VPP is held normally high, and is pulsed to +21V. While EA/VPP is at 21V, the ALE/$\overline{\text{PROG}}$ pin, which is normally being held high, is pulsed low for 50 msec. Then EA/VPP is returned to high. This is illustrated in Figure 8. Detailed timing specifications are provided in the EPROM Programming and Verification Characteristics section of this data sheet.

Program Memory Security

The program memory security feature is developed around a "security bit" in the 8744H EPROM array. Once this "hidden bit" is programmed, electrical access to the contents of the entire program memory array becomes impossible. Activation of this feature is accomplished by programming the 8744H as described in "Programming the EPROM" with the exception that P2.6 is held at a TTL high rather than a TTL low. In addition, Port 1 and P2.0-P2.3 may be in any state. Figure 9 illustrates the security bit programming configuration. Deactivating the security feature, which again allows programmability of the EPROM, is accomplished by exposing the EPROM to ultraviolet light. This exposure, as described in "Erasure Characteristics," erases the entire EPROM array. Therefore, attempted retrieval of "protected code" results in its destruction.

Program Verification

Program Memory may be read only when the "security feature" has not been activated. Refer to Figure 10 for Program Verification setup. To read the Program Memory, the following procedure can be used. The unit must be running with a 4 to 6 MHz oscillator. The address of a Program Memory location to be read is applied to Port 1 and pins P2.0-P2.3 of Port 2. Pins P2.4-P2.6 and $\overline{\text{PSEN}}$ are held at TTL low, while the ALE/$\overline{\text{PROG}}$, RST, and $\overline{\text{EA}}$/VPP pins are held at TTL high. (These are all TTL levels except RST, which requires 2.5V for high.) Port 0 will be the data output lines. P2.7 can be used as a read strobe. While P2.7 is held high, the Port 0 pins float. When P2.7 is strobed low, the contents of the addressed location will appear at Port 0. External pullups (e.g., 10K) are required on Port 0 during program verification.

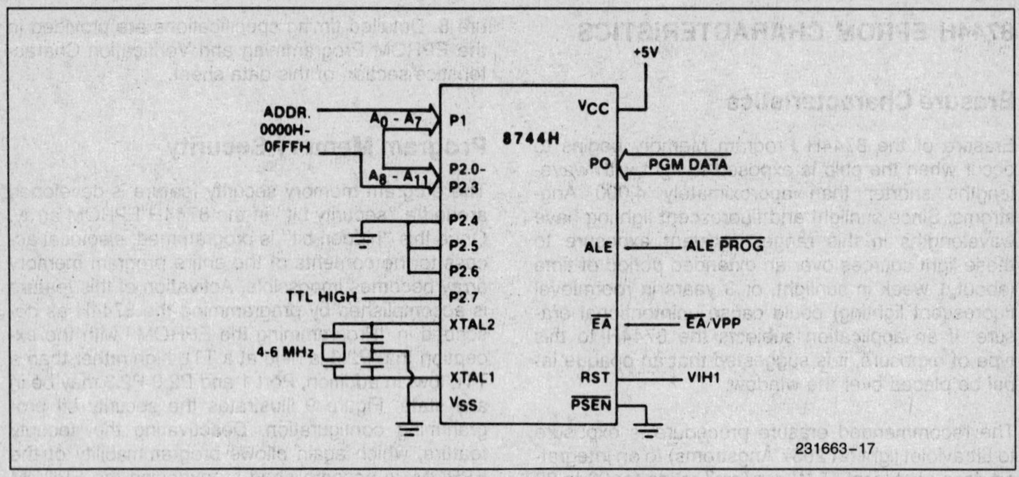

Figure 8. Programming Configuration

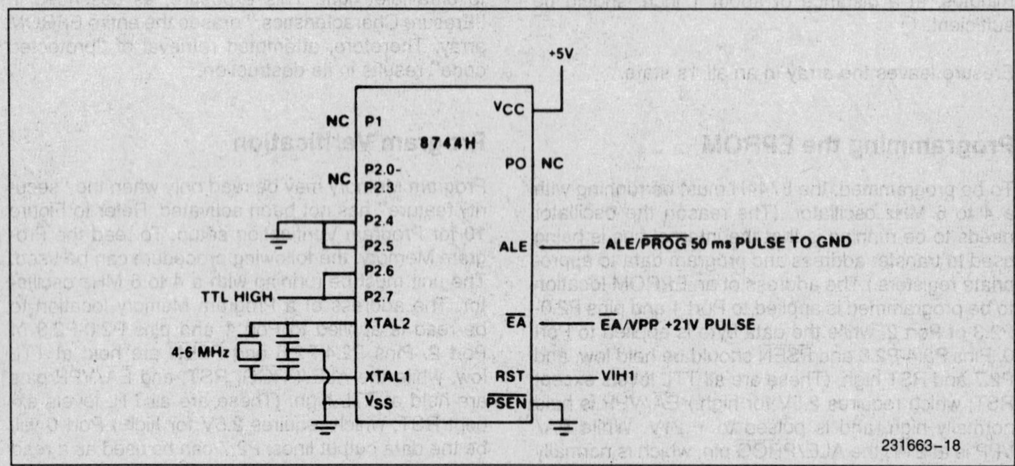

Figure 9. Security Bit Programming Configuration

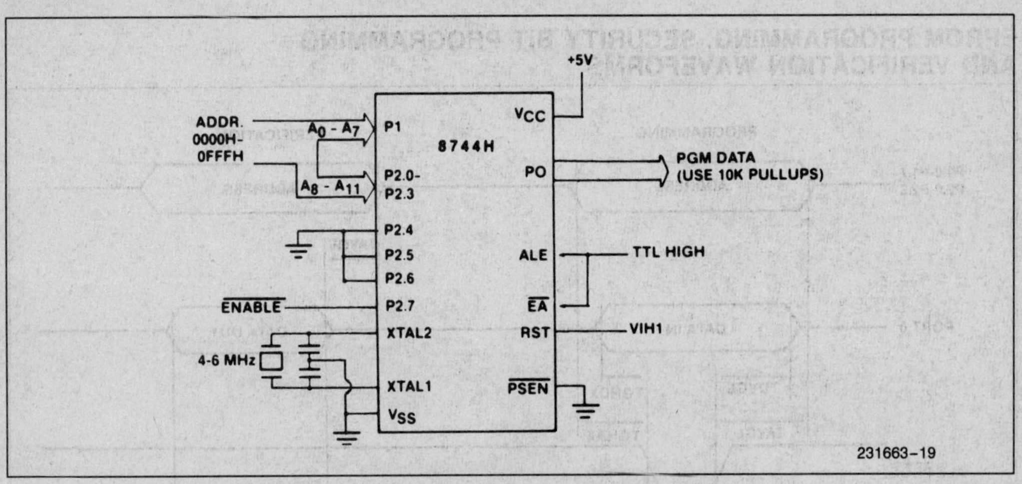

Figure 10. Program Verification Configuration

EPROM PROGRAMMING, SECURITY BIT PROGRAMMING AND VERIFICATION CHARACTERISTICS

TA = 21°C to 27°C, V_{CC} = 4.5V to 5.5V, V_{SS} = 0V

Symbol	Parameter	Min	Max	Units
V_{PP}	Programming Supply Voltage	20.5	21.5	V
IPP	Programming Current		30	mA
1/TCLCL	Oscillator Frequency	4	6	MHz
TAVGL	Address Setup to $\overline{\text{PROG}}$	48TCLCL		
TGHAX	Address Hold after $\overline{\text{PROG}}$	48TCLCL		
TDVGL	Data Setup to $\overline{\text{PROG}}$	48TCLCL		
TGHDX	Data Hold after $\overline{\text{PROG}}$	48TCLCL		
TEHSH	$\overline{\text{ENABLE}}$ High to Vpp	48TCLCL		
TSHGL	V_{PP} Setup to $\overline{\text{PROG}}$	10		μsec
TGHSL	V_{PP} Hold after $\overline{\text{PROG}}$	10		μsec
TGLGH	$\overline{\text{PROG}}$ Width	45	55	msec
TAVQV	Address to Data Valid		48TCLCL	
TELQV	$\overline{\text{ENABLE}}$ to Data Valid		48TCLCL	
TEHQZ	Data Float after $\overline{\text{ENABLE}}$	0	48TCLCL	

16

EPROM PROGRAMMING, SECURITY BIT PROGRAMMING AND VERIFICATION WAVEFORMS

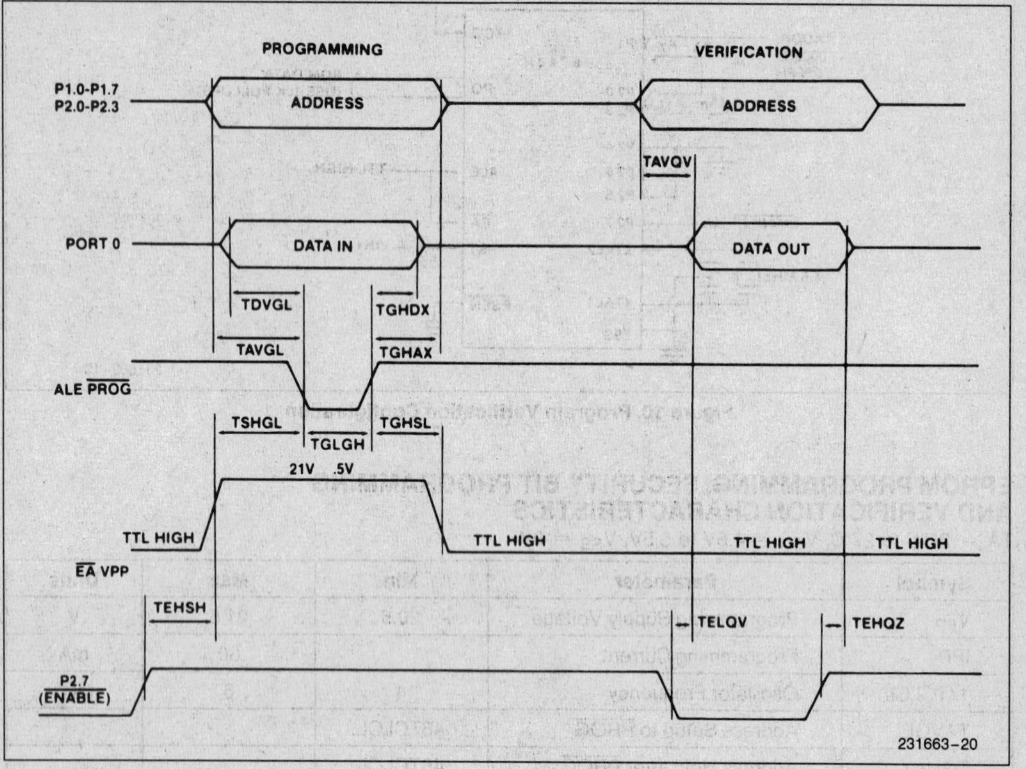

PROGRAMMING

VERIFICATION

P1.0-P1.7
P2.0-P2.3

ADDRESS

ADDRESS

TAVQV

PORT 0

DATA IN

DATA OUT

TDVGL

TGHDX

TAVGL

TGHAX

ALE $\overline{\text{PROG}}$

TSHGL

TGLGH

TGHSL

21V .5V

TTL HIGH

TTL HIGH

TTL HIGH

TTL HIGH

$\overline{\text{EA}}$ VPP

TEHSH

TELQV

TEHQZ

$\overline{\text{P2.7}}$
$\overline{\text{(ENABLE)}}$

231663-20

Service and Support 17

iRUG DESCRIPTION

iRUG is the Intel Real-Time User's Group. It is an incorporation chartered to establish a forum for users of the iRMX and iRMK operating systems and to promote and encourage development of Intel based software.

Benefits of membership include: access to the user's library of software tools and utilities; membership in local and international chapters; access to the group bulletin board; receipt of quarterly international magazines; opportunity to present papers and conduct workshops; invitations to seminars devoted to the use of Intel products.

The user's library, maintained by iRUG, contains software programs written and submitted by members and Intel employees. Programs available range from file or directory manipulation commands and terminal attribute selection utilities to dynamic logon, background job facilities and basic communication utilities.

Local and international iRUG chapters provide a forum for members to meet other Intel Real-Time system users in an informal setting. At local meetings and the annual international seminar, members can discuss their ideas, share their experiences and techniques, and give feedback to Intel for future improvements and features of Intel products and those supplied by other companies.

The "Intel Forum" sponsors iRUG Special Interest Group (SIG) on the CompuServe Information Service. The message facility (bulletin board) allows members to leave and receive messages from other members. These might include problems and solutions regarding the iRMX operating system or new techniques to be shared.

"The Human Interface" is iRUG's quarterly international magazine. It serves as a supplement to chapter meetings by providing: library listings, information on the latest releases of products; officer messages; member SPRs; vendor ads; release and update plans; and technical articles from the members.

For Information Contact:

iRUG
P.O. Box 91130
Portland OR 97291
1-800-255-iRUG

280678–1

INTEL SYSTEMS SERVICE AND SUPPORT

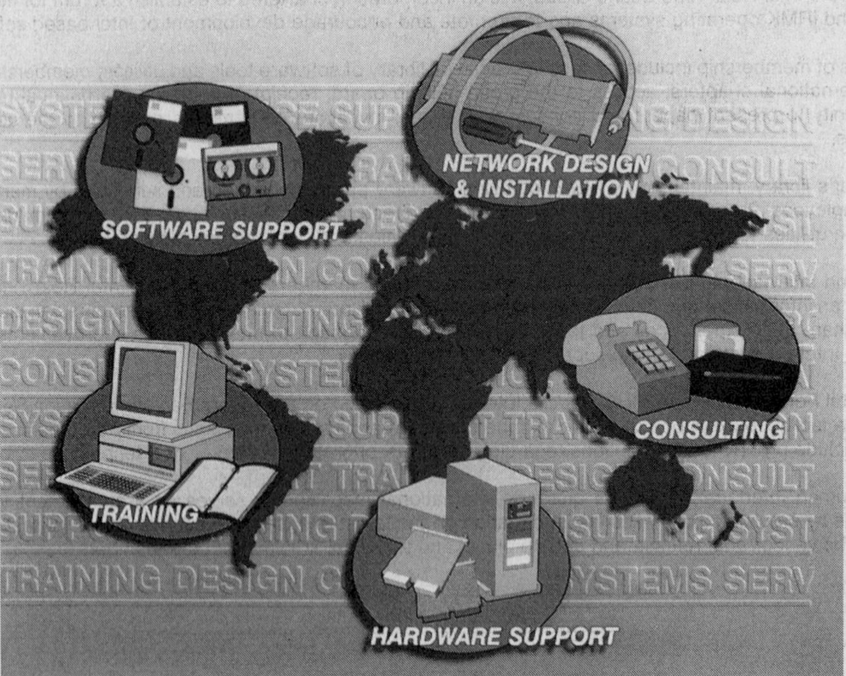

280695-1

WORLDWIDE SERVICE AND SUPPORT FROM INTEL

Intel's service and support offerings include everything you need to keep your Intel equipment—and yourself—in peak performance at all times. For you there's hands-on training to get you up to speed quickly and reduce development time. We also offer consulting services, software support, and networking assistance. For your equipment we have a variety of flexible repair programs to keep your systems up and running night and day. Hardware, software, boards or systems . . . if Intel's name is on it, Intel stands behind it.

WORLDWIDE CUSTOMER SERVICES

- Over one hundred Intel service and training centers worldwide
- Hardware maintenance program with prompt, worldwide response
- Software support that includes updates, telephone hotline support, troubleshooting guides, and *:COMMENTS*, a technical newsletter
- Consulting by Intel System Engineering Services for both hardware and software design solutions
- Hands-on training workshops on Intel systems hardware, operating systems, tools, and networking products
- Network design, installation, and maintenance

December 1990
Order Number: 280695-002

FEATURES

CONVENIENT, FLEXIBLE HARDWARE MAINTENANCE OPTIONS

Intel offers a wide variety of hardware support programs, from 24-hour on-site protection to economical carry-in repair. Our goal: to keep your systems running with the greatest economy and convenience. Consider all the options:

- **On-site Coverage.** An Intel customer engineer will repair your equipment at your site during normal business hours.
- **Extended Coverage.** Companies with critical applications choose this program, which offers on-site repair up to 24 hours a day, seven days a week.
- **Carry-in Service.** An economical option for small system users that saves you transportation costs.
- **Mail-in Service.** If time is not at issue, you can save even more by mailing in your part to an Intel Repair Center.
- **Per-call Service.** If your service needs are infrequent, this option gives you access to Intel expertise on a time and materials basis.

COMPREHENSIVE SOFTWARE SUPPORT

Everything you need to stay up-to-date on the latest improvements to your Intel software is available through Intel's software support services: Technical Information Phone Service (TIPS), software updates, Troubleshooting Guides, and *;COMMENTS*, a technical newsletter.

- **Technical Information Phone Service (TIPS).** TIPS puts you in touch instantly with Intel's software engineering staff to solve critical problems quickly.
- **Software Updates.** As Intel enhances its software, it keeps you up to date with the latest updates and documentation.
- **Troubleshooting Guides.** Intel Troubleshooting Guides provide information on problem workarounds and solutions.
- *;COMMENTS.* We also publish *;COMMENTS*, a monthly newsletter full of programming techniques, technical product information, and application solutions.

SYSTEMS ENGINEERING CONSULTING SERVICES

Intel Systems Engineers have the experience and engineering expertise with Intel chips, boards, systems, software and tools, so they can save you valuable development time. They can work at your site or from a local Intel office, helping you get your application to market sooner, boost your productivity and ensure compatibility with future Intel projects.

Intel Systems Engineers can work with you to:

- Guide your development effort
- Provide solutions to your problems
- Help you utilize new products more effectively
- Create your new applications
- Provide you with personalized training
- Customize an Intel product to fit your needs

With an Intel Systems Engineer on your team you receive service on a flexible basis—available when and where you need it!

HANDS-ON TRAINING THAT REDUCES DEVELOPMENT TIME

Intel offers in-depth training workshops on all its hardware and software products, from microcontrollers to operating systems. Customers tell us over and over that one to ten days spent with Intel saves weeks of self-study—that's weeks off your development schedule.

We routinely deliver workshops at Intel training centers all over the world, or we can come to your site. We'll even customize our standard courses to better fit your unique application and design needs.

Intel classes offered continuously around the world include:

- **Microprocessor and Microcontroller Workshops.** Programming the 8080, 8086, 386™, 486™ microprocessors, and i860 and 80960 microcontrollers for your next application.
- **Operating Systems, Languages, and Tools.** Learn the fundamentals and advanced points of programming iRMX®, iRMK™, XENIX(*), PL/M(*), and UNIX(*) Operating Systems, or developing applications for Intel microprocessors using Intel development tools.
- **Local-area Networking.** Technical workshops on Intel and non-Intel networking products.
- **End-user Workshops.** Introductory and advanced instruction on office automation, system administration and network administration.

intel®

FEATURES

TOTAL COVERAGE OF YOUR NETWORK NEEDS

Intel has the answer to all your networking needs. We provide assistance in network design (both physical and logical), component selection, installation, system administrator and user training, on-site network management, and maintenance.

We specialize in networking multiple departments, buildings and sites. We can help you understand the various network topologies and protocols, establish mainframe connections, automate your factory, and implement portable networks.

FLEXIBLE AND ACCESSIBLE

Intel has structured its support and service program in such a way that we're flexible and accessible enough to match your unique needs. Wherever in the world you are. And we mean wherever you are. Intel has more than one hundred service and training centers in thirty countries on six continents. Wherever you are, Intel speaks your language: service.

Let Intel build a support program specifically suited for your needs. Call or write us today for more information: In the U.S.A. call: **1-800-INTEL-4-U**. Worldwide: refer to the sales list on the back of this document.

IntelTechDirect™

280954-1

COMPLETE PRODUCT SUPPORT FOR FAST TIME TO MARKET

IntelTechDirect™, Intel's OEM support program provides Original Equipment Manufactures with all the assistance they need to get their Intel386™ and i486™ platform products to market quickly. Program components include an electronic bulletin board open 24 hours a day, seven days a week. Telephone assistance during normal business hours. All designed to help you be successful, for fast time to market and customer satisfaction.

STANDARD FEATURES

- Phone action line support (iPALS) during normal business hours
- Electronic bulletin board problem resolution (open 24 hours a day, seven days a week)
- Electronic access to Intel's OEM Platforms engineering database
- Monthly subscription service to Intel's product update bulletin (iPUB)
- Electronic access to Intel's product update bulletins (iPUB)
- Product documentation in OEM-requested format

*MS-DOS™ is a trademark of Microsoft, Inc.
386™ and i486™ are trademarks of Intel Corporation.

October 1991
Order Number: 280954-003

IntelTechDirect™

INTEL PHONE ACTION LINE SUPPORT (iPALS)

280954-2

- Technical assistance for Intel386 and i486 Microcomputer platform products.
- 24-hour response to questions

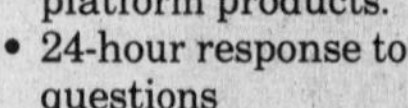

The Intel Phone Action Line Support (iPALS) is an 8-hour-a-day, five-day-a-week telephone action line for Intel386 and i486 platform MicroComputer products. iPALS personnel are trained to answer both technical and business questions about Intel's product offerings, and are committed to responding within 24 hours. iPALS is available to any OEM by subscribing to IntelTechDirect.

INTEL PRODUCT ASSISTANCE NETWORK (iPAN)

280954-3

- On-line problem resolution, with 24-hour response.
- Electronic access to engineering database
- Electronic access to Intel's Product Update Bulletins
- Worldwide access through direct-dial
- Access speeds up to 9600 baud
- Keyword search via main menu

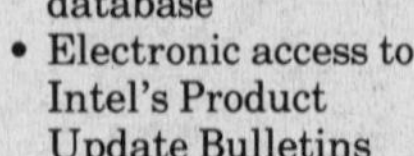

The Intel Product Assistance Network (iPAN) is an electronic information retrieval service that allows OEMs to review our on-line product database, enter questions, and view Intel's Product Update Bulletin service. Questions are responded to within 24 hours. The database also includes tips on workarounds, product technical information, and benchmark data.

The iPAN database is available to OEMs by purchasing IntelTechDirect along with their Intel platform purchase. iPAN can be accessed using a 1200, 2400 or 9600-baud modem and any standard terminal communications software. All IntelTechDirect subscribers receive an iPAN user's manual, and an iPAN user access code.

INTEL PRODUCT UPDATE BULLETIN (iPUB)

280954-4

- Monthly product updates
- Intel386 and i486 MicroComputer product histories
- Intel386 and i486 MicroComputer BIOS histories
- Software available from Intel
- Documentation updates and order number
- Hardware and software compatibility information
- Spare parts order information

The Intel Product Update Bulletin (iPUB) is a monthly subscription service which documents engineering changes and technical information on the Intel386 and i486 MicroComputer product family. Information contained in iPUB includes board and system product histories, software and hardware compatibility information and spare parts order information.

iPUB is distributed electronically through iPAN and via monthly mailings. Every IntelTechDirect subscriber receives an OEM binder and a one-year subscription to the service. The iPUB notebook constitutes a comprehensive resource for OEMs integrating Intel386 and i486 MicroComputer products.

ORDERING INFORMATION

Service	Description	Order Code
iPAN	Product Assistance Network	TECHDIRECT
iPALS	Phone Action Line Support	
iPUB	Intel Product Update Bulletin	
TRL	Technical Reference Library	TRL

For more information or the number of your nearest Intel sales office, call 800-548-4725 (good in the U.S. and Canada).

UNITED STATES, Intel Corporation
3065 Bowers Ave., Santa Clara, CA 95051
Tel: (408) 765-8080

VALUE-ADDED DISTRIBUTION

280979–1

CUSTOMIZED PRODUCTS AND SERVICES FROM INTEL AND ITS VALUE-ADDED DISTRIBUTORS

Intel's Value-Added Distribution program is designed to provide complete solutions for companies requiring custom system configurations. From Intel you get leading-edge technology, training and comprehensive product service. From Intel Value-Added Distributors (VADs) you get engineering expertise, flexible manufacturing capabilities, and customized solutions. And Intel's strict VAD certification program assures that you have selected a quality distributor who has invested in people and facilities to meet your quality standards. Our certification program, the first in the industry, defines requirements in areas of design, quality and manufacturing.

COMPETITIVE ADVANTAGES

- Certified Value-Added Distribution Centers staffed with design and manufacturing experts
- Application Technical Specialists to help tune designs
- Custom solutions based on Intel technology
- Third-party hardware and software selection assistance
- Project management expertise
- Integration design, testing and evaluation
- Custom inventory control, shipping, and service arrangements
- Quality delivery records

*UNIX is a registered trademark of AT&T Bell Laboratories. MS-DOS is a trademark of Microsoft. iRMX, 386, i486 are trademarks of Intel Corp.

October 1990
Order Number: 280979-002

VALUE-ADDED DISTRIBUTION

PRODUCT DESIGN SUPPORT

Design and integration support can begin as early as you want. Our nationwide network of sales offices and technical support centers are staffed with Intel-certified Application Technical Specialists who are experts on Intel architectures and on integrating Intel products into custom configurations. Your Application Technical Specialist can work with you to evaluate your needs, make suggestions that will save you money, improve the quality of your product and accelerate your production time to market.

If your design solution requires third-party add-in boards, peripherals or software, our VADs can help with supplier qualification. They have established relationships with hundreds of suppliers and can quickly match your needs with pre-qualified companies that conform to your quality standards. They can also test for your unique peripheral requirements.

In today's regulation sensitive environment, Intel's certified VADs can provide FCC, U.L., and DOC (Canadian) certification assistance, as well as European regulatory compliance submittal and testing.

Project management assistance is also available. Our VADs can take on the coordination of your entire product's production and provide drop-shipment to your customer's site. You make all the final decisions; they take care of the day-to-day details.

In short, your VAD Center representative or branch office sales person will sit down with you, listen to and understand your needs, then work with you to develop a creative, cost-effective solution.

PRODUCTION AND MANUFACTURING EXCELLENCE

Together, Intel VADs have invested millions of dollars in state-of-the-art integration facilities and trained personnel. These facilities are there to quickly help you turn your product ideas into a reality.

Intel's VAD certification program, the first one of its kind in the industry, ensures that all our VADs conform to Intel's rigorous Quality and Reliability standards. They employ the latest manufacturing and process control techniques to ensure top quality and a smooth production flow. Their manufacturing facilities can adapt to your changing needs and can ramp up or cut back production as your markets dictate.

They can also perform testing and certification to make sure your products operate safely and within prescribed legal parameters. Custom diagnostics can also be generated by your VAD to assure proper performance levels at your customers installation. The quality of your product is their utmost priority.

CUSTOM HARDWARE

Intel, through its VADs, can provide both board and system-level customization, including Intel386™ and Intel486™ platforms, MicroComputer Multibus board integration, custom motherboards and backplanes, system test and burn-in, integration of third-party peripherals, multiple processor design, even custom logos, keycaps and chassis. You'll have the assurance that all the components are compatible, fully tested, and that each system will perform as expected.

CUSTOM SOFTWARE

Our VADs' wide-ranging expertise in custom software includes iRMX® real-time software reconfiguration, MS-DOS*, UNIX* operating systems and drivers, human interface software, communications software, PAL/PROM generation, custom diagnostics, networking, and many other areas. They will make sure software and hardware are tightly integrated and serve as a single, accountable source for the entire system.

And, of course, they can also supply you with off-the-shelf PC application software.

SPECIAL SERVICE OPTIONS

Intel's VADs will not only help you produce the highest quality product possible at the lowest possible cost; we can also help with shipping, inventory management and other post-production matters. Many of our VADs will warehouse finished product for you and deliver on demand—or, ship directly to your end user and install the product in any corner of the world. That kind of flexibility saves you expensive, redundant shipping costs and gets your product to your customer on time.

VALUE-ADDED DISTRIBUTION

For our OEM customers, we can also accommodate Just-In-Time delivery programs, service your end users directly, set up leasing programs, and provide configuration consulting. And of course, Intel can provide you with technical, sales and service support.

LET US BE YOUR SYSTEMS INTEGRATION PARTNER

If your success depends on suppliers who can provide complete solutions, call your local Intel sales office or Intel distributor today, and let us tell you more about our Value-Added Distributor program. Building on leading-edge Intel technology, our VADs can craft a custom solution for you that's just right for your unique needs.

MAINTENANCE VALUE FOR PC'S AND PERIPHERALS

281041-1

MAINTENANCE VALUE FOR PC'S AND PERIPHERALS

Intel Service and Support is there to help you make the most of your personal computer by teaming technical excellence and full support. Today's businesses understand the value of the work performed by Personal Computers and the people who run them. The value is greatly magnified when the PC is used as a file server on a network, or as a mainframe interface. That is why a complete service and support solution must be an integral part of any computing environment. Compared to the value of the time and work performed by people and PC's, an on site maintenance agreement is a small investment. It enables your business to maximize productivity as well as the life cycle of your PC. Intel is your single phone call solution for PC Support.

TWO LEVELS OF ON SITE PC MAINTENANCE

Intel has service expertise on virtually any type of PC and peripheral product. We match support of the microcomputer with flexibility to meet our customers needs. Two levels of PC Service are available: Full Service, for end users who require fast equipment repair, data recovery and assistance in returning your PC to full operation, and, Basic Service for technical users and cost constrained end users who require only on site parts replacement.

Full Service PC Maintenance

- Full Service end user support
  Isolate S/W and H/W problems
  Winchester data recovery
  Winchester formatted for O/S
  Assist user in recovery
  Reconfigure PC into a network
- Preventative maintenance for all PC's
- Remote PC diagnostics
- Third party peripheral support
- Next day service response
- PC upgrade service

Basic PC Maintenance

- On site parts replacement H/W service.
  S/W is billable
  Winchester exchange only
  Low level Winchester format
- Perform Preventative Maintenance on failed PC only
- Remote PC Diagnostics
- Third part peripheral support
- Second day service response

PC XT is a trademark of International Business Machines Corporation. UNIX is a trademark of AT&T.
Window is a trademark of Microsoft. OS/2 is a registered trademark of International Business Machines Corporation.
OpenNet is a trademark of Intel Corporation.

October 1990
Order Number: 281041-001

MAINTENANCE VALUE FOR PC'S AND PERIPHERALS

INTEL'S WORLD CLASS SERVICE ORGANIZATION

With over 200 Sales and Service Offices world wide, where ever you're using Intel technology, our professional staff is within close reach. Our staff of Customer Engineers is one of the best trained in the service industry, averaging 30 training days per year. With average length of employment in excess of five years, you can be assured of a seasoned trained professional maintaining your equipment. Our Customer Engineers are backed up by a network of Field Product Specialists and National Technical Support Engineers in addition to an on line Technical Data Base of product information.

Intel's technical depth is matched by a computerized world wide service management network and logistic parts system. This system occupies two mainframe computers full time. A world wide network of parts depots are automatically supplied to assure local parts availability for all equipment under contract. Parts are also stored at the over night air express company in order to provide emergency parts replacement within hours instead of days. The system tracks every service call and has built in management escalation reporting whenever an open service call exceeds Intel's quality response standards.

A complete history of every machine under contract is maintained to examine failure patterns and focus on preventative maintenance and product quality. Intel spare parts are always repaired to the highest level of engineering change order. This prevents known product deficiencies from reoccurring in your system.

Intel also operates a 24 hour a day dispatch service. In the United States the central dispatch is accessed by dialing 1-800-INTEL-4-U. Local language dispatch centers are also located in Europe and Japan. A one phone call service solution for Intel and third party products.

Intel's Regional and District Service Managers are also personally involved in assuring that all aspects of our customers service needs are met. Our managers personally conduct an annual quality audit of a random sample of our customers.

SERVICES YOU'D EXPECT FROM A TECHNOLOGY LEADER

With today's explosive change in technology, your choice of a service and support company is critical if you are to fully realize the capabilities of the products and technology. Intel support is always in tandem with technical excellence.

- Complete Networking Services, from design to installation. Network Administrator training, software integration and network management services for OpenNET™, Novell, Banyon, OS/2 Lan Manager and others.
- Knowledge delivery workshops for hands on training for over 60 courses including: OS/2 and Window, UNIX and PC Hardware design.
- Systems Engineering Services for leading edge software and hardware design services, device driver development and customized products.
- Product repair options including warranty repair, factory repair, carry in repair, time and materials repair, plus spare parts kits.

SERVICE PARTNERSHIP

Our customers and Distributors integrate and add value to the OEM Platform to address their end customer markets. In a Service Partnership with our customers and Distributors, Intel maintains the entire integrated product and attached peripherals. By bundling Intel Service into their product, a smaller company with limited resources can market and sell to new customers across the country or across the world! This Service Partnership allows companies to literally "Multiply their Markets" by using Intel's on site service and support. Just as importantly, satisfied customers are the source of repeat business, thereby increasing revenue and profit. Intel will also maintain the installed base of equipment from previous sales.

INFORMATION

For more information or to find the number of the nearest service office call 1-800-468-3548 for U.S. and Canada.

JAPAN: tel: 029747-8511

EUROPE: tel: 44-0793-696000

CUSTOM SYSTEM INTEGRATION SERVICES

272038-1

COMPLEMENT THE CAPABILITIES OF YOUR INTEGRATION CENTER WITH CUSTOM SYSTEMS BUILT FROM INTEL386 TM AND INTEL486 TM MICROCOMPUTERS

Intel Custom Systems Integration Services enable resellers like Original Equipment Manufacturers (OEMs), Distributors, Value Added Distributors (VADs), and Value Added Resellers (VARs) to order completely integrated systems assembled from a list of Intel386™ and Intel486™ microcomputers and validated hardware and software options.

These services are designed to complement the reseller's own integration capabilities. Resellers can offer high performance, fully configured systems and networks with no incremental investment in integration center capability and capacity. Resellers can increase business opportunities, while controlling overhead and support costs.

FEATURES

- Comprehensive list of pre-tested and precertified platforms and options
- Network operating system software options
- Quick delivery on configurations integrated from the standard options list
- Custom configuration and options
- Custom configuration verification and certification
- Custom integration engineering services

ADVANTAGES

- Increases reseller business opportunities by offering fully integrated systems and networks
- Increases reseller business opportunity by offering integrated systems based on leading technology like the i486™ CPU
- Increases reseller business opportunity by offering custom engineering and integration capabilities to meet unique customer requirements
- Reduces costs by complementing reseller integration capacity and capabilities

November 1991
Order Number: 272038-001

CUSTOM SYSTEM INTEGRATION SERVICES

QUICK TURNAROUND FOR STANDARD CONFIGURATIONS

Based on Intel's family of high performance microprocessors, integrated systems are configured from a robust list of i386™ and i486™ microcomputers and options like: 2.4 gigabyte preformatted disk; 2.2 gigabyte tape backup; 16 megabytes of 32-bit memory; graphic displays; and, Novell or Banyan network operating systems.

Intel provides the reseller with a set of system configuration guidelines that help qualify, specify, and properly configure systems to meet customer requirements. Configurations built from the standard certified options list are delivered within five working days.

CUSTOM INTEGRATION FOR UNIQUE CUSTOMER NEEDS

For customers with special system or option requirements, Intel provides custom integration engineering. Non-standard options are validated, tested, and configured by Intel's custom integration engineers for an additional one-time charge per option. The reseller works with Intel to establish the validation and testing criteria of a custom system or option. Delivery times are quoted for each custom configuration.

INTEL CERTIFICATION AND QUALITY STANDARDS

All Intel custom integrated systems are built to Intel's standards of quality. Integration is performed in a controlled environment and is subject to strict quality procedures. All components are inspected and tested before and after integration. All integrated components are entered into a computerized database. This database keeps critical facts at hand for planning preventive maintenance and service, for product evaluations, and for future purchases.

Intel's integration process includes system testing to meet or exceed UL, FCC, and CSA agency standards and requirements. Configurations which include a network operating system are certified to meet the specifications published by the operating system vendor.

Systems configured to custom specifications undergo pre-specified system tests to verify system performance to requirements. Tests can include network operating system installation and execution verification.

Integration consists of installing disk drives, I/O cards, tape peripherals, and memory cards. If specified, a network operating system is loaded. The entire system undergoes a minimum of one hour burn-in.

Expert integration by Intel ensures quality system performance and efficient installation.

WARRANTY

Custom integrated systems include one year mail-in or return to local Intel depot warranty. Extended maintenance and support options are available.

WORLDWIDE SERVICE AND SUPPORT

Intel offers a comprehensive range of support options for its custom integrated systems. These options include on-site installation and maintenance, repair service, spare service, network operating system support, engineering consulting, and education services.

Your Intel sales representative can structure a support program to meet your needs.

ORDERING INFORMATION

Custom integrated systems are configured and priced separately. Each Top Level Option (microcomputer platform) has a unique configuration option list. An interactive configuration utility is available to guide resellers through configuration, pricing, and ordering. Consult your local Intel sales office for configuration and ordering assistance.

TOP LEVEL OPTIONS:

NOS Ready

NWB300SX	300SX 16 MHz, 386SX NOS Ready Server
NWB302	302 25 MHz, 386DX NOS Ready Server
NWB303	303 33 MHz, 386DX NOS Ready Server
NWB401	401 25 MHz, 486, Tower, NOS Ready Server
NWB402	402 25 MHz, 486, Desk Top, NOS Ready Server
NWB403E1	403E 33 MHz, 486, Tower, NOS Ready Server

Custom

BTO30X	Custom configured 386 system
BTO40X	Custom configured 486 system

Specials

SRVRUPGRD	Standard system upgrades (Not sold standalone)
SPAREKITS	Standard spare kits for Intel microcomputer platforms

Customer Specified

XXXXX	Customer specified

NOS Loaded

BAN300SX	300SX 16 MHz, 386SX Banyan Loaded Server
BAN302	302 25 MHz, 386DX Banyan Loaded Server
BAN303	303 33 MHz, 386DX Banyan Loaded Server
BAN401	401 25 MHz, 486, Tower, Banyan Loaded Server
BAN402	402 25 MHz, 486, Desk Top, Banyan Loaded Server
BAN403EI	403E 33 MHz, 486, Tower, Banyan Loaded Server
NOV300SX	300SX 16 MHz, 386SX Novell Loaded Server
NOV302	302 25 MHz, 386DX Novell Loaded Server
NOV303	303 33 MHz, 386DX Novell Loaded Server
NOV401	401 25 MHz, 486, Tower, Novell Loaded Server
NOV402	402 25 MHz, 486, Desk Top, Novell Loaded Server
NOV403EI	403E 33 MHz, 486, Tower, Novell Loaded Server

OPTION CATEGORIES:

Client/Server Platforms
Rack Mount Platforms
Memory Chips
32 Bit Memory Boards
Hard Disk/Floppy Disc Controllers
Floppy Disc Drives
Hard Disc Drives
Tape Drives
Video Controllers
Video Monitors
Communication Devices
Network Interface Controllers
Input Devices
UPS Power Systems
Data Cables
Miscellaneous Hardware

Banyan NOS Options
Banyan SNA/BI-SYNC Options
Banyan Mail Options
Banyan Misc SW Options
Banyan Hardware Options
Novell NOS Options
Novell LAM Products
Novell PC Remote Dial-In
Novell LAN Server-to-Server
Novell Host Comm Options
Novell WAN Server-to-Server
Novell Network Mgmt
Novell Network Mail
Novell PC TCP/IP Server-to-Server

Customer Specified

ORDERING INFORMATION

ORDERING INFORMATION

For more information or the number of your nearest sales office, call 800-548-4725 (good in the U.S. and Canada.)

ON-SITE INSTALLATION AND MAINTENANCE SERVICES

272040-1

TEAMING WITH INTEL FOR FULL SUPPORT

Intel's installation and maintenance services are designed to get Intel microprocessor-based systems and the networks that they use up and running—fast. Once installed, Intel is dedicated to keeping them running at maximum efficiency, while controlling costs.

Service centers staffed by trained and certified Customer Engineers (CEs) are located throughout the United States, Canada, Europe, and Asia. CEs provide on-site service for Intel microcomputer platforms, non-Intel peripherals, and for non-Intel PCs and servers when they are connected through networks. This on-site service can be complemented with an Intel software support contract for Novell or Banyan network software. This means complete network maintenance and support from a single source.

FEATURES

- Single source of installation and maintenance for standalone and networked Intel architecture systems
- Installation and maintenance for non-Intel peripherals
- Services hours tailored to customer needs
- Service manager assigned to each maintenance account
- Certified and trained Customer Engineering specialists
- Maintenance contracts include spare parts and system updates

ADVANTAGES

- Multi-vendor network maintenance
- Optional network operating support contracts
- Increases organizational productivity by maximizing system and network uptime
- Reduces costs by providing one-stop installation and maintenance for multiple vendors
- Reduces costs by providing flexible service hours to meet customer needs
- Increases availability of critical applications on standalone and networked systems

October 1991
Order Number: 272040-001

ON-SITE INSTALLATION AND MAINTENANCE SERVICES

QUICK START SYSTEM AND NETWORK INSTALLATION

Intel specialists guarantee a successful installation by carefully planning the process. So when system or network products arrive, they can be integrated into their environment smoothly and efficiently. Intel installs and verifies standalone systems or networks which can include both Intel and non-Intel components like PCs, servers, bridges, routers and gateways.

Installation includes configuration verification, software loading and comprehensive system testing, and on-site orientation. Network installation expertise includes Novell, Banyan and UNIX*-based networks.

ON-SITE MAINTENANCE FOR PEACE OF MIND

Under the Intel Equipment Service Order (ESO), equipment is covered for all parts, materials, and labor necessary to keep the systems and networks in good running order. No additional charges are required unless services are performed outside the covered contract hours and terms, and then only the labor is billable.

Each service location maintains a pool of skilled CEs trained to diagnose and repair products listed in the ESO. Local inventories of spare parts geared to the volume and type of equipment under contract are maintained. For Intel standard service contracts, our goal is to have parts available on the first service call. If we don't have the parts, they are ordered immediately through our 24-hour, 7-day emergency parts ordering system.

FLEXIBLE SERVICE HOURS CONTROL COSTS

Intel offers options for flexible hours of coverage to match a variety of customer needs.

- Monday through Friday, 8:00 a.m. to 5:00 p.m.
- Monday through Saturday, 8:00 a.m. to 5:00 p.m.
- Seven days a week, 8:00 a.m. to 5:00 p.m.
- Monday through Friday, 8:00 a.m. to 12:00 a.m.
- Monday through Saturday, 8:00 a.m. to 12:00 a.m.
- Seven days a week, 8:00 a.m. to 12:00 a.m.
- Monday through Friday, 8:00 a.m. to 8:00 a.m. (24 hour)
- Monday through Saturday, 8:00 a.m. to 8:00 a.m. (24 hour)
- Seven days a week, 8:00 a.m. to 8:00 a.m. (24 hour)

CUSTOMER SATISFACTION

Each customer account is assigned to one of our local service managers to ensure that all aspects of installation and maintenance are planned and performed properly.

CONTINUOUS TOLL-FREE SUPPORT

Intel maintains service locations worldwide. For the U.S. and Canada, problems are reported by the customer through an Intel toll-free number. Local CEs contact the customer to isolate and identify the source of the problem. In some instances, an Intel maintenance specialist may initiate remote diagnostic sessions in order to monitor problems as they occur. If problems cannot be resolved over the phone, CEs go on-site for further assistance and problem resolution.

If a customer requests service outside of the pre-specified coverage hours, Intel will complete the service at a labor-only billable rate. This ensures maximum customer coverage at all times.

MULTI-VENDOR SYSTEM MAINTENANCE

Intel installs and maintains a wide-range of products from many vendors. The following lists the categories of products supported by Intel. Contact your local Intel sales representative for the detailed Supported Products List.

- Servers
- PC/Workstations
- LAN Interface Cards
- Gateways
- Routers
- Transceivers
- Repeaters
- Concentrators
- Hubs
- UPS
- Modems
- Video Displays
- Disk Drives
- Tape Peripherals
- FAX cards
- Comm cards
- Peripheral controller
- Pointing devices
- Scanners

ON-SITE INSTALLATION AND MAINTENANCE SERVICES

U.S. AND CANADA SERVICE LOCATIONS

Intel maintains service locations worldwide. The following is a list of service locations for the continental U.S., Alaska, Hawaii, and Canada. Contract response times are guaranteed for customer locations within 50 miles of the Intel authorized service location. Response times can be assured for coverage up to 150 miles in radius for additional costs. Please contact your Intel sales representative for a list of these charges. Service locations for other parts of the world can also be provided.

Alabama
Birmingham
Dothan
Gadsden
Huntsville
Mobile
Montgomery

Alaska
Anchorage

Arizona
Phoenix
Tuscon

Arkansas
Ft. Smith
Little Rock

California
Bakersfield
Canoga Park
El Segundo
Eureka
Fresno
Folsom
Martinez
Ontario
Orange County
Sacramento
San Diego
Salinas
San Francisco
Santa Ana
Santa Clara
Santa Maria
Santa Rosa
Ventura

Colorado
Colorado Springs
Denver
Ft. Collins
Grand Junction

Connecticut
Danbury
Stamford
Hartford

Delaware
Wilmington

Florida
Deerfield Beach
Jacksonville
Miami
Merritt Island
Orlando
Pensacola
Pompano Beach
Sarasota
Tampa

Georgia
Albany
Augusta
Macon
Norcross
Savannah

Hawaii
Honolulu

Idaho
Boise

Illinois
Champagne
Rockford
Schaumburg
Springfield
Waukegan

Indiana
Ft. Wayne
Indianapolis
South Bend

Iowa
Cedar Rapids
Davenport
Des Moines

Kansas
Overland Park
(Kansas City)
Wichita

Kentucky
Lexington
Louisville

Louisiana
Baton Rouge
Layfayette
New Orleans
Shreveport

Maine
Portland

Maryland
Annapolis Junction
Upper Marlboro

Massachusetts
Manchester
Springfield
Westford
Worchester

Michigan
Ann Arbor
Detroit
Flint
Grand Rapids
Kalamazoo
Lansing

Minnesota
Austin
Minneapolis

Mississippi
Jackson
Tupelo

Missouri
Springfield
St. Louis
Montana
Billings
Missoula

Nebraska
Omaha

Nevada
Reno

Las Vegas

New Hampshire
Keene

New Jersey
Atlantic City
Englewood Cliffs
New Brunswick
Red Bank

New Mexico
Albuquerque

New York
Albany
Buffalo
Islandia
Manhattan
Newburgh
Poughkeepsie
Rochester
Syracuse

North Carolina
Ashville
Charlotte
Fayetteville
Greensboro
New Bern
Raleigh
Wilmington

North Dakota
Fargo

Ohio
Akron
Canton
Cincinnati
Cleveland
Columbus
Dayton
Toledo
Youngstown

Oklahoma
Oklahoma City
Tulsa

Oregon
Hillsboro
Medford
Portland
Salem

Pennsylvania
Allentown

ON-SITE INSTALLATION AND MAINTENANCE SERVICES

U.S. AND CANADA SERVICE LOCATIONS (Continued)

Ft. Washington
Harrisburg

Indiana
Lewisburg
Pittsburgh
Scranton

Rhode Island
Providence

South Carolina
Charleston
Columbia
Florence
Greenville

South Dakota
Sioux Falls
Rapid City

Tennessee
Chattanooga
Jackson
Knoxville
Memphis
Nashville

Texas
Abilene
Amarillo
Austin
Beaumont
College Station
Corpus Christi
Dallas
El Paso
Galveston
Houston
Longview
Lubbock
Midland
San Antonio
Victoria
Waco
Wichita Falls

Utah
Ogden
Salt Lake City

Vermont
Burlington

Virginia
Charlottsville
Norfolk
Richmond
Roanoke

Washington
Seattle
Spokane
Tacoma

West Virginia
Ashland
Charleston

Wisconsin
Green Bay
Madison
Milwaukee

Wyoming
Casper

Canada
Calgary, Alberta
Edmonton, Alberta
Vancouver, B.C.
Vernon, B.C.
Victoria, B.C.
Winnepeg, Manitoba
Halifax, Nova Scotia
Hamilton, Ontario
London, Ontario
Ottawa, Ontario
Peterborough, Ontario
Sudbury, Ontario
Toronto, Ontario
Montreal, Quebec

intel®

NETWORK OPERATING SYSTEM SUPPORT

272039–1

NOVELL AND BANYAN* TECHNICAL SUPPORT MAXIMIZE NETWORK AVAILABILITY*

An Intel software support contract for Novell NetWare* or Banyan VINES* software means unlimited access to troubleshooting expertise any time during contracted hoursup to seven days per week, twenty-four hours per day. To keep networks current and compatible with the latest software versions, support services include access to minor releases and "patches" as made available by Novell and Banyan. This means the best assurance for maximizing network uptime.

Technical assistance is provided by Intel's System Support Engineers (SSEs) through a toll free number. SSEs are trained and certified in the NetWare and VINES network operating systems.

FEATURES

- Toll free access to certified Novell, Banyan, and Intel System Support Engineers
- Unlimited number of calls during the contracted hours
- Access to NetWare and VINES minor releases and "patches"
- Flexible contract terms to meet a variety of network environments
- Multi-vendor network operating system support

ADVANTAGES

- Reduces support complexity and costs
- Provides assurance for maximum network availability
- Reduces network "downtime" for mission critical applications
- Assures continuous software compatibility for major releases
- Assures multi-vendor problem resolution

November 1991
Order Number: 272039-001

NETWORK OPERATING SYSTEM SUPPORT

CONTINUOUS TOLL-FREE NETWORK SUPPORT

When a network software problem arises or technical assistance is required, customers call Intel's toll free support line. Calls are handled by Banyan or Novell certified System Support Engineers (SSEs) who work with the system or network administrator to isolate and identify the source of the problem. In some instances, the SSE may initiate remote diagnostic sessions in order to monitor problems as they occur. SSEs have access to a comprehensive database of technical information and direct access to Banyan's and Novell's support centers. If problems cannot be resolved over the phone, SSEs may dispatch Customer Engineers (CEs) for further on-site support.

ACCESS TO NETWORK EXPERTISE

Intel provides the resources and expertise necessary to handle a wide variety of problems related to the network operating system and the user's level of experience in recognizing sources of error. The experience necessary to diagnose problems effectively comes from comprehensive and continuous SSE and CE training and participation in vendor certification programs. Due to economies of scale, this extensive expertise is available to all holders of Intel software support contracts at very reasonable rates. This approach allows Intel contract holders to redeploy expensive support dollars to activities directly affecting their enterprise and still ensure maximum network uptime.

U.S. AND CANADA SERVICE LOCATIONS

When required, Intel dispatches Customer Engineers from the following network supported authorized locations. Contract response times are guaranteed for customer locations within 50 miles of the Intel authorized service location. Response times can be assured for coverage up to 150 miles in radius for additional costs. If the problem is determined to be customer caused, Intel may bill the customer at the current labor-only rate. All sites listed below provide NetWare support. Cities indicated by an asterisk (*) support both NetWare and VINES.

Alabama
Birmingham*
Dothan
Gadsden
Huntsville
Mobile
Montgomery

Alaska
Anchorage
Phoenix*

Arizona
Tucson

Arkansas
Ft. Smith
Little Rock

California
Bakersfield
Canoga Park*
El Segundo*
Eureka
Fresno
Folsom*
Martinez
Ontario
Orange County*
Sacramento
San Diego*
Salinas
San Francisco*
Santa Ana
Santa Clara*
Santa Maria
Santa Rosa
Ventura

Colorado
Colorado Springs
Denver*
Fort Collins
Grand Junction

Connecticut
Danbury*
Stamford
Hartford

Delaware
Wilmington*

Florida
Deerfield Beach*
Jacksonville
Miami
Merritt Island
Orlando*
Pensiacola
Pompano Beach
Sarasota
Tampa*

Georgia
Albany
Augusta
Macon
Norcross*
Savannah

Hawaii
Honolulu

Idaho
Boise

Illinois
Champaign
Rockford
Schaumburg*
Springfield
Waukegan

Indiana
Ft. Wayne
Indianapolis
South Bend

Iowa
Cedar Rapids
Davenport
Des Moines

Kansas
Overland Park
(Kansas City)*
Wichita

17

NETWORK OPERATING SYSTEM SUPPORT

U.S. AND CANADA SERVICE LOCATIONS, continued

Kentucky
Lexington*
Louisville*

Louisiana
Baton Rouge
Layfayette
New Orleans
Shreveport

Maine
Portland

Maryland
Annapolis Junction*
Upper Marlboro

Massachusetts
Manchester
Springfield
Westford*
Worchester

Michigan
Ann Arbor
Detroit*
Flint
Grand Rapids
Kalamazoo
Lansing

Minnesota
Austin
Minneapolis*

Mississippi
Jackson
Tupelo

Missouri
Springfield
St. Louis*

Montana
Billings
Missoula

Nebraska
Omaha

Nevada
Reno
Las Vegas

New Hampshire
Keene

New Jersey
Atlantic City
Englewood Cliffs*
New Brunswick
Red Bank*

New Mexico
Albuquerque*

New York
Albany
Buffalo
Islandia*
Manhattan
Newburgh
Poughkeepsie*
Rochester
Syracuse*

North Carolina
Ashville
Charlotte*
Fayetteville
Greensboro
New Bern
Raleigh*
Wilmington

North Dakota
Fargo

Ohio
Akron
Canton
Cincinnati
Cleveland*
Columbus
Dayton*
Toledo
Youngstown

Oklahoma
Oklahoma City
Tulsa

Oregon
Hillsboro*
Medford
Portland
Salem

Pennsylvania
Allentown
Ft. Washington*
Harrisburg*
Indiana
Lewisburg
Pittsburgh*
Scranton

Rhode Island
Providence

South Carolina
Charleston
Columbia*
Florence
Greenville

South Dakota
Sioux Falls
Rapid City

Tennessee
Chattanooga
Jackson
Knoxville
Memphis
Nashville*

Texas
Abilene
Amarillo
Austin*
Beaumont
College Station
Corpus Christi
Dallas*
El Paso
Galveston
Houston*
Longview
Lubbock
Midland
San Antonio
Victoria
Waco
Wichita Falls

Utah
Ogden
Salt Lake City

Vermont
Burlington

Virginia
Charlottsville
Norfolk
Richmond*
Roanoke

Washington
Seattle*
Spokane
Tacoma

West Virginia
Ashland
Charleston

Wisconsin
Green Bay
Madison
Milwaukee*

Wyoming
Casper

Canada
Calgary, Alberta
Edmonton, Alberta
Vancouver, B.C.
Vernon, B.C.
Victoria, B.C.
Winnepeg, Manitoba
Halifay, Nova Scotia
Hamilton, Ontario
London, Ontario
Ottawa, Ontario
Peterborough, Ontario
Sudbury, Ontario
Toronto, Ontario
Montreal, Quebec

ORDERING INFORMATION

Software contracts include one year of unlimited toll-free telephone support during normal business days, Monday through Friday, 8:00 a.m. to 5:00 p.m. local time. Customers receive patches, updates and minor releases provided by Banyan and Novell during the contract period. Extended coverage options are available.

BANYAN VINES

VTEAM	VINES v4.10, Team software support
VUNLIMT	VINES v4.10, unlimited (i386™/ i486™ CPU) software support
VSMP	VINES v4.10, SMP (Symmetrical MultiProcessor) software support
CNS	VINES v4.10, CNS (Corporate Network Server) software support
VEXTEND	Extends coverage to 7-days, 8:00 a.m. to 8:00 a.m. (24 hours)

NOVELL NETWARE

NET2U5	NetWare v2.2, software support for up to five users
NET2U10	NetWare v2.2, software support for up to ten users
NET2U50	NetWare v2.2, software support for up to 50 users
NET2U100	NetWare v2.2, software support for up to 100 users
NET3U20	NetWare v3.11, software support for up to 20 users
NET3U100	NetWare v3.11, software support for up to 100 users
NET3U250	NetWare v3.11, software support for up to 250 users
NEXTEND	Extends coverage to 7-days, 8:00 a.m. to 8:00 a.m. (24 hours)

17

REPAIR SERVICES FOR INTEL OEM MODULES AND PLATFORMS

272048-1

MATCHING PRODUCT EXCELLENCE WITH FULL SUPPORT

Intel offers customers of its OEM Modules and Platforms a comprehensive set of repair services that reduce the costs of system warranty, maintenance, and ownership. Repair services include module or system testing and repair, module exchange, and spare part sales. Additional support services include worldwide on-site installation and maintenance contracts for systems.

Our repair services go beyond typical "in-warranty" repair support. They include flexible "out-of-warranty" options to ensure continuous support and cost control throughout a product's life cycle. Repair services include competitive Spare Parts Sales, Standard Repair Service (DRA), Exchange Service (RRA), and Express Exchange Service (BRR). All repairs are performed to Intel's highest quality standards and include a one year warranty.

Intel repair services offer Intel OEMs, Distributors, VADs, VARs, and their customers higher ownership satisfaction and lower support costs.

FEATURES

- Flexible "in-warranty" and "out-of warranty" repair options
- Reasonable prices for spare parts
- Assures compatibility with current engineering levels
- Comprehensive failure analysis
- Quick 48 or 24 hour turnaround for parts exchange
- One year warranty on all repair services
- Optional on-site services
- Automated testing and tracking of repaired parts

ADVANTAGES

- Reduces reseller warranty and support costs
- Reduces reseller costs by eliminating fixed inventory expenses
- Increases reseller customer satisfaction by increasing system uptime
- Reduces reseller overhead by simplifying operations
- Increases reseller product integrity by maintaining systems to most recent levels

NetWare™ is a trademark of Novell Corporation.
VINES™ is a trademark of Banyan Corporation.

November 1991
Order Number: 272048-001

REPAIR SERVICES FOR INTEL OEM MODULES AND PLATFORMS

FLEXIBLE REPAIR SERVICE OPTIONS

Intel's product warranties meet or exceed the industry standard. We back our warranty with flexible repair and replacement support designed to reduce the time to repair and increase customer satisfaction. For out-of-warranty situations, Intel provides a variety of repair and spare service levels to address a range of business needs. They include carry-in repair, return to factory repair, parts exchange, and even on-site maintenance contracts.

Repair services can be custom tailored to meet unique customer needs.

WARRANTY REPAIR SERVICE

Each Intel product includes warranty repair services. Consult your local sales representative for descriptions of the warranty service included for a particular product. During the warranty period, Intel is responsible for the repair expense. All warranty repair service includes these key features:

- Free labor on materials during the warranty period
- Carry-in locations throughout the U.S. [1]
- Mall-in service direct to Intel repair centers in the U.S.
- Access to Intel repair centers in England and Japan
- Quick turnaround time on repairs

Warranty repair service is initiated by calling the Intel toll free support number for the U.S. and Canada. International customers call their local Intel sales office. Depending on the product's warranty terms, customers are given shipping or carry-in instructions and authorization control numbers. Intel performs the warranty repair and returns the module or platform promptly.

OUT-OF-WARRANTY REPAIR SERVICE

With on-going repair services, resellers can extend repair and support to customers beyond the warranty period. These services provide assurance of uninterrupted system availability for customers. Resellers and their customers can choose from a range of options most suited to their particular business needs.

Standard Repair Service: Direct Return Authorization (DRA)

This service option provides standard OEM Module or Platform repair service at the most economical rate for the Intel customer. Defective products or parts are returned to Intel, freight prepaid. Intel repairs and tests the part, and updates the repaired item with all mandatory engineering change orders. Repairs are completed within 10 days of receipt of the product. Serial number integrity is maintained for all parts. The repaired part includes a one year warranty (all parts and labor). A report is included with each repair showing the nature of the failure. There is a flat rate charged for all repairs.

Exchange Service: Return Replacement Authorization (RRA)

This service provides 48-hour parts exchange at economical rates for the Intel OEM Module and Platform customer. This service is faster than Standard Repair Service (DRA). Intel provides the customer with a replacement part after receipt of the defective part. Defective parts are returned to Intel, freight prepaid. Intel returns the replaced part at the latest mandatory engineering change order level. Replacement parts are shipped within 48-hours of receipt of the defective part. Exchanged parts carry a one year warranty. There is a flat exchange rate for each part.

Express Exchange Service: Before Return Replacement (BRR)

This service is designed as an emergency exchange option offering all of the advantages of the Exchange Service (RRA), but with a faster 24-hour turnaround. Intel provides the customer with a replacement part before receiving the defective part. Replacement parts are shipped within 24-hours of the customer request, subject to availability. Defective parts must be returned to Intel, freight prepaid, within 30 days of receiving the exchanged part, or the customer is invoiced at the current list price of the replacement part. Intel returns the exchanged part at the latest mandatory engineering change order level. Customers are advised of availability when service is requested. Exchanged parts carry a one year warranty. There is a flat exchange rate for each part.

[1] May not apply to some products. Consult your Intel sales representative for details.

REPAIR SERVICES FOR INTEL OEM MODULES AND PLATFORMS

SPARE PART SALES

Sale of spare parts for Intel OEM Modules and Platforms provides resellers with parts when and where they are neededworldwide. This service reduces the reseller's inventory and management costs. Lead times for spare part orders vary depending on product availability. A 48-hour delivery option is available for a flat rate fee, subject to product availability. Minimum per order amounts can apply. Spare sales is supported by logistics, engineering, and technical resources for optimal parts availability and management.

OPTIONAL ON-SITE SERVICES

Intel offers resellers and their customers complete on-site installation, repair, and maintenance services. These services are designed to get Intel microprocessor-based systems and the networks that they use up and runningfast. Once installed, Intel is dedicated to keeping them running at maximum efficiency, while controlling costs. On-site service can be complemented with an Intel software support contract for Novell NetWare* or Banyan VINES* network software. Service centers staffed by trained and certified Customer Engineers are located throughout the United States, Canada, Europe, and Asia. Consult your local Intel sales representative for more details about On-Site Installation and Maintenance Contracts.

INTEL QUALITY STANDARDS

Intel is dedicated to delivering repair services that offer the highest quality to meet customer business requirements and maintain product integrity. Intel uses the most innovative technologies and techniques to deliver these services, because we understand that the timeliness and quality of repairs and spares is crucial to a reseller's business.

Intel maintains substantial facilities, test equipment, and highly trained engineering talent worldwide. We use accurate diagnostic techniques for fast turnaround at reasonable costs. Repair services are performed in a controlled environment and subject to strict Intel quality procedures. All components are inspected and tested before and after repair services. Boards that pass through Intel quality assurance specifications meet exacting performance standards, including environmental extremes.

Intel stands behind the quality of service and repairs with a full 12- month warranty.

ORDERING INFORMATION

For repair service pricing, spare parts pricing, parts availability, or repair authorization in the continental United States, Alaska, Hawaii, and Canada, call the Intel toll free support line at 1-800-INTEL-4-U. Select voice prompt 1 labeled "hardware support". Follow the easy touch tone phone activated instructions to obtain information. For volume repair and spare contract pricing, or for information in Europe and Japan, contact your local Intel sales representative.

Customers requesting repair service are asked for the following information:

- Part number of module, or system type
- Serial number of module or system
- Purchase order number, if warranty period has expired
- Shipping and billing address(s)
- Customer contact name

Intel assigns an RRA, DRA, or BRR control number to each repair order. This ensures safe handling and return of the repaired part. All items returned to Intel for repair must have this control number clearly marked on the outside of the package. This control number should be used on any associated paperwork that is returned with the part. For the U.S. and Canada, return parts for repair to:

Intel Corporation
Customer Support Operations
Attention: DRA/RRA/BRR # __________
Phoenix, Arizona 85027

NORTH AMERICAN SALES OFFICES

ALABAMA

Intel Corp.
5015 Bradford Dr., #2
Huntsville 35805
Tel: (205) 830-4010
FAX: (205) 837-2640

ARIZONA

†Intel Corp.
410 North 44th Street
Suite 500
Phoenix 85008
Tel: (602) 231-0386
FAX: (602) 244-0446

CALIFORNIA

†Intel Corp.
21515 Vanowen Street
Suite 116
Canoga Park 91303
Tel: (818) 704-8500
FAX: (818) 340-1144

Intel Corp.
1 Sierra Gate Plaza
Suite 280C
Roseville 95678
Tel: (916) 782-8086
FAX: (916) 782-8153

†Intel Corp.
9665 Chesapeake Dr.
Suite 325
San Diego 92123
Tel: (619) 292-8086
FAX: (619) 292-0628

*†Intel Corp.
400 N. Tustin Avenue
Suite 450
Santa Ana 92705
Tel: (714) 835-9642
TWX: 910-595-1114
FAX: (714) 541-9157

*†Intel Corp.
San Tomas 4
2700 San Tomas Expressway
2nd Floor
Santa Clara 95051
Tel: (408) 986-8086
TWX: 910-338-0255
FAX: (408) 727-2620

COLORADO

Intel Corp.
4445 Northpark Drive
Suite 100
Colorado Springs 80907
Tel: (719) 594-6622
FAX: (303) 594-0720

*†Intel Corp.
600 S. Cherry St.
Suite 700
Denver 80222
Tel: (303) 321-8086
TWX: 910-931-2289
FAX: (303) 322-8670

CONNECTICUT

†Intel Corp.
301 Lee Farm Corporate Park
83 Wooster Heights Rd.
Danbury 06810
Tel: (203) 748-3130
FAX: (203) 794-0339

FLORIDA

†Intel Corp.
800 Fairway Drive
Suite 160
Deerfield Beach 33441
Tel: (305) 421-0506
FAX: (305) 421-2444

†Intel Corp.
5850 T.G. Lee Blvd.
Suite 340
Orlando 32822
Tel: (407) 240-8000
FAX: (407) 240-8097

GEORGIA

†Intel Corp.
20 Technology Parkway
Suite 150
Norcross 30092
Tel: (404) 449-0541
FAX: (404) 605-9762

ILLINOIS

*†Intel Corp.
Woodfield Corp. Center III
300 N. Martingale Road
Suite 400
Schaumburg 60173
Tel: (708) 605-8031
FAX: (708) 706-9762

INDIANA

†Intel Corp.
8910 Purdue Road
Suite 350
Indianapolis 46268
Tel: (317) 875-0623
FAX: (317) 875-8938

MARYLAND

*†Intel Corp.
10010 Junction Dr.
Suite 200
Annapolis Junction 20701
Tel: (301) 206-2860
FAX: (301) 206-3677
(301) 206-3678

MASSACHUSETTS

*†Intel Corp.
Westford Corp. Center
3 Carlisle Road
2nd Floor
Westford 01886
Tel: (508) 692-0960
TWX: 710-343-6333
FAX: (508) 692-7867

MICHIGAN

†Intel Corp.
7071 Orchard Lake Road
Suite 100
West Bloomfield 48322
Tel: (313) 851-8096
FAX: (313) 851-8770

MINNESOTA

†Intel Corp.
3500 W. 80th St.
Suite 360
Bloomington 55431
Tel: (612) 835-6722
TWX: 910-576-2867
FAX: (612) 831-6497

NEW JERSEY

*†Intel Corp.
Lincroft Office Center
125 Half Mile Road
Red Bank 07701
Tel: (908) 747-2233
FAX: (908) 747-0983

NEW YORK

*Intel Corp.
850 Crosskeys Office Park
Fairport 14450
Tel: (716) 425-2750
TWX: 510-253-7391
FAX: (716) 223-2561

*†Intel Corp.
2950 Express Dr., South
Suite 130
Islandia 11722
Tel: (516) 231-3300
TWX: 510-227-6236
FAX: (516) 348-7939

†Intel Corp.
300 Westage Business Center
Suite 230
Fishkill 12524
Tel: (914) 897-3860
FAX: (914) 897-3125

OHIO

*†Intel Corp.
3401 Park Center Drive
Suite 220
Dayton 45414
Tel: (513) 890-5350
TWX: 810-450-2528
FAX: (513) 890-8658

*†Intel Corp.
25700 Science Park Dr.
Suite 100
Beachwood 44122
Tel: (216) 464-2736
TWX: 810-427-9298
FAX: (804) 282-0673

OKLAHOMA

Intel Corp.
6801 N. Broadway
Suite 115
Oklahoma City 73162
Tel: (405) 848-8086
FAX: (405) 840-9819

OREGON

†Intel Corp.
15254 N.W. Greenbrier Pkwy.
Building B
Beaverton 97006
Tel: (503) 645-8051
TWX: 910-467-8741
FAX: (503) 645-8181

PENNSYLVANIA

*†Intel Corp.
925 Harvest Drive
Suite 200
Blue Bell 19422
Tel: (215) 641-1000
FAX: (215) 641-0785

*†Intel Corp.
400 Penn Center Blvd.
Suite 610
Pittsburgh 15235
Tel: (412) 823-4970
FAX: (412) 829-7578

PUERTO RICO

†Intel Corp.
South Industrial Park
P.O. Box 910
Las Piedras 00671
Tel: (809) 733-8616

TEXAS

†Intel Corp.
8911 N. Capital of Texas Hwy.
Suite 4230
Austin 78759
Tel: (512) 794-8086
FAX: (512) 338-9335

*†Intel Corp.
12000 Ford Road
Suite 400
Dallas 75234
Tel: (214) 241-8087
FAX: (214) 484-1180

*†Intel Corp.
7322 S.W. Freeway
Suite 1490
Houston 77074
Tel: (713) 988-8086
TWX: 910-881-2490
FAX: (713) 988-3660

UTAH

†Intel Corp.
428 East 6400 South
Suite 104
Murray 84107
Tel: (801) 263-8051
FAX: (801) 268-1457

WASHINGTON

†Intel Corp.
155 108th Avenue N.E.
Suite 386
Bellevue 98004
Tel: (206) 453-8086
TWX: 910-443-3002
FAX: (206) 451-9556

Intel Corp.
408 N. Mullan Road
Suite 102
Spokane 99206
Tel: (509) 928-8086
FAX: (509) 928-9467

WISCONSIN

Intel Corp.
330 S. Executive Dr.
Suite 102
Brookfield 53005
Tel: (414) 784-8087
FAX: (414) 796-2115

CANADA

BRITISH COLUMBIA

Intel Semiconductor of
Canada, Ltd.
4585 Canada Way
Suite 202
Burnaby V5G 4L6
Tel: (604) 298-0387
FAX: (604) 298-8234

ONTARIO

†Intel Semiconductor of
Canada, Ltd.
2650 Queensview Drive
Suite 250
Ottawa K2B 8H6
Tel: (613) 829-9714
FAX: (613) 820-5936

†Intel Semiconductor of
Canada, Ltd.
190 Attwell Drive
Suite 500
Rexdale M9W 6H8
Tel: (416) 675-2105
FAX: (416) 675-2438

QUEBEC

†Intel Semiconductor of
Canada, Ltd.
1 Rue Holiday
Suite 115
Tour East
Pt. Claire H9R 5N3
Tel: (514) 694-9130
FAX: 514-694-0064

†Sales and Service Office
*Field Application Location

NORTH AMERICAN DISTRIBUTORS

ALABAMA

Arrow Electronics, Inc.
1015 Henderson Road
Huntsville 35806
Tel: (205) 837-6955
FAX: (205) 721-1581

Hamilton/Avnet Electronics
4960 Corporate Drive, #135
Huntsville 35805
Tel: (205) 837-7210
FAX: (205) 721-0356

MTI Systems Sales
4950 Corporate Drive
Suite 120
Huntsville 35805
Tel: (205) 830-9526
FAX: (205) 830-9557

Pioneer/Technologies Group, Inc.
4835 University Square, #5
Huntsville 35805
Tel: (205) 837-9300
FAX: (205) 837-9358

ARIZONA

†Arrow Electronics, Inc.
4134 E. Wood Street
Phoenix 85040
Tel: (602) 437-0750
FAX: (602) 252-9109

Avnet Computer
30 South McKemy Avenue
Chandler 85226
Tel: (602) 961-6460
FAX: (602) 961-4787

Hamilton/Avnet Electronics
30 South McKemy Avenue
Chandler 85226
Tel: (602) 961-6403
FAX: (602) 961-1331

Wyle Distribution Group
4141 E. Raymond
Phoenix 85040
Tel: (602) 437-2088
FAX: (602) 437-2124

CALIFORNIA

Arrow Commercial System Group
1502 Crocker Avenue
Hayward 94544
Tel: (415) 489-5371
FAX: (415) 489-9393

Arrow Commercial System Group
14242 Chambers Road
Tustin 92680
Tel: (714) 544-0200
FAX: (714) 731-8438

†Arrow Electronics, Inc.
19748 Dearborn Street
Chatsworth 91311
Tel: (818) 701-7500
FAX: (818) 772-8930

†Arrow Electronics, Inc.
9511 Ridgehaven Court
San Diego 92123
Tel: (619) 565-4800
FAX: (619) 279-8062

†Arrow Electronics, Inc.
1180 Murphy Avenue
San Jose 95131
Tel: (408) 441-9700
FAX: (408) 453-4810

†Arrow Electronics, Inc.
2961 Dow Avenue
Tustin 92680
Tel: (714) 838-5422
FAX: (714) 838-4151

Avnet Computer
3170 Pullman Street
Costa Mesa 92626
Tel: (714) 641-4121
FAX: (714) 641-4170

Avnet Computer
1361B West 190th Street
Gardena 90248
Tel: (800) 345-3870
FAX: (213) 327-5389

Avnet Computer
755 Sunrise Blvd., #150
Roseville 95661
Tel: (916) 781-2521
FAX: (916) 781-3819

Avnet Computer
1175 Bordeaux Drive, #A
Sunnyvale 94089
Tel: (408) 743-3304
FAX: (408) 743-3348

Avnet Computer
21150 Califa Street
Woodland Hills 91376
Tel: (808) 345-3870
FAX: (818) 594-8333

†Hamilton/Avnet Electronics
3170 Pullman Street
Costa Mesa 92626
Tel: (714) 641-4100
FAX: (714) 754-6033

†Hamilton/Avnet Electronics
1175 Bordeaux Drive, #A
Sunnyvale 94089
Tel: (408) 743-3300
FAX: (408) 745-6679

†Hamilton/Avnet Electronics
4545 Viewridge Avenue
San Diego 92123
Tel: (619) 571-1900
FAX: (619) 571-8761

†Hamilton/Avnet Electronics
21150 Califa St.
Woodland Hills 91367
Tel: (818) 594-0403
FAX: (818) 594-8234

†Hamilton/Avnet Electronics
1361B West 190th Street
Gardena 90248
Tel: (213) 516-8600
FAX: (213) 217-6822

†Hamilton/Avnet Electronics
755 Sunrise Avenue, #150
Roseville 95661
Tel: (916) 925-2216
FAX: (916) 925-3478

Pioneer/Technologies Group, Inc.
134 Rio Robles
San Jose 95134
Tel: (408) 954-9100
FAX: 408-954-9113

†Wyle Distribution Group
124 Maryland Street
El Segundo 90245
Tel: (213) 322-8100
FAX: (213) 416-1151

Wyle Distribution Group
7431 Chapman Ave.
Garden Grove 92641
Tel: (714) 891-1717
FAX: (714) 891-1621

†Wyle Distribution Group
2951 Sunrise Blvd., Suite 175
Rancho Cordova 95742
Tel: (916) 638-5282
FAX: (916) 638-1491

†Wyle Distribution Group
9525 Chesapeake Drive
San Diego 92123
Tel: (619) 565-9171
FAX: (619) 365-0512

†Wyle Distribution Group
3000 Bowers Avenue
Santa Clara 95051
Tel: (408) 727-2500
FAX: (408) 727-5896

†Wyle Distribution Group
17872 Cowan Avenue
Irvine 92714
Tel: (714) 863-9953
FAX: (714) 263-0473

†Wyle Distribution Group
26010 Mureau Road, #150
Calabasas 91302
Tel: (818) 880-9000
FAX: (818) 880-5510

COLORADO

Arrow Electronics, Inc.
3254 C Frazer Street
Aurora 80011
Tel: (303) 373-5616
FAX: (303) 373-5760

†Hamilton/Avnet Electronics
9605 Maroon Circle, #200
Englewood 80112
Tel: (303) 799-7800
FAX: (303) 799-7801

†Wyle Distribution Group
451 E. 124th Avenue
Thornton 80241
Tel: (303) 457-9953
FAX: (303) 457-4831

CONNECTICUT

†Arrow Electronics, Inc.
12 Beaumont Road
Wallingford 06492
Tel: (203) 265-7741
FAX: (203) 265-7988

Avnet Computer
55 Federal Road, #103
Danbury 06810
Tel: (203) 797-2880
FAX: (203) 791-9050

†Hamilton/Avnet Electronics
55 Federal Road, #103
Danbury 06810
Tel: (203) 743-6077
FAX: (203) 791-9050

†Pioneer/Standard Electronics
112 Main Street
Norwalk 06851
Tel: (203) 853-1515
FAX: (203) 838-9901

FLORIDA

†Arrow Electronics, Inc.
400 Fairway Drive, #102
Deerfield Beach 33441
Tel: (305) 429-8200
FAX: (305) 428-3991

†Arrow Electronics, Inc.
37 Skyline Drive, #3101
Lake Mary 32746
Tel: (407) 333-9300
FAX: (407) 333-9320

Avnet Computer
3343 W. Commercial Blvd.
Bldg. C/D, Suite 107
Ft. Lauderdale 33309
Tel: (305) 979-9067
FAX: (305) 730-0368

Avnet Computer
3247 Tech Drive North
St. Petersburg 33716
Tel: (813) 573-5524
FAX: (813) 572-4324

†Hamilton/Avnet Electronics
5371 N.W. 33rd Avenue
Ft. Lauderdale 33309
Tel: (305) 484-5016
FAX: (305) 484-8369

†Hamilton/Avnet Electronics
3247 Tech Drive North
St. Petersburg 33716
Tel: (813) 573-3930
FAX: (813) 572-4329

†Hamilton/Avnet Electronics
7079 University Boulevard
Winter Park 32791
Tel: (407) 657-3300
FAX: (407) 678-1878

†Pioneer/Technologies Group, Inc.
337 Northlake Blvd., Suite 1000
Alta Monte Springs 32701
Tel: (407) 834-9090
FAX: (407) 834-0865

Pioneer/Technologies Group, Inc.
674 S. Military Trail
Deerfield Beach 33442
Tel: (305) 428-8877
FAX: (305) 481-2950

GEORGIA

Arrow Commercial System Group
3400 C. Corporate Way
Duluth 30136
Tel: (404) 623-8825
FAX: (404) 623-8802

†Arrow Electronics, Inc.
4250 E. Rivergreen Pkwy., #E
Duluth 30136
Tel: (404) 497-1300
FAX: (404) 476-1493

Avnet Computer
3425 Corporate Way, #G
Duluth 30136
Tel: (404) 623-5452
FAX: (404) 476-0125

Hamilton/Avnet Electronics
3425 Corporate Way, #G
Duluth 30136
Tel: (404) 446-0611
FAX: (404) 446-1011

Pioneer/Technologies Group, Inc.
4250 C. Rivergreen Parkway
Duluth 30136
Tel: (404) 623-1003
FAX: (404) 623-0665

ILLINOIS

†Arrow Electronics, Inc.
1140 W. Thorndale Rd.
Itasca 60143
Tel: (708) 250-0500

Avnet Computer
1124 Thorndale Avenue
Bensenville 60106
Tel: (708) 860-8573
FAX: (708) 773-7976

†Hamilton/Avnet Electronics
1130 Thorndale Avenue
Bensenville 60106
Tel: (708) 860-7700
FAX: (708) 860-8530

MTI Systems
1140 W. Thorndale Avenue
Itasca 60143
Tel: (708) 250-8222
FAX: (708) 250-8275

†Pioneer/Standard Electronics
2171 Executive Dr., Suite 200
Addison 60101
Tel: (708) 495-9680
FAX: (708) 495-9831

INDIANA

†Arrow Electronics, Inc.
7108 Lakeview Parkway West Dr.
Indianapolis 46268
Tel: (317) 299-2071
FAX: (317) 299-2379

Avnet Computer
485 Gradle Drive
Carmel 46032
Tel: (317) 575-8029
FAX: (317) 844-4964

Hamilton/Avnet Electronics
485 Gradle Drive
Carmel 46032
Tel: (317) 844-9333
FAX: (317) 844-5921

†Pioneer/Standard Electronics
9350 Priority Way West Dr.
Indianapolis 46250
Tel: (317) 573-0880
FAX: (317) 573-0979

†Certified VAD

NORTH AMERICAN DISTRIBUTORS (Contd.)

IOWA

Hamilton/Avnet Electronics
2335A Blairsferry Rd., N.E.
Cedar Rapids 52402
Tel: (319) 362-4757
FAX: (319) 393-7050

KANSAS

Arrow Electronics, Inc.
8208 Melrose Dr., Suite 210
Lenexa 66214
Tel: (913) 541-9542
FAX: (913) 541-0328

Avnet Computer
15313 W. 95th Street
Lenexa 61219
Tel: (913) 541-7989
FAX: (913) 541-7904

†Hamilton/Avnet Electronics
15313 W. 95th
Overland Park 66215
Tel: (913) 888-1055
FAX: (913) 541-7951

KENTUCKY

Hamilton/Avnet Electronics
805 A. Newtown Circle
Lexington 40511
Tel: (606) 259-1475
FAX: (606) 252-3238

MARYLAND

Arrow Commercial Systems Group
200 Perry Parkway
Gaithersburg 20877
Tel: (301) 670-1600
FAX: (301) 670-0188

†Arrow Electronics, Inc.
8300 Guilford Road, #H
Columbia 21046
Tel: (301) 995-6002
FAX: (301) 995-6201

Avnet Computer
7172 Columbia Gateway Dr., #G
Columbia 21045
Tel: (301) 995-0020
FAX: (301) 995-3515

†Hamilton/Avnet Electronics
7172 Columbia Gateway Dr., #F
Columbia 21045
Tel: (301) 995-3554
FAX: (301) 995-3515

†North Atlantic Industries
Systems Division
7125 Riverwood Dr.
Columbia 21046
Tel: (301) 290-3999

†Pioneer/Technologies Group, Inc.
15810 Gaither Road
Gaithersburg 20877
Tel: (301) 921-0660
FAX: (301) 670-6746

MASSACHUSETTS

Arrow Electronics, Inc.
25 Upton Dr.
Wilmington 01887
Tel: (508) 658-0900
FAX: (508) 694-1754

Avnet Computer
10 D Centennial Drive
Peabody 01960
Tel: (508) 532-9886
FAX: (508) 532-9660

†Hamilton/Avnet Electronics
10D Centennial Drive
Peabody 01960
Tel: (508) 531-7430
FAX: (508) 532-9802

†Pioneer/Standard Electronics
44 Hartwell Avenue
Lexington 02173
Tel: (617) 861-9200
FAX: (617) 863-1547

Wyle Distribution Group
15 Third Avenue
Burlington 01803
Tel: (617) 272-7300
FAX: (617) 272-6809

MICHIGAN

†Arrow Electronics, Inc.
19880 Haggerty Road
Livonia 48152
Tel: (313) 665-4100
FAX: (313) 462-2686

Avnet Computer
2876 28th Street, S.W., #5
Grandville 49418
Tel: (616) 531-9607
FAX: (616) 531-0059

Avnet Computer
41650 Garden Road
Novi 48375
Tel: (313) 347-1820
FAX: (313) 347-4067

Hamilton/Avnet Electronics
2876 28th Street, S.W., #5
Grandville 49418
Tel: (616) 243-8805
FAX: (616) 531-0059

Hamilton/Avnet Electronics
41650 Garden Brook Rd., #100
Novi 48375
Tel: (313) 347-4270
FAX: (313) 347-4021

†Pioneer/Standard Electronics
4505 Broadmoor S.E.
Grand Rapids 49512
Tel: (616) 698-1800
FAX: (616) 698-1831

†Pioneer/Standard Electronics
13485 Stamford
Livonia 48150
Tel: (313) 525-1800
FAX: (313) 427-3720

MINNESOTA

†Arrow Electronics, Inc.
10120A West 76th Street
Eden Prairie 55344
Tel: (612) 829-5588
FAX: (612) 942-7803

Avnet Computer
10000 West 76th Street
Eden Prairie 55344
Tel: (612) 829-0025
FAX: (612) 944-2781

†Hamilton/Avnet Electronics
12400 Whitewater Drive
Minnetonka 55343
Tel: (612) 932-0600
FAX: (612) 932-0613

†Pioneer/Standard Electronics
7625 Golden Triange Dr., #G
Eden Prairie 55344
Tel: (612) 944-3355
FAX: (612) 944-3794

MISSOURI

†Arrow Electronics, Inc.
2380 Schuetz Road
St. Louis 63141
Tel: (314) 567-6888
FAX: (314) 567-1164

Avnet Computer
739 Goddard Avenue
Chesterfield 63005
Tel: (314) 537-2725
FAX: (314) 537-4248

†Hamilton/Avnet Electronics
741 Goddard
Chesterfield 63005
Tel: (314) 537-1600
FAX: (314) 537-4248

NEW HAMPSHIRE

Avnet Computer
2 Executive Park Drive
Bedford 03102
Tel: (603) 624-6630
FAX: (603) 624-2402

NEW JERSEY

†Arrow Electronics, Inc.
4 East Stow Road
Unit 11
Marlton 08053
Tel: (609) 596-8000
FAX: (609) 596-9632

†Arrow Electronics, Inc.
6 Century Drive
Parsipanny 07054
Tel: (201) 538-0900
FAX: (201) 538-4962

Avnet Computer
1-B Keystone Ave., Bldg. 36
Cherry Hill 08003
Tel: (609) 424-8961
FAX: (609) 751-2502

Avnet Computer
10 Industrial Road
Fairfield 07006
Tel: (201) 882-2879
FAX: (201) 808-9251

†Hamilton/Avnet Electronics
1 Keystone Ave., Bldg. 36
Cherry Hill 08003
Tel: (609) 424-0110
FAX: (609) 751-2552

†Hamilton/Avnet Electronics
10 Industrial
Fairfield 07006
Tel: (201) 575-3390
FAX: (201) 575-5839

†MTI Systems Sales
6 Century Drive
Parsippany 07054
Tel: (201) 539-6496
FAX: (201) 539-6430

†Pioneer/Standard Electronics
14-A Madison Rd.
Fairfield 07006
Tel: (201) 575-3510
FAX: (201) 575-3454

NEW MEXICO

Alliance Electronics Inc.
10510 Research Avenue
Albuquerque 87123
Tel: (505) 292-3360
FAX: (505) 275-6392

Avnet Computer
7801 Academy Road
Bldg. 1, Suite 204
Albuquerque 87109
Tel: (505) 828-9725
FAX: (505) 828-0360

†Hamilton/Avnet Electronics
7801 Academy Rd. N.E.
Bldg. 1, Suite 204
Albuquerque 87108
Tel: (505) 765-1500
FAX: (505) 243-1395

NEW YORK

†Arrow Electronics, Inc.
3375 Brighton Henrietta Townline Rd.
Rochester 14623
Tel: (716) 427-0300
FAX: (716) 427-0735

Arrow Electronics, Inc.
20 Oser Avenue
Hauppauge 11788
Tel: (516) 231-1000
FAX: (516) 231-1072

Avnet Computer
933 Motor Parkway
Hauppauge 11788
Tel: (516) 231-9040
FAX: (516) 434-7426

Avnet Computer
2060 Townline
Rochester 14623
Tel: (716) 272-9306
FAX: (716) 272-9685

†Hamilton/Avnet Electronics
933 Motor Parkway
Hauppauge 11788
Tel: (516) 231-9800
FAX: (516) 434-7426

†Hamilton/Avnet Electronics
2060 Townline Rd.
Rochester 14623
Tel: (716) 292-0730
FAX: (716) 292-0810

Hamilton/Avnet Electronics
103 Twin Oaks Drive
Syracuse 13120
Tel: (315) 437-2641
FAX: (315) 432-0740

MTI Systems
50 Horseblock Road
Brookhaven 11719
Tel: (516) 924-9400
FAX: (516) 924-1103

MTI Systems
1 Penn Plaza
250 W. 34th Street
New York 10119
Tel: (212) 643-1280
FAX: (212) 643-1288

Pioneer/Standard Electronics
68 Corporate Drive
Binghamton 13904
Tel: (607) 722-9300
FAX: (607) 722-9562

†Pioneer/Standard Electronics
60 Crossway Park West
Woodbury, Long Island 11797
Tel: (516) 921-8700
FAX: (516) 921-2143

†Pioneer/Standard Electronics
840 Fairport Park
Fairport 14450
Tel: (716) 381-7070
FAX: (716) 381-5955

NORTH CAROLINA

†Arrow Electronics, Inc.
5240 Greensdairy Road
Raleigh 27604
Tel: (919) 876-3132
FAX: (919) 878-9517

Avnet Computer
2725 Millbrook Rd., #123
Raleigh 27604
Tel: (919) 790-1735
FAX: (919) 872-4972

Hamilton/Avnet Electronics
5250-77 Center Dr. #350
Charlotte 28217
Tel: (704) 527-2485
FAX: (704) 527-8058

†Hamilton/Avnet Electronics
3510 Spring Forest Drive
Raleigh 27604
Tel: (919) 878-0819

Pioneer/Technologies Group, Inc.
9401 L-Southern Pine Blvd.
Charlotte 28210
Tel: (704) 527-8188
FAX: (704) 522-8564

Pioneer Technologies Group, Inc.
2810 Meridian Parkway, #148
Durham 27713
Tel: (919) 544-5400
FAX: (919) 544-5885

OHIO

Arrow Commercial System Group
284 Cramer Creek Court
Dublin 43017
Tel: (614) 889-9347
FAX: (614) 889-9680

†Arrow Electronics, Inc.
6573 Cochran Road, #E
Solon 44139
Tel: (216) 248-3990
FAX: (216) 248-1106

Arrow Electronics, Inc.
8200 Washington Village Dr.
Centerville 45458
Tel: (513) 435-5563
FAX: (513) 435-2049

†Certified VAD

NORTH AMERICAN DISTRIBUTORS (Contd.)

OHIO (Contd.)

Avnet Computer
7764 Washington Village Dr.
Dayton 45459
Tel: (513) 439-6756
FAX: (513) 439-6719

Avnet Computer
30325 Bainbridge Rd., Bldg. A
Solon 44139
Tel: (216) 349-2505
FAX: (216) 349-1894

†Hamilton/Avnet Electronics
7760 Washington Village Dr.
Dayton 45459
Tel: (513) 439-6733
FAX: (513) 439-6711

†Hamilton/Avnet Electronics
30325 Bainbridge
Solon 44139
Tel: (800) 543-2984
FAX: (216) 349-1894

Hamilton/Avnet Electronics
2600 Corp Exchange Drive, #180
Columbus 43231
Tel: (614) 882-7004
FAX: (614) 882-8650

MTI Systems Sales
23404 Commerce Park Road
Beachwood 44122
Tel: (216) 464-6688
FAX: (216) 464-3564

†Pioneer/Standard Electronics
4433 Interpoint Boulevard
Dayton 45424
Tel: (513) 236-9900
FAX: (513) 236-8133

†Pioneer/Standard Electronics
4800 E. 131st Street
Cleveland 44105
Tel: (216) 587-3600
FAX: (216) 663-1004

OKLAHOMA

Arrow Electronics, Inc.
12111 East 51st Street, #101
Tulsa 74146
Tel: (918) 252-7537
FAX: (918) 254-0917

†Hamilton/Avnet Electronics
12121 E. 51st St., Suite 102A
Tulsa 74146
Tel: (918) 664-0444
FAX: (918) 250-8763

OREGON

†Almac Electronics Corp.
1885 N.W. 169th Place
Beaverton 97006
Tel: (503) 629-8090
FAX: 503-645-0611

Avnet Computer
9409 Southwest Nimbus Ave.
Beaverton 97005
Tel: (503) 627-0900
FAX: (503) 526-6242

†Hamilton/Avnet Electronics
9409 S.W. Nimbus Ave.
Beaverton 97005
Tel: (503) 627-0201
FAX: (503) 641-4012

Wyle
9640 Sunshine Court
Bldg. G, Suite 200
Beaverton 97005
Tel: (503) 643-7900
FAX: (503) 646-5466

PENNSYLVANIA

Avnet Computer
213 Executive Drive, #320
Mars 16046
Tel: (412) 772-1888
FAX: (412) 772-1890

Hamilton/Avnet Electronics
213 Executive, #320
Mars 16045
Tel: (412) 281-4152
FAX: (412) 772-1890

Pioneer/Technologies Group, Inc.
259 Kappa Drive
Pittsburgh 15238
Tel: (412) 782-2300
FAX: (412) 963-8255

†Pioneer/Technologies Group, Inc.
500 Enterprise Road
Keith Valley Business Center
Horsham 19044
Tel: (215) 674-4000
FAX: (215) 674-3107

TENNESSEE

Arrow Commercial System Group
3635 Knight Road, #7
Memphis 38118
Tel: (901) 367-0540
FAX: (901) 367-2081

TEXAS

Arrow Electronics, Inc.
3220 Commander Drive
Carrollton 75006
Tel: (214) 380-6464
FAX: (214) 248-7208

Avnet Computer
4004 Beltline, Suite 200
Dallas 75244
Tel: (214) 308-8181
FAX: (214) 308-8129

Avnet Computer
1235 North Loop West, #525
Houston 77008
Tel: (713) 867-7500
FAX: (713) 861-6851

†Hamilton/Avnet Electronics
1826-F Kramer Lane
Austin 78758
Tel: (800) 772-5668
FAX: (512) 832-4315

†Hamilton/Avnet Electronics
4004 Beltline, #200
Dallas 75244
Tel: (214) 308-8111
FAX: (214) 308-8109

†Hamilton/Avnet Electronics
1235 N. Loop West, #521
Houston 77008
Tel: (713) 240-7733
FAX: (713) 861-6541

†Pioneer/Standard Electronics
1826-D Kramer Lane
Austin 78758
Tel: (512) 835-4000
FAX: (512) 835-9829

†Pioneer/Standard Electronics
13765 Beta Road
Dallas 75244
Tel: (214) 386-7300
FAX: (214) 490-6419

†Pioneer/Standard Electronics
10530 Rockley Road, #100
Houston 77099
Tel: (713) 495-4700
FAX: (713) 495-5642

†Wyle Distribution Group
1810 Greenville Avenue
Richardson 75081
Tel: (214) 235-9953
FAX: (214) 644-5064

Wyle Distribution Group
4030 West Braker Lane, #330
Austin 78758
Tel: (512) 345-8853
FAX: (512) 345-9330

Wyle Distribution Group
11001 South Wilcrest, #100
Houston 77099
Tel: (713) 879-9953
FAX: (713) 879-6540

UTAH

Arrow Electronics, Inc.
1946 W. Parkway Blvd.
Salt Lake City 84119
Tel: (801) 973-6913

Avnet Computer
1100 E. 6600 South, #150
Salt Lake City 84121
Tel: (801) 266-1115
FAX: (801) 266-0362

Avnet Computer
17761 Northeast 78th Place
Redmond 98052
Tel: (206) 867-0160
FAX: (206) 867-0161

†Hamilton/Avnet Electronics
1100 East 6600 South, #120
Salt Lake City 84121
Tel: (801) 972-2800
FAX: (801) 263-0104

†Wyle Distribution Group
1325 West 2200 South, #E
West Valley 84119
Tel: (801) 974-9953
FAX: (801) 972-2524

WASHINGTON

†Almac Electronics Corp.
14360 S.E. Eastgate Way
Bellevue 98007
Tel: (206) 643-9992
FAX: (206) 643-9709

†Hamilton/Avnet Electronics
17761 N.E. 78th Place, #C
Redmond 98052
Tel: (206) 241-8555
FAX: (206) 241-5472

Wyle Distribution Group
15385 N.E. 90th Street
Redmond 98052
Tel: (206) 881-1150
FAX: (206) 881-1567

WISCONSIN

Arrow Electronics, Inc.
200 N. Patrick Blvd., Ste. 100
Brookfield 53005
Tel: (414) 792-0150
FAX: (414) 792-0156

Avnet Computer
20875 Crossroads Circle, #400
Waukesha 53186
Tel: (414) 784-8205
FAX: (414) 784-6006

†Hamilton/Avnet Electronics
28875 Crossroads Circle, #400
Waukesha 53186
Tel: (414) 784-4510
FAX: (414) 784-9509

Pioneer/Standard Electronics
120 Bishops Way #163
Brookfield 53005
Tel: (414) 784-3480

ALASKA

Avnet Computer
1400 West Benson Blvd.
Suite 400
Anchorage 99503
Tel: (907) 274-9899
FAX: (907) 277-2639

CANADA

ALBERTA

Avnet Computer
2816 21st Street Northeast
Calgary T2E 6Z2
Tel: (403) 291-3284
FAX: (403) 250-1591

Zentronics
6815 8th Street N.E., #100
Calgary T2E 7H
Tel: (403) 295-8838
FAX: (403) 295-8714

BRITISH COLUMBIA

†Hamilton/Avnet Electronics
8610 Commerce Court
Burnaby V5A 4N6
Tel: (604) 420-4101
FAX: (604) 420-5376

Zentronics
11400 Bridgeport Rd., #108
Richmond V6X 1T2
Tel: (604) 273-5575
FAX: (604) 273-2413

ONTARIO

Arrow Electronics, Inc.
36 Antares Dr., Unit 100
Nepean K2E 7W5
Tel: (613) 226-6903
FAX: (613) 723-2018

†Arrow Electronics, Inc.
1093 Meyerside, Unit 2
Mississauga L5T 1M4
Tel: (416) 670-7769
FAX: (416) 670-7781

Avnet Computer
Canada System Engineering
Group
3688 Nashua Dr., Unit 6
Mississuaga L4V 1M5
Tel: (416) 672-8638
FAX: (416) 677-5091

Avnet Computer
6845 Rexwood Road
Units 7–9
Mississuaga L4V 1M4
Tel: (416) 672-8638
FAX: (416) 672-8650

Avnet Computer
190 Colonade Road
Nepean K2E 7J5
Tel: (613) 727-7529
FAX: (613) 226-1184

†Hamilton/Avnet Electronics
6845 Rexwood Rd., Units 3–5
Mississauga L4T 1R2
Tel: (416) 677-7432
FAX: (416) 677-0940

†Hamilton/Avnet Electronics
190 Colonade Road
Nepean K2E 7J5
Tel: (613) 226-1700
FAX: (613) 226-1184

†Zentronics
1355 Meyerside Drive
Mississauga L5T 1C9
Tel: (416) 564-9600
FAX: (416) 564-3127

†Zentronics
155 Colonade Rd., South
Unit 17
Nepean K2E 7K1
Tel: (613) 226-8840
FAX: (613) 226-6352

QUEBEC

Arrow Electronics Inc.
1100 St. Regis Blvd.
Dorval H9P 2T5
Tel: (514) 421-7411
FAX: (514) 421-7430

Arrow Electronics, Inc.
500 Boul. St-Jean-Baptiste Ave.
Quebec H2E 5R9
Tel: (418) 871-7500
FAX: (418) 871-6816

Avnet Computer
2795 Rue Halpern
St. Laurent H4S 1P8
Tel: (514) 335-2483
FAX: (514) 335-2481

†Hamilton/Avnet Electronics
2795 Halpern
St. Laurent H4S 1P8
Tel: (514) 335-1000
FAX: (514) 335-2481

†Zentronics
520 McCaffrey
St. Laurent H4T 1N3
Tel: (514) 737-9700
FAX: (514) 737-5212

†Certified VAD

EUROPEAN SALES OFFICES

FINLAND

Intel Finland OY
Ruosilantie 2
00390 Helsinki
Tel. (358) 0 544 644
FAX: (358) 0 544 030

FRANCE

Intel Corporation S.A.R.L.
1, Rue Edison-BP 303
78054 St. Quentin-en-Yvelines
Cedex
Tel: (33) (1) 30 57 70 00
FAX: (33) (1) 30 64 60 32

GERMANY

Intel GmbH
Dornacher Strasse 1
8016 Feldkirchen bei Muenchen
Tel: (49) 089/90992-0
FAX: (49) 089/9043948

ISRAEL

Intel Semiconductor Ltd.
Atidim Industrial Park-Neve Sharet
P.O. Box 43202
Tel-Aviv 61430
Tel: (972) 03 498080
FAX: (972) 03 491870

ITALY

Intel Corporation Italia S.p.A.
Milanofiori Palazzo E
20094 Assago
Milano
Tel: (39) (02) 89200950
FAX: (39) (2) 3498464

NETHERLANDS

Intel Semiconductor B.V.
Postbus 84130
3009 CC Rotterdam
Tel: (31) 10 407 11 11
FAX: (31) 10 455 4688

SPAIN

Intel Iberia S.A.
Zubaran, 28
28010 Madrid
Tel: (34) 308 25 52
FAX: (34) 410 7570

SWEDEN

Intel Sweden A.B.
Dalvagen 24
171 36 Solna
Tel: (46) 8 734 01 00
FAX: (46) 8 278085

UNITED KINGDOM

Intel Corporation (U.K.) Ltd.
Pipers Way
Swindon, Wiltshire SN3 1RJ
Tel: (44) (0793) 696000
FAX: (44) (0793) 641440

EUROPEAN DISTRIBUTORS/REPRESENTATIVES

AUSTRIA

Bacher Electronics GmbH
Rotenmuehlgasse 26
A-1120 Wien
Tel: 43 222 81356460
FAX: 43 222 834276

BELGIUM

Inelco Belgium S.A.
Oorlogskruisenlaan 94
B-1120 Bruxelles
Tel: 32 2 244 2811
FAX: 32 2 216 4301

FRANCE

Almex
48, Rue de l'Aubepine
B.P. 102
92164 Antony Cedex
Tel: 33 1 4096 5400
FAX: 33 1 4666 6028

Lex Electronics
Silic 585
60 Rue des Gemeaux
94663 Rungis Cedex
Tel: 33 1 4978 4978
FAX: 33 1 4978 0596

Metrologie
Tour d'Asnieres
4, Avenue Laurent Cely
92606 Asnieres Cedex
Tel: 33 1 4790 6240
FAX: 33 1 4790 5947

Tekelec-Airtronic
Cite Des Bruyeres
Rue Carle Vernet
BP 2
92310 Sevres
Tel: 33 1 4623 2425
FAX: 33 1 4507 2191

GERMANY

E2000 Vertriebs-AG
Stahlgruberring 12
8000 Muenchen 82
Tel: 49 89 420010
FAX: 49 89 42001209

Jermyn GmbH
Im Dachsstueck 9
6250 Limburg
Tel: 49 6431 5080
FAX: 49 6431 508289

Metrologie GmbH
Steinerstrasse 15
8000 Muenchen 70
Tel: 49 89 724470
FAX: 49 89 72447111

Proelectron Vertriebs GmbH
Max-Planck-Strasse 1-3
6072 Dreieich
Tel: 49 6103 304343
FAX: 49 6103 304425

Rein Electronik GmbH
Loetscher Weg 66
4054 Nettetal 1
Tel: 49 2153 7330
FAX: 49 2153 733513

GREECE

Pouliadis Associates Corp.
5 Koumbari Street
Kolonaki Square
10674 Athens
Tel: 30 1 360 3741
FAX: 30 1 360 7501

IRELAND

Micro Marketing
Tany Hall
Eglinton Terrace
Dundrum
Dublin
Tel: 0001 989 400
FAX: 0001 989 8282

ISRAEL

Eastronics Ltd.
Rozanis 11
P.O.B. 39300
Tel Baruch
Tel-Aviv 61392
Tel: 972 3 475151
FAX: 972 3 475125

ITALY

Celdis Spa
Via F.11i Gracchi 36
20092 Cinisello Balsamo
Milano
Tel: 39 2 66012003
FAX: 39 2 6182433

Intesi Div. Della Deutsche
Divisione ITT
Industries GmbH
P.I. 06550110156
Milanofiori Palazzo E5
20094 Assago (Milano)
Tel: 39 2 824701
FAX: 39 2 8242631

Lasi Elettronica S.p.A.
P.I. 00839000155
Viale Fulvio Testi, N.280
20126 Milano
Tel: 39 2 66101370
FAX: 39 2 66101385

Telcom s.r.l. – Divisione MDS
Via Trombetta
Zona Marconi
Strada Cassanese
Segrate – Milano
Tel: 39 2 2138010
FAX: 39 2 216061

NETHERLANDS

Koning en Hartman B.V.
Energieweg 1
2627 AP Delft
Tel: 31 15 609 906
FAX: 31 15 619 194

PORTUGAL

ATD Electronica LDA
Rua Dr. Faria de
Vasconcelos, 3a
1900 Lisboa
Tel: 351 1 8472200
FAX: 351 1 8472197

SPAIN

ATD Electronica
Plaza Ciudad de Viena, 6
28040 Madrid
Tel: 34 1 534 4000/09
FAX: 34 1 534 7663

Metrologia Iberica
Ctra De Fuencarral N.80
28100 Alcobendas
Madrid
Tel: 34 1 6538611
FAX: 34 1 6517549

SCANDINAVIA

OY Fintronic AB
Heikkilantie 2a
SF-00210 Helsinki
Tel: 358 0 6926022
FAX: 358 0 6821251

ITT Multikomponent A/S
Naverland 29
DK-2600 Glostrup
Denmark
Tel: 010 45 42 451822
FAX: 010 45 42 457624

Nordisk Elektronik A/S
Postboks 122
Smedsvingen 4
N-1364 Hvalstad
Norway
Tel: 47 2 846210
FAX: 47 2 846545

Nordisk Electronik AB
Box 36
Torshamnsgatan 39
S-16493 Kista
Sweden
Tel: 46 8 7034630
FAX: 46 8 7039845

SWITZERLAND

Industrade A.G.
Hertistrasse 31
CH-8304 Wallisellen
Tel: 41 1 8328111
FAX: 41 1 8307550

TURKEY

EMPA
80050 Sishane
Refik Saydam Cad No. 89/5
Istanbul
Tel: 90 1 143 6212
FAX: 90 1 143 6547

UNITED KINGDOM

Access Elect Comp Ltd.
Jubilee House
Jubilee Road
Letchworth
Hertfordshire
SG6 1QH
Tel: 0462 480888
FAX: 0462 682467

Bytech Components Ltd.
12a Cedarwood
Chineham Business Park
Crockford Lane
Basingstoke
Hants RG12 1RW
Tel: 0256 707107
FAX: 0256 707162

Bytech Systems
Unit 3
The Western Centre
Western Road
Bracknell
Berks RG12 1RW
Tel: 0344 55333
FAX: 0344 867270

Metrologie
Rapid House
Oxford Road
High Wycombe
Bucks
Herts HP11 2EE
Tel: 0494 474147
FAX: 0494 452144

Jermyn
Vestry Estate
Otford Road
Sevenoaks
Kent TN14 5EU
Tel: 0732 450144
FAX: 0732 451251

MMD
3 Bennet Court
Bennet Road
Reading
Berkshire RG2 0QX
Tel: 0734 313232
FAX: 0734 313255

Rapid Silicon
3 Bennet Court
Bennet Road
Reading
Berks RG2 0QX
Tel: 0734 752266
FAX: 0734 312728

Metro Systems
Rapid House
Oxford Road
High Wycombe
Bucks HP11 2EE
Tel: 0494 474171
FAX: 0494 21860

YUGOSLAVIA

H.R. Microelectronics Corp.
2005 de la Cruz Blvd.
Suite 220
Santa Clara, CA 95050
U.S.A.
Tel: (408) 988-0286
FAX: (408) 988-0306

INTERNATIONAL SALES OFFICES

AUSTRALIA

Intel Australia Pty. Ltd.
Unit 13
Allambie Grove Business Park
25 Frenchs Forest Road East
Frenchs Forest, NSW, 2086
Sydney
Tel: 61-2-975-3300
FAX: 61-2-975-3375

Intel Australia Pty. Ltd.
711 High Street
1st Floor
East Kw. Vic., 3102
Melbourne
Tel: 61-3-810-2141
FAX: 61-3-819 7200

BRAZIL

Intel Semiconductores do Brazil LTDA
Avenida Paulista, 1159-CJS 404/405
01311 - Sao Paulo - S.P.
Tel: 55-11-287-5899
TLX: 11-37-557-ISDB
FAX: 55-11-287-5119

CHINA/HONG KONG

Intel PRC Corporation
15/F, Office 1, Citic Bldg.
Jian Guo Men Wai Street
Beijing, PRC
Tel: (1) 500-4850
TLX. 22947 INTEL CN
FAX: (1) 500-2953

Intel Semiconductor Ltd.*
10/F East Tower
Bond Center
Queensway, Central
Hong Kong
Tel: (852) 844-4555
FAX: (852) 868-1989

INDIA

Intel Asia Electronics, Inc.
4/2, Samrah Plaza
St. Mark's Road
Bangalore 560001
Tel: 91-812-215773
TLX: 953-845-2646 INTEL IN
FAX: 091-812-215067

JAPAN

Intel Japan K.K.
5-6 Tokodai, Tsukuba-shi
Ibaraki, 300-26
Tel: 0298-47-8511
FAX: 0298-47-8450

Intel Japan K.K.*
Hachioji ON Bldg.
4-7-14 Myojin-machi
Hachioji-shi, Tokyo 192
Tel: 0426-48-8770
FAX: 0426-48-8775

Intel Japan K.K.*
Bldg. Kumagaya
2-69 Hon-cho
Kumagaya-shi, Saitama 360
Tel: 0485-24-6871
FAX: 0485-24-7518

Intel Japan K.K.*
Kawa-asa Bldg.
2-11-5 Shin-Yokohama
Kohoku-ku, Yokohama-shi
Kanagawa, 222
Tel: 045-474-7661
FAX: 045-471-4394

Intel Japan K.K.*
Ryokuchi-Eki Bldg.
2-4-1 Terauchi
Toyonaka-shi, Osaka 560
Tel: 06-863-1091
FAX: 06-863-1084

Intel Japan K.K.
Shinmaru Bldg.
1-5-1 Marunouchi
Chiyoda-ku, Tokyo 100
Tel: 03-3201-3621
FAX: 03-3201-6850

Intel Japan K.K.
Green Bldg.
1-16-20 Nishiki
Naka-ku, Nagoya-shi
Aichi 460
Tel: 052-204-1261
FAX: 052-204-1285

KOREA

Intel Korea, Ltd.
16th Floor, Life Bldg.
61 Yoido-dong, Youngdeungpo-Ku
Seoul 150-010
Tel: (2) 784-8186
FAX: (2) 784-8096

SINGAPORE

Intel Singapore Technology, Ltd.
101 Thomson Road #08-03/06
United Square
Singapore 1130
Tel: (65) 250-7811
FAX: (65) 250-9256

TAIWAN

Intel Technology Far East Ltd.
Taiwan Branch Office
8th Floor, No. 205
Bank Tower Bldg.
Tung Hua N. Road
Taipei
Tel: 000-2-5144202
FAX: 886-2-717-2455

INTERNATIONAL DISTRIBUTORS/REPRESENTATIVES

ARGENTINA

Dafsys S.R.L.
Chacabuco, 90-6 Piso
1069-Buenos Aires
Tel: 54-1-34-7726
FAX: 54-1-34-1871

AUSTRALIA

Email Electronics
15-17 Hume Street
Huntingdale, 3166
Tel: 011-61-3-544-8244
TLX: AA 30895
FAX: 011-61-3-543-8179

NSD-Australia
205 Middleborough Rd.
Box Hill, Victoria 3128
Tel: 03 8900970
FAX: 03 8990819

BRAZIL

Microlinear
Largo do Arouche, 24
01219 Sao Paulo, SP
Tel: 5511-220-2215
FAX: 5511-220-5750

CHILE

Sisteco
Vecinal 40 – Las Condes
Santiago
Tel: 562-234-1644
FAX: 562-233-9895

CHINA/HONG KONG

Novel Precision Machinery Co., Ltd.
Room 728 Trade Square
681 Cheung Sha Wan Road
Kowloon, Hong Kong
Tel: (852) 360-8999
TWX: 32032 NVTNL HX
FAX: (852) 725-3695

GUATEMALA

Abinitio
11 Calle 2 – Zona 9
Guatemala City
Tel: 5022-32-4104
FAX: 5022-32-4123

INDIA

Micronic Devices
Arun Complex
No. 65 D.V.G. Road
Basavanagudi
Bangalore 560 004
Tel: 011-91-812-600-631
011-91-812-611-365
TLX: 9538458332 MDBG

Micronic Devices
No. 516 5th Floor
Swastik Chambers
Sion, Trombay Road
Chembur
Bombay 400 071
TLX: 9531 171447 MDEV

Micronic Devices
25/8, 1st Floor
Bada Bazaar Marg
Old Rajinder Nagar
New Delhi 110 060
Tel: 011-91-11-5723509
011-91-11-589771
TLX: 031-63253 MDND IN

Micronic Devices
6-3-348/12A Dwarakapuri Colony
Hyderabad 500 482
Tel: 011-91-842-226748

S&S Corporation
1587 Kooser Road
San Jose, CA 95118
Tel: (408) 978-6216
TLX: 820281
FAX: (408) 978-8635

JAMAICA

MC Systems
10-12 Grenada Crescent
Kingston 5
Tel: (809) 929-2638
(809) 926-0188
FAX: (809) 926-0104

JAPAN

Asahi Electronics Co. Ltd.
KMM Bldg. 2-14-1 Asano
Kokurakita-ku
Kitakyushu-shi 802
Tel: 093-511-6471
FAX: 093-551-7861

CTC Components Systems Co., Ltd.
4-8-1 Dobashi, Miyamae-ku
Kawasaki-shi, Kanagawa 213
Tel: 044-852-5121
FAX: 044-877-4268

Dia Semicon Systems, Inc.
Flower Hill Shinmachi Higashi-kan
1-23 Shinmachi, Setagaya-ku
Tokyo 154
Tel: 03-3439-1600
FAX: 03-3439-1601

Okaya Koki
2-4-18 Sakae
Naka-ku, Nagoya-shi 460
Tel: 052-204-8315
FAX: 052-204-8380

Ryoyo Electro Corp.
Konwa Bldg.
1-12-22 Tsukiji
Chuo-ku, Tokyo 104
Tel: 03-3546-5011
FAX: 03-3546-5044

KOREA

J-Tek Corporation
Dong Sung Bldg. 9/F
158-24, Samsung-Dong, Kangnam-Ku
Seoul 135-090
Tel: (822) 557-8039
FAX: (822) 557-8304

Samsung Electronics
Samsung Main Bldg.
150 Taepyung-Ro-2KA, Chung-Ku
Seoul 100-102
C.P.O. Box 8780
Tel: (822) 751-3680
TWX: KORSST K 27970
FAX: (822) 753-9065

MEXICO

PSI S.A. de C.V.
Fco. Villa esq. Ajusco s/n
Cuernavaca, MOR 62130
Tel: 52-73-13-9412
52-73-17-5340
FAX: 52-73-17-5333

NEW ZEALAND

Email Electronics
36 Olive Road
Penrose, Auckland
Tel: 011-64-9-591-155
FAX: 011-64-9-592-681

SAUDI ARABIA

AAE Systems, Inc.
642 N. Pastoria Ave.
Sunnyvale, CA 94086
U.S.A.
Tel: (408) 732-1710
FAX: (408) 732-3095
TLX: 494-3405 AAE SYS

SINGAPORE

Electronic Resources Pte, Ltd.
17 Harvey Road
#03-01 Singapore 1336
Tel: (65) 283-0888
TWX: RS 56541 ERS
FAX: (65) 289-5327

SOUTH AFRICA

Electronic Building Elements
178 Erasmus St. (off Watermeyet St.)
Meyerspark, Pretoria, 0184
Tel: 011-2712-803-7680
FAX: 011-2712-803-8294

TAIWAN

Micro Electronics Corporation
12th Floor, Section 3
285 Nanking East Road
Taipei, R.O.C.
Tel: (886) 2-7198419
FAX: (886) 2-7197916

Acer Sertek Inc.
15th Floor, Section 2
Chien Kuo North Rd.
Taipei 18479 R.O.C.
Tel: 886-2-501-0055
TWX: 23756 SERTEK
FAX: (886) 2-5012521

URUGUAY

Interfase
Zabala 1378
11000 Montevideo
Tel: 5982-96-0490
5982-96-1143
FAX: 5982-96-2965

VENEZUELA

Unixel C.A.
4 Transversal de Monte Cristo
Edf. AXXA, Piso 1, of. 1&2
Centro Empresarial Boleita
Caracas
Tel: 582-238-6082
FAX: 582-238-1816

*Field Application Location

NORTH AMERICAN SERVICE OFFICES

ALASKA

Intel Corp.
c/o TransAlaska Network
1515 Lore Rd.
Anchorage 99507
Tel: (907) 522-1776

Intel Corp.
c/o TransAlaska Data Systems
c/o GCI Operations
520 Fifth Ave., Suite 407
Fairbanks 99701
Tel: (907) 452-6264

ARIZONA

*Intel Corp.
410 North 44th Street
Suite 500
Phoenix 85008
Tel: (602) 231-0386
FAX: (602) 244-0446

*Intel Corp.
500 E. Fry Blvd., Suite M-15
Sierra Vista 85635
Tel: (602) 459-5010

ARKANSAS

Intel Corp.
c/o Federal Express
1500 West Park Drive
Little Rock 72204

CALIFORNIA

*Intel Corp.
21515 Vanowen St., Ste. 116
Canoga Park 91303
Tel: (818) 704-8500

*Intel Corp.
300 N. Continental Blvd.
Suite 100
El Segundo 90245
Tel: (213) 640-6040

*Intel Corp.
1900 Prairie City Rd.
Folsom 95630-9597
Tel: (916) 351-6143

*Intel Corp.
9665 Chesapeake Dr., Suite 325
San Diego 92123
Tel: (619) 292-8086

**Intel Corp.
400 N. Tustin Avenue
Suite 450
Santa Ana 92705
Tel: (714) 835-9642

**Intel Corp.
2700 San Tomas Exp., 1st Floor
Santa Clara 95051
Tel: (408) 970-1747

COLORADO

*Intel Corp.
600 S. Cherry St., Suite 700
Denver 80222
Tel: (303) 321-8086

CONNECTICUT

*Intel Corp.
301 Lee Farm Corporate Park
83 Wooster Heights Rd.
Danbury 06811
Tel: (203) 748-3130

FLORIDA

**Intel Corp.
800 Fairway Dr., Suite 160
Deerfield Beach 33441
Tel: (305) 421-0506
FAX: (305) 421-2444

*Intel Corp.
5850 T.G. Lee Blvd., Ste. 340
Orlando 32822
Tel: (407) 240-8000

GEORGIA

*Intel Corp.
20 Technology Park, Suite 150
Norcross 30092
Tel: (404) 449-0541

5523 Theresa Street
Columbus 31907

HAWAII

**Intel Corp.
Honolulu 96820
Tel: (808) 847-6738

ILLINOIS

**†Intel Corp.
Woodfield Corp. Center III
300 N. Martingale Rd., Ste. 400
Schaumburg 60173
Tel: (708) 605-8031

INDIANA

*Intel Corp.
8910 Purdue Rd., Ste. 350
Indianapolis 46268
Tel: (317) 875-0623

KANSAS

*Intel Corp.
10985 Cody, Suite 140
Overland Park 66210
Tel: (913) 345-2727

KENTUCKY

Intel Corp.
133 Walton Ave., Office 1A
Lexington 40508
Tel: (606) 255-2957

Intel Corp.
896 Hillcrest Road, Apt. A
Radcliff 40160 (Louisville)

LOUISIANA

Hammond 70401
(serviced from Jackson, MS)

MARYLAND

**Intel Corp.
10010 Junction Dr., Suite 200
Annapolis Junction 20701
Tel: (301) 206-2860

MASSACHUSETTS

**Intel Corp.
Westford Corp. Center
3 Carlisle Rd., 2nd Floor
Westford 01886
Tel: (508) 692-0960

MICHIGAN

*Intel Corp.
7071 Orchard Lake Rd., Ste. 100
West Bloomfield 48322
Tel: (313) 851-8905

MINNESOTA

*Intel Corp.
3500 W. 80th St., Suite 360
Bloomington 55431
Tel: (612) 835-6722

MISSISSIPPI

Intel Corp.
c/o Compu-Care
2001 Airport Road, Suite 205F
Jackson 39208
Tel: (601) 932-6275

MISSOURI

*Intel Corp.
3300 Rider Trail South
Suite 170
Earth City 63045
Tel: (314) 291-1990

Intel Corp.
Route 2, Box 221
Smithville 64089
Tel: (913) 345-2727

NEW JERSEY

**Intel Corp.
300 Sylvan Avenue
Englewood Cliffs 07632
Tel: (201) 567-0821

*Intel Corp.
Lincroft Office Center
125 Half Mile Road
Red Bank 07701
Tel: (908) 747-2233

NEW MEXICO

Intel Corp.
Rio Rancho 1
4100 Sara Road
Rio Rancho 87124-1025
(near Albuquerque)
Tel: (505) 893-7000

NEW YORK

*Intel Corp.
2950 Expressway Dr. South
Suite 130
Islandia 11722
Tel: (516) 231-3300

Intel Corp.
300 Westage Business Center
Suite 230
Fishkill 12524
Tel: (914) 897-3860

Intel Corp.
5858 East Molloy Road
Syracuse 13211
Tel: (315) 454-0576

NORTH CAROLINA

*Intel Corp.
5800 Executive Center Drive
Suite 105
Charlotte 28212
Tel: (704) 568-8966

**Intel Corp.
5540 Centerview Dr., Suite 215
Raleigh 27606
Tel: (919) 851-9537

OHIO

**Intel Corp.
3401 Park Center Dr., Ste. 220
Dayton 45414
Tel: (513) 890-5350

*Intel Corp.
25700 Science Park Dr., Ste. 100
Beachwood 44122
Tel: (216) 464-2736

OREGON

**Intel Corp.
15254 N.W. Greenbrier Pkwy.
Building B
Beaverton 97006
Tel: (503) 645-8051

PENNSYLVANIA

*†Intel Corp.
925 Harvest Drive
Suite 200
Blue Bell 19422
Tel: (215) 641-1000
1-800-468-3548
FAX: (215) 641-0785

**†Intel Corp.
400 Penn Center Blvd., Ste. 610
Pittsburgh 15235
Tel: (412) 823-4970

*Intel Corp.
1513 Cedar Cliff Dr.
Camp Hill 17011
Tel: (717) 761-0860

PUERTO RICO

Intel Corp.
South Industrial Park
P.O. Box 910
Las Piedras 00671
Tel: (809) 733-8616

TEXAS

**Intel Corp.
Westech 360, Suite 4230
8911 N. Capitol of Texas Hwy.
Austin 78752-1239
Tel : (512) 794-8086

**†Intel Corp.
12000 Ford Rd., Suite 401
Dallas 75234
Tel: (214) 241-8087

**Intel Corp.
7322 SW Freeway, Suite 1490
Houston 77074
Tel: (713) 988-8086

UTAH

Intel Corp.
428 East 6400 South
Suite 104
Murray 84107
Tel: (801) 263-8051
FAX: (801) 268-1457

VIRGINIA

*Intel Corp.
9030 Stony Point Pkwy.
Suite 360
Richmond 23235
Tel: (804) 330-9393

WASHINGTON

**Intel Corp.
155 108th Avenue N.E., Ste. 386
Bellevue 98004
Tel: (206) 453-8086

CANADA

ONTARIO

**Intel Semiconductor of Canada, Ltd.
2650 Queensview Dr., Ste. 250
Ottawa K2B 8H6
Tel: (613) 829-9714

**Intel Semiconductor of Canada, Ltd.
190 Attwell Dr., Ste. 102
Rexdale (Toronto) M9W 6H8
Tel: (416) 675-2105

QUEBEC

**Intel Semiconductor of Canada, Ltd.
1 Rue Holiday
Suite 115
Tour East
Pt. Claire H9R 5N3
Tel: (514) 694-9130
FAX: 514-694-0064

CUSTOMER TRAINING CENTERS

ARIZONA

2402 W. Beardsley Road
Phoenix 85027
Tel: (602) 869-4288
1-800-468-3548

SYSTEMS ENGINEERING OFFICES

MINNESOTA

3500 W. 80th Street
Suite 360
Bloomington 55431
Tel: (612) 835-6722

NEW YORK

2950 Expressway Dr., South
Islandia 11722
Tel: (506) 231-3300

*Carry-in locations
**Carry-in/mail-in locations